Praise for *The American Promise*

"In the preface, the following sentence appears: 'We set an ambitious goal to produce the most teachable and readable introductory American history textbook available.' I think Roark et al. have hit their mark. *The American Promise* is an excellent introductory history book."

—J. M. Simpson, *Pierce College*

"The narrative shows students that individual lives are important in history. The personal approach is appealing and shows students that they are also part of history."

—Marjorie Berman, *Red Rocks Community College*

"I believe that, after only three editions, *The American Promise* has become a classic in American history college classrooms."

—Paul Hudson, *Georgia Perimeter College*

"*The American Promise* is well written and well researched. This is a book that transcends the term 'textbook' and could be sold as a history book on its own merits."

—Allen Lee Hamilton, *St. Phillips College*

"This book is the most sensible and balanced text for the U.S. survey I know of. It is appropriate in length and detail (neither too much nor too little), and has clear chapter themes that reflect recent scholarship without becoming a slave to fashion."

—Larry Grubbs, *University of Georgia*

"In regard to scholarship I would have to say that *The American Promise* ranks at the highest levels. It provides the best blend of consistency in the presentation of historical materials, offering to students a wealth of fact and information that will serve them well in the future."

—John Elder, *University of Central Oklahoma*

The American Promise

A HISTORY OF THE UNITED STATES

Fourth Edition

James L. Roark
Emory University

Michael P. Johnson
Johns Hopkins University

Patricia Cline Cohen
University of California, Santa Barbara

Sarah Stage
Arizona State University

Alan Lawson
Boston College

Susan M. Hartmann
The Ohio State University

BEDFORD/ST. MARTIN'S
Boston ◆ New York

FOR BEDFORD/ST. MARTIN'S

Publisher for History: Mary Dougherty
Director of Development for History: Jane Knetzger
Executive Editor: William J. Lombardo
Developmental Editor: Laura Arcari
Senior Production Editor: Rosemary R. Jaffe
Senior Production Supervisor: Joe Ford
Executive Marketing Manager: Jenna Bookin Barry
Editorial Assistant: Lynn Sternberger
Production Assistants: David Ayers and Lidia MacDonald-Carr
Copyeditor: Barbara Jatkola
Text Design: Joan O'Connor
Photo Research: Pembroke Herbert/Sandi Rygiel, Picture Research Consultants & Archives, Inc.
Indexer: Leoni Z. McVey
Cover Design: Donna Lee Dennison
Cover Art: Winslow Homer, *The Country School,* 1871 (detail), oil on canvas. Saint Louis Art
  Museum, Museum Purchase.
Cartography: Mapping Specialists Limited
Composition: ICC Macmillan Inc.
Printing and Binding: RR Donnelley and Sons

President: Joan E. Feinberg
Editorial Director: Denise B. Wydra
Director of Marketing: Karen R. Soeltz
Director of Editing, Design, and Production: Marcia Cohen
Assistant Director of Editing, Design, and Production: Elise S. Kaiser
Managing Editor: Elizabeth M. Schaaf

Library of Congress Control Number: 2008923922

For information, write: Bedford/St. Martin's, 75 Arlington Street, Boston, MA 02116
  (617-399-4000)

ISBN-10: 0-312-48734-7   ISBN-13: 978-0-312-48734-8 (combined edition)
ISBN-10: 0-312-48946-3   ISBN-13: 978-0-312-48946-5 (Vol. I)
ISBN-10: 0-312-48947-1   ISBN-13: 978-0-312-48947-2 (Vol. II)

BRIEF CONTENTS

CONTENTS

CHAPTER 5

Colonial America in the Eighteenth Century, 1701–1770   112

CHAPTER 6

The British Empire and the Colonial Crisis, 1754–1775   143

CHAPTER 7
The War for America, 1775–1783   177

CHAPTER 12
The New West and Free North, 1840–1860 339

CHAPTER 13
The Slave South, 1820–1860 373

CHAPTER 25

The United States and the Second World War, 1939–1945   790

A S AUTHORS, WE ARE DEEPLY GRATIFIED that *The American Promise* has become one of the most widely adopted texts for the U.S. history survey. We are now pleased to offer *The American Promise*, Value Edition. Retaining the complete narrative of the Fourth Edition, this trade-sized black-and-white edition offers students a memorable narrative. Because of its low cost, the Value Edition allows instructors greater freedom to assign supplementary reading.

From the beginning, *The American Promise* has been shaped by our firsthand knowledge that the survey course is the most difficult to teach and the most difficult to take. Collectively, we have logged considerably more than a century in introductory American history classrooms in institutions that range from small community colleges to large research institutions. Our experience as teachers informs every aspect of our text, beginning with its framework. In our classrooms, we have found that students need **both** the structure a political narrative provides **and** the insights gained from examining social and cultural experience. To write a comprehensive, balanced account of American history, we focused on the public arena—the place where politics intersects social and cultural developments—to show how Americans confronted the major issues of their day and created far-reaching historical change.

We also thought hard about the concerns most frequently voiced by instructors: that students often find history boring, unfocused, and difficult and their textbooks lifeless and overwhelming. Getting students to open the book is one of the biggest hurdles instructors face. We asked ourselves how our text could address these concerns and engage students in ways that would help them understand and remember the main developments in American history. To make the political, social, economic, and cultural changes vivid and memorable and to portray fully the diversity of the American experience, we stitched into our narrative the voices of hundreds of contemporaries—from presidents to pipefitters, sharecroppers to suffragists—whose ideas and actions shaped their times and whose efforts still affect our lives. By incorporating a rich selection of authentic American voices, we seek to capture history as it happened and to create a compelling narrative that captures students' interests and sparks their historical imagination.

Our title, *The American Promise*, reflects our emphasis on human agency and our conviction that American history is an unfinished story. For millions, the nation has held out the promise of a better life, unfettered worship, representative government, democratic politics, and other freedoms seldom found elsewhere.

But none of these promises has come with guarantees. As we see it, much of American history is a continuing struggle over the definition and realization of the nation's promise. Abraham Lincoln, in the midst of what he termed the "fiery trial" of the Civil War, pronounced the nation "the last best hope of Earth." Kept alive by countless sacrifices, that hope has been marred by compromises, disappointments, and denials, but it lives still. We believe that *The American Promise*, Fourth Edition, with its increased attention to making history come alive, will help students become aware of the legacy of hope bequeathed to them by previous generations of Americans stretching back nearly four centuries, a legacy that is theirs to preserve and build on.

Features

Carefully chosen illustrations and maps extend and reinforce the narrative. The 155 contemporaneous **illustrations**—including paintings, photographs, and artifacts—make history tangible and emphasize the importance of material culture in the study of the past. **Comprehensive captions** for the illustrations in the book entice students to delve deeper into the text itself, and enrich the historical account. Our highly regarded **map program** rests on the old truth that "History is not intelligible without geography." Each chapter offers, on average, three **full-size maps** showing major developments in the narrative. A brief **Atlas of the Territorial Growth of the United States**, a series of maps at the end of each volume, reveals the changing cartography of the nation.

As part of our ongoing efforts to make this the most teachable and readable survey text available, chapters are constructed to preview, reinforce, and review the narrative in the most memorable and engaging means possible. Each chapter begins with a colorful **opening vignette** that invites students into the narrative with lively accounts of individuals or groups who embody the central themes of the chapter. Vignettes in this edition include, among others, Queen Isabella supporting Columbus's expedition to the New World, the Robin Johns' experiences in the Atlantic slave trade, Deborah Sampson masquerading as a man to join the Continental army, Alexander Hamilton as a polarizing figure, James T. Rapier emerging in the early 1870s as Alabama's most prominent black leader, Frances Willard participating in the creation of the Populist Party in 1892, and Congresswoman Helen Gahagan Douglas during the cold war. Each vignette ends with a **narrative overview** of all of the chapter's main topics. Major sections within each chapter have **introductory paragraphs** that preview the subsections that follow and conclude with **review questions** to help students check their comprehension of main ideas. **Runningheads** with dates and topical headings remind students of chronology, **thematic chronologies** reinforce points in the narrative, and **Glossary terms**, set in boldface type at first use, make historical terms accessible. At the end of each chapter, a **conclusion** reexamines central ideas and provides a bridge to the next chapter.

A substantial **Reviewing the Chapter** section at the end of each chapter provides step-by-step study plans to ensure student success. These chapter review guides include chapter **Timelines** that give clear chronological overviews of key events and two sets of questions that prompt students to think critically and make use of the facts they have mastered: **Review Questions** repeated from within the narrative and **Making Connections** questions that prompt students to think about broad developments. **Online Study Guide cross-references** at the end of the review section point students to free self-assessment quizzes and other study aids.

Supplements

The comprehensive collection of free and premium resources accompanying the fourth edition of the parent textbook are available also with the Value Edition, providing access to a host of practical learning and teaching aids. Many of the new media options can not only save instructors and students time and money but also add sound to the voices, movement to the images, and interactivity to the documents that help bring history to life. Cross-references in the textbook to the Online Study Guide and to the primary source reader signal the tight integration of the core text with the supplements.

For Students
Print Resources

Reading the American Past: Selected Historical Documents, **Fourth Edition.** Edited by Michael P. Johnson (Johns Hopkins University), one of the authors of *The American Promise,* and designed to complement the textbook, *Reading the American Past* provides a broad selection of over 150 primary source documents, as well as editorial apparatus to help students understand the sources. Emphasizing the important social, political, and economic themes of U.S. history courses, thirty-two new documents (at least one per chapter) were added to provide a multiplicity of perspectives on environmental, western, ethnic, and gender history and to bring a global dimension to the anthology. Available for packaging with the text and now available as an e-book (see below).

Maps in Context: A Workbook for American History. Written by historical cartography expert Gerald A. Danzer (University of Illinois, Chicago), this skill-building workbook helps students comprehend essential connections between geographic literacy and historical understanding. Organized to correspond to the typical U.S. history survey course, *Maps in Context* presents a wealth of map-centered projects and convenient pop quizzes that give students hands-on experience working with maps. Package discounts are available.

NEW Trade Books. Titles published by sister companies Farrar, Straus and Giroux; Henry Holt and Company; Hill and Wang; Picador; and St. Martin's Press are available at a 50 percent discount when packaged with Bedford/St. Martin's text-books. For more information, visit **bedfordstmartins.com/tradeup.**

NEW *The Bedford Glossary for U.S. History.* This handy supplement for the survey course gives students clear, concise definitions of the political, economic, social, and cultural terms used by historians and contemporary media alike. The terms are historically contextualized to aid comprehension. Package discounts are available.

U.S. History Matters: A Student Guide to U.S. History Online, **Second Edition.** This resource, written by Alan Gevinson, Kelly Schrum, and Roy Rosenzweig (all of George Mason University), provides an illustrated and annotated guide to 250 of the most useful Web sites for student research in U.S. history as well as advice on evalu-ating and using Internet sources. This essential guide is based on the acclaimed "History Matters" Web site developed by the American History Social Project and the Center for History and New Media. Package discounts are available.

Bedford Series in History and Culture. Over one hundred titles in this highly praised series combine first-rate scholarship, historical narrative, and important primary documents for undergraduate courses. Each book is brief, inexpensive, and focused on a specific topic or period. Package discounts are available.

Historians at Work Series. Brief enough for a single assignment yet meaty enough to provoke thoughtful discussion, each volume in this series examines a single historical question by combining unabridged selections by distinguished historians, each with a different perspective on the issue, with helpful learning aids. Package discounts are available.

New Media Resources

NEW *Reading the American Past* **e-book** featuring all of the documents in the print reader (see above). This e-book is perfect for instructors who wish to build dynamic online courses or use electronic texts and documents.

Online Study Guide at bedfordstmartins.com/roarkvalue. The popular Online Study Guide for the Fourth Edition of *The American Promise* is available to stu-dents using the Value Edition. This free and uniquely personalized learning tool helps students master themes and information presented in the textbook and improve their historical skills. Assessment quizzes let students evaluate their comprehension and provide them with customized plans for further study through a variety of activities. Instructors can monitor students' progress through the online Quiz Gradebook or receive e-mail updates.

NEW Audio Reviews for *The American Promise,* **Fourth Edition, at bedfordst martins.com/roarkvalue.** Audio Reviews are a new tool that fits easily into students' lifestyles and provides a practical new way for them to study. These twenty-five- to thirty-minute summaries of each chapter in *The American Promise* highlight the major themes of the text and help reinforce student learning.

Online Bibliography at bedfordstmartins.com/roarkvalue. Organized by book chapter and topic, the online bibliography provides an authoritative and comprehensive list of references to jump-start student research.

A Student's Online Guide to History Reference Sources at bedfordstmartins .com/roarkvalue. This Web site provides links to history-related databases, indexes, and journals, plus contact information for state, provincial, local, and professional history organizations.

The Bedford Research Room at bedfordstmartins.com/roarkvalue. The Research Room, drawn from Mike Palmquist's *The Bedford Researcher,* offers a wealth of resources—including interactive tutorials, research activities, student writing samples, and links to hundreds of other places online—to support students in courses across the disciplines. The site also offers instructors a library of helpful instructional tools.

The Bedford Bibliographer at bedfordstmartins.com/roarkvalue. *The Bedford Bibliographer,* a simple but powerful Web-based tool, assists students with the process of collecting sources and generates bibliographies in four commonly used documentation styles.

Research and Documentation Online at bedfordstmartins.com/roarkvalue. This Web site provides clear advice on how to integrate primary and secondary sources into research papers, how to cite sources correctly, and how to format in MLA, APA, *Chicago,* or CBE style.

The St. Martin's Tutorial on Avoiding Plagiarism at bedfordstmartins.com/ roarkvalue. This online tutorial reviews the consequences of plagiarism and explains what sources to acknowledge, how to keep good notes, how to organize research, and how to integrate sources appropriately. The tutorial includes exercises to help students practice integrating sources and recognize acceptable summaries.

Critical Thinking Modules at bedfordstmartins.com/roarkvalue. This Web site offers over two dozen online modules for interpreting maps, audio, visual, and textual sources, centered on events covered in the U.S. history survey.

For Instructors
Print Resources

Instructor's Resource Manual. This popular manual by Sarah E. Gardner (Mercer University) and Catherine A. Jones (Johns Hopkins University) offers both experienced and first-time instructors tools for presenting textbook material in exciting and engaging ways—learning objectives, annotated chapter outlines, lecture strategies, tips for helping students with common misconceptions and difficult topics, and suggestions for in-class activities, including using film and video, ways to start discussions, topics for debate, and analyzing primary sources. The new edition includes model answers for the questions in the book as well as a chapter-by-chapter guide to all of the supplements available with *The American Promise*. An extensive guide for first-time teaching assistants and sample syllabi are also included.

Transparencies. This set of over 160 full-color acetate transparencies includes all full-size maps and many other images from the parent textbook to help instructors present lectures and teach students important map-reading skills.

Using the Bedford Series in History and Culture in the U.S. History Survey at bedfordstmartins.com/usingseries. This online guide helps instructors integrate volumes from the highly regarded Bedford Series in History and Culture into their U.S. history survey course. The guide not only correlates themes from each series book with the survey course but also provides ideas for classroom discussions.

New Media Resources

Instructor's Resource CD-ROM. This disc provides instructors with ready-made and customizable PowerPoint multimedia presentations built around chapter outlines, maps, figures, and selected images from the parent textbook, plus jpeg versions of all maps, figures, and selected images.

Computerized Test Bank. Written by Bradford Wood (Eastern Kentucky University), Peter Lau (University of Rhode Island), and Sondra Cosgrove (Community College of Northern Nevada), the test bank provides over 80 exercises per chapter, including multiple-choice, fill-in-the-blank, map analysis, short essay, and full-length essay questions. Instructors can customize quizzes, add or edit both questions and answers, and export questions and answers to a variety of formats, including WebCT and Blackboard. The disc includes correct answers and essay outlines.

Book Companion Site at bedfordstmartins.com/roarkvalue. The companion Web site gathers all the electronic resources for *The American Promise*, including the Online Study Guide and related Quiz Gradebook, at a single Web address, providing convenient links to lecture, assignment, and research materials such as PowerPoint chapter outlines and the digital libraries at Make History.

Make History at bedfordstmartins.com/roarkvalue. Comprising the content of our five acclaimed online libraries—Map Central, the Bedford History Image Library, DocLinks, HistoryLinks, and PlaceLinks—Make History provides one-stop access to relevant digital content, including maps, images, documents, and Web links. Students and instructors alike can search this free, easy-to-use database by keyword, topic, date, or specific chapter of *The American Promise* and download the content they find. Instructors can also create entire collections of content and store them online for later use or post their collections to the Web to share with students.

Content for Course Management Systems. A variety of student and instructor resources developed for *The American Promise* is ready for use in course management systems such as Blackboard, WebCT, and other platforms. This e-content includes nearly all of the offerings from the book's Online Study Guide as well as the book's test bank.

NEW Reel Teaching. A valuable tool for enhancing media-rich lectures, short segments in VHS and DVD format are available to qualified adopters from the award-winning telecourses *Shaping America* and *Transforming America* by Dallas TeleLearning at the LeCroy Center for Educational Telecommunications.

Videos and Multimedia. A wide assortment of videos and multimedia CD-ROMs on various topics in American history is available to qualified adopters.

Acknowledgments

We gratefully acknowledge all of the helpful suggestions from those who have read and taught from the previous editions of *The American Promise*, and we hope that our many classroom collaborators will be pleased to see their influence in the fourth edition. In particular, we wish to thank the talented scholars and teachers who gave generously of their time and knowledge to review this book; their critiques and suggestions contributed greatly to the published work: Kathryn Abbot, *Western Kentucky University;* Carol Anderson, *University of Missouri, Columbia;* Melissa Anyiwo, *University of Tennessee, Chattanooga;* Janis Appier, *University of Tennessee;* Marjorie Berman, *Red Rocks Community College;* Bill Bush, *University of Nevada, Las Vegas;* Charles Byler, *Carroll College;* Dominic Carrillo, *Grossmont College;* Stephanie Cole, *University of Texas, Arlington;* Barak Cook, *University of Missouri;* Sheri David, *North Virginia Community College, Manassas;* Tracy Davis, *Victor Valley College;* Thomas Dicke, *Missouri State University;* Don Doyle, *University of South Carolina;*

Bill G. Dykes, *Temple Baptist College;* John Elder, *University of Central Oklahoma;* Karen Enloe, *Glendale Community College;* Amy Essington, *California State University, Long Beach;* Dana Frank, *University of California, Santa Cruz;* Hal Friedman, *Henry Ford Community College;* Steven Gargo, *Appleton Area Schools;* Michael Garcia, *Arapahoe Community College;* David Gerleman, *George Mason University;* Gina Estep Gompert, *Sierra College;* Larry Grubbs, *University of Georgia;* Allen Hamilton, *St. Phillips College;* Paul Hudson, *Georgia Perimeter College;* Jeffrey Irvin, *Monroe County Community College;* Frances M. Jacobson, *Tidewater Community College;* Jeanette Keith, *Bloomsburg University;* Daniel P. Kotzin, *Kutztown University;* Lou LaGrande, *St. Petersburg College;* Brad Lookingbill, *Columbia College;* Robert Martin, *University of Northern Iowa;* Suzanne Summers McFadden, *Austin Community College;* Rebecca Mead, *Northern Michigan University;* Warren Metcalf, *University of Oklahoma;* Carlos Mujal, *De Anza College;* William Murphy, *SUNY Oswego;* Cassandra Newby-Alexander, *Old Dominion;* Cynthia Clark Northrup, *University of Texas, Arlington;* Carla Pestana, *Miami University;* Caroline Pruden, *North Carolina State;* Kimber Quinney, *California State San Marcos;* Akin Reinhardt, *Towson University;* Rob Risko, *Trinity Valley Community College;* Jere Roberson, *University of Central Oklahoma;* Horacio Salinas Jr., *Laredo Community College;* Sharon Salinger, *University of California, Irvine;* Ken Shafer, *Cerritos College;* Donald R. Shaffer, *University of Northern Colorado;* John Simpson, *Pierce College;* Tiwanna Simpson, *Louisiana State University;* Sherry Smith, *Southern Methodist University;* Melissa Soto-Schwartz, *Cuyahoga Community College;* Mark Stephens, *Los Positas College;* Thomas Summerhill, *Michigan State University;* Wesley Swanson, *San Joaquin Delta College;* Stacy L. Tanner, *Georgia Southern University;* Pat Thompson, *University of Texas, San Antonio;* Stephen Tootle, *University of Northern Colorado;* Kenneth Townsend, *Coastal University;* David White, *McHenry Community College;* LeeAnn Whites, *University of Missouri, Columbia;* and Rosemary Zagarri, *George Mason University.*

A project as complex as this requires the talents of many individuals. First, we would like to acknowledge our families for their support, forbearance, and toleration of our textbook responsibilities. Pembroke Herbert and Sandi Rygiel of Picture Research Consultants, Inc., contributed their unparalleled knowledge, soaring imagination, and diligent research to make possible the extraordinary illustration program.

We would also like to thank the many people at Bedford/St. Martin's who have been crucial to this project. No one contributed more than developmental editor Laura Arcari, who managed the entire revision and oversaw the development of each chapter. The results of her dedication to excellence and commitment to creating the best textbook imaginable are evident on every page. We greatly appreciate the acute intelligence and indomitable good humor that Laura brought to this revision. We thank freelance editors Jan Fitter, Michelle McSweeney, and Terri Wise for their help with the manuscript. Thanks also go to editorial assistant Daniel Cole for his assistance managing the reviews and associate editor Marissa Zanetti, who provided unflagging assistance and who coordinated the supplements. We are also grateful to Jane Knetzger, director of development for history, and Mary Dougherty, publisher for history, for their support and guidance. For their imaginative and tireless efforts to promote the book, we want to thank Jenna Bookin Barry, executive marketing manager; John Hunger, senior history specialist; and Amanda Byrnes, senior marketing associate. With great skill and professionalism, Rosemary Jaffe, senior production editor, pulled together the many pieces related to copyediting, design, and typesetting, with the able assistance of David Ayers and Lidia MacDonald-Carr, and the guidance of managing editor Elizabeth Schaaf and assistant managing editor John Amburg. Senior production supervisor Joe Ford oversaw the manufacturing of the book. Designer Joan O'Connor, copyeditor Barbara Jatkola, and proofreaders Linda McLatchie and Stella Gelboin attended to the myriad details that help make the book shine. Leoni McVey provided an outstanding index. The book's gorgeous covers were designed by Donna Lee Dennison. Associate editor Marissa Zanetti made sure that *The American Promise* remains at the forefront of technological support for students and instructors. Editorial director Denise Wydra provided helpful advice throughout the course of the project. Finally, Charles H. Christensen, former president, took a personal interest in *The American Promise* from the start, and Joan E. Feinberg, president, guided all editions through every stage of development.

JAMES L. ROARK

Born in Eunice, Louisiana, and raised in the West, James L. Roark received his B.A. from the University of California, Davis, in 1963 and his Ph.D. from Stanford University in 1973. His dissertation won the Allan Nevins Prize. He has taught at the University of Nigeria, Nsukka; the University of Nairobi, Kenya; the University of Missouri, St. Louis; and, since 1983, Emory University, where he is Samuel Candler Dobbs Professor of American History. In 1993, he received the Emory Williams Distinguished Teaching Award, and in 2001–2002 he was Pitt Professor of American Institutions at Cambridge University. He has written *Masters without Slaves: Southern Planters in the Civil War and Reconstruction* (1977). With Michael P. Johnson, he is author of *Black Masters: A Free Family of Color in the Old South* (1984) and editor of *No Chariot Let Down: Charleston's Free People of Color on the Eve of the Civil War* (1984). He has received research assistance from the American Philosophical Society, the National Endowment for the Humanities, and the Gilder Lehrman Institute of American History. Active in the Organization of American Historians and the Southern Historical Association, he is also a fellow of the Society of American Historians.

MICHAEL P. JOHNSON

Born and raised in Ponca City, Oklahoma, Michael P. Johnson studied at Knox College in Galesburg, Illinois, where he received a B.A. in 1963, and at Stanford University in Palo Alto, California, earning a Ph.D. in 1973. He is currently professor of history at Johns Hopkins University in Baltimore, having previously taught at the University of California, Irvine; San Jose State University; and LeMoyne (now LeMoyne-Owen) College in Memphis. His publications include *Toward a Patriarchal Republic: The Secession of Georgia* (1977); with James L. Roark, *Black Masters: A Free Family of Color in the Old South* (1984) and *No Chariot Let Down: Charleston's Free People of Color on the Eve of the Civil War* (1984); *Abraham Lincoln, Slavery, and the Civil War: Selected Speeches and Writings* (2001); *Reading the American Past: Selected Historical Documents*, the documents reader for *The American Promise*; and articles that have appeared in the *William and Mary Quarterly*, the *Journal of Southern History*, *Labor History*, the *New York Review of*

Books, the *New Republic,* the *Nation,* and other journals. Johnson has been awarded research fellowships by the American Council of Learned Societies, the National Endowment for the Humanities, the Center for Advanced Study in the Behavioral Sciences and Stanford University, and the Times Mirror Foundation Distinguished Research Fellowship at the Huntington Library. He has directed a National Endowment for the Humanities Summer Seminar for College Teachers and has been honored with the University of California, Irvine, Academic Senate Distinguished Teaching Award and the University of California, Irvine, Alumni Association Outstanding Teaching Award. He won the *William and Mary Quarterly* award for best article in 2002 and the Organization of American Historians ABC-CLIO *America: History and Life* Award for best American history article in 2002. He is an active member of the American Historical Association, the Organization of American Historians, and the Southern Historical Association.

PATRICIA CLINE COHEN

Born in Ann Arbor, Michigan, and raised in Palo Alto, California, Patricia Cline Cohen earned a B.A. at the University of Chicago in 1968 and a Ph.D. at the University of California, Berkeley, in 1977. In 1976, she joined the history faculty at the University of California, Santa Barbara. In 2005–2006, she received the university's Distinguished Teaching Award. Cohen has written *A Calculating People: The Spread of Numeracy in Early America* (1982; reissued 1999) and *The Murder of Helen Jewett: The Life and Death of a Prostitute in Nineteenth-Century New York* (1998). She has also published articles on quantitative literacy, mathematics education, prostitution, and murder in journals including the *Journal of Women's History, Radical History Review,* the *William and Mary Quarterly,* and the *NWSA Journal.* Her scholarly work has received support from the National Endowment for the Humanities, the National Humanities Center, the University of California President's Fellowship in the Humanities, the Mellon Foundation, the American Antiquarian Society, the Schlesinger Library, and the Newberry Library. She is an active associate of the Omohundro Institute of Early American History and Culture, sits on the advisory council of the Society for the History of the Early American Republic, and is past president of the Western Association of Women Historians. She has served as chair of the history department, as chair of the Women's Studies Program, and as acting dean of the humanities and fine arts at the University of California at Santa Barbara. In 2001–2002, she was the Distinguished Senior Mellon Fellow at the American Antiquarian Society. Currently she is working on a book about women's health advocate Mary Gove Nichols.

SARAH STAGE

Sarah Stage was born in Davenport, Iowa, and received a B.A. from the University of Iowa in 1966 and a Ph.D. in American studies from Yale University in 1975. She has taught U.S. history for more than twenty-five years at Williams College and the University of California, Riverside. Currently she is professor of Women's Studies at Arizona State University at the West campus in Phoenix. Her books include *Female Complaints: Lydia Pinkham and the Business of Women's Medicine* (1979) and *Rethinking Home Economics: Women and the History of a Profession* (1997), which has been translated for a Japanese edition. Among the fellowships she has received are the Rockefeller Foundation Humanities Fellowship, the American Association of University Women dissertation fellowship, a fellowship from the Charles Warren Center for the Study of History at Harvard University, and the University of California President's Fellowship in the Humanities. She is at work on a book entitled *Women and the Progressive Impulse in American Politics, 1890–1914.*

ALAN LAWSON

Born in Providence, Rhode Island, Alan Lawson received his B.A. from Brown University in 1955 and his M.A. from the University of Wisconsin in 1956. After Army service and experience as a high school teacher, he earned his Ph.D. from the University of Michigan in 1967. Since winning the Allan Nevins Prize for his dissertation, Lawson has served on the faculties of the University of California, Irvine; Smith College; and, currently, Boston College. He has written *The Failure of Independent Liberalism* (1971) and coedited *From Revolution to Republic* (1976). While completing the forthcoming *Ideas in Crisis: The New Deal and the Mobilization of Progressive Experience,* he has published book chapters and essays on political economy, the cultural legacy of the New Deal, multiculturalism, and the arts in public life. He has served as editor of the *Review of Education* and the *Intellectual History Newsletter* and contributed articles to those journals as well as to the *History of Education Quarterly.* He has been active in the field of American studies as director of the Boston College American studies program and as a contributor to the *American Quarterly.* Under the auspices of the United States Information Agency, Lawson has been coordinator and lecturer for programs to instruct faculty from foreign nations in the state of American historical scholarship and teaching.

Susan M. Hartmann

Professor of history at Ohio State University, Susan M. Hartmann received her B.A. from Washington University and her Ph.D. from the University of Missouri. After specializing in the political economy of the post–World War II period and publishing *Truman and the 80th Congress* (1971), she expanded her interests to the field of women's history, publishing many articles and three books: *The Home Front and Beyond: American Women in the 1940s* (1982); *From Margin to Mainstream: American Women and Politics since 1960* (1989); and *The Other Feminists: Activists in the Liberal Establishment* (1998). Her work has been supported by the Truman Library Institute, the Rockefeller Foundation, the National Endowment for the Humanities, and the American Council of Learned Societies. At Ohio State, she has served as director of women's studies, and in 1995 she won the Exemplary Faculty Award in the College of Humanities. Hartmann has taught at the University of Missouri, St. Louis, and Boston University, and she has lectured on American history in Australia, Austria, France, Germany, Greece, Japan, Nepal, and New Zealand. She is a fellow of the Society of American Historians; has served on award committees of the American Historical Association, the Organization of American Historians, the American Studies Association, and the National Women's Studies Association; and currently is on the Board of Directors at the Truman Library Institute. Her current research is on gender and the transformation of politics since 1945.

1
CHAPTER

Ancient America
Before 1492

G EORGE McJUNKIN, the manager of the Crowfoot Ranch near Folsom, New Mexico, rode out to mend fences and to look for missing cattle after a violent rainstorm in August 1908. An American of African descent, McJunkin had been born a slave in Texas and had been riding horses since he was a boy. After he became free at the end of the Civil War in 1865, McJunkin worked as a cowboy in Colorado and New Mexico before becoming the Crowfoot manager in 1891. Now, as he rode across the ranch land he knew so well to survey damage caused by the recent storm, McJunkin noticed that floodwater had washed away the bank of a gulch called Wild Horse Arroyo and exposed a deposit of stark white bones. Curious, he dismounted and chipped away at the deposit until he uncovered an entire fossilized bone. The bone was much larger than the parched skeletons of range cattle and buffalo that McJunkin often saw, so he saved it, hoping someday to identify it.

Four years later, in 1912, McJunkin met Carl Schwachheim, a white man in Raton, New Mexico. Schwachheim, a blacksmith, shared McJunkin's curiosity about fossils, and the two men became friends. McJunkin told Schwachheim about the fossil deposit he had discovered. Ten years later, a few months after McJunkin's death, Schwachheim finally drove out to Wild Horse Arroyo and dug out several bones. But, like McJunkin, he could not identify any animal that had such big bones.

In 1926, Schwachheim delivered cattle to the stockyards in Denver, and he took some of the fossilized bones to the Denver Museum of Natural History and showed them to J. D. Figgins, a paleontologist who was an expert on fossils of ancient animals. Figgins immediately recognized the significance of the bones and a

1

George McJunkin
This photo shows McJunkin a few years after he discovered the Folsom site but about fifteen years before anyone understood the significance of his find. The fossilized bones he discovered belonged to an extinct bison species that was much larger than modern bison; the horns of the ancient animal often spanned six feet, wide enough for McJunkin's horse to have stood sideways between them.
Eastern New Mexico University, Blackwater Draw Site, Portales, New Mexico 88130.

few months later began an excavation of the Folsom site that revolutionized knowledge about the first Americans.

When Figgins began his dig at Folsom, archaeologists (individuals who examine **artifacts** left by long-vanished peoples as part of the study of **archaeology**) believed that Native Americans had arrived relatively recently in the Western Hemisphere, probably no more than three or four thousand years earlier, when, experts assumed, they had paddled small boats across the icy waters of the Bering Strait from what is now Siberia. At Folsom, Figgins learned that the bones McJunkin had first spotted belonged to twenty-three giant bison, a species known to have been extinct for at least 10,000 years. More startling, Figgins found nineteen flint spear points among the bones (Folsom points, they have since been called). Since no random natural process could have produced the finely crafted Folsom points, they seemed to prove that human beings had been alive at the same time as the giant bison. Skeptics worried that erosion, floods, earthquakes, or other geological events might have accidentally brought the old bones into proximity with possibly much younger Folsom points. But one spear point proved conclusively that the giant bison, the spear points, and the human beings who made them were contemporaries. One Folsom point remained stuck between two ribs of a giant bison, where a Stone Age hunter had plunged it more than 10,000 years earlier. No longer could anyone doubt that human beings had inhabited North America for at least ten millennia.

The Folsom discovery sparked other major finds of ancient artifacts that continue to this day. Since the 1930s, archaeologists have revolutionized our knowledge about ancient Americans. They have learned a great deal about the Folsom-era hunters who killed giant bison with flint-tipped spears, as well as about their ancestors who first arrived in North America and their descendants who built southwestern pueblos, eastern burial mounds, and much else. Most of the artifacts made by ancient Americans have been lost, destroyed by animals or natural deterioration, or they still lie buried under geological deposits that accumulated for millennia. But by careful study of the rare ancient artifacts that have survived and been discovered, archaeologists have pieced together an account of the long, complex history of ancient Americans. The story is necessarily incomplete and controversial because so much of what we would like to know about ancient Americans is simply unknowable. Evidence that would resolve uncertainties and settle disputes either no longer exists or awaits discovery. But archaeologists have learned enough in the last eighty years to understand where ancient Americans came from and many basic features of the complex **cultures** they created and passed along to their descendants, some of whom stood on the beach of a small island in the Caribbean in 1492 and watched Christopher Columbus and his men row ashore.

Archaeology and History

Archaeologists and historians share the desire to learn about people who lived in the past, but they usually employ different methods to obtain information. Both archaeologists and historians study artifacts as clues to the activities and ideas of the humans who created them. They concentrate, however, on different kinds of artifacts. Archaeologists tend to focus on physical objects such as bones, spear points, pots, baskets, jewelry, textiles, clothing, graves, and buildings. Historians direct their attention mostly to writings, including personal and private jottings such as letters and diary entries, official and public pronouncements such as laws and speeches, and an enormous variety of other documents, such as newspapers, business ledgers, and court cases. Although historians are interested in other artifacts and archaeologists do not neglect written sources if they exist, the characteristic concentration of historians on writings and archaeologists on other physical objects denotes a rough cultural and chronological boundary between the human beings studied by the two groups of scholars, a boundary marked by the use of writing.

Writing is defined as a system of symbols that record spoken language. Writing originated among ancient peoples in China, Egypt, and Central America about 8,000 years ago, within the most recent 2 percent of the 400 millennia that modern human beings (*Homo sapiens*) have existed. Writing came into use even later in most other places in the world. The ancient Americans who inhabited North America in 1492, for example, possessed many forms of symbolic representation, but not writing.

The people who lived during the millennia before writing were biologically nearly identical to us. Their DNA was the template for ours. But unlike us, they did not use writing to communicate across space and time. They invented hundreds of spoken languages; they moved across the face of the globe, learning to survive in almost every natural environment; they chose and honored leaders; they traded, warred, and worshipped; and, above all, they learned from and taught each other. Much of what we would like to know about their experiences remains unknown because it took place before writing existed. The absence of writing forever muffles their words and obscures their history.

Archaeologists specialize in learning about people who did not document their history in writing. They study the millions of artifacts these people created. They also scrutinize soil, geological strata, pollen, climate, and other environmental features to reconstruct as much as possible about the world ancient peoples inhabited. Although no documents chronicle ancient Americans' births and deaths, pleasures and pains, or victories and defeats, archaeologists have learned to make artifacts, along with their natural and human context, tell a great deal about the people who used them.

This chapter relies on studies by archaeologists to sketch a brief overview of ancient America, the long first phase of the history of the United States. Ancient Americans and their descendants resided in North America for thousands of years before Europeans arrived. They did not consider their lives a prelude to a future that included entirely unimaginable creations such as the United States or the twenty-first-century Americans who read this book. For their own reasons and in their own ways, they created societies and cultures of remarkable diversity and complexity. Because they did not use written records, their history cannot be reconstructed with the detail and certainty made possible by writing. But it is better to abbreviate and oversimplify ancient Americans' history than to ignore it.

▶**REVIEW**   Why do historians rely on the work of archaeologists to write the history of ancient America?

The First Americans

The first human beings to arrive in the Western Hemisphere emigrated from Asia. They brought with them hunting skills, weapon- and toolmaking techniques, and a full range of other forms of human knowledge developed millennia earlier in

Africa, Europe, and Asia. These first Americans hunted large mammals, such as the mammoths they had learned in Europe and Asia to kill, butcher, and process for food, clothing, building materials, and many other purposes. Most likely, these first Americans wandered into the Western Hemisphere more or less accidentally, hungry and in pursuit of their prey.

African and Asian Origins

Human beings lived elsewhere in the world for hundreds of thousands of years before they reached the Western Hemisphere. Humans lacked a way to travel to the Western Hemisphere because millions of years before humans existed anywhere on the globe, North and South America became detached from the gigantic common landmass scientists now call Pangaea. About 240 million years ago, powerful forces deep within the earth fractured Pangaea and slowly pushed the continents apart to approximately their present positions (Map 1.1). This process of continental drift encircled the land of the Western Hemisphere with large oceans that isolated it from the other continents, long before early human beings (*Homo erectus*) first appeared in Africa about 2 million years ago. (Hereafter in this chapter, the abbreviation *BP*—archaeologists' notation for "years before the present"—is used to indicate dates earlier than 2,000 years ago. Dates more recent

MAP 1.1   Continental Drift

Massive geological forces separated North and South America from other continents eons before human beings evolved in Africa in the past 1.5 million years.

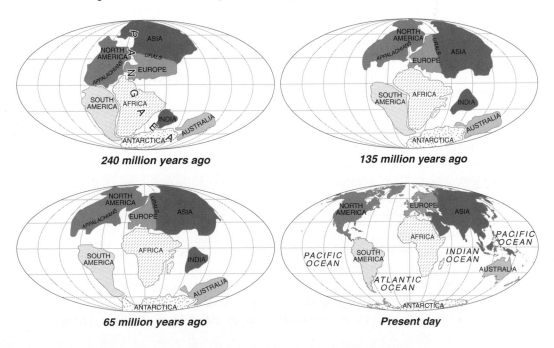

240 million years ago   *135 million years ago*

65 million years ago   *Present day*

than 2,000 years ago are indicated with the common and familiar notation *AD*—for example, AD 1492.)

More than a million and a half years after *Homo erectus* appeared, or about 400,000 BP, modern humans (*Homo sapiens*) evolved in Africa. All human beings throughout the world today are descendants of these ancient Africans. Slowly, over many millennia, *Homo sapiens* migrated out of Africa and into Europe and Asia. Unlike North and South America, Europe and Asia retained land connections to Africa, making this migration possible for *Homo sapiens*. These ancient humans traveled mostly on foot, although sometimes they navigated rivers and lakes in small boats that could not survive battering by the oceans' winds and waves. The enormous oceans isolating North and South America from the Eurasian landmass kept human beings away for roughly 97 percent of the time *Homo sapiens* have been on earth.

Two major developments made it possible for human beings to migrate to the Western Hemisphere. First, humans successfully adapted to the frigid environment near the Arctic Circle. Second, changes in the earth's climate reconnected North America to Asia.

By about 25,000 BP, *Homo sapiens* had spread from Africa throughout Europe and Asia. People, probably women, had learned to use bone needles to sew animal skins into warm clothing that permitted them to become permanent residents of extremely cold regions such as northeastern Siberia. A few of these ancient Siberians clothed in animal hides walked to North America on land that now lies submerged beneath sixty miles of water that currently separates easternmost Siberia from westernmost Alaska. During the last global cold spell—the Wisconsin glaciation, which endured from about 25,000–14,000 BP to 10,000 BP—snow piled up in glaciers, causing the sea level to drop as much as 350 feet below its current level. The falling sea level exposed what experts refer to as a land bridge between Asian Siberia and American Alaska. This land bridge, which scientists call Beringia, opened up a pathway hundreds of miles wide between the Eastern and Western Hemispheres.

Siberian hunters presumably roamed Beringia for centuries in search of game animals. Grasses and small shrubs that covered Beringia supported herds of mammoths, bison, and numerous smaller animals. As the hunters ventured farther and farther east, they eventually became pioneers of human life in the Western Hemisphere. Their migrations probably had very little influence on their own lives, which continued more or less in the age-old ways they had learned from their Siberian ancestors. Although they did not know it, their migrations revolutionized the history of the world.

Archaeologists refer to these first migrants and their descendants for the next few millennia as Paleo-Indians. They speculate that these Siberian hunters traveled in small bands of no more than twenty-five people. How many such bands arrived in North America before Beringia disappeared beneath the sea will never be known. When they came is hotly debated by experts. The first migrants probably arrived sometime after 15,000 BP. Scattered and inconclusive evidence suggests that they may have arrived several thousand years earlier. Certainly, humans who originated in Asia inhabited the Western Hemisphere by 13,500 BP.

Paleo-Indian Hunters

When humans first arrived in the Western Hemisphere, massive glaciers covered most of present-day Canada. A narrow corridor not entirely obstructed by ice ran along the eastern side of Canada's Rocky Mountains, and most archaeologists believe that Paleo-Indians probably migrated through the ice-free passageway in pursuit of game. They may also have traveled along the Pacific coast in small boats, hunting marine life and hopscotching from one desirable landing spot to another. At the southern edge of the glaciers, Paleo-Indians entered a hunters' paradise. North, Central, and South America teemed with wildlife that had never before confronted wily two-legged predators armed with razor-sharp spears. The abundance of game presumably made hunting relatively easy. Ample food permitted the Paleo-Indian population to grow. Within a thousand years or so, Paleo-Indians had migrated to the tip of South America and virtually everywhere else in the Western Hemisphere, as proved by discoveries of their spear points in numerous excavations that followed George McJunkin's Folsom find.

Early Paleo-Indians used a distinctively shaped spearhead known as a Clovis point, named for the place in New Mexico where it was first excavated. Archaeologists' discovery of Clovis points throughout North and Central America in sites occupied between 13,500 BP and 13,000 BP provides evidence that these nomadic hunters shared a common ancestry and way of life. Paleo-Indians hunted mammoths and bison—judging from the artifacts and bones that have survived from this era—but they probably also hunted smaller animals. They also likely scavenged the carcasses of mammoths and other beasts that became mired in the abundant swamps and bogs. Concentration on large animals, when possible, made

Clovis Spear Straightener

Clovis hunters used this bone spear straightener about 11,000 BP at a campsite in Arizona, where archaeologists discovered it lying among the butchered remains of two mammoth carcasses and thirteen ancient bison. Similar objects appear in ancient sites in Eurasia, but this is the only bone artifact discovered in a Clovis-era site in North America. Presumably, Clovis hunters stuck the spear shaft through the opening and then moved the straightener back and forth along the length of the shaft to remove imperfections in the weapon.

Arizona State Museum, University of Arizona.

sense because just one mammoth kill supplied hunters with meat for weeks or, if dried, for months. Some Paleo-Indians even refrigerated mammoth meat for later use by filling the intestines with stones and sinking the carcass to the bottom of an icy lake. In addition to food, mammoth kills provided hides and bones for clothing, shelter, tools, and much more.

About 11,000 BP, Paleo-Indians confronted a major crisis. The mammoths and other large mammals they hunted became extinct. The extinction was gradual, stretching over several hundred years. Scientists are not completely certain why it occurred, although environmental change probably contributed to it. About this time, the earth's climate warmed, glaciers melted, and sea levels rose. Mammoths and other large mammals probably had difficulty adapting to the warmer climate. Many archaeologists also believe, however, that Paleo-Indians probably contributed to the extinctions in the Western Hemisphere by killing large animals more rapidly than they could reproduce. Although this overkill hypothesis is disputed by some experts, similar environmental changes had occurred for millions of years without triggering the large mammal extinctions that followed the arrival of Paleo-Indian hunters. Whatever the causes, Paleo-Indian hunters faced a radical change in the natural environment within just a few thousand years of their arrival in the Western Hemisphere—namely, the extinction of large mammals that had existed for millions of years and whose presence had initially drawn Siberian hunters east across Beringia. After the extinction, Paleo-Indians literally inhabited a new world.

Paleo-Indians adapted to the drastic environmental change of the big-game extinction by making at least two important changes in their way of life. First, hunters began to prey more intensively on smaller animals. Second, Paleo-Indians devoted more energy to foraging—that is, to collecting wild plant foods such as roots, seeds, nuts, berries, and fruits. When Paleo-Indians made these changes, they replaced the apparent uniformity of the big-game-oriented Clovis culture with great cultural diversity. This diversity arose because ancient Americans adapted to the many natural environments throughout the hemisphere, ranging from icy tundra to steamy jungles.

Post-Clovis adaptations to local environments resulted in the astounding variety of Native American cultures that existed when Europeans arrived in AD 1492. By then, more than three hundred major tribes and hundreds of lesser groups inhabited North America alone. Hundreds more lived in Central and South America. These peoples spoke different languages, practiced different religions, lived in different dwellings, followed different subsistence strategies, and observed different rules of kinship and inheritance. Hundreds of other ancient American cultures had disappeared or transformed themselves as their people constantly adapted to environmental change and other challenges.

►REVIEW   Why were humans able to migrate into North America after 15,000 BP?

Archaic Hunters and Gatherers

Archaeologists use the term **Archaic** to describe both the many different hunting and gathering cultures that descended from Paleo-Indians and the long period of time when those cultures dominated the history of ancient America, roughly from 10,000 BP to somewhere between 4000 BP and 3000 BP. The term usefully describes the era in the history of ancient America that followed the Paleo-Indian big-game hunters and preceded the development of agriculture. It denotes a hunter-gatherer way of life that persisted in North America long after European colonization.

Like their Paleo-Indian ancestors, Archaic Indians hunted with spears; but they also took smaller game with traps, nets, and hooks. Unlike their Paleo-Indian predecessors, most Archaic peoples used a variety of stone tools to prepare food from wild plants. A characteristic Archaic artifact is a grinding stone used to pulverize seeds into edible form. Most Archaic Indians migrated from place to place to harvest plants and hunt animals. They usually did not establish permanent villages, although they often returned to the same river valley or fertile meadow from year to year. In certain regions with especially rich resources—such as present-day California and the Pacific Northwest—they developed permanent settlements. Many groups became highly proficient basket makers in order to collect and store plant food. But the food they harvested came from wild plants and animals, rather than from agriculture. Archaic peoples followed these practices in distinctive ways in the different environmental regions of North America.

Great Plains Bison Hunters

After the extinction of large game animals, some hunters began to concentrate on bison in the huge herds that grazed the grassy, arid plains stretching for hundreds of miles east of the Rocky Mountains. For almost a thousand years after the big-game extinctions, Archaic Indians hunted bison with Folsom points like those found at the site discovered by George McJunkin.

Like their nomadic predecessors, Folsom hunters moved constantly to maintain contact with their prey. Often two or three hunters from a band of several families would single out a few bison from a herd and creep up close enough to spear them. Great Plains hunters also developed trapping techniques that made it easier to kill large numbers of animals. At the original Folsom site, careful study of the bones McJunkin found suggests that early one winter hunters drove bison into the narrow gulch and speared twenty-three of them. At other sites, Great Plains hunters stampeded bison herds over cliffs, then slaughtered the animals that plunged to their deaths.

Bows and arrows reached Great Plains hunters from the north about AD 500. They largely replaced spears, which had been the hunters' weapons of choice for millennia. Bows permitted hunters to wound an animal from farther away, arrows made it possible to shoot repeatedly, and arrowheads were easier to make and therefore less costly to lose than the larger, heavier spear points. But these new weapons did not otherwise alter age-old techniques of bison hunting on the Great Plains. Although we tend to imagine ancient Great Plains bison hunters on horseback, in fact they hunted on foot, like their Paleo-Indian ancestors. Horses that had existed in North America millions of years earlier had long since become extinct. Horses did not return to the Great Plains until Europeans imported them in the decades after 1492. Native American bison hunters acquired them soon thereafter and quickly became expert riders.

Great Basin Cultures

Archaic peoples in the Great Basin between the Rocky Mountains and the Sierra Nevada inhabited a region of great environmental diversity. Some Great Basin Indians lived along the shores of large marshes and lakes that formed during rainy periods. They ate fish of every available size and type, catching them with bone hooks and nets. Other cultures survived in the foothills of mountains between the blistering heat on the desert floor and the cold, treeless mountain heights. Hunters killed deer, antelope, and sometimes bison, as well as smaller game such as rabbits, rodents, and snakes. These broadly defined zones of habitation changed constantly, depending largely on the amount of rain.

Despite the variety and occasional abundance of animals, Great Basin peoples relied on plants for their most important food source. Unlike meat and fish, plant food could be collected and stored for long periods to protect against shortages caused by the fickle rainfall. Many Great Basin peoples gathered ample supplies of piñon nuts as a dietary staple. By diversifying their food sources and migrating to favorable locations to collect and store them, Great Basin peoples adapted to the severe environmental challenges of the region and maintained their Archaic hunter-gatherer way of life for centuries after Europeans arrived in AD 1492.

Pacific Coast Cultures

The richness of the natural environment made present-day California the most densely settled area in all of ancient North America. The land and ocean offered such ample food that California peoples remained hunters and gatherers for hundreds of years after AD 1492. The diversity of California's environment also encouraged corresponding diversity among native peoples. The mosaic of Archaic settlements in California included about five hundred separate tribes speaking some ninety languages, each with local dialects. No other region of comparable size in North America exhibited such cultural variety.

The Chumash, one of the many California cultures, emerged in the region surrounding what is now Santa Barbara about 5000 BP. Comparatively plentiful food

Chumash Necklace

Long before the arrival of Europeans, ancient Chumash people in southern California made this elegant necklace of abalone shell. The carefully formed, polished, and assembled pieces of shell illustrate the artistry of the Chumash and their access to the rich and diverse marine life of the Pacific coast.

Natural History Museum of Los Angeles County.

resources—especially acorns—permitted Chumash people to establish relatively permanent villages. Conflict, evidently caused by competition for valuable acorn-gathering territory, frequently broke out among the villages, as documented by Chumash skeletons that display signs of violent deaths. Although few other California cultures achieved the population density and village settlements of the Chumash, all shared the hunter-gatherer way of life and reliance on acorns as a major food source.

Another rich natural environment lay along the Pacific Northwest coast. Like the Chumash, Northwest peoples built more or less permanent villages. After about 5500 BP, they concentrated on catching whales and large quantities of salmon, halibut, and other fish, which they dried to last throughout the year. They also traded with people who lived hundreds of miles from the coast. Fishing freed Northwest peoples to develop sophisticated woodworking skills. They fashioned elaborate wood carvings that denoted wealth and status, as well as huge canoes for fishing, hunting, and conducting warfare against neighboring tribes. Much of the warfare among Archaic northwesterners grew out of attempts to defend or gain access to prime fishing sites.

Eastern Woodland Cultures

East of the Mississippi River, Archaic peoples adapted to a forest environment that included many local variants, such as the major river valleys of the Mississippi, Ohio, Tennessee, and Cumberland; the Great Lakes region; and the Atlantic coast. Throughout these diverse locales, Archaic peoples followed similar survival strategies.

Woodland hunters stalked deer as their most important prey. Deer supplied Woodland peoples with food as well as hides and bones that they crafted into clothing, weapons, needles, and many other tools. Like Archaic peoples elsewhere, Woodland Indians gathered edible plants, seeds, and nuts, especially hickory nuts, pecans, walnuts, and acorns. About 6000 BP, some Woodland groups established more or less permanent settlements of 25 to 150 people, usually near a river or lake that offered a wide variety of plant and animal resources. The existence of such settlements has permitted archaeologists to locate numerous Archaic burial sites that suggest Woodland people had a life expectancy of about eighteen years. Imagine what such a short life expectancy (by modern standards) meant for Archaic Woodland people who needed to learn all the skills necessary to survive, reproduce, and adapt to change.

Around 4000 BP, Woodland cultures added two important features to their basic hunter-gatherer lifestyles: agriculture and pottery. Gourds and pumpkins that were first cultivated thousands of years earlier in Mexico spread north to Woodland peoples through trade and migration. Woodland peoples also began to cultivate local species such as sunflowers, as well as small quantities of tobacco, another import from South America. Corn was the most important plant food carried to North America by traders and migrants from Mexico, and it became a significant Woodland food crop around 2500 BP. Most likely, women learned how to plant, grow, and harvest these crops as an outgrowth of their work gathering edible wild plants. Cultivated crops added to the quantity, variety, and predictability of Woodland food sources, but they did not alter Woodland peoples' dependence on gathering wild plants, seeds, and nuts.

Like agriculture, pottery also probably originated in Mexico. Traders and migrants probably brought pots into North America along with Central and South American seeds. Pots were more durable than baskets for cooking and storage of food and water, but they were also much heavier, and therefore were shunned by nomadic peoples. The permanent settlements of Woodland peoples made the heavy weight of pots much less important than their advantages compared to leaky and fragile baskets. While pottery and agriculture introduced changes in Woodland cultures, ancient Woodland Americans retained the other basic features of their Archaic hunter-gatherer lifestyle, which persisted in most areas to 1492 and beyond.

▶REVIEW   Why did Archaic Native Americans shift from big-game hunting to foraging and smaller-game hunting?

Agricultural Settlements and Chiefdoms

Among Eastern Woodland peoples and most other Archaic cultures, agriculture supplemented, but did not replace, hunter-gatherer subsistence strategies. Reliance on wild animals and plants required most Archaic groups to remain small and mobile. But beginning about 4000 BP, distinctive southwestern cultures slowly began to depend on agriculture and to build permanent settlements. Later, around 2500 BP, Woodland peoples in the vast Mississippi valley began to

Ancient Agriculture
Dropping seeds into holes punched in cleared ground by a pointed stick, this ancient American sows a new crop while previously planted seeds—including the corn and beans immediately opposite him—bear fruit for harvest. Created by a sixteenth-century European artist, the drawing misrepresents who did the agricultural work in many ancient American cultures—namely, women rather than men.
The Pierpont Morgan Library/Art Resource, NY.

construct burial mounds and other earthworks that suggest the existence of social and political hierarchies that archaeologists term chiefdoms. Although the hunter-gatherer lifestyle never entirely disappeared, the development of agricultural settlements and chiefdoms represented important innovations to the Archaic way of life.

Southwestern Cultures

Ancient Americans in present-day Arizona, New Mexico, and southern portions of Utah and Colorado developed cultures characterized by agriculture and multi-unit dwellings called pueblos. All southwestern peoples confronted the challenge of a dry climate and unpredictable fluctuations in rainfall that made the supply of wild plant food very unreliable. These ancient Americans probably adopted agriculture in response to this basic environmental condition.

About 3500 BP, southwestern hunters and gatherers began to cultivate corn, their signature food crop. Corn had been grown in Central and South America since about 7000 BP, and it slowly traveled up to North America with migrants and traders. In the centuries after 3500 BP, corn eventually became the most important cultivated crop for ancient Americans throughout North America. In the Southwest, the demands of corn cultivation encouraged hunter-gatherers to restrict their migratory habits in order to tend the crop. A vital consideration was access to water. Southwestern Indians became irrigation experts, conserving water from streams, springs, and rainfall and distributing it to thirsty crops.

About AD 200, small farming settlements began to appear throughout southern New Mexico, marking the emergence of the Mogollon culture. Typically, a Mogollon settlement included a dozen pit houses, made by digging out a rounded pit about fifteen feet in diameter and a foot or two deep and then erecting poles to support a roof of branches or dirt. Larger villages usually had one or two bigger pit houses that may have been the predecessors of the circular *kivas*, the ceremonial rooms that became a characteristic of nearly all southwestern settlements. About AD 900, Mogollon culture began to decline, for reasons that remain obscure. Its descendants included the Mimbres people in southwestern New Mexico, who crafted spectacular pottery adorned with human and animal designs. By about AD 1250, the Mimbres culture disappeared, for reasons unknown.

Around AD 500, while the Mogollon culture prevailed in New Mexico, other ancient people migrated from Mexico to southern Arizona and established the distinctive Hohokam culture. Hohokam settlements used sophisticated grids of irrigation canals to plant and harvest crops twice a year. Hohokam settlements reflected the continuing influence of Mexican cultural practices that migrants brought with them as they traveled north. Hohokam people built sizable platform mounds and ball courts characteristic of many Mexican cultures. About AD 1400, Hohokam culture declined for reasons that remain a mystery, although the rising salinity of the soil caused by centuries of irrigation probably caused declining crop yields and growing food shortages.

North of the Hohokam and Mogollon cultures, in a region that encompassed southern Utah and Colorado and northern Arizona and New Mexico, the Anasazi culture began to flourish about AD 100. The early Anasazi built pit houses on mesa tops and used irrigation much like their neighbors to the south. Beginning around AD 1000 (again, it is not known why), some Anasazi began to move to large, multistory cliff dwellings whose spectacular ruins still exist at Mesa Verde, Colorado, and elsewhere. Other Anasazi communities—like the one whose impressive ruins can be visited at Chaco Canyon, New Mexico—erected huge, stone-walled pueblos with enough rooms to house everyone in the settlement. Pueblo Bonito at Chaco Canyon, for example, contained more than eight hundred rooms. Anasazi pueblos and cliff dwellings typically included one or more kivas used for secret ceremonies, restricted to men, that sought to communicate with the supernatural world. The alignment of buildings at Chaco with solar and lunar events (such as the spring and winter solstices) suggests that the site may have been a ceremonial center similar to sites in Mexican cultures to the south that symbolized the connections between earth and the heavens, between human beings and supernatural celestial powers.

Drought began to plague the region about AD 1130, and it lasted for more than half a century, triggering the disappearance of Anasazi culture. By AD 1200, the large Anasazi pueblos had been abandoned. The prolonged drought probably intensified conflict among pueblos and made it impossible to depend on the techniques of irrigated agriculture that had worked for centuries. Some Anasazi migrated toward regions with more reliable rainfall and settled in Hopi, Zuñi, and Acoma pueblos that their descendants in Arizona and New Mexico have occupied ever since.

Woodland Burial Mounds and Chiefdoms

No other ancient Americans created dwellings similar to pueblos, but around 2500 BP, Woodland cultures throughout the vast area drained by the Mississippi River began to build burial mounds. The size of the mounds, the labor and organization required to erect them, and differences in the artifacts buried with certain individuals suggest the existence of a social and political hierarchy that archaeologists term a chiefdom. Experts do not know the name of a single chief, nor do they know the organizational structure a chief headed. But the only way archaeologists can account for the complex and labor-intensive burial mounds and artifacts found in them is to assume that one person—whom scholars term a chief—commanded the labor and obedience of very large numbers of other people, who made up the chief's chiefdom.

Between 2500 BP and 2100 BP, Adena people built hundreds of burial mounds radiating from central Ohio. In the mounds, the Adena usually accompanied burials with grave goods that included spear points and stone pipes as well as thin sheets of mica (a glasslike mineral) crafted into shapes of birds, beasts, and human hands. Over the body and grave goods Adena people piled dirt into a mound. Sometimes burial mounds were constructed all at once, but often they were built up slowly over many years.

About 2100 BP, Adena culture evolved into the more elaborate Hopewell culture, which lasted about 500 years. Centered in Ohio, Hopewell culture extended throughout the enormous drainage of the Ohio and Mississippi rivers. Hopewell people built larger mounds than their Adena predecessors and filled them with more magnificent grave goods.

Burial was probably reserved for the most important members of Hopewell groups. Most people were cremated. Burial rituals appear to have brought many people together to honor the dead person and to help build the mound. Hopewell mounds were often one hundred feet in diameter and thirty feet high. Skeletons excavated from one mound suggest the high status of hunters; men in important graves showed signs of stress to the elbow joint caused by repetitive spear-throwing. Grave goods at Hopewell sites testify to the high quality of Hopewell crafts and to a thriving trade network that ranged from Wyoming to Florida. Archaeologists believe that Hopewell chiefs probably played an important role in this sprawling interregional trade.

Hopewell culture declined about AD 400 for reasons that are obscure. Archaeologists speculate that bows and arrows, along with increasing reliance on agriculture, made small settlements more self-sufficient and, therefore, less dependent on the central authority of the Hopewell chiefs who were responsible for the burial mounds.

Four hundred years later, another mound-building culture flourished. The Mississippian culture emerged in the floodplains of the major southeastern river systems about AD 800 and lasted until about AD 1500. Major Mississippian sites included huge mounds with platforms on top for ceremonies and for the residences of great chiefs. Most likely, the ceremonial mounds and ritual practices derived from Mexican cultural expressions that were carried north by traders and migrants. The largest Mississippian site was Cahokia, whose remnants can be seen in Illinois near the confluence of the Mississippi and Missouri rivers.

At Cahokia, more than one hundred mounds were grouped around large open plazas. Monk's Mound, the largest, covered sixteen acres at its base and was one hundred feet tall. Dwellings may have housed as many as thirty thousand inhabitants, easily qualifying Cahokia as the largest settlement in ancient North America. At Cahokia and other Mississippian sites, people evidently worshipped a sun god; the mounds probably elevated elites nearer to the sun's supernatural power. One Cahokia burial mound suggests the authority a great chief exercised. One man—presumably the chief—was buried with the bodies of more than sixty people who had been killed at the time of burial, including fifty young women who had been strangled. Such a mass sacrifice illustrates the coercive power of a Cahokia chief.

Cahokia and other Mississippian cultures dwindled by AD 1500. When Europeans arrived, most of the descendants of Mississippian cultures, like those of the Hopewell culture, lived in small dispersed villages supported by hunting and gathering supplemented by agriculture. Clearly, the conditions that caused large chiefdoms to emerge—whatever they were—had changed, and chiefs no longer commanded the sweeping powers they had once enjoyed.

►REVIEW   How did the availability of food influence the distribution of Native American population across the continent?

Native Americans in the 1490s

About thirteen millennia after Paleo-Indians first migrated to the Western Hemisphere, a new migration—this time from Europe—began in 1492 with the journey of Christopher Columbus. In the decades before 1492, Native Americans continued to employ their ancestors' time-tested survival strategies of hunting, gathering, and agriculture. Those strategies succeeded in both populating and shaping the new world Europeans encountered.

By the 1490s, Native Americans lived throughout North America, but their total population is a subject of spirited debate among scholars. Some experts claim Native Americans numbered 18 million to 20 million, while others place the population at no more than a million. A prudent estimate is about 4 million. On the eve of European colonization, the small island nation of England had about the same number of people as all of North America. The vastness of North America meant the population density was low, just 60 people per hundred square miles, compared to more than 8,000 in England. Compared to England and elsewhere in Europe, Native Americans were spread thin across the land because of their survival strategies of hunting, gathering, and agriculture.

Regions in North America with abundant resources had relatively high population. About one-fifth of Native Americans lived along the West Coast in food-rich California and the Pacific Northwest, where the population density was, respectively, six times greater and four times greater than the average for the whole continent. The food-scarce vastness of the Great Plains, Great Basin, and Arctic regions held about one-quarter of Native Americans, but the population density was extremely low, roughly one-tenth the continental average. About a quarter of Native Americans resided in the arid Southwest, where irrigation and intensive agriculture permitted a population density about twice the continental average. But even in California, the most densely inhabited region of North America, population density was just one-twentieth of England's.

The enormous Woodland region east of the Mississippi River was home to about one-third of Native Americans, whose population density approximated the continental average. Eastern Woodland peoples clustered into three broad linguistic and cultural groups: Algonquian, Iroquoian, and Muskogean.

Algonquian tribes inhabited the Atlantic seaboard, the Great Lakes region, and much of the upper Midwest (Map 1.2, page 18). The relatively mild climate along the Atlantic permitted the coastal Algonquians to grow corn and other crops as well as to hunt and fish. Around the Great Lakes and in northern New England, however, cool summers and severe winters made agriculture impractical. Instead, the Abenaki, Penobscot, Chippewa, and other tribes concentrated on hunting and fishing, using canoes both for transportation and for gathering wild rice.

Inland from the Algonquian region, Iroquoian tribes occupied territories centered in Pennsylvania and upstate New York, as well as the hilly upland regions

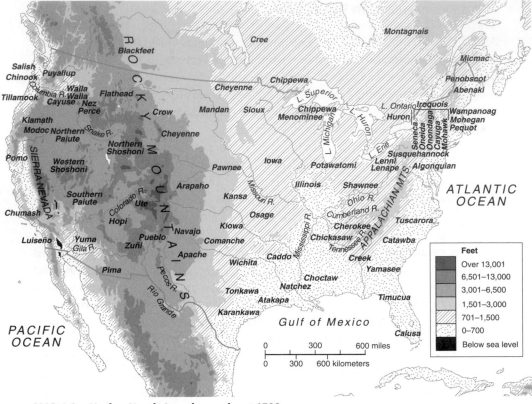

MAP 1.2   Native North Americans about 1500
Distinctive Native American peoples resided throughout the area that, centuries later, would become the United States. This map indicates the approximate location of some of the larger tribes about 1500. In the interest of legibility, many other peoples who inhabited North America at the time are omitted from the map.

of the Carolinas and Georgia. Three features distinguished Iroquoian tribes from their neighbors. First, their success in cultivating corn and other crops allowed them to build permanent settlements, usually consisting of several bark-covered longhouses up to one hundred feet long and housing five to ten families. Second, Iroquoian societies adhered to matrilineal rules of descent. Property of all sorts belonged to women. Women headed family clans and even selected the chiefs (normally men) who governed the tribes. Third, for purposes of war and diplomacy, an Iroquoian confederation—including the Seneca, Onondaga, Mohawk, Oneida, and Cayuga tribes—formed the League of Five Nations, which remained powerful well into the eighteenth century.

Muskogean peoples spread throughout the woodlands of the Southeast, south of the Ohio River and east of the Mississippi. Including the Creek, Choctaw,

Chickasaw, and Natchez tribes, Muskogeans inhabited a bountiful natural environment that provided abundant food from hunting, gathering, and agriculture. Remnants of the earlier Mississippian culture still existed in Muskogean religion. The Natchez, for example, worshipped the sun and built temple mounds modeled after those of their Mississippian ancestors.

Great Plains peoples accounted for about one out of seven Native Americans. Inhabiting the huge region west of the Eastern Woodland people and east of the Rocky Mountains, many tribes had migrated to the Great Plains within the past century or two, forced westward by Iroquoian and Algonquian tribes. Some Great Plains tribes—especially the Mandan and Pawnee—farmed successfully, growing both corn and sunflowers. But the Teton Sioux, Blackfeet, Comanche, Cheyenne, and Crow on the northern plains and the Apache and other nomadic tribes on the southern plains depended on buffalo (American bison) for their subsistence.

Southwestern cultures included about a quarter of all native North Americans. These descendants of the Mogollon, Hohokam, and Anasazi cultures lived in settled agricultural communities, many of them pueblos. They continued to grow corn, beans, and squash using methods they had refined for centuries. However, their communities came under attack by a large number of warlike Athapascan tribes who invaded the Southwest beginning around AD 1300. The Athapascans—principally Apache and Navajo—were skillful warriors who preyed on the sedentary pueblo Indians, reaping the fruits of agriculture without the work of farming.

About a fifth of all native North Americans resided along the Pacific coast. In California, abundant acorns and nutritious marine life continued to support high population densities, but they retarded the development of agriculture. Similar dependence on hunting and gathering persisted along the Northwest coast, where fishing reigned supreme. Salmon was so abundant that at The Dalles, a prime fishing site on the Columbia River on the border of present-day Oregon and Washington, Northwest peoples caught millions of pounds of salmon every summer and traded it as far away as California and the Great Plains. Although important trading centers existed throughout North America, particularly in the Southwest, it is likely that The Dalles was the largest Native American trading center in North America.

While trading was common, all native North Americans in the 1490s still depended on hunting and gathering for a major portion of their food. Most of them also practiced agriculture. Some used agriculture to supplement hunting and gathering; for others, the balance was reversed. People throughout North America used bows, arrows, and other weapons for hunting and warfare. None of them employed writing, expressing themselves instead in many other ways: drawings sketched on stones, wood, and animal skins; patterns woven in baskets and textiles; designs painted on pottery, crafted into beadwork, or carved into effigies; and songs, dances, religious ceremonies, and burial rites.

These rich and varied cultural resources of Native Americans did not include features of life common in Europe during the 1490s. Native Americans did not use wheels; sailing ships were unknown to them; they had no large domesticated animals such as horses, cows, or oxen; their use of metals was restricted to copper. However, the absence of these European conveniences mattered less to native North Americans than their own cultural adaptations to the natural environment local to each tribe and to the social environment among neighboring peoples. That great similarity—adaptation to natural and social environments—underlay all the cultural diversity among native North Americans.

It would be a mistake, however, to conclude that native North Americans lived in blissful harmony with nature and each other. Archaeological sites provide ample evidence of violent conflict among Native Americans. Skeletons bear the marks of wounds as well as of ritualistic human sacrifice and even cannibalism. Religious, ethnic, economic, and familial conflicts must have occurred, but they remain in obscurity because they left few archaeological traces. In general, fear and anxiety must have been at least as common among Native Americans as feelings of peace and security.

Native Americans not only adapted to the natural environment; they also changed it in many ways. They built thousands of structures, from small dwellings to massive pueblos and enormous mounds, permanently altering the landscape. Their gathering techniques selected productive and nutritious varieties of plants, thereby shifting the balance of local plants toward useful varieties. The first stages of North American agriculture, for example, probably resulted from Native Americans gathering wild seeds and then sowing them in a meadow for later harvest. It is almost certain that fertile and hardy varieties of corn were developed in this way, first in Mexico and later in North America. To clear land for planting corn, Native Americans set fires that burned off thousands of acres of forest.

Native Americans also used fires for hunting. Great Plains hunters often started fires to force buffalo together and make them easy to slaughter. Eastern Woodland, Southwest, and Pacific coast Indians also set fires to hunt deer and other valuable prey. Hunters crouched downwind from a brushy area while their companions set a fire upwind; as animals raced out of the burning underbrush, hunters killed them. Throughout North America, Indians started fires along the edges of woods to burn off shrubby undergrowth and encroaching tree seedlings. These burns encouraged the growth of tender young plants that attracted deer and other game animals, bringing them within convenient range of hunters' weapons. The burns also encouraged the growth of sun-loving food plants that Indians relished, such as blackberries, strawberries, and raspberries.

Because fires set by Native Americans usually burned until they ran out of fuel or were extinguished by rain or wind, enormous regions of North America were burned over. In the long run, fires created and maintained light-dappled meadows for hunting and agriculture, cleared entangling underbrush from forests, and promoted a diverse and productive natural environment. Fires, like other activities of Native Americans, shaped the landscape of North America long before Europeans arrived in 1492.

> ▶REVIEW   Why did some Native Americans set fire to the land?

The Mexica: A Meso-American Culture

The indigenous population of the New World (the Western Hemisphere) numbered roughly 80 million in the 1490s, about the same as the population of Europe. Almost all these people lived in Mexico and Central and South America. Like their much less numerous North American counterparts, they too lived in a natural environment of tremendous diversity. They too developed hundreds of cultures, far too numerous to catalog here. But among all these cultures, the Mexica stood out. (Europeans often called these people Aztecs, a name the Mexica did not use.) Their empire stretched from coast to coast across central Mexico, encompassing between 8 million and 25 million people (experts disagree about the total population). We know more about the Mexica than about any other Native American society of the time, principally because of their massive monuments and their Spanish conquerors' well-documented interest in subduing them. Their significance in the history of the New World after 1492 dictates a brief discussion of their culture and society.

The Mexica began their rise to prominence about 1325, when small bands settled on a marshy island in Lake Texcoco, the site of the future city of Tenochtitlán, the capital of the Mexican empire. Resourceful, courageous, and cold-blooded warriors, the Mexica often hired out as mercenaries for richer, more settled tribes. By 1430, the Mexica succeeded in asserting their dominance over their former allies and leading their own military campaigns in an ever-widening arc of empire building. Despite pockets of resistance, by the 1490s the Mexica ruled an empire that covered more land than Spain and Portugal combined and contained almost three times as many people.

The empire exemplified the central values of Mexican society. The Mexica worshipped the war god Huitzilopochtli. Warriors held the most exalted positions in the Mexican social hierarchy, even above the priests who performed the sacred ceremonies that won Huitzilopochtli's favor. In the almost constant battles necessary to defend and to extend the empire, young Mexican men exhibited the courage and daring that would allow them to rise in the carefully graduated ranks of warriors. The Mexica considered capturing prisoners the ultimate act of bravery. Warriors usually turned over the captives to Mexican priests, who sacrificed them to Huitzilopochtli by cutting out their hearts. The Mexica believed that human sacrifice fed the sun's craving for blood, which kept the sun aflame and prevented the fatal descent of everlasting darkness and chaos.

The empire contributed far more to Mexican society than victims for sacrifice. At the most basic level, the empire functioned as a military and political system that collected tribute from subject peoples. The Mexica forced conquered tribes to pay tribute in goods, not money. Tribute redistributed to the Mexica as much as one-third of the goods produced by conquered tribes. It included everything from candidates for human sacrifice to textiles and basic food products such as corn and beans, as well as exotic luxury items such as gold, turquoise, and rare bird feathers.

Tribute reflected the fundamental relations of power and wealth that pervaded the Mexican empire. The relatively small nobility of Mexican warriors, supported by a still smaller priesthood, possessed the military and religious power to

---

Mexican Human Sacrifice

This graphic portrait of human sacrifice was drawn by a Mexican artist in the sixteenth century. It shows the typical routine of human sacrifice practiced by the Mexica. The victim was stretched over a stone pillar, and a priest plunged a stone knife into the victim's chest, cut out the still-beating heart, and offered it to the gods. The Mexica believed that the gory ritual would help them obtain favors from supernatural powers.

Scala/Art Resource, NY; Biblioteca Nazionale, Florence, Italy.

command the obedience of thousands of non-noble Mexicans and of millions of other non-Mexicans in subjugated provinces. The Mexican elite exercised their power to obtain tribute and thereby to redistribute wealth from the conquered to the conquerors, from the commoners to the nobility, from the poor to the rich. This redistribution of wealth made possible the achievements of Mexican society that eventually amazed the Spaniards: the huge cities, fabulous temples, teeming markets, and luxuriant gardens, not to mention the storehouses stuffed with gold and other treasures.

On the whole, the Mexica did not interfere much with the internal government of conquered regions. Instead, they usually permitted the traditional ruling elite to stay in power—so long as they paid tribute. The conquered provinces received very little in return from the Mexica, except immunity from punitive raids. Subjugated communities felt exploited by the constant payment of tribute to the Mexica. By depending on military conquest and constant collection of tribute, the Mexica failed to create among their subjects a belief that Mexican domination was, at some level, legitimate and equitable. The high level of discontent among subject peoples constituted the soft, vulnerable underbelly of the Mexican empire, a fact Spanish intruders exploited after AD 1492 to conquer the Mexica.

▶**REVIEW**   How did the payment of tribute influence the Mexican empire?

Conclusion: The World of Ancient Americans

Ancient Americans shaped the history of human beings in the New World for more than twelve thousand years. They established continuous human habitation in the Western Hemisphere from the time the first big-game hunters crossed Beringia until 1492 and beyond. Much of their history remains irretrievably lost because they relied on oral rather than written communication. But much can be pieced together from artifacts they left behind, like the Folsom points among the bones discovered by George McJunkin. Ancient Americans achieved their success through resourceful adaptation to the hemisphere's many and ever-changing natural environments. They also adapted to social and cultural changes caused by human beings—such as marriages, deaths, political struggles, and warfare—but the sparse evidence that has survived renders those adaptations almost entirely unknowable. Their creativity and artistry are unmistakably documented in the artifacts they left at kill sites, camps, and burial mounds. Those artifacts sketch the only likenesses of ancient Americans we will ever have—blurred, shadowy images that are indisputably human but forever silent.

In the five centuries after 1492—just 4 percent of the time human beings have inhabited the Western Hemisphere—Europeans and their descendants began to shape and eventually to dominate American history. Native American peoples continued to influence major developments of American history for centuries after 1492. But the new wave of strangers that at first trickled and then flooded into the New World from Europe and Africa forever transformed the peoples and places of ancient America.

REVIEWING THE CHAPTER

Use the questions and timeline to review and strengthen your understanding of the chapter.

REVIEW QUESTIONS

1. Why do historians rely on the work of archaeologists to write the history of ancient America? (pp. 3–4)

2. Why were humans able to migrate into North America after 15,000 BP? (pp. 4–8)

3. Why did Archaic Native Americans shift from big-game hunting to foraging and smaller-game hunting? (pp. 9–12)

4. How did the availability of food influence the distribution of the Native American population across the continent? (pp. 12–16)

5. Why did some Native Americans set fire to the land? (pp. 17–21)

6. How did the payment of tribute influence the Mexican empire? (pp. 21–23)

MAKING CONNECTIONS

1. Explain the different approaches historians and archaeologists bring to studying people in the past. How do the different sources they draw on shape their accounts of the human past? In your answer, cite specific examples from the history of ancient America.

2. Discuss Native Americans' strategies for surviving in the varied climates of North America. How did their different approaches to survival contribute to the diversity of Native American cultures?

3. For more than twelve thousand years, Native Americans both adapted to environmental change in North America and produced significant changes in the environments around them. Discuss specific examples of Native Americans' adaptation to environmental change and the changes they caused in the North American landscape.

4. Rich archaeological and manuscript sources have enabled historians to develop a detailed portrait of the Mexica on the eve of European contact. How did the Mexica establish and maintain their expansive empire?

TIMELINE

c. 400,000 BP*	• Modern humans (*Homo sapiens*) evolve in Africa.	**c. 2500 BP**	• Eastern Woodland cultures start to build burial mounds.
c. 75,000–45,000 BP and c. 25,000–14,000 BP	• Wisconsin glaciation exposes Beringia, land bridge between Siberia and Alaska.		• Some Eastern Woodland peoples begin to cultivate corn.
		c. 2500–2100 BP	• Adena culture develops in Ohio.
c. 15,000 BP	• First humans arrive in North America.	**c. 2100 BP–AD 400**	• Hopewell culture emerges in Ohio and Mississippi valleys.
c. 13,500–13,000 BP	• Paleo-Indians in North and Central America use Clovis points to hunt big game.	**c. AD 200–900**	• Mogollon culture develops in New Mexico.
c. 11,000 BP	• Mammoths and many other big-game prey of Paleo-Indians become extinct.	**c. AD 500**	• Bows and arrows appear in North America south of Arctic.
		c. AD 500–1400	• Hohokam culture develops in Arizona.
c. 10,000–3000 BP	• Archaic hunter-gatherer cultures dominate ancient America.	**c. AD 800–1500**	• Mississippian culture flourishes in Southeast.
c. 7000 BP	• Corn cultivation begins in Central and South America.	**c. AD 1000–1200**	• Anasazi peoples build cliff dwellings at Mesa Verde and pueblos at Chaco Canyon.
c. 4000 BP	• Some Eastern Woodland peoples grow gourds and pumpkins and begin making pottery.	**c. AD 1325–1500**	• Mexica conquer neighboring peoples and establish Mexican empire.
c. 3500 BP	• Southwestern cultures begin corn cultivation.	**AD 1492**	• Christopher Columbus arrives in New World, beginning European colonization.

▶ **For an online bibliography, practice quizzes, Web sites, images, and documents related to this chapter,** see the Book Companion Site at **bedfordstmartins.com/roark.**

▶ **For firsthand accounts of this period,** see Chapter 1 in Michael Johnson, ed., *Reading the American Past,* Fourth Edition.

---

*BP is an abbreviation used by archaeologists for "years before the present."

2

CHAPTER

Europeans Encounter the New World

1492–1600

TWO BABIES WERE BORN in southern Europe in 1451, separated by about seven hundred miles and a chasm of social, economic, and political power. The baby girl, Isabella, was born in a king's castle in what is now Spain. The baby boy, Christopher, was born in the humble dwelling of a weaver near Genoa in what is now Italy. Forty-one years later, the lives and aspirations of these two people intersected in southern Spain and permanently changed the history of the world.

Isabella was named for her mother, the Portuguese second wife of King John II of Castile, whose monarchy encompassed the large central region of present-day Spain. Isabella grew up amid the swirling countercurrents of dynastic rivalries and political conflict. Her father died when she was three, and her half-brother, Henry, assumed the throne. Henry proved an ineffective ruler who made many enemies among the nobility and the clergy. When Isabella was fourteen, Henry's rivals launched a campaign to overthrow him and replace him with her brother, Alfonso.

By then, Isabella had received an excellent education from private tutors who were bishops in the Catholic Church. Her learning helped her become a strong, resolute woman whom Henry tried to control by bringing her to his court, where he could watch her. When Alfonso died in 1468, Henry's enemies shifted their support to Isabella, and the king plotted to undermine her independence by arranging her marriage to one of several eligible sons of European monarchs.

Isabella refused to accept Henry's choices for her husband and likewise refused to cooperate with Henry's enemies by rebelling and seeking to overthrow him. Instead, she maneuvered to obtain Henry's consent that she would succeed him as monarch, and then she selected Ferdinand, a man she had never met, to be her husband. A year younger than Isabella, Ferdinand was the king of Aragon, a region encompassing a triangular slice of northeastern Spain bordering France and the Mediterranean Sea. The couple married in 1469, and Isabella became queen when Henry died in 1474.

As monarchs, Isabella and Ferdinand fought to defeat other claimants to Isabella's throne, to unite the monarchies of Spain under their rule, to complete the long campaign (known as the Reconquest) to eliminate Muslim strongholds on the Iberian Peninsula, and to purify Christianity. A pious woman, Isabella encouraged the creation of the Inquisition in 1478 to identify and punish heretics, especially Jewish converts. Catholic Church officials believed that many of these converts were "false Christians" who openly embraced Christianity but secretly remained faithful to Judaism.

In the intense, decades-long campaign to defend Christianity, persecute Jews, and defeat the Muslims, Isabella and Ferdinand traveled throughout their realm, staying a month or two in one place after another, meeting local notables, hearing appeals and complaints, and impressing all with their regal splendor.

Spanish Tapestry
This detail from a sixteenth-century tapestry depicts Columbus (kneeling) receiving a box of jewels from Queen Isabella (her husband, King Ferdinand, stands slightly behind her) in appreciation for his voyages to the New World. These gifts and others signified the monarchs' elation about the immense promise of the lands and peoples that Columbus encountered.
© Julio Conoso/Corbis Sygma.

Equally at home on horseback and on the throne, Isabella enjoyed the trappings of royal luxury. Her large entourage, for example, often included a choir of twenty-five or more singers. Although Isabella understood the importance of displaying the magnificence of her royal court, she was a serious, sober ruler who supported the circulation of knowledge in the newfangled technology of print. She read Latin and had a personal library of some four hundred books, a rarity among fifteenth-century monarchs.

Tagging along in the royal cavalcade of mounted lancers, bishops, advisers, clerks, servants, and assorted hangers-on that moved around Spain in 1485 was Christopher Columbus, a deeply religious man obsessed with obtaining support for his scheme to sail west across the Atlantic Ocean to reach China and Japan. An experienced sailor, Columbus became convinced that it was possible to reach the riches of the East by sailing west. Columbus pitched his idea to the king of Portugal in 1484. The king's geography experts declared Columbus's proposal impossible: The globe was too big, the ocean between Europe and China was too wide, and no sailors or ships could possibly withstand such a long voyage.

Rejected in Portugal, Columbus made his way to the court of Isabella and Ferdinand in 1485 and joined their entourage until he finally won an audience with the monarchs in January 1486. They too rejected his plan. Columbus returned to Portugal and once again tried to interest the Portuguese king, without success. Doggedly, he went back to Spain in 1489 and managed to meet privately with Isabella, who told him to see her again as soon as her army had captured the last major Muslim stronghold at Granada. When Granada surrendered early in 1492, Isabella and Ferdinand once again asked their experts to consider Columbus's plan, and again they rejected it. But Isabella soon changed her mind. In hopes of expanding the wealth and influence of the monarchy, she summoned Columbus and in mid-April 1492 agreed to support his risky scheme.

Columbus hurriedly organized his expedition, and just before sunrise on August 3, 1492, three ships under his command caught the tide out of a harbor in southern Spain and sailed west. Barely two months later, in the predawn moon-light of October 12, 1492, Columbus glimpsed an island on the western horizon. At daybreak, he rowed ashore, and as the curious islanders crowded around, he claimed possession of the land for Isabella and Ferdinand of Spain.

Columbus's encounters in 1492 with Isabella and those islanders trans-formed the history of the world and unexpectedly made Spain the most impor-tant European power in the Western Hemisphere for more than a century. Long before 1492, other Europeans had restlessly expanded the limits of the world known to them, and their efforts helped make possible Columbus's voyage. But without Isabella's sponsorship, it is doubtful that Columbus could have made his voyage. With her support and his own unflagging determination, Columbus blazed a watery trail to a world that neither he nor anyone else in Europe knew existed. As Isabella, Ferdinand, and subsequent Spanish monarchs sought to reap the rewards of what they considered their emerging empire in the West, they created a distinctively Spanish colonial society that conquered and killed Native Americans, built new institutions, and extracted great wealth that enriched the Spanish monarchy and made Spain the envy of other Europeans.

Europe in the Age of Exploration

Historically, the East—not the West—attracted Europeans. Around the year 1000, Norsemen ventured west across the North Atlantic and founded a small fishing village at L'Anse aux Meadows on the tip of Newfoundland that lasted only a decade or so. After the world's climate cooled, choking the North Atlantic with ice, the Norse left. Viking sagas memorialized the Norse "discovery," but it had virtually no other impact in the New World or in Europe. Instead, wealthy Europeans developed a taste for luxury goods from Asia and Africa, and merchants competed to satisfy that taste. As Europeans traded with the East and with one another, they acquired new information about the world they inhabited. A few people—sailors, merchants, and aristocrats—took the risks of exploring beyond the limits of the world known to Europeans. Those risks were genuine and could be deadly. But sometimes they paid off in new information, in new opportunities, and eventually in the discovery of a world entirely new to Europeans.

Mediterranean Trade and European Expansion

From the twelfth through the fifteenth centuries, spices, silk, carpets, ivory, gold, and other exotic goods traveled overland from Persia, Asia Minor, India, and Africa and then were funneled into continental Europe through Mediterranean trade routes. Dominated primarily by the Italian cities of Venice, Genoa, and Pisa, this lucrative trade enriched Italian merchants and bankers, who fiercely defended their near **monopoly** of access to Eastern goods. The vitality of the Mediterranean trade offered few incentives to look for alternatives. New routes to the East and the discovery of new lands were the stuff of fantasy.

Preconditions for turning fantasy into reality developed in fifteenth-century Europe. In the mid-fourteenth century, Europeans suffered a catastrophic epidemic of bubonic plague. The Black Death, as it was called, killed about a third of the European population. This devastating pestilence had major long-term consequences. By drastically reducing the population, it made Europe's limited supply of food more plentiful for survivors. Many survivors inherited property from plague victims, giving them new chances for advancement. The turmoil caused by the plague also prompted many peasants to move away from their homes and seek opportunities elsewhere.

Understandably, most Europeans perceived the world as a place of alarming risks where the delicate balance of health, harvests, and peace could quickly be tipped toward disaster by epidemics, famine, and violence. Most people protected themselves from the constant threat of calamity by worshipping the supernatural, by living amid kinfolk and friends, and by maintaining good relations with the rich and powerful. But the insecurity and uncertainty of fifteenth-century European life also encouraged a few people to take greater risks, such as embarking on dangerous sea voyages through uncharted waters to points unknown.

Exploration promised fame and fortune in European societies to those who succeeded, whether they were kings or commoners. Monarchs such as Isabella who hoped to enlarge their realms and enrich their dynasties also had reasons to sponsor journeys of exploration. More territory meant more subjects who could pay more taxes, provide more soldiers, and participate in more commerce, magnifying the monarch's power and prestige. Voyages of exploration also could stabilize the monarch's regime by diverting unruly noblemen toward distant lands. Some explorers, such as Columbus, were commoners who hoped to be elevated to the aristocracy as a reward for their daring achievements.

Scientific and technological advances also helped set the stage for exploration. The invention of movable type by Johannes Gutenberg around 1450 in Germany made printing easier and cheaper, stimulating the diffusion of information, including news of discoveries, among literate Europeans. By 1400, crucial navigational aids employed by maritime explorers such as Columbus were already available: compasses; hourglasses, which allowed for the calculation of elapsed time, useful in estimating speed; and the astrolabe and quadrant, which were devices for determining latitude. Detailed sailing maps called *portulanos* illustrated shoreline topography and also noted compass headings for sailing from one port to another. Many people throughout fifteenth-century Europe knew about these and other technological advances. The Portuguese were the first to use them in a campaign to sail beyond the limits of the world known to Europeans.

A Century of Portuguese Exploration

Portugal had less than 2 percent of the population of Christian Europe, but it devoted far more energy and wealth to the geographical exploration of the world between 1415 and 1460 than all the other countries of Europe combined. Facing the Atlantic on the Iberian Peninsula, the Portuguese lived on the fringes of the thriving Mediterranean trade. As a Christian kingdom, Portugal cooperated with Spain in the Reconquest, the centuries-long drive to expel the Muslims from the Iberian Peninsula. The religious zeal that propelled the Reconquest also justified expansion into what the Portuguese considered heathen lands. A key victory came in 1415 when Portuguese forces conquered Ceuta, the Muslim bastion at the mouth of the Strait of Gibraltar that had blocked Portugal's access to the Atlantic coast of Africa.

The most influential advocate of Portuguese exploration was Prince Henry the Navigator, son of the Portuguese king (and great-uncle of Queen Isabella of Spain). From 1415 until his death in 1460, Henry collected the latest information about sailing techniques and geography, supported new crusades against the Muslims, encouraged fresh sources of trade to fatten Portuguese pocketbooks, and pushed explorers to go farther still. Both the Portuguese king and the Christian pope supported Henry's efforts to extend the Reconquest down the African coast. African expeditions also promised to wrest wheat fields from their Moroccan owners and to obtain gold, the currency of European trade. Gold was scarce in Europe because the quickening pace of commerce increased the need for currency while purchases in the East drained gold away from European markets.

Neither the Portuguese nor anybody else in Europe knew the immensity of Africa or the length or shape of its coastline, which, in reality, fronted the Atlantic for more than seven thousand miles—about five times the considerable distance from Genoa, Columbus's hometown, to Lisbon, the Portuguese capital. At first, Portuguese mariners cautiously hugged the west coast of Africa, seldom venturing beyond sight of land. By 1434, they had reached the northern edge of the Sahara Desert, where strong westerly currents swept them out to sea. They soon learned to ride those currents far away from the coast before catching favorable winds that turned them back toward land, a technique that allowed them to reach Cape Verde by 1444. To stow the supplies necessary for long periods at sea and to withstand the battering of waves in the open ocean, the Portuguese developed the caravel, a sturdy ship that became explorers' vessel of choice. In caravels, Portuguese mariners sailed into and around the Gulf of Guinea and as far south as the Congo by 1480.

Fierce African resistance confined Portuguese expeditions to coastal trading posts, where they bartered successfully for gold, slaves, and ivory. Powerful African kingdoms welcomed Portuguese trading ships loaded with iron goods, weapons, textiles, and ornamental shells. Portuguese merchants learned that establishing relatively peaceful trading posts on the coast was far more profitable than attempting the violent conquest and **colonization** of inland regions. In the 1460s, the Portuguese used African slaves to develop sugar plantations on the Cape Verde Islands, inaugurating an association between enslaved Africans and plantation labor that would be transplanted to the New World in the centuries to come.

About 1480, Portuguese explorers began a conscious search for a sea route to Asia. In 1488, Bartolomeu Dias sailed around the Cape of Good Hope at the southern tip of Africa and hurried back to Lisbon with the exciting news that it appeared to be possible to sail on to India and China. In 1498, after ten years of careful preparation, Vasco da Gama commanded the first Portuguese fleet to sail to India. Portugal quickly capitalized on the commercial potential of da Gama's new sea route. By the early sixteenth century, the Portuguese controlled a farflung commercial empire in India, Indonesia, and China (collectively referred to as the East Indies). Their new sea route to the East eliminated overland travel and allowed Portuguese merchants to charge much lower prices for the Eastern goods they imported and still make handsome profits.

Portugal's African explorations during the fifteenth century broke the monopoly of the old Mediterranean trade with the East, dramatically expanded the world known to Europeans, established a network of Portuguese outposts in Africa and Asia, and developed methods of sailing the high seas that Columbus employed on his revolutionary voyage west.

> ▶ **REVIEW**   Why did European exploration expand dramatically in the fifteenth century?

A Surprising New World in the Western Atlantic

In retrospect, the Portuguese seemed ideally qualified to venture across the Atlantic. They had pioneered the **frontiers** of seafaring, exploration, and geography for almost a century. However, Portuguese and most other experts believed that sailing west across the Atlantic to Asia was literally impossible. The European discovery of America required someone bold enough to believe that the experts were wrong and the risks were surmountable. That person was Christopher Columbus. His explorations inaugurated a geographical revolution that forever altered Europeans' understanding of the world and its peoples, including themselves. Columbus's landfall in the Caribbean originated a thriving exchange between the people, ideas, **cultures**, and institutions of the Old and New Worlds that continues to this day.

The Explorations of Columbus

Columbus went to sea when he was about fourteen, and he eventually made his way to Lisbon, where he married Felipa Moniz. Felipa's father had been raised in the household of Prince Henry the Navigator, and her family retained close ties to the prince. Through Felipa, Columbus gained access to explorers' maps and papers crammed with information about the tricky currents and winds encountered in sailing the Atlantic. Columbus himself ventured into the Atlantic frequently and at least twice sailed to the central coast of Africa.

Like other educated Europeans, Columbus believed that the earth was a sphere and that theoretically it was possible to reach the East Indies by sailing west. With flawed calculations, he estimated that Asia was only about 2,500 miles from the westernmost boundary of the known world, a shorter distance than Portuguese ships routinely sailed between Lisbon and the Congo. In fact, the shortest distance to Japan from Europe's jumping-off point was nearly 11,000 miles. Convinced by his erroneous calculations, Columbus became obsessed with a scheme to prove he was right.

In 1492, after years of unsuccessful lobbying in Portugal and Spain, plus overtures to England and France, Columbus finally won financing for his journey from the Spanish monarchs, Isabella and Ferdinand. They saw Columbus's venture as an inexpensive gamble: The potential loss was small, but the potential gain was huge. They gave Columbus a letter of introduction to China's Grand Khan, the ruler they hoped he would meet on the other side of the Atlantic.

After scarcely three months of frantic preparation, Columbus and his small fleet—the *Niña* and *Pinta*, both caravels, and the *Santa María*, a larger merchant vessel—headed west. Six weeks after leaving the Canary Islands, where he stopped for supplies, Columbus landed on a tiny Caribbean island about three hundred miles north of the eastern tip of Cuba.

Columbus claimed possession of the island for Isabella and Ferdinand and named it San Salvador, in honor of the Savior, Jesus Christ. He called the islanders "Indians," assuming that they inhabited the East Indies somewhere near Japan or China. The islanders called themselves Tainos, which in their language means "good" or "noble." The Tainos inhabited most of the Caribbean islands Columbus visited on his first voyage, as had their ancestors for more than two centuries. An agricultural people, the Tainos grew cassava, corn, cotton, tobacco, and other crops. Instead of dressing in the finery Columbus had expected to find in the East Indies, the Tainos "all . . . go around as naked as their mothers bore them," Columbus wrote. Although Columbus concluded that the Tainos "had no religion," in reality they worshipped gods they called *zemis*, ancestral spirits who inhabited natural objects such as trees and stones. The Tainos mined a little gold, but they had no riches. "It seemed to me that they were a people very poor in everything," Columbus wrote.

What the Tainos thought about Columbus and his sailors we can only surmise, since they left no written documents. At first, Columbus got the impression that the Tainos believed the Spaniards came from heaven. But after six weeks of encounters, Columbus decided that "the people of these lands do not understand me nor do I, nor anyone else that I have with me, [understand] them. And many times I understand one thing said by these Indians . . . for another, its contrary." The confused communication between the Spaniards and the Tainos suggests how strange each group seemed to the other. Columbus's perceptions of the Tainos were shaped by European attitudes, ideas, and expectations, just as the Tainos' perceptions of the Europeans were no doubt colored by their own culture.

Columbus and his men understood that they had made a momentous discovery, but they found it frustrating. Although the Tainos proved friendly, they did not have the riches Columbus expected to find in the East. For three months, Columbus cruised from island to island, looking for the king of Japan and the Grand Khan of China. In mid-January 1493, he started back to Spain, taking seven Tainos with him. Queen Isabella and King Ferdinand were overjoyed by his news. With a voyage that had lasted barely eight months, Columbus appeared to have catapulted Spain from the position of an also-ran in the race for a sea route to Asia into that of a serious challenger to Portugal, whose explorers had not yet sailed to India or China. Columbus and his Taino companions became the toast of

MAP 2.1   European Exploration in Sixteenth-Century America

This map illustrates the approximate routes of early European explorations of the New World.

the royal court. The Spanish monarchs elevated Columbus to the nobility and awarded him the title "Admiral of the Ocean Sea." The seven Tainos were baptized as Christians, and King Ferdinand became their godfather.

Soon after Columbus returned to Spain, the Spanish monarchs rushed to obtain the pope's support for their claim to the new lands in the West. When the pope, a Spaniard, complied, the Portuguese feared their own claims to recently discovered territories were in jeopardy. To protect their claims, the Portuguese and Spanish monarchs negotiated the Treaty of Tordesillas in 1494. The treaty drew an imaginary line eleven hundred miles west of the Canary Islands (Map 2.1). Land discovered west of the line (namely, the islands that Columbus discovered and any additional land that might be located) belonged to Spain; Portugal claimed land to the east (namely, its African and East Indian trading empire).

Isabella and Ferdinand moved quickly to realize the promise of their new claims. In the fall of 1493, they dispatched Columbus once again, this time with a fleet of seventeen ships and more than a thousand men who planned to locate the Asian mainland, find gold, and get rich. When Columbus returned to the island where he had left behind thirty-nine of his sailors because of a shipwreck near the end of his first voyage, he received disturbing news. In Columbus's absence, his sailors had terrorized the Tainos, kidnapping and sexually abusing their women. In retaliation, the Taino chiefs had killed all the sailors. This small episode prefigured much of what was to happen in encounters between Native Americans and Europeans in the years ahead.

Before Columbus died in 1506, he returned to the New World two more times (in 1498 and 1502) without relinquishing his belief that the East Indies were there, someplace. Other explorers continued to search for a passage to the East or some other source of profit. Before long, however, prospects of beating the Portuguese to Asia began to dim along with the hope of finding vast hoards of gold. Nonetheless, Columbus's discoveries forced sixteenth-century Europeans to think about the world in new ways. He proved that it was possible to sail from Europe to the western rim of the Atlantic and return to Europe. Most important, Columbus made clear that beyond the western shores of the Atlantic lay lands entirely unknown to Europeans.

The Geographic Revolution and the Columbian Exchange

Within thirty years of Columbus's initial discovery, Europeans' understanding of world geography underwent a revolution. An elite of perhaps twenty thousand people with access to Europe's royal courts and trading centers learned the exciting news about global geography. But it took a generation of additional exploration before they could comprehend the larger contours of Columbus's discoveries.

European monarchs hurried to stake their claims to the newly discovered lands. In 1497, King Henry VII of England, who had spurned Columbus a decade earlier, sent John Cabot to look for a "Northwest Passage" to the Indies across the North Atlantic (see Map 2.1). Cabot reached the tip of Newfoundland, which he believed was part of Asia, and hurried back to England, where he assembled a small fleet and sailed west again in 1498. But he was never heard from again. Three thousand miles to the south, a Spanish expedition landed on the northern coast of South America in 1499 accompanied by Amerigo Vespucci, an Italian businessman. In 1500, Pedro Álvars Cabral commanded a Portuguese fleet bound for the Indian Ocean that accidentally made landfall on the coast of Brazil as it looped westward into the Atlantic.

By 1500, European experts knew that several large chunks of land cluttered the western Atlantic. A few cartographers speculated that these chunks were connected to one another in a landmass that was not Asia. In 1507, Martin Waldseemüller, a German cartographer, published the first map that showed the New World separate from Asia; he named the land America, in honor of Amerigo Vespucci.

Two additional discoveries confirmed Waldseemüller's speculation. In 1513, Vasco Núñez de Balboa crossed the Isthmus of Panama and reached the Pacific Ocean. Clearly, more water lay between the New World and Asia. How much water Ferdinand Magellan discovered when he led an expedition to circumnavigate the globe in 1519. Sponsored by King Charles I of Spain, Magellan's voyage took him first to the New World, around the southern tip of South America, and into the Pacific late in November 1520. Crossing the Pacific took almost four months. By the time he reached the Philippines, his crew had been decimated by extreme hunger and thirst. Magellan himself was killed by Philippine tribesmen. A remnant of his expedition continued on to the Indian Ocean and managed to transport a cargo of spices back to Spain in 1522.

In most ways, Magellan's voyage was a disaster. One ship and 18 men crawled back from an expedition that had begun with five ships and more than 250 men. But the geographic information it provided left no doubt that America was a continent separated from Asia by the enormous Pacific Ocean. Magellan's voyage made clear that Columbus was dead wrong about the identity of what he had discovered. It was possible to sail west to reach the East Indies, but that was a terrible way to go. After Magellan, most Europeans who sailed west set their sights on the New World, not on Asia.

Columbus's arrival in the Caribbean anchored the western end of what might be imagined as a sea bridge that spanned the Atlantic, connecting the Western Hemisphere to Europe. Somewhat like the Beringian land bridge traversed by the first Americans millennia earlier, the new sea bridge reestablished a connection between the Eastern and Western Hemispheres. The Atlantic Ocean, which had previously isolated America from Europe, became an aquatic highway, thanks to sailing technology, intrepid seamen, and their European sponsors. This new sea bridge launched the **Columbian exchange**, a transatlantic trade of goods, people, and ideas that has continued ever since.

Spaniards brought novelties to the New World that were commonplace in Europe, including Christianity, iron technology, sailing ships, firearms, wheeled vehicles, horses and other domesticated animals, and much else. Unknowingly, they also smuggled along many Old World microorganisms that caused devastating epidemics of smallpox, measles, and other diseases that would kill the vast majority of Indians during the sixteenth century and continue to decimate survivors in later centuries. European diseases made the Columbian exchange catastrophic for Native Americans. In the long term, these diseases were decisive in transforming the dominant peoples of the New World from descendants of Asians, who had inhabited the hemisphere for millennia, to descendants of Europeans and Africans, the recent arrivals from the Old World by way of the newly formed sea bridge.

Ancient American goods, people, and ideas made the return trip across the Atlantic. Europeans were introduced to New World foods such as corn and potatoes that became important staples in European diets, especially for poor people. Columbus's sailors became infected with syphilis in sexual encounters with New World women and then unwittingly carried the deadly parasite back to Europe, where it may already have had a foothold.

Columbian Exchange
The arrival of Columbus in the New World started an ongoing transatlantic exchange of goods, people, and ideas. The Spaniards brought domesticated animals from the Old World, including horses, cattle, goats, chickens, cats, and sheep. The Spaniards also brought items such as cannons, guitars, and microorganisms that caused devastating epidemics of smallpox, measles, and other diseases. Ancient American people, goods, and ideas made the return trip across the Atlantic, introducing items such as corn and smoking tobacco, like the cigar puffed by an ancient Mayan lord.
Collection of Dr. Francis Robicsek.

New World tobacco created a European fashion for smoking that ignited quickly and has yet to be extinguished. But for almost a generation after 1492, this Columbian exchange did not reward the Spaniards with the riches they yearned to find.

▶ **REVIEW**   How did Columbus's landfall in the Caribbean help revolutionize Europeans' understanding of world geography?

Spanish Exploration and Conquest

During the sixteenth century, the New World helped Spain become the most powerful monarchy in both Europe and the Americas. Initially, Spanish expeditions reconnoitered the Caribbean, scouted stretches of the Atlantic coast, and established settlements on the large islands of Hispaniola, Puerto Rico, Jamaica, and Cuba. Spaniards enslaved Caribbean tribes and put them to work growing crops and mining gold. But the profits from these early ventures barely covered the costs of maintaining the settlers. After almost thirty years of exploration, the promise of Columbus's discovery seemed illusory.

In 1519, however, that promise was fulfilled, spectacularly, by Hernán Cortés's march into Mexico. By about 1545, Spanish conquests extended from northern Mexico to southern Chile, and New World riches filled Spanish treasure chests. Cortés's expedition served as the model for Spaniards' and other Europeans' expectations that the New World could yield bonanza profits for its conquerors.

The Conquest of Mexico

Hernán Cortés, who became the richest and most famous conquistador (conqueror), arrived in the New World in 1504, an obscure nineteen-year-old Spaniard seeking adventure and the chance to make a name for himself. He fought in the conquest of Cuba and elsewhere in the Caribbean. In 1519, the governor of Cuba authorized Cortés to organize an expedition to investigate rumors of a fabulously wealthy kingdom somewhere in the interior of the mainland. A charming, charismatic leader, Cortés quickly assembled a force of about six hundred men, loaded his ragtag army aboard eleven ships, and set out.

Cortés's confidence that he could talk his way out of most situations and fight his way out of the rest fortified the small band of Spaniards. But Cortés could not speak any Native American language. Landing first on the Yucatán peninsula, he had the good fortune to receive a gift from a chief of the Tobasco people. Among about twenty other women given to Cortés was a fourteen-year-old girl named Malinali, who spoke several native languages, including Mayan and Nahuatl, the language of the Mexica, the most powerful people in what is now Mexico and Central America (see chapter 1). Malinali had acquired her linguistic fluency painfully. Born into a family of the Mexican nobility, she learned Nahuatl as a young child. After her father died and her mother remarried and had a son, Malinali's stepfather sold her as a slave to Mayan-speaking Indians, who subsequently gave the slave girl to the Tobascans. Malinali, whom the Spaniards called Marina, soon learned Spanish and became Cortés's interpreter. She also became one of Cortés's several mistresses and bore him a son. (Several years later, after Cortés's wife arrived in New Spain, Cortés cast Marina aside, and she married one of his soldiers.) Although no word uttered by Marina survives in historical documents, her words were the Spaniards' essential conduit of communication with the Indians. "Without her help," wrote one of the Spaniards who accompanied Cortés, "we would not have understood the language of New Spain and Mexico." With her help, Cortés talked and fought with Indians along the Gulf coast of Mexico, trying to discover the location of the fabled kingdom. By the time Marina died at age twenty-four, the people she had grown up among—the people who had taught her languages, enslaved her, and given her to Cortés—had been conquered by the Spaniards with her help.

In the capital of the Mexican empire, Tenochtitlán, the emperor Montezuma heard rumors about some strange creatures sighted along the coast. (Montezuma and his people are often called Aztecs, but they called themselves Mexica.) He feared that the strangers were led by the god Quetzalcoatl, returning to Tenochtitlán as predicted by the Mexican religion. Montezuma sent representatives to meet with the strangers and bring them gifts fit for gods. Marina had told Cortés about Quetzalcoatl, and when Montezuma's messengers arrived, Cortés donned the regalia they had brought, almost certain proof to the Mexica that he was indeed the god they feared. The Spaniards astounded the messengers by blasting their cannons and displaying their swords.

The messengers hurried back to Montezuma with their amazing news. The emperor arranged for large quantities of food to be sent to the coast to welcome the strangers and perhaps to postpone Quetzalcoatl's dreaded arrival in the capital. Before the Mexican messengers served food to the Spaniards, they sacrificed several hostages and soaked the food in their blood. This fare disgusted the Spaniards and might have been enough to turn them back to Cuba. But along with the food, the Mexica also brought the Spaniards another gift, a "disk in the shape of a sun, as big as a cartwheel and made of very fine gold," as one of the Mexica recalled. Here was conclusive evidence that the rumors of fabulous riches heard by Cortés had some basis in fact.

In August 1519, Cortés marched inland to find Montezuma. Leading about 350 men armed with swords, lances, and muskets and supported by ten cannons, four smaller guns, and sixteen horses, Cortés had to live off the land, establishing peaceful relations with indigenous tribes when he could and killing them when he thought necessary. On November 8, 1519, Cortés reached Tenochtitlán. Montezuma came out to welcome the Spaniards. After presenting Cortés with gifts, Montezuma ushered the Spaniards to the royal palace and showered them with lavish hospitality. Quickly, Cortés took Montezuma hostage and held him under house arrest, hoping to make him a puppet through which the Spaniards could rule the Mexican empire. This uneasy peace existed for several months until one of Cortés's men led a brutal massacre of many Mexican nobles, causing the people of Tenochtitlán to revolt. They murdered Montezuma, who seemed to them a Spanish puppet, and they mounted a ferocious assault on the Spaniards. On June 30, 1520, Cortés and about a hundred other Spaniards fought their way out of Tenochtitlán and retreated about one hundred miles to Tlaxcala, a stronghold of bitter enemies of the Mexica. The friendly Tlaxcalans—who had long resented Mexican power—allowed Cortés to regroup, obtain reinforcements, and plan a strategy to conquer Tenochtitlán.

In the spring of 1521, Cortés mounted a complex campaign against the Mexican capital. The Spaniards and tens of thousands of Indian allies laid siege to the city. With a relentless, scorched-earth strategy, Cortés finally defeated the last Mexican defenders on August 13, 1521. The great capital of the Mexican empire "looked as if it had been ploughed up," one of Cortés's soldiers remembered. A few years later, one of the Mexica lamented:

> Broken spears lie in the roads;
> we have torn our hair in grief.
> The houses are roofless now, and their walls
> are red with blood. . . .
> We have pounded our hands in despair
> against the adobe walls,
> for our inheritance, our city, is lost and dead.

The Search for Other Mexicos

Lured by their insatiable appetite for gold, conquistadors quickly fanned out from Tenochtitlán in search of other sources of treasure. The most spectacular prize fell to Francisco Pizarro, who conquered the Incan empire in Peru. The Incas controlled a vast, complex region that contained more than nine million people and stretched along the western coast of South America for more than two thousand miles. In 1532, Pizarro and his army of fewer than two hundred men captured the Incan emperor Atahualpa and held him hostage. As ransom, the Incas gave Pizarro the largest treasure yet produced by the conquests: gold and silver equivalent to half a century's worth of precious-metal production in Europe. With the ransom safely in their hands, the Spaniards executed Atahualpa. The Incan treasure proved that at least one other Mexico did indeed exist, and it spurred the search for others.

Juan Ponce de León had sailed along the Florida coast in 1513. Encouraged by Cortés's success, he went back to Florida in 1521 to find riches, only to be killed in battle with Calusa Indians. A few years later, Lucas Vázquez de Ayllón explored the Atlantic coast north of Florida to present-day South Carolina. In

1526, he established a small settlement on the Georgia coast that he named San Miguel de Gualdape, the first Spanish attempt to establish a foothold in what is now the United States. This settlement was soon swept away by sickness and hostile Indians. Pánfilo de Narváez surveyed the Gulf coast from Florida to Texas in 1528. The Narváez expedition ended disastrously with a shipwreck on the Texas coast near present-day Galveston.

In 1539, Hernando de Soto, a seasoned conquistador who had taken part in the conquest of Peru, set out with nine ships and more than six hundred men to find another Peru in North America. Landing in Florida, de Soto literally slashed his way through much of southeastern North America for three years, searching for the rich, majestic civilizations he believed were there. After the brutal slaughter of many Native Americans and much hardship, de Soto died in 1542. His men buried him in the Mississippi River before turning back to Mexico, disappointed.

Tales of the fabulous wealth of the mythical Seven Cities of Cíbola also lured Francisco Vásquez de Coronado to search the Southwest and Great Plains of North America. In 1540, Coronado left northern Mexico with more than three hundred Spaniards, a thousand Indians, fifteen hundred horses, and a priest who claimed to know the way to what he called "the greatest and best of the discoveries." Cíbola turned out to be a small Zuñi pueblo of about a hundred families. When the Zuñi shot arrows at the Spaniards, Coronado attacked the pueblo and routed the defenders after a hard battle. Convinced that the rich cities must lie somewhere over the horizon, Coronado

Zuñi Defend Pueblo against Coronado
This sixteenth-century drawing by a Mexican artist shows Zuñi bowmen fighting back against the arrows of Coronado's men and the entreaties of Christian missionaries. Intended to document the support some Mexican Indians gave to Spanish efforts to extend the conquest into North America, the drawing depicts the Zuñi defender at the bottom of the pueblo aiming his arrow at a Mexican missionary armed only with a crucifix, a rosary, and a book (presumably the Bible).
Hunterian Museum Library, University of Glasgow. Glasgow University Library, Department of Special Collections.

kept moving all the way to central Kansas before deciding in 1542 that the rumors he had pursued were just that.

Juan Rodríguez Cabrillo led a maritime expedition in 1542 that sailed along the coast of California. Cabrillo died on Santa Catalina Island, offshore from present-day Los Angeles, but his men sailed on to Oregon, where a ferocious storm forced them to turn back toward Mexico.

These probes into North America by de Soto, Coronado, and Cabrillo persuaded other Spaniards that although enormous territories stretched northward, their inhabitants had little to loot or exploit. After a generation of vigorous exploration, the Spaniards concluded that there was only one Mexico and one Peru.

New Spain in the Sixteenth Century

For all practical purposes, Spain was the dominant European power in the Western Hemisphere during the sixteenth century (Map 2.2). Portugal claimed the giant territory of Brazil under the Tordesillas treaty but was far more concerned with exploiting its hard-won trade with the East Indies than in colonizing the New World. England and France were absorbed by domestic and diplomatic concerns in Europe and largely lost interest in America until late in the century. In the decades after 1519, the Spaniards created the distinctive colonial society of New Spain that showed other Europeans how the New World could be made to serve the purposes of the Old.

The Spanish monarchy claimed ownership of most of the land in the Western Hemisphere and gave the conquistadors permission to explore and plunder. The crown took one-fifth, called the "royal fifth," of any loot confiscated and allowed the conquerors to divide the rest. In the end, most conquistadors received very little after the plunder was divided among leaders such as Cortés and his favorite officers. To compensate his disappointed, battle-hardened soldiers, Cortés gave them towns the Spaniards had subdued.

The distribution of conquered towns institutionalized the system of *encomienda*, which empowered the conquistadors to rule the Indians and the lands in and around their towns. The concept of encomienda was familiar to the Spaniards, who had used it to govern regions recaptured from the Muslims during the Reconquest. In New Spain, encomienda transferred to the Spanish *encomendero* (the man who "owned" the town) the tribute that the town had previously paid to the Mexican empire.

In theory, encomienda involved a reciprocal relationship between the encomendero and "his" Indians. In return for the tribute and labor of the Indians, the encomendero was supposed to be responsible for their material well-being, to guarantee order and justice in the town, and to encourage the Indians to convert to Christianity. Catholic missionaries labored earnestly to convert the Indians to Christianity. Missionaries fervently believed that God expected them to save the Indians' souls by convincing them to abandon their old, sinful beliefs and to

MAP 2.2　New Spain in the Sixteenth Century
Spanish control spread throughout Central and South America during the sixteenth century, with the important exception of Portuguese Brazil. North America, though claimed by Spain under the Treaty of Tordesillas, remained peripheral to Spain's New World empire.

embrace the one true Christian faith. After baptizing tens of thousands of Indians, the missionaries learned that many Indians continued to worship their own gods along with the Christian God. Most friars came to believe that the Indians were lesser beings inherently incapable of fully understanding the Christian faith.

In practice, encomenderos were far more interested in what the Indians could do for them than in what they or the missionaries could do for the Indians. Encomenderos subjected the Indians to chronic overwork, mistreatment, and abuse. As one Spaniard remarked, "Everything [the Indians] do is slowly done and by compulsion. They are malicious, lying, [and] thievish." Economically, however, encomienda recognized a fundamental reality of New Spain: The most important treasure the Spaniards could plunder from the New World was not gold but uncompensated Indian labor. To exploit that labor, New Spain's richest natural resource, encomienda gave encomenderos the right to force Indians to work when, where, and how the Spaniards pleased.

Encomienda engendered two groups of influential critics. A few of the missionaries were horrified at the brutal mistreatment of the Indians. The cruelty of the encomenderos made it difficult for priests to persuade the Indians of the tender mercies of the Spaniards' God. "What will [the Indians] think about the God of the Christians," Fray Bartolomé de Las Casas asked, when they see their friends "with their heads split, their hands amputated, their intestines torn open? . . . Would they want to come to Christ's sheepfold after their homes had been destroyed, their children imprisoned, their wives raped, their cities devastated, their maidens deflowered, and their provinces laid waste?" Las Casas and other outspoken missionaries softened few hearts among the encomenderos, but they did win some sympathy for the Indians from the Spanish monarchy and royal bureaucracy. Royal officials interpreted encomenderos' brutal treatment of the Indians as part of the larger general problem of the troublesome autonomy of encomenderos. The Spanish monarchy moved to abolish encomienda in an effort to replace swashbuckling old conquistadors with royal bureaucrats as the rulers of New Spain.

One of the most important blows to encomienda was the imposition in 1549 of a reform called the *repartimiento*, which limited the labor an encomendero could command from his Indians to forty-five days per year from each adult male. The repartimiento, however, did not challenge the principle of forced labor, nor did it prevent encomenderos from continuing to cheat, mistreat, and overwork their Indians. Slowly, as the old encomenderos died, repartimiento replaced encomienda as the basic system of exploiting Indian labor.

The practice of coerced labor in New Spain grew directly out of the Spaniards' assumption that they were superior to the Indians. As one missionary put it, the Indians "are incapable of learning. . . . The Indians are more stupid than asses and refuse to improve in anything." Therefore, most Spaniards assumed, Indians' labor should be organized by and for their conquerors. The Spaniards seldom hesitated to use violence to punish and intimidate recalcitrant Indians.

From the viewpoint of Spain, the single most important economic activity in New Spain after 1540 was silver mining. Spain imported more New World gold than silver in the early decades of the century, but that changed with the discovery of major silver deposits at Potosí, Bolivia, in 1545 and Zacatecas, Mexico, in 1546. As these and other mines swung into large-scale production, an ever-growing stream of silver flowed from New Spain to Spain. Overall, exports of precious metals from New Spain during the sixteenth century were worth about twenty-five times more than hides, the next most important export. The mines required large capital investments and many miners. Typically, a few Spaniards supervised large groups of Indian miners, who were supplemented by African slaves later in the sixteenth century.

For the Spaniards, life in New Spain was relatively easy. Only a few thousand Spaniards actually fought during the conquests. Although the riches they won fell far short of their expectations, the benefits of encomienda gave them a comfortable, leisurely life that was the envy of many Spaniards back in Europe. As one colonist wrote to his brother in Spain, "Don't hesitate [to come]. . . . This land [New Spain] is as good as ours [in Spain], for God has given us more here than there, and we shall be better off."

During the century after 1492, about 225,000 Spaniards settled in the colonies. Virtually all of them were poor young men of common (non-noble) lineage who came directly from Spain. Laborers and **artisans** made up the largest proportion, but soldiers and sailors were also numerous. Throughout the sixteenth century, men vastly outnumbered women, although the proportion of women grew from about one in twenty before 1519 to nearly one in three by the 1580s.

The gender and number of Spanish settlers shaped two fundamental features of the society of New Spain. First, Europeans never made up more than 1 or 2 percent of the total population. Although the Spaniards ruled New Spain, the population was almost wholly Indian. Second, the shortage of Spanish women meant that Spanish men frequently married Indian women or used them as concubines. For the most part, the relatively few women from Spain married Spanish men, contributing to a tiny elite defined by European origins.

The small number of Spaniards, the masses of Indians, and the frequency of intermarriage created a steep social hierarchy defined by perceptions of national origin and race. Natives of Spain—*peninsulares* (people born on the Iberian Peninsula)—enjoyed the highest social status in New Spain. Below them but still within the white elite were *creoles*, the children born in the New World to Spanish men and women. Together, peninsulares and creoles made up barely 1 or 2 percent of the population. Below them on the social pyramid was a larger group of *mestizos*, the offspring of Spanish men and Indian women, who accounted for 4 or 5 percent of the population. So many of the mestizos were illegitimate that the term *mestizo* (after the Spanish word for "mixed") became almost synonymous with *bastard* in the sixteenth century. Some mestizos worked as artisans and labor overseers and lived well, and a few rose into the ranks of the elite, especially if their Indian ancestry was not obvious from their skin color. Most mestizos, however, were lumped with the Indians, the enormous bottom slab of the social pyramid.

Español con India, Mestizo.

Mestizo con Española, Castizo.

Castizo con Española, Español.

Español con Negra, Mulato.

Mixed Races

The residents of New Spain maintained a lively interest in each person's racial lineage. These eighteenth-century paintings illustrate forms of racial mixture common in the sixteenth century. In the first painting, a Spanish man and an Indian woman have a mestizo son; in the fourth, a Spanish man and a woman of African descent have a mulatto son. The many racial permutations led the residents of New Spain to develop an elaborate vocabulary of ancestry.

Bob Schalkwijk/INAH.

The society of New Spain established the precedent for what would become a pronounced pattern in the European colonies of the New World: a society stratified sharply by social origin and race. All Europeans of whatever social origin considered themselves superior to Native Americans; in New Spain, they were a dominant minority in both power and status.

The Toll of Spanish Conquest and Colonization

By 1560, the major centers of Indian civilization had been conquered, their leaders overthrown, their religion held in contempt, and their people forced to work for the Spaniards. Profound demoralization pervaded Indian society. As a Mexican poet wrote:

> Nothing but flowers and songs of sorrow
> are left in Mexico . . .
> where once we saw warriors and wise men. . . .
> We are crushed to the ground;
> we lie in ruins.
> There is nothing but grief and suffering
> in Mexico.

A Sign of Conquest
This skull of an Indian man in his fifties was excavated from the site of a Native American village in southwestern Georgia visited by de Soto's expedition in 1540. The skull shows that the man suffered a fatal sword wound above his right eye. Combined with slashed and severed arm and leg bones from the same site, the skull demonstrates the brutality de Soto employed against indigenous peoples on his journey through the Southeast. No native weapons could have inflicted the wounds left on this skull and the other bones.
Robert L. Blakely.

Adding to the culture shock of conquest and colonization was the deadly toll of European diseases. As conquest spread, the Indians succumbed to virulent epidemics of measles, smallpox, and respiratory illnesses. They had no immunity to these diseases because they had not been exposed to them before the arrival of Europeans. The isolation of the Western Hemisphere before 1492 had protected ancient Americans from the contagious diseases that had raged throughout Eurasia for millennia. The new post-1492 sea bridge eliminated that isolation, and by 1570, the Indian population of New Spain had fallen about 90 percent from what it was when Columbus arrived. The destruction of the Indians was a catastrophe unequaled in human history. A Mayan Indian recalled that when sickness struck his village, "great was the stench of the dead. . . . The dogs and vultures devoured the bodies. The mortality was terrible. . . . So it was that we became orphans. . . . We were born to die!" For most Indians, New Spain was a graveyard.

For the Spaniards, Indian deaths meant that the most valuable resource of New Spain—Indian labor—dwindled rapidly. By the last quarter of the sixteenth century, Spanish colonists felt the pinch of a labor shortage. To help supply the need for laborers, the colonists began to import African slaves. Some Africans had come to Mexico with the conquistadors; one Mexica recalled that among Cortés's men were "some black-skinned one[s] with kink[y] hair." In the years before 1550, while Indian labor was still adequate, only 15,000 slaves were imported from Africa. Even after Indian labor began to decline, the relatively high cost of African slaves kept imports low, approximately 36,000 from 1550 to the end of the century. During the sixteenth century, New Spain continued to rely primarily on a shrinking number of Indians.

Spanish Outposts in Florida and New Mexico

After the explorations of de Soto, Coronado, and Cabrillo, officials in New Spain lost interest in North America. The monarchy claimed that Spain owned North America and insisted that a few North American settlements be established to give some tangible reality to its claims. Settlements in Florida would have the additional benefit of protecting Spanish ships from pirates and privateers who lurked along the southeastern coast, waiting for the Spanish treasure fleet sailing toward Spain.

In 1565, the Spanish king sent Pedro Menéndez de Avilés to create settlements along the Atlantic coast of North America. In early September, Menéndez founded St. Augustine in Florida, the first permanent European settlement within what became the United States. By 1600, St. Augustine had a population of about five hundred, the only remaining Spanish beachhead on the vast Atlantic shoreline of North America.

More than sixteen hundred miles west of St. Augustine, the Spaniards founded another outpost in 1598. Juan de Oñate led an expedition of about five hundred people to settle northern Mexico, now called New Mexico, and claim the booty rumored to exist there. Oñate had impeccable credentials for both conquest and mining. His father had helped to discover the bonanza silver mines of Zacatecas, and his wife was Isabel Tolosa Cortés Montezuma—the granddaughter of Cortés, the conqueror of Mexico, and the great-granddaughter of Montezuma, the emperor of Mexico before conquest.

After a two-month journey from Mexico, Oñate and his companions reached pueblos near present-day Albuquerque and Santa Fe. He solemnly convened the pueblos' leaders and received their oath of loyalty to the Spanish king and to the Christian God. Oñate sent out scouting parties to find the legendary treasures of the region and to locate the ocean, which he believed must be nearby. Meanwhile, many of his soldiers planned to mutiny, and relations with the Indians deteriorated. When Indians in the Acoma pueblo revolted against the Spaniards, Oñate ruthlessly suppressed the uprising, killing eight hundred men, women, and children. Although Oñate reconfirmed the Spaniards' military superiority, he did not bring peace or stability to the region. After another pueblo revolt occurred in 1599, many of Oñate's settlers returned to Mexico, leaving New Mexico as a small, dusty assertion of Spanish claims to the North American Southwest.

▶REVIEW   Why did New Spain develop a society highly stratified by race and national origin?

The New World and Sixteenth-Century Europe

The riches of New Spain helped make the sixteenth century the Golden Age of Spain. After the deaths of Queen Isabella and King Ferdinand, their sixteen-year-old grandson became King Charles I of Spain in 1516. Three years later, just as Cortés ventured into Mexico, Charles I used judicious bribes to secure his selection as Holy Roman Emperor Charles V. His empire encompassed more than that of any other European monarch. He used the wealth of New Spain to protect his sprawling empire and promote his interests in the fierce dynastic battles of sixteenth-century Europe. He also sought to defend orthodox Christianity from the insurgent heresy of the **Protestant Reformation**. The power of the Spanish monarchy spread the clear message throughout sixteenth-century Europe that a New World empire could bankroll Old World ambitions.

The Protestant Reformation and the European Order

In 1517, Martin Luther, an obscure Catholic priest in central Germany, initiated the Protestant Reformation by publicizing his criticisms of the Catholic Church. Luther's ideas won the sympathy of many Catholics, but they were considered extremely dangerous by church officials and monarchs such as Charles V who believed with total conviction that just as the church spoke for God, they ruled for God.

Luther preached a doctrine known as *justification by faith*: Individual Christians could obtain salvation and life everlasting only by having faith that God would save them. Giving offerings to the church, following the orders of priests, or participating in church rituals would not put believers one step closer to heaven. Also, the only true source of information about God's will was the Bible, not the church. By reading the Bible, any Christian could learn as much about God's commandments as any priest. Indeed, Luther called for a "priesthood of all believers."

In effect, Luther charged that the Catholic Church was in many respects fraudulent. Luther insisted that priests were unnecessary for salvation and that they encouraged Christians to violate God's will by promoting religious practices not specifically commanded by the Bible. The church, Luther declared, had neglected its true purpose of helping individual Christians understand the spiritual realm revealed in the Bible and had wasted its resources in worldly conflicts of politics and wars. Luther hoped his ideas would reform the Catholic Church, but instead they ruptured forever the unity of Christianity in western Europe.

Charles V pledged to exterminate Luther's **Protestant** heresies. The wealth pouring into Spain from the New World fueled his efforts to defend orthodox Catholic faith against Protestants, as well as against Muslims in eastern Europe and against any nation bold or foolhardy enough to contest Spain's supremacy. As the wealthiest and most powerful monarch in Europe, Charles V, followed by his son and successor, Philip II, assumed responsibility for upholding the existing order of sixteenth-century Europe.

New World Treasure and Spanish Ambitions

Both Charles V and Philip II fought wars throughout the world during the sixteenth century. Mexican silver funneled through the royal treasury into the hands of military suppliers, soldiers, and sailors wherever in the world Spain's forces fought. New World treasure was dissipated in military adventures that served the goals of the monarchy but did little to benefit most Spaniards.

In a sense, American wealth made the Spanish monarchy too rich and too powerful among the states of Europe since it fueled grandiose Spanish ambitions. The ambitions of Charles V and Philip II were so great that the expenses of constant warfare far outstripped the revenues arriving from New Spain. To help meet military expenditures, both kings raised taxes in Spain more than fivefold during the sixteenth century. Since the nobility, by far the wealthiest class, was exempt from taxation, the burdensome new taxes fell mostly on poor peasants. The ambitions of the monarchy impoverished the vast majority of Spain's population and brought the nation to the brink of bankruptcy. When taxes failed to produce enough revenue to fight its wars, the monarchy borrowed heavily from European bankers. By the end of the sixteenth century, interest payments on royal debts swallowed two-thirds of the crown's annual revenues. In retrospect, the riches from New Spain proved a short-term blessing but a long-term curse.

But sixteenth-century Spaniards did not see it that way. As they looked at their accomplishments in the New World, they saw unmistakable signs of progress. They had added enormously to their knowledge and wealth. They had built mines, cities, Catholic churches, and even universities on the other side of the Atlantic. Their military, religious, and economic achievements gave them great pride and confidence.

Europe and the Spanish Example

The lessons of sixteenth-century Spain were not lost on Spain's European rivals. Spain proudly displayed the fruits of its New World conquests. In 1520, for example, Charles V exhibited some of the gifts Montezuma had given to Cortés. The objects astonished the German artist Albrecht Dürer, who wrote in his diary that he "marveled over the subtle ingenuity of the men in these distant lands" who created such "things which were brought to the King . . . [such as] a sun entirely of gold, a whole fathom [six feet] broad." But the most exciting news about "the men in these distant lands" was that they could serve the interests of Europeans as Spain had shown. With a few notable exceptions, Europeans saw the New World as a place for the expansion of European influence, a place where, as one Spaniard wrote, Europeans could "give to those strange lands the form of our own."

France and England tried to follow Spain's example. Both nations warred with Spain in Europe, preyed on Spanish treasure fleets, and ventured to the New World, where they too hoped to find an undiscovered passageway to the East Indies or another Mexico or Peru.

In 1524, France sent Giovanni da Verrazano to scout the Atlantic coast of North America from North Carolina to Canada, looking for a Northwest Passage (see Map 2.1). Eleven years later, France probed farther north with Jacques Cartier's voyage up the St. Lawrence River. Encouraged, Cartier returned to the region with a group of settlers in 1541, but the colony they established—like the search for a Northwest Passage—came to nothing.

English attempts to follow Spain's lead were slower but equally ill fated. Not until 1576, almost eighty years after John Cabot's voyages, did the English try again to find a Northwest Passage. This time Martin Frobisher sailed into the frigid waters of northern Canada (see Map 2.1). His sponsor was the Cathay Company, which hoped to open trade with China. Like many other explorers who preceded and followed him, Frobisher was mesmerized by the Spanish example and was sure he had found gold. But the tons of "ore" he hauled back to England proved worthless, the Cathay Company collapsed, and English interests shifted southward to the giant region on the northern margins of New Spain.

English explorers' attempts to establish North American settlements were no more fruitful than their search for a northern route to China. Sir Humphrey Gilbert led expeditions in 1578 and 1583 that made feeble efforts to found colonies in Newfoundland until Gilbert vanished at sea. Sir Walter Raleigh organized an expedition in 1585 to settle Roanoke Island off the coast of present-day North Carolina. The first group of explorers left no colonists on the island, but two years later Raleigh sent a contingent of more than one hundred settlers to Roanoke under John White's leadership. White went back to England for supplies, and when he returned to Roanoke in 1590, the colonists had disappeared, leaving only the word *Croatoan* (whose meaning is unknown) carved in a tree. The Roanoke colonists most likely died from a combination of natural causes and unfriendly Indians. By the end of the century, England had failed to secure a New World beachhead.

▶REVIEW   How did Spain's conquests in the New World shape Spanish influence in Europe?

Conclusion: The Promise of the New World for Europeans

The sixteenth century in the New World belonged to the Spaniards who employed Columbus and to the Indians who greeted him as he stepped ashore. Isabella of Spain helped initiate the Columbian exchange between the New World and the

Old that massively benefited first Spain and later other Europeans and that continues to this day. The exchange also subjected Native Americans to the ravages of European diseases and Spanish conquest. Spanish explorers, conquistadors, and colonists forced the Indians to serve the interests of Spanish settlers and the Spanish monarchy. The exchange illustrated one of the most important lessons of the sixteenth century: After millions of years, the Atlantic no longer was an impermeable barrier separating the Eastern and Western Hemispheres. After the voyages of Columbus, European sailing ships regularly bridged the Atlantic and carried people, products, diseases, and ideas from one shore to the other.

No European monarch could forget the seductive lesson taught by Spain's example: The New World could vastly enrich the Old. Spain remained a New World power for almost four centuries, and its language, religion, culture, and institutions left a permanent imprint. By the end of the sixteenth century, however, other European monarchies had begun to contest Spain's dominion in Europe and to make forays into the northern fringes of Spain's New World preserve. To reap the benefits the Spaniards enjoyed from their New World domain, the others had to learn a difficult lesson: how to deviate from Spain's example. That discovery lay ahead.

REVIEWING THE CHAPTER

Use the questions and timeline to review and strengthen your understanding of the chapter.

REVIEW QUESTIONS

1. Why did European exploration expand dramatically in the fifteenth century? (pp. 29–32)

2. How did Columbus's landfall in the Caribbean help revolutionize Europeans' understanding of world geography? (pp. 32–38)

3. Why did New Spain develop a society highly stratified by race and national origin? (pp. 38–48)

4. How did Spain's conquests in the New World shape Spanish influence in Europe? (pp. 49–51)

MAKING CONNECTIONS

1. The Columbian exchange exposed people on both sides of the Atlantic to surprising new peoples and goods. It also produced dramatic demographic and political transformations in the Old World and the New. How did the Columbian exchange lead to redistributions of power and population? Discuss these changes, being sure to cite examples from both contexts.

2. Despite inferior numbers, the Spaniards were able to conquer the Mexica and maintain control of the colonial hierarchy that followed. Why did the Spanish conquest of the Mexica succeed, and how did the Spaniards govern the conquered territory to maintain their dominance?

3. Spanish conquest in North America brought new peoples into constant contact. How did the Spaniards' and Indians' perceptions of each other shape their interactions? In your answer, cite specific examples and consider how perceptions changed over time.

4. How did the astonishing wealth generated for the Spanish crown by its conquest of the New World influence European colonial exploration throughout the sixteenth century? In your answer, discuss the ways in which it both encouraged and limited interest in exploration.

TIMELINE

1480	• Portuguese ships reach Congo.	**1521**	• Cortés conquers Mexica at Tenochtitlán.
1488	• Bartolomeu Dias rounds Cape of Good Hope.	**1532**	• Francisco Pizarro begins conquest of Peru.
1492	• Christopher Columbus lands on Caribbean island that he names San Salvador.	**1535**	• Jacques Cartier explores St. Lawrence River.
1493	• Columbus makes second voyage to New World.	**1539**	• Hernando de Soto explores southeastern North America.
1494	• Portugal and Spain negotiate Treaty of Tordesillas.	**1540**	• Francisco Vásquez de Coronado starts to explore Southwest and Great Plains.
1497	• John Cabot searches for Northwest Passage.	**1542**	• Juan Rodríguez Cabrillo explores California coast.
1498	• Vasco da Gama sails to India.	**1549**	• *Repartimiento* reforms begin to replace *encomienda*.
1513	• Vasco Núñez de Balboa crosses Isthmus of Panama.	**1565**	• St. Augustine, Florida, settled.
1517	• Protestant Reformation begins in Germany.	**1576**	• Martin Frobisher explores northern Canadian waters.
1519	• Hernán Cortés leads expedition to find wealth in Mexico. • Ferdinand Magellan sets out to sail around the world.	**1587**	• English settle Roanoke Island.
		1598	• Juan de Oñate explores New Mexico.
1520	• Mexica in Tenochtitlán revolt against Spaniards.	**1599**	• Pueblos revolt against Oñate.

▶ **For an online bibliography, practice quizzes, Web sites, images, and documents related to this chapter,** see the Book Companion Site at **bedfordstmartins.com/roark.**

▶ **For firsthand accounts of this period,** see Chapter 2 in Michael Johnson, ed., *Reading the American Past,* Fourth Edition.

3

The Southern Colonies in the Seventeenth Century

1601–1700

I N DECEMBER 1607, barely six months after arriving at Jamestown with the first English colonists, Captain John Smith was captured by warriors of Powhatan, the supreme chief of about fourteen thousand Algonquian people who inhabited the coastal plain of present-day Virginia, near the Chesapeake Bay. According to Smith, Powhatan "feasted him after their best barbarous manner." Then, Smith recalled, "two great stones were brought before Powhatan: then as many [Indians] as could layd hands on [Smith], dragged him to [the stones], and thereon laid his head, and being ready with their clubs, to beate out his braines." At that moment, Pocahontas, Powhatan's eleven-year-old daughter, rushed forward and "got [Smith's] head in her armes, and laid her owne upon his to save him from death." Pocahontas, Smith wrote, "hazarded the beating out of her owne braines to save mine, and . . . so prevailed with her father, that I was safely conducted [back] to James towne."

This romantic story of an Indian maiden rescuing a white soldier and saving Jamestown—and ultimately English **colonization** of North America—has been enshrined in the writing of American history since 1624, when Smith published his *Generall Historie of Virginia*. Historians believe that this episode happened more or less as Smith described it. But Smith did not understand why

Pocahontas acted as she did. Many commentators have claimed that her love for Smith caused her to rebel against her father's authority. Pocahontas herself left no document that explains her motives; most likely, she could not write. Everything known about her comes from the pen of Smith or other Englishmen. When their writings are considered in the context of what is known about the Algonquian society Pocahontas was born into, her actions appear in an entirely different light.

Most likely, when Pocahontas intervened to save Smith, she was a knowing participant in an Algonquian ceremony that expressed Powhatan's supremacy and his ritualistic adoption of Smith as a subordinate chief, or *werowance*. What Smith interpreted as Pocahontas's saving him from certain death was instead a ceremonial enactment of Powhatan's willingness to incorporate Smith and the white strangers at Jamestown into Powhatan's empire. The ceremony displayed Powhatan's power of life or death and his willingness to give protection to those who acknowledged his supremacy—in this case, the interlopers at Jamestown. By appearing to save Smith, Pocahontas was probably acting out Smith's new status as an adopted member of Powhatan's extended family. Rather than a rebellious, love-struck girl, Pocahontas was almost certainly a dutiful daughter playing the part prescribed for her by her father and her **culture**.

Smith went back to England about two years after the adoption ritual. In the meantime, Pocahontas frequently visited the English settlement and often brought gifts of food from her father. Powhatan routinely attached his sons and daughters to subordinate tribes as an expression of his protection and his

Pocahontas in England

Shortly after Pocahontas and her husband, John Rolfe, arrived in England in 1616, an engraver made this portrait of her dressed in English clothing suitable for a princess. Ornate, courtly clothing probably signified to English observers that Pocahontas was royalty and to Pocahontas that the English were accepting her as befitted the "Emperour" Powhatan's daughter. The mutability of Pocahontas's identity is displayed in the identification of her as "Matoaka" or "Rebecca."
Library of Congress.

Matoaks als Rebecka daughter to the mighty Prince Powhatan Emperour of Attanoughskomouck als virginia converted and baptized in the Christian faith, and wife to the wor.th Mr. Joh: Rolff.

dominance. It appears that Pocahontas's attachment to the English colonists grew out of Powhatan's attempt to treat the tribe of white strangers at Jamestown as he did other tribes in his empire—an attempt that failed.

In 1613, after relations between Powhatan and the English colonists had deteriorated into bloody raids by both parties, the colonists captured Pocahontas and held her hostage at Jamestown. Within a year, she converted to Christianity and married one of the colonists, a widower named John Rolfe. After giving birth to a son named Thomas, Pocahontas, her husband, and the new baby sailed for England in the spring of 1616. There, promoters of the Virginia colony dressed her as a proper Englishwoman and even arranged for her to go to a ball attended by the king and queen.

When John Smith heard that Pocahontas was in London, he went to see her. According to Smith, Pocahontas said, "You did promise Powhatan what was yours should bee his, and he the like to you; you called him father, being in his land a stranger, and by the same reason so must I doe you." It seems likely that Pocahontas believed her incorporation into English society was a counterpart of the adoption ritual Powhatan had staged for John Smith in Virginia back in 1607.

Pocahontas died in England in 1617. Her son, Thomas, ultimately returned to Virginia, and by the time of the American Revolution, his descendants numbered in the hundreds. But the world Thomas Rolfe and his descendants inhabited was shaped by a reversal of the power ritualized when his mother "saved" John Smith. By the end of the seventeenth century, Native Americans no longer dominated the newcomers who arrived in the Chesapeake with John Smith.

During the seventeenth century, English colonists learned how to deviate from the example of New Spain (see chapter 2) by growing tobacco, a crop Native Americans had cultivated in small quantities for centuries. The new settlers, however, grew enormous quantities of tobacco, far more than they could chew, smoke, or sniff themselves, and they exported most of it to England. Instead of incorporating Powhatan's people into their new society, the settlers encroached on Indian land and built new societies on the foundation of tobacco agriculture and transatlantic trade.

Producing large crop surpluses for export required hard labor and people who were willing—or could be forced—to do it. For the most part, the Native Americans refused to be conscripted into the colonists' fields. Instead, the settlers depended on the labor of family members, **indentured servants**, and, by the last third of the seventeenth century, African slaves. By the end of the century, the southern colonies had become sharply different both from the world dominated by Powhatan when the Jamestown settlers first arrived and from contemporary English society. In ways unimaginable to Powhatan, Pocahontas, and John Smith, the colonists paid homage to the international market and the English monarch by working mightily to make a good living growing crops for sale to the Old World.

An English Colony on the Chesapeake

When James I became king of England in 1603, he eyed North America as a possible location for English colonies that could be as profitable as the Spanish colonies. Although Spain claimed all of North America under the 1494 Treaty of Tordesillas (see chapter 2), King James believed that England could encroach on the outskirts of Spain's New World empire. In 1588, England had succcessfully defended itself from the Spanish Armada, a large fleet of warships launched to invade England and bring it under Spanish rule. Now England's success in defending itself suggested that it might flex its muscles overseas and build new colonies in North America in the areas Spain could not defend.

In 1606, London investors—including, as they called themselves, "knightes, gentlemen, merchauntes, and other adventurers"—organized the Virginia Company, a joint-stock company. English merchants had pooled their capital and shared risks for many years by using joint-stock companies for trading voyages to Europe, Asia, and Africa. The Virginia Company, however, had larger ambitions: to establish a colony in North America that might somehow benefit England as Spain's New World empire had rewarded Spain. King James granted the company more than six million acres in North America. In effect, the king's **land grant** was a royal license to poach on both Spanish claims and Powhatan's chiefdom.

The Virginia Company investors hoped to found an empire that would strengthen England both overseas and at home. Richard Hakluyt, a strong proponent of colonization, claimed that a colony would provide work for swarms of poor "valiant youths rusting and hurtfull by lack of employment" in England. Colonists could buy English goods and supply products that England now had to import from other nations. More trade and more jobs would benefit many people in England, but the Virginia Company investors risked their capital because they fervently hoped to reap quick profits from the new colony.

Enthusiastic reports from the Roanoke voyages twenty years earlier (see chapter 2) claimed that in Virginia, "the earth bringeth foorth all things in aboundance . . . without toile or labour." Even if these reports were exaggerated, investors reasoned, maybe some valuable exotic crop could be grown profitably in this Eden. Maybe rich lodes of gold and silver awaited discovery, as they had in New Spain. Or maybe quick and easy profits could be grabbed in an occasional raid on the gold and silver stashed in the holds of Spanish ships that cruised up the Atlantic coast on their way to Spain. Such hopes failed to address the difficulties of adapting European desires and expectations to the New World already inhabited by Native Americans. The Jamestown settlement struggled to survive for nearly two decades, until the royal government replaced the private Virginia Company, which never earned a penny for its investors.

The Fragile Jamestown Settlement

In December 1606, the ships *Susan Constant*, *Discovery*, and *Godspeed* carried 144 Englishmen toward Virginia. They arrived at the mouth of the Chesapeake Bay on April 26, 1607. That night while the colonists rested on shore, one of them later recalled, a band of Indians "creeping upon all foure, from the Hills like Beares, with their Bowes in their mouthes," attacked and dangerously wounded two men. The attack gave the colonists an early warning that the North American wilderness was not quite the paradise described by the Virginia Company's publications in England. A few weeks later, they went ashore on a small peninsula in the midst of Powhatan's chiefdom. With the memory of their first night in America fresh in their minds, they quickly built a fort, the first building in the settlement they named Jamestown.

The Jamestown fort showed the colonists' awareness that they needed to protect themselves from Indians and Spaniards. Spain employed spies to stay informed about the new English colony. Spain planned to wipe out Jamestown when the time was ripe, but that time never came. Powhatan's people defended Virginia as their own. For weeks, the settlers and Powhatan's warriors skirmished repeatedly. English muskets and cannons repelled Indian attacks on Jamestown, but the Indians' superior numbers and knowledge of the Virginia wilderness made it risky for the settlers to venture far beyond the peninsula. Late in June 1607, Powhatan sensed a stalemate and made peace overtures.

The settlers soon confronted dangerous, invisible threats: disease and starvation. During the summer, many of the Englishmen lay "night and day groaning in every corner of the Fort most pittiful to heare," wrote George Percy, one of the settlers. By September, fifty of the colonists had died. The colonists increased their misery by bickering among themselves, leaving crops unplanted and food supplies shrinking. "For the most part [the settlers] died of meere famine," Percy wrote; "there were never Englishmen left in a forreigne Countrey in such miserie as wee were in this new discovered Virginia."

Powhatan's people came to the rescue of the weakened and demoralized Englishmen. Early in September 1607, they began to bring corn to the colony for barter. Accustomed to eating food derived from wheat, the settlers at first did not like corn. An English botanist expressed the common prejudice against corn as a food "of the barbarous Indians which know no better . . . a more convenient food for swine than for man." The famished Jamestown colonists soon overcame their prejudice against corn. Captain John Smith recalled that the settlers were so hungry "they would have sould their soules" for half a basket of Powhatan's corn. When the many baskets of corn from Powhatan's people proved insufficient to keep the colonists fed, the settlers sent Smith to trade (and plunder) for corn with Indians living upriver from Jamestown. His efforts managed to keep 38 of the original settlers alive until a fresh supply of food and 120 more colonists arrived from England in January 1608.

It is difficult to exaggerate the fragility of the early Jamestown settlement. Although the Virginia Company sent hundreds of new settlers to Jamestown each year, each of them eager to find the paradise promised by the company, few survived. During the "starving time" winter of 1609–10, food became so short that one or two famished settlers resorted to eating their recently deceased neighbors. When a new group of colonists arrived in 1610, they found only 60 of the 500 previous settlers still alive. When told they might be taken back to England, the survivors responded with "a general acclamation, and shoutte of joy," an observer wrote. The Virginia Company continued to pour people into the colony, promising in a 1609 pamphlet that "the place will make them rich." But most settlers went instead to an early grave.

Cooperation and Conflict between Natives and Newcomers

Powhatan's people stayed in contact with the English settlers but maintained their distance. The Virginia Company boasted that the settlers bought from the Indians "the pearles of earth [corn] and [sold] to them the pearles of heaven [Christianity]." In fact, few Indians converted to Christianity, and the English devoted scant effort to proselytizing. Marriage between Indian women and English men also was rare, despite the acute shortage of English women in Virginia in the early years. Few settlers other than John Smith troubled to learn the Indians' language.

Powhatan's people regarded the English with suspicion, for good reason. Although the settlers often made friendly overtures to the Indians, they did not hesitate to use their guns and swords to enforce English notions of proper Indian behavior. More than once, the Indians refused to trade their corn to the settlers, evidently hoping to starve them out. Each time, the English broke the boycott by attacking the uncooperative Indians, pillaging their villages, and confiscating their corn.

The Indians retaliated against English violence, but for fifteen years they did not organize an all-out assault on the European intruders, probably for several reasons. Although Christianity held few attractions for the Indians, the power of the settlers' God impressed them. One chief told John Smith that "he did believe that our [English] God as much exceeded theirs as our guns did their bows and arrows." Powhatan probably concluded that these powerful strangers would make better allies than enemies. As allies, the English strengthened Powhatan's dominance over the tribes in the region. They also traded with his people, usually exchanging European goods for corn. Native Virginians had some copper weapons and tools before the English arrived, but they quickly recognized the superiority of the intruders' iron and steel knives, axes, and pots, and they traded eagerly to obtain them.

The trade that supplied the Indians with European conveniences provided the English settlers with a necessity: food. But why were the settlers unable to feed themselves for more than a decade? First, as the staggering death rate suggests, many settlers were too sick to be productive members of the colony. Second, very few farmers came to Virginia in the early years. Instead, most of the newcomers were gentlemen and their servants. In John Smith's words, these men "never did know what a day's work was." The proportion of gentlemen in Virginia in the early years was six times greater than in England, a reflection of the Virginia Company's urgent need for investors and settlers. The company explained in a 1610 pamphlet that nobody should think that the colony "excludeth Gentlemen . . . for though they cannot digge, use the square, nor practise the axe and chizell, yet [they know] . . . how to employ the force of knowledge, the exercise of counsel, the operation and power of their best breeding and qualities." In Virginia, English gentlemen's breeding and quality proved worthless for growing corn, catching fish, or even hunting deer. John Smith declared repeatedly that in Virginia "there is no country to pillage [as in New Spain]. . . . All you can expect from [Virginia] must be by labor." For years, however, colonists clung to English notions that gentlemen should not work with their hands and tradesmen should work only in trades for which they had been trained. These ideas made more sense in labor-rich England than in labor-poor Virginia. In the meantime, the colonists depended on the Indians' corn for food.

The persistence of the Virginia colony created difficulties for Powhatan's chiefdom. Steady contact between natives and newcomers spread European diseases among the Indians, who suffered deadly epidemics in 1608 and between 1617 and 1619. The settlers' insatiable appetite for corn introduced other tensions within Powhatan's villages. To produce enough corn for their own survival and for trade with the English required the Indians to spend more time and effort growing crops. Since Native American women did most of the agricultural work, their burden increased along with the cultural significance of their chief crop. The corn surplus grown by Indian women was bartered for desirable English goods such as iron pots, which replaced the baskets and ceramic jugs Native Americans had used for millennia. Growing enough corn to feed the English boosted the workload of Indian women and altered age-old patterns of village life. But from the Indians' viewpoint, the most important fact about the always-hungry English colonists was that they were not going away.

Powhatan died in 1618, and his brother Opechancanough replaced him as supreme chief. In 1622, Opechancanough organized an all-out assault on the English settlers. As an English colonist observed, "When the day appointed for the massacre arrived [March 22], a number of savages visited many of our people in their dwellings, and while partaking with them of their meal[,] the savages, at a given signal, drew their weapons and fell upon us murdering and killing everybody they could reach[,] sparing neither women nor children, as well inside as outside the dwellings." In all, the Indians killed 347 colonists, nearly a third of the English population. But the attack failed to dislodge the colonists. In the aftermath, the settlers unleashed a murderous campaign of Indian extermination that in a few years pushed the Indians beyond the small circumference of white settlement. Before 1622, the settlers knew that the Indians, though dangerous, were necessary to keep the colony alive. After 1622, most colonists considered the Indians their perpetual enemies.

From Private Company to Royal Government

The 1622 uprising came close to achieving Opechancanough's goal of pushing the colonists back into the Atlantic—so close that it prompted a royal investigation of affairs in Virginia. The investigators discovered that the appalling mortality among the colonists was caused more by disease and mismanagement than by Indian raids. In 1624, King James revoked the charter of the Virginia Company and made Virginia a royal colony, subject to the direction of the

---

Advertisement for Jamestown Settlers

Virginia imported thousands of indentured servants to labor in the tobacco fields, but the colony also advertised in 1631 for settlers like those pictured here. The notice features men and women equally, although men heavily outnumbered women in the Chesapeake region.

Harvard Map Collection, Pusey Library, Harvard University.

royal government rather than to the company's private investors, an arrangement that lasted until 1776.

The king now appointed the governor of Virginia and his council, but most other features of local government established under the Virginia Company remained intact. In 1619, for example, the company had inaugurated the House of Burgesses, an assembly of representatives (called burgesses) elected by the colony's inhabitants. (Historians do not know exactly which settlers were considered inhabitants and were thus qualified to vote.) Under the new royal government, laws passed by the burgesses had to be approved by the king's bureaucrats in England rather than by the company. Otherwise, the House of Burgesses continued as before, acquiring distinction as the oldest representative legislative assembly in the English colonies. Under the new royal government, all free adult men in Virginia could vote for the House of Burgesses, giving it a far broader and more representative constituency than the English House of Commons.

The demise of the Virginia Company marked the end of the first phase of colonization of the Chesapeake region. From the first 105 adventurers in 1607, the population had grown to about 1,200 by 1624. Despite mortality rates higher than during the worst epidemics in London, new settlers still came. Their arrival and King James's willingness to take over the struggling colony reflected a fundamental change in Virginia. After years of fruitless experimentation, it was becoming clear that English settlers could make a fortune in Virginia by growing tobacco.

►**REVIEW**   Why did Powhatan pursue largely peaceful relations with the Jamestown settlement?

A Tobacco Society

Tobacco grew wild in the New World, and Native Americans used it for thousands of years before Europeans arrived. Columbus observed Indians smoking tobacco on his first voyage to the New World. Many other sixteenth-century European explorers noticed the Indians' habit of "drinking smoke." During the sixteenth century, Spanish colonists in the New World sent tobacco to Europe, where it was an expensive luxury used sparingly by a few. During the next century, English colonists in North America sent so much tobacco to European markets that it became an affordable indulgence used often by many people.

Initially, the Virginia Company had no plans to grow and sell tobacco. "As for tobacco," John Smith wrote, "we never then dreamt of it." John Rolfe—Pocahontas's husband-to-be—planted West Indian tobacco seeds in 1612 and learned that they flourished in Virginia. By 1617, the colonists had grown enough tobacco to send the first commercial shipment to England, where it sold for a high price. After that, Virginia pivoted from a colony of rather aimless adventurers who had difficulty growing enough corn to feed themselves into a society of dedicated **planters** who grew as much tobacco as possible.

Dedicated they were. By 1700, nearly 100,000 colonists lived in the Chesapeake region, encompassing Virginia, Maryland, and northern North Carolina (Map 3.1). They exported more than 35 million pounds of tobacco, a fivefold increase in

MAP 3.1   Chesapeake Colonies in the Seventeenth Century

The association between land and water in the settlement of the Chesapeake in the seventeenth century is illustrated by this map. The fall line indicates the limit of navigable water, where rapids and falls prevented farther upstream travel. Although Delaware had excellent access to navigable water, it was claimed and defended by the Dutch colony at New Amsterdam (discussed in chapter 4) rather than by the English settlements in Virginia and Maryland shown on this map.

Tobacco Wrapper
This wrapper labeled a container of "Virginia Planters Best Tobacco." It shows a colonial planter supervising slaves, who hold hoes they used to chop weeds that robbed the leafy tobacco plants of nutrients and moisture. The planter enjoys a pipe in the shade of an umbrella held by a slave. After the tobacco was harvested and dried, it was pressed tightly into barrels, like those shown here, for shipment overseas.
Colonial Williamsburg Foundation.

per capita production since 1620. Clearly, Chesapeake colonists mastered the demands of tobacco agriculture, and the "Stinkinge Weede" (a seventeenth-century Marylander's term for tobacco) also mastered the colonists. Settlers lived by the rhythms of tobacco agriculture, and their endless need for labor attracted droves of English indentured servants to work in the tobacco fields.

Tobacco Agriculture

A demanding crop, tobacco required close attention and a great deal of hand labor year-round. Primitive tools and methods made this intensive cycle of labor taxing. Like the Indians, the colonists "cleared" fields by cutting a ring of bark from each tree (a procedure known as *girdling*), thereby killing the tree. Girdling brought sunlight to clearings but left fields studded with tree stumps, making the use of plows impractical. Instead, colonists used heavy hoes to till their tobacco fields. To plant, a visitor observed, they "just make holes [with a stick] into which they drop the seeds," much as the Indians did. Growing tobacco with such methods left little time for idleness, but the colonists enjoyed the fruits of their labor. "Everyone smokes while working or idling," one traveler reported, including "men, women, girls, and boys, from the age of seven years."

The English settlers worked hard because their labor promised greater rewards in the Chesapeake region than in England. One colonist proclaimed that "the dirt of this Province affords as great a profit to the general Inhabitant, as the Gold of Peru doth to . . . the Spaniard." Although he exaggerated, it was true that a hired man could expect to earn two or three times more in Virginia's tobacco fields than in England. Better still, in Virginia land was so abundant that it was extremely cheap, compared to land in England. By the mid-seventeenth century, common laborers could buy a hundred acres for less than their annual wages—an impossibility in England. New settlers who paid their own transportation to the Chesapeake received a grant of fifty acres of free land (termed a *headright*). The Virginia Company initiated headrights to encourage settlement, and the royal government continued them for the same reason.

A Servant Labor System

Headrights, cheap land, and high wages gave poor English folk powerful incentives to immigrate to the New World. Yet many potential immigrants could not scrape together the money to pay for a trip across the Atlantic. Their poverty and the colonists' crying need for labor formed the basic context for the creation of a servant labor system.

About 80 percent of the immigrants to the Chesapeake during the seventeenth century were indentured servants. Twenty Africans arrived in Virginia in 1619, and they probably were enslaved, although scanty records make it uncertain. Until the 1670s, however, only a small number of slaves labored in Chesapeake tobacco fields. (Large numbers of slaves came in the eighteenth century, as chapter 5 explains.) A few indentured servants of African descent served out their terms of servitude and became free. A few slaves purchased their way out of bondage and lived as free people, even owning land and using the local courts to resolve disputes, much as freed white servants did. A small number of Native Americans also became servants. But the overwhelming majority of indentured servants were white immigrants from England. Instead of a slave society, the seventeenth-century Chesapeake region was fundamentally a society of white servants and ex-servants.

To buy passage aboard a ship bound for the Chesapeake, an English immigrant had to come up with about £5, roughly a year's wages for an English servant or laborer. Earning wages at all was difficult in England since job opportunities were shrinking. Many country landowners needed fewer farmhands because they shifted from growing crops to raising sheep in newly enclosed fields. Unemployed people drifted into seaports such as Bristol, Liverpool, and London, where they learned about the plentiful jobs in North America.

Unable to pay for their trip across the Atlantic, poor immigrants agreed to a contract called an *indenture*, which functioned as a form of credit. By signing an indenture, an immigrant borrowed the cost of transportation to the Chesapeake from a merchant or ship captain in England. To repay this loan, the indentured person agreed to work as a servant for four to seven years in North America. Once the indentured person arrived in the colonies, the merchant or ship captain sold his right to the immigrant's labor to a local tobacco planter. To obtain the servant's labor, the planter paid about twice the cost of transportation and agreed to provide the servant with food and shelter during the term of the indenture. When the indenture expired, the planter owed the former servant "freedom dues," usually a few barrels of corn and a suit of clothes.

Ideally, indentures allowed poor immigrants to trade their most valuable assets—their freedom and their ability to work—for a trip to the New World and a period of servitude followed by freedom in a land of opportunity. Planters reaped more immediate benefits. Servants meant more hands to grow more tobacco. A planter expected a servant to grow enough tobacco in one year to cover the price the planter paid for the indenture. Servants' labor during the remaining three to six years of the indenture promised a handsome profit for the planter. No wonder one Virginian declared, "Our principall wealth . . . consisteth in servants." But roughly half of all servants became sick and died before serving out their indentures, reducing planters' gains and destroying servants' hopes. Planters still profited, however, since they received a headright of fifty acres of land from the colonial government for every newly purchased servant.

About three out of four servants were men between the ages of fifteen and twenty-five when they arrived in the Chesapeake. Typically, they shared the desperation of sixteen-year-old Francis Haires, who indentured himself for seven years because, according to his contract, "his father and mother and All friends [are] dead and he [is] a miserable wandering boy." Like Francis, most servants had no special training or skills, although the majority had some experience with agricultural work. "Hunger and fear of prisons bring to us onely such servants as have been brought up to no Art or Trade," one Virginia planter complained. A skilled craftsman could obtain a shorter indenture, but few risked coming to the colonies since their prospects were better in England.

Women were almost as rare as skilled craftsmen in the Chesapeake and more ardently desired. In the early days of the tobacco boom, the Virginia Company shipped young single women servants to the colony as prospective wives for male settlers willing to pay "120 weight [pounds] of the best leaf tobacco for each of them," in effect getting both a wife and a servant. The company reasoned that, as one official wrote in 1622, "the plantation can never flourish till families be planted, and the respect of wives and children fix the people on the soil." The company's efforts as a marriage broker proved no more successful than its other ventures. Women remained a small minority of the Chesapeake population until late in the seventeenth century.

The servant labor system perpetuated the gender imbalance. Although female servants cost about the same as males and generally served for the same length of time, only about one servant in four was a woman. Planters preferred male servants for field work, although many servant women hoed and harvested tobacco fields. Most women servants also did household chores such as cooking, washing, cleaning, gardening, and milking.

Servants—whether men or women, whites or blacks, English or Africans—tended to work together and socialize together. During the first half century of settlement, racial intermingling occurred, although the small number of blacks made it infrequent. Courts punished sexual relations between blacks and whites, but the number of court cases shows that sexual desire readily crossed the color line. In general, the commonalities of servitude caused servants—regardless of their race and gender—to consider themselves apart from free people, whose ranks they longed to join eventually.

Servant life was harsh by the standards of seventeenth-century England and even by the **frontier** standards of the Chesapeake. Unlike servants in England, Chesapeake servants had no control over who purchased their labor—and thus them—for the period of their indenture. Many servants were bought and sold several times before their indenture expired. A Virginia servant protested in 1623 that his master "hath sold me for £150 sterling like a damnd slave." A ship captain reported in 1625 that "servants were sold here [in Virginia] upp and downe like horses." But tobacco planters' need for labor muffled such complaints about treating servants as property.

For servants, the promise of indentured servitude that loomed large in their decision to leave England and immigrate to the Chesapeake often withered when they confronted the rigors of labor in the tobacco fields. James Revel, an eighteen-year-old thief punished by being indentured to a Virginia tobacco planter, chronicled what happened when he arrived at his new master's plantation:

> My Europian clothes were took from me,
> Which never after I again could see.
> A canvas shirt and trowsers then they gave,
> With a hop-sack frock in which I was to slave:
> No shoes nor stockings had I for to wear,
> Nor hat, nor cap, both head and feet were bare.
> Thus dress'd into the Field I next must go,
> Amongst tobacco plants all day to hoe,
> At day break in the morn our work began,
> And so held to the setting of the Sun.

Severe laws aimed to keep servants in their place. Punishments for petty crimes stretched servitude far beyond the original terms of indenture. Christopher Adams, for example, had to serve three extra years for running away for six months. Richard Higby received six extra years of servitude for killing three hogs. After midcentury, the Virginia legislature added three or more years to the indentures of most servants by requiring them to serve until they were twenty-four years old.

Women servants were subject to special restrictions and risks. They were prohibited from marrying until their servitude had expired. A servant woman, the law assumed, could not serve two masters at the same time: one who owned her indentured labor and another who was her husband. However, the predominance of men in the Chesapeake population inevitably pressured women to engage in sexual relations. About a third of immigrant women were pregnant when they married. Pregnancy and childbirth sapped a woman's strength, and a new child diverted her attention, reducing her usefulness as a servant. As a rule, if a woman servant gave birth to a child, she had to serve two extra years and pay a fine. However, for some servant women, premarital pregnancy was a path out of servitude: The father of an unborn child sometimes purchased the indenture of the servant mother-to-be, then freed and married her.

Harsh punishments reflected four fundamental realities of the servant labor system. First, planters' hunger for labor caused them to demand as much labor as they could get from their servants, including devising legal ways to extend the period of servitude. Second, servants hoped to survive their servitude and use their freedom to obtain land and start a family. Third, servants' hopes frequently conflicted with planters' demands. Since servants saw themselves as free people in a temporary status of servitude, they often made grudging, halfhearted workers. Finally, planters put up with this contentious arrangement because the alternatives were less desirable.

Planters could not easily hire free men and women because land was readily available and free people preferred to work on their own land, for themselves. Nor could planters depend on much labor from family members. The preponderance of men in the population meant that families were few, were started late, and thus had few children. And, until the 1680s and 1690s, slaves were expensive and hard to come by. Before then, masters who wanted to expand their labor force and grow more tobacco had few alternatives to buying indentured servants.

Cultivating Land and Faith

Villages and small towns dotted the rural landscape of seventeenth-century England, but in the Chesapeake, acres of wilderness were interrupted here and there by tobacco farms. Tobacco was such a labor-intensive crop that one field worker could tend only about two acres of the plants in a year (an acre is slightly smaller than a football field), plus a few more acres for food crops. A successful farmer needed a great deal more land, however, because tobacco quickly exhausted the fertility of the soil. Since each farmer cultivated only 5 or 10 percent of his land at any one time, a "settled" area comprised swatches of cultivated land surrounded by forest. Arrangements for marketing tobacco also contributed to the dispersion of settlements. Tobacco planters sought land that fronted a navigable river in order to minimize the work of transporting the heavy barrels of tobacco onto ships. A settled region thus resembled a lacework of farms stitched around waterways.

Most Chesapeake colonists were nominally **Protestants**. Attendance at Sunday services and conformity to the doctrines of the Church of England were required of all English men and women. Few clergymen migrated to the Chesapeake, however, and too few of those who did were models of righteousness and piety. Certainly, some colonists took their religion seriously. Church courts punished fornicators, censured blasphemers, and served notice on parishioners who spent Sundays "goeing a fishing." But on the whole, religion did not awaken the zeal of Chesapeake settlers, certainly not as it did the zeal of New England settlers in these same years (see chapter 4). What quickened the pulse of most Chesapeake folk was a close horse race, a bloody cockfight, or—most of all—an exceptionally fine tobacco crop. The religion of the Chesapeake colonists was Anglican, but their faith lay in the turbulent, competitive, high-stakes gamble of survival as tobacco planters.

The situation was similar in the Catholic colony of Maryland. In 1632, England's King Charles I granted his Catholic friend Lord Baltimore about six and a half million acres in the northern Chesapeake region. In return, the king specified that Lord Baltimore pay him the token rent of "two Indian arrowheads" a year. Lord Baltimore intended to create a refuge for Catholics, who suffered severe discrimination in England. He fitted out two ships, the *Ark* and the *Dove*, gathered about 150 settlers, and sent them to the new colony, where they arrived on March 25, 1634. However, Maryland failed to live up to Baltimore's hopes. The colony's population grew very slowly for twenty years, and most settlers were Protestants rather than Catholics. The religious turmoil of the **Puritan** Revolution in England (discussed in chapter 4) spilled across the Atlantic, creating conflict between Maryland's few Catholics—most of them wealthy and prominent—and the Protestant majority, most of them neither wealthy nor prominent. During the 1660s, Maryland began to attract settlers as readily as Virginia, mostly Protestants. Although Catholics and the Catholic faith continued to exert influence in Maryland, the colony's society, economy, politics, and culture became nearly indistinguishable from Virginia's. Both colonies shared a devotion to tobacco, the true faith of the Chesapeake.

▶ **REVIEW**   Why did the vast majority of European immigrants to the Chesapeake come as indentured servants?

The Evolution of Chesapeake Society

The system of indentured servitude sharpened inequality in Chesapeake society by the mid-seventeenth century, propelling social and political polarization that culminated in 1676 with Bacon's Rebellion. The rebellion prompted reforms that stabilized relations between elite planters and their lesser neighbors and paved the way for a social hierarchy that muted differences of landholding and wealth and amplified racial differences. Amid this social and political evolution, one thing did not change: Chesapeake colonists' dedication to growing tobacco.

Social and Economic Polarization

The first half of the seventeenth century in the Chesapeake was the era of the **yeoman**—a farmer who owned a small plot of land sufficient to support a family and tilled largely by servants and a few family members. A small number of elite planters had larger estates and commanded ten or more servants. But for the first several decades, few men lived long enough to accumulate a fortune sufficient to set them much apart from their neighbors. Until midcentury, the principal division in Chesapeake society was less between rich and poor planters than between free farmers and unfree servants. Although these two groups contrasted sharply in their legal and economic status, their daily lives had many similarities. Servants looked forward to the time when their indentures would expire and they would become free and eventually own land. On the whole, a rough, frontier equality characterized free families in the Chesapeake until about 1650.

Three major developments splintered that equality during the third quarter of the century. First, as planters grew more and more tobacco, the ample supply depressed tobacco prices in European markets. Cheap tobacco reduced planters' profits and made it more difficult for freed servants to save enough to become landowners. Second, because the mortality rate in the Chesapeake colonies declined, more and more servants survived their indentures, and landless freemen became more numerous and grew more discontented. Third, declining mortality also encouraged the formation of a planter elite. By living longer, the most successful planters compounded their success. The wealthiest planters also began to serve as merchants, marketing crops for their less successful neighbors, importing English goods for sale, and giving credit to hard-pressed customers.

By the 1670s, the society of the Chesapeake had become polarized. Landowners—the planter elite and the more numerous yeoman planters—clustered around one pole. Landless colonists, mainly freed servants, gathered at the other. Each group eyed the other with suspicion and mistrust. For the most part, planters saw landless freemen as a dangerous rabble rather than as fellow colonists with legitimate grievances. Governor William Berkeley feared the political threat to the governing elite posed by "six parts in seven [of Virginia colonists who] . . . are poor, indebted, discontented, and armed."

Government Policies and Political Conflict

In general, government and politics strengthened the distinctions in Chesapeake society. The most vital distinction separated servants and masters, and the colonial government enforced it with an iron fist. Poor men such as William Tyler complained that "nether the Governor nor Counsell could or would doe any poore men right, but that they would shew favor to great men and wronge the poore." Most Chesapeake colonists, like most Europeans, assumed that "great men" should bear the responsibilities of government. Until 1670, all freemen could vote, and they routinely elected prosperous planters to the legislature. No former servant served in either the governor's council or the House of Burgesses after 1640. Yet Tyler and other poor Virginians believed that the "great men" used their government offices to promote their selfish personal interests, rather than governing impartially.

As discontent mounted among the poor during the 1660s and 1670s, colonial officials tried to keep political power in safe hands. Beginning in 1661, for example,

Inside a Poor Planter's House
This photo shows a carefully documented reconstruction of the interior of a poor planter's house at Historic St. Mary's City, Maryland. The wall of this one-room dwelling with a loft features a window with a shutter but no glass. When the shutter was closed, the only source of light was a candle or a fire. Notice the rustic, unfinished bench, table, walls, and dirt floor. These meager furnishings were usually accompanied by a storage chest and some bedding but not a bed.
Image courtesy of Historic St. Mary's City.

Governor Berkeley did not call an election for the House of Burgesses for fifteen years. In 1670, the House of Burgesses outlawed voting by poor men, permitting only men who headed a household and were landowners to vote.

The king also began to tighten the royal government's control of trade and to collect substantial revenue from the Chesapeake. A series of navigation acts funneled the colonial trade exclusively into the hands of English merchants and shippers. The Navigation Acts of 1650 and 1651 specified that colonial goods had to be transported in English ships with predominantly English crews. A 1660 act required colonial products to be sent only to English ports, and a 1663 law stipulated further that all goods sent to the colonies must pass through English ports and be carried in English ships manned by English sailors. Taken together, these navigation acts reflected the English government's **mercantilist** assumptions about the colonies: What was good for England should determine colonial policy.

Assumptions about mercantilism also underlay the import duty on tobacco inaugurated by the Navigation Act of 1660. The law assessed an import tax of two pence on every pound of colonial tobacco brought into England, about the price a Chesapeake tobacco farmer received. The tax gave the king a major financial interest in the size of the tobacco crop. During the 1660s, these tobacco import taxes yielded about a quarter of all English customs revenues, an impressive sign of the growing importance of the Chesapeake colonies in England's Atlantic empire.

Bacon's Rebellion

Colonists, like residents of European monarchies, accepted social hierarchy and inequality as long as they believed that government officials ruled for the general good. When rulers violated that precept, ordinary people felt justified in rebelling. In 1676, Bacon's Rebellion erupted as a dispute over Virginia's Indian policy. Before it was over, the rebellion convulsed Chesapeake politics and society, leaving in its wake death, destruction, and a legacy of hostility between the great planters and their poorer neighbors.

Opechancanough, the Algonquian chief who had led the Indian uprising of 1622 in Virginia, mounted another surprise attack in 1644 and killed about five hundred Virginia colonists in two days. During the next two years of bitter fighting, the colonists eventually gained the upper hand, capturing and murdering the old chief. The treaty that concluded the war established policies toward the Indians that the government tried to maintain for the next thirty years. The Indians relinquished all claims to land already settled by the English. Wilderness land beyond the fringe of English settlement was supposed to be reserved exclusively for Indian use. The colonial government hoped to minimize contact between settlers and Indians and thereby maintain the peace.

If the Chesapeake population had not grown, the policy might have worked. But the number of land-hungry colonists, especially poor, recently freed servants, continued to multiply. In their quest for land, they pushed beyond the treaty limits of English settlement and encroached steadily on Indian land. During the 1660s and 1670s, violence between colonists and Indians repeatedly flared along the advancing frontier. The government, headquartered in the tidewater region near the coast, far from the danger of Indian raids, took steps to calm the disputes and reestablish the peace. Frontier settlers thirsted for revenge against what their leader, Nathaniel Bacon, termed "the protected and Darling Indians." Bacon proclaimed his "Design not only to ruine and extirpate all Indians in Generall but all Manner of Trade and Commerce with them." Indians were not the only enemies Bacon and his men singled out. Bacon also urged the colonists to "see what spounges have suckt up the Publique Treasure." He charged that "Grandees," or elite planters, operated the government for their private gain, a charge that made sense to many colonists. Bacon crystallized the grievances of the small planters and poor farmers against both the Indians and the colonial rulers in Jamestown.

Hoping to maintain the fragile peace on the frontier in 1676, Governor Berkeley pronounced Bacon a rebel, threatened to punish him for treason, and called for new elections of burgesses who, Berkeley believed, would endorse his get-tough policy. To Berkeley's surprise, the elections backfired. Almost all the old burgesses were voted out of office, and they were replaced by local leaders, including Bacon. The legislature was now in the hands of minor grandees who, like Bacon, chafed at the rule of the elite planters.

In June 1676, the new legislature passed a series of reform measures known as Bacon's Laws. Among other changes, the laws gave local settlers a voice in setting tax levies, forbade officeholders from demanding bribes or other extra fees for carrying out their duties, placed limits on holding multiple offices, and restored the vote to all freemen. Under pressure, Berkeley pardoned Bacon and authorized his campaign of Indian warfare. But elite planters soon convinced Berkeley that Bacon and his men were a greater threat than Indians.

When Bacon learned that Berkeley had once again branded him a traitor, he declared war against Berkeley and the other grandees. For three months, Bacon's forces fought the Indians, sacked the grandees' plantations, and attacked Jamestown. Berkeley's loyalists retaliated by plundering the homes of Bacon's supporters. The fighting continued until late October, when Bacon unexpectedly died, most likely from dysentery, and several English ships arrived to bolster Berkeley's strength. With the rebellion crushed, Berkeley hanged several of Bacon's allies and destroyed farms that belonged to Bacon's supporters.

The rebellion did nothing to dislodge the grandees from their positions of power. If anything, it strengthened them. When the king learned of the turmoil in the Chesapeake and its devastating effect on tobacco exports and customs duties, he ordered an investigation. Royal officials replaced Berkeley with a governor more attentive to the king's interests, nullified Bacon's Laws, and instituted an export tax on every hogshead of tobacco as a way of paying the expenses of government without having to obtain the consent of the tightfisted House of Burgesses.

In the aftermath of Bacon's Rebellion, tensions between great planters and small farmers gradually lessened. Bacon's Rebellion showed, a governor of Virginia said, that it was necessary "to steer between . . . either an Indian or a civil war." The ruling elite concluded that it was safer for the colonists to fight the Indians than to fight each other, and the government made little effort to restrict settlers' encroachment on Indian land. Tax cuts also were welcomed by all freemen. The export duty on tobacco imposed by the king allowed the colonial government to reduce taxes by 75 percent between 1660 and 1700. In the long run, however, the most important contribution to political stability was the declining importance of the servant labor system. During the 1680s and 1690s, fewer servants arrived in the Chesapeake, partly because of improving economic conditions in England. Accordingly, the number of poor, newly freed servants also declined, reducing the size of the lowest stratum of free society. In 1700, as many as one-third of the free colonists still worked as tenants on land owned by others, but the social and political distance between them and the great planters did not seem as important as it had been in 1660. The main reason was that by 1700, the Chesapeake was in the midst of transition to a slave labor system that minimized the differences between poor farmers and rich planters and magnified the differences between whites and blacks.

▶ **REVIEW**   Why did Chesapeake colonial society become increasingly polarized between 1650 and 1670?

Religion and Revolt in the Spanish Borderland

While English colonies in the Chesapeake grew and prospered with the tobacco trade, the northern outposts of the Spanish empire in New Mexico and Florida stagnated. Instead of attracting settlers and growing crops for export, New Mexico and Florida appealed to Spanish missionaries seeking to harvest Indian souls. The missionaries baptized thousands of Indians in Spanish North America during the seventeenth century, but they also planted the seeds of Indian uprisings against Spanish rule.

Few Spaniards came to New Spain's northern borderland during the seventeenth century. Only about fifteen hundred Spaniards lived in Florida, and roughly twice as many inhabited New Mexico. One royal governor complained that "no [Spaniard] comes . . . to plow and sow [crops], but only to eat and loaf." In both colonies, Indians outnumbered Spaniards ten or twenty to one.

Royal officials seriously considered eliminating both colonies because their costs greatly exceeded their benefits. Every three years, a caravan from Mexico brought wagons full of goods to outposts in New Mexico. Florida required even larger subsidies because it housed a garrison of soldiers as well as missionaries, who persuaded the Spanish government that instead of being losing propositions, the colonies represented golden opportunities to convert heathen Indians to Christianity. Stirrups adorned with Christian crosses on soldiers' saddles proclaimed the faith behind the Spaniards' swords, and vice versa. Royal officials hoped that the missionaries' efforts would pacify the Indians and be a relatively cheap way to preserve Spanish footholds in North America.

Dozens of missionaries came to Florida and New Mexico, as one announced, to free the Indians "from the miserable slavery of the demon and from the obscure darkness of their idolatry." The missionaries believed that the Indians' religious beliefs and rituals were idolatrous devil worship and that their way of life was barbaric. The missionaries followed royal instructions that Indians should be taught "to

Spanish Stirrup
This seventeenth-century stirrup used by Spaniards on the northern frontier of New Spain illustrates the use of elaborate ornamentation and display to convey a sense of Spanish power. It is no accident that the stirrup is in the shape of a Christian cross, a vivid symbol of the Spaniards' belief in the divine source of their authority.
© George H. H. Huey.

live in a civilized manner, clothed and wearing shoes . . . [and] given the use of . . . bread, linen, horses, cattle, tools, and weapons, and all the rest that Spain has had." In effect, the missionaries sought to convert the Indians not just into Christians but also into surrogate Spaniards.

The missionaries supervised the building of scores of Catholic churches across Florida and New Mexico. Typically, they conscripted Indian women and men to do the construction. Adopting practices common elsewhere in New Spain, the missionaries forced the Indians both to work and to pay tribute in the form of food, blankets, and other goods. Although the missionaries congratulated themselves on the many Indians they converted, their coercive methods subverted their goals. A missionary reported that an Indian in New Mexico asked him, "If we [missionaries] who are Christians caused so much harm and violence [to Indians], why should they become Christians?"

The Indians retaliated repeatedly against Spanish exploitation, but the Spaniards suppressed the violent uprisings by taking advantage of the disunity among the Indians, much as Cortés did in the conquest of Mexico (see chapter 2). In 1680, however, Pueblo Indians organized a unified revolt under the leadership of Popé, who ordered his followers, as one recounted, to "break up and burn the images of the holy Christ, the Virgin Mary, and the other saints, the crosses, and everything pertaining to Christianity." During the Pueblo Revolt, the Indians desecrated churches, killed two-thirds of the Spanish missionaries, and drove the Spaniards out of New Mexico to present-day El Paso, Texas. The Spaniards managed to return to New Mexico by the end of the seventeenth century, but only by curtailing the missionaries and reducing labor exploitation. Florida Indians never mounted a unified attack on Spanish rule, but they too organized sporadic uprisings and resisted conversion, causing a Spanish official to report by the end of the seventeenth century that "the law of God and the preaching of the Holy Gospel have now ceased."

▶ **REVIEW**   Why did the Pueblo Indians revolt against Spanish missionaries in 1680?

Toward a Slave Labor System

During the sixteenth century, Spaniards and Portuguese in the New World supplemented Indian laborers with enslaved Africans. On this foundation, European colonizers built African slavery into the most important form of coerced labor in the New World. During the seventeenth century, English colonies in the West Indies followed the Spanish and Portuguese examples and developed sugar plantations with slave labor. In the English North American colonies, however, a slave labor system did not emerge until the last quarter of the seventeenth century. During the 1670s, settlers from Barbados brought slavery to the new English mainland colony of Carolina, where the imprint of the West Indies remained strong for decades. In Chesapeake tobacco fields at about the same time, slave labor began to replace servant labor, marking the transition toward a society of freedom for whites and slavery for Africans.

The West Indies: Sugar and Slavery

The most profitable part of the English New World empire in the seventeenth century lay in the Caribbean (Map 3.2). The tiny island of Barbados, colonized in the 1630s, was the jewel of the English West Indies. During the 1640s, Barbadian

---

MAP 3.2 The West Indies and Carolina in the Seventeenth Century

Although Carolina was geographically close to the Chesapeake colonies, it was culturally closer to the West Indies in the seventeenth century because its early settlers—both blacks and whites—came from Barbados. South Carolina maintained strong ties to the West Indies for more than a century, long after the arrival of many later settlers from England, Ireland, France, and elsewhere.

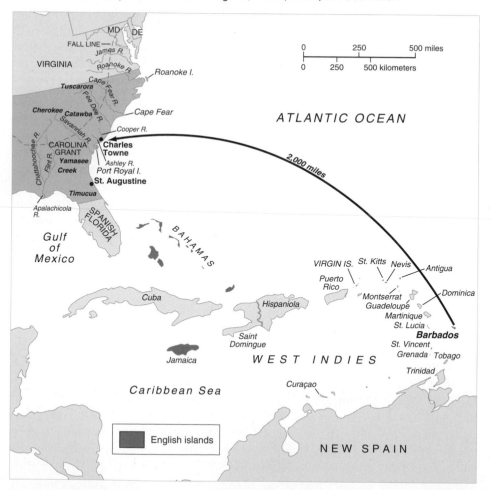

planters began to grow sugarcane with such success that a colonial official pro-claimed Barbados "the most flourishing Island in all those American parts, and I verily believe in all the world for the production of sugar." Sugar commanded high prices in England, and planters rushed to grow as much as they could. By midcentury, annual sugar exports from the English Caribbean totaled about 150,000 pounds; by 1700, exports reached nearly 50 million pounds.

Sugar transformed Barbados and other West Indian islands. Poor farmers could not afford the expensive machinery that extracted and refined sugarcane juice. Planters with the necessary capital to grow sugar got rich. By 1680, the wealthiest Barbadian sugar planters were, on average, four times richer than tobacco grandees in the Chesapeake. The sugar grandees differed from their Chesapeake counterparts in another crucial way: The average sugar baron in Barbados owned 115 slaves in 1680.

African slaves planted, cultivated, and harvested the sugarcane that made West Indian planters wealthy. Beginning in the 1640s, Barbadian planters pur-chased thousands of slaves to work their plantations, and the African population on the island mushroomed. During the 1650s, when blacks made up only 3 per-cent of the Chesapeake population, they had already become the majority on Barbados. By 1700, slaves constituted more than three-fourths of the island's population.

For slaves, work on a sugar plantation was a life sentence to brutal, unremit-ting labor. Slaves suffered high death rates. Since slave men outnumbered slave women two to one, few slaves could form families and have children. These grim realities meant that in Barbados and elsewhere in the West Indies, the slave population did not grow by natural reproduction. Instead, planters continually purchased enslaved Africans. Although sugar plantations did not gain a foothold in North America in the seventeenth century, the West Indies nonethe-less exerted a powerful influence on the development of slavery in the mainland colonies.

Carolina: A West Indian Frontier

The early settlers of what became South Carolina were immigrants from Barbados. In 1663, a Barbadian planter named John Colleton and a group of seven other men obtained a charter from England's King Charles II to establish a colony south of the Chesapeake and north of the Spanish territories in Florida. The men, known as "proprietors," hoped to siphon settlers from Barbados and other colonies and encourage them to develop a profitable export crop comparable to West Indian sugar and Chesapeake tobacco. Following the Chesapeake example, the proprietors offered headrights of up to 150 acres of land for each settler. In 1670, they established the colony's first permanent English settlement, Charles Towne (later spelled Charleston) (see Map 3.2).

As the proprietors had planned, most of the early settlers were from Barbados. In fact, Carolina was the only seventeenth-century English colony to be settled principally by colonists from other colonies rather than from England. The Barbadian immigrants brought their slaves with them. More than a fourth of the early settlers were slaves, and as the colony continued to attract settlers from Barbados, the black population multiplied. By 1700, slaves made up about half the population of Carolina. The new colony's close association with Barbados caused English officials to refer routinely to "Carolina in ye West Indies."

The Carolinians experimented unsuccessfully to match their semitropical climate with profitable export crops of tobacco, cotton, indigo, and olives. In the mid-1690s, colonists identified a hardy strain of rice and took advantage of the knowledge of rice cultivation among their many African slaves to build rice plantations. Settlers also sold livestock and timber to the West Indies, as well as another "natural resource": They captured and enslaved several thousand local Indians and sold them to Caribbean planters. Both economically and socially, seventeenth-century Carolina was a frontier outpost of the West Indian sugar economy.

Slave Labor Emerges in the Chesapeake

By 1700, more than eight out of ten people in the southern colonies of English North America lived in the Chesapeake. Until the 1670s, almost all Chesapeake colonists were white people from England. By 1700, however, one out of eight people in the region was a black person from Africa. A few black people had lived in the Chesapeake since the 1620s, but the black population grew fivefold between 1670 and 1700 as hundreds of tobacco planters made the transition from servant to slave labor.

For planters, slaves had several obvious advantages over servants. Although slaves cost three to five times more than servants, slaves never became free. Since the mortality rate had declined by the 1680s, planters could reasonably expect slaves to live longer than a servant's period of indenture. Slaves also promised to be a perpetual labor force, since children of slave mothers inherited the status of slavery.

Slaves had another important advantage over servants: They could be controlled politically. Bacon's Rebellion had demonstrated how disruptive former servants could be when their expectations were not met. A slave labor system promised to avoid the political problems caused by the servant labor system. Slavery kept discontented laborers in permanent servitude, and their color was a badge of their bondage.

The slave labor system polarized Chesapeake society along lines of race and status: All slaves were black, and nearly all blacks were slaves; almost all free people were white, and all whites were free or only temporarily bound in indentured servitude. Unlike Barbados, however, the Chesapeake retained a vast white majority. Among whites, huge differences of wealth and status still existed. By 1700, more than three-quarters of white families had neither servants nor slaves. Nonetheless, poor white farmers enjoyed the privileges of free status. They could own property, get married, have families, and bequeath their property and their freedom to their descendants; they could move when and where they wanted; they could associate freely with other people; they could serve on juries, vote, and hold political office; and they could work, loaf, and sleep as they chose. These privileges of freedom—none of them possessed by slaves—made lesser white folk feel they had a genuine stake in the existence of slavery, even if they did not own a single slave. By emphasizing the privileges of freedom shared by all white people, the slave labor system reduced the tensions between poor folk and grandees that had plagued the Chesapeake region in the 1670s.

In contrast to slaves in Barbados, most slaves in the seventeenth-century Chesapeake colonies had frequent and close contact with white people. Slaves and white servants performed the same tasks on tobacco plantations, often working side by side in the fields. Slaves took advantage of every opportunity to slip away from white supervision and seek out the company of other slaves. Planters often feared that slaves would turn such seemingly innocent social pleasures to political ends, either to run away or to conspire to strike against their masters. Slaves often did run away, but they were usually captured or returned after a brief absence. Despite planters' nightmares, slave insurrections did not occur.

Although slavery resolved the political unrest caused by the servant labor system, it created new political problems. By 1700, the bedrock political issue in the southern colonies was keeping slaves in their place, at the end of a hoe. The slave labor system in the southern colonies stood roughly midway between the sugar plantations and black majority of Barbados to the south and the small farms and homogeneous villages that developed in seventeenth-century New England to the north (see chapter 4).

▶ **REVIEW**   Why had slave labor largely displaced indentured servant labor by 1700 in Chesapeake tobacco production?

Conclusion: The Growth of English Colonies Based on Export Crops and Slave Labor

By 1700, the colonies of Virginia, Maryland, and Carolina were firmly established. The staple crops they grew for export provided a livelihood for many, a fortune for a few, and valuable revenues for shippers, merchants, and the English monarchy. Their societies differed markedly from English society in most respects, yet the colonists considered themselves English people who happened to live in

North America. They claimed the same rights and privileges as English men and women, while they denied those rights and privileges to Native Americans and African slaves.

The English colonies also differed from the example of New Spain. Settlers and servants flocked to English colonies, in contrast to Spaniards who trickled into New Spain. Few English missionaries sought to convert Indians to Protestant Christianity, unlike the numerous Catholic missionaries in the Spanish settlements in New Mexico and Florida. Large quantities of gold and silver never materialized in English North America. English colonists never adopted the system of *encomienda* (see chapter 2) because the Indians in these areas were too few and too hostile and their communities too small and decentralized compared with those of the Mexica. Yet some forms of coerced labor and racial distinction that developed in New Spain had North American counterparts, as English colonists employed servants and slaves and defined themselves as superior to Indians and Africans.

By 1700, the remnants of Powhatan's people still survived. As English settlement pushed north, west, and south of the Chesapeake Bay, the Indians faced the new colonial world that Powhatan and Pocahontas had encountered when John Smith and the first colonists had arrived at Jamestown. By 1700, the many descendants of Pocahontas's son, Thomas, as well as other colonists and Native Americans, understood that the English had come to stay.

REVIEWING THE CHAPTER

Use the questions and timeline to review and strengthen your understanding of the chapter.

REVIEW QUESTIONS

1. Why did Powhatan pursue largely peaceful relations with the Jamestown settlement? (pp. 57–62)

2. Why did the vast majority of European immigrants to the Chesapeake come as indentured servants? (pp. 62–69)

3. Why did Chesapeake colonial society become increasingly polarized between 1650 and 1670? (pp. 69–73)

4. Why did the Pueblo Indians revolt against Spanish missionaries in 1680? (pp. 74–75)

5. Why had slave labor largely displaced indentured servant labor by 1700 in Chesapeake tobacco production? (pp. 75–79)

MAKING CONNECTIONS

1. Given the extraordinary vulnerability of the Jamestown settlement in its first two decades, why did its sponsors and settlers not abandon it? In your answer, discuss the challenges the settlement faced and the benefits different participants in England and the New World hoped to derive from their efforts.

2. Tobacco dominated European settlement in the seventeenth-century Chesapeake. How did tobacco agriculture shape the region's development? In your answer, be sure to address the demographic and geographic features of the colony.

3. Bacon's Rebellion highlighted significant tensions within Chesapeake society. What provoked the rebellion, and what did it accomplish? In your answer, be sure to consider causes and results in the colonies and in England.

4. In addition to making crucial contributions to the economic success of seventeenth-century English colonies, Native Americans and enslaved Africans influenced colonial politics. Describe how European colonists' relations with these populations contributed to political friction and harmony within the colony.

TIMELINE

1588	• England defeats Spanish Armada.	**1632**	• King Charles I grants Lord Baltimore land for colony of Maryland.
1606	• Virginia Company receives royal charter.	**1634**	• Colonists begin to arrive in Maryland.
1607	• English colonists found Jamestown settlement; Pocahontas "rescues" John Smith.	**1640s**	• Barbados colonists begin to grow sugarcane with labor of African slaves.
1607–10	• Starvation plagues Jamestown.	**1644**	• Opechancanough leads second Indian uprising against Virginia colonists.
1612	• John Rolfe begins to plant tobacco in Virginia.	**1660**	• Navigation Act requires colonial tobacco to be shipped to English ports.
1617	• First commercial tobacco shipment leaves Virginia for England. • Pocahontas dies in England.	**1663**	• Royal charter granted for Carolina colony.
1618	• Powhatan dies; Opechancanough becomes chief of the Algonquians.	**1670**	• Charles Towne, South Carolina, founded.
1619	• First Africans arrive in Virginia. • House of Burgesses begins to meet in Virginia.	**1670– 1700**	• Slave labor system emerges in Carolina and Chesapeake colonies.
1622	• Opechancanough leads first Indian uprising against Virginia colonists.	**1676**	• Bacon's Rebellion.
1624	• Virginia becomes royal colony.	**1680**	• Pueblo Revolt.

▶ **For an online bibliography, practice quizzes, Web sites, images, and documents related to this chapter,** see the Book Companion Site at **bedfordstmartins.com/roark.**

▶ **For firsthand accounts of this period,** see Chapter 3 in Michael Johnson, ed., *Reading the American Past,* Fourth Edition.

4
CHAPTER

The Northern Colonies in the Seventeenth Century
1601–1700

ROGER WILLIAMS AND HIS WIFE, MARY, arrived in Massachusetts in February 1631. Fresh from a superb education at Cambridge University, the twenty-eight-year-old Williams was "a godly [Puritan] minister," noted Governor John Winthrop. Winthrop's Boston church asked Williams to become its minister, but he refused because the church had not openly rejected the corrupt Church of England. New England's premier Puritan church was not pure enough for Williams.

Williams and his wife moved to Plymouth colony for two years. While there, he spent a great deal of time among the Narragansett Indians. "My soul's desire was to do the natives good," he said. Williams believed that "Nature knows no difference between Europeans and [Native] Americans in blood, birth, [or] bodies . . . God having made of one blood all mankind." He sought to learn about the Indians' language, religion, and **culture**, without trying to convert them to Christianity. Williams insisted that the colonists respect the Indians' religion and culture since all human beings—Christians and non-Christians alike—should live according to their consciences as revealed to them by God.

Williams condemned English colonists for their "sin of unjust usurpation" of Indian land. He believed that their claims were legally, morally, and spiritually invalid. In contrast, Massachusetts officials defended colonists' settlement on Indian land. If land "lies common, and hath never been replenished or subdued, [it] is free to any that possess or improve it," Governor Winthrop explained. Besides, he said, "if we leave [the Indians] sufficient [land] for their use, we may lawfully take the rest, there being more than enough for them and us." Winthrop's arguments prevailed, but Williams refused to knuckle under. "God Land," he said, "[is] as great a God with us English as God Gold was with the Spaniards." Although New Englanders claimed to worship the one true God in heaven, Williams declared,

---

America's First Book

The first book printed in what is now the United States, this well-thumbed copy of *The Whole Booke of Psalmes Faithfully Translated into English Metre* was published in Cambridge, Massachusetts, in 1640. The famous Twenty-third Psalm begins near the bottom of the left-hand page and concludes on the facing page.

Roger Foley/Library of Congress.

"the truth is the great Gods of this world are God-belly, God-peace, God-wealth, God-honour, [and] God-pleasure."

The governor of Plymouth colony, William Bradford, praised Williams as "a man godly and zealous, having many precious parts" and also "some strange opinions." Most New England leaders considered Williams a bit much. One minister censured him for his "self-conceited, and unquiet, and unlamblike frame of . . . Spirit." Williams, however, continued to proclaim his opinions and to refuse to submit lamblike to New England orthodoxy.

In 1633, Williams became the minister of the church in Salem, Massachusetts. Like other New England Puritans, the members of the Salem church had solemnly agreed to "**Covenant** with the Lord and one with another; and doe bynd our selves in the presence of God, to walke together in all his waies, according as he is pleased to reveale himself unto us in his Blessed word of truth [the Bible]." Most New England Puritans believed that churches and governments should enforce both godly belief and behavior according to biblical rules. They claimed that "the Word of God is . . . clear." In contrast, Williams believed that the Bible shrouded the Word of God in "mist and fog." Williams pointed out that devout and pious Christians could and did differ about what the Bible said and what God expected. That observation led him to denounce the emerging New England order as impure, ungodly, and tyrannical.

Williams also disagreed with the New England government's requirement that everyone attend church services. He argued that forcing people who were not Christians to attend church was wrong in four major ways. First, Williams preached, it was akin to requiring "a dead child to suck the breast, or a dead man [to] feast." The only way for any person to become a true Christian was by God's gift of faith revealed to the person's conscience. Second, churches should be reserved exclusively for those already converted, separating "holy from unholy . . . [and] godly from ungodly." He said requiring everybody to attend church was "False Worshipping" that promoted "spiritual drunkenness and whoredom, a soul sleep and a soul sickness." Third, the government had no business ruling on spiritual matters. Williams termed New England's regulation of religious behavior "spiritual rape" that inevitably would lead governments to use coercion and violence to enforce the government's misguided ways. Finally, Williams believed that governments should tolerate all religious beliefs because only God knows the Truth; no person and no religion can understand God with absolute certainty. "I commend that man," Williams wrote, "whether Jew, or Turk, or Papist, or whoever, that steers no otherwise than his conscience dares." In Williams's view, toleration of religious belief and liberty of conscience were the only paths to religious purity and political harmony.

New England's leaders denounced Williams's arguments. One minister wrote that Williams sought "liberty to enfranchise all false Religions," which was "the greatest impiety in the World." Genuine **liberty**, he said, was "to contend earnestly for the Truth; to preserve unity of Spirit, Faith, ordinances, to be all like minded, of one accord." Like-minded New Englanders banished Williams for his "extreme and dangerous" opinions. He escaped from an attempt to ship him back to England and in the winter of 1636 spent fourteen weeks walking south to Narragansett Bay, "exposed to the mercy of an howling Wilderness in Frost and Snow." There he founded the colony of Rhode Island, which enshrined "Liberty of Conscience" as a fundamental ideal and became a refuge for other dissenters.

Although New England's leaders expelled Williams from their holy commonwealth, his dissenting ideas arose from orthodox Puritan doctrines. By urging believers to search for evidence of God's grace, **Puritanism** encouraged the faithful to listen for God's whisper of Truth and faith. Puritanism combined rigid insistence on conformity to God's law and aching uncertainty about how to identify and act upon it. Despite the best efforts of New England's leaders to define their way as God's Way, Puritanism inspired believers such as Roger Williams to draw their own conclusions and stick to them.

During the seventeenth century, New England's Puritan zeal—exemplified by Roger Williams and his persecutors—cooled. The goal of founding a holy New England faded. Late in the century, new "middle" colonies—New York, New Jersey, and Pennsylvania—featuring greater religious and ethnic diversity than New England were founded. Religion remained important throughout all the colonies, but it competed with the growing faith that the promise of a better life required less focus on salvation and more attention to worldly concerns of family, work, and trade.

As settler populations increased throughout the English mainland colonies, settlements encroached on Indian land, causing violent conflict to flare up repeatedly. Political conflict also arose among colonists, particularly in response to major political upheavals in England. By the end of the seventeenth century, the English monarchy exerted greater control over North America and the rest of its Atlantic empire. The lifeblood of the empire, however, remained the continual flow of products, people, and ideas that pulsed between England and the colonies, energizing both.

Puritan Origins: The English Reformation

The religious roots of the Puritans who founded New England reached back to the Protestant Reformation, which arose in Germany in 1517 (see chapter 2). The **Reformation** spread quickly to other countries, but the English church initially remained within the Catholic fold and continued its allegiance to the pope in Rome. King Henry VIII, who reigned from 1509 to 1547, understood that the Reformation offered him an opportunity to break with Rome and take control of the church in England. In 1534, Henry formally initiated the English Reformation. At his insistence, Parliament passed the Act of Supremacy, which outlawed the Catholic Church and proclaimed the king "the only supreme head on earth of the Church of England." Henry seized the vast properties of the Catholic Church in

England as well as the privilege of appointing bishops and others in the church hierarchy.

In the short run, the English Reformation allowed Henry VIII to achieve his political goal of controlling the church. In the long run, however, the Reformation brought to England the political and religious turmoil that Henry had hoped to avoid. Henry himself sought no more than a halfway Reformation. Protestant doctrines held no attraction for Henry; in almost all matters of religious belief and practice, he remained an orthodox Catholic. Many English Catholics wanted to revoke the English Reformation; they hoped to return the Church of England to the pope and to restore Catholic doctrines and ceremonies. But many other English people insisted on a genuine, thoroughgoing Reformation; these people came to be called Puritans.

During the sixteenth century, Puritanism was less an organized movement than a set of ideas and religious principles that appealed strongly to many dissenting members of the Church of England. They sought to purify the Church of England by eliminating what they considered the offensive features of Catholicism. For example, they demanded that the church hierarchy be abolished and that ordinary Christians be given greater control over religious life. They wanted to do away with the rituals of Catholic worship and instead emphasize an individual's relationship with God developed through Bible study, prayer, and introspection. Although there were many varieties and degrees of Puritanism, all Puritans shared a desire to make the English church thoroughly Protestant.

The fate of **Protestantism** waxed and waned under the monarchs who succeeded Henry VIII. When he died in 1547, the advisers of the new king, Edward VI—the nine-year-old son of Henry and his third wife, Jane Seymour—initiated religious reforms that moved in a Protestant direction. The tide of reform reversed in 1553 when Edward died and was succeeded by Mary I, the daughter of Henry and Catherine of Aragon, his first wife. Mary was a steadfast Catholic, and shortly after becoming queen, she married Philip II of Spain, Europe's most powerful guardian of Catholicism. Mary attempted to restore the pre-Reformation Catholic Church. She outlawed Protestantism in England and persecuted those who refused to conform, sentencing almost three hundred to burn at the stake.

The tide turned again in 1558 when Mary died and was succeeded by Elizabeth I, the daughter of Henry and his second wife, Anne Boleyn. During her long reign, Elizabeth reaffirmed the English Reformation and tried to position the English church between the extremes of Catholicism and Puritanism. Like her father, she was less concerned with theology than with politics. Above all, she desired a church that would strengthen the monarchy and the nation. By the time Elizabeth died in 1603, many people in England looked on Protestantism as a defining feature of national identity.

When Elizabeth's successor, James I, became king, English Puritans petitioned for further reform of the Church of England. James authorized a new translation of the Bible, known ever since as the King James version. However, neither James I nor his son Charles I, who became king in 1625, was receptive to the ideas of Puritan reformers. James and Charles moved the Church of England away from Puritanism. They enforced conformity to the Church of England and punished dissenters, both ordinary Christians and ministers. In 1629, Charles I dissolved Parliament—where Puritans were well represented—and initiated aggressive anti-Puritan policies. Many Puritans despaired about continuing to defend their faith in England and began to make plans to emigrate. Some left for Europe, others for the West Indies. The largest number set out for America.

►**REVIEW**   Why did Henry VIII initiate the English Reformation?

Puritans and the Settlement of New England

Puritans who emigrated aspired to escape the turmoil and persecution of England and to build a new, orderly, Puritan version of England. Puritans established the first small settlement in New England in 1620, followed a few years later by additional settlements by the Massachusetts Bay Company. Allowed self-government through royal charter, these Puritans were in a unique position to direct the new colonies according to their faith. Their faith shaped the colonies they established in almost every way. Although many New England colonists were not Puritans, Puritanism remained a paramount influence in New England's religion, politics, and community life during the seventeenth century.

The Pilgrims and Plymouth Colony

One of the first Protestant groups to emigrate, later known as Pilgrims, espoused a heresy known as separatism. These Separatists sought to withdraw—or separate—from the Church of England, which they considered hopelessly corrupt. In 1608, they moved to Holland; by 1620, they realized that they could not live and worship there as they had hoped. William Bradford, a leader of the group, recalled that "many of their children, by . . . the great licentiousness of youth in [Holland], and the manifold temptations of the place, were drawn away by evil examples." Bradford and other Separatists believed that America promised to better protect their children's piety and preserve their community. Separatists obtained permission to settle in the extensive territory granted to the Virginia Company (see chapter 3). To finance their journey, they formed a joint-stock company with English investors. The investors provided the capital; the Separatists provided their labor and lives and received a share of the profits for seven years. In August 1620, the Pilgrim families boarded the *Mayflower*, and after eleven weeks at sea, all but one of the 102 immigrants arrived at the outermost tip of Cape Cod, in present-day Massachusetts.

The Pilgrims realized immediately that they had landed far north of the Virginia grants and had no legal authority to settle in the area. To provide order and security as well as a claim to legitimacy, they drew up the Mayflower Compact on the day they arrived. They pledged to "covenant and combine ourselves together into a civil Body Politick, for our better Ordering and Preservation." The signers (all men) agreed to enact and obey necessary and just laws.

The Pilgrims settled at Plymouth and elected William Bradford their governor. That first winter "was most sad and lamentable," Bradford wrote later. "In two or three months' time half of [our] company died . . . being the depth of winter, and wanting houses and other comforts [and] being infected with scurvy and other diseases."

In the spring, Wampanoag Indians rescued the floundering Plymouth settlement. First Samoset, then Squanto befriended the settlers. Both of them had learned English from previous contacts with sailors and fishermen who had visited the coast to dry fish and make repairs years before the Plymouth settlers arrived. Samoset arranged for the Pilgrims to meet and establish good relations with Massasoit, the Wampanoag chief whose territory included Plymouth. Squanto, Bradford recalled, "was a special instrument sent of God for their [the Pilgrims'] good. . . . He directed them how to set their corn, where to take fish, and to procure other commodities, and was also their pilot to bring them to unknown places." With the Indians' guidance, the Pilgrims managed to harvest enough food to guarantee their survival through the coming winter, an occasion they celebrated in the fall of 1621 with a feast of thanksgiving attended by Massasoit and other Wampanoags.

Still, the Plymouth colony remained precarious. Only seven dwellings were erected that first year; half the original colonists died; and a new group of threadbare, sickly settlers arrived in November 1621, requiring the colony to adopt stringent food rationing. The colonists quarreled with their London investors, who became frustrated when Plymouth failed to produce the expected profits. These struggles to survive constantly frustrated the London investors, but the Pilgrims persisted, living simply and coexisting in relative peace with the Indians. They paid the Wampanoags when settlers gradually encroached on Indian land. By 1630, Plymouth had become a small permanent settlement, but it failed to attract many other English Puritans.

The Founding of Massachusetts Bay Colony

In 1629, shortly before Charles I dissolved Parliament, a group of Puritan merchants and country gentlemen obtained a royal charter for the Massachusetts Bay Company. The charter provided the usual privileges granted to joint-stock companies, including land for **colonization** that spanned present-day Massachusetts, New Hampshire, Vermont, Maine, and upstate New York. In addition, a unique provision of the charter permitted the government of the Massachusetts Bay Company to be

Seal of Massachusetts Bay Colony
In 1629, the Massachusetts Bay Company designed this seal depicting an Indian man inviting English settlers to "come over and help us." Of course, such an invitation was never issued. The seal was an attempt to lend an aura of altruism to the Massachusetts Bay Company's colonization efforts. In reality, colonists in Massachusetts and elsewhere were far less interested in helping Indians than in helping themselves. For the most part, that suited the Indians, who wanted no "help" from the colonists.
Courtesy of Massachusetts Archives.

located in the colony rather than in England. This provision allowed Puritans to exchange their status as a harassed minority in England for self-government in Massachusetts.

To lead the emigrants, the stockholders of the Massachusetts Bay Company elected John Winthrop, a prosperous lawyer and landowner, to serve as governor. In March 1630, eleven ships crammed with seven hundred passengers sailed for Massachusetts; six more ships and another five hundred emigrants followed a few months later. Winthrop's fleet arrived in Massachusetts Bay in early June. Unlike the Separatists, Winthrop's Puritans aspired to reform the corrupt Church of England (rather than separate from it) by setting an example of godliness in the New World. Winthrop and a small group chose to settle on the peninsula that became Boston, and other settlers clustered at promising locations nearby.

In a sermon to his companions aboard the *Arbella* while they were still at sea—probably the most famous sermon in American history—Winthrop proclaimed the cosmic significance of their journey. The Puritans had "entered into a covenant" with God to "work out our salvation under the power and purity of his holy ordinances," Winthrop declared. This sanctified agreement with God meant that the Puritans had to make "extraordinary" efforts to "bring into familiar and constant practice" religious principles that most people in England merely preached. To achieve their pious goals, the Puritans had to subordinate their individual interests to the common good. "We must be knit together in this work as one man," Winthrop preached. "We must delight in each other, make others' conditions our own, rejoice together, mourn together, labor and suffer together."

The stakes could not be higher, Winthrop told his listeners: "We must consider that we shall be as a city upon a hill. The eyes of all people are upon us."

That belief shaped seventeenth-century New England as profoundly as tobacco shaped the Chesapeake. Winthrop's vision of a city on a hill fired the Puritans' fierce determination to keep their covenant and live according to God's laws, unlike the backsliders and compromisers who accommodated to the Church of England. Their determination to adhere strictly to God's plan charged nearly every feature of life in seventeenth-century New England with a distinctive, high-voltage piety.

The new colonists, as Winthrop's son John wrote later, had "all things to do, as in the beginning of the world." Unlike the early Chesapeake settlers, the first Massachusetts Bay colonists encountered few Indians because the local population had been almost entirely exterminated by an epidemic probably caused by contact with Europeans more than a decade earlier. Still, as in the Chesapeake, the colonists fell victim to deadly ailments. More than two hundred settlers died during the first year, including one of Winthrop's sons and eleven of his servants. About the same number returned to England on the first outbound ship in the spring of 1631. But Winthrop maintained a confidence that proved infectious. He wrote to his wife, "I like so well to be heer as I do not repent my comminge. . . . I would not have altered my course, though I had forseene all these Afflictions." And each year from 1630 to 1640, ship after ship followed in the wake of Winthrop's fleet. In all, more than twenty thousand new settlers came, their eyes focused on the Puritans' city on a hill.

Often, when the Church of England cracked down on a Puritan minister in England, he and many of his followers moved together to New England. Smaller groups of English Puritans moved to the Chesapeake, Barbados, and elsewhere in the New World, including New Amsterdam (present-day New York). By 1640, New England had one of the highest ratios of preachers to population in all of Christendom. A few ministers sought to carry the message of Christianity to the Indians, accompanied by instructions replacing what missionary John Eliot termed the Indians' "unfixed, confused, and ungoverned . . . life, uncivilized and unsubdued to labor and order." For the most part, however, the colonists focused less on saving Indians' souls than on saving their own.

The occupations of New England immigrants reflected the social origins of English Puritans. On the whole, the immigrants came from the middle ranks of English society. The vast majority of immigrants were either farmers or tradesmen, including carpenters, tailors, and textile workers. Indentured servants, whose numbers dominated the Chesapeake settlers, accounted for only about a fifth of those headed for New England. Most New England immigrants paid their way to Massachusetts, even though the journey often took their life savings. They were encouraged by the promise of bounty in New England reported in Winthrop's letter to his son: "Here is as good land as I have seen there [in England]. . . . Here can be no want of anything to those who bring means to raise [it] out of the earth and sea."

In contrast to Chesapeake newcomers, New England immigrants usually arrived as families. In fact, more Puritans came with family members than did any other group of immigrants in all of American history. A ship that left Weymouth, England, in 1635, for example, carried 106 passengers, 98 of whom belonged to one of 14 families typically comprising a husband, a wife, children, and sometimes a servant. Unlike immigrants to the Chesapeake, women and children made up a solid majority in New England.

As Winthrop reminded the first settlers in his *Arbella* sermon, each family was a "little commonwealth" that mirrored the hierarchy among all God's creatures. Just as humankind was subordinate to God, so young people were subordinate to their elders, children to their parents, and wives to their husbands. The immigrants' family ties reinforced their religious beliefs with universally understood notions of hierarchy and mutual dependence. Whereas immigrants to the Chesapeake were disciplined mostly by the coercions of servitude and the caprices of the tobacco market, immigrants to New England entered a social order defined by the interlocking institutions of family, church, and community.

▶**REVIEW**   Why did the Puritans immigrate to North America?

The Evolution of New England Society

The New England colonists, unlike their counterparts in the Chesapeake, settled in small towns, usually located on the coast or by a river. Massachusetts Bay colonists founded 133 towns during the seventeenth century, each with one or more churches. Church members' fervent piety, buttressed by the institutions of local government, enforced remarkable religious and social conformity in the small New England settlements. During the century, tensions within the Puritan faith and changes in New England communities splintered religious orthodoxy and weakened Puritan zeal. By 1700, however, Puritanism still maintained a distinctive influence in New England.

Church, Covenant, and Conformity

Puritans believed that the church consisted of men and women who had entered a solemn covenant with one another and with God. Winthrop and three other men signed the original covenant of the first Boston church in 1630, agreeing to "Promisse, and bind our selves, to walke in all our wayes according to the Rule of the Gospell, and in all sincere Conformity to His holy Ordinaunces." Each new member of the covenant had to persuade existing members that she or he had fully experienced conversion. By 1635, the Boston church had added more than 250 names to the four original subscribers to the covenant.

Puritans embraced a distinctive version of Protestantism derived from **Calvinism**, the doctrines of John Calvin, a sixteenth-century Swiss Protestant theologian. Calvin insisted that Christians strictly discipline their behavior to conform to God's commandments announced in the Bible. Like Calvin, Puritans believed in **predestination**—the idea that the all-powerful God, before the creation of the world, decided which few human souls would receive eternal life. Only God knows the identity of these fortunate, predestined individuals—the "elect" or "saints." Nothing a person did in his or her lifetime could alter God's inscrutable choice or provide assurance that the person was predestined for salvation with the elect or damned to hell with the doomed multitude. The gloomy inevitability and exclusivity of predestination contrasted sharply with Catholic doctrines that all human beings could potentially be granted eternal life by God, acting through the Catholic Church.

Despite the looming uncertainty about God's choice of the elect, Puritans believed that if a person lived a rigorously godly life—constantly winning the daily battle against sinful temptations—his or her behavior was likely to be a hint, a visible sign, that he or she was one of God's chosen few. Puritans thought that "sainthood" would become visible in individuals' behavior, especially if they were privileged to know God's Word as revealed in the Bible.

The connection between sainthood and saintly behavior, however, was far from certain. Some members of the elect, Puritans believed, had not heard God's Word as revealed in the Bible, and therefore their behavior did not necessarily signal their sainthood. One reason Puritans required all town residents to attend church services was to enlighten anyone who was ignorant of God's Truth. The slippery relationship between saintly behavior—observable by anybody—and God's predestined election—invisible and unknowable to anyone—caused Puritans to worry constantly that individuals who acted like saints were fooling themselves and others. Nevertheless, Puritans thought that "visible saints"—persons who passed their demanding tests of conversion and church membership—probably, though not certainly, were among God's elect.

Members of Puritan churches ardently hoped that God had chosen them to receive eternal life and tried to demonstrate saintly behavior. Their covenant bound them to help each other attain salvation and to discipline the entire community by saintly standards. Church members kept an eye on the behavior of everybody in town. Infractions of morality, order, or propriety were reported to Puritan elders, who summoned the wayward to a church inquiry. By overseeing every aspect of life, the visible saints enforced a remarkable degree of righteous conformity in Puritan communities. Total conformity, however, was never achieved. Ardent Puritans differed among themselves; non-Puritans shirked orthodox rules. But Puritan doctrine spelled out the fiery punishment for failure to conform: A servant in Roxbury declared that "if hell were ten times hotter, [I] had rather be there than [I] would serve [my] master."

Sabbath Breakers

These seventeenth-century prints show some of the punishments to which Sabbath breakers could be subjected by man and God. In the upper illustration, a person who gathered sticks on the Sabbath is stoned to death as Puritans believed the Bible commanded. In the lower print, three women who broke the Sabbath by preparing flax to be spun and woven into linen suffer God's retribution when they are burned to death.

Divine Examples of God's Severe Judgements upon Sabbath-Breakers (London, 1671).

Remember that thou keepe holy ye Sabboth Day
The profane Isralite, that durst assay,
In gathering sticks, to breake the Sabboth day,
Is stunde to death, for like Contumacy
The Lord hath sworne, that every Soule shall dye.

A Woman and her two Daughters pill and dry flax on the Lords day, are all burnt

Despite the central importance of religion, churches played no direct role in the civil government of New England communities. Puritans did not want to mimic the Church of England, which they considered a puppet of the king rather than an independent body that served the Lord. They were determined to insulate New England churches from the contaminating influence of the civil state and its merely human laws. Although ministers were the most highly respected figures in New England towns, they were prohibited from holding government office.

Puritans had no qualms, however, about their religious beliefs influencing New England governments. As much as possible, the Puritans tried to bring public life into conformity with their view of God's law. For example, fines were issued for Sabbath-breaking activities such as working, traveling, playing a flute, smoking a pipe, and visiting neighbors.

Puritans mandated other purifications of what they considered corrupt English practices. They refused to celebrate Christmas or Easter because the Bible did not mention either one. They outlawed religious wedding ceremonies;

couples were married by a magistrate in a civil ceremony (the first wedding in Massachusetts performed by a minister occurred in 1686). They prohibited elaborate clothing and finery such as lace trim and short sleeves—"whereby the nakedness of the arm may be discovered." They banned cards, dice, shuffleboard, and other games of chance, as well as music and dancing. The distinguished minister Increase Mather insisted that "Mixt or Promiscuous Dancing . . . of Men and Women" could not be tolerated since "the unchaste Touches and Gesticulations used by Dancers have a palpable tendency to that which is evil." On special occasions, Puritans proclaimed days of fasting and humiliation, which, as one preacher boasted, amounted to "so many Sabbaths more."

Government by Puritans for Puritanism

It is only a slight exaggeration to say that seventeenth-century New England was governed by Puritans for Puritanism. The charter of the Massachusetts Bay Company empowered the company's stockholders, known as freemen, to meet as a body known as the General Court and make the laws needed to govern the company's affairs. The colonists transformed this arrangement for running a joint-stock company into a structure for governing the colony. Hoping to ensure that godly men would decide government policies, the General Court expanded the number of freemen in 1631 to include all male church members. Only freemen had the right to vote for governor, deputy governor, and other colonial officials. As new settlers were recognized as freemen, the size of the General Court grew too large to meet conveniently. So in 1634, the freemen in each town agreed to send two deputies to the General Court to act as the colony's legislative assembly. All other men were classified as "inhabitants," and they had the right to vote, hold office, and participate fully in town government.

A "town meeting," composed of a town's inhabitants and freemen, chose the selectmen and other officials who administered local affairs. New England town meetings routinely practiced a level of popular participation in political life that was unprecedented elsewhere in the world during the seventeenth century. Almost every adult man could speak out in town meetings and fortify his voice with a vote. However, all women—even church members—were prohibited from voting, and towns did not permit "contrary-minded" men to become or remain inhabitants. Although town meeting participants wrangled from time to time, widespread political participation tended to reinforce conformity to Puritan ideals.

One of the most important functions of New England government was land distribution. Settlers who desired to establish a new town entered a covenant and petitioned the General Court for a grant of land. The court granted town sites to suitably pious petitioners but did not allow settlement until the Indians who inhabited a grant agreed to relinquish their claim to the land, usually in exchange for manufactured goods. For instance, William Pynchon purchased the site of

Springfield, Massachusetts, from the Agawam Indians for "eighteen fathams [arm's lengths] of Wampum, eighteen coates, 18 hatchets, 18 hoes, [and] 18 knives."

Having obtained their grant, town founders apportioned land among themselves and any newcomers they permitted to join them. Normally, each family received a house lot large enough for an adjacent garden as well as one or more strips of agricultural land on the perimeter of the town. Although there was a considerable difference between the largest and smallest family plots, most clustered in the middle range—roughly fifty to one hundred acres—resulting in a more nearly equal distribution of land in New England than in the Chesapeake.

The physical layout of New England towns encouraged settlers to look inward toward their neighbors, multiplying the opportunities for godly vigilance. Most people considered the forest that lay just beyond every settler's house an alien environment that was interrupted here and there by those oases of civilization, the towns. Footpaths connecting one town to another were so rudimentary that even John Winthrop once got lost within half a mile of his house and spent a sleepless night in the forest, circling the light of his small campfire and singing psalms.

The Splintering of Puritanism

Almost from the beginning, John Winthrop and other leaders had difficulty enforcing their views of Puritan orthodoxy. In England, persecution as a dissenting minority had unified Puritan voices in opposition to the Church of England. In New England, the promise of a godly society and the Puritans' emphasis on individual Bible study led New Englanders toward different visions of godliness. Puritan leaders, however, interpreted dissent as an error caused either by a misguided believer or by the malevolent power of Satan. Whatever the cause, errors could not be tolerated. As one Puritan minister proclaimed, "The Scripture saith . . . there is no Truth but one."

Shortly after banishing Roger Williams, Winthrop confronted another dissenter, this time a devout Puritan woman steeped in Scripture and absorbed by religious questions: Anne Hutchinson. The mother of fourteen children, Hutchinson served her neighbors as a skilled midwife. After she settled into her new home in Boston in 1634, women gathered there to hear her weekly lectures on recent sermons. As one listener observed, she was a "Woman that Preaches better Gospell then any of your black-coates . . . [from] the Ninneversity." As the months passed, Hutchinson began to lecture twice a week, and crowds of sixty to eighty women and men gathered to listen to her.

Hutchinson expounded on the sermons of John Cotton, her favorite minister. Cotton stressed what he termed the "covenant of grace"—the idea that individuals could be saved only by God's grace in choosing them to be members of the elect. Cotton contrasted this familiar Puritan doctrine with the "covenant of works," the erroneous belief that a person's behavior—one's works—could win God's favor and ultimately earn a person salvation. Belief in the covenant of works and in the possibility of salvation for all was known as Arminianism. Cotton's sermons strongly hinted that many Puritans, including ministers, embraced Arminianism, which claimed—falsely, Cotton declared—that human beings could influence God's will. Anne Hutchinson agreed with Cotton. Her lectures emphasized her opinion that many of the colony's leaders affirmed the Arminian covenant of works. Like Cotton, she preached that only God's covenant of grace led to salvation.

The meetings at Hutchinson's house alarmed her nearest neighbor, John Winthrop, who believed that she was subverting the good order of the colony. In 1637, Winthrop had formal charges brought against Hutchinson and denounced her lectures as "not tolerable nor comely in the sight of God nor fitting for your sex." He told her, "You have stept out of your place, you have rather bine a Husband than a Wife and a preacher than a Hearer; and a Magistrate than a Subject."

In court, Winthrop interrogated Hutchinson, fishing for a heresy he could pin on her. Winthrop and other Puritan elders referred to Hutchinson and her followers as **antinomians**, people who believed that Christians could be saved by faith alone and did not need to act in accordance with God's law as set forth in the Bible and as interpreted by the colony's leaders. Hutchinson nimbly defended herself against the accusation of antinomianism. Yes, she acknowledged, she believed that men and women were saved by faith alone; but no, she did not deny the need to obey God's law. "The Lord hath let me see which was the clear ministry and which the wrong," she said. Finally, Winthrop had cornered her. How could she tell which ministry was which? "By an immediate revelation," she replied, "by the voice of [God's] own spirit to my soul." Winthrop spotted in this statement the heresy of prophecy, the view that God revealed his will directly to a believer instead of exclusively through the Bible, as every right-minded Puritan knew.

In 1638, the Boston church formally excommunicated Hutchinson. The minister decreed, "I doe cast you out and . . . deliver you up to Satan that you may learne no more to blaspheme[,] to seduce and to lye. . . . I command you . . . as a Leper to withdraw your selfe out of the Congregation." Banished, Hutchinson and her family moved first to Roger Williams's Rhode Island and then to present-day New York, where she and most of her family were killed by Indians.

The strains within Puritanism exemplified by Anne Hutchinson and Roger Williams caused communities to splinter repeatedly during the seventeenth century. Thomas Hooker, a prominent minister, clashed with Winthrop and other leaders over the composition of the church. Hooker argued that men and women who lived godly lives should be admitted to church membership even if they had not experienced conversion. This issue, like most others in New England, had both religious and political dimensions, for only church members could vote in Massachusetts. In 1636, Hooker led an exodus of more than eight hundred colonists from Massachusetts to the Connecticut River valley, where they founded

Hartford and neighboring towns. In 1639, the towns adopted the Fundamental Orders of Connecticut, a quasi-constitution that could be altered by the vote of freemen, who did not have to be church members, though nearly all of them were.

Other Puritan churches divided and subdivided throughout the seventeenth century as acrimony developed over doctrine and church government. Sometimes churches split over the appointment of a controversial minister. Sometimes families who had a long walk to the meetinghouse simply decided to form their own church nearer their houses. These schisms arose from ambiguities and tensions within Puritan belief. As the colonies matured, other tensions developed as well.

Religious Controversies and Economic Changes

A revolutionary transformation in the fortunes of Puritans in England had profound consequences in New England. Disputes between King Charles I and Parliament, dominated by Puritans, escalated in 1642 to civil war in England, a conflict known as the Puritan Revolution. Parliamentary forces led by the staunch Puritan Oliver Cromwell were victorious, executing Charles I in 1649 and proclaiming England a Puritan republic. From 1649 to 1660, England's rulers were not monarchs who suppressed Puritanism but believers who championed it. In a half century, English Puritans had risen from a harassed group of religious dissenters to a dominant power in English government.

When the Puritan Revolution began, the stream of immigrants to New England dwindled to a trickle, creating hard times for the colonists. They could no longer consider themselves a city on a hill setting a godly example for humankind. English society was being reformed by Puritans in England, not New England. Furthermore, when immigrant ships became rare, the colonists faced sky-high prices for scarce English goods and few customers for their own colonial products. As they searched to find new products and markets, they established the enduring patterns of New England's economy.

New England's rocky soil and short growing season ruled out cultivating the southern colonies' crops of tobacco and rice that found a ready market in Atlantic ports. Exports that New Englanders could not get from the soil they took instead from the forest and the sea. During the first decade of settlement, colonists traded with the Indians for animal pelts, which were in demand in Europe. By the 1640s, fur-bearing animals had become scarce unless traders ventured far beyond the **frontiers** of English settlement. Trees from the seemingly limitless forests of New England proved a longer-lasting resource. Masts for ships and staves for barrels of Spanish wine and West Indian sugar were crafted from New England timber.

But the most important New England export was fish. During the turmoil of the Puritan Revolution, English ships withdrew from the rich North Atlantic fishing grounds, and New England fishermen quickly took their place. Dried, salted codfish found markets in southern Europe and the West Indies. The fish trade also stimulated colonial shipbuilding and trained generations of fishermen, sailors, and merchants, creating a commercial network that endured for more than a century. But this export economy remained peripheral to most New England colonists. Their lives revolved around their farms, their churches, and their families.

Although immigration came to a standstill in the 1640s, the population continued to boom, doubling every twenty years. In New England, almost everyone married, and women often had eight or nine children. Long, cold winters minimized the warm-weather ailments of the southern colonies and reduced New England mortality. The descendants of the immigrants of the 1630s multiplied, boosting the New England population to roughly equal that of the southern colonies (Figure 4.1).

During the second half of the seventeenth century, under the pressures of steady population growth and integration into the Atlantic economy, the red-hot piety of the founders cooled. After 1640, the population grew faster than church membership. All residents attended sermons on pain of fines and punishment, but many could not find seats in the meetinghouses. Boston's churches in 1650 could house only about a third of the city's residents. By the 1680s, women were the majority of church members throughout New England. In some towns, only 15 percent of the adult men were members. A growing fraction of New Englanders, especially men, embraced what one historian has termed "horse-shed Christianity": They attended sermons but loitered outside near the horse shed, gossiping about the weather, fishing, their crops, or the

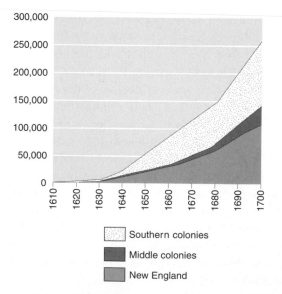

FIGURE 4.1   Population of the English North American Colonies in the Seventeenth Century
The colonial population grew at a steadily accelerating rate during the seventeenth century. New England and the southern colonies each accounted for about half the total colonial population until after 1680, when growth in Pennsylvania and New York contributed to a surge in the population of the middle colonies.

Southern colonies

Middle colonies

New England

scandalous behavior of neighbors. This slackening of piety led the Puritan minister Michael Wigglesworth to ask, in verse,

> How is it that I find
>   In stead of holiness Carnality,
> In stead of heavenly frames an Earthly mind,
>   For burning zeal luke-warm Indiferency,
> For flaming love, key-cold Dead-heartedness,
>   For temperance (in meat, and drinke, and cloaths) excess?
> Whence cometh it, that Pride, and Luxurie
>   Debate, Deceit, Contention, and Strife,
> False-dealing, Covetousness, Hypocrisie
>   (With such Crimes) amongst them are so rife,
> That one of them doth over-reach another?
>   And that an honest man can hardly trust his Brother?

Most alarming to Puritan leaders, many of the children of the visible saints of Winthrop's generation failed to experience conversion and attain full church membership. Puritans tended to assume that sainthood was inherited—that the children of visible saints were probably also among the elect. Acting on this premise, churches permitted saints to baptize their infant sons and daughters, symbolically cleansing them of their contamination with original sin. As these children grew up during the 1640s and 1650s, however, they seldom experienced the inward transformation that signaled conversion and qualification for church membership. The problem of declining church membership and the watering-down of Puritan orthodoxy became urgent during the 1650s when the children of saints, who had grown to adulthood in New England but had not experienced conversion, began to have children themselves. Their sons and daughters—the grandchildren of the founders of the colony—could not receive the protection that baptism afforded against the terrors of death because their parents had not experienced conversion.

Puritan churches debated what to do. To allow anyone, even the child of a saint, to become a church member without conversion was an unthinkable retreat from fundamental Puritan doctrine. In 1662, a synod of Massachusetts ministers reached a compromise known as the **Halfway Covenant**. Unconverted children of saints would be permitted to become "halfway" church members. Like regular church members, they could baptize their infants. But unlike full church members, they could not participate in communion or have the voting privileges of church membership. The Halfway Covenant generated a controversy that sputtered through Puritan churches for the remainder of the century. With the Halfway Covenant, Puritan churches came to terms with the lukewarm piety that had replaced the founders' burning zeal.

Nonetheless, New England communities continued to enforce piety with holy rigor. Beginning in 1656, small bands of Quakers—or members of the Society of Friends, as they called themselves—began to arrive in Massachusetts. Many of their beliefs were at odds with orthodox Puritanism. Quakers believed that God spoke directly to each individual through an "inner light," and that individuals needed neither a preacher nor the Bible in order to discover God's Word. Maintaining that all human beings were equal in God's eyes, Quakers refused to conform to mere temporal powers such as laws and governments unless God requested otherwise. For example, Quakers refused to observe the Sabbath because, they insisted, God had not set aside any special day for worship, expecting believers to worship faithfully every day. Women often took a leading role in Quaker meetings, in contrast to Puritan congregations, where women usually outnumbered men but remained subordinate.

New England communities treated Quakers with ruthless severity. Some Quakers were branded on the face "with a red-hot iron with [an] H. for heresie." When Quakers refused to leave Massachusetts, Boston officials hanged four of them between 1659 and 1661.

New Englanders' partial success in realizing the promise of a godly society ultimately undermined the intense appeal of Puritanism. In the pious Puritan communities of New England, leaders tried to eliminate sin. In the process, they diminished the sense of utter human depravity that was the wellspring of Puritanism. By 1700, New Englanders did not doubt that human beings sinned, but they were more concerned with the sins of others than with their own.

Witch trials held in Salem, Massachusetts, signaled the erosion of religious confidence and assurance. In 1692, the frenzied Salem proceedings accused more than one hundred people of witchcraft, a capital crime. The Salem court executed nineteen accused witches, signaling enduring belief in the supernatural origins of evil and gnawing doubt about the strength of Puritan New Englanders' faith.

▶**REVIEW**   Why did Massachusetts Puritans adopt the Halfway Covenant?

The Founding of the Middle Colonies

South of New England and north of the Chesapeake, a group of middle colonies were founded in the last third of the seventeenth century. Before the 1670s, few Europeans settled in the region. For the first two-thirds of the seventeenth century, the most important European outpost in the area was the relatively small Dutch colony of New Netherland. By 1700, however, the English monarchy had seized New Netherland, renamed it New York, and encouraged the creation of a Quaker colony led by William Penn. Unlike the New England colonies, the middle colonies of New York, New Jersey, and Pennsylvania originated as

land grants by the English monarch to one or more proprietors, who then possessed both the land and the extensive, almost monarchical, powers of government. These middle colonies attracted settlers of more diverse European origins and religious faiths than were found in New England.

From New Netherland to New York

In 1609, the Dutch East India Company dispatched Henry Hudson to search for a Northwest Passage to the Orient. Hudson sailed along the Atlantic coast and ventured up the large river that now bears his name until it dwindled to a stream that obviously did not lead to China. A decade later, the Dutch government granted the West India Company—a group of Dutch merchants and shippers—exclusive rights to trade with the Western Hemisphere. In 1626, Peter Minuit, the resident director of the company, purchased Manhattan Island from the Manhate Indians for trade goods worth the equivalent of a dozen beaver pelts. New Amsterdam, the small settlement established at the southern tip of Manhattan Island, became the principal trading center in New Netherland and the colony's headquarters.

Unlike the English colonies, New Netherland did not attract many European immigrants. Like New England and the Chesapeake colonies, New Netherland never realized its sponsors' dreams of great profits. The company tried to stimulate immigration by granting patroonships—allotments of eighteen miles of land along the Hudson River—to wealthy stockholders who would bring fifty families to the colony and settle them as serflike tenants on their huge domains. Only one patroonship succeeded; the others failed to attract settlers, and the company eventually recovered much of the land.

Though few in number, New Netherlanders were remarkably diverse, especially compared with the homogeneous English settlers to the north and south. Religious dissenters and immigrants from Holland, Sweden, France, Germany, and elsewhere made their way to the colony. A minister of the Dutch Reformed Church complained to his superiors in Holland that several groups of Jews had recently arrived, adding to the religious mixture of "Papists, Mennonites and Lutherans among the Dutch [and] many Puritans . . . and many other atheists . . . who conceal themselves under the name of Christians."

The West India Company struggled to govern the motley colonists. Peter Stuyvesant, governor from 1647 to 1664, tried to enforce conformity to the Dutch Reformed Church, but the company declared that "the consciences of men should be free and unshackled," making a virtue of New Netherland necessity. The company never permitted the colony's settlers to form a representative government. Instead, the company appointed government officials who established policies, including taxes, that many colonists deeply resented.

In 1664, New Netherland became New York. Charles II, who became king of England in 1660 when Parliament restored the monarchy, gave his brother James,

New Amsterdam
The settlement on Manhattan Island appears in the background of this 1673 portrait of New Amsterdam. In the foreground, the Dutch artist placed native inhabitants, drawing them in such a way that they resemble Africans rather than Lenni Lenape (Delaware) Indians. The artist probably had never seen Indians, had never been to New Amsterdam, and depended on artistic conventions about the appearance of Africans to create his Native Americans. The portrait contrasts orderly, efficient, businesslike New Amsterdam with the exotic natural environment of America.
© Collection of the New-York Historical Society.

the Duke of York, an enormous grant of land that included New Netherland. Of course, the Dutch colony did not belong to the king of England, but that legal technicality did not deter the king or his brother. The duke quickly organized a small fleet of warships, which appeared off Manhattan Island in late summer 1664, and demanded that Stuyvesant surrender. With little choice, he did.

As the new proprietor of the colony, the Duke of York exercised almost the same unlimited authority over the colony as had the West India Company. The duke never set foot in New York, but his governors struggled to impose order on the unruly colonists. Like the Dutch, the duke permitted "all persons of what Religion soever, quietly to inhabit . . . provided they give no disturbance to the publique peace, nor doe molest or disquiet others in the free exercise of their religion." This policy of religious toleration was less an affirmation of liberty of conscience than a recognition of the reality of the most heterogeneous colony in seventeenth-century North America.

New Jersey and Pennsylvania

The creation of New York led indirectly to the founding of two other middle colonies, New Jersey and Pennsylvania. In 1664, the Duke of York subdivided his grant and gave the portion between the Hudson and Delaware rivers to two of his friends. The proprietors of this new colony, New Jersey, quarreled and called in a prominent English Quaker, William Penn, to arbitrate their dispute. Penn eventually worked out a settlement that continued New Jersey's proprietary government. In the process, Penn became intensely interested in what he termed a "holy experiment" of establishing a genuinely Quaker colony in America.

Unlike most Quakers, William Penn came from an eminent family. His father had served both Cromwell and Charles II and had been knighted. Born in 1644, the younger Penn trained for a military career, but the ideas of dissenters from the reestablished Church of England appealed to him, and he became a devout Quaker. By 1680, he had published fifty books and pamphlets and spoken at countless public meetings, although he had not won official toleration for Quakers in England.

The Quakers' concept of an open, generous God who made his love equally available to all people manifested itself in behavior that continually brought them into conflict with the English government. Quaker leaders were ordinary men and women, not specially trained preachers. Quakers allowed women to assume positions of religious leadership. "In souls there is no sex," they said. Since all people were equal in the spiritual realm, Quakers considered social hierarchy false and evil. They called everyone "friend" and shook hands instead of curtsying or removing their hats—even when meeting the king. These customs enraged many non-Quakers and provoked innumerable beatings and worse. Penn was jailed four times for such offenses, once for nine months.

Despite his many run-ins with the government, Penn remained on good terms with Charles II. Partly to rid England of the troublesome Quakers, in 1681 Charles made Penn the proprietor of a new colony of some 45,000 square miles called Pennsylvania.

Toleration and Diversity in Pennsylvania

Quakers flocked to Pennsylvania in numbers exceeded only by the great Puritan migration to New England fifty years earlier. Between 1682 and 1685, nearly eight thousand immigrants arrived, most of them from England, Ireland, and Wales.

They represented a cross section of the **artisans**, farmers, and laborers who predominated among English Quakers. Quaker missionaries also encouraged immigrants from the European continent, and many came, giving Pennsylvania greater ethnic diversity than any other English colony except New York. The Quaker colony prospered, and the capital city, Philadelphia, soon rivaled New York as a center of commerce. By 1700, the city's five thousand inhabitants participated in a thriving trade exporting flour and other food products to the West Indies and importing English textiles and manufactured goods.

Penn was determined to live in peace with the Indians who inhabited the region. His Indian policy expressed his Quaker ideals and contrasted sharply with the hostile policies of the other English colonies. As he explained to the chief of the Lenni Lenape (Delaware) Indians, "God has written his law in our hearts, by which we are taught and commanded to love and help and do good to one another . . . [and] I desire to enjoy [Pennsylvania lands] with your love and consent." Penn instructed his agents to obtain the Indians' consent by purchasing their land, respecting their claims, and dealing with them fairly.

Penn declared that the first principle of government was that every settler would "enjoy the free possession of his or her faith and exercise of worship towards God." Accordingly, Pennsylvania tolerated Protestant sects of all kinds as well as Roman Catholics. All voters and officeholders had to be Christians, but the government did not compel settlers to attend religious services, as in Massachusetts, or to pay taxes to maintain a state-supported church, as in Virginia.

Despite its toleration and diversity, Pennsylvania was as much a Quaker colony as New England was a stronghold of Puritanism. Penn had no hesitation about using civil government to enforce religious morality. One of the colony's first laws provided severe punishment for "all such offenses against God, as swearing, cursing, lying, profane talking, drunkenness, drinking of healths, [and] obscene words . . . which excite the people to rudeness, cruelty, looseness, and irreligion."

As proprietor, Penn had extensive powers, subject only to review by the king. He appointed a governor, who maintained the proprietor's power to veto any laws passed by the colonial council, which was elected by property owners who possessed at least one hundred acres of land or who paid taxes. The council had the power to originate laws and administer all the affairs of government. A popularly elected assembly served as a check on the council; its members had the authority to reject or approve laws framed by the council.

Penn stressed that the exact form of government mattered less than the men who served in it. In Penn's eyes, "good men" staffed Pennsylvania's government because Quakers dominated elective and appointive offices. Quakers, of course, differed among themselves. Members of the assembly struggled to win the right to debate and amend laws, especially tax laws. They finally won the battle in 1701 when a new Charter of Privileges gave the proprietor the power to appoint the council and in turn stripped the council of all its former powers and gave them to the assembly, which became the only single-house legislature in all the English colonies.

> ▶ **REVIEW**   How did Quaker ideals shape the colony of Pennsylvania?

The Colonies and the English Empire

Proprietary grants to faraway lands were a cheap way for the king to reward friends. As the colonies grew, however, the grants became more valuable. After 1660, the king took initiatives to channel colonial trade through English hands and to consolidate royal authority over colonial governments. Occasioned by such economic and political considerations and triggered by King Philip's War between colonists and Native Americans, these initiatives defined the basic relationship between the colonies and England that endured until the American Revolution (Map 4.1, page 106).

Royal Regulation of Colonial Trade

English economic policies toward the colonies were designed to yield customs revenues for the monarchy and profitable business for English merchants and shippers. Also, the policies were intended to divert the colonies' trade from England's enemies, especially the Dutch and the French.

The Navigation Acts of 1650, 1651, 1660, and 1663 (see chapter 3) set forth two fundamental rules governing colonial trade. First, goods shipped to and from the colonies had to be transported in English ships using primarily English crews. Second, the Navigation Acts listed ("enumerated," in the language of the time) colonial products that could be shipped only to England or to other English colonies. While these regulations prevented Chesapeake **planters** from shipping their tobacco directly to the European continent, they interfered less with the commerce of New England and the middle colonies, whose principal exports— fish, lumber, and flour—were not enumerated and could legally be sent directly to their most important markets in the West Indies.

By the end of the seventeenth century, colonial commerce was defined by regulations that subjected merchants and shippers to royal supervision and gave them access to markets throughout the English empire. In addition, colonial commerce received protection from the English navy. By 1700, colonial goods (including those from the West Indies) accounted for one-fifth of all English imports and for two-thirds of all goods reexported from England to the European continent. In turn, the colonies absorbed more than one-tenth of English exports. The commercial regulations gave economic value to England's proprietorship of the American colonies.

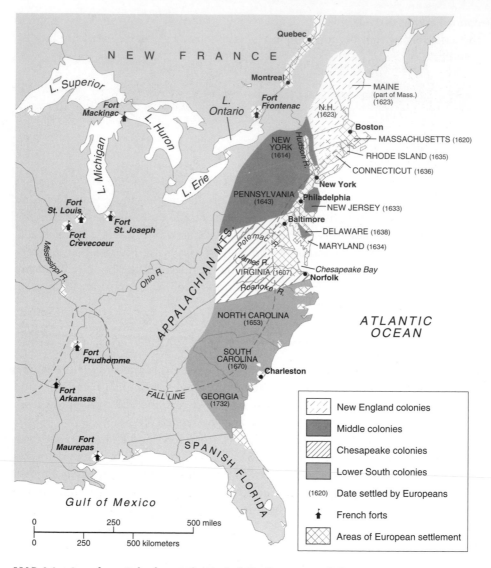

MAP 4.1 American Colonies at the End of the Seventeenth Century
By the end of the seventeenth century, settlers inhabited a narrow band of land that stretched more or less continuously from Boston to Norfolk, with pockets of settlement farther south. The colonies' claims to enormous tracts of land to the west were contested by Native Americans as well as by France and Spain.

King Philip's War and the Consolidation of Royal Authority

The monarchy also took steps to exercise greater control over colonial governments. Virginia had been a royal colony since 1624; Maryland, South Carolina, and the middle colonies were proprietary colonies with close ties to the crown.

Wampanoag War Club
This seventeenth-century war club was used to kill King Philip, according to the Anglican missionary who obtained it from Indians early in the eighteenth century. Although the missionary's tale is probably a legend, the club is certainly a seventeenth-century Wampanoag weapon that might well have been used in King Philip's War. The heavy ball carved into the head of the club could deliver a disabling, even fatal, blow.
Courtesy of the Fruitlands Museums, Harvard, Massachusetts.

The New England colonies possessed royal charters, but they had developed their own distinctively Puritan governments. Charles II, whose father, Charles I, had been executed by Puritans in England, took a particular interest in harnessing the New England colonies more firmly to the English empire. The occasion was a royal investigation following King Philip's War.

In 1675, warfare between Indians and colonists erupted in the Chesapeake and New England. Massachusetts settlers had massacred hundreds of Pequot Indians in 1637, but they had established relatively peaceful relations with the more potent Wampanoags. In the decades that followed, New Englanders steadily encroached on Indian land, and in 1675 the Wampanoags struck back with attacks on settlements in western Massachusetts. Metacomet—the chief of the Wampanoags (and son of Massasoit), whom the colonists called King Philip—probably neither planned the attacks nor masterminded a conspiracy with the Nipmucks and the Narragansetts, as the colonists feared. But when militias from Massachusetts and other New England colonies counterattacked all three tribes, a deadly sequence of battles killed more than a thousand colonists and thousands more Indians. The Indians destroyed thirteen English settlements and partially burned another half dozen. By the spring of 1676, Indian warriors ranged freely within seventeen miles of Boston. The colonists finally defeated the Indians, principally with a scorched-earth policy of burning their food supplies. King Philip's War left the New England colonists with an enduring hatred of Indians, a large war debt, and a devastated frontier. And in 1676, an agent of the king arrived to investigate whether New England was abiding by English laws.

Not surprisingly, the king's agent found all sorts of deviations from English rules, and the monarchy decided to govern New England more directly. In 1684, an

English court revoked the Massachusetts charter, the foundation of the distinctive Puritan government. Two years later, royal officials incorporated Massachusetts and the other colonies north of Maryland into the Dominion of New England. To govern the dominion, the English sent Sir Edmund Andros to Boston. Some New England merchants cooperated with Andros, but most colonists were offended by his flagrant disregard of such Puritan traditions as keeping the Sabbath. Worst of all, the Dominion of New England invalidated all land titles, confronting every landowner in New England with the horrifying prospect of losing his or her land.

Events in England, however, permitted Massachusetts colonists to overthrow Andros and retain title to their property. When Charles II died in 1685, he was succeeded by his brother James II, a zealous Catholic. James's aggressive campaign to appoint Catholics to government posts engendered such unrest that in 1688, a group of Protestant noblemen in Parliament invited the Dutch ruler William III of Orange, James's son-in-law, to claim the English throne. When William III landed in England at the head of a large army, James fled to France and William III and his wife, Mary II (James's daughter), became corulers in the relatively bloodless "Glorious Revolution," reasserting Protestant influence in England and its empire. Rumors of the revolution raced across the Atlantic and emboldened colonial uprisings against royal authority in Massachusetts, New York, and Maryland.

In Boston in 1689, rebels tossed Andros and other English officials in jail, destroyed the Dominion of New England, and reestablished the former charter government. New Yorkers followed the Massachusetts example. Under the leadership of Jacob Leisler, rebels seized the royal governor in 1689 and ruled the colony for more than a year. That same year in Maryland, the Protestant Association, led by John Coode, overthrew the colony's pro-Catholic government, fearing it would not recognize the new Protestant king.

But these rebel governments did not last. When King William III's governor of New York arrived in 1691, he executed Leisler for treason. Coode's men ruled Maryland until the new royal governor arrived in 1692 and ended both Coode's rebellion and Lord Baltimore's proprietary government. In Massachusetts, John Winthrop's city on a hill became another royal colony in 1691. The new charter said that the governor of the colony would be appointed by the king rather than elected by the colonists' representatives. But perhaps the most unsettling change was the new qualification for voting. Possession of property replaced church membership as a prerequisite for voting in colony-wide elections. Wealth replaced God's grace as the defining characteristic of Massachusetts citizenship.

Much as colonists chafed under increasing royal control, they still valued English protection from hostile neighbors. While the northern colonies were distracted by the Glorious Revolution, French forces from the fur-trading regions along the Great Lakes and in Canada attacked villages in New England and New York. Known as King William's War, the conflict with the French was a colonial outgrowth of William's war against France in Europe. The war dragged on until 1697 and ended inconclusively in both Europe and the colonies. But it made clear to many colonists that along with English royal government came a welcome measure of military security.

▶ **REVIEW**   Why did the Glorious Revolution in England lead to uprisings in the American colonies?

Conclusion: An English Model of Colonization in North America

By 1700, the diverse English colonies in North America had developed along lines quite different from the example New Spain had set in 1600. In the North American colonies, English immigrants and their descendants created societies of settlers unlike the largely Indian societies in New Spain ruled by a tiny group of Spaniards. Although many settlers came to North America from other parts of Europe and a growing number of Africans arrived in bondage, English laws, habits, ideas, and language dominated all the colonies.

Economically, the English colonies thrived on agriculture and trade instead of mining silver and exploiting Indian labor as in New Spain. Southern colonies grew huge crops of tobacco and rice with the labor of indentured servants and slaves, while farmers in the middle colonies planted wheat and New England fishermen harvested the sea. Although servants and slaves could be found throughout the North American colonies, many settlers depended principally on the labor of family members. Relations between settlers and Native Americans often exploded in bloody warfare, but Indians seldom served as an important source of labor for settlers, as they did in New Spain.

Protestantism prevailed in the North American settlements, relaxed in some colonies and straitlaced in others. The convictions of Puritanism that motivated John Winthrop and others to build a new England in the colonies became muted as the New England colonies matured and dissenters such as Roger Williams multiplied. Catholics, Quakers, Anglicans (members of the Church of England), Jews, and others settled in the middle and southern colonies, creating considerable religious toleration, especially in Pennsylvania and New York.

Politics and government differed from colony to colony, although the imprint of English institutions and practices existed everywhere. And everywhere, local settlers who were free adult white men had an extraordinary degree of political influence, far beyond that of colonists in New Spain or ordinary citizens in England. A new world of settlers that Columbus could not have imagined, that Powhatan only glimpsed, had been firmly established in English North America by 1700. During the next half century, that English colonial world would undergo surprising new developments built on the achievements of the seventeenth century.

REVIEWING THE CHAPTER

Use the questions and timeline to review and strengthen your understanding of the chapter.

REVIEW QUESTIONS

1. Why did Henry VIII initiate the English Reformation? (pp. 85–87)

2. Why did the Puritans immigrate to North America? (pp. 87–91)

3. Why did Massachusetts Puritans adopt the Halfway Covenant? (pp. 91–100)

4. How did Quaker ideals shape the colony of Pennsylvania? (pp. 100–105)

5. Why did the Glorious Revolution in England lead to uprisings in the American colonies? (pp. 105–9)

MAKING CONNECTIONS

1. How did the religious dissenters who flooded into the northern colonies address the question of religious dissent in their new homes? Comparing two colonies, discuss their different approaches and the implications of those approaches for colonial development.

2. In his sermon aboard the *Arbella*, John Winthrop spoke of the Massachusetts Bay Colony as "a city upon a hill." What did he mean? How did this expectation influence life in New England during the seventeenth century? In your answer, be sure to consider the relationship between religious and political life in the colony.

3. Religious conflict and political turmoil battered England in the seventeenth century. How did political developments in England affect life in the colonies? In your answer, consider the establishment of the colonies and the crown's attempts to exercise authority over them.

4. Although both were settled by the English, colonial New England was dramatically different from the colonial Chesapeake. How did they differ and why? In your answer, consider the economies, systems of governance, and patterns of settlement in each colony.

TIMELINE

1534	• King Henry VIII breaks with Roman Catholic Church.	**1656**	• Quakers arrive in Massachusetts and are persecuted there.
1609	• Henry Hudson searches for Northwest Passage.	**1660**	• Monarchy restored in England; Charles II becomes king.
1620	• Plymouth colony founded.	**1662**	• Many Puritan congregations adopt Halfway Covenant.
1626	• Manhattan Island purchased and New Amsterdam founded.	**1664**	• English seize Dutch colony; rename it New York.
1629	• Massachusetts Bay Company receives royal charter.		• Colony of New Jersey created.
1630	• John Winthrop leads Puritan settlers to Massachusetts Bay.	**1675**	• King Philip's War.
1636	• Rhode Island colony established.	**1681**	• William Penn receives charter for colony of Pennsylvania.
	• Connecticut colony founded.	**1686**	• Dominion of New England created.
1638	• Anne Hutchinson excommunicated.	**1688**	• England's Glorious Revolution; William III and Mary II become new rulers.
1642	• Puritan Revolution inflames England.	**1692**	• Salem witch trials.
1649	• English Puritans win civil war and execute Charles I.		

▶ **For an online bibliography, practice quizzes, Web sites, images, and documents related to this chapter,** see the Book Companion Site at **bedfordstmartins.com/roark.**

▶ **For firsthand accounts of this period,** see Chapter 4 in Michael Johnson, ed., *Reading the American Past,* Fourth Edition.

5
CHAPTER

Colonial America in the Eighteenth Century
1701–1770

T HE BROTHERS AMBOE ROBIN JOHN and Little Ephraim Robin John and their cousin Ancona Robin John lived during the 1750s and 1760s in Old Calabar on the Bight of Biafra in West Africa. The Robin Johns were part of a slave-trading dynasty headed by their kinsman Grandy King George, one of the most powerful leaders of the Efik people. Grandy King George owned hundreds of slaves whom he employed to capture and trade for still more slaves in the African interior. He sold these captives to captains of European slave ships seeking to fill their holds with human cargo for the transatlantic voyage to the sugar, tobacco, and rice fields in the New World. During the half century after 1725, Old Calabar exported about 80,000 slaves, almost all of them aboard British ships. It was a major contributor to the massive flow of more than 1.2 million slaves from the Bight of Biafra to the New World during the eighteenth century.

Grandy King George nearly monopolized the Old Calabar slave trade during the 1760s, allowing him to live in luxury, surrounded by fine British trade goods such as gold-headed canes, fancy mirrors, lace-trimmed clothing, and pewter chamber pots. British slave ship captains and Grandy King George's African rivals resented his choke hold on the supply of slaves and in 1767 conspired to trap the king and the Robin Johns, seize hundreds of their slaves, and destroy the king's monopoly. In the bloody melee, Grandy King George suffered

Slave Ship Model
The African slave trade existed to satisfy the New World's demand for labor and Europe's appetite for such New World products as sugar, tobacco, and rice. African men, women, and children were kidnapped or captured in wars—typically by other Africans—and enslaved. Uprooted from their homes, they were usually taken to coastal enclaves where African traders and European ship captains negotiated prices, made deals, and often branded the newly enslaved people. Jammed into the holds of slave ships, enslaved Africans made the dreaded Middle Passage to the New World. This model of a slave ship was used in parliamentary debates by antislavery leaders in Britain to demonstrate the inhumanity of shipping people as if they were cargo.
Wilberforce House, Hull City Museums and Art Galleries, UK/Bridgeman Art Library.

eleven musket wounds but managed to escape. Other members of his family were less fortunate. Amboe Robin John was beheaded by the leader of the African attackers. Little Ephraim and Ancona Robin John were enslaved, packed aboard the ship *Duke of York* with more than 330 other slaves, and transported across the Atlantic to the West Indian island of Dominica, which the British had recently acquired from the French.

Unlike most slaves, the Robin Johns understood, spoke, and even wrote English, an essential skill they had learned as slave traders in Old Calabar. A French physician bought the Robin Johns and, according to Ancona, "treated [them] . . . upon ye whole not badly." After seven months, the Robin Johns heard that a certain ship captain would take them back to Africa. They escaped from their owner and boarded the captain's ship "determined to get home," Little Ephraim wrote. But the captain took them to Virginia instead and sold them as slaves to a merchant who traded between the Chesapeake and Bristol, England. Their new owner, John Thompson, "would tie me up & whip me many times for nothing at all," Ancona testified, adding that Thompson "was exceedingly badly man ever I saw." After Thompson died in 1772, the Robin Johns heard that a slave ship from Old Calabar had recently arrived in Virginia, and the captain promised to take them back to Africa if they would run away and come aboard his ship. Instead, he took the Robin Johns to Bristol and sought to sell them as slaves yet again.

While imprisoned "in this Deplorable condition" on a ship in Bristol harbor, the Robin Johns managed to smuggle letters to a Bristol slave trader they had known and dealt with in Old Calabar. With help from him and other English sympathizers, the Robin Johns appeared before Lord Mansfield, the chief justice of England, and appealed for their freedom on the grounds that they "were free people . . . [who] had not done anything to forfeit our liberty" and were thus unjustly enslaved. After complex negotiations, they won legal recognition of their freedom.

As free Africans in Bristol, the Robin Johns converted to Christianity under the ministry of the famous Methodists John and Charles Wesley, who wrote that the Robin Johns "received both the outward and visible signs of the inward & spiritual grace in a wonderful manner & measure." Although the Robin Johns had many friends and admirers among English Methodists, they longed to return to Africa. In 1774, they sailed from Bristol as free men on another slave ship bound for Old Calabar, where they resumed their careers as slave traders.

The Robin Johns' unrelenting quest to escape enslavement and redeem their freedom was shared but not realized by millions of Africans who were victims of slave traders such as Grandy King George and numberless merchants, ship captains, and colonists. They came involuntarily to the New World; in contrast, tens of thousands of Europeans voluntarily crossed the Atlantic to seek opportunities in North America—opportunities many purchased by agreeing to several years of contractual servitude. Both groups illustrate the undertow of violence and deceit just beneath the surface of eighteenth-century Atlantic commerce linking Britain, Africa, the West Indies, and British North America. In the flux and uncertainty of the eighteenth-century world, many, like the Robin Johns, turned to the consolations of religious faith as a source of meaning and hope in an often cruel and unforgiving society.

The flood of free and unfree migrants crossing the Atlantic contributed to unprecedented population growth in eighteenth-century British North America. In contrast, the Spanish and French colonies remained thinly populated outposts of European empires interested principally in maintaining a toehold in the vast continent. While adaptations to varied natural, economic, and social environments reinforced regional differences among New England, the middle colonies, and the southern colonies, other commercial, cultural, and political trends built common experiences, aspirations, and assumptions among the British colonists. These unifying trends would lay the groundwork for what would become in 1776 the United States of America.

A Growing Population and Expanding Economy in British North America

The most important fact about eighteenth-century British America is its phenomenal population growth: In 1700, colonists numbered about 250,000; by 1770, they tallied well over 2 million. An index of the emerging significance of colonial North America is that in 1700, there were nineteen people in England for every American colonist; by 1770, there were only three. The eightfold growth of the colonial population signaled the maturation of a distinctive colonial society. That society was by no means homogeneous. Colonists of different ethnic groups, races, and religions lived in varied environments under thirteen different colonial governments, all of them part of the British empire.

In general, the growth and diversity of the eighteenth-century colonial population derived from two sources: immigration and natural increase (growth through reproduction). Natural increase contributed about three-fourths of the population growth, immigration about one-fourth. Immigration shifted the ethnic and racial balance among the colonists, making them by 1770 less

"Dummy Board" of Phyllis, a New England Slave
This life-size portrait of a slave woman named Phyllis, a mulatto who worked as a domestic servant, was painted sometime before 1753. Known as a "dummy board," it was propped against a wall or placed in a doorway or window to suggest that the residence was occupied and to discourage thieves. Although tens of thousands of slaves were brought from Africa to British North America during the eighteenth century, Phyllis was probably not one of them. Instead, she was most likely born in the colonies of mixed black and white parentage.
Courtesy of Historic New England.

English and less white than ever before. Fewer than 10 percent of eighteenth-century immigrants came from England; about 36 percent were Scots-Irish, mostly from northern Ireland; 33 percent arrived from Africa, almost all of them slaves; nearly 15 percent had left the many German-language principalities (the nation of Germany did not exist until 1871); and almost 10 percent came from Scotland. In 1670, more than 9 out of 10 colonists were of English ancestry, and only 1 out of 25 was of African ancestry. By 1770, only about half of the colonists were of English descent, while more than 20 percent descended from Africans. Thus, by 1770, the people of the colonies had a distinctive colonial—rather than English—profile.

The booming population of the colonies hints at a second major feature of eighteenth-century colonial society: an expanding economy. In 1700, after almost a century of settlement, nearly all the colonists lived within fifty miles of the Atlantic coast. The almost limitless wilderness stretching westward made land relatively cheap. Land in the colonies commonly sold for a fraction of its price in the Old World. The abundance of land in the colonies made labor precious, and the colonists always needed more. The colonists' insatiable demand for labor was the fundamental economic environment that sustained the mushrooming population. Economic historians estimate that free colonists (those who were not **indentured servants** or slaves) had a higher standard of living than the majority of people elsewhere in the Atlantic world. The unique achievement of the eighteenth-century colonial economy was this modest economic welfare of the vast bulk of the free population.

▶ **REVIEW**   How did the North American colonies achieve the remarkable population growth of the eighteenth century?

New England: From Puritan Settlers to Yankee Traders

The New England population grew sixfold during the eighteenth century but lagged behind the growth in the other colonies. Why did New England fail to keep pace? Most immigrants chose other destinations because of New England's relatively densely settled land and because Puritan orthodoxy made these colonies comparatively inhospitable to religious dissenters and those indifferent to religion. As the population grew, many settlers in search of farmland dispersed from towns, and Puritan communities lost much of their cohesion. Nonetheless, networks of economic exchange laced New Englanders to their neighbors, to Boston merchants, and to the broad currents of Atlantic commerce.

In many ways, trade became a faith that competed strongly with the traditions of **Puritanism**.

Natural Increase and Land Distribution

The New England population grew mostly by natural increase, much as it had during the seventeenth century. Nearly every adult woman married. Most married women had children—often many children, thanks to the relatively low mortality rate in New England. The perils of childbirth gave wives a shorter life expectancy than husbands, but wives often lived to have six, seven, or eight babies. When a wife died, her husband usually remarried quickly. Anne Franklin and her husband, Josiah, a soap and candle maker in Boston, had seven children. Four months after Anne died, Josiah married his second wife, Abiah, and the couple had ten more children, including their son Benjamin, who became one of the most prominent colonial leaders of the eighteenth century.

The growing New England population pressed against a limited amount of land. Compared to colonies farther south, New England had less land for the expansion of settlement. Moreover, as the northernmost group of British colonies, New England had a contested northern and western **frontier**. Powerful Native Americans, especially the Iroquois and Mahican tribes, jealously guarded their territory. The French (and Catholic) colony of New France also menaced the British (and mostly **Protestant**) New England colonies when provoked by colonial or European disputes.

During the seventeenth century, New England towns parceled out land to individual families. In most cases, the original settlers practiced partible inheritance (that is, they subdivided land more or less equally among sons). By the eighteenth century, the original land allotments had to be further subdivided to accommodate grandsons and great-grandsons, and many plots of land became too small to support a family. Sons who could not hope to inherit sufficient land to farm had to move away from the town where they were born.

During the eighteenth century, colonial governments in New England abandoned the seventeenth-century policy of granting land to towns. Needing revenue, the governments of both Connecticut and Massachusetts sold land directly to individuals, including speculators. Now money, rather than membership in a community bound by a church **covenant**, determined whether a person could obtain land. The new land policy eroded the seventeenth-century pattern of settlement. As colonists moved into western Massachusetts and Connecticut and north into present-day New Hampshire and Maine, they tended to settle on individual farms rather than in the towns and villages that characterized the seventeenth century. New Englanders still depended on their relatives and neighbors for help in clearing land, raising a house, worshipping God, and having a good time. But far more than in the seventeenth century, they regulated their behavior in newly settled areas by their own individual choices.

Farms, Fish, and Atlantic Trade

A New England farm was a place to get by, not to get rich. New England farmers grew food for their families, but their fields did not produce a huge marketable surplus. Instead of one big crop, farmers grew many small ones. If they had extra, they sold to or traded with neighbors. Poor roads made travel difficult, time-consuming, and expensive, especially with bulky and heavy agricultural goods. The one major agricultural product the New England colonies exported— livestock—walked to market on its own legs. By 1770, New Englanders had only one-fourth as much wealth per capita as free colonists in the southern colonies.

As consumers, New England farmers participated in a diversified commercial economy that linked remote farms to markets throughout the Atlantic world. Merchants large and small stocked imported goods—British textiles, ceramics, and metal goods; Chinese tea; West Indian sugar; and Chesapeake tobacco. Farmers' needs for comfortable shoes, warm coats, sturdy carts, and solid buildings supported local shoemakers, tailors, wheelwrights, and carpenters. Larger towns, especially Boston, housed skilled tradesmen such as cabinetmakers, silversmiths, and printers. Shipbuilders tended to do better than other **artisans** because they served the most dynamic sector of the New England economy.

Many New Englanders made their fortunes at sea, as they had since the seventeenth century. Fish accounted for more than a third of New England's eighteenth-century exports; livestock and timber made up another third. The West Indies absorbed two-thirds of all New England's exports. Slaves on Caribbean sugar plantations ate dried, salted codfish caught by New England fishermen, filled barrels crafted from New England timber with molasses and refined sugar, and loaded those barrels aboard ships bound ultimately for Europeans with a sweet tooth. Almost all of the rest of New England's exports went to Britain and continental Europe (Map 5.1). This Atlantic commerce benefited the entire New England economy, providing jobs for laborers and tradesmen, as well as for ship captains, clerks, merchants, and sailors.

Merchants dominated Atlantic commerce. The largest and most successful merchants lived in Boston at the hub of trade between local folk and the international market. Merchants not only bought and sold goods, but they also owned and insured the ships that carried the merchandise throughout the Atlantic world. Shrewd, diligent, and lucky merchants could make a fortune. The magnificence of a wealthy Boston merchant's home stunned John Adams, a thrifty Massachusetts lawyer who became a leader during the American Revolution and ultimately the second president of the United States. To Adams, the merchant's house seemed fit "for a noble Man, a Prince," furnished with "Turkey Carpets, ... painted Hangings, ... Marble Tables, ... rich Beds ... , [and a] beautiful Chimney Clock, ... [in all] the most magnificent of any Thing I have ever seen." Such luxurious Boston homes contrasted with the modest dwellings of Adams and other New Englanders, an indication of the polarization

MAP 5.1   Atlantic Trade in the Eighteenth Century
This map illustrates the economic outlook of the colonies in the eighteenth century—east toward
the Atlantic world rather than west toward the interior of North America. The long distances involved
in the Atlantic trade and the uncertainties of ocean travel suggest the difficulties Britain experienced
governing the colonies and regulating colonial commerce.

of wealth that developed in Boston and other seaports during the eighteenth century. By 1770, the richest 5 percent of Bostonians owned about half the city's
wealth; the poorest two-thirds of the population owned less than one-tenth.

While the rich got richer and everybody else had a smaller share of the total
wealth, the incidence of genuine poverty did not change much. About 5 percent
of New Englanders qualified for poor relief throughout the eighteenth century.
Overall, colonists were better off than most people in England. A Connecticut
traveler wrote from England in 1764, "We in New England know nothing of
poverty and want, we have no idea of the thing, how much better do our poor
people live than 7/8 of the people on this much famed island."

The contrast with English poverty had meaning because the overwhelming majority of New Englanders traced their ancestry to England. New England was more homogeneously English than any other colonial region. People of African ancestry (almost all of them slaves) numbered more than 15,000 by 1770, but they barely diversified the region's 97 percent white majority. Most New Englanders had no hesitation about acquiring slaves, and many Puritan ministers owned one or two. In the Narragansett region of Rhode Island, large landowners imported numerous slaves to raise livestock. But most New Englanders had little use for slaves on their family farms. Instead, slaves concentrated in towns, especially Boston, where most of them worked as domestic servants and laborers.

By 1770, the population, wealth, and commercial activity of New England differed from what they had been in 1700. Ministers still enjoyed high status, but Yankee traders had replaced Puritan saints as the symbolic New Englanders. Atlantic commerce competed with religious convictions in ordering New Englanders' daily lives.

▶ **REVIEW**　　Why did settlement patterns in New England change from the seventeenth to the eighteenth century?

The Middle Colonies: Immigrants, Wheat, and Work

In 1700, almost twice as many people lived in New England as in the middle colonies of Pennsylvania, New York, New Jersey, and Delaware. But by 1770, the population of the middle colonies had multiplied tenfold—mainly from an influx of German, Irish, Scottish, and other immigrants—and nearly equaled the population of New England. Immigrants made the middle colonies a uniquely diverse society. By 1800, barely one-third of Pennsylvanians and less than half the total population of the middle colonies traced their ancestry to England.

German and Scots-Irish Immigrants

Germans made up the largest contingent of migrants from the European continent to the middle colonies. By 1770, about 85,000 Germans had arrived in the colonies. Their fellow colonists often referred to them as "Pennsylvania Dutch," an English corruption of *Deutsch*, the word the immigrants used to describe themselves.

Most German immigrants came from what is now southwestern Germany, where, one observer noted, peasants were "not as well off as cattle elsewhere." Devastating French invasions of Germany during Queen Anne's War (1702–1713) made bad conditions worse and triggered the first large-scale migration. German immigrants included numerous artisans and a few merchants, but the great majority were farmers and laborers. Economically, they represented "middling folk," neither the poorest (who could not afford the trip) nor the better-off (who did not want to leave).

By the 1720s, Germans who had established themselves in the colonies wrote back to their friends and relatives, as one reported, "of the civil and religious liberties [and] privileges, and of all the goodness I have heard and seen." Such letters prompted still more Germans to pull up stakes and embark for America, to exchange the miserable certainties of their lives in Europe for the uncertain attractions of life in the middle colonies.

Similar motives propelled the Scots-Irish, who considerably outnumbered German immigrants. The term *Scots-Irish* was another misleading label coined in the colonies. Immigrants labeled "Scots-Irish" actually hailed from northern Ireland, Scotland, and northern England. Like the Germans, the Scots-Irish were Protestants, but with a difference. Most German immigrants worshipped in Lutheran or German Reformed churches; many others belonged to dissenting sects such as the Mennonites, Moravians, and Amish, whose adherents sought relief from persecution they had suffered in Europe for their refusal to bear arms and to swear oaths, practices they shared with the Quakers. In contrast, the Scots-Irish tended to be militant Presbyterians who seldom hesitated to bear arms or swear oaths. Like German settlers, however, Scots-Irish immigrants were clannish, residing when they could among relatives or neighbors from the old country.

In the eighteenth century, wave after wave of Scots-Irish immigrants arrived, beginning in 1717, cresting every twelve or fifteen years thereafter, and culminating in a flood of immigration in the years just before the American Revolution. Deteriorating economic conditions in northern Ireland, Scotland, and England pushed many toward America. Most of the immigrants were farm laborers or tenant farmers fleeing droughts, crop failures, high food prices, or rising rents. They came, they told inquisitive British officials, because of "poverty," "tyranny of landlords," and their desire to "do better in America."

Both Scots-Irish and Germans probably heard the common saying "Pennsylvania is heaven for farmers [and] paradise for artisans," but they almost certainly did not fully understand the risks of their decision to leave their native lands. Ship captains, aware of the hunger for labor in the colonies, eagerly signed up the penniless emigrants as "redemptioners," a variant of indentured servants. A captain would agree to provide transportation to Philadelphia, where redemptioners would obtain the money to pay for their passage by borrowing it from a friend or relative who was already in the colonies or, as most did, by selling themselves as servants. Many redemptioners traveled in family groups, unlike impoverished Scots-Irish emigrants, who usually traveled alone and paid for their passage by contracting as indentured servants before they sailed to the colonies.

Redemptioners and indentured servants were packed aboard ships "as closely as herring," one migrant observed. Seasickness compounded by exhaustion, poverty, poor food, bad water, inadequate sanitation, and tight quarters encouraged the spread of disease. On the sixteen immigrant ships arriving in Philadelphia in 1738, over half the passengers died en route. When one ship finally approached land, a traveler wrote, "everyone crawls from below to the deck . . . and people cry for joy, pray, and sing praises and thanks to God." Unfortunately, their troubles were far from over. Redemptioners and indentured servants had to stay on board until somebody came to purchase their labor. Unlike indentured servants, redemptioners negotiated independently with their purchasers about their period of servitude. Typically, a healthy adult redemptioner agreed to four years of labor. Indentured servants commonly served five, six, or seven years. Children usually had to serve as indentured servants until they reached twenty-one.

Pennsylvania: "The Best Poor [White] Man's Country"

New settlers, whether free or in servitude, poured into the middle colonies because they perceived unparalleled opportunities, particularly in Pennsylvania, "the best poor Man's Country in the World," as an indentured servant wrote in 1743. Although the servant reported that "the Condition of bought Servants is very hard" and masters often failed to live up to their promise to provide decent food and clothing, opportunity abounded because there was more work to be done than workers to do it.

Most servants toiled in Philadelphia, New York City, or one of the smaller towns or villages. Artisans, small manufacturers, and shopkeepers prized the labor of male servants. Female servants made valuable additions to households, where nearly all of them cleaned, washed, cooked, or minded children. From the masters' viewpoint, servants were a bargain. A master could purchase five or six years of a servant's labor for approximately the wages a common laborer would earn in four months. Wageworkers could walk away from their jobs when they pleased, and they did so often enough to be troublesome for employers. Servants, however, could not walk away; they were legally bound to work for their masters until their terms expired.

Since a slave cost at least three times as much as a servant, only affluent colonists could afford the long-term investment in slave labor. Like many other prosperous urban residents, Benjamin Franklin purchased a few slaves after he became wealthy. But most farmers in the middle colonies used family labor, not slaves. Wheat, the most widely grown crop, did not require more labor than farmers could typically muster from relatives, neighbors, and a hired hand or two. Consequently, although people of African ancestry (almost all slaves) increased to more than 30,000 in the middle colonies by 1770, they accounted for only about 7 percent of the total population and much less outside the cities.

Most slaves, like the Robin Johns, came to the middle colonies and New England after a stopover in the West Indies. Very few came directly from Africa. Enough slaves arrived to prompt colonial assemblies to pass laws that punished slaves much more severely than servants for the same transgressions. "For the least trespass," an indentured servant reported, slaves "undergo the severest Punishment." In practice, both servants and slaves were governed more by their masters than by the laws. But in cases of abuse, servants could and did charge masters with violating the terms of their indenture contracts. The terms of a slave's bondage were set forth in a master's commands, not in a written contract.

Small numbers of slaves managed to obtain their freedom, though few of them as dramatically as the Robin Johns. But free African Americans did not escape whites' firm convictions about black inferiority and white supremacy. Whites' racism and blacks' lowly social status made African Americans scape-goats for European Americans' suspicions and anxieties. In 1741, when arson

---

Bethlehem, Pennsylvania
This view of the small community of Bethlehem, Pennsylvania, in 1757 dramatizes the profound transformation of the natural landscape wrought in the eighteenth century by human labor. Founded by Moravian immigrants in 1740, Bethlehem must have appeared at first like the dense woods on the upper left horizon. In less than twenty years, precisely laid-out orchards and fields replaced forests and glades. Few eighteenth-century communities were as orderly as Bethlehem, but many effected a comparable transformation of the environment.

Print Collection, Miriam and Ira D. Wallack Division of Art, Prints and Photographs, The New York Public Library. Astor, Lenox, and Tilden Foundations.

and several unexplained thefts plagued New York City, officials suspected a murderous slave conspiracy. On the basis of little evidence other than the slaves' "insolence" (refusal to conform fully to whites' expectations of servile behavior), city authorities had thirteen slaves burned at the stake and eighteen others hanged. Although slaves were certifiably impoverished, they were not among the poor for whom the middle colonies were reputed to be the best country in the world.

Immigrants swarmed to the middle colonies because of the availability of land. The Penn family encouraged immigration to bring in potential buyers for their enormous tracts of land in Pennsylvania. From the beginning, Pennsylvania followed a policy of negotiating with Indian tribes to purchase additional land. This policy reduced the violent frontier clashes more common elsewhere in the colonies. Yet the Penn family did not shrink from pushing its agreements with Indians to the limit and beyond. In a dispute with tribes on the northern Delaware River in 1737, the Penns pulled out a document showing that local Indians had granted the colonists land that stretched as far as a man could walk in a day and a half. Under the terms of this infamous "Walking Purchase," the Penns sent out three runners, two of whom collapsed before the thirty-six hours expired. The third runner raced more than sixty miles, doubling the size of the Penns' claim.

Few colonists drifted beyond the northern boundaries of Pennsylvania. Owners of the huge estates in New York's Hudson valley preferred to rent rather than sell their land, and therefore they attracted fewer immigrants. The Iroquois dominated the lucrative fur trade of the St. Lawrence valley and eastern Great Lakes, and they vigorously defended their territory from colonial encroachment. Few settlers chose to risk having their scalps lifted by Iroquois warriors in northern New York when they could settle instead in the comparatively safe environs of Pennsylvania.

The price of farmland depended on soil quality, access to water, distance from a market town, and extent of improvements. One hundred acres of improved land that had been cleared, plowed, fenced, and ditched, and perhaps had a house and barn built on it, cost three or four times more than the same acreage of uncleared, unimproved land. Since the cheapest land always lay at the margin of settlement, would-be farmers tended to migrate to promising areas just beyond already improved farms. From Philadelphia, settlers moved north along the Delaware River and west along the Schuylkill and Susquehanna rivers. By midcentury, settlement had reached the eastern slopes of the Appalachian Mountains, and newcomers spilled south down the fertile valley of the Shenandoah River into western Virginia and the Carolinas. Thousands of settlers migrated from the middle colonies through this back door to the South.

Farmers made the middle colonies the breadbasket of North America. They planted a wide variety of crops to feed their families, but they grew wheat in abundance. Flour milling was the number one industry and flour the number one export, constituting nearly three-fourths of all exports from the middle colonies.

Pennsylvania flour fed residents in other colonies, in southern Europe, and, above all, in the West Indies (see Map 5.1). For farmers, the grain market in the Atlantic world proved risky but profitable. Grain prices rose steadily after 1720. By 1770, a bushel of wheat was worth twice as much (adjusted for inflation) as it had been fifty years earlier.

The standard of living in rural Pennsylvania was probably higher than in any other agricultural region of the eighteenth-century world. The comparatively widespread prosperity of all the middle colonies permitted residents to indulge in a half-century shopping spree for British imports. The middle colonies' per capita consumption of imported goods from Britain more than doubled between 1720 and 1770, far outstripping the per capita consumption of British goods in New England and the southern colonies.

At the crossroads of trade in wheat exports and British imports stood Philadelphia. By 1776, Philadelphia had a larger population than any other city in the entire British empire except London. Merchants occupied the top stratum of Philadelphia society. In a city where only 2 percent of the residents owned enough property to qualify to vote, merchants built grand homes and dominated local government. Many of Philadelphia's wealthiest merchants were Quakers. Quaker traits of industry, thrift, honesty, and sobriety encouraged the accumulation of wealth. A colonist complained that a Quaker "prays for his neighbor on First Days [the Sabbath] and then preys on him the other six."

The ranks of merchants reached downward to aspiring tradesmen such as Benjamin Franklin. After he started to publish the *Pennsylvania Gazette* in 1728, Franklin opened a shop, run mostly by his wife, Deborah, that sold a little bit of everything: cheese, codfish, coffee, goose feathers, sealing wax, soap, and now and then a slave. In 1733, Franklin began to publish *Poor Richard's Almanack*, which preached the likelihood of long-term rewards for tireless labor. The *Almanack* sold thousands of copies, quickly becoming Franklin's most profitable product.

The popularity of *Poor Richard's Almanack* suggests that many Pennsylvanians thought less about the pearly gates than about their pocketbooks. Poor Richard's advice that "God gives all Things to Industry" might be considered the motto for the middle colonies. The promise of a worldly payoff made work a secular faith. Poor Richard advised, "Work as if you were to live 100 years, Pray as if you were to die Tomorrow."

William Penn's Quaker utopia became a center of worldly affluence whose most famous citizen, Franklin, was neither a Quaker nor a utopian. Quakers remained influential, but Franklin spoke for most colonists with his aphorisms of work, discipline, and thrift that echoed Quaker rules for outward behavior. Franklin's maxims did not look to the Quakers' divine inner light for guidance. They depended instead on the spark of ambition and the glow of gain.

▶ **REVIEW**   Why did immigrants flood into Pennsylvania during the eighteenth century?

The Southern Colonies: Land of Slavery

Between 1700 and 1770, the population of the southern colonies of Virginia, Maryland, North Carolina, South Carolina, and Georgia grew almost ninefold. By 1770, about twice as many people lived in the South as in either the middle colonies or New England. As elsewhere, natural increase and immigration accounted for the rapid population growth. Many Scots-Irish and German immigrants funneled from the middle colonies into the southern backcountry. Other immigrants were indentured servants (mostly English and Scots-Irish) who followed their seventeenth-century predecessors. But slaves made the most striking contribution to the booming southern colonies, transforming the racial composition of the population. Slavery became the defining characteristic of the southern colonies during the eighteenth century, shaping the region's economy, society, and politics.

The Atlantic Slave Trade and the Growth of Slavery

The number of southerners of African ancestry (nearly all of them slaves) rocketed from just over 20,000 in 1700 to well over 400,000 in 1770. The black population increased nearly three times faster than the South's briskly growing white population. Consequently, the proportion of southerners of African ancestry grew from 20 percent in 1700 to 40 percent in 1770.

Southern colonists clustered into two distinct geographic and agricultural zones. The colonies in the upper South, surrounding the Chesapeake Bay, specialized in growing tobacco, as they had since the early seventeenth century. Throughout the eighteenth century, nine out of ten southern whites and eight out of ten southern blacks lived in the Chesapeake region. The upper South retained a white majority during the eighteenth century.

In the lower South, a much smaller cluster of colonists inhabited the coastal region and specialized in the production of rice and indigo (a plant used to make blue dye). Lower South colonists made up only 5 percent of the total population of the southern colonies in 1700 but inched upward to 15 percent by 1770. South Carolina was the sole British colony along the southern Atlantic coast until 1732, when Georgia was founded. (North Carolina, founded in 1711, was largely an extension of the Chesapeake region.) Blacks in South Carolina, in contrast to every other British mainland colony, outnumbered whites almost two to one; in some low-country districts, the ratio of blacks to whites exceeded ten to one.

The enormous growth in the South's slave population occurred through natural increase and the flourishing Atlantic slave trade (Table 5.1). Slave ships brought almost 300,000 Africans to British North America between 1619 and 1780. Of these Africans, 95 percent arrived in the South and 96 percent arrived during the eighteenth century. Unlike indentured servants or redemptioners, these Africans did not choose to come to the colonies. Like the Robin Johns, most of them had been born into free families in villages located within a

TABLE 5.1	SLAVE IMPORTS, 1451–1870
Estimated Slave Imports to the Western Hemisphere	
1451–1600	275,000
1601–1700	1,341,000
1701–1810	6,100,000
1811–1870	1,900,000

few hundred miles of the West African coast. Although they shared African origins, they came from many different African **cultures**, including Akan, Angolan, Asante, Bambara, Gambian, Igbo, Mandinga, and others. They spoke different languages, worshipped different deities, observed different rules of kinship, grew different crops, and recognized different rulers.

The most important experience they had in common was enslavement. Captured in war, kidnapped, or sold into slavery by other Africans, they were brought to the coast, sold to African traders like the Robin Johns who assembled slaves for resale, and sold again to European or colonial slave traders or ship captains, who packed two hundred to three hundred or more aboard ships that carried them on the **Middle Passage** across the Atlantic and then sold them yet again to a colonial slave merchant or a southern **planter**.

Olaudah Equiano published an account of his enslavement that hints at the stories that might have been told by the millions of other Africans swept up in the slave trade. Equiano wrote that he was born in 1745 in the interior of what is now Nigeria. "I had never heard of white men or Europeans, nor of the sea," he recalled. One day when he was eleven years old, he was kidnapped by Africans,

Olaudah Equiano
This portrait shows Equiano more than a decade after he had bought his freedom. The portrait evokes Equiano's successful acculturation to the customs of eighteenth-century England. His clothing and hairstyle reflect the fashions of a respectable young Englishman. Equiano's embrace of English culture did not cause him to forsake his African roots. He honored his dual identity by campaigning against slavery.
Library of Congress.

who sold him to other Africans, who in turn eventually sold him to a slave ship on the coast. Equiano feared that he was "going to be killed" and "eaten by those white men with horrible looks, red faces, and loose hair." Once the ship set sail, many of the slaves, crowded together in suffocating heat fouled by filth of all descriptions, died from sickness. "The shrieks of the women and the groans of the dying rendered the whole a scene of horror almost inconceivable," Equiano recalled. Most of the slaves on the ship were sold in Barbados, but Equiano and other leftovers were shipped off to Virginia, where he "saw few or none of our native Africans and not one soul who could talk to me." Equiano felt isolated and "exceedingly miserable" because he "had no person to speak to that I could understand." Finally, the captain of a tobacco ship bound for England purchased Equiano, and he traveled as a slave between North America, England, and the West Indies for ten years until he succeeded in buying his freedom in 1766.

Only about 15 percent of the slaves brought into the southern colonies came aboard ships from the West Indies, as Equiano and the Robin Johns did. All the other slaves brought into the southern colonies came directly from Africa, and almost all the ships that brought them (roughly 90 percent) belonged to British merchants. Most of the slaves on board were young adults, with men usually outnumbering women two to one. Children under the age of fourteen, like Equiano, typically accounted for no more than 10 to 15 percent of a cargo.

Mortality during the Middle Passage varied considerably from ship to ship. On average, about 15 percent of the slaves died, but sometimes half or more perished. The average mortality among the white crew of slave ships was often nearly as bad. In general, the longer the voyage lasted, the more people died. Recent studies suggest that many slaves succumbed not only to virulent epidemic diseases such as smallpox and dysentery, but also to acute dehydration caused by fluid loss from perspiration, vomiting, and diarrhea combined with a severe shortage of drinking water.

Normally, an individual planter purchased at any one time a relatively small number of newly arrived Africans, or "new Negroes," as they were called. New Negroes were often profoundly depressed, demoralized, and disoriented. Planters expected their other slaves—either those born into slavery in the colonies (often called "country-born" or "creole" slaves) or Africans who had arrived earlier—to help new Negroes become accustomed to their strange new surroundings.

Planters' preferences for slaves from specific regions of Africa aided slaves' acculturation (or "seasoning," as it was called) to the routines of bondage in the southern colonies. Chesapeake planters preferred slaves from Senegambia, the Gold Coast, or—like Equiano and the Robin Johns—the Bight of Biafra, which combined accounted for 40 percent of all Africans imported to the Chesapeake. South Carolina planters favored slaves from the central African Congo and Angola regions, the origin of about 40 percent of the African slaves they imported. Although slaves within each of these regions spoke many different languages, enough linguistic and cultural similarities existed that they could usually communicate with other Africans from the same region.

Seasoning acclimated new Africans to the physical as well as the cultural environment of the southern colonies. Slaves who had just endured the Middle Passage were poorly nourished, weak, and sick. In this vulnerable state, they encountered the alien diseases of North America without having developed a biological arsenal of acquired immunities. As many as 10 to 15 percent of newly arrived Africans, sometimes more, died during their first year in the southern colonies. Nonetheless, the large number of newly enslaved Africans made the influence of African culture in the South stronger in the eighteenth century than ever before—or since.

While newly enslaved Africans poured into the southern colonies, slave mothers bore children, which caused the slave population in the South to grow rapidly. Slave owners encouraged these births. Thomas Jefferson explained, "I consider the labor of a breeding [slave] woman as no object, that a [slave] child raised every 2 years is of more profit than the crop of the best laboring [slave] man." Although slave mothers loved and nurtured their children, the mortality rate among slave children was high, and the ever-present risk of being separated by sale brought grief to many slave families. Nonetheless, the growing number of slave babies set the southern colonies apart from other New World slave societies, where mortality rates were so high that deaths exceeded births. The high rate of natural increase in the southern colonies meant that by the 1740s, the majority of southern slaves were country-born.

Slave Labor and African American Culture

Southern planters expected slaves to work from sunup to sundown and beyond. George Washington wrote that his slaves should "be at their work as soon as it is light, work til it is dark, and be diligent while they are at it." The conflict between the masters' desire for maximum labor and the slaves' reluctance to do more than necessary made the threat of physical punishment a constant for eighteenth-century slaves. Masters preferred black slaves to white indentured servants, not just because slaves served for life but also because colonial laws did not limit the force masters could use against slaves. As a traveler observed in 1740, "A new negro . . . [will] let a hundred men show him how to hoe, or drive a wheelbarrow; he'll still take the one by the bottom and the other by the wheel and . . . often die before [he] can be conquered." Slaves, the traveler noted, resisted their masters' demands because of their "greatness of soul"— their stubborn unwillingness to conform to their masters' definition of them as merely slaves.

Some slaves escalated their acts of resistance to direct physical confrontation with the master, the mistress, or an overseer. But a hoe raised in anger, a punch in the face, or a desperate swipe with a knife led to swift and predictable retaliation by whites. Throughout the southern colonies, the balance of physical power rested securely in the hands of whites.

Rebellion occurred, however, at Stono, South Carolina, in 1739. Before dawn on a September Sunday, a group of about twenty slaves attacked a country store, killed the two storekeepers, and confiscated the store's guns, ammunition, and powder. Enticing other slaves to join, the group plundered and burned more than half a dozen plantations and killed more than twenty white men, women, and children. A mounted force of whites quickly suppressed the rebellion. They placed the rebels' heads atop mileposts along the road, grim reminders of the consequences of rebellion. The Stono rebellion illustrated that eighteenth-century slaves had no chance of overturning slavery and very little chance of defending themselves in any bold strike for freedom. After the rebellion, South Carolina legislators enacted repressive laws designed to guarantee that whites would always have the upper hand. No other similar uprisings occurred during the colonial period.

Slaves maneuvered constantly to protect themselves and to gain a measure of autonomy within the boundaries of slavery. In Chesapeake tobacco fields, most slaves were subject to close supervision by whites. In the lower South, the task system gave slaves some control over the pace of their work and some discretion in the use of the rest of their time. A "task" was typically defined as a certain area of ground to be cultivated or a specific job to be completed. A slave who completed the assigned task might use the remainder of the day, if any, to work in a garden, fish, hunt, spin, weave, sew, or cook. When masters sought to boost productivity by increasing tasks, slaves did what they could to defend their customary work assignments.

Eighteenth-century slaves also planted the roots of African American lineages that branch out to the present. Slaves valued family ties, and, as in West African societies, kinship structured slaves' relations with one another. Slave parents often gave a child the name of a grandparent, aunt, or uncle. In West Africa, kinship identified a person's place among living relatives and linked the person to ancestors in the past and to descendants in the future. Newly imported African slaves usually arrived alone, like Equiano, without kin. Often slaves who had traversed the Middle Passage on the same ship adopted one another as "brothers" and "sisters." Likewise, as new Negroes were seasoned and incorporated into existing slave communities, established families often adopted them as "fictive" kin.

When possible, slaves expressed many other features of their West African origins in their lives on New World plantations. They gave their children traditional dolls and African names such as Cudjo or Quash, Minda or Fuladi. They grew food crops they had known in Africa, such as yams and okra. They constructed huts with mud walls and thatched roofs similar to African residences. They fashioned banjos, drums, and other musical instruments, held dances, and observed funeral rites that echoed African practices. In these and many other ways, slaves drew upon their African heritages as much as the oppressive circumstances of slavery permitted.

Tobacco, Rice, and Prosperity

Slaves' labor bestowed prosperity on their masters, British merchants, and the monarchy. The southern colonies supplied 90 percent of all North American exports to Britain. Rice exports from the lower South exploded from less than half a million pounds in 1700 to eighty million pounds in 1770, nearly all of it grown by slaves. Exports of indigo also boomed. Together, rice and indigo made up three-fourths of lower South exports, nearly two-thirds of them going to Britain and most of the rest to the West Indies, where sugar-growing slaves ate slave-grown rice. Tobacco was by far the most important export from British North America; by 1770, it represented almost one-third of all colonial exports and three-fourths of all Chesapeake exports. And under the provisions of the Navigation Acts (see chapter 4), nearly all of it went to Britain, where the monarchy collected a lucrative tax on each pound. British merchants then reexported more than 80 percent of the tobacco to the European continent, pocketing a nice markup for their troubles.

These products of slave labor made the southern colonies by far the richest in North America. The per capita wealth of free whites in the South was four times greater than that in New England and three times that in the middle colonies. At the top of the wealth pyramid stood the rice grandees of the lower South and the tobacco gentry of the Chesapeake. These elite families commonly resided on large estates in handsome mansions adorned by luxurious gardens, all maintained and supported by slaves. The extravagant lifestyle of one gentry family astonished a young tutor from New Jersey, who noted that during the winter months, the family kept twenty-eight large fires roaring, requiring six oxen to haul four cartloads stacked with slave-cut firewood to the house every day. In contrast, **yeoman** families—who supported themselves on small plots of land without slaves—cut their own firewood and normally warmed themselves around just one fire.

The vast differences in wealth among white southerners engendered envy and occasional tension between rich and poor, but remarkably little open hostility. In private, the planter elite spoke disparagingly of humble whites, but in public the planters acknowledged their lesser neighbors as equals, at least in belonging to the superior—in their minds—white race. Looking upward, white yeomen and tenants (who owned neither land nor slaves) sensed the gentry's condescension and veiled contempt. But they also appreciated the gentry for granting favors, upholding white supremacy, and keeping slaves in their place. Although racial slavery made a few whites much richer than others, it also gave those who did not get rich a powerful reason to feel similar (in race) to those who were so different (in wealth).

The slaveholding gentry dominated the politics and economy of the southern colonies. In Virginia, only adult white men who owned at least one hundred acres of unimproved land or twenty-five acres of land with a house could vote. This property-holding requirement prevented about 40 percent of white men in Virginia from voting for representatives to the House of Burgesses. In South Carolina, the property requirement was only fifty acres of land, and therefore most adult white men qualified to vote. In both colonies, voters elected members of the gentry to serve in the colonial legislature. The gentry passed elected political offices from generation to generation, almost as if they were hereditary. Politically, the gentry built a self-perpetuating oligarchy—rule by the elite few—with the votes of their many humble neighbors.

The gentry also set the cultural standard in the southern colonies. They entertained lavishly, gambled regularly, and attended Anglican (Church of England) services more for social than for religious reasons. Above all, they cultivated the leisurely pursuit of happiness. They did not condone idleness, however. Their many pleasures and responsibilities as plantation owners kept them busy. Thomas Jefferson, a phenomenally productive member of the gentry, recalled that his earliest childhood memory was of being carried on a pillow by a family slave—a powerful image of the slave hands supporting the gentry's leisure and achievement.

►REVIEW   How did slavery influence the society and economy of the southern colonies?

Unifying Experiences

The societies of New England, the middle colonies, and the southern colonies became more sharply differentiated during the eighteenth century, but colonists throughout British North America also shared unifying experiences that eluded settlers in the Spanish and French colonies. The first was economic. All three British colonial regions had their economic roots in agriculture. Colonists sold their distinctive products in markets that, in turn, offered to consumers throughout British North America a more or less uniform array of goods. A second unifying experience was a decline in the importance of religion. Some settlers called for a revival of religious intensity, but most people focused less on religion and more on the affairs of the world than they had in the seventeenth century. Third, white inhabitants throughout British North America became aware that they shared a distinctive identity as *British* colonists. Thirteen different governments presided over these North American colonies, but all of them answered to the British monarchy. British policies governed not only trade but also military and diplomatic relations with the Indians, French, and Spanish arrayed along colonial borderlands. Royal officials who expected loyalty from the colonists often had difficulty obtaining obedience. The British colonists asserted their prerogatives as British subjects to defend their special colonial interests.

Commerce and Consumption

Eighteenth-century commerce whetted colonists' appetites to consume. Colonial products spurred the development of mass markets throughout the Atlantic world. Huge increases in the supply of colonial tobacco and sugar brought the price of these small luxuries within the reach of most free whites. Colonial goods brought into focus an important lesson of eighteenth-century commerce: Ordinary people, not just the wealthy elite, would buy the things that they desired in addition to what they absolutely needed. Even news, formerly restricted mostly to a few people through face-to-face conversations or private letters, became an object of public consumption through the innovation of newspapers. With the appropriate stimulus, market demand seemed unlimited.

The Atlantic commerce that took colonial goods to markets in Britain brought objects of consumer desire back to the colonies. British merchants and manufacturers recognized that colonists made excellent customers, and the Navigation Acts gave British exporters privileged access to the colonial market. By midcentury, export-oriented industries in Britain were growing ten times faster than firms attuned to the home market. Most British exports went to the vast European market, where potential customers outnumbered those in the colonies by more than one hundred to one. But as European competition stiffened, colonial markets became increasingly important. British exports to North America multiplied eightfold between 1700 and 1770, outpacing the rate of population growth after midcentury. When the colonists' eagerness to consume exceeded their ability to pay, British exporters willingly extended credit, and colonial debts soared.

Imported mirrors, silver plate, spices, bed and table linens, clocks, tea services, wigs, books, and more infiltrated parlors, kitchens, and bedrooms throughout the colonies. Despite the many differences among the colonists, the consumption of British exports built a certain material uniformity across region, religion, class, and status. Consumption of British exports made the colonists look and feel more British even though they lived at the edge of a wilderness an ocean away from Britain.

The rising tide of colonial consumption had other less visible but no less important consequences. Consumption presented women and men with a novel array of choices. In many respects, the choices might appear trivial: whether to buy knives and forks, teacups, or a clock. But such small choices confronted eighteenth-century consumers with a big question: What do you want? As colonial consumers defined and expressed their desires with greater frequency during the eighteenth century, they became accustomed to thinking of themselves as individuals who had the power to make decisions that influenced the quality of their lives—attitudes of significance in the hierarchical world of eighteenth-century British North America.

Religion, Enlightenment, and Revival

Eighteenth-century colonists could choose from almost as many religions as consumer goods. Virtually all of the bewildering variety of religious denominations represented some form of Christianity, almost all of them Protestant. Slaves made up the largest group of non-Christians. A few slaves converted to Christianity in Africa or after they arrived in North America, but most continued to embrace elements of indigenous African religions. Roman Catholics concentrated in Maryland as they had since the seventeenth century, but even there they were outnumbered by Protestants.

The varieties of Protestant faith and practice ranged across a broad spectrum. The middle colonies and the southern backcountry included militant Baptists and Presbyterians. Huguenots who had fled persecution in Catholic France peopled congregations in several cities. In New England, old-style Puritanism splintered into strands of Congregationalism that differed over fine points of theological doctrine. The Congregational Church was the official established church in New England, and all residents paid taxes for its support. Throughout the plantation South and in urban centers such as Charleston, New York, and Philadelphia, prominent colonists belonged to the Anglican Church, which received tax support in the South. But dissenting faiths grew everywhere, and in most colonies their adherents won the right to worship publicly, although the established churches retained official support.

Many educated colonists became deists, looking for God's plan in nature more than in the Bible. Deists shared the ideas of eighteenth-century European **Enlightenment** thinkers, who tended to agree that science and reason could disclose God's laws in the natural order. In the colonies as well as in Europe, Enlightenment ideas encouraged people to study the world around them, to think for themselves, and to ask whether the disorderly appearance of things masked the principles of a deeper, more profound natural order. From New England towns to southern drawing rooms, individuals met to discuss such matters. Philadelphia was the center of these conversations, especially after the formation of the American Philosophical Society in 1769, an outgrowth of an earlier group organized by Benjamin Franklin, who was a deist. Leading colonial thinkers such as Franklin and Thomas Jefferson, among many other members, communicated with each other seeking both to understand nature and to find ways to improve society. Franklin's interest in electricity, stoves, and eyeglasses exemplified the shift of focus among many eighteenth-century colonists from heaven to the here and now.

Most eighteenth-century colonists went to church seldom or not at all, although they probably considered themselves Christians. A minister in Charleston observed that on the Sabbath, "the Taverns have more Visitants than the Churches." In the leading colonial cities, church members were a small minority of eligible adults, no more than 10 to 15 percent. Anglican parishes in the

South rarely claimed more than one-fifth of eligible adults as members. In some regions of rural New England and the middle colonies, church membership embraced two-thirds of eligible adults, while in other areas, only one-quarter of the residents belonged to a church. The dominant faith overall was religious indifference. As a late-eighteenth-century traveler observed, "Religious indifference is imperceptibly disseminated from one end of the continent to the other."

The spread of religious indifference, of deism, of denominational rivalry, and of comfortable backsliding profoundly concerned many Christians. A few despaired that, as one wrote, "religion . . . lay a-dying and ready to expire its last breath of life." To combat what one preacher called the "dead formality" of church services, some ministers set out to convert nonbelievers and to revive the piety of the faithful with a new style of preaching that appealed more to the heart than to the head. Historians have termed this wave of revivals the **Great Awakening**. In Massachusetts during the mid-1730s, the fiery Puritan minister Jonathan Edwards reaped a harvest of souls by reemphasizing traditional Puritan doctrines of humanity's utter depravity and God's vengeful omnipotence. The title of Edwards's most famous sermon, "Sinners in the Hands of an Angry God," conveys the flavor of his message. In Pennsylvania and New Jersey, William Tennent led revivals that dramatized spiritual rebirth with accounts of God's miraculous powers, such as raising Tennent's son from the dead.

The most famous revivalist in the eighteenth-century Atlantic world was George Whitefield. An Anglican, Whitefield preached well-worn messages of sin and salvation to large audiences in England using his spellbinding, unforgettable voice. Whitefield visited the North American colonies seven times, staying for more than three years during the mid-1740s and attracting tens of thousands to his sermons, including Benjamin Franklin and Olaudah Equiano. Whitefield's preaching transported many in his audience to emotion-choked states of religious ecstasy. About one revival he wrote, "The bitter cries and groans were enough to pierce the hardest heart. Some of the people were as pale as death; others were wringing their hands; others lying on the ground; others sinking into the arms of their friends; and most lifting their eyes to heaven, and crying to God for mercy. They seemed like persons . . . coming out of their graves to judgment."

Whitefield's successful revivals spawned many lesser imitations. Itinerant preachers, many of them poorly educated, toured the colonial backcountry after midcentury, echoing Whitefield's medium and message as best they could. Bathsheba Kingsley, a member of Jonathan Edwards's flock, preached the revival message informally—as did an unprecedented number of other women throughout the colonies—causing her congregation to brand her a "brawling woman" who had "gone quite out of her place."

The revivals awakened and refreshed the spiritual energies of thousands of colonists struggling with the uncertainties and anxieties of eighteenth-century America. The conversions at revivals did not substantially boost the total number of church members, however. After the revivalists moved on, the routines and pressures of everyday existence reasserted their primacy in the lives of many converts. But the revivals communicated the important message that every soul mattered, that men and women could choose to be saved, that individuals had the power to make a decision for everlasting life or death. Colonial revivals expressed in religious terms many of the same democratic and egalitarian values expressed in economic terms by colonists' patterns of consumption. One colonist noted the analogy by referring to itinerant revivalists as "Pedlars in divinity." Like consumption, revivals contributed to a set of common experiences that bridged colonial divides of faith, region, class, and status.

Borderlands and Colonial Politics in the British Empire

The plurality of peoples, faiths, and communities that characterized the North American colonies arose from the somewhat haphazard policies of the eighteenth-century British empire. Since the Puritan Revolution of the mid-seventeenth century, British monarchs had valued the colonies' contributions to trade and encouraged their growth and development. Unlike Spain and France—whose policies of excluding Protestants and foreigners kept the population of their North American colonial territories tiny—Britain kept the door to its colonies open to anyone, and tens of thousands of non-British immigrants settled in the North American colonies and raised families. The open door did not extend to trade, however, as the seventeenth-century Navigation Acts restricted colonial trade to British ships and traders. These policies evolved because they served the interests of the monarchy and of influential groups in Britain and the colonies. The policies also gave the colonists a common framework of political expectations and experiences.

At a minimum, British power defended the colonists from Indian, French, and Spanish enemies on their borders—as well as from foreign powers abroad. Each colony organized a militia, and privateers sailed from every port to prey on foreign ships. But the British navy and army bore ultimate responsibility for colonial defense.

Royal officials warily eyed the small North American settlements of New France and New Spain for signs of threats to the colonies. Alone, neither New France nor New Spain jeopardized British North America, but with Indian allies, they could become a potent force that kept colonists on their guard (Map 5.2). Native Americans' impulse to defend their territory from colonial incursions warred with their desire for trade, which tugged them toward the settlers. As a colonial official observed in 1761, "A modern Indian cannot subsist without Europeans. . . . [The European goods that were] only conveniency at first [have] now become necessity." To obtain such necessities as guns, ammunition, clothing, sewing utensils, and much more that was manufactured largely by the British, Indians trapped beavers, deer, and other fur-bearing animals throughout the interior.

MAP 5.2   Zones of Empire in Eastern North America
The British zone was much more densely settled than the zones under French, Spanish, and Indian control. The comparatively large number of British colonists made them more secure than the relatively few colonists in the vast regions claimed by France and Spain. Yet the British colonists were not powerful enough to dominate and had to guard against attacks by powerful Indian groups allied with the French or Spanish.

Colonial traders and their respective empires competed to control the fur trade. British, French, Spanish, and Dutch officials monitored the trade to prevent their competitors from deflecting the flow of furs toward their own markets. Indians took advantage of this competition to improve their own prospects, playing one trader and empire off against another. The Iroquois, for example, promised the French exclusive access to the furs and territory of the Great Lakes region and at the same time made the same pledge of exclusive rights to the British. Indian tribes and confederacies also competed among themselves for favored trading rights with one colony or another, a competition colonists encouraged.

The shifting alliances and complex dynamics of the fur trade struck a fragile balance along the frontier. The threat of violence from all sides was ever present, and the threat became reality often enough for all parties to be prepared for the worst. In the Yamasee War of 1715, Yamasee and Creek Indians—with French encouragement—mounted a coordinated attack against colonial settlements in South Carolina and inflicted heavy casualties. The Cherokee Indians, traditional enemies of the Creeks, refused to join the attack. Instead, they protected their access to British trade goods by allying with the colonists and turning the tide of battle, thus triggering a murderous rampage of revenge by the colonists against the Creek and Yamasee tribes.

Relations between Indians and colonists differed from colony to colony and from year to year. But the British colonists' nagging perceptions of menace on the frontier kept them continually hoping for help from the British to keep the Indians at bay and to maintain the essential flow of trade. In 1754, the British colonists' endemic competition with the French flared into the Seven Years' War (also known as the French and Indian War), which would inflame the frontier for years (see chapter 6). Before the 1760s, neither the British colonists nor the British themselves developed a coherent policy toward the Indians. But both agreed that Indians made deadly enemies, profitable trading partners, and powerful allies. As a result, the British and their colonists kept an eye on the Spanish empire to the west and relations with the Indians there.

Russian hunters in search of seals and sea otters ventured along the Pacific coast from Alaska to California and threatened to become a permanent presence on New Spain's northern frontier. To block Russian access to present-day California, officials in New Spain mounted a campaign to build forts (called *presidios*) and missions there.

In 1769, an expedition headed by a military man, Gaspar de Portolá, and a Catholic priest, Junípero Serra, traveled north from Mexico to present-day San Diego, where they founded the first California mission, San Diego de Alcalá. They soon journeyed all the way to Monterey, which became the capital of Spanish California. There Portolá established a presidio in 1770 "to defend us from attacks by the Russians," he wrote. The same year, Serra founded Mission San Carlos Borroméo de Carmelo in Monterey to convert the Indians and recruit them to work to support the soldiers and other Spaniards in the presidio. By 1772, Serra had founded other missions along the path from San Diego to Monterey.

One Spanish soldier praised the work of the missionaries, writing that "with flattery and presents [the missionaries] attract the savage Indians and persuade them to adhere to life in society and to receive instruction for a knowledge of the Catholic faith, the cultivation of the land, and the arts necessary for making the instruments most needed for farming." Yet for the Indians, the Spaniards' California missions had horrendous consequences, as they had elsewhere in the Spanish borderlands. European diseases decimated Indian populations, Spanish soldiers raped Indian women, and missionaries beat Indians and subjected them to near slavery. Indian uprisings against the Spaniards occurred repeatedly, but the presidios and missions endured as feeble projections of the Spanish empire along the Pacific coast.

Mission Carmel
This eighteenth-century drawing portrays a reception for a Spanish visitor at Mission Carmel in what is now Carmel, California. Lines of mission Indians, dressed in robes, flank the entrance to the chapel, where a priest and his assistants await the visitor. The reception ritual dramatized the strict hierarchy that governed relations between Spanish missionaries, ruling officials, and the subordinate Indians.
University of California at Berkeley, Bancroft Library.

British attempts to exercise political power in their colonial governments met with success so long as British officials were on or very near the sea. Colonists acknowledged—although they did not always readily comply with—British authority to collect customs duties, inspect cargoes, and enforce trade regulations. But when royal officials tried to wield their authority on land in the internal affairs of the colonies, they invariably encountered colonial resistance. A governor appointed by the king in each of the nine royal colonies (Rhode Island and Connecticut selected their own governors) or by the proprietors in Maryland and Pennsylvania headed the government of each colony. The British envisioned colonial governors as mini-monarchs able to exert influence in the colonies much as the king did in Britain. But colonial governors were not kings, and the colonies were not Britain.

Eighty percent of colonial governors had been born in England, not in the colonies. Some governors stayed in England, close to the source of royal patronage, and delegated the grubby details of colonial affairs to subordinates. Even the best-intentioned colonial governors had difficulty developing relations of trust and respect with influential colonists because their terms of office averaged just five years and could be terminated at any time. Colonial governors controlled few patronage positions to secure political friendships in the colonies. Officials who administered the colonial customs service, for example, received their appointments through patronage networks centered in England rather than from colonial governors. In obedience to Britain, colonial governors fought incessantly with the colonists' assemblies. They battled over governors' vetoes of colonial legislation, removal of colonial judges, creation of new courts, dismissal of the representative assemblies, and other local issues. Some governors developed a working relationship with the colonists' assemblies. But during the eighteenth century, the assemblies gained the upper hand.

Since British policies did not clearly define the colonists' legal powers, colonial assemblies seized the opportunity to make their own rules. Gradually, the assemblies established a strong tradition of representative government analogous, in their eyes, to the British Parliament. Voters often returned the same representatives to the assemblies year after year, building continuity in power and leadership that far exceeded that of the governor. By 1720, colonial assemblies had won the power to initiate legislation, including tax laws and authorizations to spend public funds. Although all laws passed by the assemblies (except in Maryland, Rhode Island, and Connecticut) had to be approved by the governor and then by the Board of Trade in Britain, the difficulties in communication about complex subjects over long distances effectively ratified the assemblies' decisions. Years often passed before colonial laws were repealed by British authorities, and in the meantime, the assemblies' laws prevailed.

The heated political struggles between royal governors and colonial assemblies that occurred throughout the eighteenth century taught colonists a common set of political lessons. They learned to employ traditionally British ideas of representative government to defend their own colonial interests. They learned that power in the British colonies rarely belonged to the British government.

> ▶**REVIEW**   What experiences tended to unify the colonists in British North America during the eighteenth century?

Conclusion: The Dual Identity of British North American Colonists

During the eighteenth century, a society that was both distinctively colonial and distinctively British emerged in British North America. Tens of thousands of immigrants and slaves like the Robin Johns gave the colonies an unmistakably colonial complexion and contributed to the colonies' growing population and expanding economy. People of different ethnicities and faiths sought their for-tunes in the colonies, where land was cheap, labor was dear, and—as Benjamin Franklin preached—work promised to be rewarding. Indentured servants and redemptioners risked a temporary period of bondage for the potential reward of better opportunities in the colonies than on the Atlantic's eastern shore. Slaves endured lifetime servitude, which they neither chose nor desired but from which their masters greatly benefited.

Identifiably colonial products from New England, the middle colonies, and the southern colonies flowed to the West Indies and across the Atlantic. Back came unquestionably British consumer goods along with fashions in ideas, faith, and politics. The bonds of the British empire required colonists to think of them-selves as British subjects and, at the same time, encouraged them to consider their status as colonists.

People of European origin in the North American colonies of Spain and France did not share in the emerging political identity of the British colonists. They also did not participate in the cultural, economic, social, and religious changes experi-enced by their counterparts in British North America. Unlike the much more numerous colonists in British North America, North American Spanish and French colonists did not develop societies that began to rival the European empires that sponsored and supported them.

By 1750, British colonists in North America could not imagine that their dis-tinctively dual identity—as British and as colonists—would soon become a source of intense conflict. But by 1776, colonists in British North America had to choose whether they were British or American.

REVIEWING THE CHAPTER

Use the questions and timeline to review and strengthen your understanding of the chapter.

REVIEW QUESTIONS

1. How did the North American colonies achieve the remarkable population growth of the eighteenth century? (pp. 115–16)

2. Why did settlement patterns in New England change from the seventeenth to the eighteenth century? (pp. 116–20)

3. Why did immigrants flood into Pennsylvania during the eighteenth century? (pp. 120–25)

4. How did slavery influence the society and economy of the southern colonies? (pp. 126–32)

5. What experiences tended to unify the colonists in British North America during the eighteenth century? (pp. 132–40)

MAKING CONNECTIONS

1. Colonial products such as tobacco and sugar transformed consumption patterns on both sides of the Atlantic in the eighteenth century. How did consumption influence the relationship between the American colonies and Britain? In your answer, consider how it might have strengthened and weakened connections.

2. Why did the importance of religion decline throughout the colonies from the seventeenth to the eighteenth century? How did American colonists respond to these changes?

3. How did different colonies attempt to manage relations with the Indians? How did the Indians attempt to manage relationships with the Europeans? In your answer, consider disputes over territory and trade.

4. Varied immigration patterns contributed to important differences between the British colonies. Compare and contrast patterns of immigration to the middle and southern colonies. Who came, and how did they get there? How did they shape the economic, cultural, and political character of each colony?

TIMELINE

1702	• Queen Anne's War triggers German migration to North America.	1745	• Olaudah Equiano born.
1711	• North Carolina founded.	1750s	• Colonists begin to move down Shenandoah Valley.
1715	• Yamasee War.	1754	• Seven Years' War begins.
1717	• Scots-Irish immigration increases.	1769	• American Philosophical Society founded.
1730s	• Jonathan Edwards promotes Great Awakening.		• First California mission, San Diego de Alcalá, established.
1732	• Georgia founded.	1770	• Mission and presidio established at Monterey, California.
1733	• Benjamin Franklin begins to publish *Poor Richard's Almanack*.		• British North American colonists number more than two million.
1739	• Stono rebellion.	1775	• Indians destroy San Diego mission.
1740s	• George Whitefield preaches religious revival in North America. • Majority of southern slaves are country-born.		

▶ **For an online bibliography, practice quizzes, Web sites, images, and documents related to this chapter,** see the Book Companion Site at **bedfordstmartins.com/roark.**

▶ **For firsthand accounts of this period,** see Chapter 5 in Michael Johnson, ed., *Reading the American Past,* Fourth Edition.

6
CHAPTER

The British Empire and the Colonial Crisis

1754–1775

I N 1771, THOMAS HUTCHINSON became the royal governor of the colony of Massachusetts. Unlike most royal governors, who were British aristocrats sent over by the king for short tours of duty, Hutchinson was a fifth-generation American. A Harvard-educated member of the Massachusetts elite, from a family of successful merchants, Hutchinson had served two decades in the Massachusetts general assembly. In 1758, he was appointed lieutenant governor, and in 1760 he also became chief justice of the colony's highest court. He lived in the finest mansion in Boston. Wealth, power, and influence were his in abundance. He was proud of his connection to the British empire and loyal to his king.

Hutchinson had the misfortune to be a loyal colonial leader during the two very tumultuous decades leading up to the American Revolution. He worked hard to keep the British and colonists aligned in interests, even promoting a plan to unify the colonies into a single defensive unit (the Albany Plan of Union) to ward off Indian wars. The plan of union failed, and a major war ensued—the Seven Years' War, pitting the British and colonists against the French and their Indian allies in the backcountry of the American colonies. When the war ended and the British government began to think about taxing colonists to pay for it, Hutchinson had no doubt that the new British policies were legitimate. Unwise, perhaps, in their specific formulation, but certainly legitimate.

Not everyone in Boston shared his opinion. Fervent, enthusiastic crowds protested against a succession of British taxation policies enacted after 1763—the

143

Sugar Act, the Stamp Act, the Townshend duties, the Tea Act, all landmark events on the road to the American Revolution. But Hutchinson maintained his steadfast loyalty to Britain. His love of order and tradition inclined him to unconditional support of the British empire, and he was, by nature, a measured and cautious man. "My temper does not incline to enthusiasm," he once wrote.

Privately, he lamented the stupidity of the British acts that provoked trouble, but his sense of duty required him to defend the king's policies, however misguided. Quickly, he became an inspiring villain to the emerging revolutionary movement. Governor Hutchinson came to personify all that was wrong with British and colonial relations. The man not inclined to enthusiasm unleashed popular enthusiasm all around him. He never appreciated that irony.

In another irony, Thomas Hutchinson was actually one of the first Americans to recognize the difficulties of maintaining full rights and privileges for colonists so far from their supreme government, the king and Parliament in Britain. In 1769, when British troops occupied Boston in an effort to provide civil order, he wrote privately to a friend in England, "There must be an abridgement of what are called English liberties. . . . I doubt whether it is possible to project a system of government in which a colony three thousand miles distant from the parent state shall enjoy all the liberty of the parent state." What he could not imagine was the possibility of giving up the parent state and creating an independent government closer to home.

Governor Hutchinson was a loyalist; in the 1750s, most English-speaking colonists were affectionately loyal to Britain. But the Seven Years' War, which Britain and its colonies fought together as

Thomas Hutchinson
The only formal portrait of Thomas Hutchinson still in existence shows an assured young man in ruffles and hair ribbons. One other portrait of him hung in his summer house outside Boston; a revolutionary crowd mutilated it and stabbed out the eyes. In 1775, Hutchinson fled to Britain, the country he regarded as his cultural home, only to realize how very American he was.
Courtesy of the Massachusetts Historical Society.

allies, shook that affection, and imperial policies in the decade following the war (1763 to 1773) shattered it completely. Over the course of that decade, colonists insistently raised serious questions about American liberties and rights, especially over the issues of taxation and representation. Many came to believe what Thomas Hutchinson could never credit—that a tyrannical Britain had embarked on a course to enslave the colonists by depriving them of their traditional English liberties.

The opposite of **liberty** was slavery, a condition of nonfreedom and coercion. Political rhetoric about liberty, tyranny, and slavery heated up emotions of white colonists during the many crises of the 1760s and 1770s. But this rhetoric turned out to be a two-edged sword. The call for an end to tyrannical slavery meant one thing when sounded by Boston merchants whose commercial shipping rights had been revoked; the same call meant something quite different in 1775 when sounded by black Americans locked in the bondage of slavery.

All of this was set in motion by the Seven Years' War. The British victory at first fortified loyalty to the mother country, but its aftermath, taxation, stirred up discussions of rights, fueled white colonists' fear of enslavement by king and Parliament, and produced a potent political vocabulary with unexpected consequences.

The Seven Years' War, 1754–1763

For the first fifty years of the eighteenth century, Britain was at war intermittently with France or Spain. Often the colonists in America experienced reverberations from these conflicts, most acutely along the French **frontier** in northern New England, which bumped up against New France, an area of French settlement along the St. Lawrence River with population centers at Montreal and Quebec. In the 1750s, international tensions mounted again, but this time over events originating in America. The conflict began in 1754 over contested land in the Ohio Valley, variously claimed by Virginians, Pennsylvanians, the French, and the Indians already living there. The result was the costly Seven Years' War (its British name), which spread in 1756 to encompass much of Europe, the Caribbean, and even India. The American colonists experienced nearly ten years of warfare, not seven, in what they called the French and Indian War. (In Canada, it is called the War of the Conquest, marking the takeover of French Canada by the British.) British and American soldiers shared the hardships of battle and the glory of victory over the French and Indians. But the immense costs of the war— in money, death, and desire for revenge by losers and even winners—laid the groundwork for the imperial crisis of the 1760s between the British and Americans.

French-British Rivalry in the Ohio Country

For several decades, French traders had cultivated alliances with the Indian tribes in the Ohio Country, a frontier region they regarded as part of New France (Map 6.1). Cementing their relationships with gifts, the French established a profitable trade of manufactured goods for beaver furs. But in the 1740s, aggressive Pennsylvania traders traveled west and began to infringe on their territory, underselling French traders and threatening to reorient Indian loyalties. Adding to the tensions, a group of wealthy Virginians, including the brothers Lawrence and Augustine Washington, also asserted claim to the same large territory. The Virginians formed the Ohio Company in 1747 and obtained a **land grant** from the British king to some five hundred square miles of land, including the strategically important forks of the Ohio River (present-day Pittsburgh). In contrast to the French, who had no plans to settle colonists in the Ohio Country, the Virginians were primarily interested in land speculation, fueled by an exploding Anglo-American population seeking new land.

In response to these incursions, the French sent soldiers to build a series of military forts to secure their trade routes and to create a western barrier to American population expansion. In 1753, the royal governor of Virginia, Robert Dinwiddie, himself a shareholder in the Ohio Company, sent a messenger to warn the French that they were trespassing on Virginia land.

The messenger on this dangerous mission was George Washington, younger half-brother of the Ohio Company leaders. Though only twenty-one, Washington was an ambitious youth whose imposing height (six feet two) and air of silent competence convinced the governor he could do the job. The middle child in a family of eight, Washington did not stand to inherit great wealth, so he sought to gain public reputation and impress the Virginia elite by volunteering for this perilous duty. Accompanied by six other Virginians, only one of whom spoke French, Washington delivered Dinwiddie's message to a French outpost near Lake Erie in late 1753 and returned home with crucial intelligence about French military plans.

Impressed, Dinwiddie appointed the youth to lead a small military expedition west to assert and, if need be, defend Virginia's claim. Imperial officials in London, concerned about the French fortifications, had authorized the governor "to repell force by force," but only if the French attacked first. By early 1754, the French had built Fort Duquesne at the forks of the Ohio River; Washington's difficult assignment was to chase the French away without actually being the aggressor.

In the spring of 1754, Washington set out with 160 Virginians, soon accompanied by a contingent of Mingo Indians, who opposed the increasing French military presence in the Ohio Country. Washington's game plan was not well formed, and he followed the lead of Tanaghrisson, the Mingo chief, who guided a detachment of Virginians in the early-morning hours to a very small encampment of French soldiers in the woods. The French, just rising, suddenly feared attack, and

MAP 6.1   European Areas of Influence and the Seven Years' War, 1754–1763

In the mid-eighteenth century, France, Britain, and Spain claimed vast areas of North America, many of them already inhabited by various Indian peoples. The early flash points of the Seven Years' War were in regions of disputed claims where the French had allied with powerful native groups—the Iroquois and the Algonquian tribes—to put pressure on the westward-moving British and Americans.

in a few panicked minutes, both sides commenced shooting. This May morning marked the violent start of the Seven Years' War. Who fired first was later a matter of dispute, but fourteen Frenchmen (and no Virginians) were wounded. Washington, lacking a translator, struggled to communicate with the injured French commander, who himself was on a diplomatic mission to deliver a message to the Virginians. But Tanaghrisson and his men intervened to kill and then scalp the wounded men, starting with the commander, probably with the strategic aim of inflaming hostilities between the French and the colonists.

This sudden massacre violated Washington's instructions to avoid being the aggressor and raised the stakes considerably. Fearing retaliation, Washington ordered his men to fortify their position; the flimsy "Fort Necessity" was the result. Reinforcements amounting to several hundred more Virginians arrived; but the Mingos, sensing disaster and displeased by Washington's style of command, fled. (Tanaghrisson later said, "The Colonel was a good-natured man, but had no experience; he took upon him to command the Indians as his slaves, [and] would by no means take advice from the Indians.") In early July, more than six hundred French soldiers aided by one hundred Shawnee and Delaware warriors attacked Fort Necessity, killing or wounding a third of Washington's men. The message was clear: The French would not depart from the disputed territory.

The Albany Congress and Intercolonial Defense

Even as Virginians, Frenchmen, and Indians fought and died in the Ohio Country, British imperial leaders hoped to prevent a larger war. One obvious strategy was to strengthen British alliances with seemingly neutral Indian tribes. To this end, British authorities directed the governor of New York to convene a colonial conference.

In June and July of 1754, twenty-four delegates from seven colonies met in Albany, New York. Also attending were Iroquois Indians of the Six Nations, a confederacy of tribes (Mohawk, Oneida, Onondaga, Cayuga, Seneca, and Tuscarora) inhabiting the central and western parts of present-day New York. Albany was the traditional meeting place of the Covenant Chain, a trade alliance first created in 1692 between New York leaders and Mohawk Indians, the most easterly of the Six Nations. In 1753, the aged and venerable Mohawk leader Hendrick accused the New York colonials of breaking the Covenant Chain. A prime goal of the Albany Congress was to repair trade relations with the Mohawk and secure their help— or at least their neutrality—against the French threat.

Two delegates at the congress had more ambitious plans. Benjamin Franklin of Pennsylvania and Thomas Hutchinson of Massachusetts, both rising political stars in their home colonies, coauthored the Albany Plan of Union, a proposal for a unified colonial government limited to war and defense policies. In the course of the meeting, the Albany delegates learned of Washington's defeat at Fort Necessity and understood instantly the escalating risk of war with France; they approved the plan. Key features included a president general appointed by the crown and a grand council of forty-eight representatives, all to meet annually to consider questions of war, peace, and trade with the Indians. The writers of the Albany Plan humbly reaffirmed Parliament's authority; this was no bid for enlarged autonomy of the colonies.

To Franklin's surprise, not a single colony approved the Albany Plan. The Massachusetts assembly feared it was "a Design of gaining power over the Colonies," especially the power of taxation. Others objected that it would be impossible to agree on unified policies toward scores of quite different Indian tribes. The British government never backed the Albany Plan either, which perplexed both Franklin and Hutchinson. Instead, British authorities centralized dealings with Indians by appointing, in 1755, two superintendents of Indian affairs, one for the northern and another for the southern colonies, each with exclusive powers to negotiate treaties, trade, and land sales with all tribes.

The Indians at the Albany Congress were not impressed with the Albany Plan either. The Covenant Chain alliance with the Mohawk tribe was reaffirmed, but the other nations left without pledging to help the British battle the French. At this very early point in the Seven Years' War, the Iroquois figured that the French military presence around the Great Lakes would discourage the westward push of American colonists and therefore better serve their interests.

The War and Its Consequences

By 1755, Washington's frontier skirmish had turned into a major mobilization of British and American troops against the French. At first, the British hoped for quick victory on three fronts. General Edward Braddock, recently arrived from England, planned to rout the French at Fort Duquesne in western Pennsylvania. In Massachusetts, Governor William Shirley aimed his soldiers at Fort Niagara, critically located between Lakes Erie and Ontario. And William Johnson, a New Yorker recently appointed superintendent of Indian affairs, led forces north toward Lake Champlain, in an effort to push the French back to Canada (see Map 6.1). Unfortunately for the British, the French were prepared to fight and had cemented respectful alliances with many Indian tribes from Canada down through the Great Lakes region and into the Ohio Country.

Braddock's march west was the first of a series of disasters for the British. Accompanied by George Washington and his Virginia soldiers, Braddock led 2,000 troops into the backcountry in July 1755, expecting an easy victory with his big artillery and overwhelming numbers. Indian guidance and support amounted to a mere 8 Oneida warriors. One day short of Fort Duquesne, in heavy woods where their cannons were useless, the British were ambushed by 250 French soldiers aided by 640 Indian warriors, including Ottawas, Ojibwas, Potawatomis, Shawnees, and Delawares. In the bloody Battle of the Monongahela, named for a nearby river, nearly a thousand on the British side were killed or wounded. Washington was unhurt, though two horses in succession were shot out from under him; General Braddock was killed. Washington's bravery in battle caused the governor of Virginia to promote him to commander of the Virginia army. At age twenty-two, Washington was beginning to realize his ambitions.

News of Braddock's defeat caused the other two British armies, then hacking their way through the dense forests of northern New York, to retreat from action. For the next two years, the British stumbled badly on the American front. They lacked adequate troops and supplies, and they received scant help from the American colonial assemblies. Most Indian tribes actively supported the French, figuring that sparsely populated fur trading French settlements were better for them than the fast-growing, westward-pushing American colonies.

What finally turned the war around was the rise to power of William Pitt, who became Britain's prime minister in 1757. Willing to commit massive resources to fight France and its ally Spain throughout the world, he paid colonial assemblies to raise and equip provincial soldiers, and he mounted military assaults in Europe, Canada, and the Caribbean. In America, British and American troops captured Forts Duquesne, Niagara, and Ticonderoga by 1759. Next, the British navy sailed up the St. Lawrence River to the isolated French cities of Quebec and Montreal. The decisive victory on the North American continent was the capture of the seemingly invincible fortress city of Quebec in September 1759 by the young British general James Wolfe. Montreal surrendered in 1760.

The American colonists rejoiced, but the worldwide war was not over yet. Battles continued in the Caribbean, where the French sugar islands Martinique and Guadeloupe fell to the British. Battles raged in Austria and Prussia and extended to India. In 1762, the British laid siege to Spanish Cuba because Spain was France's ally in the global conflict. The costly water invasion of Havana required some four thousand provincial soldiers from New York and New England. By the end of 1762, the fighting was over. France and Spain capitulated, and the Treaty of Paris was signed in 1763.

The triumph was sweet but short-lived. The complex peace negotiations reorganized the map of North America but stopped short of providing Britain with the full spoils of victory. Britain gained control of Canada, eliminating the French threat from the north and west. British and American title to the eastern half of North America, precisely what Britain had claimed before the war, was confirmed. But all French territory west of the Mississippi River, including New Orleans, was transferred to Spain as compensation for Spain's assistance to France during the war. Stranger still, Cuba was returned to Spain, and Martinique and Guadeloupe were returned to France (Map 6.2).

In truth, the French islands in the Caribbean were hardly a threat to Americans, for they provided a profitable trade in smuggled molasses. The main threat to the colonists came instead from the Indians. The Treaty of Paris ignored them and assigned their lands to British rule. With the French gone, the Indians lost the advantage of having two opponents to play off against each other, and they now

MAP 6.2   North America after the Seven Years' War
In the peace treaty of 1763, France ceded its interior territory but retained fishing rights and islands in the far north and several sugar islands in the Caribbean. Much of France's claim to Louisiana went not to Britain but to Spain.

had to cope with the westward-moving Americans. Indian policy would soon become a serious point of contention between the British government and the colonists.

Britain's version of the victory of 1763 awarded all credit to the mighty British army, successful despite inadequate support by ungrateful colonists. Worse still, some colonists had engaged in smuggling—notably a lively trade in beaver pelts with French fur traders and an illegal molasses trade in the Caribbean. American traders, grumbled the British leaders, were really traitors. William Pitt was convinced that the illegal trade "principally, if not alone, enabled France to sustain and protract this long and expensive war."

Colonists read the lessons of the war differently. American colonial soldiers had turned out in force, they claimed, but had been relegated to grunt work by arrogant British leaders and subjected to unexpectedly harsh military discipline, ranging from floggings to executions. One soldier recalled watching three New

England soldiers endure whippings of eight hundred lashes for some "trifling offense" at the hands of the British. Americans bristled at stories of British disdain, such as the remark of the impetuous General Wolfe, the British hero of Quebec, who said the American soldiers were "contemptible dogs." General Braddock had foolishly bragged to Benjamin Franklin that "these savages may, indeed, be a formidable enemy to your raw American militia, but upon the king's regular and disciplined troops, sir, it is impossible they should make any impression." Braddock's defeat "gave us Americans," Franklin wrote, "the first suspicion that our exalted ideas of the prowess of British regulars had not been well founded."

The human costs of the war were etched especially sharply in the minds of New England colonists. About one-third of all Massachusetts men between fifteen and thirty had seen service. Many families lost loved ones, a cost not soon forgotten. The assault on Havana in Cuba, for example, took the lives of some two thousand Americans, half the provincial force that had been sent there.

The enormous expense of the war caused by Pitt's no-holds-barred military strategy cast another huge shadow over the victory. By 1763, Britain's national debt, double what it had been when Pitt took office, posed a formidable challenge to the next decade of leadership in Britain.

British Leadership, Pontiac's Uprising, and the Proclamation of 1763

In 1760, in the middle of the Seven Years' War, twenty-two-year-old George III came to the British throne. Timid and insecure, the new king trusted only his Scottish tutor, the Earl of Bute, an outsider to power circles in London, and made him head of his cabinet of ministers. Bute committed blunders and did not last long, but he made one significant decision—to keep a standing army in the colonies after the last battle was over in 1760. In both financial and political terms, this was a costly move.

The ostensible reason for stationing British troops in America was to maintain the peace between the colonists and the Indians. This was not a misplaced concern. The defeat and withdrawal of the French from North America had left their Indian allies—who did not accept defeat—in a state of alarm. Just three months after the Treaty of Paris was signed in 1763, Pontiac, chief of the Ottawa tribe in the northern Ohio region, attacked the British garrison near Detroit. Six more attacks on forts quickly followed, and frontier settlements were also raided by nearly a dozen tribes from western New York, the Ohio Valley, and the Great Lakes region. By the fall, every fort west of Detroit had been captured; more than four hundred British soldiers were dead and another two thousand colonists killed or taken captive. Pontiac's uprising was quelled in December 1763 by the combined efforts of British and colonial soldiers, but tensions remained high.

To minimize the violence, the British government issued the Proclamation of 1763, forbidding colonists to settle west of the Appalachian Mountains. The

Proclamation chiefly aimed to separate Indians and settlers, but it also limited trade with Indians to traders licensed by colonial governors, and it forbade private sales of Indian land. The Proclamation's language took care not to identify western lands as belonging to the Indians. Instead, it spoke of Indians "who live under our protection" on "such parts of our Dominions and Territories as, not having been ceded to or purchased by Us, are reserved to them, as their Hunting Grounds." Other parts of the Proclamation of 1763 referred to American and even French colonists in Canada as "our loving subjects," entitled to English rights and privileges. In contrast, the Indians were clearly rejected as British subjects, and instead described more vaguely as "Tribes of Indians with whom We are connected." Of course, the British were not really well connected with any Indians, nor did they wish connections to form among the tribes. As William Johnson, the superintendent of northern Indian affairs, advised in 1764, "It will be expedient to treat with each nation separately . . . for could they arrive at a perfect union, they must prove very dangerous Neighbours."

The 1763 boundary proved impossible to enforce. Surging population growth had already sent many hundreds of settlers west of the Appalachians, and land speculators, such as those of Virginia's Ohio Company, had no desire to lose opportunities for profitable resale of their land grants. Bute's decision to post a standing army in the colonies was thus a cause for concern among western settlers, eastern speculators, and Indian tribes alike.

▶ **REVIEW** How did the Seven Years' War erode relations between colonists and British authorities?

The Sugar and Stamp Acts, 1763–1765

Lord Bute lost power in 1763, and the young King George turned to a succession of leaders throughout the 1760s, searching for a prime minister he could trust. A half dozen ministers in seven years took turns dealing with one basic, underlying British reality: A huge war debt, amounting to £123 million and growing due to interest, needed to be serviced, and the colonists, as British subjects, should help to pay it off. To many Americans, however, that proposition seemed in deep violation of what they perceived to be their rights and liberties as British subjects, and it created resentment that eventually erupted in rebellion. The first provocative revenue acts were the work of Sir George Grenville, prime minister from 1763 to 1765.

Grenville's Sugar Act

To find revenue, George Grenville scrutinized the customs service, which monitored the shipping trade and collected all import and export duties in both Britain and America. Grenville found that the salaries of customs officers cost the government four times what was collected in revenue. The shortfall was due in part to bribery and smuggling, so Grenville began to insist on rigorous attention to paperwork and a strict accounting of collected duties.

The hardest duty to enforce was the one imposed by the Molasses Act of 1733—a stiff tax of six pence per gallon on any molasses purchased from non-British sources. The purpose of the tax was to discourage trade with French Caribbean islands and redirect the molasses trade to British sugar islands, but it did not work. French molasses remained cheap and abundant because French **planters** on Martinique and Guadeloupe had no use for it. A by-product of sugar production, molasses was a key ingredient in rum, a drink the French scorned. Rum-loving Americans were eager to buy French molasses, and they had ignored the tax law for decades.

Grenville's ingenious solution was the Revenue Act of 1764, popularly dubbed the "Sugar Act." It lowered the duty on French molasses to three pence, making it more attractive for shippers to obey the law, and at the same time raised penalties for smuggling. The act appeared to be in the tradition of navigation acts meant to regulate trade, but Grenville's actual intent was to raise revenue. He was using an established form of law for new ends and accomplishing his goal by the novel means of lowering a duty.

The Sugar Act toughened enforcement policies. From now on, all British naval crews could act as impromptu customs officers, boarding suspicious ships and seizing cargoes found to be in violation. Smugglers caught without proper paperwork would be prosecuted, not in a friendly civil court with a local jury but in a vice-admiralty court located in Halifax, Nova Scotia, where a single judge presided. The implication was that justice would be sure and severe.

Grenville hoped that the new Sugar Act would reform American smugglers into law-abiding shippers and in turn generate income for the empire. Unfortunately, the decrease in duty was not sufficient to offset the attractions of smuggling. The vigilant customs officers made bribery harder to accomplish, and several ugly confrontations occurred in port cities. Reaction to the Sugar Act foreshadowed questions about Britain's right to tax Americans, but in 1764 objections to the act came principally from Americans in the shipping trades inconvenienced by the law.

From the British point of view, the Proclamation of 1763 and the Sugar Act seemed to be reasonable efforts to administer the colonies. To the Americans, however, the British supervision appeared to be a disturbing intrusion into the long colonial practice of centering taxation powers in colonial assemblies composed of elected representatives. Philadelphian Benjamin Franklin, living in London as the agent for Pennsylvania, warned that "two distinct Jurisdictions or Powers of Taxing cannot well subsist together in the same country. If a Tax is propos'd with us, how dare we venture to lay it, as the next Ship perhaps may bring us an Account of some heavy Tax propos'd by you?"

The Stamp Act

By his second year in office, Grenville had made almost no dent in the national debt. Continued evasion prevented the Sugar Act from becoming the money-maker he had hoped it would be. So in February 1765, he escalated his revenue program with the Stamp Act, precipitating a major conflict between Britain and the colonies over Parliament's right to tax. The Stamp Act imposed a tax on all paper used for official documents—newspapers, pamphlets, court documents, licenses, wills, ships' cargo lists—and required an affixed stamp as proof that the tax had been paid. Unlike the Sugar Act, which regulated trade, the Stamp Act was designed plainly and simply to raise money. It affected nearly everyone who used any taxed paper, but most of all those in the business and legal communities, who relied heavily on official documents.

Grenville was no fool. Anticipating that the stamp tax would be unpopular—Thomas Hutchinson had forewarned him—he delegated the administration of the act to Americans, to avoid taxpayer hostility toward British enforcers. In each colony, local stamp distributors would be hired at a handsome salary of 8 percent of the revenue collected.

English tradition held that taxes were a gift of the people to their monarch, granted by the people's representatives. This view of taxes as a freely given gift preserved an essential concept of English political theory: the idea that citizens have the liberty to enjoy and use their property without fear of confiscation. The king could not demand money; only the House of Commons could grant it. Grenville quite agreed with the notion of taxation by consent, but he argued that the colonists were already "virtually" represented in Parliament. The House of Commons, he insisted, represented all British subjects, wherever they were.

Colonial leaders emphatically rejected this view, arguing that **virtual representation** could not withstand the stretch across the Atlantic. The stamp tax itself, levied by a distant Parliament on unwilling colonies, illustrated the problem. Daniel Dulany, a Maryland lawyer, wrote a best-selling pamphlet explaining that virtual representation was "a mere cob-web, spread to catch the unwary, and entangle the weak."

Resistance Strategies and Crowd Politics

News of the Stamp Act arrived in the colonies in April 1765, seven months before it was to take effect on November 1. There was time, therefore, to object. Governors were unlikely to challenge the law, for most of them owed their office to the king. Instead, the colonial assemblies took the lead; eight of them held discussions on the Stamp Act.

Virginia's assembly, the House of Burgesses, was the first. At the end of its May session, after two-thirds of the members had left, Patrick Henry, a young political newcomer, presented a series of resolutions on the Stamp Act that were debated and passed, one by one. They became known as the Virginia Resolves.

Henry's resolutions inched the assembly toward radical opposition to the Stamp Act. The first three stated the obvious: that Virginians were British citizens, that they enjoyed the same rights and privileges as Britons, and that self-taxation was one of those rights. The fourth resolution noted that Virginians had always taxed themselves, through their representatives in the House of Burgesses. The fifth took a radical leap by pushing the other four unexceptional statements to one logical conclusion—that the Virginia assembly alone had the right to tax Virginians.

Two more fiery resolutions were debated as Henry pressed the logic of his case to the extreme. The sixth resolution denied legitimacy to any tax law originating outside Virginia, and a seventh boldly called anyone who disagreed with these propositions an enemy of Virginia. This was too much for the other representatives. They voted down resolutions six and seven and later rescinded their vote on number five as well.

Their caution hardly mattered, however, because newspapers in other colonies printed all seven Virginia Resolves, creating the impression that a daring first challenge to the Stamp Act had occurred. Consequently, other assemblies were willing to consider even more radical questions, such as this: By what authority could Parliament legislate for the colonies without also taxing them? No one disagreed, in 1765, that Parliament had legislative power over the

---

Newspapers Protest the Stamp Act

From New Hampshire to South Carolina, papers issued on October 31, 1765, used dark black mourning lines and funereal language to herald the date the Stamp Act went into effect. The editor of the *Pennsylvania Journal* designed his paper to look like a tombstone, with coffins and skulls throughout its four pages. All colonial newspapers resumed publication within a week or two, defiantly operating without stamps. One stampless editor wrote, "The press is the test of truth, the bulwark of public safety, the guardian of freedom."
Library of Congress.

colonists, who were, after all, British subjects. Several assemblies advanced the argument that there was a distinction between *external* taxes, imposed to regulate trade, and *internal* taxes, such as a stamp tax or a property tax, which could only be self-imposed.

Reaction to the Stamp Act ran far deeper than political debate in assemblies. Every person whose livelihood required official paper had to decide whether to comply with the act. There were only three options: boycotting, which was within the law but impractical because of the reliance on paper; defying the law and using unstamped paper; or preventing distribution of the stamps at the source, before the law took effect, thus ensuring universal noncompliance.

The first organized resistance to the Stamp Act began in Boston in August 1765 under the direction of town leaders, chief among them Samuel Adams, John Hancock, and Ebenezer Mackintosh. The first two had Harvard educations and were elected officials in Boston. Adams, in his forties, had shrewd political instincts and a gift for organizing. Hancock, though not yet thirty, had recently inherited his uncle's mercantile shipping business and was one of the wealthiest men in Massachusetts. Mackintosh, the same age as Hancock, was a shoemaker and highly experienced street activist. Many other artisans, tradesmen, printers, tavern keepers, dockworkers, and sailors—the middling and lower orders— mobilized in resistance to the Stamp Act, taking the name "Sons of Liberty" from an impassioned speech given in Parliament by a member opposed to the act.

The plan hatched in Boston called for a large street demonstration highlighting a ritualized mock execution designed to convince Andrew Oliver, the designated stamp distributor, to resign. With no distributor, no stamps could be sold. On August 14, 1765, a crowd of two thousand to three thousand demonstrators, led by Mackintosh, hung an effigy of Oliver in a tree and then paraded it around town before finally beheading and burning it. In hopes of calming tensions, the royal governor Francis Bernard took no action. The flesh-and-blood Oliver stayed in hiding; the next day he resigned his office in a well-publicized announcement. The Sons of Liberty were elated.

The demonstration provided lessons for everyone. Oliver learned that stamp distributors would be very unpopular people. Governor Bernard, with no police force to call on, learned the limitations of his power to govern. The demonstration's leaders learned that street action was effective. And hundreds of ordinary men not only learned what the Stamp Act was all about but also gained pride in their ability to have a decisive impact on politics.

Twelve days later, a second crowd action showed how well these lessons had been learned. On August 26, a crowd visited the houses of three detested customs and admiralty court officials, breaking windows and raiding wine cellars. A fourth target was the finest dwelling in Massachusetts, owned by Andrew Oliver's stiff-necked brother-in-law, Thomas Hutchinson. Rumors abounded that Hutchinson had urged Grenville to adopt the Stamp Act. Although he had actually done the opposite, Hutchinson refused to set the record straight, saying curtly, "I am not obliged to give an answer to all the questions that may be put me by every lawless person." The crowd attacked his house and, after removing his furniture and personal effects, demolished it. By daybreak only the exterior walls were standing. Governor Bernard gave orders to call out the militia, but he was told that many militiamen were among the crowd.

The destruction of Hutchinson's house brought a temporary halt to protest activities in Boston. The town meeting issued a statement of sympathy for Hutchinson, but a large reward for the arrest and conviction of rioters failed to produce a single lead. Hutchinson assumed that Mackintosh had led the attack, under orders issued by Samuel Adams, but Adams denied involvement and professed shock at the "truly mobbish Nature" of the violence.

Nonetheless, the opponents of the Stamp Act in Boston had triumphed; no one volunteered to replace Oliver as distributor. When the Stamp Act took effect on November 1, customs officers were unable to prevent ships lacking properly stamped clearance papers from passing through the harbor. Hutchinson, as chief justice of the Massachusetts court, could not tolerate this defiance of the law, but he could not bring the lawbreakers to justice in his court. So he did the only thing he could do as a principled man: He resigned his judgeship. He remained lieutenant governor, however, and within five years he would agree to become the royal governor.

Liberty and Property

Boston's crowd actions of August sparked similar eruptions by groups calling themselves Sons of Liberty in nearly fifty towns throughout the colonies, and stamp distributors everywhere hastened to resign. One Connecticut distributor was forced by a crowd to throw his hat and powdered wig in the air while shouting a cheer for "Liberty and property!" This man fared better than another Connecticut stamp agent, who was nearly buried alive by Sons of Liberty. Only when the thuds of dirt sounded on his coffin did he have a sudden change of heart, shouting out his resignation to the crowd above. Luckily, he was heard. In Charleston, South Carolina, the stamp distributor resigned after crowds burned effigies and chanted "Liberty! Liberty!"

Some colonial leaders, disturbed by the riots, sought a more moderate challenge to parliamentary authority. Twenty-seven delegates representing nine colonial assemblies met in New York City in October 1765 as the Stamp Act Congress. For two weeks, the men hammered out a petition about taxation addressed to the king and Parliament. Their statement closely resembled the first five Virginia Resolves, claiming that taxes were "free gifts of the people," which only the people's representatives could give. They dismissed virtual representation: "The people of these colonies are not, and from their local circumstances, cannot be represented in the House of Commons." At the same time, the delegates carefully affirmed their subordination to Parliament and monarch in deferential language. (Even so, the elected president of the congress, wealthy Timothy Ruggles of Hardwick,

Massachusetts, refused to sign the document, fearing it was too radical. When he returned home, his townsmen challenged his lukewarm attitude, ending his long career in politics.) Although the Stamp Act Congress's deference to the king defined a moderate path, the mere fact of its meeting advanced a radical potential— the notion of intercolonial political action.

The rallying cry of "Liberty and property" made perfect sense to many white Americans of all social ranks, who feared that the Stamp Act threatened their traditional right to liberty as British subjects. In this case, the liberty in question was the right to be taxed only by representative government. "Liberty and property" came from a trinity of concepts—"life, liberty, property"—that had come to be regarded as the birthright of freeborn British subjects since at least the seventeenth century. A powerful tradition of British political thought invested representative government with the duty to protect individual lives, liberties, and property (possessions or money) against potential abuse by royal authority. Up to 1765, Americans had consented to accept Parliament as a body that in some way represented them. But now, in this matter of taxation via stamps, Parliament seemed a distant body that had failed to protect Americans' liberty and property against royal authority.

Alarmed, some Americans began to speak and write about a plot by British leaders to enslave them. The opposite of liberty was slavery, the condition of being under the control of someone else. A Maryland writer warned that if the colonies lost "the right of exemption from all taxes without their consent," that loss would "deprive them of every privilege distinguishing freemen from slaves." In Virginia, a group of planters headed by Richard Henry Lee issued a document called the Westmoreland Resolves, claiming that the Stamp Act was an attempt "to reduce the people of this country to a state of abject and detestable slavery." The opposite meanings of *liberty* and *slavery* were utterly clear to white Americans, but they stopped short of applying similar logic to the half million black Americans they held in bondage. Many blacks, however, could see the contradiction. When a crowd of Charleston blacks paraded with shouts of "Liberty!" just a few months after white Sons of Liberty had done the same, the town militia turned out to break up the demonstration.

Teapots for Patriots
Colonists could purchase commemorative teapots to celebrate the repeal of the Stamp Act. This pot was a British import. Can you think of any reason why a British pottery manufacturer might also have celebrated the repeal of the Stamp Act? Remember that in 1765, the symbolic significance of tea lay several years in the future. During the political struggles over tea in 1770–1774, no British manufacturer is known to have made a souvenir teapot for the American market.
Peabody Essex Museum, Salem, Massachusetts.

Politicians and merchants in Britain reacted with distress to the American demonstrations and petitions. Merchants particularly feared trade disruptions and pressured Parliament to repeal the Stamp Act. By late 1765, yet another new minister, the Marquess of Rockingham, headed the king's cabinet and sought a way to repeal the act without losing face. The solution came in March 1766—the Stamp Act was repealed—but with it came the Declaratory Act, which asserted Parliament's right to legislate for the colonies "in all cases whatsoever." Perhaps the stamp tax had been inexpedient, but the power to tax—one prime case of a legislative power—was stoutly upheld.

▶REVIEW   Why did the Sugar Act and the Stamp Act draw fierce opposition from colonists?

The Townshend Acts and Economic Retaliation, 1767–1770

Rockingham did not last long as prime minister. By the summer of 1766, George III had persuaded William Pitt to resume that position. Pitt appointed Charles Townshend to be chancellor of the exchequer, the chief financial minister. Facing both the old war debt and the continuing cost of stationing British troops in America, Townshend turned again to taxation. But his knowledge of the changing political climate in the colonies was limited, and his simple yet naive idea to raise revenue touched off coordinated boycotts of British goods in 1768 and 1769. Even women were politicized as self-styled "Daughters of Liberty." Boston led the uproar, causing the British to send peacekeeping soldiers to assist the royal governor. The stage was thus set for the first fatalities in the brewing revolution.

The Townshend Duties

Townshend proposed new taxes in the old form of a navigation act. Officially called the Revenue Act of 1767, it established new duties on tea, glass, lead, paper, and painters' colors imported into the colonies, to be paid by the importer but passed on to consumers in the retail price. A year before, the duty on French molasses had been reduced from three pence to one pence per gallon, and finally the Sugar Act was pulling in a tidy revenue of about £45,000 annually. So it was not unreasonable to suppose that duties on additional trade goods might also improve the cash flow. Townshend assumed that external taxes on transatlantic trade would be more acceptable to Americans than internal taxes, such as the stamp tax.

The Townshend duties were not especially burdensome, but the principle they embodied—taxation through trade duties—looked different to the colonists in the wake of the Stamp Act crisis. Although Americans once distinguished between external and internal taxes, accepting external duties as presumably wise governmental policy designed to direct the flow of trade, that distinction was wiped out by an external tax meant only to raise money. John Dickinson, a Philadelphia lawyer, articulated this view in a series of articles titled *Letters from a Farmer in Pennsylvania*, widely reprinted in the winter of 1767–68. "We are taxed without our consent. . . . We are therefore—SLAVES," Dickinson wrote, calling for "a total denial of the power of Parliament to lay upon these colonies any 'tax' whatever."

A controversial provision of the Townshend duties directed that some of the revenue generated would pay the salaries of royal governors. Before 1767, local assemblies set the salaries of their own officials, giving them significant influence over crown-appointed officeholders. Townshend wanted to strengthen the governors' position as well as to curb the growing independence of the assemblies.

The New York assembly, for example, seemed too defiant to Townshend. It had refused to enforce a British rule of 1765 called the Quartering Act, which directed the colonies to furnish shelter and provisions for the British army left in place after the Seven Years' War. The assembly argued that the Quartering Act was really a tax measure because it required New Yorkers to pay money by order of Parliament. Townshend came down hard on the assembly. He orchestrated a parliamentary order, the New York Suspending Act, which declared all the assembly's acts null and void until it met its obligations to the army. Both measures—the new way to pay royal governors' salaries and the suspension of the governance functions of the New York assembly—struck a chill throughout the colonies. Many wondered whether legislative government was at all secure.

Massachusetts again took the lead in protesting the Townshend duties. Samuel Adams, an elected member of the provincial assembly, argued that any form of parliamentary taxation was unjust because Americans were not represented in Parliament. Further, he argued that the new way to pay governors' salaries subverted the proper relationship between the people and their rulers. The assembly circulated a letter with Adams's arguments to other colonial assemblies for their endorsement. As with the Stamp Act Congress of 1765, colonial assemblies were starting to coordinate their protests.

In response to Adams's letter, the new man in charge of colonial affairs in Britain, Lord Hillsborough, instructed Massachusetts governor Bernard to dissolve the assembly if it refused to repudiate the letter. The assembly refused, by a vote of 92 to 17, and Bernard carried out his instruction. In the summer of 1768, Boston was in an uproar.

Nonconsumption and the Daughters of Liberty

The Boston town meeting had already passed resolutions, termed "nonconsumption agreements," calling for a boycott of all British-made goods. Dozens of other towns passed similar resolutions in 1767 and 1768. For example, prohibited purchases in the town of New Haven, Connecticut, included carriages, furniture, hats, clothing, lace, clocks, and textiles. The idea was to encourage home manufacture and to hurt trade, causing London merchants to pressure Parliament for repeal of the duties.

Nonconsumption agreements were very hard to enforce. With the Stamp Act, there was one hated item, a stamp, and a limited number of official distributors. In contrast, an agreement to boycott all British goods required coordination on many fronts, from shippers to merchants to consumers. It also required serious personal sacrifice. Some merchants were wary of nonconsumption because it hurt their pocketbooks, and a few continued to import in readiness for the end of nonconsumption (or to sell on the side to people choosing to ignore nonconsumption). In Boston, such merchants found themselves blacklisted in newspapers and broadsides.

A more direct blow to trade came from nonimportation agreements, but it proved more difficult to get merchants to agree to these. There was always the risk that merchants in other colonies might continue to trade with the British and thus receive handsome profits if neighboring colonies prohibited trade. Not until late 1768 could Boston merchants agree to suspend trade through a nonimportation agreement lasting one year starting January 1, 1769. Sixty signed the agreement. New York merchants soon followed suit, as did Philadelphia and Charleston merchants in 1769.

Doing without British products, whether luxury goods, tea, or textiles, no doubt was a hardship. But it also presented an opportunity, for many of the British products specified in nonconsumption agreements were household goods traditionally under the control of the "ladies." By 1769, male leaders in the patriot cause clearly understood that women's cooperation in nonconsumption and home manufacture was beneficial to their cause. The Townshend duties thus provided an unparalleled opportunity for encouraging female patriotism. During the Stamp Act crisis, Sons of Liberty took to the streets in protest. During the difficulties of 1768 and 1769, the concept of "Daughters of Liberty" emerged to give shape to a new idea—that women might play a role in public affairs.

Any woman could express affiliation with the colonial protest through conspicuous boycotts of British-made goods. In Boston, more than three hundred women signed a petition to abstain from tea, "sickness excepted," in order to "save this abused Country from Ruin and Slavery." A Philadelphia woman inscribed some "patriotic poesy" in praise of women boycotters in her notebook in 1768, ending with the lines, "Stand firmly resolved and bid Grenville to see, / That rather than Freedom, we'll part with our Tea." A nine-year-old girl visiting the royal governor's house in New Jersey took the tea she was offered, curtsied, and tossed the beverage out a nearby window.

Homespun cloth became a prominent symbol of patriotism. A young Boston girl learning to spin called herself "a daughter of liberty," noting that

"I chuse to wear as much of our own manufactory as pocible." A stylish matron in Massachusetts who pieced together a patchwork petticoat sewn from dozens of old remnants was deemed exemplary and therefore newsworthy by a Boston newspaper. In the boycott period of 1768 to 1770, newspapers reported on spinning matches, or bees, in some sixty New England towns, in which women came together in public to make yarn. Nearly always, the bee was held at the local minister's house, and the yarn produced was charitably handed over to him for distribution to the poor. Newspaper accounts variously called the spinners "Daughters of Liberty" or "Daughters of Industry."

This surge of public spinning was related to the politics of the boycott, which infused traditional women's work with new political purpose. But the women spinners were not equivalents of the Sons of Liberty. The Sons marched in streets, burned effigies, threatened hated officials, and celebrated anniversaries of their successes with raucous drinking and feasting in taverns. The Daughters manifested their patriotism quietly, in ways marked by piety, industry, and charity. The difference was due in part to cultural ideals of gender, which prized masculine self-assertion but feminine selflessness. It also was due to class. The Sons were a cross-class alliance, with leaders from the middling orders reliant on men and boys of the lower ranks to fuel their crowds. The Daughters, dusting off spinning wheels and shelving their teapots, were genteel ladies used to buying British goods. The difference between the Sons and Daughters also speaks to two views of how best to challenge authority. Which was the more effective strategy: violent threats and street actions, or the self-disciplined, self-sacrificing boycott of goods?

On the whole, the anti-British boycotts were a success. Imports fell by more than 40 percent; British merchants felt the pinch and let Parliament know it. In Boston, the Hutchinson family also endured losses, but even more alarming to the rigid lieutenant governor, Boston seemed overrun with anti-British sentiment. The Sons of Liberty staged annual rollicking celebrations of the Stamp Act riot, and both Hutchinson and Governor Bernard concluded that British troops were necessary to restore order.

Military Occupation and "Massacre" in Boston

In the fall of 1768, three thousand uniformed troops arrived to occupy Boston. The soldiers drilled conspicuously on the Common, played loud music on the Sabbath, and in general grated on the nerves of Bostonians. Although the situation was frequently tense, no major troubles occurred during that winter and through most of 1769. But as January 1, 1770, approached, marking the end of the nonimportation agreement, it was clear that some merchants—such as Thomas Hutchinson's two sons, both importers—were ready to break the boycott.

Trouble began in January, when a crowd defaced the door of the Hutchinson brothers' shop by "Hillsborough paint," a potent mixture of human excrement and urine. In February, a crowd surrounded the house of customs official Ebenezer Richardson, who panicked and fired a musket, accidentally killing a young boy passing on the street. The Sons of Liberty mounted a massive funeral procession to mark this first instance of violent death in the struggle with Britain.

For the next week, tension gripped Boston. The climax came on Monday evening, March 5, 1770, when a crowd taunted eight British soldiers guarding the customs house. Onlookers threw snowballs and rocks and dared the soldiers to fire; finally one did. After a short pause, someone yelled "Fire!" and the other soldiers shot into the crowd, hitting eleven men, killing five of them.

The Boston Massacre, as the event quickly became called, was over in minutes. In the immediate aftermath, Hutchinson (now acting governor after Bernard's recall to Britain) showed courage in addressing the crowd from the balcony of the statehouse. He quickly removed the regiments to an island in the harbor to prevent further bloodshed, and he jailed Captain Thomas Preston and his eight soldiers for their own protection, promising they would be held for trial.

The Sons of Liberty staged elaborate martyrs' funerals for the five victims. Significantly, the one nonwhite victim shared equally in the public's veneration. Crispus Attucks, a sailor and rope maker in his forties, was the son of an African man and a Natick Indian woman. A slave in his youth, he was at the time of his death a free laborer at the Boston docks. Attucks was one of the first American partisans to die in the American Revolution, and certainly the first African American.

The trial of the eight soldiers came in the fall of 1770. They were defended by two young Boston attorneys, Samuel Adams's cousin John Adams and Josiah Quincy. Because Adams and Quincy had direct ties to the leadership of the Sons of Liberty, their decision to defend the British soldiers at first seems odd. But Adams was deeply committed to the idea that even unpopular defendants deserved a fair trial. Samuel Adams respected his cousin's decision to take the case, for there was a tactical benefit as well. It showed that the Boston leadership was not lawless but could be seen as defenders of British liberty and law.

The five-day trial, with dozens of witnesses, resulted in acquittal for Preston and for all but two of the soldiers, who were convicted of manslaughter, branded on the thumbs, and released. Nothing materialized in the trial to indicate a conspiracy or concerted plan to provoke trouble by either the British or the Sons of Liberty. To this day, the question of responsibility for the Boston Massacre remains obscure.

▶**REVIEW**   Why did British authorities send troops to occupy Boston in the fall of 1768?

The Tea Party and the Coercive Acts, 1770–1774

In the same week as the Boston Massacre, yet another new British prime minister, Frederick North, acknowledged the harmful impact of the boycott on trade and recommended repeal of the Townshend duties. A skillful politician, Lord North took office in 1770 and kept it for twelve years; at last King George had stability at the helm. Seeking peace with the colonies and prosperity for British merchants, North persuaded Parliament to remove all the duties except the tax on tea, kept as a symbol of Parliament's power.

The renewal of trade and the return of cooperation between Britain and the colonies gave men like Thomas Hutchinson hope that the worst of the crisis was behind them. For nearly two years, peace seemed possible, but tense incidents in 1772, followed by a renewed struggle over the tea tax in 1773, precipitated a full-scale crisis that by 1775 resulted in war.

The Calm before the Storm

Repeal of the Townshend duties brought an end to nonimportation, despite the tax on tea. Trade boomed in 1770 and 1771, driven by pent-up demand. Moreover, the leaders of the popular movement seemed to be losing their power. Samuel Adams, for example, ran for a minor local office in Boston and lost to a conservative merchant.

Then in 1772, several incidents again brought the conflict with Britain into sharp focus. One was the burning of the *Gaspée*, a Royal Navy ship pursuing suspected smugglers off the coast of Rhode Island. A British investigating commission failed to arrest anyone but announced that it would send suspects, if any were found, to Britain for trial on charges of high treason. This ruling seemed to fly in the face of the traditional English right to trial by a jury of one's peers.

When news of the *Gaspée* investigation spread, it was greeted with disbelief in other colonies. Patrick Henry, Thomas Jefferson, and Richard Henry Lee in the Virginia House of Burgesses proposed that a network of standing committees be established to link the colonies and pass along alarming news. By mid-1773, every colonial assembly except Pennsylvania's had a "committee of correspondence."

Another British action in 1772 further spread the communications network. Lord North proposed to pay the salaries of superior court justices out of the tea revenue, similar to Townshend's plan for paying royal governors. The Boston town meeting, fearful that judges would now be in the pockets of their new paymasters, established a committee of correspondence and urged all Massachusetts towns to do likewise. The first vital message, circulated in December 1772, attacked the judges' salary policy as the latest proof of a British plot to undermine traditional "liberties": unjust taxation, military occupation, massacre, now capped by the subversion of justice. By the spring of 1773, more than half the towns in

Massachusetts had set up committees of correspondence, providing local forums for debate. These committees politicized ordinary townspeople, sparking a revolutionary language of rights and constitutional duties. They also bypassed the official flow of power and information through the colony's royal government.

The final incident shattering the relative calm of the early 1770s was the Tea Act of 1773. Americans had resumed buying the taxed British tea, but they were also smuggling large quantities of Dutch tea, cutting into the sales of Britain's East India Company. So Lord North proposed legislation giving favored status to the East India Company, allowing it to sell tea directly to government agents rather than through public auction to independent merchants. The hope was to lower the price of the East India tea, including the duty, below that of smuggled Dutch tea, motivating Americans to obey the law.

Tea in Boston Harbor

In the fall of 1773, news of the Tea Act reached the colonies. Parliamentary legislation to make tea inexpensive struck many colonists as an insidious plot to trick Americans into buying large quantities of the duted tea. The real goal, some argued, was the increased revenue, which would be used to pay the royal governors and judges. The Tea Act was thus a painful reminder of Parliament's claim to the power to tax and legislate for the colonies.

But how to resist the Tea Act? Nonimportation was not viable, because the tea trade was too lucrative to expect all merchants to give it up willingly. Consumer boycotts had proved ineffective, because it was impossible to distinguish between duted tea (the object of the boycott) and smuggled tea (illegal but politically clean) once it was in the teapot. The act's appointment of tea agents, parallel to the Stamp Act distributors, suggested one solution. In every port city, revived Sons of Liberty pressured tea agents to resign; without agents, governors yielded, and tea cargoes either landed without paperwork or were sent home.

Governor Hutchinson, however, would not bend any rules. Three ships bearing tea arrived in Boston in November 1773. They cleared customs and unloaded their other cargoes but not the tea. Sensing the town's extreme tension, the captains wished to return to England, but Hutchinson would not grant them clearance to leave without paying the tea duty. Also, there was a time limit on the stay allowed in the harbor. After twenty days, the duty had to be paid, or local authorities would confiscate the tea.

For the full twenty days, pressure built in Boston. Daily mass meetings energized citizens from Boston and surrounding towns, alerted by the committees of correspondence. On the final day, December 16, when for a final time Hutchinson refused clearance for the ships, a large crowd gathered at Old South Church to debate a course of action. No solution emerged at that meeting, but immediately following it, somewhere between 100 and 150 men, thinly disguised as Indians, boarded the ships and dumped thousands of pounds of tea into the water while a

Tossing the Tea
This engraving from an English book published in 1789 recounts the history of North America from its settlement to "becoming united, free, and independent states." Men on the ship break into the chests and dump the contents; a few are depicted in Indian disguise. A large crowd on the shore looks on. This event was not dubbed the "Tea Party" until the 1830s, when a later generation celebrated the illegal destruction of the tea and made heroes out of the few surviving participants.
Library of Congress.

crowd of 2,000 watched. John Adams rejoiced over the bold destruction of the tea in a diary entry the following day: "There is a Dignity, a Majesty, a Sublimity, in this last Effort of the Patriots, that I greatly admire. . . . This Destruction of the Tea is so bold, so daring, so firm, intrepid and inflexible, and it must have so important Consequences."

The Coercive Acts

Lord North's response was swift and stern: He persuaded Parliament to issue the Coercive Acts, four laws meant to punish Massachusetts for destroying the tea. In America, those laws, along with a fifth one, the Quebec Act, were soon known as the Intolerable Acts.

The first act, the Boston Port Act, closed Boston harbor to all shipping as of June 1, 1774, until the destroyed tea was paid for. Britain's objective was to halt the commercial life of the city.

The second act, the Massachusetts Government Act, altered the colony's charter, underscoring Parliament's claim to supremacy over Massachusetts. The royal governor's powers were greatly augmented, and the council became an appointive, rather than elective, body. Further, the governor could now appoint all judges, sheriffs, and officers of the court. No town meeting beyond the annual spring election of town selectmen could be held without the governor's approval, and every agenda item likewise required prior approval. Every Massachusetts town was affected.

The third Coercive Act, the Impartial Administration of Justice Act, stipulated that any royal official accused of a capital crime—for example, Captain Preston and his soldiers at the Boston Massacre—would be tried in a court in Britain. It did not matter that Preston had received a fair trial in Boston. What this act ominously suggested was that down the road, more Captain Prestons and soldiers might be firing into unruly crowds.

The fourth act amended the 1765 Quartering Act and permitted military commanders to lodge soldiers wherever necessary, even in private households. In a related move, Lord North appointed General Thomas Gage, commander of the Royal Army in New York, governor of Massachusetts. Thomas Hutchinson was out, relieved at long last of his duties. Military rule, including soldiers, returned once more to Boston.

Ill timed, the fifth act—the Quebec Act—had nothing to do with the four Coercive Acts, but it fed American fears. It confirmed the continuation of French civil law and government form, as well as Catholicism, for Quebec—all an affront to **Protestant** New Englanders recently denied their own representative government. The act also gave Quebec control of disputed land (and control of the lucrative fur trade) throughout the Ohio Valley, land also claimed by Virginia, Pennsylvania, and a number of Indian tribes.

The five Intolerable Acts spread alarm in all the colonies. If Britain could squelch Massachusetts—change its charter, suspend local government, inaugurate military rule, and on top of that give Ohio to Catholic Quebec—what liberties were secure? Fearful royal governors in half a dozen colonies dismissed the sitting assemblies, adding to the sense of urgency. A few of the assemblies defiantly continued to meet in new locations. Through the committees of correspondence, colonial leaders arranged to convene in Philadelphia in September 1774 to respond to the crisis.

Beyond Boston: Rural Massachusetts

By the time delegates assembled in Philadelphia, all of Massachusetts had arrived at the brink of open insurrection. With a British general occupying the governorship and some three thousand troops controlling Boston, the revolutionary momentum shifted from urban radicals to rural farmers who protested the Massachusetts Government Act in dozens of spontaneous, dramatic showdowns. In some towns, the last authorized town meeting simply continued to meet, as a dodge against the prohibition on new meetings, while more defiant towns just ignored the law. Gage's call for elections for a new provincial assembly under his control sparked elections for a competing and unauthorized assembly. In all counties except one, crowds of hundreds and even thousands of armed men converged to prevent the opening of county courts run by crown-appointed jurists. No judges were physically harmed, but they were forced to resign and made to doff their judicial wigs or run a humiliating gantlet. In Suffolk County, the courts met in troop-filled Boston, making mass intimidation of judges impossible. One by one, however, the citizen jurors called to serve in court refused. By late August 1774, farmers and artisans all over Massachusetts had effectively taken local control away from the crown.

In this early phase of the struggle, confrontations did not lead to bloodshed. But one incident, the Powder Alarm, nearly provoked violence and showed just how ready New England farmers were to take up arms. Gage sent troops to capture a supply of gunpowder just outside Boston on September 1, and in the surprise and scramble of the attack, false news spread that the troops had fired on men defending the powder, killing six. Within twenty-four hours, thousands of armed men from Massachusetts and Connecticut set out on foot for Boston to avenge the first blood spilled. Once the error was corrected and the crisis defused, the men returned home peaceably. But Gage could no longer doubt the speed, size, and determination of the rebellious subjects he was told to subdue.

All this had occurred without orchestration by Boston radicals, Gage reported. But British leaders found it hard to believe, as one put it, that "a tumultuous Rabble, without any Appearance of general Concert, or without any Head to advise, or Leader to conduct" could pull off such effective resistance. Repeatedly in the years to come, the British would seriously underestimate their opponents.

Ordinary Massachusetts citizens, unfettered by the crown, began serious planning for the crisis everyone assumed would come. Town militias acquired two pounds of gunpowder per man "in case of invasion." Judges who had been willing crown appointees recanted and confessed their errors—or started packing to leave. The new provincial assembly convinced towns to withhold tax money from the royal governor and divert it to military supplies. Gage beefed up fortifications around Boston, sent armed soldiers to stop meetings that quickly dispersed, and in general rattled his sword loudly. Any bolder action would have to wait until he could acquire a larger army.

The First Continental Congress

Every colony except Georgia sent delegates to Philadelphia in September 1774 to discuss the looming crisis in what was later called the First Continental Congress. The gathering included notables such as Samuel Adams and John Adams from Massachusetts and George Washington and Patrick Henry from Virginia. A few colonies purposely sent men who opposed provoking Britain, such as Pennsylvania's Joseph Galloway, to keep the congress from becoming too radical.

Delegates sought to articulate their liberties as British subjects and the powers Parliament held over them, and they debated possible responses to the Coercive Acts. Some wanted a total ban on trade with Britain to force repeal, while others, especially southerners dependent on tobacco and rice exports, opposed halting trade. Samuel Adams and Patrick Henry were eager for a ringing denunciation of all parliamentary control. The conservative Joseph Galloway proposed a plan (quickly defeated) to create a secondary parliament in America to assist the British Parliament in ruling the colonies.

The congress met for seven weeks and produced a declaration of rights couched in traditional language: "We ask only for peace, liberty and security. We wish no diminution of royal prerogatives, we demand no new rights." But from Britain's point of view, the rights assumed already to exist were radical. Chief among them was the claim that Americans were not represented in Parliament and so each colonial government had the sole right to govern and tax its own people. The one slight concession to Britain was a carefully worded agreement that the colonists would "cheerfully consent" to trade regulations for the larger good of the empire—so long as trade regulation was not a covert means of raising revenue.

To put pressure on Britain, the delegates agreed to a staggered and limited boycott of trade—imports prohibited this year, exports the following, and rice totally exempted (to keep South Carolinians happy). To enforce the boycott, they called for a Continental Association, with chapters in each town variously called committees of public safety or of inspection, to monitor all commerce and punish suspected violators of the boycott (sometimes with a bucket of tar and a bag of feathers). Its work done in a month, the congress disbanded in October, with agreement to convene a second time in May 1775.

The committees of public safety, the committees of correspondence, the regrouped and defiant colonial assemblies, and the Continental Congress were all political bodies functioning without any constitutional authority. British officials did not recognize them as legitimate, but many Americans who supported the patriot cause instantly accepted them. A key reason for the stability of such unauthorized governing bodies was that they were composed of many of the same men who had held elective office before.

Britain's severe reaction to Boston's destruction of the tea finally succeeded in making many colonists from New Hampshire to Georgia realize that the problems of British rule went far beyond questions of taxation. The Coercive Acts infringed on liberty and denied self-government; they could not be ignored. With one colony already subordinated to military rule and a British army at the ready in Boston, the threat of a general war was on the doorstep.

▶REVIEW   Why did Parliament pass the Coercive Acts in 1774?

Domestic Insurrections, 1774–1775

Before the Second Continental Congress could meet, violence and bloodshed came to Massachusetts, raising the stakes considerably. General Thomas Gage, military commander and royal governor, knew that it would take more than a mere show of force to subdue the domestic insurrection unfolding in Massachusetts. He requested more soldiers and, under pressure from above, initiated a march on the towns of Lexington and Concord in April 1775. As in the Powder Alarm of 1774, New England farmers were ready, justifying their preparations for war as a defense of their homes and liberties against an intrusive power bent on enslaving them. To the south, a different and inverted version of the same story began to unfold, as thousands of enslaved black men and women seized an unprecedented opportunity to mount a different kind of insurrection—against planter-patriots who looked over their shoulders uneasily whenever they called out for liberty from the British.

Lexington and Concord

During the winter of 1774–75, Americans pressed on with boycotts. Optimists hoped to effect a repeal of the Coercive Acts; pessimists started stockpiling arms and ammunition. In Massachusetts, gunpowder and shot were secretly stored, and militia units known as minutemen prepared to respond at a minute's notice to any threat from the British troops in Boston.

Thomas Gage soon realized how desperate the British position was. The people, Gage wrote Lord North, were "numerous, worked up to a fury, and not a Boston rabble but the freeholders and farmers of the country." Gage requested twenty thousand reinforcements. He also strongly advised repeal of the Coercive Acts, but leaders in Britain could not admit failure. Instead, they ordered Gage in mid-April 1775 to arrest the troublemakers immediately, before the Americans got better organized.

Gage quickly planned a surprise attack on a suspected ammunition storage site at Concord, a village eighteen miles west of Boston. Near midnight on April 18, 1775, British soldiers moved west across the Charles River. Boston silversmith Paul Revere and William Dawes, a tanner, raced ahead to alert the minutemen. When the soldiers got to Lexington, a village five miles east of Concord, they were met by some seventy armed men assembled on the village green. The British commander barked out, "Lay down your arms, you damned rebels, and disperse." The militiamen hesitated and began to comply, turning to leave the green, but then someone—nobody knows who—fired. In the next two minutes, more firing left eight Americans dead and ten wounded.

The British units continued their march to Concord, any pretense of surprise gone. Three companies of minutemen nervously occupied the town center but offered no challenge to the British as they searched in vain for the ammunition.

Finally, at Old North Bridge in Concord, troops and minutemen exchanged shots, killing two Americans and three British soldiers.

By now, both sides were very apprehensive. The British had failed to find the expected arms, and the Americans had failed to stop their raid. As the British returned to Boston along a narrow road, militia units in hiding attacked from the sides of the road in the bloodiest fighting of the day. In the end, 273 British soldiers were wounded or dead; the toll for the Americans stood at about 95. It was April 19, 1775, and the war had begun.

Rebelling against Slavery

News of the battles of Lexington and Concord spread rapidly. Within eight days, Virginians had heard of the fighting, and, as Thomas Jefferson reflected, "a phrenzy of revenge seems to have seized all ranks of people." The royal governor of Virginia, Lord Dunmore, removed a large quantity of gunpowder from the Williamsburg powder house and put it on a ship in the dead of night, out of reach of any frenzied Virginians. Next, he threatened to arm slaves, if necessary, to ward off attacks by colonists.

This was an effective threat; Dunmore understood full well how to produce panic among the planters. He did not act on his warning until November 1775, when he issued an official proclamation promising freedom to defecting able-bodied slaves who would fight for the British. Although Dunmore wanted to scare the planters, he had no intention of liberating all the slaves or starting a real slave rebellion. Female, young, and elderly slaves were not welcome behind British lines, and many were sent back to face irate masters. Astute blacks noticed that Dunmore neglected to free his own slaves. A Virginia barber named Caesar declared that "he did not know any one foolish enough to believe him [Dunmore], for if he intended to do so, he ought first to set his own free."

By December 1775, around fifteen hundred slaves in Virginia had fled to Lord Dunmore, who armed them and called them his "Ethiopian Regiment." Camp diseases quickly set in: dysentery, typhoid fever, and, worst of all, small-pox. When Dunmore sailed for England in mid-1776, he took just three hundred black survivors with him. But the association of freedom with the British authorities had been established, and throughout the war, thousands more southern slaves made bold to run away as soon as they heard the British army was approaching.

In the northern colonies as well, slaves clearly recognized the evolving political struggle with Britain as an ideal moment to bid for freedom. A twenty-one-year-old Boston domestic slave employed biting sarcasm in a 1774 newspaper essay to call attention to the hypocrisy of local slave owners: "How well the Cry for Liberty, and the reverse Disposition for exercise of oppressive Power over others agree,—I humbly think it does not require the Penetration of a Philosopher to Determine." This extraordinary young woman, Phillis Wheatley, had already

Phillis Wheatley's Title Page

Phillis, born in Africa, was sold to John Wheatley of Boston at age seven. Remarkably gifted, she published her first poem at age twelve, in 1766. By age sixteen, she could read the Bible with ease and composed many poems. In 1773, her master took her to London, where this book was published, gaining her great literary notice. Wheatley's achievement captured the attention of American leaders, and in 1776 she met with George Washington. The Wheatleys freed Phillis, but limited resources, an unhappy marriage, and the early deaths of her children blunted the promise of her early years.

Library of Congress.

gained international recognition through a book of poems, endorsed by Governor Thomas Hutchinson and Boston merchant John Hancock and published in London in 1773. Possibly neither man fully appreciated the irony of his endorsement, however, for Wheatley's poems spoke of "Fair Freedom" as the "Goddess long desir'd" by Africans enslaved in America. At the urging of his wife, Wheatley's master freed the young poet in 1775.

Wheatley's poetic ideas about freedom found concrete expression among other discontented groups. Some slaves in Boston petitioned Thomas Gage, promising to fight for the British if he would liberate them. Gage turned them down. In Ulster County, New York, along the Hudson River, two blacks were overheard discussing gunpowder, and thus a plot unraveled that involved at least twenty slaves in four villages discovered to have ammunition stashed away.

In Maryland, soon after the news of the Lexington battle arrived, blacks exhibited impatience with their status as slaves, causing one Maryland planter to report that "the insolence of the Negroes in this county is come to such a height, that we are under a necessity of disarming them. . . . We took about eighty guns, some bayonets, swords, etc." In North Carolina, a planned uprising was uncovered, and scores of slaves were arrested. Ironically, it was the revolutionary committee of public safety that ordered the whippings to punish this quest for liberty.

By 1783, when the Revolutionary War ended, as many as twenty thousand blacks had voted against slavery with their feet by seeking refuge with the British army. Most failed to achieve the liberation they were seeking. The British generally used them for menial labor, and disease, especially smallpox, devastated encampments of runaways. But some eight thousand to ten thousand persisted through the war and later, under the protection of the British army, left America to start new lives of freedom in Canada's Nova Scotia or Africa's Sierra Leone.

> ▶REVIEW   How did enslaved people in the colonies react to the stirrings of revolution?

Conclusion: How Far Does Liberty Go?

The Seven Years' War set the stage for the imperial crisis of the 1760s and 1770s by creating distrust between Britain and its colonies and by running up a huge deficit in the British treasury. The years 1763 to 1775 brought repeated attempts by the British government to subordinate the colonies into taxpaying partners in the larger scheme of empire.

American resistance grew slowly but steadily over those years. In 1765, loyalist Thomas Hutchinson shared with patriot Samuel Adams the belief that it was exceedingly unwise for Britain to assert a right to taxation, because Parliament did not adequately represent Americans. By temperament and office, Hutchinson had to uphold British policy. Adams, in contrast, protested the policy and made political activists out of thousands in the process.

By 1775, events propelled many Americans to the conclusion that a concerted effort was afoot to deprive them of all their liberties, the most important of which were the right to self-taxation, the right to live free of an occupying army, and the right to self-rule. Hundreds of minutemen converged on Concord, prepared to die for those liberties. April 19 marked the start of their rebellion.

Another rebellion under way in 1775 was doomed to be short-circuited. Black Americans who had experienced actual slavery listened to shouts of "Liberty!" from white crowds and appropriated the language of revolution swirling around them that spoke to their deepest needs and hopes. Defiance of authority was indeed contagious.

The emerging leaders of the patriot cause were mindful of a delicate balance they felt they had to strike. To energize the American public about the crisis with Britain, they had to politicize masses of men—and eventually women, too—and infuse them with a keen sense of their rights and liberties. But in so doing, they became fearful of the unintended consequences of teaching a vocabulary of rights and liberties. They worried that the rhetoric of enslavement might go too far.

The question of how far the crisis could be stretched before something snapped was largely unexamined in 1765. Patriot leaders in that year wanted a correction, a restoration of an ancient liberty of self-taxation that Parliament seemed to be ignoring. But events from 1765 to 1775 convinced many that a return to the old ways was impossible. Challenging Parliament's right to tax had led, step by step, to challenging Parliament's right to legislate over the colonies in any matter. If Parliament's sovereignty was set aside, who actually had authority over the American colonies? By 1775, with the outbreak of fighting and the specter of slave rebellions, American leaders turned to the king for the answer to that question.

REVIEWING THE CHAPTER

Use the questions and timeline to review and strengthen your understanding of the chapter.

REVIEW QUESTIONS

1. How did the Seven Years' War erode relations between colonists and British authorities? (pp. 145–53)

2. Why did the Sugar Act and the Stamp Act draw fierce opposition from colonists? (pp. 153–60)

3. Why did British authorities send troops to occupy Boston in the fall of 1768? (pp. 160–64)

4. Why did Parliament pass the Coercive Acts in 1774? (pp. 165–70)

5. How did enslaved people in the colonies react to the stirrings of revolution? (pp. 171–74)

MAKING CONNECTIONS

1. In the mid-eighteenth century, how did Native Americans influence relations between European nations? Between Britain and the colonies?

2. Why did disputes over taxation figure so prominently in the deteriorating relations between Britain and the colonies? In your answer, refer to specific disputed British attempts to raise revenue and the colonial response.

3. How did the colonists organize to oppose British power so effectively? In your answer, discuss the role of communication in facilitating the colonial resistance, being sure to cite specific examples.

TIMELINE

1747	• Ohio Company of Virginia formed.
1754	• Seven Years' War begins in North America. • Albany Congress proposes Plan of Union (never implemented).
1755	• Braddock defeated in western Pennsylvania.
1757	• William Pitt fully commits Britain to war effort.
1759	• Quebec falls to British.
1760	• Montreal falls to British. • George III becomes British king.
1763	• Treaty of Paris ends Seven Years' War. • Pontiac's uprising. • Proclamation of 1763. • Paxton Boys massacre friendly Indians in Pennsylvania.
1764	• Parliament enacts Revenue (Sugar) Act.
1765	• Parliament enacts Stamp Act. • Virginia Resolves challenge Stamp Act. • Dozens of crowd actions by Sons of Liberty. • Stamp Act Congress meets.
1766	• Parliament repeals Stamp Act and passes Declaratory Act.
1767	• Parliament enacts Townshend duties.
1768	• British station troops in Boston.
1769	• Merchants sign nonimportation agreements.
1770	• Boston Massacre. • Parliament repeals Townshend duties.
1772	• British navy ship *Gaspée* burned. • Committees of correspondence begin forming.
1773	• Parliament passes Tea Act. • Dumping of tea in Boston harbor.
1774	• Parliament passes Coercive Acts (Intolerable Acts). • Powder Alarm shows colonists' readiness to bear arms. • First Continental Congress meets; Continental Association formed.
1775	• Battles of Lexington and Concord. • Lord Dunmore promises freedom to defecting slaves.

▶ **For an online bibliography, practice quizzes, Web sites, images, and documents related to this chapter,** see the Book Companion Site at **bedfordstmartins.com/roark.**

▶ **For firsthand accounts of this period,** see Chapter 6 in Michael Johnson, ed., *Reading the American Past,* Fourth Edition.

7
CHAPTER

The War for America
1775–1783

IKE MANY OF THE MEN who fought in the Revolutionary War on the American side, Robert Shurtliff of Massachusetts enlisted in the Continental army in 1782 for several different reasons. Early in the war, a desire to fight British oppression motivated many recruits, especially those from Massachusetts, the colony under direct attack. But late in the war, deciding to enlist required more than idealism, and even the promise of a pay envelope and future frontier acreage no longer sufficed. To meet their draft quotas, towns offered cash bounties as high as $50 in silver. Young, single, poor, and unsettled in life, Shurtliff responded to that powerful incentive. Tall (five feet seven) and muscular, with an adventurous disposition, the young recruit readily won assignment in the army's elite light infantry unit.

Shurtliff's reported age was eighteen, not unusual for the new recruits of 1782 in the seventh year of a difficult war. Some quarter of a million soldiers, ages sixteen to sixty, served in either the Continental army or state militia units, and as the war wound down, manpower was in short supply. Beardless boys populated Washington's army—boys who had been just ten years old when the British marched on Lexington. The need for an army of thousands persisted well past the decisive American victory at Yorktown in the fall of 1781 because the British army refused to end its occupation of New York City until a peace treaty was signed. Consequently, the Americans had to field an army to hold the British in check. For nearly two years after Yorktown, Washington's force of 10,000 men camped along the Hudson River north of the city, skirmishing with the enemy.

That is, 10,000 men and 1 woman. In fact, "Robert Shurtliff" was actually Deborah Sampson, age twenty-three, from Middleborough, Massachusetts. For

177

Deborah Sampson
In the mid-1790s, Deborah Sampson sat for this small portrait. An engraved copy of it illustrated *The Female Review*, a short book about Sampson's unusual military career and life published in 1797. Sampson, by then a wife and mother, displays femininity in this picture. Sampson the soldier had used a cloth band to compress her breasts; Sampson the matron wore a satin band to define her bustline.
Rhode Island Historical Society.

seventeen months, Sampson masqueraded as a man, marching through the woods, handling and firing a musket, and spending seemingly interminable time in camp. Misrepresenting her age enabled her to blend in with the beardless boys, as did her unusual competence as a soldier. With privacy at a minimum, she faced constant risks of discovery. Soldiers slept six to a tent, "spooning" their bodies together for warmth. Yet somehow, Sampson managed to escape detection. Certainly, she was helped by the poor standards of hygiene of the day. With no centralized shower or bathing facilities, she was not compelled to disrobe in front of her comrades.

Although many thousands of women served the army as cooks, laundresses, and caregivers, they were never allowed in combat positions. Not only was Sampson defrauding the military (and the town that had paid her bounty), but she was also violating a biblical prohibition on cross-dressing that was punishable under Massachusetts law. Why did she run this risk?

A hard-luck childhood had left Sampson both impoverished and unusually plucky. By the time she was five, her father had deserted the family, causing her mother to place her children in foster care. Deborah lived with a succession of families, learning household skills appropriate to a servant's life. More unusually, she also learned to plow a field and to read and write. Freed from servitude at age eighteen, she earned a living as a weaver and then a teacher, both low-wage jobs but also ones without supervising bosses. Marriage would have been her normal next step, but either lack of inclination or a wartime shortage of men kept her single and "masterless," something few women could claim to be in the eighteenth century. But like most single females, she was also poor, and the $50 bounty enticed her to enlist.

Sampson was unmasked after seventeen months of service, when she suffered a battle-related injury, and the treatment revealed her sex. She was discharged immediately, but her fine record kept her superiors from prosecuting her for cross-dressing. Sampson spent many years seeking a pension from the government to compensate her for her war injury, but to no avail.

What eventually made Sampson famous was not her war service alone, but her effort to capitalize on it by selling her story to the public. In 1797, now a middle-aged mother of three, she cooperated with a young author to tell her life story (a blend of fact and fiction) in a short book. During 1802–1803, she reenacted her wartime masquerade on a speaking tour of New England and New York. Once again, she was crossing gender boundaries, since women normally did not speak from public stages (except as actresses) or travel without a male escort.

Except for her disguised sex, Sampson's Revolutionary War experience was similar to that of most Americans. Disruptions caused by the war affected everyone's life, whether in military service or on the home front. Wartime shortages of all kinds caused women and children to step in and replace male labor. Soldiers fought for ideas, but they also fought to earn money. Hardship was widely endured. And Sampson's quest for personal independence—freedom from the constraints of being female—was echoed in the general quest for political independence that many Americans identified as a major goal of the war.

Political independence was not everyone's primary goal, however, at least not at first. For more than a year after the war began, the Continental Congress in Philadelphia resisted declaring America's independence. Some delegates were cautiously hoping for reconciliation with Britain. Yet with fighting already under way, the congress had to raise an army, finance it, and seek alliances with foreign countries—all while exploring diplomatic channels for peace.

When King George III rejected all peace overtures, Americans loudly declared their independence, and the war moved into high gear. In part a classic war with professional armies and textbook battles, the Revolutionary War was also a civil war and at times even a brutal **guerrilla war** between committed rebels and loyalists. It also had complex ethnic dimensions, pitting some Indian tribes allied with the British against others allied with the Americans. And it provided an unprecedented opportunity for enslaved African Americans to win their freedom, some by joining the British, who openly encouraged slaves to desert their masters, and others by joining the Continental army or state militias, fighting alongside white Americans.

The Second Continental Congress

On May 10, 1775, nearly one month after the fighting at Lexington and Concord, the Second Continental Congress assembled in Philadelphia. The congress immediately set to work on two crucial and seemingly contradictory tasks: to raise and supply an army and to explore reconciliation with Britain. To do the former, they needed soldiers and a commander to come to the aid of the Massachusetts militiamen, they needed money, and they needed to work out a declaration of war. To do the latter, however, they needed diplomacy to approach the king. But the king was not receptive, and by 1776, as the war progressed and hopes of reconciliation faded, delegates at the congress began to ponder the treasonous act of declaring independence—said by some to be plain common sense.

Assuming Political and Military Authority

Like members of the First Continental Congress (see chapter 6), the delegates to the second were well-established figures in their home colonies, but they still had to learn to know and trust each other; they did not always agree. The Adams cousins John and Samuel defined the radical end of the spectrum, favoring independence. John Dickinson of Pennsylvania, no longer the eager revolutionary who had dashed off *Letters from a Farmer* back in 1767, was now a moderate, seeking reconciliation with Britain. Benjamin Franklin, fresh off a ship from an eleven-year residence in London, was feared by some to be a British spy. Mutual suspicions flourished easily when the undertaking was so dangerous, opinions were so varied, and a misstep could spell disaster.

Most of the delegates were not yet prepared to break with Britain. Several legislatures instructed their delegates to oppose independence. Some felt that government without a king was unworkable, while others feared it might be suicidal to lose Britain's protection against its traditional enemies, France and Spain. Colonies that traded actively with Britain feared undermining their economies. Probably the vast majority of ordinary Americans were unable to envision independence. From the Stamp Act of 1765 to the Coercive Acts of 1774 (see chapter 6), the constitutional struggle with Britain had turned on the issue of parliamentary power. During that decade, almost no one had questioned the legitimacy of the monarchy.

The few men at the Continental Congress who did think that independence was desirable were, not surprisingly, from Massachusetts. Their colony had been stripped of civil government under the Coercive Acts, their capital was occupied by the British army, and blood had been shed at Lexington and Concord. Even so, those men knew that it was premature to push for a break with Britain. John Adams wrote to his wife, Abigail, in June 1775: "America is a great, unwieldy body. Its progress must be slow. It is like a large fleet sailing under convoy. The fleetest sailors must wait for the dullest and slowest."

As slow as the American colonies were in sailing toward political independence, they needed to take swift action to coordinate a military defense, for the Massachusetts countryside was under threat of further attack. Even the hesitant moderates in the congress agreed that a military buildup was necessary. Around the country, militia units from New York to Georgia collected arms and drilled on village greens in anticipation. On June 14, the congress voted to create the Continental army. Choosing the commander in chief offered an opportunity to demonstrate that this was no local war of a single rebellious colony. The congress bypassed Artemas Ward from Massachusetts, a veteran of the Seven Years' War, then already commanding the soldiers massed around Boston, and instead chose a Virginian, George Washington. Washington's appointment sent the clear message to Britain that there was widespread commitment to war beyond New England.

Next the congress drew up a document titled "A Declaration on the Causes and Necessity of Taking Up Arms," which rehearsed familiar arguments about the tyranny of Parliament and the need to defend English liberties. This declaration was first drafted by a young Virginia **planter**, Thomas Jefferson, a newcomer to the congress and a radical on the question of independence. The moderate John Dickinson, fearing that the declaration would offend Britain and rule out reconciliation, was allowed to rewrite it. However, he left intact much of Jefferson's highly charged language about choosing "to die freemen rather than to live slaves." Even a man as reluctant for independence as Dickinson acknowledged the necessity of military defense against an invading army.

To pay for the military buildup, the congress authorized a currency issue of $2 million. The Continental dollars were merely paper; they did not represent gold or silver, for the congress owned no precious metals. The delegates somewhat naively expected that the currency would be accepted as valuable on trust as it spread in the population through the hands of soldiers, farmers, munitions suppliers, and beyond.

In just two months, the Second Continental Congress had created an army, declared war, and issued its own currency. It had taken on the major functions of a legitimate government, both military and financial, without any legal basis for its authority, for it had not—and would not for a full year—declare independence from the authority of the king.

Pursuing Both War and Peace

Three days after the congress approved a Continental army, one of the bloodiest battles of the Revolution occurred. The British commander in Boston, Thomas Gage, had recently received troop reinforcements, three talented generals (William Howe, John Burgoyne, and Henry Clinton), and new instructions to root out the rebels around Boston. But before Gage could take the offensive, the Americans fortified the hilly terrain of Charlestown, a peninsula just north of Boston, on the night of June 16, 1775.

The British generals could have nipped off the peninsula where it met the mainland, to box in the Americans. But General Howe insisted on a bold frontal assault, sending his 2,500 soldiers across the water and up the hill in an intimidating but potentially costly attack. The American troops, 1,400 strong, listened to the British drummers pacing the uphill march and held their fire until the British were about twenty yards away. At that distance, the musket volley was sure and deadly, and the British turned back. Twice more, General Howe sent his men up the hill and received the same blast of firepower; each time they had to step around the bodies of men felled in the previous attempts.

On the third assault, the British took the hill, mainly because the American ammunition supply gave out, and the defenders quickly retreated. The battle of Bunker Hill was thus a British victory, but an expensive one. The dead numbered 226 on the British side, with more than 800 wounded; the Americans suffered 140 dead, 271 wounded, and 30 captured. As General Clinton later remarked, "It was a dear bought victory; another such would have ruined us."

Instead of pursuing the fleeing Americans, Howe pulled his army back to Boston, unwilling to risk more raids into the countryside. If the British had had any grasp of the basic instability of the American units gathered around Boston, they might have pushed westward and perhaps decisively defeated the Continental army in its infancy. Instead, they lingered in Boston, abandoning it without a fight nine months later. Howe used the time in Boston to inoculate his army against smallpox, because a new epidemic of the deadly disease was spreading in port cities along the Atlantic. Inoculation worked by producing a light but real (and therefore risky) case of smallpox, followed by lifelong immunity. Howe's instinct was right: From 1775 to 1782, the years coinciding with the American Revolution, some 130,000 people on the American continent, most of them Indians, died of smallpox. Nearly 500 uninoculated Bostonians contracted smallpox, and Howe booted them out of Boston, causing American leaders to fear that the British intended to spread the disease as a "weapon of defense."

A week after Bunker Hill, when General Washington arrived to take charge of the new Continental army, he found enthusiastic but undisciplined troops. Sanitation was an unknown concept, with inadequate latrines fouling the campground. Drunkenness on duty was common, and soldiers came and went at will. The amazed general attributed the disarray to the New England custom of letting militia units elect their own officers, a custom he felt undermined deference. A captain from a Connecticut regiment was spotted shaving one of his own men, an inappropriate gesture of personal service by a superior officer. But in civilian life the captain was a barber; he had been elected an officer by the men of his town, who saw nothing strange in his practicing his trade in the camp. Washington quickly imposed more hierarchy and authority. "Discipline is the soul of the army," he stated.

While military plans moved forward, the Second Continental Congress pursued its second, contradictory objective: reconciliation with Britain. Delegates from the middle colonies (Pennsylvania, Delaware, and New York), whose merchants depended on trade with Britain, urged that channels for negotiation remain open. In July 1775, congressional moderates led by John Dickinson engineered an appeal to the king called the Olive Branch Petition. The petition affirmed loyalty to the monarchy and blamed all the troubles on the king's ministers and on Parliament. It proposed that the American colonial assemblies

Continental Army Uniform

In 1775, the Continental Congress faced the daunting prospect of fielding an army to fight the largest military force in the world. Money was scarce, and uniforms were hard to come by. At first, enlisted men wore brown work clothes, but this did not allow for easy categorization of soldiers by their units. When General Washington finally issued dress specifications, he chose dark blue and then specified the colors to be used for the facings and linings of the coat to establish the rank and the unit of each soldier. These differences distinguished officers from ordinary soldiers so that the military hierarchy could be maintained at all times.

National Museum of American History, Smithsonian Institution, Washington, D.C.

be recognized as individual parliaments, under the umbrella of the monarchy. By late fall 1775, however, reconciliation was out of the question. King George III rejected the Olive Branch Petition and heatedly condemned the Americans, calling them rebels and traitors. Thereafter, it was hard to blame only the king's ministers, and not the king himself, for the conflict.

Thomas Paine, Abigail Adams, and the Case for Independence

Pressure for independence started to mount in January 1776, when a pamphlet titled *Common Sense* appeared in Philadelphia. Thomas Paine, its author, was an English **artisan** and coffeehouse intellectual who had befriended Benjamin Franklin in London. He came to America in the fall of 1774 with letters of introduction from Franklin to several Philadelphia printers. He landed a job with the *Pennsylvania Magazine* and soon met delegates from the Second Continental Congress. With their encouragement, he wrote *Common Sense* to lay out a lively and compelling case for complete independence.

In simple yet forceful language, Paine elaborated on the absurdities of the British monarchy. Why should one man, by accident of birth, claim extensive power over others? he asked. A king might be foolish or wicked. "One of the strongest natural proofs of the folly of hereditary right in kings," Paine wrote, "is that nature disapproves it; otherwise she would not so frequently turn it into ridicule by giving mankind *an ass for a lion*." Calling the British king an ass broke through the automatic deference most Americans still had for the monarchy. To replace monarchy, Paine advocated **republican** government, based on the consent of the people. Rulers, according to Paine, were only representatives of the people, and the best form of government relied on frequent elections to achieve the most direct **democracy** possible.

Paine's pamphlet sold more than 150,000 copies in a matter of weeks. Newspapers reprinted it; men read it aloud in taverns and coffeehouses; John Adams, a delegate in Philadelphia, sent a copy to his wife, Abigail, who passed it around to neighbors in Braintree, Massachusetts. New Englanders desired independence, but other colonies, under no immediate threat of violence, remained cautious.

Abigail Adams was impatient not only for independence but also for other legal changes that would revolutionize the new country. In a series of astute letters to her husband, she outlined obstacles and gave advice. She worried that southern slave owners might shrink from a war in the name of **liberty**: "I have sometimes been ready to think that the passion for Liberty cannot be Equally strong in the Breasts of those who have been accustomed to deprive their fellow Creatures of theirs." And in March 1776, she expressed her hope that women's legal status would improve under the new government: "In the new Code of Laws which I suppose it will be necessary for you to make I desire you would Remember the Ladies, and be more generous and favourable to them than your ancestors." Her chief concern was husbands' legal dominion over wives: "Do not put such unlimited power into the hands of the Husbands," she advised. "Remember all Men would be tyrants if they could." Abigail Adams anticipated a more radical end to tyranny than did Thomas Paine.

The Continental Congress was, in fact, not rewriting family law; that task was left to individual states in the 1780s. John Adams lightly dismissed his wife: "As to your extraordinary Code of Laws, I cannot but Laugh." Men were too smart to repeal their "Masculine Systems," John assured her, needing structured male dominance to avoid the "despotism of the petticoat." To a male politician and friend, Adams privately rehearsed the reasons why women (and men who were free blacks, or young, or propertyless) should remain excluded from political participation. Even though he concluded that nothing should change, at least Abigail's letter had forced him to ponder the exclusion, something few men—or women—did in 1776. Urgent talk of political independence was seen as radical enough. Few could imagine even more radical change in social and political relations.

The Declaration of Independence

In addition to Paine's *Common Sense*, another key factor hastening official independence was the prospect of an alliance with France, Britain's archrival. France was willing to provide military supplies and naval power, but not without firm assurance that the Americans would separate from Britain. News that the British were negotiating to hire German mercenary soldiers further solidified support for independence. By May, all but four colonies were agitating for a declaration. The holdouts were Pennsylvania, Maryland, New York, and South Carolina, the latter two containing large loyalist populations. An exasperated Virginian wrote to his friend in the congress, "For God's sake, why do you dawdle in the Congress so strangely? Why do you not at once declare yourself a separate independent state?" But a more pessimistic southerner feared that independence was "in truth a delusive bait which men inconsiderably snatch at, without knowing the hook to which it is affixed."

In early June, Richard Henry Lee of the Virginia delegation introduced a resolution calling for independence. The moderates still commanded enough support to postpone a vote on the measure until July, so they could go home and consult about this extreme step. In the meantime, the congress appointed a committee, with Thomas Jefferson and others, to draft a longer document setting out the case for independence.

On July 2, after intense politicking, all but one state voted for independence; New York abstained. The congress then turned to the document drafted by Jefferson and his committee. Jefferson began with a preamble that articulated philosophical principles about natural rights, equality, the right of revolution, and the consent of the governed as the only true basis for government. He then listed more than two dozen grievances against King George. The congress merely glanced at the political philosophy, finding nothing exceptional in it. The ideas about natural rights and the consent of the governed were seen as "self-evident truths," just as the document claimed. In itself, this absence of comment showed a remarkable transformation in political thinking since the end of the Seven Years' War. The single phrase declaring the natural equality of "all men" was also passed over without comment; no one elaborated on its radical implications.

For two days, the congress wrangled over the list of grievances, especially the issue of slavery. Jefferson had included an impassioned statement blaming the king for slavery, which delegates from Georgia and South Carolina struck out. They had no intention of denouncing their labor system as an evil practice. But the congress let stand another of Jefferson's fervent grievances, blaming the king for mobilizing "the merciless Indian Savages" into bloody **frontier** warfare, a reference to Pontiac's uprising (see chapter 6).

On July 4, the amendments to Jefferson's text were complete, and the congress formally adopted the document. (See appendix I, page A-1.) A month later, the delegates gathered to sign the official parchment copy, handwritten by an exacting scribe. Four men, including John Dickinson, declined to sign; several others "signed with regret . . . and with many doubts," according to John Adams. The document was then printed, widely distributed, and read aloud in celebrations everywhere. A crowd in New York listened to a public reading of it and then toppled a lead statue of George III on horseback to melt it down for bullets. On July 15, the New York delegation switched from abstention to endorsement, making the vote on independence unanimous.

Printed copies of the Declaration of Independence did not include the sign-ers' names, for they had committed treason, a crime punishable by death. On the day of signing, they indulged in gallows humor. When Benjamin Franklin paused before signing to look over the document, John Hancock of Massachusetts teased him, "Come, come, sir. We must be unanimous. No pulling different ways. We must all hang together." Franklin replied, "Indeed we must all hang together. Otherwise we shall most assuredly hang separately."

▶ **REVIEW**   Why were many Americans reluctant to pursue independence from Britain?

The First Year of War, 1775–1776

Both sides approached the war for America with uneasiness. The Americans, with inexperienced militias, opposed the mightiest military power in the world. Also, their country was not unified; many remained loyal to Britain. The British faced serious obstacles as well. Their disdain for the fighting abilities of the Americans required reassessment in light of the Bunker Hill battle. The logistics of supplying an army with food across three thousand miles of water were daunting. And since the British goal was to regain allegiance, not to destroy and conquer, the army was often constrained in its actions. These patterns—undertrained American troops and British troops strangely unwilling to press their advantage—played out re-peatedly in the first year of war when the Americans invaded Canada, the British invaded New York, and the two sides chased each other up and down the length of New Jersey.

The American Military Forces

Americans claimed that the initial months of war were purely defensive, trig-gered by the British army's invasion. But the war also quickly became a rebellion, an overthrowing of long-established authority. As both defenders and rebels, Americans were generally highly motivated to fight, and the potential manpower that could be mobilized was in theory very great.

Local defense in the colonies had long rested with a militia requiring partici-pation from able-bodied men over age sixteen. When the main threat to public safety was the occasional Indian attack, the local militia made sense. But such attacks were now mostly limited to the frontier. Southern militias trained with potential slave rebellions in mind, but these, too, were rare. The annual muster day in most communities had evolved into a holiday of drinking, marching, and shooting practice with small fowling guns or muskets.

Militias were best suited for limited engagements and not for extended wars requiring military campaigns far from home. In forming the Continental army, the congress set enlistment at one year, but army leaders soon learned

Backcountry Riflemen

A German officer with the British army drew this sketch of two American riflemen, dressed in rustic hunting shirts and leggings. Their celebrated ability to hit small targets at great distances made the riflemen a terror to the British. General Washington worried that they were too undisciplined to make good soldiers, but others suggested that the trademark hunting shirt should become the Continental army uniform for all soldiers, just for the fear it provoked in the enemy. The picture depicts a fixed bayonet on each rifle, but only muskets had bayonets. Artistic errors aside, the debt of western riflemen to Indian apparel is evident.

Anne S. K. Brown Military Collection, Brown University Library.

that was inadequate to train soldiers and carry out campaigns. A three-year enlistment earned a new soldier a $20 bonus, while men who committed for the duration of the war were promised a postwar **land grant** of one hundred acres. For this inducement to be effective, of course, recruits had to believe that the Americans would win. Over the course of the war, some 230,000 men spent time in military service, amounting to roughly one-quarter of the white male population over age sixteen.

Women also served in the Continental army, cooking, washing, and nursing the wounded. The British army established a ratio of one woman to every ten men; in the Continental army, the ratio was set at one woman to fifteen men. Close to 20,000 "camp followers," as they were called, served during the war, probably most of them wives of men in service. Children tagged along as well, and babies were born in the camps and on the road.

Black Americans were at first excluded from the Continental army, by slave owner George Washington's orders. But as manpower needs increased, the northern states welcomed free blacks into service; slaves in some states could serve with their masters' permission. About 5,000 black men served in the Revolutionary War on the rebel side, nearly all from the northern states. Black Continental soldiers sometimes were segregated into separate units; two battalions from Rhode Island were entirely black. Just under 300 blacks joined regiments from Connecticut. Whereas some of these men were **draftees**, others were clearly inspired by the ideals of freedom being voiced in a war against tyranny. For example, twenty-three blacks gave "Liberty," "Freedom," or "Freeman" as their surname at the time of enlistment. (Southern slaves did not join the Continental army, but in large numbers they deserted their owners for the protection of the British instead.)

Military service helped politicize Americans during the early stages of the war. In early 1776, independence was a risky idea, potentially treasonous. But as the war heated up and recruiters demanded commitment, some Americans discovered that apathy had its dangers as well. Anyone who refused to serve ran the risk of being called a traitor to the cause. Military service became a prime way of defining and demonstrating political allegiance.

The American army was at times raw and inexperienced, and often woefully undermanned. It never had the precision and discipline of European professional armies. But it was never as bad as the British continually assumed. The British would learn that it was a serious mistake to underrate the enemy.

The British Strategy

The American strategy was straightforward—to repulse and defeat an invading army. The British strategy was not nearly so clear. Britain wanted to put down a rebellion and restore monarchical power in the colonies, but the question was how to accomplish this. A decisive defeat of the Continental army was essential but not sufficient to end the rebellion, for the British would still have to contend with an armed and motivated insurgent population.

Furthermore, there was no single political nerve center whose capture would spell certain victory. The Continental Congress moved from place to place, staying just out of reach of the British. During the course of the war, the British captured and occupied every major port city, but that brought no serious loss to the Americans, 95 percent of whom lived in the countryside.

Britain's delicate task was to restore the old governments, not to destroy an enemy country. Hence, the British generals were reluctant to ravage the countryside, confiscate food, or burn villages and towns. There were thirteen distinct political entities to capture, pacify, and then restore to the crown, and they stretched in a long line from New Hampshire to Georgia. Clearly, a large land army was required for the job. Without the willingness to seize food from the locals, the British needed hundreds of supply ships bringing food for storage— hence their desire to capture the ports. The British strategy also assumed that many Americans remained loyal to the king and would come to their aid. Without substantial numbers of loyal subjects, the plan to restore old royal governments made no sense.

The overall British plan was a divide-and-conquer approach, focusing first on New York, the state judged to harbor the greatest number of loyal subjects. New York offered a geographic advantage as well: Control of the Hudson River would allow the British to isolate those troublesome New Englanders. British armies could descend from Canada and move up from New York City along the Hudson River into western Massachusetts. Squeezed between a naval blockade on the eastern coast and army raids in the west, Massachusetts could be driven to surrender. New Jersey and Pennsylvania would fall in line, the British thought, due to loyalist strength. Virginia was a problem, like Massachusetts, but the British were confident that the Carolinas would help them isolate and subdue Virginia.

Quebec, New York, and New Jersey

In late 1775, an American expedition was swiftly launched to capture the cities of Montreal and Quebec before British reinforcements could arrive (Map 7.1, page 190). This offensive was a clear sign that the war was not purely a reaction to the invasion of Massachusetts. The two cities were symbolic as well as strategic goals, having been sites of bloody contest in the Seven Years' War (see chapter 6). A force of New York Continentals commanded by General Richard Montgomery took Montreal easily in September 1775 and then advanced on Quebec. Meanwhile, a second contingent of Continentals led by Colonel Benedict Arnold moved north through Maine to Quebec, a punishing trek through freezing rain with woefully inadequate supplies; many men died. Arnold's determination to get to Quebec was heroic, but in human costs, the campaign was a tragedy. Arnold and Montgomery jointly attacked Quebec in December but failed to take the city. Worse yet, they encountered smallpox, which killed more men than had been felled by the British.

The main action of the first year of the war came not in Canada, however, but in New York, so crucial to Britain. In August 1776, some 45,000 British troops (including 8,000 German mercenaries, called Hessians) landed south of New York City, under the command of General Howe. General Washington had anticipated that New York would be Howe's target and had moved his army, numbering about 20,000, south from Massachusetts. The battle of Long Island, in late August 1776, pitted the well-trained British "redcoats" (common slang referring to the red British uniforms) against a very green Continental army. Howe attacked, inflicting many casualties (1,500 dead and wounded) and spreading panic among the American soldiers, who fled to the western edge of Long Island. A British general called it "a field day," as though the battle had been a military parade. "If a good bleeding can bring those Bible-faced Yankees to their senses, the fever of independency should soon abate," he said. Howe failed to press forward, however, perhaps remembering the costly victory of Bunker Hill, and Washington evacuated his troops to Manhattan Island in the dead of a foggy night.

Washington knew it would be hard to hold Manhattan, so he withdrew farther north to two forts on either side of the Hudson River. For two months, the armies engaged in limited skirmishing, but in November, Howe finally captured

MAP 7.1   The War in the North, 1775–1778

After the early battles in Massachusetts in 1775, rebel forces invaded Canada but failed to capture Quebec. A large British army landed in New York in August 1776, turning New Jersey into a continual battle site in 1777 and 1778. Burgoyne arrived from England to secure Canada and made his attempt to pinch off New England along the Hudson River, but he was stopped at Saratoga in 1777 in the key battle of the early war.

Fort Washington and Fort Lee, taking nearly 3,000 prisoners. Washington retreated quickly across New Jersey into Pennsylvania. Yet again Howe unaccountably failed to press his advantage. Had he attacked Washington's army at Philadelphia, he probably would have taken the city. Instead, he parked his German troops in winter quarters along the Delaware River. Perhaps he knew that many of the Continental soldiers' enlistment periods ended on December 31, so he felt confident that the Americans would not attack him. But he was wrong.

On December 25, near midnight, as sleet and hail rained down, Washington stealthily moved his large army across the icy Delaware River and in the early morning made a quick capture of the unsuspecting German soldiers encamped at Trenton. This impressive victory lifted the sagging morale of the patriot side. For the next two weeks, Washington remained on the offensive, capturing supplies in a clever attack on British units at Princeton on January 3. Soon he was safe in Morristown, in northern New Jersey, where he settled his troops in for the winter. Washington finally had time to administer mass smallpox inoculations and see his men through the abbreviated course of the disease. Future recruits also would face inoculation.

All in all, in the first year of declared war, the rebellious Americans had a few isolated moments to feel proud of but also much to worry about. The very inexperienced Continental army had barely hung on in the New York campaign. Washington had shown exceptional daring and admirable restraint, but what really saved the Americans may have been the repeated reluctance of the British to follow through militarily when they had the advantage.

▶REVIEW   Why did the British exercise restraint in their efforts to defeat the rebellious colonies?

The Home Front

Battlefields alone did not determine the outcome of the war. Struggles on the home front were equally important. In 1776, each community contained small numbers of highly committed people on both sides and far larger numbers who were uncertain about whether independence was worth a war. Both persuasion and force were used to gain the allegiance of the many neutrals. Revolutionaries who took control of local government often used it to punish loyalists and intimidate neutrals, while loyalists worked to reestablish British authority. The struggle to secure political allegiance was complicated greatly by a shaky wartime economy. The creative financing of the fledgling government brought hardships as well as opportunities, forcing Americans to confront new manifestations of virtue and corruption.

Patriotism at the Local Level

Committees of correspondence, of public safety, and of inspection dominated the political landscape in patriot communities. These committees took on more than customary local governance; they enforced boycotts, picked army draftees, and policed suspected traitors. They sometimes invaded homes to search for contraband goods such as British tea or textiles.

Loyalists were dismayed by the increasing show of power by patriots. A man in Westchester, New York, described his response to intrusions by committees: "Choose your committee or suffer it to be chosen by a half dozen fools in your neighborhood—open your doors to them—let them examine your tea-cannisters and molasses-jugs, and your wives' and daughters' petty coats—bow and cringe and tremble and quake—fall down and worship our sovereign lord the mob. . . . Should any pragmatical committee-gentleman come to my house and give himself airs, I shall show him the door." Oppressive or not, the local committees were rarely challenged. Their persuasive powers convinced many middle-of-the-road citizens that neutrality was not a comfortable option.

Another group new to political life—white women—increasingly demonstrated a capacity for patriotism as wartime hardships dramatically altered their work routines. Many wives whose husbands were away on military or political service took on masculine duties. Their competence to tend farms and make business decisions encouraged some to assert competence in politics as well. Abigail Adams managed the family farm in Massachusetts while John Adams was away for several years doing politics, in which Abigail took a keen interest. Eliza Wilkinson managed a South Carolina plantation and talked revolutionary politics with women friends. "None were greater politicians than the several knots of ladies who met together," she remarked, alert to the unusual turn female conversations had taken. "We commenced perfect statesmen."

Women from prominent Philadelphia families took more direct action, forming the Ladies Association in 1780 to collect money for Continental soldiers. A published broadside, "The Sentiments of an American Woman," defended their female patriotism: "The time is arrived to display the same sentiments which animated us at the beginning of the Revolution, when we renounced the use of teas [and] when our republican and laborious hands spun the flax." The broadside's author was Esther Reed, wife of Pennsylvania's governor.

Even young girls found ways to participate in the rebellion. Three feisty fifteen-year-olds on Martha's Vineyard, an island south of Massachusetts, decided to destroy a cherished liberty pole in their town rather than let a British navy captain take it to replace a broken spar on his ship. (Liberty poles, like liberty trees, had come to symbolize Americans' quest for liberty.) The town's leaders capitulated to the captain's demand that they sell him the tall, mastlike pole or face violent attack. Under cover of night, the girls drilled holes in the pole; deposited gunpowder in the holes, using rags as fuses; and touched off an explosion with hot coals. The pole was ruined for any naval use but saved as a symbol. Town leaders were so totally mystified by the act of destruction that the angry navy captain left without launching an attack. More than fifty years later, the aged and poor Mary Daggett Hillman petitioned the U.S. Congress for a reward for her bold deed.

The Loyalists

Around one-fifth of the American population remained loyal to the crown in 1776, and another two-fifths were probably neutral. With proper cultivation, this large base might have sustained the British empire in America, if only the British army leaders had known how to use it. In general, loyalists had strong cultural and economic ties to England; they thought that social stability depended on a government anchored by monarchy and aristocracy. Perhaps most of all, they feared democratic tyranny. They understood that dissolving the automatic respect that subjects had for their king could lead to a society where deference to one's social betters might come under challenge. Patriots seemed to them to be unscrupulous, violent, self-interested men who simply wanted power for themselves.

The most visible loyalists (called Tories by their enemies) were royal officials, not only governors such as Thomas Hutchinson of Massachusetts but also local judges and customs officers. Wealthy merchants gravitated toward loyalism to maintain the trade protections of navigation acts and the British navy. Conservative urban lawyers admired the stability of British law and order. Some colonists chose loyalism simply to oppose traditional adversaries. For example, backcountry farmers in the Carolinas tended to be loyalists out of resentment over the political and economic power of the lowlands gentry, generally of patriot persuasion. And, of course, southern slaves had their own resentments against the white slave-owning class and looked to Britain for hope of freedom.

Many Indian tribes hoped to remain neutral at the war's start, seeing the conflict as a civil war between English and American brothers. Eventually, however, most were drawn in, many taking the British side. The powerful Iroquois confederacy divided: The Mohawk, Cayuga, Seneca, and Onondaga peoples lined up with the British; the Oneida and Tuscarora tribes aided Americans. One young Mohawk leader, Thayendanegea (known also by his English name, Joseph Brant), traveled to England in 1775 to complain to King George about American settlers cheating his people of land. "It is very hard when we have let the King's subjects have so much of our lands for so little value," he wrote, "they should want to cheat us in this manner of the small spots we have left for our women and children to live on. We are tired out in making complaints & getting no redress." Brant pledged Indian support for the king in exchange for protection from encroaching settlers. In the Ohio Country, parts of the Shawnee and Delaware tribes started out pro-American but shifted to the British side by 1779 in the face of repeated betrayals by American settlers and soldiers.

Joseph Brant
The Mohawk leader Thayendanegea, called Joseph Brant by the Americans, had been educated in English ways at Eleazar Wheelock's New England school (which became Dartmouth College in 1769). In 1775, the thirty-four-year-old Brant traveled to England with another Mohawk to negotiate the tribe's support for the British. During his extended stay in London, he had his portrait painted by the English artist George Romney. National Gallery of Canada.

Pockets of loyalism thus existed everywhere—in the middle colonies, in the backcountry of the southern colonies, and out beyond the Appalachian Mountains in Indian country. Even New England towns at the heart of the turmoil, such as Concord, Massachusetts, had a small and increasingly silenced core of loyalists who refused to countenance armed revolution. On occasion, husbands and wives, fathers and sons disagreed completely on the war.

Loyalists were most vocal between 1774 and 1776, when the possibility of a full-scale rebellion against Britain was still uncertain. Loyalists challenged the emerging patriot side in pamphlets and newspapers. In New York City, 547 loyalists signed and circulated a broadside titled "A Declaration of Dependence," in rebuttal to the congress's July 4, 1776, declaration. The broadside denounced the "most unnatural, unprovoked Rebellion that ever disgraced the annals of Time."

Speeches delivered by ministers in the pulpit and others at open-air meetings bolstered the loyalist cause. At a backcountry rally in South Carolina in 1775, a loyalist warned listeners of the superior might of the British army and of the damage to trade that war would bring. Most effectively, he played on white farmers' resentment of coastal planters' wealth and political power. It is ironic, he said, that "the charge of our intending to enslave you should come oftenest from the mouths of those lawyers who in your southern provinces, at least, have long made you slaves to themselves."

Who Is a Traitor?

The rough treatment that loyalists experienced at the hands of the revolutionaries seemed to substantiate their worst fears. In June 1775, the First Continental Congress declared all loyalists to be traitors. Over the next year, state laws defined as treason acts such as joining or provisioning the British army, saying or printing anything that undermined patriot morale, or discouraging men from enlisting in the Continental army. Punishments ranged from house arrest and suspension of voting privileges to confiscation of property and deportation. And sometimes self-appointed committees of Tory-hunters bypassed the judicial niceties and terrorized loyalists, raiding their houses or tarring and feathering them.

Were wives of loyalists also traitors? When loyalist families fled the country, their property was typically confiscated. In the rare case that a wife stayed behind, courts usually allowed her to keep one-third of the property, the amount due her if widowed, and confiscated the rest, so long as she was known to be "a steady and true and faithful friend to the American states," in the case of one Connecticut woman. But even when a wife fled with her husband, was she necessarily a loyalist, too? If the husband insisted, was she not obligated to leave with him? Such questions were adjudicated in lawsuits after the Revolution, when descendants of refugee loyalists tried to regain property that had entered the family through the mother's inheritance or marriage dowry. In one well-publicized Massachusetts case in 1805, the outcome confirmed the traditional view of women as political blank slates. The American son of loyalist refugee Anna Martin recovered her dowry property on the grounds that she had no independent will to be a loyalist.

Tarring and feathering, property confiscation, deportation, terrorism—to the loyalists, such denials of liberty of conscience and of freedom to own private property proved that democratic tyranny was more to be feared than the monarchical variety. A Boston loyalist named Mather Byles aptly expressed this point: "They call me a brainless Tory, but tell me . . . which is better—to be ruled by one tyrant three thousand miles away, or by three thousand tyrants not a mile away?" Byles was soon sentenced to deportation.

Throughout the war, probably 7,000 to 8,000 loyalists fled to England, and 28,000 found closer haven in Canada. But many chose to remain in the new United States and tried to swing with the changing political winds. In some instances, that proved difficult. In New Jersey, for example, 3,000 Jerseyites felt protected (or scared) enough by the occupying British army in 1776 to swear an oath of allegiance to the king. But then General Howe drew back to New York City, leaving them to the mercy of local patriot committees. British strategy depended on using loyalists to hold occupied territory, but the New Jersey experience showed how poorly that strategy was carried out.

Financial Instability and Corruption

Wars cost money—for arms and ammunition, for food and uniforms, for soldiers' pay. The Continental Congress printed money, but its value quickly deteriorated because the congress held no reserves of gold or silver to back the currency. In practice, it was worth only what buyers and sellers agreed it was worth. When the dollar eventually bottomed out at one-fortieth of its face value, a loaf of bread that once sold for two and a half cents then sold for a dollar. States, too, were printing paper money to pay for wartime expenses, further complicating the economy.

As the currency depreciated, the congress turned to other means to procure supplies and labor. One method was to borrow **hard money** (gold or silver coins) from wealthy men in exchange for certificates of debt (public securities) promising repayment with interest. The certificates of debt were similar to present-day **government bonds**. To pay soldiers, the congress issued land grant certificates, written promises of acreage usually located in frontier areas such as central Maine or eastern Ohio. Both the public securities and the land grant certificates quickly became forms of negotiable currency. A soldier with no cash, for example, could sell his land grant certificate to get food for his family. These certificates soon depreciated, too.

Depreciating currency inevitably led to rising prices, as sellers compensated for the falling value of the money. The wartime economy of the late 1770s, with its unreliable currency and price inflation, was extremely demoralizing to Americans everywhere. In 1778, in an effort to impose stability, local committees of public safety began to fix prices on essential goods such as flour. Inevitably, some turned this unstable situation to their advantage. Money that fell fast in value needed to be spent quickly; being in debt was suddenly advantageous because the debt could be repaid in devalued currency. A brisk black market sprang up in prohibited luxury imports, such as tea, sugar, textiles, and wines, even though these items came from Britain. A New Hampshire delegate to the congress denounced the violation of the homespun association agreements of just a few years before: "We are a crooked and perverse generation, longing for the fineries and follies of those Egyptian task masters from whom we have so lately freed ourselves."

▶**REVIEW**   How did the patriots promote support for their cause in the colonies?

The Campaigns of 1777–1779: The North and West

In early 1777, the Continental army faced bleak choices. General Washington had skillfully avoided outright defeat, but the minor victories in New Jersey lent only faint optimism to the American side. Meanwhile, British troops moved south from Quebec, aiming to isolate New England from the rest of the colonies by taking control of the Hudson River. Their presence drew the Continental army up into central New York, polarizing Indian tribes of the Iroquois nation and turning the Mohawk Valley into a bloody war zone. By 1779, tribes in western New York and in Indian country in the Ohio Valley were fully involved in the Revolutionary War; most sided with the British and against the Americans. The Americans had some success in this period, such as the victory at Saratoga, but the involvement of Indians and the continuing strength of the British forced the American government to look toward France for help.

Burgoyne's Army and the Battle of Saratoga

In 1777, British general John Burgoyne assumed command of an army of 7,800 soldiers in Canada and began the northern squeeze on the Hudson River valley. His goal was to capture Albany, near the intersection of the Hudson and Mohawk rivers (see Map 7.1). Accompanied by 1,000 "camp followers" (cooks, laundresses, and musicians) and some 400 Indian warriors, Burgoyne's army did not travel light. In addition to food and supplies for 9,200 people, the army carried food for the 400 horses hauling heavy artillery. Burgoyne also carted thirty trunks of personal belongings, including fine wines and elegant clothing.

In July, Burgoyne captured Fort Ticonderoga with ease. Some 3,000 American troops stationed there spotted the approaching British and abandoned the fort without a fight. The British continued to move south, but the large army moved slowly on primitive roads through heavily forested land. Burgoyne lost a month hacking his way south; meanwhile, his supply lines back to Canada were severely stretched. Soldiers sent out to forage for food were beaten back by local militia units.

The logical second step in isolating New England should have been to advance troops up the Hudson from New York City to meet Burgoyne, who was expecting them. George Washington expected this move, too, in light of American surveillance indicating that General Howe in Manhattan was readying his men for a major expedition in August 1777. But Howe surprised everyone by sailing south, to attack Philadelphia.

Now Burgoyne could only hope for crucial support to arrive from the west, along the Mohawk River in central New York. Close to 1,000 soldiers, including British regulars, German mercenaries, Canadians, and refugee loyalists, sailed from Montreal to Lake Ontario under the leadership of British general Barry St. Leger. Once in New York, a thousand Mohawk and Seneca Indians joined them, along with hundreds more local loyalists fighting against their rebel neighbors. St. Leger believed, wrongly, that the large community of Palatine Germans in the Mohawk Valley also would be heavily loyalist, so he expected little trouble getting to Albany. These Germans were descendants of some 10,000 immigrants who had come to New York around 1710 from the Palatinate, a region of Germany near the Rhine River.

A hundred miles west of their goal, in August 1777, the British encountered a small force of American Continental soldiers at Fort Stanwix who refused to surrender. On August 3, the British laid siege to the fort, causing local militia units forty miles away to rush to the aid of the Continentals. The 800 militiamen were mostly Palatine Germans, joined by 40 Oneida Indians. St. Leger dispatched the Mohawks and Senecas, under the leadership of the Mohawk chief Joseph Brant, and a loyalist regiment to stop the militia. Brant, with his detailed knowledge of the terrain, selected as the site of the ambush a deep ravine that the militia would have to traverse. On August 6, as the thirsty militiamen drank at Oriskany Creek in the ravine, the Indians and loyalists opened fire and inflicted heavy losses, killing nearly 500 out of 840 Americans and Indians. On Brant's side, some 90 men were killed. The battle of Oriskany was notable not only for its high death rate but also for the fact that all the combatants were American-born.

While the Oriskany battle raged, the Continentals at Fort Stanwix repelled the British and Indians besieging them and forced the attackers to retreat (see Map 7.1). Taken together, the Oriskany and Fort Stanwix battles were complexly multiethnic, pitting Indians against Indians, German Americans (the Palatines) against German mercenaries, New York patriots against New York loyalists, and English Americans against British soldiers.

The British retreat at Fort Stanwix was complete when the American general Benedict Arnold in Albany mobilized troops to chase St. Leger back to Canada, depriving General Burgoyne of the reinforcements he expected to carry out his Hudson River strategy. Camped at a small village called Saratoga, Burgoyne was isolated, with food supplies dwindling and men deserting. His adversary at Albany, General Horatio Gates, began moving 7,000 Continental soldiers toward him. Burgoyne decided to attack first because every day his army weakened. The British prevailed, but at the great cost of 600 dead or wounded redcoats. Three weeks later, an American attack on Burgoyne's forces at Saratoga cost the British another 600 men and most of their cannons. General Burgoyne finally surrendered to the American forces on October 17, 1777.

Americans on the side of the rebellion were jubilant. After the battle of Saratoga, the first decisive victory for the Continental army, a popular dance called "General Burgoyne's Surrender" swept through the country, and bookies in the major cities set odds at five to one that the war would be won in six months.

General Howe, meanwhile, had succeeded in occupying Philadelphia in September 1777. Figuring that the Saratoga loss was balanced by the capture of Philadelphia, the British government proposed a negotiated settlement—not including independence—to end the war. The American side refused.

Patriot optimism was not well-founded. Spirits ran high, but supplies of arms and food ran precariously low. Washington moved his troops into winter quarters at Valley Forge, just west of Philadelphia. Quartered in drafty huts, the men lacked blankets, boots, stockings, and food. Some 2,000 men at Valley Forge died of disease; another 2,000 deserted over the bitter six-month encampment.

Washington blamed the citizenry for lack of support, and indeed, evidence of corruption and profiteering was abundant. Army suppliers too often provided defective food, clothing, and gunpowder. When a shipment of blankets arrived, they turned out to be one-quarter their customary size. Preserved meat arrived rotten because the brine had been drained from the barrels in order to lighten the load and thereby reduce transportation costs. Selfishness and greed seemed to infect the American side. As one Continental officer said, "The people at home are destroying the Army by their conduct much faster than Howe and all his army can possibly do by fighting us."

The War in the West: Indian Country

Burgoyne's defeat in the fall of 1777 and Washington's long stay at Valley Forge up to June 1778 might suggest that the war paused for a time; and it did, on the Atlantic coast. But in the interior western areas—the Mohawk Valley, the Ohio Valley, and Kentucky—the war of Indians against the American pro-independence side was heating up. For native tribes, the struggle was not about taxation, representation, or monarchical rule; it was about independence, freedom, and land.

The ambush and slaughter at Oriskany in August 1777 marked the beginning of three years of terror for the inhabitants of the Mohawk Valley. Loyalists and Indians together engaged in many raids on farms throughout 1778, capturing or killing the residents. In retaliation, American militiamen destroyed Joseph Brant's home village, Onaquaga, but failed to capture any warriors; several children in hiding were killed. A month later, Brant's warriors attacked the town of Cherry Valley, killing 32 townspeople and 16 soldiers and taking 71 people captive.

The following summer, General Washington authorized a campaign to wreak "total destruction and devastation" on all the Iroquoian villages of central New York. Some 4,500 troops commanded by General John Sullivan carried out a deliberate campaign of terror in the fall of 1779. Forty Indian towns met with total obliteration; the soldiers looted and torched the dwellings, then burned cornfields and orchards. In a few towns, women and children were slaughtered; but in most, the inhabitants managed to escape, fleeing to the British at Fort Niagara. Thousands of Indian refugees, sick and starving, camped around the fort in one of the most miserable winters on record.

Much farther to the west, beyond Fort Pitt, another complex story of alliances and betrayals between American militiamen and Indians unfolded. Some 150,000 native people lived between the Appalachian Mountains and the Mississippi River, and by 1779, neutrality was no longer an option. Most sided with the British, who maintained a major garrison at Fort Detroit, but a portion of the Shawnee and Delaware tribes at first sought peace with the Americans. In mid-1778, the Delaware chief White Eyes negotiated a treaty at Fort Pitt, pledging Indian support for the Americans in exchange for supplies and trade goods. But escalating violence undermined the agreement. That fall, when American soldiers killed two friendly Shawnee chiefs, Cornstalk and Red Hawk, the Continental Congress hastened to apologize, as did the governors of Pennsylvania and Virginia, but the soldiers who stood trial for the murders were acquitted. Two months later, White Eyes, still nominally an ally and an informant for the Americans, died under mysterious circumstances, almost certainly murdered by militiamen, who repeatedly had trouble honoring distinctions between allied and enemy Indians.

In far western North Carolina (today's Tennessee), a frontier war zone heated up in the South in 1779, when militias attacked Cherokee settlements, destroying thirty-six villages and burning fields and livestock. Indian raiders from north of the Ohio River, in alliance with the British, repeatedly attacked white settlements such as Boonesborough (in present-day Kentucky) that had sprouted up in defiance of the Proclamation of 1763 (Map 7.2). In retaliation, a

MAP 7.2   The Indian War in the West, 1777–1782

The American Revolution involved many Indian tribes, most of them supporting the British. Iroquois Indians, with British aid, attacked American towns in New York's Mohawk Valley throughout 1778. In 1779, the Continental army destroyed forty Iroquois villages in central New York. Shawnee and Delaware Indians to the west of Fort Pitt tangled with American militia units in 1779, while tribes supported by the British at Fort Detroit skirmished with Kentucky settlers. Fighting continued in the west through 1782.

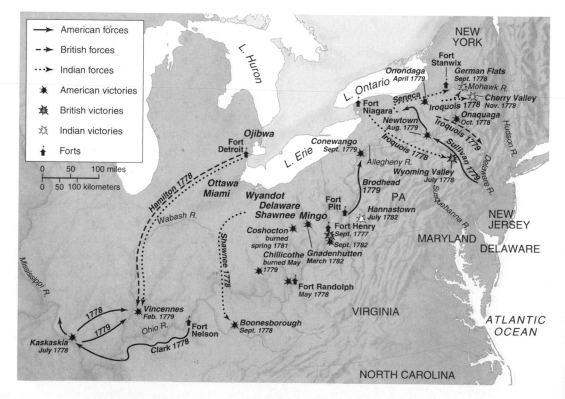

young Virginian, George Rogers Clark, led Kentucky militiamen into what is now Illinois, his men attacking and taking the British fort at Kaskaskia. Clark's men wore native clothing—hunting shirts and breech cloths—but their dress was not a sign of solidarity with the Indians. When they attacked British-held Fort Vincennes in 1779, Clark's troops tomahawked Indian captives and threw their still-live bodies into the river in a gory spectacle witnessed by the redcoats. "To excel them in barbarity is the only way to make war upon Indians," Clark announced. And, he might have added, it was a good way to terrorize British soldiers as well.

By 1780, very few Indians remained neutral. Violent raids by Americans drove Indians into the arms of the British at Detroit and Niagara, or into the arms of the Spanish, who still held much of the land west of the Mississippi River. Said one officer on the Sullivan campaign, "Their nests are destroyed but the birds are still on the wing." For those who stayed near their native lands, chaos and confusion prevailed. Rare as it was, Indian support for the American side occasionally emerged out of a strategic sense that the Americans were unstoppable in their westward pressure and that it was better to work out an alliance than to lose in a war. But American treatment of even friendly Indians showed that there was no winning strategy for them.

The French Alliance

On their own, the Americans could not have defeated Britain, especially as pressure from hostile Indians increased. Essential help arrived as a result of the victory at Saratoga, which convinced the French to enter the war; a formal alliance was signed in February 1778. France recognized the United States as an independent nation and promised full military and commercial support throughout the war. Most crucial was the French navy, which could challenge Britain's transatlantic shipment of supplies and troops and aid the Americans in taking and holding prisoners of war.

Although France had been waiting for a promising American victory to justify a formal declaration of war, the French had been providing aid to the Americans in the form of cannons, muskets, gunpowder, and highly trained military advisers since 1776. Still, monarchical France was understandably cautious about endorsing a democratic revolution attacking the principles of kingship. For France, the main attraction of an alliance was the opportunity it provided to defeat archrival Britain. A victory would also open pathways to trade and perhaps result in France acquiring the coveted British West Indies. Even American defeat would not be a full disaster for France if the war lasted many years and drained Britain of men and money.

French support materialized slowly. The navy arrived off the Virginia coast in July 1778 but then sailed south to the West Indies to defend the French sugar-producing islands. French help would prove indispensable to the American victory, but the alliance's first months brought no dramatic victories, and some Americans grumbled that the partnership would prove worthless.

▶ **REVIEW**   Why did the Americans need assistance from the French to ensure victory?

The Southern Strategy and the End of the War

When France joined the war, some British officials wondered whether the fight was worth continuing. A troop commander, arguing for an immediate negotiated settlement, shrewdly observed that "we are far from an anticipated peace, because the bitterness of the rebels is too widespread, and in regions where we are masters the rebellious spirit is still in them. The land is too large, and there are too many people. The more land we win, the weaker our army gets in the field." The commander of the British navy argued for abandoning the war, and even Lord North, the prime minister, agreed. But the king was determined to crush the rebellion, and he encouraged a new strategy for victory focusing on the southern colonies, thought to be more persuadably loyalist. It was a brilliant but desperate plan, and ultimately unsuccessful. Southern colonists were not all that loyal and in fact were willing to engage in guerrilla warfare against the British. The southern strategy thus led to a British defeat at Yorktown and the end of the war.

Georgia and South Carolina

The new strategy called for British forces to abandon New England and focus on the South, with its valuable crops—tobacco, rice, and indigo—and its large slave population, potentially a powerful destabilizing factor that might keep rebellious white southerners in line. Georgia and the Carolinas appeared to hold large numbers of loyalists, providing a base for the British to recapture the southern colonies one by one, moving north to the more problematic middle colonies and saving prickly New England for last.

Georgia, the first target, fell at the end of December 1778 (Map 7.3). A small army of British soldiers occupied Savannah and Augusta, and a new royal governor and loyalist assembly were quickly installed. Taking Georgia was easy because the bulk of the Continental army was in New York and New Jersey, keeping an eye on General Henry Clinton, Howe's replacement as commander in chief, and the French were in the West Indies. The British in Georgia quickly organized twenty loyal militia units, and 1,400 Georgians swore an oath of allegiance to the king. So far, the southern strategy looked as if it might work.

Next came South Carolina. The Continental army put ten regiments into the port city of Charleston to defend it from attack by British troops shipped south from New York under the command of General Clinton. For five weeks in early

MAP 7.3   The War in the South, 1780–1781
After taking Charleston in May 1780, the British advanced into South Carolina and North Carolina, leaving a bloody civil war in their wake. When the American general Horatio Gates and his men fled from the humiliating battle of Camden, Gates was replaced by General Nathanael Greene and General Daniel Morgan, who pulled off major victories at King's Mountain and Cowpens. The British general Cornwallis then moved north and invaded Virginia but was overpowered at Yorktown in the fall of 1781.

1780, the British laid siege to the city, then took it in May 1780, sending 3,300 American soldiers (a tremendous loss) into British captivity. Again, the king's new strategy seemed to be on target.

Clinton returned to New York, leaving the task of pacifying the rest of South Carolina to General Charles Cornwallis and 4,000 troops. A bold commander, Lord Cornwallis quickly chased out the remaining Continentals and established military rule of South Carolina by midsummer. He purged rebels from government office and disarmed rebel militias. The export of South Carolina's main crop, rice, resumed, and as in Georgia, pardons were offered to Carolinians who swore loyalty oaths to the crown and then proved their loyalty by taking up arms for the British.

By August, American troops arrived from the North to strike back at Cornwallis. General Gates, the hero of the battle of Saratoga, led 3,000 troops, half of them experienced Continental soldiers and others newly recruited militiamen, into battle against Cornwallis at Camden, South Carolina, on August 16 (see Map 7.3). The militiamen panicked at the sight of the approaching enemy cavalry; men threw down unfired muskets and ran. When regiment leaders tried to regroup the next day, only 700 soldiers showed up; a thousand Americans were dead or wounded, another thousand captured, and three hundred were still in flight. The battle of Camden was a devastating defeat, the worst of the entire war; prospects seemed very grim for the Americans.

Britain's southern strategy succeeded in 1780 in part because of information about American troop movements secretly passed on to the British by an American traitor: Benedict Arnold. The hero of several American battles, Arnold was a brilliant military talent but also a deeply insecure man who never felt he got his due in either honor or financial reward. Sometime in 1779, he opened secret negotiations with General Clinton in New York, trading information for money and hinting that he could deliver far more of value. When General Washington made him commander of West Point, a new fort sixty miles north of New York City on the Hudson River, Arnold's plan crystallized. West Point controlled the Hudson; its easy capture by the British might well have meant victory in the war.

Arnold's plot to sell a West Point victory to the British was foiled in the fall of 1780 when Americans captured the man carrying plans of the fort's defense from Arnold to Clinton. News of Arnold's treason created shock waves. Arnold represented all of the patriots' worst fears about themselves: greedy self-interest, like that of the war profiteers; the unprincipled abandonment of war aims, like that of turncoat southern Tories; panic, like that of the terrified soldiers at Camden. Plus, the war was going badly for the Americans; what if Arnold's choice to switch sides was really the smart choice? All these deeply troubling questions could be submerged by making Arnold into a moral monster. His treachery was publicly and ritually denounced in a kind of displacement of the anxieties of the moment. Vilifying Arnold allowed Americans to stake out a wide distance between themselves and dastardly conduct. It inspired a renewal of patriotism at a particularly low moment.

The Other Southern War: Guerrillas

Shock over Gates's defeat at Camden and Arnold's treason revitalized rebel support in western South Carolina, an area that Cornwallis believed to be pacified and loyal. The backcountry of the South soon became the site of guerrilla warfare.

In hit-and-run attacks, both sides burned and ravaged not only opponents' property but the property of anyone claiming to be neutral. Loyalist militia units organized by the British were met by fierce rebel militia units who figured they had little to lose. In South Carolina, some 6,000 men became active partisan fighters, and they entered into at least twenty-six engagements with loyalist units. Some were classic battles, but on other occasions the fighters were more like bandits than soldiers. Guerrilla warfare soon spread to Georgia and North Carolina. Both sides committed murders and atrocities and plundered property, clear deviations from standard military practice.

The British southern strategy depended on sufficient loyalist strength to hold reconquered territory as Cornwallis's army moved north. The backcountry civil war proved this assumption false. The Americans won few major battles in the South, but they ultimately succeeded by harassing the British forces and preventing them from foraging for food. Cornwallis moved the war into North Carolina in the fall of 1780, not because he thought South Carolina was secure—it was not—but because the North Carolinians were supplying the South Carolina rebels with arms and men (see Map 7.3). Then news of a brutal massacre of loyalist units by 1,400 frontier riflemen at the battle of King's Mountain, in western South Carolina, sent him hurrying back. The British were stretched too thin to hold on to even two of their onetime colonies.

Surrender at Yorktown

By early 1781, the war was going very badly for the British. Their defeat at King's Mountain was quickly followed by a second major defeat at the battle of Cowpens in South Carolina in January 1781. Cornwallis moved back to North Carolina again and thence to Virginia, where he captured Williamsburg in June. A raiding party proceeded to Charlottesville, the seat of government, capturing members of the Virginia assembly but not Governor Thomas Jefferson, who escaped the soldiers by a mere ten minutes. (More than a dozen of Jefferson's slaves chose this moment to seek refuge with the British.) These minor victories allowed Cornwallis to imagine that he was gaining the upper hand in Virginia. He next marched to Yorktown, near the Chesapeake Bay, to await the arrival of backup troops by ship from New York City, still held by the British.

At this juncture, the French-American alliance came into play. Already, French regiments commanded by the Comte de Rochambeau had joined General Washington in Newport, Rhode Island, in mid-1780, and now in 1781 warships under the Comte de Grasse sailed from France. Washington, Rochambeau, and de Grasse fixed their attention on the Chesapeake Bay in Virginia. The French fleet got there ahead of the British troop ships from New York; a five-day naval battle left the French navy in clear control of the Virginia coast. This proved to be the decisive factor, because it eliminated the possibility of reinforcements for Cornwallis's army, dug in at Yorktown, and made rescue by the British navy impossible.

"The Ballance of Power," 1780

This cartoon was published in England soon after Spain and the Netherlands declared an alliance with France to support the war in America. On the left, Britannia, a figure representing Great Britain, cannot be moved by all the lightweights on the right: France, Spain, the Netherlands, and America, represented by an Indian who wails, "My Ingratitude is Justly punished." The poem printed below the cartoon predicts a British victory, but, nine months after it appeared, the British surrendered at Yorktown.

Print Collection, Miriam and Ira D. Wallach Division of Art, Prints, and Photographs, The New York Public Library. Astor, Lenox, and Tilden Foundations.

On land, General Cornwallis and his 7,500 troops faced a combined French and American army numbering more than 16,000. For twelve days, the Americans and French bombarded the British fortifications at Yorktown; Cornwallis ran low on food and ammunition. An American observer keeping a diary noted that "the enemy, from want of forage, are killing off their horses in great numbers. Six or seven hundred of these valuable animals have been killed, and their carcasses are almost continually floating down the river." Realizing that escape was impossible, Cornwallis signaled his intention to surrender. On October 19, 1781, he formally capitulated.

What began as a promising southern strategy in 1778 turned into a discouraging defeat by 1781. British attacks in the South had energized American resistance, as did the timely exposure of Benedict Arnold's treason. The arrival of the French fleet sealed the fate of Cornwallis at the battle of Yorktown, and major military operations came to a halt.

The Losers and the Winners

The surrender at Yorktown proved to be the decisive end to the war with Britain, but it took two years for the principals to realize that. Frontier areas in Kentucky, Ohio, and Illinois still blazed with battles and sieges pitting Americans against various Indian tribes. The British army still occupied three coastal cities, including New York City with 13,000 soldiers, causing the Continental army at an augmented strength of 10,000 to remain in the field, stationed north of the city near West Point and Newburgh, New York. Occasional skirmishes broke out, like the one in which light infantryman Deborah Sampson saw action and sustained a wound, thereby revealing her cross-gender masquerade.

The peace treaty took six months to negotiate. Commissioners from America, Britain, and France met in Paris and worked out eighty-two articles of peace. The first article went to the heart of the matter: "His Britannic Majesty acknowledges the said United States to be free Sovereign and independent States." Other articles set the western boundary of the new country at the Mississippi River and guaranteed that creditors on both sides could collect debts owed them in sterling money, a provision especially important to British merchants. Britain agreed to withdraw its troops quickly; more than a decade later, this promise still had not been fully kept. The Treaty of Paris was signed on September 2, 1783.

Like the treaty ending the Seven Years' War, this treaty failed to recognize the Indians as players in the conflict. As one American told the Shawnee people, "Your Fathers the English have made Peace with us for themselves, but forgot you their Children, who Fought with them, and neglected you like Bastards." Indian lands were assigned to the victors as though they were uninhabited. Some Indian refugees fled west into present-day Missouri and Arkansas, and others, such as Joseph Brant's Mohawks, relocated to Canada. But significant numbers remained within the new United States, occupying their traditional homelands in areas west and north of the Ohio River. For them, the Treaty of Paris brought no peace at all; their longer war against the Americans would extend at least until 1795 and for some until 1813. The Indians' ally, Britain, conceded defeat, but the Indians did not.

With the treaty finally signed, the British began their evacuation of New York, Charleston, and Savannah, a process complicated by the sheer numbers involved—soldiers, fearful loyalists, and runaway slaves by the thousands. In New York City, more than 27,000 soldiers and 30,000 loyalists sailed on hundreds of ships for England in the late fall of 1783. In a final act of mischief, on the November day when the last ships left, the losing side raised the British flag at the southern tip of Manhattan, cut away the ropes used to hoist it, and greased the flagpole.

▶REVIEW   Why did the British southern strategy ultimately fail?

Conclusion: Why the British Lost

The British began the war for America convinced that they could not lose. They had the best-trained army and navy in the world; they were familiar with the landscape from the Seven Years' War; they had the willing warrior-power of most of the native tribes of the backcountry; and they easily captured every port city of consequence in America. Probably one-fifth of the population was loyalist, and another two-fifths were undecided. Why, then, did the British lose?

One continuing problem the British faced was the uncertainty of supplies. Unwilling to ravage the countryside, the army depended on a steady stream of supply ships from home. Insecurity about food helps explain their reluctance to pursue the Continental army aggressively. A further obstacle was their continual misuse of loyalist energies. Any plan to repacify the colonies required the cooperation of the loyalists, as well as new support from the many neutrals. But repeatedly, the British failed to back the loyalists, leaving them to the mercy of vengeful rebels. In the South, they allowed loyalist militias to engage in vicious guerrilla warfare that drove away potential converts among the rest of the population.

French aid looms large in any explanation of the British defeat. Even before the formal alliance, French artillery and ammunition proved vital for the Continental army. After 1780, the French army brought a new infusion of troops to a war-weary America, and the French navy made the Yorktown victory possible. Finally, the British abdicated civil power in the colonies in 1775 and 1776, when royal officials fled to safety, and they never really regained it. For seven years, the Americans created their own government structures, from the Continental Congress to local committees and militias. Staffed by many who before 1775 had been the political elites, these new government agencies had remarkably little trouble establishing their authority to rule. The basic British goal—to turn back the clock to imperial rule—receded into impossibility as the war dragged on.

The war for America had lasted just over six years, from Lexington to Yorktown; negotiations and the evacuation took two more. It profoundly disrupted the lives of Americans everywhere. It was a war for independence from Britain, but it was more. It was a war that required men and women to think about politics and the legitimacy of authority. The precise disagreement with Britain about representation and political participation had profound implications for the kinds of governance the Americans would adopt, both in the moment of emergency and in the longer run of the late 1770s and early 1780s when states began to write their constitutions. The rhetoric employed to justify the revolution against Britain put words such as *liberty, tyranny, slavery, independence,* and *equality* into common usage. These words carried far deeper meanings than a mere complaint over taxation without representation. The Revolution unleashed a dynamic of equality and liberty that was largely unintended and unwanted by many of the American leaders of 1776. But that dynamic emerged as a potent force in American life in the decades to come.

REVIEWING THE CHAPTER

Use the questions and timeline to review and strengthen your understanding of the chapter.

REVIEW QUESTIONS

1. Why were many Americans reluctant to pursue independence from Britain? (pp. 179–86)

2. Why did the British exercise restraint in their efforts to defeat the rebellious colonies? (pp. 186–91)

3. How did the patriots promote support for their cause in the colonies? (pp. 191–96)

4. Why did the Americans need assistance from the French to ensure victory? (pp. 196–202)

5. Why did the British southern strategy ultimately fail? (pp. 202–8)

MAKING CONNECTIONS

1. Even before the colonies had committed to independence, they faced the likelihood of serious military conflict. How did they mobilize for war? In your answer, discuss specific challenges they faced, noting any unintended consequences of their solutions.

2. Congress's adoption of the Declaration of Independence confirmed a decisive shift in the conflict between the colonies and Britain. Why did the colonies make this decisive break in 1776? In your answer, discuss some of the arguments for and against independence.

3. The question of whether the colonists' loyalty would be to the new government or to the old king was pivotal during the Revolutionary War. Discuss the importance of loyalty in the outcome of the conflict. In your answer, consider both military and political strategy.

4. American colonists and British soldiers were not the only participants in the Revolutionary War. Discuss the role of Native Americans in the war. How did they shape the conflict? What benefits did they hope to gain? Did they succeed?

TIMELINE

1775
- Second Continental Congress convenes.
- British win battle of Bunker Hill.
- King George rejects Olive Branch Petition.
- Americans lose battle of Quebec.

1776
- *Common Sense* published.
- British evacuate Boston.
- **July 4.** Congress adopts Declaration of Independence.
- British take Manhattan.

1777
- British take Fort Ticonderoga.
- Ambush at Oriskany.
- Americans hold Fort Stanwix.
- British occupy Philadelphia.
- British surrender at Saratoga.
- Continental army endures winter at Valley Forge.

1778
- France enters war on American side.
- American militiamen destroy Mohawk chief Joseph Brant's village.
- White Eyes negotiates treaty with Americans; later mysteriously dies.

1779
- Militias attack Cherokee settlements in far western North Carolina.
- Americans destroy forty Iroquois villages in New York.
- Americans take Forts Kaskaskia and Vincennes.

1780
- Philadelphia Ladies Association raises money for soldiers.
- British take Charleston, South Carolina.
- French army arrives in Newport, Rhode Island.
- British win battle of Camden.
- Benedict Arnold exposed as traitor.
- Americans win battle of King's Mountain.

1781
- British forces invade Virginia.
- French fleet blockades Chesapeake Bay.
- Cornwallis surrenders at Yorktown; concedes British defeat.

1783
- Treaty of Paris ends war; United States gains all land to Mississippi River.

▶ **For an online bibliography, practice quizzes, Web sites, images, and documents related to this chapter,** see the Book Companion Site at **bedfordstmartins.com/roark.**

▶ **For firsthand accounts of this period,** see Chapter 7 in Michael Johnson, ed., *Reading the American Past,* Fourth Edition.

8
CHAPTER

Building a Republic
1775–1789

JAMES MADISON GRADUATED from Princeton College in New Jersey in 1771, not knowing what to do next with his life. Certainly, the twenty-year-old had an easy fallback position. As the firstborn son of a wealthy plantation owner, he could return home to the foothills of Virginia and wait to inherit substantial land and a large force of slaves. But Madison was an intensely studious young man, uninterested in farming and reluctant to leave the collegiate environment. Five years at boarding school had given him fluency in Greek, Latin, French, and mathematics, and three years at Princeton had acquainted him with the great thinkers, both ancient and modern. Driven by a thirst for learning, young Madison slept only five hours a night, perhaps undermining his health. Protesting that he was too ill to travel, he hung around Princeton for six months after graduation.

In 1772, he returned home, still adrift. He tried studying law, but his unimpressive oratorical talents discouraged him. Instead, he swapped reading lists and ideas about political theory by letter with a Princeton classmate, prolonging his student life. While Madison struggled for direction, the powerful winds before the storm of the American Revolution swirled through the colonies. In May 1774, he traveled north to deliver his brother to boarding school and was in Philadelphia when the startling news broke that Britain had closed the port of Boston in retaliation for the destruction of the tea. Turbulent protests over the Coercive Acts turned him into a committed revolutionary.

Back in Virginia, Madison joined his father on the newly formed committee of public safety. For a few days in early 1775, the twenty-four-year-old took up musket practice, but his continued poor health ruled out the soldier's life. His special talent lay in the science of politics, and in the spring of 1776, he gained election to the Virginia Convention, a Revolutionary assembly replacing the defunct royal government. The convention's main task was to hammer out a state constitution with innovations such as frequent elections and limited executive power. Shy, self-effacing, and still learning the ropes, Madison mostly stayed on the sidelines, but Virginia's elder statesmen noted the young man's logical, thoughtful contributions. When his county failed to return him to the assembly in the next election, he was appointed to the governor's council, where he spent two years gaining experience in a wartime government.

In early 1780, Madison represented Virginia in the Continental Congress. Not quite twenty-nine, unmarried, and supported by his father's money, he was free of the burdens that made distant political service difficult for so many others. He stayed in the North for three years, working with men such as Alexander Hamilton of New York and Robert Morris of Pennsylvania as the congress wrestled with the chaotic economy and the ever-precarious war effort. In one crisis, Madison's negotiating skills proved crucial: He broke the deadlock over the ratification of the Articles of Confederation by arranging for the cession of Virginia's vast western lands. Those lands would soon appear on maps as the Northwest Territory, calling forth a series of western land ordinances, planned out by Madison's friend Thomas Jefferson, that exemplified the promise and high hopes for the future of the new confederation government. But more often, service in the congress proved frustrating to Madison because the confederation government seemed to lack essential powers, chief among them the power to tax.

James Madison, by Charles Willson Peale
This miniature portrait, made in 1783 when James Madison was thirty-two, shows him with natural hair (no wig) and a boyishly smooth face. Madison commissioned the portrait on the occasion of his engagement to Kitty Floyd, the sixteen-year-old daughter of a New York delegate to the Continental Congress. Madison's portrait was mounted in a brooch so that his lady love might wear it on her person. The romance came to an end when Kitty jilted Madison for a younger man. It would be eleven years before Madison found success in love, marrying Dolley Payne Todd, seventeen years his junior, at the age of forty-three.
Library of Congress.

Madison resumed a seat in the Virginia assembly in 1784. But he did not retreat to a local point of view as so many other state politicians of the decade did. The difficult economic hardships created by heavy state taxation programs—which in Massachusetts led to a full-fledged rebellion against state government—spurred Madison to pursue means to strengthen the government of the thirteen new states. In this, he was in the minority: It was by no means clear to many Americans that the Articles of Confederation needed any major revamping.

Madison thought it did. He worked hard to bring about an all-state convention in Philadelphia in the late spring of 1787, where he took the lead in steering the delegates to a complete rewrite of the structure of the national government, investing it with considerably greater powers. True to form, Madison spent the months before the convention in feverish study of the great thinkers he had read in college, searching out the best way to constitute a government on **republican** principles. His lifelong passion for scholarly study, seasoned by a dozen years of energetic political experience, paid off handsomely. The United States Constitution was the result.

By the end of the 1780s, James Madison had had his finger in every kind of political pie, on the local, state, confederation, and finally national level. He had transformed himself from a directionless and solitary youth into one of the leading political thinkers of the Revolutionary period. His personal history over the 1780s was deeply entwined with the path of the emerging United States.

The Articles of Confederation

For five years after declaring independence, the Second Continental Congress continued to meet in Philadelphia and other cities without any formal constitutional basis. Delegates first had to work out a plan of government that embodied Revolutionary principles. With monarchy gone, where would sovereignty lie? What would be the nature of representation? Who would hold the power of taxation? Who should vote; who should rule? The resulting plan, called the Articles of Confederation, proved to be surprisingly difficult to implement, mainly because the thirteen states had serious disagreements about how to manage areas to the west whose political ownership was contested. Once the Articles were finally ratified and the confederation was formally constituted, that arena of government seemed to many to be far less relevant or interesting than the state governments.

Congress, Confederation, and the Problem of Western Lands

Only after declaring independence did the Continental Congress turn its attention to creating a written document that would specify what powers the congress had and by what authority it existed. There was widespread agreement on key government powers: pursuing war and peace, conducting foreign relations, regulating trade, and running a postal service. But there was serious disagreement about the powers of the congress over the western boundaries of the states. Virginia and Connecticut, for example, had old colonial charters that located their western boundaries at the Mississippi River. States without extensive land claims insisted on redrawing those colonial boundaries.

This was no mere quarrel over lines on a map. In the 1780s, more than 100,000 Americans had moved west of the Appalachian Mountains, and another 100,000 were moving from eastern towns to newly opened land in northern Vermont and western New York and Pennsylvania, as well as to Kentucky, Georgia, and beyond. Who owned the land, who protected it, who governed it? These were major and pressing questions.

For more than a year, the congress tinkered with drafts of the Articles of Confederation, reaching agreement only in November 1777. The Articles defined the union as a loose confederation of states, characterized as "a firm league of friendship" existing mainly to foster a common defense. The structure of the government paralleled that of the existing Continental Congress. There was no national executive (that is, no president) and no national judiciary. The congress was composed of two to seven delegates from each state, selected annually by the state legislatures and prohibited from serving more than three years out of any six. The actual number of delegates was not critical, since each state delegation cast a single vote.

Routine decisions in the congress required a simple majority of seven states; for momentous decisions, such as declaring war, nine states needed to agree. To approve or amend the Articles required the unanimous consent both of the thirteen state delegations and of the thirteen state legislatures. The congressional delegates undoubtedly thought they were guaranteeing that no individual state could be railroaded by the other twelve in fundamental constitutional matters. But what this requirement really did was to hamstring the government. Any single state could—and did—hold the rest of the country hostage to its demands.

On the delicate question of taxes, needed to finance the war, the Articles provided an ingenious but ultimately troublesome solution. Each state was to contribute in proportion to the property value of the state's land. Large and populous states would give more than small or sparsely populated states. The actual taxes would be levied by the state legislatures, not by the congress, to preserve the Revolution's principle of taxation only by direct representation. However, no mechanism was created to compel states to contribute their fair share.

The lack of centralized authority in the confederation government was exactly what many state leaders wanted in the late 1770s. A league of states with rotating personnel, no executive branch, no power of taxation, and a requirement of unanimity for any major change seemed to be a good way to avoid the kind of tyranny experienced under the rule of the British monarchy.

Yet there were problems. The requirement for unanimous approval, for example, stalled the acceptance of the Articles for four additional years. The key dispute involved the problem of land claims west of the existing states (Map 8.1). Five states, all lacking land claims—Maryland, Delaware, New Jersey,

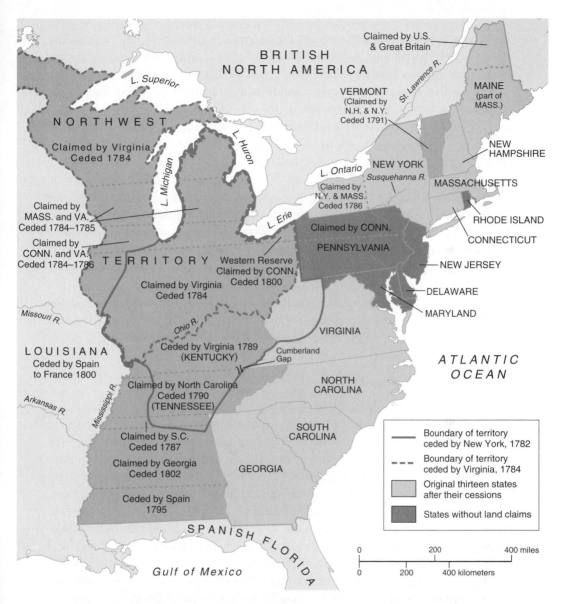

MAP 8.1   Cession of Western Lands, 1782–1802

The thirteen new states found it hard to ratify the Articles of Confederation without settling their con-
flicting land claims in the West, an area larger than the original states and occupied by Indian tribes.
The five states objecting to the Articles' silence over western lands policy were Maryland, Delaware,
New Jersey, Rhode Island, and Pennsylvania.

Rhode Island, and Pennsylvania—insisted that the congress control western lands as a national domain that would eventually constitute new states. The other eight states refused to yield their colonial-era claims and opposed giving the congress power to alter boundaries. In all the heated debate, few seemed to remember that those same western lands were inhabited by many thousands of Indians not party to the disputes.

The eight land-claiming states were ready to sign the Articles of Confederation in 1777. Three states without claims, Rhode Island, Pennsylvania, and New Jersey, eventually capitulated and signed, "not from a Conviction of the Equality and Justness of it," said a New Jersey delegate, "but merely from an absolute Necessity there was of complying to save the Continent." But Delaware and Maryland continued to hold out, insisting on a national domain policy. In 1779, the disputants finally compromised: Any land a state volunteered to relinquish would become the national domain. When James Madison and Thomas Jefferson ceded Virginia's huge land claim in 1781, the Articles were at last unanimously approved.

The western lands issue demonstrated that powerful interests divided the thirteen new states. The apparent unity of purpose inspired by fighting the war against Britain papered over sizable cracks in the new confederation.

Running the New Government

No fanfare greeted the long-awaited inauguration of the new government. The congress continued to sputter along, its problems far from solved by the signing of the Articles. Lack of a quorum often hampered day-to-day activities. The Articles required representation from seven states to conduct business and a minimum of two men from each state's delegation. But some days, fewer than fourteen men in total showed up. State legislatures were slow to select delegates, and many of those appointed were reluctant to attend, especially if they had wives and children at home. Consequently, some of the most committed delegates were young bachelors, such as James Madison, and men in their fifties and sixties whose families were grown, such as Samuel Adams.

Many politicians preferred to devote their energies to state governments, especially when the congress seemed deadlocked or, worse, irrelevant. It also did not help that the congress had no permanent home. During the war, when the British army threatened Philadelphia, the congress relocated to small Pennsylvania towns such as Lancaster and York and then to Baltimore. After hostilities ceased, the congress moved from Trenton to Princeton to Annapolis to New York City.

To address the difficulties of an inefficient congress, executive departments of war, finance, and foreign affairs were created in 1781 to handle purely administrative functions. When the department heads were ambitious—as was Robert Morris, a wealthy Philadelphia merchant who served as superintendent of finance—they could exercise considerable executive power. The Articles of Confederation had deliberately refrained from setting up an executive branch, but a modest one was being invented by necessity.

> ▶**REVIEW**   Why was the confederation government's authority so limited?

The Sovereign States

In the first decade of independence, the states were sovereign and all-powerful. Relatively few functions, such as declaring war and peace, had been transferred to the confederation government. As Americans discarded their British identity, they thought of themselves instead as Virginians or New Yorkers or Rhode Islanders. Familiar and close to home, state governments claimed the allegiance of citizens and became the arena in which the Revolution's innovations would first be tried. States defined who was a voter, and they also defined who would be free. The question of slavery quickly became a front-burner issue, as all the states were forced to figure out whether or how Revolutionary ideals could coexist with lifelong bondage for African Americans. Northern states had more success ending inconsistency than did southern states, where slavery was deeply entrenched in the economy.

The State Constitutions

In May 1776, the congress recommended that all states draw up constitutions based on "the authority of the people." By 1778, ten states had done so, and three more (Connecticut, Massachusetts, and Rhode Island) had adopted and updated their original colonial charters. Having been denied unwritten British **liberties**, Americans wanted written contracts that guaranteed basic principles.

A shared feature of all the state constitutions was the conviction that government ultimately rests on the consent of the governed. Political writers in the late 1770s embraced the concept of republicanism as the underpinning of the new governments. Republicanism meant more than popular elections and representative institutions. For some, republicanism invoked a way of thinking about who leaders should be: autonomous, virtuous citizens who placed civic values above private interests. For others, it suggested direct **democracy**, with nothing standing in the way of the will of the people. For all, it meant government that promoted the people's welfare.

Widespread agreement about the virtues of republicanism went hand in hand with the idea that republics could succeed only in relatively small units. Distant government could easily become tyrannical; that was the lesson of the 1760s. Nearly every state continued the colonial practice of a two-chamber assembly but greatly augmented the powers of the lower house, since it was closer to the people. Two states, Pennsylvania and Georgia, abolished the more elite upper house altogether, and most states severely limited the term and pow-ers of the governor. The lower houses of the state legislatures, with annual elec-tions and guaranteed rotation in office, could be most responsive to popular majorities. If a representative displeased his constituents, he could be out of office in a matter of months. James Madison's unsuccessful attempt to win reelection to the Virginia assembly in 1777 offers an example of quick rotation in office. He was sure he had lost because he had failed to campaign in the traditional style, with the abundant liquor and glad-handing that his constituents had come to expect. Shy and retiring, Madison was not capable of running for election in this manner. His series of increasingly significant political posts from 1778 to 1787 all came as a result of appointment, not popular election.

Six of the state constitutions included bills of rights—lists of basic individual liberties that government could not abridge. Virginia debated and passed the first bill of rights in June 1776, and many of the other states borrowed from it. Its lan-guage bears a close resemblance to the wording of the Declaration of Indepen-dence, which Thomas Jefferson was drafting that same June in Philadelphia: "That all men are by nature equally free and independent, and have certain inherent rights, of which, when they enter into a state of society, they cannot by any com-pact deprive or divest their posterity; namely, the enjoyment of life and liberty, with the means of acquiring and possessing property, and pursuing and obtaining happiness and safety." Along with these inherent rights went more specific rights to freedom of speech, freedom of the press, and trial by jury.

Who Are "the People"?

When the Continental Congress called for state constitutions based on "the authority of the people," and when the Virginia bill of rights granted "all men" cer-tain rights, who was meant by "the people"? Who exactly were the citizens of this new country, and how far would the principle of democratic government extend? Different people answered these questions differently, but in the 1770s certain lim-its to full political participation by all Americans were widely agreed upon.

One limit was defined by property. In nearly every state, candidates for the highest offices had to meet substantial property qualifications. In Maryland, a candidate for governor had to be worth £5,000, a large sum of money. Voters in Maryland had to own fifty acres of land or £30, a barrier to one-third of adult white males. In the most democratic state, Pennsylvania, voters and candidates needed to be taxpayers, owning enough property to owe taxes. Only property owners were presumed to possess the necessary independence of mind to make wise political choices. Are not propertyless men, asked John Adams, "too little acquainted with public affairs to form a right judgment, and too dependent upon other men to have a will of their own?" In addition, the requirement drew logic from the claim that propertyless men should not have a voice in decisions about tax levies since they paid no taxes.

Property qualifications probably **disfranchised** from one-quarter to one-half of adult white males in all the states. Not all of them took their nonvoter status quietly. One Maryland man wondered what was so special about being worth £30: "Every poor man has a life, a personal liberty, and a right to his earnings; and is in danger of being injured by government in a variety of ways." Why then restrict such a man from voting? Others pointed out that propertyless men were fighting and dying in the Revolutionary War; surely they were expressing an active concern about politics. Finally, a few radical voices challenged the notion that owning property transformed men into good citizens. Perhaps it did the opposite: The richest men might well be greedy and selfish and therefore bad citizens. But ideas like this were outside the mainstream. The writers of the new constitutions, themselves men of property, viewed the right to own and preserve property as a central principle of the Revolution.

Another exclusion from voting—women—was so ingrained that few stopped to question it. Yet the logic of allowing propertied females to vote did occur to at least two well-placed women. Abigail Adams wrote to her husband, John, in 1782, "Even in the freest countrys our property is subject to the controul and disposal of our partners, to whom the Laws have given a sovereign Authority. Deprived of a voice in Legislation, obliged to submit to those Laws which are imposed upon us, is it not sufficient to make us indifferent to the publick Welfare?" A wealthy Virginia widow named Hannah Corbin wrote to her brother, Richard Henry Lee, to complain of her taxation without the corresponding representation. Her letter no longer exists, but his reply does: "You complain that widows are not represented, and that being temporary possessors of the estates, ought not to be liable to the tax." Yet, he continued, women would be "out of character . . . to press into those tumultuous assemblies of men where the business of choosing representatives is conducted."

Only three states specified that voters had to be male, so powerful was the unspoken assumption that only men could vote. Still, in one state, small numbers of women began to turn out at the polls in the 1780s. New Jersey's constitution of 1776 enfranchised all free inhabitants worth more than £50, language that in theory opened the door to free blacks as well as unmarried women who met the property requirement. (Married women owned no property, for by law their husbands held title to everything, and few free blacks would meet the property qualification.) Little fanfare accompanied this radical shift, and some historians have inferred that the inclusion of unmarried women and blacks was an oversight. Yet other parts of the **suffrage** clause pertaining to residency and property were extensively debated when it was put in the state constitution, and no objections were raised at that time to its gender- and race-free language. Thus other historians have concluded that the law was intentionally inclusive. In 1790, a revised election law used the words *he or she* in reference to voters, making woman suffrage explicit. As one New Jersey legislator declared, "Our Constitution gives this right to maids or widows *black* or *white*." However, that legislator was complaining, not bragging, so his expansive words should not be taken as a sign that egalitarian suffrage was an accepted fact.

In 1790, only about 1,000 free black adults of both sexes lived in New Jersey, a state with a population of 184,000. The number of unmarried adult white women was probably also small, mainly widows. In view of the property requirement, the voter bloc enfranchised under this law could not have been decisive in elections. Still, this highly unusual situation lasted until 1807, when a new state law specifically disfranchised both blacks and women. Henceforth, independence of mind, that essential precondition of voting, was redefined to be sex- and race-specific.

In the 1780s, voting everywhere was class-specific, due to the property restrictions. John Adams urged the framers of the Massachusetts constitution not even to discuss the scope of suffrage but simply to adopt the traditional colonial property qualifications. If suffrage is brought up for debate, he warned, "there will be no end of it. New claims will arise; women will demand a vote; lads from twelve to twenty-one will think their rights not enough attended to; and every man who has not a farthing, will demand an equal voice with any other." Adams was astute enough to anticipate complaints about excluding women, youths, and poor men from political life, but it did not even occur to him to worry about another group: slaves.

Equality and Slavery

Restrictions on political participation did not mean that propertyless people enjoyed no civil rights and liberties. The various state bills of rights applied to all individuals who had, as the Virginia bill so carefully phrased it, "enter[ed] into a state of society." No matter how poor, a free person was entitled to life, liberty, property, and freedom of conscience. Unfree people, however, were another matter.

The author of the Virginia bill of rights was George Mason, a plantation owner with 118 slaves. When he penned the sentence "All men are by nature equally free and independent," he did not have slaves in mind; he instead was asserting that Americans (meaning white Americans) were the equals of the British and could not be denied the liberties of British citizens. But other Virginia legislators worried that the words could be construed to apply to slaves. So they added the phrase specifying that rights belonged only to people who had entered civil society. As one wrote, with relief, "Slaves, not being constituent members of our society, could never pretend to any benefit from such a maxim."

One month later, the Declaration of Independence used essentially the same phrase about equality, this time without the modifying clause about entering society. Two state constitutions, for Pennsylvania and Massachusetts, also included the inspiring language about equality without limiting it, as had Virginia. When the Massachusetts constitution was sent around to be ratified, town by town, the town of Hardwick suggested rewording the phrase "All men are born free and equal" to read "All men, whites and blacks, are born free and equal." The clear

Paul Cuffe's Silhouette

Captain Paul Cuffe of Martha's Vineyard was the son of a Wampanoag Indian woman and an African man who had purchased his own freedom. During the American Revolution, he endured several months of imprisonment by the British. After the war, he protested that Massachusetts taxed free blacks who lacked the privilege of voting. In his career as a shipbuilder and mariner, Cuffe traveled extensively. By 1812, when this engraving was made, Cuffe had explored the African country of Sierra Leone as a possible site for resettlement of American blacks and had met with African kings, English dukes, and an American president.

Library of Congress.

endorsement of racial equality was not implemented.

The only other state to draft language about equality was Vermont, whose 1777 constitution explicitly outlawed slavery and based its logic on the equality phrase of the Declaration. (Vermont had very few slaves within its borders and did not win recognition as a state until 1791, due to competing claims to its territory by New York and New Hampshire.) Reluctance to include equality language in other state bills of rights and constitutions indicates an uneasy recognition that such language might indeed threaten the institution of slavery.

Northern enslaved blacks challenged their bondage in petitions citing Revolutionary ideals of equality. In 1773, four enslaved men in Massachusetts petitioned the state legislature for their "natural right" to freedom, offering a plan to resettle in Africa. Three years later, several more Massachusetts slaves presented their claim to a "natural & unalienable right to that freedom which the great Parent of the Universe hath bestowed equally on all mankind." Their modest request, for freedom for their children at age twenty-one, met with rejection. In 1779, similar petitions in Connecticut and New Hampshire also were unsuccessful. In 1780, seven Massachusetts freemen, including the mariner brothers Paul and John Cuffe, refused to pay taxes for three years on the grounds that they could not vote and so were not represented. The Cuffe brothers went to jail for tax evasion, but their petition to the state legislature spurred the extension of suffrage to taxpaying free blacks in 1783.

Legal Changes to Slavery, 1777–1804

Another way to bring the issue before lawmakers was to sue in court. In 1781, a woman called Mum Bett was the first to win freedom in a Massachusetts court, basing her case on the just-passed state constitution that declared "all men are born free and equal." Later that year, another Massachusetts slave, Quok Walker, charged his master with assault and battery, arguing that he was de facto a free man under that same constitutional phrase. Walker won the case and was set free, a decision confirmed in an appeal to the state's superior court in 1783. Several similar cases followed, and by 1789 slavery had been effectively abolished by a series of judicial decisions in Massachusetts.

Legal wheels sometimes turned far more slowly. Pennsylvania politicians ended slavery by a gradual **emancipation** law in 1780. Only infants born to a slave mother on or after March 1, 1780, would be freed, but not until age twenty-eight. Thus no current slave in Pennsylvania would in theory gain freedom until 1808; well into the nineteenth century, those blacks born before 1780 would still be slaves. Not until 1847 did Pennsylvania fully abolish slavery. But slaves did not wait for such slow implementation. Untold numbers in Pennsylvania simply ran away from their owners and claimed their freedom, sometimes with the help of sympathetic whites. One estimate holds that more than half of young slave men in Philadelphia took flight in the 1780s and joined the ranks of free blacks. Owners generally did not pursue them. By 1790, free blacks outnumbered slaves in Pennsylvania by nearly two to one.

Rhode Island and Connecticut adopted gradual emancipation laws in 1784. In 1785, New York expanded the terms under which individual owners could free slaves, but only in 1799 did the state adopt a gradual emancipation law; New Jersey followed suit in 1804. These were the two northern states with the largest number of slaves: New York in 1800 with 20,000, New Jersey with more than 12,000. In contrast, slaves in Pennsylvania numbered just 1,700. Gradual emancipation illustrates the tension between radical and conservative implications of republican ideology. Republican government protected people's liberties and property, yet slaves were both people and property. Gradual emancipation balanced the civil rights of blacks and the property rights of their owners by delaying the promise of freedom.

South of Pennsylvania, in Delaware, Maryland, and Virginia, where slavery was so important to the economy, emancipation bills were rejected. All three states, however, eased legal restrictions and allowed individual acts of emancipation for adult slaves below the age of forty-five under new manumission laws passed in 1782 (Virginia), 1787 (Delaware), and 1790 (Maryland). By 1790, close to 10,000 newly freed Virginia slaves had formed local free black communities complete with schools and churches.

In the deep South—the Carolinas and Georgia—freedom for slaves was unthinkable among whites. Yet several thousand slaves had defected to the British during the war, and between 3,000 and 4,000 shipped out of Savannah and Charleston, destined for freedom. Adding northern blacks evacuated from New York City in 1783, the probable total of emancipated blacks who left the United States was between 8,000 and 10,000. Some went to Canada, some to England, and some to Sierra Leone, on the west coast of Africa. Many hundreds took refuge with the Seminole and Creek Indians, becoming permanent members of their communities in Spanish Florida and western Georgia.

All these instances of emancipation were gradual, small, and certainly incomplete, but their symbolic importance was enormous. Every state from Pennsylvania north acknowledged explicitly that slavery was fundamentally inconsistent with Revolutionary ideology. On some level, white southerners also understood this, but their inability to imagine a free biracial society prevented them from taking much action. George Washington owned 390 slaves and freed not one of them in the 1780s, even when his friend the French general Lafayette urged him to do so as a model for others. In his will, written in 1799, the guilt-stricken Washington provided for the eventual freedom of his slaves—but only after his wife, Martha, died. One year after his death, Martha Washington freed them, preferring loss of income to the uneasy situation of her life being the only barrier to her slaves' freedom.

Emancipation in the 1780s, limited as it was, shows that the phrase of the Declaration of Independence—"all men are created equal"—was beginning to acquire real force as a basic principle. Yet a geographical pattern was taking shape: From the 1780s on, the North was associated with freedom and the South with slavery, with profound consequences for the next two centuries of American history.

▶**REVIEW**   How did states determine who would be allowed to vote?

The Confederation's Problems

After the Revolution concluded in 1783, the confederation government turned to its three main and interrelated areas of concern: paying down the large war debt, making formal peace with the Indians, and dealing with western settlement. The debt was a vexing problem, since the Articles of Confederation lacked the power to tax. Western lands provided a promising source of income, once it was clear who owned them and who could sell them. Virginia's cession of its vast western territory in 1781 had opened the way for the ratification of the Articles, but there were still conflicts over territory, most crucially in the area that is now western New York, where Massachusetts and tribes of the Iroquois confederacy had legitimate claims. In the years from 1784 to 1786, the congress struggled mightily with these issues. Some leaders were gripped by a sense of crisis, fearing that the Articles of Confederation were too weak. Others defended the Articles as the best guarantee of individual liberty, because real governance occurred at the state level, closer to the people. A major outbreak of civil disorder in western Massachusetts quickly crystallized the debate and propelled the critics of the Articles into decisive and far-reaching action.

Financial Chaos and Paper Money

Seven years of war produced a chaotic economy in the 1780s. The confederation and the individual states had run up huge war debts, financed by printing paper money and borrowing from private sources. Some $400 million to $500 million in paper currency had been injected into the economy, and prices and wages fluctuated wildly. Private debt and rapid expenditure flourished, as people quickly bought what goods they could with the depreciating currency. In many localities, legal suits between debtors and creditors quadrupled over prewar levels. A laborer in central Massachusetts, William Manning, described the economic trouble brewing: "With the prices of labor and produce falling very fast, creditors began calling for old debts and saying that they would not take payment in paper money. . . . Property was selling almost every day by execution [court-ordered foreclosures] for less than half its value. The jails were crowded with debtors." A serious postwar depression settled in by the mid-1780s and did not lift until the 1790s.

The confederation government itself was in a terrible financial fix. Continental dollars had lost almost all value: In 1781, it took 146 of them to buy what one dollar had bought in 1775. Desperate times required desperate measures. The congress chose Robert Morris, Philadelphia merchant and newly reelected delegate, to be superintendent of finance. Morris had a gift for financial dealings but had resigned from the congress in 1778 amid accusations that he had unfairly profited from public service. Now his talents were again needed, and from 1781 to 1784, he took charge of the confederation's economic problems.

To augment the government's revenue, Morris first proposed a 5 percent impost (an import tax). Since the Articles of Confederation did not authorize taxation, an amendment was needed, but unanimous agreement proved impossible. Rhode Island and New York, whose bustling ports provided ample state revenue, preferred to keep their money and simply refused to agree to a national impost.

Morris's next idea was the creation of the Bank of North America. This private bank would enjoy a special relationship with the confederation, holding the government's **hard money** (gold and silver coins) as well as private deposits, and providing it with short-term loans. The bank's contribution to economic stability came in the form of banknotes, pieces of paper inscribed with a dollar value. Unlike paper money, banknotes were backed by hard money in the bank's vaults and thus would not depreciate. Morris hoped this form of money would retain value; the congress agreed and voted to approve the bank in 1781. But the bank had limited success curing the confederation's economic woes because it issued very little currency; its charter was allowed to expire in 1786.

If Morris could not resuscitate the economy in the 1780s, probably no one could have done it. Because the Articles of Confederation reserved most economic functions to the states, the congress was helpless to tax trade, control inflation, curb the flow of state-issued paper money, or pay the mounting public debt.

However, the confederation had one source of enormous potential wealth: the huge western territories, attractive to the fast-growing white population but inhabited by Indians.

The Treaty of Fort Stanwix

Since the Indians had not been party to the Treaty of Paris of 1783, the confederation government needed to formalize a treaty with them to conclude hostilities and secure land cessions. The most pressing problem was the land inhabited by the Iroquois League of Six Nations, now urgently claimed by the states of New York and Massachusetts based on colonial charters granted by the king (see Map 8.1). Both states hoped to ease heavy war debts by selling land to speculators and settlers. The Massachusetts claim was legally stronger because its charter predated New York's by four decades, but New York felt entitled because it bordered the territory. The dispute in the congress between the two states was so tense that it struck a southern delegate as "the seeds of dissension which I think will not end without a civil war."

The congress tried to solve the dispute by calling the Six Nations to a meeting in October 1784 at Fort Stanwix, on the upper reaches of the Mohawk River. The Articles of Confederation gave the congress (as opposed to individual states) the right to manage diplomacy, war, and "all affairs with the Indians, not members of any of the States." But New York leaders seized on this ambiguous language to claim that the Iroquois were in fact "members" of their state and that New York alone should negotiate with them.

To scoop both the congress and Massachusetts, New York's governor called his own meeting with the Iroquois at Fort Stanwix in September. Suspecting that New York's claim to authority might be superseded by the congress, the most important chiefs declined to come. Instead, they sent deputies who lacked the authority to negotiate. The Mohawk leader Joseph Brant shrewdly identified the problem of divided authority that afflicted the confederation government: "Here lies some Difficulty in our Minds, that there should be two separate bodies to manage these Affairs." No deal was struck with New York.

Three weeks later, U.S. commissioners opened proceedings at Fort Stanwix with the Seneca chief Cornplanter and Captain Aaron Hill, a Mohawk leader. Six hundred Indians from the six tribes attended the meeting. The U.S. commissioners came with a security detail of one hundred New Jersey militiamen.

The Americans demanded a return of prisoners of war; recognition of the confederation's authority to negotiate, rather than that of individual states; and an all-important cession of a strip of land from Fort Niagara due south, which established U.S.-held territory adjacent to the border with Canada. This crucial change enclosed the Iroquois land within the United States and made it impossible for the Indians to claim to be *between* the United States and Canada. When the tribal leaders balked, one of the commissioners sternly replied, "You are mistaken in supposing that, having been excluded from the treaty between the United States and the King of England, you are become a free and independent nation and may make what terms you please. It is not so. You are a subdued people."

In the end, the treaty was signed, gifts were given, and six high-level Indian hostages were kept at the fort awaiting the release of the American prisoners taken during the war, most of whom were women and children. In addition, a significant side deal sealed for $5,000 the release of much of the Seneca tribe's claim to the Ohio Valley to the United States. This move was a major surprise and disappointment to the Delaware, Mingo, and Shawnee Indians who lived there. In the months to come, the Iroquois and other tribes not at the meeting tried to disavow the Treaty of Fort Stanwix as a document signed under coercion by virtual hostages. But the confederation government ignored those complaints and made plans to survey and develop the Ohio Territory.

New York's governor understood that the confederation government's power to implement the treaty terms it had gained was limited. The U.S. government's financial coffers were nearly empty, and its leadership was stretched. So New York quietly began surveying and then selling the very land it had failed to secure by individual treaty with the Indians. As that fact became generally known, it pointed up the weakness of the confederation government. One Connecticut leader wondered, "What is to defend us from the ambition and rapacity of New York, when she has spread over that vast territory, which she claims and holds? Do we not already see in her the seeds of an over-bearing ambition?"

Land Ordinances and the Northwest Territory

The congress ignored western New York and turned instead to the Ohio Valley to make good on the promise of western expansion. Delegate Thomas Jefferson, charged with drafting a policy, proposed dividing the territory north of the Ohio River and east of the Mississippi—called the Northwest Territory—into nine new states with evenly spaced east-west boundaries and townships ten miles square. He at first advocated giving the land to settlers, rather than selling it, arguing that future property taxes on the improved land would be payment enough. Jefferson's aim was to encourage rapid and democratic settlement, to build a nation of freeholders (as opposed to renters), and to avoid land speculation. Jefferson also insisted on representative governments in the new states; they would not become colonies of the older states. Finally, Jefferson's draft prohibited slavery in the ten new states.

The congress adopted parts of Jefferson's plan in the Ordinance of 1784: the rectangular grid, the ten states, and the guarantee of self-government and eventual statehood. What the congress found too radical was the proposal to give away the land; the national domain was the confederation's only source of independent wealth. The slavery prohibition also failed, by a vote of seven to six states.

Jefferson's Map of the Northwest Territory
Thomas Jefferson sketched out borders for nine new states in his initial plan for the Northwest Territory in 1784 and additional anticipated states below the Ohio River. Straight lines and right angles held a strong appeal for him. But such regularity ignored inconvenient geographic features such as rivers and even more inconvenient political features such as Indian territorial claims.
William L. Clements Library.

A year later, the congress revised the legislation with procedures for mapping and selling the land. The Ordinance of 1785 called for three to five states (instead of ten) divided into townships six miles square, further divided into thirty-six sections of 640 acres, or one mile square, each section enough for four family farms. Property was thus reduced to precise and easily mappable squares. One lot in each township was earmarked for educational purposes. Land would be sold by public auction, at a minimum price of one dollar an acre, with highly desirable land bid up for more. Two further restrictions applied: The minimum purchase was 640 acres, and payment must be in hard money or in certificates of debt from Revolutionary days. This effectively meant that the land's first owners would be prosperous speculators. The grid of invariant squares further enhanced speculation, allowing buyers and sellers to operate without ever setting foot on the acreage. The commodification of land had been taken to a new level.

Speculators usually held the land for resale rather than inhabiting it. Thus they avoided direct contact with the most serious obstacle to settlement: the dozens of Indian tribes that claimed the land as their own. The treaty signed at Fort Stanwix in 1784 was followed by the Treaty of Fort McIntosh in 1785, which similarly coerced partial cessions of land from the Delaware, Huron, and Miami tribes. Finally, in 1786, a united Indian meeting near Detroit issued an ultimatum: No cession would be valid without unanimous consent of the tribes. The Indians advised the United States to "prevent your surveyors and other people from coming upon our side of the Ohio river." For two more decades, violent Indian wars in Ohio and Indiana would continue to impede white settlement (see chapter 9).

In 1787, a third land act, called the Northwest Ordinance, set forth a three-stage process by which settled territories would advance to statehood. First, the congress would appoint officials for a sparsely populated territory who would adopt a legal code and appoint local magistrates to administer justice. When the free male population of voting age and landowning status (fifty acres) reached 5,000, the territory could elect its own legislature and send a nonvoting delegate to the congress. When the population of voting citizens reached 60,000, they could write a state constitution and apply for full admission to the Union. At all three territorial stages, the inhabitants were subject to taxation to support the Union, in the same manner as were the original states.

The Northwest Ordinance of 1787 was perhaps the most important legislation passed by the confederation government. It ensured that the new United States, so recently released from colonial dependency, would not itself become a colonial power—at least not with respect to white citizens. The mechanism it established allowed for the successful and orderly expansion of the United States across the continent in the next century.

Nonwhites were not forgotten or neglected in the 1787 ordinance. The brief document acknowledged the Indian presence in the Northwest Territory and promised that "the utmost good faith shall always be observed towards the Indians; their lands and property shall never be taken from them without their consent; and, in their property, rights, and liberty, they shall never be invaded or disturbed, unless in just and lawful wars authorized by Congress." The 1787 ordinance further pledged that "laws founded in justice and humanity, shall from time to time be made for preventing wrongs being done to them, and for preserving peace and friendship with them." These promises were full of noble intentions, but they were not generally honored in the decades to come.

Jefferson's original and remarkable suggestion to prohibit slavery in the Northwest Territory resurfaced in the 1787 ordinance, passing this time without any debate. Probably the addition of a fugitive slave provision in the act set southern congressmen at ease: Escaped slaves caught north of the Ohio River would be returned south. The ordinance thus acknowledged and supported slavery even as it prohibited it in one region. Further, abundant territory south of the Ohio remained available for the spread of slavery. Still, the prohibition of slavery in the Northwest Territory perpetuated the dynamic of gradual emancipation in the North. North-South sectionalism based on slavery was slowly taking shape.

Shays's Rebellion, 1786–1787

Without an impost amendment, and with public land sales projected but not yet realized, the confederation turned to the states in the 1780s to contribute revenue voluntarily. Struggling with their own war debts, most state legislatures were reluctant to tax their constituents too heavily. Massachusetts, however, had a fiscally conservative legislature, dominated by the coastal commercial centers. For four years, the legislature passed tough tax laws that called for payment in hard money, not cheap paper. Farmers in the western two-thirds of the state found it increasingly difficult to comply and repeatedly petitioned against what they called oppressive taxation. In July 1786, when the legislature adjourned having yet again ignored their complaints, dissidents held a series of conventions and called for revisions to the state constitution to promote democracy, eliminate the elite upper house, and move the capital farther west in the state.

Still unheard in Boston, the dissidents targeted the county courts, the local symbol of state authority. In the fall of 1786, several thousand armed men marched on courthouses in six Massachusetts counties and forced bewildered judges to close their courts until the state constitution was revised. Sympathetic local militias did not intervene. The insurgents were not predominantly poor or debt-ridden farmers; they included veteran soldiers and officers in the Continental army as well as town leaders. One was a farmer and onetime army captain, Daniel Shays, from the town of Pelham.

The governor of Massachusetts, James Bowdoin, who had once organized protests against British taxes, now characterized the western dissidents as illegal rebels. He vilified Shays as the chief leader, and a Boston newspaper claimed Shays planned to burn Boston to the ground and overthrow the government, clearly an overreaction. Another former radical, Samuel Adams, took the extreme position that "the man who dares rebel against the laws of a republic ought to suffer death." Those aging revolutionaries had given little thought to the possibility that popular majorities, embodied in a state legislature, could seem to be just as oppressive as monarchs. The dissidents challenged the assumption that popularly elected governments would always be fair and just.

Members of the Continental Congress worried that the Massachusetts insurgency was spinning out of control. In October, the congress attempted to triple the size of the federal army, calling for 660 new recruits from Massachusetts and another 560 from the rest of New England; fewer than 100 enlisted in the troubled state. So Governor Bowdoin raised a private army, gaining the services of some

Two Rebel Leaders
A Boston almanac of 1787 yields the only depiction of Daniel Shays in existence. Shays is standing with another rebel leader, Job Shattuck, from the town of Groton. This particular almanac series was quite pro-Constitution in 1788, so very likely this picture was intended to mock the rebels by showing them in fancy uniforms and armed with swords, trappings beyond their presumed lowly means.
National Portrait Gallery, Smithsonian Institution/Art Resource, NY.

3,000 by paying them bounties provided by wealthy and fearful Boston merchants (and later repaid by the state).

In January 1787, the insurgents learned of the private army marching their way, and 1,500 of them moved swiftly to capture a federal armory in Springfield to gain weapons. But a militia band loyal to the state government beat them to the weapons facility and met their attack with gunfire; 4 rebels were killed and another 20 wounded. The final and bloodless encounter came at Petersham, where Bowdoin's army surprised the rebels on a freezing February morning and took 150 prisoners; the others fled into the woods. Shays took off for Canada and other leaders left the state, but more than 1,000 dissidents were rounded up and jailed.

In the end, 2 men were executed for rebellion; 16 more sentenced to hang were reprieved at the last moment on the gallows. Some 4,000 men gained leniency by confessing their misconduct and swearing an oath of allegiance to the state. A special Disqualification Act prohibited the penitent rebels from voting, holding public office, serving on juries, working as schoolmasters, or operating taverns for up to three years.

Shays's Rebellion caused leaders throughout the country to worry about the confederation's ability to handle civil disorder. Inflammatory Massachusetts newspapers wrote about bloody mob rule; perhaps, some feared, similar "combustibles" in other states were awaiting the spark that would set off a dreadful political conflagration. New York lawyer John Jay wrote to George Washington, "Our affairs seem to lead to some crisis, some revolution—something I cannot foresee or conjecture. I am uneasy and apprehensive; more so than during the war." Benjamin Franklin, in his eighties, shrewdly observed that in 1776, Americans had feared "an excess of power in the rulers" but now the problem was perhaps "a defect of obedience" in the subjects. Among such leaders, the sense of crisis in the confederation had greatly deepened.

▶**REVIEW**   Why did farmers in western Massachusetts revolt against the state legislature?

The United States Constitution

Shays's Rebellion provoked an odd mixture of fear and hope that the government under the Articles of Confederation was losing its grip on power. A small circle of Virginians decided to try one last time to augment the powers granted to the government by the Articles. Their call for a meeting to discuss trade regulation led, more quickly than they could have imagined in 1786, to a total reworking of the national government.

From Annapolis to Philadelphia

The Virginians took their lead from James Madison, now thirty-five and a member of the Virginia assembly. Madison convinced the confederation congress to allow a meeting of delegates at Annapolis, Maryland, in September 1786, to try again to revise the trade regulation powers of the Articles, but only five states participated. Like Madison, the dozen men who attended felt a foreboding of crisis, and they rescheduled the meeting for Philadelphia in May 1787. The congress reluctantly endorsed the Philadelphia meeting and limited its scope to "the sole and express purpose of revising the Articles of Confederation." But at least one representative at the Annapolis meeting had more ambitious plans. Alexander Hamilton of New York hoped the Philadelphia meeting would do whatever was necessary to strengthen the federal government. Hamilton got his wish, as the meeting soon turned into a constitutional convention.

Hamilton was, by nature, suited for such bold steps. The illegitimate son of a poor mother in the West Indies, he trained as a bookkeeper and prospered under the intellectual mentorship of a local minister. In 1773, the bright lad greatly impressed an American trader, who sent him to New York City for a college education. Hamilton soon got swept up in the military enthusiasm of 1776 and by 1777 had joined George Washington's staff, serving at the general's side through much of the Revolution. After the war, he studied law, married into a New York merchant family, and sat in the Continental Congress for two years. Despite his stigmatized and impoverished childhood, the aspiring Hamilton identified with the elite classes and their fear of democratic disorder.

The fifty-five men who assembled at Philadelphia in May 1787 were generally those who had already concluded that there were weaknesses in the Articles of Confederation. Few attended who were opposed to revising the Articles.

The Pennsylvania Statehouse

The constitutional convention assembled at the Pennsylvania statehouse during the summer of 1787. Despite the heat, the delegates nailed the windows shut to eliminate the chance of being heard by eavesdroppers, so intent were they on secrecy. The statehouse, built in the 1740s to house the colony's assembly, is now called Independence Hall, in honor of the signing of the Declaration of Independence there in 1776.
Historical Society of Pennsylvania.

Patrick Henry, author of the Virginia Resolves in 1765 and more recently state governor, refused to go to the convention, saying he "smelled a rat." Rhode Island refused to send delegates. Two New York representatives left in dismay in the middle of the convention, leaving Alexander Hamilton as the sole delegate from New York.

This gathering of white men included no **artisans** or day laborers or even farmers of middling wealth. Two-thirds of the delegates were lawyers. The majority had served in the confederation congress and knew its strengths and weaknesses; half had been officers in the Continental army. Seven men had been governors of their states and knew firsthand the frustrations of thwarted executive power. A few elder statesmen attended, such as Benjamin Franklin and George Washington, but on the whole, the delegates were young, like Madison and Hamilton.

The Virginia and New Jersey Plans

The convention worked in secrecy, so the men could freely explore alternatives without fear that their honest opinions would come back to haunt them. The Virginia delegation first laid out a fifteen-point plan for a complete restructuring of the government. This Virginia Plan was a total repudiation of the principle of a confederation of states. Largely the work of Madison, the plan set out a three-branch government composed of a two-chamber legislature, a powerful executive, and a judiciary. It practically eliminated the voices of the smaller states by pegging representation in both houses of the congress to population. The theory was that government operated directly on people, not on states. Among the breathtaking powers assigned to the congress were the rights to veto state legislation and to coerce states militarily to obey national laws. To prevent the congress from having absolute power, the executive and judiciary could jointly veto its actions.

In mid-June, a delegate from New Jersey, after caucusing with delegates from other small states, unveiled an alternative proposal. The New Jersey Plan, as it was called, maintained the existing single-house congress of the Articles of Confederation in which each state had one vote. Acknowledging the need for an executive, it created a plural presidency to be shared by three men elected by the congress from among its membership. Where it sharply departed from the existing government was in the sweeping powers it gave to the new congress: the right to tax, to regulate trade, and to use force on unruly state governments. In favoring national power over **states' rights**, it aligned itself with the Virginia Plan. But the New Jersey Plan retained the confederation principle that the national government was to be an assembly of states, not of people.

For two weeks, delegates debated the two plans, focusing on the key issue of representation. The small-state delegates conceded that one house in a two-house legislature could be apportioned by population, but they would never agree that both houses could be. Madison was equally vehement about bypassing represen-tation by state, which he viewed as the fundamental flaw in the Articles.

The debate seemed deadlocked, and for a while the convention was "on the verge of dissolution, scarce held together by the strength of a hair," according to one of the delegates. Only in mid-July did the so-called Great Compromise break the stalemate and produce the basic structural features of the emerging United States Constitution. Proponents of the competing plans agreed on a bicameral legislature. Representation in the lower house, the House of Represen-tatives, would be apportioned by population, and representation in the upper house, the Senate, would come from all the states equally. Instead of one vote per state in the upper house, as in the New Jersey Plan, the compromise provided two senators who voted independently.

Representation by population turned out to be an ambiguous concept once it was subjected to rigorous discussion. Who counted? Were slaves, for example, people or property? As people, they would add weight to the southern delega-tions in the House of Representatives, but as property they would add to the tax burdens of those states. What emerged was the compromise known as the three-fifths clause: All free persons plus "three-fifths of all other Persons" constituted the numerical base for the apportionment of representatives.

Using "all other Persons" as a substitute for "slaves" indicates the discomfort delegates felt in acknowledging in the Constitution the existence of slavery. The words *slave* and *slavery* appear nowhere in the document, but slavery figured in two other places besides the three-fifths clause. Trade regulation, for example, a power of the new House of Representatives, naturally included regulation of the slave trade. In euphemistic language, a compromise between southern and northern states specified that "the Migration or Importation of such Persons as any of the States now shall think proper to admit, shall not be prohibited by the Congress prior to the Year one thousand eight hundred and eight." A third provi-sion guaranteed the return of fugitive slaves: "No person, held to Service or Labour in one State, under the Laws thereof, escaping into another, shall, in Consequence of any Law or Regulation therein, be discharged from such Service or Labour but shall be delivered up on Claim of the party to whom such Service or Labour may be due." Slavery was nowhere named, but it was recognized, guaranteed, and thereby perpetuated by the U.S. Constitution.

Democracy versus Republicanism

The delegates in Philadelphia made a distinction between *democracy* and *republi-canism* new to American political vocabulary. Pure democracy was now taken to be a dangerous thing. As a Massachusetts delegate put it, "The evils we experi-ence flow from the excess of democracy." The delegates still favored republican institutions, but they created a government that gave direct voice to the people only in the House and that granted a check on that voice to the Senate, a body of men elected not by direct popular vote but by the state legislatures. Senators served for six years, with no limit on reelection; they were protected from the whims of democratic majorities, and their long terms fostered experience and maturity in office.

Similarly, the presidency evolved into a powerful office out of the reach of direct democracy. The delegates devised an electoral college whose only function was to elect the president and vice president. Each state's legislature would choose the electors, whose number was the sum of representatives and senators for the state, an interesting blending of the two principles of representation. The president thus would owe his office not to the Congress, the states, or the people, but to a temporary assemblage of distinguished citizens who could vote their own judgment on the candidates.

The framers had developed a far more complex form of federal government than that provided by the Articles of Confederation. To curb the excesses of democracy, they devised a government with limits and checks on all three branches of government. They set forth a powerful president who could veto Congress, but they gave Congress power to override presidential vetoes. They set up a national judiciary to settle disputes between states and citizens of different states. They separated branches of government not only by functions and by reciprocal checks but by deliberately basing the election of each branch on different universes of voters—voting citizens (the House), state legislators (the Senate), and the electoral college (the presidency).

The convention carefully listed the powers of the president and of Congress. The president could initiate policy, propose legislation, and veto acts of Congress; he could command the military and direct foreign policy; and he could appoint the entire judiciary, subject to Senate approval. Congress held the purse strings: the power to levy taxes, to regulate trade, and to coin money and control the currency. States were expressly forbidden to issue paper money. Two more powers of Congress—to "provide for the common defence and general Welfare" of the country and "to make all laws which shall be necessary and proper" for carrying out its powers—provided elastic language that came closest to Madison's wish to grant sweeping powers to the new government.

The Constitution was a product of lengthy debate and compromise; no one was entirely satisfied with every line. Madison himself, who soon became its staunchest defender, remained unsure that the most serious flaws of the Articles had been expunged. But when the final vote was taken at the Philadelphia convention in September 1787, only three dissenters refused to endorse the document. The thirty-nine who signed it (thirteen others had gone home early) no doubt wondered how to sell this plan, with its powerful executive and Congress and its deliberate limits on pure democracy, to the American public. The Constitution specified a mechanism for ratification that avoided the dilemma faced earlier by the confederation government: Nine states, not all thirteen, had to ratify it, and special ratifying conventions elected only for that purpose, not state legislatures, would make the crucial decision.

> ▶ REVIEW   Why did the government proposed by the constitutional convention employ multiple checks on each branch?

Ratification of the Constitution

Had a popular vote been taken on the Constitution in the fall of 1787, it would probably have been rejected. In the three most populous states—Virginia, Massachusetts, and New York—substantial majorities opposed a powerful new national government. North Carolina and Rhode Island refused to call ratifying conventions. Seven of the eight remaining states were easy victories for the Constitution, but securing the approval of the ninth proved difficult. Pro-Constitution forces, called Federalists, had to strategize very shrewdly to defeat anti-Constitution forces, called Antifederalists.

The Federalists

Proponents of the Constitution moved into action swiftly. To silence the criticism that they had gone beyond their charge (which indeed they had), they sent the document to the congress. The congress withheld explicit approval but resolved to send the Constitution to the states for their consideration. The pro-Constitution forces shrewdly secured another advantage by calling themselves "Federalists." By all logic, this label was more suitable for the backers of the confederation concept, because the Latin root of the word *federal* means "league." Their opponents became known as "Antifederalists," a label that made them sound defensive and negative, lacking a program of their own.

To gain momentum, the Federalists targeted the states most likely to ratify quickly. Delaware provided unanimous ratification by early December, before the Antifederalists had even begun to campaign. Pennsylvania, New Jersey, and Georgia followed within a month (Map 8.2). Delaware and New Jersey were small states surrounded by more powerful neighbors; a government that would regulate trade and set taxes according to population was an attractive proposition. Georgia sought the protection that a stronger national government would afford against hostile Indians and Spanish Florida to the south. "If a weak State with the Indians on its back and the Spaniards on its flank does not see the necessity of a General Government there must I think be wickedness or insanity in the way," said Federalist George Washington.

Another three easy victories came in Connecticut, Maryland, and South Carolina. As in Pennsylvania, merchants, lawyers, and urban artisans in general

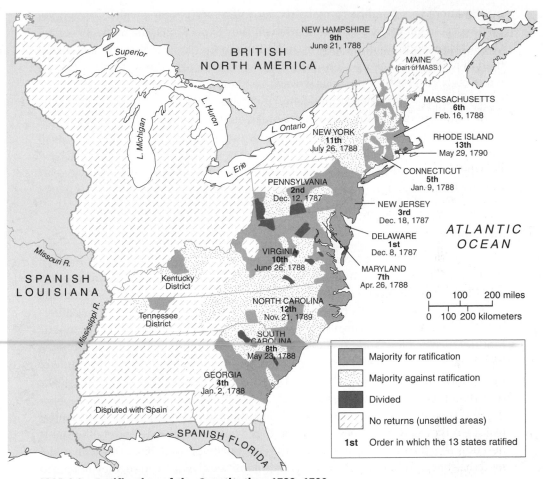

MAP 8.2   Ratification of the Constitution, 1788–1790
Populated areas cast votes for delegates to state ratification conventions. This map shows
Antifederalist strength generally concentrated in backcountry, noncoastal, and non-urban
areas, but with significant exceptions (for example, Rhode Island).

favored the new Constitution, as did large landowners and slaveholders. This
tendency for the established political elite to be Federalist enhanced the prospects
of victory, for Federalists already had power and influence disproportionate to
their number. Antifederalists in these states tended to be rural, western, and non-
commercial, men whose access to news was limited and whose participation in
state government was tenuous.

Massachusetts was the only early state that gave the Federalists difficulty.
The vote to select the ratification delegates decidedly favored the Antifederalists,
whose strength lay in the western areas of the state, home to Shays's Rebellion.
One rural delegate from Worcester County voiced widely shared suspicions:
"These lawyers and men of learning and money men that talk so finely, and gloss

over matters so smoothly, to make us poor illiterate people swallow down the pill, expect to get into Congress themselves; they expect to be the managers of the Constitution and get all the power and all the money into their own hands, and then they will swallow up all us little folks." Nevertheless, the Antifederalist lead was slowly eroded by a vigorous newspaper campaign. In the end, the Federalists won by a very slim margin and only with promises that amendments to the Constitution would be taken up in the first Congress.

By May 1788, eight states had ratified; only one more was needed. North Carolina and Rhode Island were hopeless for the Federalist cause, and New Hampshire seemed nearly as bleak. More worrisome was the failure to win over the largest and most important states, Virginia and New York.

The Antifederalists

The Antifederalists were a composite group, united mainly in their desire to block the Constitution. Although much Antifederalist strength came from backcountry areas long suspicious of eastern elites, many Antifederalist leaders came from the same social background as Federalist leaders; economic class alone did not differentiate them. Antifederalism also drew strength in states already on sure economic footing, such as New York, that could afford to remain independent. Probably the biggest appeal of antifederalism lay in the long-nurtured fear that distant power might infringe on people's liberties. The language of the earlier Revolutionary movement was not easily forgotten.

But by the time eight states had ratified, the Antifederalists faced a far harder task than they had once imagined. First, they were no longer defending the status quo now that the momentum lay with the Federalists. Second, it was difficult to defend the confederation government with its admitted flaws. Even so, they remained genuinely fearful that the new government would be too distant from the people and could thus become corrupt or tyrannical. "The difficulty, if not impracticability, of exercising the equal and equitable powers of government by a single legislature over an extent of territory that reaches from the Mississippi to the western lakes, and from them to the Atlantic ocean, is an insuperable objection to the adoption of the new system," wrote one articulate Antifederalist in a compelling and much-read political pamphlet by "A Columbia Patriot." The Columbia Patriot was the alias for Mercy Otis Warren, a Massachusetts woman whose father, brother, and husband had all been active leaders in the Revolutionary movement in Boston.

The new government was indeed distant. In the proposed House of Representatives, the only directly democratic element of the Constitution, one member represented some 30,000 people. How could that member really know or communicate with his whole constituency, the Antifederalists wondered. In contrast, one wrote, "the members of our state legislatures are annually elected—they are subject to instructions—they are chosen within small circles—they are sent but a small distance from their respective homes. Their conduct is constantly known to their constituents. They frequently see, and are seen, by the men whose servants they are."

The Antifederalists also worried that elected representatives would always be members of the elite. Such men "will be ignorant of the sentiments of the middling and much more of the lower class of citizens, strangers to their ability, unacquainted with their wants, difficulties, and distress," a Maryland man worried. None of this would be a problem under a confederation system, according to the Antifederalists, because real power would continue to reside in the state governments.

The Federalists generally agreed that the elite would be favored for election to the House of Representatives, not to mention the Senate and the presidency. That was precisely what they hoped. Federalists wanted power to flow to intelligent, virtuous, public-spirited leaders like themselves. They did not envision a government constituted of every class of people. "Fools and knaves have voice enough in government already," argued a New York Federalist, without being guaranteed representation in proportion to the total population of fools. Alexander Hamilton claimed that mechanics and laborers preferred to have their social betters represent them. The Antifederalists challenged the notion that any class could be sufficiently selfless to rule disinterestedly for others. One complained that "in reality, there will be no part of the people represented, but the rich. . . . It will literally be a government in the hands of the few to oppress and plunder the many."

Antifederalists fretted over many specific features of the Constitution. It prohibited state-issued paper money. It regulated the time and place of congressional elections, leading to fears that only one inconvenient polling place might be authorized, to disfranchise rural voters. The most widespread objection to the Constitution was its glaring omission of any guarantees of individual liberties in a bill of rights, like those contained in many state constitutions.

Despite Federalist campaigns in the large states, it was a small state—New Hampshire—that provided the decisive ninth vote for ratification, on June 21, 1788. Federalists there succeeded in getting the convention postponed from February to June and in the interim conducted an intense and successful lobbying effort on specific delegates.

The Big Holdouts: Virginia and New York

Four states still remained outside the new union, and a glance at a map demonstrated the necessity of pressing the Federalist case in the two largest, Virginia and New York (see Map 8.2). Although Virginia was home to Madison and Washington, an influential Antifederalist group led by Patrick Henry and George Mason made the outcome uncertain. The Federalists finally but barely won ratification by proposing twenty specific amendments that the new government would promise to consider.

New York voters tilted toward antifederalism out of a sense that a state so large and powerful need not relinquish so much authority to the new federal government. But New York was also home to some of the most persuasive Federalists. Starting in October 1787, Alexander Hamilton collaborated with James Madison and New York lawyer John Jay on a series of eighty-five essays on the political philosophy of the new Constitution, published in New York newspapers and later republished as *The Federalist Papers*. The essays brilliantly set out the failures of the Articles of Confederation and offered an analysis of the complex nature of federalism. In one of the most compelling essays, number 10, Madison challenged the Antifederalists' heartfelt conviction that republican government had to be small-scale. Madison argued that a large and diverse population was itself a guarantee of liberty. In a national government, no single faction could ever be large enough to subvert the freedom of other groups. "Extend the sphere, and you take in a greater variety of parties and interests; you make it less probable that a majority of the whole will have a common motive to invade the rights of other citizens," Madison asserted. He called it "a republican remedy for the diseases most incident to republican government."

At New York's ratifying convention, Antifederalists predominated, but impassioned debate and lobbying—plus the dramatic news of Virginia's ratification—finally tipped the balance to the Federalists. Still, the Antifederalists' approval of the document was delivered with a list of twenty-four individual rights they hoped would be protected and thirty-three structural changes they hoped to see in the Constitution. New York's ratification ensured the solidity and legitimacy of the new government. It took another year and a half for Antifederalists in North Carolina to come around. Fiercely independent Rhode Island held out until May 1790, and even then it ratified by only a two-vote margin.

In less than twelve months, the U.S. Constitution was both written and ratified. (See appendix I, page A-9.) An amazingly short time by twenty-first-century standards, it is even more remarkable for the late eighteenth century, with its horse-powered transportation and hand-printed communications. The Federalists had faced a formidable task, but by building momentum and assuring consideration of a **Bill of Rights**, they did indeed carry the day.

▶**REVIEW**   Why did Antifederalists oppose the Constitution?

Conclusion: The "Republican Remedy"

Thus ended one of the most intellectually tumultuous and creative periods in American history. American leaders experimented with ideas and drew up plans to embody their evolving and conflicting notions of how a society and a government ought to be formulated. There was widespread agreement that government should derive its power and authority from the people, but a narrow vision of "the people" prevailed. With limited exceptions—New Jersey, for example—free blacks and women were excluded from government. Indians, even when dubiously called "members" of a state, were outside the sovereign people authorizing government, as were all slaves. Even taking free white males as "the people," men disagreed fiercely over the degree of democracy—the amount of direct control of government by the people—that would be workable in American society.

The period began in 1775 with a confederation government that could barely be ratified because of its requirement of unanimity, but there was no reaching unanimity on the western lands, an impost, or the proper way to respond to unfair taxation in a republican state. The new Constitution offered a different approach to these problems by loosening the grip of impossible unanimity and by embracing the ideas of a heterogeneous public life and a carefully balanced government that together would prevent any one part of the public from tyrannizing another. The genius of James Madison was to anticipate that diversity of opinion was not only an unavoidable reality but a hidden strength of the new society beginning to take shape. This is what he meant in his tenth *Federalist* essay when he spoke of the "republican remedy" for the troubles most likely to befall a government where the people are the source of authority.

Despite Madison's optimism, political differences remained keen and worrisome to many. The Federalists still hoped for a society in which leaders of exceptional wisdom would discern the best path for public policy. They looked backward to a society of hierarchy, rank, and benevolent rule by an aristocracy of talent, but they created a government with forward-looking **checks and balances** as a guard against corruption, which they figured would most likely emanate from the people. The Antifederalists also looked backward, but to an old order of small-scale direct democracy and local control, where virtuous people kept a close eye on potentially corruptible rulers. Antifederalists feared a national government led by distant, self-interested leaders who needed to be held in check. In the 1790s, these two conceptions of republicanism and of leadership would be tested in real life.

REVIEWING THE CHAPTER

Use the questions and timeline to review and strengthen your understanding of the chapter.

REVIEW QUESTIONS

1. Why was the confederation government's authority so limited? (pp. 213–17)

2. How did states determine who would be allowed to vote? (pp. 217–23)

3. Why did farmers in western Massachusetts revolt against the state legislature? (pp. 223–31)

4. Why did the government proposed by the constitutional convention employ multiple checks on each branch? (pp. 231–36)

5. Why did Antifederalists oppose the Constitution? (pp. 236–40)

MAKING CONNECTIONS

1. Leaders in the new nation held that voting should be restricted to citizens who possessed independence of mind. Why? What did they mean by independence of mind? How did this principle limit voters in the early Republic?

2. Why did many Revolutionary leaders shaping the government of the new nation begin to find the principle of democracy troubling? How did they attempt to balance democracy with other concerns in the new government?

3. Twenty-first-century Americans see a profound tension between the Revolutionary ideals of liberty and equality and the persistence of American slavery. Did Americans in the late eighteenth century see a tension? In your answer, be sure to discuss factors that might have shaped varied responses, such as region, race, and class.

4. The Northwest Territory was the confederation's greatest asset. Discuss the proposals to manage settlement of the new territory. How did they shape the nation's expansion? Which proposals succeeded and which failed?

TIMELINE

1775	• Second Continental Congress begins to meet.	1784	• Gradual emancipation laws passed in Rhode Island and Connecticut. • Treaty of Fort Stanwix.
1776	• Virginia adopts state bill of rights.	1786	• Virginia adopts Statute of Religious Freedom.
1777	• Articles of Confederation sent to states.		• Shays's Rebellion begins.
1778	• State constitutions completed.		
1780	• Pennsylvania institutes gradual emancipation.	1787	• Shays's Rebellion crushed. • Northwest Ordinance. • Delaware provides manumission law.
1781	• Articles of Confederation ratified. • Creation of executive departments. • Bank of North America chartered. • Slaves Mum Bett and Quok Walker successfully sue for freedom in Massachusetts.		• Constitutional convention meets in Philadelphia.
		1788	• U.S. Constitution ratified.
		1789	• Slavery ended in Massachusetts by judicial decision.
1782	• Virginia relaxes state manumission law.	1790	• Maryland provides manumission law.
1783	• Treaty of Paris signed, ending the Revolutionary War. • Massachusetts extends suffrage to taxpaying free blacks.	1799	• Gradual emancipation law passed in New York.
		1804	• Gradual emancipation law passed in New Jersey.

▶ **For an online bibliography, practice quizzes, Web sites, images, and documents related to this chapter,** see the Book Companion Site at **bedfordstmartins.com/roark.**

▶ **For firsthand accounts of this period,** see Chapter 8 in Michael Johnson, ed., *Reading the American Past,* Fourth Edition.

9
CHAPTER

The New Nation Takes Form

1789–1800

ALEXANDER HAMILTON was just thirty-four years old when President George Washington appointed him secretary of the treasury, giving him control over all economic and domestic policy in the new nation. Young and brilliant, Hamilton had been called a "colossus" for his gigantic mental abilities by Thomas Jefferson, the new secretary of state. But he also proved to be the most polarizing figure of the 1790s, leading to the collapse of the tight political alliance that had unified Federalists in the 1780s.

Through force of personality, Hamilton overcame a disadvantaged childhood on the small West Indies island of Nevis. His parents never married. His father, the impoverished fourth son of a Scottish lord, disappeared when Alexander was nine, and his mother, a woman with a checkered past, died two years later. Jeered as a "whore child," Hamilton developed a fierce ambition to make good. After serving an apprenticeship to a merchant, he made his way to the mainland colony of New York. In a mere six months, he sufficiently mastered Greek and Latin to gain admission to King's College (now Columbia University), from which he graduated in three years. Articles he wrote for a New York newspaper brought him to the attention of General Washington, who made the twenty-year-old an officer in the Continental army and hired him as a close aide. After the war, Hamilton practiced law in New York and then played a central role at the constitutional convention in Philadelphia. His astute *Federalist* essays—more than fifty drafted in just six months—helped secure the ratification of the Constitution.

243

Alexander Hamilton, by John Trumbull
Hamilton was confident, handsome, audacious, brilliant, and very hard-working. Ever slender, in marked contrast to the more corpulent leaders of his day, he posed for this portrait in 1792, at the age of thirty-seven and at the height of his power.
Yale University Art Gallery.

Hamilton's private life was similarly upwardly mobile. Handsome and now well connected, he married Betsey Schuyler, whose father was one of the richest men in New York. He had a magnetic personality that attracted both men and women eager to experience his charm, which was on full display at dinner parties and social gatherings. Late-night events, however, never interfered with his prodigious capacity for work.

As secretary of the treasury, Hamilton quickly moved into high gear. "If a Government appears to be confident of its own powers, it is the surest way to inspire the same confidence in others," he once remarked. He immediately secured big loans from two banks and started to track tax revenues from trade, the government's main source of income. Most trade was with Britain, so Hamilton sought ways to protect Anglo-American relations. Next he tackled the country's unpaid Revolutionary War debt, writing in three months a forty-thousand-word report for Congress laying out a plan that both funded the debt and pumped millions of dollars into the U.S. economy. In short order, he drafted a bold plan for a national banking system to enhance and control the money supply. Finally, he turned his attention to industrial development, writing a richly detailed analysis of ways to promote manufacturing via government subsidies and tariff policies.

Hamilton was both visionary and practical. No one could doubt that he was a gifted man with remarkable political intuitions. It is strange, then, that this magnetic man made enemies in the 1790s, as the "Founding Fathers" of the Revolution and Constitution became competitors and even bitter rivals. To some extent, jealousy over Hamilton's talents and his access to President Washington explains the chill, but serious disagreement about political philosophy drove the divisions deeper.

Personalities clashed. Hamilton's charm no longer worked with James Madison, now a representative in Congress and at odds with Hamilton on all his plans. His charm had never worked with John Adams, the new vice president, who privately called him "the bastard brat of a Scotch pedlar," who was motivated by "disappointed Ambition and unbridled malice and revenge." Abigail Adams thought Hamilton a second Napoleon Bonaparte, an uncomplimentary reference to the belligerent leader of war-torn France. Years later, when asked why he deserted Hamilton, Madison replied, "Colonel Hamilton deserted me."

Hamilton assumed that government was safest when in the hands of "the rich, the wise, and the good"—in other words, America's commercial elite. For Hamilton, economic and political power naturally belonged together, creating an energetic force for economic growth. In contrast, Jefferson and Madison trusted most those whose livelihood was tied to the land. Agrarian values ran deep with them, and they were suspicious of get-rich-quick speculators, financiers, and manufacturing development. Differing views of European powers also loomed large in the rivalries. Whereas Hamilton was an unabashed admirer of everything British, Jefferson was enchanted by France, where he had lived in the 1780s. These loyalties governed foreign relations in the late 1790s, when the United States was in a war or near war with both of these overseas rivals.

The personal and political antagonisms of this first generation of American leaders left their mark on the young country. No one was prepared for the intense and passionate polarization that emerged over economic and foreign policy. The disagreements were articulated around particular events and policies: taxation and the public debt, a new farmers' rebellion in a western region, policies favoring commercial development, a treaty with Britain, a rebellion in Haiti, and the Quasi-War with France that led to severe strictures on ideas of sedition and free speech. But at their heart, these disagreements arose out of opposing ideological stances on the value of **democracy**, the nature of leadership, and the limits of federal power. About the only major policy development that did not replicate or intensify these antagonisms among political leaders was Indian policy in the new republic. Out in war-torn western Ohio, three forts named for Washington, Hamilton, and Jefferson symbolized the government's unified stance on Indians.

By 1800, the opposing politics ripening between Hamiltonian and Jeffersonian politicians would begin to crystallize into political parties, the Federalists and the Republicans. To the men of that day, this was an unhappy development.

The Search for Stability

After the struggles and discord of the 1780s, the most urgent task in establishing the new government under the Constitution was to secure stability. Leaders sought ways to heal old divisions and maximize unity, and the first presidential election offered the means to do that in the person of George Washington, who enjoyed widespread veneration. People trusted him to exercise the untested and perhaps elastic powers of the presidency, and his precedent-setting decisions would have a decisive impact on the success of the enterprise.

Congress had important work as well in initiating the new government. Many Antifederalists had insisted on changing the new Constitution to include a **Bill of Rights**, and Federalists now agreed. And beyond politics, cultural changes were mobilized to promote stability in the fledgling government. One important shift involved rethinking gender. Cultural commentators began to argue for the importance of a private virtue in women that would bolster the public virtue of male citizens. Despite the fact that women could not vote, **republicanism** was forcing a rethinking of women's relation to the state.

Washington Inaugurates the Government

The election of George Washington in February 1789 was quick work, the tallying of the sixty-nine unanimous votes by the electoral college a mere formality. Everyone's first choice, Washington perfectly embodied the republican ideal of disinterested, public-spirited leadership. Indeed, he cultivated that image through astute ceremonies such as the dramatic surrender of his sword to the Continental Congress at the end of the war, symbolizing the subservience of military power to the law.

With attractive modesty, Washington at first feigned reluctance to accept the presidency. He wrote his wartime confidant, Alexander Hamilton, for advice: Could he hesitate to accept but then ultimately take the office without seeming to be too ambitious? Hamilton replied that he must accept the office; public sentiment was universally for it. "No other man," Hamilton urged him, "can sufficiently unite the public opinion or can give the requisite weight to the office in the commencement of the government." The unanimous ballot for Washington supported Hamilton's claim. John Adams of Massachusetts, the vice presidential candidate, won only thirty-four votes, with the other thirty-five votes split among a variety of candidates, a result that deeply wounded Adams's pride.

Once in office, Washington calculated his moves, knowing that every step set a precedent and any misstep could be dangerous for the fragile government. How kingly should a president be? Congress debated a range of titles, such as "His Highness, the President of the United States of America and Protector of Their Liberties" and "His Majesty, the President"; Washington was known to favor "His High Mightiness." (Opponents of such lofty titles joked that the vice president should be called "His Rotundity" or "Duke of Braintree," Adams's home village in Massachusetts.) But in the end, republican simplicity prevailed. The final title was simply "President of the United States of America," and the established form of address became "Mr. President," a subdued yet dignified title in a society where only property-owning adult white males could presume to be called "Mister."

Washington's genius in establishing the presidency lay in his capacity for implanting his own reputation for integrity into the office itself. He was not a brilliant thinker or a shrewd political strategist. He was not even a particularly congenial man. In the political language of the day, he was *virtuous*, meaning that he took pains to elevate the public good over private interest and projected honesty and honor over ambition. He remained aloof, resolute, and dignified, to the point of appearing wooden at times. He encouraged pomp and ceremony to create respect for the office, traveling with six sleekly oiled white horses to pull his coach, hosting formal balls, and surrounding himself with uniformed servants. He even held weekly "levees," as European monarchs did. At these hourlong audiences granted to distinguished visitors (including women), Washington appeared attired in black velvet, with a feathered hat and a polished sword. The president and his guests bowed, avoiding the egalitarian familiarity of a handshake. But he always managed, perhaps just barely, to avoid the extreme of royal splendor.

Washington chose talented and experienced men to preside over the newly created Departments of War, Treasury, and State. For the Department of War, Washington chose General Henry Knox, former secretary of war in the confederation government. For the Treasury—an especially tough job in view of revenue conflicts during the Confederation (see chapter 8)—the president picked Alexander Hamilton, known for his general brilliance and financial astuteness. To lead the Department of State, the foreign policy arm of the executive branch, Washington chose Thomas Jefferson, a master of the intricacy of diplomatic relations and the current minister to France. For attorney general, Washington picked Edmund Randolph, a Virginian who had attended the constitutional convention but had turned Antifederalist during ratification. For chief justice of the Supreme Court, Washington designated John Jay, a New York lawyer who, along with Madison and Hamilton, had vigorously defended the Constitution in *The Federalist Papers*.

Washington liked and trusted all these men, and by 1793, in his second term, he was meeting regularly with them, thereby establishing the precedent of a presidential cabinet. (Vice President John Adams was not included; his only official duty, to preside over the Senate, he found "a punishment" because he could not participate in legislative debates. To his wife he complained, "My country has in its wisdom contrived for me the most insignificant office.") Yet deep philosophical differences separated key appointees. No one anticipated that two decades of party turbulence would emerge from the brilliant but explosive mix of Washington's first cabinet.

The Bill of Rights

An early order of business in the First Congress was the passage of a Bill of Rights. Seven states had ratified the Constitution on the condition that guarantees of individual liberties and limitations to federal power be swiftly incorporated.

The Federalists of 1787 had thought an enumeration of rights unnecessary, but in 1789 Congressman James Madison understood that healing the divisions of the 1780s was of prime importance. "It will be a desirable thing to extinguish from the bosom of every member of the community, any apprehensions that there are those among his countrymen who wish to deprive them of the liberty for which they valiantly fought and honorably bled," Madison said.

Madison pulled much of his wording of rights directly from various state constitutions with bills of rights. He enumerated guarantees of freedom of speech, press, and religion; the right to petition and assemble; and the right to be free from unwarranted searches and seizures. One amendment asserted the right to keep and bear arms in support of a "well-regulated militia," to which Madison added, "but no person religiously scrupulous of bearing arms, shall be compelled to render military service in person." That provision for what a later century would call "conscientious objector" status failed to gain acceptance in Congress.

In September 1789, Congress approved a set of twelve amendments and sent them to the states for approval; ten were eventually ratified. The First through Eighth Amendments dealt with individual liberties, and the Ninth and Tenth concerned the boundary between federal and state authority. (See the amendments to the U.S. Constitution in appendix I, page A-17.) One proposal that failed to pass suggested a formula for fine-tuning the ratio of representation as population grew; the other required that any congressional pay raise voted in would not take effect until after the next election (not until 1992 did this amendment—the Twenty-seventh—pass). The process of state ratification took another two years, but there was no serious doubt about the outcome.

Still, not everyone was entirely satisfied. State ratifying conventions had submitted some eighty proposed amendments. Congress never considered proposals to change structural features of the new government, and Madison had no intention of reopening debates about the length of the president's term or the power to levy excise taxes.

Significantly, no one complained about one striking omission in the Bill of Rights: the right to vote. Only much later was voting seen as a fundamental **liberty** requiring protection by constitutional amendment—indeed, by four amendments. The Constitution deliberately left the definition of voters to the states because of the existing wide variation in local voting practices. Most of these practices were based on property qualifications, but some touched on religion and, in one unusual case (New Jersey), on sex and race (see chapter 8, page 220).

The Republican Wife and Mother

The exclusion of women from political activity did not mean they had no civic role or responsibility. A flood of periodical articles in the 1790s by both male and female writers reevaluated courtship, marriage, and motherhood in light of republican ideals. Tyrannical power in the ruler, whether king or husband, was now

Woman's Rights in the
***Lady's Magazine*, 1792**
This frontispiece appeared in the first volume of the Philadelphia periodical the *Lady's Magazine and Repository of Entertaining Knowledge*, published in December 1792. The caption identified the kneeling figure as "the Genius of the *Lady's Magazine*." She is accompanied by "the Genius of Emulation," carrying a trumpet and a laurel wreath. (*Genius* here meant a spirit; *emulation* meant ambition to excel. Thus, the genius of emulation was the spirit of ambition—women's ambition in this case.) The spirit representing the *Lady's Magazine* kneels before Liberty, identified by her liberty cap on a pole, and presents a paper titled "Rights of Woman."
Library Company of Philadelphia.

FRONTISPIECE.

Thackara & Vallance sculp.

Publish'd at Philad.ª *Dec.ʳ 1.ˢᵗ 1792.*

declared a thing of the past. Affection, not duty, bound wives to their husbands and citizens to their government. In republican marriages, the writers claimed, women had the capacity to reform the morals and manners of men. One male author promised women that "the solidity and stability of the liberties of your country rest with you; since Liberty is never sure, 'till Virtue reigns triumphant. . . . While you thus keep our country virtuous, you maintain its independence."

Until the 1790s, public virtue was strictly a masculine quality. But another sort of virtue enlarged in importance: sexual chastity, a private asset prized as a feminine quality. Essayists of the 1790s explicitly advised young women to use sexual virtue to increase public virtue in men. "Love and courtship . . . invest a lady with more authority than in any other situation that falls to the lot of human beings," one male essayist proclaimed. If women spurned selfish suitors, they could promote good morals more than any social institution could, essayists promised.

Republican ideals also cast motherhood in a new light. Throughout the 1790s, advocates for female education, still a controversial proposition, argued that education would produce better mothers, who in turn would produce better citizens. Benjamin Rush, a Pennsylvania physician and educator, called for female education because "our ladies should be qualified . . . in instructing their sons in the principles of liberty and government." A series of published essays by Judith Sargent Murray of Massachusetts favored education that would remake women into self-confident, rational beings, poised to become the equals of men. Her first essay, published in 1790, was boldly titled "On the Equality of the Sexes." A subsequent essay on education asserted that educated women "will accustom themselves to reflection; they will investigate accurately, and reason will point their conclusion; Yet they will not be assuming; the characteristic trait [sweetness] will still remain." Even Murray had to dress her advanced ideas in the cloak of republican motherhood, justifying female education in the context of family duty.

Although women's obligations as wives and mothers were now infused with political meaning, traditional gender relations remained unaltered. The analogy between marriage and civil society worked precisely because of the self-subordination inherent in the term *virtue*. Men should put the public good first, before selfish desires, just as women must put their husbands and families first, before themselves. Women might gain literacy and knowledge, but only in the service of improved domestic duty. In Federalist America, wives and citizens alike should feel affection for and trust in their rulers; neither should ever rebel.

▶ **REVIEW**   How did political leaders in the 1790s attempt to overcome the divisions of the 1780s?

Hamilton's Economic Policies

The new government had the lucky break to be launched in relatively flush economic times. Compared to the severe financial instability of the 1780s, the 1790s brimmed with opportunity and prosperity, as seen in increased agricultural trade and improvements in transportation and banking. In 1790, the federal government moved from New York City to Philadelphia, a more central location with a substantial mercantile class. There, Alexander Hamilton, secretary of the treasury, embarked on his innovative plan to solidify the government's economic base. But controversy arose at every turn. Hamilton's plan to combine the large national debt, unpaid and unfunded, with unpaid state debts produced an early crisis in the First Congress. And his plan to raise revenues via taxation brought on the young country's first domestic conflict, the Whiskey Rebellion.

Agriculture, Transportation, and Banking

Dramatic increases in international grain prices motivated American farmers to boost agricultural production for the export trade. Europe's rising population needed grain, and the French Revolutionary and Napoleonic Wars that engulfed Europe for a dozen years after 1793 severely compromised production there. From the Connecticut River valley to the Chesapeake, farmers planted more wheat, generating new jobs for millers, coopers, dockworkers, and ship and wagon builders.

Cotton production also underwent a boom, spurred by market demand and a mechanical invention. Limited amounts of smooth-seed cotton had long been grown in the coastal areas of the South, but this variety of cotton did not prosper in the drier, inland regions. Green-seed cotton grew well inland, but its rough seeds stuck to the cotton fibers and were difficult to remove. In 1793, Yale graduate Eli Whitney visited Georgia and devised a machine called a gin that separated out the seeds. Cotton production soared—from 138,000 pounds in 1782 to 35 million in 1800—with the cleaned cotton shipped to English factories to be made into textiles.

A surge of road building also stimulated the economy. Before 1790, a series of bumpy post roads ran from Maine to Georgia, but with the establishment of the U.S. Post Office in 1792, six times as many miles of roads were quickly constructed to facilitate the transport of mail. Privately chartered companies also built roads. The first toll road in the nation was the Lancaster Turnpike of 1794, connecting Philadelphia with Lancaster, Pennsylvania. Another turnpike linked Boston with Albany, New York. Farther inland, a major road extended southwest down the Shenandoah Valley, while another joined Richmond, Virginia, with the Tennessee towns of Knoxville and Nashville.

By 1800, a dense network of dirt, gravel, or plank roadways connected cities and towns in southern New England and the Middle Atlantic states, spurring commercial stage companies to regularize and speed up passenger traffic. A trip from New York to Boston took four days; from New York to Philadelphia, less than two. In 1790, Boston had only three stagecoach companies; by 1800, there were twenty-four. Transport of goods by road was still expensive per mile compared to water transport on navigable rivers or along the coast, but at least it was possible.

A third development signaling economic resurgence was the growth of commercial banking. During the 1790s, the number of banks nationwide multiplied tenfold, from three to twenty-nine in 1800. Banks drew in money chiefly through the sale of stock. They then made loans in the form of banknotes, paper currency backed by the gold and silver that stockholders paid in. Because banks issued two or three times as much money in banknotes as they held in **hard money**, they were creating new money for the economy.

The U.S. population expanded along with economic development, propelled by large average family size and better than adequate food and land resources. As measured by the first two federal censuses, in 1790 and 1800, population grew from 3.9 million to 5.3 million, an increase of 35 percent.

The Return for SOUTH CAROLINA having been made since the foregoing Schedule was originally printed, the whole Enumeration is here given complete, except for the N. Western Territory, of which no Return has yet been published.

DISTICTS	Free white Males of 16 years and upwards, including heads of families.	Free white Males under sixteen years.	Free white Females, including heads of families.	All other free persons.	Slaves.	Total.
Vermont	22435	22328	40505	255	16	85539
N. Hampshire	36086	34851	70160	630	158	141885 ·
Maine	24384	24748	46870	538	NONE	96540
Massachusetts	95453	87289	190582	5463	NONE	378787
Rhode Island	16019	15799	32652	3407	948	68825
Connecticut	60523	54403	117448	2808	2764	237946
New York	83700	78122	152320	4654	21324	340120
New Jersey	45251	41416	83287	2762	11423	184139
Pennsylvania	110788	106948	206363	6537	3737	434373
Delaware	11783	12143	22384	3899	8887	59094
Maryland	55915	51339	101395	8043	103036	319728
Virginia	110936	116135	215046	12866	292627	747610
Kentucky	15154	17057	28922	114	12430	73677
N. Carolina	69988	77506	140710	4975	100572	393751
S. Carolina	35576	37722	66880	1801	107094	249073
Georgia	13103	14044	25739	398	29264	82548
	807094	791850	1541263	59150	694280	3893635

Total number of Inhabitants of the United States exclusive of S. Western and N. Territory.	Free white Males of 21 years and upwds.	Free Males under 21 years of age.	Free white Females.	All other Persons.	Slaves.	Total
S. W. territory	6271	10277	15365	361	3417	35691
N. Ditto	—	—	—	—	—	—

1790 Census Page

This page shows the results of the first federal census in 1790, mandated by the U.S. Constitution as the means by which representation in Congress and taxation on the states would be determined. Notice the five classifications: free white males age sixteen or older, free white males under age sixteen, free white females, all other free persons, and slaves. Because the Constitution considered slaves as three-fifths of a person, slaves were counted separately. Separating white males into two age groups provided a measure of military strength.

U.S. Census Bureau.

The Public Debt and Taxes

The upturn in the economy, plus the new taxation powers of the government, suggested that the government might soon repay its wartime debt, amounting to more than $52 million owed to foreign and domestic creditors. Much of the debt originated when the Continental Congress needed supplies and manpower but had no independent source of revenue. Soldiers paid in government IOUs often sold them for as little as 15 percent of their face value, reflecting the widespread belief that the confederation government could never make good on them.

Treasury Secretary Hamilton attacked the debt problem in his *Report on Public Credit* in January 1790. He recommended that the debt be funded—but not repaid immediately—at full value. This meant that old certificates of debt would be rolled over into new bonds, which would earn interest until they were retired several years later. There would still be a public debt, but it would be secure, supported by citizens' presumed confidence in the new government. The bonds would circulate as owners bought and sold them, in effect injecting millions of dollars of new money into the economy. "A national debt if not excessive will be to us a national blessing; it will be a powerfull cement of our union," Hamilton wrote to a financier. The holders of the national debt would be investors in the country, men with a direct financial stake in the success of the new government. The debt was the "price of liberty," he further argued, and had to be honored, not repudiated. But not paid off either: Hamilton's goal was to make the new country creditworthy, not debt-free.

Funding the debt in full was controversial mainly because a large part of the old debt had been bought up cheaply by speculators in the late 1780s, and Hamilton's report touched off another round of turbulent speculation. (Hamilton himself held no certificates; he was careful to divest himself of anything that posed a conflict of interest. However, his father-in-law had certificates with a face value of $60,000.) Philadelphia and New York speculators sent agents deep into backcountry regions looking for certificates of debt whose unwary owners were ignorant about the proposed face-value funding.

Hamilton compounded controversy with a second breathtaking proposal: to add to the federal debt another $25 million that some state governments still owed to individuals. During the war, all the states had obtained supplies by issuing IOUs to farmers, merchants, and moneylenders. Some states, such as Virginia and New York, had paid off these debts entirely. Others, such as Massachusetts, had partially paid them off through heavy taxation of the people. About half the states had made little headway. Hamilton called for the federal government to assume these state debts and combine them with the federal debt, in effect consolidating federal power over the states. This large-scale debt consolidation—called *assumption* at the time—struck critics as expensive, unnecessary, unfair, and, worse, a power grab by the new government to subordinate the states.

Congressman James Madison strenuously objected to putting windfall profits in the pockets of speculators. Up to this point, he and Hamilton had been friends, but they broke over this issue of "discrimination"—of whether or not to discriminate between original and later debt holders. Madison proposed a complex scheme to pay both the original holders of the federal debt and the speculators, each at fair fractions of the face value. Hamilton countered that tracking the history of traded certificates would be impossible. When the vote on discrimination was tallied, Madison lost by a vote of 36 to 13. Madison also strongly objected to assumption of all the states' debts. His Virginia constituents had responsibly paid down their state debt, but now they would be taxed to pay the debts of other states. Furthermore, a large debt was dangerous, Madison warned, especially because it would lead to high taxation. Secretary of State Jefferson also was fearful of Hamilton's proposals. "No man is more ardently intent to see the public debt soon and sacredly paid off than I am. This exactly marks the difference between Colonel Hamilton's views and mine, that I would wish the debt paid tomorrow; he wishes it never to be paid, but always to be a thing where with to corrupt and manage the legislature."

A solution to this impasse over assumption arrived when Jefferson invited Hamilton and Madison to dinner. Good food evidently softened their animosity;

Hamilton secured the reluctant Madison's promise to restrain his opposition. In return, Hamilton pledged to back efforts to locate the nation's new capital city in the South, along the Potomac River, an outcome that was sure to please Virginians. In early July, Congress voted for the Potomac site, and in late July, Congress passed the debt package, assumption and all.

The First Bank of the United States and the *Report on Manufactures*

The second and third major elements of Hamilton's economic plan were his proposal to create a national Bank of the United States and his program to encourage domestic manufacturing. Arguing that banks were the "nurseries of national wealth," Hamilton modeled his bank plan on European central banks, such as the Bank of England, a private corporation that used its government's money to invigorate the British economy. According to Hamilton's bold plan, the central bank was to be capitalized at $10 million, a sum larger than all the hard money in the entire nation. The federal government would hold 20 percent of the bank's stock, making the bank in effect the government's fiscal agent, holding its revenues derived from import duties, land sales, and various other taxes. The other 80 percent of the bank's capital would come from private investors, who could buy stock in the bank with either hard money (silver or gold) or federal securities. Because of its size and the privilege of being the only national bank, the central bank would help stabilize the economy by exerting prudent control over credit, interest rates, and the value of the currency. The bank had twenty-five directors, five appointed by the government and the other twenty chosen from the bank's stockholders, sure to be merchants from the world of high finance.

Concerned that a few rich bankers might have undue influence over the economy, Madison tried but failed to stop the plan in Congress; it passed by a vote of 39 to 20 in the House, with the principal division one of North versus South. The Senate passed it easily, so bank opponents next looked to the president to veto it. Secretary of State Jefferson advised President Washington that the Constitution did not permit Congress to charter banks. Hamilton, however, pointed out that the Constitution gave Congress specific powers to regulate commerce and a broad right "to make all laws which shall be necessary and proper for carrying into execution the foregoing powers." Washington sided with Hamilton and signed the Bank of the United States into law in February 1791, with a charter allowing it to operate for twenty years.

When the bank's privately held stock went on sale in Philadelphia, Boston, and New York City in July, it sold out in a few hours, touching off an immediate mania of speculation in resale that lasted for more than a month and drew in many hundreds of urban merchants and artisans. A discouraged Madison reported that in New York, "the Coffee House is an eternal buzz with the gamblers," some of them self-interested congressmen intent on "public plunder."

Stock prices shot upward, then crashed in mid-August. Hamilton shrewdly managed to cushion the crash to an extent, but Jefferson worried about the risk to morality inherent in gambling in stocks: "The spirit of gaming, once it has seized a subject, is incurable. The tailor who has made thousands in one day, tho' he has lost them the next, can never again be content with the slow and moderate earnings of his needle."

The third key component of Hamilton's plan was issued in December 1791 in the *Report on Manufactures*, a proposal to encourage the production of American-made goods and thus make the country less reliant on European imports, a dependence that had proved crippling during the Revolution. Domestic manufacturing was in its infancy, and Hamilton aimed to mobilize the new powers of the federal government to grant subsidies to manufacturers and to impose moderate tariffs on those same products from overseas. This would protect the nascent industries at home and give them extra incentive to get established. Hamilton's plan targeted manufacturing of iron goods, arms and ammunition, coal, textiles, wood products, and glass. Among the blessings of manufacturing, he counted the new employment opportunities that would open to children and unmarried young women, who he felt were underutilized in agricultural societies. The *Report on Manufactures*, however, was never approved by Congress, and indeed never even voted on. Many confirmed agriculturalists in Congress remained cautious about endorsing manufacturing, fearing that it would prove to be a curse rather than a blessing. Madison and Jefferson in particular were deeply alarmed by the prospect of stretching the "general welfare" clause of the Constitution to include public subsidies to private businesses.

The Whiskey Rebellion

Hamilton's plan to restore public credit required new taxation to pay the interest on the large national debt, swollen to some $77 million. Hamilton did not propose a general increase in import duties, in deference to the merchant class, nor did he propose land taxes, which would have fallen hardest on the nation's wealthiest landowners. Instead, he convinced Congress in 1791 to pass a 25 percent excise tax on whiskey, to be paid by farmers when they brought their grain to the distillery, then passed on to individual whiskey consumers in the form of higher prices. Members of Congress from eastern areas favored the tax—especially those from New England, where the favorite drink was rum. A New Hampshire representative cheerfully observed that the country would be "drinking down the national debt," an idea he evidently found acceptable. Virginia representative James Madison took a different but approving view of the tax, which he hoped might promote "sobriety and thereby prevent disease and untimely deaths."

Not surprisingly, the new excise tax proved unpopular with cash-short grain farmers in the western regions and whiskey drinkers everywhere. In 1791, farmers in the western parts of Pennsylvania, Virginia, Maryland, and the Carolinas, as well as throughout Kentucky, forcefully conveyed to Congress their resentment of Hamilton's tax. One farmer complained that he already paid half his grain to the local distillery for distilling his rye, and now the distiller was taking the new whiskey tax out of the farmer's remaining half. This "reduces the balance to less than one-third of the original quantity. If this is not an oppressive tax, I am at a loss to describe what is so," the farmer wrote. Congress responded with modest modifications to the tax in 1792, but even so, discontent was rampant.

Simple evasion of the law was the most common response; the tax proved hard to collect. In some places, crowds threatened to tar and feather federal tax collectors, and some distilleries underreported their production. Four counties in Pennsylvania established committees of correspondence and held assemblies to carry their message to Congress. President Washington issued a warning that the protests had to stop, and for a time, things cooled down. Still, noncompliance continued, and an embarrassed Hamilton admitted to Congress that the revenue was far less than anticipated. But rather than abandon the law, he tightened up the prosecution of tax evaders.

In western Pennsylvania, Hamilton had one ally, a stubborn tax collector named John Neville, who refused to quit even after a group of spirited farmers burned him in effigy. In May 1794, Neville filed charges against seventy-five farmers and distillers for tax evasion. In July, he and a federal marshal were ambushed in Allegheny County by a group of forty men. Neville's house was then burned to the ground by a crowd estimated at five hundred, and one man in the crowd was killed. At the end of July, seven thousand Pennsylvania farmers planned a march—or perhaps an attack, some thought—on Pittsburgh to protest the hated tax.

The governor of Pennsylvania refused to call out the militia, preferring to allow arrests and judicial authority to handle illegal acts. In response, President Washington nationalized the Pennsylvania militia and set out, with Hamilton at his side urging him on, at the head of thirteen thousand soldiers. (This event remains the only time in the country's history that a president in military uniform led an army in anticipated action.) A worried Philadelphia newspaper criticized the show of force: "Shall Pennsylvania be converted into a human slaughter house because the dignity of the United States will not admit of conciliatory measures? Shall torrents of blood be spilled to support an odious excise system?" But in the end, no blood was spilled. By the time the army arrived in late September, the demonstrators had dispersed. No battles were fought, and no shots were exchanged. Twenty men were rounded up as rebels and charged with high treason, but only two were convicted, and both were soon pardoned by Washington.

Had the federal government overreacted? Thomas Jefferson thought so; he saw the event as a replay of Shays's Rebellion of 1786, when a protest against government taxation had been met with unreasonable government force (see chapter 8). The rebel farmers agreed; they felt entitled to protest oppressive taxation. Hamilton and Washington, however, thought that laws passed by a republican government must be obeyed. The Whiskey Rebellion presented an opportunity for the new federal government to flex its muscles and stand up to civil disorder.

▶ **REVIEW**   Why were Hamilton's economic policies controversial?

Conflicts West, East, and South

While the whiskey rebels challenged federal leadership from within the country, disorder threatened the United States from external sources as well. From 1790 onward, serious trouble brewed in three directions. To the west, a powerful confederation of Indian tribes in the Ohio Country resisted white encroachment, resulting in a brutal war. At the same time, conflicts between the major European powers forced Americans to take sides and nearly thrust the country into another war, this time across the Atlantic. And to the south, a Caribbean slave rebellion raised fears that racial war would be imported to the United States. Despite these conflicts, and the grave threats they posed to the young country, Washington won reelection to the presidency unanimously in the fall of 1792.

To the West: The Indians

In the 1783 Treaty of Paris, Britain had yielded all land east of the Mississippi River to the United States without regard to the resident Indian population. The 1784 Treaty of Fort Stanwix (see chapter 8) had attempted to solve that omission by establishing terms between the new confederation government and native peoples, but the key tribes of the Ohio Valley—the Shawnee, Delaware, and Miami—had not been involved in those negotiations. To confuse matters further, British troops still occupied a half dozen forts in the northwest, protecting an ongoing fur trade between British traders and Indians and thereby sustaining Indians' claims to that land.

The doubling of the American population from two million in 1770 to nearly four million in 1790 greatly intensified the pressure for western land. Several thousand settlers a year moved down the Ohio River in the mid-1780s. Most headed for Kentucky, on the south bank of the river, but some eyed the forests to the north, in Indian country. By the late 1780s, government land sales in eastern Ohio had commenced, although actual settlement lagged.

Meanwhile, the U.S. army entered the western half of Ohio, where white settlers did not dare to go. Fort Washington, built on the Ohio River in 1789 at the site of present-day Cincinnati, became the command post for three major invasions of Indian country (Map 9.1, page 258). General Josiah Harmar, under orders to subdue the Indians of western Ohio, marched with 1,400 men into Ohio's

MAP 9.1   Western Expansion and Indian Land Cessions to 1810
By the first decade of the nineteenth century, intense Indian wars had resulted in significant cessions of land to the U.S. government by treaty.

northwest region in the fall of 1790, burning Indian villages. His inexperienced troops were ambushed by Miami and Shawnee Indians led by their chiefs, Little Turtle and Blue Jacket. Harmar lost one-eighth of his soldiers.

Harmar's defeat—so humiliating that he was court-martialed—spurred efforts to clear Ohio for permanent American settlement. General Arthur St. Clair, the military governor of the Northwest Territory, had pursued peaceful tactics in the 1780s, signing treaties with Indians for land in eastern Ohio—dubious treaties, as it happened, since the Indian negotiators were not authorized to yield land. In the wake of Harmar's bungled operation, St. Clair geared up for military action, and in the fall of 1791, he led two thousand men (accompanied by two hundred women camp followers) north from Fort Washington to claim Ohio territory from the Miami and Shawnee tribes. Along the route, St. Clair's men quickly built two forts, named for Hamilton and Jefferson. However, when the Indians attacked at daybreak on November 4, at the headwaters of the Wabash River, St. Clair's army was not protected by fortifications.

Before noon, 55 percent of the Americans were dead or wounded; only three of the women escaped alive. "The savages seemed not to fear anything we could do," wrote an officer afterward. "They could skip out of reach of bayonet and return, as they pleased. The ground was literally covered with the dead. . . . It appeared as if the officers had been singled out, as a very great proportion fell. The men being thus left with few officers, became fearful, despaired of success, gave up the fight." The Indians captured valuable weaponry, scalped and dismembered the dying, and pursued fleeing survivors for miles. With more than nine hundred lives lost, this was the most stunning American loss in the history of the U.S.-Indian wars. President Washington fumed that St. Clair "was worse than a murderer" and demanded his resignation. An angry Congress issued subpoenas and launched its first-ever investigation of the executive branch, looking beyond St. Clair to learn what had gone wrong. Grisly tales of St. Clair's defeat became instantly infamous, increasing the level of terror that Americans brought to their confrontations with the Indians.

Washington doubled the U.S. military presence in Ohio and appointed a new commander, General Anthony Wayne of Pennsylvania, nicknamed "Mad Anthony" for his headstrong, hard-drinking style of leadership. About the Ohio natives, Wayne wrote, "I have always been of the opinion that we never should have a permanent peace with those Indians until they were made to experience our superiority." With some 3,500 men, Wayne established two new military camps, Fort Greenville and Fort Recovery, deep in Indian territory in western Ohio, the latter on the site of St. Clair's defeat. Wayne's men had to pick through skeletal remains to build the fort.

Throughout 1794, Wayne's army engaged in skirmishes with Shawnee, Delaware, and Miami Indians. Chief Little Turtle of the Miami tribe advised negotiation; in his view, Wayne's large army looked overpowering. But Blue Jacket of the Shawnees counseled continued warfare, and his view prevailed. The decisive action came in August 1794 at the battle of Fallen Timbers, near the Maumee River where a recent tornado had felled many trees. The confederated Indians— mainly Ottawas, Potawatomis, Shawnees, and Delawares and numbering around eight hundred—ambushed the Americans but were underarmed, and Wayne's troops made effective use of their guns and bayonets. The Indians withdrew and sought refuge at nearby Fort Miami, still held by the British. Their former allies,

Treaty of Greenville, 1795
This painting by an unknown artist of the 1790s depicts the signing of the Treaty of Greenville in 1795.
The treaty was signed by General Anthony Wayne, Chief Little Turtle of the Miami tribe, and Chief
Tarhe the Crane of the Wyandot tribe. An Indian gestures as if to dictate terms to the Americans, but in
fact the treaty was most favorable to the United States. Although Indians from a dozen Ohio tribes
came to the signing of the treaty, this picture shows unrealistically open spaces and very few Indians.
Chicago Historical Society.

however, locked the gate and refused protection. The surviving Indians fled to
the woods, their ranks decimated.

Fallen Timbers was a major defeat for the Indians. The Americans had destroyed cornfields and villages on the march north, and with winter approaching, the Indians' confidence was sapped. They reentered negotiations in a much
less powerful bargaining position. In 1795, about a thousand Indians representing nearly a dozen tribes met with Wayne and other American emissaries to
work out the Treaty of Greenville. The Americans offered treaty goods (calico
shirts, axes, knives, blankets, kettles, mirrors, ribbons, thimbles, and abundant
wine and liquor casks) worth $25,000 and promised additional shipments every
year. The government's idea was to create a dependency on American goods to
keep the Indians friendly. In exchange, the Indians ceded most of Ohio to the
Americans; only the northwest part of the territory was reserved solely for the
Indians.

The treaty brought temporary peace to the region; however, it did not restore a peaceful life to the Indians. The annual allowance from the United States too often came in the form of liquor. "More of us have died since the Treaty of Greenville than we lost by the years of war before, and it is all owing to the introduction of liquor among us," said Chief Little Turtle in 1800. "This liquor that they introduce into our country is more to be feared than the gun and tomahawk."

Across the Atlantic: France and Britain

While Indian battles engaged the American military in the west, another war overseas to the east was also closely watched. Since 1789, revolution had been raging in France. In its first five years, the general American reaction was positive, for it was flattering to think that the American Revolution had inspired imitation in France. As monarchy and privilege were overthrown in the name of republicanism in France, towns throughout America celebrated the victory of the French people with civic feasts and public festivities. Dozens of pro-French political clubs, called democratic or republican societies, sprang up around the country. The societies mobilized farmers and mechanics, issued circular letters, injected pro-French (and anti-British) feelings into local elections, and in general heightened popular participation and public interest in foreign policy.

Many American women also joined in the pro-French enthusiasm. Clothing accessories provided a striking way to make a political statement, leading some women to sport a sash and an ornamental French cockade made with ribbons of red, white, and blue—a badge of solidarity with revolutionary France. Pro-French headgear for committed women included an elaborate turban, leading one horrified Federalist newspaper editor to chastise the "fiery frenchified dames" thronging Philadelphia's streets. Staged female celebrations of France's new liberty occurred in New England, Pennsylvania, and the South, where one most extraordinary event made the columns of South Carolina's *Charleston City Gazette and Daily Advertiser* in 1793. It centered on a public marriage ceremony uniting two women as partners, one French and one American, who repudiated their husbands "on account of ill treatment" and pledged mutual "union and friendship." A militia fired a salute to seal the pledge, while male dignitaries beamed on the women and their blended multichild family. Most likely, this ceremony was not the country's first civil union but instead a richly metaphorical piece of street theater in which the spurned husbands represented Britain. The paper did not report names for the two women but did print recognizably local names of male sponsors and officiants.

Anti–French Revolution sentiments also ran deep. Vice President John Adams, who lived in France in the 1780s, said he trembled for the outcome. Radicals in France worried him, just as radicals in America did. "Too many Frenchmen, after the example of too many Americans, pant for the equality of persons and property," Adams said. "The impracticability of this, God Almighty has decreed, and the advocates for liberty, who attempt it, will surely suffer for it."

Support for the French Revolution remained a matter of personal conviction until 1793, when Britain and France went to war and French versus British loyalty became a critical foreign policy debate. France had helped America substantially during the American Revolution, and the confederation government had signed an alliance in 1778 promising aid if France were ever under attack. Some Americans, optimistic about the eventual outcome of the French Revolution, wanted to deliver on that promise. Others, including those shaken by the report of the guillotining of thousands of French people, as well as those with strong commercial ties to Britain, sought ways to stay neutral. In particular, the startling news of the beheading of King Louis XVI and Queen Marie Antoinette quickly dampened the uncritical enthusiasm for everything French. Those who fondly remembered the excitement and risk of the American Revolution were still likely to regard France with optimism. But the reluctant revolutionaries of the 1770s and 1780s, who had worried about excessive democracy and social upheaval in America, deplored the far greater violence occurring in the name of republicanism as France in 1793 moved into the Reign of Terror, with its surge of executions.

In May 1793, President Washington issued the Neutrality Proclamation, which contained friendly assurances to both sides. But tensions at home flared in response to official neutrality. "The cause of France is the cause of man, and neutrality is desertion," wrote H. H. Brackenridge, a congressman from western Pennsylvania, voicing the sentiments of thousands. The Neutrality Proclamation fit Washington's goal of staying out of European wars. Yet American ships continued to trade between the French West Indies and France. In late 1793 and early 1794, the British expressed their displeasure by capturing more than three hundred of these vessels near the West Indies. Clearly, something had to be done to assert American power.

President Washington sent John Jay, the chief justice of the Supreme Court and a man of strong pro-British sentiments, to England to negotiate commercial relations in the British West Indies and secure compensation for the seizure of American ships. In addition, Jay was supposed to resolve several long-standing problems. Southern **planters** wanted reimbursement for the slaves lured away by the British army during the war, and western settlers wanted Britain to vacate the frontier forts still occupied because of their proximity to the Indian fur trade.

Jay returned from his diplomatic mission in 1795 with a treaty that no one could love. First, the treaty failed to address the captured cargoes or the lost property in slaves. Second, it granted the British a lenient eighteen months to withdraw from the frontier forts, as well as continued rights in the fur trade. (Even with the delay, however, the provision disheartened the Indians just then negotiating the Treaty of Greenville in Ohio. It was a significant factor in their decision to make peace.) Finally, the Jay Treaty called for repayment with interest of the debts that some American planters still owed to British firms dating from the

Revolutionary War. In exchange for such generous terms, Jay secured limited trading rights in the West Indies and agreement that some issues—boundary disputes with Canada and the damage and loss claims of shipowners—would be decided later by arbitration commissions.

The Senate debated the treaty in secrecy, knowing how explosive its terms would be, and passed it by a vote of 20 to 10. President Washington signed it, but with misgivings. When newspapers published the terms of the treaty, powerful opposition emerged from Maine to Georgia. In Massachusetts, this graffiti appeared on a wall: "Damn John Jay! Damn everyone who won't damn John Jay! Damn everyone who won't stay up all night damning John Jay!" Bonfires in many places burned effigies of Jay and copies of the treaty. A newspaper in New Jersey used graphic imagery to explain to its readers the implications of the Jay Treaty:

> The nation has been secretly, I will not say treacherously, divorced from France, and most clandestinely married to Great Britain: we are taken from the embraces of a loving wife, and find ourselves in the arms of a detestable and abandoned whore, covered with crimes, rottenness, and corruption.

When Alexander Hamilton appeared at a public meeting in New York City to defend the treaty, he was hissed and booed, and several stones were thrown at him. Within days, he was challenging opponents to fights, but no one took up his challenge. A Connecticut newspaper, in reporting with cautious approval on unmarried females voting in a New Jersey election, openly wondered whether "a certain treaty" might have "obtained better terms" had it been negotiated by a widow instead of "a MALE minister," intended as a clear insult to Jay's competence.

Some representatives in the House, led by Madison, tried to undermine the Senate's approval by insisting on a separate vote on the funding provisions of the treaty, on the grounds that the House controlled all money matters. Finally, in 1796, the House approved funds to implement the various commissions mandated by the treaty, but by only a three-vote margin. The vote in both houses of Congress divided along the same lines as the Hamilton-Jefferson split on economic policy. It was the most bitter political split yet in the country's short history.

To the South: The Haitian Revolution

In addition to the Indian wars in Ohio and the European wars across the Atlantic, a third bloody conflict to the south polarized and even terrorized many Americans in the 1790s. The western third of the large Caribbean island of Hispaniola, just to the east of Cuba, became engulfed in revolution starting in 1791. The eastern portion of the island was a Spanish colony called Santo Domingo; the western part, in bloody conflagration, was the French Saint Domingue. War raged in Saint Domingue for more than a decade, resulting in 1804 in the birth of the Republic of Haiti, the first and only independent black state to arise out of a successful slave revolution.

The Haitian Revolution was a complex event involving many participants, including the diverse local population and, eventually, three European countries. Some 30,000 whites ruled the island in 1790, running sugar and coffee plantations with close to half a million enslaved blacks, two-thirds of them of African birth. The white French colonists were not the only plantation owners, however. About 28,000 free, mixed-race people (*gens de couleur*) also lived in Saint Domingue; they owned one-third of the island's plantations and nearly a quarter of the slave labor force. Despite their economic status, these mixed-race planters were barred from political power, but they aspired to it.

The French Revolution of 1789 was the immediate catalyst for rebellion in this already tense society. First, white colonists challenged the white royalist government in an effort to link Saint Domingue with the new revolutionary government in France. Next, the mixed-race planters rebelled in 1791, demanding equal civil rights with the whites. No sooner was this revolt viciously suppressed than another part of the island exploded as thousands of enslaved blacks armed with machetes and torches wreaked devastation and slaughter. In 1793, the civil war escalated to include French, Spanish, and British troops fighting the inhabitants and also each other. Slaves led by Toussaint L'Ouverture in alliance with Spain occupied the northern regions of the island, leaving a thousand plantations in ruins and tens of thousands of people dead. Thousands of white and mixed-race planters, along with some of their slaves, fled to Spanish Louisiana and southern cities in the United States.

White Americans followed the revolution in fascinated horror through newspapers and refugees' accounts. A few sympathized with the impulse for liberty, but many more shuddered at the violent atrocities. White refugees were welcomed in Charleston, Norfolk, and Richmond; but French-speaking blacks, whether free or slave, were eventually barred from entry in all southern states except Virginia. White southerners clearly feared that violent black insurrection might be imported from Haiti into their own society.

Many black American slaves also followed the revolution, hearing about it from dockworkers; black sailors; anxious whites, who spoke of it over dinner or in taverns, where blacks waited on tables; and French-speaking blacks themselves, who arrived in Virginia ports in significant numbers after 1793. Amazing news—the success of the first massive revolution by slaves—traveled quickly in this oral **culture**. Southern whites complained of behaviors among slaves that might prefigure plots and conspiracies, such as increased insolence and higher runaway rates.

The Haitian Revolution provoked naked fear of a race war in white southerners. Jefferson, agonizing over the contagion of liberty in 1797, wrote another Virginia slaveholder that "if something is not done, and soon done, we shall be the murderers of our own children . . . ; the revolutionary storm, now sweeping the globe, will be upon us, and happy if we make timely provision to give it an easy passage over our land. From the present state of things in Europe and America, the day which brings our combustion must be near at hand; and only a single spark is wanting to make that day to-morrow."

Jefferson's cataclysmic fears were not shared by New Englanders. Timothy Pickering of Massachusetts, in Washington's cabinet since 1795, chastised the inconsistent Jefferson for supporting French revolutionaries while condemning black Haitians fighting for freedom just because they had "a skin not colored like our own." Not that Pickering supported either type of violent revolutionary—he did not. But he and his political allies, soon to be called the Federalists, were far more willing to contemplate trade and diplomatic relations with the emerging black republic of Haiti.

▶**REVIEW**   Why did the United States feel vulnerable to international threats in the 1790s?

Federalists and Republicans

By the mid-1790s, polarization over the French Revolution, Haiti, the Jay Treaty, and Hamilton's economic plans had led to two distinct and consistent rival political groups: Federalists and Republicans. Politicians and newspapers adopted these labels, words that summarized conflicting political positions. Federalist leaders supported Britain in foreign policy and commercial interests at home, while Republicans rooted for liberty in France and worried about monarchical Federalists at home. The labels did not yet describe full-fledged political parties, which were still thought to be a sign of failure of the experiment in government. Washington's decision not to seek a third term led to serious partisan electioneering in the presidential and congressional elections of 1796. Federalist John Adams won the presidency, but party strife accelerated over failed diplomacy in France, bringing the United States to the brink of war. Pro-war and antiwar antagonism created a major crisis over political free speech, militarism, and fears of sedition and treason.

The Election of 1796

Washington struggled to appear to be above party politics, and in his farewell address, he stressed the need to maintain a "unity of government" reflecting a unified body politic. He also urged the country to "steer clear of permanent alliances with any portion of the foreign world." The leading contenders for his position, John Adams of Massachusetts and Thomas Jefferson of Virginia, in theory agreed with him, but around them raged a party contest split along pro-British versus pro-French lines.

Adams and Jefferson were not adept politicians in the modern sense, skilled in the arts of persuasion and intrigue. Bruised by his conflicts with Hamilton, Jefferson had resigned as secretary of state in 1793 and retreated to Monticello, his home in Virginia. Adams's job as vice president kept him closer to the political action, but his personality often put people off. He was temperamental, thin-skinned, and quick to take offense.

The leading Federalists informally caucused and chose Adams as their candidate, with Thomas Pinckney of South Carolina to run with him. The Republicans settled on Aaron Burr of New York to pair with Jefferson. The Constitution did not anticipate parties and tickets. Instead, each electoral college voter could cast two votes for any two candidates, but on only one ballot. The top vote-getter became president, and the next-highest assumed the vice presidency. (This procedural flaw was corrected by the Twelfth Amendment, adopted in 1804.) With only one ballot, careful maneuvering was required to make sure the chief rivals for the presidency did not land in the top two spots.

Into that maneuverable moment stepped Alexander Hamilton. No longer in the cabinet, Hamilton had returned to his law practice in 1795, but he kept a firm hand on political developments. Hamilton did not trust Adams; he preferred Pinckney, and he tried to influence electors to throw their support to the South Carolinian. But his plan backfired: Adams was elected president with 71 electoral votes; Jefferson came in second with 68 and thus became vice president. Pinckney got 59 votes, while Burr trailed with 30.

Adams's inaugural speech pledged neutrality in foreign affairs and respect for the French people, which made Republicans hopeful. To please Federalists, Adams retained three cabinet members from Washington's administration—the secretaries of state, treasury, and war. But the three were Hamilton loyalists, passing off Hamilton's judgments and advice as their own to the unwitting Adams. Vice President Jefferson extended a conciliatory hand to Adams when the two old friends met in Philadelphia, still the capital. They even took temporary lodging in the same boardinghouse, as if expecting to work closely together. But the Hamiltonian cabinet ruined the honeymoon. Jefferson's advice was spurned, and he withdrew from active counsel of the president.

The XYZ Affair

From the start, Adams's presidency was in crisis. France retaliated for the British-friendly Jay Treaty by abandoning its 1778 alliance with the United States. French privateers—armed private vessels—started detaining American ships carrying British goods; by March 1797, more than three hundred American vessels had been seized. To avenge these insults, Federalists started murmuring openly about war with France. Adams preferred negotiations and dispatched a three-man commission to France in the fall of 1797. When the three commissioners arrived in Paris, French officials would not receive them. Finally, the French minister of foreign affairs, Talleyrand, sent three French agents—unnamed and later known to the American public as X, Y, and Z—to the American commissioners with the information that $250,000 might grease the wheels of diplomacy and a $12 million loan to the French government would be the price of a peace treaty. Incensed, the commissioners brought news of the bribery attempt to the president.

Americans reacted to the XYZ affair with shock and anger. Even staunch pro-French Republicans began to reevaluate their allegiance. The Federalist-dominated Congress appropriated money for an army of ten thousand soldiers and repealed all prior treaties with France. In 1798, twenty naval warships launched the United States into its first undeclared war, called the Quasi-War by historians to underscore its uncertain legal status. The main scene of action was the Caribbean, where more than one hundred French ships were captured.

There was no home-front unity in this time of undeclared war; antagonism only intensified between Federalists and Republicans. Because there seemed to be very little chance of a land invasion by France, leading Republicans feared, with some justification, that the Federalists' real aim might be to raise the army to threaten domestic dissenters. Some claimed that Hamilton had masterminded the army buildup and was lobbying to be second in command, behind the aging Washington. President Adams was increasingly mistrustful, but his cabinet backed the military buildup, and Adams was too weak politically to prevail. He was, moreover, beginning to suspect that his cabinet was more loyal to Hamilton than to the president.

Republican newspapers heaped abuse on Adams. Pro-French mobs roamed the capital, and Adams, fearing for his personal safety, stocked weapons in his presidential quarters. Federalists, too, went on the offensive. In Newburyport, Massachusetts, they lit a huge bonfire and burned issues of the state's Republican newspapers. One Federalist editor ominously declared that "he who is not for us is against us."

The Alien and Sedition Acts

With tempers so dangerously high, and fears that political dissent was perhaps akin to treason, Federalist leaders moved to muffle the opposition. In mid-1798, Congress hammered out the Sedition Act, which not only made conspiracy and revolt illegal but also penalized speaking or writing anything that defamed the president or Congress. Criticizing government leaders became a criminal offense. One Federalist in Congress justified his vote for the law this way: "Let gentlemen look at certain papers printed in this city and elsewhere, and ask themselves whether an unwarrantable and dangerous combination does not exist to overturn and ruin the government by publishing the most shameless falsehoods against

Cartoon of the Matthew Lyon Fight in Congress
The political tensions of 1798 were not merely intellectual. At a February session in Congress, Roger Griswold, a Connecticut Federalist, called Matthew Lyon, a Vermont Republican, a coward. Name-calling degenerated into a brawl. The honorable way to avenge insults in Virginia's planter class was to negotiate a duel, but Lyon, a Scots-Irish immigrant, came from a different class and culture. Rough-and-tumble fighting was his first response to insult.
Library of Congress.

the representatives of the people." In all, twenty-five men, almost all Republican newspaper editors, were charged with sedition; twelve were convicted.

Congress also passed two Alien Acts. The first extended the waiting period for an alien to achieve citizenship from five to fourteen years and required all aliens to register with the federal government. The second empowered the president in time of war to deport or imprison without trial any foreigner suspected of being a danger to the United States. The clear intent of these laws was to harass French immigrants already in the United States and to discourage others from coming.

Republicans strongly opposed the Alien and Sedition Acts on the grounds that they were in conflict with the Bill of Rights, but they did not have the votes to revoke the acts in Congress, nor could the federal judiciary, dominated by Federalist judges, be counted on to challenge them. Jefferson and Madison turned to the state legislatures, the only other competing political arena, to press their opposition. Each man drafted a set of resolutions condemning the acts and had the legislatures of Virginia and Kentucky present them to the federal government in late fall 1798. The Virginia and Kentucky Resolutions tested the novel argument that state legislatures have the right to judge the constitutionality of federal laws and to **nullify** laws that infringe on the liberties of the people as defined in the Bill of Rights. The resolutions made little dent in the Alien and Sedition Acts, but the idea of a state's right to nullify federal law did not disappear. It would resurface several times in decades to come, most notably in a major tariff dispute in 1832 and in the sectional arguments that led to the Civil War.

Amid all the war hysteria and sedition fears in 1798, President Adams regained his balance. He was uncharacteristically restrained in pursuing opponents under the Sedition Act, and he finally refused to declare war on France, as extreme Federalists wished. No doubt he was beginning to realize how much he had been the dupe of Hamilton. He also shrewdly realized that France was not eager for war and that a peaceful settlement might be close at hand. In January 1799, a peace initiative from France arrived in the form of a letter assuring Adams that diplomatic channels were open again and that new commissioners would be welcomed in France. Adams accepted this overture and appointed new negotiators. By late 1799, the Quasi-War with France had subsided, and in 1800 the negotiations resulted in a treaty declaring "a true and sincere friendship" between the United States and France. But Federalists were not pleased; Adams lost the support of a significant part of his own party and sealed his fate as the first one-term president of the United States.

The election of 1800 was openly organized along party lines. The self-designated national leaders of each group met to handpick their candidates for president and vice president. Adams's chief opponent was Thomas Jefferson. When the election was finally over, President Jefferson mounted the inaugural platform to announce, "We are all republicans, we are all federalists," an appealing rhetoric of harmony appropriate to an inaugural address. But his formulation perpetuated a denial of the validity of party politics, a denial that ran deep in the founding generation of political leaders.

▶ **REVIEW**   Why did Congress pass the Alien and Sedition Acts in 1798?

Conclusion: Parties Nonetheless

American political leaders began operating the new government in 1789 with great hopes of unifying the country and overcoming selfish factionalism. The enormous trust in President Washington was the central foundation for those hopes, and Washington did not disappoint, becoming a model "Mr. President" with a blend of integrity and authority. Stability was further aided by easy passage of the Bill of Rights (to appease Antifederalists) and by attention to cultivating a virtuous citizenry of upright men supported and rewarded by republican womanhood. Yet the hopes of the honeymoon period soon turned to worries and then fears as major political disagreements flared up.

At the core of the conflict was a group of talented men—Hamilton, Madison, Jefferson, and Adams—so recently allies but now opponents. They diverged over Hamilton's economic program, over relations with the British and the Jay Treaty, over the French and Haitian revolutions, and over preparedness for war abroad and free speech at home. Hamilton was perhaps the driving force in these conflicts, but the antagonism was not about mere personality. Parties were taking shape not around individuals, but around principles, such as ideas about what constituted enlightened leadership, how powerful the federal government should be, who was the best ally in Europe, and when oppositional political speech turned into treason. The Federalists were pro-British, pro-commerce, and ever alarmed about the potential excesses of democracy. The Republicans celebrated, up to a point, the radical republicanism of France and opposed the Sedition Act as an alarming example of an overbearing government cutting off freedom of speech.

When Jefferson in his inaugural address of 1800 offered his conciliatory assurance that Americans were at the same time "all republicans" and "all federalists," he probably mystified some listeners. Possibly, he meant to suggest that both groups shared two basic ideas—the value of republican government, in which power derived from the people, and the value of the unique federal system of shared governance structured by the Constitution. But by 1800, *Federalist* and *Republican* defined competing philosophies of government. To at least some of his listeners, Jefferson's assertion of harmony across budding party lines could only have seemed bizarre. For the next two decades, these two groups would battle each other, each fearing that the success of the other might bring the demise of the country. And for the next two decades, leaders continued to worry that partisan spirit itself was a bad thing.

REVIEWING THE CHAPTER

Use the questions and timeline to review and strengthen your understanding of the chapter.

REVIEW QUESTIONS

1. How did political leaders in the 1790s attempt to overcome the divisions of the 1780s? (pp. 245–50)

2. Why were Hamilton's economic policies controversial? (pp. 250–57)

3. Why did the United States feel vulnerable to international threats in the 1790s? (pp. 257–65)

4. Why did Congress pass the Alien and Sedition Acts in 1798? (pp. 265–69)

MAKING CONNECTIONS

1. Why did the Federalist alliance fracture in the 1790s? Why was this development troubling to the nation? In your answer, cite specific ideological and political developments that compromised cooperation.

2. What provoked the Whiskey Rebellion? How did the government respond? In your answer, discuss the foundations and precedents of the conflict, as well as the significance of the government's response.

3. Americans held that virtue was pivotal to the success of their new nation. What did they mean by virtue? How did they hope to ensure that their citizens and their leaders possessed virtue?

4. The domestic politics of the new nation were profoundly influenced by conflicts beyond the nation's borders. Discuss how conflicts abroad contributed to domestic political developments in the 1790s.

TIMELINE

1789	• George Washington inaugurated first president. • French Revolution begins. • First Congress meets. • Fort Washington erected in western Ohio.	**1793**	• Napoleonic Wars break out between France and Britain. • Washington issues Neutrality Proclamation. • Eli Whitney invents cotton gin.
1790	• Congress approves Hamilton's debt plan. • Judith Sargent Murray publishes "On the Equality of the Sexes." • Shawnee and Miami Indians in Ohio defeat General Josiah Harmar.	**1794**	• Whiskey Rebellion. • Battle of Fallen Timbers.
		1795	• Treaty of Greenville. • Jay Treaty.
1791	• States ratify Bill of Rights. • Congress and president charter Bank of the United States. • Ohio Indians defeat General Arthur St. Clair. • Congress passes whiskey tax. • Haitian Revolution begins. • Hamilton issues *Report on Manufactures*.	**1796**	• Federalist John Adams elected second president.
		1797	• XYZ affair.
		1798	• Quasi-War with France erupts. • Alien and Sedition Acts. • Virginia and Kentucky Resolutions.
		1800	• Republican Thomas Jefferson elected third president.

▶ **For an online bibliography, practice quizzes, Web sites, images, and documents related to this chapter,** see the Book Companion Site at **bedfordstmartins.com/roark.**

▶ **For firsthand accounts of this period,** see Chapter 9 in Michael Johnson, ed., *Reading the American Past,* Fourth Edition.

10
CHAPTER

Republicans in Power
1800–1824

T HE NAME TECUMSEH translates as "Shooting Star," a fitting name for the
Shawnee chief who reached meteoric heights of fame among Indians during
Thomas Jefferson's presidency. From Canada south to Georgia and from the
Atlantic west to the Mississippi, Tecumseh was accounted a charismatic leader,
for which white Americans praised (and also feared) him. Graceful, eloquent,
compelling, and astute: Tecumseh was all these and more. A gifted natural
commander, he was equal parts politician and warrior.

The Ohio Country, where Tecumseh was born in 1768, was home to about a
dozen Indian tribes, including the Shawnee, recently displaced from the South.
During the Revolutionary War, the region became a battleground with the "Big
Knives," as the Shawnee people called the Americans. Tecumseh's childhood was
marked by repeated violence and the loss of his father and two brothers in battle.
Five times between 1774 and 1782, the boy fled raids by American soldiers that
left his home in flames and his village destroyed. The Treaty of Paris in 1783
brought no peace to Indian country. American settlers pushed west, and the youthful Tecumseh honed his warrior skills by ambushing pioneers running flatboats
down the Ohio River. He fought at the battle of Fallen Timbers, a major Indian
defeat in 1794, but avoided the 1795 negotiations of the Treaty of Greenville, in
which half a dozen dispirited tribes ceded much of Ohio to the Big Knives. In
frustration, he watched as seven treaties between 1802 and 1805 whittled away
more Indian land.

Some Indians, resigned and tired, looked for ways to accommodate, taking
up farming, trade, and even intermarriage with the Big Knives. Others spent their
treaty payments on alcohol. Tecumseh's younger brother Tenskwatawa led an

Tecumseh
This 1848 engraving of Tecumseh
is adapted from an earlier drawing
that no longer exists, sketched by
a French trader in Indiana named
Pierre Le Dru in a live sitting
with the Indian leader in 1808.
The engraver has given Tecumseh
a British army officer's uniform,
showing that he fought on the
British side in the War of 1812.
Library of Congress.

embittered life of idleness and drink. But Tecumseh rejected assimilation and inebriation and instead campaigned for a return to ancient ways. Donning traditional animal-skin garb, he traveled around the Great Lakes region after 1805, persuading tribes to join his pan-Indian confederacy. The American territorial governor of Indiana, William Henry Harrison, reported, "For four years he has been in constant motion. You see him today on the Wabash, and in a short time hear of him on the shores of Lake Erie or Michigan, or on the banks of the Mississippi, and wherever he goes he makes an impression favorable to his purpose." In 1811, the leader named Shooting Star traveled among tribes in the South while an especially brilliant comet illuminated the night sky.

Even his dissolute brother was born anew. After a near-death experience in 1805, Tenskwatawa revived and recounted a startling vision of meeting the Master of Life. Renaming himself the Prophet, he urged Indians everywhere to regard whites as children of the Evil Spirit, destined to be destroyed. Tecumseh and the Prophet established a new village called Prophetstown, located in present-day Indiana, offering a potent blend of spiritual regeneration and political unity that attracted thousands of followers. Governor Harrison admired and feared Tecumseh, calling him "one of those uncommon geniuses which spring up occasionally to produce revolutions."

President Thomas Jefferson worried about an organized Indian confederacy and its potential for a renewed alliance with the British in Canada. Those worries became a reality during Jefferson's second term in office (1805–1809). Although his first term (1801–1805) brought notable successes, such as the Louisiana Purchase and the Lewis and Clark expedition, his second term was consumed by the threat of war with either Britain or France, in a replay of the late-1790s tensions. When war came in 1812, the enemy was Britain, bolstered by a reenergized Indian-British alliance. Among the causes of the war were insults over international shipping rights, the capture of U.S. vessels, and the impressment of American sailors. But the war also derived compelling strength from Tecumseh's confederacy, now pledged to help the British in Canada. Significant battles pitted U.S. soldiers against Indians in the Great Lakes, Tennessee, and Florida.

In the end, the War of 1812 settled little between the United States and Britain, but it was tragically conclusive for the Indians. Eight hundred warriors led by Tecumseh helped defend Canada against U.S. attacks, but the British did not reciprocate when the Indians were under threat. Tecumseh died on Canadian soil at the battle of the Thames in the fall of 1813. No Indian leader with his star power would emerge again east of the Mississippi.

The briefly unified Indian confederacy under Tecumseh had no counterpart in the young Republic's confederation of states, where widespread unity and enthusiasm behind a single leader proved impossible to achieve. Republicans did battle with Federalists during the Jefferson and Madison administrations, but then Federalists doomed their party by opposing the War of 1812 and after 1815 ceased to be a major force in political life. The next two presidents, James Monroe and John Quincy Adams, congratulated themselves on the Federalists' demise and Republican unity, but in fact divisions within their own party were extensive. Wives of politicians increasingly inserted themselves into this dissonant mix, managing their husbands' politicking and jockeying for power in the Capitol and enabling them to appear above the fray and maintain the fiction of a nonpartisan state. That it was a fiction became sharply apparent in the most serious political crisis of this period, the Missouri Compromise of 1820.

Jefferson's Presidency

The nerve-wracking election of 1800, decided in the House of Representatives, enhanced fears that party divisions would ruin the country. A panicky Federalist newspaper in Connecticut predicted that Jefferson's victory would produce a bloody civil war and usher in an immoral reign of "murder, robbery, rape, adultery and incest." Similar fears were expressed in the South, where a frightful slave uprising seemed a possible outcome of Jefferson's victory. But nothing nearly so dramatic occurred. Jefferson later called his election the "revolution of 1800," referring to his repudiation of monarchical practices, his undoing of Federalist judicial appointments, and his cutbacks in military spending and taxes.

Jefferson did radically transform the presidency, away from the Federalists' vision of a powerful executive branch and toward **republican** simplicity and limited government. Yet even Jefferson found that circumstances sometimes required him to draw on the expansive powers of the presidency. The rise of

Napoleon in France brought France and Britain into open warfare again in 1803, creating unexpected opportunities and challenges for Jefferson. One major opportunity arrived in the spectacular purchase from France of the Louisiana Territory; a significant challenge arose when pirates threatened American ships off the north coast of Africa and when British and French naval forces nipped at American ships—and American honor—in the Atlantic Ocean.

Turbulent Times: Election and Rebellion

The result of the election of 1800 remained uncertain from polling time in November to repeated roll call votes in the House of Representatives in February 1801. Federalist John Adams, never secure in his leadership of the Federalist Party, was no longer in the presidential race once it got to the House. Instead, the contest was between Jefferson and his running mate, Senator Aaron Burr of New York. Republican voters in the electoral college slipped up, giving Jefferson and Burr an equal number of votes, an outcome possible because of the single balloting to choose both president and vice president. (To fix this problem, the Twelfth Amendment to the Constitution, adopted four years later, provided for distinct ballots for the two offices.) The vain and ambitious Burr declined to concede, so the Federalist-dominated House of Representatives took up its constitutional mandate to choose which Republican would become president.

Each state delegation had one vote, and a candidate needed nine votes to win. Some Federalists preferred Burr, believing that his character flaws made him especially susceptible to Federalist pressure. But the influential Alexander Hamilton, though no friend of Jefferson, recognized that the high-strung Burr would be more dangerous than Jefferson in the presidency. Jefferson was a "contemptible hypocrite" in Hamilton's opinion, but at least he was not corrupt. Jefferson received the votes of eight states on the first ballot. Thirty-six ballots and six days later, he got the critical ninth vote, as well as a tenth. This election demonstrated a remarkable feature of the new constitutional government: No matter how hard fought the campaign, the leadership of the nation could shift from one group to a distinctly different group in a peaceful transfer of power effected by ballots, not bullets.

As the country struggled over its white leadership crisis, a twenty-four-year-old blacksmith named Gabriel, the slave of Thomas Prossor, plotted rebellion in Virginia. Inspired by the Haitian Revolution (see chapter 9), and perhaps directly informed of it by French slaves new to the Richmond area, Gabriel was said to be organizing a thousand slaves to march on the state capital of Richmond and take the governor, James Monroe, hostage. On the appointed day, however, a few nervous slaves went to the authorities, and within days, scores of implicated conspirators were jailed and brought to trial.

One of the jailed rebels compared himself to the most venerated icon of the early Republic: "I have nothing more to offer than what General Washington would have had to offer, had he been taken by the British and put to trial by them." Such talk invoking the specter of a black George Washington worried white Virginians, and in September and October 1800, twenty-seven black men were hanged for allegedly contemplating rebellion. Finally, President Jefferson advised Governor Monroe that the hangings had gone far enough. "The world at large will forever condemn us if we indulge a principle of revenge," Jefferson wrote.

The Jeffersonian Vision of Republican Simplicity

Jefferson sidestepped the problem of slavery and turned his attention to establishing his administration in clear contrast to the Federalists. For his inauguration, held in the village optimistically called Washington City, he dressed in everyday clothing, to strike a tone of republican simplicity, and he walked to the Capitol for the modest swearing-in ceremony. Once in office, he continued to emphasize unfussy frugality. He scaled back Federalist building plans for Washington and cut the government budget. He wore plain clothes, appearing "neglected but not slovenly," according to one onlooker. He cultivated a casual style, wearing slippers to greet important guests, avoiding the formality of state parties and liveried servants. Jefferson's apparent carelessness was very deliberate.

Martha Washington and Abigail Adams had received the wives of government officials at weekly teas, thereby creating and cementing social relations in the governing class. But Jefferson, a longtime widower, disdained female gatherings and avoided the women of Washington City. He abandoned George Washington's practice of holding weekly formal receptions, limiting these drop-in gatherings to just two a year. His preferred social event was the small dinner party with carefully chosen politicos, either all Republicans or all Federalists (and all male). At these intimate dinners, the president demonstrated his version of statecraft, exercising influence and strengthening informal relationships that would help him govern.

Jefferson's paramount goal was to roll back federal power. He was no Antifederalist. He had supported the Constitution in 1788, although he had qualms about the unrestricted reelection allowed to the president. But events of the 1790s had caused him to worry about the stretching of powers in the executive branch. Jefferson had watched with distrust as Hamiltonian policies refinanced the public debt, established a national bank, and secured commercial ties with Britain (see chapter 9). These policies seemed to Jefferson to promote the interests of greedy speculators at the expense of the rest of the country. Jefferson was not at all anticommerce, but financial schemes that seemed merely to allow rich men to become richer were corrupt and worthless, he believed, and their promotion by the federal government was not authorized by the Constitution. In Jefferson's vision, the source of true **liberty** in America was the independent farmer, someone who owned and worked his land both for himself and for the market.

Jefferson set out to dismantle Federalist innovations. He reduced the size of the army by a third, leaving only three thousand soldiers, and he kept the navy small, with just half a dozen ships. Peacetime defense, he felt, should rest with "a well-disciplined militia," not a standing army. With the consent of Congress, he abolished all federal internal taxes based on population or whiskey. A national tax on population had been tried just once, in 1798, and had proved as burdensome and expensive as taking a census. Government revenue would now derive solely from customs duties and from the sale of western land. This strategy was of particular benefit to the South, because the three-fifths clause of the Constitution counted slaves for both representation and taxation. The South could exercise its extra influence in the House of Representatives without the threat of extra taxes. By the end of his first term, Jefferson had deeply reduced Hamilton's cherished national debt.

A properly limited federal government, according to Jefferson, was responsible merely for running a postal system, maintaining the federal courts, staffing lighthouses, collecting customs duties, and conducting a census once every ten years. Government jobs were kept to a minimum. The president had just one private secretary, a young man named Meriwether Lewis, to help with his correspondence, and Jefferson paid him out of his own pocket. The Department of State employed only 8 people: Secretary James Madison, 6 clerks, and a messenger. The Treasury Department was by far the largest unit, with 73 revenue commissioners, auditors, and clerks, plus 2 watchmen. The entire payroll of the executive branch amounted to a mere 130 people in 1801.

The Judiciary and the Midnight Judges

One large set of government workers lay beyond Jefferson's command. His predecessor, John Adams, had seized the few weeks between his election defeat and Jefferson's inauguration to appoint 217 Federalists to various judicial, diplomatic, and military posts.

Most of this windfall of appointments came to Adams as a result of the Judiciary Act of 1801, passed in the final month of his presidency. Its predecessor, the Judiciary Act of 1789, had established a six-man Supreme Court and six circuit courts. The new law authorized sixteen circuit courts, each headed by a new judge. If he acted quickly, Adams could appoint sixteen circuit court judges with lifetime tenure, plus dozens more attorneys, marshals, and clerks for each court. The 1801 act also reduced the Supreme Court from six to five justices. Prior to its passage, however, Adams appointed solidly Federalist Virginian John Marshall to a vacant sixth seat. After the 1801 act became law, a future president would not be able to fill the next empty seat.

In the last weeks of February 1801, Adams and Marshall worked feverishly to secure agreements from the new appointees. In view of the slowness of the mail, achieving 217 acceptances was astonishing. The two men were at work until

9 p.m. on the last night Adams was president, signing and delivering commissions (appointment papers) to the new officeholders.

The appointment of the "midnight judges" infuriated the Republicans. Jefferson, upon taking office, immediately canceled the appointments of the non-tenured men and refused to honor the few appointments that had not yet been delivered. One of them was addressed to William Marbury, who soon decided to sue the new secretary of state, James Madison, for failure to make good on the appointment. This action gave rise to a landmark Supreme Court case, *Marbury v. Madison*, decided in 1803. The Court, presided over by John Marshall, ruled that although Marbury's commission was valid and the new president should have delivered it, the Court could not compel him to do so. What made the case significant was little noted at the time: The Court found that the grounds of Marbury's suit, resting in the Judiciary Act of 1789, were in conflict with the Constitution. For the first time, the Court acted to disallow a law on the grounds that it was unconstitutional. John Marshall quietly established the concept of judicial review; the Supreme Court in effect assumed the legal authority to **nullify** acts judged in conflict with the Constitution.

The Promise of the West: The Louisiana Purchase and the Lewis and Clark Expedition

The reach of the *Marbury* decision went largely unnoticed in 1803 because the president and Congress were preoccupied with other major issues, among them the acquisition of the Louisiana Territory. Up through the Seven Years' War (see chapter 6), France claimed but only lightly settled a large expanse of land west of the Mississippi River, only to lose it to Spain in the 1763 Treaty of Paris. Spain never sent adequate forces to control or settle the land, and Spanish power in North America remained precarious everywhere outside New Orleans. Meanwhile, American farming families were settling Kentucky and Tennessee, along rivers emptying into the upper Mississippi, and for a time, the Spanish allowed them to ship their agricultural produce downriver and even encouraged American settlements across the river, in an effort to augment the population. By 1801, Americans made up a sizable minority of the population around the lower Mississippi. Publicly, Jefferson protested the luring of Americans to Spanish territory, but privately he welcomed it as a potential move toward appropriating territory immediately west of the Mississippi. He wrote, "I wish a hundred thousand of our inhabitants would accept the invitation; it will be the means of delivering to us peaceably, what may otherwise cost us a war."

Jefferson's fears of war were not unrealistic. In 1802, the Spanish governor revoked American shipping privileges through or past New Orleans. Congressmen began muttering about taking the city by force. Talk of war, especially in Federalist newspapers, became commonplace.

In the same year, rumors reached Jefferson that Spain had struck a secret bargain with France to hand over a large part of Spain's trans-Mississippi territory to Napoleon in exchange for some land in Italy. Spain had proved a weak western neighbor, but France was another story. Jefferson was so alarmed that he instructed Robert R. Livingston, America's minister in France, to try to buy New Orleans. At first, the French denied they owned the city. But when Livingston hinted that the United States might simply seize it if buying was not an option, the French negotiator suddenly asked him to name his price for the entire Louisiana Territory, from the Gulf of Mexico north to Canada. Livingston stalled, and the Frenchman made suggestions: $125 million? $60 million? Livingston shrewdly stalled some more, and within days the French sold the entire territory for the bargain price of $15 million (Map 10.1). The French, motivated sellers, needed cash because of their impending war with Britain and the recent failure, despite committing twenty thousand troops, to prevent Haitian independence.

MAP 10.1   The Louisiana Purchase and the Lewis and Clark Expedition

Robert Livingston's bargain buy of 1803 far exceeded his initial assignment to acquire the city of New Orleans. The Indians who inhabited the vast region, unaware that their land had been claimed by either the French or the Americans, got their first look at Anglo-American and African American men when the Lewis and Clark expedition explored the territory in 1804–1806.

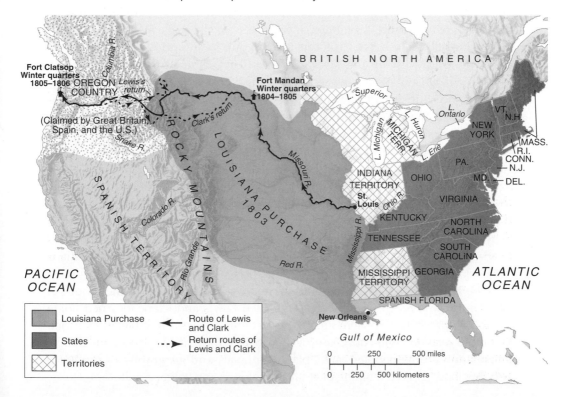

Jefferson and most of Congress were delighted with the outcome of the diplomatic mission. Still, Jefferson had some qualms about the Louisiana Purchase. The price was right, and the enormous territory fulfilled Jefferson's dream of abundant farmland for future generations. But by what authority expressed in the Constitution could he justify the purchase? His frequent criticism of Hamilton's stretching of the Constitution came back to haunt him. His legal reasoning told him he needed a constitutional amendment to authorize the addition of territory; more expedient minds told him the treaty-making powers of the president were sufficient. Expediency won out. In late 1803, the American army took formal control of the Louisiana Territory, and the United States grew by 828,000 square miles.

Even before the Louisiana Purchase, Jefferson had eyed the trans-Mississippi West with intense curiosity. In early 1803, he had arranged congressional funding for a secret scientific and military mission into Spanish and Indian territory. Jefferson appointed twenty-eight-year-old Meriwether Lewis, his personal secretary, to head the expedition, instructing him to investigate Indian **cultures,** to collect plant and animal specimens, and to chart the geography of the West. Congress had more traditional goals in mind: The expedition was to scout locations for military posts, open commercial agreements for the fur trade, and locate any possible waterway between the East and West coasts.

For his co-leader, Lewis chose Kentuckian William Clark, a veteran of the 1790s Indian wars. Together, they handpicked a crew of forty-five, including expert rivermen, gunsmiths, hunters, interpreters, a cook, and a slave named York, who belonged to Clark. The explorers left St. Louis in the spring of 1804, working their way northwest up the Missouri River. They camped for the winter at a Mandan village in what is now central North Dakota. The Mandan Indians were familiar with British and French traders from Canada, but the black man York created a sensation. Reportedly, the Indians rubbed moistened fingers over the man's skin to see if the color was painted on.

The following spring, the explorers headed west, accompanied by a sixteen-year-old Shoshoni woman named Sacajawea. Kidnapped by Mandans at about age ten, she had been sold to a French trapper as a slave/wife. Hers was not a unique story among Indian women; such women knew several languages, making them valuable translators and mediators. Further, Sacajawea and her new baby allowed the American expedition to appear peaceful to suspicious tribes. As Lewis wrote in his journal, "No woman ever accompanies a war party of Indians in this quarter."

The Lewis and Clark expedition reached the Pacific Ocean at the mouth of the Columbia River in November 1805. When Lewis and Clark returned home the following year, they were greeted as national heroes. They had established favorable relations with dozens of Indian tribes; they had collected invaluable information on the peoples, soils, plants, animals, and geography of the West; and they had inspired a nation of restless explorers and solitary imitators.

Challenges Overseas: The Barbary Wars

The inspiring opportunity of westward exploration was matched at the same time by a frustrating challenge from the Middle East, leading to the first declaration of war against the United States. For well over a century, four Muslim states on the northern coast of Africa—Morocco, Algiers, Tunis, and Tripoli—called the Barbary States by Americans, controlled all Mediterranean shipping traffic by demanding large annual payments (called "tribute") for safe passage. Countries electing not to pay the tribute found their ships at risk for seizure, with cargoes plundered and crews captured and sold into slavery. Up to 1776, American ships flew the British flag and thus were protected. Once independent, the United States began to pay the tribute, which rose by the mid-1790s to $50,000 a year. The trade was apparently worth maintaining. About a hundred American merchant ships annually traversed the Mediterranean, trading lumber, tobacco, sugar, and rum for regional delicacies such as raisins, figs, capers, and opium, the last an essential ingredient in many medicines. Some 20 percent of all American exports went to the Middle East.

In May 1801, when the pasha (military head) of Tripoli failed to secure a large increase in his tribute, he declared war on the United States. Jefferson had long considered such payments extortion, and he sent four warships to the Mediterranean to protect U.S. shipping. From 1801 to 1803, U.S. frigates engaged in skirmishes with Barbary privateers.

Then, in late 1803, the USS *Philadelphia* ran aground near Tripoli harbor. Its three-hundred-man crew was captured along with the ship. In retaliation, seventy men led by navy lieutenant Stephen Decatur sailed into the harbor after dark, guided by an Arabic-speaking pilot to fool harbor sentries. They drew up to the *Philadelphia*, boarded it, and set it on fire, then escaped. Decatur was an instant hero in America. A second foray into the harbor to try to blow up the entire Tripoli fleet with a bomb-laden boat failed when the explosives detonated prematurely; eleven Americans were killed.

In 1804, William Eaton, an American officer stationed in Tunis, felt the humiliation of his country's ineffectiveness. He wrote to Secretary of State James Madison to ask for a thousand marines to invade Tripoli. Madison rejected the plan and another scheme to ally with the pasha's exiled brother to effect a regime change. On his own, Eaton contacted the brother, assembled a force of four hundred men (more than three hundred Egyptian mercenaries and a handful of marines), and marched them over five hundred miles of desert for a surprise attack on Tripoli's second-largest city. Amazingly, he succeeded. The pasha of Tripoli yielded, released the prisoners taken from the *Philadelphia*, and negotiated a treaty with the United States. Peace with the other Barbary States came in a second treaty in 1812.

The Barbary Wars of 1801–1805 cost Jefferson's government more money than the tribute demanded. But the honor of the young country was thought to be at stake. At political gatherings, the slogan "Millions for defense, but not a cent for tribute" became a popular toast.

More Transatlantic Troubles: Impressment and Embargo

Jefferson easily retained the presidency in the election of 1804, with his 162 electoral votes trouncing the 14 won by the Federalist candidate, Charles Cotesworth Pinckney of South Carolina. But governing in his second term was not easy, due to seriously escalating tensions between the United States and both France and Britain. Beginning in 1803, both European rivals, embroiled in a war with each other, repeatedly warned the United States not to ship arms to the other. Britain acted on these threats in 1806, stopping U.S. ships to inspect cargoes for military aid to France and seizing suspected deserters from the British navy, along with many Americans. Ultimately, 2,500 sailors were "impressed" (taken by force) by the British. In retaliation, Jefferson convinced Congress to pass nonimportation laws banning certain British-made goods.

One incident made the usually cautious Jefferson nearly belligerent. In June 1807, the American ship *Chesapeake*, harboring some British deserters, was ordered to stop by the British frigate *Leopard*. The *Chesapeake* refused, and the *Leopard* opened fire, killing three Americans—right at the mouth of the Chesapeake Bay, well within U.S. territory. In response, Congress passed the Embargo Act of 1807, banning all importation of British goods into the country. Though surely a drastic measure, the embargo was meant to forestall war: The goal was to make Britain suffer. All foreign ports were declared off-limits to American merchants, to discourage illegal trading through secondary ports. Jefferson was convinced that Britain needed America's agricultural products far more than America needed British goods. He also was wary of Federalist shipowners who might circumvent the ban.

The Embargo Act of 1807 was a disaster. From 1790 to 1807, U.S. exports had increased fivefold, but the embargo brought commerce to a standstill. In New England, the heart of the shipping industry, unemployment rose. Grain plummeted in value, river traffic halted, tobacco rotted in the South, and cotton went unpicked. Protest petitions flooded Washington. The federal government suffered, too, for import duties were a significant source of revenue. Jefferson paid political costs as well. The Federalist Party, in danger of fading away after its weak showing in the election of 1804, began to revive.

▶ **REVIEW**   How did Jefferson attempt to undo the Federalist innovations of earlier administrations?

The Madisons in the White House

In mid-1808, Jefferson indicated that he would not run for a third term. Secretary of State James Madison got the nod from the Republican caucuses—informal political groups that orchestrated the selection of candidates for state and local elections. The Federalist caucuses again chose Charles Cotesworth Pinckney, their candidate in 1804. Madison won, but Pinckney received 47 electoral votes, nearly half of Madison's total. Support for the Federalists remained centered in New England, and Republicans still held the balance of power nationwide.

As president, James Madison continued Jefferson's policy of economic pressure on Britain and France with a modified embargo, but he broke new ground in the domestic management of the executive office, with the aid of his astute and talented wife, Dolley Madison. Under her leadership, the president's house was designated the White House—something close to a palace, but a palace many Americans were welcome to visit. Under his leadership, the country went to war in 1812 with Britain and with Tecumseh's Indian confederacy. In 1814, British forces burned the White House and Capitol nearly to the ground.

Women in Washington City

During her first eight years in Washington, as wife of the highest-ranking cabinet officer, Dolley Madison developed elaborate social networks that, in the absence of a First Lady, constituted the top level of female politicking in the highly political city. Although women could not vote and supposedly left politics to men, the women of Washington took on several overtly political functions that greased the wheels of the affairs of state. They networked through dinners, balls, receptions, and the intricate custom of "calling," in which men and women paid brief visits and left calling cards at each other's homes. Webs of friendship and influence in turn facilitated female political lobbying. It was not uncommon for women in this social set to write letters of recommendation for men seeking government work. Hostessing was no trivial or leisured business; it significantly influenced the federal government's patronage system.

When James Madison became president, Dolley Madison, called by some the "presidentress," struck a balance between queenliness and republican openness. She dressed the part in resplendent clothes, choosing a plumed velvet turban for her headdress at her husband's inauguration. She opened three large, elegant rooms in the executive mansion for a weekly party called "Mrs. Madison's crush" or "squeeze." In contrast to George and Martha Washington's stiff, brief receptions, the Madisons' parties went on for hours, with scores or even hundreds of guests milling about, talking, and eating. Members of Congress, cabinet officers, distinguished guests, envoys from foreign countries, and their womenfolk attended with regularity. Even people who hated parties—or these gatherings in particular—attended. Mrs. Madison's "squeeze" was an essential event for gaining political access, trading information, and establishing informal channels that would smooth the governing process.

In 1810–1811, the Madisons' house acquired its present name, the White House, probably in reference to its white-painted sandstone exterior. In 1810, a Baltimore newspaper heralded the name as "the people's name" for the people's

Dolley Madison, by Gilbert Stuart
The "presidentress" of the Madison administration sat for this official portrait in 1804. She wears an empire-style dress, at the height of French fashion in 1804 and a style worn by many women at the coronation of the emperor Napoleon in Paris.
© White House Historical Association.

house, because the words were simple and commonplace. The many guests at the weekly parties experienced simultaneously the splendor of the executive mansion and the atmosphere of republicanism that made it accessible to so many. Dolley Madison, ever an enormous political asset to her rather shy husband, understood well the symbolic function of the White House to enhance the power and legitimacy of the presidency.

Indian Troubles in the West

While the Madisons cemented alliances at home, difficulties with Britain and France overseas and with Indians in the old Northwest Territory continued to increase. The Shawnee chief Tecumseh actively solidified his confederacy, while the more northern tribes renewed their ties with supportive British agents and fur traders in Canada, a potential source of food and weapons. If the United States went to war with Britain, there would clearly be serious repercussions on the **frontier**.

Shifting demographics raised the stakes for both sides. The 1810 census counted some 230,000 Americans in Ohio only seven years after it achieved statehood. Another 40,000 Americans inhabited the territories of Indiana, Illinois, and Michigan. The Indian population of the entire region (the old Northwest Territory) was much smaller, probably about 70,000, a number unknown (because uncounted) to the Americans but certainly gauged by Tecumseh during his extensive travels.

Up to 1805, Indiana's territorial governor, William Henry Harrison, had negotiated a series of treaties in a divide-and-conquer strategy aimed at extracting Indian lands for paltry payments. But with the rise to power of Tecumseh and his brother Tenskwatawa, the Prophet, Harrison's strategy faltered. A fundamental part of Tecumseh's message was the assertion that all Indian lands were held in common by all the tribes. "No tribe has the right to sell [these lands], even to each other, much less to strangers . . . ," Tecumseh said. "Sell a country! Why not sell the air, the great sea, as well as the earth? Didn't the Great Spirit make them all for the use of his children?" In 1809, while Tecumseh was away on a recruiting trip, Harrison assembled the leaders of the Potawatomi, Miami, and Delaware tribes to negotiate the Treaty of Fort Wayne. After promising (falsely) that this was the last cession of land the United States would seek, Harrison secured three million acres at about two cents per acre.

When he returned, Tecumseh was furious with both Harrison and the tribal leaders. Leaving his brother in charge at Prophetstown on Tippecanoe River, the Shawnee chief left to seek alliances with tribes in the South. In November 1811, Harrison decided to attack Prophetstown with a thousand men. The two-hour battle resulted in the deaths of sixty-two Americans and forty Indians before the Prophet's forces fled the town, which Harrison's men set on fire. The battle of Tippecanoe was heralded as a glorious victory for the Americans, but Tecumseh was now more ready than ever to make war on the United States.

The War of 1812

The Indian conflicts in the old Northwest Territory soon merged into the wider conflict with Britain, now known as the War of 1812. Between 1809 and 1812, President Madison teetered between declaring either Britain or France America's primary enemy, as attacks by both countries on American ships continued. In 1809, Congress replaced Jefferson's stringent embargo with the Non-Intercourse Act, which prohibited trade only with Britain and France and their colonies, thus opening up other trade routes to alleviate somewhat the anguish of shippers, farmers, and **planters**. By 1811, the country was seriously divided and in a deep quandary. To some, the United States seemed, appropriately, on the verge of war. To others, war with either Britain or France meant disaster for commerce.

A new Congress arrived in Washington in March 1811. Several dozen of the younger Republican members were eager to avenge the insults from abroad. Thirty-four-year-old Henry Clay from Kentucky and twenty-nine-year-old John C. Calhoun from South Carolina became the center of a group informally known as the **War Hawks**. They saluted Harrison's victory at Tippecanoe and urged the country to war. Mostly lawyers by profession, they came from the West and South and welcomed a war with Britain both to justify attacks on the Indians and to bring an end to impressment. Many were also expansionists, looking to occupy Florida and threaten Canada. Clay was elected Speaker of the House, an extraordinary honor for a newcomer. Calhoun won a seat on the Foreign Relations Committee. The War Hawks approved major defense expenditures, and the army soon quadrupled in size.

In June 1812, Congress declared war on Great Britain in a vote divided along sectional lines: New England and some Middle Atlantic states opposed the war, while the South and West were strongly for it. Ironically, Britain had just announced that it would stop the search and seizure of American ships, but the war momentum would not be slowed. The Foreign Relations Committee issued an elaborate justification titled *Report on the Causes and Reasons for War*, written mainly by Calhoun and containing extravagant language about Britain's "lust for power," "unbounded tyranny," and "mad ambition." These were fighting words in a war that was in large measure about insult and honor.

The War Hawks proposed an invasion of Canada, confidently predicting victory in four weeks. Instead, the war lasted two and a half years, and Canada never fell. The northern invasion turned out to be a series of blunders that revealed America's grave unpreparedness for war against the unexpectedly powerful British and Indian forces. Detroit quickly fell, as did Fort Dearborn, site of the future Chicago (Map 10.2). By the fall of 1812, the outlook was grim.

MAP 10.2   The War of 1812
During the War of 1812, battles were fought along the Canadian border and in the Chesapeake region. The most important American victory came in New Orleans two weeks after a peace agreement had been signed in England.

Worse, the New England states dragged their feet in raising troops, and some New England merchants carried on illegal trade with Britain. While President Madison fumed about Federalist disloyalty, Bostonians drank India tea in Liverpool cups. The fall presidential election pitted Madison against DeWitt Clinton of New York, nominally a Republican but able to attract the Federalist vote. Clinton picked up all of New England's electoral votes, with the exception of Vermont's, and also took New York, New Jersey, and part of Maryland. Madison won in the electoral college, 128 to 89, but his margin of victory was considerably smaller than in 1808.

In late 1812 and early 1813, the tide began to turn in the Americans' favor. First came some reassuring victories at sea. Then the Americans attacked York (now Toronto), the capital of Upper Canada, and burned it in April 1813. A few months later, Commodore Oliver Hazard Perry defeated the British fleet at the western end of Lake Erie. Emboldened, General Harrison drove an army into Canada from Detroit and in October 1813 defeated the British and Indians at the battle of the Thames, where Tecumseh was killed.

The Indians in the South who had allied with Tecumseh's confederacy were also plunged into all-out war. Some fifty villages, home to 10,000 Creek Indians in the southern region of the Mississippi Territory, put up a spirited fight against American militia for ten months in 1813–1814. Even without Tecumseh's recruitment trip of 1811 or the War of 1812, the Creeks had grievances aplenty, sparked by American settlers moving into their territory. Using guns obtained in the panhandle of Spanish Florida, the Creeks mounted a strong defense. But the Creek War ended suddenly in March 1814, when a general named Andrew Jackson led 2,500 Tennessee militiamen in a bloody attack called the Battle of Horseshoe Bend. More than 550 Indians were killed, and several hundred more died trying to escape across a river. Later that year, General Jackson extracted from the defeated Creek tribe a treaty relinquishing thousands of square miles of their land to the United States.

Washington City Burns: The British Offensive

In August 1814, British ships sailed into the Chesapeake Bay, landing 5,000 troops and throwing the capital into a panic. Families evacuated, banks hid their money, and government clerks carted away boxes of important papers. Dolley Madison, with dinner for guests cooking over the fire, fled with her husband's papers and a portrait of George Washington. British commanders ate Mrs. Madison's meal before burning her house. They also burned the Capitol, a newspaper office, and a well-stocked arsenal. Instead of trying to hold the city, the British headed north and attacked Baltimore, but a fierce defense by the Maryland militia thwarted that effort.

In another powerful offensive that same month, British troops marched from Canada into New York State, but a series of mistakes cost them a naval skirmish

Remains of the President's House
This watercolor sketch documents the burning of the White House in Washington in August 1814, when the British attacked the city. The walls still stood, but the interior had been gutted by the fire.
Library of Congress.

at Plattsburgh on Lake Champlain, and they retreated to Canada. Five months later, another large British army landed in lower Louisiana and, in early January 1815, encountered General Andrew Jackson and his militia just outside New Orleans. Jackson's forces dramatically carried the day. The British suffered between 2,000 and 3,000 casualties, the Americans fewer than 80. Jackson became an instant hero. The battle of New Orleans was the most glorious victory the Americans had experienced, allowing some Americans to boast that the United States had won a second war of independence from Britain. No one in the United States knew that negotiators in Europe had signed a peace agreement two weeks earlier.

The Treaty of Ghent, signed in December 1814, settled few of the surface issues that had led to war. Neither country could claim victory, and no land changed hands. Instead, the treaty reflected a mutual agreement to give up certain goals. The Americans dropped their plea for an end to impressments, which in any case subsided as soon as Britain and France ended their war in 1815. They also gave up any claim to Canada; the British agreed to abandon aid to the Indians. Nothing was said about shipping rights. The most concrete result was a plan for a commission to determine the exact boundary between the United States and Canada.

Antiwar Federalists in New England could not gloat over the war's ambiguous conclusion, because of an ill-timed and seemingly unpatriotic move on their part. The region's leaders had convened a secret meeting in Hartford, Connecticut, in December 1814, to discuss dramatic measures to curb the South's power. They proposed amending the Constitution to abolish the three-fifths clause as a basis of representation; to specify that congressional powers to impose embargoes, admit states, or declare war should require a two-thirds vote instead of a simple majority; and to limit the president to one term and prohibit the election of successive presidents from the same state. The cumulative effect of these proposals would have been to reduce the South's political power and break the monopoly held by Virginians on the presidency. New England wanted to make sure that no sectional party could again lead the country into war against the clear interests of another. The Federalists at Hartford even discussed secession from the Union but rejected that path. Coming just as peace was achieved, however, the Hartford Convention suddenly looked very unpatriotic. The Federalist Party never recovered its grip, and within a few years, it was reduced to a shadow of its former self, even in New England.

No one really won the War of 1812. Americans celebrated as though they had, however, with parades and fireworks. The war gave rise to a new spirit of **nationalism**. The paranoia over British tyranny evident in the 1812 declaration of war was laid to rest, replaced by pride in a more equal relationship with the old mother country. Indeed, in 1817 the two countries signed the Rush-Bagot disarmament treaty (named after its two negotiators), which limited each country to a total of four naval vessels, each with just a single cannon, to patrol the vast watery border between them. The Rush-Bagot treaty was perhaps the most successful disarmament treaty for a century to come.

The biggest winners in the War of 1812 were the young men, once called War Hawks, who took up the banner of the Republican Party and carried it in new, expansive directions. These young politicians favored trade, western expansion, internal improvements, and the energetic development of new economic markets. The biggest losers of the war were the Indians. Tecumseh was dead, his brother the Prophet was discredited, the prospects of an Indian confederacy were dashed, the Creeks' large homeland was seized, and the British protectors were gone.

▶**REVIEW**   Why did Congress declare war on Great Britain in 1812?

Women's Status in the Early Republic

General esteem for Dolley Madison's pioneering role as "presidentress" showed that at the pinnacles of power, elite women of the early nineteenth century could be a visible and even active presence in civic affairs. But as with the 1790s cultural compromise that endorsed female education chiefly so that women could be better wives and mothers (see chapter 9), Mrs. Madison and her female circle practiced politics in service to their husbands' careers. Any argument for an independently grounded "rights of woman" movement fizzled after the English feminist Mary Wollstonecraft was exposed as an unwed mother.

From 1800 to 1825, key institutions central to the shaping and constraining of women's lives—the legal system, marriage, and religion—proved fairly, but not completely, resistant to change. State legislatures and the courts grappled with the legal dependency of married white women in a country whose defining (and symbolic) characteristic for men was independence. Marriage laws for whites continued to support unequal power between men and women, but this was far less true for blacks. Religious organizations struggled to redefine the role of women in church governance, at a time when church membership rates for women were skyrocketing beyond those for men. The most dramatic opportunity for women came with the flowering of female academies, whose rigorous curricula fostered high-level literacy and rational thought. Even when advertised as institutions to prepare girls to be intelligent mothers, many academies built up their students' self-confidence and implanted expectations that their knowledge and mental training would find a use beyond the kitchen and nursery.

Women and the Law

The Anglo-American view of women, implanted in English common law, was that wives had no independent legal or political personhood. The legal doctrine of *feme covert* (covered woman) held that a wife's civic life was completely subsumed by her husband's. A wife was obligated to obey her husband; her property was his, her domestic and sexual services were his, and even their children were legally his. Women had no right to keep their wages, to make contracts, or to sue or be sued. Any crime committed by a wife in the presence of her husband was chargeable to him, with two exceptions: treason against the state and keeping a brothel. The fundamental assumption of coverture was that husbands did—and ought to—control their wives.

State legislatures generally passed up the opportunity to rewrite the laws of domestic relations even though they redrafted other British laws in light of republican principles. The standard and much consulted legal treatise on family law, published in 1816, was titled *The Law of Baron and Feme*—meaning "the law of lord and woman." The title perfectly captured how lawyers framed husband-wife power relations: unequal and unchallenged.

The one aspect of family law that changed in the early Republic was divorce. Before the Revolution, only New England jurisdictions recognized a limited right to divorce; by 1820, every state except South Carolina did so. However, divorce was uncommon and difficult and in many states could be obtained only by petition to the state's legislature, a daunting obstacle for many ordinary people.

A mutual wish to terminate a marriage was never sufficient grounds for a legal divorce. A New York judge affirmed that "it would be aiming a deadly blow at public morals to decree a dissolution of the marriage contract merely because the parties requested it. Divorces should never be allowed, except for the protection of the innocent party, and for the punishment of the guilty." States upheld the institution of marriage both to protect persons they thought of as naturally dependent (women and children) and to regulate the use and inheritance of property. (Unofficial self-divorce, desertion, and bigamy were remedies that ordinary people sometimes chose to get around the strictness of marriage law. But powerful social sanctions against such behavior usually prevailed.) Legal enforcement of marriage as an unequal relationship played a major role in maintaining gender inequality in the nineteenth century.

Single adult women could own and convey property, make contracts, initiate lawsuits, and pay taxes. They could not vote (except in New Jersey before 1807), serve on juries, or practice law, so their civil status was limited. Single women's economic status was often limited as well, by custom as much as by law. Unless they had inherited adequate property or could live with married siblings, single adult women in the early Republic were very often poor.

None of the legal institutions that structured white gender relations applied to black slaves. As property themselves, slaves could not freely consent to any contractual obligations, including marriage. The protective features of state-sponsored unions were thus denied to black men and women in slavery, who were controlled by a more powerful authority: the slave owner. But this also meant that slave unions did not establish unequal power relations between partners, backed by the force of law, as did marriages among the free.

Women and Church Governance

In most **Protestant** denominations around 1800, white women made up the majority of congregants, as they had for some time. Yet the church hierarchy— ordained ministers and elders—was exclusively male, and the governance of most denominations rested in men's hands.

There were some exceptions, however. In Baptist congregations in New England, women served along with men on church governance committees, deciding on the admission of new members, voting on hiring ministers, and even debating doctrinal points. Quakers, too, had a history of recognizing women's spiritual talents. Quaker women who felt a special call were accorded the status of minister, which meant they were capable of leading and speaking in Quaker meetings.

Between 1790 and 1820, a small and highly unusual set of women emerged who actively engaged in open preaching. Most were from Freewill Baptist groups centered in New England and upstate New York. Others came from small Methodist sects, and yet others rejected any formal religious affiliation. Probably fewer than a hundred such women existed, but several dozen traveled beyond

Women and the Church: Jemima Wilkinson
In this early woodcut, Jemima Wilkinson, "the Publick Universal Friend," wears a clerical collar and body-obscuring robe, in keeping with the claim that the former Jemima was now a person without gender. Her hair is pulled back tight on her head and curled at the neck in a masculine style of the 1790s.
Rhode Island Historical Society.

their local communities, creating converts and controversy. They spoke from the heart, without prepared speeches, often exhibiting trances and claiming to exhort (counsel or warn) rather than to preach. None of these women were ordained ministers with official credentials to preach or perform baptisms.

The best-known exhorting woman was Jemima Wilkinson, who called herself "the Publick Universal Friend." After a near-death experience from a high fever in 1776, Wilkinson proclaimed her body no longer female or male but the incarnation of the "Spirit of Light." She dressed in men's clothes, wore her hair in a masculine style, shunned gender-specific pronouns, and preached openly in Rhode Island and Philadelphia. In the early nineteenth century, Wilkinson withdrew to a settlement called New Jerusalem in western New York with some 250 followers. Her fame was sustained by periodic newspaper articles that fed public curiosity about her lifelong transvestism and her unfeminine forcefulness.

The decades from 1790 to the 1820s marked a period of unusual confusion, ferment, and creativity in American religion. New denominations blossomed, new styles of religiosity gripped adherents, and an extensive periodical press devoted to religion popularized all manner of theological and institutional innovations. Congregations increasingly attracted vibrant female participation, often eclipsing the percentage of male congregants. In such a climate, the age-old tradition of gender subordination came into question here and there among the most radically **democratic** of the churches. But the presumption of male authority over women was deeply entrenched in American culture. Even denominations that had allowed women to participate in church governance began to pull back, and most churches reinstated patterns of hierarchy along gender lines.

Female Education

Starting in the North and eventually spreading to the South, states and localities began investing in public schools to foster an educated citizenry deemed essential to the good functioning of a republic. Young girls attended such schools, called district schools, sometimes along with boys or, in rural areas, more often in separate summer sessions. Basic literacy and numeracy formed the curriculum taught to white children aged roughly six to eleven. By 1830, girls had made rapid gains, in many places approaching male literacy rates. (Far fewer schools addressed the needs of free black children, whether male or female.)

More advanced education for girls was provided by a growing number of private academies, which attracted teenage girls with parents willing and able to invest in their education. Judith Sargent Murray, the Massachusetts author who had called for an equality of the sexes around 1790 (see chapter 9), predicted in 1800 that "a new era in female history" would emerge because "female academies are everywhere establishing." Some dozen female academies were established in the 1790s, and by 1830 that number had grown to nearly two hundred. Many of the earliest female academies were in New England and Pennsylvania, but others soon followed in the South, for example in Salem and Warrenton, North Carolina; in Lexington, Kentucky; and in Columbia, South Carolina. Candidates for admission were primarily daughters of elite families, as well as those of middling families with elite or intellectual aspirations, such as ministers' daughters.

The curriculum in the three-year course of study included both ornamental arts and solid academics. The ornamental program developed the skills of female gentility: drawing, needlework, music, dancing, and conversing in French. The academic subjects typically advanced well beyond prior levels of female education to include English grammar, literature, history, the natural sciences, geography, and elocution (the art of effective public speaking). Academy catalogs show that by the 1820s, the courses and reading lists at the top female academies equaled those at male colleges such as Harvard, Yale, Dartmouth, and Princeton. The girls at these academies studied Latin, rhetoric, logic, theology, moral philosophy, algebra, geometry, and even chemistry and physics.

The most rigorous schools called themselves seminaries, to set themselves a notch above the academies. The two best-known female seminaries were the Troy Female Seminary in New York, founded by Emma Willard in 1821, and the Hartford Seminary in Connecticut, founded by Catharine Beecher in 1822. Both schools prepared their students to teach. This was especially true of the Hartford Seminary, where half the students did not have a father (thus making them legally orphans) and hence were in special need of practical training for employment. Willard and

Beecher argued that women made better teachers than men. Author Harriet Beecher Stowe, educated at her sister's school and then a teacher there, agreed: "If men have more knowledge they have less talent at communicating it. Nor have they the patience, the long-suffering, and gentleness necessary to superintend the formation of character."

The most immediate value of advanced female education lay in the self-cultivation and confidence it provided. Following the model of male colleges, female graduation exercises required speeches, recitations, and demonstrations of learning from each student, generally performed in front of a mixed-sex audience of family, friends, and local notables. Here, their elocution studies paid off; they had learned the art of persuasion along with correct pronunciation and the skill of fluent speaking. Many schools took care to assure parents that their pupils would retain a pleasing female modesty. Female pedantry or intellectual immodesty triggered the stereotype of the "bluestocking," a British term of hostility for a too-learned woman, doomed to fail in the marriage market.

By the mid-1820s, the total annual enrollment at the female academies and seminaries equaled the male enrollment at the five dozen male colleges in the United States. Both groups accounted for only about 1 percent of their age cohorts in the country at large, indicating that advanced education was clearly limited to a privileged few. Among the men, this group disproportionately filled the future rosters of ministers, lawyers, judges, political leaders, and writers of influence and note. Most female graduates in time married and raised families, but first many of them became teachers at academies and district schools. And a large number of the women became authors, contributing essays, stories, and poetry to newspapers and periodicals; editing publications; and publishing novels. The new attention to the training of female minds laid the foundation for major changes in the gender system as girl students of the 1810s matured into adult women of the 1830s.

▶REVIEW   How did the civil status of American women and men differ in the early Republic?

Monroe and Adams

With the elections of 1816 and 1820, Virginians continued their hold on the presidency. In 1816, James Monroe beat Federalist Rufus King of New York, garnering 183 electoral votes to King's 34. In 1820, Monroe was reelected with all but one electoral vote. That near unanimity did not necessarily reflect voter satisfaction, however, for barely one-quarter of eligible voters went to the polls. At the state level, elections for governors, congressmen, and state assemblymen engaged voters as never before, and a drive for universal white male suffrage sparked political debate in all the states that maintained property qualifications for voting.

After Monroe's first victory, the apparent collapse of the Federalist Party at the national level led one overly optimistic newspaper to proclaim the arrival of the "Era of Good Feelings," as though a period of one-party government was destined to be harmonious. The harmony did not last long. Monroe and his aloof wife, Elizabeth, sharply curtailed social gatherings at the White House, driving the hard work of social networking into different and competing channels. Ill feelings were stirred by a sectional crisis over the admission of Missouri to the Union, and foreign policy questions involving European claims to Latin America animated sharp disagreements as well. The election of 1824 brought forth an abundance of candidates, all claiming to be Republicans. The winner was John Quincy Adams, in an election decided by the House of Representatives and, many believed, a backroom bargain. Put to the test of practical circumstances, the one-party political system failed and then fractured.

From Property to Democracy

Presidential elections occurred at a remove from ordinary voters, since the electoral college (or occasionally the House of Representatives) ultimately chose the president. But state elections were another matter, generating widespread popular involvement and driving an insistent pressure for greater democratization that ultimately spilled over into presidential elections from 1824 on.

In the 1780s, twelve of the original thirteen states enacted property qualifications for voting, usually specified at a minimum (and sometimes substantial) threshold. This policy was based on the time-honored theory that only male freeholders—landowners, as distinct from tenants or servants—had sufficient independence of mind and attachment to community to be entrusted with the vote. Of course, not everyone accepted that restricted idea of the people's role in government (see chapter 8). In the 1790s, Vermont entered the Union as the first state to enfranchise all adult males, and four other states soon substituted "taxpayer" for "freeholder." This change in terminology broadened suffrage considerably, since owning a few acres or even just a cow required the paying of taxes in many states. These were early signs of the trend toward greater democratization that gripped all the states between 1800 and 1830. Petitions and lively newspaper exchanges finally led to a series of state constitutional conventions, where questions of suffrage, balloting procedures, apportionment, and representation were hotly debated. Both political philosophy and practical politics were entwined in these debates: Who are "the people" in a government founded on **popular sovereignty**, and whose party or interest group gains the most from expanded suffrage?

For underpopulated western states entering the Union before 1830, a further consideration was whether a restrictive property qualification made any sense if it kept the voter pool extremely small. Congress had set a fifty-acre freehold as the threshold for voting in several territories, but in Illinois, fewer than three hundred men met that test at the time of statehood. When Indiana, Illinois, and Mississippi became states, their constitutions granted suffrage to all taxpayers. Five additional new western states abandoned property and taxpayer qualifications altogether.

The most heated battles over extending suffrage occurred in East Coast states, where expanding numbers of commercial men, renters, and mortgage holders of all classes contended with entrenched landed political elites who, not surprisingly, tended to favor the status quo. From 1800 to 1812, seven of the original eastern states debated suffrage reform, which then passed in three but failed in four. After the War of 1812, states again took up the issue of democracy. Contentious state constitutional conventions in Massachusetts, Connecticut, and New York finally abolished the freehold qualification and opened the franchise to all whites who paid any tax or rendered militia service.

The defenders of substantial freehold qualifications put up a fight and in several states managed to delay expanded suffrage for two more decades. But it was increasingly hard to persuade the **disfranchised** that landowners alone had a stake in government. Proponents of the status quo began to argue instead that the "industry and good habits" necessary to achieve a propertied status in life were what gave landowners the right character to vote. Opponents fired back blistering attacks. One delegate to New York's constitutional convention said, "More integrity and more patriotism are generally found in the labouring class of the community than in the higher orders." Owning land was no more predictive of wisdom and good character than it was of a person's height or strength, said another.

Both sides of the debate generally agreed that character mattered, and many ideas for ensuring an electorate of proper wisdom came up for discussion. The exclusion of paupers and felons convicted of "infamous crimes" found favor in legislation in many states. Literacy tests and raising the voting age to a figure in the thirties were debated but ultimately discarded. The exclusion of women required no discussion in the constitutional conventions, so firm was the legal power of *feme covert*. But in one exceptional moment, at the Virginia convention in 1829, a delegate who wondered aloud why unmarried women over the age of twenty-one could not vote was quickly silenced with the argument that all women lacked the "free agency and intelligence" necessary for wise voting.

Free black men's enfranchisement was another story, generating much discussion at all the conventions. Under existing freehold qualifications, a small number of propertied black men could vote; universal or taxpayer suffrage would inevitably enfranchise many more. Many delegates at the various state conventions spoke against that extension, claiming that blacks as a race lacked prudence, independence, and knowledge. With the exception of New York, which retained the existing property qualification for black voters as it removed it for whites, the general pattern was one of expanded suffrage for whites and a total eclipse of suffrage for blacks.

The Missouri Compromise

The politics of race lay at the heart of one of the most divisive issues to confront the Monroe administration. In February 1819, Missouri applied for statehood. Since 1815, four other states had joined the Union (Indiana, Mississippi, Illinois, and Alabama), following the blueprint laid out by the Northwest Ordinance of 1787. But Missouri posed a problem. Although much of its area was on the same latitude as the free state of Illinois, its territorial population included ten thousand slaves brought there by southern white planters.

Missouri's unusual combination of geography and demography led a New York congressman, James Tallmadge Jr., to propose two amendments to the statehood bill. The first stipulated that slaves born in Missouri after statehood would be free at age twenty-five, and the second declared that no new slaves could be imported into the state. Tallmadge modeled the first amendment on New York's gradual **emancipation** law of 1799. It did not strip slave owners of their current property, and it allowed them full use of the labor of newborn slaves well into their prime productive years. Still, southerners in Congress objected, because in the long run the amendments would make Missouri a free state, presumably no longer allied with southern economic and political interests. Just as southern economic power rested on slave labor, southern political power drew extra strength from the slave population because of the three-fifths rule. In 1820, the South owed seventeen of its seats in the House of Representatives to its slave population.

Tallmadge's amendments passed in the House by a close and sharply sectional vote of North against South. The ferocious debate led a Georgia representative to observe that the question had started "a fire which all the waters of the ocean could not extinguish. It can be extinguished only in blood." The Senate, with an even number of slave and free states, voted down the amendments, and Missouri statehood was postponed until the next congressional term.

In 1820, a compromise emerged. Maine, once part of Massachusetts, applied for statehood as a free state, balancing against Missouri as a slave state. The Senate further agreed that the southern boundary of Missouri—latitude 36°30′—extended west, would become the permanent line dividing slave from free states, guaranteeing the North a large area where slavery was banned (Map 10.3, page 298). The House also approved the compromise, thanks to expert deal brokering by Kentucky's Henry Clay, who earned the nickname "the Great Pacificator" for his superb negotiating skills. The whole package passed because seventeen northern congressmen decided that minimizing sectional conflict was the best course and voted with the South.

President Monroe and former president Jefferson at first worried that the Missouri crisis would reinvigorate the Federalist Party as the party of the North. But even ex-Federalists agreed that the split between free and slave states was too dangerous a fault line to be permitted to become a shaper of national politics. When new parties did develop in the 1830s, they took pains to bridge geography,

MAP 10.3   The Missouri Compromise, 1820
After a difficult battle in Congress, Missouri entered the Union in 1821 as part of a package of compromises. Maine was admitted as a free state to balance slavery in Missouri, and a line drawn at
latitude 36°30' put most of the rest of the Louisiana Territory off-limits to slavery in the future.

each party developing a presence in both North and South. Monroe and Jefferson
also worried about the future of slavery. Both understood slavery to be deeply
problematic, but, as Jefferson said, "we have the wolf by the ears, and we can neither hold him, nor safely let him go. Justice is in one scale, and self-preservation
in the other."

The Monroe Doctrine

New foreign policy challenges arose even as Congress struggled with the slavery
issue. In 1816, U.S. troops led by General Andrew Jackson invaded Spanish Florida
in search of Seminole Indians harboring escaped slaves. Once there, Jackson declared himself the commander of northern Florida, demonstrating his power in
1818 by executing two British men who he claimed were dangerous enemies. In
asserting rule over the territory, and surely in executing the two British subjects on
Spanish land, Jackson had gone too far. Privately, President Monroe was distressed
and pondered court-martialing Jackson, prevented only by Jackson's immense

popularity as the hero of the battle of New Orleans. Instead, John Quincy Adams, the secretary of state, negotiated with Spain the Adams-Onís Treaty, which delivered Florida to the United States in 1819. In exchange, the Americans agreed to abandon any claim to Texas or Cuba. Southerners viewed this as a large concession, having eyed both places as potential acquisitions for future slave states.

Spain at that moment was preoccupied with its colonies in South America. One after another, Chile, Colombia, Peru, and finally Mexico declared themselves independent in the early 1820s. To discourage Spain or France from reconquering these colonies, Monroe formulated a declaration of principles on South America. Incorporated into his annual message to Congress in December 1823, the declaration became known in later years as the **Monroe Doctrine**. The president warned that "the American Continents, by the free and independent condition which they have assumed and maintain, are henceforth not to be considered as subjects for future colonization by any European power." Any attempt to interfere in the Western Hemisphere would be regarded as "the manifestation of an unfriendly disposition towards the United States." In exchange for noninterference by Europeans, Monroe pledged that the United States would stay out of European struggles. At that time, Monroe did not intend his statement to lay a foundation for U.S. intervention in South America. Indeed, the small American navy could not realistically defend Chile or Peru against Spain or France. The doctrine was Monroe's idea of sound foreign policy, but it did not have the force of law.

The Election of 1824

Monroe's nonpartisan administration was the last of its kind, a throwback to eighteenth-century ideals, led by the last president to wear a powdered wig and knee breeches. Monroe's cabinet contained men of sharply different philosophies, all calling themselves Republicans. Secretary of State John Quincy Adams represented the urban Northeast; South Carolinian John C. Calhoun spoke for the planter aristocracy as secretary of war; and William H. Crawford of Georgia, secretary of the treasury, was a proponent of Jeffersonian **states' rights** and limited federal power. Even before the end of Monroe's first term, these men and others began to maneuver for the election of 1824.

Crucially helping them to maneuver were their wives, who accomplished some of the work of modern campaign managers by courting men—and women—of influence. The parties not thrown by Elizabeth Monroe were now given all over town by women whose husbands were jockeying for political favor. Louisa Catherine Adams remodeled her house and had a party every Tuesday night for guests numbering in the hundreds. The somber Adams lacked charm— "I am a man of reserved, cold, austere, and forbidding manners," he once wrote— but his abundantly charming (and hardworking) wife made up for that. She attended to the etiquette of social calls, sometimes making two dozen in a morning, and counted sixty-eight members of Congress as her regular Tuesday guests.

Since 1800, the congressional caucus of each party had met to identify and lend its considerable but still informal support to the party's leading candidate. In 1824, with only one party alive—and alive with five serious candidates—the caucus system splintered. Since such a large number of candidates reduced the chances of anyone securing a majority in the electoral college, many expected that the final election would be decided by the House of Representatives. Having sixty-eight members of Congress on one's regular guest list was thus smart politics.

John Quincy Adams (and Louisa Catherine) very much wanted the presidency, an ambition fed by John's sense of rising to his father's accomplishment. Candidate Henry Clay, Speaker of the House and a man of vast congressional experience, had engaged in high-level diplomacy in negotiating the Treaty of Ghent with Britain in 1814. Clay promoted his "American System," a package of protective tariffs to encourage manufacturing and federal expenditures for extensive internal improvements such as roads and canals. Treasurer William Crawford was a favorite of Republicans from Virginia and New York, even after he suffered an incapacitating stroke in mid-1824. Calhoun was another serious contender, having served in Congress and in several cabinets. Like Clay, he favored internal improvements and protective tariffs, which gained him support in northern states.

The final candidate was an outsider and a latecomer: General Andrew Jackson of Tennessee. Jackson had much less national political experience than the others, having served one year in the House and two in the Senate. His fame derived from his reputation as a military leader. In January 1824, on the anniversary of the battle of New Orleans, the Adamses threw a spectacular ball with five hundred guests in honor of General Jackson. No doubt Adams hoped that some of Jackson's charisma would rub off on him; he was not yet thinking of Jackson as a rival for office. But later in 1824, Jackson's supporters put his name in play, and voters in the West and South reacted with

JOHN Q ADAMS

Election Sewing Box from 1824
Women could express their support for presidential candidate John Quincy Adams by purchasing a sewing box emblazoned with his face. The top of the box (not visible here) has a velvet pincushion printed with the slogan "Be Firm for Adams."
Collection of Janice L. and David J. Frent.

enthusiasm. Calhoun soon dropped out of the race and shifted his attention to winning the vice presidency.

The 1824 election was the first presidential contest in which candidates' popularity with ordinary voters could be measured. Along with expanding the suffrage to nearly all white males, the recent conventions to rewrite the state constitutions had put the power to choose members of the electoral college directly in the hands of voters. (Only six states out of the full twenty-four kept that power in the hands of the state legislature.) Jackson was by far the most popular candidate with voters, winning 153,544 votes. Adams was second with 108,740, Clay won 47,136 votes, and the debilitated Crawford garnered 46,618. This was still not a large voter turnout, probably amounting to just over a quarter of adult white males. But in its tortured outcome, the election of 1824 forever changed popular voting for the presidency. Partisanship energized the electorate; apathy and a low voter turnout would not recur until the twentieth century.

In the electoral college, Jackson received 99 votes, Adams 84, Crawford 41, and Clay 37. Jackson did not have a majority, so the election went to the House of Representatives, for the second (and last) time in American history. Each state delegation had one vote; according to the Twelfth Amendment to the Constitution, passed in 1804, only the top three candidates could enter the runoff. Thus Henry Clay was out of the race and in a position to bestow his support on another candidate.

Jackson's supporters later characterized the election of 1824 as the "corrupt bargain." Clay backed Adams, and Adams won by one vote in the House, in a vote in February 1825. Clay's support made sense on several levels. Despite strong mutual dislike, he and Adams agreed on issues such as federal support to build roads and canals, and Clay was uneasy with Jackson's volatile temperament and unstated political views and with Crawford's diminished capacity. What made Clay's decision look "corrupt" was that immediately after the election, Adams offered to appoint Clay secretary of state—and Clay accepted.

In fact, there probably was no concrete bargain; Adams's subsequent cabinet appointments demonstrated his lack of political astuteness. But Andrew Jackson felt that the election had been stolen from him, and he wrote bitterly that "the Judas of the West [Clay] has closed the contract and will receive the thirty pieces of silver."

The Adams Administration

John Quincy Adams, like his father, was a one-term president. His career had been built on diplomacy, not electoral politics, and despite his wife's deftness in the art of political influence, his own political horse sense was not well developed. With his cabinet choices, he welcomed his opposition into his inner circle. He asked Crawford to stay on in the Treasury. He retained an openly pro-Jackson postmaster general even though that position controlled thousands of nationwide patronage appointments. He even asked Jackson to become secretary of war. With Calhoun as vice president (elected without opposition by the electoral college) and Clay at the State Department, the whole argumentative crew would have been thrust into the executive branch. Crawford and Jackson had the good sense to decline the appointments.

Adams had lofty ideas for federal action during his presidency, and the plan he put before Congress was so sweeping that it took Henry Clay aback. Adams called for federally built roads, canals, and harbors. He proposed a national university in Washington as well as government-sponsored scientific research. He wanted to build observatories to advance astronomical knowledge and to promote precision in timekeeping, and he backed a decimal-based system of weights and measures. In all these endeavors, Adams believed he was continuing the Jefferson and Madison legacy, using the powers of government to advance knowledge. But his opponents feared he was too Hamiltonian, using federal power inappropriately to advance commercial interests.

Whether he was more truly Federalist or Republican was a moot point. Lacking the give-and-take political skills required to gain congressional support, Adams was unable to implement much of his program. He scorned the idea of courting voters to gain support and using the patronage system to enhance his power. He often made appointments (to posts such as customs collectors) to placate enemies rather than reward friends. A story of a toast offered to the president may well have been mythical, but as humorous folklore it made the rounds during his term and came to summarize Adams's precarious hold on leadership. A dignitary raised a glass and said, "May he strike confusion to his foes," to which another voice scornfully chimed in, "as he has already done to his friends."

▶ **REVIEW**   How did the collapse of the Federalist Party influence the administrations of James Monroe and John Quincy Adams?

Conclusion: Republican Simplicity Becomes Complex

The Jeffersonian Republicans tried at first to undo much of what the Federalists had created in the 1790s, but their promise of a simpler government gave way to the complexities of domestic and foreign issues. The sudden acquisition of the Louisiana Purchase promised land and opportunity to settlers but also complicated the country's political future with the issues central to the Missouri Compromise. Antagonism from both foreign and Indian nations led to complex and costly policies such as embargoes, treaties, and military action, culminating in the War of 1812, a war motivated less by concrete economic or political issues than by questions of honor. Its conclusion at the battle of New Orleans allowed Americans to foster the illusion that they had fought a second war of independence.

The War of 1812 was the Indians' second *lost* war for independence. Tecumseh's vision of an unprecedentedly large confederacy of Indian tribes that would halt westward expansion by white Americans was cut short by the war and by his death. Without British support, the Indians probably could not have successfully challenged for long the westward dynamic of American settlement. But when Canada was under attack, the British valued its defense more than they valued their promises to help the Indians.

The war elevated to national prominence General Andrew Jackson, whose popularity with voters in the 1824 election surprised traditional politicians—and their politically astute wives—and threw the one-party rule of Republicans into a tailspin. John Quincy Adams had barely assumed office in 1825 before the election campaign of 1828 was off and running. Appeals to the people—the mass of white male voters—would be the hallmark of all elections after 1824. It was a game Adams could not easily play.

Politics in this entire period was a game that women could not play either. Except for the political wives of Washington, women, whether white or free black, had no place in government. Male legislatures maintained women's *feme covert* status, keeping wives dependent on husbands. A few women found a pathway to greater personal autonomy through religion. Meanwhile, the routine inclusion of girls in public schools and the steady spread of female academies planted seeds that would blossom into a major transformation of gender in the 1830s and 1840s.

The War of 1812 started another chain of events that would prove momentous in later decades. Jefferson's long embargo and Madison's wartime trade stoppages gave strong encouragement to American manufacturing, momentarily protected from competition with British factories. When peace returned in 1815, the years of independent development burst forth into a period of sustained economic growth that continued nearly unabated into the mid-nineteenth century.

REVIEWING THE CHAPTER

Use the questions and timeline to review and strengthen your understanding of the chapter.

REVIEW QUESTIONS

1. How did Jefferson attempt to undo the Federalist innovations of earlier administrations? (pp. 274–82)

2. Why did Congress declare war on Great Britain in 1812? (pp. 282–89)

3. How did the civil status of American women and men differ in the early Republic? (pp. 289–94)

4. How did the collapse of the Federalist Party influence the administrations of James Monroe and John Quincy Adams? (pp. 294–302)

MAKING CONNECTIONS

1. When Jefferson assumed the presidency following the election of 1800, he expected to transform the national government. Describe his republican vision and his successes and failures in implementing it. Did subsequent Republican presidents advance the same objectives?

2. How did the United States expand and strengthen its control of territory in North America in the early nineteenth century? Discuss the roles of diplomacy, military action, and political leadership in contributing to this development.

3. Regional tensions emerged as a serious danger to the American political system in the early nineteenth century. Discuss specific conflicts that had regional dimensions. How did Americans resolve, or fail to resolve, these tensions?

4. Women were denied equality in public life, yet some were able to exert considerable influence. How did they do so? In your answer, discuss the legal, political, and educational status of women in the early Republic.

TIMELINE

1789	• Judiciary Act establishes six Supreme Court justices.	1809	• Treaty of Fort Wayne. • Non-Intercourse Act.
1800	• Republicans Thomas Jefferson and Aaron Burr tie in electoral college. • Fears of slave rebellion led by Gabriel in Virginia result in twenty-seven executions.	1811	• Battle of Tippecanoe.
		1812	• United States declares war on Great Britain.
1801	• Judiciary Act reduces Supreme Court justices to five, increases number of circuit courts. • House of Representatives elects Thomas Jefferson president after thirty-six ballots.	1813	• Tecumseh dies at battle of the Thames.
		1814	• British attack Washington, D.C. • Treaty of Ghent. • New England Federalists meet at Hartford Convention.
1803	• *Marbury v. Madison.* • Britain and France warn United States not to ship war-related goods to each other. • United States purchases Louisiana Territory.	1815	• Battle of New Orleans.
		1816	• Republican James Monroe elected president.
		1819	• Adams-Onís Treaty.
1804–1806	• Lewis and Clark expedition goes to Pacific Ocean.	1820	• Missouri Compromise.
		1821	• Troy Female Seminary founded.
1807	• British attack and search *Chesapeake.* • Embargo Act.	1823	• Monroe Doctrine asserted.
1808	• Republican James Madison elected president; Dolley Madison soon dubbed "presidentress."	1825	• John Quincy Adams elected president by House of Representatives.

▶ **For an online bibliography, practice quizzes, Web sites, images, and documents related to this chapter,** see the Book Companion Site at **bedfordstmartins.com/roark.**

▶ **For firsthand accounts of this period,** see Chapter 10 in Michael Johnson, ed., *Reading the American Past,* Fourth Edition.

11
CHAPTER

The Expanding Republic
1815–1840

P RESIDENT ANDREW JACKSON was the dominant figure of his age, yet his precarious childhood little foretold the fame, fortune, and influence he would enjoy in the years after 1815. Jackson was born in the Carolina backcountry in 1767. His Scots-Irish father had recently died, leaving a poor, struggling mother to support three small boys. During the Revolution, Andrew followed his brothers into the militia, where both died of disease, as did his mother. Orphaned at fourteen, Jackson drifted around, drinking, gambling, and brawling.

Then at seventeen, his prospects began to improve. He studied under a lawyer for three years and moved to Nashville, a **frontier** community full of opportunities for a young man with legal training and an aggressive temperament. He became a public prosecutor, married into a leading family, and acquired land and slaves. When Tennessee became a state in 1796, Jackson, then twenty-nine, was elected to Congress and served a single term. In 1802, he became major general of the Tennessee militia, cultivating a fierce style of military leadership.

Jackson captured national attention in 1815 by leading the United States to victory at the battle of New Orleans. With little else to celebrate about the War of 1812, many Americans seized on the Tennessee general as the champion of the day. Songs, broadsides, and an admiring biography set him up as the original self-made man—the parentless child magically responsible for his own destiny. Jackson seemed to have created himself—a gritty, forceful personality extracting opportunities from the dynamic, turbulent frontier.

Jackson was more than a man of action, however. He was also strong-willed, reckless, and quick to anger, impulsively challenging men to duels, sometimes on slight pretexts. In one legendary fight in 1806, Jackson deliberately let his opponent, an expert marksman, shoot first. The bullet hit him in a rib, but Jackson masked all sign of injury under a loose cloak and an immobile face. He then took careful aim at the astonished man and killed him. Such steely courage chilled his political opponents.

Jackson's image as a tough frontier hero set him apart from the learned and privileged gentlemen from Virginia and Massachusetts who had occupied the presidency up to 1828. When he lost the 1824 election to John Quincy Adams, an infuriated Jackson vowed to fight a rematch. He won in 1828 and again in 1832, capturing large majorities. His appeal stretched across the urban working classes of the East, frontier voters of the West, and slaveholders in the South, who all saw something of themselves in Jackson. Once elected, he brought a combative style to politics and enlarged the powers of the presidency.

The confidence and even recklessness of Jackson's personality mirrored the new confidence of American society in the years after 1815. An entrepreneurial spirit gripped the country, producing a market revolution of unprecedented scale. Old social hierarchies eroded; ordinary men dreamed of moving high up the ladder of success, just as Jackson had done. Stunning advances in transportation and economic productivity fueled such dreams and propelled thousands to move west or to cities. Urban growth and technological change fostered the diffusion of a distinctive and vibrant public

Ship's Figurehead of Andrew Jackson
Carved in 1834 and affixed to the bow of a revered navy frigate, this figurehead of Andrew Jackson symbolized national pride by putting "the image of the most popular man of the West upon the favorite ship of the East," according to the commodore who commissioned it. But when Jackson introduced a new, strict banking policy, his popularity in the urban East quickly plummeted. In protest, an ardent Whig stole on board and decapitated the figurehead. The commodore, himself alert to symbolic actions, wrapped the headless statue in a flag and sent it to New York City, where woodworkers fashioned a new head in 1835. The figurehead was then reattached to the ship.
Museum of the City of New York, Gift of the Seawanhaka Corinthian Yacht Club.

culture, spread mainly through the increased circulation of newspapers, which allowed popular opinions to coalesce and intensify. Jackson's sudden nation-wide celebrity was a case in point.

Expanded communication transformed politics dramatically. Sharp disagreements over the best way to promote individual **liberty**, economic opportunity, and national prosperity in the new market economy defined key differences between Jackson and Adams and the parties they gave rise to in the 1830s. The process of party formation brought new habits of political participation and party loyalty to many thousands more adult white males. Religion became democratized as well. A nationwide **evangelical** revival brought its adherents the certainty that salvation and perfection were now available to all.

As president from 1829 to 1837, Jackson presided over all these changes, fighting some and supporting others in his vigorous and volatile way. As with his own stubborn personality, there was a dark underside to the confidence and expansiveness of American society. Steamboats blew up, banks and businesses periodically collapsed, alcoholism rates soared, Indians were killed or relocated farther west, and slavery continued to expand. The brash confidence that turned some people into rugged, self-promoting, Jackson-like individuals inspired others to think about the human costs of rapid economic expansion and thus about reforming society in dramatic ways. The common denominator was a faith that people and societies could shape their own destinies.

The Market Revolution

The return of peace in 1815 unleashed powerful forces that revolutionized the organization of the economy. Spectacular changes in transportation facilitated the movement of commodities, information, and people, while textile mills and other factories created many new jobs, especially for young unmarried women. Innovations in banking, legal practices, and tariff policies promoted swift economic growth.

This was not yet an industrial revolution, as was beginning in Britain, but a market revolution, fueled by traditional sources—water, wood, beasts of burden, and human muscle. What was new was the accelerated pace of economic activity and the scale of the distribution of goods. Men and women were drawn out of old patterns of rural self-sufficiency into the wider realm of national market relations. At the same time, the nation's money supply enlarged considerably, leading to speculative investments in commerce, manufacturing, transportation, and land. The new nature and scale of production and consumption changed Americans' economic behavior, attitudes, and expectations. But in 1819 and again in 1837 and 1839, serious crashes of the economy punctured those optimistic expectations.

Improvements in Transportation

Before 1815, transportation in the United States was slow and expensive; it cost as much to ship a crate over thirty miles of domestic roads as it did to send it across the Atlantic Ocean. The fastest stagecoach trip from Boston to New York took four days. But between 1815 and 1840, networks of roads, canals, steamboats, and finally railroads dramatically raised the speed and lowered the cost of travel. The young Andrew Jackson spent weeks traveling west from North Carolina to Nashville, Tennessee, in the 1780s along old Indian trails, but when he journeyed east in 1829, it took only days for the new president to get to Washington, D.C., by steamboat and turnpike.

Improved transportation moved goods into wider markets. It moved passengers, too, broadening their horizons and allowing young people as well as adults to take up new employment in cities and factory towns. Transportation also facilitated the flow of political information via the U.S. mail with its bargain postal rates for newspapers, periodicals, and books.

Enhanced public transport was expensive and produced uneven economic benefits, so presidents from Jefferson to Monroe were reluctant to fund it with federal dollars. Only the National Road, begun in 1806, was government sponsored. By 1818, it linked Baltimore with Wheeling, in western Virginia. In all other cases, private investors pooled resources and chartered transport companies, receiving significant subsidies and **monopoly** rights from state governments. Turnpike and roadway mileage increased dramatically after 1815, reducing shipping costs. Stagecoach companies proliferated, and travel time on main routes was cut in half.

Water travel was similarly transformed. In 1807, Robert Fulton's steam-propelled boat, the *Clermont*, churned up the Hudson River from New York City to Albany in thirty-two hours, compared with two days for the land route, touching off a steamboat craze. In 1820, a dozen boats left New York City daily, and scores more operated on midwestern rivers and the Great Lakes. A voyager on one of the first steamboats to go down the Mississippi reported that the Chickasaw Indians called the vessel a "fire canoe" and considered it "an omen of evil." By the early 1830s, more than seven hundred steamboats were in operation on the Ohio and Mississippi rivers. A journey upriver from New Orleans to Louisville, Kentucky, took only one week.

Steamboats were not benign advances, however. The urgency to cut travel time led to overstoked furnaces, sudden boiler explosions, and terrible mass fatalities. By 1838, nearly three thousand Americans had been killed in steamboat accidents, leading to initial federal attempts—at first unsuccessful—to regulate safety on ships used for interstate commerce. Environmental costs were also very high. Steamboats had to load fuel—"wood up"—every twenty miles or so, causing serious deforestation. By the 1830s, the banks of many main rivers were denuded of trees, and forests miles back from the rivers fell to the ax. As steamboats burned wood, they transferred the carbon stored in trees into the atmosphere, creating America's first significant air pollution.

Canals were another major innovation of the transportation revolution. These shallow highways of water (typically just four feet deep) allowed passage for barges and boats pulled by horses or mules trudging on a towpath along the embankment. Travel speed was slow—under five miles per hour. The economy in comparison to land travel came from increased loads. The low-friction water allowed one horse to pull a fifty-ton barge. Pennsylvania in 1815 and New York in 1817 commenced major state-sponsored canal enterprises. Pennsylvania's Schuylkill Canal stretched 108 miles west from Philadelphia when it was completed in 1826. Much more impressive was the Erie Canal, finished in 1825. It spanned 350 miles from Albany to Buffalo, New York, thus linking the port of

---

View of the Erie Canal at Lockport
The Erie Canal struck many as the eighth wonder of the world when it was completed in 1825, not only for its length of 350 miles but also for the eighty-three locks required to move boats over the combined ascent and descent of 680 feet. The biggest challenge of the route came at Lockport, New York, where five double locks were constructed to move boats in stages up and down the steep 60-foot elevation.
Library of Congress.

New York City (via the Hudson River) with the entire Great Lakes region. Wheat and flour moved east, household goods and tools moved west, and passengers went in both directions. By the 1830s, the cost of shipping by canal fell to less than a tenth of the cost of overland transport, and New York City quickly blossomed into the premier commercial city in the United States.

In the 1830s, private railroad companies began to give canals stiff competition, and by the 1840s railroads eclipsed canal boats as passenger conveyances, leaving them to haul freight only. The nation's first railroad, the Baltimore and Ohio, laid thirteen miles of track in 1829. During the 1830s, three thousand more miles of track materialized nationwide, the result of a speculative fever in railroad construction masterminded by bankers, locomotive manufacturers, and state legislators, who provided subsidies, charters, and land rights-of-way. Rail lines in the 1830s were generally short, on the order of twenty to one hundred miles. They did not yet provide an efficient distribution system for goods, but passengers flocked to experience the marvelous speeds of fifteen to twenty miles per hour. Railroads and other advances in transportation made possible enormous change by unifying the country culturally and economically.

Factories, Workingwomen, and Wage Labor

Transportation advances promoted the expansion of manufacturing after 1815, creating an ever-expanding market for goods. The two leading industries, textiles and shoes, altered methods of production and labor relations. Textile production was greatly spurred by the development of water-driven machinery, built near fast-coursing rivers. Shoe manufacturing, still using the power and skill of human hands, involved only a reorganization of production. Both mechanized and manual manufacturing pulled young women into wage-earning labor for the first time.

The earliest factory was built by English immigrant Samuel Slater in Pawtucket, Rhode Island, in the 1790s. It featured a mechanical spinning machine that produced thread and yarn. By 1815, nearly 170 spinning mills had been built along streams and rivers in lower New England. In British manufacturing cities, entire families worked in factories where wages were low and conditions unhealthy. In contrast, American factories targeted young women as employees. Mill girls provided cheap labor because of their limited employment options and because they would soon "retire" to marriage, to be replaced by fresh recruits earning a beginner's wage.

In 1821, a group of Boston entrepreneurs founded the town of Lowell, Massachusetts, on the Merrimack River. There, they centralized all aspects of cloth production: combing, shrinking, spinning, weaving, and dyeing. By 1830, the eight mills in Lowell employed more than five thousand young women, most between the ages of sixteen and twenty-three. A key innovation was the close moral supervision of these workers, who lived in company-owned boarding-houses. Corporation rules required church attendance and prohibited drinking and unsupervised courtship; dorms were locked at 10 p.m. The typical mill worker earned $2 to $3 for a seventy-hour week. That was more than a seamstress or domestic servant could earn but less than a young man's wages. The job consisted of tending noisy power looms in rooms kept hot and humid—ideal conditions for thread but not for people.

Despite the discomforts, young women embraced factory work as a means to earn spending money and build savings before marriage. Also welcome was the unprecedented, though still limited, personal freedom of living in an all-female social space, away from parents and domestic tasks. In the evening, the women could engage in self-improvement activities, such as attending lectures or writing for the company's periodical, the *Lowell Offering.*

In the mid-1830s, worldwide changes in the cotton market impelled mill owners to speed up work and lower wages. The workers protested, emboldened by their communal living arrangement and by their relative independence as temporary employees. In 1834 and again in 1836, hundreds of women at Lowell went out on strike. All over New England, female mill workers led strikes and formed unions. In 1834, women at a mill in Dover, New Hampshire, denounced their owners for trying to turn them into "slaves": "However freely the epithet of 'factory slaves' may be bestowed upon us, we will never deserve it by a base and cringing submission to proud wealth or haughty insolence." Their assertiveness surprised many, but in the end their bargaining power was undercut by the ease with which factory owners could replace them. In the 1840s, owners began to shift to immigrant families as their primary labor source.

Other manufacturing enterprises of the 1820s and 1830s, such as shoemaking, innovated by employing women in ever-larger numbers. New modes of organizing the work allowed manufacturers to step up production, control waste and quality, and decrease wages by hiring women, including wives. Male shoemakers still cut the leather and made the soles, but now the stitching of the upper parts of the shoes, called shoebinding, became women's work, performed at home so that it could be done in conjunction with domestic chores. Although women's wages were lower than men's, shoebinders were in the vanguard of a new trend as wage-earning wives, contributing additional cash to family income.

In the economically turbulent 1830s, shoebinder wages fell. The fact that shoebinders worked at home, in isolation, was a serious hindrance to organized protest. In Lynn, Massachusetts, a major shoemaking center, women used female church networks to organize resistance, communicating via religious newspapers. The Lynn shoebinders who demanded higher wages in 1834 built on a collective sense of themselves as women even though they did not work together daily. "Equal rights should be extended to all—to the weaker sex as well as the stronger," they wrote in a document establishing the Female Society of Lynn.

In the end, the Lynn shoebinders' protests failed to achieve wage increases. Isolated workers all over New England continued to accept low wages, and even in Lynn, many women shied away from organized protest, preferring to situate their work in the context of family duty (helping their husbands to finish the shoes) instead of market relations.

Bankers and Lawyers

Entrepreneurs such as the Lowell factory owners relied on innovations in the banking system to finance their ventures. Between 1814 and 1816, the number of state-chartered banks in the United States more than doubled, from fewer than 90 to 208. By 1830, there were 330, and by 1840 hundreds more. Banks stimulated the economy by making loans to merchants and manufacturers and by enlarging the money supply. Borrowers were issued loans in the form of banknotes— certificates unique to each bank—which were used as money for all transactions. Neither federal nor state governments issued paper money, so banknotes became the country's currency.

In theory, a note could always be traded in at a bank for its **hard-money** equivalent in gold or silver. This transaction was known as a "specie payment." A note from a solid local bank might be worth exactly what it was written for, but the face value of a note from a distant or questionable bank would be discounted. Buying and selling banknotes in this era required knowledge and caution. Not surprisingly, counterfeiting flourished.

Bankers exercised great power over the economy, deciding who would get loans and what the discount rates would be. The most powerful bankers sat on the board of directors for the second Bank of the United States, headquartered in Philadelphia. The twenty-year charter of the first Bank of the United States had expired in 1811. The second Bank of the United States, with eighteen branches throughout the country, opened for business in 1816 under another twenty-year charter. The rechartering of this bank would be a major issue in Andrew Jackson's reelection campaign in 1832.

Accompanying the market revolution was a revolution in commercial law, fashioned by politicians to enhance the prospects of private investment. In 1811, states started to rewrite their laws of incorporation (allowing the chartering of businesses by states), and the number of corporations expanded rapidly, from about twenty in 1800 to eighteen hundred by 1817. Incorporation protected individual investors from being held liable for corporate debts. State lawmakers also wrote laws of eminent domain, empowering states to buy land for roads and canals even from unwilling sellers. They drafted legislation on contributory negligence, relieving employers of the responsibility for workplace injuries. In such ways, entrepreneurial lawyers of the 1820s and 1830s created the legal foundation for an economy that would give priority to ambitious individuals interested in maximizing their own wealth.

Not everyone applauded these developments. Andrew Jackson, himself a skillful lawyer turned politician, spoke for a large and mistrustful segment of the population when he warned about the potential abuses of power "which the moneyed interest derives from a paper currency which they are able to control, from the multitude of corporations with exclusive privileges which they have succeeded in obtaining in the different states, and which are employed altogether for their benefit." Jacksonians believed that ending government-granted privileges was the way to maximize individual liberty and economic opportunity.

Booms and Busts

One aspect of the economy that the lawyer-politicians could not control was the threat of financial collapse. The boom years from 1815 to 1818 exhibited a volatility that resulted in the first sharp, large-scale economic downturn in U.S. history. Americans called this downturn a "panic," and the pattern was repeated in the 1830s. Rapidly rising consumer demand stimulated price increases, and speculative investment opportunities offering the possibility of high payoffs abounded—in bank stocks, western land sales, urban real estate, and commodities markets. High inflation made some people wealthy but created hardships for workers on fixed incomes.

When the bubble burst in 1819, the overnight rich suddenly became the overnight poor. Some blamed the panic of 1819 on the second Bank of the United States, which had failed to exercise control over the state banks. Many of those state banks had suspended specie payments—the exchange of gold or silver for banknotes—in their eagerness to expand the economic bubble. By mid-1818, when the Bank of the United States started to call in its loans and insisted that the state banks do likewise, the contracting of the money supply sent tremors throughout the economy. The crunch was made worse by a financial crisis in Europe in the spring of 1819. Overseas, prices for American cotton, tobacco, and wheat plummeted by more than 50 percent. Thus, when the Bank of the United States and the state banks called in their outstanding loans, American debtors involved in the commodities trade could not come up with the money. The number of business and personal bankruptcies skyrocketed. The intricate web of credit and debt relationships meant that almost everyone with even a toehold in the new commercial economy was affected by the panic. Thousands of Americans lost their savings and property, and unemployment estimates suggest that half a million people lost their jobs.

Recovery took several years. Unemployment rates fell, but bitterness lingered, ready to be stirred up by politicians in the decades to come. The dangers of a system that was dependent on extensive credit were clear to many. In one folksy formulation that circulated around 1820, a farmer compared credit to "a man pissing in his breeches on a cold day to keep his arse warm—very comfortable at first but I dare say . . . you know how it feels afterwards."

By the mid-1820s, the economy was back on track, driven by increases in productivity, consumer demand for goods, and international trade, as well as a restless and calculating people moving goods, human labor, and investment capital in expanding circles of commerce. Despite the panic of 1819, credit financing continued to fuel the system. With the growth of manufacturing and transportation networks, buyers and sellers operated in a much larger arena, using credit transactions on paper instead of moving actual (and scarce) hard money around. A merchant in Ohio who bought goods in New York City on credit hoped to repay the loan with interest when he sold the merchandise—often on credit—for a profit. Slave owners might obtain loans to purchase additional land or slaves, using currently owned slaves as collateral. A network of credit and debt relations grew dense by the 1830s in a system that encouraged speculation and risk taking. A pervasive optimism about continued growth supported the elaborate system, but a single business failure could produce many innocent victims. Well after the panic of 1819, an undercurrent of anxiety about rapid economic change continued to shape the political views of many Americans.

> ▶ **REVIEW**   Why did the United States experience a market revolution after 1815?

The Spread of Democracy

Just as the market revolution held out the promise, if not the reality, of economic opportunity for all who worked, the political transformation of the 1830s held out the promise of political opportunity for hundreds of thousands of new voters. During Andrew Jackson's presidency (1829–1837), the second American party system took shape. Not until 1836, however, would the parties have distinct names and consistent programs transcending the particular personalities running for office. Over those years, more men could and did vote, responding to new methods of arousing voter interest. In 1828, Jackson's charismatic personality defined his party, and his victory over incumbent president John Quincy Adams turned on questions of character. Once in office, Jackson championed ordinary citizens against the power elite—**democracy** versus aristocracy in Jackson's terminology. A lasting contribution of the Jackson years was the notion that politicians needed to have the common touch in their dealings with voters.

Popular Politics and Partisan Identity

The election of 1828 was the first presidential contest in which the popular vote determined the outcome. In twenty-two out of twenty-four states, voters—not state legislatures—designated the number of electors committed to a particular candidate. More than a million voters participated in the election—three times the number in 1824 and nearly half the free male population, reflecting the high stakes that voters perceived in the Adams-Jackson rematch. Throughout the 1830s, voter turnout continued to rise and reached 70 percent in some localities, partly due to the disappearance of property qualifications in all but three states and partly due to heightened political interest.

The 1828 election inaugurated new campaign styles. State-level candidates routinely gave speeches at rallies, picnics, and banquets. Adams and Jackson still declined such appearances as undignified, but Henry Clay of Kentucky, campaigning for Adams, earned the nickname "the Barbecue Orator." Campaign rhetoric became more informal and even blunt. The Jackson camp established many Hickory Clubs, trading on Jackson's popular nickname, "Old Hickory," from a common Tennessee tree suggesting resilience and toughness. (Jackson was the first presidential candidate to have an affectionate and widely used nickname.)

Partisan newspapers in ever-larger numbers defined issues and publicized political personalities as never before. Improved printing technology and rising literacy rates fueled a great expansion of newspapers of all kinds. Party leaders dispensed subsidies and other favors to secure the support of papers, even in remote towns and villages. In New York State, where party development was most advanced, a pro-Jackson group called the Bucktails controlled fifty weekly publications. Stories from the leading Jacksonian paper in Washington, D.C., were reprinted two days later in a Boston or Cincinnati paper, for example, as fast as the mail stage could carry them. Presidential campaigns were now coordinated in a national arena.

Politicians at first identified themselves as Jackson or Adams men, honoring the fiction of Republican Party unity. By 1832, however, the terminology had evolved to National Republicans, favoring federal action to promote commercial development, and Democratic Republicans, who promised to be responsive to the will of the majority. Between 1834 and 1836, National Republicans came to be called Whigs, while Jackson's party became simply the Democrats.

The Election of 1828 and the Character Issue

The campaign of 1828 was the first national election in which scandal and character questions reigned supreme. They became central issues because voters used them to comprehend the kind of public officer each man would make. Character issues conveyed in shorthand larger questions about morality, honor, and discipline. Jackson and Adams presented two radically different styles of manhood.

John Quincy Adams was vilified by his opponents as an elitist, a bookish academic, and perhaps even a monarchist. Critics pointed to his White House billiard table and ivory chess set as symbols of his aristocratic degeneracy. They also attacked his "corrupt bargain" of 1824—the alleged election deal between Adams and Henry Clay (see chapter 10). Adams's supporters returned fire with fire. They played on Jackson's fatherless childhood to portray him as the bastard son of a prostitute. Worse, the cloudy circumstances around his marriage to Rachel Donelson Robards in 1791 gave rise to the story that Jackson was a seducer and an adulterer, having married a woman whose divorce from her first husband was not entirely legal. Pro-Adams newspapers howled that Jackson was sinful and impulsive, while portraying Adams as pious, learned, and virtuous.

Editors in favor of Adams played up Jackson's violent temper, as evidenced by the many duels, brawls, and canings in which he had been involved. Jackson's supporters used the same stories to project Old Hickory as a tough frontier hero who knew how to command obedience. As for learning, Jackson's rough frontier education gave him a "natural sense," wrote a Boston editor, that "can never be acquired by reading books—it can only be acquired, in perfection, by reading men."

Jackson won a sweeping victory, 56 percent of the popular vote and 178 electoral votes to Adams's 83. Old Hickory took most of the South and West and carried Pennsylvania and New York as well; Adams carried the remainder of the East. Jackson's vice president was John C. Calhoun, who had just served as vice president under Adams but had broken with Adams's policies.

After 1828, national politicians no longer deplored the existence of political parties. They were coming to see that parties mobilized and delivered voters, sharpened candidates' differences, and created party loyalty that surpassed loyalty to individual candidates and elections. Adams and Jackson clearly symbolized the competing ideas of the emerging parties: a moralistic, top-down party (the Whigs) ready to make major decisions to promote economic growth competing against a contentious, energetic party (the Democrats) ready to embrace liberty-loving individualism.

Jackson's Democratic Agenda

Before the inauguration in March 1829, Rachel Jackson died. Certain that the ugly campaign had hastened his wife's death, the president went into deep mourning, his depression worsened by constant pain from the bullet still lodged in his chest from the 1806 duel and by mercury poisoning from the medicines he took. At sixty-two years old, Jackson carried only 140 pounds on his six-foot-one frame. His adversaries doubted that he would make it to a second term. His supporters, however, went wild at the inauguration. Thousands cheered his ten-minute inaugural address, the shortest in history. An open reception at the White House turned into a near riot as well-wishers jammed the premises, used windows as doors, stood on furniture for a better view of the great man, and broke thousands of dollars' worth of china and glasses.

During his presidency, Jackson continued to offer unprecedented hospitality to the public. Twenty spittoons newly installed in the East Room of the White House accommodated the tobacco chewers among the throngs that arrived daily to see the president. The courteous Jackson, committed to his image as president of the "common man," held audiences with unannounced visitors throughout his two terms.

Jackson's appointments marked a departure from past presidential policy. Earlier presidents had tried to lessen party conflict by including men of different factions in their cabinets, but Jackson would have only loyalists, a political tactic followed by most later presidents. For secretary of state, the key job, he tapped New Yorker Martin Van Buren, one of the shrewdest politicians of the day. Throughout the federal government, from postal clerks to ambassadors, Jackson removed competent civil servants and installed party loyalists. "To the victor belong the spoils," said a Democratic senator from New York, expressing his approval of patronage-driven appointments. Jackson's approach to **civil service** employment got tagged the **spoils system**; it was a concept the president strenuously defended.

Jackson's agenda quickly emerged. He favored a Jeffersonian limited federal government, fearing that intervention in the economy inevitably favored some groups at the expense of others. He therefore opposed federal support of transportation and grants of monopolies and charters that privileged wealthy investors. Like Jefferson, he anticipated the rapid settlement of the country's interior, where land sales would spread economic democracy to settlers. Thus, establishing a federal policy to remove the Indians from this area was a priority for Jackson. Unlike Jefferson, Jackson exercised his presidential veto power over Congress. In 1830, he vetoed a highway project in Maysville, Kentucky—Henry Clay's home state—that Congress had voted to support with federal dollars. The Maysville Road veto articulated Jackson's principled stand that citizens' federal tax dollars could be spent only on projects of a "general, not local" character. In all, Jackson used the veto twelve times; all previous presidents had exercised that right a total of nine times.

▶ **REVIEW**   Why did Andrew Jackson defeat John Quincy Adams so dramatically in the 1828 election?

Jackson Defines the Democratic Party

In his two terms as president, Andrew Jackson worked to implement his vision of a politics of opportunity for all white men. To open land for white settlement, he favored the relocation of all eastern Indian tribes. He dramatically confronted John C. Calhoun and South Carolina when that state tried to nullify the tariff of 1828. Disapproving of all government-granted privilege, Jackson challenged what he called the "monster" Bank of the United States and took it down to defeat. In all this, he greatly enhanced the power of the presidency.

Indian Policy and the Trail of Tears

Probably nothing defined Jackson's presidency more than his efforts to solve what he saw as the Indian problem. Thousands of Indians lived in the South and the old Northwest, and not a few remained in New England and New York. Jackson, who rose to fame fighting the Creek and Seminole tribes in the 1810s, declared in 1829, in his first message to Congress, that removing the Indians to territory west of the Mississippi was the only way to save them. White civilization destroyed Indian resources and thus doomed the Indians, he claimed: "That this fate surely awaits them if they remain within the limits of the states does not admit of a doubt. Humanity and national honor demand that every effort should be made to avert so great a calamity." Jackson never publicly wavered from this seemingly noble theme, returning to it in his next seven annual messages.

Prior administrations had experimented with different Indian policies. Starting in 1819, Congress granted $10,000 a year to various missionary associations eager to "civilize" native peoples by converting them to Christianity and encouraging English literacy and agricultural practices. Missionaries also promoted white gender customs, but Indian women were reluctant to embrace practices that accorded them less power than their tribal systems did. The federal government also had pursued aggressive treaty making with many tribes, dealing with the Indians as if they were foreign nations (see chapter 10, page 284).

Andrew Jackson as "the Great Father"
In 1828, a new process of cheap commercial lithography found immediate application in a colorful presidential campaign aimed at capturing popular votes, and with it, a rich tradition of political cartoons was born. Jackson inspired at least five dozen satirical cartoons centering on caricatures of him. Strikingly, only one of them featured his Indian policy, controversial as it was, and only a single copy still exists. William L. Clements Library.

Privately, Jackson thought it was "absurd" to treat the Indians as foreigners; he saw them as subjects of the United States. Jackson also did not approve of assimilation; that way lay extinction, he said. In his 1833 message to Congress, he wrote, "They have neither the intelligence, the industry, the moral habits, nor the desire of improvement which are essential. . . . Established in the midst of a superior race . . . they must necessarily yield to the force of circumstances and ere long disappear." Congress backed Jackson's goal and passed the Indian Removal Act of 1830, appropriating $500,000 to relocate eastern tribes west of the Mississippi. About 100 million acres of eastern land would be vacated for eventual white settlement under this act authorizing ethnic expulsion (Map 11.1).

Jackson's explanation that removal would save the Indians from extinction was in part formulated in response to the widespread controversy generated by the act. Newspapers, public lecturers, and local clubs debated Jackson's proposed

MAP 11.1   Indian Removal and the Trail of Tears

The federal government under President Andrew Jackson pursued a vigorous policy of Indian removal in the 1830s. Tribes were forcibly moved west to land known as Indian Territory (present-day Oklahoma). As many as a quarter of the Cherokee Indians died on the route known as the Trail of Tears in 1838.

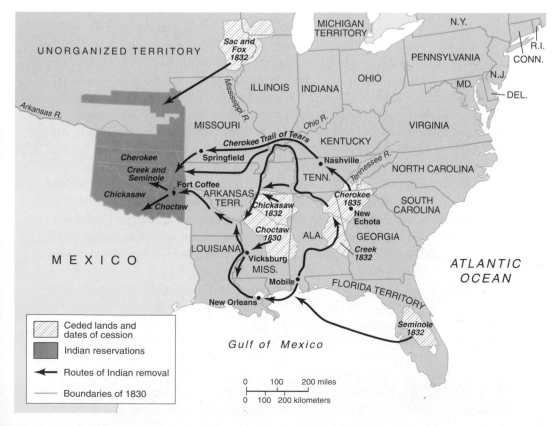

policy, and in an unprecedented move, thousands of northern white women launched a petition drive to protest the expulsion law. The right to petition for redress of grievances, part of the Constitution's First Amendment, had long been used by individual women acting on personal cause, as when a widow requested a benefit based on a dead husband's military service. But mass petitioning by women was something new; it challenged the prevailing assumptions that women were not political actors and should let their husbands speak for them. Between 1830 and 1832, women's petitions rolled into Washington, arguing specifically that the Cherokee Indians of Georgia were a sovereign people, on the road to Christianity and with a right to stay on their land. The petitions had little effect on Jackson's policy.

For the northern tribes, their numbers diminished by years of war, gradual removal was already well under way. But not all the Indians went quietly. In 1832 in western Illinois, Black Hawk, a leader of the Sauk and Fox Indians who had fought in alliance with Tecumseh in the War of 1812 (see chapter 10, page 287), resisted removal. Volunteer militias attacked and chased the Indians into south-ern Wisconsin, where, after several skirmishes and a deadly battle (later called the Black Hawk War), Black Hawk was captured and about four hundred of his people were massacred.

The southern tribes proved even more resistant to removal. The powerful Creek, Chickasaw, Choctaw, and Cherokee tribes refused to relocate. A second Seminole War broke out in Florida as the Indians there—a mixture of Seminoles and escaped black slaves who had intermarried with the tribe—took up arms against relocation in 1836–1837.

The Cherokee tribe of Georgia responded with a unique legal challenge to being treated as subjects. More than any other southern tribe, the seventeen thou-sand Cherokees had incorporated white political and economic practices into their tribal life. Spurred by dedicated missionaries, they had adopted written laws, including, in 1827, a constitution modeled on the U.S. Constitution. Two hundred of the wealthiest Cherokees had intermarried with whites and had adopted white styles of housing, dress, and cotton agriculture, including the ownership of a thousand slaves. They had developed a written alphabet and published a newspaper and Christian prayer books in their language. These features helped make their cause attractive to the northern white women who petitioned the government on their behalf.

In 1831, after Georgia announced that it would subject the Indians to state law and seize their property, the Cherokee tribe appealed to the U.S. Supreme Court to restrain Georgia. Chief Justice John Marshall found for Georgia on the grounds that the tribe did not have standing to sue. When Georgia jailed two missionaries under an 1830 state law forbidding missionary aid to Indians without permission, the tribe brought suit again, naming one of the missionaries as plain-tiff. In the 1832 case *Worcester v. Georgia*, the Supreme Court upheld the territorial sovereignty of the Cherokee people, recognizing their existence as "a distinct community, occupying its own territory, in which the laws of Georgia can have no force." Ignoring the Court's decision, an angry President Jackson pressed the Cherokee tribe to move west: "If they now refuse to accept the liberal terms offered, they can only be liable for whatever evils and difficulties may arise. I feel conscious of having done my duty to my red children."

The Cherokee tribe remained in Georgia for two more years without significant violence. Then, in 1835, a small, unauthorized faction of the tribe signed a treaty selling all the tribal lands to the state, which rapidly resold the land to whites. Chief John Ross, backed by several thousand Cherokees, petitioned the U.S. Congress to ignore the bogus treaty. "By the stipulations of this instrument," he wrote, "we are stripped of every attribute of freedom and eligibility for legal self-defense. Our property may be plundered before our eyes; violence may be committed on our persons; even our lives may be taken away. . . . We are denationalized; we are **disfranchised**."

Most of the Cherokees refused to move, so in May 1838, the deadline for voluntary evacuation, federal troops sent by Jackson's successor, Martin Van Buren, arrived to remove them. Under armed guard, the Cherokees embarked on a 1,200-mile journey west that came to be called the Trail of Tears. A newspaperman in Kentucky described the forced march: "Even aged females, apparently, nearly ready to drop into the grave, were traveling with heavy burdens attached to the back. . . . They buried fourteen to fifteen at every stopping place." Nearly a quarter of the Cherokees died en route. The survivors joined the fifteen thousand Creek, twelve thousand Choctaw, five thousand Chickasaw, and several thousand Seminole Indians also forcibly relocated to Indian Territory (which became the state of Oklahoma in 1907).

In his farewell address to the nation in 1837, Jackson professed his belief in the benefit of Indian removal: "This unhappy race . . . are now placed in a situation where we may well hope that they will share in the blessings of civilization and be saved from the degradation and destruction to which they were rapidly hastening while they remained in the states." Perhaps Jackson genuinely believed that exile to the West was necessary to save these Indian cultures from destruction. But for the forcibly removed tribes, the costs of relocation were high.

The Tariff of Abominations and Nullification

Jackson's Indian policy happened to harmonize with the principle of **states' rights**: The president supported Georgia's right to ignore the Supreme Court's decision in *Worcester v. Georgia*. But in another pressing question of states' rights, Jackson contested South Carolina's attempt to ignore federal tariff policy.

Federal tariffs as high as 33 percent on imports such as textiles and iron goods had been passed in 1816 and again in 1824, in an effort to favor new American manufacturers and shelter them from foreign competition, as well as to raise federal revenue. Some southern congressmen opposed the steep tariffs, fearing they would decrease overseas shipping and hurt cotton exports. During John Quincy Adams's administration (1825–1829), tariff policy generated heated debate. In 1828, Congress passed a revised tariff that came to be known as the Tariff of Abominations. A bundle of conflicting duties—some as high as 50 percent—the legislation contained provisions that pleased and angered every economic and sectional interest. Drafted mostly by southern congressmen, who loaded it with duties on raw materials needed by New England manufacturers, it also contained protectionist elements favored by those same manufacturers.

South Carolina in particular suffered from the Tariff of Abominations. Worldwide prices for cotton had declined in the late 1820s, and the falloff in shipping caused by the high tariffs further hurt the South. In 1828, a group of South Carolina politicians headed by John C. Calhoun advanced a doctrine called **nullification**. The Union, they argued, was a confederation of states that had yielded some but not all power to the federal government. When Congress overstepped its powers, states had the right to nullify Congress's acts. As precedents, they pointed to the Virginia and Kentucky Resolutions of 1798, which had attempted to invalidate the Alien and Sedition Acts (see chapter 9). Congress had erred in using tariff policy as an instrument to benefit specific industries, the South Carolinians claimed; tariffs should be used only to raise revenue.

On assuming the presidency in 1829, Jackson ignored the South Carolina statement of nullification and shut out Calhoun, his new vice president, from influence or power. Tariff revisions in early 1832 brought little relief to the South. Sensing futility, Calhoun resigned the vice presidency in 1832 and accepted election by the South Carolina legislature to a seat in the U.S. Senate, where he could better argue his state's antitariff stance. Strained to their limit, the South Carolina leaders took the radical step of declaring the federal tariffs null and void in their state as of February 1, 1833. Finally, the constitutional crisis was out in the open.

Opting for a dramatic confrontation, Jackson sent armed ships to Charleston harbor and threatened to invade the state. He pushed through Congress a bill, called the Force Bill, defining the Carolina stance as treason and authorizing military action to collect federal tariffs. At the same time, Congress moved quickly to pass a revised tariff that was more acceptable to the South. The conciliating Senator Henry Clay rallied support for a moderate bill that gradually reduced tariffs down to the 1816 level. On March 1, 1833, Congress passed both the new tariff and the Force Bill. South Carolina responded by withdrawing its nullification of the old tariff—and then nullifying the Force Bill. It was a symbolic gesture, since Jackson's show of muscle was no longer necessary. Both sides were satisfied with the immediate outcome. Federal power had prevailed over a dangerous assertion of states' rights, and South Carolina got the lower tariff it wanted.

Yet the question of federal power versus states' rights was far from settled. The implied threat behind nullification was secession, a position articulated in 1832 by some South Carolinians whose concerns went beyond tariff policy. In the 1830s, the political moratorium on discussions of slavery agreed on at the time of the Missouri Compromise (see chapter 10) was coming unglued, and new northern voices opposed to slavery gained increasing attention. If and when a northern-dominated federal government decided to end slavery, the South Carolinians thought, the South might want to nullify such laws, or even remove itself from the Union.

The Bank War and Economic Boom

Along with the tariff and nullification, President Jackson fought another political battle, over the Bank of the United States. After riding out the panic of 1819, the bank finally prospered. It handled the federal government's deposits, extended credit and loans, and issued banknotes—by 1830, the most stable currency in the country. Now having twenty-nine branches, it benefited the whole nation. Jackson, however, did not find the bank's functions sufficiently valuable to offset his criticism of the concept of a national bank. In his first two annual messages to Congress, in 1829 and 1830, he claimed that the bank concentrated undue economic power in the hands of a few.

National Republican (Whig) senators Daniel Webster and Henry Clay decided to force the issue. They convinced the bank to apply for charter renewal in 1832, well before the fall election, even though the existing charter ran until 1836. They fully expected that Congress's renewal would force Jackson to follow through on his rhetoric with a veto, that the unpopular veto would cause Jackson to lose the election, and that the bank would survive on an override vote by a new Congress swept into power on the anti-Jackson tide.

At first, the plan seemed to work. The bank applied for rechartering, Congress voted to renew, and Jackson, angry over being manipulated, issued his veto. But it was a brilliantly written veto, full of fierce language about the privileges of the moneyed elite who oppress the democratic masses in order to enrich themselves. "Many of our rich men have not been content with equal protection and equal benefits, but have besought us to make them richer by act of Congress," Jackson wrote.

Clay and his supporters found Jackson's economic ideas so absurd and his language of class antagonism so shocking that they distributed thousands of copies of the bank veto as campaign material for their own party. A confident Henry Clay headed his party's ticket for the presidency. But the plan backfired. Jackson's translation of the bank controversy into a language of class antagonism and egalitarian ideals resonated with many Americans. Old Hickory won the election easily, gaining 55 percent of the popular vote and 219 electoral votes to Clay's 49. Jackson's party still controlled Congress, so no override was possible. The second Bank of the United States would cease to exist after 1836.

Jackson, however, wanted to destroy the bank sooner. Calling it a "monster," he ordered the sizable federal deposits to be removed from its vaults and redeposited into Democratic-inclined state banks. In retaliation, the Bank of the

United States raised interest rates and called in loans. This action caused a brief decline in the economy in 1833 and actually enhanced Jackson's claim that the bank was too powerful for the good of the country.

Unleashed and unregulated, the economy went into high gear in 1834. Just at this moment, an excess of silver from Mexican mines made its way into American banks, giving bankers license to print ever more banknotes. From 1834 to 1837, inflation soared; prices of basic goods rose more than 50 percent. States quickly chartered hundreds of new private banks. Each bank issued its own bank-notes and set interest rates as high as the market would bear. Entrepreneurs borrowed and invested money, much of it funneled into privately financed railroads and canals. With money cheap, the webs of credit and debt relationships that were the hallmark of the American economy grew denser yet.

The market in western land sales heated up. In 1834, about 4.5 million acres of the public domain had been sold, the highest annual volume since 1818. By 1836, the total reached an astonishing 20 million acres. Some of this was southern land in Mississippi and Louisiana, which slave owners rushed to bring under cultivation, but much more was in the North, where land offices were deluged with buyers. The Jackson administration worried that the purchasers were overwhelmingly eastern capitalists, land speculators instead of self-reliant **yeoman** farmers who intended to settle on the land.

In one respect, the economy attained an admirable goal: The national debt disappeared, and, for the first and only time in American history, from 1835 to 1837 the government had a monetary surplus. But much of that surplus consisted of questionable bank currencies—"bloated, diseased" currencies, in Jackson's vivid terminology. While the boom was on, however, few stopped to worry about the consequences if and when the bubble burst.

▶ **REVIEW**   Why did Jackson promote Indian removal?

Cultural Shifts, Religion, and Reform

The growing economy, moving steadily upward in the 1820s and then booming in the mid-1830s, transformed far more than just productive activity. For increasing numbers of families, especially in the commercialized Northeast, standards of living rose, consumption patterns changed, and the nature and location of work altered. All of these changes had a direct impact on the duties of men and women and on the training of youths for the economy of the future.

Along with economic change came an unprecedented revival of evangelical religion known as the **Second Great Awakening**. Just as universal male **suffrage** allowed all white men to vote, democratized religion offered salvation to all who chose to embrace it. Among the most serious adherents of evangelical **Protestantism**

were men and women of the new merchant classes, whose self-discipline in pursuing market ambitions meshed well with the message of self-discipline in pursuit of
spiritual perfection. Not content with individual perfection, many of these people
sought to perfect society as well, by defining excessive alcohol consumption, non-
marital sex, and slavery as three major evils of modern life in need of correction.

The Family and Separate Spheres

The centerpiece of new ideas about gender relations was the notion that husbands found their status and authority in the new world of work, leaving wives
to tend the hearth and home. Sermons, advice books, periodicals, and novels reinforced the idea that men and women inhabited **separate spheres** and had separate duties. "To woman it belongs . . . to elevate the intellectual character of her
household [and] to kindle the fires of mental activity in childhood," wrote
Mrs. A. J. Graves in a popular book titled *Advice to American Women*. For men, in
contrast, "the absorbing passion for gain, and the pressing demands of business,
engross their whole attention." In particular, the home, now the exclusive domain
of women, was sentimentalized as the source of intimacy, love, and safety, a
refuge from the cruel and competitive world of market relations.

Some new aspects of society gave substance to this formulation of separate
spheres. Men's work was undergoing profound change after 1815 and increasingly brought cash to the household, especially in the manufacturing and urban
Northeast. Farmers and tradesmen sold products in a market, and bankers, book-
keepers, shoemakers, and canal diggers got pay envelopes. Furthermore, many
men performed jobs outside the home, at an office or store. For men who were
not farmers, work indeed seemed newly disconnected from life at home.

A woman's domestic role was more complicated than the cultural prescriptions indicated. Although the vast majority of married white women did not hold
paying jobs, the home continued to be a site of time-consuming labor. But the advice books treated household tasks as loving familial duties; housework as *work*
was thereby rendered invisible in an economy that evaluated work by how much
cash it generated. In reality, wives contributed directly to family income in many
ways. Some took in boarders; others engaged in outwork, earning pay for shoebinding, hatmaking, or needlework done at home. Wives in the poorer classes of
society, including most free black wives, did not have the luxury of husbands
earning adequate wages; for them, work as servants or laundresses helped augment family income.

Idealized notions about the feminine home and the masculine workplace
gained acceptance in the 1830s (and well beyond) because of the cultural dominance of the middle and upper classes of the Northeast, expressed through books
and periodicals that reflected these gender ideals. Men seeking manhood through
work and pay would embrace competition and acquisitiveness, while women
established femininity through dutiful service to home and family. This particular

formulation of gender difference helped smooth the path for the first generation of Americans experiencing the market revolution, and both men and women of the middle classes benefited. Men were set free to pursue wealth, and women gained moral authority within the home. Beyond white families of the middle and upper classes, however, these new gender ideals had limited applicability. Despite their apparent dominance in printed material of the period, they were never all-pervasive.

The Education and Training of Youths

The market economy, with its new expectations for men and women, required expanded opportunities for training youths of both sexes. By the 1830s, in both the North and South, state-supported public school systems were the norm, designed to produce pupils able, by age twelve or fourteen, to read, write, and participate in marketplace calculations. Girls usually received the same basic education as boys. Literacy rates for white females climbed dramatically, rivaling the rates for white males for the first time. The fact that taxpayers paid for children's education created an incentive to seek an inexpensive teaching force. By the 1830s, school districts began replacing male teachers with young females, for, as a Massachusetts state report on education put it, "females can be educated cheaper, quicker, and better, and will teach cheaper after they are qualified." Like mill workers, female teachers were in their late teens and regarded the work as temporary. Many were trained in private female academies, now numbering in the hundreds (see chapter 10).

Advanced education continued to expand in the 1830s, with an additional two dozen colleges for men and several more female seminaries offering education on a par with the male colleges. Mount Holyoke Seminary in western Massachusetts, founded by educator Mary Lyon in 1837, developed a rigorous scientific curriculum drawing on resources from the science program at nearby Amherst College. And Oberlin College in Ohio, founded by Presbyterians in 1835, became the first coeducational college when it opened its doors to women in 1837. Oberlin's goal was to train young men for the ministry and to prepare young women to be ministers' wives.

Still, only a very small percentage of young people attended institutions of higher learning. The vast majority of male youths left public school at age fourteen to apprentice in specific trades or to embark on business careers by seeking entry-level clerkships, abundant in the growing urban centers. Young girls also headed for mill towns or for cities in unprecedented numbers, seeking work in the expanding service sector as seamstresses and domestic servants. Changes in patterns of youth employment meant that large numbers of youngsters escaped the watchful eyes of their parents. Moralists fretted about the dangers of unsupervised youths, and following the lead of the Lowell mill owners, some established apprentices' libraries and uplifting lecture series to keep young people

Women Graduates of Oberlin College, Class of 1855
Oberlin College, founded in Ohio by evangelical and abolitionist activists in the 1830s, admitted men and women, both white and black. Instruction was not coeducational; the women attended classes in the separate Ladies' Department. By 1855, as this daguerreotype shows, black women had integrated the Ladies' Department.
Oberlin College Archives, Oberlin, Ohio.

honorably occupied. Advice books published by the hundreds instructed youths in the virtues of hard work and delayed gratification.

The Second Great Awakening

A newly invigorated version of Protestantism gained momentum in the 1820s and 1830s as the economy reshaped gender and age relations. The earliest manifestations of this fervent piety appeared in 1801 in Kentucky, when a crowd of ten thousand people camped out on a hillside at Cane Ridge for a revival meeting that lasted several weeks. By the 1810s and 1820s, "camp meetings" had spread to the Atlantic seaboard states, finding especially enthusiastic audiences in western New York and Pennsylvania. The outdoor settings permitted huge attendance, which itself intensified the emotional impact of the experience. "For more than a half mile, I could see people on their knees before God in humble prayer," recalled one Cane Ridge worshipper.

The gatherings attracted women and men hungry for a more immediate access to spiritual peace, one not requiring years of soul-searching. One eyewitness at a revival reported that "some of the people were singing, others praying, some crying for mercy. . . . At one time I saw at least five hundred swept down in a moment as if a battery of a thousand guns had been opened upon them, and then immediately followed shrieks and shouts that rent the very heavens."

From 1800 to 1820, church membership doubled in the United States, much of it among the evangelical groups. Methodists, Baptists, and Presbyterians formed the core of the new movement; Episcopalians, Congregationalists, Unitarians, Dutch Reformed, Lutherans, and Catholics maintained strong skepticism about the emotional enthusiasm. Women more than men were attracted to the evangelical movement, and wives and mothers typically recruited husbands and sons to join them.

The leading exemplar of the Second Great Awakening was a lawyer turned minister named Charles Grandison Finney. Finney lived in western New York, where the completion of the Erie Canal in 1825 fundamentally altered the social and economic landscape overnight. Towns swelled with new inhabitants who brought in remarkable prosperity along with other, less admirable side effects, such as prostitution, drinking, and gaming. Finney saw New York canal towns as especially ripe for evangelical awakening. In Rochester, New York, he sustained a six-month revival through the winter of 1830–31, generating thousands of converts.

Finney's message was directed primarily at women and men of the business classes. He argued that a reign of Christian perfection loomed, one that required public-spirited outreach to the less-than-perfect to foster their salvation. Evangelicals promoted Sunday schools to bring piety to children; they battled to end mail delivery, stop public transport, and close shops on Sundays to honor the Sabbath. Many women formed missionary societies, which distributed millions of Bibles and religious tracts. Through such avenues, evangelical religion offered women expanded spheres of influence. Finney adopted the tactics of Jacksonian-era politicians—publicity, argumentation, rallies, and speeches—to sell his cause. His object, he said, was to get Americans to "vote in the Lord Jesus Christ as the governor of the Universe."

The Temperance Movement and the Campaign for Moral Reform

The evangelical disposition—a combination of faith, energy, self-discipline, and righteousness—animated vigorous campaigns to eliminate alcohol abuse and eradicate sexual sin. Millions of Americans took the temperance pledge to abstain from strong drink, and thousands became involved in efforts to end prostitution.

Alcohol consumption had risen steadily in the decades up to 1830, when the average person over age thirteen annually consumed an astonishing nine gallons of hard liquor plus thirty gallons of hard cider, beer, and wine. All classes imbibed. A lively saloon culture fostered masculine camaraderie along with extensive alcohol consumption among laborers, while in elite homes, the after-dinner whiskey or sherry was commonplace. Colleges before 1820 routinely served students a pint of ale with meals, and the army and navy included rum in the standard daily ration.

Organized opposition to drinking first surfaced in the 1810s among health and religious reformers. In 1826, Lyman Beecher, a Connecticut minister of an "awakened" church, founded the American Temperance Society, which warned that drinking led to poverty, idleness, crime, and family violence. Adopting the methods of evangelical ministers, temperance lecturers traveled the country expounding the damage of drink. By 1833, some six thousand local affiliates of the American Temperance Society boasted more than a million members. Middle-class drinking began a steep decline. One powerful tool of persuasion was the temperance pledge, which many manufacturers and business owners began to require of employees.

In 1836, leaders of the **temperance movement** regrouped into a new society, the American Temperance Union, which demanded total abstinence of its adherents. The intensified war against alcohol moved beyond individual moral suasion into the realm of politics, as reformers sought to deny taverns liquor licenses. By 1845, temperance advocates had put an impressive dent in alcohol consumption, which diminished to one-quarter of the per capita consumption of 1830. In 1851, Maine became the first state to ban entirely the manufacture and sale of all alcoholic beverages.

More controversial than temperance was a social movement called "moral reform," which first aimed at public morals in general but quickly narrowed to a campaign to eradicate sexual sin, especially prostitution. In 1833, a group of Finneyite women started the New York Female Moral Reform Society. Its members insisted that uncontrolled male sexual expression posed a serious threat to society in general and to women in particular. The society's nationally distributed newspaper, the *Advocate of Moral Reform*, was the first major paper in the country that was written, edited, and typeset by women. In it, they condemned men who visited brothels or seduced innocent women. Within five years, more than four thousand auxiliary groups of women had sprung up, mostly in New England, New York, Pennsylvania, and Ohio.

In its analysis of the causes of licentiousness and its conviction that women had a duty to speak out about unspeakable things, the Moral Reform Society pushed the limits of what even the men in the evangelical movement could tolerate. Yet these women did not regard themselves as radicals. They were simply pursuing the logic of a gender system that defined home protection and morality as women's special sphere and a religious conviction that called for the eradication of sin.

Organizing against Slavery

More radical still was the movement in the 1830s to abolish the sin of slavery. The abolitionist movement had its roots in Great Britain in the late 1700s. Previously, the American Colonization Society, founded in 1817 by some Maryland and Virginia **planters**, aimed to promote gradual individual **emancipation** of slaves followed by **colonization** in Africa. By the early 1820s, several thousand ex-slaves had been transported to Liberia on the West African coast. But not surprisingly, newly freed men and women were often not eager to emigrate; their African roots were three or more generations in the past. Colonization was too gradual (and expensive) to have much impact on American slavery.

Around 1830, northern challenges to slavery surfaced with increasing frequency and resolve, beginning in free black communities. In 1829, a Boston printer named David Walker published *An Appeal . . . to the Coloured Citizens of the World*, which condemned racism, invoked the egalitarian language of the Declaration of Independence, and hinted at racial violence if whites did not change their prejudiced ways. In 1830, at the inaugural National Negro Convention meeting in Philadelphia, forty blacks from nine states discussed the racism of American society and proposed emigration to Canada. In 1832, a twenty-eight-year-old black woman named Maria Stewart delivered public lectures for black audiences in Boston on slavery and racial prejudice. Although her arguments against slavery were welcomed, her voice—that of a woman—created problems even among her sympathetic audiences. Few American-born women had yet engaged in public speaking beyond theatrical performances or religious prophesying. Stewart was breaking a social taboo, an offense made more challenging by her statements suggesting that black women should rise above housework: "How long shall the fair daughters of Africa be compelled to bury their minds and talents beneath a load of iron pots and kettles?" She retired from the platform in 1833 but took up writing and published her lectures in a national publication called the *Liberator*, giving them much wider circulation.

The *Liberator*, founded in 1831 in Boston, took antislavery agitation to new heights. Its founder and editor, an uncompromising twenty-six-year-old white printer named William Lloyd Garrison, advocated immediate abolition: "On this subject, I do not wish to think, or speak, or write, with moderation. No! No! Tell a man whose house is on fire to give a moderate alarm; tell him to moderately rescue his wife from the hands of the ravisher; tell the mother to gradually extricate her babe from the fire into which it has fallen;—but urge me not to use moderation in a cause like the present."

In 1832, Garrison's supporters started the New England Anti-Slavery Society. Similar groups were organized in Philadelphia and New York in 1833. Soon a dozen antislavery newspapers and scores of antislavery lecturers were spreading the word and inspiring the formation of new local societies, which numbered thirteen hundred by 1837. Entirely confined to the North, their membership totaled a quarter of a million men and women.

Many white northerners were not prepared to embrace the abolitionist call for emancipation, immediate or gradual. They might oppose slavery as a blot on the country's ideals or as a rival to the **free-labor** system of the North, but at the same time most white northerners remained antiblack and therefore antiabolition. From 1834 to 1838, there were more than a hundred eruptions of serious mob violence against abolitionists or free blacks. On one occasion, antislavery

Abolitionist Purses
Female antislavery societies raised many thousands of dollars to support the abolitionist cause by selling handcrafted items at giant antislavery fairs. Items were often emblazoned with abolitionist mot-
toes, such as "Let My People Go," "Liberty," and "Loose the Bonds of Wickedness." These silk
drawstring bags are decorated with pictures of the "hapless slave woman," an object of compassion.
The Daughters of the American Revolution Museum, Washington, D.C. Gift of Mrs. Erwin L. Broecker.

headquarters in Philadelphia and a black church and orphanage were burned to
the ground. In another incident, Illinois abolitionist editor Elijah Lovejoy was
killed by a rioting crowd attempting to destroy his printing press.

Women played a prominent role in abolition, just as they did in moral reform
and evangelical religion. They formed women's auxiliaries and held fairs to sell
handmade crafts to support male lecturers in the field. They circulated antislavery
petitions, presented to the U.S. Congress with tens of thousands of signatures. Up
to 1835, women's petitions were framed as respectful memorials to Congress about
the evils of slavery, but by mid-decade these petitions called for Congress to outlaw
slavery in the District of Columbia (the only area under Congress's sole power). By
1836, women were signing petitions using urgent and strident abolitionist language. They were asserting their claim to be heard on political issues without their
husbands' permission and their privilege to instruct members of Congress.

Garrison particularly welcomed women's activity. When a southern plantation daughter named Angelina Grimké wrote to him about her personal repug-
nance for slavery, Garrison published the letter in the *Liberator* and brought her
overnight fame. In 1837, Grimké and her older sister, Sarah, became antislavery
lecturers targeting women, but their powerful eyewitness speeches attracted men
as well, causing leaders of the Congregational Church in Massachusetts to warn
all ministers not to let the Grimké sisters use their pulpits. Like Maria Stewart, the
Grimkés had violated a gender norm by presuming to instruct men.

In the late 1830s, the cause of abolition divided the nation as no other issue did. Even among abolitionists, significant divisions emerged. The Grimké sisters, radicalized by the public reaction to their speaking tour, began to write and speak about woman's rights. They were opposed by moderate abolitionists who were unwilling to mix the new and controversial issue of woman's rights with their first cause, the rights of blacks. A few radical men, such as Garrison, embraced woman's rights fully, working to get women leadership positions in the national antislavery group.

The many men and women active in reform movements in the 1830s found their initial inspiration in evangelical Protestantism's dual message: Salvation was open to all, and society needed to be perfected. Their activist mentality squared well with the interventionist tendencies of the party forming in opposition to Andrew Jackson's Democrats. Generally, reformers gravitated toward the Whig Party, the males as voters and the females as rallying supporters in the 1830s campaigns.

▶ **REVIEW**   How did evangelical Protestantism contribute to the social reform movements of the 1830s?

Van Buren's One-Term Presidency

By the mid-1830s, a vibrant and tumultuous political culture occupied center stage of American life. A colorful military hero had left his stamp on the nation, for good or for ill, but both by custom and by the old man's infirmity, another reelection of Andrew Jackson was out of the question. The northerner Martin Van Buren, Old Hickory's vice president and handpicked successor, inherited a strong Democratic organization, but he faced doubts from slave-owning Jacksonians as well as opposition from increasingly combative Whigs. Abolitionist tactics had pushed slavery into the political debate, but Van Buren managed to defuse that conflict somewhat and even use it to his advantage. What could not be forestalled, however, was the collapse of the economic boom so celebrated by both Democrats and Whigs. The shattering panic of 1837, followed by another panic in 1839, brought the country its worst economic depression yet. The difficult times did not let up for six years.

The Politics of Slavery

Sophisticated party organization was Martin Van Buren's specialty. Nicknamed "the Little Magician" and "the Red Fox" for his consummate political skills, the redheaded New Yorker had built his career by pioneering many of the loyalty-enhancing techniques the Democrats used in the 1830s. After serving as senator and then governor, he became Jackson's secretary of state in 1828. Four years later, he replaced South Carolinian John C. Calhoun as Jackson's running mate. His eight years in the volatile Jackson administration required the full measure of his political deftness as he sought repeatedly to save Jackson from both his enemies and his own obstinacy.

Jackson made it known that he favored Van Buren for the nomination in 1836, but starting in 1832, the major political parties had moved to formal nominating conventions to choose their candidates. To help ensure a Van Buren victory, Democratic leaders agreed to hold their nominating convention a year early, in 1835. The convention voted unanimously for the vice president, to the dismay of his archrival, Calhoun, who tried to discredit Van Buren among southern proslavery Democrats. Van Buren spent the next year assuring them that he was a "northern man with southern principles."

This should not have been hard for the vice president. His Dutch family hailed from the Hudson River counties where New York slavery had once flourished, and his own family had owned at least one slave as late as the 1810s, although he chose not to broadcast that fact. (Slavery was only gradually phased out in New York starting in 1799; see chapter 8, page 221.) Calhoun's partisans whipped up controversy over Van Buren's support of suffrage for New York's propertied free blacks at the 1821 state convention on suffrage. Van Buren's partisans developed a proslavery spin by emphasizing that the Little Magician had argued that the mass of "poor, degraded blacks" were incapable of voting; he had merely favored retaining the existing stiff property qualifications for the handful of elite blacks who had always voted in New York, while simultaneously removing all such qualifications for white men.

Calhoun was able to stir up trouble for Van Buren because in 1835, southerners were increasingly alarmed by the rise of northern antislavery sentiment. When, in late 1835, abolitionists prepared to circulate in the South a million pamphlets condemning slavery, a mailbag of their literature was hijacked at the post office in Charleston, South Carolina, and ceremoniously burned along with effigies of leading abolitionists. President Jackson condemned the theft but issued approval for individual postmasters to exercise their own judgment about whether to allow incendiary materials to reach their destination. Abolitionists saw this as undue censorship of the mail.

The petitioning tactics of abolitionists escalated sectional tensions. As petitions demanding Congress to "purify" the site of the national government by outlawing slavery in the District of Columbia grew into the hundreds, proslavery congressmen sought to short-circuit the appeals by passing a "**gag rule**" in 1836. The gag rule prohibited entering the documents into the public record on the grounds that what the abolitionists prayed for was unconstitutional and, further, an assault on the rights of white southerners, as one South Carolina representative put it.

Van Buren shrewdly seized on both mail censorship and the gag rule to express his prosouthern sympathies. Abolitionists were "fanatics," he repeatedly claimed, possibly under the influence of "foreign agents" (British abolitionists). He dismissed the issue of abolition in the District of Columbia as "inexpedient" and said that if he was elected president, he would not allow any interference in southern "domestic institutions."

The Election of 1836

The Democrats had evolved from a coalition into a party, and Martin Van Buren had a clear shot at the presidency. Although the elections of 1824, 1828, and 1832 clearly bore the stamp of Jackson's personality, by 1836 the party apparatus was sufficiently developed to support itself. Local and state committees existed throughout the country. Democratic candidates ran in every state election, succeeding even in old Federalist states such as Maine and New Hampshire. More than four hundred newspapers declared themselves Democratic.

Van Buren was a backroom politician, not a popular public figure, and the Whigs hoped that he might be defeatable. In many states, Whigs had captured high office in 1834, shedding the awkward National Republican label and developing statewide organizations to rival those of the Democrats. However, no figure yet commanded nationwide support, and so three regional candidates opposed Van Buren in 1836. Senator Daniel Webster of Massachusetts could deliver New England, home to reformers, merchants, and manufacturers; Senator Hugh Lawson White of Tennessee attracted proslavery voters still suspicious of the northern Magician; and the aging General William Henry Harrison, now residing in Ohio and memorable for his Indian war heroics in 1811, pulled in the western, anti-Indian vote. Not one of the three candidates had the ability to win the presidency, but together they came close to denying Van Buren a majority vote. Van Burenites called the three-Whig strategy a deliberate plot to derail the election and move it to the House of Representatives, setting the stage perhaps for another allegedly stolen election, as in 1824 (see chapter 10).

In the end, Van Buren won the election of 1836 by 170 electoral votes, while the other three received a total of 113. The popular vote told a somewhat different story. Van Buren's narrow majorities, where he won, were far below those Jackson had commanded. Although Van Buren had pulled together a national Democratic Party, with wins in both the North and the South, he had done it at the cost of committing northern Democrats to the proslavery agenda. And running three candidates had maximized the Whigs' success by drawing Whigs into office at the state level.

Two Panics and the Election of 1840

The day Martin Van Buren took office in March 1837, the financial markets were already quaking; by April, the country was plunged into crisis. The causes of the panic of 1837 were multiple and far-ranging. Bad harvests in Europe and a large trade imbalance between Britain and the United States caused the Bank of England to raise its interest rates in 1836 and to start calling in loans to American merchants, demanding money and not banknotes in payment. Failures in various crop markets and a 30 percent downturn in cotton prices on the international market fed the growing disaster. Cotton merchants in the South could no longer meet their obligations to creditors in New York City, and brokerage firms in the nation's financial capital began to fail—ninety-eight of them in March and April 1837 alone. Frightened citizens thronged the banks to try to get their money out, and businesses rushed to liquefy their remaining assets to pay off debts. Prices of stocks, bonds, and real estate fell 30 to 40 percent. The familiar events of the panic of 1819 unfolded again, with terrifying rapidity, and the credit market tumbled like a house of cards.

Some Whig leaders were certain that Jackson's antibank and hard-money policies were responsible for the ruin. New Yorker Philip Hone, a wealthy Whig, called the Jackson administration "the most disastrous in the annals of the country" for its "wicked interference" in banking and monetary matters. Others framed the devastation as retribution for an immoral frenzy of speculation that had gripped the nation. A religious periodical in Boston hoped that Americans would now moderate their greed: "We were getting to be almost insane upon the subject of wealth. . . . We were getting to think that there was no end to the wealth, and could be no check to the progress of our country; that economy was not needed, that prudence was weakness." In this view, the panic was a wake-up call, a blessing in disguise. Others identified the competitive, profit-maximizing capitalist economic system as the cause of the wrecked economy and looked across the Atlantic, to Britain and France, for new socialist ideas calling for the common ownership of land and of the means of production. American socialists were not large in number during this period, but they were vocal and imaginative, and in the early 1840s, several thousand developed utopian alternatives (see chapter 12, page 366).

The panic of 1837 subsided somewhat by 1838, as banks suspended payouts in hard money, stopping the outflow of deposits and even resuming loan activity. But in 1839, another run on the banks and ripples of business failures deflated the economy, creating a second panic. President Van Buren called a special session of Congress to consider creating an independent treasury system to perform some of the functions of the defunct Bank of the United States. Such a system, funded by government deposits, would deal only in hard money, forcing commercial banks to restrict their issuance of paper currency, and it would not make loans, thus avoiding the danger of speculative meddling in the economy. In short, an independent treasury system could exert a powerful moderating influence on inflation and the credit market without being directly involved in the market. But Van Buren encountered strong resistance in Congress, even among Democrats. The treasury system finally won approval in 1840, but by then Van Buren's chances of winning a second term in office were virtually nil because of the tumultuous economy.

In 1840, the Whigs settled on William Henry Harrison to oppose Van Buren. The campaign drew on voter involvement as no presidential campaign ever had. The Whigs borrowed tricks from the Democrats: Harrison was touted as a common man born in a log cabin (in reality, he was born on a Virginia plantation), and raucous campaign parades featured toy log cabins held aloft. His Indian-fighting days, now thirty years behind him, were played up to give him a Jacksonian aura. Whigs staged festive rallies all over the country, drumming up mass appeal with candlelight parades and song shows, and women participated in rallies as never before. Some 78 percent of eligible voters cast ballots—the highest percentage ever in American history. Harrison took 53 percent of the popular vote and won a resounding 234 electoral college votes to Van Buren's 60. A Democratic editor lamented, "We have taught them how to conquer us!"

▶ **REVIEW**   How did slavery figure as a campaign issue in the election of 1836?

Conclusion: The Age of Jackson or the Era of Reform?

Harrison's election closed a decade that had brought the common man and democracy to the forefront of American politics. Economic transformations loom large in explaining the fast-paced changes of the 1830s. Transportation advances put goods and people in circulation, augmenting urban growth and helping to create a national culture, and water-powered manufacturing began to change the face of wage labor. Trade and banking mushroomed, and western land once occupied by Indians was auctioned off in a landslide of sales. Two periods of economic downturn—including the panic of 1819 and the panics of 1837 and 1839—offered sobering lessons about speculative fever.

Andrew Jackson symbolized this age of opportunity for many. His fame as an aggressive general, Indian fighter, champion of the common man, and defender of slavery attracted growing numbers of voters to the emergent Democratic Party, which championed personal liberty, free competition, and egalitarian opportunity for all white men.

Jackson's constituency was challenged by a small but vocal segment of the population troubled by serious moral problems that Jacksonians preferred to ignore. Reformers drew sustenance from the message of the Second Great Awakening: that all men and women were free to choose salvation and that personal and societal sins could be overcome. Reformers targeted personal vices (illicit sex and intemperance) and social problems (prostitution, poverty, and slavery), and joined forces with evangelicals and wealthy lawyers and merchants (North and South) who appreciated a national bank and protective tariffs. The Whig Party was the party of activist moralism and state-sponsored entrepreneurship. Whig voters were, of course, male, but thousands of reform-minded women broke new ground by signing political petitions on the issues of Indian removal and slavery.

National politics in the 1830s were more divisive than at any time since the 1790s. The new party system of Democrats and Whigs reached far deeper into the electorate than had the Federalists and Republicans. Stagecoaches and steamboats carried newspapers from the cities to the backwoods, politicizing voters and creating party loyalty. Politics acquired immediacy and excitement, causing nearly four out of five white men to cast ballots in 1840.

High rates of voter participation would continue into the 1840s and 1850s. Unprecedented urban growth, westward expansion, and early industrialism marked those decades, sustaining the Democrat-Whig split in the electorate. But critiques of slavery, concerns for free labor, and an emerging protest against women's second-class citizenship complicated the political scene of the 1840s, leading to third-party political movements. One of these third parties, called the Republican Party, would achieve dominance in 1860 with the election of an Illinois lawyer, Abraham Lincoln, to the presidency.

REVIEWING THE CHAPTER

Use the questions and timeline to review and strengthen your understanding of the chapter.

REVIEW QUESTIONS

1. Why did the United States experience a market revolution after 1815? (pp. 307–14)

2. Why did Andrew Jackson defeat John Quincy Adams so dramatically in the 1828 election? (pp. 314–17)

3. Why did Jackson promote Indian removal? (pp. 317–24)

4. How did evangelical Protestantism contribute to the social reform movements of the 1830s? (pp. 324–32)

5. How did slavery figure as a campaign issue in the election of 1836? (pp. 332–36)

MAKING CONNECTIONS

1. Describe the market revolution that began in the 1810s. How did it affect Americans' work and domestic lives? In your answer, be sure to consider how gender contributed to these developments.

2. Andrew Jackson's presidency coincided with important changes in American politics. Discuss how Jackson benefited from, and contributed to, the vibrant political culture of the 1830s. Cite specific national developments in your answer.

3. Describe Andrew Jackson's response to the "Indian problem" during his presidency. How did his policies revise or continue earlier federal policies toward Native Americans? How did Native Americans respond to Jackson's actions?

4. While a volatile economy buffeted the United States in the 1830s, some Americans looked to reform the nation. Discuss the objectives and strategies of two reform movements. What was the relationship of these reform movements to larger political and economic trends of the 1830s?

TIMELINE

1807	• Robert Fulton's *Clermont* sets off steamboat craze.	**1832**	• Massacre of Sauk and Fox Indians under Chief Black Hawk.
1816	• Second Bank of the United States chartered.		• *Worcester v. Georgia.* • Jackson vetoes charter renewal of Bank of the United States.
1817	• American Colonization Society founded.		• New England Anti-Slavery Society founded.
1818	• National Road links Baltimore to western Virginia.	**1833**	• Nullification of federal tariffs declared in South Carolina.
1819	• Economic panic.		• New York and Philadelphia antislavery societies founded.
1821	• Mill town of Lowell, Massachusetts, founded.		• New York Female Moral Reform Society founded.
1825	• Erie Canal completed in New York.		
1826	• American Temperance Society founded. • Schuylkill Canal completed in Pennsylvania.	**1834**	• Female mill workers strike in Lowell, Massachusetts, and again in 1836.
1828	• Congress passes Tariff of Abominations. • Democrat Andrew Jackson elected president.	**1836**	• Democrat Martin Van Buren elected president. • American Temperance Union founded.
1829	• David Walker's *Appeal . . . to the Coloured Citizens of the World* published. • Baltimore and Ohio Railroad begun.	**1837**	• Economic panic.
		1838	• Trail of Tears: Cherokees forced to relocate west.
1830	• Indian Removal Act; women's petitions for Indian rights begin.	**1839**	• Economic panic.
1831	• William Lloyd Garrison starts *Liberator*. • Charles Grandison Finney preaches in Rochester, New York.	**1840**	• Whig William Henry Harrison elected president.

▶ **For an online bibliography, practice quizzes, Web sites, images, and documents related to this chapter,** see the Book Companion Site at **bedfordstmartins.com/roark.**

▶ **For firsthand accounts of this period,** see Chapter 11 in Michael Johnson, ed., *Reading the American Past,* Fourth Edition.

12
CHAPTER

The New West and Free North

1840–1860

E ARLY IN NOVEMBER 1842, Abraham Lincoln and his new wife, Mary, moved into their first home in Springfield, Illinois, a rented room measuring eight by fourteen feet on the second floor of the Globe Tavern. A busy blacksmith shop next door filled the Lincolns' room with the clamor of iron being pounded into horseshoes and other useful objects. The small, noisy room above the tavern was the nicest place that Abraham Lincoln had ever lived; it was the worst place that Mary Todd Lincoln had ever inhabited. She had grown up in Lexington, Kentucky, attended by slaves in the elegant home of her father, a prosperous merchant, banker, and politician. When she came to Illinois as a young single woman, she lived with relatives, who were among the local elite. Less than twenty years after their marriage, in March 1861, the Lincolns moved into what would prove to be their last home, the presidential mansion in Washington, D.C.

Abraham Lincoln climbed from the Globe Tavern to the White House by relentless work, unslaked ambition, and immense talent—traits he had honed since boyhood. Lincoln and many others celebrated his rise from humble origins as an example of the opportunities that beckoned in the free-labor economy of the North and West. They attributed his spectacular ascent to his individual qualities and tended to ignore the help he received from Mary and many others.

Born in a Kentucky log cabin in 1809, Lincoln grew up on small, struggling farms as his family migrated west. His father, Thomas, had left Virginia, where he had been born, and settled in Kentucky. Thomas Lincoln never learned to read and, as his son recalled, "never did more in the way of writing than to bunglingly sign his own name." Lincoln's mother, Nancy, could neither read nor write. In December 1816, Thomas Lincoln moved his young family from Kentucky to the Indiana wilderness. They lived for two frozen months in a crude lean-to while Thomas, a skilled carpenter, built a cabin. On the Indiana farmstead, Abraham learned the arts of agriculture practiced by families throughout the nation. Although only eight years old, he "had an axe put into his hands at once" and used it "almost constantly" for the next fifteen years, as he recalled later. He worked for neighbors for twenty-five cents a day and gave the money to his father. When he could be spared from work, the boy attended school, less than a year in all. "There was absolutely nothing to excite ambition for education," Lincoln recollected. In contrast, Mary Todd received ten years of schooling in Lexington's best private academies for young women.

In 1830, Thomas Lincoln decided to move farther west. The Lincolns hitched up the family oxen and headed to central Illinois, where they built another log cabin. The next spring, Thomas moved yet again, but this time Abraham stayed behind and set out on his own, a "friendless, uneducated, penniless boy," as he described himself.

By dogged striving, Abraham Lincoln gained an education and the respect of his Illinois neighbors, although a steady income eluded him for years. Mary Todd had many suitors, including Stephen A. Douglas, Lincoln's eventual political rival. She told a friend that she "would rather marry a good man—a man of mind—with hope and bright prospects ahead for position—fame and power."

Abraham Lincoln's Patent
In 1849, Abraham Lincoln applied for a patent based on this model illustrating his idea of using inflatable rubberized bags (the long white objects under the lower deck) to lift riverboats over stretches of shallow water. His desire to solve practical problems grew out of his firm belief "that heads and hands should cooperate as friends," a key ingredient of the widespread free-labor ideology. Lincoln received his patent, becoming the only patent holder ever to serve as president.
Smithsonian Institution, National Museum of American History.

After she married Lincoln, she said, "Intellectually my husband towers above Douglas . . . [and he] has no equal in the United States." The newlyweds received help from Mary's father, including eighty acres of land and a yearly allowance of about $1,100 for six years that helped them move out of their room above the Globe Tavern. Abraham eventually built a thriving law practice in Springfield, Illinois, and served in the state legislature and then in Congress. Mary helped him in many ways, rearing their sons, tending their household, and integrating him into her wealthy and influential extended family in Illinois and Kentucky. Mary also shared Abraham's keen interest in politics and ambition for power and prestige. With Mary's encouragement and support, Abraham's political success ultimately propelled them into the White House, where he became the first president born west of the Appalachian Mountains.

Like Lincoln, millions of Americans believed they could make something of themselves, whatever their origins, so long as they were willing to work. Individuals who refused to work—who were lazy, undisciplined, or foolish—had only themselves to blame if they failed. Work was a prerequisite for success, not a guarantee. This emphasis on work highlighted the individual efforts of men and tended to slight the many crucial contributions of women, family members, neighbors, and friends to the successes of men like Lincoln. In addition, the rewards of work were skewed toward white men and away from women and free African Americans. Nonetheless, the promise of rewards from hard work spurred efforts that shaped the contours of America, pushing the boundaries of the nation south to the Rio Grande, north to the Great Lakes, and ever westward to the Pacific Ocean. During Lincoln's presidency, Abraham and Mary talked about moving west to California at the end of his term. The economic, political, and geographic expansion that the Lincolns exemplified raised anew the question of whether slavery should also move west, the question that Lincoln and other Americans confronted again and again following the Mexican-American War, yet another outgrowth of the nation's ceaseless westward movement.

Economic and Industrial Evolution

During the 1840s and 1850s, Americans experienced a profound economic transformation that had been under way since the start of the nineteenth century. Since 1800, the total output of the U.S. economy had multiplied twelvefold. Four fundamental changes in American society fueled this remarkable economic growth.

First, millions of Americans—Abraham Lincoln among them—moved from farms to towns and cities. Even so, 80 percent of the nation's 31 million people remained in rural areas in 1860. Second, the number of Americans who worked in factories, mainly in urban centers, grew to about 20 percent of the labor force by 1860. This trend contributed to the nation's economic growth because, in general, factory workers produced twice as much (per unit of labor) as agricultural workers.

Third, a shift from waterpower to steam as a source of energy raised productivity, especially in factories and transportation. In the 1840s, mines in Pennsylvania, Ohio, and elsewhere began to excavate millions of tons of coal for industrial fuel, accelerating the shift to steam power. Between 1840 and 1860, coal production multiplied eightfold, cutting prices in half and permitting coal-fired steam engines to power ever more factories, railroads, and ships. Nonetheless, by 1860 coal supplied less than a fifth of the nation's energy consumption, and the muscles of people and work animals still provided thirty times more energy for manufacturing than steam.

A fourth fundamental change propelling America's economic development was the rise in agricultural productivity, which nearly doubled during Lincoln's lifetime. More than any other single factor, agricultural productivity spurred the nation's economic growth. While cities, factories, and steam engines multiplied throughout the nation—particularly in the North and West—the roots of the United States' economic growth lay in agriculture.

Historians often refer to this cascade of changes in farms, cities, factories, power, and transportation as an industrial revolution. However, these changes did not cause an abrupt discontinuity in America's economy or society. The United States remained overwhelmingly agricultural. Old methods of production continued alongside the new. The changes in the American economy during the 1840s and 1850s might better be termed "industrial evolution."

Agriculture and Land Policy

A French traveler in the United States noted that Americans had "a general feeling of hatred against trees." Although the traveler exaggerated, his observation contained an important truth. Trees limited agricultural productivity because farmers had to spend a great deal of time and energy clearing land for planting. But as farmers pushed westward in a quest for cheap land, they encountered the Midwest's comparatively treeless prairie, where they could spend less time with an ax and more time with a plow and hoe. Rich prairie soils yielded bumper crops, enticing farmers such as the Lincolns to migrate to the Midwest by the tens of thousands between 1830 and 1860. The populations of Indiana, Illinois, Michigan, Wisconsin, and Iowa exploded tenfold between 1830 and 1860, four times faster than the growth of the nation as a whole. Lincoln's home state of Illinois added more people during the 1850s than any other state in the Union.

Laborsaving improvements in farm implements also hiked agricultural productivity. The cast-iron plow in use since the 1820s proved too weak for the thick turf and dense soil of the midwestern prairie. In 1837, John Deere patented a strong, smooth steel plow that sliced through prairie soil so cleanly that farmers called it the "singing plow." Deere's company became the leading plow manufacturer in the Midwest, turning out more than ten thousand plows a year by the late 1850s. Energy for plowing still came from human and animal muscles, but better plows permitted farmers to break more ground and plant more crops.

Improvements in wheat harvesting also multiplied farmers' productivity. In 1850, most farmers harvested wheat by hand, cutting two or three acres a day with backbreaking labor. In the 1840s, Cyrus McCormick and others experimented with designs for mechanical reapers, and by the 1850s, a McCormick reaper that cost between $100 and $150 allowed a farmer to harvest twelve acres a day. Farmers had purchased about eighty thousand reapers by 1860, but most continued to cut their grain by hand. Still, improved reapers and plows, usually powered by horses or oxen, allowed farmers to cultivate more land, doubling the corn and wheat harvests between 1840 and 1860.

Federal land policy made possible the agricultural productivity that fueled the nation's economy. Up to 1860, the United States continued to be land-rich and labor-poor. Territorial acquisitions made the nation a great deal richer in land, adding more than a billion acres with the Louisiana Purchase (see chapter 10) and the annexation of Florida, Oregon, and vast territories following the Mexican-American War (see page 359). The federal government made most of this land available for purchase to attract settlers and to generate revenue. Wily speculators found ways to claim large tracts of the most desirable plots and sell them to settlers at a generous markup. But millions of ordinary farmers bought federal land for just $1.25 an acre, or $50 for a forty-acre farm that could support a family. Millions of other farmers could not afford that much. They squatted on unclaimed federal land, carved out a farm, and, if they still lacked funds to buy the land after a few years, usually moved farther west to squat on federal land elsewhere. By making land available to millions of Americans on relatively easy terms, the federal government achieved the goal of attracting settlers to the new territories in the West, which in due course joined the Union as new states. Above all, federal land policy created the basic precondition for the increase in agricultural productivity that underlay the nation's impressive economic growth.

Manufacturing and Mechanization

Changes in manufacturing arose from the nation's land-rich, labor-poor economy. Britain and other European countries had land-poor, labor-rich economies; there, meager opportunities in agriculture kept factory laborers plentiful and wages low. In the United States, western expansion and government land policies buoyed agriculture, keeping millions of people on the farm and thereby limiting the supply of workers for manufacturing and elevating wages. Because of this relative shortage of workers, manufacturers searched constantly for ways to save labor.

Mechanization allowed manufacturers to produce more with less labor. The practice of manufacturing and then assembling interchangeable parts spread from gun making to other industries and became known as the "American system." Mechanization became so integral to American manufacturing that some machinists specialized in what was called the machine tool industry, which made parts for machinery. Standardized parts produced by machine allowed manufacturers to employ unskilled workers who were much cheaper and more readily available than highly trained craftsmen. A visitor to a Springfield, Massachusetts, gun factory in 1841 noted, for example, that unskilled workers "in every machine shop and manufactory throughout the country" could now make guns because standardized parts made the trained gunsmith's "skill of the eye and the hand, [previously] acquired by practice alone . . . no longer indispensable." Even in heavily mechanized industries, factories remained fairly small; few had more than twenty or thirty employees.

Manufacturing and agriculture meshed into a dynamic national economy. New England led the nation in manufacturing, shipping goods such as guns, clocks, plows, and axes west and south, while southern and western states sent commodities such as wheat, pork, whiskey, tobacco, and cotton north and east. Manufacturers specialized in producing for the gigantic domestic market rather than for export. British goods dominated the international market and, on the whole, were cheaper and better than American-made products. U.S. manufacturers supported tariffs to minimize British competition, but their best protection from British competitors was to strive harder to please their American customers, most of them farmers. The burgeoning national economy was further fueled by the growth of the railroads, which served to link farmers and factories in new ways.

Railroads: Breaking the Bonds of Nature

Railroads incorporated the most advanced developments of the age. A Swedish visitor in 1849 noticed that American schoolboys drew sketches of locomotives, always in motion, belching smoke. Railroads captured Americans' imaginations because they seemed to break the bonds of nature. When canals and rivers froze in winter or became impassable during summer droughts, trains steamed ahead. When becalmed sailing ships went nowhere, locomotives kept on chugging, averaging over twenty miles an hour during the 1850s. Above all, railroads gave cities not blessed with canals or navigable rivers a way to compete for rural trade.

By 1850, trains steamed along 9,000 miles of track, almost two-thirds of it in New England and the Middle Atlantic states. By 1860, several railroads spanned the Mississippi River, connecting frontier farmers to the nation's 30,000 miles of track, approximately as much as in all of the rest of the world combined. In 1857, for example, France had 3,700 miles of track; England and Wales had a total of 6,400 miles. The massive expansion of American railroads helped catapult the nation into position as the world's second-greatest industrial power (after Great Britain).

In addition to speeding transportation, railroads propelled the growth of other industries, such as iron and communications. Iron production grew five times faster than the population during the decades up to 1860, in part to meet the demand for rails, wheels, axles, locomotives, and heavy, gravity-defying iron bridges. Railroads also stimulated the fledgling telegraph industry. In 1844, Samuel F. B. Morse persuasively demonstrated the potential of his telegraph by transmitting a series of dots and dashes that instantly conveyed an electronic message along forty miles of wire strung between Washington, D.C., and Baltimore. By 1861, more than fifty thousand miles of wire stretched across the continent to the Pacific Ocean, often alongside railroad tracks, making trains safer and more efficient and accelerating communications of all sorts.

Private corporations built and owned almost all railroads, in contrast to government ownership of railroads common in other industrial nations. But privately owned American railroads received massive government aid, especially federal **land grants**. Up to 1850, the federal government had granted a total of seven million acres of federal land to various turnpike, highway, and canal projects. In 1850, Congress approved a precedent-setting grant to railroads of six square miles of federal land for each mile of track laid. By 1860, Congress had granted railroads more than twenty million acres of federal land, thereby underwriting construction costs and promoting the expansion of the rail network, the settlement of federal land, and the integration of the domestic market.

The railroad boom of the 1850s signaled the growing industrial might of the American economy. But railroads, like other industries, succeeded because they served both farms and cities. Older forms of transportation remained significant. By 1857, for example, trains carried only about one-third of the mail; most of the rest still went by stagecoach or horseback. In 1860, most Americans were far more familiar with horses than with locomotives.

The economy of the 1840s and 1850s linked an expanding, westward-moving population in farms and cities with muscles, animals, machines, steam, and railroads. Abraham Lincoln cut trees, planted corn, and split rails as a young man before he moved to Springfield, Illinois, and became a successful attorney who defended, among others, railroad corporations. His mobility—westward, from farm to city, from manual to mental labor, and upward—illustrated the direction of economic change and the opportunities that beckoned enterprising individuals.

> ►REVIEW   Why did the United States become a leading industrial power in the nineteenth century?

Free Labor: Promise and Reality

The nation's impressive economic performance did not reward all Americans equally. Native-born white men tended to do better than immigrants. With few exceptions, women were excluded from opportunities open to men. Tens of thousands of women worked as seamstresses, laundresses, domestic servants, factory hands, and teachers but had little opportunity to aspire to higher-paying jobs. In the North and West, slavery was slowly eliminated in the half century after the American Revolution, but most free African Americans were relegated to dead-end jobs as laborers and servants. Discrimination against immigrants, women, and free blacks did not trouble most white men. With certain notable exceptions, they considered it proper and just.

The Free-Labor Ideal: Freedom Plus Labor

During the 1840s and 1850s, leaders throughout the North and West emphasized a set of ideas that seemed to explain why the changes under way in their society benefited some people more than others. They referred again and again to the advantages of what they termed **free labor**. (The word *free* referred to laborers who were not slaves. It did not mean laborers who worked for nothing.) By the 1850s, free-labor ideas described a social and economic ideal that accounted for both the successes and the shortcomings of the economy and society taking shape in the North and West.

Free-labor spokesmen celebrated hard work, self-reliance, and independence. They proclaimed that the door to success was open not just to those who inherited wealth or status but also to self-made men such as Abraham Lincoln. Free labor, Lincoln argued, was "the just and generous, and prosperous system, which opens the way for all—gives hope to all, and energy, and progress, and improvement of condition to all." Free labor permitted farmers and artisans to enjoy the products of their own labor, and it also benefited wageworkers. "The prudent, penniless beginner in the world," Lincoln asserted, "labors for wages awhile, saves a surplus with which to buy tools or land, for himself; then labors on his own account another while, and at length hires another new beginner to help him." Wage labor was the first rung on the ladder toward eventual self-employment and hiring others.

The free-labor ideal affirmed an egalitarian vision of human potential. Lincoln and other spokesmen stressed the importance of universal education to permit "heads and hands [to] cooperate as friends." Throughout the North and West, communities supported public schools to make the rudiments of learning available to young children. By 1860, many cities and towns boasted that up to 80 percent of children ages seven to thirteen attended school at least for a few weeks each year. In rural areas, where the labor of children was more difficult to spare, schools typically enrolled no more than half the school-age children. Lessons included more than arithmetic, penmanship, and a smattering of other subjects. Textbooks and teachers—most of whom were young women—drummed into students the lessons of the free-labor system: self-reliance, discipline, and, above all else, hard work. "Remember that all the ignorance, degradation, and misery in the world is the result of indolence and vice," one textbook intoned. In school and out, free-labor ideology emphasized labor as much as freedom.

Economic Inequality

The free-labor ideal made sense to many Americans, especially in the North and West, because it seemed to describe their own experiences. Lincoln frequently referred to his humble beginnings as a hired laborer and implicitly invited his listeners to consider how far he had come. In 1860, his wealth of $17,000 easily placed him in the top 5 percent of the population. The opportunities presented by the expanding economy made a few men much, much richer. In 1860, the nation had about forty millionaires. Most Americans, however, measured success in far more modest terms. The average wealth of adult white men in the North in 1860 barely topped $2,000. Nearly half of American men had no wealth at all; about 60 percent owned no land. Because property possessed by married women was normally considered to belong to their husbands, women had less wealth than men. Free African Americans had still less; 90 percent of them were propertyless.

Free-labor spokesmen considered these economic inequalities a natural outgrowth of freedom—the inevitable result of some individuals being more able and willing to work and luckier. These inequalities also demonstrate the gap between the promise and the performance of the free-labor ideal. Economic growth permitted many men to move from being landless squatters to landowning farmers and from being hired laborers to independent, self-employed producers. But many more Americans remained behind, landless and working for wages. Even those who realized their aspirations often had a precarious hold on their independence. Bad debts, market volatility, crop failure, sickness, or death could quickly eliminate a family's gains.

Seeking out new opportunities in pursuit of free-labor ideals created restless social and geographic mobility. Whereas fortunate people such as Abraham Lincoln rose far beyond their social origins, others shared the misfortune of a merchant who, an observer noted, "has been on the sinking list all his life." In search of better prospects, roughly two-thirds of the rural population moved every decade, and population turnover in cities was even greater. This constant coming and going weakened community ties to neighbors and friends and threw individuals even more on their own resources in times of trouble.

Immigrants and the Free-Labor Ladder

The risks and uncertainties of free labor did not deter millions of immigrants from entering the United States during the 1840s and 1850s. Almost 4.5 million immigrants arrived between 1840 and 1860, six times more than had come during the previous two decades. The half million immigrants who came in 1854 accounted for nearly 2 percent of the entire U.S. population, a higher proportion than in any other single year of the nation's history. By 1860, foreign-born residents made up about one-eighth of the U.S. population, a fraction that held steady well into the twentieth century.

Nearly three out of four immigrants who arrived in the United States between 1840 and 1860 came from Germany or Ireland. The vast majority of the 1.4 million Germans who entered during these years were skilled tradesmen and their families. They left Germany to escape deteriorating economic conditions, and they had little difficulty finding work in the expanding U.S. economy. German immigrants settled most heavily in the Midwest. German butchers, bakers, beer makers, carpenters, shopkeepers, machinists, and others tended to congregate in cities. Roughly a quarter of German immigrants were farmers, most of whom scattered throughout the Midwest, although some settled in Texas. On the whole, German Americans settled into that middle stratum of sturdy independent producers celebrated by free-labor spokesmen; relatively few Germans occupied the bottom rung of the free-labor ladder as wage laborers or domestic servants.

Irish immigrants, in contrast, entered at the bottom of the free-labor ladder and struggled to climb up. Nearly 1.7 million Irish immigrants arrived between 1840 and 1860, nearly all of them desperately poor and often weakened by hunger and disease. Potato blight struck Ireland in 1845 and returned repeatedly in subsequent years, spreading a catastrophic famine throughout the island. Many of the lucky ones, half-starved, crowded into the holds of ships and set out for America, where they congregated in northeastern cities. As one immigrant group declared, "All we want

Irish Laborer
Landless, jobless, and confronting famine in Ireland, tens of thousands of Irish laborers, like the young man photographed here, immigrated to the United States in the 1850s. They frequently encountered prejudice because of their appearance, language, religion, and what respectable folk considered their rowdy habits. Undeterred, most Irish immigrants found jobs as laborers and servants, and formed thriving communities in many American cities.

Unknown photographer, from *Ireland in Old Photos* compiled by Sean Sexton, Bullfinch Press Book © 1994.

is to get out of Ireland; we must be better anywhere than here." Death trailed after them. So many died crossing the Atlantic that ships from Ireland were often termed "coffin ships."

Roughly three out of four Irish immigrants worked as laborers or domestic servants. Irish men dug canals, loaded ships, laid railroad track, and took what other work they could find. Irish women hired out to cook, wash and iron, mind children, and clean house. Almost all Irish immigrants were Catholic, a fact that set them apart from the overwhelmingly **Protestant** native-born residents. Many natives regarded the Irish as hard-drinking, obstreperous, half-civilized folk. Such views lay behind the discrimination reflected in job announcements that commonly stated, "No Irish need apply." Despite such prejudices, native residents hired Irish immigrants because they accepted low pay and worked hard.

In America's labor-poor economy, Irish laborers could earn more in one day than in several weeks in Ireland, if they could find work there. In America, one immigrant explained in 1853, there was "plenty of work and plenty of wages plenty to eat and no land lords thats enough what more does a man want." But some immigrants wanted more, especially respect and decent working conditions. One immigrant complained that he was "a slave for the Americans as the generality of the Irish . . . are."

Such testimony illustrates that the free-labor system, whether for immigrants or native-born laborers, often did not live up to the optimistic vision outlined by Abraham Lincoln and others. Many wage laborers could not realistically aspire to become independent, self-sufficient property holders, despite the claims of free-labor proponents.

▶REVIEW   How did the free-labor ideal account for economic inequality?

The Westward Movement

In the 1840s, the nation's swelling population, booming economy, and boundless confidence propelled a new era of rapid westward migration. Until then, the overwhelming majority of Americans lived east of the Mississippi River. Native Americans inhabited the plains, deserts, and rugged coasts to the west. The British claimed the Oregon Country, and the Mexican flag flew over the vast expanse of the Southwest. But by 1850, the boundaries of the United States stretched to the Pacific, and the nation had more than doubled in size. By 1860, the great migration had carried four million Americans west of the Mississippi River.

Frontier settlers took the land and then, with the exception of the Mormons, lobbied their government to acquire the territory they had settled. The human cost of aggressive expansionism was high. The young Mexican nation lost a war and half of its territory. Two centuries of Indian wars east of the Mississippi ended during the 1830s, but the fierce struggle between native inhabitants and invaders continued for another half century in the West. Americans believed it was their destiny to conquer the continent.

Manifest Destiny

Most Americans believed that the superiority of their institutions and white **culture** bestowed on them a God-given right to spread their civilization across the continent. They imagined the West as a howling wilderness, empty and undeveloped. If they recognized Indians and Mexicans at all, they dismissed them as primitive drags on progress who would have to be redeemed, shoved aside, or exterminated. The West provided young men especially an arena in which to "show their manhood." The sense of uniqueness and mission was as old as the Puritans, but by the 1840s, the conviction of superiority had been bolstered by the United States' amazing success. Most Americans believed that the West needed the civilizing power of the hammer and the plow, the ballot box and the pulpit, which had transformed the East.

In 1845, a New York political journal edited by John L. O'Sullivan coined the term **manifest destiny** as the latest justification for white settlers to take the land they coveted. O'Sullivan called on Americans to resist any foreign power—British, French, or Mexican—that attempted to thwart "the fulfillment of our manifest destiny to overspread the continent allotted by Providence for the free development of our yearly multiplying millions . . . [and] for the development of the great experiment of liberty and federative self-government entrusted to us." Almost overnight, the magic phrase *manifest destiny* swept the nation and provided an ideological shield for conquering the West.

As important as national pride and racial arrogance were to manifest destiny, economic gain made up its core. Land hunger drew hundreds of thousands of average Americans westward. Some politicians, moreover, had become convinced that national prosperity depended on capturing the rich trade of the Far East. To trade with Asia, the United States needed the Pacific coast ports that stretched from San Diego to Puget Sound. No one was more eager to extend American trade in the Pacific than Missouri senator Thomas Hart Benton. "The sun of civilization must shine across the sea: socially and commercially," he declared. The United States and Asia must "talk together, and trade together. Commerce is a great civilizer." In the 1840s, American economic expansion came wrapped in the rhetoric of uplift and civilization.

Oregon and the Overland Trail

The Oregon Country—a vast region bounded on the west by the Pacific Ocean, on the east by the Rocky Mountains, on the south by the forty-second parallel, and on the north by Russian Alaska—caused the pulse of American expansionists to race. But the British also coveted the area. They argued that their claim lay with Sir Francis Drake's discovery of the Oregon coast in 1579. Americans countered with historic claims of their own. Unable to agree, the United States and Great Britain decided in 1818 on "joint occupation" that would leave Oregon "free and open" to settlement by both countries. A handful of American fur traders and "mountain men" roamed the region in the 1820s, but expansionists soon made the Oregon Country an early target of manifest destiny.

By the late 1830s, settlers began to trickle along the Oregon Trail, following a path blazed by the mountain men (Map 12.1). The first wagon trains headed west in 1841, and by 1843 about 1,000 emigrants a year set out from Independence, Missouri. By 1869, when the first transcontinental railroad was completed, approximately 350,000 migrants had traveled west to the Pacific in wagon trains.

MAP 12.1   Major Trails West
In the 1830s, wagon trains began snaking their way to the Southwest and the Pacific coast. Deep ruts, some of which can still be seen today, soon marked the most popular routes.

Emigrants encountered the Plains Indians, a quarter of a million Native Americans who populated the area between the Rocky Mountains and the Mississippi River. Some were farmers who lived peaceful, sedentary lives, but a majority—the Sioux, Cheyenne, Shoshoni, and Arapaho of the central plains and the Kiowa, Wichita, and Comanche of the southern plains—were horse-mounted, nomadic, nonagricultural peoples whose warriors symbolized the "savage Indian" in the minds of whites.

Horses, which had been brought to North America by Spaniards in the sixteenth century, permitted the Plains tribes to become highly mobile hunters of buffalo. They came to depend on buffalo for nearly everything—food, clothing, shelter, and fuel. Competition for buffalo led to war between the tribes. Young men were introduced to warfare early, learning to ride ponies at breakneck speed while firing off arrows and, later, rifles with astounding accuracy. "A Comanche on his feet is out of his element," observed western artist George Catlin, "but the moment he lays his hands upon his horse, his *face* even becomes handsome, and he gracefully flies away like a different being."

The Plains Indians struck fear in the hearts of whites on the wagon trains. But Native Americans had far more to fear from whites. Indians killed fewer than four hundred emigrants on the trail between 1840 and 1860, while whites brought alcohol and deadly epidemics of smallpox, measles, cholera, and scarlet fever. Moreover, whites killed the buffalo, often slaughtering them for sport. The buffalo still numbered some twelve million in 1860, but the herds were shrinking rapidly, intensifying conflict among the Plains tribes.

Emigrants insisted that the federal government provide them with more protection. The government responded by constructing a chain of forts along the Oregon Trail (see Map 12.1). More important, it adopted a new Indian policy: "concentration." First, the government rescinded the "permanent" buffer it had granted the Indians west of the ninety-fifth meridian, which was only two hundred to three hundred miles west of the Mississippi River. Then, in 1851, it called the Plains tribes to a conference at Fort Laramie, Wyoming. Some ten thousand Indians showed up, hopeful that something could be done to protect them from the ravages of the wagon trains. Instead, U.S. government negotiators persuaded the chiefs to sign agreements that cleared a wide corridor for wagon trains by restricting Native Americans to specific areas that whites promised they would never violate. This policy of concentration became the seedbed for the subsequent policy of reservations. But whites would not keep out of Indian territory, and Indians would not easily give up their traditional ways of life. Struggle for control of the West meant warfare for decades to come.

Still, Indians threatened emigrants less than life on the trail did. The men, women, and children who headed west each spring could count on at least six months of grueling travel. With nearly two thousand miles to go and traveling no more than fifteen miles a day, the pioneers endured parching heat, drought, treacherous rivers, disease, physical and emotional exhaustion, and, if the snows

Pioneer Family on the Trail West
In 1860, W. G. Chamberlain photographed these unidentified travelers momentarily at rest by the upper Arkansas River in Colorado. We do not know their fates, but we can only hope that they fared better than the Sager family, whose seven children were orphaned during the seven-month crossing in 1844.
Denver Public Library, Western History Division #F3226.

closed the mountain passes before they got through, freezing and starvation. Women sometimes faced the dangers of trailside childbirth. It was said that a person could walk from Missouri to the Pacific stepping only on the graves of those who had died heading west. Such tribulations led one miserable woman, trying to keep her children dry in a rainstorm and to calm them as they listened to Indian shouts, to wonder "what had possessed my husband, anyway, that he should have thought of bringing us away out through this God forsaken country."

Men usually found Oregon "one of the greatest countries in the world." From "the Cascade mountains to the Pacific, the whole country can be cultivated," exclaimed one eager settler. When women reached Oregon, they found a wilderness. Neighbors were few and far between, and things were in a "primitive state." One young wife set up housekeeping with her new husband with only one stew kettle and three knives. Necessity blurred the traditional division between men's and women's work. "I am maid of all traids," one busy woman remarked in 1853. Work seemed unending. "I am a very old woman," declared twenty-nine-year-old Sarah Everett. "My face is thin sunken and wrinkled, my hands bony withered and hard." Another settler observed, "A woman that can not endure almost as much as a horse has no business here." Yet despite the ordeal of the trail and the difficulties of starting from scratch, emigrants kept coming.

The Mormon Exodus

Not every wagon train heading west was bound for the Pacific Slope. One remarkable group of religious emigrants halted near the Great Salt Lake in what was then Mexican territory. The Mormons deliberately chose the remote site as a refuge. After years of persecution in the East, they fled west to find religious freedom and communal security.

In 1830, Joseph Smith Jr., who was only twenty-four, published *The Book of Mormon* and founded the Church of Jesus Christ of Latter-Day Saints (the Mormons). A decade earlier, the upstate New York farm boy had begun to experience revelations that were followed, he said, by a visit from an angel who led him to golden tablets buried near his home. With the aid of magic stones, Smith translated the mysterious language on the tablets to produce *The Book of Mormon*. It told the story of an ancient Hebrew civilization in the New World and predicted the appearance of an American prophet who would reestablish Jesus Christ's undefiled kingdom in America. Converts, attracted to the promise of a pure faith in the midst of **antebellum** America's social turmoil and rampant materialism, flocked to the new church.

Neighbors branded Mormons heretics and drove Smith and his followers from New York to Ohio, then to Missouri, and finally in 1839 to Nauvoo, Illinois, where they built a prosperous community. But a rift in the church developed after Smith sanctioned "plural marriage" (polygamy). Non-Mormons caught wind of the controversy and eventually arrested Smith and his brother. On June 27, 1844, a mob stormed the jail and shot both men dead.

The embattled church turned to an extraordinary new leader, Brigham Young, who immediately began to plan a great exodus. In 1846, traveling in 3,700 wagons, 12,000 Mormons made their way to eastern Iowa. The following year, they arrived at their new home beside the Great Salt Lake. Young described the region as a barren waste, "the paradise of the lizard, the cricket and the rattlesnake." Within ten years, however, the Mormons developed an irrigation system that made the desert bloom. They accomplished the feat through cooperative labor, not the individualistic and competitive enterprise common among most emigrants. Under Young's stern leadership, the Mormons built a thriving community.

In 1850, the Mormon kingdom was annexed to the United States as Utah Territory. The nation's attention focused on Utah in 1852 when Brigham Young announced that many Mormons practiced polygamy. Although only one Mormon man in five had more than one wife (Young had twenty-three), Young's statement caused a popular outcry that forced the U.S. government to establish its authority in Utah. In 1857, 2,500 U.S. troops invaded Salt Lake City in what was known as the Mormon War. The bloodless occupation illustrates that most Americans viewed the Mormons as a threat to American morality, law, and institutions. The invasion did not dislodge the Mormon Church from its central place in Utah, however, and for years to come, most Americans perceived the Mormon settlement as strange and suitably isolated.

The Mexican Borderlands

In the Mexican Southwest, westward-moving Anglo-American pioneers confronted northern-moving Spanish-speaking frontiersmen. On this frontier as elsewhere, national cultures, interests, and aspirations collided. Since 1821, when Mexico won its independence from Spain, the Mexican flag had flown over the vast expanse that stretched from the Gulf of Mexico to the Pacific and from the Oregon Country to Guatemala. Mexico's borders remained ill defined, and its northern provinces were sparsely populated. Moreover, severe problems plagued the young nation: civil wars, economic crises, quarrels with the Roman Catholic Church, and devastating raids by the Comanche, Apache, and Kiowa. Mexico found it increasingly difficult to defend its borderlands, especially when faced with a northern neighbor convinced of its superiority and bent on territorial acquisition.

The American assault began quietly. In the 1820s, Anglo-American trappers, traders, and settlers drifted into Mexico's far northern provinces. Santa Fe, a remote outpost in the province of New Mexico, became a magnet for American enterprise. Each spring, American traders gathered at Independence, Missouri, for the long trek southwest along the Santa Fe Trail (see Map 12.1). They crammed their wagons with inexpensive American manufactured goods and returned home with Mexican silver, furs, and mules.

The Mexican province of Texas attracted a flood of Americans who had settlement, not long-distance trade, on their minds. Wanting to populate and develop its northern territory, the Mexican government granted the American Stephen F. Austin a huge tract of land along the Brazos River. In the 1820s, Austin became the first Anglo-American *empresario* (colonization agent) in Texas, offering land at only ten cents an acre. Thousands of Americans poured across the border. Most were Southerners who brought cotton and slaves with them.

By the 1830s, the settlers had established a thriving plantation economy in Texas. Americans numbered 35,000, while the *Tejano* (Spanish-speaking) population was less than 8,000. Few Anglo-American settlers were Roman Catholic, spoke Spanish, or cared about assimilating into Mexican culture. Afraid of losing Texas to the new arrivals, the Mexican government in 1830 banned further immigration to Texas from the United States and outlawed the introduction of additional slaves. The Anglo-Americans complained loudly and made it increasingly clear that they wanted to be rid of the "despotism of the sword and the priesthood" and to govern themselves. In Mexico City, however, General Antonio López de Santa Anna seized political power and set about restoring order to the northern frontier.

Faced with what they considered tyranny, the Texan settlers rebelled. Santa Anna ordered the Mexican army northward and in February 1836 arrived at the outskirts of San Antonio. Commanded by Colonel William B. Travis from Alabama, the rebels included the Tennessee frontiersman David Crockett and the Louisiana adventurer James Bowie, as well as a handful of Tejanos. They took refuge in a former Franciscan mission known as the Alamo. Santa Anna sent wave after wave of his 2,000-man army crashing against the walls until the attackers finally broke through and killed all 187 rebels. A few weeks later, outside the small town of Goliad, Mexican forces surrounded and captured a garrison of Texans. Following orders from Santa Anna, Mexican firing squads executed almost 400 of the men as "pirates and outlaws." In April 1836, at San Jacinto, General Sam Houston's army adopted the massacre of Goliad as a battle cry and crushed Santa Anna's troops in a predawn attack. The Texans had succeeded in establishing the Lone Star Republic, and the following year, the United States recognized the independence of Texas from Mexico.

Earlier, in 1824, in an effort to increase Mexican migration to the thinly settled province of California, the Mexican government granted *ranchos*—huge estates devoted to cattle raising—to new settlers. *Rancheros* ruled over near-feudal empires worked by Indians whose condition sometimes approached that of slaves. Not satisfied, the *rancheros* coveted the vast lands controlled by the Franciscan missions. In 1834, they persuaded the Mexican government to confiscate the missions and make their lands available to new settlement, a development that accelerated the decline of the California Indians. Devastated by disease, the Indians, who had numbered approximately 300,000 when the Spanish arrived in 1769, had declined to half that number by 1846.

Despite the efforts of the Mexican government, California in 1840 counted a population of only 7,000 Mexican settlers. Non-Mexican settlers numbered only 380, but among them were Americans who championed manifest destiny. They sought to woo American emigrants to California. In the 1840s, wagon after wagon left the Oregon Trail to head southwest on the California Trail (see Map 12.1). As the trickle of Americans became a river, Mexican officials grew alarmed. As a New York newspaper put it in 1845, "Let the tide of emigration flow toward California and the American population will soon be sufficiently numerous to play the Texas game." Only a few Americans in California wanted a war for independence, but many dreamed of living again under the U.S. flag.

The U.S. government made no secret of its desire to acquire California. In 1835, President Andrew Jackson tried unsuccessfully to purchase it. In 1846, American settlers in the Sacramento Valley took matters into their own hands. Prodded by John C. Frémont, a former army captain and explorer who had arrived with a party of sixty buckskin-clad frontiersmen spoiling for a fight, the Californians raised an independence movement known as the Bear Flag Revolt. By then, James K. Polk, a champion of aggressive expansion, sat in the White House.

▶ **REVIEW** Why did westward migration expand dramatically in the mid-nineteenth century?

Expansion and the Mexican-American War

Although emigrants acted as the advance guard of American empire, there was nothing automatic about the U.S. annexation of territory in the West. Acquiring territory required political action. In the 1840s, the politics of expansion became entangled with sectionalism and the slavery question. Texas, Oregon, and the Mexican borderlands thrust the United States into dangerous diplomatic crises with Great Britain and Mexico.

Aggravation between Mexico and the United States escalated to open antagonism in 1845 when the United States annexed Texas. Absorbing territory still claimed by Mexico ruptured diplomatic relations between the two countries and set the stage for war. But it was President James K. Polk's insistence on having Mexico's other northern provinces that made war certain. The war was not as easy as Polk anticipated, but it ended in American victory and the acquisition of a new American West.

The Politics of Expansion

Texans had sought admission to the Union almost since winning their independence from Mexico in 1836. Almost constant border warfare between Mexico and the Republic of Texas in the decade following the revolution underscored the precarious nature of independence. Any suggestion of adding another slave state to the Union outraged most Northerners, however. Although Northerners applauded westward expansion, they imagined the expansion of American liberty, not the spread of slavery. Annexing Texas also risked precipitating war, because Mexico had never relinquished its claim to its lost province.

President John Tyler, who became president in April 1841 when William Henry Harrison died one month after taking office, understood that Texas was a dangerous issue. Adding to the danger, Great Britain began sniffing around Texas, apparently contemplating adding the young republic to its growing empire. Tyler, an ardent expansionist, decided to risk annexing the Lone Star Republic.

In April 1844, John C. Calhoun, Tyler's secretary of state, laid an annexation treaty before the Senate. But when Calhoun linked annexation to the defense of slavery, he doomed the treaty. Howls of protest erupted across the North. In Massachusetts, future senator Charles Sumner deplored the "insidious" plan to annex Texas and carve from it "great slaveholding states." The Senate soundly rejected the treaty, and it appeared that Tyler had succeeded only in inflaming sectional conflict. In Texas, one newspaper observed that a "general gloom seems to rest over every section of the Republic."

The issue of Texas had not died down by the 1844 election. In an effort to appeal to northern voters, the Whig nominee for president, Henry Clay, came out against the immediate annexation of Texas. "Annexation and war with Mexico are identical," he declared. The Democrats chose Tennessean James K. Polk, who was as strongly in favor of the annexation of Texas as Clay was against it. To make annexation palatable to Northerners, the Democrats shrewdly yoked Texas to Oregon, thus tapping the desire for expansion in the free states of the North as well as in the slave states of the South. The Democratic platform called for the "reannexation of Texas" and the "reoccupation of Oregon." The suggestion that the United States was merely reasserting existing rights was poor history but good politics.

When Clay finally recognized the popularity of expansion, he waffled, hinting that under certain circumstances, he might accept the annexation of Texas. His retreat won little support in the South and succeeded only in alienating antislavery opinion in the North. James G. Birney, the candidate of the fledgling Liberty Party, picked up the votes of thousands of disillusioned Clay supporters. In the November election, Polk received 170 electoral votes and Clay 105. New York's 35 electoral votes proved critical to Clay's defeat. A shift of just one-third of Birney's 15,000 votes to Clay would have given Clay the state and the presidency.

On March 4, 1845, in his inaugural address, Polk confirmed his faith in America's manifest destiny and aggressive **nationalism**. "This heaven-favored land," he declared, enjoyed the "most admirable and wisest system of well-regulated self-government . . . ever devised by human minds." He asked, "Who shall assign limits to the achievements of free minds and free hands under the protection of this glorious Union?"

The nation did not have to wait for Polk's inauguration in March 1845 to see results from his victory. One month after the election, President Tyler announced that the triumph of the Democratic Party provided a mandate for the annexation of Texas "promptly and immediately." In February 1845, after a fierce debate between antislavery and proslavery forces, Congress approved a joint resolution offering the Republic of Texas admission to the United States. Texas entered as the fifteenth slave state.

Tyler delivered Texas, but Polk had promised Oregon, too. Westerners particularly demanded that the new president make good on the Democrats' pledge "Fifty-four Forty or Fight"—that is, all of Oregon, right up to Alaska (54°40′ was the southern latitude of Russian Alaska). But Polk was close to war with Mexico and could not afford a war with Britain over U.S. claims in Canada. After the initial bluster, he muted the all-of-Oregon refrain and renewed an old offer to divide Oregon along the forty-ninth parallel. When Britain accepted the compromise, some Americans cried betrayal, but most celebrated the agreement that gave the nation an enormous territory peacefully. When the Senate finally approved the treaty in June 1846, the United States and Mexico were already at war.

The Mexican-American War, 1846–1848

From the day he entered the White House, Polk craved Mexico's remaining northern provinces: California and New Mexico, land that today makes up California, Nevada, Utah, most of New Mexico and Arizona, and parts of Wyoming and Colorado. Polk hoped to buy the territory, but when the Mexicans refused to sell, he concluded that military force would be needed to realize the United States' manifest destiny.

Polk had already ordered General Zachary Taylor to march his 4,000-man army 150 miles south from its position on the Nueces River, the southern boundary of Texas according to the Mexicans, to the banks of the Rio Grande, the boundary claimed by Texans (Map 12.2). Viewing the American advance as aggression, the Mexican general in Matamoros ordered Taylor back to the Nueces. Taylor refused, and on April 25, Mexican cavalry attacked a party of American soldiers, killing or wounding sixteen and capturing the rest. Even

---

MAP 12.2 The Mexican-American War, 1846–1848

American and Mexican soldiers skirmished across much of northern Mexico, but the major battles took place between the Rio Grande and Mexico City.

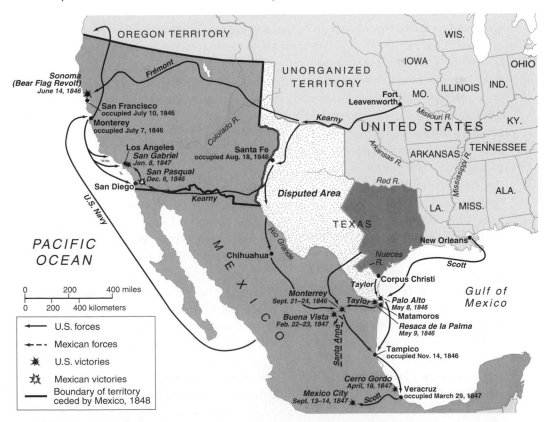

before news of the battle arrived in Washington, Polk had obtained his cabinet's approval of a war message.

On May 11, 1846, the president told Congress, "Mexico has passed the boundary of the United States, has invaded our territory, and shed American blood upon American soil." Thus "war exists, and, notwithstanding all our efforts to avoid it, exists by the act of Mexico herself." Congress passed a declaration of war and began raising an army. Despite years of saber rattling toward Mexico and Britain, the U.S. army was pitifully small, only 8,600 soldiers. Faced with the nation's first foreign war, against a Mexican army that numbered more than 30,000, Polk called for volunteers. Of the men who rushed to the colors, 40 percent were immigrants. Eventually, more than 112,000 white Americans (blacks were banned) joined the army to fight in Mexico.

Despite the flood of volunteers, the war divided the nation. Northern Whigs in particular condemned the war as the bullying of a weak neighbor. The Massachusetts legislature claimed that the war was being fought for the "triple object of extending slavery, of strengthening the slave power, and of obtaining control of the free states." On January 12, 1848, a gangly freshman Whig representative from Illinois rose from his back-row seat in the House of Representatives to deliver his first important speech in Congress. Before Abraham Lincoln sat down, he had questioned Polk's intelligence, honesty, and sanity. The president simply ignored the upstart representative, but antislavery, antiwar Whigs kept up the attack throughout the conflict. In their effort to undercut national support, they labeled it "Mr. Polk's War."

Since most Americans backed the war, it was not really Polk's war, but the president acted as if it were. Although he had no military experience, he directed the war personally. He planned a short war in which U.S. armies would occupy Mexico's northern provinces and defeat the Mexican army in a decisive battle or two, after which Mexico would sue for peace and the United States would keep the territory its armies occupied.

At first, Polk's strategy seemed to work. In May 1846, Zachary Taylor's troops drove south from the Rio Grande and routed the Mexican army, first at Palo Alto, then at Resaca de la Palma (see Map 12.2). "Old Rough and Ready," as Taylor was affectionately known among his adoring troops, became an instant war hero. Polk rewarded Taylor for his victories by making him commander of the Mexican campaign.

A second prong of the campaign to occupy Mexico's northern provinces centered on Colonel Stephen Watts Kearny, who led a 1,700-man army from Missouri into New Mexico. Without firing a shot, U.S. forces took Santa Fe in August 1846. Polk then ordered Kearny to California. Pushing on with only 300 troops, Kearny marched into San Diego three months later, encountering a major Mexican rebellion against American rule. In January 1847, after several clashes and severe losses, the U.S. forces occupied Los Angeles. California and New Mexico were in American hands.

By then, Taylor had driven deep into the interior of Mexico. In September 1846, after a five-day siege and house-to-house fighting, he took the fortified city of Monterrey. With reinforcements and fresh supplies, Taylor pushed his 5,000 troops southwest, where the Mexican hero of the Alamo, General Antonio López de Santa Anna, was concentrating an army of 21,000. On February 23, 1847, Santa Anna's troops attacked Taylor at Buena Vista. Superior American artillery and accurate musket fire won the day, but the Americans suffered heavy casualties, including Henry Clay Jr., the son of the man who had opposed Texas annexation for fear it would precipitate war. The Mexicans suffered even greater losses (some 3,400 dead, wounded, and missing, compared with 650 Americans). During the night, Santa Anna withdrew his battered army, much to the "profound disgust of the troops," one Mexican officer remembered. "They are filled with grief that they were going to lose the benefit of all the sacrifices that they had made; that the conquered field would be abandoned, and that the victory would be given to the enemy." Retreat, he complained, fed the belief "that it was impossible to conquer the Americans."

The series of uninterrupted victories in northern Mexico certainly fed the American troops' sense of superiority. "No American force has ever thought of being defeated by any amount of Mexican troops," one soldier declared. The Americans worried about other hazards, however. "I can assure you that fighting is the least dangerous & arduous part of a soldier's life," one young man declared. Letters home told of torturous marches across arid wastes alive with tarantulas, scorpions, and rattlesnakes. Others recounted dysentery, malaria, smallpox, cholera, and yellow fever. Of the 13,000 American soldiers who died (some 50,000 Mexicans perished), fewer than 2,000 fell to Mexican bullets and shells. Disease killed most of the others. Medicine was so primitive and conditions so harsh that, as one Tennessee man observed, "nearly all who take sick die."

Victory in Mexico

Although the Americans won battle after battle, President Polk's strategy misfired. Despite heavy losses on the battlefield, Mexico refused to trade land for peace. One American soldier captured the Mexican mood: "They cannot submit to be deprived of California after the loss of Texas, and nothing but the conquest of their Capital will force them to such a humiliation." Polk had arrived at the same conclusion. The president tapped another general to carry the war to Mexico City. While Taylor occupied the north, General Winfield Scott would land his army on the Gulf coast of Mexico and march 250 miles inland to the capital. Polk's plan entailed enormous risk because Scott would have to cut himself off from supplies and lead his men deep into enemy country against a much larger army.

After months of careful planning, an amphibious landing on March 9, 1847, near Veracruz put some 10,000 American troops ashore without the loss of a single life. After a siege of two weeks and furious shelling, Veracruz surrendered on March 29, 1847. In early April 1847, the U.S. army moved westward, following

Mexican Family

This family had its portrait taken in 1847, in the middle of the war. Mexican civilians were vulnerable to atrocities committed by the invading army. Volunteers, a large portion of the American troops, received little training and resisted discipline. Generals Zachary Taylor and Winfield Scott gradually tamed the volunteers with stern military justice.

Mexican Family, unknown, ca. 1847. Daguerreotype, Amon Carter Museum, Fort Worth, Texas.

the path blazed more than three centuries earlier by Hernán Cortés to "the halls of the Montezumas" (see chapter 2).

After the defeat at Buena Vista, Santa Anna had returned to Mexico City. He rallied his ragged troops and marched them east to set a trap for Scott in the mountain pass at Cerro Gordo. Knifing through Mexican lines, the Americans almost captured Santa Anna, who fled the field on foot. So complete was the victory that Scott gloated to Taylor, "Mexico no longer has an army." But Santa Anna, ever resilient, again rallied the Mexican army. Some 30,000 troops took up defensive positions on the outskirts of Mexico City and began melting down church bells to cast new cannons.

In August, Scott began his assault on the Mexican capital. The fighting proved the most brutal of the war. Santa Anna backed his army into the city, fighting each step of the way. At the battle of Churubusco, the Mexicans took 4,000 casualties in a single day and the Americans more than 1,000. At the castle of Chapultepec, American troops scaled the walls and fought the Mexican defenders hand to hand. After Chapultepec, Mexico City officials persuaded Santa Anna to evacuate the city to save it from destruction, and on September 14, 1847, General Winfield Scott rode in triumphantly. The ancient capital of the Aztecs had fallen once again to an invading army.

On February 2, 1848, American and Mexican officials signed the Treaty of Guadalupe Hidalgo in Mexico City. Mexico agreed to give up all claims to Texas north of the Rio Grande and to cede the provinces of New Mexico and California—more than 500,000 square miles—to the United States (see Map 12.2). The United States agreed to pay Mexico $15 million and to assume $3.25 million in claims that American citizens had against Mexico. Some Americans clamored for all of Mexico, some for none of it, but in March 1848, the Senate ratified the treaty. Polk had his Rio Grande border, his Pacific ports, and all the land that lay between.

The American triumph had enormous consequences. Less than three-quarters of a century after its founding, the United States had achieved its self-proclaimed manifest destiny to stretch from the Atlantic to the Pacific (Map 12.3).

MAP 12.3 Territorial Expansion by 1860

Less than a century after its founding, the United States spread from the Atlantic seaboard to the Pacific coast. War, purchase, and diplomacy had gained a continent.

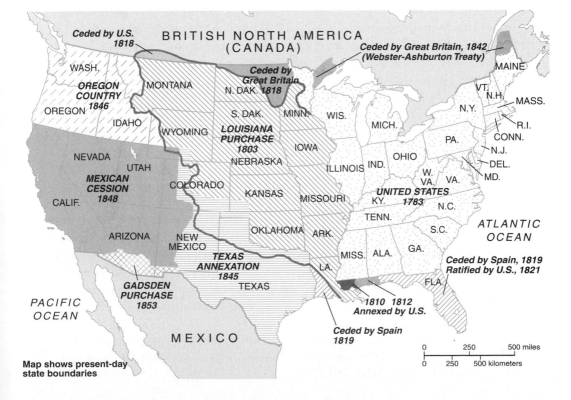

It would enter the industrial age with vast new natural resources and a two-ocean economy, while Mexico faced a sharply diminished economic future. Mexicans neither forgot nor forgave Americans for tearing away the northern half of their country. In 1915, in south Texas, Tejanos killed dozens of white farmers in a violent effort to return the American Southwest to Mexico. The wave of lynchings and vigilantism that followed cost thousands of Tejanos their lives.

Golden California

Another consequence of the Mexican defeat in the war with the United States was that California gold poured into American, not Mexican, pockets. On a cold January morning in 1848, just weeks before the formal transfer of territory, James Marshall discovered gold in the American River in the foothills of the Sierra Nevada. Marshall's discovery set off the California gold rush, one of the wildest mining stampedes in the world's history. Between 1849 and 1852, more than 250,000 "forty-niners," as the would-be miners were known, descended on the Golden State. In less than two years, Marshall's discovery transformed California from foreign territory to statehood.

News of gold quickly spread around the world. Soon, a stream of men, of various races and nationalities, all bent on getting rich, arrived in California, where they remade the quiet world of Mexican ranches into a raucous, roaring mining and town economy. Forty-niners rarely had much money or mining experience, but as one witness observed, "No capital is required to obtain this gold, as the laboring man wants nothing but his pick, shovel, and tin pan, with which to dig and wash the gravel; and many frequently pick gold out of the crevices of rock with their butcher knives in pieces from one to six ounces." Only a few struck it rich, and life in the goldfields was nasty, brutish, and often short. Men faced miserable living conditions, sometimes sheltering in holes and brush lean-tos. They also faced cholera and scurvy, exorbitant prices for food (eggs cost a dollar apiece), deadly encounters with claim jumpers, and endless backbreaking labor. An individual with gold in his pocket could find only temporary relief in the saloons, card games, dogfights, gambling dens, and brothels that flourished in the mining camps.

By 1853, San Francisco had grown into a raw, booming city of 50,000 that depended as much on gold as did the mining camps inland. Like all the towns that dotted the San Joaquin and Sacramento valleys, it suffered from overcrowding, fire, crime, and violence. But enterprising individuals had learned that there was money to be made tending to the needs of the miners. Hotels, saloons, restaurants, laundries, and shops and stores of all kinds exchanged services and goods for miners' gold.

In 1851, the Committee of Vigilance determined to bring order to the city. Members pledged that "no thief, burglar, incendiary or assassin shall escape punishment, either by the quibbles of the law, the insecurity of prisons, the carelessness or corruption of the police, or a laxity of those who pretended to administer justice." Lynchings proved that the committee meant business. In time, merchants, **artisans**, and professionals made the city their home and brought their families from back east. Gradually, gunfights declined and theaters sprouted, but many years would pass before anyone pacified San Francisco.

Establishing civic order on a turbulent frontier was made more difficult by Anglo bigotry and by the welter of nationalities, ethnicities, and races drawn to California. The Chinese attracted special scrutiny. By 1851, 25,000 Chinese lived in California, and their religion, language, dress, queues (long pigtails), eating habits, and opium convinced many Anglos that they were not fit citizens of the Golden State. As early as 1852, opponents demanded a halt to Chinese immigration. Chinese leaders in San Francisco fought back. Admitting deep cultural differences, they insisted that "in the important matters we are good men. We honor our parents; we take care of our children; we are industrious and peaceable; we trade much; we are trusted for small and large sums; we pay our debts; and are honest, and of course must tell the truth." Their protestations offered little protection, however, and racial violence braided with forty-niner optimism and energy.

Westward expansion did not stop at the California shore. California's ports were connected to a vast trade network throughout the Pacific. American seafarers and merchants traded furs, hides and tallow, and lumber and engaged in whaling and the China trade. Still, as California's first congressional representative observed, the state was separated "by thousands of miles of plains, deserts, and almost impossible mountains" from the rest of the Union. Some dreamers imagined a railroad that would someday connect the Golden State with the booming agriculture and thriving industry of the East. Others imagined an America transformed not by transportation, but by progressive individual and institutional reform.

▶**REVIEW**   Why was the annexation of Texas such a controversial policy?

Reforming Self and Society

While manifest destiny, the Mexican-American War, and the California gold rush transformed the nation's geography, many Americans sought personal and social reform. The emphasis on self-discipline and individual effort at the core of the free-labor ideal led Americans to believe that insufficient self-control caused the major social problems of the era. **Evangelical** Protestants struggled to control individuals' propensity to sin, and **temperance** advocates exhorted drinkers to control their urge for alcohol. In the midst of the worldly disruptions of geographic expansion and economic change, evangelicals brought more Americans than ever before into churches. Historians estimate that church members accounted for about one-third of the American population by 1850. Most Americans remained outside churches, as did Abraham Lincoln. But the influence of evangelical religion reached far beyond those who belonged to churches. The evangelical temperament—a conviction of righteousness coupled with energy, self-discipline, and faith that the world could be improved—animated most reformers.

A few activists pointed out that certain fundamental injustices lay beyond the reach of individual self-control. Transcendentalists and utopians believed that perfection could be attained only by rejecting the competitive, individualistic values of mainstream society. Woman's rights activists and abolitionists sought to reverse the subordination of women and to eliminate the enslavement of blacks by changing laws and social institutions as well as attitudes and customs. They confronted the daunting challenge of repudiating widespread assumptions about male supremacy and white supremacy and somehow subverting the entrenched institutions that reinforced those assumptions: the family and slavery.

The Pursuit of Perfection: Transcendentalists and Utopians

A group of New England writers that came to be known as transcendentalists believed that individuals should conform neither to the dictates of the materialistic world nor to the dogma of formal religion. Instead, people should look within themselves for truth and guidance. The leading transcendentalist, Ralph Waldo Emerson—an essayist, poet, and lecturer—proclaimed that the power of the solitary individual was nearly limitless. Henry David Thoreau, Margaret Fuller, and other transcendentalists agreed with Emerson that "if the single man plant himself indomitably on his instincts, and there abide, the huge world will come round to him." In many ways, the inward gaze and confident egoism of transcendentalism represented less an alternative to mainstream values than an exaggerated form of the rampant individualism of the age.

Unlike transcendentalists who sought to turn inward, a few reformers tried to change the world by organizing utopian communities as alternatives to prevailing social arrangements. Although these communities never attracted more than a few thousand people, the activities of their members demonstrated both dissatisfaction with the larger society and their efforts to realize their visions of perfection. Some communities functioned as retreats for those who did not want to sever ties with the larger society. Brook Farm, organized in 1841 in West Roxbury, Massachusetts, briefly provided a haven for a few literary and artistic New Englanders trying to balance bookish pursuits with manual labor.

Other communities set out to become models of perfection that they hoped would point the way toward a better life for everyone. During the 1840s, more than two dozen communities organized around the ideas of Charles Fourier, a French critic of contemporary society. Members of Fourierist phalanxes, as these communities were called, believed that individualism and competition were evils that denied the basic truth that "men . . . are brothers and not competitors."

Phalanxes aspired to replace competition with harmonious cooperation based on communal ownership of property. But Fourierist communities failed to realize their lofty goals, and few survived more than two or three years.

The Oneida community went beyond the Fourierist notion of communalism. John Humphrey Noyes, the charismatic leader of Oneida, believed that American society's commitment to private property made people greedy and selfish. Noyes claimed that the root of private property lay in marriage, in men's conviction that their wives were their exclusive property. Drawing from a substantial inheritance, Noyes organized the Oneida community in New York in 1848 to abolish marital property rights through the practice of what he called "complex marriage." Sexual intercourse was not restricted to married couples but was permitted between any consenting man and woman in the community. Noyes also required all members to relinquish their economic property to the community, which developed a lucrative business manufacturing animal traps. Oneida's sexual and economic communalism attracted several hundred members, but most of their neighbors considered Oneidans adulterers, blasphemers, and worse. Yet the practices that set Oneida apart from its mainstream neighbors strengthened the community, and it survived long after the Civil War.

Woman's Rights Activists

Women participated in the many reform activities that grew out of evangelical churches. Women church members outnumbered men two to one and worked to put their religious ideas into practice by joining peace, temperance, antislavery, and other societies. Involvement in reform organizations gave a few women activists practical experience in such political arts as speaking in public, running a meeting, drafting resolutions, and circulating petitions. Along with such experience came confidence. The abolitionist Lydia Maria Child pointed out in 1841 that "those who urged women to become missionaries and form tract societies . . . have changed the household utensil to a living energetic being and they have no spell to turn it into a broom again."

In 1848, about three hundred reformers led by Elizabeth Cady Stanton and Lucretia Mott gathered at Seneca Falls, New York, for the first national woman's rights convention in the United States. As Stanton recalled, "The general discontent I felt with women's portion as wife, mother, housekeeper, physician, and spiritual guide, [and] the wearied anxious look of the majority of women impressed me with a strong feeling that some active measure should be taken to right the wrongs of society in general, and of women in particular." The Seneca Falls Declaration of Sentiments set an ambitious agenda to right the wrongs of women and society. The declaration proclaimed that "the history of mankind is a history of repeated injuries and usurpations on the part of man toward woman, having in direct object the establishment of an absolute tyranny over her." In the style of the Declaration of Independence (see appendix I, page A-1), the Seneca

Falls declaration denounced men who "endeavored in every way . . . to destroy her confidence in her own powers, to lessen her self-respect, and to make her willing to lead a dependent and abject life." The declaration demanded that women "have immediate admission to all the rights and privileges which belong to them as citizens of the United States," particularly the "inalienable right to the elective franchise."

Nearly two dozen other woman's rights conventions assembled before 1860, repeatedly calling for **suffrage** and an end to discrimination against women. But women had difficulty receiving a respectful hearing, much less achieving legislative action. No state came close to permitting women to vote. Politicians and editorialists held that a woman's place was in the home, rearing her children and civilizing her man. Even so, the Seneca Falls declaration served as a path-breaking manifesto of dissent against male supremacy and of support for woman suffrage, and it inspired many women to challenge the barriers that limited their opportunities.

Bloomers and Woman's Emancipation
This 1851 British cartoon lampoons bloomers, the trouserlike garment worn beneath shortened skirts by two cigar-smoking American women. Bloomers were promoted by woman's rights activists as an alternative to the uncomfortable dresses worn by fashionable women, suggested here by the clothing of the British women on the right. Critics, as suggested by the cartoon, ridiculed "bloomerism" as unfeminine.
Miriam and Ira D. Wallach Division of Art, Prints and Photographs, The New York Public Library. Astor, Lenox and Tilden Foundations.

BLOOMERISM—AN AMERICAN CUSTOM.

Stanton and other activists sought fair pay and expanded employment opportunities for women by appealing to free-labor ideology. Woman's rights advocate Paula Wright Davis pointed out that "every able bodied Man, inured to Labor . . . is worth a dollar a day and can readily command it. . . . But the sister of this same faithful worker, equally careful, intelligent, and willing to do anything honest and reputable for a living . . . [is] fortunate if . . . she can earn five or six dollars per month." Davis urged Americans to stop discriminating against able and enterprising women: "Let [women] . . . open a Store, . . . plant and tend an Orchard, . . . learn any of the lighter mechanical Trades, . . . study for a Profession, . . . be called to the lecture-room, [and] . . . the Temperance rostrum . . . [and] let her be appointed [to serve in the Post Office]." Some women pioneered in these and many other occupations during the 1840s and 1850s. Woman's rights activists also succeeded in protecting married women's rights to their own wages and property in New York in 1860. But discrimination against women persisted, as most men believed that free-labor ideology required no compromise of male supremacy.

Abolitionists and the American Ideal

During the 1840s and 1850s, abolitionists continued to struggle to draw the nation's attention to the plight of slaves and the need for emancipation. Former slaves such as Frederick Douglass, Henry Bibb, and Sojourner Truth lectured to reform audiences throughout the North about the cruelties of slavery. Abolitionists published newspapers, held conventions, and petitioned Congress, but they never attracted a mass following among white Americans. Many white Northerners became convinced that slavery was wrong, but they still believed that blacks were inferior. Many other white Northerners shared the common view of white Southerners that slavery was necessary and even desirable. The geographic expansion of the nation during the 1840s offered abolitionists an opportunity to link their unpopular ideal to a goal that many white Northerners found much more attractive—limiting the geographic expansion of slavery, an issue that moved to the center of national politics during the 1850s (see chapter 14).

Black leaders rose to prominence in the abolitionist movement during the 1840s and 1850s. African Americans had actively opposed slavery for decades, but a new generation of leaders came to the forefront in these years. Frederick Douglass, Henry Highland Garnet, William Wells Brown, Martin R. Delany, and others became impatient with white abolitionists' appeals to the conscience of the white majority. In 1843, Garnet proclaimed that slaves had "little hope of Redemption without the shedding of blood" and urged them to choose "Liberty or Death" and rise in insurrection against their masters, an idea that alienated almost all white people and carried little influence among slaves. To express their own uncompromising ideas, black abolitionists founded their own newspapers and held their own antislavery conventions, although they still cooperated with sympathetic whites.

The commitment of black abolitionists to battling slavery grew out of their own experiences with white supremacy. The 250,000 free African Americans in the North and West constituted less than 2 percent of the total population. They confronted the humiliations of racial discrimination in nearly every arena of daily life. Only Maine, Massachusetts, New Hampshire, and Vermont permitted black men to vote; New York imposed a special property-holding requirement on black—but not white—voters, effectively excluding most black men from the **franchise**. The pervasive racial discrimination both handicapped and energized black abolitionists. Some cooperated with the American Colonization Society's efforts to send freed slaves and other black Americans to Liberia in West Africa. Others sought to move to Canada, Haiti, or someplace else, convinced that, as an African American from Michigan wrote, "it is impracticable, not to say impossible, for the whites and blacks to live together, and upon terms of social and civil equality, under the same government." Most black American leaders refused to embrace emigration and worked against racial prejudice in their own communities, organizing campaigns against segregation, particularly in transportation and education. Their most notable success came in 1855 when Massachusetts integrated its public schools. Elsewhere, white supremacy continued unabated.

Outside the public spotlight, free African Americans in the North and West contributed to the antislavery cause by quietly aiding fugitive slaves. Harriet Tubman escaped from slavery in Maryland in 1849 and repeatedly risked her freedom and her life to return to the South to escort slaves to freedom. When the opportunity arose, free blacks in the North provided fugitive slaves with food, a safe place to rest, and a helping hand. An outgrowth of the antislavery sentiment and opposition to white supremacy that unified nearly all African Americans in the North, this "underground railroad" ran mainly through black neighborhoods, black churches, and black homes.

▶**REVIEW**   Why were women especially prominent in many nineteenth-century reform efforts?

Conclusion: Free Labor, Free Men

During the 1840s and 1850s, a cluster of interrelated developments—steam power, railroads, and the growing mechanization of agriculture and manufacturing—meant greater economic productivity, a burst of output from farms and factories, and prosperity for many. Diplomacy and war handed the United States 1.2 million square miles and more than 1,000 miles of Pacific coastline. One prize of manifest destiny, California, almost immediately rewarded its new owners with tons of gold. To most Americans, new territory and vast riches were appropriate accompaniments to the nation's stunning economic progress.

To Northerners, industrial evolution confirmed the choice they had made to eliminate slavery and promote free labor as the key to independence, equality, and prosperity. Like Abraham Lincoln, millions of Americans could point to their personal experiences as evidence of the practical truth of the free-labor ideal. But millions of others had different stories to tell. They knew that in the free-labor system, poverty and wealth continued to rub shoulders. By 1860, more than half of the nation's free-labor workforce still toiled for someone else. Free-labor enthusiasts denied that the problems were inherent in the country's social and economic systems. Instead, they argued, most social ills—including poverty and dependency—sprang from individual deficiencies. Consequently, many reformers focused on self-control and discipline, on avoiding sin and alcohol. Other reformers focused on woman's rights and slavery. They challenged widespread conceptions of male supremacy and black inferiority, but neither group managed to overcome the prevailing free-labor ideology, based on individualism, racial prejudice, and notions of male superiority.

By midcentury, the nation was half slave and half free, and each region was animated by different economic interests, cultural values, and political aims. Not even the victory over Mexico could bridge the deepening divide between North and South.

REVIEWING THE CHAPTER

Use the questions and timeline to review and strengthen your understanding of the chapter.

REVIEW QUESTIONS

1. Why did the United States become a leading industrial power in the nineteenth century? (pp. 341–45)

2. How did the free-labor ideal account for economic inequality? (pp. 345–49)

3. Why did westward migration expand dramatically in the mid-nineteenth century? (pp. 349–57)

4. Why was the annexation of Texas such a controversial policy? (pp. 357–65)

5. Why were women especially prominent in many nineteenth-century reform efforts? (pp. 365–70)

MAKING CONNECTIONS

1. Varied political, economic, and technological factors promoted westward migration in the mid-nineteenth century. Considering these factors, discuss migration to two different regions (for instance, Texas, Oregon, Utah, or California). What drew migrants to the region? How did the U.S. government contribute to their efforts?

2. How did the ideology of manifest destiny contribute to the mid–nineteenth-century drive for expansion? Discuss its implications for individual migrants and the nation. In your answer, consider how manifest destiny built on, or revised, earlier understandings of the nation's history and racial politics.

3. The Mexican-American War reshaped U.S. borders and more. Discuss the consequences of the war for national political and economic developments in subsequent decades. What resources did the new territory give the United States? How did debate over annexation revive older political disputes?

4. Some nineteenth-century reform movements drew on the free-labor ideal, while others challenged it. Discuss the free-labor ideal in relation to two reform movements (such as abolitionism and utopian communalism). How did they draw on the ideal to pursue specific reforms? How did these minority movements try to influence national developments?

TIMELINE

1836	• Texas declares independence from Mexico.	**1847**	• Mormons settle in Utah.
1837	• John Deere patents steel plow.	**1848**	• Treaty of Guadalupe Hidalgo.
1840s	• Practical mechanical reapers created.		• Oneida community organized in New York. • First U.S. woman's rights convention takes place at Seneca Falls, New York.
1841	• First wagon trains head west on Oregon Trail. • Vice President John Tyler becomes president when William Henry Harrison dies. • Brook Farm organized.	**1849**	• California gold rush begins.
		1850	• Mormon community annexed to United States as Utah Territory.
1844	• Democrat James K. Polk elected president. • Samuel F. B. Morse demonstrates telegraph.	**1851**	• Conference in Laramie, Wyoming, marks the beginning of government policy of concentration.
1845	• Term *manifest destiny* coined. • United States annexes Texas, which enters Union as slave state. • Potato blight in Ireland spurs immigration to United States.	**1855**	• Massachusetts integrates public schools.
		1857	• U.S. troops invade Salt Lake City in Mormon War.
1846	• Bear Flag Revolt in California. • Congress declares war on Mexico. • United States and Great Britain agree to divide Oregon Country.		

▶ **For an online bibliography, practice quizzes, Web sites, images, and documents related to this chapter,** see the Book Companion Site at **bedfordstmartins.com/roark.**

▶ **For firsthand accounts of this period,** see Chapter 12 in Michael Johnson, ed., *Reading the American Past,* Fourth Edition.

13

CHAPTER

The Slave South

1820–1860

N AT TURNER WAS BORN A SLAVE in Southampton County, Virginia, in October 1800. People in his neighborhood claimed that he had always been different. His parents noticed special marks on his body, which they said were signs that he was "intended for some great purpose." His master said that he learned to read without being taught. As an adolescent, he adopted an austere lifestyle of Christian devotion and fasting. In his twenties, he received visits from the "Spirit," the same spirit, he believed, that had spoken to the ancient prophets. In time, Turner began to interpret these things to mean that God had appointed him an instrument of divine vengeance for the sin of slaveholding.

In the early morning of August 22, 1831, he set out with six trusted friends—Hark, Henry, Sam, Nelson, Will, and Jack—to punish slave owners. Turner struck the first blow, an ax to the head of his master, Joseph Travis. The rebels killed all of the white men, women, and children they encountered in each household they attacked. By noon, they had visited eleven farms and slaughtered fifty-seven whites. Along the way, they had added fifty or sixty men to their army. Word spread quickly, and soon the militia and hundreds of local whites gathered in response. By the next day, whites had captured or killed all of the rebels except Turner, who hid out for about ten weeks before being captured in nearby woods. Within a week, he was tried, convicted, and executed. By then, forty-five slaves had stood trial, twenty had been convicted and hanged, and another ten had been banished from Virginia. Frenzied whites had killed another hundred or more blacks—insurgents and innocent bystanders—in their counterattack against the rebellion.

Horrid Massacre in Virginia
There are no known contemporary images of Nat Turner. This woodcut simply imagines the rebellion as a nightmare in which black brutes took the lives of innocent whites. Although there was never another rebellion as large as Turner's, images of black violence continued to haunt white imaginations. Library of Congress.

Virginia's governor, John Floyd, asked how Turner's band of "assassins and murderers" could have assaulted the "unsuspecting and defenseless" citizens of "one of the fairest counties in the Commonwealth." White Virginians prided themselves on having the "mildest" slavery in the South, but sixty black rebels on a rampage challenged the comforting theory of the contented slave. Nonetheless, whites found explanations that allowed them to feel safer. They placed the blame on outside agitators. In 1829, David Walker, a freeborn black man living in Boston, had published his *Appeal . . . to the Coloured Citizens of the World*, an invitation to slaves to rise up in bloody rebellion, and copies had fallen into the hands of Virginia slaves. Moreover, on January 1, 1831, in Boston, the Massachusetts abolitionist William Lloyd Garrison had published the first issue of the *Liberator*, his fiery newspaper. White Virginians also dismissed the rebellion's leader, Nat Turner, as insane. "He is a complete fanatic, or plays his part admirably," wrote Thomas R. Gray, the lawyer who was assigned to defend Turner.

In the months following the insurrection, white Virginians debated the future of slavery in their state. Although some expressed substantial doubts, the Virginia legislature reaffirmed the state's determination to preserve black bondage. Delegates passed a raft of laws strengthening the institution of slavery and further restricting free blacks. A thirty-year-old professor at the College of William and Mary, Thomas R. Dew, published a vigorous defense of slavery that became the bible of Southerners' proslavery arguments. More than ever, the nation was divided along the "Mason-Dixon line," the surveyors' mark that in colonial times had established the boundary between Maryland and Pennsylvania but half a century later divided the free North and the slave South.

Black slavery increasingly molded the South into a distinctive region. In the decades after 1820, Southerners, like Northerners, raced westward, but unlike Northerners who spread small farms and free labor, Southerners spread slavery, cotton, and plantations. Geographic expansion meant that slavery became more vigorous and profitable than ever, embraced more people, and increased the South's political power. **Antebellum** Southerners included diverse people who at times found themselves at odds with one another—not only slaves and free people but also women and men; Indians, Africans, and Europeans; and aristocrats and common folk. Nevertheless, beneath this diversity, a distinctively southern society and **culture** were forming. The South became a slave society, and most white Southerners were proud of it.

The Growing Distinctiveness of the South

From the earliest settlements, inhabitants of the southern colonies had shared a great deal with northern colonists. Most whites in both sections were British and **Protestant**, spoke a common language, and shared an exuberant pride in their victorious revolution against British rule. The creation of the new nation under the Constitution in 1789 forged strong political ties that bound all Americans. The beginnings of a national economy fostered economic interdependence and communication across regional boundaries. White Americans everywhere celebrated the achievements of the prosperous young nation, and they looked forward to its seemingly boundless future.

Despite these national similarities, Southerners and Northerners grew increasingly different. The French political observer Alexis de Tocqueville believed he knew why. "I could easily prove," he asserted in 1831, "that almost all the differences which may be noticed between the character of the Americans in the Southern and Northern states have originated in slavery." Slavery made the South different, and it was the differences between the North and South, not the similarities, that increasingly shaped antebellum American history.

Cotton Kingdom, Slave Empire

In the first half of the nineteenth century, millions of Americans migrated west. In the South, the stampede began after the Creek War of 1813–1814, which divested the Creek Indians of 24 million acres and initiated the government campaign to remove Indian people living east of the Mississippi River to the West (see chapters 10 and 11). Eager slaveholders seeking virgin acreage for new plantations, struggling farmers looking for patches of land for small farms, herders and drovers pushing their hogs and cattle toward fresh pastures—anyone who was restless and ambitious felt the pull of Indian land. Southerners pushed westward relentlessly, until by midcentury the South encompassed nearly a million square miles. Contemporaries spoke of this vast region as the Lower South, those states where cotton was dominant, and the Upper South, where cotton was less important.

The South's climate and geography were ideally suited for the cultivation of cotton. Advancing Southerners encountered a variety of terrain, soil, and weather, but cotton's requirements are minimal: two hundred frost-free days from planting to picking and plentiful rain, conditions found in much of the South. By the 1830s, cotton fields stretched from southern Virginia to central Texas. Heavy southern and westward migration led to statehood for Arkansas in 1836 and for Texas and Florida in 1845. Production soared from 300,000 bales in 1830 to nearly 5 million in 1860, when the South produced three-fourths of the world's supply. The South—especially that tier of states from South Carolina west to Texas—had become the cotton kingdom (Map 13.1).

The cotton kingdom was also a slave empire. The South's cotton boom rested on the backs of slaves, who grew 75 percent of the crop on plantations, toiling in gangs in broad fields under the direct supervision of whites. As cotton agriculture expanded westward, whites shipped more than 300,000 slaves out of the old seaboard states. Victims of this brutal but thriving domestic slave trade marched hundreds of miles to new plantations in the Lower South. Cotton, slaves, and plantations moved west together.

The slave population grew enormously. Southern slaves numbered fewer than 700,000 in 1790, about 2 million in 1830, and almost 4 million by 1860, an increase of almost 600 percent in seven decades. By 1860, the South contained more slaves than all the other slave societies in the New World combined. The extraordinary growth was not the result of the importation of slaves, which the federal government outlawed in 1808. Instead, the slave population grew through natural reproduction. By the nineteenth century, most slaves were native-born Southerners. In comparison, Cuba and Brazil, slave societies that kept their slave trades open until the mid-nineteenth century, had more African-born slaves and thus stronger ties to Africa.

The South in Black and White

By 1860, one in every three Southerners was black (approximately 4 million blacks and 8 million whites). In the Lower South states of Mississippi and South Carolina, blacks were the majority. The contrast with the North was striking: In 1860, only one Northerner in seventy-six was black (about 250,000 blacks to 19 million whites).

The presence of large numbers of African Americans had profound consequences for the South. Southern culture—language, food, music, religion, and even accents—was in part shaped by blacks. But the most direct consequence of the South's biracialism was southern whites' commitment to white supremacy. Northern whites believed in racial superiority, too, but they lived in a society in

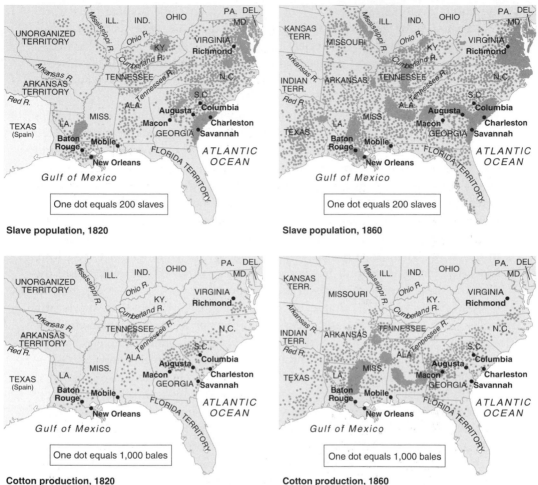

MAP 13.1   Cotton Kingdom, Slave Empire: 1820 and 1860
As the production of cotton soared, the slave population increased dramatically. Slaves continued to toil in tobacco and rice fields along the Atlantic seaboard, but increasingly they worked on cotton plantations in Alabama, Mississippi, and Louisiana.

which blacks made up barely 1 percent of the population. Their dedication to white supremacy lacked the intensity and urgency increasingly felt by white Southerners who lived among millions of blacks. White Southerners despised blacks because they considered them members of an inferior race, further degraded by their status as slaves. They also feared blacks because they realized that slaves had every reason to hate them and to strike back, as Nat Turner had.

Attacks on slavery after 1820—from blacks and a handful of white antislavery advocates within the South and from abolitionists outside—jolted southern slaveholders into a distressing awareness that they lived in a dangerous and fragile world. As the only slave society embedded in an egalitarian, democratic republic, the South made extraordinary efforts to strengthen slavery. State legislatures constructed slave codes (laws) that required the total submission of slaves to their masters and to white society in general. As the Louisiana code stated, a slave "owes his master . . . a respect without bounds, and an absolute obedience." The laws underlined the authority of all whites, not just masters. Any white could "correct" slaves who did not stay "in their place."

Intellectuals joined legislators in the campaign to strengthen slavery. Beginning in earnest in the 1820s, the South's academics, writers, and clergy constructed a proslavery argument that sought to unify the region's whites around slavery and provide ammunition for the emerging war of words with northern abolitionists. With the intellectuals' guidance, white Southerners gradually moved away from defending slavery as a "necessary evil"—the halfhearted argument popular in Jefferson's day—and toward a full-throated, aggressive defense of slavery as a "positive good." John C. Calhoun, an influential southern politician, declared that in the states where slavery had been abolished, "the condition of the African, instead of being improved, has become worse," while in the slave states, the Africans "have improved greatly in every respect."

Slavery's champions employed every imaginable defense. In the South, slaves were legal property, and wasn't the protection of property the bedrock of American **liberty**? They also used historical evidence to endorse slavery. Weren't the great civilizations—such as those of the Hebrews, Greeks, and Romans— slave societies? They argued that the Bible, properly interpreted, also sanctioned slavery. Old Testament patriarchs owned slaves, they observed, and in the New Testament, Paul returned the runaway slave Onesimus to his master. Some proslavery spokesmen played on the fears of Northerners and Southerners alike by charging that giving blacks equal rights would lead to the sexual mixing of the races, or **miscegenation**. Others attacked the economy and society of the North. George Fitzhugh of Virginia argued that behind the North's grand slogan of **free labor** lay a heartless philosophy: "Every man for himself, and the devil take the hindmost." Gouging capitalists exploited wageworkers unmercifully, Fitzhugh declared, and he contrasted the North's vicious free-labor system with the humane relations that he claimed prevailed between masters and slaves because slaves were valuable capital that masters sought to protect.

But at the heart of the defense of slavery lay the claim of black inferiority. Black enslavement was both necessary and proper, antebellum defenders argued, because Africans were lesser beings. Rather than exploitative, slavery was a mass civilizing effort that lifted lowly blacks from barbarism and savagery, taught them disciplined work, and converted them to soul-saving Christianity. According to Virginian Thomas R. Dew, most slaves were grateful. He declared that "the slaves of a good master are his warmest, most constant, and most devoted friends."

Black slavery encouraged whites to unify around race rather than to divide by class. The grubbiest, most tobacco-stained white man could proudly proclaim his superiority to all blacks and his equality with the most refined southern patrician.

Because of racial slavery, Georgia attorney Thomas R. R. Cobb observed, every white Southerner "feels that he belongs to an elevated class. It matters not that he is no slaveholder; he is not of the inferior race; he is a freeborn citizen." Consequently, the "poorest meets the richest as an equal; sits at his table with him; salutes him as a neighbor; meets him in every public assembly, and stands on the same social platform." In the South, Cobb boasted, "there is no war of classes."

In reality, slavery did not create perfect harmony among whites or ease every strain along class lines. But by providing every antebellum white Southerner membership in the ruling race, slavery helped whites bridge differences in wealth, education, and culture. Slavery meant white dominance, white superiority, and white equality.

The Plantation Economy

As important as slavery was in unifying white Southerners, only about a quarter of the white population lived in slaveholding families. Most slaveholders owned fewer than five slaves. Only about 12 percent of slave owners owned twenty or more, the number of slaves that historians consider necessary to distinguish a **planter** from a farmer. Although they were hugely outnumbered, planters nevertheless dominated the southern economy. In 1860, 52 percent of the South's slaves lived and worked on plantations. Plantation slaves produced more than 75 percent of the South's export crops, the backbone of the region's economy. Slavery was dying elsewhere in the New World (only Brazil and Cuba still defended slavery at midcentury), but slave plantations increasingly dominated southern agriculture.

The South's major cash crops—tobacco, sugar, rice, and cotton—grew on plantations. Tobacco, the original plantation crop in North America, had shifted westward in the nineteenth century from the Chesapeake to Tennessee and Kentucky. Large-scale sugar production began in 1795, when Étienne de Boré built a modern sugar mill in what is today New Orleans, and sugar plantations were confined almost entirely to Louisiana. Commercial rice production began in the seventeenth century, and like sugar, rice was confined to a small geographic area, a narrow strip of coast stretching from the Carolinas into Georgia.

Tobacco, sugar, and rice were labor-intensive crops that relied on large numbers of slaves to do the backbreaking work. Most phases of tobacco cultivation—planting, transporting, thinning, picking off caterpillars, cutting, drying, packing—required laborers to stoop or bend down. Work on sugarcane plantations was reputed to be the most physically demanding. During the harvest, slaves worked eighteen hours a day, and so hard was the slaves' task that one visitor concluded that "nothing but 'involuntary servitude' could go through the toil and suffering required to produce sugar." Working in water and mud in the heat of a Carolina summer regularly threatened slaves involved in rice production with malaria, yellow fever, and other diseases. As a consequence, blacks accounted for 90 percent of the population in the coastal area.

The Cotton Gin
The South could grow cotton in unimaginable quantities, but cotton stuck to seeds was useless in British textile mills. In 1793, Eli Whitney, a Northerner who was living on a Savannah River plantation, built a simple device for separating the cotton from the seed. Widespread use of the cotton gin broke the bottleneck in the commercial production of cotton and eventually bound millions of African Americans to slavery.
Smithsonian Institution, Washington, D.C.

If tobacco, sugar, and rice were the princes of plantation agriculture, cotton was the king. Cotton became commercially significant in the 1790s after the invention of a new cotton gin by Eli Whitney dramatically increased the production of raw cotton. Cotton was relatively easy to grow and took little capital to get started—just enough to purchase land, seed, and simple tools. Thus, small farmers as well as planters grew the white fluffy stuff. But planters, whose fields were worked by slaves, produced three-quarters of the South's cotton, and cotton made planters rich.

Plantation slavery also enriched the nation. By 1840, cotton accounted for more than 60 percent of American exports. Much of the profit from the sale of cotton overseas returned to planters, but some went to northern middlemen who bought, sold, insured, warehoused, and shipped cotton to the mills in Great Britain and elsewhere. As one New York merchant observed, "Cotton has enriched all through whose hands it has passed." As middlemen invested their profits in the booming northern economy, industrial development received a burst of much-needed capital. Furthermore, southern plantations benefited northern industry by providing an important market for textiles, agricultural tools, and other manufactured goods.

The economies of the North and South steadily diverged. While the North developed a mixed economy—agriculture, commerce, and manufacturing—the South remained overwhelmingly agricultural. Since planters were earning healthy profits, they saw little reason to diversify. Year after year, they funneled the profits they earned from land and slaves back into more land and slaves. With its capital flowing into agriculture, the South did not develop many factories. By 1860, only 10 percent of the nation's industrial workers lived in the South. Some cotton mills sprang up, but the region that produced 100 percent of the nation's cotton manufactured less than 7 percent of its cotton textiles.

Without significant economic diversification, the South developed fewer cities than the North and West. In 1860, it was the least urban region in the country. Whereas nearly 37 percent of New England's population lived in cities, less than 12 percent of Southerners were urban dwellers. Southern cities also differed from those elsewhere in the nation. They were mostly port cities on the periphery of the region and busy principally with exporting the agricultural products of plantations in the interior. Urban merchants provided agriculture with indispensable services, such as hauling, insuring, and selling cotton, rice, and sugar, but they were the tail on the plantation dog. Southern cities could claim something no northern city desired: 140,000 slaves in 1860. In some southern cities, slaves made up half the population, and they worked in nearly every conceivable occupation, helping the southern economy thrive.

Because the South had so few cities and industrial jobs, it attracted relatively small numbers of European immigrants. Seeking economic opportunity, not competition with slaves (whose labor would keep wages low), immigrants steered well north of the South's slave-dominated, agricultural economy. In 1860, 13 percent of all Americans were born abroad. But in nine of the fifteen slave states, only 2 percent or less of the population was foreign-born. As in the North, immigrants were concentrated in the cities.

Not every Southerner celebrated the region's plantation economy. Critics lambasted the excessive commitment to cotton and slaves and bemoaned what one called the "deplorable scarcity" of factories. Diversification, reformers promised, would make the South economically independent and more prosperous. State governments encouraged economic development by helping to create banking systems that supplied credit for a wide range of projects and by constructing railroads, but they also failed to create some of the essential services modern economies required. By the mid-nineteenth century, for example, no southern legislature had created a statewide public school system. The dominant slaveholders failed to see any benefit in educating small farmers, especially with their tax money. Despite the flurry of railroad building, the South's mileage in 1860 was less than half that of the North. Moreover, whereas railroads crisscrossed the North carrying manufactured goods as well as agricultural products, most railroads in the South ran from port cities back into farming areas and were built to export cotton.

Northerners claimed that slavery was a backward and doomed labor system, but few Southerners perceived economic weakness in their region. In fact, planters' pockets were never fuller than in the 1850s. Compared with Northerners, Southerners invested less of their capital in industry, transportation, and public education. Planters' decisions to reinvest in agriculture ensured the momentum of the plantation economy and the political and social relationships rooted in it.

►**REVIEW**   Why did the nineteenth-century southern economy remain primarily agricultural?

Masters, Mistresses, and the Big House

Nowhere was the contrast between northern and southern life more vivid than on the plantations of the South. Located on a patchwork of cleared fields and dense forests, a plantation typically included a "big house" and a slave quarter. Scattered about were numerous outbuildings, each with a special function. Near the big house were the kitchen, storehouse, smokehouse (for curing and preserving meat), and hen coop. More distant were the barns, toolsheds, **artisans'** workshops, and overseer's house. Large plantations sometimes had an infirmary and a chapel for slaves. Depending on the crop, there was a tobacco shed, a rice mill, a sugar refinery, or a cotton gin house. Lavish or plain, plantations everywhere had an underlying similarity.

The plantation was the home of masters, mistresses, and slaves. Slavery shaped the lives of all the plantation's inhabitants, from work to leisure activities, but it affected each differently. A hierarchy of rigid roles and duties governed relationships. Presiding was the master, who ruled his wife, children, and slaves, none of whom had many legal rights and all of whom were designated by the state as dependents under his dominion and protection.

Plantation Masters

Whereas smaller planters supervised the labor of their slaves themselves, larger planters hired overseers who went to the fields with the slaves, leaving the planters free to concentrate on marketing, finance, and general affairs of the plantation. Planters also found time to escape to town to discuss cotton prices, to the courthouse and legislature to debate politics, and to the woods to hunt and fish.

Increasingly in the nineteenth century, planters characterized their mastery in terms of what they called "Christian guardianship" and what historians have called **paternalism**. The concept of paternalism denied that the form of slavery practiced in the South was brutal and exploitative. Instead, it defined southern slavery as a set of reciprocal obligations between masters and slaves. In exchange for the slaves' labor and obedience, masters provided basic care and necessary guidance. As owners of blacks, masters argued, they had the responsibility of caring for a childlike, dependent people. In 1814, Thomas Jefferson captured the essence of the advancing ideal: "We should endeavor, with those whom fortune has thrown on our hands, to feed & clothe them well, protect them from ill usage, require such reasonable labor only as is performed voluntarily by freemen, and be led by no repugnancies to abdicate them, and our duties to them." A South Carolina rice planter insisted, "I manage them as my children."

Paternalism was part propaganda and part self-delusion. But it was also economically shrewd. Masters increasingly recognized slaves as valuable assets, particularly after the nation closed its external slave trade in 1808. They realized that the expansion of the slave labor force could come only from natural reproduction. As one planter declared in 1849, "It behooves those who own them to make them last as long as possible." Another planter instructed his overseer to pay attention to "whatever tends to promote their health and render them prolific."

One consequence of this paternalism and economic self-interest was a small improvement in slaves' welfare. Diet improved, although nineteenth-century slaves still ate mainly fatty pork and cornmeal. Housing improved, although the cabins still had cracks large enough, slaves said, for cats to slip through. Clothing improved, although slaves seldom received much more than two crude outfits a year and perhaps a pair of cheap shoes. In the fields, workdays remained sunup to sundown, but planters often provided a rest period in the heat of the day. And most owners ceased the colonial practice of punishing slaves by branding and mutilation.

Paternalism should not be mistaken for "Ol' Massa's" kindness and goodwill. It encouraged better treatment because it made economic sense to provide at least minimal care for valuable slaves. Nor did paternalism require that planters put aside their whips. They could flail away and still claim that they were only fulfilling their responsibilities as guardians of their naturally lazy and at times insubordinate dependents. State laws gave masters nearly "uncontrolled authority over the body" of the slave, according to one North Carolina judge. Paternalism offered slaves some informal protection against the most brutal punishments, but whipping remained the planters' essential form of coercion.

With its notion that slavery imposed on masters a burden and a duty, paternalism provided slaveholders with a means of rationalizing their rule. But it also provided some slaves with leverage in controlling the conditions of their lives. Slaves learned to manipulate the slaveholder's need to see himself as a good and decent master. To avoid a reputation as a cruel tyrant, planters sometimes negotiated with slaves, rather than just resorting to the whip. Masters sometimes granted slaves small garden plots in which they could work for themselves after working all day in the fields, or they gave slaves a few days off and a dance when they had gathered the last of the cotton.

The Virginia statesman Edmund Randolph argued that slavery created in white southern men a "quick and acute sense of personal liberty" and a "disdain for every abridgement of personal independence." Indeed, prickly individualism and aggressive independence became crucial features of the southern concept of honor. Social standing, political advancement, and even self-esteem rested on an honorable reputation. Defending honor became a male passion. Andrew Jackson's mother reportedly told her son, "Never tell a lie, nor take what is not your own, nor sue anybody for slander or assault and battery. *Always settle them cases yourself.*" Among planters, such advice sometimes led to duels. Dueling arrived from Europe in the eighteenth century. It died out in the North, but in the South, even after legislatures banned it, gentlemen continued to defend their honor with pistols at ten paces.

Southerners also expected an honorable gentleman to be a proper patriarch. Nowhere in America was masculine power more accentuated. Slavery buttressed

Southern Man with Children and Their Mammy
Obviously prosperous, this patriarch poses around 1848 with his young daughters
and their nurse. The black woman is clearly a servant, a status indicated by her race
and her attire. The death of the mother might account for the inclusion of the slave
woman in the family circle. Her presence signals her importance in the household.
Fathers left the raising of daughters to mothers and nurses.
Collection of the J. Paul Getty Museum, Malibu, CA.

the power of white men, and planters brooked no opposition from any of their
dependents, black or white. The master's absolute dominion sometimes led to
miscegenation. Laws prohibited interracial sex, and some masters practiced self-
restraint. Others merely urged discretion. How many trips masters and their sons
made to slave cabins is impossible to tell, but as long as slavery gave white men
extraordinary power, slave women were forced to submit to the sexual appetites
of the men who owned them.

Individualistic impulses were strong among planters, but duty to family was
paramount. In time, as the children of one elite family married the children of
another, ties of blood and kinship, as well as economic interest and ideology,
linked planters to one another. Conscious of what they shared as slaveholders,
planters worked together to defend their common interests. The values of the big
house—slavery, honor, male domination—washed over the boundaries of plantations and flooded all of southern life.

Plantation Mistresses

Like their northern counterparts, southern ladies were expected to possess the feminine virtues of piety, purity, chastity, and obedience within the context of marriage, motherhood, and domesticity. Southerners also expected ladies to mirror all that was best in plantation society. Countless toasts praised the southern lady as the perfect complement to her husband, the commanding patriarch. She was physically weak, "formed only for the less laborious occupations," and thus dependent on male protection. To gain this protection, she was naturally modest and delicate, possessed beauty and grace, and cultivated refinement and charm.

For women, this image of the southern lady was no blessing. Chivalry—the South's romantic ideal of male-female relationships—glorified the lady while it subordinated her. Chivalry's underlying assumptions about the weakness of women and the protective authority of men resembled the paternalistic defense of slavery. Indeed, the most articulate spokesmen for slavery also vigorously defended the subordination of women. George Fitzhugh insisted that "a woman, like children, has but one right and that is the right to protection. The right to protection involves the obligation to obey. A husband, a lord and master, nature designed for every woman. . . . If she be obedient she stands little danger of maltreatment." Just as the slaveholder's mastery was written into law, so too were the paramount rights of husbands. Married women lost almost all their property rights to their husbands. Women throughout the nation found divorce difficult, but southern women found it almost impossible.

Daughters of planters confronted chivalry's demands at an early age. Their education aimed at fitting them to become southern ladies. At their private boarding schools, they read literature, learned languages, and studied the appropriate drawing-room arts. Elite women began courting at a young age and married early. Kate Carney exaggerated only slightly when she despaired in her diary: "Today, I am seventeen, getting quite old, and am not married." Yet marriage meant turning their fates over to their husbands and making enormous efforts to live up to their region's lofty ideal. One mother warned her daughter: "A single life has fewer troubles; but then it is not the one for which our maker designed us."

Proslavery ideologues claimed that slavery freed white women from drudgery. Surrounded "by her domestics," declared Thomas R. Dew, "she ceases to be a mere beast of burden" and "becomes the cheering and animating center of the family circle." In reality, however, having servants required the plantation mistress to work long hours. Like her husband, she had managerial responsibilities. She managed the big house, directly supervising as many as a dozen slaves. But unlike her husband, the mistress had no overseer. All house servants answered directly to her. She assigned them tasks each morning, directed their work throughout the day, and punished them when she found fault. In addition to supervising a complex household, she had responsibility for the henhouse and dairy. On some plantations, she directed the slave hospital and nursery and rationed supplies for the slave quarter. Women also bore the dangers of childbearing and the responsibilities of child rearing. Southern ladies did not often lead lives of leisure.

Whereas masters used their status as slaveholders as a springboard into public affairs, mistresses' lives were circumscribed by the plantation. Masters left the plantation when they pleased, but mistresses needed chaperones to travel. When they could, they went to church, but women spent most days at home, where they often became lonely. In 1853, Mary Kendall wrote how much she enjoyed her sister's letter: "For about three weeks I did not have the pleasure of seeing one white female face, there being no white family except our own upon the plantation." In their few leisure hours, plantation mistresses read and wrote letters, but they preferred the company of friends. Grand parties and balls occasionally broke the daily routine, but the burden of planning and supervising the preparation of the food and drink fell on mistresses.

As members of slaveholding families, mistresses lived privileged lives. But they also had significant grounds for discontent. No feature of plantation life generated more anguish among mistresses than miscegenation. A perceptive observer of plantation society, Mary Boykin Chesnut of Camden, South Carolina, confided in her diary, "Ours is a monstrous system, a wrong and iniquity. Like the patriarchs of old, our men live all in one house with their wives and their concubines; and the mulattos one sees in every family partly resemble the white children. Any lady is ready to tell you who is the father of all the mulatto children in everybody's household but her own. Those, she seems to think drop from the clouds."

Most planters' wives, including Chesnut, accepted slavery. After all, the mistress's world rested on slave labor, just as the master's did. By acknowledging the realities of male power, mistresses enjoyed the rewards of their class and race. But these rewards came at a price. Still, the heaviest burdens of slavery fell not on those who lived in the big house, but on those who toiled to support them.

▶REVIEW   Why did the ideology of paternalism gain currency among planters in the nineteenth century?

Slaves and the Quarter

On most plantations, only a few hundred yards separated the big house and the slave quarter. The distance was short enough to ensure whites easy access to the labor of blacks, yet great enough to provide slaves with some privacy. Out of eyesight and earshot of the big house, slaves drew together and built lives of their own. They created families, worshipped God, and developed an African American community. Individually and collectively, slaves found subtle and not so subtle ways to resist their bondage.

Despite the rise of plantations, a substantial minority of slaves lived and worked elsewhere. Most labored on small farms, where they wielded a hoe alongside another slave or two and perhaps their master. But by 1860, almost half a million slaves (one in eight) did not work in agriculture at all. Some were employed in towns and cities as domestics, day laborers, bakers, barbers, tailors, and more. Others, far from urban centers, toiled as fishermen, lumbermen, and railroad workers. Slaves could also be found in most of the South's factories. Nevertheless, a majority of slaves (52 percent) counted plantations as their workplaces and homes.

Work

An ex-slave named Albert Todd recalled, "Work was a religion that we were taught." Whites enslaved blacks for their labor, and all slaves who were capable of productive labor worked. Young children were introduced to the world of work as early as age five or six. Ex-slave Carrie Hudson recalled that children who were "knee high to a duck" were sent to the fields to carry water to thirsty workers or to protect ripening crops from hungry birds. Others helped in the slave nursery, caring for children even younger than themselves, or in the big house, where they swept floors or shooed flies in the dining room. When slave boys and girls reached the age of eleven or twelve, masters sent most of them to the fields, where they learned farmwork by laboring alongside their parents. After a lifetime of labor, old women left the fields to care for the small children and spin yarn, and old men moved on to mind livestock and clean stables.

The overwhelming majority of plantation slaves worked as field hands. Planters sometimes assigned men and women to separate gangs, the women working at lighter tasks and the men doing the heavy work of clearing and breaking the land. But women also did heavy work. "I had to work hard," Nancy Boudry remembered, and "plow and go and split wood just like a man." The backbreaking labor and the monotonous routines caused one ex-slave to observe that the "history of one day is the history of every day."

A few slaves (about one in ten) became house servants. Nearly all of those (nine out of ten) were women. They cooked, cleaned, babysat, washed clothes, and did the dozens of other tasks the master and mistress required. House servants enjoyed somewhat less physically demanding work than field hands, but they were constantly on call, with no time that was entirely their own. Since no servant could please constantly, most bore the brunt of white frustration and rage. Ex-slave Jacob Branch of Texas remembered, "My poor mama! Every washday old Missy give her a beating."

Even rarer than house servants were skilled artisans. In the cotton South, no more than one slave in twenty (almost all men) worked in a skilled trade. Most were blacksmiths and carpenters, but slaves also worked as masons, mechanics, millers, and shoemakers. Slave craftsmen took pride in their skills and often exhibited the independence of spirit that caused slaveholder James H. Hammond of South Carolina to declare in disgust that when a slave became a skilled artisan, "he is more than half freed." Skilled slave fathers took pride in teaching their crafts to their sons. "My pappy was one of the black smiths and worked in the shop," John Mathews remembered. "I had to help my pappy in the shop when I was a child and I learnt how to beat out the iron and make wagon tires, and make plows."

Rarest of all slave occupations was that of slave driver. Probably no more than one male slave in a hundred worked in this capacity. These men were well named, for their primary task was driving other slaves to work harder in the fields. In some drivers' hands, the whip never rested. Ex-slave Jane Johnson of South Carolina called her driver the "meanest man, white or black, I ever see." But other drivers showed all the restraint they could. "Ole Gabe didn't like that whippin' business," West Turner of Virginia remembered. "When Marsa was there, he would lay it on 'cause he had to. But when old Marsa wasn't lookin', he never would beat them slaves."

Normally, slaves worked from what they called "can to can't," from "can see" in the morning to "can't see" at night. Even with a break at noon for a meal and rest, it made for a long day. For slaves, Lewis Young recalled, "work, work, work, 'twas all they do."

Family, Religion, and Community

From dawn to dusk, slaves worked for the master, but at night, when the labor was done, and all day Sunday and usually Saturday afternoon, slaves were left largely to themselves. Bone tired perhaps, they nonetheless used the time and space to develop and enjoy what mattered most: family, religion, and community.

In the quarter, slaves became husbands and wives, mothers and fathers, sons and daughters, preachers and singers, storytellers and conjurers. Over the generations, they created a community and a culture that buoyed them up during long hours in the fields and brought them joy and hope in the few hours they had to themselves.

One of the most important consequences of slaves' limited autonomy was the preservation and persistence of the family. Though severely battered, the black family survived slavery. No laws recognized slave marriage, and therefore no master or slave was legally obligated to honor the bond. Nevertheless, plantation records show that slave marriages were often long-lasting. Because the slave population in the South grew primarily through natural reproduction, sex ratios were approximately equal by the nineteenth century. Young men and women in the quarter fell in love, married, and set up housekeeping in cabins of their own. The primary cause of the ending of slave marriages was death, just as it was in white families. But the second most frequent cause was the sale of the husband or wife, something no white family ever had to fear. Precise figures are unavailable, but in the years 1820 to 1860, research suggests that sales destroyed at least 300,000 slave marriages.

In 1858, a South Carolina slave named Abream Scriven wrote a letter to his wife, who lived on a neighboring plantation. "My dear wife," he began, "I take

Slave Quarter, South Carolina
On large plantations, several score of African Americans lived in cabins that were often arranged along what slaves called "the street." The dwellings in this picture of a South Carolina planta- tion were better built than the typical rickety, one-room, dirt-floored slave cabin. Almost certainly posed, this photograph shows the inhabitants of the slave quarter. During the daylight hours of the workweek, when most men and women labored in the fields, the quarter was mostly empty. At night and on Sundays, it was a busy place.
Collection of the New-York Historical Society.

the pleasure of writing you . . . with much regret to inform you I am Sold to man by the name of Peterson, a Treader and Stays in New Orleans." Scriven promised to send some things when he got to his new home in Louisiana, but he admitted that he was not sure how he would "get them to you and my children." He asked his wife to "give my love to my father and mother and tell them good Bye for me. And if we do not meet in this world I hope to meet in heaven. . . . My dear wife for you and my children my pen cannot express the griffe I feel to be parted from you all." He closed with words no master would have permitted in a slave's marriage vows: "I remain your truly husband until Death." The letter makes clear Scriven's love for his family; it also demonstrates slavery's massive assault on family life in the quarter.

Despite their inability to fulfill the traditional roles of provider and protector, fathers gained status by doing what they could to help their families. Slave fathers and mothers divided responsibilities in the quarter along traditional gender lines: Women cooked, sewed, and cleaned; men hunted, raised hogs, cultivated gardens, and made furniture for their cabins. Slaves held their parents in high esteem, grateful for the small bits of refuge from the rigors of slavery their parents provided when they were children.

Religion also provided slaves with a refuge and a reason for living. Before the American Revolution, Baptists and Methodists began trying to convert slaves from their African beliefs. **Evangelicals** offered an emotional "religion of the heart" to which blacks (and many whites as well) responded enthusiastically. By the mid-nineteenth century, perhaps as many as one-quarter of all slaves claimed church membership, and many of the rest would not have objected to being called Christians.

Planters promoted Christianity in the quarter because they believed that the slaves' salvation was part of their obligation and that religion made slaves more obedient. South Carolina slaveholder Charles Colcock Jones, the leading missionary to the slaves, published his *Catechism for Colored Persons* in 1834. In it, he instructed slaves "to count their Masters 'worthy of all honour,' as those whom God has placed over them in this world." But slaves laughed up their sleeves at such messages. "That old white preacher just was telling us slaves to be good to our masters," one ex-slave said with a chuckle. "We ain't cared a bit about that stuff he was telling us 'cause we wanted to sing, pray, and serve God in our own way."

Meeting in their cabins or secretly in the woods, slaves created an African American Christianity that served their needs, not the masters'. Laws prohibited teaching slaves to read, but a few could read enough to struggle with the Bible. They interpreted the Christian message themselves. Rather than obedience, their faith emphasized justice. Slaves believed that God kept score and that the accounts of this world would be settled in the next. "The idea of a revolution in the conditions of the whites and blacks is the corner-stone" of the slaves' religion, recalled one ex-slave. But the slaves' faith also spoke to their experiences in this world. In the Old Testament, they discovered Moses, who delivered his people from slavery, and in the New Testament, they found Jesus, who offered salvation to all. Jesus' message of equality provided a potent antidote to the planters' claim that blacks were an inferior people whom God condemned to slavery.

Christianity did not entirely drive out traditional African beliefs. Even slaves who were Christians sometimes continued to believe that conjurers, witches, and spirits possessed the power to injure and protect. Moreover, slaves' Christian music, preaching, and rituals reflected the influence of Africa, as did many of their secular activities, such as wood carving, quilt making, and storytelling. But by the mid-nineteenth century, black Christianity had assumed a central place in slaves' quest for freedom. In the words of one spiritual, "O my Lord delivered Daniel / O why not deliver me too?"

Resistance and Rebellion

Slaves did not suffer slavery passively. They were, as whites said, "troublesome property." Slaves understood that accommodation to what they could not change was the price of survival, but in a hundred ways, they protested their bondage. Theoretically, the master was all-powerful and the slave powerless. But sustained by their families, religion, and community, slaves engaged in day-to-day resistance against their enslavers.

The spectrum of slave resistance ranged from mild to extreme. Telling a pointed story by the fireside in a slave cabin was probably the mildest form of protest. But when the weak got the better of the strong, as they did in tales of Br'er Rabbit and Br'er Fox (*Br'er* is a contraction of *Brother*), listeners could enjoy the thrill of a vicarious victory over their masters. Protest in the fields was riskier and included putting rocks in their cotton bags before having them weighed, feigning illness, and pretending to be so thickheaded that they could not understand the simplest instruction. Slaves broke so many hoes that owners outfitted the tools with oversized handles. Slaves so mistreated the work animals that masters switched from horses to mules, which could absorb more abuse. Although slaves worked hard in the master's fields, they also sabotaged his interests.

Running away was a common form of protest. Some runaways sought the ultimate prize: freedom in the North or in Canada. Over the decades, thousands of slaves, almost all from the Upper South, made it. But escape from the Lower South was almost impossible, except in Texas, where several hundred slaves found freedom in Mexico. Overwhelmingly young, unattached men, runaways could hope only to escape for a few days. Seeking temporary respite from hard labor or avoiding punishment, they usually stayed close to their plantations, keeping to the deep woods or swamps and slipping back into the quarter at night to get food. "Lying out," as it was known, usually ended when the runaway, worn-out and ragged, gave up or was finally chased down by slave-hunting dogs.

Although resistance was common, outright rebellion—a violent assault on slavery by large numbers of slaves—was very rare. Major rebellions were more common elsewhere in the New World. The scarcity of revolts in the South is not evidence of the slaves' contentedness, however. Rather, conditions gave rebels almost no chance of success. By 1860, whites in the South outnumbered blacks two to one and were heavily armed. Moreover, communication between plantations was difficult, and the South provided little protective wilderness into which rebels could retreat and defend themselves. Rebellion, as Nat Turner's experience showed, was virtual suicide.

Despite the rarity of slave revolts, whites believed that they were surrounded by conspiracies to rebel. In 1822, whites in Charleston accused Denmark Vesey, a free black carpenter, of conspiring with plantation slaves to slaughter Charleston's white inhabitants. The authorities rounded up scores of suspects, who, prodded by torture and the threat of death, implicated others in the plot "to riot in blood, outrage, and rapine." Although the city fathers never found any weapons and Vesey and most of the accused steadfastly denied the charges of conspiracy, officials hanged thirty-five black men, including Vesey, and banished another thirty-seven blacks from the state.

Masters boasted that their slaves were "instinctively contented," but steady resistance and occasional rebellion proved otherwise. Slaves did not have the power to end their bondage, but by asserting themselves, they affirmed their humanity and worth. By resisting their masters' will, slaves became actors in the plantation drama, helping establish limits beyond which planters and overseers hesitated to go.

Still, slavery blunted and thwarted African Americans' hopes and aspirations. Slavery broke some and crippled others. But slavery's destructive power had to contend with the resiliency of the human spirit. Slaves fought back physically, culturally, and spiritually. They not only survived bondage, but they also created in the quarter a vibrant African American culture and community that sustained them through more than two centuries of slavery and what came after.

▶**REVIEW**   What types of resistance did slaves participate in, and why did slave resistance rarely take the form of rebellion?

Black and Free: On the Middle Ground

Not every black Southerner was a slave. In 1860, some 260,000 (approximately 6 percent) of the region's 4.1 million African Americans were free. What is surprising is not that their numbers were small but that they existed at all. "Free black" seemed increasingly a contradiction to most white Southerners. According to the emerging racial thinking, blacks were supposed to be slaves. Blacks who were free stood out, and whites made them more and more targets of oppression. Free blacks stood precariously between slavery and full freedom, on what a young free black artisan in Charleston characterized in 1848 as "a middle ground." But they made the most of their freedom, and a few found success despite the restrictions placed on them by white Southerners.

Precarious Freedom

The population of free blacks swelled after the Revolution, when the natural rights philosophy of the Declaration of Independence and the egalitarian message of evangelical Protestantism joined to challenge slavery. A brief flurry of

emancipation visited the Upper South, where the ideological assault on slavery coincided with a deep depression in the tobacco economy. Some masters freed their slaves outright; others permitted favorite slaves to buy their freedom by working after hours to accumulate money for self-purchase. By 1810, free blacks in the South numbered more than 100,000, a fact that worried white Southerners, who, because of the cotton boom, wanted more slaves, not more free blacks.

In the 1820s and 1830s, state legislatures acted to stem the growth of the free black population and to shrink the liberty of those blacks who had gained their freedom. Some laws denied masters the right to free their slaves. Other laws humiliated and restricted free blacks by subjecting them to special taxes, requiring them to register annually with the state or to choose a white guardian, prohibiting them from interstate travel, denying them the right to have schools and to participate in politics, and requiring them to carry "freedom papers" to prove they were not slaves. Increasingly, whites subjected free blacks to the same laws as slaves. They could not testify under oath in a court of law or serve on juries. Like slaves, they were liable to whipping and the treadmill, where they were made to walk on the moving steps of a wheel until they fell, exhausted. Free blacks were forbidden to strike whites, even to defend themselves. "Free negroes belong to a degraded caste of society," a South Carolina judge said in 1848. "They are in no respect on a perfect equality with the white man. . . . They ought, by law, to be compelled to demean themselves as inferiors."

The elaborate system of regulations confined most free African Americans to a constricted life of poverty and dependence. Typically, free blacks were rural, uneducated, unskilled agricultural laborers and domestic servants. Opportunities of all kinds—for work, education, or community—were slim. Planters looked on free blacks as degraded parasites, likely to set a bad example for slaves. They believed that free blacks subverted the racial subordination that was the essence of slavery.

Achievement despite Restrictions

Despite increasingly harsh laws and stepped-up persecution, free African Americans made the most of the advantages their status offered. Unlike slaves, free blacks could legally marry. They could protect their families from arbitrary disruption and pass on their heritage of freedom to their children. Freedom also meant that they could choose occupations and own property. For most, these economic rights proved only theoretical, for a majority of the South's free blacks remained propertyless.

Still, some free blacks escaped the poverty and degradation whites thrust on them. Particularly in urban areas—especially the cities of Charleston, Mobile, and New Orleans—a small elite of free blacks emerged. Urban whites enforced many of the restrictive laws only sporadically, allowing free blacks room to maneuver. The elite consisted overwhelmingly of light-skinned African Americans who worked at skilled trades, and their customers were prominent whites who appreciated their able, respectful service. The free black elite operated schools for their children and traveled in and out of their states, despite laws forbidding both activities. They worshipped with whites (in separate seating) in the finest churches and lived scattered about in white neighborhoods, not in ghettos. And like elite whites, some owned slaves. Blacks could own blacks because they had the right to own property, which in the South included human property. Of the 3,200 black slaveholders (barely 1 percent of the free black population), most owned only a few slaves, who were sometimes family members whom they could not legally free. Others owned slaves in large numbers and exploited them for labor.

One free black slave owner was William Ellison of South Carolina. Ellison was born a slave in 1790, but he bought his freedom in 1816 and moved to a thriving plantation district about one hundred miles north of Charleston. He set up business as a cotton gin maker, a trade he had learned as a slave, and by 1835 he was prosperous enough to purchase the home of a former governor of the state. By the time of his death in 1861, he had become a cotton planter, with sixty-three slaves and an 800-acre plantation.

Most free blacks neither became slaveholders like Ellison nor sought to raise a slave rebellion, as whites accused Denmark Vesey of doing. Rather, most free blacks simply tried to preserve their freedom, which was under increasing attack. Unlike blacks in the North whose freedom was secure, free blacks in the South clung to a precarious freedom by seeking to impress whites with their reliability, economic contributions, and good behavior.

> ►REVIEW   Why did many state legislatures pass laws restricting free blacks' rights in the 1820s and 1830s?

The Plain Folk

Like most free blacks, most whites in the South did not own slaves, not even one. In 1860, more than six million of the South's eight million whites lived in slaveless households. Some slaveless whites lived in cities and worked as artisans, mechanics, and traders. Others lived in the country and worked as storekeepers, parsons, and schoolteachers. But most "plain folk" were small farmers. Perhaps three out of four were **yeomen**, small farmers who owned their own land. As in the North, farm ownership provided a family with an economic foundation, social respectability, and political standing. Unlike their northern counterparts, however, southern yeomen lived in a region whose economy and society were increasingly dominated by unfree labor.

In an important sense, the South had more than one white yeomanry. The huge southern landscape provided space enough for two yeoman societies, separated roughly along geographical lines. Yeomen throughout the South had much in common, but the life of a small farm family in the plantation belt—the flatlands that spread from South Carolina to east Texas—differed from the life of a family in the upcountry—the area of hills and mountains. And some rural, slaveless whites were not yeomen; they owned no land at all and were sometimes desperately poor.

Plantation Belt Yeomen

Plantation belt yeomen lived within the orbit of the planter class. Small farms actually outnumbered plantations in that great arc of fertile cotton land known as the cotton belt, which stretched from South Carolina to Texas, but they were dwarfed in importance. Small farmers grew mainly food crops, particularly corn, but they also devoted a portion of their land to cotton. With only family labor to draw upon, they produced only a few 400-pound bales each year, whereas large planters measured their crop in hundreds of bales. The small farmers' cotton tied them to planters. Unable to afford cotton gins or baling presses of their own, they relied on helpful neighborhood slave owners to gin and bale their cotton. With no link to merchants in the port cities, plantation belt yeomen also turned to better-connected planters to ship and sell their cotton.

A dense network of relationships laced small farmers and planters together in patterns of reciprocity and mutual obligation. Planters hired out surplus slaves to ambitious yeomen who wanted to expand cotton production. They sometimes chose overseers from among the sons of local farm families. Plantation mistresses sometimes nursed ailing neighbors. In rural counties, adult white males, often yeomen, rode in slave patrols, which nightly scoured country roads to make certain that no slaves were moving about without permission. Family ties could span class lines, making rich and poor kin as well as neighbors. On Sundays, plantation dwellers and plain folk came together in church to worship and afterward lingered to gossip and to transact small business.

Plantation belt yeomen may have envied, and at times even resented, wealthy slaveholders, but in general small farmers learned to accommodate. Planters made accommodation easier by going out of their way to behave as good neighbors and avoid direct exploitation of slaveless whites in their community. As a consequence, rather than raging at the oppression of the planter regime, the typical plantation belt yeoman sought entry into it. He dreamed of adding acreage to his farm, buying a few slaves of his own, and retiring from exhausting field work.

Upcountry Yeomen

By contrast, the hills and mountains of the South resisted the spread of slavery and plantations. In the western parts of Virginia, North Carolina, and South Carolina; in northern Georgia and Alabama; and in eastern Tennessee and Kentucky, the higher elevation, colder climate, rugged terrain, and poor transportation made it difficult for commercial agriculture to make headway. As a result, yeomen dominated these isolated areas, and planters and slaves were scarce.

Gathering Corn in Virginia, circa 1870
In this romanticized agricultural scene, painter Felix O. C. Darley depicts members of a white farm family gathering its harvest by hand. In reality, growing corn was hard work. Even yeomen who grew considerable amounts of cotton also grew lots of corn, usually producing about twice the corn they needed for their families and livestock and marketing the rest. The artist, however, is less concerned with realism than with extolling rural family labor as virtuous and noble. Darley surrounds the southern yeomen with an aura of republican independence, dignity, and freedom.
Warner Collection of Gulf States Paper Corporation.

At the core of this distinctive upcountry society was the independent farm family working its own patch of land; raising hogs, cattle, and sheep; and seeking self-sufficiency and independence. Toward that end, all members of the family worked, their tasks depending on their sex and age. Husbands labored in the fields, and with their sons, they cleared, plowed, planted, and cultivated primarily food crops. Though pressed into field labor at harvesttime, wives and daughters of upcountry yeomen, like those of plantation belt yeomen, worked in and about the cabin most of the year. One upcountry farmer remembered that his mother "worked in the house cooking, spinning, weaving [and doing] patchwork." Women also tended the vegetable garden, kept a cow and some chickens, preserved food, cleaned their homes, fed their families, and cared for their children. Male and female tasks were equally crucial to the farm's success, but as in other white southern households, the domestic sphere was subordinated to the will of the male patriarch.

The typical upcountry yeoman also grew a little cotton or tobacco, but production for home consumption was more important than production for the market. Not much currency changed hands in the upcountry. Barter was common. A yeoman might trade his small cotton or tobacco crop to a country store owner for a little salt, lead shot, needles, and nails. Or he might swap extra sweet potatoes for a plow from a blacksmith or for leather from a tanner. Networks of exchange and mutual assistance tied individual homesteads to the larger community. Farm families also joined together in logrolling, house and barn raising, and cornhusking.

Even the hills had some plantations and slaves, but they existed in much smaller numbers than in the plantation belt. The few upcountry folks who owned slaves usually had only two or three. As a result, slaveholders had much less direct social and economic power, and yeomen had more. But the upcountry did not oppose slavery. As long as upcountry plain folk were free to lead their own lives, they defended slavery and white supremacy just as staunchly as other white Southerners.

Poor Whites

Hardworking, landholding small farmers made up the majority of white Southerners. But Northerners had a different image of southern society. They believed that slavery had condemned most whites to poverty, brutality, and backwardness. One antislavery advocate charged that the South harbored three classes: "the slaves on whom devolves all the regular industry, the slaveholders who reap all the fruits, and an idle and lawless rabble who live dispersed over vast plains little removed from absolute barbarism." Critics called this third class a variety of derogatory names: hillbillies, crackers, rednecks, and poor white trash. According to critics, poor whites were not just whites who were poor. They were also supposedly ignorant, diseased, and degenerate. Even slaves were known to chant, "I'd rather be a nigger an' plow ol' Beck / Than a white hillbilly with a long red neck."

Contrary to northern opinion, only about one in four nonslaveholding rural white men was landless and very poor. Some worked as tenants, renting land and struggling to make a go of it. Others survived by herding pigs and cattle. And still others worked for meager wages, ditching, mining, logging, and laying track for railroads. A Georgian remembered that his "father worked by the day when ever he could get work."

Some poor white men earned reputations for mayhem and violence. One visitor claimed that a "bowie-knife was a universal, and a pistol a not at all unusual companion." Edward Isham, an illiterate roustabout, spent about as much time fighting as he did working. When he wasn't engaged in ear-biting, eye-gouging free-for-alls, he was fighting with sticks, shovels, rocks, axes, tomahawks, knives, and guns. Working at what he could find, he took up with and abandoned many women, gambled, drank, stole, had run-ins with the law, and eventually murdered a respected slaveholder, for which he was hanged in 1860.

Unlike Isham, most poor white men did not engage in ferocious behavior but instead lived responsible lives. They sat at the bottom of the white pecking order, but they were ambitious people eager to climb into the yeomanry. The Lipscomb family illustrates the possibility of upward mobility. In 1845, Smith and Sally Lipscomb and their children abandoned their worn-out land in South Carolina for Benton County, Alabama. "Benton is a mountainous country but ther is a heep of good levil land to tend in it," Smith wrote back to his brother. Alabama, Smith said, "will be better for the rising generation if not for ourselves but I think it will be the best for us all that live any length of time." Indeed, primitive living conditions made life precarious. All of the Lipscombs fell ill, but all recovered, and the entire family went to work. Because they had no money to buy land, they squatted on seven unoccupied acres. With the help of neighbors, they built a 22-by-24-foot cabin, a detached kitchen, and two stables. From daylight to dark, Smith and his sons worked the land. Nature cooperated, and they produced enough food for the table and several bales of cotton. The women worked as hard in the cabin, and Sally contributed to the family's income by selling homemade shirts and socks. In time, the Lipscombs bought land and joined the Baptist church, completing their transformation to respectable yeomen.

Many poor whites succeeded in climbing the economic ladder, but in the 1850s upward mobility slowed. The cotton boom of that decade caused planters to expand their operations, driving the price of land beyond the reach of poor families. Whether they gained their own land or not, however, poor whites shared common cultural traits with yeomen farmers.

The Culture of the Plain Folk

Situated on scattered farms and in tiny villages, rural plain folk lived isolated, local lives. Bad roads and a lack of newspapers meant that everyday life revolved around family, a handful of neighbors, the local church, and perhaps a country store. Work occupied most hours, but plain folk still found time for pleasure. "Dancing they are all fond of," a visitor to North Carolina discovered, "especially when they can get a fiddle, or bagpipe." They also loved their tobacco. One visitor complained that the "use of tobacco is almost universal." Men smoked and chewed (and spat), while women dipped snuff. But the truly universal pastimes among men and boys were fishing and hunting. A traveler in Mississippi recalled that his host sent "two of his sons, little fellows that looked almost too small to shoulder a gun," for food. "One went off towards the river and the other struck into the forest, and in a few hours we were feasting on delicious venison, trout and turtle."

Plain folk did not usually associate "book learning" with the basic needs of life. A northern woman visiting the South in the 1850s observed, "Education is not extended to the masses here as at the North." Private academies charged fees that yeomen could not afford, and public schools were scarce. Although most people managed to pick up a basic knowledge of the "three R's," approximately one southern white man in five was illiterate in 1860, and the rate for white women was even higher. "People here prefer talking to reading," a Virginian remarked. Telling stories, reciting ballads, and singing hymns were important activities in yeoman culture.

Plain folk everywhere spent more hours in revival tents than in classrooms. Not all rural whites were religious, but many were, and the most characteristic feature of their evangelical Christian faith was the revival. The greatest of the early-nineteenth-century revivals occurred in 1801 at Cane Ridge, Kentucky, where some twenty thousand people gathered to listen to evangelical preachers who spoke day and night for a week. Ministers sought to save souls by bringing individuals to a personal conviction of sin. Revivalism crossed denominational lines, but Baptists and Methodists adopted it most readily and by midcentury had become the South's largest religious groups. By emphasizing free choice and individual worth, the plain folk's religion was hopeful and affirming. Hymns and spirituals provided guides to right and wrong—praising humility and steadfastness, condemning drunkenness and profanity. Above all, hymns spoke of the eventual release from worldly sorrows and the assurance of eternal salvation.

▶ **REVIEW**   Why did yeomen dominate the upcountry?

The Politics of Slavery

By the mid-nineteenth century, all southern white men—planters and plain folk alike—had gained the vote. But even after the South's politics became **democratic** for the white male population, political power remained unevenly distributed. The nonslaveholding white majority wielded less political power than their numbers indicated. The slaveholding white minority wielded more. Self-conscious, cohesive, and with a well-developed sense of class interest, slaveholders busied themselves with party politics, campaigns, and officeholding and made demands of state governments. As a result, they received significant benefits. Nonslaveholding whites were concerned mainly with preserving their liberties and keeping their taxes low. Collectively, they asked government for little of an economic nature, and they received little.

Slaveholders sometimes worried about nonslaveholders' loyalty to slavery, but since the eighteenth century, the majority of whites had accepted the planters' argument that the existing social order served *all* Southerners' interests. Slavery rewarded every white man—no matter how poor—with membership in the South's white ruling class. It also provided the means by which nonslaveholders might someday advance into the ranks of the planters. White men in the South fought furiously about many things, but they agreed that they should take land from Indians, promote agriculture, uphold white supremacy and masculine privilege, and defend slavery from its enemies.

The Democratization of the Political Arena

The political reforms that swept the nation in the first half of the nineteenth century reached deeply into the South. Southern politics became democratic politics—for white men. Southerners eliminated the wealth and property requirements that had once restricted political participation. Beginning in the 1810s, Southerners began expanding **suffrage** until, by the 1850s, every state had extended the right to vote to all adult white males. Most southern states also removed the property requirements for holding state offices. To be sure, undemocratic features lingered. Plantation districts still wielded disproportionate power in several state legislatures. Nevertheless, southern politics took place within an increasingly democratic political structure.

White male suffrage ushered in an era of vigorous electoral competition. Eager voters rushed to the polls to exercise their new rights. High turnouts—often approaching 80 percent—became a hallmark of southern electoral politics. As politics became aggressively democratic, it also grew fiercely partisan. From the 1830s to the 1850s, Whigs and Democrats battled for the electorate's favor. In the South, both parties presented themselves as the plain white folk's best friend. All candidates declared their fervent commitment to **republican** equality and pledged to defend the people's liberty. Each party sought to portray the other as a collection of rich, snobbish, selfish men who had antidemocratic designs up their silk sleeves. Each, in turn, claimed for itself the mantle of humble "servant of the people."

The Whig and Democratic parties sought to serve the people differently, however. Whigs favored government intervention in the economy, and Democrats tended to oppose it. Whigs generally backed state support of banks, railroads, and corporations, arguing that government aid would stimulate the economy, enlarge opportunity, and thus increase the general welfare. Democrats emphasized the threat to individual liberty that government intervention posed, claiming that granting favors to special economic interests would result in concentrated power, which would in turn jeopardize the common man's opportunity and equality. Beginning with the panic of 1837, the parties clashed repeatedly on concrete economic and financial issues.

Planter Power

Whether Whig or Democrat, southern officeholders were likely to be slave owners. The power slaveholders exerted over slaves did not translate directly into political authority over whites, however. In the nineteenth century, political power could be won only at the ballot box, and almost everywhere nonslaveholders were in the majority. Yet year after year, proud and noisily egalitarian common men elected wealthy slaveholders.

By 1860, the percentage of slave owners in state legislatures ranged from 41 percent in Missouri to nearly 86 percent in North Carolina. Legislators not only tended
to own slaves; they also often owned large numbers. The percentage of planters (individuals with twenty or more slaves) in southern legislatures in 1860 ranged from
5.3 percent in Missouri to 55.4 percent in South Carolina. In North Carolina, where
only 3 percent of the state's white families belonged to the planter class, more than
36 percent of state legislators were planters. The democratization of politics in the
nineteenth century meant that more ordinary citizens participated in elections, but
yeomen and artisans remained rare sights in the halls of southern legislatures.

Upper-class dominance of southern politics reflected the elite's success in
persuading the white majority that what was good for slaveholders was also
good for them. In reality, the South had, on the whole, done well by the plain folk.
Most had farms of their own. They participated as equals in a democratic political
system. They enjoyed an elevated social status, above all blacks and in theory
equal to all other whites. They commanded patriarchal authority over their
households. And as long as slavery existed, they could dream of joining the
planter class. Slaveless white men found much to celebrate in the slave South.

Most slaveholders took pains to win the plain folk's trust and to nurture their
respect. One South Carolinian told his wealthy neighbor that he had a bright
political future because he never thought himself "too good to sit down & talk to a
poor man." South Carolinian Mary Boykin Chesnut complained about the fawning
attention her slaveholding husband showed to poor men, including one who had
"mud sticking up through his toes." Smart candidates found ways to convince wary
plain folk of their democratic convictions and egalitarian sentiments, whether they
were genuine or not. When young John A. Quitman ran for a seat in the Mississippi
legislature, he amazed a boisterous crowd of small farmers at one campaign stop by
not only entering but winning contests in jumping, boxing, wrestling, and sprint-
ing. For his finale, he outshot the area's champion marksman. Then, demonstrating
his deft political touch, he gave his prize, a fat ox, to the defeated rifleman. The electorate showed its approval by sending Quitman to the state capital.

Georgia politics illustrate how well planters protected their interests in state
legislatures. In 1850, about half of the state's revenues came from taxes on slaves,
the characteristic form of planter wealth. However, the tax rate on slaves was trifling, only about one-fifth the rate on land. Moreover, planters benefited far more
than other groups from public spending. Financing railroads—which carried cotton to market—was the largest state expenditure. The legislature also established
low tax rates on land, the characteristic form of yeoman wealth, which meant that
the typical yeoman's annual tax bill was small. Still, relative to their wealth, large
slaveholders paid less than did other whites. Relative to their numbers, they got
more in return. A sympathetic slaveholding legislature protected planters' interests and gave the impression of protecting the small farmers' interests as well.

The South's elite defended slavery in other ways. In the 1830s, whites decided
that slavery was too important to debate. "So interwoven is [slavery] with our

interest, our manners, our climate and our very being," one man declared in 1833, "that no change can ever possibly be effected without a civil commotion from which the heart of a patriot must turn with horror." To end free speech on the slavery question, powerful whites dismissed slavery's critics from college faculties, drove them from pulpits, and hounded them from political life. Sometimes antislavery Southerners fell victim to vigilantes and mob violence. One could defend slavery; one could even delicately suggest mild reforms. But no Southerner could any longer safely call slavery evil or advocate its destruction.

In the South, therefore, the rise of the common man occurred alongside the continuing, even growing, power of the planter class. Rather than pitting slaveholders against nonslaveholders, elections remained an effective means of binding the region's whites together. Elections affirmed the sovereignty of white men, whether planter or plain folk, and the subordination of African Americans. Those twin themes played well among white women as well. Though unable to vote, white women supported equality for whites and slavery for blacks. In the antebellum South, the politics of slavery helped knit together all of white society.

▶ REVIEW   How did planters benefit from their control of state legislatures?

Conclusion: A Slave Society

By the early nineteenth century, northern states had either abolished slavery or put it on the road to extinction, while southern states were aggressively building the largest slave society in the New World. Regional differences increased over time, not merely because the South became more and more dominated by slavery, but also because developments in the North rapidly propelled it in a very different direction.

One-third of the South's population was enslaved by 1860. Bondage saddled blacks with enormous physical and spiritual burdens: hard labor, harsh treatment, broken families, and, most important, the denial of freedom itself. Although degraded and exploited, they were not defeated. Out of African memories and New World realities, blacks created a life-affirming African American culture that sustained and strengthened them. Their families, religion, and community provided antidotes to white racist ideas and even to white power. Defined as property, they refused to be reduced to things. Perceived as inferior beings, they rejected the notion that they were natural slaves. Slaves engaged in a war of wills with masters who sought their labor, while the slaves themselves sought to live dignified, autonomous lives.

By the mid-nineteenth century, slavery was crucial to the South's distinctiveness and to the loyalty and regional identification of its whites. The South was not merely a society with slaves; it had become a slave society. Slavery shaped the region's economy, culture, social structure, and politics. Whites south of the Mason-Dixon line believed that racial slavery was necessary and just. By making all blacks a pariah class, all whites gained a measure of equality and harmony.

Racism did not erase stress along class lines, nor did the other features of southern life that helped confine class tensions: the wide availability of land, rapid economic mobility, the democratic nature of political life, and patriarchal power among all white men. Anxious slaveholders continued to worry that yeomen would defect from the proslavery consensus. But during the 1850s, a far more ominous division emerged—that between "slave states" and "free states."

REVIEWING THE CHAPTER

Use the questions and timeline to review and strengthen your understanding of the chapter.

REVIEW QUESTIONS

1. Why did the nineteenth-century southern economy remain primarily agricultural? (pp. 375–81)

2. Why did the ideology of paternalism gain currency among planters in the nineteenth century? (pp. 382–86)

3. What types of resistance did slaves participate in, and why did slave resistance rarely take the form of rebellion? (pp. 386–92)

4. Why did many state legislatures pass laws restricting free blacks' rights in the 1820s and 1830s? (pp. 392–94)

5. Why did yeomen dominate the upcountry? (pp. 394–99)

6. How did planters benefit from their control of state legislatures? (pp. 399–402)

MAKING CONNECTIONS

1. By the mid-nineteenth century, the South had become a "cotton kingdom." How did cotton's profitability shape the region's antebellum development? In your answer, discuss the region's distinctive demographic and economic features.

2. How did southern white legislators and intellectuals attempt to strengthen the institution of slavery in the 1820s? What prompted them to undertake this work? In your answer, be sure to explore regional and national influences.

3. Although bondage restricted slaves' autonomy and left slaves vulnerable to extreme abuse, they resisted slavery. Discuss the variety of ways in which slaves attempted to lessen the harshness of slavery. What were the short- and long-term effects of their efforts?

4. Despite vigorous political competition in the South, by 1860 legislative power was largely concentrated in the hands of a regional minority—slaveholders. Why were slaveholders politically dominant? In your answer, be sure to consider how the region's biracialism contributed to its politics.

TIMELINE

1808	• External slave trade outlawed.
1810s–1850s	• Suffrage extended throughout South to all adult white males.
1813–1814	• Creek War opens Indian land to white settlement.
1820s–1830s	• Southern legislatures enact slave codes to strengthen slavery. • Southern legislatures enact laws to restrict growth of free black population. • Southern intellectuals begin to fashion systematic defense of slavery.
1829	• *Appeal . . . to the Coloured Citizens of the World* published.
1830	• Southern slaves number approximately two million.
1831	• Nat Turner's slave rebellion. • First issue of *Liberator* published.
1834	• *Catechism for Colored Persons* published.
1836	• Arkansas admitted to Union as slave state.
1840	• Cotton accounts for more than 60 percent of nation's exports.
1845	• Texas and Florida admitted to Union as slave states.
1860	• Southern slaves number nearly four million, one-third of South's population.

▶ **For an online bibliography, practice quizzes, Web sites, images, and documents related to this chapter,** see the Book Companion Site at **bedfordstmartins.com/roark.**

▶ **For firsthand accounts of this period,** see Chapter 13 in Michael Johnson, ed., *Reading the American Past,* Fourth Edition.

14
CHAPTER

The House Divided

1846–1861

O THER THAN TWENTY CHILDREN, John Brown did not have much to show for his life in 1859. Grizzled, gnarled, and fifty-nine years old, he had for decades lived like a nomad, hauling his large family back and forth across six states as he tried desperately to better himself. He turned his hand to farming, raising sheep, running a tannery, and selling wool, but failure dogged him. The world had given John Brown some hard licks, but it had not budged his conviction that slavery was wrong and ought to be destroyed. He had learned to hate slavery at his father's knee, and in the wake of the fighting that erupted over the issue in Kansas in the 1850s, his beliefs turned violent. On May 24, 1856, he led an eight-man antislavery posse in the midnight slaughter of five allegedly proslavery men at Pottawatomie, Kansas. He told Mahala Doyle, whose husband and two oldest sons he killed, that if a man stood between him and what he thought right, he would take that man's life as calmly as he would eat breakfast.

After the killings, Brown slipped out of Kansas and reemerged in the East. More than ever, he was a man on fire for abolition. He spent thirty months begging money from New Englanders to support his vague plan for military operations against slavery. He captivated the genteel easterners, particularly the Boston elite. They were awed by his iron-willed determination and courage, but most could not accept violence. "These men are all talk," Brown declared. "What is needed is action—action!" But the hypnotic-eyed Brown convinced a handful of people that God had touched him for a great purpose, and they donated enough money for him to gather a small band of antislavery warriors.

On the night of October 16, 1859, Brown took his war against slavery into the South. With only twenty-one men, including five African Americans, he invaded

John Brown

In this 1859 photograph, John Brown appears respectable, even statesmanlike, but contemporaries debated his mental state and moral character, and the debate still rages. Critics argue that he was a bloody terrorist, a religious fanatic who believed that he was touched by God for a great purpose, one for which he was willing to die. Admirers see a resolute and selfless hero, a rare white man who believed that black people were the equals of whites, and a shrewd political observer who recognized that only a full-scale revolt of the oppressed would end slavery in America.

National Portrait Gallery, Smithsonian Institution/Art Resource, NY.

Harpers Ferry, Virginia. His band quickly seized the town's armory and rifle works, but the invaders were immediately surrounded, first by local militia and then by Colonel Robert E. Lee, who commanded the U.S. troops in the area. When Brown refused to surrender, federal soldiers charged with bayonets. Seventeen men, two of whom were slaves, lost their lives. Although a few of Brown's raiders escaped, federal forces killed ten (including two of his sons) and captured seven, among them Brown.

"When I strike, the bees will begin to swarm," Brown told Frederick Douglass a few months before the raid. As slaves rushed to Harpers Ferry, he said, he would arm them with the pikes he carried with him and with weapons stolen from the armory. They would then fight a war of liberation. Brown, however, neglected to inform the slaves that he had arrived in Harpers Ferry, and the few who knew of his arrival wanted nothing to do with his enterprise. "It was not a slave insurrection," Abraham Lincoln observed. "It was an attempt by white men to get up a revolt among slaves, in which the slaves refused to participate. In fact, it was so absurd that the slaves, with all their ignorance, saw plainly enough it could not succeed."

Although Brown's raid ended in utter defeat, white Southerners viewed it as proof of their growing suspicion that Northerners actively sought to incite slaves in bloody rebellion. For more than a decade, Northerners and Southerners had accused one another of hostile intentions, and by 1859, emotions were raw. Sectional tension was as old as the Constitution, but hostility had escalated with the outbreak of war with Mexico in May 1846 (see chapter 12). Only three months after the war began, national expansion and the slavery issue intersected when Representative David Wilmot introduced a bill to prohibit slavery in any territory that might be acquired as a result of the war. After that, the problem of slavery in the territories became the principal wedge that divided the nation.

"Mexico is to us the forbidden fruit," South Carolina senator John C. Calhoun declared at the war's outset. "The penalty of eating it [is] to subject our institutions to political death." For a decade and a half, the slavery issue intertwined with the fate of former Mexican land, poisoning the national political debate. Slavery proved powerful enough to transform party politics into sectional politics. Rather than Whigs and Democrats confronting one another across party lines, Northerners and Southerners eyed one another hostilely across the Mason-Dixon line. Sectional politics encouraged the South's separatist impulses. Southern separatism, a fitful tendency before the Mexican-American War, gained strength with each confrontation. As the nation lurched from crisis to crisis, southern disaffection and alienation mounted, and support for compromise and conciliation eroded. The era began with a crisis of Union and ended with the Union in even graver peril. As Abraham Lincoln predicted in 1858, "A house divided against itself cannot stand."

The Bitter Fruits of War

Between 1846 and 1848, the nation grew by 1.2 million square miles, an incredible two-thirds. The gold rush of 1849 transformed the sleepy **frontier** of California into a booming, thriving economy (see chapter 12). The 1850s witnessed new "rushes," for gold in Colorado and silver in Nevada's Comstock Lode. People from around the world flocked to the West, where they produced a vibrant agriculture as well as tons of gold and silver. But it quickly became clear that Northerners and Southerners had very different visions of the West, particularly the place of slavery in its future.

History provided contradictory precedents for handling slavery in the territories. In 1787, the Northwest Ordinance banned slavery north of the Ohio River. In 1803, slavery was allowed to remain in the newly acquired Louisiana Territory. The Missouri Compromise of 1820 prohibited slavery in part of that territory but allowed it in the rest. In 1846, when the war with Mexico suggested new territory for the United States, politicians offered various plans. But when the war ended in 1848, Congress had made no headway in solving the issue of slavery in the land acquired from Mexico, called the Mexican cession. In 1850, Congress patched together a settlement, one that Americans hoped would be permanent.

The Wilmot Proviso and the Expansion of Slavery

In the years leading up to the Civil War, Americans focused not on slavery where it existed, but on the possibility that slavery might expand into areas where it did not exist. Most Americans agreed that the Constitution left the issue of slavery to the individual states to decide. Northern states had done away with slavery, while southern states had retained it. But what about slavery in the nation's territories? The Constitution states that "Congress shall have power to . . . make all needful rules and regulations respecting the territory . . . belonging to the United States." The debate about slavery, then, turned toward Congress.

The spark for the national debate was provided in August 1846 by a young Democratic representative from Pennsylvania, David Wilmot, who proposed that Congress bar slavery from all lands acquired in the war with Mexico. The Mexicans had already abolished slavery in their country, and Wilmot declared, "God forbid that we should be the means of planting this institution upon it."

Regardless of party affiliation, Northerners lined up behind the Wilmot Proviso. Many supported **free soil**, by which they meant territory in which slavery would be prohibited, on the basis of egalitarian principles. They wanted to preserve the West for **free labor**, for hardworking, self-reliant free men, not for slaveholders and slaves. But support also came from those who were simply anti-South. New slave territories would eventually mean new slave states, and they opposed magnifying the political power of Southerners. Wilmot himself said he saw his proposal as a means of blunting "the *power* of slaveholders" in the national government.

Additional support for free soil came from Northerners who were hostile to blacks and wanted to reserve new land for whites. Wilmot understood what one Indiana man put bluntly: "The American people are emphatically a *Negro-hating* people." Wilmot himself blatantly encouraged racist support when he declared, "I would preserve for free white labor a fair country, a rich inheritance, where the sons of toil, of my own race and own color, can live without the disgrace which association with negro slavery brings upon free labor." It is no wonder that some called the Wilmot Proviso the "White Man's Proviso."

The thought that slavery might be excluded outraged almost all white Southerners. They regarded the West as a ladder for economic and social opportunity. They also believed that the exclusion of slavery was a slap in the face to veterans of the Mexican-American War, at least half of whom were Southerners. "When the war-worn soldier returns home," one Alabaman asked, "is he to be told that he cannot carry his property to the country won by his blood?"

In addition, southern leaders understood the need for political parity with the North to protect the South's interests, especially slavery. The need seemed especially urgent in the 1840s, when the North's population and wealth were booming. James Henry Hammond of South Carolina predicted that ten new states would be carved from the acquired Mexican land. If free soil won, the North would "ride over us roughshod" in Congress, he claimed. "Our only safety is in *equality* of POWER."

The two sides squared off in the nation's capital. Because Northerners had a majority in the House, they easily passed the Wilmot Proviso. In the Senate, however, where slave states outnumbered free states fifteen to fourteen,

Southerners defeated it in 1847. Senator John C. Calhoun of South Carolina denied that Congress had the constitutional authority to exclude slavery from the nation's territories. He argued that the territories were the "joint and common property" of all the states and that Congress could not justly deprive any state of equal rights in the territories and therefore could not bar citizens of one state from migrating with their property (including slaves) to the territories. Whereas Wilmot demanded that Congress slam shut the door to slavery, Calhoun called on Congress to hold the door wide open.

In 1847, Senator Lewis Cass of Michigan offered a compromise through the doctrine of **popular sovereignty**, by which the people who settled the territories would decide for themselves slavery's fate. This solution, Cass argued, sat squarely in the American tradition of **democracy** and local self-government. It had the added attraction of removing the incendiary issue of the expansion of slavery from the nation's capital and lodging it in distant, sleepy territorial legislatures, where it would excite fewer passions.

Popular sovereignty's most attractive feature was its ambiguity about the precise moment when settlers could determine slavery's fate. Northern advocates believed that the decision on slavery could be made as soon as the first territorial legislature assembled. With free-soil majorities likely because of the North's greater population, they would shut the door to slavery almost before the first slave arrived. Southern supporters declared that popular sovereignty guaranteed that slavery would be unrestricted throughout the entire territorial period. Only at the very end, when settlers in a territory drew up a constitution and applied for statehood, could they decide the issue of slavery. By then, slavery would have sunk deep roots. As long as the matter of timing remained vague, popular sovereignty gave hope to both sides.

When Congress ended its session in 1848, no plan had won a majority in both houses. Northerners who demanded no new slave territory anywhere, ever, and Southerners who demanded entry for their slave property into all territories, or else, staked out their extreme positions. Unresolved in Congress, the territorial question naturally became an issue in the presidential election of 1848.

The Election of 1848

When President Polk, worn-out and ailing, chose not to seek reelection, the Democratic convention nominated Lewis Cass of Michigan, the man most closely associated with popular sovereignty. But in an effort to keep peace between their proslavery and antislavery factions, the Democrats adopted a platform that avoided a firm position on slavery in the territories. The Whigs followed a different strategy and nominated a Mexican-American War hero, General Zachary Taylor. The Whigs bet that the combination of a military hero and total silence on the slavery issue would unite their divided party, and thus they declined to adopt a party platform. Taylor, who owned more than one hundred slaves on planta-tions in Mississippi and Louisiana, was hailed by Georgia politician Robert Toombs as a "Southern man, a slaveholder, a cotton **planter**."

Antislavery Whigs balked and looked for an alternative. The time seemed ripe for a major political realignment. Senator Charles Sumner called for "one grand Northern party of Freedom," and in the summer of 1848, antislavery Whigs and antislavery Democrats founded the Free-Soil Party. Nearly fifteen thousand noisy Free-Soilers gathered in Buffalo, New York, where they nomi-nated a Democrat, Martin Van Buren, for president and a Whig, Charles Francis Adams, for vice president. The platform boldly proclaimed, "Free soil, free speech, free labor, and free men."

The November election dashed the hopes of the Free-Soilers. Although they succeeded in making slavery the campaign's central issue, they did not carry a single state. The major parties went through contortions to present their candi-dates favorably in both North and South, and their evasions succeeded. Taylor won the all-important electoral vote, 163 to 127, carrying eight of the fifteen slave states and seven of the fifteen free states. (Wisconsin had entered the Union earlier in 1848 as the fifteenth free state.) Northern voters proved that they were not yet ready for Sumner's "one grand Northern party of Freedom," but the struggle over slavery in the territories had shaken the major parties badly.

Debate and Compromise

Southern slaveholder Zachary Taylor entered the White House in March 1849 and almost immediately shocked the nation by championing a free-soil solution to the Mexican cession. Believing that he could avoid further sectional strife if California and New Mexico skipped the territorial stage, he sent agents west to persuade the settlers to apply for admission to the Union as states. Predominantly antislavery, the settlers began writing free-state constitutions. "For the first time," Mississip-pian Jefferson Davis lamented, "we are about permanently to destroy the balance of power between the sections."

Congress convened in December 1849, beginning one of the most contentious and most significant sessions in its history. President Taylor urged Congress to admit California as a free state immediately and to admit New Mexico, which lagged behind a few months, as soon as it applied. Southerners exploded. In their eyes, Taylor had betrayed his region. A North Carolinian declared that Southern-ers who would "consent to be thus degraded and enslaved, ought to be whipped through their fields by their own negroes."

Into this rancorous scene stepped Senator Henry Clay of Kentucky, known as "the Great Pacificator," the architect of Union-saving compromises in the Missouri and **nullification** crises (see chapters 10 and 11). Clay offered a series of resolutions meant to answer and balance "all questions in controversy between the free and slave states, growing out of the subject of slavery." Admit California as a free state, he proposed, but organize the rest of the Southwest without restrictions on slavery. Require Texas to abandon its claim to parts of New Mexico, but compensate it by assuming its preannexation debt. Abolish the domestic slave trade in Washington, D.C., but confirm slavery itself in the nation's capital. Reassert Congress's lack of authority to interfere with the interstate slave trade and enact a more effective fugitive slave law.

Both antislavery advocates and "fire-eaters" (as radical Southerners who urged secession from the Union were called) savaged Clay's plan. Senator Salmon P. Chase of Ohio ridiculed it as "sentiment for the North, substance for the South." Senator Henry S. Foote of Mississippi denounced it as more offensive to the South than the speeches of abolitionists William Lloyd Garrison, Wendell Phillips, and Frederick Douglass combined. The most ominous response came from John C. Calhoun, who charged that unending northern agitation on the slavery question had "snapped" many of the "cords which bind these states together in one common Union." He argued that the fragile political unity of North and South depended on continued equal representation in the Senate, which Clay's plan for a free California destroyed. "As things now stand," he said in February 1850, the South "cannot with safety remain in the Union."

After Clay and Calhoun had spoken, it was time for the third member of the "great triumvirate," Senator Daniel Webster of Massachusetts, to address the Senate. Like Clay, Webster sought to build a constituency for compromise. He told Northerners that the South had legitimate complaints that required attention. But he told Southerners that secession from the Union would mean civil war. He appealed for an end to taunts and reckless proposals and, to the dismay of many Northerners, mentioned by name the Wilmot Proviso. A legal ban on slavery in the territories was unnecessary, he said, because the harsh climate effectively prohibited the expansion of cotton and slaves into the new American Southwest. "I would not take pains uselessly to reaffirm an ordinance of nature, nor to re-enact the will of God," Webster declared.

Free-Soil forces recoiled from what they saw as Webster's desertion. In Boston, clergyman and abolitionist Theodore Parker could only conclude that "the Southern men" must have offered Webster the presidency. In Washington, Senator William H. Seward of New York responded that Webster's and Clay's compromise with slavery was "radically wrong and essentially vicious." He flatly rejected Calhoun's argument that Congress lacked the constitutional authority to exclude slavery from the territories. In any case, Seward said, in the most sensational moment in his address, there was a "higher law than the Constitution"— the law of God—to ensure freedom in all the public domain. Claiming that God was a Free-Soiler did nothing to cool the superheated political atmosphere.

In May, a Senate committee produced a bill that joined Clay's resolutions into a single comprehensive package, known as the Omnibus Bill because it was a vehicle on which "every sort of passenger" could ride. Clay bet that a majority of Congress wanted compromise and that the members would vote for the package, even though it contained provisions they disliked, to gain an overall settlement of sectional issues. But the omnibus strategy backfired. Free-Soilers and proslavery Southerners voted down the comprehensive plan.

Fortunately for those who favored a settlement, Senator Stephen A. Douglas, a rising Democratic star from Illinois, stepped in. He broke the bill into its various parts and skillfully ushered each through Congress. The agreement Douglas won in September 1850 was very much the one Clay had proposed in January. California entered the Union as a free state. New Mexico and Utah became territories where slavery would be decided by popular sovereignty. Texas accepted its boundary with New Mexico and received $10 million from the federal government. Congress ended the slave trade in the District of Columbia but enacted a more stringent fugitive slave law. In September, Millard Fillmore, who had become president when Zachary Taylor died in July, signed into law each bill, collectively known as the Compromise of 1850 (Map 14.1).

Actually, the Compromise of 1850 was not a true compromise at all. Douglas's parliamentary skill, not a spirit of conciliation, was responsible for the legislative success. Still, the nation breathed a sigh of relief, for the Compromise preserved the Union and peace for the moment. Daniel Webster declared, "We have gone through the most important crisis that has occurred since the foundation of the government." But others recognized that the Compromise

---

MAP 14.1 The Compromise of 1850

The patched-together sectional agreement was both clumsy and unstable. Few Americans—in either North or South—supported all five parts of the Compromise.

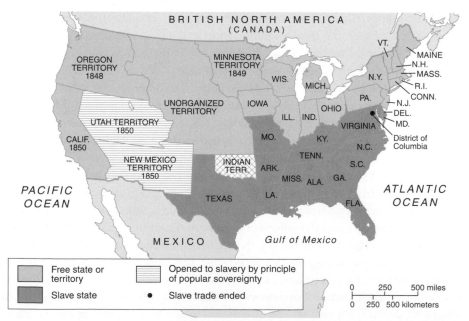

scarcely touched the deeper conflict over slavery. Free-Soiler Salmon Chase observed, "The question of slavery in the territories has been avoided. It has not been settled."

> ▶**REVIEW**   Why did response to the Wilmot Proviso split along sectional rather than party lines?

The Sectional Balance Undone

The Compromise of 1850 began to come apart almost immediately. The thread that unraveled it was not slavery in the Southwest, the crux of the disagreement, but runaway slaves in New England, a part of the settlement that had previously received relatively little attention. Instead of restoring calm, the Compromise brought the horrors of slavery into the North.

Millions of Northerners who had never seen a runaway slave confronted slavery in the early 1850s. Harriet Beecher Stowe's *Uncle Tom's Cabin*, a novel that vividly depicts the brutality and heartlessness of the South's "peculiar institution," aroused passions so deep that many found goodwill toward white Southerners nearly impossible to achieve. But no groundswell of antislavery sentiment compelled Congress to reopen the slavery controversy. Instead, politicians did it themselves. Four years after Congress delicately stitched the sectional compromise together, it ripped the threads out. With the Kansas-Nebraska Act, it again posed the question of slavery in the territories, the deadliest of all sectional issues.

The Fugitive Slave Act

The Fugitive Slave Act proved the most explosive of the Compromise measures. The issue of runaways was as old as the Constitution, which contained a provision for the return of any "person held to service or labor in one state" who escaped to another. In 1793, a federal law gave muscle to the provision by authorizing slave owners to enter other states to recapture their slave property. Proclaiming the 1793 law a license to kidnap free blacks, northern states in the 1830s began passing "personal liberty laws" that provided fugitives with some protection.

Some northern communities also formed vigilance committees to help runaways and to obstruct white Southerners who came north to reclaim them. Each year, a few hundred slaves escaped into free states and found friendly northern "conductors" who put them aboard the "underground railroad," which was not a railroad at all but a series of secret "stations" (hideouts) on the way to Canada. Harriet Tubman, an escaped slave from Maryland, returned to the South more than a dozen times and guided more than three hundred slaves to freedom in this way.

The Modern Medea
In 1855, a slave family—Robert Garner; his twenty-two-year-old wife, Margaret; their four children; and his parents—fled Kentucky. Margaret's owner tracked them to a cabin in Ohio. Thinking that all was lost and that her children would be returned to slavery, Margaret cut the throat of her two-year-old daughter. She was turning on her other children when slave catchers burst in and captured her. Abolitionists claimed that the act revealed the horror of slavery and the tragic heroism of slave mothers. Defenders of slavery argued that the deed proved that slaves were savages. In 1867, Thomas Satterwhite Noble painted a defiant Margaret Garner standing over the bodies of two boys. Noble's departure from history was demanded by his allusion to the Greek myth about Medea killing her two children to spite her husband.
Harper's Weekly, May 18, 1867/Picture Research Consultants & Archives.

Furious about northern interference, Southerners in 1850 insisted on the stricter fugitive slave law that was passed as part of the Compromise. To seize an alleged slave, a slaveholder simply had to appear before a commissioner and swear that the runaway was his. The commissioner earned $10 for every black returned to slavery but only $5 for those set free. Most galling to Northerners, the law stipulated that all citizens were expected to assist officials in apprehending runaways.

Theodore Parker, the clergyman and abolitionist, denounced the law as "a hateful statute of kidnappers." In Boston in February 1851, an angry crowd overpowered federal marshals and snatched a runaway named Shadrach from a courtroom, put him on the underground railroad, and whisked him off to Canada. Three years later, when another Boston crowd rushed the courthouse in a failed attempt to rescue Anthony Burns, who had recently fled slavery in

Richmond, a guard was shot dead. Martha Russell was among the angry crowd that watched Burns being escorted to the ship that would return him to Virginia. "Did you ever feel every drop of blood in you boiling and seething, throbbing and burning, until it seemed you should suffocate?" she asked. "I have felt all this today. I have seen that poor slave, Anthony Burns, carried back to slavery!"

To white Southerners, it seemed that fanatics of the "higher law" creed had whipped Northerners into a frenzy of massive resistance. Actually, the overwhelming majority of fugitives claimed before federal commissioners were reenslaved peacefully. Spectacular rescues such as the one that saved Shadrach were rare. But brutal enforcement of the unpopular law had a radicalizing effect in the North, particularly in New England. And to Southerners it seemed that Northerners had betrayed the Compromise. "The continued existence of the United States as one nation," warned the *Southern Literary Messenger*, "depends upon the full and faithful execution of the Fugitive Slave Bill."

Uncle Tom's Cabin

The spectacle of shackled African Americans being herded south seared the conscience of every Northerner who witnessed such a scene. But even more Northerners were turned against slavery by a fictional account, a novel. Harriet Beecher Stowe, a Northerner who had never stepped foot on a plantation, made the South's slaves into flesh-and-blood human beings almost more real than life.

A member of a famous clan of preachers, teachers, and reformers, Stowe despised the slave catchers and wrote to expose the sin of slavery. Published as a book in 1852, *Uncle Tom's Cabin, or Life among the Lowly* became a blockbuster hit and sold 300,000 copies in its first year and more than 2 million copies within ten years. Stowe's characters leaped from the page. Here was the gentle slave Uncle Tom, a Christian saint who forgave those who beat him to death; the courageous slave Eliza, who fled with her child across the frozen Ohio River; and the fiendish overseer Simon Legree, whose Louisiana plantation was a nightmare of torture and death. Mother of seven children, Stowe aimed her most powerful blows at slavery's destructive impact on the family. Her character Eliza succeeds in keeping her son from being sold away, but other mothers are not so fortunate. When told that her infant has been sold, Lucy drowns herself. Driven half mad by the sale of a son and daughter, Cassy decides "never again [to] let a child live to grow up!" She gives her third child an opiate and watches as "he slept to death."

In the North, common people and literary giants alike shed tears and sang praises to *Uncle Tom's Cabin*. The poet Henry Wadsworth Longfellow judged it "one of the greatest triumphs recorded in literary history." What Northerners accepted as truth, Southerners denounced as slander. Virginian George F. Holmes proclaimed Stowe a member of the "Woman's Rights" and "Higher Law" schools and dismissed the novel as a work of "intense fanaticism." Although it is impossible to measure precisely the impact of a novel on public opinion, *Uncle Tom's Cabin* clearly helped to crystallize northern sentiment against slavery and to confirm white Southerners' suspicion that they no longer had any sympathy in the free states.

Other writers—ex-slaves who knew life in slave cabins firsthand—also produced stinging indictments of slavery. Solomon Northup's compelling *Twelve Years a Slave* (1853) sold 27,000 copies in two years, and the powerful *Narrative of the Life of Frederick Douglass, as Told by Himself* (1845) eventually sold more than 30,000 copies. But no work touched the North's conscience like the novel by a free white woman. A decade after its publication, when Stowe visited Abraham Lincoln at the White House, he reportedly said, "So you are the little woman who wrote the book that made this great war."

The Kansas-Nebraska Act

As the 1852 election approached, the Democrats and Whigs sought to close the sectional rifts that had opened within their parties. For their presidential nominee, the Democrats turned to Franklin Pierce of New Hampshire. Pierce's most valuable asset was his well-known sympathy with southern views on public issues. His leanings caused northern critics to include him among the "doughfaces," northern men malleable enough to champion southern causes. The Whigs were less successful in bridging differences. Adopting the formula that had proved successful in 1848, they chose another Mexican-American War hero, General Winfield Scott of Virginia. But the Whigs' northern and southern factions were hopelessly divided, and the party suffered a humiliating defeat. The Democrat Pierce carried twenty-seven states to Scott's four and won the electoral college vote 254 to 42. In the afterglow of the Compromise of 1850, the Free-Soil Party lost almost half of the voters who had turned to it in the tumultuous political atmosphere of 1848.

Eager to leave the sectional controversy behind, the new president turned swiftly to foreign expansion. **Manifest destiny** remained robust. Pierce's major objective was Cuba, which was owned by Spain and in which slavery flourished, but his clumsy diplomatic efforts galvanized antislavery Northerners, who blocked Cuba's acquisition to keep more slave territory from entering the Union. Pierce's fortunes improved in Mexico. In 1853, he sent diplomat James Gadsden to negotiate a $15 million purchase of some 30,000 square miles of land south of the Gila River in present-day Arizona and New Mexico (see Map 12.3, page 363). The Gadsden Purchase stemmed from the dream of a transcontinental railroad to California and Pierce's desire for a southern route through Mexican territory. The booming population of the Pacific coast made it obvious that the vast, loose-jointed Republic needed a railroad to bind it together. Talk of a railroad ignited rivalries in cities from New Orleans to Chicago as they maneuvered to become the eastern terminus. The desire for a transcontinental railroad evolved into a sectional contest, which by the 1850s inevitably involved slavery.

No one played the railroad game more enthusiastically than Illinois's Democratic senator Stephen A. Douglas. He badly wanted the transcontinental railroad for Chicago and his home state, and his chairmanship of the Senate Committee on Territories provided him with an opportunity. Any railroad that ran west from Chicago would pass through a region that Congress in 1830 had designated a "permanent" Indian reserve. Douglas proposed giving this vast area between the Missouri River and the Rocky Mountains an Indian name, Nebraska, and then throwing the Indians out. Once the region achieved territorial status, whites could survey and sell the land, establish a civil government, and build a railroad.

Nebraska lay within the Louisiana Purchase and, according to the Missouri Compromise of 1820, was closed to slavery (see chapter 10). Since Douglas could not count on New England to back western economic development, he needed southern votes to pass his Nebraska legislation. But Southerners had no incentive to create another free territory or to help a northern city win the transcontinental railroad. Southerners, however, agreed to help organize Nebraska for a price: nothing less than repeal of the Missouri Compromise. Southerners insisted that Congress organize Nebraska according to popular sovereignty. That meant giving slavery a chance in Nebraska Territory and reopening the dangerous issue of slavery expansion, which Douglas himself had so ably helped to resolve only four years earlier.

In January 1854, Douglas introduced his bill to organize Nebraska Territory, leaving to the settlers themselves the decision about slavery. At southern insistence, and even though he knew it would "raise a hell of a storm," Douglas added an explicit repeal of the Missouri Compromise. Indeed, the Nebraska bill did raise a storm of controversy. Free-Soilers branded Douglas's plan "a gross violation of a sacred pledge" and an "atrocious plot" to transform free land into a "dreary region of despotism, inhabited by masters and slaves."

Undaunted, Douglas skillfully shepherded the explosive bill through Congress in May 1854. Nine-tenths of the southern members (Whigs and Democrats) and half of the northern Democrats cast votes in favor of the bill. Like Douglas, most northern supporters believed that popular sovereignty would make Nebraska free territory. Ominously, however, half of the northern Democrats broke with their party and opposed the bill. In its final form, the Kansas-Nebraska Act divided the huge territory in two: Nebraska west of the free state of Iowa and Kansas west of the slave state of Missouri (Map 14.2, page 418). With this act, the government pushed the Plains Indians farther west, making way for farmers and railroads.

▶ **REVIEW**   Why did the Fugitive Slave Act provoke such strong opposition in the North?

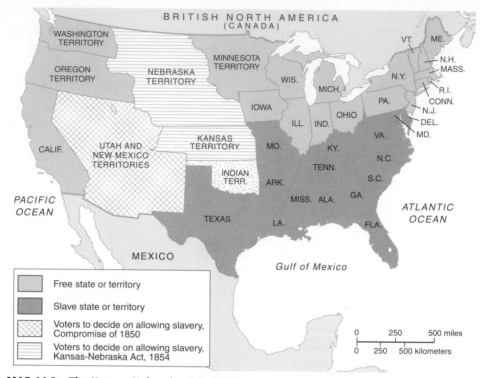

MAP 14.2   The Kansas-Nebraska Act, 1854
Americans hardly thought twice about dispossessing the Indians of land guaranteed them by treaty, but many worried about the outcome of repealing the Missouri Compromise and opening up the region to slavery.

Realignment of the Party System

The Kansas-Nebraska Act marked a fateful escalation of the sectional conflict. Douglas's controversial measure had several consequences, none more crucial than the realignment of the nation's political parties. Since the rise of the Whig Party in the early 1830s, Whigs and Democrats had organized and channeled political conflict in the nation. This party system dampened sectionalism and strengthened the Union. To achieve national political power, the Whigs and Democrats had to retain their strength in both North and South. Strong northern and southern wings required that each party compromise and find positions acceptable to both wings.

The Kansas-Nebraska controversy shattered this stabilizing political system. In place of two national parties with bisectional strength, the mid-1850s witnessed the development of one party heavily dominated by one section and another party entirely limited to the other section. Rather than "national" parties, the country had what one critic disdainfully called "geographic" parties. Parties now sharpened ideological and policy differences between the sections and no longer muffled moral issues such as slavery. The new party system also thwarted political compromise and instead promoted political polarization that further jeopardized the Union.

The Old Parties: Whigs and Democrats

Distress signals could be heard from the Whig camp as early as the Mexican-American War, when members clashed over the future of slavery in annexed Mexican lands. By 1852, the Whig Party could please its proslavery southern wing or its antislavery northern wing but not both. The Whigs' miserable showing in the election of 1852 made clear that they were no longer a strong national party. By 1856, after more than two decades of contesting the Democrats, they were hardly a party at all.

The collapse of the Whig Party left the Democrats as the country's only national party. Although the Democrats were not immune to the disruptive pressures of the territorial question, they discovered in popular sovereignty a doctrine that many Democrats could support. Even so, popular sovereignty very nearly undid the party. When Stephen Douglas applied the doctrine to the part of the Louisiana Purchase where slavery had been barred, he divided northern Democrats and destroyed the dominance of the Democratic Party in the free states. After 1854, the Democrats became a southern-dominated party. Nevertheless, the Democrats, unlike the Whigs, remained a national political organization. Gains in the South more than balanced Democratic losses in the North. During the 1850s, Democrats elected two presidents and won majorities in Congress in almost every election.

The breakup of the Whigs and the disaffection of significant numbers of northern Democrats set many Americans politically adrift. As they searched for new political harbors, Americans found that the death of the old party system created a multitude of fresh political alternatives. The question was which party would attract the drifters.

The New Parties: Know-Nothings and Republicans

Dozens of new political organizations vied for voters' attention. Out of the confusion, two emerged as true contenders. One grew out of the slavery controversy, a spontaneous coalition of indignant antislavery Northerners. The other arose from an entirely different split in American society, between Roman Catholic immigrants and native **Protestants**.

The tidal wave of immigrants that broke over America from 1845 to 1855 produced a nasty backlash among Protestant Americans, who believed that the American Republic was about to drown in a sea of Roman Catholics from Ireland and Germany. Most immigrants became Democrats because they perceived that party as more tolerant of newcomers than were the Whigs. But in the 1850s, they met sharp political opposition when **nativists** (individuals who were anti-immigrant) began to organize, first into secret fraternal societies and then in

1854 into a political party. Recruits swore never to vote for either foreign-born or Roman Catholic candidates and not to reveal any information about the organization. When questioned, they said, "I know nothing." Officially, they were the American Party, but most Americans called them Know-Nothings.

The Know-Nothings exploded onto the political stage in 1854 and 1855 with a series of dazzling successes. They captured state legislatures in the Northeast, West, and South and claimed dozens of seats in Congress. Their greatest triumph came in Massachusetts, a favorite destination for Irish immigrants. Know-Nothings elected the Massachusetts governor, all of the state senators, all but two of the state representatives, and all of the congressmen. Members of the Democratic and Whig parties described the phenomenal success of the Know-Nothings as a "tornado," a "hurricane," and "a freak of political insanity." By 1855, an observer might reasonably have concluded that the Know-Nothings had emerged as the successor to the Whigs.

The Know-Nothings were not the only new party making noise, however. One of the new antislavery organizations provoked by the Kansas-Nebraska Act called itself the Republican Party. The Republicans attempted to unite all the dissidents and political orphans—Whigs, Free-Soilers, anti-Nebraska Democrats, even Know-Nothings—who opposed the extension of slavery into any territory of the United States.

Know-Nothing Banner
Convinced that the incendiary issue of slavery had blinded Americans to the greater dangers of uncontrolled immigration and foreign influence, the Know-Nothing Party nominated Millard Fillmore for president in 1856. This banner's appeal to "Native Americans" refers to native-born Americans, but bona fide Native Americans—American Indians— also faced an invasion, and to them it made little difference whether the aggressors were fresh off the boat or born in the USA.
Milwaukee County Historical Society.

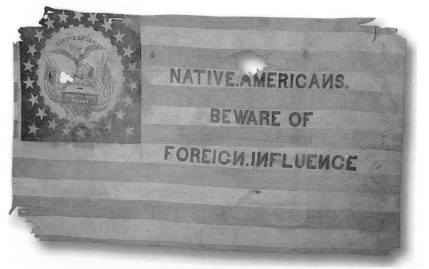

The Republican creed tapped into the basic beliefs and values of the northern public. Slavery, the Republicans argued, degraded the dignity of white labor by associating work with blacks and servility. Three-quarters of the South's white population, claimed one Republican, "retire to the outskirts of civilization, where they live a semi-savage life, sinking deeper and more hopelessly into barbarism with every succeeding generation." They warned that the insatiable slaveholders of the South, whom antislavery Northerners called the "Slave Power," were conspiring through their control of the Democratic Party to expand slavery, subvert **liberty**, and undermine the Constitution. Only if slavery was restricted to the South, Republicans believed, could the system of free labor flourish elsewhere. The ideal of free labor respected the dignity of work and provided anyone willing to toil a chance for a decent living and advancement (see chapter 12). In the North, one Republican declared in 1854, "every man holds his fortune in his own right arm; and his position in society, in life, is to be tested by his own individual character." These powerful images of liberty and opportunity attracted a wide range of Northerners to the Republican cause (Figure 14.1).

FIGURE 14.1   Changing Political Landscape, 1848–1860

The polarization of American politics between free states and slave states occurred in little more than a decade.

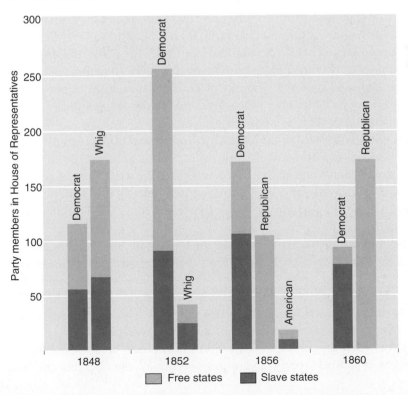

Women as well as men rushed to the new Republican Party. Indeed, three women helped found the party in Ripon, Wisconsin, in 1854. Although women could not vote before the Civil War and suffered from a raft of other legal handicaps, they nevertheless participated in partisan politics by writing campaign literature, marching in parades, giving speeches, and working to influence voters. Women's antislavery fervor attracted them to the Republican Party, and participation in party politics in turn nurtured the woman's rights movement. Susan B. Anthony, who attended Republican meetings throughout the 1850s, found that her political activity made her **disfranchisement** all the more galling. She and other women worked throughout the country to secure both woman suffrage and the right of married women to control their own property.

The Election of 1856

The election of 1856 revealed that the Republicans had become the Democrats' main challenger, and slavery in the territories, not nativism, was the election's principal issue. When the Know-Nothings insisted on a platform that endorsed the Kansas-Nebraska Act, most of the Northerners walked out, and the party came apart. The few Know-Nothings who remained nominated ex-president Millard Fillmore.

The Republicans adopted a platform that focused almost exclusively on "making every territory free." When they labeled slavery a "relic of barbarism," they signaled that they had written off the South. For president, they nominated the dashing soldier and California adventurer John C. Frémont, "Pathfinder of the West." Frémont lacked political credentials, but his wife, Jessie, the daughter of Senator Thomas Hart Benton of Missouri, knew the political map as well as her husband knew the western trails. Though careful to maintain a proper public image, the vivacious young mother and antislavery zealot helped attract voters and draw women into politics.

The Democrats, successful in 1852 in bridging sectional differences by nominating a northern man with southern principles, chose another "doughface," James Buchanan of Pennsylvania. They took refuge in the ambiguity of popular sovereignty and portrayed the Republicans as extremists ("Black Republican Abolitionists") whose support for the Wilmot Proviso risked pushing the South out of the Union.

The Democratic strategy carried the day for Buchanan, but Frémont did astonishingly well. Buchanan won 174 electoral votes against Frémont's 114 and Fillmore's 8. Campaigning under the banner "Free soil, Free men, Frémont," the Republican carried all but five of the states north of the Mason-Dixon line. The election made clear that the Whigs had disintegrated, the Know-Nothings would not ride nativism to national power, and the Democrats were badly strained. But the big news was what the press called the "glorious defeat" of the Republicans. Despite being a brand-new party and purely sectional, the Republicans had seriously challenged for national power. Sectionalism had fashioned a new party system, one that spelled danger for the Republic. Indeed, war had already broken out between proslavery and antislavery forces in distant Kansas Territory.

▶REVIEW   Why did the Whig Party disintegrate in the 1850s?

Freedom under Siege

Events in Kansas Territory in the mid-1850s provided the young Republican organization with an enormous boost and help explain its strong showing in the election of 1856. Republicans organized around the premise that the slaveholding South provided a profound threat to "free soil, free labor, and free men," and now Kansas reeled with violence that Republicans argued was southern in origin. Kansas, Republicans claimed, opened a window to southern values and intentions. Republicans also pointed to the brutal beating by a Southerner of a respected northern senator on the floor of Congress. Even the Supreme Court, in the Republicans' view, reflected the South's drive toward tyranny and minority rule in its decision in the *Dred Scott* case. Then, in 1858, the issues dividing North and South received an extraordinary airing in a senatorial contest in Illinois, when the nation's foremost Democrat debated a resourceful Republican.

"Bleeding Kansas"

Three days after the House of Representatives approved the Kansas-Nebraska Act in 1854, Senator William H. Seward of New York boldly challenged the South. "Come on then, Gentlemen of the Slave States," he cried, "since there is no escaping your challenge, I accept it in behalf of the cause of freedom. We will engage in competition for the virgin soil of Kansas, and God give the victory to the side which is stronger in numbers as it is in right." Because of Stephen Douglas, popular sovereignty would determine whether Kansas became slave or free. Free-state and slave-state settlers both sought a majority at the ballot box, claimed God's blessing, and kept their rifles ready.

In both North and South, emigrant aid societies sprang up to promote settlement from free states or slave states. The most famous, the New England Emigrant Aid Company, sponsored some 1,240 settlers in 1854 and 1855. In the South, tiny rural communities from Virginia to Texas raised money to support proslavery settlers. Missourians, already bordered on the east by the free state of Illinois and on the north by the free state of Iowa, especially thought it important to secure Kansas for slavery. Thousands of rough frontiersmen, egged on by Missouri senator David Rice Atchison, invaded Kansas. "There are eleven hundred coming over from

Platte County to vote," Atchison reported, "and if that ain't enough we can send five thousand—enough to kill every God-damned abolitionist in the Territory." Not surprisingly, proslavery candidates swept the territorial elections in November 1854. When Kansas's first territorial legislature met, it enacted a raft of proslavery laws. Antislavery men, for example, were barred from holding office or serving on juries. Ever-pliant President Pierce endorsed the work of the fraudulently elected legislature. Free-soil Kansans did not. They elected their own legislature, which promptly banned both slaves and free blacks from the territory. Organized into two rival governments and armed to the teeth, Kansans verged on civil war.

Fighting broke out on the morning of May 21, 1856, when several hundred proslavery men raided the town of Lawrence, the center of free-state settlement. Only one man died, but the "Sack of Lawrence," as free-soil forces called it, inflamed northern opinion. Elsewhere in Kansas, news of events in Lawrence provoked John Brown, a free-soil settler, to "fight fire with fire." Announcing that "it was better that a score of bad men should die than that one man who came here to make Kansas a Free State should be driven out," he led the posse that massacred five allegedly proslavery settlers along Pottawatomie Creek. After that, **guerrilla war** engulfed the territory.

Armed Settlers Near Lawrence, Kansas
Armed with rifles, knives, swords, and pistols, these tough antislavery men gathered for a photograph near Lawrence in 1856.
Kansas State Historical Society.

Just as "Bleeding Kansas" gave the fledgling Republican Party fresh ammunition for its battle against the "Slave Power," so too did an event that occurred in the national capital. In May 1856, Senator Charles Sumner of Massachusetts delivered a speech titled "The Crime against Kansas," which included a scalding personal attack on South Carolina senator Andrew P. Butler. Sumner described Butler as a "Don Quixote" who had taken as his mistress "the harlot, slavery." Preston Brooks, a young South Carolina member of the House and a kinsman of Butler's, felt compelled to defend the honor of both his aged relative and his state. On May 22, Brooks entered the Senate, where he found Sumner working at his desk. He beat Sumner over the head with his cane until Sumner lay bleeding and unconscious on the floor. Brooks resigned his seat in the House, only to be promptly reelected. In the North, the southern hero became an archvillain. Like "Bleeding Kansas," "Bleeding Sumner" provided the Republican Party with a potent symbol of the South's "twisted and violent civilization."

The *Dred Scott* Decision

Political debate over slavery in the territories became so heated in part because the Constitution lacked precision on the issue. Only the Supreme Court speaks definitively about the meaning of the Constitution, and in 1857, in the case of *Dred Scott v. Sandford*, the Court announced its judgment of the issue of slavery in the territories. The Court's decision demonstrated that it enjoyed no special immunity from the sectional and partisan passions that convulsed the land.

In 1833, John Emerson, an army doctor, bought the slave Dred Scott in St. Louis, Missouri, and took him as his personal servant to Fort Armstrong, Illinois. Two years later, Scott accompanied Emerson when he transferred to Fort Snelling in Wisconsin Territory. Emerson eventually returned Scott to St. Louis, where in 1846, Scott, with the help of white friends, sued to prove that he and his family were legally entitled to their freedom. Scott based his claim on his travels and residences. He argued that living in Illinois, a free state, and Wisconsin, a free territory, had made his family free, and that they remained free even after returning to Missouri, a slave state.

In 1857, the U.S. Supreme Court ruled in the case. Chief Justice Roger B. Taney hated Republicans and detested racial equality, and the Court's majority decision, which he wrote, reflected those prejudices. First, the Court ruled that Dred Scott could not legally claim violation of his constitutional rights because he was not a citizen of the United States. In 1787, when the Constitution was written, Taney said, blacks "were regarded as beings of an inferior order . . . so far inferior, that they had no rights which the white man was bound to respect." Second, the laws of Dred Scott's home state, Missouri, determined his status, and thus his travels in free areas did not make him free. Third, Congress's power to make "all needful rules and regulations" for the territories did not include the right to prohibit slavery. The Court explicitly declared the Missouri Compromise unconstitutional, even though it had already been voided by the Kansas-Nebraska Act.

The Taney Court's extreme proslavery decision outraged Republicans. By denying the federal government the right to exclude slavery in the territories, it cut the legs out from under the Republican Party. Moreover, as the *New York Tribune* lamented, the decision cleared the way for "all our Territories . . . to be ripened into Slave States." Particularly frightening to African Americans in the North was the Court's declaration that free blacks were not citizens and had no rights.

The Republican rebuttal to the *Dred Scott* ruling relied heavily on the dissenting opinion of Justice Benjamin R. Curtis. Scott *was* a citizen of the United States, Curtis argued. At the time of the writing of the Constitution, free black men could vote in five states and participated in the ratification process. Scott *was* free. Because slavery was prohibited in Wisconsin, the "involuntary servitude of a slave, coming into the Territory with his master, should cease to exist." The Missouri Compromise *was* constitutional. The Founders had meant exactly what they said: Congress had the power to make "*all* needful rules and regulations" for the territories, including barring slavery.

In a seven-to-two decision, the Court rejected Curtis's arguments, thereby validating an extreme statement of the South's territorial rights. John C. Calhoun's claim that Congress had no authority to exclude slavery became the law of the land. White Southerners cheered, but the *Dred Scott* decision actually strengthened the young Republican Party. Indeed, that "outrageous" decision, one Republican argued, was "the best thing that could have happened." It provided dramatic evidence of the Republicans' claim that a hostile "Slave Power" conspired against northern liberties. Only the capture of the Supreme Court by the "slavocracy," Republicans argued, could explain the tortured and historically inaccurate decision.

As for Dred Scott, although the Court rejected his suit, he did in the end gain his freedom. In May 1857, a white man purchased and freed Scott and his family. On September 17, 1858, Dred Scott died in obscurity. Nevertheless, his case changed the political landscape and brought new Republican politicians to the fore.

Prairie Republican: Abraham Lincoln

By reigniting the sectional flames, the *Dred Scott* case provided Republican politicians with fresh challenges and fresh opportunities. Abraham Lincoln had long since put behind him his hardscrabble log-cabin beginnings in Kentucky and Indiana. He lived in a fine two-story house in Springfield, Illinois, and earned good money as a lawyer. The law provided Lincoln's living, but politics was his life. "His ambition was a little engine that knew no rest," observed his law partner William Herndon. Lincoln had served as a Whig in the Illinois state legislature and in the House of Representatives, but he had not held public office since 1849.

The disintegration of the Whig Party meant that Lincoln had no political home. His credo—opposition to "the *extension* of slavery"—made the Republicans his only choice, and in 1856 Lincoln joined the party. Convinced that slavery was a "monstrous injustice," a "great moral wrong," and an "unqualified evil to the negro, the white man, and the State," Lincoln condemned Douglas's Kansas-Nebraska Act of 1854 for giving slavery a new life. He accepted that the Constitution permitted slavery in those states where it existed, but he believed that Congress could contain its spread. Penned in, Lincoln believed, plantation slavery would wither, and in time Southerners would end slavery themselves. By providing fresh land for slavery in the territories, Douglas had put it "on the high road to extension and perpetuity."

Lincoln held what were, for his times, moderate racial views. Like a majority of Republicans, Lincoln defended black humanity without challenging white supremacy. Although he denounced slavery as immoral, he also viewed black equality as impractical and unachievable. "Negroes have natural rights . . . as other men have," he said, "although they cannot enjoy them here." Insurmountable white prejudice made it impossible to extend full citizenship and equality to blacks in America, he believed. Freeing blacks and allowing them to remain in this country would lead to a race war. In Lincoln's mind, social stability and black progress required that slavery end and that blacks leave the country.

Lincoln envisioned the western territories as "places for poor people to go to, and better their conditions." The "*free* labor system," he said, "opens the way for all—gives hope to all, and energy, and progress, and improvement of condition to all." But slavery's expansion threatened free men's basic right to succeed. The Kansas-Nebraska Act and the *Dred Scott* decision persuaded him that slaveholders were engaged in a dangerous conspiracy to nationalize slavery. The next step, Lincoln warned, would be "another Supreme Court decision, declaring that the Constitution of the United States does not permit a State to exclude slavery from its limits." Unless the citizens of Illinois woke up, he warned, the Supreme Court would make "Illinois a slave State."

In Lincoln's view, the nation could not "endure, permanently half slave and half free." Either opponents of slavery would arrest its spread and place it on the "course of ultimate extinction," or its advocates would see that it became legal in "*all* the States, *old* as well as *new*—*North* as well as *South*." Lincoln's convictions that slavery was wrong, that Congress must stop its spread, and that it must be put on the road to extinction formed the core of the Republican ideology. Lincoln so impressed his fellow Republicans in Illinois that in 1858, they chose him to challenge the nation's premier Democrat, who was seeking reelection to the U.S. Senate.

The Lincoln-Douglas Debates

When Stephen Douglas learned that the Republican Abraham Lincoln would be his opponent for the Senate, he confided in a fellow Democrat: "He is the strong man of the party—full of wit, facts, dates—and the best stump speaker, with his droll ways and dry jokes, in the West. He is as honest as he is shrewd, and if I beat him my victory will be hardly won."

Not only did Douglas have to contend with a formidable foe, but he also carried the weight of a burden not of his own making. The previous year, the nation's economy had experienced a sharp downturn. Prices had plummeted, thousands of businesses had failed, and unemployment had risen. As a Democrat, Douglas had to go before the voters as a member of the party whose policies stood accused of causing the panic of 1857.

Douglas's response to another crisis in 1857, however, helped shore up his standing in Illinois. Proslavery forces in Kansas met in the town of Lecompton, drafted a proslavery constitution, and applied for statehood. Everyone knew that free-soilers outnumbered proslavery settlers, but President Buchanan instructed Congress to admit Kansas as the sixteenth slave state. Republicans denounced the "Lecompton swindle." Senator Douglas broke with the Democratic administration and came out against the Lecompton constitution; Congress killed the Lecompton bill. (When Kansans reconsidered the Lecompton constitution in an honest election, they rejected it six to one. Kansas entered the Union in 1861 as a free state.) By denouncing the fraudulent proslavery constitution, Douglas declared his independence from the South and, he hoped, made himself acceptable at home.

A relative unknown and a decided underdog in the Illinois election, Lincoln challenged Douglas to debate him face-to-face. The two met in seven communities for what would become a legendary series of debates. To the thousands who stood straining to see and hear, they must have seemed an odd pair. Douglas was five feet four inches tall, broad, and stocky; Lincoln was six feet four inches tall, angular, and lean. Douglas was in perpetual motion, darting across the platform, shouting, and jabbing the air; Lincoln stood still and spoke deliberately. Douglas wore the latest fashions and dazzled audiences with his flashy vests; Lincoln wore good suits but managed to look rumpled anyway. The differences in physical appearance and style, however, were of little importance. The men debated the central issues of the age—slavery and freedom—and showed the citizens of Illinois (and much of the nation because of widespread press coverage) the difference between an anti-Lecompton Democrat and a true Republican.

Lincoln badgered Douglas with the question of whether he favored the spread of slavery. He tried to force Douglas into the damaging admission that the Supreme Court had repudiated Douglas's own territorial solution, popular sovereignty. In the debate at Freeport, Illinois, Douglas admitted that settlers could not now pass legislation barring slavery, but he argued that they could ban slavery just as effectively by not passing protective laws, such as those found in slave states. Southerners condemned Douglas's "Freeport Doctrine" and charged him with trying to steal the victory they had gained with the *Dred Scott* decision. Lincoln chastised his opponent for his "don't care" attitude about slavery, for "blowing out the moral lights around us."

Douglas worked the racial issue. He called Lincoln an abolitionist and an egalitarian enamored of "our colored brethren." Put on the defensive, Lincoln came close to staking out positions on race that were as **conservative** as Douglas's. Lincoln reaffirmed his faith in white rule: "I will say, then, that I am not, nor ever have been, in favor of bringing about in any way the social and political equality of the white and black race." But unlike Douglas, who told racist jokes, Lincoln was no negrophobe. He tried to steer the debate back to what he considered the true issue: the morality and future of slavery. "Slavery is wrong," Lincoln repeated, because "a man has the right to the fruits of his own labor."

As Douglas predicted, the election was hard-fought and closely contested. Until the adoption of the Seventeenth Amendment in 1911, citizens voted for state legislators, who in turn selected U.S. senators. Since Democrats won a slight majority in the Illinois legislature, the members returned Douglas to the Senate. But the debates thrust Lincoln, the prairie Republican, into the national spotlight.

▶ **REVIEW**   Why did the *Dred Scott* decision strengthen northern suspicions of a "Slave Power" conspiracy?

The Union Collapses

Lincoln's thesis that the "slavocracy" conspired to make slavery a national institution now seems exaggerated. But from the northern perspective, the Kansas-Nebraska Act, the Brooks-Sumner affair, the *Dred Scott* decision, and the Lecompton constitution amounted to irrefutable evidence of the South's aggressiveness. White Southerners, of course, saw things differently. They were the ones who were under siege, they declared. Signs were everywhere that the North planned to use its numerical advantage to attack slavery, and not just in the territories. Republicans had made it clear that they were unwilling to accept the *Dred Scott* ruling as the last word on the issue of slavery expansion. And John Brown's attempt to incite a slave insurrection in Virginia in 1859 proved that Northerners were unwilling to be bound by Christian decency and reverence for life.

Threats of secession increasingly laced the sectional debate. Talk of leaving the Union had been heard for years, but until the final crisis, Southerners had used secession as a ploy to gain concessions within the Union, not to destroy it. Then the 1850s delivered powerful blows to Southerners' confidence that they could remain Americans and protect slavery. When the Republican Party won the White House in 1860, many Southerners concluded that they would have to leave.

The Aftermath of John Brown's Raid

For his attack on Harpers Ferry, John Brown stood trial for treason, murder, and incitement of slave insurrection. "To hang a fanatic is to make a martyr of him and fledge another brood of the same sort," cautioned one southern newspaper.

But on December 2, 1859, Virginia executed Brown. In life, Brown was a ne'er-do-well, but he died with courage and dignity. He told his wife that he was "determined to make the utmost possible out of a defeat." He told the court: "If it is deemed necessary that I should forfeit my life for the furtherance of the ends of justice, and mingle my blood further with the blood of . . . millions in this slave country whose rights are disregarded by wicked, cruel, and unjust enactments, I say, let it be done."

After Brown's heroic death, northern denunciation of Brown as a dangerous fanatic gave way to grudging respect. Some even celebrated his "splendid martyrdom." Abolitionist Lydia Maria Child likened Brown to Christ and declared that he made "the scaffold . . . as glorious as the Cross of Calvary." Some abolitionists explicitly endorsed Brown's resort to violence. Abolitionist William Lloyd Garrison, who usually professed pacifism, announced, "I am prepared to say 'success to every slave insurrection at the South and in every country.'"

Most Northerners did not advocate bloody rebellion, however. Like Lincoln, they concluded that Brown's noble antislavery ideals could not "excuse violence, bloodshed, and treason." Still, when many in the North marked John Brown's execution with tolling bells, hymns, and prayer vigils, white Southerners contemplated what they had in common with people who "regard John Brown as a martyr and a Christian hero, rather than a murderer and robber." Georgia senator Robert Toombs announced solemnly that Southerners must "never permit this Federal government to pass into the traitorous hands of the black Republican party." At that moment, the presidential election was only months away.

Republican Victory in 1860

Events between Brown's hanging and the presidential election only heightened sectional hostility and estrangement. A southern business convention meeting in Nashville shocked the nation (including many Southerners) by calling for the reopening of the African slave trade, closed since 1808 and considered an abomination everywhere in the Western world. Chief Justice Taney provoked new indignation when the Supreme Court ruled northern personal liberty laws unconstitutional and reaffirmed the Fugitive Slave Act. Then, the normally routine business of electing a Speaker of the House threatened to turn bloody as Democrats and Republicans battled over control of the office. After two months of acrimonious debate left the House deadlocked, one congressman observed that the "only persons who do not have a revolver and a knife are those who have two revolvers." A last-minute compromise may have averted a shootout. Finally, Mississippian Jefferson Davis demanded that the Senate adopt a federal slave code for the territories, a goal of extreme proslavery Southerners for several years. Not only was Congress powerless to block slavery's spread, he argued, but it was obligated to offer slavery all "needful protection."

When the Democrats converged on Charleston for their convention in April 1860, fire-eating Southerners denounced Stephen Douglas and demanded a platform that included federal protection of slavery in the territories. But northern Democrats knew that northern voters would not stomach a federal slave code. When the delegates approved a platform with popular sovereignty, representatives from the entire Lower South and Arkansas stomped out of the convention. The remaining Democrats adjourned to meet a few weeks later in Baltimore, where they nominated Douglas for president.

When southern Democrats met, they nominated Vice President John C. Breckinridge of Kentucky and approved a platform with a federal slave code. Southern moderates, however, refused to support Breckinridge. They formed the Constitutional Union Party to provide voters with a Unionist choice. Instead of adopting a platform and confronting the slavery question, the Constitutional Union Party merely approved a vague resolution pledging "to recognize no political principle other than *the Constitution . . . the Union . . . and the Enforcement of the Laws.*" For president, they picked former senator John Bell of Tennessee.

The Republicans smelled victory, but they estimated that they needed to carry nearly all the free states to win. To make their party more appealing, they expanded their platform beyond antislavery. They hoped that free homesteads, a protective tariff, a transcontinental railroad, and a guarantee of immigrant political rights would provide an economic and social agenda broad enough to unify the North. While reasserting their commitment to stop the spread of slavery, they also denounced John Brown's raid as "among the gravest of crimes" and confirmed the security of slavery in the South.

Republicans cast about for a moderate candidate to go with their even-handed platform. The foremost Republican, William H. Seward, had made enemies with his radical "higher law" doctrine and "irrepressible conflict" speech. Lincoln, however, since bursting onto the national scene in 1858, had demonstrated his clear purpose, good judgment, and solid Republican credentials. That, and his residence in Illinois, a crucial state, made him attractive to the party. On the third ballot, the delegates chose Lincoln. Defeated by Douglas in a state contest less than two years earlier, Lincoln now stood ready to take him on for the presidency.

The election of 1860 was like none other in American politics. It took place in the midst of the nation's severest crisis. Four major candidates crowded the presidential field. Rather than a four-cornered contest, however, the election broke into two contests, each with two candidates. In the North, Lincoln faced Douglas; in the South, Breckinridge confronted Bell. So outrageous did Southerners consider the Republican Party that they did not even permit Lincoln's name to appear on the ballot in ten of the fifteen slave states.

An unprecedented number of voters cast their ballots on November 6, 1860. Approximately 82 percent of eligible northern men and nearly 70 percent of eligible southern men went to the polls. Lincoln swept all of the eighteen free states except New Jersey, which split its electoral votes between him and Douglas. Although Lincoln received only 39 percent of the popular vote, he won easily in the electoral college with 180 votes, 28 more than he needed for victory. Lincoln did not win because his opposition was splintered. Even if the votes of his three opponents had been combined, Lincoln would still have won. He won because his votes were concentrated in the free states, which contained a majority of electoral votes. Ominously, however, Breckinridge, running on a southern-rights platform, won the entire Lower South, plus Delaware, Maryland, and North Carolina.

Secession Winter

The telegraphs had barely stopped tapping out the news of Lincoln's victory when anxious Southerners began debating what to do. Although Breckinridge had carried the South, a vote for "southern rights" was not necessarily a vote for secession. Besides, slightly more than half of the Southerners who had voted had cast ballots for Douglas and Bell, two stout defenders of the Union.

Southern Unionists tried to calm the fears that Lincoln's election triggered. Let the dust settle, they pleaded. Former congressman Alexander Stephens of Georgia asked what Lincoln had done to justify something as extreme as secession. Had he not promised to respect slavery where it existed? In Stephens's judgment, the fire-eater cure would be worse than the Republican disease. Secession might lead to war, which would loosen the hinges of southern society, possibly even open the door to slave insurrection. "Revolutions are much easier started than controlled," he warned. "I consider slavery much more secure in the Union than out of it."

Secessionists emphasized the dangers of delay. "Mr. Lincoln and his party assert that this doctrine of equality applies to the negro," former Georgia governor Howell Cobb declared, "and necessarily there can exist no such thing as property in our equals." Lincoln's election without a single electoral vote from the South meant that Southerners were no longer able to defend themselves within the Union, Cobb argued. Why wait, he said, for Lincoln to appoint abolitionist judges, marshals, customs collectors, and postmasters to federal posts throughout the South? As for war, there would be none. The Union was a voluntary compact, and Lincoln would not coerce patriotism. If Northerners did resist with force, secessionists argued, one southern woodsman could whip five of Lincoln's greasy mechanics.

For all their differences, southern whites agreed that they had to defend slavery. John Smith Preston of South Carolina spoke for the overwhelming majority when he declared, "The South cannot exist without slavery." They disagreed about whether the mere presence of a Republican in the White House made it necessary to exercise what they considered a legitimate right to secede.

"The Union Is Dissolved!"
On December 20, 1860, the *Charleston Mercury* put out this special edition of the paper to celebrate South Carolina's secession from the Union. Six weeks earlier, upon hearing the news that Lincoln had won the presidency, it had predicted as much. "The tea has been thrown overboard," the *Mercury* announced. "The revolution of 1860 has been initiated."
Chicago Historical Society.

The debate about what to do was briefest in South Carolina; it seceded from the Union on December 20, 1860. By February 1861, the six other Lower South states marched in South Carolina's footsteps. In some states, the vote was close. In general, slaveholders spearheaded secession, while nonslaveholders in the Piedmont and mountain counties, where slaves were relatively few, displayed the greatest attachment to the Union. On February 4, 1861, representatives from South Carolina, Georgia, Florida, Alabama, Mississippi, Louisiana, and Texas met in Montgomery, Alabama, where three days later they celebrated the birth of the Confederate States of America. Jefferson Davis became president, and Alexander Stephens, who had spoken so eloquently about the dangers of revolution, became vice president. In March 1861, Stephens declared that the Confederacy's "cornerstone" was "the great truth that the negro is not equal to the white man; that slavery, subordination to the superior race, is his natural and moral condition."

Lincoln's election had split the Union. Now secession split the South. Seven slave states seceded during the winter, but the eight slave states of the Upper

South rejected secession, at least for the moment. The Upper South had a smaller stake in slavery. Barely half as many white families in the Upper South held slaves (21 percent) as in the Lower South (37 percent). Slaves represented twice as large a percentage of the population in the Lower South (48 percent) as in the Upper South (23 percent). Consequently, whites in the Upper South had fewer fears that Republican ascendancy meant economic catastrophe, social chaos, and racial war. Lincoln would need to do more than just be elected to provoke them into secession.

The nation had to wait until March 4, 1861, when Lincoln took office, to see what he would do. (Presidents-elect waited four months to take office until 1933, when the Twentieth Amendment to the Constitution shifted the inauguration to January 20.) After his election, Lincoln chose to stay in Springfield and to say nothing. "Lame-duck" president James Buchanan sat in Washington and did nothing. Buchanan demonstrated, William H. Seward said mockingly, that "it is the President's duty to enforce the laws, unless somebody opposes him." I Congress, efforts at cobbling together a peace-saving compromise came to nothing.

Lincoln began his inaugural address with reassurances to the South. He had "no lawful right" to interfere with slavery where it existed, he declared again, adding for emphasis that he had "no inclination to do so." In filling federal posts, he would not "force obnoxious strangers" on the South. Conciliatory about slavery, Lincoln proved inflexible about the Union. The Union, he declared, was "perpetual." Secession was "anarchy" and "legally void." The Constitution required him to execute the law "in all the States." He would hold federal property, collect federal duties, and deliver the mail.

The decision for civil war or peace rested in the South's hands, Lincoln said. "You can have no conflict, without being yourselves the aggressors. *You* have no oath registered in Heaven to destroy the government, while *I* shall have the most solemn one to 'preserve, protect, and defend' it." What Confederates in Charleston held in their hands at that very moment were the cords for firing the cannons aimed at the federal garrison at Fort Sumter.

▶**REVIEW**   Why did some southern states secede immediately after Lincoln's election?

Conclusion: Slavery, Free Labor, and the Failure of Political Compromise

As their economies, societies, and **cultures** diverged in the nineteenth century, Northerners and Southerners expressed different concepts of the American promise and the place of slavery within it. Their differences crystallized into political form in 1846 when David Wilmot proposed banning slavery in any territory won in the Mexican-American War. "As if by magic," a Boston news-paper observed, "it brought to a head the great question that is about to divide the American people." Discovery of gold and other precious metals in the West added urgency to the controversy over slavery in the territories. Although Congress addressed the issue with the Compromise of 1850, the Fugitive Slave Act quickly brought conflict between free and slave states. Matters worsened with the 1852 publication of *Uncle Tom's Cabin*, which further hardened northern sentiments against slavery and confirmed southern suspicions of northern ill will. The bloody violence that erupted in Kansas in 1856 and the incendiary *Dred Scott* decision in 1857 further eroded hope for a solution to this momentous question.

During the extended crisis of the Union that stretched from 1846 to 1861, the slavery question braided with national politics. The traditional Whig and Demo-cratic parties struggled to hold together, as new parties, most notably the Repub-lican Party, emerged. Politicians fixed their attention on the expansion of slavery, but from the beginning, the nation recognized that the controversy had less to do with slavery in the territories than with the future of slavery in America.

For more than seventy years, statesmen had found compromises that accepted slavery and preserved the Union. But as each section grew increasingly committed to its labor system and the promise it provided, Americans discovered that accom-modation had limits. In 1859, John Brown's militant antislavery pushed white Southerners to the edge. In 1860, Lincoln's election convinced whites in the Lower South that slavery and the society they had built on it were at risk in the Union, and they seceded. In his inaugural address, Lincoln pleaded, "We are not enemies but friends. We must not be enemies." By then, however, seven southern states had ceased to sing what he called "the chorus of the Union." It remained to be seen whether disunion would mean war.

REVIEWING THE CHAPTER

Use the questions and timeline to review and strengthen your understanding of the chapter.

REVIEW QUESTIONS

1. Why did response to the Wilmot Proviso split along sectional rather than party lines? (pp. 407–13)

2. Why did the Fugitive Slave Act pro-voke such strong opposition in the North? (pp. 413–17)

3. Why did the Whig Party disintegrate in the 1850s? (pp. 418–23)

4. Why did the *Dred Scott* decision strengthen northern suspicions of a "Slave Power" conspiracy? (pp. 423–29)

5. Why did some southern states secede immediately after Lincoln's election? (pp. 429–34)

MAKING CONNECTIONS

1. The process of compromise that had successfully contained tensions between slave and free states since the nation's founding collapsed with secession. Why did compromise fail at this moment? In your answer, address specific political conflicts and attempts to solve them between 1846 and 1861.

2. In the 1850s, many Americans supported popular sovereignty as the best solution to the explosive question of slavery in the western territories. Why was this solution so popular, and why did it ultimately prove inadequate? In your answer, be sure to address popular sovereignty's varied critics as well as its champions.

3. In the 1840s and 1850s, the United States witnessed the realignment of its long-standing two-party system. Why did the old system fall apart, what emerged to take its place, and how did this process contribute to the coming of the Civil War?

4. Abraham Lincoln believed that he had staked out a moderate position on the question of slavery, avoiding the extremes of immediate abolitionism and calls for unlimited protection of slavery. Why, then, did some southern states determine that his election necessitated the radical act of secession?

TIMELINE

1820	• Missouri Compromise.	1856	• "Bleeding Kansas." • Preston Brooks canes Charles Sumner. • Pottawatomie massacre. • Democrat James Buchanan elected president.
1846	• Wilmot Proviso introduced in Congress.		
1847	• Wilmot Proviso defeated in Senate. • Compromise of "popular sovereignty" offered.		
		1857	• *Dred Scott* decision. • Congress rejects Lecompton constitution. • Panic of 1857.
1848	• Free-Soil Party founded. • Whig Zachary Taylor elected president.		
1849	• California gold rush.	1858	• Abraham Lincoln and Stephen A. Douglas debate slavery; Douglas wins Senate seat.
1850	• Taylor dies; Vice President Millard Fillmore becomes president. • Compromise of 1850 becomes law.	1859	• John Brown raids Harpers Ferry, Virginia.
1852	• *Uncle Tom's Cabin* published. • Democrat Franklin Pierce elected president.	1860	• Republican Abraham Lincoln elected president. • South Carolina secedes from Union.
1853	• Gadsden Purchase.		
1854	• American (Know-Nothing) Party emerges. • Kansas-Nebraska Act. • Republican Party founded.	1861	• Six other deep South states secede. • Confederate States of America formed. • Lincoln takes office.

▶ **For an online bibliography, practice quizzes, Web sites, images, and documents related to this chapter,** see the Book Companion Site at **bedfordstmartins.com/roark.**

▶ **For firsthand accounts of this period,** see Chapter 14 in Michael Johnson, ed., *Reading the American Past,* Fourth Edition.

15

CHAPTER

The Crucible of War

1861–1865

O N THE RAINY NIGHT OF SEPTEMBER 21, 1862, in Wilmington, North Carolina, twenty-four-year-old William Gould and seven other black men crowded into a small boat on the Cape Fear River and quietly pushed away from the dock. Knowing that the authorities would sound the alarm for eight runaway slaves at daybreak, they rowed hard throughout the night. By dawn, the runaways had traveled twenty-eight miles to where the river flowed into the Atlantic Ocean. They plunged into the swells and made for the Union navy patrolling offshore to disrupt the flow of goods in and out of Wilmington, a major Confederate port. At 10:30 that morning, the USS *Cambridge* took the men aboard.

Astonishingly, on the same day that Gould reached the federal ship, President Abraham Lincoln announced to his cabinet in Washington, D.C., that he intended to issue a proclamation of **emancipation** freeing the slaves in the Confederate states. Because the proclamation would not take effect until January 1863, Gould was not legally free in the eyes of the U.S. government. But the U.S. navy, suffering from a shortage of sailors, cared little about the formal status of runaway slaves. Within days, all eight runaways became sailors "for three years," Gould said, "first taking the Oath of Allegiance to the Government of Uncle Samuel."

Unlike most slaves, William Gould could read and write, and he began making almost daily entries in a remarkable diary, apparently the only diary kept during the war by a sailor who had been a slave. In some ways, Gould's naval experience looked like that of a white sailor. He found duty on a ship in the blockading squadron both boring and exhilarating. He often recorded comments such as "All hands painting, cleaning" and "Cruised as usual." But long days of tedious work were sometimes interrupted by a "period of daring exploit" as enemy ships

The Crew of the USS *Hunchback*
African Americans served as sailors in the federal military long before they were permitted to become soldiers. Blacks initially served only as coal heavers, cooks, and stewards, but within a year, some black sailors joined their ships' gun crews. The *Hunchback* was one of the Union's innovative ironclad ships.
National Archives.

engaged in combat. When Gould's ship closed on one Confederate vessel, he declared that "we told them good morning in the shape of a shot." In a five-day period in 1862, his ship and two other blockaders captured four blockade runners and ran another aground. In October 1863, Gould transferred to the USS *Niagara* and sailed for European waters to search for Confederate cruisers abroad.

But Gould's Civil War experience was shaped by his race. Most white Northerners fought to preserve their government and society, while most black men in the Union military saw service as an opportunity to fight slavery. From the beginning, Gould linked union and freedom, which he called "the holiest of all causes."

Nevertheless, Gould witnessed a number of racial incidents on federal ships. "There was A malee [melcc] on Deck between the white and colard [colored] men," he declared. Later, when a black regiment came aboard, "they were treated verry rough by the crew," he observed. The white sailors "refused to let them eat off the mess pans and called them all kinds of names[;] . . . in all they was treated shamefully." Recording another incident, Gould stated, "This Morning four or fiv[e] white fellows beat Jerry Jones (co[lored]). He was stabd in his left shoulder. Verry bad."

Still, Gould was proud of his service in the navy and monitored the progress of racial equality during the war. On shore leave in 1863, he cheered the "20th Regmt of U.S. (collard) Volunteers, the first collard Regement raised in New York pronounce[d] by all to be A splendid Regement." In March 1865, he celebrated the "passage of an amendment of the Con[sti]tution prohibiting slavery througho[ut] the United States." And a month later, he thrilled to the "Glad Tidings that the Stars and Stripe[s] had been planted over the Capital of the D—nd Confederacy by the invincible Grant." He added, we must not forget the "Mayrters to the cau[se] of Right and Equality."

Slaves like the eight runaways from Wilmington took the first steps toward making the war for union also a war for freedom. Early in the fighting, black abolitionist Frederick Douglass challenged the friends of freedom to "*be up and doing;—now is your time.*" But for the first eighteen months of the war, Union soldiers fought solely to uphold the Constitution and preserve the nation. With the Emancipation Proclamation, however, the northern war effort took on a dual purpose: to save the Union and to free the slaves.

Even if the Civil War had not touched slavery, the conflict still would have transformed America. As the world's first modern war, it mobilized the entire populations of North and South, harnessed the productive capacities of both economies, and produced battles that fielded 200,000 soldiers and created casualties in the tens of thousands. The carnage lasted four years and cost the nation an estimated 633,000 lives, nearly as many as in all of its other wars combined. The war helped mold the modern American nation-state, and the federal government emerged with new power and responsibility over national life. The war encouraged industrialization. It tore families apart and pushed women into new work and roles. But because the war for union also became a war against slavery, the northern victory had truly revolutionary meaning. Defeat and emancipation destroyed the slave society of the Old South and gave birth to a different southern society.

Recalling the Civil War years, Frederick Douglass said, "It is something to couple one's name with great occasions." It *was* something—for William Gould and millions of other Americans. Whether they fought for the Confederacy or the Union, whether they labored behind the lines to supply Yankee or rebel soldiers, whether they prayed for the safe return of Northerners or Southerners, all Americans experienced the crucible of war. But the war affected no group more than the 4 million African Americans who saw its beginning as slaves and emerged as free people.

"And the War Came"

Abraham Lincoln faced the worst crisis in the history of the nation: disunion. He revealed his strategy on March 4, 1861, in his inaugural address, which was firm yet conciliatory. First, he sought to stop the contagion of secession by avoiding any act that would push the skittish Upper South (North Carolina, Virginia, Maryland, Delaware, Kentucky, Tennessee, Missouri, and Arkansas) out of the Union. Second, he sought to buy time so that emotions could cool by reassuring the seceding Lower South (South Carolina, Georgia, Florida, Alabama, Mississippi, Louisiana, and Texas) that the Republicans would not abolish slavery. Lincoln believed that Unionists there would assert themselves and overturn the secession decision. Always, Lincoln denied the right of secession and upheld the Union.

His counterpart, Jefferson Davis, fully intended to establish the Confederate States of America as an independent republic. To achieve permanence, Davis had to sustain the secession fever that had carried the Lower South out of the Union. Even if the Lower South held firm, however, the Confederacy would remain weak without additional states. Davis watched for opportunities to add new stars to the Confederate flag.

Neither man sought war; both wanted to achieve their objectives peacefully. As Lincoln later observed, "Both parties deprecated war, but one of them would *make* war rather than let the nation survive, and the other would *accept* war rather than let it perish. And the war came."

Attack on Fort Sumter

Major Robert Anderson and some eighty U.S. soldiers occupied Fort Sumter, which was perched on a tiny island at the entrance to Charleston harbor. The fort with its American flag became a hated symbol of the nation that Southerners had abandoned, and they wanted federal troops out. Sumter was also a symbol to Northerners, a beacon affirming federal sovereignty in the seceded states.

Lincoln decided to hold Fort Sumter, but to do so, he had to provision it, for Anderson was running dangerously short of food. In the first week of April 1861, Lincoln authorized a peaceful expedition to bring supplies, but not military reinforcements, to the fort. The president understood that he risked war, but his plan honored his inaugural promises to defend federal property and to avoid using military force unless first attacked. Masterfully, Lincoln had shifted the fateful decision of war or peace to Jefferson Davis.

On April 9, Jefferson Davis and his cabinet met to consider the situation in Charleston harbor. The territorial integrity of the Confederacy demanded the end of the federal presence, Davis argued. But his secretary of state, Robert Toombs of Georgia, pleaded against military action. "Mr. President," he declared, "at this time it is suicide, murder, and will lose us every friend at the North. You will wantonly strike a hornet's nest which extends from mountain to ocean, and legions now quiet will swarm out and sting us to death." Davis rejected Toombs's prophecy and sent word to Confederate troops in Charleston to take the fort before the relief expedition arrived. Thirty-three hours of bombardment on April 12 and 13 reduced the fort to rubble. Miraculously, not a single Union soldier died. On April 14, with the fort ablaze, Major Anderson offered his surrender and lowered the U.S. flag. The Confederates had Fort Sumter, but they also had war.

On April 15, when Lincoln called for 75,000 militiamen to serve for ninety days to put down the rebellion, several times that number rushed to defend the flag. Democrats responded as fervently as Republicans. Stephen A. Douglas, the recently defeated Democratic candidate for president, pledged his support. "There are only two sides to the question," he said. "Every man must be for the United States or against it. There can be no neutrals in this war, *only patriots—or traitors*." But the people of the Upper South found themselves torn.

The Upper South Chooses Sides

The Upper South faced a horrendous choice: either to fight against the Lower South or to fight against the Union. Many who only months earlier had rejected secession now embraced the Confederacy. To vote against southern independence was one thing, to fight fellow Southerners another. Thousands felt betrayed, believing that Lincoln had promised to achieve a peaceful reunion by waiting patiently for Unionists to retake power in the seceding states. One man furiously denounced the conflict as a "politician's war," conceding that "this is no time now to discuss the causes, but it is the duty of all who regard Southern institutions of value to side with the South, make common cause with the Confederate States and sink or swim with them."

One by one, the states of the Upper South jumped off the fence. In April and May 1861, Virginia, Arkansas, Tennessee, and North Carolina joined the Confederacy (Map 15.1, page 442). But in the border states of Delaware, Maryland, Kentucky, and Missouri, Unionism triumphed. Only in Delaware, where slaves accounted for less than 2 percent of the population, was the victory easy. In Maryland, Unionism needed a helping hand. Rather than allow the state to secede and make Washington, D.C., a federal island in a Confederate sea, Lincoln suspended the writ of habeas corpus, essentially setting aside constitutional guarantees that protect citizens from illegal and arbitrary arrest and detention, and he ordered U.S. troops into Baltimore. Maryland's legislature rejected secession.

The struggle turned violent in the West. In Missouri, Unionists won a narrow victory, but southern-sympathizing **guerrilla** bands roamed the state for the duration of the war, terrorizing civilians and soldiers alike. In Kentucky, Unionists also narrowly defeated secession, but the prosouthern minority claimed otherwise. The Confederacy, not especially careful about counting votes, eagerly made Missouri and Kentucky the twelfth and thirteenth stars on the Confederate flag.

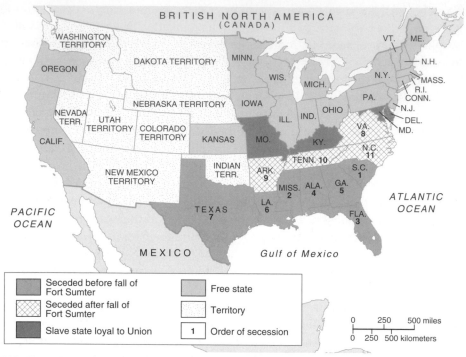

MAP 15.1 Secession, 1860–1861

After Lincoln's election, the fifteen slave states debated what to do. Seven states quickly left the Union, four left after the firing on Fort Sumter, and four remained loyal to the Union.

Throughout the border states, but especially in Kentucky, the Civil War divided families. Seven of Henry Clay's grandsons fought: four for the Confederacy and three for the Union. Lincoln understood that the border states—particularly Kentucky—contained indispensable resources, population, and wealth and also controlled major rivers and railroads. "I think to lose Kentucky is nearly the same as to lose the whole game," Lincoln said. "Kentucky gone, we can not hold Missouri, nor, as I think, Maryland. These all against us, . . . we would as well consent to separation at once."

In the end, only eleven of the fifteen slave states joined the Confederate States of America. Moreover, the four seceding Upper South states contained significant numbers of people who felt little affection for the Confederacy. Dissatisfaction was so rife in the western counties of Virginia that in 1863, citizens there voted to create the separate state of West Virginia, loyal to the Union. Still, the acquisition of four new states greatly strengthened the Confederacy's drive for national independence.

▶ **REVIEW** Why did both the Union and the Confederacy consider control of the border states crucial?

The Combatants

Only slaveholders had a direct economic stake in preserving slavery (estimated at some $3 billion in 1860), but most whites in the Confederacy defended the institution, the way of life built on it, and the Confederacy itself. The degraded and subjugated status of blacks elevated the status of the poorest whites. "It matters not whether slaves be actually owned by many or by few," one Southerner declared. "It is enough that one simply belongs to the superior and ruling race, to secure consideration and respect." Moreover, Yankee "aggression" was no longer a mere threat; it was real and at the South's door. Southern whites equated the secession of 1861 with the declaration of independence from tyrannical British rule in 1776. As one Georgia woman observed, Southerners wanted "nothing from the North but—to *be let alone.*"

For Northerners, rebel "treason" threatened to destroy the best government on earth. The South's failure to accept the **democratic** election of a president and its firing on the nation's flag challenged the rule of law, the authority of the Constitution, and the ability of the people to govern themselves. As an Indiana soldier told his wife, a "good government is the best thing on earth. Property is nothing without it, because it is not protected; a family is nothing without it, because they cannot be educated." Only a Union victory, Lincoln declared, would secure America's promise "to elevate the condition of man."

Northerners and Southerners rallied behind their separate flags, fully convinced that they were in the right and that God was on their side. But no one could argue that the South's resources and forces equaled the North's. A glance at the census figures contradicted such a notion. Yankees took heart from their superior power, but the rebels believed they had advantages that nullified every northern strength. Both sides mobilized swiftly in 1861, and each devised what it believed would be a winning military and diplomatic strategy.

How They Expected to Win

The balance sheet of northern and southern resources reveals enormous advantages for the Union (Figure 15.1, page 444). The twenty-three states remaining in the Union had a population of 22.3 million; the eleven Confederate states had a population of only 9.1 million, of whom 3.67 million (40 percent) were slaves. The North's economic advantages were even more overwhelming. So mismatched were the Union and the Confederacy that the question becomes, Was not the South's cause lost before Confederates fired the first rounds at Fort Sumter? The answer quite simply is "no." Southerners expected to win—for some good reasons—and they came very close to doing so.

Southerners knew they bucked the military odds, but hadn't the **liberty-**loving colonists in 1776 also done so? "Britain could not conquer three million," a Louisianan proclaimed, and "the world cannot conquer the South." How could

Total population	71% / 29%	2.4 to 1
Free males	81% / 19%	4.3 to 1
Wealth produced	75% / 25%	3 to 1
Industrial workers	92% / 8%	11.5 to 1
Factory production	91% / 9%	10.1 to 1
Textile production	93% / 7%	13.3 to 1
Firearms production	97% / 3%	32.3 to 1
Railroad mileage	71% / 29%	2.4 to 1
Iron production	94% / 6%	15.7 to 1
Coal production	97% / 3%	32.3 to 1
Livestock	60% / 40%	1.5 to 1
Farm acreage	75% / 25%	3 to 1
Wheat	81% / 19%	4.3 to 1
Corn	67% / 33%	2 to 1
Cotton	4% / 96%	1 to 24
Merchant ship tonnage	90% / 10%	9 to 1
Naval ship tonnage	96% / 4%	24 to 1

☐ Union   ■ Confederacy

FIGURE 15.1   Resources of the Union and Confederacy
The Union's enormous statistical advantages failed to convince Confederates that their cause was doomed.

anyone doubt the outcome of a contest between lean, hard, country-born rebel warriors defending family, property, and liberty, and soft, flabby, citified Yankee mechanics waging an unconstitutional war?

The South's confidence also rested on its belief that northern prosperity depended on the South's cotton. It followed that without cotton, New England textile mills would stand idle. And without southern **planters** purchasing northern manufactured goods, northern factories would drown in their own unsold goods. And without the foreign exchange earned by the overseas sales of cotton, the financial structure of the entire Yankee nation would collapse. A Virginian spoke for most Confederates when he declared that in the South's ability to "withhold the benefits of our trade, we hold a power over the North more powerful than a powerful army in the field."

Cotton would also make Europe a powerful ally of the Confederacy, Southerners reasoned. After all, they said, Britain's economy (and, to a lesser degree, France's) also depended on cotton. Of the 900 million pounds of cotton Britain imported annually, more than 700 million pounds came from the South. If the supply was interrupted, sheer economic need would make Britain (and perhaps France) a Confederate ally. And because the British navy ruled the seas, the North would find Britain a formidable foe.

Southerners' confidence may seem naive today, but even tough-minded European military observers picked the South to win. Offsetting the Union's power was the Confederacy's expanse. The North, Europeans predicted, could not conquer the vast territory (750,000 square miles) extending from the Potomac to the Rio Grande. To defeat the South, the Union would need to raise and equip a massive invading army and protect supply lines that would stretch farther than any in modern history.

Indeed, the South enjoyed major advantages, and the Confederacy devised a military strategy to exploit them. It recognized that a Union victory required the North to defeat and subjugate the South, but a Confederate victory required only that the South stay at home, blunt invasions, avoid battles that risked annihilating its army, and outlast the North's will to fight. When an opportunity presented itself, the South would strike the invaders. Like the American colonists, the South could win independence by not losing the war.

If the North did nothing, the South would by default establish itself as a sovereign nation. The Lincoln administration, therefore, adopted an offensive strategy that applied pressure at many points. Lincoln declared a naval blockade of the Confederacy to deny the South the advantages offered by its most valuable commodity—cotton. Without the sale of cotton abroad, the South would have far fewer dollars to pay for war goods. Even before the North could mount an effective blockade, however, Jefferson Davis decided voluntarily to cease exporting cotton. He wanted to create a cotton "famine" that would enfeeble the northern economy and precipitate European intervention. But the cotton famine Davis created devastated the South, not the North, and left Europe on the diplomatic sidelines. Lincoln also ordered the Union army into Virginia, at the same time planning a march through the Mississippi valley that would cut the Confederacy in two. This ambitious strategy took advantage of the Union's superior resources.

Neither side could foresee the magnitude and duration of the war. Americans thought of war in terms of their most recent experience, the Mexican-American War of the 1840s. In Mexico, fighting had taken place between relatively small armies, had cost relatively few lives, and had inflicted only light damage on the countryside. On the eve of the Civil War, they could not know that four ghastly years of bloodletting lay ahead.

Lincoln and Davis Mobilize

Mobilization required effective political leadership, and at first glance, the South appeared to have the advantage. Jefferson Davis brought to the Confederate presidency a distinguished political career, including experience in the U.S. Senate.

He was also a West Point graduate, a combat veteran and authentic hero of the Mexican-American War, and a former secretary of war. Dignified and ramrod straight, with "a jaw sawed in steel," Davis appeared to be everything a nation could want in a wartime leader.

In contrast, Abraham Lincoln brought to the White House one lackluster term in the House of Representatives and almost no administrative experience. His sole brush with anything military was as a captain in the militia in the Black Hawk War, a brief struggle in Illinois in 1832 in which whites expelled the last Indians from the state. Lincoln later joked about his service in the Black Hawk War as the time when he survived bloody encounters with mosquitoes and led raids on wild onion patches. The lanky, disheveled Illinois lawyer-politician looked anything but military or presidential in his bearing.

Davis, however, proved to be less than he appeared. Although he worked hard, he had no gift for military strategy yet intervened often in military affairs. He was an even less able political leader. Quarrelsome and proud, he had an acid tongue that made enemies the Confederacy could ill afford. He insisted on dealing with every scrap of paper that came across his desk, and he grew increasingly unbending and dogmatic. The Confederacy's intimidating problems might have defeated an even more talented leader, however. For example, **state sovereignty**, which was enshrined in the Confederate constitution, made Davis's task of organizing a new nation and fighting a war difficult in the extreme.

With Lincoln, in contrast, the North got far more than met the eye. He proved himself a master politician and a superb leader. When forming his cabinet, Lincoln appointed the ablest men, no matter that they were often his chief rivals and critics. He appointed Salmon P. Chase secretary of the treasury, knowing that Chase had presidential ambitions. As secretary of state, he chose his chief opponent for the Republican nomination in 1860, William H. Seward. Despite his civilian background, Lincoln displayed an innate understanding of military strategy. No one was more crucial in mapping the Union war plan. Further, Lincoln wrote beautifully and through letters and speeches reached out to the North's people, helping to galvanize them in defense of the nation he called "the last best hope of earth."

Lincoln and Davis began gathering their armies. Confederates had to build almost everything from scratch, and Northerners had to channel their superior numbers and industrial resources to the purposes of war. On the eve of the war, the federal army numbered only 16,000 men, most of them scattered over the West subjugating Indians. One-third of the officers followed the example of the Virginian Robert E. Lee, resigning their commissions and heading south. The U.S. navy was in better shape. Forty-two ships were in service, and a large merchant marine would in time provide more ships and sailors for the Union cause. Possessing a much weaker navy, the South pinned its hopes on its armies.

The Minié Ball

The Union army was one of the best-equipped armies in history, but none of its weaponry proved more vital than a French innovation by Captain Claude Minié. In 1848, Minié created an inch-long bullet that would spin at great speed as it left the muzzle. The spin gave the bullet greater distance and accuracy. Bullets caused more than 90 percent of battle wounds, and minié balls proved extremely destructive to human bodies on impact.

Picture Research Consultants & Archives.

The Confederacy made prodigious efforts to build new factories to produce tents, blankets, shoes, and its gray uniforms, but many rebel soldiers slept in the open air without proper clothes and sometimes without shoes. Even when factories managed to produce what the soldiers needed, southern railroads often could not deliver the goods. And each year, more railroads were captured, destroyed, or left in disrepair. Food production proved less of a problem, but food sometimes rotted before it reached the soldiers. The one bright spot was the Confederacy's Ordnance Bureau, headed by Josiah Gorgas, a near miracle worker when it came to manufacturing gunpowder, cannons, and rifles. In April 1864, Gorgas proudly observed: "Where three years ago we were not making a gun, a pistol nor a sabre, no shot nor shell . . . —a pound of powder—we now make all these in quantities to meet the demands of our large armies."

Recruiting and supplying huge armies required enormous new revenues. At first, the Union and the Confederacy sold war bonds, which essentially were loans from patriotic citizens. In addition, both sides turned to taxes. The North raised one-fifth of its wartime revenue from taxes; the South raised only one-twentieth. Eventually, both began printing paper money. Inflation soared, but the Confederacy suffered more because it financed a greater part of its wartime costs through the printing press. Prices in the Union rose by about 80 percent during the war, while inflation in the Confederacy topped 9,000 percent.

Within months of the bombardment of Fort Sumter, both sides found men to fight and ways to supply and support them. But the underlying strength of the northern economy gave the Union the decided advantage. With their military and industrial muscles beginning to ripple, Northerners became itchy for action. They wanted an invasion that once and for all would smash the rebellion. Horace Greeley's *New York Tribune* began to chant: "Forward to Richmond! Forward to Richmond!"

▶**REVIEW**　　Why did the South believe it could win the war despite numerical disadvantages?

Battling It Out, 1861–1862

During the first year and a half of the war, armies fought major campaigns in both East and West. Because the rival capitals—Richmond and Washington, D.C.— were only ninety miles apart and each was threatened more than once with capture, the eastern campaign was especially dramatic. But the battles in the West proved more decisive. As Yankee and rebel armies pounded each other on land, the navies fought on the seas and on the rivers of the South. In Europe, Confederate and U.S. diplomats competed for advantage in the corridors of power. All the while, casualty lists on both sides reached appalling lengths.

Stalemate in the Eastern Theater

Irvin McDowell, commanding general of the Union army assembling outside Washington, had no thought of taking his raw recruits into battle during the summer of 1861. Lincoln, however, ordered him to prepare his 35,000 troops for an attack on the 20,000 Confederates defending Manassas, a railroad junction in Virginia about thirty miles southwest of Washington. On July 21, the Union army forded Bull Run, a branch of the Potomac River, and engaged the southern forces (Map 15.2). But fast-moving southern reinforcements blunted the Union attack and then counterattacked. What began as an orderly Union retreat turned into a panicky stampede. Demoralized federal troops ran over shocked civilians as the soldiers raced back to Washington.

By Civil War standards, the casualties (wounded and dead) at Bull Run (or Manassas, as Southerners called the battle) were light, about 2,000 Confederates and 1,600 Federals. The significance of the battle lay in the lessons Northerners and Southerners drew from it. For Southerners, it confirmed the superiority of rebel fighting men and the inevitability of Confederate nationhood. Manassas was "*one of the decisive battles of the world*," a Georgian proclaimed. It "*has* secured our independence." While victory elevated southern pride, defeat sobered Northerners. It was a major setback, admitted the *New York Tribune*, but "let us go to work, then, with a will." Bull Run taught Lincoln that victory would be neither quick nor easy. Within four days of the disaster, the president authorized the enlistment of 1 million men for three years.

Lincoln also found a new general, replacing McDowell with young George B. McClellan. Having been born in Philadelphia of well-to-do parents and graduated from West Point second in his class, the thirty-four-year-old McClellan believed that he was a great soldier and that Lincoln was a dunce, the "original Gorilla." A superb administrator and organizer, McClellan came to Washington as commander of the newly named Army of the Potomac. McClellan energetically whipped his dispirited army into shape but was reluctant to send his soldiers into battle. For all his energy, McClellan lacked decisiveness. Lincoln wanted a general who would advance, take risks, and fight, but McClellan went

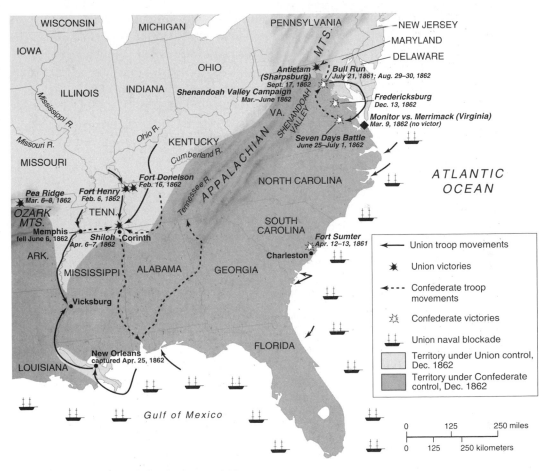

MAP 15.2   The Civil War, 1861–1862
While most eyes were focused on the eastern theater, especially the ninety-mile stretch of land between Washington, D.C., and the Confederate capital of Richmond, Virginia, Union troops were winning strategic victories in the West.

into winter quarters. "If General McClellan does not want to use the army I would like to *borrow* it," Lincoln declared in frustration.

Finally, in May 1862, McClellan launched his long-awaited offensive. He transported his highly polished army, now 130,000 strong, to the mouth of the James River and began slowly moving up the Yorktown peninsula toward Richmond. When he was within six miles of the Confederate capital, General Joseph Johnston hit him like a hammer. In the assault, Johnston was wounded and was replaced by Robert E. Lee, who would become the South's most celebrated general. Lee named his command the Army of Northern Virginia.

The contrast between Lee and McClellan could hardly have been greater. McClellan brimmed with conceit and braggadocio; Lee was courteous and reserved.

On the battlefield, McClellan grew timid and irresolute, and Lee became audaciously, even recklessly, aggressive. And Lee had at his side in the peninsula campaign military men of real talent: Thomas J. Jackson, nicknamed "Stonewall" for holding the line at Manassas, and James E. B. ("Jeb") Stuart, a dashing twenty-nine-year-old cavalry commander who rode circles around Yankee troops.

Lee's assault initiated the Seven Days Battle (June 25–July 1) and began McClellan's march back down the peninsula. By the time McClellan reached the safety of the Union navy, 30,000 men from both sides had died or been wounded. Although Southerners suffered twice the casualties of Northerners, Lee had saved Richmond and achieved a strategic success. Lincoln wired McClellan to abandon the peninsula campaign and replaced him with General John Pope.

In August, north of Richmond, at the second battle of Bull Run, Lee's smaller army battered Pope's forces and sent them scurrying back to Washington. Lincoln ordered Pope to Minnesota to pacify the Indians and restored McClellan to command. Lincoln had not changed his mind about McClellan's capacity as a warrior, but he reluctantly acknowledged that "if he can't fight himself, he excels in making others ready to fight."

Lee could fight, and sensing that he had the enemy on the ropes, Lee sought to land the knockout punch. He pushed his army across the Potomac and invaded Maryland. A victory on northern soil would dislodge Maryland from the Union, Lee reasoned, and might even cause Lincoln to sue for peace. On September 17, 1862, McClellan's forces engaged Lee's army at Antietam Creek (see Map 15.2).

The Dead of Antietam

In October 1862, photographer Mathew Brady opened an exhibition at his New York gallery that shocked the nation. Titled The Dead of Antietam, the exhibition consisted of ninety-five photographs that presented the battle of Antietam as the soldiers saw it. The photograph included here shows fallen Confederate soldiers along a rail fence on the Hagerstown Pike.
Library of Congress.

Earlier, a Union soldier had found a copy of Lee's orders to his army wrapped around some cigars dropped by a careless Confederate officer, so McClellan had a clear picture of Lee's position. McClellan's characteristic caution, however, cost him the opportunity to destroy the opposing army. Still, he did severe damage. With "solid shot . . . cracking skulls like eggshells," according to one observer, the armies went after each other. At Miller's Cornfield, the firing was so intense that "every stalk of corn in the . . . field was cut as closely as could have been done with a knife." By nightfall, 6,000 men lay dead or dying on the battlefield, and 17,000 more had been wounded. The battle of Antietam would be the bloodiest day of the war. More American soldiers died in a single day than died in the entire Revolutionary War. Instead of being the war-winning fight Lee had anticipated when he came north, Antietam sent the battered Army of Northern Virginia limping back home. McClellan claimed to have saved the North, but Lincoln again removed him from command of the Army of the Potomac and appointed General Ambrose Burnside.

Though bloodied, Lee found an opportunity in December to punish the enemy at Fredericksburg, Virginia, where Burnside's 122,000 Union troops faced 78,500 Confederates dug in behind a stone wall on the heights above the Rappahannock River. Half a mile of open ground separated the armies. "A chicken could not live on that field when we open on it," a Confederate artillery officer predicted. Yet Burnside ordered a frontal assault. When the shooting ceased, the Federals counted nearly 13,000 casualties, the Confederates fewer than 5,000. The battle of Fredericksburg was one of the Union's worst defeats. As 1862 ended, the North seemed no nearer to ending the rebellion than it had been when the war began. Rather than checkmate, military struggle in the East had reached stalemate.

Union Victories in the Western Theater

While most eyes focused on events in the East, the decisive early encounters of the war were taking place between the Appalachian Mountains and the Ozarks (see Map 15.2). The West's rivers—the Mississippi, the Tennessee, and the Cumberland—became the keys to the military situation. Looking northward along the three rivers, Southerners spied Missouri and Kentucky, states they claimed but did not control. Looking southward, Northerners saw that if they controlled the Mississippi River, they would split Arkansas, Louisiana, and Texas from the Confederacy. Moreover, the Cumberland and Tennessee rivers penetrated Tennessee, one of the Confederacy's main producers of food, mules, and iron—all vital resources.

Before Union forces could march on Tennessee, they needed to secure Missouri to the west. Union troops commanded by General Samuel R. Curtis swept across Missouri to the border of Arkansas, where in March 1862, they encountered General Earl Van Dorn's 16,000-man Confederate army, which included three regiments of Indians from the Five Civilized Tribes in Indian Territory. Although Indians fought on both sides during the war, Native Americans who sided with the South hoped that the Confederacy would grant them more independence than had the United States. Curtis's victory at the battle of Pea Ridge left Missouri free of Confederate troops, but Missouri was not free of Confederate guerrillas. Guerrilla bands led by the notorious William Clarke Quantrill and "Bloody Bill" Anderson burned, tortured, scalped, and murdered Union civilians and soldiers until the final year of the war.

Even farther west, Confederate armies sought to fulfill Jefferson Davis's vision of a slaveholding empire stretching all the way to the Pacific. Both sides recognized the immense value of the gold and silver mines of California, Nevada, and Colorado. A quick strike by Texas troops took Santa Fe, New Mexico, in the winter of 1861–62. Then in March 1862, a band of Colorado miners ambushed and crushed southern forces at Glorieta Pass, outside Santa Fe. Confederate military failures in the far West meant that there would be no Confederate empire beyond Texas.

The principal western battles took place in Tennessee, where General Ulysses S. Grant emerged as the key northern commander. Grant had graduated from West Point and served bravely in Mexico. When the Civil War began, he was a thirty-nine-year-old dry-goods clerk in Galena, Illinois. Gentle at home, he became pugnacious on the battlefield. "The art of war is simple," he said. "Find out where your enemy is, get at him as soon as you can and strike him as hard as you can, and keep moving on." Grant's philosophy of war as attrition would take a huge toll in human life, but it played to the North's strength: superiority in manpower. In his private's uniform and slouch hat, Grant did not look much like a general. But Lincoln, who did not look much like a president, learned his worth. Later, to critics who wanted the president to sack Grant because of his drinking, Lincoln would say, *"I can't spare this man. He fights."*

In February 1862, operating in tandem with U.S. navy gunboats, Grant captured Fort Henry on the Tennessee River and Fort Donelson on the Cumberland (see Map 15.2). Defeat forced the Confederates to withdraw from all of Kentucky and most of Tennessee, but Grant followed. On April 6, General Albert Sidney Johnston's army surprised him at Shiloh Church in Tennessee. Grant's troops were badly mauled the first day, but Grant remained cool and brought up reinforcements throughout the night. The next morning, the Union army counterattacked, driving the Confederates before it. The battle of Shiloh was terribly costly to both sides; there were 20,000 casualties, among them General Johnston. Grant later said that after Shiloh, he "gave up all idea of saving the Union except by complete conquest."

Although no one knew it at the time, Shiloh ruined the Confederacy's bid to control the theater of operations in the West. In short order, the Yankees captured the strategic town of Corinth, Mississippi; the river city of Memphis; and the South's largest city, New Orleans. By the end of 1862, the far West and most—but not all—of the Mississippi valley lay in Union hands. At the same time, the outcome of the struggle in another theater of war was also becoming clearer.

The Atlantic Theater

Both sides recognized the importance of the naval theater in the Atlantic. When the war began, the U.S. navy's blockade fleet consisted of about three dozen ships to patrol more than 3,500 miles of southern coastline, and rebel merchant ships were able to slip in and out of southern ports nearly at will. Taking on cargoes in the Caribbean, sleek Confederate blockade runners brought in vital supplies— guns and medicine. But with the U.S. navy commissioning a new blockader almost weekly, the naval fleet eventually numbered 150 ships on duty, and the Union navy dramatically improved its score.

Unable to build a conventional navy equal to the expanding U.S. fleet, the Confederates experimented with a radical new maritime design: the ironclad war- ship. At Norfolk, Virginia, they layered the wooden hull of the frigate *Merrimack* with two-inch-thick armor plate. Rechristened *Virginia*, the ship steamed out in March 1862 and sank two wooden federal ships, killing at least 240 Union sailors (see Map 15.2). When the *Virginia* returned to finish off the federal blockaders the next morning, it was challenged by the *Monitor*, a federal ironclad of even more radical design, topped with a revolving turret holding two eleven-inch guns. On March 9, the two ships hurled shells at each other for two hours, but neither could penetrate the other's armor, and the battle ended in a draw.

The Confederacy never found a way to break the Union blockade despite exploring many naval innovations, including a new underwater vessel—the sub- marine. It placed its greatest hope in destroying enough Union ships to force the blockading squadrons to withdraw to protect the northern merchant marine. The British-built Confederate cruiser *Alabama* sank or captured sixty-four Union merchant ships before the USS *Kearsarge* sank it off the coast of France in 1864. But each month, the Union fleet tightened its noose. By 1863, the South had abandoned its embargo policy and desperately wanted to ship cotton to pay for imports of arms, bullets, shoes, and uniforms needed to fight the war. The grow- ing effectiveness of the federal blockade, a southern naval officer observed, "shut the Confederacy out from the world, deprived it of supplies, weakened its military and naval strength." By 1865, the blockaders were intercepting about half of the southern ships attempting to break through. The Confederacy was sealed off, with devastating results.

International Diplomacy

What the Confederates could not achieve on the seas, they sought to achieve through international diplomacy. Confederates and Unionists both recognized that the world was watching the struggle in North America. Nationalists every- where understood that the American Civil War involved issues central to their own nation-building efforts. The Confederates rested their claims to separate nationhood on the principles of self-determination and rightful rebellion against tyrannical power, and they desperately wanted Europe to intervene. The Lincoln administration explained why the Union had to be preserved and Europe had to remain neutral. "The question," Lincoln explained, is "whether a constitutional republic, or a democracy—a government of the people, by the same people—can or cannot, maintain its territorial integrity, against its own domestic foes."

More practically, the Confederates based their hope for European support on King Cotton. In theory, cotton-starved European nations would have no choice but to break the Union blockade and recognize the Confederacy. Southern hopes were not unreasonable, for at the height of the "cotton famine" in 1862, when 2 million British workers were unemployed, Britain tilted toward recognition. Along with several other European nations, Britain granted the Confederacy "belligerent" status, which enabled it to buy goods and build ships in European ports. But no country challenged the blockade or recognized the Confederate States of America as a nation, a bold act that probably would have drawn that country into war with the United States and perhaps tipped the balance in the South's favor.

King Cotton diplomacy failed for several reasons. A bumper cotton crop in 1860 meant that the warehouses of British textile manufacturers bulged with surplus cotton throughout 1861. In 1862, when a cotton shortage did occur, European manufacturers found new sources in India, Egypt, and elsewhere. In addition, the development of a brisk trade between the Union and Britain— British war materiel for American grain and flour—helped offset the decline in textiles and encouraged Britain to remain neutral.

Europe's temptation to intervene disappeared for good in 1862. Union military successes in the West made Britain and France think twice about linking their fates to the struggling Confederacy. Moreover, in September 1862, five days after the Union victory at Antietam, Lincoln announced a new policy that made an alliance with the Confederacy an alliance with slavery—a commitment the French and British, who had outlawed slavery in their empires and looked forward to its eradication worldwide, were not willing to make. After 1862, the South's cause was linked irrevocably with slavery and reaction, and the Union's cause was linked with freedom and democracy. As the great English liberal John Stuart Mill declared, a Confederate victory "would give courage to the enemies of progress and damp the spirits of its friends all over the civilized world." The Union, not the Confederacy, had won the diplomatic stakes.

▶REVIEW   Why did the Confederacy's bid for international support fail?

Union *and* Freedom

For a year and a half, Lincoln insisted that the North fought strictly to save the Union and not to abolish slavery. Despite Lincoln's repeated pronouncements, however, the war for union became a war for African American freedom. Each month the conflict dragged on, it became clearer that the Confederate war machine depended heavily on slavery. Rebel armies used slaves to build fortifications, haul materiel, tend horses, and perform camp chores. On the home front, slaves labored in ironworks and shipyards, and they grew the food that fed both soldiers and civilians. Slavery undergirded the Confederacy as certainly as it had the Old South. Union military commanders and politicians alike gradually realized that to defeat the Confederacy, the North would have to destroy slavery. "I am a slow walker," Lincoln said, "but I never walk back."

From Slaves to Contraband

Lincoln detested human bondage, but as president he felt compelled to act prudently in the interests of the Union. He doubted his right under the Constitution to tamper with the "domestic institutions" of any state, even states in rebellion. An astute politician, Lincoln worked within the tight limits of public opinion. The issue of black freedom was particularly explosive in the loyal border states, where slaveholders threatened to jump into the arms of the Confederacy at even the hint of emancipation. Black freedom also raised alarms in the free states. The Democratic Party gave notice that emancipation would make the war strictly a Republican affair. Democrats marched under the banner "The Constitution As It Is, the Union As It Was."

Moreover, many white Northerners were not about to risk their lives to satisfy what they considered abolitionist "fanaticism." "We Won't Fight to Free the Nigger," one popular banner read. They feared that emancipation would propel "two or three million semi-savages" northward, where they would crowd into white neighborhoods, compete for white jobs, and mix with white "sons and daughters." Thus, emancipation threatened to dislodge the loyal slave states from the Union, alienate the Democratic Party, deplete the armies, and perhaps even spark race warfare.

Yet proponents of emancipation pressed Lincoln as relentlessly as the antiemancipation forces. Abolitionists argued that by seceding, Southerners had forfeited their right to the protection of the Constitution, and that Lincoln could—as the price of their treason—legally confiscate their property in slaves. When Lincoln refused, abolitionists scalded him. Frederick Douglass labeled him "the miserable tool of traitors and rebels." Abolitionists won increasing numbers of converts during the war, especially among the radical faction of the Republican Party.

The Republican-dominated Congress declined to leave slavery policy entirely in President Lincoln's hands. In August 1861, Congress approved the Confiscation Act, which allowed the seizure of any slave employed directly by the Confederate military. It also fulfilled the **free-soil** dream of prohibiting slavery in the territories and abolished slavery in Washington, D.C. Democrats and border-state representatives voted against even these mild measures, but Congress's attitude was clearly stiffening against slavery.

Human Contraband

This photograph shows a black family approaching Union lines in 1862, seeking sanctuary with the federal army. Most slaves fled with little more than the clothes on their backs, but not all escaped slavery empty-handed. The mules, wagon, and goods seen here could have been purchased during slavery, "borrowed" from their former master, or found during flight. Refugees who possessed draft animals and a wagon had many more economic opportunities than those who did not.

National Archives.

Slaves, not politicians, became the most insistent force for emancipation. By escaping their masters by the tens of thousands and running away to Union lines, they forced slavery on the North's wartime agenda. Runaways precipitated a series of momentous decisions. Were the runaways now free, or were they still slaves who, according to the fugitive slave law, had to be returned to their masters? At first, Yankee military officers sent the fugitives back. But Union armies needed laborers, and some officers accepted the runaways and put them to work. At Fort Monroe, Virginia, General Benjamin F. Butler refused to turn them over to their owners, calling them "contraband of war," meaning "confiscated property." Congress made Butler's practice national policy in March 1862 when it forbade returning fugitive slaves to their masters. Slaves were still not legally free, but there was a tilt toward emancipation.

Lincoln's policy of noninterference with slavery gradually crumbled. To calm Northerners' racial fears, Lincoln offered **colonization**, the deportation of African Americans from the United States to Haiti, Panama, or elsewhere. In the summer of 1862, he defended colonization to a delegation of black visitors to the White House. He told them that deep-seated racial prejudice made it impossible for blacks to achieve equality in this country. One of the visiting African Americans told the president, "This is our country as much as it is yours, and we will not leave." Congress voted a small amount of money to underwrite colonization, but after one miserable experiment on a small island in the Caribbean, practical limitations and black opposition sank further efforts.

While Lincoln was developing his own initiatives, he snuffed out actions that he believed would jeopardize northern unity. He was particularly alert to Union commanders who tried to dictate slavery policy from the field. In August 1861, when John C. Frémont, former Republican presidential nominee and now commander of federal troops in Missouri, freed the slaves belonging to Missouri rebels, Lincoln forced the general to revoke his edict and then removed him from command. The following May, when General David Hunter freed the slaves in Georgia, South Carolina, and Florida, Lincoln countermanded his order. Events moved so rapidly, however, that Lincoln found it impossible to control federal policy on slavery.

From Contraband to Free People

On August 22, 1862, Lincoln replied to an angry abolitionist who demanded that he attack slavery. "My paramount objective in this struggle *is* to save the Union," Lincoln said deliberately, "and is *not* either to save or destroy slavery. If I could save the Union without freeing *any* slave I would do it, and if I could save it by freeing *all* the slaves I would do it; and if I could save it by freeing some and leaving others alone I would also do that." Instead of simply restating his old position that union was the North's sole objective, Lincoln announced that slavery was no longer untouchable and that he would emancipate every slave if doing so would preserve the Union.

By the summer of 1862, events were tumbling rapidly toward emancipation. On July 17, Congress adopted the second Confiscation Act. The first had confiscated slaves employed by the Confederate military; the second declared all slaves of rebel masters "forever free of their servitude." In theory, this breathtaking measure freed most Confederate slaves, for slaveholders formed the backbone of the rebellion. Congress had traveled far since the war began.

Lincoln had, too. On July 21, the president informed his cabinet that he was ready "to take some definitive steps in respect to military action and slavery." The next day, he read a draft of a preliminary emancipation proclamation that promised to free *all* the slaves in the seceding states on January 1, 1863. Lincoln described emancipation as an "act of justice," but it was the lengthening casualty lists that finally brought him around. Emancipation, he declared, was "a military necessity, absolutely essential to the preservation of the Union." Only freeing the slaves would "strike at the heart of the rebellion." On September 22, Lincoln issued his preliminary Emancipation Proclamation promising freedom to slaves in areas still in rebellion on January 1, 1863.

The limitations of the proclamation—it exempted the loyal border states and the Union-occupied areas of the Confederacy—caused some to ridicule the act. The *Times* (London) observed cynically, "Where he has no power Mr. Lincoln will set the negroes free, where he retains power he will consider them as slaves." But Lincoln had no power to free slaves in loyal states, and invading Union armies would liberate slaves in the Confederacy as they advanced.

By presenting emancipation as a "military necessity," Lincoln hoped he had disarmed his **conservative** critics. Emancipation would deprive the Confederacy of valuable slave laborers, shorten the war, and thus save lives. Democrats, however, fumed that the "shrieking and howling abolitionist faction" had captured the White House and made it "a nigger war." Democrats made political hay out of Lincoln's action in the November 1862 elections, gaining thirty-four congressional seats. House Democrats quickly proposed a resolution branding emancipation "a high crime against the Constitution." The Republicans, who maintained narrow majorities in both houses of Congress, beat it back.

As promised, on New Year's Day 1863, Lincoln issued the final Emancipation Proclamation. In addition to freeing the slaves in the rebel states, the edict also committed the federal government to the fullest use of African Americans to defeat the Confederate enemy.

War of Black Liberation

Even before Lincoln proclaimed freedom a Union war aim, African Americans in the North had volunteered to fight. But the War Department, doubtful of their abilities and fearful of white reaction to serving side by side with them, refused to make black men soldiers. Instead, the army employed black men as manual laborers; black women sometimes found employment as laundresses and cooks. The navy, however, accepted blacks from the outset, including runaway slaves such as William Gould.

As the Union experienced manpower shortages, Northerners gradually and reluctantly turned to African Americans to fill the Union army's blue uniforms. With the Militia Act of July 1862, Congress authorized enrolling blacks in "any military or naval service for which they may be found competent." After the Emancipation Proclamation, whites—like it or not—were fighting and dying for black freedom, and few insisted that blacks remain out of harm's way behind the lines. Indeed, whites insisted that blacks share the danger, especially after March 1863, when Congress resorted to the **draft** to fill the Union army.

The military was far from color-blind. The Union army established segregated black regiments, paid black soldiers $10 per month rather than the $13 it paid whites, refused blacks the opportunity to become commissioned officers, punished blacks as if they were slaves, and assigned blacks to labor battalions rather than to combat units. Still, when the war ended, 179,000 African American men had served in the Union military, approximately 10 percent of the total army. An astounding 71 percent of black men ages eighteen to forty-five in the free states wore Union blue, a participation rate that was substantially higher than that of white men. More than 130,000 black soldiers came from the slave states, perhaps 100,000 of them ex-slaves.

In time, whites allowed blacks to put down their shovels and to shoulder rifles. At the battles of Port Hudson and Milliken's Bend on the Mississippi River and at Fort Wagner in Charleston harbor, black courage under fire finally dispelled notions that African Americans could not fight. More than 38,000 black soldiers died in the Civil War, a mortality rate that was higher than that of white troops. Blacks played a crucial role in the triumph of the Union and the destruction of slavery in the South.

▶ **REVIEW**   Why did the Union change policy in 1863 to allow black men to serve in the army?

The South at War

By seceding, Southerners brought on themselves a firestorm of unimaginable fury. Monstrous losses on the battlefield nearly bled the Confederacy to death. White Southerners on the home front also suffered, even at the hands of their own government. Efforts by the Davis administration in Richmond to centralize power in order to fight the war effectively convinced some men and women that the Confederacy had betrayed them. Wartime economic changes hurt everyone, some more than others. By 1863, planters and **yeomen** who had stood together began to drift apart. Most disturbing of all, slaves became open participants in the destruction of slavery and the Confederacy.

Revolution from Above

As a Confederate general observed, Southerners were engaged in a total war "in which the whole population and the whole production . . . are to be put on a war footing, where every institution is to be made auxiliary to war." Jefferson Davis faced the task of building an army and navy from scratch, supplying them from factories that were scarce and anemic, and paying for it all from a treasury that did not exist. Finding eager soldiers proved easiest. Hundreds of officers defected from the U.S. army, and hundreds of thousands of eager young rebels volunteered to follow them. Very quickly, the Confederacy developed formidable striking power.

The Confederacy's economy and finances proved tougher problems. Because of the Union blockade, the government had no choice but to build an industrial sector itself. Government-owned clothing and shoe factories, mines, arsenals, and powder works sprang up. The government also harnessed private companies, such as the huge Tredegar Iron Works in Richmond, to the war effort. Paying for the war became the most difficult task. A flood of paper money caused debilitating inflation. By 1863, people in Charleston paid ten times more for food than they had paid at the start of the war. By Christmas 1864, a Confederate soldier's monthly pay no longer bought a pair of socks. Despite bold measures, the Davis administration failed to transform the agricultural economy into a modern industrial one. The Confederacy manufactured much more than most people imagined possible, but it never produced all that the South needed. Each month, the gap between the North's and the South's production widened.

Richmond's war-making effort brought unprecedented government intrusion into the private lives of Confederate citizens. In April 1862, the Confederate Congress passed the first **conscription** (draft) law in American history. All able-bodied white males between the ages of eighteen and thirty-five (later seventeen and fifty) were liable to serve in the rebel army. The government adopted a policy of impressment, which allowed officials to confiscate food, horses, wagons, and whatever else they wanted from private citizens and to pay for them at below-market rates. After March 1863, the Confederacy legally impressed slaves, employing them as military laborers.

War necessitated much of the government's unprecedented behavior, but citizens found it arbitrary and inequitable. Richmond's centralizing efforts ran head-on into the South's traditional values of **states' rights** and unfettered individualism. The states lashed out at what Georgia governor Joseph E. Brown denounced as the "dangerous usurpation by Congress of the reserved right of the States." Richmond and the states struggled for control of money, supplies, and soldiers, with damaging consequences for the war effort. Individuals also remembered that Davis had promised to defend southern "liberty" against Republican "despotism."

Hardship Below

Hardships on the home front fell most heavily on the poor. Salt—necessary for preserving meat—shot up from $2 to $60 a bag during the first year of the war. Flour, which cost three or four cents a pound in 1861, cost thirty-five cents in 1863. The draft stripped yeoman farms of men, leaving the women and children to grow what they ate. Government agents took 10 percent of farmwives' harvests as a "tax-in-kind" on agriculture. Like inflation, shortages afflicted the entire population, but the rich lost luxuries while the poor lost necessities. In the spring of 1863, bread riots broke out in a dozen cities and villages across the South. In Richmond, a mob of nearly a thousand hungry women broke into shops and took what they needed.

"Men cannot be expected to fight for the Government that permits their wives & children to starve," a southern leader observed in November 1862. Although a few wealthy individuals shared their bounty and the Confederate and state governments made efforts at social welfare, every attempt fell short. In late 1864, one desperate farmwife told her husband, "I have always been proud of you, and since your connection with the Confederate army, I have been prouder of you than ever before. I would not have you do anything wrong for the world, but before God, Edward, unless you come home, we must die." When the war ended, one-third of the soldiers had already gone home. A Mississippi deserter explained, "We are poor men and are willing to defend our country but our families [come] first."

Yeomen perceived a profound inequality of sacrifice. They called it "a rich man's war and a poor man's fight." The draft law permitted a man who had money to hire a substitute to take his place. Moreover, the "twenty-Negro law" exempted one white man on every plantation with twenty or more slaves. The government intended this law to provide protection for white women and to see that slaves tended the crops, but yeomen perceived it as rich men evading military service. A Mississippian complained that stay-at-home planters sent their slaves into the fields to grow cotton while in plain view "poor soldiers' wives are plowing with *their own* hands to make a subsistence for themselves and children— while their husbands are suffering, bleeding and dying for their country." In fact, most slaveholders went off to war, but the extreme suffering of common folk and the relative immunity of planters fueled class animosity.

The Richmond government hoped that the crucible of war would mold a region into a nation. Officials and others worked to promote a southern **nationalism** that would "excite in our citizens an ardent and enduring attachment to our Government and its institutions." Clergymen assured their

Maria Isabella ("Belle") Boyd, Spy

Most southern white women served the Confederate cause by sewing uniforms, knitting socks, and nursing the sick and wounded. But Belle Boyd became a spy. Her first act for the Confederacy came in 1861, when she shot a drunken federal soldier who insulted her mother. Soon Boyd was eavesdropping on Union officers' conversations and slipping messages to Confederate armies. Imprisoned several times for spying, Boyd took up a theatrical career when the war ended.

Courtesy Warren Rifles Confederate Museum, Front Royal, VA.

congregations that God had blessed slavery and the new nation. Patriotic song-writers, poets, authors, and artists extolled southern **culture**. Jefferson Davis asked citizens to observe national days of fasting and prayer. But these efforts failed to win over thousands of die-hard Unionists, and friction between yeomen and planters increased rather than decreased. The war also threatened to rip the south-ern social fabric along its racial seam.

The Disintegration of Slavery

The legal destruction of slavery was the product of presidential proclamation, congressional legislation, and eventually constitutional amendment, but the practical destruction of slavery was the product of war—what Lincoln called war's "friction and abrasion." War exposed the illusion of slave contentment. Slaves took advantage of the upheaval to reach for freedom. Some half a million of the South's 4 million slaves ran away to Union military lines. More than 100,000 runaways took up arms as federal soldiers and sailors and attacked slav-ery directly. Other men and women stayed in the slave quarter, where they staked their claim to more freedom.

War disrupted slavery in a dozen ways. Almost immediately, it called the master away, leaving the mistress to assume responsibility for the plantation. But mistresses could not maintain traditional standards of slave discipline in war-time, and the balance of power shifted. Slaves got to the fields late, worked indif-ferently, and quit early. Some slaveholders responded violently; most saw no alternative but to strike bargains—offering gifts or part of the crop—to keep slaves at home and at work. An Alabama woman complained that she "begged . . . what little is done." Slaveholders had believed that they "knew" their slaves, but they learned that they did not. When the war began, a North Carolina woman praised her slaves as "diligent and respectful." When it ended, she said, "As to the idea of a *faithful servant, it is all a fiction.*"

As military action sliced through the South's farms and plantations, some slaveholders fled, leaving their slaves behind. Many more took their slaves with them, but flight meant additional chaos and offered slaves new opportunities to resist bondage. Whites' greatest fear—retaliatory violence—rarely occurred, however. Slaves who stayed home steadily undermined white mastery and ex-panded control over their own lives.

▶**REVIEW**   How did wartime hardship in the South contribute to class animosity?

The North at War

Although the North was largely untouched by the fighting, Northerners could not avoid being touched by the war. Almost every family had a son, husband, father, or brother in uniform. Moreover, total war blurred the distinction between home front and battlefield. As in the South, men marched off to fight, but preserving the country was also women's work. For civilians as well as soldiers, for women as well as men, war was transforming.

The need to build and fuel the Union war machine boosted the economy. The Union sent nearly 2 million men into the military and still increased production in almost every area. But because the rewards and burdens of patriotism were distributed unevenly, the North experienced sharp, even violent, divisions. Workers confronted employers, whites confronted blacks, and Democrats confronted Republicans. Still, Northerners on the home front remained fervently attached to the Union.

The Government and the Economy

When the war began, the United States had no national banking system, no national currency, and no federal income or excise taxes. But the secession of eleven slave states cut the Democrats' strength in Congress in half and destroyed their capacity to resist Republican economic programs. The Legal Tender Act of February 1862 created a national currency—paper money that Northerners called "greenbacks." With the passage of the National Banking Act in February 1863, Congress established a system of national banks that by the 1870s had largely replaced the **antebellum** system of decentralized state banks. Congress also enacted a series of sweeping tax laws. The Internal Revenue Act created the Bureau of Internal Revenue to collect taxes. In addition, Congress enacted a higher tariff to increase revenue and protect manufacturers against foreign competition. By revolutionizing the country's banking, monetary, and tax structures, the Republicans generated enormous economic power.

The Republicans' wartime legislation also aimed at integrating the West more thoroughly into the Union. In May 1862, Congress approved the Homestead Act, which offered 160 acres of public land to settlers who would live and labor on it. The Homestead Act bolstered western loyalty and in time resulted in more than a million new farms. The Pacific Railroad Act in July 1862 provided massive federal assistance for building a transcontinental railroad that ran from Omaha to San Francisco when completed in 1869. Congress further bound East and West by subsidizing the Pony Express mail service and a transcontinental telegraph.

Two additional initiatives had long-term consequences for agriculture and industry. Congress created the Department of Agriculture and passed the Land-Grant College Act (also known as the Morrill Act after its sponsor, Representative Justin Morrill of Vermont), which set aside public land to support universities that emphasized "agriculture and mechanical arts." The Lincoln administration immeasurably strengthened the North's effort to win the war, but its ideas also permanently changed the nation.

Women and Work on the Home Front

More than a million farm men were called to the military, so farm women added men's chores to their own. "I met more women driving teams on the road and saw more at work in the fields than men," a visitor to Iowa reported in the fall of 1862. Rising production testified to their success in plowing, planting, and harvesting. Rapid mechanization assisted farm women in their new roles. Cyrus McCormick sold 165,000 of his reapers during the war years. The combination of high prices for farm products and increased production ensured that war and prosperity joined hands in the rural North.

A few industries, such as textiles (which depended on southern cotton), declined during the war, but many more grew. Huge profits prompted one Pennsylvania ironmaster to remark, "I am in no hurry for peace." With orders pouring in and a million nonfarmworkers at war, unemployment declined and wages often rose. The boom proved friendlier to owners than to workers, however. Inflation and taxes cut so deeply into workers' paychecks that their standard of living actually fell.

In cities, women stepped into jobs vacated by men, particularly in manufacturing, and also into essentially new occupations such as government secretaries and clerks. Women made up about one-quarter of the manufacturing workforce when the war began and one-third when it ended. As more and more women entered the workforce, employers cut wages. In 1864, New York seamstresses working fourteen-hour days earned only $1.54 a week. Urban workers resorted increasingly to strikes to wrench decent salaries from their employers, but their protests rarely succeeded. Nevertheless, tough times failed to undermine the patriotism of most workers.

Most middle-class white women stayed home and contributed to the war effort in traditional ways. They sewed, wrapped bandages, and sold homemade goods at local fairs to raise money to aid the soldiers. Other women expressed their patriotism in an untraditional way—as wartime nurses. Thousands of women on both sides defied prejudices about female delicacy and volunteered to nurse the wounded. Many northern female volunteers worked through the U.S. Sanitary Commission, a civilian organization that bought and distributed clothing, food, and medicine and recruited doctors and nurses.

Some volunteers went on to become paid military nurses. For example, Dorothea Dix, well known for her efforts to reform insane asylums, was named superintendent of female nurses in April 1861. Eventually, some 3,000 women served under her. Most nurses worked in hospitals behind the battle lines, but some, like Clara Barton, who later founded the American Red Cross, worked in battlefield units. At Antietam, as Barton was giving a wounded man a drink, a bullet ripped through her sleeve, striking and killing the soldier. Women who served in the war went on to lead the postwar movement to establish training schools for female nurses.

Politics and Dissent

At first, the bustle of economic and military mobilization seemed to silence politics, but bipartisan unity did not last. Within a year, Democrats were labeling the Republican administration a "reign of terror," and Republicans were calling Democrats the party of "Dixie, Davis, and the Devil." Democrats denounced Republican policies—emancipating the slaves, subsidizing private business, and expanding federal power—as unconstitutional, arguing that the "Constitution is as binding in war as in peace."

In September 1862, in an effort to stifle opposition to the war, Lincoln placed under military arrest any person who discouraged enlistments, resisted the draft, or engaged in "disloyal" practices. Before the war ended, his administration imprisoned nearly 14,000 individuals, most in the border states. The campaign fell short of a reign of terror, for the majority of the prisoners were not northern Democratic opponents but Confederates, blockade runners, and citizens of foreign countries, and most of those arrested gained quick release. Still, the administration's heavy-handed tactics did suppress free speech.

When the Republican-dominated Congress enacted the draft law in March 1863, Democrats had another grievance. The law required that all men between the ages of twenty and forty-five enroll and make themselves available for a lottery that would decide who went to war. What poor men found particularly galling were provisions that allowed a draftee to hire a substitute or simply to pay a $300 fee and get out of his military obligation. As in the South, common folk could be heard chanting, "A rich man's war and a poor man's fight."

Linking the draft and emancipation, Democrats argued that Republicans employed an unconstitutional means (the draft) to achieve an unconstitutional end (emancipation). In the summer of 1863, antidraft, antiblack mobs went on rampages in northern cities. In New York City, Democratic Irish workingmen— crowded into filthy tenements, gouged by inflation, enraged by the draft, and dead set against fighting to free blacks—erupted in four days of rioting. The draft riots killed at least 105 people, most of them black, and left the Colored Orphan Asylum a smoking ruin.

Racist mobs failed to achieve their purpose: the subordination of African Americans. Free black leaders had lobbied aggressively for emancipation, and after Lincoln's proclamation, they fanned out over the North agitating for equality. They won a few small victories. Illinois and Iowa overturned laws that excluded blacks from entering those states. Illinois and Ohio began permitting blacks to testify in court. But significant progress toward black equality would have to wait until the war ended.

▶ **REVIEW**   Why was the U.S. Congress able to pass such a bold legislative agenda during the war?

Grinding Out Victory, 1863–1865

In the early months of 1863, the Union's prospects looked bleak, and the Confederate cause stood at high tide. Then, in July 1863, the tide began to turn. The military man most responsible for this shift was Ulysses S. Grant. Lifted from obscurity by his successes in the West, Grant became the "great man of the day, perhaps of the age," one man observed in July 1864. Elevated to supreme command, Grant knit together a powerful war machine that integrated a sophisticated command structure, modern technology, and complex logistics and supply systems. But the arithmetic of this plain man remained unchanged: Killing more of the enemy than he kills of you equaled "the complete overthrow of the rebellion."

The North ground out the victory battle by bloody battle. The balance tipped in the Union's favor in 1863, but Southerners were not deterred. The fighting escalated in the last two years of the war. As national elections approached in the fall of 1864, Lincoln expected a war-weary North to reject him. Instead, northern voters declared their willingness to continue the war in the defense of the ideals of union and freedom.

Vicksburg and Gettysburg

Vicksburg, Mississippi, situated on the eastern bank of the Mississippi River, stood between Union forces and complete control of the river. Impenetrable terrain made the city impossible to take from the north. To get his army south of Vicksburg, Grant marched it down the swampy western bank of the Mississippi. Union forces crossed the Mississippi, marched north more than one hundred miles, and attacked the city. Confederates beat back the assault, and in May, Grant decided to lay siege to the city and starve out the enemy. Civilian residents of Vicksburg moved into caves to escape the incessant Union bombardment, and as the siege dragged on, they ate mules and rats to survive.

After six weeks, on July 4, 1863, nearly 30,000 rebels marched out of Vicksburg, stacked their arms, and surrendered unconditionally. A Yankee captain wrote home to his wife: "The backbone of the Rebellion is this day broken. The Confederacy is divided. . . . Vicksburg is ours. The Mississippi River is opened, and Gen. Grant is to be our next President."

On the same Fourth of July, word arrived that Union forces had crushed General Lee at Gettysburg, Pennsylvania (Map 15.3). Emboldened by his victory at Chancellorsville in May and hoping to relieve Virginia of the burden of the fighting, Lee and his 75,000-man army had invaded Pennsylvania. On June 28, Union forces under General George G. Meade intercepted the Confederates at the small town of Gettysburg, where Union soldiers occupied the high ground. Three days of furious fighting involving 165,000 troops could not dislodge the Federals from the hills. Lee ached for a decisive victory, and on July 3 he ordered a major assault against the Union center on Cemetery Ridge. Open, rolling fields provided the dug-in Yankees with three-quarters of a mile of clear vision, and they raked the

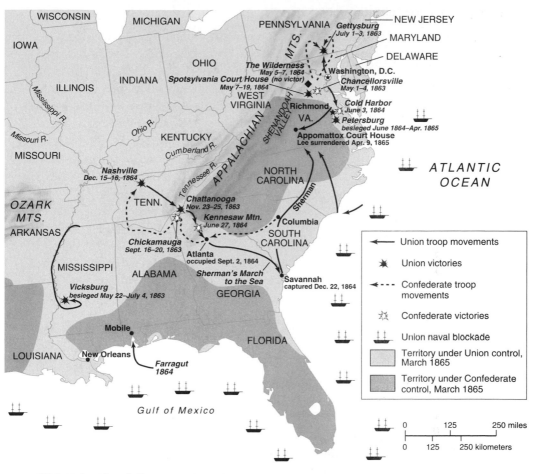

MAP 15.3 The Civil War, 1863–1865

Ulysses S. Grant's victory at Vicksburg divided the Confederacy at the Mississippi River. William Tecumseh Sherman's march from Chattanooga to Savannah divided it again. In northern Virginia, Robert E. Lee fought fiercely, but Grant's larger, better-supplied armies prevailed.

mile-wide line of Confederate soldiers under General George E. Pickett with cannon and rifle fire. Gettysburg cost Lee more than one-third of his army— 28,000 casualties. "It's all my fault," he lamented. In a drenching rain on the night of July 4, 1863, he marched his battered army back to Virginia.

The twin disasters at Vicksburg and Gettysburg proved to be the turning point of the war. The Confederacy could not replace the nearly 60,000 soldiers who were captured, wounded, or killed. Lee never launched another major offensive north of the Mason-Dixon line. It is hindsight, however, that permits us to see the pair of battles as decisive. At the time, the Confederacy still controlled the heartland of the South, and Lee still had a vicious sting. War-weariness threatened to erode the North's will to win before Union armies could destroy the Confederacy's ability to go on.

Grant Takes Command

Toward the end of September 1863, Union general William Rosecrans placed his army in a dangerous situation in Chattanooga, Tennessee, where he had retreated after defeat at the battle of Chickamauga earlier in the month (see Map 15.3). Rebels surrounded the disorganized bluecoats and threatened to starve them into submission. Grant, now commander of Union forces between the Mississippi River and the Appalachians, arrived in Chattanooga in October. Within weeks, he opened an effective supply line, broke the siege, and routed the Confederate army. The victory at Chattanooga on November 25 opened the door to Georgia. It also confirmed Lincoln's estimation of Grant. In March 1864, the president asked Grant to come east to become the general in chief of all Union armies.

In Washington, General Grant implemented his grand strategy for a war of attrition. He ordered a series of simultaneous assaults from Virginia all the way to Louisiana. Two actions proved particularly significant. In one, General William Tecumseh Sherman, whom Grant appointed his successor to command the western armies, plunged southeast toward Atlanta. In the other, Grant, who took control of the Army of the Potomac, went head-to-head with Lee for almost four straight weeks in Virginia.

Grant and Lee met in the first week of May 1864 in northern Virginia in a dense tangle of scrub oaks and small pines. Often unable to see more than ten paces, the armies pounded away at each other until approximately 18,000 Yankees and 11,000 rebels had fallen. The savagery of the battle of the Wilderness did not compare with that at Spotsylvania Court House a few days later. Frenzied men fought hand to hand for eighteen hours in the rain. One veteran remembered men "piled upon each other in some places four layers deep, exhibiting every ghastly phase of mutilation." Spotsylvania cost Grant another 18,000 casualties and Lee 10,000, but the Yankee bulldog would not let go. Grant kept moving and tangled with Lee again at Cold Harbor, where he suffered 13,000 additional casualties to Lee's 5,000.

Twice as many Union soldiers as rebel soldiers died in four weeks of fighting in Virginia in May and June, but because Lee had only half as many troops as Grant, his losses were equivalent to Grant's. Grant knew that the South could not replace the losses. Moreover, the campaign carried Grant to the outskirts of Petersburg, just south of Richmond, where he abandoned the costly tactic of the frontal assault and began a siege that immobilized both armies and dragged on for nine months.

Simultaneously, Sherman invaded Georgia. Grant instructed Sherman to "get into the interior of the enemy's country as far as you can, inflicting all the damage you can against their War resources." In early May, Sherman moved 100,000 men south against 65,000 rebels. Skillful maneuvering, constant skirmishing, and one pitched battle, at Kennesaw Mountain, brought Sherman to Atlanta, which fell on September 2.

Intending to "make Georgia howl," Sherman marched out of Atlanta on November 15 with 62,000 battle-hardened veterans, heading for Savannah,

285 miles away on the Atlantic coast. One veteran remembered, "[We] destroyed all we could not eat, stole their niggers, burned their cotton & gins, spilled their sorghum, burned & twisted their R. Roads and raised Hell generally." Sherman's "March to the Sea" aimed at destroying the will of the southern people. A few weeks earlier, General Philip H. Sheridan had carried out his own scorched-earth campaign in the Shenandoah Valley, complying with Grant's order to turn the valley into "a barren waste . . . so that crows flying over it for the balance of this season will have to carry their provender [food] with them." When Sherman's troops entered an undefended Savannah in mid-December, the general telegraphed Lincoln that he had "a Christmas gift" for him. A month earlier, Union voters had bestowed on the president an even greater gift.

The Election of 1864

In the summer of 1864, with Sherman temporarily checked outside Atlanta and Grant bogged down in the siege of Petersburg, the Democratic Party smelled victory in the fall elections. Rankled by a seemingly never-ending war, inflation, the draft, the attack on civil liberties, and the commitment to blacks, Northerners appeared ready for a change. Lincoln himself concluded, "It seems exceedingly probable that this administration will not be re-elected."

The Democrats were badly divided, however. "Peace" Democrats insisted on an armistice, while "war" Democrats supported the conflict but opposed Republican means of fighting it. The party tried to paper over the chasm by nominating a war candidate, General George McClellan, but adopting a peace platform that demanded that "immediate efforts be made for a cessation of hostilities." Republicans denounced the peace plank as a cut-and-run plan that "virtually proposed to surrender the country to the rebels in arms against us."

The capture of Atlanta on September 2 turned the political tide in favor of the Republicans. Lincoln received 55 percent of the popular vote, but his electoral margin was a whopping 212 to McClellan's 21. The Republicans also gained large margins over the Democrats in the congressional elections. Lincoln's party won a resounding victory, one that gave him a mandate to continue the war until slavery and the Confederacy were dead.

The Confederacy Collapses

As 1865 dawned, military disaster littered the Confederate landscape. With the destruction of John B. Hood's army at Nashville in December 1864, the interior of the Confederacy lay in Yankee hands (see Map 15.3). Sherman's troops, resting momentarily in Savannah, eyed South Carolina hungrily. Farther north, Grant had Lee's army pinned down in Petersburg, a few miles from Richmond.

Some Confederates turned their backs on the rebellion. News from the battlefield made it difficult not to conclude that the Yankees had beaten them. Soldiers' wives begged their husbands to return home to keep their families from starving, and the stream of deserters grew dramatically. In most cases, when white South-erners lost the will to continue, it was not because they lost faith in independence but because they had been battered into submission. Despite the deep divisions within the Confederacy, white Southerners had demonstrated a remarkable en-durance for their cause. Half of the 900,000 Confederate soldiers had been killed or wounded, and ragged, hungry women and children had sacrificed throughout one of the bloodiest wars then known to history.

The end came with a rush. On February 1, 1865, Sherman's troops stormed out of Savannah into South Carolina, the "cradle of the Confederacy." In Virginia, Lee abandoned Petersburg on April 2, and Richmond fell on April 3. Grant pursued Lee until he surrendered on April 9, 1865, at Appomattox Court House, Virginia. Grant offered generous peace terms. He allowed Lee's men to return home and to keep their horses to help "put in a crop to carry themselves and their families through the next winter." With Lee gone, the remaining Confederate armies lost hope and gave up within two weeks. After four years, the war was over.

No one was more relieved than Lincoln, but his celebration was restrained. He told his cabinet that his postwar burdens would weigh almost as heavily as those of wartime. Seeking a distraction, Lincoln attended Ford's The-atre on the evening of Good Friday, April 14, 1865. John Wilkes Booth, an actor with southern sympathies, slipped into the president's box and shot Lincoln in the head. He died at 7:22 the following morning. Vice President Andrew Johnson became president. The man who had led the nation through the war would not lead it during the postwar search for a just peace.

► **REVIEW**   Why were the siege of Vicksburg and the battle of Gettysburg crucial to the outcome of the war?

Conclusion: The Second American Revolution

A transformed nation emerged from the crucible of war. Antebellum America was decentralized politically and loosely integrated economically. To bend the resources of the country to a Union victory, Congress enacted legislation that reshaped the nation's political and economic character. It created a national currency and banking system and turned to free land, a transcontinental railroad, and miles of telegraph lines to bind the West to the rest of the nation. Congress also established the sovereignty of the federal government and permanently increased its power. To most citizens before the war, Washington meant the local post office and little more. During the war, the federal government drafted, taxed, and judged Americans in unprecedented ways. The massive changes brought about by the war—the creation of a national government, a national economy, and a national spirit—led one historian to call the American Civil War the "Second American Revolution."

The Civil War also had a profound effect on individual lives. When the war began in 1861, millions of men dropped their hoes, hammers, and pencils; put on blue or gray uniforms; and fought and suffered for what they passionately believed was right. The war disrupted families, leaving women at home with additional responsibilities while offering new opportunities to others for wartime work in factories, offices, and hospitals. It offered blacks new and more effective ways to resist slavery and agitate for equality.

The war devastated the South. Three-fourths of southern white men of military age served in the Confederate army, and at least half of them were captured, wounded, or killed or died of disease. The war destroyed two-fifths of the South's livestock, wrecked half of the farm machinery, and blackened dozens of cities and towns. The immediate impact of the war on the North was more paradoxical. The struggle cost the North a heavy price: 373,000 lives. But rather than devastating the land, the war set the countryside and cities humming with business activity. The radical shift in power from South to North signaled a new direction in American development: the long decline of agriculture and the rise of industrial capitalism.

Most revolutionary of all, the war ended slavery. Ironically, the South's war to preserve slavery destroyed it. Nearly 200,000 black men, including ex-slave William Gould, dedicated their wartime service to its eradication. Because slavery was both a labor and a racial system, the institution was entangled in almost every aspect of southern life. Slavery's uprooting inevitably meant fundamental change. But the full meaning of abolition remained unclear in 1865. Determining the new economic, political, and social status of nearly 4 million ex-slaves would be the principal task of reconstruction.

REVIEWING THE CHAPTER

Use the questions and timeline to review and strengthen your understanding of the chapter.

REVIEW QUESTIONS

1. Why did both the Union and the Confederacy consider control of the border states crucial? (pp. 440–42)

2. Why did the South believe it could win the war despite numerical disadvantages? (pp. 443–47)

3. Why did the Confederacy's bid for international support fail? (pp. 448–54)

4. Why did the Union change policy in 1863 to allow black men to serve in the army? (pp. 454–59)

5. How did wartime hardship in the South contribute to class animosity? (pp. 459–62)

6. Why was the U.S. Congress able to pass such a bold legislative agenda during the war? (pp. 462–65)

7. Why were the siege of Vicksburg and the battle of Gettysburg crucial to the outcome of the war? (pp. 466–70)

MAKING CONNECTIONS

1. Despite loathing slavery, Lincoln embraced emancipation as a war objective late and with great caution. Why? In your answer, trace the progression of Lincoln's position, considering how legal, political, military, and moral concerns influenced his policies.

2. The Emancipation Proclamation did not accomplish the destruction of slavery on its own. How did a war over union bring about the end of slavery? In your answer, consider the direct actions of slaves and Union policymakers as well as indirect factors within the Confederacy.

3. In addition to restoring the Union and destroying slavery, what other significant changes did the war produce on the home front and in the nation's capital? In your answer, discuss economic, governmental, and social developments, being attentive to regional variations.

4. Brilliant military strategy alone did not determine the outcome of the war; victory also depended on generating revenue, materiel mobilization, diplomacy, and politics. In light of these considerations, explain why the Confederacy believed it would succeed and why it ultimately failed.

TIMELINE

1861
- **April.** Attack on Fort Sumter.
- **April–May.** Four Upper South states join Confederacy.
- **July.** Union forces routed in first battle of Bull Run.
- **August.** First Confiscation Act.

1862
- **February.** Grant captures Fort Henry and Fort Donelson.
- **March.** Confederates defeated at battle of Glorieta Pass.
- Union victory at battle of Pea Ridge.
- **April.** Battle of Shiloh in Tennessee ends Confederate bid to control Mississippi valley.
- Confederate Congress authorizes draft.
- **May.** Homestead Act.
- **May–July.** Union forces defeated during Virginia peninsula campaign.
- **July.** Second Confiscation Act.
- Militia Act.
- **September.** Battle of Antietam stops Lee's advance into Maryland.

1863
- **January.** Emancipation Proclamation becomes law.
- **February.** National Banking Act.
- **March.** Congress authorizes draft.
- **July.** Fall of Vicksburg to Union forces.
- Lee defeated at battle of Gettysburg.
- New York City antidraft riots.

1864
- **March.** Grant appointed Union general in chief.
- **May–June.** Wilderness campaign.
- **September.** Fall of Atlanta to Sherman.
- **November.** Lincoln reelected.
- **December.** Fall of Savannah to Sherman.

1865
- **April 2–3.** Fall of Petersburg and Richmond.
- **April 9.** Lee surrenders to Grant.
- **April 15.** Lincoln dies from bullet wound; Vice President Andrew Johnson becomes president.

▶ **For an online bibliography, practice quizzes, Web sites, images, and documents related to this chapter,** see the Book Companion Site at **bedfordstmartins.com/roark.**

▶ **For firsthand accounts of this period,** see Chapter 15 in Michael Johnson, ed., *Reading the American Past,* Fourth Edition.

16
CHAPTER

Reconstruction
1863–1877

I N 1856, JOHN RAPIER, a free black barber in Florence, Alabama, urged his four freeborn sons to flee the increasingly repressive and dangerous South. Searching for a color-blind society, three of the brothers scattered to New York, California, and Panama. The fourth, James T. Rapier, chose Canada, where he went to live with his uncle in a largely black community and studied Greek and Latin in a log schoolhouse. After his conversion at a Methodist revival, James wrote to his father: "I have not thrown a card in 3 years[,] touched a woman in 2 years[,] smoked nor drunk any Liquor in going on 2 years." And he vowed, "I will endeavor to do my part in solving the problems [of African Americans] in my native land."

The approaching Union victory in the Civil War gave James Rapier the opportunity to redeem his pledge. Defeat promised to turn the South upside down. With the Confederacy dead and slavery gone, blacks could push for equality. A few months before the war ended, after eight years of exile, the twenty-seven-year-old Rapier returned to the South. He participated in a freedmen's convention in Tennessee and then went home to Alabama, where he presided over the first political gathering of former slaves in the state. The Alabama freedmen produced a petition that called on the federal government to thoroughly reconstruct the South, to grant blacks the vote, and to guarantee free speech, free press, free schools, and equal rights for all men, regardless of color.

Rapier soon discovered that Alabama's whites found it agonizingly difficult to accept defeat and black freedom. They responded to the revolutionary changes under the banner "White Man—Right or Wrong—Still the White Man!" In 1868, when Rapier and other Alabama blacks vigorously supported the Republican

James T. Rapier

Only two years after emancipation, ex-slaves in the United States gained full political rights and wielded far more political power than former bondsmen anywhere else in the New World. Black suffrage sent fourteen African American congressmen to Washington, D.C., during Reconstruction, among them James T. Rapier of Alabama. Temporarily at least, he and his black colleagues helped shape post-emancipation society.

Alabama Department of Archives and History.

presidential candidate, former Union general Ulysses S. Grant, the recently organized Ku Klux Klan went on a bloody rampage of whipping, burning, and shooting. In September, a mob of 150 outraged whites scoured Rapier's neighborhood seeking four black politicians they claimed were trying to "Africanize Alabama." They caught and hanged three, but the "nigger carpetbagger from Canada" escaped. Badly shaken, Rapier considered fleeing the state, but he decided to stay and fight.

Tall, handsome, knowledgeable, and quick-witted, Rapier emerged in the early 1870s as Alabama's most prominent black leader. He demanded that the federal government end the violence against ex-slaves and guarantee their civil rights. He called for debt relief for black sharecroppers and tenant farmers, the end of racial segregation in public places, and land for freedmen. In 1872, he won election to the House of Representatives and joined six other black congressmen in Washington, D.C. Even those who sought to destroy him and overthrow so-called "Negro rule" admitted that Rapier was "the best intellect under a colored skin in Alabama." Defeated for reelection in 1874 in a fraudulent campaign of violence and ballot box stuffing, Rapier turned to cotton farming, generously giving thousands of dollars of his profits to black schools and churches.

Rapier's black constituents celebrated him as a hero, but in the eyes of dominant whites, he was "nothing but a nigger." Embittered by persistent black poverty and illiteracy, demoralized by continuing racial violence and a federal government that refused to stop it, Rapier again chose exile. Kansas attracted him because of its millions of acres of cheap land and because it was, before the war, home to that fiery enemy of slavery John Brown. After more than a dozen trips scouting the possibilities in Kansas, Rapier purchased land and urged Alabama's blacks to escape with him. Buoyant and confident when he returned to Alabama in 1865, he had over the years grown profoundly pessimistic that blacks could ever achieve equality and prosperity in the South. In 1883, however, before he could leave Alabama, Rapier died of tuberculosis at the age of forty-five.

In 1865, Carl Schurz had foreseen many of the troubles Rapier would encounter in the postwar South. A Union general who undertook a fact-finding mission to the former Confederate states immediately after the war, Schurz concluded that the Civil War was "a revolution but half accomplished." Northern victory had freed the slaves, but it had not changed former slaveholders' minds about blacks' unfitness for freedom. Left to themselves, Schurz believed, whites would "introduce some new system of forced labor, not perhaps exactly slavery in its old form but something similar to it." To defend their freedom, Schurz concluded, blacks would need federal protection, land of their own, and voting rights. Until whites "cut loose from the past, it will be a dangerous experiment to put Southern society upon its own legs."

As Schurz discovered, the end of the war did not mean peace. The United States was one of only two societies in the New World in which slavery ended in bloody war. (The other was Haiti, where a slave revolt that began in 1791 eventually swept slavery away.) Not surprisingly, racial turmoil continued in the South after the armies quit fighting in 1865. The nation entered one of its most chaotic and conflicted eras—Reconstruction, a violent period that would define the defeated South's status within the Union and the meaning of freedom for ex-slaves.

The place of the South within the nation and the extent of black freedom were determined not only in Washington, D.C., where the federal government played an active role, but also in the state legislatures and county seats of the South, where blacks participated in the process. Moreover, on farms and plantations from Virginia to Texas, ex-slaves struggled to become free people while ex-slaveholders clung to the Old South.

In the midst of Reconstruction's racial flux and economic chaos, a small band of crusading women sought to achieve gender equality. Their attempts to secure voting rights for women as well as blacks were blunted, and they soon turned their attention solely to the feminist cause.

Reconstruction witnessed a gigantic struggle to determine the consequences of Confederate defeat and **emancipation**. In the end, white Southerners prevailed. Their **New South** was a different South from the one to which most whites wished to return but also vastly unlike the one of which James Rapier dreamed.

Wartime Reconstruction

Reconstruction did not wait for the end of war. As the odds of a northern victory increased, thinking about reunification quickened. Immediately, a question arose: Who had authority to devise a plan for reconstructing the Union? President Abraham Lincoln believed firmly that reconstruction was a matter of executive responsibility. Congress just as firmly asserted its jurisdiction. Fueling the argument about who had the authority to set the terms of reconstruction were significant differences about the terms themselves. Lincoln's primary aim was the restoration of national unity, which he sought through a program of speedy, forgiving political reconciliation. Congress feared that the president's program amounted to restoring the old southern ruling class to power. It wanted greater assurances of white loyalty and greater guarantees of black rights.

In their eagerness to formulate a plan for political reunification, neither Lincoln nor Congress gave much attention to the South's land and labor problems. But as the war rapidly eroded slavery and traditional plantation agriculture, Yankee military commanders in the Union-occupied areas of the Confederacy had no choice but to oversee the emergence of a new labor system.

"To Bind Up the Nation's Wounds"

On March 4, 1865, President Lincoln delivered his second inaugural address. He surveyed the history of the long, deadly war and then looked ahead to peace. "With malice toward none; with charity for all; with firmness in the right, as God gives us to see the right," Lincoln said, "let us strive on to finish the work we are in; to bind up the nation's wounds . . . to do all which may achieve and cherish a just, and a lasting peace." Lincoln had contemplated reunion for nearly two years. While deep compassion for the enemy guided his thinking about peace, his plan for reconstruction aimed primarily at shortening the war and ending slavery.

In his Proclamation of Amnesty and Reconstruction, issued in December 1863, Lincoln offered a full pardon to rebels willing to renounce secession and to accept emancipation. (Pardons were valuable because they restored all property, except slaves, and full political rights.) His offer excluded only high-ranking Confederate military and political officers and a few other groups. When merely 10 percent of a state's voting population had taken an oath of allegiance, the state could organize a new government. Lincoln's plan did not require ex-rebels to extend social or political rights to ex-slaves, nor did it anticipate a program of long-term federal assistance to freedmen. Clearly, the president looked forward to the speedy restoration of the broken Union.

Lincoln's easy terms enraged abolitionists such as Wendell Phillips of Boston, who charged that the president "makes the negro's freedom a mere sham." He "is willing that the negro should be free but seeks nothing else for him," Phillips declared. He compared Lincoln to the most passive of the Civil War generals: "What McClellan was on the battlefield—'Do as little hurt as possible!'—Lincoln is in civil affairs—'Make as little change as possible!'" Phillips and other northern radicals called instead for a thorough overhaul of southern society. Their ideas proved to be too drastic for most Republicans during the war years, but Congress agreed that Lincoln's plan was inadequate. In July 1864, Congress put forward a plan of its own.

Congressman Henry Winter Davis of Maryland and Senator Benjamin Wade of Ohio jointly sponsored a bill that demanded that at least half of the voters in a conquered rebel state take the oath of allegiance before reconstruction could begin. Moreover, the Wade-Davis bill banned all ex-Confederates from participating in the drafting of new state constitutions. Finally, the bill guaranteed the equality of freedmen before the law. Congress's reconstruction would be neither as quick nor as forgiving as Lincoln's. When Lincoln exercised his right not to sign the bill and let it die instead, Wade and Davis charged the president with usurpation of power. They warned Lincoln to confine himself to "his executive duties—to obey and execute, not make the laws—to suppress by arms armed rebellion, and leave political organization to Congress."

Undeterred, Lincoln continued to nurture the formation of loyal state governments under his own plan. Four states—Louisiana, Arkansas, Tennessee, and Virginia—fulfilled the president's requirements, but Congress refused to seat representatives from the "Lincoln states." In his last public address in April 1865, Lincoln defended his plan but for the first time expressed publicly his endorsement of **suffrage** for southern blacks, at least "the very intelligent, and . . . those who serve our cause as soldiers." The announcement demonstrated that Lincoln's thinking about reconstruction was still evolving. Four days later, he was dead.

Land and Labor

Of all the problems raised by the North's victory in the war, none proved more critical than the South's transition from slavery to **free labor**. As federal armies invaded and occupied the Confederacy, hundreds of thousands of slaves became free workers. Union armies controlled vast territories in the South where legal title to land had become unclear. The wartime Confiscation Acts punished "traitors" by taking away their property. The question of what to do with federally occupied land and how to organize labor on it engaged former slaves, former slaveholders, Union military commanders, and federal government officials long before the war ended.

Up and down the Mississippi valley, occupying federal troops announced a new labor code. The code required slaveholders to sign contracts with ex-slaves and to pay wages. It obligated employers to provide food, housing, and medical care. It outlawed whipping, but it reserved to the army the right to discipline blacks who refused to work. The code required black laborers to enter into contracts, work diligently, and remain subordinate and obedient. Military leaders clearly had no intention of promoting a social or economic revolution. Instead, they sought to restore plantation agriculture with wage labor. The effort resulted in a hybrid system that one contemporary called "compulsory free labor," something that satisfied no one. Depending on one's point of view, it provided either too little or too much of a break with the past.

Planters complained because the new system fell short of slavery. Blacks could not be "transformed by proclamation," a Louisiana sugar planter warned. Yet under the new system, blacks "are expected to perform their new obligations without coercion, & without the fear of punishment which is essential to stimulate the idle and correct the vicious." Without the right to whip, he argued, the new labor system did not have a chance.

African Americans found the new regime too reminiscent of slavery to be called free labor. Its chief deficiency, they believed, was the failure to provide them with land of their own. "What's the use of being free if you don't own land enough to be buried in?" one man asked. Freedmen believed they had a moral right to land because they and their ancestors had worked it without compensation for more than two centuries. Moreover, several wartime developments led them to believe that the federal government planned to undergird black freedom with landownership.

In January 1865, General William Tecumseh Sherman set aside part of the coast south of Charleston for black settlement. He devised the plan to relieve himself of the burden of thousands of impoverished blacks who trailed desperately after his army. By June 1865, some 40,000 freedmen sat on 400,000 acres of "Sherman land." In addition, in March 1865, Congress passed a bill establishing the Bureau of Refugees, Freedmen, and Abandoned Lands. The Freedmen's Bureau, as it was called, distributed food and clothing to destitute Southerners and eased the transition of blacks from slaves to free persons. Congress also authorized the agency to divide abandoned and confiscated land into 40-acre plots, to rent them to freedmen, and eventually to sell them "with such title as the United States can convey." By June 1865, the bureau had situated nearly 10,000 black families on a half million acres abandoned by fleeing planters. Hundreds of thousands of other ex-slaves eagerly anticipated farms of their own.

Despite the flurry of activity, wartime reconstruction failed to produce agreement about whether the president or Congress had the authority to devise and direct policy or what proper policy should be. As Lincoln anticipated, the nation faced postwar dilemmas almost as trying as those of the war.

The African American Quest for Autonomy

Ex-slaves never had any doubt about what they wanted from freedom. They had only to contemplate what they had been denied as slaves. Slaves had to remain on their plantations; freedom allowed blacks to go wherever they pleased. Thus, in the first heady weeks after emancipation, freedmen often abandoned their plantations just to see what was on the other side of the hill. Slaves had to be at work in the fields by dawn; freedom permitted blacks to taste the formerly forbidden pleasure of sleeping through a sunrise. Freedmen also tested the etiquette of racial subordination. "Lizzie's maid passed me today when I was coming from church *without speaking to me*," huffed one plantation mistress.

To whites, emancipation looked like pure anarchy. Blacks, they said, had reverted to their natural condition: lazy, irresponsible, and wild. Without the discipline of slavery, whites predicted, blacks would go the way of "the Indian and the buffalo." Actually, former slaves were experimenting with freedom, but they could not long afford to roam the countryside, neglect work, and casually provoke whites. Soon, most were back at work in whites' kitchens and fields.

But other items on ex-slaves' agenda of freedom endured. They continued to dream of land and economic independence. "The way we can best take care of ourselves is to have land," one former slave declared in 1865, "and turn it and till it by our own labor." Another explained that he wanted land, "not a Master or owner[,] Neither a driver with his Whip."

Antebellum southern whites had deliberately kept blacks illiterate, and freedmen wanted to learn to read and write. Many black soldiers had become literate in the Union army, and they understood the value of the pen and book. "I wishes the Childern all in School," one black veteran asserted. "It is beter for them then to be their Surveing a mistes [mistress]."

Moreover, bondage had denied slaves secure family lives, and the restoration of their families became a persistent black aspiration. Thousands of black men and women took to the roads in 1865 to look for kin who had been sold away or to free those who were being held illegally as slaves. A black soldier from Missouri wrote his daughters that he was coming for them. "I will have you if it cost me my life," he declared. "Your Miss Kitty said that I tried to steal you," he told them. "But I'll let her know that god never intended for a man to steal his own flesh and blood." And he swore that "if she meets me with ten thousand soldiers, she [will] meet her enemy."

Another hunger was for independent worship. African Americans greeted freedom with a mass exodus from white churches, where they had been required to worship when slaves. Some joined the newly established southern branches of all-black northern churches, such as the African Methodist Episcopal Church. Others formed black versions of the major southern denominations, Baptists and Methodists. Slaves had comprehended their tribulations through the lens of their deeply felt Christian faith, and freedmen continued to interpret the events of the Civil War and reconstruction as people of faith. One black woman thanked Lincoln for the Emancipation Proclamation, declaring, "When you are dead and in Heaven, in a thousand years that action of yours will make the Angels sing your praises I know it."

> ►**REVIEW**   Why did Congress object to Lincoln's wartime plan for reconstruction?

Presidential Reconstruction

Abraham Lincoln died on April 15, 1865, just hours after John Wilkes Booth shot him at a Washington, D.C., theater. Chief Justice Salmon P. Chase immediately administered the oath of office to Vice President Andrew Johnson of Tennessee.

Congress had adjourned in March, which meant that legislators were away from Washington when Lincoln was killed. They would not reconvene until December. Throughout the summer and fall, therefore, the "accidental president" made critical decisions about the future of the South without congressional advice. Like Lincoln, Johnson believed that responsibility for restoring the Union lay with the president. With dizzying speed, he drew up and executed a plan of reconstruction.

Congress returned to the capital in December to find that, as far as the president and former Confederates were concerned, reconstruction was already decided. Most Republicans, however, thought Johnson's modest demands of ex-rebels made a mockery of the sacrifice of Union soldiers. Instead of honoring the dead by insisting on "a new birth of freedom," as Lincoln had promised in his 1863 speech at Gettysburg, Johnson had acted as midwife to the rebirth of the Old South and the stillbirth of black **liberty**. To let his program stand, Republican legislators said, would mean that the North's dead had indeed died in vain. They proceeded to dismantle it and substitute a program of their own, one that southern whites found ways to resist.

Johnson's Program of Reconciliation

Born in 1808 in Raleigh, North Carolina, Andrew Johnson was the son of illiterate parents. Self-educated and ambitious, Johnson moved to Tennessee, where he worked as a tailor, accumulated a fortune in land, acquired five slaves, and built a career in politics championing the South's common white people and assailing its "illegitimate, swaggering, bastard, scrub aristocracy." The only senator from a Confederate state to remain loyal to the Union, Johnson held the planter class responsible for secession. Less than two weeks before he became president, he made it clear what he would do to planters if he ever had the chance: "I would arrest them—I would try them—I would convict them and I would hang them."

Despite such statements, Johnson was no friend of the Republicans. A southern Democrat all his life, Johnson occupied the White House only because the Republican Party in 1864 had needed a vice presidential candidate who would appeal to loyal, Union-supporting Democrats. Johnson favored traditional Democratic causes, vigorously defending **states' rights** (but not secession) and opposing Republican efforts to expand the power of the federal government. A steadfast defender of slavery, Johnson had owned slaves until 1862, when Tennessee rebels, angry at his Unionism, confiscated them. He only grudgingly accepted emancipation. When he did, it was more because he hated planters than sympathized with slaves. "Damn the negroes," he said. "I am fighting those traitorous aristocrats, their masters." At a time when the nation confronted the future of black Americans, the new president harbored unshakable racist convictions. Africans, Johnson said, were "inferior to the white man in point of intellect—better calculated in physical structure to undergo drudgery and hardship."

Like Lincoln, Johnson stressed reconciliation between the Union and the defeated Confederacy and rapid restoration of civil government in the South. Like Lincoln, he promised to pardon most, but not all, ex-rebels. Johnson recognized the state governments created by Lincoln but set out his own requirements for restoring the other rebel states to the Union. All that the citizens of a state had to do was to renounce the right of secession, deny that the debts of the Confederacy were legal and binding, and ratify the Thirteenth Amendment abolishing slavery, which became part of the Constitution in December 1865. Johnson's plan ignored Lincoln's acceptance near the end of his life of some form of limited black voting.

Johnson's eagerness to restore relations with southern states and his lack of sympathy for blacks also led him to return to pardoned ex-Confederates all confiscated and abandoned land, even if it was in the hands of freedmen. Reformers were shocked. They had expected the president's hatred of planters to mean the permanent confiscation of the South's plantations and the distribution of the land to loyal freedmen. Instead, his instructions canceled the promising beginnings made by General Sherman and the Freedmen's Bureau to settle blacks on land of their own. As one freedman observed, "Things was hurt by Mr. Lincoln getting killed."

White Southern Resistance and Black Codes

In the summer of 1865, delegates across the South gathered to draw up the new state constitutions required by Johnson's plan of reconstruction. Rather than take their medicine, delegates choked on even the president's mild requirements. Refusing to renounce secession, the South Carolina and Georgia conventions merely "repudiated" their secession ordinances, preserving in principle their right to secede. South Carolina and Mississippi refused to disown their Confederate war debts. Mississippi rejected the Thirteenth Amendment outright, and Alabama rejected it in part. Despite these defiant acts, Johnson did nothing. By failing to draw a hard line, he rekindled southern resistance. White Southerners began to think that by standing up for themselves they—not victorious Northerners—would shape reconstruction. In the fall of 1865, newly elected southern legislators set out to reverse what they considered the "retreat into barbarism" that followed emancipation.

State governments across the South adopted a series of laws known as *black codes*, which made a travesty of black freedom. The codes sought to keep ex-slaves subordinate to whites by subjecting them to every sort of discrimination. Several states made it illegal for blacks to own a gun. Mississippi made insulting gestures and language by blacks a criminal offense. The codes barred blacks from jury duty. Not a single southern state granted any black—no matter how educated, wealthy, or refined—the right to vote.

At the core of the black codes, however, lay the matter of labor. Faced with the death of slavery, legislators sought to hustle freedmen back to the plantations.

South Carolina attempted to limit blacks to either farmwork or domestic service by requiring them to pay annual taxes of $10 to $100 to work in any other occupation. Mississippi declared that blacks who did not possess written evidence of employment could be declared vagrants and be subject to involuntary plantation labor. Most states allowed judges to bind black children—orphans and others whose parents they deemed unable to support them—to white employers. Under these so-called apprenticeship laws, courts bound thousands of black children to work for planter "guardians."

Johnson refused to intervene. A staunch defender of states' rights, he believed that the citizens of every state, even those who attempted to destroy the Union, should be free to write their own constitutions and laws. Moreover, since Johnson was as eager as other white Southerners to restore white supremacy and black subordination, the black codes did not offend him.

But Johnson also followed the path that he believed would offer him the greatest political return. A **conservative** Tennessee Democrat at the head of a northern Republican Party, he began to look southward for political allies. Despite tough talk about punishing traitors, he personally pardoned fourteen thousand wealthy or high-ranking ex-Confederates. By pardoning powerful whites, by acquiescing in the black codes, and by accepting governments even when they failed to satisfy his minimal demands, he won useful southern friends.

In the fall elections of 1865, white Southerners dramatically expressed their mood. To represent them in Congress, they chose former Confederates, not loyal Unionists. Of the eighty senators and representatives they sent to Washington, fifteen had served in the Confederate army, ten of them as generals.

Confederate Flag Dress

While politicians debated the future of the South, white Southerners were coming to grips with the reality of Confederate defeat. They began to refer to their failure to secede from the Union as the "Lost Cause." They enshrined the memory of former Confederates, and they made a fetish of the Confederate flag, as shown by this dress, made from material embossed with the flag.

Valentine Museum, Cook Collection.

Another sixteen had served in civil and judicial posts in the Confederacy. Nine others had served in the Confederate Congress. One—Alexander Stephens—had been vice president of the Confederacy. In December, this remarkable group arrived on the steps of the nation's Capitol building to be seated in Congress. As one Georgian remarked, "It looked as though Richmond had moved to Washington."

Expansion of Federal Authority and Black Rights

Southerners had blundered monumentally. They had assumed that what Andrew Johnson was willing to accept, Republicans would accept as well. But southern intransigence compelled even moderates to conclude that ex-rebels were a "generation of vipers," still untrustworthy and dangerous. So angry were Republicans with the rebels that the federal government refused to supply artificial limbs to disabled Southerners, as they did for Union veterans.

The black codes became a symbol of southern intentions to "restore all of slavery but its name." Northerners were hardly saints when it came to racial justice, but black freedom had become a hallowed war aim. "We tell the white men of Mississippi," the *Chicago Tribune* roared, "that the men of the North will convert the State of Mississippi into a frog pond before they will allow such laws to disgrace one foot of the soil in which the bones of our soldiers sleep and over which the flag of freedom waves."

The moderate majority of the Republican Party wanted only assurance that slavery and treason were dead. They did not champion black equality or the confiscation of plantations or black voting, as did the radicals, a minority within the party. But southern obstinacy had succeeded in forging unity (at least temporarily) among Republican factions. In December 1865, exercising Congress's right to determine the qualifications of its members, Republicans refused to seat the southern representatives. Rather than accept Johnson's claim that the "work of restoration" was done, Congress challenged his executive power. Congressional Republicans enjoyed a three-to-one majority over the Democrats, and if they could agree on a program of reconstruction, they could easily pass legislation and even override presidential vetoes.

Senator Lyman Trumbull of Illinois declared that the president's policy meant that the ex-slave would "be tyrannized over, abused, and virtually reenslaved without some legislation by the nation for his protection." Early in 1866, the moderates produced two bills that strengthened the federal shield. The first, the Freedmen's Bureau bill, prolonged the life of the agency established by the previous Congress. Since the end of the war, it had distributed food, supervised labor contracts, and sponsored schools for freedmen. Arguing that the Constitution never contemplated a "system for the support of indigent persons," President Andrew Johnson vetoed the bill. Congress failed by a narrow margin to override the president's veto.

The moderates designed their second measure, the Civil Rights Act, to nullify the black codes by affirming African Americans' rights to "full and equal benefit of all laws and proceedings for the security of person and property as is enjoyed by white citizens." The act boldly required the end of legal discrimination in state laws and represented an extraordinary expansion of black rights and federal authority. The president argued that the civil rights bill amounted to "unconstitutional invasion of states' rights" and vetoed it. In essence, he denied that the federal government possessed the authority to protect the civil rights of blacks.

In April 1866, an incensed Republican Party again pushed the civil rights bill through Congress and overrode the presidential veto. In July, it passed another Freedmen's Bureau bill and overrode Johnson's veto. For the first time in American history, Congress had overridden presidential vetoes of major legislation. As a worried South Carolinian observed, Johnson had succeeded in uniting the Republicans and probably touched off "a fight this fall such as has never been seen."

▶**REVIEW**   How did the North respond to the passage of black codes in the southern states?

Congressional Reconstruction

By the summer of 1866, President Andrew Johnson and Congress had dropped their gloves and stood toe-to-toe in a bare-knuckle contest unprecedented in American history. Johnson made it clear that he would not budge on either constitutional issues or policy. Moderate Republicans responded by amending the Constitution. But the obstinacy of Johnson and white Southerners pushed Republican moderates ever closer to the radicals and to acceptance of additional federal intervention in the South. In time, Congress debated whether to give the ballot to black men. Congress also voted to impeach the president. Outside of Congress, blacks championed color-blind voting rights, while women sought to make voting sex-blind as well.

The Fourteenth Amendment and Escalating Violence

In June 1866, Congress passed the Fourteenth Amendment to the Constitution, and two years later it gained the necessary ratification of three-fourths of the states. The most important provisions of this complex amendment made all native-born or naturalized persons American citizens and prohibited states from abridging the "privileges and immunities" of citizens, depriving them of "life, liberty, or property without due process of law," and denying them "equal protection of the laws." By making blacks national citizens, the amendment provided a national guarantee of equality before the law. In essence, it protected blacks against violation by southern state governments.

The Fourteenth Amendment also dealt with voting rights. It gave Congress the right to reduce the congressional representation of states that withheld suffrage from some of its adult male population. In other words, white Southerners could either allow black men to vote or see their representation in Washington slashed.

Whatever happened, Republicans stood to benefit from the Fourteenth Amendment. If southern whites granted voting rights to freedmen, Republicans, entirely a northern party, would gain valuable black votes, establish a wing in the South, and secure their national power. If whites refused, representation of southern Democrats would plunge, and Republicans would still gain political power.

The Fourteenth Amendment's suffrage provisions completely ignored the small band of politicized and energized women who had emerged from the war demanding "the ballot for the two disenfranchised classes, negroes and women." Founding the American Equal Rights Association in 1866, Susan B. Anthony and Elizabeth Cady Stanton lobbied for "a government by the people, and the whole people; for the people and the whole people." They felt betrayed when their old antislavery allies, who now occupied positions of national power, proved to be fickle and refused to work for their goals. "It was the Negro's hour," Frederick Douglass later explained. Senator Charles Sumner suggested that woman suffrage could be "the great question of the future."

The Fourteenth Amendment dashed women's expectations. It provided for punishment of any state that excluded voters on the basis of race but not on the basis of sex. The amendment also introduced the word *male* into the Constitution when it referred to a citizen's right to vote. Stanton predicted that "if that word 'male' be inserted, it will take us a century at least to get it out."

Tennessee approved the Fourteenth Amendment in July, and Congress promptly welcomed the state's representatives and senators back. Had President Johnson counseled other southern states to ratify this relatively mild amendment and warned them that they faced the fury of an outraged Republican Party if they refused, they might have listened. Instead, Johnson advised Southerners to reject the Fourteenth Amendment and to rely on him to trounce the Republicans in the fall congressional elections.

Johnson had decided to make the Fourteenth Amendment the overriding issue of the 1866 congressional elections and to gather its white opponents into a new conservative party, the National Union Party. The president's strategy suffered a setback when whites in several southern cities went on rampages against blacks— an escalation of the violence that had never really ceased. When a mob in New Orleans assaulted delegates to a black suffrage convention, thirty-four blacks died. In Memphis, white mobs crashed through the black sections of town, killing at least forty-six people. The slaughter shocked Northerners and renewed skepticism about Johnson's claim that southern whites could be trusted. "Who doubts that the Freedmen's Bureau ought to be abolished forthwith," a New Yorker observed sarcastically, "and the blacks remitted to the paternal care of their old masters, who 'understand the nigger, you know, a great deal better than the Yankees can.'"

The 1866 elections resulted in an overwhelming Republican victory in which the party retained its three-to-one congressional majority. Johnson had bet that Northerners would not support federal protection of black rights and that a racist backlash would blast the Republican Party. But the war was still fresh in northern minds, and as one Republican explained, southern whites "with all their intelligence were traitors, the blacks with all their ignorance were loyal."

Radical Reconstruction and Military Rule

The 1866 election should have taught southern whites the folly of relying on Andrew Johnson to guide them through reconstruction. But when Johnson continued to urge Southerners to reject the Fourteenth Amendment, every southern state except Tennessee voted it down. "The last one of the sinful ten," thundered Representative James A. Garfield of Ohio, "has flung back into our teeth the magnanimous offer of a generous nation." After the South rejected the moderates' program, the radicals seized the initiative.

Each act of defiance by southern whites had boosted the standing of the radicals within the Republican Party. Except for freedmen themselves, no one did more to make freedom the "mighty moral question of the age." Radicals such as Massachusetts senator Charles Sumner and Pennsylvania representative Thaddeus Stevens did not speak with a single voice, but they united in demanding civil and political equality. They insisted on extending to ex-slaves the same opportunities that northern working people enjoyed under the free-labor system. Southern states were "like clay in the hands of the potter," Stevens declared in January 1867, and he called on Congress to begin reconstruction all over again.

In March 1867, Congress overturned the Johnson state governments and initiated military rule of the South. The Military Reconstruction Act (and three subsequent acts) divided the ten unreconstructed Confederate states into five military districts. Congress placed a Union general in charge of each district and instructed him to "suppress insurrection, disorder, and violence" and to begin political reform. After the military had completed voter registration, which would include black men, voters in each state would elect delegates to conventions that would draw up new state constitutions. Each constitution would guarantee black suffrage. When the voters of each state had approved the constitution and the state legislature had ratified the Fourteenth Amendment, the state could submit its work to Congress. If Congress approved, the state's senators and representatives could be seated, and political reunification would be accomplished.

Radicals proclaimed the provision for black suffrage "a prodigious triumph," for it extended far beyond the limited suffrage provisions of the Fourteenth Amendment. Republicans united in the conviction that only the voting power of ex-slaves could bring about a permanent revolution in the South. Indeed, suffrage provided blacks with a powerful instrument of change and self-protection. When combined with the **disfranchisement** of thousands of ex-rebels, it promised to cripple any neo-Confederate resurgence and guarantee Republican state governments in the South.

Despite its bold suffrage provision, the Military Reconstruction Act of 1867 disappointed those who advocated the confiscation and redistribution of southern plantations to ex-slaves. Thaddeus Stevens, who believed that at bottom reconstruction was an economic problem, agreed with the freedman who said, "Give us our own land and we take care of ourselves, but without land, the old masters can hire us or starve us, as they please." But most Republicans believed they had already provided blacks with what they needed: equal legal rights and the ballot. If blacks were to get forty acres, as some freedmen had in 1865 when Sherman distributed forty-acre lots, they would have to gain the land themselves.

Declaring that he would rather sever his right arm than sign such a formula for "anarchy and chaos," Andrew Johnson vetoed the Military Reconstruction Act. Congress overrode his veto the very same day, dramatizing the shift in power from the executive to the legislative branch of government. With the passage of the Reconstruction Acts of 1867, congressional reconstruction was virtually completed. Congress left whites owning most of the South's land but, in a departure that justified the term "radical reconstruction," had given black men the ballot. In 1867, the nation began an unprecedented experiment in interracial **democracy**—at least in the South, for Congress's plan did not touch the North. But before the spotlight swung away from Washington to the South, the president and Congress had one more scene to play.

Impeaching a President

Despite his defeats, Andrew Johnson had no intention of yielding control of reconstruction. In a dozen ways, he sabotaged Congress's will and encouraged southern whites to resist. He issued a flood of pardons to undermine efforts at political and economic change. He waged war against the Freedmen's Bureau by removing officers who sympathized too much with ex-slaves. And he replaced Union generals eager to enforce Congress's Reconstruction Acts with conservative men eager to defeat them. Johnson claimed that he was merely defending the "violated Constitution." At bottom, however, the president subverted congressional reconstruction to protect southern whites from what he considered the horrors of "Negro domination."

When Congress realized that overriding Johnson's vetoes did not ensure that it got its way, it looked for other ways to exert its will. According to the Constitution, the House of Representatives can impeach and the Senate can try any federal official for "treason, bribery, or other high crimes and misdemeanors." Radicals argued that Johnson's abuse of constitutional powers and his failure to fulfill constitutional obligations to enforce the law were impeachable offenses. Moderates interpreted the constitutional provision to mean violation of criminal statutes. As long as Johnson refrained from breaking the law, **impeachment** remained a faint hope.

Then, in August 1867, Johnson suspended Secretary of War Edwin M. Stanton from office. As required by the Tenure of Office Act, which demanded the approval of the Senate for the removal of any government official who had been appointed with Senate approval, the president requested the Senate to consent to the dismissal. When the Senate balked, Johnson removed Stanton anyway. "Is the President crazy, or only drunk?" asked a dumbfounded Republican moderate. "I'm afraid his doings will make us all favor impeachment."

News of Johnson's open defiance of the law convinced every Republican in the House to vote for a resolution impeaching the president. Supreme Court chief justice Salmon Chase presided over the Senate trial, which lasted from March until May 1868. Chase refused to allow Johnson's opponents to raise broad issues of misuse of power and forced them to argue their case exclusively on the narrow legal grounds of Johnson's removal of Stanton. Johnson's lawyers argued that the president had not committed a criminal offense, that the Tenure of Office Act was unconstitutional, and that in any case it did not apply to Stanton, who had been appointed by Lincoln. When the critical vote came, 35 senators voted guilty and 19 not guilty. The impeachment forces fell one vote short of the two-thirds needed to convict.

Although Johnson survived, he did not come through the ordeal unscathed. After his trial, he called a truce, and for the remaining ten months of his term, congressional reconstruction proceeded unhindered by presidential interference. Without interference from Johnson, Congress revisited the suffrage issue.

The Fifteenth Amendment and Women's Demands

In February 1869, Republicans passed the Fifteenth Amendment to the Constitution, which prohibited states from depriving any citizen of the right to vote because of "race, color, or previous condition of servitude." The Reconstruction Acts of 1867 already required black suffrage in the South; the Fifteenth Amendment extended black voting nationwide. Partisan advantage played an important role in the amendment's passage. Gains by northern Democrats in the 1868 elections worried Republicans, and black voters now represented the balance of power in several northern states. By giving the ballot to northern blacks, Republicans could lessen their political vulnerability. As one Republican congressman observed, "Party expediency and exact justice coincide for once."

Some Republicans, however, found the final wording of the Fifteenth Amendment "lame and halting." Rather than absolutely guaranteeing the right to vote, the amendment merely prohibited exclusion on grounds of race. The distinction would prove to be significant. In time, inventive white Southerners would devise tests of literacy and property and other apparently nonracial measures that would effectively disfranchise blacks yet not violate the Fifteenth Amendment. But an amendment that fully guaranteed the right to vote courted defeat outside the South. Rising antiforeign sentiment—against the Chinese in

Major Reconstruction Legislation, 1865–1875

1865

Thirteenth Amendment (ratified 1865)	Abolishes slavery.

1865 and 1866

Freedmen's Bureau Acts	Establish the Freedmen's Bureau to distribute food and clothing to destitute Southerners and help freedmen with labor contracts and schooling.
Civil Rights Act of 1866	Affirms the rights of blacks to enjoy "full and equal benefit of all laws and proceedings for the security of person and property as is enjoyed by white citizens" and effectively requires the end of legal discrimination in state laws.
Fourteenth Amendment (ratified 1868)	Makes native-born blacks citizens and guarantees all citizens "equal protection of the laws." Threatens to reduce representatives of a state that denies suffrage to any of its male inhabitants.

1867

Military Reconstruction Acts	Impose military rule in the South, establish rules for readmission of ex-Confederate states to the Union, and require those states to guarantee the vote to black men.

1869

Fifteenth Amendment (ratified 1870)	Prohibits racial discrimination in voting rights in all states in the nation.

1875

Civil Rights Act of 1875	Outlaws racial discrimination in transportation, public accommodations, and juries.

California and European immigrants in the Northeast—caused states to resist giving up total control of suffrage requirements. (Because the vast majority of Native Americans became citizens only in 1924, the Fifteenth Amendment had little immediate impact on Indian voting.) In March 1870, after three-fourths of the states had ratified it, the Fifteenth Amendment became part of the Constitution. Republicans generally breathed a sigh of relief, confident that black suffrage was "the last great point that remained to be settled of the issues of the war."

Woman suffrage advocates, however, were sorely disappointed with the Fifteenth Amendment's failure to extend voting rights to women. Although women fought hard to include the word *sex* (as they had fought hard to keep the word *male* out of the Fourteenth Amendment), the amendment denied states the right to forbid suffrage only on the basis of race. Elizabeth Cady Stanton and Susan B. Anthony condemned the Republicans' "negro first" strategy and pointed out that women remained "the only class of citizens wholly unrepresented in the government." Black enfranchisement provoked racist statements from Stanton, who wondered aloud why ignorant black men should legislate for educated and cultured white women. Increasingly, activist women concluded that woman "must not put her trust in man." The Fifteenth Amendment severed the early **feminist** movement from its abolitionist roots. Over the next several decades, women would establish an independent suffrage crusade that drew millions of women into political life.

Republicans took enough satisfaction in the Fifteenth Amendment to promptly scratch the "Negro question" from the agenda of national politics. Even that steadfast crusader for equality Wendell Phillips concluded that the black man now held "sufficient shield in his own hands. . . . Whatever he suffers will be largely now, and in future, his own fault." Northerners had no idea of the violent struggles that lay ahead.

▶ **REVIEW**   Why did Johnson urge the southern states to reject the Fourteenth Amendment?

The Struggle in the South

Northerners believed they had discharged their responsibilities with the Reconstruction Acts and the amendments to the Constitution, but Southerners knew that the battle had just begun. Black suffrage established the foundation for the rise of the Republican Party in the South. Gathering together outsiders and outcasts, southern Republicans won elections, wrote new state constitutions, and formed new state governments.

Challenging the established class for political control was dangerous business. Equally dangerous were the confrontations that took place on farms and plantations in the southern countryside, where blacks sought to give practical, everyday meaning to their newly won legal and political equality. Ex-masters had their own ideas about the social and economic arrangements that should replace slavery. Freedom remained contested territory, and Southerners fought pitched battles with one another to determine the contours of their new world.

Freedmen, Yankees, and Yeomen

African Americans made up the majority of southern Republicans. After gaining voting rights in 1867, nearly every eligible black man registered to vote. Almost all black men registered as Republicans, grateful to the party that had freed them and granted them the **franchise**. In Monroe, Alabama, black men participating in their first political meeting pressed toward the speaker, crying "God bless you" and "Bless God for this." Black women, like white women, remained disfranchised but mobilized along with black men. In the 1868 presidential election, they bravely wore buttons supporting the Republican candidate, Ulysses S. Grant. Southern blacks did not have identical political priorities, but they united in their desire for education and equal treatment before the law.

Northern whites who made the South their home after the war were a second element of the South's Republican Party. Conservative white Southerners called them "carpetbaggers," men so poor that they could stuff all their earthly belongings in a single carpet-sided suitcase and swoop southward like buzzards to "fatten on our misfortunes." But most Northerners who moved south were restless, relatively well-educated young men who looked upon the South as they did the West—as a promising place to make a living. They expected that the South without slavery would prosper, and they wanted to be part of it. Northerners in the southern Republican Party consistently supported programs that encouraged vigorous economic development along the lines of the northern free-labor model.

Southern whites made up the third element of the South's Republican Party. Approximately one out of four white Southerners voted Republican. The other three condemned the one who did as a traitor to his region and his race and called him a "scalawag," a term for runty horses and low-down, good-for-nothing rascals. **Yeoman** farmers accounted for the majority of southern white Republicans. Some were Unionists who emerged from the war with bitter memories of Confederate persecution. Others were small farmers who wanted to end state governments' favoritism toward plantation owners. Yeomen usually supported initiatives for public schools and for expanding economic opportunity in the South.

The South's Republican Party, then, was made up of freedmen, Yankees, and yeomen—an improbable coalition. The mix of races, regions, and classes inevitably meant friction as each group maneuvered to define the party. But Reconstruction represents an extraordinary moment in American politics: Blacks and whites joined together in the Republican Party to pursue political change. Formally, of course, only men participated in politics—casting ballots and holding offices—but women also played a part in the political struggle by joining in parades and rallies, attending stump speeches, and even campaigning.

Reconstruction politics was not for cowards. Activity on behalf of Republicans in particular took courage. Most whites in the South condemned reconstruction politics as illegitimate and felt justified in doing whatever they could to stamp out Republicanism. Violence against blacks—the "white terror"—took brutal institutional form in 1866 with the formation in Tennessee of the Ku Klux Klan, a social club of Confederate veterans that quickly developed into a paramilitary organization supporting Democrats. The Klan went on a rampage of whipping, hanging, shooting, burning, and throat-cutting to defeat Republicans and restore white supremacy. Rapid demobilization of the Union army after the war left only twenty thousand troops to patrol the entire South, a vast territory. Without effective military protection, southern Republicans had to take care of themselves.

Republican Rule

In the fall of 1867, southern states held elections for delegates to state constitutional conventions, as required by the Reconstruction Acts. About 40 percent of the white electorate stayed home because they had been disfranchised or because

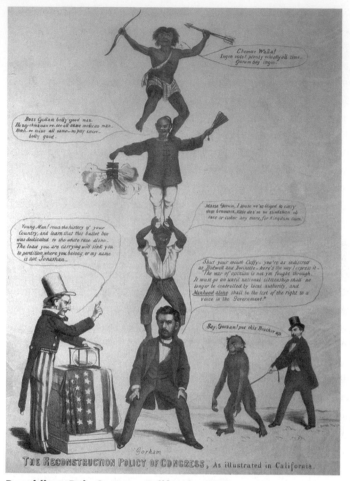

Republican Rule Cartoon, California, 1867
This racist Democratic cartoon from California ridicules Republican sup-
port of black suffrage, and it links black voting with the enfranchisement of
Chinese immigrants and Native Americans. Uncle Sam, on the left, admon-
ishes George C. Gorham, Republican candidate for governor: "Young
Man! Read the history of your Country, and learn that this ballot box
was dedicated to the white race alone." The black man, Chinese man, and
Indian all speak in dialects that confirm white racial stereotypes.
Library of Congress.

they had decided to boycott politics. Republicans won three-fourths of the seats.
About 15 percent of the Republican delegates to the conventions were Northerners who had moved south, 25 percent were African Americans, and 60 percent
were white Southerners. As a British visitor observed, the delegate elections
reflected "the mighty revolution that had taken place in America." But Democrats described the state conventions as zoos of "baboons, monkeys, mules . . . and

other jackasses." In fact, the conventions brought together serious, purposeful men who hammered out the legal framework for a new order.

The reconstruction constitutions introduced two broad categories of changes in the South: those that reduced aristocratic privilege and increased democratic equality and those that expanded the state's responsibility for the general welfare. In the first category, the constitutions adopted universal male suffrage, abolished property qualifications for holding office, and made more offices elective and fewer appointed. In the second category, they enacted prison reform; made the state responsible for caring for orphans, the insane, and the deaf and mute; and exempted debtors' homes from seizure.

These forward-looking state constitutions provided blueprints for a new South but stopped short of the specific reforms advocated by some. Despite the wishes of virtually every former slave, no southern constitution confiscated and redistributed land. And despite the prediction of Unionists that unless all former Confederates were banned from politics they would storm back and wreck reconstruction, no state constitution disfranchised ex-rebels wholesale.

Democrats, however, were blind to the limits of the Republican program. They thought they faced wild revolution. According to Democrats, Republican victories initiated "black and tan" (ex-slave and mulatto) governments across the South. But the claims of "Negro domination" had almost no validity. Although four out of five Republican voters were black men, more than four out of five Republican officeholders were white. Southerners sent fourteen black congressmen and two black senators to Washington, but only 6 percent of Southerners in Congress during Reconstruction were black. With the exception of South Carolina, where blacks briefly held a majority in one house of the legislature, no state experienced "Negro rule," despite black majorities in the populations of some states.

In almost every state, voters ratified the new constitutions and swept Republicans into power. When the former Confederate states ratified the Fourteenth Amendment, Congress readmitted them. Southern Republicans then turned to a staggering array of problems. Wartime destruction—burned cities, shattered bridges, broken levees—still littered the landscape. The South's share of the nation's wealth had fallen from 30 percent to only 12 percent. Manufacturing limped along at a fraction of prewar levels, agricultural production remained anemic, and the region's railroads lay devastated. Without the efforts of the Freedmen's Bureau, black and white Southerners would have starved. Making matters worse, racial harassment and reactionary violence dogged Southerners who sought reform. In this desperate context, Republicans struggled to breathe life into their new state governments.

Republican activity focused on three areas—education, civil rights, and economic development. Every state inaugurated a system of public education. Before the Civil War, whites had deliberately kept slaves illiterate, and planter-dominated governments rarely spent tax money to educate the children of

Students at a Freedmen's School in Virginia, circa 1870s
"The people are hungry and thirsty after knowledge," a former slave observed immediately after the Civil War. The students at this Virginia school stand in front of their log-cabin classroom reading books. For people long forbidden to learn to read and write, literacy symbolized freedom.
Valentine Museum, Cook Collection.

yeomen. By 1875, half of Mississippi's and South Carolina's eligible children (the majority of whom were black) were attending school. Despite underfunding and dilapidated facilities, literacy rates rose sharply. Although public schools were racially segregated, education remained for many blacks a tangible, deeply satisfying benefit of freedom and Republican rule.

State legislatures also attacked racial discrimination and defended civil rights. Republicans especially resisted efforts to segregate blacks from whites in public transportation. Mississippi levied fines of up to $1,000 and three years in jail for railroads and steamboats that pushed blacks, regardless of their ability to pay, into "smoking cars" or to lower decks. Refined, well-off blacks took particular aim at hotels and theaters that denied "full and equal rights." An exasperated Mississippian complained: "Education amounts to nothing, good behavior counts for nothing, even money cannot buy for a colored man or woman decent treatment and the comforts that white people claim and can obtain." But passing color-blind laws was one thing; enforcing them was another. Despite the laws, segregation—later called **Jim Crow**—developed at white insistence and became a feature of southern life long before the end of the Reconstruction era.

Republican governments also launched ambitious programs of economic development. They envisioned a South of diversified agriculture, roaring factories, and booming towns. Republican legislatures chartered scores of banks and industrial companies, appropriated funds to fix ruined levees and drain swamps, and went on a railroad-building binge. These efforts fell far short of solving the South's economic troubles, however. Republican spending to stimulate economic growth also meant rising taxes and enormous debt that drained funds from schools and other programs.

The southern Republicans' record, then, was mixed. To their credit, the biracial party took up under trying circumstances an ambitious agenda to change the South. Money was scarce, the Democrats continued their harassment, and factionalism threatened the Republican Party from within. However, corruption infected Republican governments in the South. Public morality reached new lows everywhere in the nation after the Civil War, and the chaos and disruption of the postwar South proved fertile soil for bribery, fraud, and influence peddling. Despite problems and shortcomings, however, the Republican Party made headway in its efforts to purge the South of aristocratic privilege and racist oppression. Republican governments had less success in overthrowing the long-established white oppression of black farm laborers in the rural South.

White Landlords, Black Sharecroppers

In the countryside, clashes occurred daily between ex-slaves who wished to escape slave labor and ex-masters who wanted to reinstitute old ways. Except for having to put down the whip and pay subsistence wages, planters had not been required to offer many concessions to emancipation. They continued to believe that African Americans were inherently lazy and would not work without coercion. Whites moved quickly to restore the antebellum world of work gangs, white overseers, field labor for black women and children, clustered cabins, minimal personal freedom, and even whipping whenever they could get away with it.

Ex-slaves resisted every effort to turn back the clock. They argued that if any class could be described as "lazy," it was the planters, who, as one ex-slave noted, "lived in idleness all their lives on stolen labor." Land of their own would anchor their economic independence, they believed, and end planters' interference in their personal lives. They could then, for example, make their own decisions about whether women and children would labor in the fields. Indeed, within months after the war, perhaps one-third of black women abandoned field labor to work on chores in their own cabins just as poor white women did. With freedom to decide how to use family time, hundreds of thousands of black children enrolled in school. But landownership proved to be beyond the reach of most blacks once the federal government abandoned plans to redistribute Confederate property. Without land, ex-slaves had little choice but to work on plantations.

Although they were forced to return to the planters' fields, freedmen resisted efforts to restore slavelike conditions. In his South Carolina neighborhood, David Golightly Harris discovered that few freedmen were "willing to hire by the day, month or year." Instead of working for wages, "the negroes all seem disposed to rent land," which would increase their independence from whites. By rejecting wage labor, by striking, and by abandoning the most reactionary employers, blacks sought to force concessions. Out of this tug-of-war between white landlords and black laborers emerged a new system of southern agriculture.

Sharecropping was a compromise that offered both ex-masters and ex-slaves something but satisfied neither. Under the new system, planters divided their cotton plantations into small farms of twenty-five to thirty acres that freedmen rented, paying with a share of each year's crop, usually half. Sharecropping gave blacks more freedom than the system of wages and labor gangs and released them from the day-to-day supervision of whites. Black families abandoned the old slave quarters and scattered over plantations, building separate cabins for themselves on the patches of land they rented. Black families now decided who would work, for how long, and how hard. Still, most blacks remained dependent on white landlords, who had the power to expel them at the end of each growing season. For planters, sharecropping offered a way to resume agricultural production, but it did not allow them to restore the old slave plantation.

Sharecropping introduced a new figure—the country merchant—into the agricultural equation. Landlords supplied sharecroppers with land, mules, seeds, and tools, but blacks also needed credit to obtain essential food and clothing before they harvested their crops. Thousands of small crossroads stores sprang up to offer credit. Under an arrangement called a crop lien, a merchant would advance goods to a sharecropper in exchange for a *lien*, or legal claim, on the farmer's future crop. Some merchants charged exorbitant rates of interest, as much as 60 percent, on the goods they sold. At the end of the growing season, after the landlord had taken half of the farmer's crop for rent, the merchant took most of the rest. Sometimes, the farmer's debt to the merchant exceeded the income he received from his remaining half of the crop, and the farmer would have no choice but to borrow more from the merchant and begin the cycle all over again.

An experiment at first, sharecropping spread quickly and soon dominated the cotton South. Lien merchants forced tenants to plant cotton, which was easy to sell, instead of food crops. The result was excessive production of cotton and falling cotton prices, developments that cost thousands of small white farmers their land and pushed them into the great army of sharecroppers. The new share-cropping system of agriculture took shape just as the political power of Republicans in the South began to buckle under Democratic pressure.

▶**REVIEW**   Why was the Republican Party in the South a coalition party?

Reconstruction Collapses

By 1870, after a decade of war and reconstruction, Northerners wanted to turn to their own affairs and put "the southern problem" behind them. Increasingly, practical, business-minded men came to the forefront of the Republican Party, replacing the band of reformers and idealists who had been prominent in the 1860s. While northern commitment to defend black freedom eroded, southern commitment to white supremacy intensified. Without northern protection, southern Republicans were no match for the Democrats' economic coercion, political corruption, and bloody violence. One by one, Republican state governments fell in the South. The election of 1876 both confirmed and completed the collapse of reconstruction.

Grant's Troubled Presidency

In 1868, the Republican Party's presidential nomination went to Ulysses S. Grant, the North's favorite general. Hero of the Civil War and a supporter of congressional reconstruction, Grant was the obvious choice. His Democratic opponent, Horatio Seymour of New York, ran on a platform that blasted congressional reconstruction as "a flagrant usurpation of power . . . unconstitutional, revolutionary, and void." The Republicans answered by "waving the **bloody shirt**"— that is, they reminded voters that the Democrats were "the party of rebellion." During the campaign, the Ku Klux Klan erupted in a reign of terror, murdering hundreds of southern Republicans. Violence in the South cost Grant votes, but he gained a narrow 309,000-vote margin in the popular vote and a substantial victory (214 votes to 80) in the electoral college.

Grant hoped to forge a policy that secured both justice for blacks and sectional reconciliation. But he took office at a time when a majority of white Northerners had grown weary of the "Southern Question" and were increasingly willing to let southern whites manage their own affairs. Moreover, Grant had doubts about his preparation for the White House. "To go into the Presidency opens altogether a new field to me, in which there is to be a new strife to which I am not trained," he admitted. Indeed, Grant was not as good a president as he was a general. The talents he had demonstrated on the battlefield—decisiveness, clarity, and resolution—were less obvious in the White House. Able advisers might have helped, but he

Grant and Scandal

This anti-Grant cartoon by Thomas Nast shows the president falling headfirst into the barrel of fraud and corruption that tainted his administration. During Grant's eight years in the White House, many members of his administration failed him. Sometimes duped, sometimes merely loyal, Grant stubbornly defended wrongdoers, even to the point of perjuring himself to keep an aide out of jail.

Library of Congress.

surrounded himself with fumbling kinfolk and old cronies from his army days. He also made a string of dubious appointments that led to a series of damaging scandals. Charges of corruption tainted his vice president, Schuyler Colfax, and brought down two of his cabinet officers. Grant's dogged loyalty to liars and cheats only compounded the damage. Though never personally implicated in any scandal, Grant was aggravatingly naive and blind to the rot that filled his administration. Congressman James A. Garfield declared: "His imperturbability is amazing. I am in doubt whether to call it greatness or stupidity."

In 1872, anti-Grant Republicans bolted and launched the Liberal Party. To clean up the graft and corruption, Liberals proposed ending the **spoils system**, by which victorious parties rewarded loyal workers with public office, and replacing it with a nonpartisan **civil service** commission that would oversee competitive examinations for appointment to office. Moreover, they demanded that the federal government remove its troops from the South and restore "home rule" (southern white control). Democrats liked the Liberals' southern policy and endorsed the Liberal presidential candidate, Horace Greeley, the longtime editor of the *New York Tribune*. However, the nation still felt enormous affection for the man who had saved the Union and reelected Grant with 56 percent of the popular vote.

Grant's ambitions for his administration extended beyond reconstruction, but not even foreign affairs could escape the problems of the South. The annexation of Santo Domingo in the Caribbean was Grant's greatest passion. He argued that the acquisition of this tropical land would permit the United States to expand its trade and also provide a new home for the South's blacks, who were so desperately harassed by the Klan. Aggressive foreign policy had not originated with the Grant administration. Lincoln's and Johnson's secretary of state, William H. Seward, had thwarted French efforts to set up a puppet empire under Maximilian in Mexico, and his purchase of Alaska ("Seward's Ice Box") from Russia in 1867 for only $7 million fired Grant's **imperialist** ambition. But in the end, Grant could not convince Congress to approve the treaty annexing Santo Domingo. The South preoccupied Congress and undermined Grant's initiatives.

Northern Resolve Withers

Although Grant genuinely wanted to see blacks' civil and political rights protected, he understood that most Northerners had grown weary of reconstruction. Average citizens wanted to shift their attention to other issues, especially after the nation slipped into a devastating economic depression in 1873. More than eighteen thousand businesses collapsed, leaving more than a million workers without jobs. Northern businessmen who wanted to invest in the South believed that recurrent federal intrusion was itself a major cause of instability in the region. Republican leaders began to question the wisdom of their party's alliance with the South's lower classes—its small farmers and sharecroppers. Grant's secretary of the interior, Jacob D. Cox of Ohio, proposed allying with the "thinking and influential native southerners . . . the intelligent, well-to-do, and controlling class."

Congress, too, wanted to leave reconstruction behind, but southern Republicans made that difficult. When the South's Republicans begged for federal protection from Klan violence, Congress enacted three laws in 1870 and 1871 that were intended to break the back of white terrorism. The severest of the three, the Ku Klux Klan Act (1871), made interference with voting rights a felony and authorized the use of the army to enforce it. Intrepid federal marshals arrested thousands of Klansmen, and the government came close to destroying the Klan but did not end terrorism against blacks. Congress also passed the Civil Rights Act of 1875, which boldly outlawed racial discrimination in transportation, public accommodations, and juries. But federal authorities never enforced the law aggressively, and segregated facilities remained the rule throughout the South.

By the early 1870s, the Republican Party had lost its principal spokesmen for African American rights to death or defeat at the polls. Others in Congress concluded that the quest for black equality was mistaken or hopelessly naive. In May 1872, Congress restored the right of officeholding to all but three hundred ex-rebels. In the opinion of many, traditional white leaders offered the best hope for honesty, order, and prosperity in the South.

Underlying the North's abandonment of reconstruction was unyielding racial prejudice. During the war, Northerners had learned to accept black freedom, but deep-seated prejudice prevented many from following freedom with equality. Even the actions they took on behalf of blacks often served partisan political advantage. Northerners generally supported Indiana senator Thomas A. Hendricks's harsh declaration that "this is a white man's Government, made by the white man for the white man."

The U.S. Supreme Court also did its part to undermine reconstruction. The Court issued a series of decisions that significantly weakened the federal government's ability to protect black Southerners under the Fourteenth and Fifteenth Amendments. In the *Slaughterhouse* cases (1873), the Court distinguished between national and state citizenship and ruled that the Fourteenth Amendment protected only those rights that stemmed from the federal government, such as voting in federal elections and interstate travel. Since the Court decided that most rights derived from the states, it sharply curtailed the federal government's authority to protect black citizens. Even more devastating, the *United States v. Cruikshank* ruling (1876) said that the reconstruction amendments gave Congress the power to legislate against discrimination only by states, not by individuals. The "suppression of ordinary crime," such as assault, remained a state responsibility. The Supreme Court did not declare reconstruction unconstitutional but undermined its legal foundation.

The mood of the North found political expression in the election of 1874, when for the first time in eighteen years the Democrats gained control of the House of Representatives. As one Republican observed, the people had grown tired of the "negro question, with all its complications, and the reconstruction of Southern States, with all its interminable embroilments." Reconstruction had come apart. The people were tired of it. Grant grew increasingly unwilling to enforce it. Congress gradually abandoned it. The Supreme Court busily denied the constitutionality of significant parts of it. Rather than defend reconstruction from its southern enemies, Northerners steadily backed away from the challenge. After the early 1870s, southern blacks faced the forces of reaction largely on their own.

White Supremacy Triumphs

Republican state and local governments in the South attracted more bitterness and hatred than any other political regimes in American history. In the eyes of the majority of whites, Republican rule meant intolerable insults: Black militiamen patrolled town streets, black laborers negotiated contracts with former masters, black maids stood up to former mistresses, black voters cast ballots, and black legislators such as James T. Rapier enacted laws. The northern retreat from reconstruction permitted southern Democrats to harness this white rage to politics. Taking the name "Redeemers," they promised to replace "bayonet rule" (some federal troops continued to be stationed in the South) with "home rule." They branded Republican governments a carnival of extravagance, waste, and fraud and promised that honest, thrifty Democrats would supplant the irresponsible tax-and-spend Republicans. Above all, Redeemers swore to save southern civilization from a descent into African "barbarism" and "Negro rule." As one man put it, "We must render this either a white man's government, or convert the land into a Negro man's cemetery."

Southern Democrats adopted a two-pronged racial strategy to overthrow Republican governments. First, they sought to polarize the parties around color. They went about gathering all the South's white voters into the Democratic Party, leaving the Republicans to depend on blacks. The "straight-out" appeal to whites promised great advantage because whites made up a majority of the population in every southern state except Mississippi, South Carolina, and Louisiana.

To dislodge whites from the Republican Party, Democrats fanned the flames of racial prejudice. A South Carolina Democrat crowed that his party appealed to the "proud Caucasian race, whose sovereignty on earth God has proclaimed." Ostracism also proved effective. Local newspapers published the names of whites who kept company with blacks. So complete was the ostracism that one of its victims said, "No white man can live in the South in the future and act with any other than the Democratic party unless he is willing and prepared to live a life of social isolation."

Democrats also exploited the severe economic plight of small white farmers by blaming it on Republican financial policy. Government spending soared during reconstruction, and small farmers saw their tax burden skyrocket. "This is tax time," South Carolinian David Golightly Harris observed. "We are nearly all on our head about them. They are so high & so little money to pay with." Farmers without enough cash to pay their taxes began "selling every egg and chicken they can get." In 1871, Mississippi reported that one-seventh of the state's land—3.3 million acres—had been forfeited for nonpayment of taxes. The small farmers' economic distress had a racial dimension. Because few freedmen succeeded in acquiring land, they rarely paid taxes. In Georgia in 1874, blacks made up 45 percent of the population but paid only 2 percent of the taxes. From the perspective of a small white farmer, Republican rule meant that he was paying more taxes and paying them to aid blacks. Democrats asked whether it was not time for hard-pressed yeomen to join the white man's party.

If racial pride, social isolation, and Republican financial policies proved insufficient to drive yeomen from the Republican Party, Democrats turned to terrorism. "Night riders" targeted white Republicans as well as blacks for murder and assassination. "A dead Radical is very harmless," South Carolina Democratic leader Martin Gary told his followers. By the 1870s, only a handful of white Republicans remained.

The second prong of Democratic strategy aimed at the complete intimidation of black Republicans, especially local leaders. Emanuel Fortune, whom the Klan drove from Jackson County, Florida, declared: "The object of it is to kill out the leading men of the republican party . . . men who have taken a prominent stand." Violence expanded to all black voters and escalated to unprecedented levels. In 1873, a clash between black militiamen and gun-toting whites killed two white men and an estimated seventy black men in Louisiana. The whites slaughtered half of the black men after they surrendered. Although the federal government indicted more than one hundred of the white men, local juries failed to convict even one.

Even before adopting the all-out white supremacist tactics of the 1870s, Democrats had already taken control of the governments of Virginia, Tennessee, and North Carolina. The new campaign brought fresh gains. The Redeemers retook Georgia in 1871, Texas in 1873, and Arkansas and Alabama in 1874. Mississippi became a scene of open, unrelenting, and often savage intimidation of black voters and their few remaining white allies. As the state election approached in 1876, Governor Adelbert Ames appealed to Washington for federal troops to control the violence, only to hear from the attorney general that the "whole public are tired of these annual autumnal outbreaks in the South." Abandoned, Mississippi Republicans succumbed to the Democratic onslaught in the fall elections. By the election of 1876, only three Republican state governments—in Florida, Louisiana, and South Carolina—survived in the South (Map 16.1).

An Election and a Compromise

The centennial year of 1876 witnessed one of the most tumultuous elections in American history. Its chaos and confusion provided a fitting conclusion to the experiment known as reconstruction. The election took place in November, but not until March 2 of the following year did the nation know who would be inaugurated president on March 4. The Democrats nominated New York's governor, Samuel J. Tilden, who immediately targeted the corruption of the Grant administration and the despotism of Republican reconstruction. The Republicans put forward Rutherford B. Hayes, governor of Ohio. Privately, Hayes considered "bayonet rule" a mistake but concluded that waving the "bloody shirt"—reminding voters that the Democrats were the "party of rebellion"—remained the Republicans' best political strategy.

On election day, Tilden tallied 4,288,590 votes to Hayes's 4,036,000. But in the all-important electoral college, Tilden fell one vote short of the majority required for victory. The electoral votes of three states—South Carolina, Louisiana, and

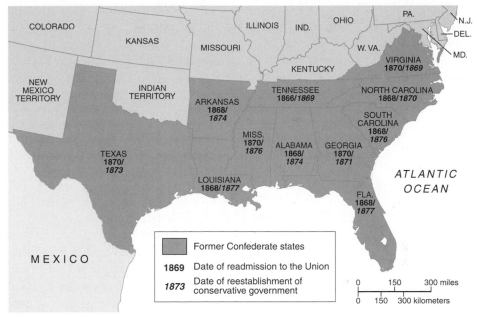

MAP 16.1   The Reconstruction of the South
Myth has it that Republican rule of the former Confederacy was not only harsh but long. In most states, however, conservative southern whites stormed back into power in months or just a few years. By the election of 1876, Republican governments could be found in only three states, and they soon fell.

Florida, the only remaining Republican governments in the South—remained in doubt because both Republicans and Democrats in those states claimed victory. To win, Tilden needed only one of the nineteen contested votes. Hayes had to have all of them.

Congress had to decide who had actually won the elections in the three southern states and thus who would be president. The Constitution provided no guidance for this situation. Moreover, Democrats controlled the House, and Republicans controlled the Senate. Congress created a special electoral commission to arbitrate the disputed returns. All of the commissioners voted their party affiliation, giving every state to the Republican Hayes and putting him over the top in electoral votes.

Some outraged Democrats vowed to resist Hayes's victory. Rumors flew of an impending coup and renewed civil war. But the impasse was broken when negotiations behind the scenes between Hayes's lieutenants and some moderate southern Democrats resulted in an informal understanding known as the Compromise of 1877. In exchange for a Democratic promise not to block Hayes's inauguration and to deal fairly with the freedmen, Hayes vowed to refrain from using the army to uphold the remaining Republican regimes in the South and to provide the South with substantial federal subsidies for internal improvements. Two days later, the nation celebrated Hayes's peaceful inauguration.

Stubborn Tilden supporters bemoaned the "stolen election" and damned "His Fraudulency," Rutherford B. Hayes. Old-guard radicals such as William Lloyd Garrison denounced Hayes's bargain as a "policy of compromise, of credulity, of weakness, of subserviency, of surrender." But the nation as a whole celebrated, for the country had weathered a grave crisis. The last three Republican state governments in the South fell quickly once Hayes abandoned them and withdrew the U.S. army. Reconstruction came to an end.

▶REVIEW   How did the Supreme Court undermine the Fourteenth and Fifteenth Amendments?

Conclusion: "A Revolution But Half Accomplished"

In 1865, when General Carl Schurz visited the South, he discovered "a revolution but half accomplished." White Southerners resisted the passage from slavery to free labor, from white racial despotism to equal justice, and from white political **monopoly** to biracial democracy. The old elite wanted to get "things back as near to slavery as possible," Schurz reported, while African Americans such as James T. Rapier and some whites were eager to exploit the revolutionary implications of defeat and emancipation.

The northern-dominated Republican Congress pushed the revolution along. Although it refused to provide for blacks' economic welfare, Congress employed constitutional amendments to require ex-Confederates to accept legal equality and share political power with black men. Congress was not willing to extend such power to women. Conservative southern whites fought ferociously to recover their power and privilege. When Democrats regained control of politics, whites used both state power and private violence to wipe out many of the gains of Reconstruction, leading one observer to conclude that the North had won the war but the South had won the peace.

The Redeemer counterrevolution, however, did not mean a return to slavery. Northern victory in the Civil War ensured abolition, and ex-slaves gained the freedom to not be whipped or sold, to send their children to school, to worship in their own churches, and to work independently on their own rented farms. Even sharecropping, with all its hardships, provided more autonomy and economic welfare than bondage had. It was limited freedom, to be sure, but it was not slavery.

The Civil War and emancipation set in motion the most profound upheaval in the nation's history, and nothing whites did entirely erased its revolutionary impact. War destroyed the largest slave society in the New World. The world of masters and slaves succumbed to that of landlords and sharecroppers, a world in which old lines of racial dominance continued, though with greater freedom for blacks. War also gave birth to a modern nation-state. For the first time, sovereignty rested uncontested in the federal government, and Washington increased its role in national affairs. When the South returned to the Union, it did so as a junior partner. The victorious North now possessed the power to establish the nation's direction, and it set the nation's compass toward the expansion of industrial capitalism and the final conquest of the West.

Despite massive changes, the Civil War remained only a "half accomplished" revolution. By not fulfilling the promises the nation seemed to hold out to black Americans at war's end, Reconstruction represents a tragedy of enormous proportions. The failure to protect blacks and guarantee their rights had enduring consequences. Almost a century after Reconstruction, the nation would embark on what one observer called a "second reconstruction." The solid achievements of the Thirteenth, Fourteenth, and Fifteenth Amendments to the Constitution would provide a legal foundation for the renewed commitment. It is worth remembering, though, that it was only the failure of the first reconstruction that made the modern civil rights movement necessary.

REVIEWING THE CHAPTER

Use the questions and timeline to review and strengthen your understanding of the chapter.

REVIEW QUESTIONS

1. Why did Congress object to Lincoln's wartime plan for reconstruction? (pp. 475–79)

2. How did the North respond to the passage of black codes in the southern states? (pp. 479–84)

3. Why did Johnson urge the southern states to reject the Fourteenth Amendment? (pp. 484–90)

4. Why was the Republican Party in the South a coalition party? (pp. 490–97)

5. How did the Supreme Court undermine the Fourteenth and Fifteenth Amendments? (pp. 497–504)

MAKING CONNECTIONS

1. Reconstruction succeeded in advancing black civil rights but failed to secure them over the long term. Why and how did the federal government retreat from defending African Americans' civil rights in the 1870s? In your answer, cite specific actions by Congress and the Supreme Court.

2. Why was distributing plantation land to former slaves such a controversial policy? In your answer, discuss why landownership was important to freedmen and why Congress rejected redistribution as a general policy.

3. At the end of the Civil War, it remained to be seen exactly how emancipation would transform the South. How did emancipation change political and labor organization in the region? In your answer, discuss how ex-slaves exercised their new freedoms and how white Southerners attempted to limit them.

4. The Republican Party shaped Reconstruction through its control of Congress and state legislatures in the South. How did the identification of the Republican Party with Reconstruction policy affect the party's political fortunes in the 1870s? In your answer, be sure to address developments on the federal and state levels.

TIMELINE

1863	• Proclamation of Amnesty and Reconstruction.	**1869**	• Congress approves Fifteenth Amendment.
1864	• Wade-Davis bill.	**1871**	• Ku Klux Klan Act.
1865	• Freedmen's Bureau established. • President Abraham Lincoln shot; dies on April 15; succeeded by Andrew Johnson. • Black codes enacted. • Thirteenth Amendment becomes part of Constitution.	**1872**	• Liberal Party formed; calls for end of government corruption. • President Grant reelected.
		1873	• Economic depression sets in for remainder of decade. • *Slaughterhouse* cases.
1866	• Congress approves Fourteenth Amendment. • Civil Rights Act. • American Equal Rights Association founded. • Ku Klux Klan founded.	**1874**	• Democrats win majority in House of Representatives.
		1875	• Civil Rights Act.
		1876	• *United States v. Cruikshank.*
1867	• Military Reconstruction Act. • Tenure of Office Act.	**1877**	• Republican Rutherford B. Hayes assumes presidency; Reconstruction era ends.
1868	• Impeachment trial of President Johnson. • Republican Ulysses S. Grant elected president.		

▶ **For an online bibliography, practice quizzes, Web sites, images, and documents related to this chapter,** see the Book Companion Site at **bedfordstmartins.com/roark.**

▶ **For firsthand accounts of this period,** see Chapter 16 in Michael Johnson, ed., *Reading the American Past,* Fourth Edition.

17
CHAPTER

The Contested West
1870–1900

T O CELEBRATE INDIAN CITIZENSHIP DAY in 1892, students at Hampton Institute's Indian boarding school in Virginia staged a pageant honoring the four hundredth anniversary of the "discovery" of the New World. Students appeared dressed as the nation's heroes—among them Christopher Columbus, Miles Standish, and George Washington. Halfway through the program, the pageant finally honored some Native American heroes, but the Indians selected—Samoset, Pocahontas—all came from the distant past in lands east of the Appalachians. There was no mention of Crazy Horse, Sitting Bull, or Geronimo—Indians who resisted white encroachment and appropriation of their land in the West. Only two years earlier, the massacre of more than two hundred Miniconjou Sioux at Wounded Knee, South Dakota, marked the end of three decades of war against the Indians in the trans-Mississippi West. The Indian wars left the Native American population in the continental United States at 250,000 according to the census of 1900 (admittedly an undercount), down from estimates as high as 15 million at the time of first contact with Europeans. Not only had the population been decimated by war and disease, but Indian lands had shrunk so much that by 1890 Euro-Americans controlled 97.5 percent of the territory formerly occupied by Native Americans.

The Hampton pageant could not entirely ignore a catastrophe of this magnitude. Yet it managed to end on a note of reconciliation with a student proclaiming:

> You have taken our rivers and fountains
>   And the plains where we loved to roam,—
> Banish us not to the mountains
>   And the lonely wastes for home!

507

Our clans that were strongest and bravest,
   Are Broken and powerless through you:
Let us join the great tribe of the white men,
   As brothers to dare and to do!

How the actors felt about the lines they spoke we cannot know. But the pageant clearly reflected the values and beliefs that Indian boarding schools hoped to inculcate in their pupils at the end of the nineteenth century.

Indian schools constituted the cultural battleground of the Indian wars in the West, their avowed purpose "to destroy the Indian in him and save the man." In 1877, Congress appropriated funds for Indian education, reasoning "it was less expensive to educate Indians than to kill them." Hampton Institute, created in 1868 to school newly freed slaves, accepted its first Indian students in 1878. Although many Indian schools operated on the reservations, authorities much

---

Hampton Pageant, 1892
The Indian students in this picture are dressed for Columbia's Roll Call, a pageant at Hampton Institute honoring the nation's heroes on Indian Citizenship Day, 1892. Among those portrayed are Christopher Columbus, Pocahontas, George Washington, and, in the center, a student dressed as Columbia, symbol of the Republic, draped in the American flag.
Courtesy of Hampton University Archives.

preferred boarding facilities that isolated students from the "contamination" of tribal values.

Many Native American parents resisted sending their children away. When all else failed, the military kidnapped the children and sent them off to school. An agent at the Mescalero Apache Agency in Arizona Territory reported in 1886 how "it became necessary to visit the camps unexpectedly with a detachment of police, and seize such children as were proper and take them away to school, willing or unwilling." The parents put up a struggle. "Some hurried their children off to the mountains or hid them away in camp, and the police had to chase and capture them like so many wild rabbits," the agent observed. "This unusual proceeding created quite an outcry. The men were sullen and muttering, the women loud in their lamentations, and the children almost out of their wits with fright."

Once at school, the children were stripped and scrubbed, their clothing and belongings confiscated, their hair hacked off and doused with kerosene to kill lice. Issued stiff new uniforms, shoes, and what one boy recalled as the "torture" of woolen long underwear, the children often lost not only their possessions but also their names: Hehakaavita (Yellow Elk) became Thomas Goodwood; Polingaysi Qoyawayma became Elizabeth White.

The curriculum featured agricultural and manual arts for boys and domestic skills for girls, training designed to make Indians "willing workers" who would no longer be a burden to the government. The Carlisle Indian School in Pennsylvania, founded in 1879, became the model for later institutions. To encourage assimilation, Carlisle pioneered the "outing system"—sending students to live with white families during summer vacations. The policy reflected the school's slogan, "To civilize the Indian, get him into civilization. To keep him civilized, let him stay." Some graduates, like the two Omaha sisters Susan and Suzette LaFlesche, put their education to work to champion Indian rights. But many entered a dismal netherworld—never accepted in white society as equals but no longer at home on the reservation.

Merrill Gates, a member of the Board of Indian Commissioners, summed up the goal of Indian education: "To get the Indian out of the blanket and into trousers,—and trousers with a pocket in them, *and with a pocket that aches to be filled with dollars!*" Gates's faith in the "civilizing" power of the dollar reflected the unabashed materialism of his age. In 1871, author Mark Twain published *Roughing It*, a chronicle of his days spent in mining towns in California and Nevada. There he found the same corrupt politics, vulgar display, and mania for speculation that he later skewered in *The Gilded Age* (1873), a biting satire of greed and corruption in the nation's capital. Far from being an antidote to the meretricious values of the East—an innocent idyll out of place and time—the American West, with its get-rich-quick ethos and its addiction to gambling and speculation, played an integral part in the politics and economics of the Gilded Age.

"West" has always been a relative term. Until the gold rush of 1849 focused attention on California, the West for settlers lay beyond the Appalachians, east of the Mississippi in the area drained by the Ohio River. But by 1860, "West" increasingly referred to the land across the Mississippi, from the Great Plains to the Pacific Ocean. The expansion of U.S. domination into the trans-Mississippi West and the displacement of Native Americans and their **culture** point to the cruel paradox that the promise that drew miners and settlers into the West meant conquest and subjugation for Indian peoples. With its rich natural resources and land, the West became fiercely contested terrain, not only for the Indians who struggled to preserve their sovereignty and their cultural identity but also among competing groups of Anglos, Hispanics, and a host of others who followed the promise of land and riches into the West.

All the major themes of U.S. history in the era following the Civil War played themselves out under western skies. The expansion of U.S. empire; the consolidation of business in mining, ranching, and commercial farming; corruption and cupidity in territorial government; vicious ethnic and racial animosity whether in the form of Chinese exclusion or prejudice against Mexicans and Mormons; and the exploitation of natural resources that led to the decimation of the great bison herds, the despoliation of the landscape and the pollution of rivers with mining wastes; and pitched battles between workers and bosses—all marked western variants of the major currents in American political, social, and economic history in the period from 1870 to 1900.

Conquest and Empire in the West

While the European powers expanded their authority and wealth through *imperialism* and *colonialism*, establishing far-flung empires abroad, the United States focused its attention on the West. American *exceptionalism* has stressed how the history of the United States differs from that of western European nations, and America's preoccupation with its western **frontier** has often been cited as a case in point. Yet recent historians have argued that the process by which the United States expanded its borders in the nineteenth century can best be understood in terms of imperialism and colonialism—language applied to European powers in this period that makes explicit how expansion in the American West involved the conquest, displacement, and rule over native peoples. The federal government, through chicanery and conquest, pushed the Indians off their land (Map 17.1). Removed to Indian Territory or confined on reservations, Indians became wards of the federal government, their culture assaulted by policies designed to force assimilation. Through the lens of colonialism, we can see how the United States' commitment to an imperialist, expansionist ideology resulted in the displacement of Native Americans and the establishment of new territories and eventually states. The colonizing of the West was a dynamic process in which Native Americans actively resisted, contested, and adapted to colonial rule.

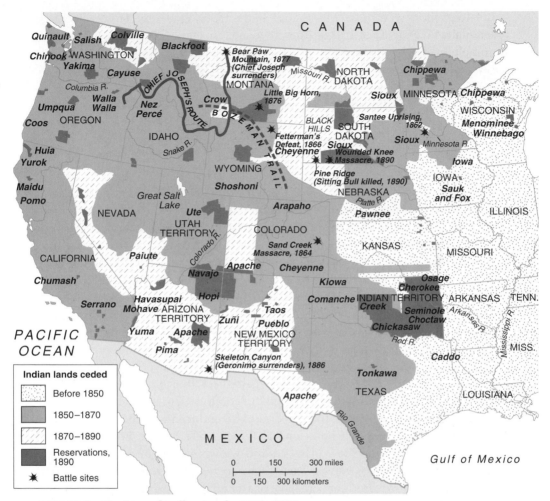

MAP 17.1   The Loss of Indian Lands, 1850–1890

By 1890, western Indians were isolated on small, scattered reservations. Native Americans had struggled to retain their land in major battles, from the Santee Uprising in Minnesota in 1862 to the massacre at Wounded Knee, South Dakota, in 1890.

Indian Removal and the Reservation System

From the first encounter, when Christopher Columbus mistakenly identified Native Americans as "Indians," Euro-Americans have used the term as if it designated a homogeneous race, disregarding the fact that Native Americans once included more than five hundred distinct tribal entities with different languages, myths, religions, and physical appearance. Beginning in the early days of the Republic, Americans advocated a policy of Indian removal. With plenty of land open in the West, the government removed eastern tribes—often against their will—to territory west of the Mississippi. In the 1830s, President Andrew Jackson pushed the Five Civilized Tribes—the Cherokee, Choctaw, Chickasaw, Creek, and Seminole peoples—off their land in the southern United States. Jackson's Indian removal forced thousands of men, women, and children to leave their homes in Georgia and Tennessee and walk hundreds of miles west. So many died of hunger, exhaustion, and disease along the way that the Cherokees called their path "the trail on which we cried." At the end of this trail of tears stood land set aside as Indian Territory (present-day Oklahoma). Here, the government promised, the Indians could remain "as long as grass shall grow" (see chapter 11). But hunger for western land soon negated that promise.

Manifest destiny—the belief that the United States had a "God-given" right to aggressively spread the values of white civilization and expand the nation from ocean to ocean—dictated U.S. policy. In the name of manifest destiny, Americans forced the removal of the Five Civilized Tribes to Oklahoma; colonized Texas and won its independence from Mexico in 1836; conquered California, Arizona, New Mexico, and parts of Utah and Colorado in the Mexican-American War of 1846–1848; and invaded Oregon in the 1840s (see chapter 12). But by the mid-nineteenth century, western land no longer seemed inexhaustible, and instead of removing Indians to the West, the government sought control of Indian lands and promised in return to pay annuities and put the Indians on lands reserved for their use—*reservations*. This policy won the support of both friends of the Indians, who feared for their survival, and Indian haters, who coveted their land and wished to confine them to the least desirable areas in the West. The Navajo, like the Cherokee, endured a forced march, called the "Long Walk," from their homeland to the desolate Bosque Redondo Reservation in New Mexico in 1864. "This ground we were brought on, it is not productive," complained the Navajo leader Barboncito. "We plant but it does not yield. All the stock we brought here have nearly all died."

By midcentury, settlers in unprecedented numbers crossed the Great Plains on their way to the goldfields of California or the rich farmland of Washington and Oregon. In their path stood a solid wall of Indian land, stretching from Minnesota to Texas, much of it granted through the policy of Indian removal. As the *United States Magazine* observed, "Now the removed tribes are precisely in the center of this path." The "Indian problem" needed to be solved—through treaties if possible or coercion if necessary. In 1851, some ten thousand Plains Indians came together at Fort Laramie in Wyoming to negotiate a treaty that ceded a wide swath of their land to allow passage of the wagon trains. In return, the government promised that the rest of the Indian land would remain inviolate. It was yet another promise the government would not keep.

The Indians who "touched the pen" to the Treaty of Fort Laramie hoped to preserve their culture in the face of the white onslaught, which already had decimated their population and despoiled their environment. White invaders cut down trees, miners polluted streams, and hunters killed off bison and small game. Whites brought alcohol, guns, and something even more deadly—disease. Smallpox was the biggest killer of Native Americans in the West. Epidemics spread from Mexico up to Canada. Between 1780 and 1870, the population of the Plains tribes declined by half. Cholera, diphtheria, measles, scarlet fever, and other contagious diseases also took their toll. "If I could see this thing, if I knew where it came from, I would go there and fight it," a Cheyenne warrior anguished. Disease shifted the balance of power on the plains from Woodland agrarian tribes like the Mandan and Hidatsa (who died at the rate of 79 percent) to the Lakota Sioux, who fled the contagion of villages to take up life as equestrian (horse-riding) nomads on the western plains. As the Sioux pushed west, they displaced weaker tribes.

The Indian wars in the West marked the last resistance of a Native American population devastated by disease and demoralized by the removal policy pursued by the federal government. More accurately called "settlers' wars" (since they began with "peaceful settlers," often miners, overrunning Native American land), the wars flared up again only a few years after the signing of the Fort Laramie treaty. The Dakota Sioux in Minnesota went to war in 1862. For years, under the leadership of Chief Little Crow, the Dakota, also known as the Santee, had pursued a policy of accommodation, ceding land in return for the promise of annuities. But with his people on the verge of starvation (the local Indian agent told the hungry Dakota, "Go and eat grass"), Little Crow reluctantly led his angry warriors in a desperate campaign against the intruders, killing more than 1,000 settlers. American troops quelled what was called the Great Sioux Uprising (also called the Santee Uprising) and marched 1,700 Sioux to Fort Snelling, where 400 Indians were put on trial for murder and 38 died in the largest mass execution in American history.

On the southern plains, the conflict reached its nadir in November 1864 at the Sand Creek Massacre in Colorado Territory. There Colonel John M. Chivington and his Colorado militia descended on a village of Cheyenne, mostly women and children. Their leader, Black Kettle, raised a white flag and an American flag to signal surrender, but the charging cavalry ignored his signal and butchered 270 Indians. Chivington watched as his men scalped and mutilated their victims and later justified the killing of Indian children with the terse remark, "Nits make lice." The city of Denver treated Chivington and his men as heroes, but a congressional inquiry castigated the soldiers for their "fiendish malignity" and condemned the "savage cruelty" of the massacre. To escape court-martial, Chivington resigned his commission and left the army. To Americans like Chivington, fed theories of racial superiority, the Indians constituted, in the words of one Colorado militia major, "an obstacle to civilization . . . [and] should be exterminated."

After the Civil War, President Ulysses S. Grant faced the prospect of an Indian war on the Great Plains. Reluctant to spend more money and sacrifice more lives in battle, Grant adopted a "peace policy," advocating reservations as a way to segregate and control the Indians while opening up land to white settlers.

General William Tecumseh Sherman summed up the new Indian policy suc-
cinctly: "Remove all to a safe place and then reduce them to a helpless condition."
The army herded the Indians onto reservations (see Map 17.1), where the U.S.
Bureau of Indian Affairs—a badly managed, weak agency, often acting through
corrupt agents—supposedly ministered to their needs. When Indians refused to
give up their hunting grounds and move onto reservations, the army launched
military campaigns to "bring in" bands who would not accept confinement.

Poverty and starvation stalked the reservations. Confined by armed force,
the Indians eked out an existence on stingy government rations. These once
proud peoples found themselves dependent on government handouts and the
assistance of Indian agents who, in the words of Paiute Sarah Winnemucca, did
"nothing but fill their pockets." Winnemucca launched a lecture campaign in the
United States and Europe, denouncing the government's reservation policy.

Indian reservations became cultural battlegrounds. Styled as stepping-stones
on the road to "civilization," they closely resembled colonial societies where
native populations, ruled by outside bureaucrats, saw their culture assaulted, their
religious practices outlawed, their children sent away to school, and their way
of life attacked in the name of progress and civilization. Even the most well-
meaning reformers, the self-styled "friends of the Indians," championed reservations as the best route to assimilation. These reformers, many of them easterners
with little experience in the West, held the romantic notion that the Indians, if
given a chance, would settle down peacefully and become farmers. Reservations
would provide a classroom of civilization where Indians could be taught to speak
English, to worship a Christian god, to give up hunting for farming, and to reject
tribal ways. In the face of this assault, Indians found ways to resist and hold on to
their cultural identity.

The Decimation of the Great Bison Herds
and the Fight for the Black Hills

By the nineteenth century, more than two hundred years of contact with whites
had utterly transformed Native American societies. Indians had been pushed off
their lands east of the Mississippi and moved west. Through trade with the Spanish
and French, Indians had acquired horses and guns. The Sioux, hunting on horseback, staked their survival on the buffalo (American bison). But the great herds,
once numbering as many as thirty million, fell into decline. A host of environmental and human factors contributed to the destruction of the bison. The dynamic
ecology of the Great Plains, with its drought, fires, and blizzards, combined with
the ecological imperialism of humans (Indian buffalo robe traders as well as whites
and their cattle), put increasing pressure on the bison. By the 1850s, a combination
of drought and commerce had driven the great herds onto the far western plains.

After the Civil War, the accelerating pace of industrial expansion brought
about the near extinction of the bison. Industrial demand for heavy leather

"Slaughtered for the Hide"
Harper's Weekly in 1874 featured this illustration of a buffalo hunter skinning a carcass on the south-western plains. By 1872, the Santa Fe railroad reached Kansas, making Dodge City the center for the shipment of buffalo hides to the East, where they were made into leather belting used to run the nation's machinery. In a matter of months, hunters decimated the great southern bison herds.
Library of Congress.

belting used in machinery and the development of larger, more accurate rifles contributed to the slaughter of the bison. The nation's growing transcontinental rail system cut the range in two and divided the herds. For the nomadic tribes of the plains, the buffalo constituted a way of life—a source of food, fuel, and shelter and a central part of their religion and rituals. To the railroads, the bison were a nuisance, at best a cheap source of meat for their workers and a target for sport. Buffalo hunters hired by the railroads, joined by sport hunters, fired from railroad cars just for the thrill of the kill. "It will not be long before all the buffaloes are extinct near and between the railroads," Ohio senator John Sherman prophesied in 1868. The army took credit for the conquest of the Plains Indians, but victory came about largely as a result of the decimation of the great bison herds. General Philip Sheridan acknowledged as much when he applauded white hide hunters for "destroying the Indians' commissary." With their food supply gone, Indians had to choose between starvation and the reservation. "A cold wind blew across the prairie when the last buffalo fell," the great Sioux leader Sitting Bull lamented, "a death wind for my people."

On the southern plains in 1867, more than five thousand warring Comanches, Kiowas, and Southern Arapahos gathered at Medicine Lodge Creek in Kansas to negotiate a treaty. Satak, or Sitting Bear, a prominent Kiowa chief and medicine man, explained why the Indians sought peace: "In the far-distant past . . . the world seemed large enough for both the red man and the white man." But, he observed, "its broad plains seem now to contract, and the white man grows jealous of his red brother." To preserve their land from white encroachment, the Indians signed the Treaty of Medicine Lodge, agreeing to move to a reservation. But after 1870, hide hunters poured into the region, and within a decade, they had nearly exterminated the southern bison herds. Luther Standing Bear recounted the sight and stench: "I saw the bodies of hundreds of dead buffalo lying about, just wasting, and the odor was terrible. . . . They were letting our food lie on the plains to rot."

On the northern plains, the fever for gold fueled the conflict between Indians and Euro-Americans. In 1866, the Cheyenne united with the Sioux in Wyoming to protect their hunting grounds in the Powder River valley, which were threatened by the construction of the Bozeman Trail connecting Fort Laramie with the goldfields in Montana. Captain William Fetterman, who had boasted that with eighty men he could ride through the Sioux nation, was killed along with all of his troops in an Indian attack. The Sioux's impressive victories led to the second Treaty of Fort Laramie in 1868, in which the United States agreed to abandon the Bozeman Trail and guaranteed the Indians control of the Black Hills, land sacred to the Lakota Sioux. The treaty was full of contradictions—in one breath promising to preserve Indian land and in the next forcing the tribes to relinquish all territory outside their reservations. A controversial provision of the treaty guaranteed the Indians access to their traditional hunting grounds "so long as the buffalo may range thereon in such numbers as to justify the chase." With the bison facing extermination, the provision was ominous. Yet the government's fork-tongued promises induced some of the tribes to accept the treaty. The great Sioux chief Red Cloud led many of his people onto the reservation. Red Cloud soon regretted his decision. "Think of it!" he told a visitor to the Pine Ridge Reservation. "I, who used to own . . . country so extensive that I could not ride through it in a week . . . must tell Washington when I am hungry. I must beg for that which I own." Several Sioux chiefs, among them Crazy Horse of the Oglala band and Sitting Bull of the Hunkpapa, refused to sign the treaty. Crazy Horse said that he wanted no part of the "piecemeal penning" of his people.

In 1874, the discovery of gold in the Black Hills of the Dakotas led the government to break its promise to Red Cloud. Miners began pouring into the region, and the Northern Pacific Railroad made plans to lay track. Lieutenant Colonel George Armstrong Custer, whose troopers found gold in the area, trumpeted news of the strike. At first, the government offered to purchase the Black Hills. But to the Lakota Sioux the Black Hills were sacred—"the heart of everything that is." They refused to sell. The army responded by issuing an ultimatum ordering all Lakota Sioux and Northern Cheyenne bands onto the Pine Ridge Reservation and threatening to hunt down those who refused.

In the summer of 1876, the army launched a three-pronged attack led by Custer, General George Crook, and Colonel John Gibbon. Crazy Horse stopped

Crook at the Battle of the Rosebud. Custer, leading the second prong of the army's offensive, divided his troops and ordered an attack. On June 25, he spotted signs of the Indians' camp and crying "Hurrah Boys, we've got them," led 265 men of the Seventh Cavalry into the largest Indian camp ever assembled on the Great Plains. Nomadic bands of Sioux, Cheyenne, and Arapaho had come together for a summer buffalo hunt and camped along the banks of the Greasy Grass River (whites called it the Little Big Horn). Indian warriors led by Sitting Bull and Crazy Horse set upon Custer and his men and quickly annihilated them. "It took us about as long as a hungry man to eat his dinner," the Cheyenne chief Two Moons recalled. Gibbon arrived two days later to discover the carnage. "Custer's Last Stand," as the Battle of the Little Big Horn was styled in myth, turned out to be the last stand for the Sioux. The Indians' nomadic way of life meant they could not remain a combined force for long. The bands that had massed at the Little Big Horn scattered, and the army hunted them down. "Wherever we went," wrote the Oglala holy man Black Elk, "the soldiers came to kill us." Crazy Horse was killed in 1877, and Sitting Bull surrendered four years later, in 1881. The government took the Black Hills and confined the Lakota to the Great Sioux Reservation. The Sioux never accepted the loss of the Black Hills. In 1923, they filed suit, demanding the return of the land taken illegally from them. After a protracted court battle lasting nearly sixty years, the U.S. Supreme Court ruled in 1980 that the government had illegally abrogated the Treaty of Fort Laramie and upheld an award of $122.5 million in compensation to the tribes. The Sioux refused the settlement and continue to press for the return of the Black Hills.

The Dawes Act and Indian Land Allotment

In the 1880s, the practice of rounding up Indians and herding them onto reservations lost momentum in favor of allotment—a new policy designed to encourage assimilation through farming and the ownership of private property. Americans vowing to avenge Custer urged the government to get tough with the Indians. Reservations, they argued, took up too much good land that white settlers could put to better use. At the same time, those sympathetic to the Indians were appalled at the desperate poverty on the reservations and feared for the Indians' survival. Helen Hunt Jackson, in her classic work *A Century of Dishonor* (1881), convinced many readers that the Indians had been treated unfairly. "Our Indian policy," the *New York Times* concluded, "is usually spoliation behind the mask of benevolence."

Reformers pressed for change. The Indian Rights Association, a group of mainly white easterners formed in 1882, campaigned for the dismantling of the reservations, now viewed as obstacles to progress. To "cease to treat the Indian as a red man and treat him as a man" meant putting an end to tribal communalism and fostering individualism. "Selfishness," declared Senator Henry Dawes of Massachusetts, "is at the bottom of civilization." The solution to the "Indian problem" called for "allotment in severalty"—the institution of private property.

Dawes promised to grant Indians full citizenship and promote economic self-sufficiency by making them trade their tribal lands for individual farms.

In 1887, Congress passed the Dawes Allotment Act, dividing up reservations and allotting parcels of land to individual Indians as private property. Each Indian household was eligible to receive 160 acres of land from reservation property. Only those Indians who took allotments earned citizenship. Since Indian land far surpassed the acreage needed for allotments, the government reserved the right to sell the "surplus" to white settlers—a goal those less benevolent in their attitudes toward the Indians had no trouble supporting. The Dawes Act effectively reduced Indian land from 138 million acres to a scant 48 million. The legislation, in the words of one critic, worked "to despoil the Indians of their lands and to make them vagabonds on the face of the earth." Sitting Bull put it bluntly: "The life of white men is slavery. They are prisoners in towns or farms." He concluded, "I have seen nothing that a white man has, houses or railways or clothing or food, that is as good as the right to move in open country, and live in our own fashion." The Dawes Act completed the dispossession of the western Indian peoples and dealt a crippling blow to traditional tribal culture. It remained in effect until 1934, when the United States restored the right of Native Americans to own land communally (see chapter 24).

Indian Resistance and Survival

Faced with the extinction of their entire way of life, different groups of Indians responded in different ways in the waning decades of the nineteenth century. Some tribes, including the Crow, Arikara, Pawnee, and Shoshoni, fought alongside the U.S. army against their old enemies the Sioux. The Crow chief Plenty Coups explained why he allied with the United States: "Not because we loved the white man . . . or because we hated the Sioux . . . but because we plainly saw that this course was the only one which might save our beautiful country for us." The Crow and Shoshoni got to stay in their homelands and avoided the fate of other tribes shipped to reservations far away.

Indians who refused to stay on reservations risked being hunted down—a clear indication that reservations were intended to keep Indians in, not to keep whites out, as the friends of the Indians had intended. The Nez Percé war of 1877 is perhaps the most harrowing example of the army's policy. In 1863, the government dictated a treaty drastically reducing Nez Percé land. Most of the chiefs refused to sign the treaty and did not move to the reservation. In 1877, the army issued an ultimatum—come in to the reservation or be hunted down. Some eight hundred Nez Percé people, many of them women and children, fled across the mountains of Idaho, Wyoming, and Montana, heading for the safety of Canada. At the end of their 1,300-mile trek, 50 miles from freedom, they stopped to rest in the snow. The army's Indian scouts spotted their tepees, and the soldiers attacked. Yellow Wolf recalled their plight: "Children crying with cold. No fire.

There could be no light. Everywhere the crying, the death wail." After a five-day siege, the Nez Percé leader, Chief Joseph, surrendered. His speech, reported by a white soldier, would become famous. "I am tired of fighting," he said as he surrendered his rifle. "Our chiefs are killed. It is cold and we have no blankets. The little children are freezing to death. . . . I am tired. My heart is sick and sad. From where the sun now stands, I will fight no more forever."

In the Southwest, the Apaches resorted to armed resistance. They roamed the Sonoran Desert of southern Arizona and northern Mexico, perfecting a hit-and-run **guerrilla warfare** that terrorized white settlers and bedeviled the army in the 1870s and 1880s. General George Crook combined a policy of dogged pursuit with judicious diplomacy. Crook relied on Indian scouts to track the raiding parties, recruiting nearly two hundred, including Apaches along with Navajos and Paiutes. By 1882, Crook had succeeded in persuading most of the Apaches to settle on the San Carlos Reservation in Arizona Territory. A desolate piece of desert inhabited by scorpions and rattlesnakes, San Carlos, in the words of one Apache, was "the worst place in all the great territory stolen from the Apaches."

Geronimo, a respected shaman (medicine man) of the Chiricahua Apache, refused to stay at San Carlos and repeatedly led raiding parties in the early 1880s. His warriors attacked ranches to obtain ammunition and horses. Among Geronimo's band was Lozen, a woman who rode with the warriors, armed with a rifle and a cartridge belt. The sister of a great chief who described her as being as "strong as a man, braver than most, and cunning in strategy," Lozen never married and remained a warrior in Geronimo's band even after her brother's death. In the spring of 1885, Geronimo and his followers, including Lozen, went on a ten-month offensive, moving from the Apache sanctuary in the Sierra Madre to raid and burn ranches and towns on both sides of the Mexican border. General Crook caught up with Geronimo in the fall and persuaded him to return to San Carlos, only to have him slip away on the way back to the reservation. Chagrined, Crook resigned his post. General Nelson Miles, Crook's replacement, adopted a policy of hunt and destroy.

Geronimo's band of thirty-three Apaches, including women and children, managed to elude Miles's troops for more than five months. In the end, this small band fought two thousand soldiers to a stalemate. After months of pursuit, Lieutenant Leonard Wood, a member of Miles's spit-and-polish cavalry, discarded his horse and most of his clothes until he was reduced to wearing nothing "but a pair of canton flannel drawers, and an old blue blouse, a pair of moccasins and a hat without a crown."

Eventually, Miles's scouts cornered Geronimo in 1886. Caught between Mexican regulars and the U.S. army, Geronimo agreed to march north with the soldiers and negotiate a settlement. "We have not slept for six months," he admitted, "and we are worn out." Although fewer than three dozen Apaches had been considered "hostile," when General Miles induced them to surrender, the government rounded up nearly five hundred Apaches, including the scouts who had helped track Geronimo, and sent them as prisoners to Florida. By 1889, more than a quarter of them had died, some due to illnesses contracted in the damp lowland climate and some by suicide. Their plight roused public opinion, and in 1892 they were moved to Fort Sill in Oklahoma and later to New Mexico.

Geronimo lived to become something of a celebrity. He appeared at the St. Louis Exposition in 1904, and he rode in President Theodore Roosevelt's inaugural parade in 1905. In a newspaper interview, he confessed, "I want to go to my old home before I die. . . . Want to go back to the mountains again. I asked the Great White Father to allow me to go back, but he said no." None of the Apaches were permitted to return to Arizona; when Geronimo died in 1909, he was buried in Oklahoma.

On the plains, many tribes turned to a nonviolent form of resistance—a compelling new religion called the Ghost Dance. The Paiute shaman Wovoka, drawing on a cult that had developed in the 1870s, combined elements of Christianity and traditional Indian religion to found the Ghost Dance religion in 1889. Wovoka claimed that he had received a vision in which the Great Spirit spoke through him to all Indians, prophesying that if they would unite in the Ghost Dance ritual, whites would be destroyed in an apocalypse. The shaman promised that Indian warriors slain in battle would return to life and that buffalo once again would roam the land unimpeded. This religion, born of despair with its message of hope, spread like wildfire over the plains. The Ghost Dance was performed in Idaho, Montana, Utah, Wyoming, Colorado, Nebraska, Kansas, the Dakotas, and Indian Territory by tribes as diverse as the Sioux, Arapaho, Cheyenne, Pawnee, and Shoshoni. Dancers often went into hypnotic trances, dancing until they dropped from exhaustion.

The Ghost Dance was nonviolent, but it frightened whites, especially when the Sioux taught that wearing a white ghost shirt made Indians immune to soldiers' bullets. Soon whites began to fear an uprising. "Indians are dancing in the snow and are wild and crazy," wrote the Bureau of Indian Affairs agent at the Pine Ridge Reservation in South Dakota. Frantic, he pleaded for reinforcements. "We are at the mercy of these dancers. We need protection, and we need it now." President Benjamin Harrison dispatched several thousand federal troops to Sioux country to handle any outbreak.

In December 1890, when Sitting Bull joined the Ghost Dance, he was killed by Indian police as they tried to arrest him at his cabin on the Standing Rock Reservation. His people, fleeing the scene, joined with a larger group of Miniconjou Sioux, who were apprehended by the Seventh Cavalry, Custer's old regiment, near Wounded Knee Creek, South Dakota. As the Indians laid down their arms, a shot rang out, and the soldiers opened fire. In the ensuing melee, Indian men, women, and children were mowed down in minutes by the army's brutally efficient Hotchkiss rapid-fire guns. More than two hundred Sioux lay dead or dying in the snow. Settler Jules Sandoz surveyed the scene the day after the massacre at Wounded Knee. "Here in ten minutes an entire community was as the buffalo that bleached on the plains," he wrote. "There was something loose in the world that hated joy and happiness as it hated brightness and color, reducing everything to drab agony and gray."

It had taken Euro-Americans 250 years to wrest control of the eastern half of the United States from the Indians. It took them less than forty years to take the western half. The subjugation of the American Indians marked the first chapter in a national mission of empire that would later lead to overseas imperialistic adventures in Asia, Latin America, the Caribbean, and the Pacific Islands.

▶ **REVIEW**　　How did the slaughter of the bison contribute to the Plains Indians' removal to reservations?

Gold Fever and the Mining West

Mining stood at the center of the United States' quest for empire in the West. The California gold rush of 1849 touched off the frenzy. The four decades following witnessed equally frenetic rushes for gold and other metals, most notably on the Comstock Lode in Nevada and later in New Mexico, Colorado, the Dakotas, Montana, Idaho, Arizona, and Utah. Each rush built on the last, producing new technologies and innovations in financing as hordes of miners, eager to strike it rich, moved from one boomtown to the next. Mining in the West, however, was a story not only of boom and bust but also of community building and the development of territories into states. At first glance, the mining West may seem much different from the East, but by the 1870s, the term "urban industrialism" described Virginia City, Nevada, as accurately as it did Pittsburgh or Cleveland. And the diverse peoples drawn to the West by the promise of mining riches made the region the most cosmopolitan in the nation. A close look at mining on the Comstock Lode indicates some of the patterns and paradoxes of western mining. And a look at territorial government uncovers striking parallels with corruption and cupidity in politics east of the Mississippi.

Mining on the Comstock Lode

By 1859, refugees from California's played-out goldfields flocked to the Washoe basin in Nevada. There prospectors found the gold they sought mired in blackish sand they called "that blasted blue stuff." Eventually, an enterprising miner had the stuff assayed, and it turned out the Washoe miners had stumbled on the richest vein of silver ore on the continent—the legendary Comstock Lode, named for prospector Henry Comstock.

To exploit even potentially valuable silver claims required capital and expensive technology well beyond the means of the prospector. An active San Francisco stock market sprang up to finance operations on the Comstock. Shrewd businessmen soon recognized that the easiest way to get rich was not to mine at all but to sell their claims or to form mining companies and sell shares of stock. The most unscrupulous mined the wallets of gullible investors by selling shares in bogus mines to stockholders to whom the very word *Comstock* conjured up images of riches. Speculation, misrepresentation, and outright thievery ran rampant. In twenty years, more than $300 million poured from the earth in Nevada alone. A little stayed in Virginia City, but a great deal more went to speculators in California, some of whom got rich without ever leaving San Francisco.

The promise of gold and silver drew thousands to the mines of the West, the honest as well as the unprincipled. As Mark Twain observed, the Comstock attracted an international array of immigrants. "All the peoples of the earth had representative adventures in the Silverland," he wrote. Irish, Chinese, Germans, English, Scots, Welsh, Canadians, Mexicans, Italians, Scandinavians, French, Swiss, Chileans, and other South and Central Americans came to share in the bonanza. With them came a sprinkling of Russians, Poles, Greeks, Japanese, Spaniards, Hungarians, Portuguese, Turks, Pacific Islanders, and Moroccans, as well as other North Americans, African Americans, and American Indians. This polyglot population, typical of mining boomtowns, made Virginia City in the 1870s more cosmopolitan than New York or Boston. In the part of Utah Territory that eventually became Nevada, as many as 30 percent of the people came from outside the United States, compared to 25 percent in New York and 21 percent in Massachusetts.

Irish immigrants formed the largest ethnic group in the mining district. In Virginia City, fully one-third of the population claimed at least one parent from Ireland. Irish and Irish American women constituted the largest group of women on the Comstock. As servants, boardinghouse owners, and washerwomen, they made up a significant part of the workforce. In contrast, the Chinese community, composed of 642 men in 1870, remained overwhelmingly male. Virulent anti-Chinese sentiment barred the men from work in the mines, but despite the violent anti-Asian rhetoric, the mining community came to depend on Chinese labor. Many boardinghouses and affluent homes employed a Chinese cook or servant along with an Irish parlor maid.

As was so often the case in the West, where Euro-American ambitions clashed with Native American ways, the discovery of precious metals on the Comstock spelled disaster for the Indians. No sooner had the miners struck pay dirt than they demanded army troops to "hunt Indians" and establish forts to protect transportation to and from the diggings. This sudden and dramatic intrusion left Nevada's native tribes—the Northern Paiute and Bannock Shoshoni—exiles in their own land. At first they resisted, but over time they made peace with the invaders and proved resourceful in finding ways to adapt and preserve their culture and identity despite the havoc wrought by western mining and settlement.

In 1873, Comstock miners uncovered a new vein of ore, a veritable cavern of gold and silver. This "Big Bonanza" speeded the transition from small-scale industry to corporate **oligopoly**, creating a radically new social and economic environment. The Comstock became a laboratory for new mining technology, a place of industry and engineers. Huge stamping mills pulverized rock with pistonlike hammers driven by steam engines. Enormous engines known as Cornish pumps sucked water from the mine shafts, and huge ventilators circulated air in the underground chambers. No backwoods mining camp, Virginia City was an industrial center, with more than 1,200 stamping mills working on average a ton of ore every day. Almost 400 men worked in milling, nearly 300 labored in manufacturing industries, and roughly 3,000 toiled in the mines. The Gould and Curry mine covered sixty acres. Most of the miners who came to the Comstock ended up as laborers for the big companies, although they sometimes worked their own small "rat hole" mines on their time off, still hoping to strike it rich.

The miner's job was filled with peril. Descending deep into the earth, down 1,500 to 3,000 feet where temperatures rose to 120 degrees, stripped-down miners on the Comstock Lode retreated to "cooling-off rooms" where the company provided barrels of ice water to bring down the miners' body temperature. Death stalked the mines and came in many forms—fires, floods, cave-ins, bad air, falling timbers, and misfired explosives.

New technology eliminated some of the dangers of mining but often created new ones. In the hard-rock mines of the West, accidents in the 1870s disabled one out of every thirty miners and killed one in eighty. Ross Moudy, who worked as a miner in Cripple Creek, Colorado, recalled how a stockholder visiting the mine nearly fell to his death. The terrified visitor told the miner next to him that "instead of being paid $3 a day, they ought to have all the gold they could take out." Moudy's biggest worry was carbon dioxide, which often filled the tunnels because of poor ventilation. "Many times," he confessed, "I have been carried out unconscious." Those who avoided accidents still breathed air so dangerous that respiratory diseases eventually disabled them. After a year on the job, Moudy joined a labor union "because I saw it would help me to keep in work and for protection in case of accident or sickness." The union provided good sick benefits and hired nurses, "so if one is alone and sick he is sure to be taken care of." On the Comstock Lode, because of the difficulty of obtaining skilled labor, the richness of the ore, and the need for a stable workforce, labor unions formed early and held considerable bargaining power. Comstock miners commanded $4 a day, the highest wage in the mining West.

The mining towns of the "Wild West" are often portrayed as lawless outposts, filled with saloons and rough gambling dens and populated almost exclusively by men, except for the occasional dance-hall floozy. The truth is more complex, as Virginia City's development attests. An established urban community built to serve an industrial giant, Virginia City in its first decade boasted churches, schools, theaters, an opera house, and hundreds of families. By 1870, women composed 30 percent of the population, and 75 percent of the women listed their occupation in the census as housekeeper. Many of them made money on the side by providing lodging and by cooking or sewing and doing laundry for bachelor miners. Mary McNair Mathews, a widow from Buffalo, New York, who lived on the Comstock in the 1870s, worked as a teacher, nurse, seamstress, laundress, and lodging-house operator. She later published a book on her adventures.

By 1875, Virginia City boasted a population of 25,000 people, making it one of the largest cities between St. Louis and San Francisco. A must-see stop on the way west, the Queen of the Comstock hosted American presidents as well as legions of lesser dignitaries. No rough outpost of the Wild West, Virginia City represented, in the words of a recent chronicler, "the distilled essence of America's newly established course—urban, industrial, acquisitive, and materialistic, on the move, 'a living polyglot' of cultures that collided and converged." In short, Virginia City formed an integral part of a new urban, industrial America.

Territorial Government

The federal government practiced a policy of benign neglect when it came to territorial government in the West. The president appointed a governor, a secretary, and two to four judges, along with an attorney and a marshal. In Nevada Territory, that meant that a handful of officials governed an area the size of New England. Originally a part of the larger Utah Territory, Nevada, propelled by mining interests, moved on the fast track to statehood, entering the Union in 1864, long before its population or its development merited statehood.

More typical were the territories extant in 1870—New Mexico, Utah, Washington, Colorado, Dakota, Arizona, Idaho, Montana, and Wyoming. These areas remained territories for inordinately long periods ranging from twenty-three to sixty-two years. While awaiting statehood, they were subject to territorial governors who were underpaid, often unqualified, and largely ignored in Washington. The vast majority of territorial appointments were given to men because of their party loyalty. Most governors had no knowledge of the areas they served, little notion of their duties, and limited ability to perform them.

In theory, territorial governors received adequate salaries, as high as $3,500 in an era when the average workingman earned less than $500 a year. In practice, the funds rarely arrived in a timely fashion, and more than one governor found that he had to pay government expenses out of his own pocket. As one cynic observed, "Only the rich or those having 'no visible means of support,' can afford to accept office." John C. Frémont, the governor of Arizona Territory, was so poor he complained to Washington that he could not inspect the Grand Canyon because he didn't have enough money to keep a horse.

Territorial governors with fewer scruples accepted money from special-interest groups such as mine owners or ranchers. Nearly all territorial appointees tried to make ends meet by maintaining business connections with the East or by taking advantage of investment opportunities in the West. Distance and the lack of funds made it difficult to summon officers from Washington to investigate charges of corruption. Officials who ventured west to look into malfeasance often felt intimidated by gun-packing westerners. One judge sent to New Mexico Territory in 1871 reported that he "stayed three days, made up his mind that it would be dangerous to do any investigating, . . . and returned to his home without any action." Underfunded and overlooked, victims of political cronyism and prey to local interests, territorial governments were rife with conflicts of interest and corruption, mirroring the self-serving political and economic values of the country as a whole in the rush for riches that followed the Civil War.

The Diverse Peoples of the West

The West of the late nineteenth century was a polyglot place, as much so as the big cities of the East. The parade of peoples who came to the West included immigrants from Europe, Asia, and Canada, not to mention New Englanders, Mormons, African Americans, Mexicans, and Latinos. The sheer number of peoples who mingled in the West produced a complex blend of racism and prejudice. One historian has noted, not entirely facetiously, that there were at least eight oppressed "races" in the West—Indians, Latinos, Chinese, Japanese, blacks, Mormons, strikers, and radicals.

African Americans who ventured out to the territories faced hostile settlers determined to keep the West "for whites only." In response, they formed all-black communities such as Nicodemas, Kansas. That settlement, founded by thirty black Kentuckians in 1877, grew to a community of seven hundred by 1880. Isolated and often separated by great distances, small black settlements grew up throughout the West, in Nevada, Utah, and the Pacific Northwest as well as in Kansas. Black soldiers who served in the West during the Indian wars often stayed on as settlers. Called "buffalo soldiers" because Native Americans thought their hair resembled that of the buffalo, these black troops numbered up to 25,000. The army pitted people of color against one another, using black soldiers to fight the Apaches in Arizona Territory and to help subdue the Sioux in the Dakotas.

Hispanic peoples had lived in Texas and the Southwest since Juan de Oñate led pioneer settlers up the Rio Grande in 1598. Hispanics had occupied the Pacific coast since San Diego was founded in 1769. Overnight, they were reduced to a "minority" after the United States annexed Texas in 1845 and took land stretching to California after the Mexican-American War ended in 1848. At first, the Hispanic owners of large *ranchos* in California, New Mexico, and Texas greeted conquest as an economic opportunity—new markets for their livestock and buyers for their lands. But racial prejudice soon ended their optimism. Californios (Mexican residents of California), who had been granted American citizenship by the Treaty of Guadalupe Hidalgo (1848), faced discrimination by Anglos who sought to keep them out of California's mines and commerce. Whites illegally squatted on *rancho* land while protracted litigation over Spanish and Mexican **land grants** forced the

Californios into court. Although the U.S. Supreme Court eventually validated most of their claims, it took so long—seventeen years on average—that many Californios sold their property to pay taxes and legal bills. The city of Oakland, California, sits on what was once a 19,000-acre ranch owned by the Peralta family, who lost the land to Anglos. Swindles, chicanery, and intimidation dispossessed scores of Californios. Many ended up segregated in urban barrios (neighborhoods) in their own homeland. Their percentage of California's population declined from 82 percent in 1850 to 19 percent in 1880 as Anglos migrated to the state. In New Mexico and Texas, Mexicans remained a majority of the population but became increasingly impoverished as Anglos dominated business and took the best jobs. Skirmishes between Hispanics and whites in northern New Mexico over the fencing of the open range lasted for decades. Groups of Hispanics with names such as *Las Manos Negras* (the Black Hands) cut fences and burned barns. In Texas, violence along the Rio Grande pitted Tejanos (Mexican residents of Texas) against the Texas Rangers, who saw their role as "keeping Mexicans in their place."

Like the Mexicans, the Mormons faced prejudice and hostility. The followers of Joseph Smith, the founder and prophet of the Church of Jesus Christ of Latter-Day Saints, fled west to avoid religious persecution. They believed that they had a divine right to the land, and their messianic militancy contributed to making them outcasts. The Mormon practice of polygamy (a man taking more than one wife) became a convenient point of attack for those who hated and feared the group. After Smith was killed by an Illinois mob in 1844, Brigham Young led the flock, which numbered more than 20,000, over the Rockies to the valley of the Great Salt Lake in Utah Territory. The Mormons quickly set to work irrigating the desert. They relied on cooperation and communalism, a strategy that excluded competition from those outside the faith. The church controlled water supplies, stores, insurance companies, and later factories and mining smelters. By 1882, the Mormons had built Salt Lake City, a thriving metropolis of more than 150,000 residents.

The Mormon practice of polygamy (Brigham Young had twenty-seven wives) had come under attack as early as 1857, when U.S. troops occupied Salt Lake City (see chapter 12). To counter criticism of polygamy, the Utah territorial legislature gave women the right to vote in 1870, the first universal woman suffrage act in the nation. (Wyoming had granted suffrage to white women in 1869.) Although woman's rights advocates argued that the newly enfranchised women would "do away with the horrible institution of polygamy," it remained in force. Not until 1890 did the church hierarchy give in to pressure to renounce polygamy. The fierce controversy over polygamy postponed statehood for Utah until 1896.

The Chinese suffered brutal treatment at the hands of employers and other laborers. Drawn by the promise of gold, more than 20,000 Chinese had joined the rush to California by 1852. Miners determined to keep "California for Americans" succeeded in passing prohibitive foreign license laws to keep the Chinese out of the mines. But Chinese immigration continued. In the 1860s, when

Chinese Workers
Chinese section hands are shown here in 1898 shoveling dirt for the North Pacific Coast Railroad in Corte Madera, California. Charles Crocker was the first railroad executive to hire Chinese laborers to work on the Central Pacific railroad in the 1860s, reasoning that the race that built the Great Wall could build tracks through the Sierra Nevada.
California Historical Society, FN-25345.

white workers moved on to find riches in the bonanza mines of Nevada, Chinese laborers took jobs abandoned by the whites. Railroad magnate Charles Crocker hired Chinese gangs to work on the Central Pacific, reasoning that the race that built the Great Wall could lay tracks across the treacherous Sierra Nevada. Some 12,000 Chinese, representing 90 percent of Crocker's workforce, completed America's first transcontinental railroad in 1869.

By 1870, more than 63,000 Chinese immigrants lived in America, 77 percent of them in California. A 1790 federal statute that limited naturalization to "white persons" was modified after the Civil War to extend naturalization to blacks ("persons of African descent"). But the Chinese and other Asians continued to be denied access to citizenship. As perpetual aliens, they constituted a reserve army of transnational industrial laborers that many saw as a threat to American labor. For the most part, the Chinese did not displace white workers but instead found work as railroad laborers, cooks, servants, and farmhands while white workers sought out more lucrative fields. In the 1870s, when California and the rest of the nation weathered a major economic depression, the Chinese became easy scapegoats. California workingmen rioted and fought to keep Chinese workers out of the state, claiming they were "coolie labor"—involuntary contract laborers recruited by business interests determined to keep wages at rock bottom.

In 1876, the Workingmen's Party formed to fight for Chinese exclusion. Racial and cultural animosities stood at the heart of anti-Chinese agitation. Denis Kearney, the fiery San Francisco leader of the movement, made clear this racist bent when he urged legislation to "expel every one of the moon-eyed lepers." Nor was California alone in its anti-immigrant **nativism**. As the country confronted growing ethnic and racial diversity with the rising tide of global immigration in the decades following the Civil War, many questioned the principle of racial equality at the same time they argued against the assimilation of "nonwhite" groups. In this climate, Congress passed the Chinese Exclusion Act in 1882, effectively barring Chinese immigration and becoming a precedent for further immigration restrictions. The Chinese Exclusion Act led to a sharp drop in the Chinese population—from 105,465 in 1880 to 89,863 in 1900—because Chinese immigrants, overwhelmingly male, did not have families to sustain their population. Eventually, Japanese immigrants, including women as well as men, replaced the Chinese, particularly in agriculture. As "nonwhite" immigrants, they could not become naturalized citizens, but their children born in the United States claimed the rights of citizenship. Japanese parents, seeking to own land, purchased it in their children's names. Although anti-Asian prejudice remained strong in California and elsewhere in the West, Asian immigrants formed an important part of the economic fabric of the western United States.

The American West in the nineteenth century witnessed more than its share of conflict and bloodshed. Violent prejudice against the Chinese and other Asian immigrants remained common. But violence also broke out between cattle ranchers and sheep ranchers, between ranchers and farmers, between striking miners and their bosses, among rival Indian groups, and between whites and Indians. At issue was who would control the vast resources of the emerging region.

▶ REVIEW   How did industrial technology change mining in Nevada?

Land Fever

After the Civil War, Americans by the hundreds of thousands packed up and moved west, goaded if not by the hope of striking gold, then by the promise of owning land. In the three decades following 1870, more land was settled than in all the previous history of the country. Between 1876 and 1900, eight new western states entered the Union—Colorado, Montana, North and South Dakota, Washington, Idaho, Wyoming, and Utah—leaving only three territories—

Railroad Locomotive
After the Civil War, the locomotive replaced the covered wagon, enabling settlers to travel from Chicago or St. Louis to the West Coast in two days. The first transcontinental railroad, completed in 1869, soon led to the creation of competing systems, so that by the 1880s, travelers going west could choose from four railroad lines. In this photograph, men and women perched on a locomotive celebrate the completion of a section of track.
Library of Congress.

Oklahoma, New Mexico, and Arizona. The agrarian West shared with the mining West a persistent restlessness, an equally pervasive addiction to speculation, and a penchant for exploiting natural resources and labor.

Two factors stimulated the land rush in the trans-Mississippi West. The Homestead Act of 1862 promised 160 acres free to any citizen or prospective citizen, male or female, who settled on the land for five years. Even more important, transcontinental railroads opened up new areas and actively recruited settlers. After the completion of the first transcontinental railroad in 1869, homesteaders abandoned the covered wagon, and by the 1880s they could choose from four competing rail lines and make the trip in a matter of days.

Although the country was rich in land and resources, not all who wanted to own land achieved their goal. A growing number of Americans found themselves forced to work for wages on land they would never own. During the transition from the family farm to large commercial farming, small farms gave way to vast spreads worked by migrant labor or paid farmworkers. Just as industry corporatized and consolidated in the East, the period from 1870 to 1900 witnessed corporate consolidation in mining, ranching, and agriculture.

Moving West: Homesteaders and Speculators

A Missouri homesteader remembered packing as her family pulled up stakes and headed west to Oklahoma in 1890. "We were going to God's Country," she wrote. "You had to work hard on that rocky country in Missouri. I was glad to be leaving it. . . . We were going to a new land and get rich."

People who ventured west searching for "God's Country" faced hardship, loneliness, and deprivation. To carve a farm from the raw prairie of Iowa, the plains of Nebraska, or the forests of the Pacific Northwest took more than fortitude and backbreaking toil. It took luck. Blizzards, tornadoes, grasshoppers, hailstorms, drought, prairie fires, accidental death, and disease were only a few of the catastrophes that could befall even the best farmer. Homesteaders on free land still needed as much as $1,000 for a house, a team of farm animals, a well, fencing, and seed. Poor farmers called "sodbusters" did without even these basics, living in dugouts carved into hillsides and using muscle instead of machinery.

"Father made a dugout and covered it with willows and grass," one Kansas girl recounted. When it rained, the dugout flooded, and "we carried the water out in buckets, then waded around in the mud until it dried." Rain wasn't the only problem. "Sometimes the bull snakes would get in the roof and now and then one would lose his hold and fall down on the bed. . . . Mother would grab the hoe . . . and after the fight was over Mr. Bull Snake was dragged outside." The sod house, a step up from the dugout, had walls cut from blocks of sod and a roof of sod, lumber, or tin. In requiring that homesteaders "settle" on the land for five years to achieve ownership, the government did not stipulate a specific size or manner of construction for homesteads. In the Dakotas, homesteaders often erected claim shacks, some as small as eight by ten feet.

For women on the frontier, obtaining simple daily necessities such as water and fuel meant backbreaking labor. Out on the plains, where water was scarce, women often had to trudge to the nearest creek or spring. "A yoke was made to place across [Mother's] shoulders, so as to carry at each end a bucket of water," one daughter recollected, "and then water was brought a half mile from spring to house." Gathering fuel was another heavy chore. Without ready sources of coal or firewood, settlers on the plains turned to what substitutes they could scavenge—twigs, tufts of grass, corncobs, sunflower stalks. But by far the most prevalent fuel was "chips"— chunks of dried cattle and buffalo dung, found in abundance on the plains.

Despite the hardships, some homesteaders succeeded in building comfortable lives. The sod hut made way for a more substantial house; the log cabin yielded to a white clapboard home with a porch and a rocking chair. And the type and quality of the family diet improved. "Our living at first was very scanty," recalled one Kansas woman, "mostly corn coarsely ground and made into hominy." Then the family raised a crop of wheat and ground it into flour. "We would invite the neighbors proudly telling them we have 'flour doings.'" When the farmwife began to raise chickens, the family added "chicken fixings" to its diet, "and when we could have 'flour doings' and 'chicken fixings' at the same meal we felt we were on the road to prosperity."

For others, the promise of the West failed to materialize. Already by the 1870s, much of the best land had been taken. Too often, homesteaders found that only the least desirable tracts were left—poor land, far from markets, transportation, and society. Speculators held the lion's share of the land. "There is plenty of land for sale in California," one migrant complained in 1870, but "the majority of the available lands are held by speculators, at prices far beyond the reach of a poor man."

The railroads, flush from land grants provided by the state and federal governments, owned huge swaths of land in the West and actively recruited settlers. Altogether, the land grants totaled approximately 180 million acres—an area almost one-tenth the size of the United States (Map 17.2). Many farmers who

---

MAP 17.2   Federal Land Grants to Railroads and the Development of the West, 1850–1900
Generous federal land grants meant that railroads could sell the desirable land next to the track at a profit or hold it for speculation. Railroads received more than 180 million acres, an area as large as Texas. Notice how the cattle trails connect with major railheads in Dodge City, Abilene, and Kansas City and to mining towns in Montana, Nevada, Colorado, and New Mexico.

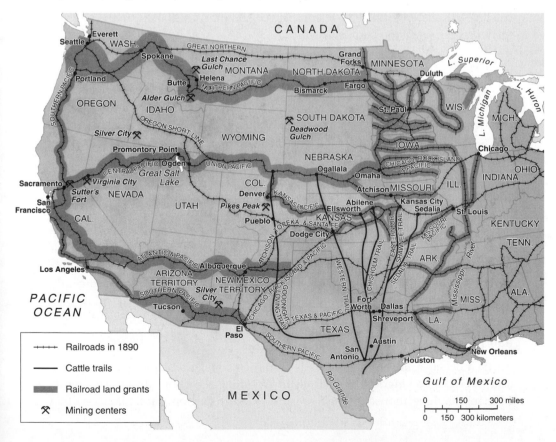

went west ended up buying land from the railroads or from the speculators and land companies that quickly followed the railroads into the West. Of the 2.5 million farms established between 1860 and 1900, homesteading accounted for only one in five; the vast majority of farmland sold for a profit.

As land grew scarce on the prairie in the 1870s, farmers began to push farther west, moving into western Kansas, Nebraska, and eastern Colorado—the region called the Great American Desert by settlers who had passed over it on their way to California and Oregon. Many agricultural experts warned that the semiarid land (where less than twenty inches of rain fell annually) would not support a farm on the 160 acres allotted to homesteaders, but their words of caution were drowned out by the extravagant claims of western promoters, many employed by the railroads to sell off their land grants. "Rain follows the plow" became the slogan of western boosters, who insisted that cultivation would alter the climate of the region and bring more rainfall.

Instead, drought followed the plow. Droughts were a cyclical fact of life on the Great Plains. Plowed up, the dry topsoil blew away in the wind. A period of relatively good rainfall in the early 1880s encouraged farming; then a protracted drought in the late 1880s and early 1890s sent starving farmers reeling back from the plains. Thousands left, some in wagons carrying the slogan "In God we trusted, in Kansas we busted." A popular ballad bitterly summed up the plight of the worst off, those too poor to leave.

> But here I am stuck and here I must stay
> My money's all gone and I can't get away;
> There's nothing will make a man hard and profane
> Like starving to death on a government claim.

Fever for fertile land set off a series of spectacular land runs in Oklahoma. When two million acres of land in former Indian Territory opened for settlement in 1889, thousands of homesteaders massed on the border. At the opening pistol shot, "with a shout and a yell the swift riders shot out, then followed the light buggies or wagons," a reporter wrote. "Above all, a great cloud of dust hover[ed] like smoke over a battlefield." By nightfall, Oklahoma boasted two tent cities with more than ten thousand residents. In the last frenzied land rush on Oklahoma's Cherokee strip in 1893, several settlers were killed in the stampede, and nervous men guarded their claims with rifles. As public land grew scarce, the hunger for land grew fiercer for both farmers and ranchers.

Ranchers and Cowboys

Cattle ranchers followed the railroads onto the plains, establishing between 1865 and 1885 a cattle kingdom from Texas to Wyoming. Cowboys drove huge herds, as many as three thousand head of cattle, that grazed on public lands as they

Barbed Wire Machine

Joseph Glidden's original barbing machine, patented in 1874, consisted of an old-fashioned coffee mill with its casing cut away and its grinder altered to cut and coil small lengths of wire. The barbs were strung by hand between strands of plain wire. Despite its flimsiness, barbed wire could contain cattle, as master promoter John "Bet a Million" Gates demonstrated by corralling a herd of Texas longhorns in downtown San Antonio in 1879. Ellwood House Museum, De Kalb, Illinois.

followed cattle tracks like the Chisholm Trail from Texas to railheads in Kansas. From there, the cattle traveled by boxcar to Chicago, where they sold for as much as $45 a head. More than a million and a half Texas longhorns went to market before the range began to close in the 1880s.

Barbed wire revolutionized the cattle business and sounded the death knell for the open range. In 1874, Joseph F. Glidden, an Illinois sheriff, invented and patented barbed wire. Gambler and promoter John "Bet a Million" Gates made his fortune by corralling a herd of Texas longhorns in downtown San Antonio, proving the merit of the flimsy-looking wire he went on to market profitably. As the largest ranches in Texas began to fence, nasty fights broke out between big ranchers and "fence cutters," who resented the end of the free range. One old-timer observed, "Those persons, Mexicans and Americans, without land but who had cattle were put out of business by fencing." Fencing forced small-time ranchers who owned land but could not afford to buy barbed wire or sink wells to sell out for the best price they could get. The displaced ranchers, many of them Mexicans, ended up as wageworkers on the huge spreads owned by Anglos or by European syndicates.

On the range, the cowboy gave way to the cattle king and, like the miner, became a wage laborer. Many cowboys were African Americans (as many as five thousand in Texas alone). Writers of western literature chose to ignore the presence of black cowboys like Deadwood Dick (Nat Love), who was portrayed as a white man in the dime novels of the era. Cowboy life was hard, and like many other dissatisfied workers in the East, cowboys organized labor unions in the 1880s and mounted strikes in both Texas and Wyoming.

By 1886, cattle overcrowded the range. Severe blizzards during the winters of 1886–87 and 1887–88 decimated the herds. "A whole generation of cowmen," wrote one chronicler, "went dead broke." Fencing worsened the situation. During blizzards, cattle stayed alive by keeping on the move. But when they ran up against barbed wire fences, they froze to death. In the aftermath of the "Great Die Up," new labor-intensive forms of cattle ranching replaced the open-range model.

Tenants, Sharecroppers, and Migrants

Many who followed the American promise into the West prospered, but landownership proved an elusive goal for many others—among them freed slaves, immigrants from Europe and Asia, and Mexicans in California and on the Texas border. In the post–Civil War period, as agriculture became a big business tied to national and global markets, an increasing number of laborers worked land that they would never own.

In the southern United States, farmers labored under particularly heavy burdens (see chapter 16). The Civil War wiped out much of the region's capital, which had been invested in slaves, and crippled the plantation economy. Newly freed slaves rarely obtained land of their own and often ended up as farm laborers. "The colored folks stayed with the old boss man and farmed and worked on the plantations," a black Alabama sharecropper observed bitterly. "They were still slaves, but they were free slaves." Some freed people did manage to pull together enough resources to go west. In 1879, more than fifteen thousand black "Exodusters" moved from Mississippi and Louisiana to take up land in Kansas.

Many Mexicans who held land grants from the former Spanish or Mexican governments found themselves in the aftermath of the Mexican-American War in the new state of California (1850), which demanded that they prove their claims in court. The protracted legal battles over their land claims drove many *rancheros* (Mexican ranchers), discouraged by the wait, to sell out to Anglos.

California's Mexican cowboys, or *vaqueros*, commanded decent wages throughout the Southwest. Skilled horsemen, the vaqueros boasted that five of them could do the work of thirty Anglo cowboys. The vocabulary of ranching, with words such as *rodeo, lasso, lariat*, and *rancho*, testified to the centrality of the vaqueros' place in the cattle industry. But in the 1870s, when the coming of the railroads ended the long cattle drives and large feedlots began to replace the open range, the value of their skills declined. Many vaqueros ended up as migrant laborers, often on land their families had once owned. Similarly, in Texas, Tejanos found themselves displaced. After the heyday of cattle ranching ended in the late 1880s, cotton production rose in the southeastern regions of the state. Ranchers turned their pastures into sharecroppers' plots and hired displaced cowboys, most of them Mexicans, as seasonal laborers for as little as seventy-five cents a day. Within ten years, ranch life in southern Texas gave way to a growing army of agricultural wageworkers.

Land **monopoly** and large-scale farming fostered tenancy and migratory labor on the West Coast. By the 1870s, less than 1 percent of California's population owned half the state's available agricultural land. The rigid economics of large-scale commercial agriculture and the seasonal nature of the crops spawned a ragged army of migratory agricultural laborers. Derisively labeled "blanket men" or "bindle stiffs," these transients worked the fields in the growing season and wintered in the flophouses of San Francisco. Wheat farming in California in the 1870s and 1880s exhausted the land and was replaced, with the introduction of irrigation, by fruit and sugar beet farming. Most of the California farm laborers were Chinese immigrants until the Chinese Exclusion Act of 1882 forced big growers to look to other groups, primarily Mexicans, Filipinos, and Japanese, for farm labor.

Commercial Farming and Industrial Cowboys

In the late nineteenth century, America's population remained overwhelmingly rural. The 1870 census showed that nearly 80 percent of the nation's people lived on farms and in villages of fewer than 8,000 inhabitants. By 1900, the figure had dropped to 66 percent. At the same time, the number of farms rose. Rapid growth in the West increased the number of the nation's farms from 2 million in 1860 to more than 5.7 million in 1900.

Despite the hardships individual farmers experienced on the plains, new technology and farming techniques revolutionized American farm life. Mechanized plows and reapers halved the time and labor cost of production and made it possible to cultivate vast tracts of land. Urbanization provided farmers with expanding markets for their produce, and railroads carried crops to markets thousands of miles away. Even before the opening of the twentieth century, American agriculture had entered the era of what would come to be called **agribusiness**— farming as a big business—with the advent of huge commercial farms.

As farming moved onto the prairies and plains, mechanization took command. Steel plows, reapers, mowers, harrows, seed drills, combines, and threshers replaced human muscle. Horse-drawn implements gave way to steam-powered machinery. By 1880, a single combine could do the work of twenty men, vastly increasing the acreage a farmer could cultivate. Mechanization spurred the growth of bonanza wheat farms, some more than 100,000 acres, in California and the Red River Valley of North Dakota and Minnesota. This agricultural revolution meant that Americans raised more than four times the corn, five times the hay, and seven times the wheat and oats they had before the Civil War. Much of this new production went to feed people as far away as England and Germany.

Like cotton farmers in the South, western grain and livestock farmers increasingly depended on foreign markets for their livelihood. A fall in global market prices meant that a farmer's entire harvest went to pay off debts. In the depression that followed the panic of 1893, many heavily mortgaged farmers lost their land to creditors. As a Texas cotton farmer complained, "By the time the World

Gets their Liveing out of the Farmer as we have to Feed the World, we the Farmer has nothing Left but a Bear Hard Liveing."

Commercial farming, along with mining, represented another way in which the West developed its own brand of industrialism. The far West's industrial economy sprang initially from California gold and the vast territory that came under American control following the Mexican-American War. In the ensuing rush on land and resources, environmental factors interacted with economic and social forces to produce enterprises as vast in scale and scope as anything found in the East. Two Alsatian immigrants, Henry Miller and Charles Lux, pioneered the West's mix of agriculture and industrialism.

Beginning as meat wholesalers, Miller and Lux quickly expanded their business to encompass cattle, land, and land reclamation projects such as dams and irrigation systems. With a labor force of migrant workers, a highly coordinated corporate system, and large sums of investment capital, the firm of Miller & Lux became one of America's industrial behemoths. Already by 1870, Miller & Lux owned well over 300,000 acres of grazing land in California's central San Joaquin Valley, over half of it derived from former Mexican land grants. Its industrial-sized wheat operations in California bore little resemblance to any previous form of agriculture. Eventually, these "industrial cowboys" grazed a herd of 100,000 cattle on 1.25 million acres of company land in three western states (California, Oregon, and Nevada) and employed more than 1,200 migrant laborers on their corporate ranches. By 1900, Miller & Lux controlled capital and labor to a degree far surpassing that of most eastern manufacturing firms.

Miller & Lux developed remarkably dynamic investment strategies and corporate structures to control not only California land but water rights as well. The state's largest land speculators, Miller & Lux employed an army of lobbyists to serve its interests in Sacramento. Although the specific components of the Miller & Lux business may have differed from those of industries in the East, the company nonetheless shared the main characteristics of other modern enterprises: corporate consolidation, ownership of resources and raw materials, and schemes to minimize labor costs and stabilize the workforce. Miller & Lux dealt with the labor problem by offering free meals to migratory workers, thus keeping wages low while winning goodwill among an army of unemployed who competed for the work. When the company's Chinese cooks rebelled at washing the dishes resulting from the free meals, the migrant laborers were forced to eat after the ranch hands and use their dirty plates. By the 1890s, more than eight hundred migrants followed what came to be known as the "Dirty Plate Route" on Miller & Lux ranches throughout California.

Since the days of Thomas Jefferson, agrarian life had been linked with the highest ideals of a democratic society. Now agrarianism itself had been transformed. The farmer was no longer a self-sufficient **yeoman** but often a businessman or a wage laborer tied to a global market. And even as farm production soared, industrialization outstripped it. More and more farmers left the fields for urban factories or found work in the "factories in the fields" of the new industrialized agribusiness. Now that the future seemed to lie not with the small farmer but with industrial enterprises, was democracy itself at risk? This question would ignite a farmers' revolt in the 1880s and dominate political debate in the 1890s.

▶ **REVIEW**   Why did many homesteaders find it difficult to acquire good land in the West?

Conclusion: The Mythic West

Even as the Old West was changing, the mythic West was being born. The prince of the dime novel, Buffalo Bill, became its icon. Born William F. Cody, the real-life Buffalo Bill had panned for gold, ridden for the Pony Express, scouted for the army, and earned his nickname hunting buffalo for the railroad. The masterful showman formed a touring Wild West company in 1883. Part circus, part theater, the Wild West extravaganza featured exhibitions of riding, shooting, and roping and presented dramatic reenactments of great moments in western lore. The star of the show, Annie Oakley (Phoebe Moses), dubbed "Little Miss Sure Shot," delighted the crowd by shooting a dime out of her husband's hand. For years, the centerpiece of Buffalo Bill's Wild West show was a reenactment of Custer's Last Stand featuring real Indians wearing war paint and feathered headdresses. Some of them, including Sitting Bull, who traveled with the show in 1885, had fought at Little Big Horn. At the end of the mock battle, Buffalo Bill galloped in through a cloud of dust and dramatically mouthed the words "Too late!" Highly dubious as history, as spectacle the Wild West show was unbeatable. At the World's Columbian Exposition in 1893, crowds numbering tens of thousands packed the bleachers to cheer. By the turn of the twentieth century, the high drama of the struggle for the West had become little more than a thrilling but harmless entertainment.

While Buffalo Bill's show entertained the crowds on the Midway, across the fairgrounds historian Frederick Jackson Turner addressed the American Historical Association on "The Significance of the Frontier in American History." Turner noted that by 1890, the census could no longer discern a clear frontier line. His tone was elegiac: "The existence of an area of free land, its continuous recession, and the advance of settlement westward," he observed, "explained American development" and was inextricably linked to what was best and unique in America. Of course, land in the West had never been empty or free; nor were the whites who moved westward its only inhabitants. The pastoral agrarianism Turner celebrated belied the urban, industrial West found on the Comstock and in the commercial farms of California. Nevertheless, Turner's "frontier thesis" became one of the most enduring myths of the American West.

The real West was no less dramatic than the mythic West. Between 1860 and 1900, the United States developed an empire in the West that filled the map of the continent with states and territories all the way to the Pacific. Native Americans ended up dispossessed, forced onto reservations, and later put out to farm on 160-acre plots. At the same time, whites sought to erase tribal identity and force assimilation. As miners poured into the West, giant mining operations like those on the Comstock replaced the prospector with his burro and pan. Agriculture, too, became increasingly mechanized and commercial; huge farms totaling thousands of acres were tilled by machine and the muscle of hired workers. With its consolidated mining companies and burgeoning agribusiness, the West developed its own brand of urban industrialism.

In the decades following the Civil War, as the United States pursued empire in the American West, new problems replaced the old issues of slavery and sectionalism. The growing power of big business, the exploitation of labor and natural resources, corruption in politics, and ethnic and racial tensions exacerbated by colonial expansion and unparalleled immigration dominated the debates of the day in both East and West. As the nineteenth century ended, Americans had more questions than answers. Could the American promise survive in the new world of corporations, wage labor, and mushrooming cities? Neither out of place nor out of time, the West contributed its share to both the promise and the problems of the era Mark Twain would brand the Gilded Age.

REVIEWING THE CHAPTER

Use the questions and timeline to review and strengthen your understanding of the chapter.

REVIEW QUESTIONS

1. How did the slaughter of the bison contribute to the Plains Indians' removal to reservations? (pp. 510–21)

2. How did industrial technology change mining in Nevada? (pp. 521–28)

3. Why did many homesteaders find it difficult to acquire good land in the West? (pp. 528–37)

MAKING CONNECTIONS

1. Westward migration brought settlers into conflict with Native Americans. What was the U.S. government's policy toward Indians in the West, and how did it evolve over time? How did the Indians resist and survive white encroachment? In your answer, discuss the cultural and military features of the conflict.

2. The economic and industrial developments characteristic of the East after the Civil War also made their mark on the West. How did innovations in business and technology transform mining and agriculture in the West? In your answer, be sure to consider effects on production and the consequences for the lives of miners and agricultural laborers.

3. Settlers from all over the world came to the American West seeking their fortunes but found that opportunity was not equally available to all. In competition for work and land, why did Anglo-American settlers usually have the upper hand? How did legal developments contribute to this circumstance?

TIMELINE

1851	• First Treaty of Fort Laramie.	**1881**	• Sitting Bull surrenders.
1862	• Homestead Act. • Great Sioux Uprising (Santee Uprising).	**1882**	• Chinese Exclusion Act. • Indian Rights Association formed.
1864	• Sand Creek Massacre.	**1883**	• Buffalo Bill Cody begins touring.
1867	• Treaty of Medicine Lodge.	**1886**	• Geronimo surrenders.
1868	• Second Treaty of Fort Laramie.	**1886– 1888**	• Severe blizzards decimate cattle herds.
1869	• First transcontinental railroad completed.		
1870	• Hunters begin to decimate bison herds. • Henry Miller and Charles Lux develop agricultural empire in California.	**1887**	• Dawes Allotment Act.
		1889	• Rise of Ghost Dance. • Two million acres in Oklahoma opened for settlement.
1873	• "Big Bonanza" on Comstock Lode.		
1874	• Discovery of gold in Black Hills.	**1890**	• Sitting Bull killed. • Massacre at Wounded Knee, South Dakota. • Gold discovered in Cripple Creek, Colorado.
1876	• Battle of the Little Big Horn.		
1877	• Chief Joseph surrenders. • Crazy Horse surrenders and is later arrested and killed.		
		1893	• Last land rush takes place in Oklahoma Territory.
1878	• Indian students enroll at Hampton Insti- tute in Virginia.	**1900**	• Census finds 66 percent of population lives in rural areas, compared to 80 percent in 1870.
1879	• Carlisle Indian School opens in Pennsylvania. • More than fifteen thousand Exodusters move to Kansas.		

▶ **For an online bibliography, practice quizzes, Web sites, images, and documents related to this chapter,** see the Book Companion Site at **bedfordstmartins.com/roark.**

▶ **For firsthand accounts of this period,** see Chapter 17 in Michael Johnson, ed., *Reading the American Past,* Fourth Edition.

18
CHAPTER

Business and Politics in the Gilded Age
1870–1895

O NE NIGHT OVER DINNER, humorist and author Mark Twain and his friend Charles Dudley Warner teased their wives about the popular novels they read. When the two women challenged them to write something better, they set to work. Warner supplied the sentimental melodrama, while Twain "hurled in the facts." The result was a runaway best seller, uneven as fiction but offering a savage satire of the "get-rich-quick" era that forever after would be known by the book's title, *The Gilded Age* (1873).

Twain left no one unscathed in the novel—political hacks, Washington lobbyists, Wall Street financiers, small-town boosters, wildcat miners, and the "great putty-hearted public" that tolerated the plunder. Underneath the glitter of the Gilded Age, as Twain's title implied, lurked baser stuff. Twain had witnessed up close the corrupt partnership of business and politics in the administration of Ulysses S. Grant. Drawing on this experience, he described how a lobbyist could get an appropriation bill through Congress:

> Why the matter is simple enough. A Congressional appropriation costs money. Just reflect, for instance. A majority of the House Committee, say $10,000 apiece—$40,000; a majority of the Senate Committee, the same each—say $40,000; a little extra to one or two chairmen of one or two such committees, say $10,000 each—$20,000; and there's $100,000 of the money gone, to begin with. Then, seven male lobbyists, at $3,000 each—$21,000; one female lobbyist, $3,000; a high moral Congressman or Senator here and there—the high moral

ones cost more, because they give tone to a measure—say ten of these at $3,000 each, is $30,000; then a lot of small fry country members who won't vote for anything whatever without pay—say twenty at $500 apiece, is $10,000 altogether; lot of jimcracks for Congressmen's wives and children—those go a long way—you can't spend too much money in that line—well, those things cost in a lump, say $10,000—along there somewhere;—and then comes your printed documents. . . . Oh, my dear sir, printing bills are destruction itself. Ours, so far amount to—let me see— . . . well, never mind the details, the total in clean numbers foots up $118,254.42 thus far!

In Twain's satire, Congress is for sale to the highest bidder. The unseemly intimacy between government and business meant that more often than not, senators, representatives, and even members of the executive branch were on the payroll of business interests, if not in their pockets. The corrupt interplay of business and politics raised serious questions about the health of American **democracy**.

The Gilded Age seemed to tarnish all who touched it. No one would learn that lesson better than Twain, who, even as he attacked it as an "era of incredible rottenness," fell prey to its enticements. Born Samuel Langhorne Clemens, he grew up in a rough Mississippi River town, where he first became a journeyman printer and then a riverboat pilot. Taking the pen name Mark Twain, he moved west and gained fame chronicling mining booms in California and Nevada. In 1866, he came east to launch a career as an author, public speaker, and itinerant humorist. Twain played to packed houses, but his work was judged too vulgar for the genteel tastes of the time because he wrote about common people and used common language. His masterpiece, *The Adventures of Huckleberry Finn*, was banned in Boston when it appeared in 1884.

Huckleberry Finn's creator eventually stormed the citadels of polite society, hobnobbing with the wealthy and living in increasingly expensive and

Mark Twain
Popular author Mark Twain (Samuel Langhorne Clemens) wrote acerbically about the excesses of the Gilded Age in his novel of that name written with Charles Dudley Warner and published in 1873. No one knew the meretricious lure of the era better than Twain, who succumbed to a get-rich-quick scheme that led him to the brink of bankruptcy.
Newberry Library.

elegant style. Succumbing to the money fever of his age, Twain plunged into one scheme after another in the hope of making millions. The Paige typesetting machine proved his downfall. Twain invested heavily in this elaborate invention that promised to mechanize typesetting. The idea was a good one; a competing invention, the Linotype, eventually replaced hand type. The Paige machine, however, proved too complicated and temperamental to be practical. By the 1890s, Twain faced bankruptcy. Only the help of his friend Standard Oil millionaire Henry H. Rogers enabled him to begin his dogged climb out of debt.

Twain's tale was common in an age when the promise of wealth led as many to ruin as to riches. In the Gilded Age, fortunes were made and lost with dizzying frequency. Wall Street panics, like those in 1873 and 1893, periodically interrupted the boom times and plunged the country into economic depression. But with railroads and cities to be built and industry expanding on every level, the mood of the country remained buoyant.

The rise of industrialism in the United States and the interplay of business and politics strike the key themes in the Gilded Age. In the decades from 1870 to 1890, the transition from a rural, agricultural economy to urban industrialism, global in its reach, transformed American society. The growth of old industries and the creation of new ones, along with the rise of big business, signaled the coming of age of industrial capitalism. With new times came new economic and political issues. Old divisions engendered by sectionalism and slavery still influenced politics. But increasingly, economic issues such as the tariff and monetary policy shaped party politics. And as concern grew over the power of big business and the growing chasm between the rich and the poor, many Americans looked to the government for solutions.

Perhaps nowhere were the hopes and fears that industrialism inspired more evident than in the public's attitude toward the great business moguls of the day, men like Jay Gould, Andrew Carnegie, John D. Rockefeller, and J. P. Morgan. These larger-than-life figures not only dominated business but also sparked the popular imagination as the heroes and villains in the high drama of industrialization. At no other period in U.S. history would the industrial giants and the businesses they built (and sometimes wrecked) loom so large in American life.

Old Industries Transformed, New Industries Born

In the years following the Civil War, the scale and scope of American industry expanded dramatically. Old industries like iron transformed into modern industries typified by the behemoth U.S. Steel. Discovery and invention stimulated new industries from oil refining to electric light and power. The expansion of the nation's rail system in the decades after the Civil War played the key role in the transformation of the American economy. New rail lines created a national market and fueled a new **consumer culture** that enabled businesses to expand from a regional to a nationwide scale. The railroads became America's first big business.

Jay Gould, Andrew Carnegie, John D. Rockefeller, and other business leaders pioneered new strategies to seize markets and consolidate power in the rising railroad, steel, and oil industries. Always with an eye to the main chance, these business tycoons set the tone in the get-rich-quick era of freewheeling capitalism that came to be called the Gilded Age.

Railroads: America's First Big Business

In the decades following the Civil War, the United States built the greatest railroad network in the world. The first transcontinental railroad was completed in 1869 when the tracks of the Union Pacific and Central Pacific railroads came together at Promontory Point, Utah, linking new markets in the West to the nation's economy. Between 1870 and 1880, the amount of track in the country doubled, and it nearly doubled again in the following decade. By 1900, the nation boasted more than 193,000 miles of railroad track—more than in all of Europe and Russia combined (Map 18.1).

MAP 18.1   Railroad Expansion, 1870–1890
Railroad mileage nearly quadrupled between 1870 and 1890, with the greatest growth occurring in the trans-Mississippi West. New transcontinental lines—the Great Northern, Northern Pacific, Southern Pacific, and Atlantic and Pacific—were completed in the 1880s. Small feeder lines fed into the great transcontinental systems, knitting the nation together.

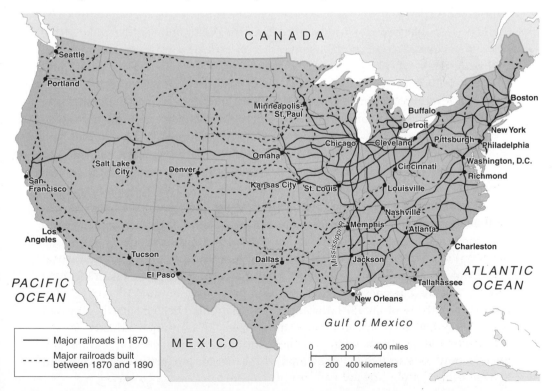

To understand how the railroads developed and came to dominate American life, there is no better place to start than with the career of Jay Gould, who pioneered the expansion of America's railway system and became the era's most notorious speculator. Jason "Jay" Gould bought his first railroad before he turned twenty-five. It was only sixty-two miles long, in bad repair, and on the brink of failure, but within two years, he sold it at a profit of $130,000.

Gould, by his own account, knew little about railroads and cared less about their operation. The secretive Gould operated in the stock market like a shark, looking for vulnerable railroads, buying enough stock to take control, and threatening to undercut his competitors until they bought him out at a high profit. The railroads that fell into his hands fared badly and often went bankrupt. Gould's genius lay in cleverly buying and selling railroad stock, not in providing transportation. In the 1880s, he moved to put together a second transcontinental railroad. To defend their interests, his competitors had little choice but to adopt his strategy of expansion and consolidation, which in turn encouraged railroad building and stimulated a national market.

The dramatic growth of the railroads created the country's first big business. Before the Civil War, even the largest textile mill in New England employed no more than 800 workers. In contrast, the Pennsylvania Railroad by the 1870s boasted a payroll of more than 55,000 workers. Capitalized at more than $400 million, the Pennsylvania Railroad constituted the largest private enterprise in the world.

The Republican Party, firmly entrenched in Washington in the wake of the Civil War, worked closely with business interests, subsidizing the transcontinental railroad system with **land grants** of a staggering 100 million acres of public land and $64 million in tax incentives and direct aid. States and local communities joined the railroad boom, knowing that only those towns and villages along the tracks would grow and flourish. The combined federal and state giveaway amounted to more than 180 million acres, an area larger than Texas. The land grants diminished the amount of public land available to homesteaders and allowed the railroads to increase their profits by selling excess land to the settlers who followed the railroads west.

A revolution in communication accompanied and supported the growth of the railroads. The telegraph, developed by Samuel F. B. Morse, marched across the continent alongside the railroad. By transmitting coded messages along electrical wire, the telegraph formed the "nervous system" of the new industrial order. Telegraph service quickly replaced Pony Express mail carriers in the West and transformed business by providing instantaneous communication. Again Jay Gould took the lead. In 1879, through stock manipulation, he seized control of Western Union, the company that monopolized the telegraph industry. By the end of the century, the telegraph carried 63 million messages a year and made it increasingly easy to move money around the world. Financiers in London and

New York, Paris and Brussels, could follow the markets on ticker tape and transfer funds by wire.

The railroads soon fell on hard times. Already by the 1870s, lack of planning led to overbuilding. On the eastern seaboard, railroads competed fiercely for business. A manufacturer in an area served by competing railroads could get substantially reduced shipping rates in return for promises of steady business. Because railroad owners lost money through this kind of competition, they tried to set up agreements, or "pools," to end cutthroat competition by dividing up territory and setting rates. But these informal gentlemen's agreements invariably failed because men like Jay Gould, intent on undercutting all competitors, refused to play by the rules.

Not all the early railroad builders proved as unscrupulous as Gould. James J. Hill built the Great Northern Railroad and built it well. Entering the railroad business too late to benefit from land grants or subsidies, Hill had to plan carefully to maximize returns to his investors. As a result, the Great Northern, completed in 1893, became one of the few major railroads able to weather the depression that began that same year. In contrast, speculators like Gould could more accurately be called wreckers rather than builders. Through speculation, they ruined the Erie Railroad by gambling with its stock on Wall Street to line their own pockets. Novelist Charles Dudley Warner described how they operated:

> [They fasten upon] some railway that is prosperous, pays dividends, pays a liberal interest on its bonds, and has a surplus. They contrive to buy, no matter at what cost, a controlling interest in it, either in its stock or its management. Then they absorb its surplus; they let it run down so that it pays no dividends and by-and-by cannot even pay its interest; then they squeeze the bondholders, who may be glad to accept anything that is offered out the wreck, and perhaps then they throw the property into the hands of a receiver, or consolidate it with some other road at a value enormously greater than it cost them in stealing it. Having in one way or another sucked it dry, they look around for another road.

Such machinations relied on the stock market, which played a key role in the growth of industrial capitalism. In the past, capital traditionally took tangible form in property, whether in land or in slaves. After the Civil War, corporate capitalism, in which companies incorporated and sold stock to the public, displaced older forms of business organization such as partnerships. Increasingly, capital took the form of stocks in railroads, mines, or ranches. The relationship between shares of stock and actual value, then as now, was never clear-cut. In the worst cases, unscrupulous brokers peddled stocks in nonexistent mines to buyers looking to get rich quick. But the volatility of the market and the manipulations of speculators meant that even shareholders in solid companies fell prey to boom-and-bust cycles in the stock market. As the scale and complexity of the financial system increased, the line between investment and speculation blurred, leading to the exuberant era of risk and speculation Twain skewered as the Gilded Age.

Discomfort with this new state of affairs, in which the nation's financial markets seemed more concerned with paper profits than with building tangible wealth, colored the public's reaction to speculators like Jay Gould. When he died in 1892, the press described Gould as "the world's richest man," estimating his fortune at more than $100 million. His competitor "Commodore" Cornelius Vanderbilt, who built the New York Central Railroad, judged Gould "the smartest man in America." But to the public, he was, as he himself admitted shortly before his death, "the most hated man in America."

Andrew Carnegie, Steel, and Vertical Integration

If Jay Gould was the man Americans loved to hate, Andrew Carnegie became one of America's heroes. Unlike Gould, for whom speculation was the game and wealth the goal, Carnegie turned his back on speculation and worked to build something enduring—Carnegie Steel, the biggest steel business in the world during the Gilded Age.

The growth of the steel industry proceeded directly from railroad building. The first railroads ran on iron rails, which cracked and broke with alarming frequency. Steel, both stronger and more flexible than iron, remained too expensive for use in rails until Englishman Henry Bessemer developed a way to make steel more cheaply from pig iron. Andrew Carnegie, among the first to champion the new "King Steel," came to dominate the emerging industry.

Carnegie, a Scottish immigrant, landed in New York in 1848 at the age of twelve. He rose from a job cleaning bobbins in a textile factory to become one of the richest men in America. Before he died, he gave away more than $300 million, most notably to public libraries. His generosity, combined with his own rise from poverty, burnished his public image. But Carnegie had a darker side: He was a harsh taskmaster who made nearly inhuman demands on his employees.

When Carnegie was a teenager, his skill as a telegraph operator caught the attention of Tom Scott, superintendent of the Pennsylvania Railroad. Scott hired Carnegie, soon promoted him, and lent him the money for his first foray into Wall Street investment. A millionaire before his thirtieth birthday, Carnegie turned away from speculation and struck out on his own to reshape the iron and steel industry. "My preference was always manufacturing," he wrote. "I wished to make something tangible." By applying the lessons of cost accounting and efficiency that he had learned from twelve years with the Pennsylvania Railroad, Carnegie turned steel into the nation's first manufacturing big business.

In 1872, Andrew Carnegie acquired one hundred acres in Braddock, Pennsylvania, on the outskirts of Pittsburgh, convenient to two railroad lines and fronted by the Monongahela River, a natural highway to Pittsburgh and the Ohio River and to the coal and iron mines farther north. There Carnegie built the largest, most up-to-date Bessemer steel plant in the world and began turning out steel at a furious rate. At that time, steelmakers produced about 70 tons a week. Within two decades, Carnegie's blast furnaces poured out an incredible 10,000 tons a week. He soon cut the cost of making rails by more than half, from $58 to $25 a ton. His formula for success was simple: "Cut the prices, scoop the market, run the mills full; watch the costs and profits will take care of themselves." And they did. By 1900, Carnegie Steel earned $40 million a year.

To guarantee the lowest costs and the maximum output, Carnegie pioneered a system of business organization called **vertical integration**. All aspects of the business were under Carnegie's control—from the mining of iron ore, to its transport on the Great Lakes, to the production of steel. Vertical integration, in the words of one observer, meant that "from the moment these crude stuffs were dug out of the earth until they flowed in a stream of liquid steel in the ladles, there was never a price, profit, or royalty paid to any outsider."

Always Carnegie kept his eyes on the account books, looking for ways to cut costs. The great productivity Carnegie encouraged came at a high price. He deliberately pitted his managers against one another, firing the losers and rewarding the winners with a share in the company. Workers achieved the output Carnegie demanded by enduring low wages, dangerous working conditions, and twelve-hour days six days a week. One worker, commenting on the contradiction between Carnegie's generous philanthropy in endowing public libraries and his tightfisted labor policy, observed, "After working twelve hours, how can a man go to a library?"

By 1900, Andrew Carnegie had become the best-known manufacturer in the nation, and the age of iron had yielded to an age of steel. Steel from Carnegie's mills supported the elevated trains in New York and Chicago, formed the skeleton of the Washington Monument, supported the first steel bridge to span the Mississippi, and girded America's first skyscrapers. Carnegie steel armored the naval fleet that helped make the United States a world power. As a captain of industry, Carnegie's only rival was the titan of the oil industry, John D. Rockefeller.

John D. Rockefeller, Standard Oil, and the Trust

Edwin Drake's discovery of oil in Pennsylvania in 1859 sent thousands rushing to the oil fields in search of "black gold." In the days before the automobile and gasoline, crude oil was refined into lubricating oil for machinery and kerosene for lamps, the major source of lighting in nineteenth-century houses before the invention of gas lamps or electric lighting. The amount of capital needed to buy or build an oil refinery in the 1860s and 1870s remained relatively low—less than $25,000, or roughly what it cost to lay one mile of railroad track. With start-up costs so low, the new petroleum industry experienced riotous competition among many small refineries. Ultimately, John D. Rockefeller and his Standard Oil Company succeeded in controlling nine-tenths of the oil-refining business.

"What a Funny Little Government"
The power wielded by John D. Rockefeller and the Standard Oil Company is captured in this political cartoon by Horace Taylor from 1900. Rockefeller is pictured holding the White House and the Treasury Department in the palm of his hand, while in the background the U.S. Capitol has been converted into an oil refinery. Rockefeller held so much power that many feared democracy itself was threatened in the Gilded Age.
Collection of The New-York Historical Society.

Rockefeller grew up the son of a shrewd Yankee who peddled quack cures for cancer. Under his father's rough tutelage, he learned how to drive a hard bargain. "I trade with the boys and skin 'em and just beat 'em every time I can," "Big Bill" Rockefeller boasted. "I want to make 'em sharp." John D. learned his lessons well. In 1865, at the age of twenty-five, he controlled the largest oil refinery in Cleveland. Like a growing number of business owners, Rockefeller abandoned partnership or single proprietorship to embrace the corporation as the business structure best suited to maximize profit and minimize personal liability. In 1870, he incorporated his oil business, founding the Standard Oil Company, a behemoth so huge it served as the precursor not only of today's ExxonMobil but also of Amoco, Chevron, Sunoco, and ConocoPhillips.

As the largest refiner in Cleveland, Rockefeller demanded secret rebates from the railroads in exchange for his steady business. Rebates enabled Rockefeller to drive out his competitors through predatory pricing. The railroads, facing the pressures of cutthroat competition, needed Rockefeller's business so badly that they gave him a share of the rates that his competitors paid. A Pennsylvania Railroad official later confessed that Rockefeller extracted such huge rebates that the railroad, which could not risk losing his business, sometimes ended up paying him to transport Standard's oil. Secret deals, predatory pricing, and rebates enabled Rockefeller to undercut his competitors and pressure competing refiners to sell out or face ruin. Because Rockefeller operated under the cloak of secrecy, the unsuspecting public knew nothing about the extent of Standard Oil's holdings until a New York State inquiry in 1888 revealed the reach of Rockefeller's oil empire.

To gain legal standing for Standard Oil's secret deals, Rockefeller in 1882 pioneered a new form of corporate structure—the **trust**. The trust differed markedly from Carnegie's vertical approach in steel. Instead of attempting to control all aspects of the oil business, from the well to the consumer, Rockefeller used **horizontal integration** to control the refining process. Several trustees held stock in various refinery companies "in trust" for Standard's stockholders. This elaborate stock swap allowed the trustees to coordinate policy among the refineries, giving Rockefeller a virtual **monopoly** on the oil-refining business. The Standard Oil trust, valued at more than $70 million, paved the way for trusts in sugar, whiskey, matches, and many other products.

When the federal government responded to public pressure to outlaw the trust as a violation of free trade, Standard Oil changed tactics and reorganized as a **holding company**. Instead of stockholders in competing companies acting through trustees to set prices and determine territories, the holding company simply brought competing companies under one central administration. No longer technically separate businesses, they could act in concert without violating antitrust laws that forbade companies from forming "combinations in restraint of trade."

As Standard Oil's empire grew, Rockefeller ended the independence of the refinery operators and closed inefficient plants. Next he moved to control sources of crude oil and took charge of the transportation and marketing of petroleum products. By the 1890s, Standard Oil ruled more than 90 percent of the oil business, employed 100,000 people, and was the biggest, richest, most feared, and most admired business organization in the world.

John D. Rockefeller enjoyed enormous success in business, but he was not well liked by the public. Before he died in 1937 at the age of ninety-eight, Rockefeller had become the country's first billionaire. But despite his modest habits, his pious Baptist faith, and his many charitable gifts, he never shared in the public affection that Carnegie enjoyed. Editor and journalist Ida M. Tarbell's "History of the Standard Oil Company," which ran for three years (1902–1905) in serial form in *McClure's Magazine*, largely shaped the public's harsh view of Rockefeller. Tarbell had grown up in the Pennsylvania oil region, and her father had owned one of the small refineries gobbled up by Standard Oil. Her devastatingly thorough history chronicled the methods Rockefeller had used to take over the oil industry. Publicly, Rockefeller refused to respond to her allegations, although in private he dubbed her "Miss Tarball." "If I step on that worm I will call attention to it," he explained. "If I ignore it, it will disappear." Yet by the time Tarbell finished publishing her story, Rockefeller slept with a loaded revolver by his bed in fear of would-be assassins. Standard Oil and the man who created it had become the symbol of heartless monopoly.

Mass Marketing, Advertising, and Consumer Culture

By the 1880s, the railroad made possible a national market for consumer goods. Manufacturers integrated methods of mass production with mass distribution to achieve the first large-scale consumer businesses in the United States. These enterprises came to dominate many of the nation's most vital industries. Successful organizational changes in the meatpacking and food processing industries enabled manufacturers to reap huge profits from products like hot dogs and ketchup.

What Carnegie did for steel, Gustavus Swift did for meatpacking. Until well after the Civil War, cattle moved out of the West on the hoof to be slaughtered by local butchers. Swift, who first visited Chicago in 1875 to buy beef for a Boston company, realized that it would be more efficient to slaughter cattle in the Midwest and transport the meat to the East in refrigerated railway cars. He put together a vertically integrated meatpacking business that controlled the entire process—from the purchase of cattle for slaughter to the mass distribution of meat to retailers and consumers. Through high quality, low prices, and effective advertising, Swift won over consumers who at first worried about buying meat from anyone but the local butcher. The success of Swift & Company led the older meatpackers, including Philip Armour, to build similarly integrated businesses to compete.

Swift's transformation of the beef industry had far-reaching consequences. In the West, it stimulated the rise of commercial cattle ranching, which in turn led to overgrazing and contributed to the near extinction of the bison and the ultimate conquest of Native American tribes (see chapter 17). A national market created a complicated web, an intricate tangle of competition and dependency.

Just as Swift combined mass production with mass distribution in meatpacking, Henry John Heinz transformed the processed food industry. In 1880, Heinz, struggling to recover from bankruptcy after the depression of the 1870s, produced pickles, sauces, and condiments in his factory outside Pittsburgh. By adopting new, more efficient methods of canning and bottling, he built a network of sales offices to advertise his fifty-seven varieties and sell them across the nation. To ensure a steady flow of vegetables and other foodstuffs, he created a large buying and storing organization to contract with local farmers. By 1888, Heinz was rich, and ketchup had become an American staple. Using similar methods, other food processors, including Quaker Oats, Campbell Soup, and

Borden, coordinated mass production with mass distribution to produce low-priced, packaged consumer goods for the national market.

The Gilded Age witnessed the rise of a mass consumer culture. The same economic transformations that made life difficult for ordinary workers paradoxically helped them as consumers. Mass production slashed prices and made available a wide array of new products, from Coca-Cola to kerosene. Although the meager pay of many workers meant a struggle to make ends meet, the more comfortable middle class could choose from a wide array of goods, including new products such as Gillette safety razors, Duke cigarettes, and Kodak cameras.

Advertising played a vital role. Just as the railroad made possible a national market, advertising stimulated the rise of a new consumer culture. Advances in printing enabled magazines and newspapers to subsidize their costs by selling advertising. By the 1870s, more than eight thousand newspapers circulated in the United States, and many magazines reached a nationwide audience at the cost of just five cents an issue. The *Ladies' Home Journal* boasted half a million subscribers in the 1880s. In its pages, advertisements, sprinkled among the articles and advice, tempted readers to buy new products such as Jell-O, Uneeda biscuits, and Hershey chocolate bars. An essential part of the consumer culture, advertising turned the old law of supply and demand on its head by enticing people to buy things they did not need or had never needed before. Electric lights and telephones soon numbered among the new products Americans demanded.

New Inventions: The Telephone and Electricity

Although many Americans disliked and distrusted industrial giants such as Gould and Rockefeller, they admired inventors. The second half of the nineteenth century was an age of invention. Men like Thomas Alva Edison and Alexander Graham Bell became folk heroes. But no matter how dramatic the inventors or the inventions, the new electric and telephone industries pioneered by Edison and Bell soon eclipsed their inventors and fell under the control of bankers and industrialists.

Alexander Graham Bell came to America from Scotland at the age of twenty-four with a passion to find a way to teach the deaf to speak (his wife and mother were deaf). Instead, he developed a way to transmit voice over wire—the telephone. Bell's invention astounded the world when he demonstrated it at the Philadelphia Centennial Exposition in 1876. Dumbfounded by the display, the emperor of Brazil cried out, "My God, it talks!" In 1880, Bell's company, American Bell, pioneered "long lines" (long-distance telephone service), creating American Telephone and Telegraph (AT&T) as a subsidiary. In 1900, AT&T became the parent company of the system as a whole, controlling Western Electric, which manufactured and installed the equipment, and coordinating the Bell regional divisions. This complicated organizational structure meant that Americans could communicate not only locally but also across the country. And unlike a telegraph message, which had to be written out and taken to a telegraph station, sent over the wire, and then delivered by hand to the recipient, the telephone connected both parties immediately and privately. Bell's invention proved a boon to business, contributing to speed and efficiency. The number of telephones soared, reaching 310,000 in 1895 and more than 1.5 million in 1900.

Even more than Alexander Graham Bell, inventor Thomas Alva Edison embodied the old-fashioned virtues of Yankee ingenuity and rugged individualism that Americans most admired. A self-educated dynamo, he worked twenty hours a day in his laboratory in Menlo Park, New Jersey, vowing to turn out "a minor invention every ten days and a big thing every six months or so." He almost made good on his promise. At the height of his career, he averaged a patent every eleven days and invented such "big things" as the phonograph, the motion picture camera, and the filament for the incandescent lightbulb.

Edison, in competition with George W. Westinghouse, pioneered the use of electricity as an energy source. By the late nineteenth century, electricity had become a part of American urban life. It powered trolley cars and lighted factories, homes, and office buildings. Indeed, electricity became so prevalent in urban life that it symbolized the city, whose bright lights contrasted with rural America, left largely in the dark because private enterprise judged it not profitable enough to run electric lines to outlying farms and ranches.

While Americans thrilled to the new electric cities and the changes wrought by inventors, the day of the inventor quietly yielded to the heyday of the corporation. In 1892, the electric industry consolidated. Reflecting a nationwide trend in business, Edison General Electric dropped the name of its inventor, becoming simply General Electric (GE). For years, an embittered Edison refused to set foot inside a GE building. General Electric could afford to overlook the slight. A prime example of the trend toward business consolidation taking place in the 1890s, GE soon dominated the market.

▶REVIEW   How did John D. Rockefeller gain control of 90 percent of the oil-refining business by 1890?

From Competition to Consolidation

Even as Rockefeller and Carnegie built their empires, the era of the "robber barons," as they were dubbed by their detractors, was drawing to a close. Increasingly, businesses replaced partnerships and sole proprietorships with the anonymous corporate structure that would come to dominate the twentieth century. At the same time, mergers led to the creation of huge new corporations.

Banks and financiers played a key role in this consolidation, so much so that the decades at the turn of the twentieth century can be characterized as a period of **finance capitalism**—investment sponsored by banks and bankers. When the depression that followed the panic of 1893 bankrupted many businesses, bankers stepped in to bring order and to reorganize major industries. During these years, a new social philosophy based on the theories of naturalist Charles Darwin helped to justify consolidation and to inhibit state or federal regulation of business. A **conservative** Supreme Court further frustrated attempts to control business by consistently declaring unconstitutional legislation designed to regulate railroads or to outlaw trusts and monopolies.

J. P. Morgan and Finance Capitalism

John Pierpont Morgan, the preeminent finance capitalist of the late nineteenth century, loathed competition and sought whenever possible to eliminate it by substituting consolidation and central control. Morgan's passion for order made him the architect of business mergers. The son of a prominent banker, J. P. Morgan inherited along with his wealth the stern business code of the old-fashioned merchant bankers, men who valued character and reputation. Aloof and silent, Morgan looked down on the climbers and the speculators with a haughtiness that led his rivals to call him "Jupiter," after the ruler of the Roman gods. At the turn of the twentieth century, he dominated American banking, exerting an influence so powerful that his critics charged he controlled a vast "money trust."

Morgan acted as a power broker in the reorganization of the railroads and the creation of industrial giants such as General Electric and U.S. Steel. When the railroads fell on hard times in the 1890s, he used his access to capital to rescue embattled, wrecked, and ruined companies. Morgan quickly took over the struggling railroads and moved to eliminate competition by creating what he called "a community of interest" among the managers he handpicked. By the time he finished reorganizing the railroads, Morgan had concentrated the nation's rail lines in the hands of a few directors who controlled two-thirds of the nation's track.

Banker control of the railroads rationalized, or coordinated, the industry. But stability came at a high price. To keep investors happy and to guarantee huge profits from the sale of stock, Morgan heavily "watered" the stock of the railroads, issuing more shares than the assets of the company warranted. J. P. Morgan & Co. made millions of dollars from commissions and from blocks of stock acquired through reorganization. The flagrant overcapitalization created by the watered stock hurt the railroads in the long run, saddling them with enormous debt. Equally harmful was the management style of the Morgan directors. Bankers, not railroad men, they aimed at short-term profit and discouraged the continued technological and organizational innovation needed to run the railroads effectively.

In 1898, Morgan moved into the steel industry, directly challenging Andrew Carnegie. Morgan supervised the mergers of several smaller steel companies, which soon expanded from the manufacture of finished goods to compete head-to-head with Carnegie in steel production. The pugnacious Carnegie cabled his partners in the summer of 1900: "Action essential: crisis has arrived . . . have no fear as to the result; victory certain."

The press trumpeted news of the impending fight between the feisty Scot and the haughty Wall Street banker, but what the papers called the "battle of the giants" in the end proved little more than the wily maneuvering of two business-men so adept that even today it is difficult to say who won. For all his belliger-ence, the sixty-six-year-old Carnegie yearned to retire to Skibo Castle, his home in Scotland. He may well have welcomed Morgan's bid for power. Morgan, who disdained haggling, agreed to pay Carnegie's asking price, $480 million (the equivalent of about $9.6 billion in today's currency). According to legend, when Carnegie later teased Morgan, saying that he should have asked $100 million more, Morgan replied, "You would have got it if you had."

Morgan's acquisition of Carnegie Steel signaled the passing of one age and the arrival of another. Carnegie represented the old entrepreneurial order, Morgan the new corporate world. The banker quickly moved to pull together Carnegie's chief competitors to form a huge new corporation, United States Steel, known today as USX. Created in 1901 and capitalized at $1.4 billion, U.S. Steel

---

Homestead Steelworks

The Homestead steelworks, outside Pittsburgh, is pictured shortly after J. P. Morgan bought out Andrew Carnegie and created U.S. Steel, the precursor of today's USX. Try to count the smokestacks in the picture. Air pollution on this scale posed a threat to the health of citizens and made for a dismal landscape. Workers complained that trees would not grow in Homestead.

Hagley Museum & Library.

was the largest corporation in the world. Yet for all its size, it did not hold a monopoly in the steel industry. Significant small competitors, such as Bethlehem Steel, remained independent, creating a competitive system called an **oligopoly**, in which several companies control production. The smaller manufacturers simply followed the lead of U.S. Steel in setting prices and dividing the market so that each company held a comfortable share. Many other industries, such as meatpacking, also functioned as oligopolies. Although oligopoly did not entirely eliminate competition, it did effectively blunt it.

When J. P. Morgan died in 1913, his estate totaled $68 million, not counting an estimated $50 million in art treasures. Andrew Carnegie, who gave away more than $300 million before his death six years later, is said to have quipped, "And to think he was not a rich man!" But Carnegie's gibe missed the mark. The quest for power, not wealth, had motivated J. P. Morgan, and his power could best be measured not in the millions he owned but in the billions he controlled. Even more than Carnegie or Rockefeller, Morgan left his stamp on the twentieth century and formed the model for corporate consolidation that economists and social scientists soon justified with a new social theory known as **social Darwinism**.

Social Darwinism and the Gospel of Wealth

John D. Rockefeller Jr., the son of the founder of Standard Oil, once remarked to his Baptist Bible class that the Standard Oil Company, like the American Beauty rose, resulted from "pruning the early buds that grew up around it." The elimination of smaller, inefficient units, he said, was "merely the working out of a law of nature and a law of God." The comparison of the business world to the natural world gave rise to a theory of society based on the law of evolution formulated by British naturalist Charles Darwin. In his monumental work *On the Origin of Species* (1859), Darwin theorized that in the struggle for survival, adaptation to the environment triggered among species a natural selection process that led to evolution. Drawing on Darwin's work, Herbert Spencer in Britain and William Graham Sumner in the United States developed the theory of social Darwinism. Crudely applying Darwin's theory to human society, the social Darwinists concluded that progress came about as a result of relentless competition in which the strong survived and the weak died out.

In social terms, the idea of the "survival of the fittest" had profound significance, as Sumner, a professor of political economy at Yale University, made clear in his 1883 book, *What Social Classes Owe to Each Other*. "The drunkard in the gutter is just where he ought to be, according to the fitness and tendency of things," Sumner insisted. Conversely, "millionaires are the product of natural selection," and although "they get high wages and live in luxury," Sumner claimed, "the bargain is a good one for society."

Social Darwinists equated wealth and power with "fitness" and believed that the unfit should be allowed to die off to advance the progress of humanity.

Any efforts by the rich to aid the poor would only tamper with the rigid laws of nature and slow down evolution. Social Darwinism acted to curb social reform while at the same time glorifying great wealth. In an age when Rockefeller and Carnegie amassed hundreds of millions of dollars (billions in today's currency) and the average worker earned $500 a year (about $8,800 today), social Darwinism justified economic inequality.

Andrew Carnegie softened some of the harshness of social Darwinism in his essay "The Gospel of Wealth," published in 1889. The millionaire, Carnegie wrote, acted as a "mere trustee and agent for his poorer brethren, bringing to their service his superior wisdom, experience, and ability to administer, doing for them better than they could or would do for themselves." Carnegie preached philanthropy and urged the rich to "live unostentatious lives" and "administer surplus wealth for the good of the people." His **gospel of wealth** earned much praise but won few converts. Most millionaires followed the lead of J. P. Morgan, who contributed to charity but ostentatiously amassed private treasures in his marble library.

Social Darwinism nicely suited an age in which the gross inequalities accompanying industrialization seemed to cry out for action. Assuaging the nation's conscience, social Darwinism justified neglect of the poor in the name of "race progress." With so many of the poor coming from different races and ethnicities, social Darwinism fueled racism. A new "scientific racism" purported to prove "Anglo-Saxons" superior to all other groups. In an era noted for greed and crass materialism, social Darwinism buttressed the status quo and provided reassurance to comfortable, white Americans that all was as it should be. Even the gospel of wealth, which mitigated the harshest dictates of social Darwinism, insisted that Americans lived in the best of all possible worlds and that the rich were the natural rulers.

Laissez-Faire and the Supreme Court

Social Darwinism, with its emphasis on the free play of competition and the survival of the fittest, encouraged the economic theory of **laissez-faire** (French for "let it alone"). Business argued that government should not meddle in economic affairs, except to protect private property. A conservative Supreme Court agreed. During the 1880s and 1890s, the Court increasingly reinterpreted the Constitution to protect business from taxation, regulation, labor organization, and antitrust legislation.

In a series of landmark decisions, the Court used the Fourteenth Amendment, originally intended to protect freed slaves from state laws violating their rights, to protect corporations. The Fourteenth Amendment declares that no state can "deprive any person of life, liberty, or property, without due process of law." In 1886, in *Santa Clara County v. Southern Pacific Railroad*, the Court insisted that corporations be considered "persons." Reasoning that legislation designed to regulate corporations deprived them of "due process," the Court struck down state laws regulating railroad rates, declared income tax unconstitutional, and judged labor unions a "conspiracy in restraint of trade." The Court insisted on elevating the rights of property over all other rights. According to Justice Stephen J. Field, the Constitution "allows no impediments to the acquisition of property." Field, born into a wealthy New England family, spoke with the bias of the privileged class to whom property rights were sacrosanct. Imbued with this ideology, the Court refused to impede corporate consolidation and did nothing to curb the excesses of big business. Only in the arena of politics did Americans tackle the issues raised by corporate capitalism.

▶ **REVIEW**   Why did the ideas of social Darwinism appeal to many Americans in the late nineteenth century?

Politics and Culture

One could easily argue that politics, not baseball, constituted America's pastime in the Gilded Age. For many Americans, politics provided a source of identity, a means of livelihood, and a ready form of entertainment. No wonder voter turnout averaged a hefty 77 percent (compared to 60 percent in the 2004 presidential election). A variety of factors contributed to the complicated interplay of politics and **culture**. Patronage provided an economic incentive for voter participation, but ethnicity, religion, sectional loyalty, race, and gender all influenced the political life of the period.

Political Participation and Party Loyalty

Patronage—the **spoils system**—proved a strong motivation for party loyalty among many voters. Political parties in power doled out federal, state, and local government jobs to their loyal supporters. With hundreds of thousands of jobs to be filled, the choice of party affiliation could mean the difference between a paycheck and an empty pocket. Money greased the wheels of this system of patronage, dubbed the spoils system from the adage "to the victor go the spoils." Party bosses expected jobholders to kick back from 2 to 4 percent of their salaries to support the party's electoral campaigns. With their livelihoods tied to their party identity, government employees in particular had an incentive to vote in great numbers during the Gilded Age.

Political affiliation provided a powerful sense of group identity for many voters proud of their loyalty to the Democrats or the Republicans. Democrats, who traced the party's roots back to Thomas Jefferson, called theirs "the party of the fathers." The Republican Party, founded in the 1850s, still claimed strong loyalties as a result of its alignment with the Union during the Civil War. Noting the power of old sectional loyalties, one of the party faithful observed, "Iowa will go Democratic when Hell goes Methodist." Both Republicans in the North and Democrats in the South employed a tactic called "waving the **bloody shirt**"—reminding voters which side they had fought for in the Civil War.

Politics also provided entertainment and spectacle for voters and nonvoters alike in an age before mass recreation and amusement, particularly in rural areas. Political parties sponsored parades, rallies, speeches, picnics, torchlight processions, and Fourth of July fireworks, attracting millions of Americans. Outside the big cities, only religious revivals and traveling shows could compete.

Religion and ethnicity also played a significant role in politics. In the North, **Protestants** from the old-line denominations, particularly Presbyterians and Methodists, flocked to the Republican Party, which championed a series of moral reforms, including local laws requiring businesses to close in observance of the Sabbath. In the burgeoning cities, the Democratic Party courted immigrants and working-class Catholic and Jewish voters charging, rightly, that Republican moral crusades often masked attacks on immigrant culture.

Sectionalism and the New South

After the end of Reconstruction, most white voters in the former Confederate states remained loyal Democrats, voting for Democratic candidates in every presidential election for the next seventy years. Labeling the Republican Party the agent of "Negro rule," Democrats urged white southerners to "vote the way you shot." Yet the so-called solid South proved far from solid on the state and local levels. The economic plight of the South led to shifting political alliances and to third-party movements that challenged Democratic attempts to define politics along race lines and maintain the Democratic Party as the white man's party.

The South's economy, devastated by the war, foundered at the same time the North experienced an unprecedented industrial boom. Soon an influential group of southerners called for a **New South** modeled on the industrial North. Henry Grady, the ebullient young editor of the *Atlanta Constitution*, used his paper's substantial influence (it boasted the largest circulation of any weekly in the country) to extol the virtues of a new industrial South. Part bully, part booster, Grady exhorted the South to use its natural advantages—cheap labor and abundant natural resources—to go head-to-head in competition with northern industry.

Grady's message fell on receptive ears. Many southerners, men and women, black and white, joined the national migration from farm to city, leaving the old plantations to molder and decay. With the end of military rule in 1877, southern Democrats took back state governments, calling themselves "Redeemers." Yet rather than restore the economy of the old **planter** class, they embraced northern promoters who promised prosperity and profits.

The railroads came first, opening up the region for industrial development. Southern railroad mileage grew fourfold from 1865 to 1890 (see Map 18.1). The number of cotton spindles also soared, as textile mill owners abandoned New England in search of the cheap labor and proximity to raw materials promised in the South. By 1900, the South had become the nation's leading producer of cloth, and more than 100,000 southerners, many of them women and children, worked in the region's textile mills.

The New South prided itself most on its iron and steel industry, which grew up in the area surrounding Birmingham, Alabama. During this period, the smokestack replaced the white-pillared plantation as the symbol of the New South. Andrew Carnegie toured the region in 1889 and observed, "The South is Pennsylvania's most formidable industrial enemy." But southern industry remained controlled by northern investors, who had no intention of letting the South beat the North at its own game. Elaborate mechanisms rigged the price of southern steel, inflating it, as one northern insider confessed, "for the purpose of protecting the Pittsburgh mills and in turn the Pittsburgh steel users." Similarly, in the extractive industries—lumber and mining—investors in the North and abroad, not southerners, reaped the lion's share of the profits.

In only one industry did the South truly dominate—tobacco. Capitalizing on the invention of a machine for rolling cigarettes, the American Tobacco Company, founded by the Duke family of North Carolina, eventually dominated the industry. As cigarettes replaced chewing tobacco in popularity at the turn of the twentieth century, a booming market developed for Duke's "ready mades." Soon the company sold 400,000 cigarettes a day.

In practical terms, the industrialized New South proved an illusion. Much of the South remained agricultural, caught in the grip of the insidious crop lien system (see chapter 16). White southern farmers, desperate to get out of debt, sometimes joined with African Americans to pursue their goals politically. Southerners used this strategy in a variety of ways. Between 1865 and 1900, voters in every state south of the Mason-Dixon line experimented with political alliances that crossed the color line. In Virginia, the "Readjusters," a coalition of blacks and whites determined to "readjust" (lower) the state debt and spend more money on public education, captured state offices from 1879 to 1883. In southern politics, the interplay of race and gender made coalitions like the Readjusters a potent threat to the status quo.

Gender, Race, and Politics

Gender—society's notion of what constitutes acceptable masculine or feminine behavior—influenced politics throughout the nineteenth century. From the early days of the Republic, citizenship had been defined in male terms. Citizenship and its prerogatives (voting and officeholding) served as a badge of manliness and rested on its corollary, patriarchy—the power and authority men exerted over their wives and families. With the advent of universal (white) male **suffrage** in the early nineteenth century, gender eclipsed class as the defining feature of citizenship; men's dominance over women provided the common thread that knit all white men together politically. The concept of **separate spheres** dictated political participation for men only. Once the public sphere of political participation became equated with manhood, women found themselves increasingly restricted to the private sphere of home and hearth.

Gender permeated politics in other ways, especially in the tangled skein of the New South. Cross-racial alliances like the Readjusters rested on the belief that universal political rights (voting, officeholding, patronage) could be extended to black males in the public sphere without eliminating racial barriers in the private sphere. Democrats, for their part, fought back by trying to convince voters that black voting would inevitably lead to **miscegenation** (racial mixing). Black male political power and sexual power, they warned, went hand in hand. Ultimately, their arguments prevailed, and many whites returned to the Democratic fold to protect "white womanhood" and with it white supremacy.

The notion that black men threatened white southern womanhood reached its most vicious form in the practice of lynching—the killing and mutilation of black men by white mobs. By 1892, the practice had become so prevalent that a courageous black woman, Ida B. Wells, launched an antilynching movement. That

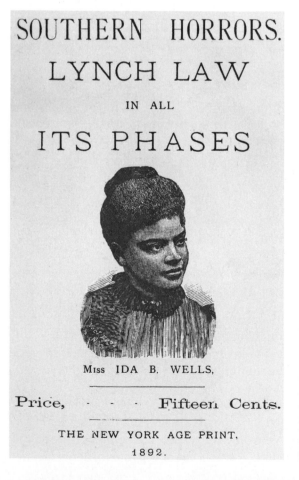

SOUTHERN HORRORS.

LYNCH LAW

IN ALL

ITS PHASES

Miss IDA B. WELLS,

Price,   · · ·   Fifteen Cents.

THE NEW YORK AGE PRINT,

1892.

year, a white mob lynched a friend of Wells's whose grocery store competed too successfully with a white-owned store. Wells shrewdly concluded that lynching served "as an excuse to get rid of Negroes who were acquiring wealth and property and thus keep the race terrorized." She began to collect data on

Ida B. Wells

Ida B. Wells began her antilynching campaign in 1892 after a friend's murder led her to examine the problem of lynching in the South. She spread her message in lectures and pamphlets like this one, distributed for fifteen cents. Wells brought the horror of lynching to a national and international audience. She later became a founding member of the National Association for the Advancement of Colored People (NAACP).

Manuscript, Archives and Rare Books Division, Schomburg Center for Research in Black Culture, The New York Public Library, Astor, Lenox, and Tilden Foundations.

lynching and discovered that in the decade between 1882 and 1892, lynching rose in the South by an overwhelming 200 percent, with more than 241 people killed. The vast increase in lynching testified to the retreat of the federal government following Reconstruction and to white southerners' determination to maintain supremacy through terrorism and intimidation. Wells struck back.

As the first salvo in her attack, Wells put to rest the "old threadbare lie that Negro men assault white women." As she pointed out, violations of black women by white men, which were much more frequent than black attacks on white women, went unnoticed and unpunished. Wells articulated lynching as a problem of race and gender. She insisted that the myth of black attacks on white southern women masked the reality that mob violence had more to do with economics and the shifting social structure of the South than with rape. She demonstrated in a sophisticated way how the southern patriarchal system, having lost its control over blacks with the end of slavery, used its control over women to circumscribe the liberty of black men.

Wells's strong stance immediately resulted in reprisal. While she was traveling in the North, vandals ransacked her office in Tennessee and destroyed her printing equipment. Yet the warning that she would be killed on sight if she ever returned to Memphis only stiffened her resolve. As she wrote in her autobiography, *Crusade for Justice* (1928), "Having lost my paper, had a price put on my life and been made an exile . . . , I felt that I owed it to myself and to my race to tell the whole truth now that I was where I could do so freely."

Antilynching became a lifelong commitment that took Wells twice to Britain, where she placed lynching on the international agenda. As a reporter, first for the *New York Age* and later for the *Chicago Inter-Ocean*, she used every opportunity to hammer home her message. Wells's activities mobilized other black women, including Victoria Earle Matthews and Maritcha Lyons, who were already engaged in social reform and self-improvement. They hosted a testimonial dinner for Wells in New York in 1892 that led to the organization of a black women's club, the Women's Loyal Union. The club became the spearhead for the creation of the National Association of Colored Women (NACW) in 1896. The organization's first president, Mary Church Terrell of Washington, D.C., urged her followers to "promote the welfare of our race, along all the lines that tend to its development and advancement." Taking as their motto "Lifting as we climb," the women of the NACW attacked myriad issues, including health care, housing, education, and the promotion of a positive image of the race. The NACW played a critical role in Wells's antilynching campaign by lobbying for legislation to make lynching a federal crime. Beginning in 1894 and continuing for decades, antilynching bills were introduced in Congress only to be defeated by southern opposition.

Lynching did not end during Ida B. Wells's lifetime, but Wells's forceful voice brought the issue to national prominence. At her funeral in 1931, black leader W. E. B. Du Bois eulogized Wells as the woman who "began the awakening of the conscience of the nation." Wells's determined campaign against lynching provided just one example of women's political activism during the Gilded Age. The suffrage and **temperance movements**, along with the growing popularity of women's clubs, dramatized how women refused to be relegated to a separate sphere that kept them out of politics.

Women's Activism

No one better recognized the potency of the gendered notion of political rights than Elizabeth Cady Stanton, who lamented the introduction of the word *male* into the Fourteenth Amendment (see chapter 16). The explicit linking of manhood with citizenship and voting rights in the Constitution marked a major setback for reformers who supported the vote for women. In 1869, Stanton along with Susan B. Anthony formed the National Woman Suffrage Association (NWSA), the first independent woman's rights organization in the United States (see chapter 20).

Women found ways to act politically long before they voted and cleverly used their moral authority as wives and mothers to move from the domestic sphere into the realm of politics. The extraordinary activity of women's clubs in the period following the Civil War provides just one example. Women's clubs proliferated from the 1860s to the 1890s, often in response to the exclusionary policies of men's organizations. In 1868, newspaper reporter Jane Cunningham Croly (pen name Jennie June) founded the Sorosis Club in New York City after the New York Press Club denied entry to women journalists wishing to attend a banquet honoring the British author Charles Dickens. In 1890, Croly brought state and local clubs together under the umbrella of the General Federation of Women's Clubs (GFWC). Not wanting to alienate southern women, the GFWC barred black women's clubs from joining, despite their vehement objections. Women's clubs soon turned from literary pursuits to politics and reform. "Very early," wrote an officer of the GFWC, "club women became unwilling to discuss Dante and Browning over the teacups in some ladies' drawing room . . . while unsightly heaps of rubbish flanked the paths over which they had passed." Women's clubs resolved to devote themselves to "civic usefulness," endorsing an end to child labor, supporting the eight-hour workday, and helping pass pure food and drug legislation.

The temperance movement (the movement to end drunkenness) attracted by far the largest number of organized women in the late nineteenth century. By the late 1860s and 1870s, the liquor business flourished, with about one saloon for every fifty males over the age of fifteen. During the winter of 1873–74, temperance women adopted a radical new tactic. Armed with Bibles and singing hymns, they marched on taverns and saloons and refused to leave until the proprietors signed a pledge to quit selling liquor. Known as the Woman's Crusade, the movement spread like a prairie fire through small towns in Ohio, Indiana, Michigan, and Illinois and soon moved east into New York, New England, and Pennsylvania. Before it was over, more than 100,000 women had marched in more than 450 cities and towns.

The women's tactics may have been new, but the temperance movement dated back to the 1820s. Originally, the movement was led by Protestant men who organized clubs to pledge voluntary abstinence from liquor. By the 1850s, temperance advocates won significant victories when states, starting with Maine, passed laws to prohibit the sale of liquor (known as "Maine laws"). The Woman's Crusade dramatically brought the issue of temperance back into the national spotlight and led to the formation of a new organization, the Woman's Christian Temperance Union (WCTU) in 1874. Composed entirely of women, the WCTU advocated total abstinence from alcohol. The drunken, abusive husband and father epitomized the evils of a society in which women remained second-class citizens, dependent on men for their livelihood. Temperance provided women with a respectable outlet for their increasing resentment of women's inferior status and their growing recognition of women's capabilities. In its first five years, the WCTU relied on education and moral suasion, but when Frances Willard became president in 1879, she politicized the organization (see chapter 20). When the women of the WCTU joined with the Prohibition Party (formed in 1869 by a group of **evangelical** clergymen), one wag observed, "Politics is a man's game, an' women, childhern, and prohyibitionists do well to keep out iv it." By sharing power with women, the Prohibitionist men violated the old political rules and risked attacks on their honor and manhood.

Temperance, club work, antilynching, and suffrage constituted only a few of women's political causes. Even though they could not yet vote, women found ways to affect the political process. Like men, they displayed strong party loyalties and rallied around traditional Republican and Democratic candidates. Third parties courted women, recognizing that their volunteer labor and support could be key assets in party building. Nevertheless, despite growing political awareness among women, politics, particularly presidential politics, remained—like chewing tobacco—an exclusively male prerogative.

►**REVIEW**   How did race and gender influence politics?

Presidential Politics

Why do the great industrialists—Rockefeller, Morgan, Carnegie—jump vividly from the pages of the past while the presidents of that period remain so pallid? The presidents from Rutherford B. Hayes (1877–1881) to William McKinley (1897–1901) are indeed forgotten men, largely because little was expected of them. Until the 1890s, few Americans thought the president or the national government had any role to play in addressing the problems accompanying the nation's industrial transformation. The dominant creed of laissez-faire, coupled with the dictates of social Darwinism, warned government to leave business alone (except to encourage it with tariffs and subsidies). Still, presidents in the

Gilded Age grappled with corruption and party strife and struggled toward the creation of new political ethics designed to replace patronage with a **civil service** system that promised to award jobs on the basis of merit, not party loyalty.

Corruption and Party Strife

The political corruption and party factionalism that characterized the administration of Ulysses S. Grant (1869–1877) continued to trouble the nation in the 1880s. The spoils system—awarding jobs for political purposes—remained the driving force in party politics at all levels of government in the Gilded Age. Pro-business Republicans generally held a firm grip on the White House, while Democrats had better luck in Congress. Both parties relied on patronage to cement party loyalty. Reformers eager to replace the spoils system with civil service faced an uphill battle.

A small but determined group of reformers championed a new ethics that would preclude politicians from getting rich from public office. The selection of U.S. senators particularly concerned them. Under the Constitution, senators were selected by state legislatures, not directly elected by the voters. Powerful business interests often contrived to control state legislatures and through them U.S. senators. As journalist Henry Demarest Lloyd quipped, Standard Oil "had done everything to the Pennsylvania legislature except to refine it." The "oil combination," he charged, virtually owned Pennsylvania's two senators. Nothing prevented a senator from collecting a paycheck from any of the great corporations. So many did so that political cartoonists often portrayed senators as huge money bags labeled with the names of the corporations they served. Nelson Aldrich, the powerful Republican senator from Rhode Island (whose daughter married John D. Rockefeller Jr.), did not object to being called "the senator from Standard Oil." In this climate, a constitutional amendment calling for the direct election of senators faced stiff opposition from entrenched interests.

Republican president Rutherford B. Hayes, whose disputed election in 1876 signaled the end of Reconstruction in the South, tried to steer a middle course between spoilsmen and reformers. Although the Democratic press ridiculed him as "Rutherfraud" because he had not been popularly elected (see chapter 16), Hayes proved a hardworking, well-informed executive who wanted peace, prosperity, and an end to party strife. Yet the Republican Party remained divided into factions led by strong party bosses who boasted that they could make or break any president.

Fiery and dynamic party bosses who harbored their own presidential ambitions dominated politics on the national scene. Foremost among the Republicans stood Senator Roscoe Conkling of New York, a master spoilsman who ridiculed civil service as "snivel service." He and his followers, called the "Stalwarts," represented the Grant faction of the party. Conkling's archrival, Senator James G. Blaine of Maine, led the "Half Breeds." Not as openly corrupt as the Grant wing of the party, the Half Breeds and their champion were nevertheless tainted with charges of corruption. A third group, called the "Mugwumps," consisted primarily of reform-minded Republicans from Massachusetts and New York who deplored the spoils system and advocated civil service reform. The name "Mugwump" came from the Algonquian word for chief, but critics used the term derisively, punning that the Mugwumps straddled the fence on issues of party loyalty, "with their mug on one side and wump on the other."

President Hayes's middle course pleased no one, and he soon managed to alienate all factions of his party. No one was surprised when he announced that he would not seek reelection in 1880. To avoid choosing among its factions, the Republican Party in 1880 nominated a dark-horse candidate, Representative James A. Garfield from Ohio. To appease Conkling, they picked Stalwart Chester A. Arthur as the vice presidential candidate. The Democrats made an attempt to overcome sectionalism and establish a national party by selecting as their presidential standard-bearer an old Union general, Winfield Scott Hancock. But as one observer noted, "It is a peculiarly constituted party that sends rebel brigadiers to Congress because of their rebellion, and then nominates a Union General as its candidate for president because of his loyalty." Hancock garnered only lukewarm support, receiving just 155 electoral votes to Garfield's 214, although the popular vote was less lopsided.

Garfield's Assassination and Civil Service Reform

"My God," Garfield swore after only a few months in office, "what is there in this place that a man should ever want to get into it?" Garfield, like Hayes, faced the difficult task of remaining independent while pacifying the party bosses and placating the reformers. As the federal bureaucracy grew to nearly 150,000 jobs, thousands of office seekers swarmed to the nation's capital, each clamoring for a position. In the days before Secret Service protection, the White House door stood open to all comers. Garfield took a fatalistic view. "Assassination," he told a friend, "can no more be guarded against than death by lightning, and it is best not to worry about either."

On July 2, 1881, less than four months after taking office, Garfield was shot. His assailant, Charles Guiteau, though clearly insane, turned out to be a disappointed office seeker who claimed to be motivated by political partisanship. He told the police officer who arrested him, "I did it; I will go to jail for it; Arthur is president, and I am a Stalwart." Throughout the hot summer, the country kept a deathwatch as Garfield lingered. When he died in September, Chester A. Arthur became president.

The press almost universally condemned Republican factionalism for creating the political climate that produced Guiteau and led to the second political assassination in a generation. Stalwart Roscoe Conkling saw his hopes for the White House dashed. Attacks on the spoils system increased, and the public joined the chorus calling for reform. But reformers faced stiff opposition from those who recognized that civil service had class and ethnic biases. At a time when few men achieved more than a grammar school education, written civil service examinations threatened to undo political advances made by Irish Americans and return government to an educated Yankee elite. As one opponent pointed out, "George Washington could not have passed examination for a clerk-ship," noting that "in his will written by his own hand, he spells clothes, cloathes."

Reform came with the passage of the Pendleton Civil Service Act in 1883. Both parties claimed credit for the act, which established a permanent Civil Service Commission consisting of three members appointed by the president. Some fourteen thousand jobs came under a merit system that required examinations for office and made it impossible to remove jobholders for political reasons. Half of the postal jobs and most of the customhouse jobs, the largest share of the spoilsmen's bounty, passed to the control of the Civil Service Commission. The new law also prohibited federal jobholders from contributing to political campaigns, thus drying up the major source of the party bosses' revenue. Soon business interests stepped in to replace officeholders as the nation's chief political contributors. Ironically, civil service reform thus gave business an even greater influence in political life.

Reform and Scandal: The Campaign of 1884

With Conkling's downfall, James G. Blaine assumed leadership of the Republican Party and at long last captured the presidential nomination in 1884. A magnetic Irish American politician, Blaine inspired such devotion that his supporters called themselves Blainiacs. But Mugwumps like editor Carl Schurz insisted that Blaine "wallowed in spoils like a rhinoceros in an African pool." They bolted the party and embraced the Democrats' presidential nominee, the stolid Grover Cleveland, reform governor of New York. The burly, beer-drinking Cleveland distinguished himself from an entire generation of politicians by the simple motto "A public office is a public trust." First as mayor of Buffalo and later as governor of New York, he built a reputation for honesty, economy, and administrative efficiency. The Democrats, who had not won the presidency since 1856, had high hopes for his candidacy, especially after the Mugwumps threw their support to Cleveland, insisting that "the paramount issue this year is moral rather than political."

The Mugwumps soon regretted their words. The 1884 contest degenerated so far into scandal and nasty mudslinging that one disgusted journalist styled it "the vilest campaign ever waged." In July, Cleveland's hometown paper, the *Buffalo Telegraph*, dropped the bombshell that the candidate had fathered an illegitimate child in an affair with a local widow. Cleveland, a bachelor, stoically accepted responsibility for the child, perhaps to save the reputation of his married law partner, who may have been the actual father (and whose daughter Cleveland later married). Crushed by the scandal, the Mugwumps tried to argue the difference between public and private morality. But robbed of their moral righteousness, they lost much of their enthusiasm. "Now I fear it has resolved itself into a choice of two evils," one weary reformer confessed. At public rallies, Blaine's partisans taunted Cleveland, chanting, "Ma, Ma, where's my Pa?" Silent but fuming, Cleveland waged his campaign in the traditional fashion by staying home.

While Cleveland sat at home, Blaine launched a whirlwind national tour. On a last-minute stop in New York City, the exhausted candidate committed a misstep that may have cost him the election. He overlooked a remark by a supporter, a local clergyman who cast a slur on Catholic voters by styling the Democrats as the party of "Rum, Romanism, and Rebellion." Linking drinking (rum) and Catholicism (Romanism) offended Irish Catholic voters, whom Blaine had counted on to desert the Democratic Party and support him because of his Irish background.

With less than a week to go until the election, Blaine had no chance to recover from the negative publicity. He lost New York State by fewer than 1,200 votes and with it the election. In the final tally, Cleveland defeated Blaine by a scant 23,005 votes nationwide but won with 219 electoral votes to Blaine's 182, ending twenty-five years of Republican control of the presidency. Cleveland's followers had the last word. To the chorus of "Ma, Ma, where's my Pa?" they retorted, "Going to the White House, ha, ha, ha."

▶ **REVIEW**   How did the question of civil service reform contribute to divisions within the Republican Party?

Economic Issues and Party Realignment

Four years later, in the election of 1888, fickle voters turned Cleveland out, electing Republican Benjamin Harrison, the grandson of President William Henry Harrison. Then, in the only instance in America's history when a president once defeated at the polls returned to office, the voters brought Cleveland back in the election of 1892. What factors account for such a surprising turnaround? Personalities played a part. The stubborn Cleveland, newly married, refused to campaign in 1888. Although he won more popular votes than Harrison, he lost in the electoral college. Once in office, Harrison proved to be a cold and distant leader, prompting critics to call him "the human iceberg." But new issues as well as personalities increasingly swayed the voters. The 1880s witnessed a remarkable political realignment as a set of economic concerns replaced appeals to Civil

War sectional loyalties. The tariff, federal regulation of the railroads and trusts, and the campaign for **free silver** restructured American politics.

The Tariff and the Politics of Protection

The tariff became a potent political issue in the 1880s. The concept of a protective tariff to raise the price of imported goods and stimulate American industry dated back to Alexander Hamilton in the founding days of the Republic. Congress enacted the first tariff following the War of 1812. The Republicans turned the tariff to political ends in 1861 by enacting a measure that both raised revenues for the Civil War and rewarded their industrial supporters, who wanted protection from foreign competition. After the war, the pro-business Republicans continued to revise and enlarge the tariff. Manufactured goods such as steel and textiles, and some agricultural products, including sugar and wool, benefited from protection. Most farm products, notably wheat and cotton, did not. By the 1880s, the tariff produced more than $2.1 billion in revenue. The high tariff not only paid off the nation's Civil War debt and funded pensions for Union soldiers, but it also created a huge surplus that sat idly in the Treasury's vaults while the government argued about how (or even whether) to spend it.

To many Americans, particularly southern and midwestern farmers who sold their crops in a world market but had to buy goods priced artificially high because of the protective tariff, the answer was simple: Reduce the tariff. Advocates of free trade and moderates agitated for tariff reform. But those who benefited from the tariff—industrialists insisting that America's "infant industries" needed protection and some westerners producing protected raw materials such as wool, hides, and lumber—firmly opposed lowering the tariff. Many argued that workers, too, benefited from high tariffs that protected American wages by giving American products an edge over imported goods.

The Republican Party seized on the tariff question to forge a new national coalition. "Fold up the bloody shirt and lay it away," Blaine advised a colleague in 1880. "It's of no use to us. You want to shift the main issue to protection." By encouraging an alliance among industrialists, labor, and western producers of raw materials—groups seen to benefit from the tariff—Blaine hoped to solidify the North, Midwest, and West against the solidly Democratic South. Although the tactic failed for Blaine in the presidential election of 1884, it worked for the Republicans four years later. Cleveland, who had straddled the tariff issue in the election of 1884, startled the nation in 1887 by calling for tariff reform. Cleveland attacked the tariff as a tax levied on American consumers by powerful industries. And he pointed out that high tariffs impeded the expansion of American markets abroad at a time when American industries needed to expand if they were to keep growing. The Republicans countered by arguing that "tariff tinkering" would only unsettle prosperous industries, drive down wages, and shrink the farmers' home market. Republican Benjamin Harrison, who supported the high tariff, ousted Cleveland from the White House in 1888, carrying all the western and northern states except Connecticut and New Jersey.

Back in power, the Republicans brazenly passed the highest tariff in the nation's history in 1890. The new tariff, sponsored by Republican representative William McKinley of Ohio and signed into law by Harrison, stirred up a hornet's nest of protest across the United States. The American people had elected Harrison to preserve protection but not to enact a higher tariff. Democrats condemned the McKinley tariff and labeled the Republican Congress that passed it the "Billion Dollar Congress" for its carnival of spending, which depleted the nation's surplus by enacting a series of pork barrel programs shamelessly designed to bring federal money to congressmen's own constituents. In the congressional election of 1890, angry voters swept the hapless Republicans, including tariff sponsor McKinley, out of office. Two years later, Harrison himself was defeated. Grover Cleveland, whose call for tariff revision had cost him the election in 1888, triumphantly returned to the White House vowing to lower the tariff. Such were the changes in the political winds whipped up by the tariff issue.

However real the contest between Republicans and Democrats over the economic advantages of the tariff, the debate masked deeper divisions in American society. Conflict between workers and farmers on the one side and bankers and corporate giants on the other erupted throughout the 1880s and came to a head in the 1890s. Both sides of the tariff debate spoke to concern over class conflict when they insisted that their respective plans, whether McKinley's high tariff or Cleveland's tariff reform, would bring prosperity and harmony. For their part, many working people shared the sentiment voiced by one labor leader that the tariff was "only a scheme devised by the old parties to throw dust in the eyes of laboring men."

Railroads, Trusts, and the Federal Government

American voters may have divided on the tariff, but increasingly they agreed on the need for federal regulation of the railroads and federal legislation to curb the power of the "trusts" (a term loosely applied to all large business combinations). As early as the 1870s, angry farmers in the Midwest who suffered from the unfair shipping practices of the railroads organized to fight for railroad regulation. The Patrons of Husbandry, or the Grange, founded in 1867 as a social and educational organization for farmers, soon became an independent political movement. By electing Grangers to state office, farmers made it possible for several midwestern states to pass laws in the 1870s and 1880s regulating the railroads. At first the Supreme Court ruled in favor of state regulation (*Munn v. Illinois*, 1877). But in 1886, the Court reversed itself, ruling that because railroads crossed state boundaries, they fell outside state jurisdiction (*Wabash v. Illinois*). With more than three-fourths of railroads crossing state lines, the Supreme Court's decision effectively quashed the states' attempts at railroad regulation.

Anger at the *Wabash* decision finally led to the first federal law regulating the railroads, the Interstate Commerce Act, passed in 1887 during Cleveland's first administration. The act established the nation's first federal regulatory agency, the Interstate Commerce Commission (ICC), to oversee the railroad industry. In its early years, the ICC was never strong enough to pose a serious threat to the railroads. It could not, for example, end rebates to big shippers. In its early decades, the ICC proved more important as a precedent than effective as a watchdog.

Concern over the growing power of the trusts led Congress to pass the Sherman Antitrust Act in 1890. The act outlawed pools and trusts, ruling that businesses could no longer enter into agreements to restrict competition. It did nothing to restrict huge holding companies such as Standard Oil, however, and proved to be a weak sword against the trusts. In the following decade, the government successfully struck down only six trusts but used the law four times against labor by outlawing unions as a "conspiracy in restraint of trade." In 1895, the Supreme Court dealt the antitrust law a crippling blow in *United States v. E. C. Knight Company*. In its decision, the Court ruled that "manufacture" did not constitute "trade." This semantic quibble drastically narrowed the law, in this case allowing the American Sugar Refining Company, which had bought out a number of other sugar companies (including E. C. Knight) and controlled 98 percent of the production of sugar, to continue its virtual monopoly.

Both the ICC and the Sherman Antitrust Act testified to the nation's concern about corporate abuses of power and to a growing willingness to use federal measures to intervene on behalf of the public interest. As corporate capitalism became more and more powerful, public pressure toward government intervention grew. Yet not until the twentieth century would more active presidents sharpen and use these weapons effectively against the large corporations.

The Fight for Free Silver

While the tariff and regulation of the trusts gained many backers, the silver issue stirred passions like no other issue of the day. On one side stood those who believed that gold constituted the only honest money. Although other forms of currency circulated, notably paper money such as banknotes and greenbacks, the government's support of the **gold standard** meant that anyone could redeem paper money for gold. Many who supported the gold standard were eastern creditors who did not wish to be paid in devalued dollars. On the opposite side stood a coalition of western silver barons and poor farmers from the West and South who called for free silver. The mining interests, who had seen the silver bonanza in the West drive down the price of the precious metal, wanted the government to buy silver and mint silver dollars. Farmers from the West and South who had suffered from deflation during the 1870s and 1880s

U.S. Currency
Gold remained the nation's standard currency, but silver supporters, including farmers and western mining interests, demanded the minting of silver dollars and the issuance of silver certificates. On the left is a dollar gold piece.
The American Numismatic Assn.; Picture Research Consultants & Archives.

hoped that increasing the money supply with silver dollars, thus causing infla-tion, would give them some relief by enabling them to pay off their debts with cheaper dollars.

During the depression following the panic of 1873, critics of hard money organized the Greenback Labor Party, an alliance of farmers and urban wage laborers. The Greenbackers favored issuing paper currency not tied to the gold supply, citing the precedent of the greenbacks issued during the Civil War. The government had the right to define what constituted legal tender, the Greenback-ers reasoned: "Paper is equally money, when . . . issued according to law." They proposed that the nation's currency be based on its wealth—land, labor, and capital—and not simply on its reserves of gold. The Greenback Labor Party cap-tured more than a million votes and elected fourteen members to Congress in 1878. Although conservatives considered the Greenbackers dangerous cranks, their views eventually prevailed in the 1930s, when the country abandoned the gold standard.

After the Greenback Labor Party collapsed, proponents of free silver came to dominate the monetary debate in the 1890s. Advocates of free silver pointed out that until 1873, the country had enjoyed a system of bimetallism—the minting of both silver and gold into coins. In that year, at the behest of those who favored gold, the Republican Congress had voted to stop buying and minting silver, an act silver supporters denounced as the "crime of '73." By sharply contracting the money supply at a time when the nation's economy was burgeoning, the

Republicans had enriched bankers and investors at the expense of cotton and wheat farmers and industrial wageworkers. In 1878 and again in 1890, with the Sherman Silver Purchase Act, Congress took steps to ease the tight money policy and appease advocates of silver by passing legislation requiring the government to buy silver and issue silver certificates. Though good for the mining interests, the laws did little to promote the inflation desired by farmers. Soon they began to call for "the free and unlimited coinage of silver," a plan whereby nearly all the silver mined in the West would be minted into coins circulated at the rate of sixteen ounces of silver to one ounce of gold.

By the 1890s, the silver issue crossed party lines. The Democrats hoped to use it to achieve a union between western and southern voters. Unfortunately for them, Democratic president Grover Cleveland remained a staunch conservative in money matters and supported the gold standard as vehemently as any Republican. After a panic on Wall Street in the spring of 1893, Cleveland called a special session of Congress and bullied the legislature into repealing the Silver Purchase Act because he believed it threatened economic confidence. Repeal proved disastrous for Cleveland, not only economically but also politically. It did nothing to bring prosperity and dangerously divided the country. Angry farmers, furious at the president's harsh monetary policy, warned Cleveland not to travel west of the Mississippi River if he valued his life.

Panic and Depression

President Cleveland had scarcely begun his second term in office in 1893 when he faced a deep economic depression, the worst the country had yet seen. In the face of economic disaster, Cleveland clung to the economic orthodoxy of the gold standard. In the winter of 1894–95, the president walked the floor of the White House, sleepless over the prospect that the United States might go bankrupt. Individuals and investors, rushing to trade in their banknotes for gold, strained the country's monetary system. The Treasury's gold reserves dipped so low that unless they could be buttressed, the unthinkable might happen: The U.S. Treasury might not be able to meet its obligations.

At this juncture, J. P. Morgan stepped in and suggested a plan. A group of bankers would purchase gold abroad and supply it to the Treasury. Cleveland knew that such a scheme would unleash a thunder of protest, yet to save the gold standard, the president had no choice but to turn to Morgan for help. A storm of controversy erupted over the deal. The press claimed that Cleveland had lined his own pockets and rumored that Morgan had made $8.9 million. Neither allegation was true. Cleveland had not profited a penny, and Morgan made far less than the millions his critics claimed.

But if President Cleveland's action managed to salvage the gold standard, it did not save the country from hardship. The winter of 1894–95 was one of the worst times in American history. People faced unemployment, cold, and hunger. A firm believer in limited government, Cleveland insisted that nothing could be done to help. "I do not believe that the power and duty of the General Government ought to be extended to the relief of individual suffering which is in no manner properly related to the public service or benefit." Nor did it occur to Cleveland that his great faith in the gold standard prolonged the depression, favored creditors over debtors, and caused immense hardship for millions of Americans.

> ►REVIEW   Why were Americans split on the question of the tariff and currency?

Conclusion: Business Dominates an Era

The gold deal between J. P. Morgan and Grover Cleveland underscored a dangerous reality: The federal government was so weak that its solvency depended on a private banker. This lopsided power relationship signaled the dominance of business in the era Mark Twain satirically but accurately characterized as the Gilded Age. Perhaps no other era in American history spawned greed, corruption, and vulgarity on so grand a scale—an era when speculators like Jay Gould not only built but wrecked businesses to turn paper profits; an era when business boasted openly of buying politicians, who in turn lined their pockets at the public's expense.

Nevertheless, the Gilded Age was not without its share of solid achievements. In these years, America made the leap into the industrial age. Factories and refineries poured out American steel and oil at unprecedented rates. Businessmen like Carnegie, Rockefeller, and Morgan developed new strategies to consolidate American industry. New inventions, including the telephone and electric light and power, changed Americans' everyday lives. And the rise of mass marketing and advertising created a new consumer culture. By the end of the nineteenth century, the country had achieved industrial maturity. It boasted the largest, most innovative, most productive economy in the world. Its citizens enjoyed the highest standard of living on the globe. No other era in the nation's history witnessed such a transformation.

Yet the changes that came with these developments worried many Americans and gave rise to the era's political turmoil. Race and gender profoundly influenced American politics, leading to new political alliances. Fearless activist Ida B. Wells fought racism in its most brutal form—lynching. Women's organizations championed causes, notably suffrage and temperance, and challenged prevailing views of woman's proper sphere. Reformers fought corruption by instituting civil service. And new issues—the tariff, the regulation of the trusts, and currency reform—restructured the nation's politics.

The Gilded Age witnessed a nation transformed. Where dusty roads and cattle trails once sprawled across the continent, steel rails now bound the country together. Cities grew exponentially, not only with new inhabitants from around the globe but also with new bridges, subways, and skyscrapers. The nation's workers and the great cities they labored to build are the focus of Chapter 19.

REVIEWING THE CHAPTER

Use the questions and timeline to review and strengthen your understanding of the chapter.

REVIEW QUESTIONS

1. How did John D. Rockefeller gain control of 90 percent of the oil-refining business by 1890? (pp. 542–52)

2. Why did the ideas of social Darwinism appeal to many Americans in the late nineteenth century? (pp. 552–57)

3. How did race and gender influence politics? (pp. 557–63)

4. How did the question of civil service reform contribute to divisions within the Republican Party? (pp. 563–67)

5. Why were Americans split on the question of the tariff and currency? (pp. 567–73)

MAKING CONNECTIONS

1. Late-nineteenth-century industrialization depended on developments in technology and business strategy. What were some of the key innovations in both arenas? How did they facilitate the maturation of American industry? How did the railroads contribute to the growth of American industry? In your answer, discuss the drawbacks and benefits of these developments.

2. By the 1870s, several new concerns had displaced slavery as the defining question of American politics. What were these new issues, and how did they shape new regional, economic, and racial alliances and rivalries? In your answer, consider the part political parties played in this process.

3. Energetic political activity characterized Gilded Age America, both within formal party politics and beyond. How did the activism of women denied the vote contribute to the era's electoral politics? In your answer, be sure to cite specific examples of political action.

4. The U.S. Congress and the Supreme Court facilitated the concentration of power in the hands of private business concerns during the Gilded Age. Citing specific policies and court decisions, discuss how government helped augment the power of big business in the late nineteenth century.

TIMELINE

1869	• First transcontinental railroad completed. • National Woman Suffrage Association (NWSA) founded.	**1881**	• Garfield assassinated; Vice President Chester A. Arthur becomes president.
1870	• John D. Rockefeller incorporates Standard Oil Company.	**1882**	• John D. Rockefeller develops the trust.
		1883	• Pendleton Civil Service Act.
1872	• Andrew Carnegie builds the largest, most up-to-date Bessemer steel plant in the world.	**1884**	• Democrat Grover Cleveland elected president.
		1886	• *Wabash v. Illinois.*
1873	• U.S. government stops minting silver. • Wall Street panic leads to major economic depression. • Woman's Crusade begins.	**1887**	• Interstate Commerce Act.
		1888	• Republican Benjamin Harrison elected president.
1874	• Woman's Christian Temperance Union (WCTU) founded.	**1890**	• McKinley tariff. • General Federation of Women's Clubs (GFWC) founded. • Sherman Antitrust Act.
1876	• Alexander Graham Bell demonstrates telephone.		
1877	• Republican Rutherford B. Hayes sworn in as president. • "Redeemers" come to power in South. • *Munn v. Illinois.*	**1892**	• Ida B. Wells launches antilynching campaign.
		1893	• Wall Street panic touches off national depression.
1879	• Thomas Alva Edison perfects lightbulb.	**1895**	• J. P. Morgan bails out U.S. Treasury.
1880	• Republican James A. Garfield elected president.	**1901**	• U.S. Steel incorporated for $1.4 billion.

▶ **For an online bibliography, practice quizzes, Web sites, images, and documents related to this chapter,** see the Book Companion Site at **bedfordstmartins.com/roark.**

▶ **For firsthand accounts of this period,** see Chapter 18 in Michael Johnson, ed., *Reading the American Past,* Fourth Edition.

19
CHAPTER

The City and Its Workers

1870–1900

"**A** TOWN THAT CRAWLED now stands erect, and we whose backs were bent above the hearths know how it got its spine," boasted a steelworker surveying New York City. Where once wooden buildings stood rooted in the mire of unpaved streets, cities of stone and steel sprang up in the last decades of the nineteenth century. The labor of millions of workers, many of them immigrants, laid the foundations for urban America.

No symbol better represented the new urban landscape than the Brooklyn Bridge, opened in May 1883 and quickly hailed as "one of the wonders of the world." The great bridge soared over the East River in a single mile-long span. Begun in 1869, the bridge was the dream of builder John Roebling, who died in a freak accident almost as soon as construction began.

The building of the Brooklyn Bridge took fourteen years and cost the lives of thirty men. Nearly three hundred workers labored around the clock in three shifts, six days a week, most for $2 a day. To sink the foundation deep into the riverbed, common laborers tunneled down through mud and debris, working in reinforced wooden boxes called caissons, which were open at the bottom and pressurized to keep the water from flooding in. Before long, the workers experienced a mysterious malady they called "bends" because it left them doubled over in pain after they came to the surface. (Scientists later discovered that nitrogen bubbles trapped in the bloodstream caused the condition and that it could be prevented if the men came up slowly to allow for decompression.)

Construction of the Brooklyn Bridge
This photograph shows the cables of the Brooklyn Bridge being put in place. The
wooden footpath that leads to the gothic tower provided access for the workers.
The bridge took fourteen years to build and cost the lives of thirty men.
© Bettmann/Corbis.

The first death occurred when the caisson reached a depth of seventy-one
feet. On April 22, 1872, a heavyset German immigrant named John Meyers complained that he did not feel well and headed home to his boardinghouse. Before
he could reach his bed, he collapsed and died. Eight days later, another man
dropped dead, and the entire workforce in the caissons went out on strike.
Conditions had become so hazardous, so terrifying that the workers demanded a
higher wage for fewer hours of work.

One worker, Frank Harris, remembered the men's fear of working in the caissons. As a scrawny sixteen-year-old from Ireland, Harris started to work a few
days after landing in America. He described how the men went into a coffinlike
"air-lock" to acclimate to the pressure of the compressed air in the caissons:

> When the air was fully compressed, the door of the air-lock opened at a touch
> and we all went down to work with pick and shovel on the gravelly bottom.
> My headaches soon became acute. The six of us were working naked to the
> waist in the small iron chamber with the temperature of about 80 degrees
> Fahrenheit: In five minutes the sweat was pouring from us, and all the while
> we were standing in icy water that was only kept from rising by the terrific
> pressure. No wonder the headaches were blinding.

Harris recalled the big Swede who headed the work gang telling him that "I could stay as long as I liked, but he advised me to leave at the end of a month: It was too unhealthy." By the fifth day, Harris experienced terrible shooting pains in his ears, and fearing he might go deaf, he quit. Like Harris, many immigrant workers walked off the job, often as many as a hundred a week. But a ready supply of immigrants meant that the work never slowed or stopped; new workers eagerly entered the caissons, where they could earn in a day more than they made in a week in Ireland or Italy.

Washington Roebling, who took over as chief engineer after his father's death, routinely worked twelve to fourteen hours six days a week. Soon he, too, fell victim to the bends and ended up an invalid, directing the completion of the bridge through a telescope from his window in Brooklyn Heights. His wife, Emily Warren Roebling, acted as site superintendent and general engineer of the project. At the dedication of the bridge, Roebling turned to his wife and said, "I want the world to know that you, too, are one of the Builders of the Bridge."

Arching 130 feet above the East River, the bridge carried a roadway for vehicles and above it a pedestrian walkway. Together, they pierced massive granite towers at each end through two huge Gothic arches. Roebling intended the bridge to stand as "a great work of art" as well as "a successful specimen of advanced Bridge engineering." Generations of artists and poets have testified to his success.

At the end of the nineteenth century, the Brooklyn Bridge stood as a symbol of many things: the industrial might of the United States; the labor of the nation's immigrants; the ingenuity and genius of its engineers and inventors; the rise of iron and steel; and most of all, the ascendancy of urban America. Poised on the brink of the twentieth century, the nation was shifting inexorably from a rural, agricultural society to an urban, industrial nation. In the nation's cities, tensions would erupt into conflict as workers squared off to fight for their rights to organize into labor unions and demand safer working conditions, shorter hours, and better pay. And the explosive growth of the cities would foster political corruption as unscrupulous bosses and entrepreneurs cashed in on the building boom. Immigrants, political bosses, middle-class managers, poor laborers, and the very rich populated the burgeoning cities, crowding the streets, laboring in the stores and factories, and taking their leisure at the new ballparks, amusement parks, dance halls, and municipal parks that dotted the urban landscape. As the new century dawned, the city and its workers moved to center stage in American life.

The Rise of the City

"We cannot all live in cities, yet nearly all seem determined to do so," New York editor Horace Greeley complained. The last three decades of the nineteenth century witnessed an urban explosion. Cities and towns grew more than twice as rapidly as the total population. Among the fastest-growing cities, Chicago expanded at a me-teoric rate, from 100,000 in 1860 to over a million by 1890, doubling its population each decade. By 1900, the number of cities with more than 100,000 inhabitants had jumped from eighteen in 1870 to thirty-eight. Most of the nation's largest cities were east of the Mississippi, although St. Louis and San Francisco both ranked among the top ten urban areas in 1900. And in the far West, Los Angeles mush-roomed from a sleepy village of 5,000 in 1870 to a metropolis of more than 100,000 a scant thirty years later. By 1900, the United States boasted three cities with more than a million inhabitants—New York, Chicago, and Philadelphia.

Patterns of global migration contributed to the rise of the city. In the port cities of the East Coast, more than fourteen million people arrived, many from southern and eastern Europe, and huddled together in dense urban ghettos. The word *slum* entered the American vocabulary and with it growing concern over the rising tide of newcomers. In the city, the widening gap between rich and poor became more visible, exacerbated by changes in the city landscape brought about by advances in transportation and technology.

The Urban Explosion, a Global Migration

The United States grew up in the country and moved to the city, or so it seemed by the end of the nineteenth century. Between 1870 and 1900, eleven million people moved into cities. Burgeoning industrial centers such as Pittsburgh, Chicago, New York, and Cleveland acted as giant magnets, attracting workers from the country-side. But migrants to the cities were by no means limited to rural Americans. Worldwide in scope, the movement from rural areas to urban industrial centers attracted millions of immigrants to American shores in the waning decades of the nineteenth century.

By the 1870s, the world could be conceptualized as three interconnected geographic regions. At the center stood an industrial core bounded by Chicago and St. Louis in the west; Toronto, Glasgow, and Berlin in the north; Warsaw in the east; and Milan, Barcelona, Richmond, and Louisville in the south. Surrounding this industrial core lay a vast agricultural domain encompassing Canada, much of Scandinavia, Russia and Poland, Hungary, Greece, Italy and Sicily, southern Spain, the South and the western plains of America, central and northern Mexico, the hin-terlands of northern China, and the southern islands of Japan. Capitalist develop-ment in the late nineteenth century shattered traditional patterns of economic activity in this rural periphery. As old patterns broke down, these rural areas exported, along with other raw materials, new recruits for the industrial labor force.

Beyond this second circle lay an even larger third world including the Caribbean, Central and South America, the Middle East, Africa, India, and most of Asia. Ties between this part of the world and the industrial core strengthened in the late nineteenth century, but most of the people living there stayed put. They worked on plantations and railroads, in mines and ports, as part of a huge export network managed by foreign powers that staked out spheres of influence and colonies in this vast region.

In the 1870s, railroad expansion and low steamship fares gave the world's peoples a newfound mobility that enabled industrialists to draw on a global population for cheap labor. When Andrew Carnegie opened his first steel mill in 1872, his superintendent hired workers he called "buckwheats"—young American boys just off the farm. By the 1890s, however, Carnegie's workforce was liberally sprinkled with other rural boys—Hungarians and Slavs who had migrated to the United States, willing to work for low wages.

Altogether, more than 25 million immigrants came to the United States between 1850 and 1920. They came from all directions: east from Asia, south from Canada, north from Latin America, and west from Europe (Map 19.1). Part of a worldwide migration, immigrants traveled to South America and Australia as well as to the United States. Yet more than 70 percent of all European immigrants chose North America as their destination.

MAP 19.1   The Impact of Immigration, to 1910

Immigration flowed in all directions—south from Canada, north from Mexico and Latin America, east from Asia to Seattle and San Francisco, and west from Europe to East Coast port cities including Boston and New York.

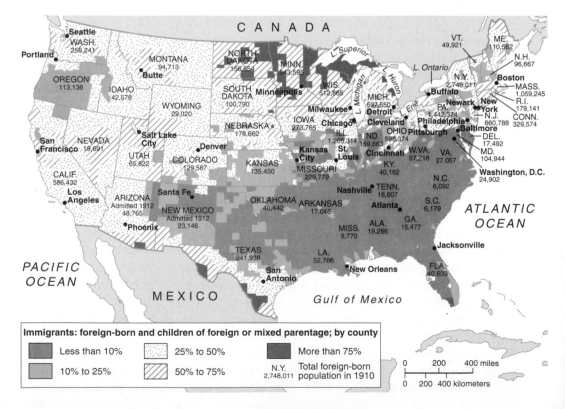

The largest number of immigrants to the United States came from the British Isles and from German-speaking lands. The vast majority of immigrants were white; Asians accounted for fewer than one million immigrants, and other people of color numbered even fewer. Yet ingrained racial prejudices increasingly influenced the country's perception of immigration patterns. One of the classic formulations of the history of European immigration divided immigrants into two distinct waves that have been called the "old" and the "new" immigration. According to this formulation, before 1880 the majority of immigrants came from northern and western Europe, with Germans, Irish, English, and Scandinavians making up approximately 85 percent of the newcomers. After 1880, the pattern shifted, with more and more ships carrying passengers from southern and eastern Europe. Italians, Hungarians, eastern European Jews, Turks, Armenians, Poles, Russians, and other Slavic peoples accounted for more than 80 percent of all immigrants by 1896. Implicit in the distinction was an invidious comparison between "old" pioneer settlers and "new" unskilled proletarians. Yet this sweeping generalization spoke more to perception than to reality. In fact, many of the earlier immigrants from Ireland, Germany, and Scandinavia came not as settlers or farmers, but as wage laborers, much like the Italians and Slavs who followed them.

The "new" immigration resulted from a number of factors. Improved economic conditions in western Europe coupled with increased immigration to Australia and Canada slowed the flow of immigrants coming into the United States from northern and western Europe. At the same time, economic depression in southern Italy, the persecution of Jews in eastern Europe, and a general desire to avoid **conscription** into the Russian army led many people from southern and eastern Europe to move to the United States. The need of America's industries for cheap, unskilled labor during prosperous years also stimulated immigration.

Steamship companies courted immigrants—a highly profitable, self-loading cargo. By the 1880s, the price of a ticket from Liverpool had dropped to less than $25. Agents from the large lines traveled throughout Europe drumming up business. Colorful pamphlets and posters advertised America as the land of promise. Would-be immigrants eager for information about the United States relied on letters from friends and relatives, advertisements, and word of mouth—sources that were not always dependable or truthful. Even photographs proved deceptive: Workers dressed in their Sunday best looked more prosperous than they actually were to relatives in the old country, where only the very wealthy wore white collars or silk dresses. No wonder people left for the United States believing, as one Italian immigrant observed, "that if they were ever fortunate enough to reach America, they would fall into a pile of manure and get up brushing the diamonds out of their hair."

Most of the newcomers stayed in the nation's cities. By 1900, almost two-thirds of the country's immigrant population resided in cities, many too poor to move on. (The average laborer immigrating to the United States carried only about $21.50.) Although the foreign-born population rarely outnumbered the native-born population, taken together immigrants and their American-born children did constitute a majority, particularly in the nation's largest cities: Philadelphia, 55 percent; Boston, 66 percent; Chicago, 75 percent; and New York City, an amazing 80 percent in 1900.

Not all the newcomers came to stay. Perhaps eight million European immigrants—most of them young men—worked for a year or a season and then returned to their homelands. Immigration officers called these young male immigrants, many of them Italians, "birds of passage" because they followed a regular pattern of migration to and from the United States. By 1900, almost 75 percent of the new immigrants were young, single men.

Women generally had less access to funds for travel and faced tighter family control. Because they stood to make less money than men, their prospective wages rarely merited the expense of long-distance travel. The traditional sexual division of labor relied on women's unpaid domestic labor and care of the very young and the very old. For these reasons, women most often came to the United States as wives, mothers, or daughters, not as single wage laborers. Only among the Irish did women immigrants outnumber men by a small margin from 1871 to 1891.

Jews from eastern Europe most often came with their families and came to stay. Beginning in the 1880s, a wave of violent **pogroms**, or persecutions, in Russia and Poland prompted the departure of more than a million Jews in the next two decades. Most of the Jewish immigrants settled in the port cities of the East, creating distinct ethnic enclaves. Hester Street in the heart of New York City's Lower East Side rang with the calls of pushcart peddlers and vendors hawking their wares, from pickles to feather beds.

Racism and the Cry for Immigration Restriction

Ethnic diversity and racism played a role in dividing skilled workers (those with a craft or specialized ability) from the globe-hopping proletariat of unskilled workers (those who supplied muscle or tended machines). As industrialists mechanized to replace skilled workers with lower-paid, unskilled labor, they drew on immigrants, particularly those from southern and eastern Europe, who had come to the United States in the hope of bettering their lives. Skilled workers, frequently members of older immigrant groups from northern or western Europe, criticized the newcomers. One Irish worker complained, "There should be a law . . . to keep all the Italians from comin' in and takin' the bread out of the mouths of honest people."

The Irish worker's resentment of the new Italian immigrants brings into focus the impact of racism on America's immigrant laborers. Throughout the nineteenth century and into the twentieth, members of the educated elite as well as the uneducated viewed ethnic and even religious differences as racial characteristics, referring to the Polish or the Jewish "race." Americans judged "new" immigrants of southern and eastern European "races" as inferior to those of

Anglo-Teutonic "stock." Each wave of newcomers was deemed somehow inferior to the established residents. The Irish who criticized the Italians so harshly
had themselves been stigmatized as a lesser "race" a generation earlier.

Immigrants not only brought their own religious and racial prejudices to the
United States but also absorbed the popular prejudices of American **culture**.
Social Darwinism, with its strongly racist overtones, decreed that whites stood at
the top of the evolutionary ladder. But who was "white"? Skin color supposedly
served as a marker for the "new" immigrants—"swarthy" Italians; dark-haired,
olive-skinned Jews. But even blond, blue-eyed Poles were not considered white.
The social construction of "race" is nowhere more apparent than in the testimony
of an Irish dockworker who boasted that he hired only "white men" to load
cargo, a category that he insisted excluded "Poles and Italians." For the new
immigrants, Americanization and assimilation would prove inextricably part of
becoming "white."

Racism took its most blatant form in the treatment of African Americans and
Asians. Like other migrants from the rural periphery, African American men in
the South—former slaves and the children of slaves—found work as "human machines." The labor gang system used in many industries reached brutal extremes
in the South, where private employers contracted prison labor, mostly African
Americans jailed for such minor crimes as vagrancy. Shackled together in chains
as they worked under the watchful eyes of armed guards, these men stood on the
bottom rung of labor's ladder. A Georgia man who escaped the brutal chain gang
system remarked, "Call it slavery, peonage, or what not, the truth is we lived in a
hell on earth." Eager to escape bigotry and poverty, many African Americans fled
to the North.

For African Americans, the cities of the North promised not just economic
opportunity but also an end to institutionalized segregation and persecution. **Jim
Crow** laws—restrictions that segregated blacks—became common throughout
the South in the decades following Reconstruction. Intimidation and lynching
(essentially pogroms against black people) terrorized blacks throughout the
South (see chapter 18). "To die from the bite of frost is far more glorious than at
the hands of a mob," proclaimed the *Defender*, Chicago's largest African American newspaper. In the 1890s, many blacks moved north, settling for the most part
in the growing cities. Racism relegated them to poor jobs and substandard living
conditions, but by 1900 New York, Philadelphia, and Chicago had the largest
black communities in the nation. Although the most significant African American
migration out of the South would occur during and after World War I, the great
exodus was already under way.

On the West Coast, Asian immigrants became scapegoats of the changing
economy. After California's gold rush of the mid-1800s, many Chinese who had
come to work "on the gold mountain" found jobs on the country's transcontinental railroads. When the railroad work ended, they most often took work other
groups shunned, including domestic service. But hard times in the 1870s made

them a target for disgruntled workers. Prohibited from owning land, the Chinese migrated to the cities. In 1870, San Francisco housed a Chinese population estimated at 12,022, and it continued to grow until passage of the Chinese Exclusion Act in 1882 (see chapter 17). For the first time in the nation's history, U.S. law excluded an immigrant group on the basis of race. Some Chinese managed to come to America using a loophole that allowed relatives to join their families. In contrast, the nation's small Japanese community of about 3,000 expanded rapidly after 1890, until pressures to keep out all Asians led in 1910 to the creation of

---

Russian Immigrant Family

A Russian immigrant family is shown leaving Ellis Island in 1900. The white slips of paper pinned to their coats indicate that they have been processed. The paucity of their possessions testifies to the struggles they would face in their new country. Ellis Island opened the year this photograph was taken, replacing the old immigration station at Castle Garden in lower Manhattan.

Keystone-Mast Collection, UCR/California Museum of Photography, University of California, Riverside.

an immigration station at Angel Island in San Francisco Bay. Asian immigrants were detained there, sometimes for months, and many were deported as "undesirables." Their sad stories can be read in the graffiti on the barracks walls. One immigrant from Heungshan (Macao) wrote:

> There are tens of thousands of poems on these walls.
> They are all cries of suffering and sadness.

On the East Coast, the volume of immigration from Europe in the last two decades of the century proved unprecedented. In 1888 alone, more than half a million Europeans landed in America, 75 percent of them in New York City. The Statue of Liberty, a gift from the people of France erected in 1886, stood sentinel in the harbor. The nation's response to the new immigrants was best summed up in the verse inscribed at Liberty's base, penned by a young Jewish girl named Emma Lazarus:

> Give me your tired, your poor,
> Your huddled masses yearning to breathe free,
> The wretched refuse of your teeming shore,
> Send these, the homeless, tempest-tost to me,
> I lift my lamp beside the golden door!

The tide of immigrants to New York City soon swamped the immigration office at Castle Garden in lower Manhattan. An imposing new brick facility opened on Ellis Island in New York harbor in 1900. Its overcrowded halls became the gateway to the United States for millions.

To many Americans, the "new" immigrants seemed uneducated, backward, and uncouth—impossible to assimilate. "These people are not Americans," editorialized the popular journal *Public Opinion*, "they are the very scum and offal of Europe." Terence V. Powderly, head of the broadly inclusive Knights of Labor, complained that the newcomers "herded together like animals and lived like beasts."

Blue-blooded Yankees led by Senator Henry Cabot Lodge of Massachusetts formed an unlikely alliance with organized labor to press for immigration restrictions. Lodge and his old-stock followers championed a literacy test, knowing that the vast majority of Italian and Slavic peasants were unable to read. In 1896, Congress approved a literacy test for immigrants, but President Grover Cleveland promptly vetoed it. "It is said," the president reminded Congress, "that the quality of recent immigration is undesirable. The time is quite within recent memory when the same thing was said of immigrants, who, with their descendants, are now numbered among our best citizens." Cleveland's veto forestalled immigration restriction but did not stop anti-immigrant forces from seeking to close the gates. They would continue to press for restrictions until they achieved their goal in the 1920s (see chapter 23).

The Social Geography of the City

During the Gilded Age, cities experienced demographic and technological changes that greatly altered the social geography of the city. Cleveland, Ohio, provides a good example. In the 1870s, Cleveland was a small city, in both population and area. Oil magnate John D. Rockefeller could, and often did, walk from his large brick house on Euclid Avenue to his office downtown. On his way, he passed the small homes of his clerks and other middle-class families. Behind these homes ran miles of alleys crowded with the dwellings of Cleveland's working class. Farther out, on the shores of Lake Erie, close to the factories and foundries, clustered the shanties of the city's poorest laborers.

Within two decades, the Cleveland that Rockefeller knew no longer existed. The coming of mass transit transformed the walking city. In its place emerged a central business district surrounded by concentric rings of residences organized by ethnicity and income. First the horsecar in the 1870s and then the electric streetcar in the 1880s made it possible for those who could afford the five-cent fare to work downtown and flee after work to the "cool green rim" of the city, with its single-family homes, lawns, gardens, and trees. By the early twentieth century, more than half of Cleveland's residents rode streetcars to work. Unable to afford even a few cents for streetcar fare, the city's poor crowded into the inner city or lived "back of the yards" near the factories where they worked. This pattern of development repeated throughout the country as urban congestion and suburban sprawl forever altered the social geography of the city. Social segregation—the separation of rich and poor, and of ethnic and old-stock Americans—was one of the major social changes engendered by the rise of the industrial metropolis, evident not only in Cleveland but in cities across the nation.

Race and ethnicity affected the way cities evolved. Newcomers to the burgeoning cities faced hostility and not surprisingly sought out their kin and country folk as they struggled to survive. Distinct ethnic neighborhoods often formed around a synagogue or church. Blacks typically experienced the greatest residential segregation, but every large city had its ethnic enclaves—Little Italy, Chinatown, Bohemia Flats, Germantown—where English was rarely spoken.

In 1890, Jacob Riis, a young police reporter, took his notebook and camera into the tenements of New York City. The result was the best-selling book *How the Other Half Lives* (1890). Riis invited his readers into a Bottle Alley tenement:

> Here is a "flat" [made up] of "parlor" and two pitch-dark coops called bedrooms. Truly the bed is all there is room for. The family tea-kettle is on the stove, doing duty for the time being as a wash-boiler. . . . One, two, three beds are there, if the old boxes and heaps of foul straw can be called by that name; a broken stove with a crazy pipe from which the smoke leaks at every joint, a table of rough boards propped up on boxes, piles of rubbish in the corner. The closeness and smell are appalling.

Poverty, crowding, dirt, and disease constituted the daily reality of New York City's immigrant poor. Riis's book, like his photographs, presented a world of black and white. There were many layers to the population Riis labeled the "other half," distinctions deepened by ethnicity, religion, race, and gender. *How the Other Half Lives* is best read as a social reformer's call to action rather than as an accurate portrayal of the city's poor. But by taking his camera into the hovels of the poor, Riis opened the nation's eyes to conditions in the tenements.

Riis's audience shivered at his revelations about the "other half." But middle-class Americans worried equally about the excesses of the wealthy. They feared the class antagonism fueled by the growing chasm between rich and poor so visible in the nation's cities. Many people shared Riis's view that "the real danger to society comes not only from the tenements, but from the ill-spent wealth which reared them."

The excesses of the Gilded Age's newly minted millionaires were nowhere more visible than in the lifestyle of the Vanderbilts. "Commodore" Cornelius Vanderbilt, the uncouth ferryman who built the New York Central Railroad, died in 1877, leaving his son $90 million. William Vanderbilt doubled that sum, and his two sons proceeded to spend it on Fifth Avenue mansions and "cottages" in Newport, Rhode Island, which, with their marble and gold leaf, sought to rival the palaces of Europe. In 1883, Alva Vanderbilt (Mrs. William Vanderbilt) launched herself into New York society by throwing a costume party so lavish that not even old New York society, which turned up its nose at the nouveau riche, could resist an invitation. Dressed as a Venetian princess, the hostess greeted her twelve hundred guests. But her sister-in-law Alice Vanderbilt stole the show by appearing as that miraculous new invention, the electric light, resplendent in a white satin evening dress studded with diamonds. The *New York World* speculated that Alva Vanderbilt's party cost more than a quarter of a million dollars (more than $4 million today).

Such ostentatious displays of wealth became especially alarming when they were coupled with disdain for the well-being of ordinary people. When a reporter in 1882 asked William Vanderbilt whether he considered the public good when running his railroads, he shot back, "The public be damned." The fear that America had become a **plutocracy**—a society ruled by the rich—gained credence from the fact that the wealthiest 1 percent of the population owned more than half the real and personal property in the country. (A century later, the top 1 percent controlled less than a quarter of the property.) As the new century dawned, reformers would form a **progressive movement** to address the problems of urban industrialism and the substandard living and working conditions it produced.

▶ REVIEW   Why did American cities experience explosive growth in the late nineteenth century?

At Work in Industrial America

The number of industrial wageworkers in the United States exploded in the second half of the nineteenth century, more than tripling from 5.3 million in 1860 to 17.4 million in 1900. These workers toiled in a variety of settings. Many skilled workers and **artisans** still earned a living in small workshops. But with the rise of corporate capitalism, large factories, mills, and mines increasingly dotted the landscape. Sweatshops and outwork, the contracting of piecework to be performed in the home, provided work experiences different from those of factory operatives (machine tenders) and industrial workers. Pick-and-shovel labor, whether on the railroads or in the building trades, constituted yet another kind of work. Managers and other white-collar employees, as well as women "typewriters" and salesclerks, formed a new white-collar segment of America's workforce. The best way to get a sense of the diversity of workers and workplaces is to look at the industrial nation at work.

America's Diverse Workers

Common laborers formed the backbone of the American labor force. They built the railroads and subways, tunneled under New York's East River to anchor the Brooklyn Bridge, and helped lay the foundation of industrial America. These "human machines" stood at the bottom of the country's economic ladder and generally came from the most recent immigrant groups. Initially, the Irish wielded the picks and shovels that built American cities, but by the turn of the century, as the Irish bettered their lot, Slavs and Italians took up their tools.

At the opposite end of labor's hierarchy stood skilled craftsmen like iron puddler James J. Davis, a Welsh immigrant. Using brains along with brawn, puddlers took the melted pig iron in the heat of the furnace and, with long poles, formed the cooling metal into 200-pound balls, relying on eye and intuition to make each ball uniform. Davis compared the task to baking bread: "I am like some frantic baker in the inferno kneading a batch of iron bread for the devil's breakfast. My spoon weighs twenty-five pounds, my porridge is pasty iron, and the heat of my kitchen is so great that if my body was not hardened to it, the ordeal would drop me in my tracks."

Possessing such a skill meant earning good wages, up to $7 a day, when there was work. But often no work could be found. Much industry and manufacturing in the nineteenth century remained seasonal; few workers could count on year-round pay. In addition, two major depressions only twenty years apart, beginning in 1873 and 1893, spelled unemployment and hardship for all workers. In an era before unemployment insurance, workers' compensation, or old-age pensions, even the best worker could not guarantee security for his family. "The fear of ending in the poor-house is one of the terrors that dog a man through life," Davis confessed.

Skilled workers like Davis wielded power on the shop floor. Employers attempted to limit workers' control by replacing people with machines, breaking down skilled work into ever smaller tasks that could be performed by unskilled factory operatives. New England's textile mills provide a classic example of the effects of mechanized factory labor in the nineteenth century. Mary, a weaver at the mills in Fall River, Massachusetts, told her story to the *Independent* magazine. She went to work in the 1880s at the age of twelve. By then, mechanization of the looms had reduced the job of the weaver to watching for breaks in the thread. "At first the noise is fierce, and you have to breathe the cotton all the time, but you get used to it," Mary told her interviewer. "When the bobbin flies out and a girl gets hurt, you can't hear her shout—not if she just screams, you can't. She's got to wait, 'till you see her. . . . Lots of us is deaf."

During the 1880s, the number of foreign-born mill workers almost doubled. At the Amoskeag textile mill in New Hampshire, foreign-born workers, many French Canadians, constituted more than half of the workforce. At Fall River, Mary and her Scots-Irish family resented the new immigrants. "The Polaks learn weavin' quick," she remarked, using a common derogatory term to identify a rival group. "They just as soon live on nothin' and work like that. But it won't do 'em much good for all they'll make out of it." Employers encouraged racial and ethnic antagonism because it inhibited labor organization.

The majority of factory operatives in the textile mills were young, unmarried women like Mary. They worked from six in the morning to six at night six days a week, and they took home about $1 a day. The seasonal nature of the work also drove wages down. "Like as not your mill will 'shut down' three months," and "some weeks you only get two or three days' work," Mary recounted. After twenty years of working in the mill, Mary's family had not

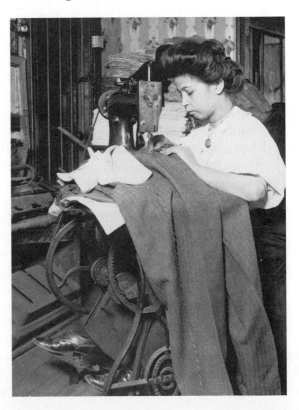

Sweatshop Worker
Sweatshop workers endured crowded and often dangerous conditions. Most were young women, like the one shown here sewing pants in New York City. Young working girls earned little money but prided themselves on their independence.
George Eastman House.

been able to scrape together enough money to buy a house: "We saved some, but something always comes."

Mechanization transformed the garment industry as well. With the introduction of the foot-pedaled sewing machine in the 1850s and the use of mechanical cloth-cutting knives in the 1870s, independent tailors were replaced with workers hired by contractors to sew pieces of cloth into clothing. Working in sweatshops, small rooms hired for the season or even in the contractor's own tenement, women and children formed an important segment of garment workers. Discriminated against in the marketplace, where they earned less than men, women generally worked for wages only eight to ten years, until they married.

Sadie Frowne, a sixteen-year-old Polish Jew, went to work in a Brooklyn sweatshop in the 1890s. Frowne sewed for eleven hours a day in a room twenty feet long and fourteen feet wide containing fourteen machines. "The machines go like mad all day, because the faster you work the more money you get," she recalled. Paid by the piece, she earned about $4.50 a week and, by rigid economy, tried to save $2. Young and single, Frowne typified the woman wage earner in the late nineteenth century. In 1890, the average workingwoman was twenty-two and had been working since the age of fifteen, laboring twelve hours a day six days a week and earning less than $6 a week.

The Family Economy: Women and Children

In 1890, the average male worker earned $500 a year, about $8,000 in today's dollars. Many working-class families, whether native-born or immigrant, lived in or near poverty, their economic survival dependent on the contributions of all family members, regardless of sex or age. One statistician estimated that in 1900, as many as 64 percent of working-class families relied on income other than the husband's wages to make ends meet. The paid and unpaid work of women and children proved essential for family survival and economic advancement.

In the cities, boys as young as six years old plied their trades as bootblacks and newsboys. Often working under an adult contractor, these children earned as little as fifty cents a day. Many of them were homeless—orphaned or cast off by their families. "We wuz six, and we ain't got no father," a child of twelve told reporter Jacob Riis. "Some of us had to go." So out he went to work on his own. In New York City, the Children's Aid Society tried to better the situation of the city's youngest workers by establishing lodging houses. To encourage "self sufficiency and self respect," the boys were expected to pay their way—six cents for a bed, six for a breakfast of bread and coffee, and six for a supper of pork and beans. Lodged in dormitories that sometimes held more than a hundred berths, the boys had to be on good behavior. A sign at the entrance admonished, "Boys who swear and chew tobacco cannot sleep here."

Child labor increased decade by decade after 1870. The percentage of children under fifteen engaged in paid labor did not drop until after World War I. The 1900 census estimated that 1,750,178 children ages ten to fifteen were employed, an increase of more than a million over thirty years. Children in this age range constituted more than 18 percent of the industrial labor force. Many younger children not counted by the census worked in mills, in factories, and on the streets.

In the late nineteenth century, the number of women workers also rose sharply, with their most common occupation changing slowly from domestic service to factory work and then to office work. In 1870, the census listed 1.5 million women working for wages in nonagricultural occupations. By 1890, the number had more than doubled, with 3.7 million women working for pay. Women's working patterns varied considerably according to race and ethnicity. White married women, even among the working class, rarely worked for wages outside the home. In 1890, only 3 percent were employed. Nevertheless, married women found ways to contribute to the family economy. Families often took in boarders or lodgers, which meant extra housework. In many Italian families, piecework such as making artificial flowers allowed married women to contribute to the family economy without leaving their homes. Black women, married and unmarried, worked for wages in much greater numbers than white women. The 1890 census showed that 25 percent of married African American women were employed, often as domestics in the houses of white families.

Working-class families joined together in the struggle to make ends meet. Women's labor, paid and unpaid, and children's meager wages could mean the difference between eating and going hungry. Meanwhile, industrial capitalism created new "white-collar" jobs in management, offices, and department stores.

Managers and White Collars

In the late nineteenth century, business expansion and consolidation led to a managerial revolution, creating a new class of managers. As skilled workers saw their crafts replaced by mechanization, some moved into management positions. "The middle class is becoming a salaried class," a writer for the *Independent* magazine observed, "and is rapidly losing the economic and moral independence of former days." As large business organizations consolidated, corporate development separated management from ownership, and the job of directing the firm became the province of salaried executives and managers, the majority of whom were white men drawn from the 8 percent of Americans who held high school diplomas. In 1880, the middle managers at the Chicago, Burlington, and Quincy Railroad earned between $1,500 and $4,000 a year; senior executives, generally recruited from the college-educated elite, took home $4,000 or more; and the company's general manager made $15,000 a year, approximately thirty times what the average worker earned. (Today's top CEOs earn as much as 411 times more than the average worker.) At the top of the economic pyramid, the great industrialists like Andrew Carnegie and John D. Rockefeller amassed fortunes calculated today in the billions.

Until late in the century, when engineering schools began to supply recruits, many skilled workers moved from the shop floor to positions of considerable responsibility. The career of William "Billy" Jones provides a glimpse of a skilled ironworker turned manager. Jones, the son of a Welsh immigrant, grew up in the heat of the blast furnaces, where he started working as an apprentice at the age of ten. When Andrew Carnegie opened his steelworks on the outskirts of Pittsburgh in 1872, he hired Jones as his plant superintendent. By all accounts, Jones was the best steel man in the industry. "Good wages and good workmen" was his motto. Carnegie constantly tried to force down workers' pay, but Jones succeeded in shortening the shift from twelve to eight hours a day by convincing Carnegie that shorter hours would reduce absenteeism and accidents. Jones himself demanded and received a "hell of a big salary." Carnegie paid him $25,000—the same salary as the president of the United States—a stupendous sum in the 1870s, which made Jones perhaps the most successful manager to move up from the shop floor. He did not have long to enjoy his newfound wealth. Jones died in 1889 when a blast furnace exploded, adding his name to the estimated 35,000 killed each year in industrial accidents.

"Typewriters" and Salesclerks

In the decades after the Civil War, as businesses became larger and more far-flung, the need for more elaborate and exact records, as well as the greater volume of correspondence, led to the hiring of more office workers. Mechanization transformed business as it had industry and manufacturing. The adding machine, the cash register, and the typewriter came into general use in the 1880s. Employers seeking literate workers soon turned to nimble-fingered women. Educated men had many other career choices, but for middle-class white women, secretarial work constituted one of very few areas where they could put their literacy to use for wages.

Sylvie Thygeson was typical of the young women who went to work as secretaries. Thygeson grew up in an Illinois prairie town. When her father died in 1884, she went to work as a country schoolteacher at the age of sixteen, immediately after graduating high school. Quickly learning that teaching school did not pay a living wage, she mastered typing and stenography and found work as a secretary to help support her family. According to her account, she made "a fabulous sum of money." Nevertheless, she gave up her job after a few years when she met and married her husband.

Called "typewriters," women workers like Thygeson were seen as indistinguishable from the machines they operated. Far from viewing their jobs as dehumanizing, women typewriters took pride in their work and relished the economic independence it afforded them. By the 1890s, secretarial work was the overwhelming choice of white, native-born women, who constituted more than

90 percent of the female clerical force. Not only considered more genteel than factory work or domestic labor, office work also meant more money for shorter hours. Boston's clerical workers made more than $6 a week in 1883, compared with less than $5 for women working in manufacturing.

As a new **consumer culture** came to dominate American urban life in the late nineteenth century, department stores offered another employment opportunity for women in the cities. Boasting ornate facades, large plate-glass display windows, and marble and brass fixtures, stores such as Macy's in New York, Wanamaker's in Philadelphia, and Marshall Field in Chicago stood as monuments to the material promise of the era. Within these palaces of consumption, cash girls, stock clerks, and wrappers earned as little as $3 a week, while at the top of the scale, buyers like Belle Cushman of the fancy goods department at Macy's earned $25 a week, an unusually high salary for a woman in the 1870s.

In all stores, saleswomen were subject to harsh and arbitrary discipline. Sitting was forbidden, and conversation with other clerks led to instant dismissal. The women worked under the watchful eyes of male supervisors called floorwalkers, who commanded salaries twice as high as the typical saleswoman. Yet salesclerks counted themselves a cut above factory workers. Their work was neither dirty nor dangerous, and even when they earned less than factory workers, they felt a sense of superiority.

▶ **REVIEW**   How did business expansion and consolidation change workers' occupations in the late nineteenth century?

Workers Organize

By the late nineteenth century, industrial workers were losing ground in the workplace. In the fierce competition to lower prices and cut costs, industrialists like Andrew Carnegie invested heavily in new machinery that enabled managers to replace skilled workers with unskilled labor. The erosion of skills and the redefinition of labor as mere "machine tending" left the worker with a growing sense of individual helplessness that served as a spur to collective action. In the 1870s and 1880s, labor organizations grew, and the Knights of Labor and the American Federation of Labor attracted workers. Convinced of the inequity of the wage-labor system, labor organizers spoke eloquently of abolishing class privileges and monopoly. The rhetoric frightened many middle-class Americans and led them to equate the labor movement with the specter of violence and **anarchism**. Strikes particularly underscored the tensions produced by rapid industrialization. In 1877, in the midst of a depression that left many workers destitute, labor flexed its muscle in the Great Railroad Strike and showed the power of collective action.

The Great Railroad Strike of 1877

Economic depression following the panic of 1873 threw as many as three million people out of work. Those who were lucky enough to keep their jobs watched as pay cuts eroded their wages until they could no longer feed their families. In the summer of 1877, the Baltimore and Ohio (B&O) Railroad announced a 10 percent wage reduction and at the same time declared a 10 percent dividend to its stockholders. Angry brakemen in West Virginia, whose wages had already fallen from $70 to $30 a month, walked out on strike. One B&O worker described the hardship that drove him to take such desperate action: "We eat our hard bread and tainted meat two days old on the sooty cars up the road, and when we come home, find our children gnawing bones and our wives complaining that they cannot even buy hominy and molasses for food."

The West Virginia brakemen's strike touched off the Great Railroad Strike of 1877, a nationwide uprising that spread rapidly to Pittsburgh and Chicago, St. Louis and San Francisco (Map 19.2). Within a few days, nearly 100,000 railroad workers walked off the job. The spark of rebellion soon led an estimated 500,000 laborers to join the train workers. In Reading, Pennsylvania, militiamen refused to fire on the strikers, saying, "We may be militiamen, but we are workmen first." Rail traffic ground to a halt; the nation lay paralyzed.

MAP 19.2   The Great Railroad Strike of 1877

Starting in West Virginia and Pennsylvania, the strike spread as far north as Albany, New York, and as far west as San Francisco, bringing rail traffic to a standstill. Called the Great Uprising, the strike heralded the beginning of a new era of working-class protest and trade union organization.

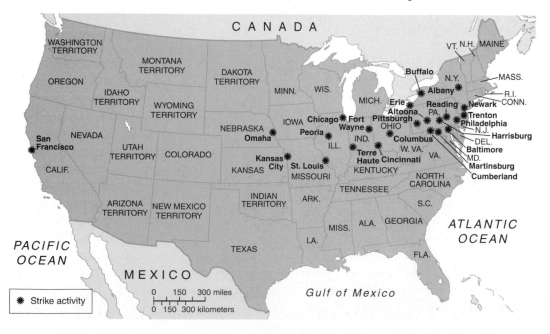

Violence erupted as the strike spread. In Pittsburgh, strikers clashed with militia brought in from Philadelphia, who arrogantly boasted they would clean up "the workingmen's town." Opening fire on the crowd, the militia killed twenty people. Angry workers retaliated by reducing an area two miles long beside the tracks to smoldering rubble. Before the day ended, twenty more workers had been shot, and the railroad had sustained property damage totaling $2 million.

Within eight days, the governors of nine states, acting at the prompting of the railroad owners and managers, defined the strike as an "insurrection" and called for federal troops. President Rutherford B. Hayes, after hesitating briefly, called out the army. By the time the troops arrived, the violence had run its course. Federal troops did not shoot a single striker in 1877. But they struck a blow

---

Destruction from the Great Railroad Strike of 1877
The devastation caused in Pittsburgh during the strike shocked many Americans. When militiamen fired on striking workers, killing more than twenty, the mob retaliated by destroying a two-mile area along the track, causing $2 million in property damage. Curious pedestrians came out to view the destruction. Carnegie Library of Pittsburgh.

against labor by acting as strikebreakers—opening rail traffic, protecting non-striking "scab" train crews, and maintaining peace along the line. In three weeks, the strike was over.

Although the Great Railroad Strike was spontaneous and unorganized, it frightened the authorities and upper classes like nothing before in U.S. labor history, fueling their hostility toward labor organization. They quickly tried to blame the tiny, radical Workingmen's Party for the strike and predicted a bloody uprising. "Any hour the mob chooses it can destroy any city in the country—that is the simple truth," wrote future secretary of state John Hay to his wealthy father-in-law.

Although many middle-class Americans initially sympathized with the conditions that led to the strike, they condemned the strikers for the violence and property damage that occurred. The *New York Times* editorialized about the "dangerous classes," and the *Independent* magazine offered the following advice on how to deal with "rioters":

> If the club of a policeman, knocking out the brains of the rioter, will answer then well and good; but if it does not promptly meet the exigency, then bullets and bayonets . . . constitutes [*sic*] the one remedy and one duty of the hour.

"The strikes have been put down by force," President Hayes noted in his diary on August 5. "But now for the real remedy. Can't something be done by education of the strikers, by judicious control of the capitalists, by wise general policy to end or diminish the evil? The railroad strikers, as a rule, are good men, sober, intelligent, and industrious." While Hayes acknowledged the workers' grievances, most businessmen and industrialists did not and fought the idea of labor unions, arguing that workers and employers entered into contracts as individuals and denying the right of unions to bargain collectively for their workers. For their part, workers quickly recognized that they held little power individually and flocked to join unions. As labor leader Samuel Gompers noted, the strike served as an alarm bell to labor "that sounded a ringing message of hope to us all."

The Knights of Labor and the American Federation of Labor

The Knights of Labor, the first mass organization of America's working class, proved the chief beneficiary of labor's newfound consciousness. The Noble and Holy Order of the Knights of Labor had been founded in 1869 by Uriah Stephens, a Philadelphia garment cutter. A secret society of workers, the Knights envisioned a "universal brotherhood" of all workers, from common laborers to master craftsmen. The organization's secrecy and ritual served to bind Knights together at the same time that it discouraged company spies and protected members from reprisals.

Although the Knights played no active role in the 1877 railroad strike, membership swelled as a result of the growing interest in labor organizing that accompanied the strike. In 1878, the Knights abandoned secrecy and launched an ambitious campaign to organize workers regardless of skill, sex, race, or nationality. The Knights of Labor attempted to bridge the boundaries of ethnicity, gender, ideology, race, and occupation in a badly fragmented society. Under the leadership of Leonora Barry, who served as general investigator for women's work from 1886 to 1890, the Knights recruited teachers, waitresses, housewives, and domestics along with factory and sweatshop workers. Women composed perhaps 20 percent of the membership. The Knights also made good on its vow to include African Americans, organizing more than 95,000 black workers. That the Knights of Labor often fell short of its goals to unify the working class proved less surprising than the scope of its efforts.

Under the direction of Grand Master Workman Terence V. Powderly, the Knights became the dominant force in labor during the 1880s. The organization advocated a kind of workers' **democracy** that embraced reforms such as public ownership of the railroads, an income tax, equal pay for women workers, and the abolition of child labor. A loose mix of ideology, unionism, culture, fraternalism, and mysticism, the Knights called for one big union to create a cooperative commonwealth that would supplant the wage system and remove class distinctions. Only the "parasitic" members of society—gamblers, stockbrokers, lawyers, bankers, and liquor dealers—were denied membership.

In theory, the Knights of Labor opposed strikes. Powderly championed arbitration and preferred to use boycotts. But in practice, much of the organization's appeal came from a successful strike the Knights mounted in 1885 against railroads controlled by Jay Gould. The Knights won a sweeping victory, including the revocation of a 15 percent pay cut. Despite the reservations of its leadership, the Knights became a militant labor organization that won passionate support from working people with the slogan "An injury to one is the concern of all."

The Knights of Labor was not without rivals. Many skilled workers belonged to craft unions organized by trade. Among the largest and richest of these unions stood the Amalgamated Association of Iron and Steel Workers, founded in 1876 and counting twenty thousand skilled workers as members. Trade unionists spurned the broad reform goals of the Knights and focused on workplace issues. Samuel Gompers, a cigar maker born in London of Dutch Jewish ancestry, promoted what he called "pure and simple" unionism. More hardheaded than Powderly, Gompers embraced class struggle—the implacable enmity between workers and employers posited by European **socialist** Karl Marx—and wielded the strike as the workers' most effective weapon. Gompers founded the Organized Trades and Labor Unions in 1881 and reorganized it in 1886 into the American Federation of Labor (AFL), which coordinated the activities of craft unions throughout the United States. His plan was simple:

Organize skilled workers such as machinists and locomotive engineers—those with the most bargaining power—and use strikes to gain immediate objectives such as higher pay and better working conditions. Gompers at first drew few converts. The AFL had only 138,000 members in 1886, compared with 730,000 for the Knights of Labor. But events soon brought down the Knights, and Gompers's brand of unionism came to prevail.

Haymarket and the Specter of Labor Radicalism

While the AFL and the Knights of Labor competed for members, more radical labor groups, including socialists and anarchists, believed that reform was futile and called instead for social revolution. Both groups, sensitive to criticism that they preferred revolution in theory to improvements here and now, rallied around the popular issue of the eight-hour day.

Since the 1840s, labor had sought to end the twelve-hour workday, which was standard in industry and manufacturing. By the mid-1880s, it seemed clear to many workers that labor shared too little in the new prosperity of the decade, and pressure mounted for the eight-hour day. Labor rallied to the popular issue and launched major rallies in cities across the nation. Supporters of the movement set May 1, 1886, as the date for a nationwide general strike in support of the eight-hour workday.

All factions of the nascent labor movement came together in Chicago on May Day for what was billed as the largest demonstration to date. A group of labor radicals led by anarchist Albert Parsons, a *Mayflower* descendant, and August Spies, a German socialist, spearheaded the eight-hour movement in Chicago. Chicago's Knights of Labor rallied to the cause even though Terence Powderly and the union's national leadership, worried about the increasing activism of the rank and file, refused to endorse the movement for shorter hours. Samuel Gompers was on hand, too, to lead the city's trade unionists, although he privately urged the AFL assemblies not to participate in the general strike.

Gompers's skilled workers were labor's elite. Many still worked in small shops where negotiations between workers and employers took place in an environment tempered by personal relationships. Well dressed in their frock coats and starched shirts, the AFL's skilled workers stood in sharp contrast to the dispossessed workers out on strike across town at Chicago's huge McCormick reaper works. There strikers watched helplessly as the company brought in strikebreakers to take their jobs and marched the "scabs" to work under the protection of the Chicago police and security guards supplied by the Pinkerton Detective Agency. Cyrus McCormick Jr., son of the inventor of the mechanical reaper, viewed labor organization as a threat to his power as well as to his profits; he was determined to smash the union.

During the May Day rally, 45,000 workers paraded peacefully down Michigan Avenue in support of the eight-hour day, many singing the song that had become the movement's anthem:

We mean to make things over; we're tired of toil for naught
But bare enough to live on: never an hour for thought.
We want to feel the sunshine; we want to smell the flowers;
We're sure that God has willed it, and we mean to have eight hours.
Eight hours for work, eight hours for rest, eight hours for what we will!

Trouble came two days later, when strikers attacked scabs outside the McCormick works and police opened fire, killing or wounding six men. Angry radicals rushed out a circular urging workers to "arm yourselves and appear in full force" at a rally in Haymarket Square.

On the evening of May 4, the turnout at Haymarket was disappointing. No more than two or three thousand gathered in the drizzle to hear Spies, Parsons, and the other speakers. Mayor Carter Harrison, known as a friend of labor, mingled conspicuously in the crowd, pronounced the meeting peaceable, and went home to bed. A short time later, police captain John "Blackjack" Bonfield, who had made his reputation cracking skulls, marched his men into the crowd, by now fewer than three hundred people, and demanded that it disperse. Suddenly, someone threw a bomb into the police ranks. After a moment of stunned silence, the police drew their revolvers. "Fire and kill all you can," shouted a police lieutenant. When the melee ended, seven policemen and an unknown number of others lay dead. An additional sixty policemen and thirty or forty civilians suffered injuries.

News of the "Haymarket riot" provoked a nationwide convulsion of fear, followed by blind rage directed at anarchists, labor unions, strikers, immigrants, and the working class in general. Eight men, including Parsons and Spies, went on trial in Chicago, although witnesses testified that none of them had thrown the bomb. "Convict these men," thundered the state's attorney, Julius S. Grinnell, "make examples of them, hang them, and you save our institutions." Although the state could not link any of the defendants to the Haymarket bombing, the jury nevertheless found them all guilty. Four were executed, one committed suicide, and three received prison sentences. On the gallows, August Spies spoke for the Haymarket martyrs: "The time will come when our silence will be more powerful than the voices you throttle today."

In 1893, Governor John Peter Altgeld, after a thorough investigation, pardoned the three remaining Haymarket anarchists. He denounced the trial as a shameless travesty of justice. The governor's action brought on a storm of protest and cost him his political career.

The bomb blast at Haymarket had lasting repercussions. To commemorate the death of the Haymarket martyrs, labor made May 1 an annual international celebration of the worker. But the Haymarket bomb, in the eyes of one observer, proved "a godsend to all enemies of the labor movement." It effectively scotched the eight-hour-day movement and dealt a blow to the Knights of Labor, already wracked by internal divisions.

With the labor movement everywhere under attack, many skilled workers turned to the American Federation of Labor. Gompers's narrow economic strategy made sense at the time and enabled one segment of the workforce—the skilled—to organize effectively and achieve tangible gains. But the nation's unskilled workers remained untouched by the AFL's brand of trade unionism. The vast majority of America's workers would have to wait another forty years before a mainstream labor union, the Congress of Industrial Organizations (CIO), moved to organize the unskilled (see chapter 24).

> ▶ **REVIEW**   Why did the fortunes of the Knights of Labor rise in the late 1870s and decline in the 1890s?

At Home and at Play

The growth of urban industrialism not only dramatically altered the workplace but also transformed home and family life and gave rise to new forms of commercialized leisure. Industrialization redefined the very concepts of work and home. Increasingly, men went out to work for wages, while most white married women stayed home, either working in the home without pay—cleaning, cooking, and rearing children—or supervising paid domestic servants who did the housework.

Domesticity and "Domestics"

The separation of the workplace and the home that marked the shift to industrial society redefined the home as a "haven in the heartless world," presided over by a wife and mother who made the household her **separate sphere**. The growing separation of workplace and home led to a new ideology, one that sentimentalized the home and women's role in it. The cultural ideology that dictated woman's place in the home has been called the **cult of domesticity**, a phrase used to prescribe an ideal of middle-class, white womanhood that dominated the period from 1820 to the end of the nineteenth century (see chapter 11).

The cult of domesticity and the elaboration of the middle-class home led to a major change in patterns of hiring household help. The live-in servant, or domestic, became a fixture in the North, replacing the hired girl of the previous century. (The South continued to rely on black female labor, first slave and later free.) In American cities by 1870, 15 to 30 percent of all households included live-in domestic servants, more than 90 percent of them women. By the mid-nineteenth century, native-born women increasingly took up other work and left domestic service to immigrants. In the East, the maid was so often Irish that "Bridget" became a generic term for female domestics.

Servants by all accounts resented the long hours and lack of privacy. "She is liable to be rung up at all hours," one study reported. "Her very meals are not secure from interruption, and even her sleep is not sacred." No wonder tension between domestic servants and their female employers proved endemic. Furthermore, going into service carried a social stigma. As one young woman observed, "If a girl goes into the kitchen she is sneered at and called 'the Bridget,' but if she goes behind the counter she is escorted by gentlemen." Domestic service became the occupation of last resort, a "hard and lonely life" in the words of one servant girl.

For women of the white middle class, domestics were a boon, freeing them from household drudgery and giving them more time to spend with their children or to pursue club work or reform. Thus, while domestic service supported the cult of domesticity, it created for those women who could afford it opportunities that expanded their horizons outside the home in areas such as women's clubs and the temperance and suffrage movements.

As if to emphasize the new role of the home as a refuge and a haven in the decades after the Civil War, the typical middle-class dwelling itself became more embellished architecturally and its interior more cluttered. Possession of such a home, indeed of any home, marked the gulf between the working poor and the middle class. Homeowners constituted only 36 percent of the U.S. housing population in 1900, compared with 67 percent today.

The gap between working-class austerity and the trappings associated with middle-class respectability becomes apparent in the comparison of two households. Margaret Byington, a reformer who undertook a scientific survey of Homestead, the Carnegie mill town outside Pittsburgh, recounted her visit with the family of a Slavic worker. The family lived in a two-room tenement, and Byington found the young mother doing the family laundry in a big washtub set on a chair in the middle of the room, struggling to keep her two babies from tumbling into the scalding water. Byington noted the sparse furnishings:

> On one side of the room was a huge puffy bed, with one feather tick to sleep on and another for covering; near the window stood a sewing machine; in the corner, an organ,—all these, besides the inevitable cook stove upon which in the place of honor was simmering the evening's soup. Upstairs in a second room, a boarder and the man of the house were asleep. Soon they would get up and turn their beds over to two more boarders, who were out at work.

Compare the Slavic family's household with the description of a middle-class home taken from *The Gilded Age*, the 1873 novel by Mark Twain and Charles Dudley Warner:

> Every room has its book-cases or book-shelves, and was more or less a library; upon every table was liable to be a litter of new books, fresh periodicals and daily newspapers. There were plants in the sunny windows and some choice

engravings on the walls, with bits of color in oil or watercolors; the piano was sure to be open and strewn with music; and there were photographs and little souvenirs here and there of foreign travels.

In the eyes of Byington and many middle-class reformers, the Slavs' crowded tenement, with its boarders and its lack of privacy, scarcely qualified as a "home." Yet for all the obvious differences between the households, one can see in the workers' two feather ticks, sewing machine, and organ the same urge for sociability and impulse toward comfort apparent in the middle-class home.

Mill Towns and Company Towns

Mill towns like the one Byington studied became a feature of the industrial landscape in the nineteenth century. Many, like Homestead, grew up haphazardly. By 1892, eight thousand people lived in Homestead, transforming a rural village into a bustling mill town that belied its pastoral name. As the steelworks expanded, they encroached on the residential area, pushing the homes out of the flatlands along the Monongahela River. Workers moved into the hills and ravines. In an area called the Hollow, shanties hung precariously on the hillsides. These small, boxlike dwellings—many no larger than two rooms—housed the unskilled laborers from the mills.

Elsewhere, particularly in New England and the South, the company itself planned and built the town. The Amoskeag textile mill in Manchester, New Hampshire, was a self-contained world laid out according to a master plan conceived in the 1830s. Such planned communities rested on the notion of benevolent corporate paternalism. Viewing the workers as the "corporation's children," Amoskeag's owners sought to socialize their increasingly immigrant workforce to the patterns of industrial work and to instill loyalty to the company, curb labor unrest, and prevent unionization.

By the 1880s, Amoskeag employed tens of thousands of workers, housing 35 percent of them in corporation tenements. "The corporations," as workers called them, were three- to five-story attached brick houses. Workers paid the equivalent of $1 per month for company housing. To qualify, families had to have more than one member working in the mill, a requirement that encouraged child labor. The substantial brick row houses with high ceilings and hardwood floors offered a striking contrast to the ramshackle shanties of Homestead. But through its housing, the mill exerted a powerful hold over the lives of its workers. "If you told the boss to go to hell, you might as well move out of the city," one mill worker acknowledged.

In western mining towns, companies exerted control not only over the housing of employees but over their religious and social lives as well. In Ludlow, a mining town in Colorado controlled by the Rockefeller family, the local minister was hired and supported by the company. Such ironfisted control was designed to prevent labor unions from gaining a foothold. Rockefeller hired spies to infiltrate the town, hang out at the local saloons, and report on any union activity.

Control by the mill owners reached its height in company towns south of the Mason-Dixon line. "Practically speaking," a federal investigator observed, "the company owns everything and controls everybody in the mill village." These largely nameless company towns, with their company-controlled stores, churches, schools, and houses, offer a classic example of social control over workers. Paid in company currency, or scrip, workers had no choice but to patronize the company store, where high prices led to a mounting spiral of debt that reduced the workers to virtual captives of the company. At the turn of the century, 92 percent of southern textile workers' families lived in company towns.

The mill towns and company towns of the United States provide only the most dramatic examples of the ways in which industrialization and the rise of corporate capitalism changed the landscape of the country and altered traditional patterns of work and home life.

Cheap Amusements

Growing class divisions manifested themselves in patterns of leisure as well as in work and home life. The poor and working class took their leisure, when they had any, not in the crowded tenements that housed their families, but increasingly in the cities' new dance halls, music houses, ballparks, and amusement arcades, which by the 1890s formed a familiar part of the urban landscape.

Saloons played a central role in workers' lives, often serving informally as political headquarters, employment agencies, and union halls. But not all the working class thronged to saloons. Recreation varied according to ethnicity, religion, gender, and age. For many immigrants, social life revolved around the family. Weddings, baptisms, birthdays, and bar mitzvahs constituted the chief celebrations. Men spent more time away from home in neighborhood clubs, saloons, and fraternal orders than did women, who were largely barred from these establishments. An exception was the German beer garden, which welcomed the entire family.

The growing anonymity of urban industrial society posed a challenge to traditional rituals of courtship. Adolescent working girls no longer met prospective husbands only through their families. Fleeing crowded tenements, the young sought each other's company in dance halls and other commercial retreats. Scorning proper introductions, working-class youths "picked up" partners at dance halls, where drinking was part of the evening's entertainment. Young workingwomen, who rarely could afford more than trolley fare when they went out, counted on being "treated" by men, a transaction that often implied sexual payback. Young women's need to negotiate sexual encounters if they wished to participate in commercial amusements blurred the line between respectability and promiscuity and made the dance halls a favorite target of reformers who feared they lured girls into prostitution.

For men, baseball became a national pastime in the 1870s—then, as now, one force in urban life capable of uniting a city across class lines. Cincinnati mounted the first entirely paid team, the Red Stockings, in 1869. Soon professional teams proliferated in cities across the nation, and Mark Twain hailed baseball as "the very symbol, the outward and visible expression, of the drive and push and rush and struggle of the raging, tearing, booming nineteenth century."

The increasing commercialization of entertainment in the late nineteenth century can best be seen at Coney Island. A two-mile stretch of sand nine miles from Manhattan by trolley or steamship, Coney Island in the 1870s and 1880s attracted visitors to its beaches, dance pavilions, and penny arcades, where they consumed treats ranging from oysters to saltwater taffy. In the 1890s, Coney Island was transformed into the site of some of the largest and most elaborate amusement parks in the country. Promoter George Tilyou built Steeplechase Park in 1897, advertising "10 hours of fun for 10 cents." With its mechanical thrills and funhouse laughs, the amusement park encouraged behavior that one schoolteacher aptly described as "everyone with the brakes off." By 1900, as many as a million New Yorkers flocked to Coney Island on any given weekend, making the amusement park the unofficial capital of a new mass culture.

▶REVIEW   How did urban industrialism shape the world of leisure?

City Growth and City Government

Private enterprise, not planners, built the cities of the United States. Boosters, builders, businessmen, and politicians all had a hand in creating the modern metropolis. With a few notable exceptions, such as Washington, D.C., and Savannah, Georgia, there was no such thing as a comprehensive city plan. Cities simply mushroomed, formed by the dictates of private enterprise and the exigencies of local politics. With the rise of the city came the need for public facilities, transportation, and services that would tax the imaginations of America's architects and engineers and set the scene for the rough-and-tumble of big-city government, politics, and politicians.

Building Cities of Stone and Steel

Skyscrapers and mighty bridges dominated the imagination and the urban landscape. Less imposing but no less significant were the paved streets, the parks and public libraries, and the subways and sewers. In the late nineteenth century, Americans rushed to embrace new technology of all kinds, making their cities the most modern in the world.

Structural steel made enormous advances in building possible. A decade after the completion of the Brooklyn Bridge, engineers used the new technology to construct the Williamsburg Bridge three miles to the north. More prosaic and utilitarian than its neighbor, the new bridge was never as acclaimed, but it was longer by four feet and completed in half the time. It became the model for future building as the age of steel supplanted the age of stone and iron.

Skyscrapers forever changed the cityscape. Competition for space in Manhattan pushed the city up into the air even before the use of steel. The invention of Elisha Otis's elevator (called a "safety hoister") in the 1850s led to the construction of cast-iron buildings with elevators that carried passengers as high as ten stories. But until the advent of structural steel in the 1880s, no building in Manhattan topped the spire of Wall Street's Trinity Church.

Chicago, not New York, gave birth to the modern skyscraper. Rising from the ashes of the Great Fire of 1871, which destroyed three square miles and left eighteen thousand people homeless, Chicago offered a generation of skilled architects and engineers the chance to experiment with new technologies. Commercial architecture became an art form at the hands of a skilled group of architects who together constituted the "Chicago school." Men of genius such as Louis Sullivan and John Wellborn Root gave Chicago some of the world's finest commercial buildings. Employing the dictum "Form follows function," they built startlingly modern structures. A fitting symbol of modern America, the skyscraper expressed the domination of corporate power.

Alongside the skyscrapers rose new residential apartments for the rich and middle class. The "French flat"—apartments with the latest plumbing and electricity—gained popularity in the 1880s as affluent city dwellers overcame their distaste for multifamily housing (which carried the stigma of the tenement) and gave in to "flat fever." Fashionable new apartments boasted modern luxuries such as telephones, central heating, and elevators. The convenience of apartment living appealed particularly to women. "Housekeeping isn't fun," cried one New York woman. "Give us flats!" In 1883 alone, more than one thousand new apartments went up in Chicago.

The flush toilets, bathtubs, and lavatories of the new apartments would not have been possible without major improvements in city sewers and water mains. In the absence of proper sewage disposal, contaminated water wreaked havoc in big cities. In 1882, an outbreak of typhoid fever caused by the city's polluted water killed more than twenty thousand people in Chicago. To end this scourge, enlightened city engineers created and expanded municipal sewage systems and devised ingenious ways to bring clean water to the urban population. By the 1890s, the residents of U.S. cities demanded and received, at the twist of a faucet, water for their bathtubs, toilets, and even their lawn sprinklers. Those who could afford it enjoyed a standard of living that was the envy of civilization.

Across the United States, municipal governments undertook public works on a scale never before seen. They paved streets, built sewers and water mains, replaced gas lamps with electric lights, ran trolley tracks on the old horsecar lines, and dug underground to build subways, tearing down the unsightly elevated tracks that had clogged city streets. In San Francisco, Andrew Smith Hallidie mastered the city's hills, building a system of cable cars in 1873. Boston completed the nation's first subway system in 1897, and New York and Philadelphia soon followed.

Cities became more beautiful with the creation of urban public parks to complement the new buildings that quickly filled city lots. Much of the credit for America's greatest parks goes to one man—landscape architect Frederick Law Olmsted. The indefatigable Olmsted designed parks in Atlanta, Boston, Brooklyn, Hartford, Detroit, Chicago, and Louisville, as well as the grounds for the U.S. Capitol. But he is best remembered for the creation of New York City's Central Park. Completed in 1873, it became the first landscaped public park in the United States. Olmsted and his partner, Calvert Vaux, directed the planting of more than five million trees, shrubs, and vines to transform the eight hundred acres between 59th and 110th streets into an oasis for urban dwellers. We want a place, he wrote, where people "may stroll for an hour, seeing, hearing, and feeling nothing of the bustle and jar of the streets."

American cities did not overlook the mind in their efforts at improvement. They created a comprehensive free public school system that educated everyone from the children of the middle class to the sons and daughters of immigrant workers. The exploding urban population strained the system and led to crowded and inadequate facilities. In 1899, more than 544,000 pupils attended school in New York's five boroughs. Schools in Boston, New York, Chicago, and San Francisco, as well as those in other cities and towns, provided the only classrooms in the world where students could attend secondary school free of charge.

In addition to schools, the cities built libraries to educate their citizens. In the late nineteenth century, American cities created the most extensive free public library system in the world. In 1895, the Boston Public Library opened its bronze doors under the inscription "Free to All." Designed in the style of a Renaissance palazzo, with more than 700,000 books on the shelves ready to be checked out, the library earned the description "a palace of the people."

Despite the Boston Public Library's legend "Free to All," the poor did not share equally in the advantages of city life. The parks, the libraries, and even the subways and sewers benefited some city dwellers more than others. Few library cards were held by Boston's laborers, who worked six days a week and found the library closed on Sunday. And in the 1890s, there was nothing central about New York's Central Park. It was a four-mile walk from the tenements of Hester Street to the park's entrance at 59th Street and Fifth Avenue. Cities spent more money on plumbing improvements for affluent apartment dwellers than on public baths and lodging houses for the down-and-out. Even the uniform subway fare, which enabled Boston and New York riders to travel anywhere in the system for five cents, worked to the advantage of middle-class commuters but not the downtown poor. Then, as now, the comfortable majority, not the indigent minority, reaped a disproportionate share of the benefits in the nation's big cities.

Any story of the American city, it seems, must be a tale of two cities—or, given the cities' great diversity, a tale of many cities within each metropolis. At the turn of the twentieth century, a central paradox emerged: The enduring monuments of America's cities—the bridges, skyscrapers, parks, and libraries— stood as the undeniable achievements of the same system of municipal government that reformers dismissed as boss-ridden, criminal, and corrupt.

City Government and the "Bosses"

The physical growth of the cities required the expansion of public services and the creation of entirely new facilities: streets, subways, elevated trains, bridges, docks, sewers, and public utilities. There was work to be done and money to be made. The professional politician—the colorful big-city boss—became a phenomenon of urban growth. Though corrupt and often criminal, the boss saw to the building of the city and provided needed social services for the new residents. Yet not even the big-city boss could be said to rule the unruly city. The governing of America's cities resembled more a tug-of-war than boss rule.

The most notorious of all the city bosses was William Marcy Tweed of New York. At midcentury, Boss Tweed's Democratic Party "machine" held sway. A machine was really no more than a political party organized at the grassroots level. Its purpose was to win elections and reward its followers, often with jobs on the city's payroll. New York's citywide Democratic machine, Tammany Hall, commanded an army of party functionaries. At the bottom were district captains. In return for votes, they provided services for their constituents, everything from a scuttle of

Tammany Bank
This cast-iron bank, a campaign novelty, bears the name of the New York City Democratic machine. It conveys its political reform message graphically: When you put a penny in the politician's hand, he puts it in his pocket. Tammany Hall dominated city politics for more than a century, dispensing contracts and franchises worth millions of dollars and padding the pockets of Tammany politicians.
Collection of Janice L. and David J. Frent.

coal in the winter to housing for an evicted family. At the top were powerful ward bosses who distributed lucrative franchises for subways and streetcars. They formed a shadow government, more powerful than the city's elected officials. The only elected office Tweed ever held was alderman. But as chairman of the Tammany general committee, he wielded more power than the mayor. Through the use of bribery and graft, he kept the Democratic Party together and ran the city. "As long as I count the votes," he shamelessly boasted, "what are you going to do about it?"

The cost of Tweed's rule was staggering. The construction of New York City's courthouse, budgeted at $250,000, ended up costing the taxpayers $14 million. The inflated sum represented bribery, kickbacks, and the greasing of many palms. The excesses of the Tweed ring soon led to a clamor for reform and cries of "Throw the rascals out." Cartoonist Thomas Nast pilloried Tweed in the pages of *Harper's Weekly*. His cartoons, easily understood even by those who could not read, did the boss more harm than hundreds of outraged editorials. Tweed's rule ended in 1871. Eventually, he was tried and convicted and later died in jail.

New York was not the only city to experience bossism and corruption. The British visitor James Bryce concluded in 1888, "There is no denying that the government of cities is the one conspicuous failure of the United States." More than 80 percent of the nation's thirty largest cities experienced some form of boss rule in the decades around the turn of the twentieth century. However, infighting among powerful ward bosses often meant that no single boss enjoyed exclusive power in the big cities.

Urban reformers and proponents of good government (derisively called "goo goos" by their rivals) challenged machine rule and sometimes succeeded in electing reform mayors. But the reformers rarely managed to stay in office for long. Their detractors called them "mornin' glories," observing that they "looked lovely in the mornin' and withered up in a short time." The bosses enjoyed continued success largely because the urban political machines helped the cities' immigrants and poor, who remained their staunchest allies. "What tells in holding your district," a Tammany ward boss observed, "is to go right down among the poor and help them in the different ways they need help. It's philanthropy, but it's politics, too—mighty good politics."

A few reform mayors managed to achieve success and longevity by following the bosses' model. Hazen S. Pingree of Detroit exemplified the successful reform mayor. A businessman who went into politics in the 1890s, Pingree, like most good-government candidates, promised to root out dishonesty and inefficiency. But when the depression of 1893 struck, Pingree emerged as a champion of the working class and the poor. He hired the unemployed to build schools, parks, and public baths. By providing jobs and needed services, he built a powerful political organization based on working-class support. Detroit's voters kept him in the mayor's office for four terms and then helped elect him governor twice.

While most good-government candidates harped on the Sunday closing of saloons and attacked vice and crime, Pingree demurred: "The most dangerous enemies to good government are not the saloons, the dives, the dens of iniquity and the criminals," but "the temptations which are offered to city officials when franchises are sought by wealthy corporations, or contracts are to be let for public works." Through the skillful orchestration of rewards, an astute political operator could exert powerful leverage and line up support for his party from a broad range of constituents, from the urban poor to wealthy industrialists. In 1902, when journalist Lincoln Steffens began "The Shame of the Cities," a series of articles exposing city corruption, he found that business leaders who fastidiously refused to mingle socially with the bosses nevertheless struck deals with them. "He is a self-righteous fraud, this big businessman," Steffens concluded. "I found him buying boodlers [bribers] in St. Louis, defending grafters in Minneapolis, originating corruption in Pittsburgh, sharing with bosses in Philadelphia, deploring reform in Chicago, and beating good government with corruption funds in New York."

The complexity of big-city government, apparent in the many levels of corruption that Steffens uncovered, pointed to one conclusion: For all the color and flamboyance of the big-city boss, he was simply one of many actors in the drama of municipal government. The successful boss was not an autocratic ruler but a power broker. Old-stock aristocrats, new professionals, saloonkeepers, pushcart peddlers, and politicians all fought for their interests in the hurly-burly of city government. They didn't much like each other, and they sometimes fought savagely. But they learned to live with one another. Compromise and accommodation—not boss rule—best characterized big-city government by the turn of the twentieth century, although the cities' reputation for corruption left an indelible mark on the consciousness of the American public.

White City or City of Sin?

Americans in the late nineteenth century, like Americans today, were of two minds about the city. They liked to boast of its skyscrapers and bridges, its culture and sophistication, and they prided themselves on its bigness and bustle. At the same time, they feared it as the city of sin, the home of immigrant slums, the center of vice and crime. Nowhere did the divided view of the American city take form more graphically than in Chicago in 1893.

In that year, Chicago hosted the World's Columbian Exposition, the grandest world's fair in the nation's history. The fairground, called the White City and built on the shores of Lake Michigan, offered a lesson in what Americans on the eve of the twentieth century imagined a city might be. Only five miles down the shore from Chicago, the White City seemed light-years away. Its very name celebrated a harmony and pristine beauty unknown in Chicago, with its stockyards, slums, and bustling terminals. Frederick Law Olmsted and architect Daniel Burnham supervised the transformation of a swampy wasteland into a paradise of lagoons, fountains, wooded islands, gardens, and imposing buildings.

"Sell the cookstove and come," novelist Hamlin Garland wrote to his parents on the farm. And come they did, in spite of the panic and depression that broke out only weeks after the fair opened in May 1893. In six months, fairgoers purchased more than 27 million tickets, turning a profit of nearly a half million dollars for promoters. Visitors from home and abroad strolled the elaborate grounds, visited the exhibits — everything from a model of the Brooklyn Bridge carved in soap to the latest goods and inventions. Half carnival, half culture, the great fair offered something for everyone. On the Midway Plaisance, crowds thrilled to the massive wheel built by Mr. Ferris and watched agog as Little Egypt danced the hootchy-kootchy.

In October, the fair closed its doors in the midst of the worst depression the country had yet seen. During the winter of 1894, Chicago's unemployed and homeless took over the grounds, vandalized the buildings, and frightened the city's comfortable citizens out of their wits. When reporters asked Daniel Burnham what should be done with the moldering remains of the White City, he responded, "It should be torched." And it was. In July 1894, in a clash between federal troops and striking railway workers, incendiaries set fires that leveled the fairgrounds.

In the end, the White City remained what it had always been, a dreamscape. Buildings that looked like marble were actually constructed of staff, a plaster of paris substance that began to crumble even before fire destroyed the fairgrounds. The White City was a fantasy never destined to last. Perhaps it was not so strange, after all, that the legacy of the White City could be found on Coney Island, where two new amusement parks, Luna and Dreamland, sought to combine, albeit in a more tawdry form, the beauty of the White City and the thrill of the Midway Plaisance. More enduring than the White City itself was what it represented: the emergent industrial might of the United States, at home and abroad, with its inventions, manufactured goods, and growing consumer culture.

▶**REVIEW** How did municipal governments respond to the challenges of urban expansion?

Conclusion: Who Built the Cities?

As much as the great industrialists and financiers, as much as eminent engineers like John and Washington Roebling, common workers, most of them immigrants, built the nation's cities. The unprecedented growth of urban, industrial America resulted from the labor of millions of men, women, and children who toiled in workshops and factories, in sweatshops and mines, on railroads and construction sites across America.

America's cities in the late nineteenth century teemed with life. Immigrants and blue bloods, poor laborers and millionaires, middle-class managers and corporate moguls, secretaries, salesgirls, sweatshop laborers, and society matrons lived in the cities and contributed to their growth. Town houses, tenements, and new apartment buildings jostled for space with skyscrapers and great department stores, while parks, ball fields, amusement arcades, and public libraries provided the city masses with recreation and entertainment.

Municipal governments, straining to build the new cities, experienced the rough-and-tumble of machine politics as bosses and their constituents looked to profit from city growth. Reformers deplored the graft and corruption that accompanied the rise of the cities. But they were rarely able to oust the party bosses for long because they failed to understand the services the political machines provided for their largely immigrant and poor constituents, as well as the ties between the politicians and wealthy businessmen who sought to benefit from franchises and contracts.

For America's workers, urban industrialism along with the rise of big business and corporate consolidation drastically changed the workplace. Industrialists replaced skilled workers with new machines that could be operated by cheaper, unskilled labor. And during hard times, employers did not hesitate to cut workers' already meager wages. As the Great Railroad Strike of 1877 demonstrated, when labor united, it could bring the nation to attention. Organization held out the best hope for the workers; first the Knights of Labor and later the American Federation of Labor won converts among the nation's working class.

The rise of urban industrialism challenged the American promise, which for decades had been dominated by Jeffersonian agrarian ideals. Could such a promise exist in the changing world of cities, tenements, immigrants, and huge corporations? In the great depression that came in the 1890s, mounting anger and frustration would lead workers and farmers to join forces and create a grassroots movement to fight for change under the banner of a new People's Party.

REVIEWING THE CHAPTER

Use the questions and timeline to review and strengthen your understanding of the chapter.

REVIEW QUESTIONS

1. Why did American cities experience explosive growth in the late nineteenth century? (pp. 578–87)

2. How did business expansion and consolidation change workers' occupations in the late nineteenth century? (pp. 588–93)

3. Why did the fortunes of the Knights of Labor rise in the late 1870s and decline in the 1890s? (pp. 593–600)

4. How did urban industrialism shape the world of leisure? (pp. 600–604)

5. How did municipal governments respond to the challenges of urban expansion? (pp. 604–10)

MAKING CONNECTIONS

1. Americans expressed both wonder and concern at the nation's mushrooming cities. Why did cities provoke such divergent responses? In your answer, discuss the dramatic demographic, environmental, and political developments associated with urbanization.

2. Why did patterns of immigration to the United States in the late nineteenth century change? How did Americans respond to the immigrants who arrived late in the century? In your answer, consider how industrial capitalism, nationally and globally, contributed to these developments.

3. How did urban industrialization affect Americans' lives outside of work? Describe the impact late-nineteenth-century economic developments had on home life and leisure. In your answer, consider how class, race, gender, and ethnicity contributed to diverse urban experiences.

4. When workers began to embrace organization in the late 1870s, what did they hope to accomplish? Were they successful? Why or why not? In your answer, discuss both general conditions and specific events that shaped these developments.

TIMELINE

1869	• Knights of Labor founded. • Cincinnati mounts first paid baseball team, the Red Stockings.	**1890s**	• African American migration from South begins.
1871	• Boss Tweed's rule in New York ends. • Chicago's Great Fire.	**1890**	• Jacob Riis publishes *How the Other Half Lives.*
1873	• Panic on Wall Street touches off depression. • San Francisco's cable car system opens.	**1893**	• World's Columbian Exposition. • Panic on Wall Street touches off major economic depression.
1877	• Great Railroad Strike.	**1895**	• Boston Public Library opens.
1878	• Knights of Labor organizes workers.	**1896**	• President Grover Cleveland vetoes immigrant literacy test.
1880s	• Immigration from southern and eastern Europe rises.	**1897**	• Steeplechase Park opens on Coney Island. • Nation's first subway system opens in Boston.
1882	• Chinese Exclusion Act.		
1883	• Brooklyn Bridge opens.	**1900**	• Ellis Island opens.
1886	• American Federation of Labor (AFL) founded. • Haymarket bombing.		

▶ **For an online bibliography, practice quizzes, Web sites, images, and documents related to this chapter,** see the Book Companion Site at **bedfordstmartins.com/roark.**

▶ **For firsthand accounts of this period,** see Chapter 19 in Michael Johnson, ed., *Reading the American Past,* Fourth Edition.

20

CHAPTER

Dissent, Depression, and War

1890–1900

FRANCES WILLARD TRAVELED to St. Louis in February 1892 with high hopes. She was not alone. Farmers, laborers, and reformers of all stripes flocked to Missouri to attend a meeting, in the words of one reporter, "different from any other political meeting ever witnessed in St. Louis." The cigar-chomping politicians who generally worked the convention circuit were nowhere to be seen. In their place, "mostly gray-haired, sunburned and roughly clothed men" assembled under a banner that proclaimed, "We do not ask for sympathy or pity. We ask for justice."

Political change was in the air, and Willard was there to help fashion a new reform party, one that she hoped would embrace her two passions—temperance and woman **suffrage**. As head of the Woman's Christian Temperance Union, an organization with members in every state and territory in the nation, Willard wielded considerable clout. At her invitation, twenty-eight of the country's leading reformers had already met in Chicago to draft a set of principles to bring to St. Louis. Always expedient, Willard had settled for a statement condemning the saloon rather than an endorsement for a stronger measure to prohibit the sale of alcohol. But at the convention she hoped to press the case for woman suffrage and prohibition. Willard knew it would not be easy, but in the heady atmosphere of 1892, she determined to try. No American woman before her had played such a central role in a political movement. At the height of her political power, Willard took her place among the leaders on the podium in St. Louis.

Frances Willard
The forward-thinking leader of the Woman's Christian Temperance Union
learned to ride a bicycle at age fifty-three. The bicycle became hugely popular
in the 1890s, even though traditionalists fulminated that it was unladylike for
women to straddle a bike. Willard declared bicycling a "harmless pleasure"
that encouraged "clear heads and steady hands." She brought her
progressive ideas to the People's Party convention in 1892.
Courtesy of the Frances E. Willard Memorial Library and Archives (WCTU).

Exposition Music Hall presented a colorful spectacle. "The banners of the
different states rose above the delegates throughout the hall, fluttering like the
flags over an army encamped," wrote one reporter. The fiery orator Ignatius
Donnelly attacked the money kings of Wall Street. Mary Elizabeth Lease, a veteran campaigner from Kansas known for exhorting farmers to "raise less corn
and more hell," added her powerful voice to the cause. Terence V. Powderly, head
of the Knights of Labor, called on workers to join hands with farmers against the

"nonproducing classes." Frances Willard exhorted the crowd to outlaw the liquor traffic and give the vote to women. Between speeches, the crowd sang labor songs like "Hurrah for the Toiler" and "All Hail the Power of Laboring Men."

In the course of the next few days, delegates hammered out a series of demands, breathtaking in their scope. They tackled the tough questions of the day—the regulation of business, the need for banking and currency reform, the right of labor to organize and bargain collectively, and the role of the federal government in regulating business, curbing **monopoly**, and guaranteeing **democracy**. But the new party determined to stick to economic issues and resisted endorsing either temperance or woman suffrage. As a member of the platform committee, Willard fought for both and complained of the "crooked methods . . . employed to scuttle these planks." Outmaneuvered in committee, she brought the issues to the floor of the convention, only to go down to defeat by a vote of 352 to 238.

Despite Willard's disappointment, the convention ended its work amid a chorus of cheers. According to one eyewitness, "Hats, paper, handkerchiefs, etc., were thrown into the air; . . . cheer after cheer thundered and reverberated through the vast hall reaching the outside of the building where thousands who had been waiting the outcome joined in the applause till for blocks in every direction the exultation made the din indescribable."

What was all the shouting about? The cheering crowd celebrated the birth of a new political party, officially named the People's Party. Fed up with the Democrats and Republicans, a broad coalition of groups came together in St. Louis to fight for change. They resolved to reconvene in Omaha in July to nominate candidates for the upcoming presidential election. Defeated but not willing to abandon the new party, Willard urged the nomination of a presidential candidate committed to temperance and suffrage.

The St. Louis gathering marked a milestone in one of the most turbulent decades in U.S. history. Unrest, agitation, agrarian revolt, labor strikes, a severe financial panic and depression, and a war of expansion shook the 1890s. While the two major political parties continued to do business as usual, Americans flocked to organizations including the Farmers' Alliance, the American Federation of Labor, and the Woman's Christian Temperance Union, and they worked together to create the political alliance that gave birth to the People's (or **Populist**) Party. In a decade of unrest and uncertainty, the People's Party challenged **laissez-faire** economics by insisting that the federal government play a more active role to ensure greater economic equity in industrial America. This challenge to the status quo culminated in 1896 in one of the most hotly contested presidential elections in the nation's history. At the close of the tumultuous decade, the Spanish-American War helped to bring the country together as Americans rallied to support the troops. But disagreement over American **imperialism** and overseas expansion raised questions about the nation's role on the world stage as the United States stood poised to enter the twentieth century.

The Farmers' Revolt

Hard times in the 1880s and 1890s created a groundswell of agrarian revolt. A bitter farmer wrote from Minnesota, "I settled on this Land in good Faith Built House and Barn. Broken up Part of the Land. Spent years of hard Labor in grubbing fencing and Improving." About to lose his farm to foreclosure, he lamented, "Are they going to drive us out like trespassers . . . and give us away to the Corporations?"

Farm prices fell decade after decade, even as American farmers' share of the world market grew. Wheat that sold for a dollar a bushel in 1870 dropped to sixty cents in the 1890s. Cotton plummeted from fifteen cents to five cents a pound. Corn started at forty-five cents and fell to thirty cents a bushel. In parts of Kansas, it sold for as little as ten cents, and angry farmers burned their corn for fuel rather than market it at that price. At the same time, consumer prices soared. By 1894, in Kansas alone almost half the farms had fallen into the hands of the banks because poor farmers could no longer afford to pay their mortgages.

At the heart of the problem stood a banking system dominated by eastern commercial banks committed to the **gold standard**, a railroad rate system that was capricious and unfair, and rampant speculation that drove up the price of land. In the West, farmers rankled under a system that allowed railroads to charge them exorbitant freight rates while granting rebates to large shippers (see chapter 18). The railroads' policy of charging higher rates for short hauls meant that large grain elevator companies could ship their wheat from Chicago to New York for less money than it cost a Dakota farmer to send his crop to nearby Minneapolis. In the South, lack of currency and credit drove farmers to the stopgap credit system of the crop lien, turning the entire region into "a vast pawn shop." To pay for seed and supplies, farmers had to pledge their crops to local creditors, called "furnishing merchants," whose exorbitant prices meant chronic debt and destitution for southern farmers. Determined to do something, farmers banded together to fight for change.

The Farmers' Alliance

Farm protest was not new. In the 1870s, farmers had supported the Grange and the Greenback Labor Party. And as the farmers' situation grew more desperate, they organized, forming regional alliances. The first Farmers' Alliance came together in Lampasas County, Texas, to fight "landsharks and horse thieves." During the 1880s, the movement spread rapidly. In **frontier** farmhouses in Texas, in log cabins in the backwoods of Arkansas, and in the rural parishes of Louisiana, separate groups of farmers formed similar alliances for self-help.

As the movement grew, farmers' groups consolidated into two regional alliances. The Northwestern Farmers' Alliance was active in Kansas, Nebraska, and other midwestern Granger states. The more radical Southern Farmers' Alliance got its start in Texas and spread rapidly. In the 1880s, traveling lecturers preached the Alliance message. Worn-out men and careworn women did not need to be convinced that something was wrong. Overnight, scores of local alliances sprang up, each with its own lecturer, who in turn carried the word to every crossroads in the South.

The Southern Alliance soon spread from Texas to Louisiana and Arkansas, recruiting at the amazing rate of 20,000 a month in the autumn of 1886. "The farmers seem like unto ripe fruit—you can gather them by a gentle shake of the bush," an Alliance lecturer gloated. By 1887, the Southern Farmers' Alliance had grown to more than 200,000 members, and by 1890 it counted more than 3 million members.

Determined to reach blacks as well as whites, the Southern Alliance worked with the Colored Farmers' Alliance, an African American group founded in Texas in the 1880s. Although the Colored Alliance did not always agree with the Southern Alliance, blacks and whites attempted to make common cause. As Georgia's Tom Watson, a Southern Alliance stalwart, pointed out, "The colored tenant is in the same boat as the white tenant, . . . and . . . the accident of color can make no difference in the interests of farmers, croppers, and laborers."

The Farmers' Alliance reached out to workers as well as to farmers. During the Great Southwestern Strike against Jay Gould's Texas and Pacific Railroad in 1886, the Alliance supported the strikers. The Southern Farmers' Alliance rushed food and supplies to the striking workers and issued a proclamation in support of the Knights of Labor, calling on farmers to boycott Gould's railroad.

Women rallied to the Alliance banner along with their menfolk. In Kansas, more than 30 percent of Alliance members were women. "I am going to work for prohibition, the Alliance, and for Jesus as long as I live," swore one woman. The political culture of the Alliance encouraged the inclusion of women and children and used the family as its defining symbol. As journalist Elizabeth Barr wrote, "Women with skins tanned to parchment . . . with bony hands of toil and clad in faded calico, could talk in meeting, and could talk straight to the point."

Alliance meetings combined picnic, parade, revival, country fair, and political convention into a day of socializing, eating (no drinking—the Alliance banned alcohol), playing, and education. In wagon trains a thousand strong, men and women thronged to the meetings to listen to speeches and to debate and discuss the issues raised by the prophets of the movement. Alliance lecturers aimed to do more than exhort their followers; they worked to educate them. The Alliance produced and distributed "a perfect avalanche of literature"—speeches, newspapers, books, and tracts—full of damning details about the political collusion between business and politics, along with detailed analyses of the securities and commodities markets, the tariff and international trade, and credit and currency. Secular preachers, the Alliance lecturers reached out to the illiterate, often speaking for hours under the broiling sun to educate their rapt audiences on the fine points of economics and politics.

At the heart of the Alliance movement stood a series of farmers' cooperatives. By "bulking" their cotton—that is, selling it together—farmers could negotiate a better price. And by setting up trade stores and exchanges, they sought to escape the grasp of the merchant/creditor. Through the cooperatives, the Farmers' Alliance promised to change the way farmers lived. "We are going to get out of debt and be free and independent people once more," exulted one Georgia farmer.

Cooperatives flowered throughout the South and West. In 1888, farmers scored a major victory when they defeated the jute-bagging trust in its scheme to double the price of the bags used to bale cotton. But the Alliance could not succeed in its attempts to run cooperative stores. Opposition by merchants, bankers, wholesalers, and manufacturers made it impossible for the cooperatives to get credit.

As the cooperative movement died, the Farmers' Alliance moved toward direct political action. Texas farmers drafted a set of demands in 1886 and pressured political candidates to endorse them. In 1890, the Southern Farmers' Alliance called for railroad regulation, laws against land speculation, and currency and credit reform. The Alliance urged farmers to use the platform as a "yardstick," warning that candidates must "stand up and be measured." Confounded by the failure of the Democrats and Republicans to break with commercial interests and support the farmers, Alliance leaders moved, often reluctantly, toward the formation of a third party.

The Populist Movement

In the earliest days of the Alliance movement, C. W. Macune, a leader of the Southern Farmers' Alliance, insisted, "The Alliance is a strictly white man's nonpolitical, secret business association." But by 1892, it was none of those things. Although some white southern leaders, including Macune, made it clear that they would never threaten the unity of the white vote in the South by leaving the Democratic Party, advocates of a third party carried the day at the convention of laborers, farmers, and common folk in St. Louis in 1892. There, the Farmers' Alliance gave birth to the People's Party and launched the Populist movement. "There is something at the back of all this turmoil more than the failure of crops or the scarcity of ready cash," a journalist observed in 1892.

Populism was indeed more than a set of demands and a list of economic grievances. The same spirit of religious revival that animated the Farmers' Alliance infused the People's Party. The Populists built on the work of the Farmers' Alliance to mount a critique of industrial society and a call for action. Far from being backward-looking romantics, they articulated a rational and sophisticated program that called on the government to mediate between the interests of business and agriculture.

Convinced that the money and banking systems worked to the advantage of the wealthy few, they demanded economic democracy. To help farmers get the credit they needed at reasonable rates, southern farmers hit on the ingenious idea

On the Way to a Populist Meeting in Dickinson County, Kansas
Populism was more than a political movement; it was a culture unto itself. For rural farmers, the movement provided reassurance that they were not alone, that others shared their problems, and that solutions could be found. When the Populists called a meeting, wagons came from miles around.
Kansas State Historical Society.

of a subtreasury—a plan that would allow farmers to store nonperishable crops in government storehouses until market prices rose. At the same time, borrowing against their crops, farmers would receive commodity credit from the federal government to enable them to purchase needed supplies and seed for the coming year. In the South, the subtreasury promised to get rid of the crop lien system once and for all. Although the idea would be enacted piecemeal in **progressive** and **New Deal** legislation in the twentieth century, **conservatives** in the 1890s dismissed it as far-fetched "corn tassel communism."

To the western farmer, the Populists promised land reform, championing a plan that would reclaim excessive land granted to railroads or sold to foreign investors. The Populists' boldest proposal called for government ownership of the railroads and the telegraph system to put an end to discriminatory rates. Citing examples of how the powerful railroads had corrupted the political system, the Populists did not shrink from advocating what their opponents branded state **socialism**.

In addition to economic democracy and land reform, the Populists demanded currency reform. Farmers in all sections rallied to the cry for cheaper currency, endorsing platform planks calling for **free silver** and greenbacks—attempts to increase the nation's tight money supply and thus make credit easier to obtain.

To empower the common people, the Populist platform called for the direct election of senators and for other electoral reforms, including the secret ballot and the right to initiate legislation, to recall elected officials, and to submit issues to the people by means of a referendum. Because the Populists shared common cause with labor against corporate interests, they also supported the eight-hour work-day and an end to contract labor.

Missing from the Populist platform were the moral reforms championed by the Farmers' Alliance. Prohibition was judged too divisive an issue by a party hoping to win votes from urban workers. Frances Willard speculated that party leaders kept suffrage off their platform in a desire to court more traditional south-ern voters. A political party and not a grassroots movement like the Alliance, Populism looked to a male electorate for support. Since women didn't vote, their power within the party was circumscribed, although women like Mary Elizabeth Lease participated actively in the Populist movement.

Yet the sweeping array of Populist reforms enacted in the Populist platform changed the agenda of politics for decades to come. More than just a response to hard times, Populism presented an alternative vision of American economic democracy.

> ▶ REVIEW   Why did American farmers organize alliances in the late nineteenth century?

The Labor Wars

While farmers united to fight for change, industrial laborers fought their own battles in a series of bloody strikes so fiercely waged on both sides that historians have called them the "labor wars." Coal miners struck to fight the use of convict labor in the mines of eastern Tennessee. Miners in Coeur d'Alene, Idaho, battled the bosses and founded the militant Western Federation of Miners. Railroad switchmen went on strike in Buffalo, New York, and black and white workers mounted a general strike that closed down the port of New Orleans. Industrial workers felt increasingly threatened as businesses combined into huge corpora-tions, and in the 1890s labor took a stand. At issue was the right of workers to organize and speak through unions to bargain collectively and fight for better working conditions, higher wages, shorter hours, and greater worker control in the face of increased mechanization.

Three major conflicts of the period, the lockout of steelworkers in Home-stead, Pennsylvania, in 1892; the miners' strike in Cripple Creek, Colorado, in 1894; and the Pullman strike in Illinois that same year, raised fundamental ques-tions about the rights of labor and the sanctity of private property.

The Homestead Lockout

In 1892, steelworkers in Pennsylvania squared off against Andrew Carnegie in a decisive struggle over the right to organize in the Homestead steel mills. At first glance, it seemed ironic that Carnegie became the adversary in the workers' fight for the right to unionize. Andrew Carnegie was unusual among industrialists as a self-styled friend of labor. In 1886, he had written, "The right of the workingmen to combine and to form trade unions is no less sacred than the right of the manufacturer to enter into associations and conferences with his fellows."

Yet as much as he cherished his **liberal** beliefs, Carnegie cherished his profits more. Labor unions had worked to his advantage during the years when he was building his empire. Labor strife at Homestead during the 1870s had enabled Carnegie to buy the plant from his competitors at cost and to take over the steel industry. But by the 1890s, Carnegie had beat out his competitors, and the only thing standing in the way of his control of the industry was the Amalgamated Association of Iron and Steel Workers, one of the largest and richest of the craft unions that made up the American Federation of Labor (AFL).

In 1892, when the Amalgamated attempted to renew its contract at Carnegie's Homestead mill, its leaders were told that since "the vast majority of our employees are Non union, the Firm has decided that the minority must give place to the majority." While it was true that only 800 skilled workers belonged to the elite Amalgamated, the union had long enjoyed the support of the plant's 3,000 nonunion workers. Slavs, who did much of the unskilled work, made common cause with the Welsh, Scots, and Irish skilled workers who belonged to the union. Never before had the Amalgamated been denied a contract.

Carnegie preferred not to be directly involved in the union busting that lay on the horizon, so that spring he sailed to Scotland and left Henry Clay Frick, the toughest antilabor man in the industry, in charge of the Homestead plant. By summer, a strike looked inevitable. Frick prepared by erecting a fifteen-foot fence around the plant and topping it with barbed wire. Workers aptly dubbed it "Fort Frick." To defend his fort and protect strikebreakers, Frick hired 316 mercenaries from the Pinkerton National Detective Agency at the rate of $5 per day, more than double the wage of the average Homestead worker.

The Pinkerton Agency, founded before the Civil War, came into its own in the 1880s as businessmen like Frick used Pinkerton agents as a private security force. The agents were a motley crew, recruited from all levels of society, from urban thugs to college boys. The "Pinks" earned the hatred of workers by protecting strikebreakers and acting as company spies.

On June 28, Frick locked the workers out of the mills and prepared to bring in scab workers. Hugh O'Donnell, the young Irishman who led the union, vowed to prevent strikebreakers from entering the plant. On July 6 at four in the morning, a lookout spotted two barges moving up the Monongahela River in the fog. Frick was attempting to smuggle Pinkertons into Homestead. Workers sounded the alarm, and within minutes a crowd of more than a thousand, hastily armed with rifles, hoes, and fence posts, rushed to the riverbank to meet the enemy. When the Pinkertons attempted to come ashore, gunfire broke out, and more than a dozen Pinkertons and some thirty strikers fell, killed or wounded. The Pinkertons retreated to the barges.

For twelve hours, the workers, joined by their family members, threw everything they had at the barges, from fireworks to dynamite. Finally, the Pinkertons hoisted a white flag and arranged with O'Donnell to surrender. With three workers dead and scores wounded, the crowd, numbering perhaps ten thousand, was in no mood for conciliation. As the hated "Pinks" came up the hill, they were forced to run a gantlet of screaming, cursing men, women, and children. When a young guard dropped to his knees, weeping for mercy, a woman used her umbrella to poke out his eye. One Pinkerton had been killed in the siege on the barges. In the grim rout that followed their surrender, not one avoided injury.

The "battle of Fort Frick" ended in a dubious victory for the workers. They took control of the plant and elected a council to run the community. At first, public opinion favored their cause. Newspapers urged Frick to negotiate or submit to arbitration. A congressman castigated Carnegie for "skulking in his castle in Scotland." Populists, meeting in St. Louis, condemned the use of "hireling armies."

But the action of the Homestead workers struck at the heart of the capitalist system, pitting the workers' right to their jobs against the rights of private property. The workers' insistence that "we are not destroying the property of the company—merely protecting our rights" did not prove as compelling to the courts and the state as the property rights of the mill owners. Four days after the confrontation, Pennsylvania's governor, who sympathized with the workers, nonetheless yielded to pressure from Frick and ordered eight thousand National Guard troops into Homestead to protect Carnegie's property. The strikers, thinking they had nothing to fear from the militia, welcomed the troops with a brass band. But they soon understood the reality. The troops' ninety-five-day occupation not only protected Carnegie's property but also enabled Frick to reopen the mills and bring in strikebreakers. "We have been deceived," one worker complained bitterly. "We have stood idly by and let the town be occupied by soldiers who come here, not as our protectors, but as the protectors of non-union men. . . . If we undertake to resist the seizure of our jobs, we will be shot down like dogs."

Then, in a misguided effort to ignite a general uprising, Alexander Berkman, a Russian immigrant and **anarchist**, attempted to assassinate Frick. Berkman bungled his attempt. Shot twice and stabbed with a dagger, Frick survived and showed considerable courage, allowing a doctor to remove the bullets but refusing to leave his desk until the day's work was completed. "I do not think that I shall die," Frick remarked coolly, "but whether I do or not, the Company will pursue the same policy and it will win."

After the assassination attempt, public opinion turned against the workers. Berkman was quickly tried and sentenced to prison. Although the Amalgamated and the AFL denounced his action, the incident linked anarchism and unionism, already associated in the public mind as a result of the Haymarket bombing in 1886 (see chapter 19). Hugh O'Donnell later wrote, "The bullet from Berkman's pistol, failing in its foul intent, went straight through the heart of the Homestead strike."

In the end, the workers capitulated after four and a half months. The Homestead mill reopened in November, and the men returned to work, except for the union leaders, now blacklisted in every steel mill in the country. With the owners firmly in charge, the company slashed wages, reinstated the twelve-hour day, and eliminated five hundred jobs.

In the drama of events at Homestead, the significance of what occurred often remained obscured: The workers at Homestead had been taught a lesson. They would never again, in the words of the National Guard commander, "believe the works are their's [sic] quite as much as Carnegie's." Another forty-five years would pass before steelworkers, unskilled as well as skilled, successfully unionized. In the meantime, Carnegie's production tripled, even in the midst of a depression. "Ashamed to tell you profits these days," Carnegie wrote a friend in 1899. And no wonder: Carnegie's profits had grown from $4 million in 1892 to $40 million in 1900.

The Cripple Creek Miners' Strike of 1894

Less than a year after the Homestead lockout, a panic on Wall Street in the spring of 1893 touched off a bitter economic depression. In the West, silver mines fell on hard times. Looking for work, many miners left for the goldfields of Cripple Creek, Colorado, where miners enjoyed relatively high wages—$3 a day. When conservative mine owners moved to lengthen the workday from eight to ten hours, the newly formed Western Federation of Miners (WFM) vowed to hold the line. In February 1894, the WFM threatened to strike all mines working more than eight-hour shifts. The mine owners divided: Some quickly settled with the WFM; others continued to demand ten hours, provoking a strike.

The striking miners received help from many quarters. Working miners paid $15 a month to a strike fund, and miners in neighboring districts sent substantial contributions. Because so many of the mine owners lived in nearby Colorado Springs, Cripple Creek styled itself a workers' town. The miners enjoyed the support and assistance of local businesses and grocers, who provided credit to the strikers. With these advantages, the Cripple Creek strikers could afford to hold out for their demands.

Even more significant was the solidarity of local officials. The mine owners controlled the county sheriff, but when he called up deputies to put down the strike, local officials intervened. In nearby Altman, Colorado, the mayor, city marshal, and police magistrate all belonged to the WFM. When sheriff's deputies arrived in Altman, the mayor ordered them arrested for disturbing the peace and carrying concealed weapons. The sheriff then appealed to Governor Davis H. Waite to send troops. But Waite, a Populist elected in 1892, also had strong ties to the miners and refused to use the power of the state against the peaceful strikers. Desperate, the sheriff deputized more than a thousand men and in May sent them to occupy the mines. The strikers, entrenched on Bull Hill outside of Cripple Creek, prepared for a showdown. Kathleen Welch Chapman recalled her mother's story of one confrontation where the miners managed to trick the militia and avoid bloodshed: "The men took their coats off, and their hats, and put them up in a tree and put the guns up in there . . . and oh, they just thought that the world was up there, this militia [sheriff's deputies] did, when they saw them."

After several confrontations at Bull Hill, pressure mounted for a settlement. Governor Waite asked the strikers to lay down their arms and demanded that the mine owners disperse their hired deputies. The miners agreed to arbitration and selected Waite as their sole arbitrator. By May, the recalcitrant mine owners capitulated, and the union won an eight-hour day.

Governor Waite's intervention demonstrated the pivotal power of the state in the nation's labor wars. At Cripple Creek, the WFM's union organization, divisions among the mine owners, and support from local officials combined with the restraint of Governor Waite to bring about the strike's success. Having a Populist in power made a difference. A decade later, in 1904, with Waite out of office, mine owners relied on state troops to take back control of the mines, defeating the WFM and blacklisting all of its members. In retrospect, the Cripple Creek miners' strike of 1894 proved the exception to the rule of state intervention on the side of private property. More typical was the outcome of another strike in 1894 in Pullman, Illinois.

Eugene V. Debs and the Pullman Strike

The economic depression that began in 1893 swelled the ranks of the unemployed to three million, almost half of the working population. "A fearful crisis is upon us," wrote a labor publication. "Countless thousands of our fellow men are unemployed; men, women and children are suffering the pangs of hunger." Nowhere were workers more demoralized than in the model town of Pullman, on the outskirts of Chicago.

In the wake of the Great Railroad Strike of 1877, George M. Pullman, the builder of Pullman railroad cars, had moved his plant and workers away from the "snares of the great city." In 1880, he purchased 4,300 acres nine miles south of Chicago on the shores of Lake Calumet and built a model town. He intended the company town to be orderly, clean, and with the appearance of luxury, like the Pullman Palace cars that had made his fortune. The town of Pullman boasted parks, fountains, playgrounds, an auditorium, a library, a hotel, shops, and markets, along with 1,800 units of housing. Noticeably absent was a saloon.

The housing in Pullman was clearly superior to that in neighboring areas, but workers paid a high price to live in the model town. George M. Pullman expected a 6 percent return on his investment. As a result, Pullman's rents ran 10 to 20 percent higher than housing costs in nearby communities. And a family in Pullman could never own its own home. George Pullman refused to "sell an acre under any circumstances." As long as he controlled the town absolutely, he held the powerful whip of eviction over his employees and could quickly get rid of "troublemakers." Although observers at first praised the beauty and orderliness of the town, critics by the 1890s compared Pullman's model town to a "gilded cage" for workers.

The depression brought hard times to Pullman. Workers saw their wages slashed five times between May and December 1893, with cuts totaling at least 28 percent. At the same time, Pullman refused to lower the rents in his model town, insisting that "the renting of the dwellings and the employment of workmen at Pullman are in no way tied together." When workers went to the bank to cash their paychecks, they found the rent had been taken out. One worker discovered only forty-seven cents in his pay envelope for two weeks' work. When the bank teller asked him whether he wanted to apply it to his back rent, he retorted, "If Mr. Pullman needs that forty-seven cents worse than I do, let him have it." At the same time, Pullman continued to pay his stockholders an 8 percent dividend, and the company accumulated a $25 million surplus.

At the heart of the labor problems at Pullman lay not only economic inequity but also the company's attempt to control the work process, substituting piecework for day wages and undermining skilled craftsworkers. The Pullman workers rebelled. During the spring of 1894, Pullman's desperate workers, seeking help, flocked to the ranks of the American Railway Union (ARU), led by the charismatic Eugene V. Debs. The ARU, unlike the skilled craft unions of the AFL, pledged to organize all railway workers—from engineers to engine wipers.

George Pullman responded to union organization at his plant by firing three of the union's leaders the day after they led a delegation to protest wage cuts. Angry men and women walked off the job in disgust. What began as a spontaneous protest in May 1894 quickly blossomed into a strike that involved more than 90 percent of Pullman's 3,300 workers. "We do not know what the outcome will be, and in fact we do not much care," one worker confessed. "We do know that we are working for less wages than will maintain ourselves and families in the necessaries of life, and on that proposition we refuse to work any longer." Pullman countered by shutting down the plant.

In June, the Pullman strikers appealed to the ARU to come to their aid. Debs hesitated to commit his fledgling union to a major strike in the midst of a depression. He pleaded with the workers to find another solution. When George Pullman adamantly refused arbitration, the ARU membership voted to boycott all Pullman cars. Beginning on June 29, switchmen across the United States refused to handle any train that carried Pullman cars.

The conflict escalated quickly. The General Managers Association (GMA), an organization of managers from twenty-four different railroads, acted in concert to quash the boycott. Determined to kill the ARU, they recruited strikebreakers and

National Guard Occupying Pullman, Illinois
After President Grover Cleveland called out the troops to put down the Pullman strike in 1894, the
National Guard occupied the town of Pullman to protect George M. Pullman's property. Here, guards-
men ring the Arcade building, the town shopping center, while curious men and women look on.
Chicago Historical Society.

fired all the protesting switchmen. Their tactics set off a chain reaction. Entire
train crews walked off the job in a show of solidarity with the Pullman workers.
In a matter of days, the boycott/strike spread to more than fifteen railroads and
affected twenty-seven states and territories. By July 2, rail lines from New York to
California lay paralyzed. Even the GMA was forced to concede that the railroads
had been "fought to a standstill."

The boycott remained surprisingly peaceful. Mobs stopped trains carrying
Pullman cars and forced train crews to uncouple the cars and leave them on the
sidings. In contrast to the Great Railroad Strike of 1877, no major riots broke out,
and no serious property damage occurred. Debs, in a whirlwind of activity, fired
off telegrams to all parts of the country advising his followers to avoid violence
and respect law and order. But the nation's newspapers, fed press releases by the
GMA, distorted the issues and misrepresented the strike. Across the country,
papers ran headlines like "Wild Riot in Chicago" and "Mob Is in Control."

In Washington, Attorney General Richard B. Olney, a lawyer with strong
ties to the railroads, determined to put down the strike. In his way stood the

governor of Illinois, John Peter Altgeld, who, observing that the boycott remained peaceful, refused to call out troops. To get around Altgeld, Olney convinced President Grover Cleveland that federal troops had to intervene to protect the mails. To further cripple the boycott, two conservative Chicago judges issued an injunction so sweeping that it prohibited Debs from speaking in public. By issuing the injunction, the court made the boycott a crime punishable by a jail sentence for contempt of court, a civil process that did not require a jury trial. Even the conservative *Chicago Tribune* judged the injunction "a menace to liberty . . . a weapon ever ready for the capitalist." Furious, Debs risked jail by refusing to honor it.

Olney's strategy worked. With the strikers violating a federal injunction and with the mails in jeopardy (the GMA made sure that Pullman cars were put on every mail train), Cleveland called out the army. On July 5, nearly 8,000 troops marched into Chicago. Violence immediately erupted. In one day, troops killed 25 workers and wounded more than 60. In the face of bullets and bayonets, the strikers held firm. "Troops cannot move trains," Debs reminded his followers, a fact that was borne out as the railroads remained paralyzed despite the military intervention. But if the army could not put down the boycott, the injunction could and did. Debs was arrested and imprisoned for contempt of court. With its leader in jail, its headquarters raided and ransacked, and its members demoralized, the ARU was defeated along with the boycott. Pullman reopened his factory, hiring new workers to replace many of the strikers and leaving 1,600 workers without jobs.

In the aftermath of the strike, a special commission investigated the events at Pullman, taking testimony from 107 witnesses, from the lowliest workers to George M. Pullman himself. Stubborn and self-righteous, Pullman spoke for the business orthodoxy of his era, steadfastly affirming the right of business to safeguard its interests through confederacies such as the GMA and at the same time denying labor's right to organize. "If we were to receive these men as representatives of the union," he stated, "they could probably force us to pay any wages which they saw fit."

From his jail cell, Eugene Debs reviewed the events of the Pullman strike. With the courts and the government ready to side with industrialists in the interest of defending private property, Debs realized that labor had little recourse. Strikes seemed futile, and unions remained helpless; workers would have to take control of the state itself. Debs went into jail a trade unionist and came out six months later a socialist. At first, he turned to the Populist Party, but after its demise, he formed the Socialist Party in 1900 and ran for president on its ticket five times. Debs's dissatisfaction with the status quo was shared by another group even more alienated from the political process—women.

▶ **REVIEW** Why did the strikes of the 1890s fail to produce permanent gains for workers?

Women's Activism

"Do everything," Frances Willard urged her followers in 1881. The new president of the Woman's Christian Temperance Union (WCTU) meant what she said. The WCTU followed a trajectory that was common for women in the late nineteenth century. As women organized to deal with issues that touched their homes and families, they moved into politics, lending new urgency to the cause of woman suffrage. Urban industrialism dislocated women's lives no less than men's. Like men, women sought political change and organized to promote issues central to their lives, from temperance and suffrage to antilynching (see chapter 18).

Frances Willard and the Woman's Christian Temperance Union

Frances Willard, the visionary leader of the WCTU, spoke for a group left almost entirely out of the U.S. electoral process—women. In 1890, only one state, Wyoming, allowed women to vote in national elections. But lack of the **franchise** did not mean that women were apolitical. The WCTU demonstrated the breadth of women's political activity in the late nineteenth century.

Women supported the **temperance movement** because they felt particularly vulnerable to the effects of drunkenness. Dependent on men's wages, women and children suffered when money went for drink. The drunken, abusive husband epitomized the evils of a nation in which women remained second-class citizens. Composed entirely of women, the WCTU viewed all women's interests as essentially the same—crossing class, ethnic, and racial lines—and therefore did not hesitate to use the singular *woman* to emphasize gender solidarity. Although mostly white and middle-class, WCTU members resolved to speak for their entire sex.

When Frances Willard became president in 1879, she radically changed the direction of the organization. Moving away from a religious approach, the WCTU began to view alcoholism as a disease rather than a sin, and poverty as a cause rather than a result of drink. Accordingly, social action replaced prayer as women's answer to the threat of drunkenness. By the 1890s, the WCTU worked to establish women's reformatories, promoted the hiring of female police officers, and sponsored day nurseries, industrial training schools for women, missions for the homeless, medical dispensaries, and lodging houses for the poor. At the same time, the WCTU became involved in labor issues, joining with the Knights of Labor to press for better working conditions for women workers. Describing workers in a textile mill, a WCTU member wrote in the *Union Signal*, the WCTU monthly magazine, "It is dreadful to see these girls, stripped almost to the skin . . . and running like racehorses from the beginning to the end of the day." She concluded, "The hard slavish work is drawing the girls into the saloon."

Willard capitalized on the **cult of domesticity** as a shrewd political tactic to move women into public life and gain power to ameliorate social problems. Using "home protection" as her watchword, she argued as early as 1884 that women needed the vote to protect home and family. By the 1890s, the WCTU's grassroots network of local unions had spread to all but the most isolated rural areas of the country. Strong and rich, with more than 200,000 dues-paying members, the WCTU was a formidable group.

Willard worked to create a broad reform coalition in the 1890s, embracing the Knights of Labor, the People's Party, and the Prohibition Party. Until her death in 1898, she led, if not a women's rights movement, then the first organized mass movement of women united around a women's issue. By 1900, thanks largely to the WCTU, women could claim a generation of experience in political action— speaking, lobbying, organizing, drafting legislation, and running private charitable institutions. As Willard observed, "All this work has tended more toward the liberation of women than it has toward the extinction of the saloon."

Elizabeth Cady Stanton, Susan B. Anthony, and the Movement for Woman Suffrage

Unlike the WCTU, the organized movement for woman suffrage remained small and relatively weak in the late nineteenth century. The woman's rights movement, begun by Elizabeth Cady Stanton at Seneca Falls in 1848 (see chapter 12), split in 1867 over whether the Fourteenth and Fifteenth Amendments, which granted voting rights to African American men, should have extended the vote to women as well. Stanton and her ally, Susan B. Anthony, launched the National Woman Suffrage Association (NWSA) in 1869, demanding the vote for women (see chapter 18). A more conservative group, the American Woman Suffrage Association (AWSA), formed the same year. Composed of men as well as women, the AWSA believed that women should vote in local but not national elections.

By 1890, the split had healed, and the newly united National American Woman Suffrage Association (NAWSA) launched campaigns on the state level to gain the vote for women. Twenty years had made a great change. Woman suffrage, though not yet generally supported, was no longer considered a crackpot idea. Thanks to the WCTU's support of the "home protection" ballot, suffrage had become accepted as a means to an end even when it was not embraced as a woman's natural right. The NAWSA honored Elizabeth Cady Stanton by electing her its first president, but Susan B. Anthony, who took the helm in 1892, emerged as the leading figure in the new united organization.

Stanton and Anthony, both in their seventies, were coming to the end of their public careers. Since the days of the Seneca Falls woman's rights convention, they had worked for reforms for their sex, including property rights, custody rights, and the right to education and gainful employment. But the prize of woman suffrage still eluded them. Suffragists won victories in Colorado in 1893 and Idaho in

Woman Suffrage Flag
The West led the way in the campaign for woman suffrage, with Wyoming Territory granting women the vote as early as 1869. Sparse population meant that only sixteen votes were needed in the state's territorial legislature to obtain passage of woman suffrage. This flag illustrates the number of states where women could vote in 1896— Wyoming, Colorado, Idaho, and Utah.
Smithsonian Institution, Washington, D.C.

1896. One more state joined the suffrage column in 1896 when Utah entered the Union. But women suffered a bitter defeat in a California referendum on woman suffrage that same year. Never losing faith, Susan B. Anthony remarked in her last public appearance, in 1906, "Failure is impossible." Although it would take until 1920 for all women to gain the vote with the ratification of the Nineteenth Amendment, the unification of the two woman suffrage groups in 1890 signaled a new era in women's fight for the vote just as Frances Willard's place on the platform in 1892 at the founding of the People's Party in St. Louis symbolized women's growing role in politics and reform.

▶REVIEW   How did women's temperance activism contribute to the cause of woman suffrage?

Depression Politics

The depression that began in the spring of 1893 and lasted for more than four years put nearly half of the labor force out of work, a higher percentage than during the Great Depression of the 1930s. The country swarmed with people looking for jobs. The human cost of the depression was staggering. "I Take my pen in hand to let you know that we are Starving to death," a Kansas farm woman wrote to the governor in 1894. "Last cent gone," wrote a young widow in her diary. "Children went to work without their breakfasts." The burden of feeding and sheltering the unemployed and their families fell to private charity, city government, and some of the stronger trade unions. Following the harsh dictates of **social Darwinism** and laissez-faire, the majority of America's elected officials believed that it was inappropriate for the government to intervene. But the scope of the depression made it impossible for local agencies to supply sufficient relief, and increasingly Americans called on the federal government to take action.

Armies of the unemployed marched on Washington to demand relief, and the Populist Party experienced a surge of support as the election of 1896 approached.

Coxey's Army

Masses of unemployed Americans marched to Washington, D.C., in the spring of 1894 to call attention to their plight and to urge Congress to enact a public works program to end unemployment. From as far away as Seattle, San Francisco, Los Angeles, and Denver, hundreds joined the march. Jacob S. Coxey of Massilon, Ohio, led the most publicized contingent. Coxey, a millionaire with a penchant for racehorses and high living, seemed an unlikely champion of the unemployed. Convinced that men could be put to work building badly needed roads for the nation, Coxey proposed a scheme to finance public works through non-interest-bearing bonds. "What I am after," he maintained, "is to try to put this country in a condition so that no man who wants work shall be obliged to remain idle." His plan won support from the AFL and the Populists.

Starting out from Ohio with one hundred men, "Coxey's army," as it was dubbed by journalists, swelled as it marched east through the spring snows of the Alleghenies. In Pennsylvania, Coxey recruited several hundred from the ranks of those left unemployed by the Homestead lockout. Called by Coxey the Common-weal of Christ, the army advanced to the tune of "Marching through Georgia":

> We are not tramps nor vagabonds, that's shirking honest toil,
> But miners, clerks, skilled artisans, and tillers of the soil
> Now forced to beg our brother worms to give us leave to toil,
> While we are marching with Coxey.
> Hurrah! hurrah! for the unemployed's appeal
> Hurrah! hurrah! for the marching commonweal!

On May 1, Coxey's army arrived in Washington. When Coxey defiantly marched his men onto the Capitol grounds, police set upon the demonstrators with nightsticks, cracking skulls and arresting Coxey and his lieutenants. Coxey went to jail for twenty days and was fined $5 for "walking on the grass."

Those who had trembled for the safety of the Republic heaved a sigh of relief after Coxey's arrest, hoping that it would halt the march on Washington. But other armies of the unemployed, totaling possibly as many as five thousand people, were still on their way. Too poor to pay for railway tickets, they rode the rails as "freeloaders." The more daring contingents commandeered entire trains, stirring fears of revolution. Journalists who covered the march did little to quiet the nation's fears. They delighted in military terminology, describing themselves as "war correspondents." To boost newspaper sales, they gave to the episode a tone of urgency and heightened the sense of a nation imperiled.

By August, the leaderless, tattered armies dissolved. Although the "On to Washington" movement proved ineffective in forcing federal relief legislation,

Coxey's army dramatized the plight of the unemployed and acted, in the words of one participant, as a "living, moving object lesson." Like the Populists, Coxey's army called into question the underlying values of the new industrial order and demonstrated how ordinary citizens turned to means outside the regular party system to influence politics in the 1890s.

The People's Party and the Election of 1896

Even before the depression of 1893 gave added impetus to their cause, the Populists had railed against the status quo. "We meet in the midst of a nation brought to the verge of moral, political, and material ruin," Ignatius Donnelly had declared in his keynote address at the creation of the People's Party in St. Louis in 1892. "The fruits of the toil of millions are boldly stolen to build up colossal fortunes for a few. . . . From the same prolific womb of governmental injustice we breed the two great classes—tramps and millionaires."

The fiery rhetoric frightened many who saw in the People's Party a call not to reform but to revolution. Throughout the country, the press denounced the Populists as "cranks, lunatics, and idiots." When one self-righteous editor dismissed them as "calamity howlers," Populist governor Lorenzo Lewelling of Kansas shot back, "If that is so I want to continue to howl until those conditions are improved."

The People's Party captured more than a million votes in the presidential election of 1892, a respectable showing for a new party. The Populists might have done better, but on the eve of the convention, they lost their standard-bearer when Leonidis L. Polk, president of the Southern Farmers' Alliance, died suddenly. Scrambling to find a replacement, the convention nominated General James B. Weaver of Iowa, a former Union general who had run for president on the Greenback Labor ticket in 1880. To balance the ticket, they selected an ex-Confederate as his running mate. But many southern Populists could not bring themselves to vote for a Yankee general and stayed away from the polls.

Increasingly, sectional and racial animosities threatened the unity of the People's Party. More than their alliance with the Yankee North, it was the Populists' willingness to form common cause with black farmers that made them anathema in the white South. Tom Watson of Georgia had tackled the "Negro question" head-on in 1892. Realizing that race prejudice obscured the common economic interests of black and white farmers, Watson openly courted African Americans, appearing on platforms with black speakers and promising "to wipe out the color line." When angry Georgia whites threatened to lynch a black Populist preacher, Watson rallied two thousand gun-toting Populists to the man's defense. Although many Populists remained racist in their attitudes toward African Americans, the spectacle of white Georgians riding through the night to protect a black man from lynching was symbolic of the enormous changes the Populist Party promised in the South.

The People's Party fared better in the 1894 congressional election, when, un-encumbered by a Union general, the Populists added half a million voters to their column. With the depression swelling the ranks of the disaffected, the Populists looked forward to the election of 1896.

As the presidential election approached, the depression intensified cries for reform not only from the Populists but also throughout the electorate. Depression worsened the tight money problem caused by the deflationary pressures of the gold standard. Once again, proponents of free silver (the unlimited coinage of sil-ver in addition to gold) stirred rebellion in the ranks of both the Democratic and the Republican parties. When the Republicans nominated Ohio governor William McKinley on a platform pledging the preservation of the gold standard, western advocates of free silver representing miners and farmers walked out of the con-vention. Open rebellion also split the Democratic Party as vast segments in the West and South repudiated President Grover Cleveland because of his support for gold. In South Carolina, Benjamin Tillman won his race for Congress by promising, "Send me to Washington and I'll stick my pitchfork into [Cleveland's] old ribs!"

The spirit of revolt animated the Democratic National Convention in Chicago in the summer of 1896. "Pitchfork Ben" Tillman set the tone by attacking the party's president, denouncing the Cleveland administration as "undemocratic and tyrannical." But the man of the hour was William Jennings Bryan of Nebraska, the thirty-six-year-old "boy orator from the Platte," who whipped the convention into a frenzy with his passionate call for free silver. In his keynote address, Bryan masterfully cataloged the grievances of farmers and laborers, closing his dramatic speech with a ringing exhortation: "Do not crucify mankind upon a cross of gold." Pandemonium broke loose as delegates stampeded to nominate Bryan, the youngest candidate ever to run for the presidency.

The juggernaut of free silver rolled out of Chicago and on to St. Louis, where the People's Party met a week after the Democrats adjourned. Smelling victory, many western Populists urged the party to ally with the Democrats and endorse Bryan. A major obstacle in the path of fusion, however, was Bryan's running mate, Arthur M. Sewall. A Maine railway director and bank president, Sewall, who had been placed on the ticket to appease conservative Democrats, embodied everything the Populists opposed.

Populism's regional constituencies remained as divided on tactics as they were uniform in their call for change. Western Populists, including a strong coali-tion of farmers and miners in states such as Idaho and Colorado, championed free silver as a way to put the ailing Rocky Mountain silver industry back on its feet and restore prosperity to the region. In these largely Republican states, Populists had joined forces with Democrats in previous elections and saw no problem with becoming "Popocrats" once Bryan led the Democratic ticket on a free-silver plat-form. Similarly in the Midwest, a Republican stronghold, Populists who had used fusion with the Democrats as a tactic to win elections had little trouble backing

Bryan. But in the South, where Democrats had resorted to fraud and violence to steal elections from the Populists in 1892 and 1894, support for a Democratic ticket proved especially hard to swallow. Die-hard southern Populists wanted no part of fusion.

All of these tactical differences emerged as the Populists met in St. Louis in 1896 to nominate a candidate for president. To show that they remained true to their principles, delegates first voted to support all the planks of the 1892 plat-form, added to it a call for public works projects for the unemployed, and only narrowly defeated a plank for woman suffrage. To deal with the problem of fusion, the convention selected the vice presidential candidate first. The nomina-tion of Tom Watson undercut opposition to Bryan's candidacy. And although Bryan quickly sent a telegram to protest that he would not drop Sewall as his running mate, mysteriously his message never reached the convention floor. Fusion triumphed. Watson's vice presidential nomination paved the way for the selection of Bryan by a lopsided vote. The Populists did not know it, but their cheers for Bryan signaled not a chorus of victory but the death knell of the People's Party.

Few contests in the nation's history have been as fiercely fought and as full of emotion as the presidential election of 1896. On one side stood Republican William McKinley, backed by the wealthy industrialist and party boss Mark Hanna. Hanna played on the business community's fears of Populism to raise more than $4 million for the Republican war chest, double the amount of any previous campaign. On the other side, William Jennings Bryan, with few assets beyond his silver tongue, struggled to make up in energy and eloquence what his party lacked in campaign funds. He set a new style for presidential campaigning, crisscrossing the country in a whirlwind tour, traveling more than eighteen thousand miles and delivering more than six hundred speeches in three months. According to his own reckoning, he visited twenty-seven states and spoke to more than five million Americans.

As election day approached, the silver states of the Rocky Mountains lined up solidly for Bryan. The Northeast stood solidly for McKinley. Much of the South, with the exception of the border states, abandoned the Populists and returned to the Democratic fold, leaving Tom Watson to lament that "[Populists] play Jonah while [Democrats] play the whale." The Midwest hung in the balance. Bryan intensified his campaign in Illinois, Michigan, Ohio, and Indiana. But mid-western farmers proved less receptive than western voters to the blandishments of free silver.

In the cities, Democrats charged the Republicans with mass intimidation. "Men, vote as you please," the head of New York's Steinway Piano Company reportedly announced to his workers on the eve of the election, "but if Bryan is elected tomorrow the whistle will not blow Wednesday morning." Intimidation alone did not explain the failure of urban labor to rally to Bryan. Republicans repeatedly warned workers that if the Democrats won, the inflated silver dollar would be worth only fifty cents. However much farmers and laborers might insist that they were united as producers against the nonproducing bosses, it was equally true that inflation did not offer the boon to urban laborers that it did to western farmers. For while debtors benefited from the inflated currency, which allowed them to pay off their debts with cheaper, more plentiful dollars, inflation promised no real gain to city workers and in fact might worsen their situation by leading to higher prices for food and rent. Although industrial workers in the West and South, particularly miners, voted Populist, eastern workers failed to rally to Bryan.

On election day, four out of five voters went to the polls in an unprecedented turnout. In the critical midwestern states, as many as 95 percent of the eligible voters cast their ballots. In the end, the election hinged on between 100 and 1,000 votes in several key states, including Wisconsin, Iowa, and Minnesota. Although McKinley won twenty-three states to Bryan's twenty-two, the electoral vote showed a lopsided 271 to 176 in McKinley's favor.

The biggest losers in 1896 turned out to be the Populists. On the national level, they polled fewer than 300,000 votes, a million less than in 1894. In the clamor to support Bryan, Populists in the South had drifted back to the Democratic Party. The People's Party was crushed, and with it the agrarian revolt.

But if Populism proved unsuccessful at the polls, it nevertheless set the domestic political agenda for the United States in the next decades, highlighting issues such as banking and currency reform, electoral reforms, and an enlarged role for the federal government in the economy. Meanwhile, as the decade ended, the bugle call to arms turned America's attention to foreign affairs and effectively drowned out the trumpet of reform. The struggle for social justice gave way to a war for empire as the United States asserted its power on the world stage.

▶ REVIEW Why was the People's Party unable to translate national support into victory in the 1896 election?

The United States and the World

Throughout much of the second half of the nineteenth century, U.S. interest in foreign policy took a backseat to its own expansion in the American West. Intent on its own continental expansion, the United States stood aloof while Great Britain, France, Germany, Spain, Belgium, and the increasingly powerful Japan competed for empires in Asia, Africa, Latin America, and the Pacific. Between 1870 and 1900, European nations **colonized** more than 20 percent of the world's landmass and 10 percent of the world's population.

At the turn of the twentieth century, American foreign policy consisted of two currents—**isolationism** and expansionism. Although the determination to remain aloof from European politics had been a hallmark of U.S. foreign policy since the nation's founding, Americans simultaneously believed in **manifest destiny**—the "obvious" right to expand the nation from ocean to ocean. The United States' determination to protect its sphere of influence in the Western Hemisphere at the same time it expanded its trading in Asia moved the nation away from isolationism and toward a more active role on the world stage. The push for commercial expansion joined with a sense of Christian mission to refocus the nation's attention abroad and led both to the strengthening of the **Monroe Doctrine** in the Western Hemisphere and to a new Open Door policy in Asia.

Markets and Missionaries

The depression of the 1890s provided a powerful impetus to American commercial expansion. As markets weakened at home, American businesses looked abroad for profits. As early as 1890, Captain Alfred Thayer Mahan, leader of a growing group of American expansionists, prophesied, "Whether they will or not, Americans must now begin to look outward. The growing production of the country requires it." Although not all U.S. business leaders thought it advantageous to undertake adventures abroad, the logic of acquiring new markets to absorb the nation's growing capacity for production proved convincing to many. As the depression deepened, one diplomat warned that Americans "must turn [their] eyes abroad, or they will soon look inward upon discontent."

Exports constituted a small but significant percentage of the profits of American business in the 1890s. And where American interests led, businessmen expected the government's power and influence to follow to protect their investments. America's foreign policy often appeared to be little more than a sidelight to business development. Companies like Standard Oil actively sought to use the U.S. government as their agent, often putting foreign service employees on the payroll. "Our ambassadors and ministers and consuls," wrote John D. Rockefeller appreciatively, "have aided to push our way into new markets and to the utmost corners of the world." Whether "our" referred to the United States or to Standard Oil remained ambiguous; in practice, the distinction was of little importance in late-nineteenth-century foreign policy.

America's foreign policy often appeared little more than a sidelight to business development. In Hawaii (first called the Sandwich Islands), American sugar interests fomented a rebellion in 1893, toppling the increasingly independent Queen Liliuokalani. They pushed Congress to annex the islands, which would allow planters to avoid the high McKinley tariff on sugar. When President Cleveland learned that Hawaiians opposed annexation, he withdrew the proposal from Congress. But expansionists still coveted the islands and continued to look for an excuse to push through annexation.

However compelling the economic arguments about overseas markets proved, business interests alone did not account for the new expansionism that seized the nation during the 1890s. As Mahan confessed, "Even when material interests are the original exciting cause, it is the sentiment to which they give rise, the moral tone which emotion takes that constitutes the greater force." Much of that moral tone was set by American missionaries intent on spreading the gospel of Christianity to the "heathen." No area on the globe constituted a greater challenge than China. In 1858, the Tientsin treaty admitted foreign missionaries to China. Roman Catholics from France and Protestants from Britain, Germany, and the United States rushed to convert the Chinese.

Increased missionary activity and Western enterprise touched off a series of antiforeign outbreaks in China culminating in the Boxer uprising. Although for the most part Christian missionaries proved unsuccessful, converting only 100,000 in a population of 400 million, the Chinese nevertheless resented the interference of missionaries in village life and the preference and protection they afforded their Christian converts. Opposition to foreign missionaries took the form of antiforeign secret societies, most notably the Boxers, whose Chinese name translated to "Righteous Harmonious Fist." No simple boxing club, in 1899 the Boxers began to terrorize Chinese Christians and missionaries in northwestern Shandong Province. Men and women were hacked to death with swords, burned alive in their houses, and dragged by howling mobs to their execution. With the tacit support of China's Dowager Empress, the Boxers became bolder. Under the slogan "Uphold the Ch'ing Dynasty, Exterminate the Foreigners," they marched on the cities. Their rampage eventually led to the massacre of some 30,000 Chinese converts and 250 foreign nuns, priests, and missionaries along with their families.

As the Boxers spread terror throughout northern China, some 800 Americans and Europeans sought refuge in the foreign legation buildings in Beijing (then called Peking). Along with missionaries from the countryside came thousands of their Chinese converts, fleeing the Boxers. Unable to escape and cut off from outside aid and communication, the Americans and Europeans in Beijing mounted a defense to face the Boxer onslaught. For two months, they held out under siege, eating mule and horse meat and losing 76 men in battle. American missionary Luella Miner wrote sadly, "We are isolated here as if we were on a desert island. . . . Are our Christians everywhere being slaughtered?"

Americans back home who learned of the fate of their compatriots at the hands of the Chinese showed little toleration for the cautious diplomatic approach favored by Secretary of State John Hay. In August 1900, 2,500 U.S. troops joined an international force sent to rescue the foreigners besieged in Beijing. After routing the Boxers, the troops looted the Forbidden City, home of the imperial court, forcing the Dowager Empress to flee disguised as a peasant. In 1901, the European powers imposed the humiliating Boxer Protocol, giving them the right to maintain military forces in the Chinese capital and requiring the Chinese government to pay an indemnity of $333 million for the loss of life and property resulting from the Boxer uprising.

In the aftermath of the uprising, missionaries voiced no concern at the paradox of bringing Christianity to China at gunpoint. "It is worth any cost in money, worth any cost in bloodshed," argued one bishop, "if we can make millions of Chinese true and intelligent Christians." Merchants and missionaries alike shared such moralistic reasoning. Indeed, they worked hand in hand; trade and Christianity marched into Asia together. "Missionaries," admitted the American clergyman Charles Denby, "are the pioneers of trade and commerce. . . . The missionary, inspired by holy zeal, goes everywhere and by degrees foreign commerce and trade follow."

The Monroe Doctrine and the Open Door Policy

The emergence of the United States as a world power pitted the nation against the colonial powers, particularly Germany and Japan, which posed a threat to the twin pillars of America's expansionist foreign policy—one dating back to President James Monroe in the 1820s, the other formalized in 1900 under President William McKinley. The first, the Monroe Doctrine, came to be interpreted as establishing the Western Hemisphere as an American "sphere of influence" and warned European powers to stay away or risk war. The second, the Open Door, dealt with maintaining market access to China.

American diplomacy actively worked to buttress the Monroe Doctrine, with its assertion of American hegemony (domination) in the Western Hemisphere. In the 1880s, Republican secretary of state James G. Blaine promoted hemispheric peace and trade through Pan-American cooperation but at the same time used American troops to intervene in Latin American border disputes. In 1895, Americans risked war with Great Britain to enforce the Monroe Doctrine when a conflict developed between Venezuela and British Guiana. President Cleveland asserted the U.S. prerogative to step in and mediate, reducing Venezuela to the role of mere onlooker in its own affairs. At first, Britain refused to accept U.S. mediation, and conflict seemed imminent. "Let the fight come if it must," wrote rising Republican neophyte Theodore Roosevelt, always itching to do battle. Seeing an opportunity to extend manifest destiny to the north, Roosevelt vowed, "We [will] take Canada." But the British, who feared the possibility of war in Europe and as a consequence wished to avoid conflict in Latin America, accepted the terms of U.S. mediation, resolving the Venezuelan crisis.

In Central America, where the United States kept a watchful eye on European adventures, American business triumphed in a bloodless takeover that saw French and British interests routed by behemoths such as the United Fruit Company of Boston. United Fruit virtually dominated the Central American nations of Costa Rica and Guatemala, while an importer from New Orleans turned Honduras into a "banana republic" (a country run by U.S. business interests). Thus, by 1895, the United States, through business as well as diplomacy, had successfully achieved hegemony in Latin America and the Caribbean, forcing even the British to concur with the secretary of state that "the infinite resources [of the United States] combined with its isolated position render it master of the situation and practically invulnerable as against any or all other powers."

At the same time that American foreign policy warned European powers to stay out of the Western Hemisphere, the United States competed with the colonial powers for trade in the Eastern Hemisphere. As American interests in China grew, the United States became more aggressive in defending its presence in Asia and the Pacific. The United States risked war with Germany in 1889 to guarantee the U.S. navy access to a port for refueling on the way to Asia. The United States held treaty rights to the harbor at Pago Pago in the Samoan Islands. Germany, seeking dominance over the islands, challenged the United States by sending warships to the region. But before fighting broke out, a great typhoon destroyed the German and American ships. Acceding to the will of nature, the potential combatants later divided the islands amicably in the 1899 Treaty of Berlin.

The biggest prize in Asia remained the China market. In the 1890s, China, weakened by years of internal warfare, was beginning to be partitioned into spheres of influence by Britain, Japan, Germany, France, and Russia. Concerned about the integrity of China and no less about American trade, Secretary of State John Hay in 1899–1900 wrote a series of notes calling for an "open door" policy that would ensure trade access to all and maintain Chinese sovereignty. The notes—sent to Britain, Germany, and Russia and later to France, Japan, and Italy—were greeted by the major powers with polite evasion. Nevertheless, Hay skillfully managed to maneuver the major powers into doing his bidding, and in 1900 he boldly announced the Open Door as international policy. The United States, by insisting on the Open Door policy, managed to secure access to Chinese markets, expanding its economic power while avoiding the problems of maintaining a far-flung colonial empire on the Asian mainland. But as the Spanish-American War soon demonstrated, Americans found it hard to resist the temptations of empire.

▶ **REVIEW**   Why did the United States largely abandon its isolationist foreign policy in the 1890s?

War and Empire

The Spanish-American War began as a humanitarian effort to free Cuba from Spain's colonial grasp and ended with the United States itself acquiring territory overseas and fighting a dirty **guerrilla war** with Filipino nationalists, who, like the Cubans, sought independence. Behind the contradiction stood the twin pillars of American foreign policy: The Monroe Doctrine made Spain's presence in Cuba unacceptable, and U.S. determination to keep open the door to Asia made the Philippines attractive as a stepping-stone to China.

"A Splendid Little War"

Looking back on the Spanish-American War of 1898, Secretary of State John Hay judged it "a splendid little war; begun with the highest motives, carried on with magnificent intelligence and spirit, favored by that fortune which loves the brave." At the close of a decade marred by bitter depression, social unrest, and political upheaval, the war offered Americans a chance to wave the flag and march in unison. War fever proved as infectious as the tune of a John Philip Sousa march. Few argued the merits of the conflict until it was over and the time came to divide the spoils.

The war began with moral outrage over the treatment of Cuban revolutionaries, who had launched a fight for independence against the Spanish colonial regime in 1895. In an attempt to isolate the guerrillas, the Spanish general Valeriano Weyler herded Cubans into crowded and unsanitary concentration camps, where thousands died of hunger, disease, and exposure. Starvation soon spread to the cities. Tens of thousands of Cubans died, and countless others were left without food, clothing, or shelter. By 1898, fully a quarter of the island's population had perished in the Cuban revolution.

As the Cuban rebellion dragged on, pressure for American intervention mounted. American newspapers fueled public outrage at Spain. A fierce circulation war raged in New York City between William Randolph Hearst's *Journal* and Joseph Pulitzer's *World*. Their competition provoked what came to be called "yellow journalism," named for the colored ink used in a popular comic strip. Practitioners of yellow journalism pandered to the public's appetite for sensationalism. The Cuban war provided a wealth of dramatic copy. Newspapers fed the American people a daily diet of "Butcher" Weyler and Spanish atrocities. Hearst sent artist Frederic Remington to document the horror, and when Remington wired home, "There is no trouble here. There will be no war," Hearst shot back, "You furnish the pictures and I'll furnish the war."

American interests in Cuba were, in the words of the U.S. minister to Spain, more than "merely theoretical or sentimental." American business had more than $50 million invested in Cuban sugar, and American trade with Cuba, a brisk $100 million a year before the rebellion, had dropped to near zero. Nevertheless, the business community balked, wary of a war with Spain. When industrialist Mark Hanna, the Republican kingmaker and senator from Ohio, urged restraint, a hotheaded Theodore Roosevelt exploded, "We will have this war for the freedom of Cuba, Senator Hanna, in spite of the timidity of commercial interests."

To expansionists like Roosevelt, more than Cuban independence was at stake. War with Spain opened up the prospect of expansion into Asia as well, since Spain controlled not only Cuba and Puerto Rico but also Guam and the Philippine Islands. Appointed assistant secretary of the navy in April 1897, Roosevelt worked for preparedness whenever his boss's back was turned. During the hot summer while the navy secretary vacationed, Roosevelt took the helm in his absence and audaciously ordered the U.S. fleet to Manila in the Philippines. In the event of conflict with Spain, Roosevelt put the navy in a position to capture the islands and gain an entry point to China.

President McKinley slowly moved toward intervention. In a show of American force, he dispatched the battleship *Maine* to Cuba. On the night of February 15, 1898, a mysterious explosion destroyed the *Maine*, killing 267 crew members. The source of the explosion remained unclear, but inflammatory stories in the press enraged Americans, who immediately blamed the Spanish government. Rallying to the cry "Remember the *Maine*," Congress declared war on Spain in April. In a surge of patriotism, more than 235,000 men enlisted. War brought with it a unity of purpose and national harmony that ended a decade of political dissent and strife. "In April, everywhere over this good fair land, flags were flying," wrote Kansas editor William Allen White. "At the stations, crowds gathered to hurrah for the soldiers, and to throw hats into the air, and to unfurl flags."

Soon they had something to cheer about. Five days after McKinley signed the war resolution, a U.S. navy squadron commanded by Admiral George Dewey destroyed the Spanish fleet in Manila Bay. Dewey's stunning victory caught the United States by surprise. Although naval strategists including Theodore Roosevelt had been orchestrating the move for some time, few Americans had ever heard of the Philippines. Even McKinley confessed that he could not immediately locate the archipelago on the map. He nevertheless recognized the strategic importance of the Philippines and dispatched U.S. troops to secure the islands.

The war in Cuba ended almost as quickly as it began. The first troops landed on June 22, and after a handful of battles, the Spanish surrendered on July 17. The war lasted just long enough to elevate Theodore Roosevelt to the status of bona fide war hero. Roosevelt resigned his navy post and formed the Rough Riders, a regiment composed about equally of Ivy League polo players and cowboys Roosevelt knew from his stint as a cattle rancher in the Dakotas. While the troops languished in Tampa awaiting their orders, Roosevelt and his men staged daily rodeos for the press, with the likes of New York blue blood William Tiffany busting broncs in competition with Dakota cowboy Jim "Dead Shot" Simpson. When the Rough Riders shipped out to Cuba, journalists fought for a berth with the colorful regiment. Roosevelt's charge up Kettle Hill and his role in the decisive battle of San Juan Hill made front-page news. Overnight, Roosevelt became the most famous man in America. By the time he sailed home from Cuba, a coalition of independent Republicans was already plotting his political future.

The Debate over American Imperialism

After a few brief campaigns in Cuba and Puerto Rico brought the Spanish-American War to an end, the American people woke up in possession of an empire that stretched halfway around the globe. As part of the spoils of war, the United States acquired Cuba, Puerto Rico, Guam, and the Philippines. Yielding to pressure from American sugar growers, President McKinley expanded the empire further, annexing Hawaii in July 1898.

Cuba, freed from Spanish rule, failed to gain full autonomy. Contemptuous of the Cubans, whom General William Shafter declared "no more fit for self-government than gun-powder is for hell," the U.S. government dictated a Cuban constitution in 1898. It included the so-called Platt Amendment—a series of provisions that granted the United States the right to intervene to protect Cuba's "independence," as well as the power to oversee Cuban debt so that European creditors would not find an excuse for intervention. For good measure, the United States gave itself a ninety-nine-year lease on a naval base at Guantánamo. In return, McKinley promised to implement an extensive sanitation program to clean up the island, making it more attractive to American investors.

In the formal Treaty of Paris (1898), Spain ceded the Philippines to the United States along with its former colonies of Puerto Rico and Guam (Map 20.1).

MAP 20.1   U.S. Overseas Expansion through 1900

The United States extended its interests abroad with a series of territorial acquisitions. Although Cuba was granted independence, the Platt Amendment kept the new nation firmly under U.S. control. After the Spanish-American War, the United States found that it held an empire extending halfway around the globe.

Empire did not come cheap. When Spain initially balked at these terms, the United States agreed to pay an indemnity of $20 million for the islands. Nor was the cost measured in money alone. Filipino revolutionaries under Emilio Aguinaldo, who had greeted U.S. troops as liberators, bitterly fought the new masters. It would take seven years and 4,000 American dead—almost ten times the number killed in Cuba—not to mention an estimated 20,000 Filipino casualties, to defeat Aguinaldo and secure American control of the Philippines, America's coveted stepping-stone to China.

At home, a vocal minority, mostly Democrats and former Populists, resisted the country's foray into overseas empire, judging it unwise, immoral, and unconstitutional. William Jennings Bryan, who enlisted in the army but never saw action, concluded that American expansionism only distracted the nation from problems at home. What did imperialism offer the ordinary American, Bryan asked, except "heavier taxes, Asiatic emigration and an opportunity to furnish more sons for the army." Pointing to the central paradox of the war, Representative Bourke Cockran of New York admonished, "We who have been the destroyers of oppression are asked now to become its agents." Mark Twain, lending his bitter eloquence to the cause of anti-imperialism, lamented that the United States had indeed become "yet another Civilized Power, with its banner of the Prince of Peace in one hand and its loot-basket and its butcher-knife in the other."

The anti-imperialists were soon drowned out by cries for empire. As Senator Knute Nelson of Minnesota assured his colleagues, "We come as ministering angels, not as despots." The moral tone of the age, set by social Darwinism, with its emphasis on survival

Columbia's Easter Bonnet
The United States, symbolized by the female figure of Columbia, tries on "World Power" in this cartoon from *Puck*, which appeared in 1901 after the Spanish-American War left the United States in control of Spain's former colonies in Guam, the Philippines, and Puerto Rico. The cartoon points to a new overseas direction for American foreign policy at the turn of the twentieth century.
Library of Congress.

of the fittest and Anglo-Saxon racial superiority, proved ideally suited to imperialism. Congregational minister Josiah Strong revealed the mixture of racism and missionary zeal that fueled American adventurism abroad when he remarked, "It seems to me that God, with infinite wisdom and skill, is training the Anglo Saxon race for an hour sure to come in the world's future." The *Washington Post* trumpeted, "The taste of empire is in the mouth of the people," thrilled at the prospect of "an imperial policy, the Republic renascent, taking her place with the armed nations."

> ▶REVIEW   Why did the United States declare war on Spain in 1898?

Conclusion: Rallying around the Flag

A decade of domestic strife ended amid the blare of martial music and the waving of flags. The Spanish-American War drowned out the calls for social reform that had fueled the Populist politics of the 1890s. During that decade, angry farmers facing hard times looked to the Farmers' Alliance to fight for their vision of economic democracy, workers staged bloody battles across the country to assert their rights, and women attacked drunkenness and the conditions that fostered it and mounted a suffrage movement to secure their basic political rights. In St. Louis in 1892, Frances Willard joined with other disaffected Americans to form a new People's Party to fight for change.

The bitter depression that began in 1893 led to increased labor strife. The Pullman boycott brutally dramatized the power of property and the conservatism of the laissez-faire state. Even the miners' victory in Cripple Creek, Colorado, in 1894 proved short-lived. But workers' willingness to confront capitalism on the streets of Chicago, Homestead, Cripple Creek, and a host of other sites across America eloquently testified to labor's growing determination, unity, and strength.

As the depression deepened, the sight of Coxey's army of unemployed marching on Washington to demand federal intervention in the economy signaled a growing shift in the public mind against the stand-pat politics of laissez-faire. The call for the government to take action to better the lives of workers, farmers, and the dispossessed manifested itself in the fiercely fought presidential campaign of William Jennings Bryan in 1896. With the outbreak of the Spanish-American War in 1898, the decade ended on a harmonious note with patriotic Americans rallying around the flag. Few questioned America's foray into overseas empire. The United States took its place on the world stage, buttressing its hemispheric domination with the Monroe Doctrine and employing the Open Door policy, which promised access to the riches of China. But even though

Americans basked in patriotism and contemplated empire, old grievances had not been laid to rest. The People's Party had been beaten, but the Populists' call for greater government involvement in the economy, expanded opportunities for direct democracy, and a more equitable balance of profits and power between the people and the big corporations sounded the themes that would be taken up by a new generation of progressive reformers in the first decades of the twentieth century.

REVIEWING THE CHAPTER

Use the questions and timeline to review and strengthen your understanding of the chapter.

REVIEW QUESTIONS

1. Why did American farmers organize alliances in the late nineteenth century? (pp. 616–20)

2. Why did the strikes of the 1890s fail to produce permanent gains for workers? (pp. 620–27)

3. How did women's temperance activism contribute to the cause of woman suffrage? (pp. 628–30)

4. Why was the People's Party unable to translate national support into victory in the 1896 election? (pp. 630–35)

5. Why did the United States largely abandon its isolationist foreign policy in the 1890s? (pp. 635–39)

6. Why did the United States declare war on Spain in 1898? (pp. 639–44)

MAKING CONNECTIONS

1. In the late nineteenth century, Americans clashed over the disparity of power brought about by industrial capitalism. Why did many working Americans look to the government to help advance their vision of economic justice? In your answer, discuss specific reforms working-class Americans pursued and the strategies they employed.

2. In the 1890s, workers mounted labor protests and strikes. What circumstances gave rise to these actions? How did they differ from earlier strikes, such as the Great Railroad Strike of 1877? In your answer, discuss specific actions, being sure to consider how local and national circumstances contributed to their ultimate resolution.

3. How did women's activism in the late nineteenth century help advance the cause of woman suffrage? How did women activists in the late nineteenth century differ from their predecessors? In your answer, discuss specific gains made in the late nineteenth century, as well as shifts in reformers' strategies.

4. How did the conquest of Native Americans in the West foreshadow U.S. expansion abroad? In what ways did assumptions of racial superiority evident in U.S. Indian policy affect the treatment of Cubans and Filipinos?

TIMELINE

1884	• Woman's Christian Temperance Union, headed by Frances Willard, calls for woman suffrage.	**1895**	• President Grover Cleveland defends Monroe Doctrine in border dispute between British Guiana and Venezuela.
1889	• Typhoon averts hostilities between German and U.S. ships in Samoan Islands.	**1896**	• Democrats and Populists support William Jennings Bryan for president.
1890	• National American Woman Suffrage Association (NAWSA) formed.		• Republican William McKinley elected president.
	• Wyoming enters Union with woman suffrage.	**1898**	• U.S. battleship *Maine* explodes in Havana harbor.
	• Southern Farmers' Alliance numbers three million members.		• Congress declares war on Spain.
1892	• People's (Populist) Party founded.		• Admiral George Dewey destroys Spanish fleet in Manila Bay, the Philippines.
	• Homestead lockout.		• U.S. troops defeat Spanish forces in Cuba.
1893	• Stock market crash touches off severe economic depression.		• Treaty of Paris ends war with Spain and cedes Philippines, Puerto Rico, and Guam to the United States.
	• President Grover Cleveland nixes attempt to annex Hawaii.		• United States annexes Hawaii.
1894	• Miners strike in Cripple Creek, Colorado.	**1899– 1900**	• Secretary of State John Hay enunciates Open Door policy in China.
	• Coxey's army marches to Washington, D.C.		• Boxer uprising in China.
	• Federal troops and court injunction crush Pullman boycott.	**1901**	• Boxer Protocol imposed on Chinese government.

▶ **For an online bibliography, practice quizzes, Web sites, images, and documents related to this chapter,** see the Book Companion Site at **bedfordstmartins.com/roark**.

▶ **For firsthand accounts of this period,** see Chapter 20 in Michael Johnson, ed., *Reading the American Past,* Fourth Edition.

21
CHAPTER

Progressivism from the Grass Roots to the White House

1890–1916

I N THE SUMMER OF 1889, a young woman leased the upper floor of a dilapidated mansion on Chicago's West Side in the heart of a burgeoning immigrant population. Watching as she prepared to move in, neighbors scratched their heads, wondering why the well-dressed woman, who surely could afford a better house in a better neighborhood, chose to live on South Halsted Street. Yet the house, built by Charles Hull, precisely suited the needs of Jane Addams.

For Addams, personal action marked the first step in the search for solutions to the social problems fostered by urban industrialism. Her object was twofold: She wanted to help her immigrant neighbors, and she wanted to offer an opportunity for educated women like herself to find meaningful work. As she later wrote in her autobiography, *Twenty Years at Hull-House* (1910), "I gradually became convinced that it would be a good thing to rent a house in a part of the city where many primitive and actual needs are found, in which young women who had been given over too exclusively to study might restore a balance of activity along traditional lines and learn of life from life itself." Addams's emphasis on the reciprocal relationship between the social classes made Hull House different from other philanthropic enterprises. She wished to do things with, not just for, Chicago's poor.

In the next decade, Hull House expanded from one rented floor in the old brick mansion to some thirteen buildings housing a remarkable variety of activities. Addams converted the bathrooms in the basement into public baths, opened a coffee shop and restaurant to sell take-out food to workingwomen too tired to cook after their long shifts, and sponsored a nursery and kindergarten for neighborhood children. Hull House offered classes, lectures, art exhibits, musical instruction, and college extension courses. It boasted a gymnasium, a theater, a manual training workshop, a labor museum, and the first public playground in Chicago.

But Hull House was more than a group of buildings. From the first, it attracted an extraordinary set of reformers. Some stayed for decades, as did Julia Lathrop before she went to Washington, D.C., in 1912 to head the Children's Bureau. Others, like Gerard Swope, who later became president of the General Electric Company, came for only a short time. Hull House residents pioneered the scientific investigation of urban ills. Armed with statistics, they launched campaigns to improve housing, end child labor, fund playgrounds, mediate between labor and management, and lobby for laws to protect workers.

Addams quickly learned that it was impossible to deal with urban problems without becoming involved in political action. Her determination to clean up the garbage on Halsted Street led her into politics. Piles of decaying garbage overflowed the street's wooden trash bins, breeding flies and disease. Investigation revealed that the local ward boss awarded the contract to pick up the trash as a political plum to one of his henchmen, who felt under no obligation to

Jane Addams

Jane Addams was twenty-nine years old when she founded Hull House in Chicago. She and her college roommate, Ellen Gates Starr, established America's premier social settlement. Her desire to live among the poor and her insistence that settlement house work benefited educated women such as herself as well as her immigrant neighbors separated her from the charity workers who had come before her and marked the distance from philanthropy to progressive reform.

Jane Addams Memorial Collection (JAM neg. 14), Special Collections, University of Illinois at Chicago; photographer: Max Platz.

provide adequate service. To end the graft, Addams got herself appointed garbage inspector. Out on the streets at six in the morning, she rode atop the garbage wagon to make sure it made its rounds. Addams mounted several unsuccessful political campaigns to oust the corrupt ward boss but eventually realized that bossism was a symptom and not the cause of urban blight. Recognizing that bosses stayed in power by providing jobs and services to their constituents, she moved instead to sponsor legislation to help her neighbors. Eventually, her struggle to aid the urban poor led her not only to city hall but on to the state capitol and to Washington, D.C.

Under Jane Addams's leadership, Hull House became a "spearhead for reform," part of a broader movement that contemporaries called **progressivism**. The transition from personal action to political activism that Addams personified became one of the hallmarks of this reform period, which lasted from the 1890s to World War I.

By the 1890s, it had become clear to many Americans that the **laissez-faire** approach of government toward business no longer worked. The classical **liberalism** of the nation's Founders, with its emphasis on opposition to the tyranny of centralized government, had not reckoned on the enormous private wealth and power of the Gilded Age's business giants. As the gap between rich and poor widened in the 1890s, issues of social justice challenged traditional notions of laissez-faire liberalism. The violence and militancy of the 1890s—labor strikes, farmers' revolt, **suffrage** and antilynching movements—eloquently testified to the growing polarities in society. Yet a laissez-faire state only exacerbated the inequalities of class, race, and gender. A generation of progressive reformers demanded government intervention to guarantee a more equitable society. The willingness to use the government to promote change and to counterbalance the power of private interests redefined liberalism in the twentieth century.

Faith in activism in both the political and the private realms formed a common thread that united an otherwise diverse group of progressive reformers. A sense of Christian mission inspired some. Others, fearing social upheaval, sought to remove some of the worst evils of urban industrialism—tenements, child labor, and harsh working conditions. Progressives shared a growing concern about the power of wealthy individuals and corporations and a strong dislike of the **trusts**. But often they feared the immigrant poor and sought to control and Americanize them. Along with moral fervor, a belief in technical expertise and scientific management infused progressivism and made the cult of efficiency part and parcel of the movement. All of these elements—uplift and efficiency, social justice and social control—came together in the Progressive Era and characterized the progressive movement both at the grassroots level in the cities and states and in the presidencies of Theodore Roosevelt and Woodrow Wilson.

Grassroots Progressivism

Much of progressive reform began at the grassroots level and percolated upward into local, state, and eventually national politics as reformers attacked the social problems fostered by urban industrialism. Although reform flourished in many different settings across the country, urban problems inspired the progressives' greatest efforts. In their zeal to "civilize the city," reformers founded settlement houses, professed a new Christian **social gospel**, and campaigned against vice and crime in the name of "social purity." Allying with the working class, they sought to better the lot of sweatshop garment workers and to end child labor. Their reform efforts often began on the local level but ended up being debated in state legislatures and in the U.S. Congress.

Civilizing the City

Progressives attacked the problems of the city on many fronts. The settlement house movement attempted to bridge the distance between the classes. The social gospel called for the churches to play a new role in social reformation. And the **social purity movement** campaigned to clean up vice, particularly prostitution.

The settlement house movement that began in England came to the United States in 1886 with the opening of the University Settlement House in New York City. The needs of poor urban neighborhoods provided the impetus for these social settlements. In 1893, Lillian Wald, a nurse attending medical school in New York, went to care for a woman living in a dilapidated tenement. The experience led Wald to leave medical school and recruit several other nurses to move to New York City's Lower East Side "to live in the neighborhood as nurses, identify ourselves with it socially, and . . . contribute to it our citizenship." Wald's Henry Street settlement expanded in 1895, pioneering public health nursing. Although Wald herself was Jewish, she insisted that the settlement remain independent of religious ties, making it different from the avowedly religious settlements in England.

Women, particularly college-educated women like Jane Addams and Lillian Wald, formed the backbone of the settlement house movement and stood in the vanguard of the progressive movement. Eager to use their knowledge, they often found themselves blocked from careers in medicine, law, and the clergy. (Fewer than fifteen hundred women practiced law in 1900, and women constituted only 6 percent of the medical profession.) Settlement houses gave college-educated women a place to put their talents to work in the service of society and to champion progressive reform. Largely due to women's efforts, settlements like Hull House grew in number from six in 1891 to more than four hundred in 1911. In the process, settlement house women created a new profession—social work—and stimulated a new reform movement—progressivism.

For their part, churches confronted urban social problems by enunciating a new social gospel, one that saw its mission not simply to reform individuals but to reform society. The social gospel offered a powerful corrective to **social Darwinism** and the **gospel of wealth**, which fostered the belief that riches somehow signaled divine favor. Washington Gladden, a prominent social gospel minister, challenged that view when he urged Congregationalists to turn down a gift from John D. Rockefeller, arguing that it was "tainted money." In place of the gospel of wealth, progressive clergy exhorted their congregations to put Christ's teachings to work in their daily lives. Charles M. Sheldon's popular book *In His Steps* (1898) called on men and women to Christianize capitalism by asking the question "What would Jesus do?"

For Walter Rauschenbusch, a Baptist minister working in New York's tough Hell's Kitchen neighborhood, the social gospel grew out of the depression of the 1890s, which left hundreds of thousands of people unemployed. "They wore down our threshold and they wore away our hearts," he later wrote. "One could hear human virtue cracking and crumbling all around." In *Christianity and the Social Crisis* (1907), Rauschenbusch called for churches to play a new role in promoting social justice, and many congregations across the country heeded the call.

Ministers also played an active role in the social purity movement, the campaign to attack vice. The Reverend Charles H. Parkhurst shocked his Madison Square congregation in the 1890s by donning a disguise and touring New York City's brothels to uncover the links between political corruption and urban vice. Armed with eyewitness accounts and affidavits, he demanded reform. To end the "social evil," as reformers euphemistically called prostitution, the social purity movement brought together ministers who wished to stamp out sin, doctors concerned about the spread of venereal disease, and women reformers determined to fight the double standard that made it acceptable for men to engage in premarital and extramarital sex but demanded chastity of all unmarried women. Advanced progressive reformers linked prostitution to poverty and championed higher wages for women. "Is it any wonder," asked the Chicago vice commission, "that a tempted girl who receives only six dollars per week working with her hands sells her body for twenty-five dollars per week when she learns there is a demand for it and men are willing to pay the price?"

Together, social purity reformers of all stripes waged campaigns to close red-light districts in cities across the country and lobbied for the Mann Act, passed in 1910, which made it illegal to transport women across state lines for "immoral purposes." On the state level, they struck at venereal disease by securing legislation to require a blood test for syphilis before marriage.

Attacks on alcohol went hand in hand with the push for social purity. The **temperance** campaign launched by the Woman's Christian Temperance Union (WCTU) heated up in the early twentieth century. The Anti-Saloon League, formed in 1895 under the leadership of **Protestant** clergy, campaigned for an end to the sale of liquor. Reformers pointed to links between drinking, prostitution, wife and child abuse, unemployment, and industrial accidents. The powerful liquor lobby fought back, spending liberally in election campaigns, fueling the charge that liquor corrupted the political process.

An element of **nativism** (dislike of foreigners) ran through the movement for prohibition, as it did in a number of progressive reforms. The Irish, the Italians, and the Germans were among the groups stigmatized by temperance reformers for their drinking. Progressives often failed to see the important role the tavern played in many ethnic communities. Unlike the American saloon, an almost exclusively male domain, the tavern often provided a family retreat. German Americans of all ages socialized at beer gardens after church on Sunday. Even though most workers toiled six days a week and had only Sunday for recreation and relaxation, some progressives campaigned on the local level to enforce the Sunday closing of taverns, stores, and other commercial establishments. To deny the working class access to alcohol, these progressives pushed for state legislation to outlaw the sale of liquor. By 1912, seven states were "dry."

Progressives' efforts to civilize the city demonstrated their willingness to take action; their belief that environment, not heredity alone, determined human behavior; and their optimism that conditions could be corrected through government action without radically altering America's economy or institutions. All of these attitudes characterized the progressive movement.

Progressives and the Working Class

Day-to-day contact with their neighbors made settlement house workers particularly sympathetic to labor unions. When Mary Kenney O'Sullivan complained that her bookbinders' union met in a dirty, noisy saloon, Jane Addams invited the union to meet at Hull House. And during the Pullman strike in 1894, Hull House residents organized strike relief. "Hull-House has been so unionized," grumbled one Chicago businessman, "that it has lost its usefulness and become a detriment and harm to the community." But to the working class, the support of middle-class reformers marked a significant gain.

Attempts to forge a cross-class alliance became institutionalized in 1903 with the creation of the Women's Trade Union League (WTUL). The WTUL brought together women workers and middle-class "allies." Its goal was to organize workingwomen into unions under the auspices of the American Federation of Labor (AFL). However, the AFL paid little more than lip service to unionizing women. As one workingwoman confided, "The men think that the girls should not get as good work as the men and should not make half as much money as a man." Samuel Gompers, president of the AFL, endorsed the principle of equal pay for equal work, shrewdly observing that it would help male workers more than women, since many employers hired women precisely because they could be paid less.

Although the alliance between workingwomen, primarily immigrants and daughters of immigrants, and their middle-class allies was not without tension, the WTUL helped workingwomen achieve significant gains. Its most notable

Women Strikers

Throughout the bitter winter of 1909, garment workers led a strike demanding union representation, shorter hours, better working conditions, and higher wages. The strikers, primarily young women from the Jewish and Italian immigrant communities, joined the International Ladies' Garment Workers Union and proved that women could be unionized and mount an effective strike. The women pictured here claim 30,000 are on strike, but historically the strike has been called the "uprising of the 20,000." Brown Brothers.

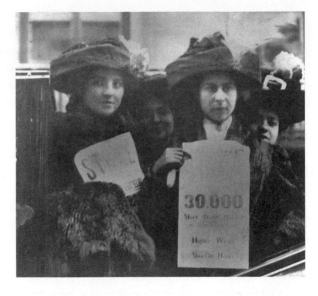

success came in 1909 in the "uprising of the twenty thousand." In November, hundreds of women employees of the Triangle Shirtwaist Company in New York City went on strike to protest low wages, dangerous and demeaning working conditions, and management's refusal to recognize their union, the International Ladies' Garment Workers Union (ILGWU). In support of the walkout, the ILGWU called for a general strike of all garment workers. An estimated twenty thousand workers, most of them teenage girls and many of them Jewish and Italian immigrants, stayed out on strike through the winter, picketing in the bitter cold. More than six hundred were arrested, and many were sent to jail for "streetwalking," a move by the authorities to try to break the spirit and impugn the morals of the striking women. By the time the strike ended in February 1910, the workers had won important demands in many shops. But they lost their bid to gain recognition for their union. The solidarity shown by the women workers proved to be the strike's greatest achievement. As Clara Lemlich, one of the strike's leaders, exclaimed, "They used to say that you couldn't even organize women. They wouldn't come to union meetings. They were 'temporary' workers. Well we showed them!"

The WTUL made enormous contributions to the strike. It provided volunteers for the picket lines, posted more than $29,000 in bail, protested police brutality, organized a parade of ten thousand strikers, took part in the arbitration conference, appealed for funds, and generated publicity for the strike. Under the leadership of the WTUL, women from every class of society, from J. P. Morgan's daughter Anne to **socialists** on New York's Lower East Side, joined the strikers in a dramatic display of cross-class alliance.

But for all its success, the uprising of the twenty thousand failed fundamentally to change conditions for women workers, as the tragic Triangle fire dramatized in 1911. A little over a year after the shirtwaist makers' strike ended, fire alarms sounded at the Triangle Shirtwaist factory. The ramshackle building, full of lint and combustible cloth, burned to rubble in half an hour. A WTUL member described the scene below on the street: "Two young girls whom I knew to be working in the vicinity came rushing toward me, tears were running from their eyes and they were white and shaking as they caught me by the arm. 'Oh,' shrieked one of them, 'they are jumping. Jumping from ten stories up! They are going through the air like bundles of clothes.'"

The terrified Triangle workers had little choice but to jump. Flames blocked one exit, and the other door had been locked to prevent workers from pilfering. The flimsy, rusted fire escape collapsed under the weight of fleeing workers, killing dozens. Trapped, 54 workers jumped from the ninth-floor windows, only to smash to their deaths on the sidewalk. Of 500 workers, 146 died and scores of others were injured. The owners of the Triangle firm went to trial for negligence, but they avoided conviction when authorities determined that the fire had been started by a careless smoker. The Triangle Shirtwaist Company reopened in another firetrap within a matter of weeks.

Outrage and a sense of futility overwhelmed Rose Schneiderman, a leading WTUL organizer, who made a bitter speech at the memorial service for the dead Triangle workers. "I would be a traitor to those poor burned bodies if I came here to talk good fellowship," she told her audience. "We have tried you good people of the public and we have found you wanting. . . . I know from my experience it is up to the working people to save themselves . . . by a strong working class movement."

The Triangle fire tested severely the bonds of the cross-class alliance. Along with Rose Schneiderman, WTUL leaders experienced a growing sense of futility. It seemed not enough to organize and to strike, particularly when the AFL paid so little attention to women workers. Increasingly, the WTUL turned its efforts to lobbying for protective legislation—laws that would limit hours and regulate working conditions for women workers.

Advocates of protective legislation won a major victory in 1908 when the U.S. Supreme Court, in *Muller v. Oregon*, reversed its previous rulings and upheld an Oregon law that limited to ten the hours women could work in a day. A mass of sociological evidence put together by Florence Kelley of the National Consumers' League and Josephine Goldmark of the WTUL demonstrated the ill effects of long hours on the health and safety of women. The data convinced the Court that long hours endangered women and therefore the entire human race. The Court's ruling set a precedent, but one that separated the well-being of women workers from that of men by arguing that women's reproductive role justified special treatment. Later generations of women fighting for equality would question the effectiveness of this strategy and argue that it ultimately closed good jobs to women. The WTUL, however, greeted protective legislation as a first step in the attempt to ensure the safety of all workers.

The National Consumers' League (NCL), like the WTUL, fostered cross-class alliance. When Florence Kelley took over the leadership of the NCL in 1899, she urged middle-class women to boycott stores and exert pressure for decent wages and working conditions for women employees, primarily saleswomen. The league published a "white list" of stores that met its standards. The NCL's tactics were widely copied abroad. Like the WTUL, the National Consumers' League increasingly promoted protective legislation to better working conditions for working women. Frustrated by the reluctance of the private sector to respond to the need for reform, progressives turned to government at all levels. Critics would later charge that the progressives assumed too easily that government regulation could best solve social problems.

Reform also fueled the fight for woman suffrage. For women like Jane Addams and Florence Kelley, involvement in social reform led inevitably to support for woman suffrage. These new suffragists emphasized the reforms that could be accomplished if women had the vote. When they talked of the need for the ballot, they often compared it to the broom. Addams insisted that in an urban, industrial society, a good housekeeper could not be sure the food she fed her family or the water and milk they drank were pure unless she became involved in politics and wielded the ballot—and not just the broom—to protect her family. The concept of municipal housekeeping encouraged women to put their talents to work in the service of society.

> ►**REVIEW**   What types of people were drawn to the progressive movement, and what motivated them?

Progressivism: Theory and Practice

Progressive reformers developed a theoretical basis for their activist approach by countering social Darwinism with a dynamic new **reform Darwinism** and by championing the uniquely American philosophy of **pragmatism**. The progressives emphasized action and experimentation. Dismissing the view that humans should leave progress to the dictates of natural selection, progressive reform Darwinists argued that human intelligence could shape change and improve society. In their zeal for action, progressives often showed an unchecked admiration for speed and efficiency that promoted **scientific management** and a new cult of efficiency. These varied strands of progressive theory found practical application in state and local politics, where reformers challenged traditional laissez-faire government.

Reform Darwinism and Social Engineering

The active, interventionist approach of the progressives directly challenged social Darwinism, with its insistence that the world operated on the principle of survival of the fittest and that human beings stood powerless in the face of the law of natural selection. Without abandoning the evolutionary framework of Darwinism, a new group of sociologists argued that evolution could be advanced more rapidly if men and women used their intellects to alter the environment. Sociologist Lester Frank Ward put it clearly in his book *Dynamic Sociology* (1883). "I insist that the time must soon come," he wrote, "when control of blind natural forces in society must give way to human foresight." Dubbed "reform Darwinism," the new sociological theory condemned the laissez-faire approach, insisting that the liberal state should play a more active role in solving social problems.

In their pursuit of reform, progressives were influenced by the work of two philosophers, William James and John Dewey, who argued for a new test for truth. They insisted that there were no eternal truths and that the real worth of any idea lay in its consequences. They called their pluralistic, relativistic philosophy "pragmatism." Dewey put his theories to the test in the classroom of his laboratory school at the University of Chicago. A pioneer in American education, he emphasized process rather than content and encouraged students to learn by doing. By championing social experimentation, the American pragmatists provided an important impetus for progressive reform.

Efficiency and *expertise* became watchwords in the progressive vocabulary. In *Drift and Mastery* (1914), journalist and critic Walter Lippmann called for skilled "technocrats" to use scientific techniques to control social change, substituting social engineering for aimless drift. Progressive reformers' emphasis on expertise inevitably fostered a kind of elitism. Unlike the **Populists**, who advocated a greater voice for the masses, progressives, for all their interest in social justice, insisted that experts be put in charge.

At its extreme, the application of expertise and social engineering took the form of scientific management, which by elevating productivity and efficiency alienated the working class. Frederick Winslow Taylor pioneered "systematized shop management." After dropping out of Harvard, Taylor went to work as a machinist at Midvale Steel in Philadelphia in the 1880s. Obsessed with making humans and machines produce more and faster, he earned a master of engineering degree in 1885 and went back to Midvale to restructure the workplace. With his stopwatch, he carefully timed workers and attempted to break down their work into its simplest components, one repetitive action after another, on the theory that productivity would increase if tasks could be simplified. An advocate of piecework, quotas, and pay incentives for productivity, Taylor insisted that unions were unnecessary. As a consulting engineer, he spread his gospel of efficiency and won many converts among corporate managers. Workers hated the monotony of systematized shop management and argued that it led to the speedup—pushing workers to produce more in less time and for less pay. But many progressives applauded the increased productivity and efficiency of Taylor's system.

Progressive Government: City and State

The politicians who became premier progressives were generally the followers, not the leaders, in a movement already well advanced at the grassroots level. Yet they left their stamp on the movement. Tom Johnson made Cleveland a model of progressive reform, Robert M. La Follette turned Wisconsin into a laboratory for progressivism, and Hiram Johnson ended the domination of the Southern Pacific Railroad in California politics.

Progressivism burst forth at every level of government in 1900, but nowhere more forcefully than in Cleveland, with the election of Thomas Loftin Johnson as mayor. A self-made millionaire by age forty, Johnson made his money in the street railroad business in Detroit. A flamboyant man who craved power and acclaim, Johnson turned his back on business and moved to Cleveland in 1899, where he began his career in politics. During his mayoral campaign, he pledged to reduce the streetcar fare from five cents to three cents. His election touched off a seven-year war between advocates of the lower fare, who believed that workers paid a disproportionate share of their meager earnings for transportation, and the street-car moguls, who argued that they couldn't meet costs with the lower fare. When Johnson responded by building his own streetcar line, his foes tore up the tracks and blocked him with court injunctions and legal delays. At the prompting of his opponents, the Ohio legislature sought to limit Johnson's mayoral power by revoking the charter of every city in the state, replacing home rule with central control from the state capitol in Columbus.

Reelected four times, Johnson fought for fair taxation and championed greater **democracy** through the use of the initiative, referendum, and recall—devices that allowed voters to have a direct say in legislative and judicial matters. Frustrated in his attempt to bring the streetcar industry to heel, he had the city buy the streetcar system and institute the three-cent fare. He also championed the municipal ownership of public utilities, a tactic that progressives called "gas and water socialism." Under Johnson's administration, Cleveland became, in the words of journalist Lincoln Steffens, the "best governed city in America."

In Wisconsin, Robert M. La Follette, who as a young congressional represen-tative had supported William McKinley, converted to the progressive cause early in the 1900s. An astute politician, La Follette capitalized on the grassroots move-ment for reform to launch his long political career, first as governor (1901–1905) and later as a U.S. senator (1906–1925). A graduate of the University of Wisconsin, La Follette brought scientists and professors into his administration and used the university, just down the street from the statehouse in Madison, as a resource in drafting legislation. As governor, he lowered railroad rates, raised railroad taxes, improved education, preached conservation, established factory regulation and workers' compensation, instituted the first direct primary in the country, and inaugurated the first state income tax. Under his leadership, Wisconsin earned the title "laboratory of democracy."

A fiery orator, "Fighting Bob" La Follette united his supporters around issues that transcended party loyalties. This emphasis on reform characterized progressivism, which attracted followers from both major parties. Democrats like Tom Johnson and Republicans like Robert La Follette could lay equal claim to the label "progressive." When La Follette moved to the U.S. Senate in 1906, he joined a coalition of insurgent progressives, Democrats and Republicans alike, who crossed party lines to work for reform.

West of the Rockies, progressivism arrived somewhat later and found a champion in Hiram Johnson of California, who served as governor from 1911 to 1917 and later as a U.S. senator. Since the 1870s, California politics had been dominated by the Southern Pacific Railroad, a corporation so rapacious that novelist Frank Norris styled it *The Octopus* (1901). Johnson ran for governor in 1910 on the promise to "kick the Southern Pacific out of politics." With the support of the reform wing of the Republican Party and the promise "to return the government to the people," he handily won. As governor, he introduced the direct primary; supported the initiative, referendum, and recall; strengthened the state's railroad commission; supported conservation; and signed an employer's liability law.

Who benefited most from Johnson's progressivism? California's entrepreneurs—large farmers, independent oil producers, and other rising businessmen who could make money more easily once Johnson curtailed the influence of the Southern Pacific. A vigorous, compelling personality with a reputation for a towering temper, Hiram Johnson proved an able governor. In 1912, he could boast that by regulating the Southern Pacific Railroad, he had saved shippers more than $2 million.

> ▶ **REVIEW**   How did progressives justify their demand for more activist government?

Progressivism Finds a President: Theodore Roosevelt

On September 6, 1901, President William McKinley was shot by Leon Czolgosz, an **anarchist**, while attending the Pan-American Exposition in Buffalo, New York. Eight days later, McKinley died. When news of his assassination reached his friend and political mentor Mark Hanna, Hanna is said to have growled, "Now that damned cowboy is president." He was speaking of Vice President Theodore Roosevelt, the colorful hero of the battle of San Juan Hill, who had indeed punched cattle in the Dakotas in the 1880s. Roosevelt's status as a Spanish-American War hero had propelled him to the governorship of New York in 1898. A moderate reformer, he had clashed with New York's Republican "Easy Boss" Tom Platt. To get rid of Roosevelt, the boss finagled to get him "kicked upstairs" as a candidate for the vice presidency in 1900. His energy and popularity added

Theodore Roosevelt
At forty-two, Theodore Roosevelt was the youngest president ever to occupy the White House. He brought to the office energy, intellect, and activism in equal measure. Roosevelt boasted that he used the presidency as a "bully pulpit"—a forum from which he advocated reforms ranging from trust-busting to conservation.
Library of Congress.

luster to the Republican ticket and helped President McKinley win a second term. As vice president, Platt and the party bosses reasoned, Roosevelt could do little harm. But one bullet proved the error of their logic.

In the first hours of his presidency, Roosevelt reassured the shocked nation that he intended "to continue absolutely unbroken" the policies of McKinley. But Roosevelt was as different from McKinley as the twentieth century was from the nineteenth. An activist and a moralist, imbued with the progressive spirit, Roosevelt would turn the White House into a "bully pulpit" advocating reforms like conservation and championing the nation's emergence as a world power. In the process, Roosevelt would work to shift the nation's center of power from Wall Street to Washington.

The Square Deal

At age forty-two, Theodore Roosevelt became the youngest man ever to move into the White House. A patrician by birth and an activist by temperament, Roosevelt brought to the job enormous talent and energy. By the time he graduated from Harvard, he was already an accomplished naturalist, an enthusiastic historian, and a naval strategist. He could have chosen from any of those promising careers. Instead, he chose politics, not a bad choice for a man who relished competition and craved power.

Roosevelt was shrewd enough to realize that the path to power did not lie in the good-government leagues formed by his well-bred friends. Instead, he apprenticed himself to the local ward boss, who held court in a grimy, smoke-filled Republican club above a Manhattan saloon. Roosevelt's rise in politics was swift and sure. He went from the New York assembly at the age of twenty-three to the presidency in less than twenty years, with time out as a cowboy in the Dakotas, police commissioner of New York City, assistant secretary of the navy, colonel of the Rough Riders, and governor of New York.

As president, Roosevelt would harness his explosive energy to strengthen the power of the federal government, putting business on notice that it could no longer count on a laissez-faire government to give it free rein. The "absolutely vital question" facing the country, Roosevelt wrote to a friend in 1901, was "whether or not the government has the power to control the trusts." The Sherman Antitrust Act of 1890 had been badly weakened by a conservative Supreme Court and by attorneys general more willing to use it against labor unions than against **monopolies**. To determine whether the law had any teeth left, Roosevelt, in one of his first acts as president, ordered his attorney general to begin a secret antitrust investigation of the Northern Securities Company.

Roosevelt trained his sights on a good target. Northern Securities had resulted from one of the most controversial mergers of the era. When Edward H. Harriman, who controlled the Union Pacific and Southern Pacific railroads, attempted to add the Northern Pacific to his holdings, James J. Hill of the Great Northern squared off against him. The result was a ruinous rate war that precipitated a panic on Wall Street, bankrupting thousands of small investors. To bring peace to the warring factions, financier J. P. Morgan stepped in and created the Northern Securities Company in 1901, linking under one management three competing railroads. This new behemoth monopolized railroad traffic in the Northwest. Small investors, still smarting from their losses, farmers worried about freight rates, and the public in general saw in Northern Securities the symbol of corporate high-handedness.

In February 1902, just five months after Roosevelt took office, Wall Street rocked with the news that the government had filed an antitrust suit against Northern Securities. As one newspaper editor sarcastically observed, "Wall Street is paralyzed at the thought that a President of the United States would sink so low as to try to enforce the law." An indignant J. P. Morgan demanded to know why he had not been consulted. "If we have done anything wrong," he told the attorney general, "send your man to my man and they can fix it up." Roosevelt, amused, later noted that Morgan "could not help regarding me as a big rival operator." In a sense, that was just what he intended. Roosevelt's thunderbolt put Wall Street on notice that the new president expected to be treated as an equal and was willing to use government as a weapon to curb business excesses. Perhaps sensing the new mood, the Supreme Court, in a significant turnaround, upheld the Sherman Act and called for the dissolution of Northern Securities in 1904.

"Hurrah for Teddy the Trustbuster," cheered the papers. Roosevelt went on to use the Sherman Act against forty-three trusts, including such giants as American Tobacco, Du Pont, and Standard Oil. Always the moralist, he insisted on a "rule of reason." He would punish "bad" trusts (those that broke the law) and leave "good" ones alone. In practice, he preferred regulation to antitrust suits. In 1903, he pressured Congress to pass the Elkins Act, outlawing railroad rebates. And he created the new cabinet-level Department of Commerce and Labor with the subsidiary Bureau of Corporations to act as a corporate watchdog.

Observing Roosevelt in action, journalist Joseph Pulitzer remarked, "He has subjugated Wall Street." Pulitzer exaggerated, but Roosevelt had masterfully asserted the moral and political authority of the executive, underscoring, in his words, the "duty of the President to act upon the theory that he is the steward of the people."

In his handling of the anthracite coal strike in 1902, Roosevelt again demonstrated his willingness to assert the authority of the presidency, this time to mediate between labor and management. In May, 147,000 coal miners in Pennsylvania went on strike. The United Mine Workers (UMW) demanded a reduction in the workday from twelve to ten hours, an equitable system of weighing each miner's output, and a 10 percent wage increase, along with recognition of the union.

When asked about the appalling conditions in the mines that led to the strike, George Baer, the mine operators' spokesman, scoffed, "The miners don't suffer, why they can't even speak English." Buttressed by social Darwinism, Baer observed that "God in his infinite wisdom" had placed "the rights and interests of the laboring man" in the hands of the capitalists, not "the labor agitators." His Olympian confidence rested on the fact that six eastern railroads owned more than 70 percent of the anthracite mines. With the power of the railroads behind them, Baer and the mine owners refused to budge.

The strike dragged on through the summer and into the fall. Hoarding and profiteering drove the price of coal from $2.50 to $6.00 a ton. Coal heated nearly every house, school, and hospital in the Northeast, and as winter approached, coal shortages touched off near riots in the nation's big cities. Labor's sympathizers called for national ownership of the coal mines. Business leaders urged Roosevelt to follow President Grover Cleveland's example in 1894 and call out federal troops to break the strike. In the face of mounting tension, Roosevelt steered a middle course by doing what no president had ever done. He stepped in to mediate, issuing a personal invitation to representatives from both sides to meet in Washington in October. His unprecedented intervention served notice that government counted itself an independent force in business and labor disputes. At the same time, it gave unionism a boost by granting the UMW a place at the table. At the meeting, Baer and the mine owners arrogantly refused to talk with the union representative—a move that angered the attorney general and insulted the president. The meeting ended in an impasse.

Beside himself with anger over the "wooden-headed obstinacy and stupidity" of management, Roosevelt threatened to seize the mines and run them with federal troops. It was a powerful bluff, one that called into question not only the supremacy of private property but also the rule of law. But the specter of federal troops being used to operate the mines quickly brought management around. At the prompting of J. P. Morgan, the mine owners agreed to arbitration ending the strike. In the end, the miners won a reduction in hours and a wage increase, but the owners succeeded in preventing formal recognition of the UMW.

Taken together, Roosevelt's actions in the Northern Securities case and the anthracite coal strike marked a dramatic departure from the presidential passivity of his predecessors in the Gilded Age. Roosevelt's actions demonstrated conclusively that government intended to act as a countervailing force to the power of the big corporations. Pleased with his role in the anthracite strike, he announced that all he had tried to do was give labor and capital a "square deal."

The phrase "Square Deal" became Roosevelt's campaign slogan in the 1904 election. But to win the presidency in his own right, Roosevelt needed to wrest control of the Republican Party from kingmaker and party boss Mark Hanna. Roosevelt adroitly used patronage to win supporters and weaken Hanna's power. The standoff never reached a climax. Hanna died of typhoid fever in 1904, leaving Roosevelt the undisputed leader of the party.

In the presidential election of 1904, Roosevelt easily defeated the Democrats, who abandoned their perennial candidate, William Jennings Bryan, to support Judge Alton B. Parker, a "safe" candidate they hoped would lure business votes away from Roosevelt. In the months before the election, the president prudently toned down his criticism of big business. Wealthy Republicans like J. P. Morgan may have grumbled privately, branding Roosevelt a class traitor, but they remained loyal to the party. Roosevelt swept into office with the largest popular majority—57.9 percent—any candidate had polled up to that time.

Roosevelt the Reformer

"Tomorrow I shall come into my office in my own right," Roosevelt is said to have remarked on the eve of his election. "Then watch out for me!" Roosevelt's stunning victory gave him a mandate for reform. He would need all the popularity and political savvy he could muster, however, to guide his reform measures through Congress. The Senate remained controlled by a staunchly **conservative** Republican "old guard," with many senators on the payrolls of the corporations Roosevelt sought to curb. Roosevelt's pet project remained railroad regulation. The Elkins Act prohibiting rebates had not worked. No one could stop big shippers like Standard Oil from wringing concessions from the railroads. Roosevelt determined that the only solution lay in giving the Interstate Commerce Commission (ICC) real power to set rates and prevent discriminatory practices. But the right to determine the price of goods or services was an age-old prerogative of private enterprise, and one that business had no intention of yielding to government.

To ensure passage of the Hepburn Act, which would increase the power of the ICC, Roosevelt worked skillfully behind the scenes. In its final form, the Hepburn Act, passed in May 1906, gave the ICC the power to set rates subject to court review. Committed progressives like La Follette judged the law a defeat for reform. Die-hard conservatives branded it a "piece of populism." Both sides exaggerated. The law left the courts too much power and failed to provide adequate means for the ICC to determine rates, but its passage proved a landmark in federal control of private industry. For the first time, a government commission had the power to investigate private business records and to set rates.

Passage of the Hepburn Act marked the high point of Roosevelt's presidency. In a serious political blunder, Roosevelt had announced on the eve of his election in 1904 that he would not run again. By 1906, he had become a "lame duck" at the very moment he enjoyed his greatest public popularity.

Always an apt reader of the public temper, Roosevelt witnessed a growing appetite for reform fed by the revelations of corporate and political wrongdoing and social injustice that filled the papers and boosted the sales of popular periodicals. Roosevelt, who wielded publicity like a weapon in his pursuit of reform, counted many of the new investigative journalists, including Jacob Riis, among his friends. But he warned them against going too far, citing the allegorical character in *Pilgrim's Progress* who was so busy raking muck that he took no notice of higher things. Roosevelt's criticism gave the American vocabulary a new word, *muckraker*, which journalists soon appropriated as a title of honor.

Muckraking, as Roosevelt well knew, provided enormous help in securing progressive legislation. In the spring of 1906, publicity generated by the muckrakers about poisons in patent medicines goaded the Senate, with Roosevelt's backing, into passing a pure food and drug bill. Opponents in the House of Representatives hoped to keep the legislation locked up in committee. There it would have died, were it not for the publication of Upton Sinclair's novel *The Jungle* (1906), with its sensational account of filthy conditions in meatpacking plants. A massive public outcry led to the passage of the Pure Food and Drug Act and the Meat Inspection Act in 1906.

In the waning years of his administration, Roosevelt allied with the more progressive elements of the Republican Party. In speech after speech, he attacked "malefactors of great wealth." Styling himself a "radical," he claimed credit for leading the "ultra conservative" party of McKinley to a position of "progressive conservatism and conservative radicalism."

When an economic panic developed in the fall of 1907, business interests quickly blamed the president. The panic of 1907 proved severe but short. Once again, J. P. Morgan stepped in to avert disaster, this time switching funds from one bank to another to prop up weak institutions. For his services, he claimed the Tennessee Coal and Iron Company, an independent steel business that had long been coveted by the U.S. Steel Corporation. Morgan dispatched his lieutenants to Washington, where they told Roosevelt that the sale of the company would aid the economy "but little benefit" U.S. Steel. Willing to take the word of a gentleman, Roosevelt tacitly agreed not to institute antitrust proceedings against U.S. Steel over the acquisition. Roosevelt later learned that Morgan had been less than candid. U.S. Steel acquired Tennessee Coal and Iron for a price well below market value, doing away with a competitor and undercutting the economy of the Southeast. Roosevelt's promise not to institute antitrust proceedings against U.S. Steel would give rise to the charge that he acted as a tool of the Morgan interests.

The charge of collusion between business and government underscored the extent to which corporate leaders like Morgan found federal regulation preferable to unbridled competition or harsher state measures. During the Progressive Era, enlightened business leaders cooperated with government in the hope of avoiding antitrust prosecution. Convinced that regulation and not trust-busting offered the best way to deal with big business, Roosevelt never acknowledged that his regulatory policies fostered an alliance between business and government that today is called corporate liberalism. Despite his harsh attacks on "malefactors of great wealth," Roosevelt's actions in the panic of 1907 demonstrated his indebtedness to Morgan, who still functioned informally as the national bank and would continue to do so until the passage of the Federal Reserve Act six years later.

Roosevelt and Conservation

In one area, Roosevelt proved indisputably ahead of his time. Robert La Follette, who thought Roosevelt a lukewarm progressive and found much to criticize in his presidency, hailed as Roosevelt's "greatest work" his efforts in the conservation of natural resources. When Roosevelt took office, some 45 million acres of land remained as government reserves. He more than tripled that number to 150 million acres, buying land and creating national parks and wildlife preserves by executive order. To conserve natural resources, he fought western cattle barons, lumber kings, mining interests, and powerful leaders in Congress, including Speaker of the House Joseph Cannon, who was determined to spend "not one cent for scenery."

As the first president to have lived and worked in the West, Roosevelt came to the White House convinced of the need for better management of the nation's rivers and forests. During the 1890s, concern for the wanton exploitation of natural resources had led Congress to pass legislation giving the president the power to "reserve" forestland from commercial development by executive proclamation. During his presidency, Roosevelt did not hesitate to wield that power. He placed the nation's conservation policy in the hands of scientifically trained experts like his chief forester, Gifford Pinchot. Pinchot fought for the principle of managed use. He desired not so much to remove land from commercial use, but to use the power of the federal government to effect long-term planning and the rational management of the nation's resources. Roosevelt and Pinchot preached conservation—the efficient use of natural resources. Willing to permit grazing, lumbering, and the development of hydroelectric power, conservationists fought private interests only when they felt business acted irresponsibly or threatened to monopolize water and electric power.

Roosevelt's conservation policies drew criticism from many quarters. Preservationists like John Muir, founder of the Sierra Club, believed the wilderness needed to be protected from all commercial exploitation. Muir soon clashed with Roosevelt, whose policy of managed use led to the destruction of the Hetch Hetchy valley in California's Yosemite National Park. Progressives also criticized the Newlands Reclamation Act of 1902, arguing that the legislation encouraged the growth of large-scale farming at the expense of small farmers. The law established the Reclamation Bureau within the Department of the Interior and provided federal funding for irrigation projects. The growing involvement of the federal government in the management of water resources, a critical issue in the West, marked another victory for the policy of federal intervention that characterized progressivism and marked the end of laissez-faire liberalism.

In 1907, Congress put the brakes on Roosevelt's conservation program by passing a law limiting his power to create forest reserves in six western states. In the days leading up to the law's enactment, Roosevelt feverishly created twenty-one new reserves and enlarged eleven more, saving sixteen million acres for posterity. Once again, Roosevelt had outwitted his adversaries. "Opponents of the forest service turned handsprings in their wrath," he wrote, "but the threats . . . were really only a tribute to the efficiency of our action." Worried that private utilities were gobbling up waterpower sites and creating a monopoly of hydroelectric power, he authorized Pinchot to withdraw 2,565 power sites from private use by designating them "ranger stations." Firm in his commitment to conservation, Roosevelt proved willing to stretch the law when it served his ends. Today, the six national parks, sixteen national monuments, and fifty-one wildlife refuges that he created bear witness to his substantial accomplishments as a conservationist (Map 21.1, page 666).

The Big Stick

Roosevelt's activism extended to his foreign policy, where he worked to buttress the nation's newly won place among world leaders. A fierce proponent of America's interests abroad, he believed that Congress was inept in foreign affairs, and he relied on executive power to pursue a vigorous foreign policy, sometimes stretching the powers of the presidency beyond legal limits. A man who relished military discipline and viewed life as a constant conflict for supremacy, Roosevelt believed that "civilized nations" should police the world and hold "backward" countries in line. In his relations with the European powers, he relied on military strength and diplomacy, a combination he aptly described with the aphorism "Speak softly but carry a big stick."

In the Caribbean, Roosevelt jealously guarded the U.S. sphere of influence defined in the **Monroe Doctrine**. In 1902, he risked war to keep Germany from intervening in Venezuela when that country's dictator borrowed money in Europe and could not repay it. Roosevelt issued an ultimatum to the German

MAP 21.1   National Parks and Forests
The national park system in the West began with Yellowstone in 1872. Grand Canyon, Yosemite, Kings Canyon, and Sequoia followed in the 1890s. During his presidency, Theodore Roosevelt added six parks—Crater Lake, Wind Cave, Petrified Forest, Lassen Volcanic, Mesa Verde, and Zion.

kaiser, warning him not to intervene in Venezuela to secure payment of the debt. Roosevelt's message was blunt—stay out of Latin America or face war with the United States. Both sides eventually backed down and agreed to arbitration.

Roosevelt's proprietary attitude toward the Western Hemisphere became evident in the case of the Panama Canal. A firm advocate of naval power and an astute naval strategist, Roosevelt had long been a supporter of a canal linking the Caribbean and the Pacific. By enabling ships to move quickly from the Atlantic to the Pacific, a canal could effectively double the U.S. navy's power. Having decided on a route across the Panamanian isthmus (a narrow strip of land connecting North and South America), then part of Colombia, Roosevelt in 1902 offered the Colombian government a one-time sum of $10 million and an annual rent of $250,000. When the government in Bogotá refused to accept the offer, Roosevelt became incensed at what he called the "homicidal corruptionists" in Colombia for trying to "blackmail" the United States. At the prompting of a group of New York investors, the Panamanians staged an uprising in 1903, and with unseemly haste the U.S. government recognized the new government within twenty-four hours. The Panamanians promptly accepted the $10 million, and the building got under way. The canal would take eleven years and $375 million to complete; it opened in 1914.

In the wake of the Panama affair, the confrontation with Germany over Venezuela, and yet another default on a European debt, this time in the Dominican Republic, Roosevelt announced in 1904 what became known as the Roosevelt Corollary to the Monroe Doctrine. Couched in the moralistic rhetoric typical of Roosevelt, the corollary declared that the United States would not intervene in Latin America as long as nations there conducted their affairs with "decency." But the United States would step in if any Latin American nation proved guilty of "brutal wrongdoing." The Roosevelt Corollary in effect made the United States the policeman of the Western Hemisphere and served notice to the European powers to keep out. To ensure the payment of debts, Roosevelt immediately put the corollary into practice by intervening in Costa Rica and by taking over the customhouse in the Dominican Republic to ensure the repayment of European debt.

In Asia, Roosevelt inherited the Open Door policy initiated by Secretary of State John Hay in 1899, designed to ensure U.S. commercial entry into China. As Britain, France, Russia, Japan, and Germany raced to secure Chinese trade and territory, Roosevelt was tempted to use force to enter the fray and gain economic or possibly territorial concessions. As a result of victory in the Spanish-American War, the United States already enjoyed a foothold in the region by virtue of its control of the Philippines. Realizing that Americans would not support an aggressive Asian policy, Roosevelt sensibly held back.

In his relations with Europe, Roosevelt sought to establish the United States, fresh from its victory over Spain, as a rising force in world affairs. When tensions flared between France and Germany in Morocco in 1905, Roosevelt mediated at a conference in Algeciras, Spain, where he worked to maintain a balance of power that helped neutralize German ambitions. His skillful mediation gained him a reputation as an astute player on the world stage and demonstrated the nation's new presence in world affairs.

Roosevelt earned the Nobel Peace Prize in 1906 for his role in negotiating an end to the Russo-Japanese War, which had broken out when the Japanese invaded Chinese Manchuria, threatening Russia's sphere of influence in the area. Once again, Roosevelt sought to maintain a balance of power, in this case working to curb Japanese expansionism. Roosevelt admired the Japanese, judging them "the most dashing fighters in the world," but he did not want Japan to become too strong in Asia. He presided over the peace conference at Portsmouth, New Hampshire, where he was able to prevent Japan from dominating Manchuria. He had no qualms, however, about initiating the Taft-Katsura agreement, which granted Japan control of the sovereign nation of Korea in exchange for a pledge that Japan would not threaten the Philippines.

When good relations with Japan were jeopardized by discriminatory legislation in California calling for segregated public schools for "Orientals," Roosevelt smoothed over the incident and negotiated the "Gentlemen's Agreement" in 1907, which allowed the Japanese to save face by voluntarily restricting immigration to the United States. To demonstrate America's naval power and counter Japan's growing bellicosity, Roosevelt dispatched the Great White Fleet, sixteen of the navy's most up-to-date battleships, on a "goodwill mission" around the world. U.S. relations with Japan improved, and in the 1908 Root-Takahira agreement, the two nations pledged to maintain the Open Door and support the status quo in the Pacific. Roosevelt's show of American force constituted a classic example of his dictum "Speak softly but carry a big stick." Political cartoonists delighted in caricaturing the president wielding a cudgel in foreign affairs, and the American public relished the image.

▶**REVIEW**   How did Roosevelt's foreign policy move the United States onto the world stage?

Progressivism Stalled

Roosevelt retired from the presidency in 1909 at age fifty and removed himself from the political scene by going on safari in Africa. He turned the White House over to his handpicked successor, William Howard Taft, a lawyer who had served as governor-general of the Philippines. In the presidential election of 1908, Taft soundly defeated the perennial Democratic candidate, William Jennings Bryan. But Taft's popular majority amounted to only half of Roosevelt's record win in 1904.

Any man would have found it difficult to follow in Roosevelt's footsteps, but Taft proved hopelessly ill suited to the task. A genial man with a talent for law, Taft had no experience in elective office, no feel for politics, and no nerve for controversy. His ambitious wife coveted the office and urged him to seek it. He would have been better off listening to his mother, who warned, "Roosevelt is a good fighter and enjoys it, but the malice of politics would make you miserable." Her words proved prophetic. Taft's presidency was marked by a progressive stalemate, a bitter break with Roosevelt, and a schism in the Republican Party.

The Troubled Presidency of William Howard Taft

Once in office, Taft proved a perfect tool in the hands of Republicans who yearned for a return to the days of a less active executive. A lawyer by training and instinct, Taft believed that it was up to the courts, not the president, to arbitrate social issues. Roosevelt had carried presidential power to a new level, often flouting the separation of powers. Taft the legalist found it difficult to condone Roosevelt's actions. Wary of the progressive insurgents in Congress, Taft relied increasingly on conservatives in the Republican Party. As a progressive senator lamented, "Taft is a ponderous and amiable man completely surrounded by men who know exactly what they want."

Taft's troubles began on the eve of his inaugural, when he called a special session of Congress to deal with the tariff, which had grown inordinately high under Republican rule. Roosevelt had been too politically astute to tackle the troublesome tariff issue, even though he knew that rates needed to be lowered. Taft blundered into the fray. The House of Representatives passed a modest downward revision and, to make up for lost revenue, imposed a small inheritance tax. Led by Senator Nelson Aldrich of Rhode Island, the conservative Senate struck down the tax and added more than eight hundred crippling amendments to the tariff. The Payne-Aldrich bill that emerged actually raised the tariff, benefiting big business and the trusts at the expense of consumers. As if paralyzed, Taft neither fought for changes nor vetoed the measure. On a tour of the Midwest in 1909, he was greeted with jeers when he claimed, "I think the Payne bill is the best bill that the Republican Party ever passed." In the eyes of a growing number of Americans, Taft's praise of the tariff made him either a fool or a liar.

Taft's legalism soon got him into hot water in the area of conservation. He undid Roosevelt's work to preserve hydroelectric power sites when he learned that they had been improperly designated as ranger stations. And when Gifford Pinchot publicly denounced Taft's secretary of the interior as a tool of western land-grabbers, Taft fired Pinchot, touching off a storm of controversy that damaged Taft and alienated Roosevelt.

When Roosevelt returned to the United States in June 1910, he received a hero's welcome and attracted a stream of visitors and reporters seeking his advice and opinions. Hurt, Taft kept his distance. By late summer, Roosevelt had taken sides with the progressive insurgents in his party. "Taft is utterly hopeless as a leader," Roosevelt confided to his son as he set out on a speaking tour of the West. Reading the mood of the country, Roosevelt began to sound more and more like a candidate.

With the Republican Party divided, the Democrats swept the congressional elections of 1910. Branding the Payne-Aldrich tariff "the mother of trusts," they captured a majority in the House of Representatives and won several key governorships. The revitalized Democratic Party could look to new leaders, among them the progressive governor of New Jersey, Woodrow Wilson.

The new Democratic majority in the House, working with progressive Republicans in the Senate, achieved a number of key reforms, including legislation to regulate mine and railroad safety, to create the Children's Bureau in the Department of Labor, and to establish an eight-hour day for federal workers. Two significant constitutional amendments—the Sixteenth Amendment, which provided for a modest graduated income tax, and the Seventeenth Amendment, which called for the direct election of senators (formerly chosen by state legislatures)—went to the states, where they would win ratification in 1913. While Congress rode the high tide of progressive reform, Taft sat on the sidelines.

In foreign policy, Taft continued Roosevelt's policy of extending U.S. influence abroad, but here, too, Taft had a difficult time following in Roosevelt's footsteps. His policy of "dollar diplomacy" championed commercial goals rather than the strategic aims Roosevelt had pursued. Taft naively assumed he could substitute "dollars for bullets." In the Caribbean, he provoked anti-American feeling by attempting to force commercial treaties on Nicaragua and Honduras and by dispatching U.S. marines to Nicaragua and the Dominican Republic in 1912 pursuant to the Roosevelt Corollary. In Asia, he openly avowed his intent to promote in China "active intervention to secure for . . . our capitalists opportunity for profitable investment." Lacking Roosevelt's understanding of power politics, Taft never recognized that an aggressive commercial policy could not exist without the willingness to use military might to back it up.

Taft faced the limits of dollar diplomacy when revolution broke out in Mexico in 1911. Under pressure to protect American investments, which amounted to more than $4 billion, he mobilized troops along the border. In the end, however, with no popular support for a war with Mexico, he had to fall back on diplomatic pressure to salvage American interests.

Taft hoped to encourage world peace through the use of a world court and arbitration. He unsuccessfully sponsored a series of arbitration treaties that Roosevelt, who prized national honor more than international law, vehemently opposed as weak and cowardly. By 1910, Roosevelt had become a vocal critic of Taft's foreign policy, which he dismissed as "maudlin folly."

The final breach between Taft and Roosevelt came in 1911, when Taft's attorney general filed an antitrust suit against U.S. Steel. In its brief against the corporation, the government cited Roosevelt's agreement with the Morgan interests in the 1907 acquisition of Tennessee Coal and Iron. The incident greatly embarrassed Roosevelt. Thoroughly enraged, he lambasted Taft's "archaic" antitrust policy and hinted that he might be persuaded to run for president again.

Progressive Insurgency and the Election of 1912

In February 1912, Roosevelt challenged Taft for the Republican nomination, announcing, "My hat is in the ring." But for all his popularity, Roosevelt no longer controlled the party machinery. Taft, with uncharacteristic strength, refused to step aside. As he bitterly told a journalist, "Even a rat in a corner will fight." Roosevelt took advantage of newly passed primary election laws and ran in thirteen states, winning 278 delegates to Taft's 48. But at the Chicago convention, Taft's bosses refused to seat the Roosevelt delegates. Fistfights broke out on the convention floor as Taft won nomination on the first ballot. Crying robbery, Roosevelt's supporters bolted the party.

Seven weeks later, in the same Chicago auditorium, the hastily organized Progressive Party met to nominate Roosevelt. Amid a thunder of applause, Jane Addams seconded Roosevelt's nomination. Full of reforming zeal, the delegates chose Roosevelt and Hiram Johnson to head the new party and approved the most ambitious platform since the Populists'. Planks called for woman suffrage, presidential primaries, conservation of natural resources, an end to child labor, a minimum wage that would include women workers, workers' compensation, social security, and a federal income tax.

Roosevelt arrived in Chicago to accept the nomination and announced that he felt "as strong as a bull moose," giving the new party a nickname and a mascot. But for all the excitement and the cheering, the new Progressive Party was doomed, and the candidate knew it. The people may have supported the party, but the politicians, even progressives like La Follette, stayed within the Republican fold. "I am under no illusion about it," Roosevelt confessed to a friend. "It is a forlorn hope." But he had gone too far to turn back. He led the Bull Moose Party into the fray, exhorting his followers in ringing biblical tones, "We shall not falter, we stand at Armageddon and do battle for the Lord."

The Democrats, delighted at the split in the Republican ranks, smelled victory. Their convention turned into a bitter fight for the nomination. After forty-six ballots, Woodrow Wilson became the party's nominee. Wilson's career in politics was nothing short of meteoric. He was elected governor of New Jersey in 1910, and after only eighteen months in office, the former professor of political science and president of Princeton University found himself running for president of the United States.

Voters in 1912 could choose among four candidates who claimed to be progressives. Taft, Roosevelt, and Wilson each embraced the label, and even the Socialist candidate, Eugene V. Debs, styled himself a progressive. That the term *progressive* could stretch to cover these diverse candidates underscored major disagreements in progressive thinking about the relationship between business and government. Taft, in spite of his trust-busting, was generally viewed as the candidate of the old guard. The real contest for the presidency was between Roosevelt and Wilson and the two political philosophies summed up in their respective campaign slogans: "The New Nationalism" and "The New Freedom."

The New Nationalism expressed Roosevelt's belief in federal planning and regulation. He accepted the inevitability of big business but demanded that government act as "a steward of the people" to regulate the giant corporations. Roosevelt called for an increase in the power of the federal government, a decrease in the power of the courts, and an active role for the president. He hoped to use an active federal government to promote social justice and democracy, replacing the laissez-faire policies of the old liberal state with a new form of liberalism.

Wilson, schooled in the Democratic principles of limited government and **states' rights**, set a markedly different course with his New Freedom. Wilson promised to use antitrust legislation to get rid of big corporations and to give small businesses and farmers better opportunities in the marketplace.

Wilson and Roosevelt fought it out, and the energy and enthusiasm of the Bull Moosers made the race seem closer than it really was. In the end, the Republican vote split, while the Democrats remained united. No candidate claimed a majority in the race. Wilson captured a bare 42 percent of the popular vote. Roosevelt and his Bull Moose Party won 27 percent, an unprecedented tally for a new party. Taft came in third with 23 percent. The Socialist Party, led by Debs, captured 6 percent. In the electoral college, however, Wilson won a decisive 435 votes, with 88 going to Roosevelt and only 8 to Taft. The Progressive Party essentially collapsed after Roosevelt's defeat. It had always been, in the words of one astute observer, "a house divided against itself and already mortgaged."

▶ **REVIEW**   Why did Roosevelt become the presidential nominee of the Progressive Party in 1912?

Woodrow Wilson and Progressivism at High Tide

Born in Virginia and raised in Georgia, Woodrow Wilson became the first southerner to be elected president since 1844 and only the second Democrat to occupy the White House since Reconstruction. Democrats who anticipated a wild celebration when Wilson took office had their hopes dashed. The son of a Presbyterian minister, Wilson was a teetotaler more given to Scripture than to celebration. He called instead for a day of prayer.

This lean, ascetic scholar was, as one biographer conceded, a man whose "political convictions were never as fixed as his ambition." Although he owed his governorship to the Democratic machine, he quickly turned his back on the bosses and put New Jersey in the vanguard of progressivism. A year into his term, Wilson had his eye on the presidency. Always able to equivocate, Wilson proved rarely able to compromise. He brought to the White House a gift for oratory, a stern will, and a set of fixed beliefs. His tendency to turn differences of opinion into personal hatreds would impair his leadership and damage his presidency. Fortunately for Wilson, he came to power with a Democratic Congress eager to do his bidding.

Although he opposed big government in his campaign, Wilson was prepared to work on the base built by Roosevelt to strengthen presidential power, exerting leadership to achieve banking reform and working through his party in Congress to accomplish the Democratic agenda. Before he was finished, Wilson presided over progressivism at high tide and lent his support not only to the platform of the Democratic Party but to many of the Progressive Party's social reforms as well.

Wilson's Reforms: Tariff, Banking, and the Trusts

In March 1913, Wilson showed off his oratorical ability by becoming the first president since John Adams to go to Capitol Hill and speak directly to Congress. With the Democratic Party firmly in control, he called for tariff reform. "The object of the tariff," Wilson told Congress, "must be effective competition." Eager to topple the high tariff, the Democratic House of Representatives hastily passed the Underwood tariff, which lowered rates by 15 percent. To compensate for lost revenue, the House approved a moderate federal income tax, made possible by ratification of the Sixteenth Amendment a month earlier. In the Senate, lobbyists for industries quietly went to work to get the tariff raised, but Wilson rallied public opinion by attacking the "industrious and insidious lobby." In the harsh glare of publicity, the Senate passed the Underwood tariff, which earned praise as "the most honest tariff since the Civil War."

Wilson next turned his attention to banking. The panic of 1907 dramatically testified to the failure of the banking system. That year, Roosevelt, like President Grover Cleveland before him, had to turn to J. P. Morgan to avoid economic catastrophe. But by the time Wilson came to office, Morgan's legendary power had come under close scrutiny. In 1913, a Senate committee investigated the "money trust," calling J. P. Morgan himself to testify. The committee uncovered an alarming concentration of banking power. J. P. Morgan and Company and its affiliates held 341 directorships in 112 corporations, controlling assets of more than $22 billion ($457 billion in today's dollars). The sensational findings created a mandate for banking reform.

The Federal Reserve Act of 1913 marked the most significant piece of domestic legislation of Wilson's presidency. It established a national banking system composed of twelve regional banks, privately controlled but regulated and supervised by the Federal Reserve Board, appointed by the president. It gave the United States its first efficient banking and currency system and, at the same time, provided for a greater degree of government control over banking. The new system made currency more elastic and credit adequate for the needs of business and agriculture. It did not, however, attempt to take control of the boom and bust cycles in the U.S. economy, which would produce the Great Depression of the 1930s.

Wilson, flushed with success, tackled the trust issue next. When Congress reconvened in January 1914, he supported the introduction of the Clayton Antitrust Act to outlaw "unfair competition"—practices such as price discrimination and interlocking directorates (directors from one corporation sitting on the board of another). By spelling out unfair practices, Wilson hoped to guide business activity back to healthy competition without resorting to regulation. Despite a grandiose preamble that stated, "The labor of human beings is not a commodity or article of commerce," the Clayton Act did not improve labor's position. Although AFL president Samuel Gompers hailed the act as the "Magna Carta of labor," the conservative courts continued to issue injunctions and to use antitrust legislation against labor unions.

In the midst of the fight for the Clayton Act, Wilson changed course and threw his support behind the creation of the Federal Trade Commission (FTC), precisely the kind of federal regulatory agency that Roosevelt had advocated in his New Nationalism platform. The FTC, created in 1914, had not only wide investigatory powers but the authority to prosecute corporations for "unfair trade practices" and to enforce its judgments by issuing "cease and desist" orders. Despite his campaign promises, Wilson's antitrust program worked to regulate rather than to break up big business.

By the fall of 1914, Wilson had exhausted the stock of ideas that made up the New Freedom. He alarmed progressives by declaring that the progressive movement had fulfilled its mission and that the country needed "a time of healing." Disgruntled progressives also disapproved of Wilson's conservative appointments. Having fought provisions in the Federal Reserve Act that would give bankers control, Wilson promptly named a banker as the first chief of the Federal Reserve Board. Appointments to the new FTC also went to conservative businessmen. The progressive penchant for expertise helps explain Wilson's choices. Believing that experts in the field could best understand the complex issues at stake, Wilson appointed bankers to oversee the banks and businessmen to regulate business.

Wilson, Reluctant Progressive

Progressives watched in dismay as Wilson repeatedly obstructed or obstinately refused to endorse further progressive reforms. He failed to support labor's demand for an end to court injunctions against labor unions. He twice threatened to veto legislation providing farm credits for nonperishable crops. He refused to support child labor legislation or woman suffrage. Wilson used the rhetoric of the New Freedom to justify his actions, claiming that his administration would condone "special privileges to none." But, in fact, his stance often reflected the interests of his small-business constituency.

In the face of Wilson's obstinacy, reform might have ended in 1913 had not politics intruded. In the congressional elections of 1914, the Republican Party, no longer split by Roosevelt's Bull Moose faction, won substantial gains. Democratic strategists, with their eyes on the 1916 presidential race, recognized that Wilson needed to pick up support in the Midwest and the West by capturing votes from former Bull Moose progressives.

Wilson responded belatedly by lending his support to reform in the months leading up to the election of 1916. In a sharp about-face, he cultivated union labor, farmers, and social reformers. To please labor, he appointed progressive Louis Brandeis to the Supreme Court. To woo farmers, he threw his support behind legislation to obtain rural credits. And he won praise from labor by supporting workers' compensation and the Keating-Owen child labor law (1916), which outlawed the regular employment of children younger than sixteen. When a railroad strike threatened in the months before the election, Wilson practically ordered Congress to establish an eight-hour day on the railroads. He had moved a long way from his position in 1912 to embrace many of the social reforms championed

Progressive Poster Condemning Child Labor

This poster attacks child labor, using a flowchart to show how industries employing children were "making human junk." Progressives' concern for poor children won them the label "child savers." Although activists worked to pass the Keating-Owen Act prohibiting child labor in 1916, the Supreme Court declared the law unconstitutional on the grounds that Congress had no right to regulate manufacturing within states.

Library of Congress.

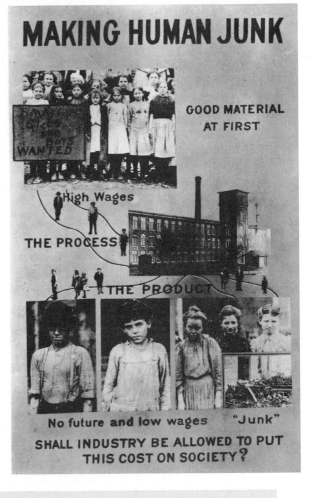

by Theodore Roosevelt. As Wilson boasted, the Democrats had "opened their hearts to the demands of social justice" and had "come very near to carrying out the platform of the Progressive Party." Wilson's shift toward reform, along with his claim that he had kept the United States out of the war in Europe (see chapter 22), helped him win reelection in 1916.

▶ REVIEW How and why did Wilson's reform program evolve during his first term?

The Limits of Progressive Reform

While progressivism called for a more active role for the liberal state, at heart it was a movement that sought reforms designed to preserve American institutions and stem the tide of more radical change. Its basic conservatism can be seen by comparing it to more radical movements of the era—socialism, radical labor, and birth control—and by looking at the groups progressive reform left behind, including women and African Americans.

Radical Alternatives

The year 1900 marked the birth of the Social Democratic Party in America, later called simply the Socialist Party. Like the progressives, the socialists were middle-class and native-born. They had broken with the older, more militant Socialist Labor Party precisely because of its dogmatic approach and immigrant constituency. The new group of socialists proved eager to appeal to a broad mass of disaffected Americans. Socialists elected mayors in Schenectady and Milwaukee, and by 1912 the party counted more than 100,000 members.

The Socialist Party chose as its presidential standard-bearer Eugene V. Debs, whose experience in the Pullman strike of 1894 convinced him that "there is no hope for the toiling masses of my countrymen, except by the pathways mapped out by Socialism." Debs would run for president five times, in every election (except 1916) from 1900 to 1920. The socialism Debs advocated preached cooperation over competition and urged men and women to liberate themselves from "the barbarism of private ownership and wage slavery." Roosevelt labeled Debs a "mere inciter to murder and preacher of applied anarchy." Debs, for his part, pointed to the conservatism that underlay Roosevelt's rhetoric. In the 1912 election, Debs indicted both old parties as "Tweedledee and Tweedledum," each dedicated to the preservation of capitalism and the continuation of the wage system. Only through socialism, he argued, could democracy exist. Styling the Socialist Party the "revolutionary party of the working class," he urged voters to rally to his standard. Debs's best showing came in 1912, when he polled 6 percent of the popular vote, capturing more than 900,000 votes.

Farther to the left of the socialists stood the Industrial Workers of the World (IWW), nicknamed the Wobblies. In 1905, Debs, along with Western Federation of Miners leader William Dudley "Big Bill" Haywood, created the IWW, "one big union" dedicated to organizing the most destitute segment of the workforce, the unskilled workers disdained by Samuel Gompers's AFL: western miners, migrant farmworkers, lumbermen, and immigrant textile workers. Haywood, a craggy-faced miner with one eye (he had lost the other in a childhood accident), was a charismatic leader and a proletarian intellectual. Seeing workers on the lowest rung of the social ladder as the victims of violent repression, the IWW unhesitatingly advocated direct action, sabotage, and the general strike—tactics designed to trigger a workers' uprising. The IWW never had more than 10,000 members at any one time, although possibly as many as 100,000 workers belonged to the union at one time or another in the early twentieth century. Nevertheless, the IWW's influence on the country extended far beyond its numbers.

In contrast to political radicals like Debs and Haywood, Margaret Sanger promoted birth control as a movement for social change. Sanger, a nurse who had worked among the poor on New York's Lower East Side, coined the term *birth control* in 1915 and launched a movement with broad social implications. Sanger and her followers saw birth control not only as a sexual and medical reform but also as a means to alter social and political power relationships and to alleviate human misery.

The desire for family limitation was widespread, and in this sense, birth control was nothing new. The birthrate in the United States had been falling

Margaret Sanger's Brownsville Birth Control Clinic
Margaret Sanger opened the first birth control clinic in the United States in the Brownsville section of Brooklyn in 1916. During the nine days it operated before police shut it down, more than four hundred women visited the clinic. Here, they are shown waiting patiently in line with their baby carriages.
Sophia Smith Collection, Smith College.

consistently throughout the nineteenth century. The average number of children per family dropped from 7.0 in 1800 to 3.6 by 1900. But the open advocacy of *contraception*, the use of artificial means to prevent pregnancy, struck many people as both new and shocking. And it was illegal. Anthony Comstock, New York City's commissioner of vice, promoted laws in the 1870s making it a felony not only to sell contraceptive devices like condoms and cervical caps but also to publish information on how to prevent pregnancy. Labeling birth control "obscene matter" meant the Post Office could seize and censor any article or pamphlet promoting birth control. Theodore Roosevelt was among those who fulminated against birth control as "race suicide," warning that the "white" population was declining while immigrants and "undesirables" continued to breed.

Convinced that women needed to be able to control their pregnancies but unsure of the best methods to do so, Sanger traveled to Europe in 1913 to learn more about contraceptive techniques. On her return, she promoted birth control in her militant **feminist** newspaper, the *Woman Rebel*. On the masthead in bold letters she proclaimed her motto: "No Gods, No Masters." The Post Office confiscated Sanger's publication and brought charges against her. Facing arrest, she fled to Europe, only to return in 1916 something of a national celebrity. In her absence, birth control had become linked with free speech and had been taken up as a liberal cause. Under public pressure, the government dropped the charges against Sanger, who undertook a nationwide tour to publicize the birth control cause.

Sanger then turned to direct action, opening the nation's first birth control clinic in the Brownsville section of Brooklyn in October 1916. Located in the heart of a Jewish and Italian immigrant neighborhood, the clinic attracted 464 clients in the nine days it remained open. On the tenth day, police shut down the clinic and threw Sanger in jail. By then, she had become a national figure, and the cause she championed had gained legitimacy, if not legality. After World War I, the birth control movement would become much less radical as Sanger turned to medical doctors for support and mouthed the racist theories of the eugenics movement. But in its infancy, the movement Sanger led was part of a radical vision for reforming the world that made common cause with the socialists and the IWW in challenging the limits of progressive reform.

Progressivism for White Men Only

The day before President Woodrow Wilson's inauguration in March 1913, the largest mass march to date in the nation's history took place as more than five thousand demonstrators took to the streets in Washington to demand the vote for women. A rowdy crowd on hand to celebrate the Democrats' triumph attacked the marchers. Men spat at the suffragists and threw lighted cigarettes and matches at their clothing. "If my wife were where you are," a burly cop told one suffragist, "I'd break her head." But for all the marching, Wilson, who didn't believe that a "lady" should vote, pointedly ignored woman suffrage in his inaugural address the next day.

The march served as a reminder that the political gains of progressivism were not spread equally throughout the population. As the twentieth century dawned, women still could not vote in most states, although they had won major victories in the West. Increasingly, however, woman suffrage had become an international movement. In Great Britain, Emmeline Pankhurst and her daughters Cristabel and Sylvia promoted a new, militant suffragism. They seized the spotlight in a series of marches, mass meetings, and acts of **civil disobedience**, which sometimes escalated into riots, violence, and arson.

Alice Paul, a Quaker social worker who had visited England and participated in suffrage activism there, returned to the United States in 1910 in time to plan the mass march on the eve of Wilson's inauguration and to lobby for a federal amendment to give women the vote. Paul's dramatic tactics alienated many in the National American Woman Suffrage Association (NAWSA). In 1916, Paul founded the militant National Woman's Party (NWP), which became the radical voice of the suffrage movement, advocating direct action such as mass marches and civil disobedience.

The NAWSA, spurred by the actions of Paul and her followers, gained new direction after Carrie Chapman Catt became president in 1915. Catt revitalized the organization with a carefully crafted "winning plan" designed to achieve suffrage in six years. While Paul and her NWP held a six-month vigil outside the White House—holding banners that read "Mr. Wilson, What Will You Do for Woman Suffrage?"—Catt led a centrally directed effort that worked on several levels. Catt's strategy was to "keep so much 'suffrage noise' going all over the country that neither the enemy [n]or friends will discover where the real battle is." Catt's "winning plan" worked. It took only four years instead of the six Catt had predicted to obtain ratification of the Nineteenth Amendment granting woman suffrage.

Women weren't the only group left out in progressive reform. Progressivism, as it was practiced in the West and South, was tainted with racism and sought to limit the rights of African and Asian Americans. Anti-Asian bigotry in the West led to a renewal of the Chinese Exclusion Act in 1902. At first, California governor Hiram Johnson stood against the strong anti-Asian prejudice of his state. Then, in 1913, he caved in to near-unanimous pressure and signed the Alien Land Law, which barred Japanese immigrants from purchasing land in California. The law was largely symbolic—ineffectual in practice because Japanese children born in the United States were U.S. citizens and property could be purchased in their names.

South of the Mason-Dixon line, the progressives' racism targeted African Americans. Progressives preached the **disfranchisement** of black voters as a "reform." During the bitter electoral fights that had pitted Populists against Democrats in the 1890s, the party of white supremacy held its power by votes purchased or coerced from African Americans. Southern progressives proposed to "reform" the electoral system by eliminating black voters. Beginning in 1890 with Mississippi, southern states curtailed the African American vote through devices such as poll taxes (fees required for voting) and literacy tests. The racist intent of southern voting legislation became especially clear after 1900 when states resorted to the grandfather clause, a legal provision that allowed men who failed a literacy test to vote if their grandfathers had cast a ballot. Grandfathering permitted southern white men to vote while excluding blacks.

The Progressive Era also witnessed the rise of **Jim Crow** laws to segregate public facilities. The new railroads precipitated segregation in the South where it had rarely existed before, at least on paper. Blacks traveling by train found themselves restricted to Jim Crow coaches even when they paid the first-class fare. Soon, separate waiting rooms, separate bathrooms, and separate dining facilities for blacks sprang up across the South. In courtrooms in Mississippi, blacks were even required to swear on a separate Bible.

In the face of this growing repression, Booker T. Washington, the preeminent black leader of the day, urged caution and restraint. A former slave, Washington had opened the Tuskegee Institute in Alabama in 1881 to teach vocational skills to African Americans. He emphasized education and economic progress for his race and urged African Americans to put aside issues of political and social equality. In an 1895 speech in Atlanta, which came to be known as the "Atlanta Compromise," he stated, "In all things that are purely social we can be as separate as the fingers, yet one as the hand in all things essential to mutual progress." Washington's accommodationist policy appealed to whites and elevated "the wizard of Tuskegee" to the role of national spokesman for African Americans.

The year after Washington proclaimed the Atlanta Compromise, the Supreme Court upheld the legality of racial segregation, affirming in *Plessy v. Ferguson* (1896) the constitutionality of the doctrine of "separate but equal." Blacks could be segregated in separate schools, restrooms, and other facilities, as long as the facilities were "equal" to those provided for whites. In actuality, facilities for blacks rarely proved equal. In the North, where racism of a different sort led to a clamor for legislation to restrict immigration, support for African American equality found few advocates. And with anti-Asian bigotry strong in the West, the doctrine of "white supremacy" found increasing support in all sections of the country.

When Theodore Roosevelt invited Booker T. Washington to dine at the White House in 1901, a storm of racist criticism erupted. One southern editor fumed that the White House "had been painted black." But Roosevelt summoned Washington to talk politics and patronage, not African American rights. Roosevelt's unquestioned racial prejudice became obvious in the Brownsville incident in 1906, when he dishonorably discharged an entire battalion of 167 black soldiers because he suspected (although there was no proof) that they were shielding the murderer of a white saloonkeeper killed in a shoot-out in the Texas town.

Woodrow Wilson brought to the White House southern attitudes toward race and racial segregation. He instituted segregation in the federal workforce, especially the Post Office, and approved segregated drinking fountains and restrooms in the nation's capital. When critics attacked the policy, Wilson insisted that segregation was "in the interest of the Negro."

A major race riot in Atlanta in 1906 called into question Booker T. Washington's strategy of uplift and accommodation. For three days in September, the streets of Atlanta ran red with blood as angry white mobs chased and cornered any blacks they happened upon, pulling passengers from streetcars and invading black neighborhoods to kill and loot. An estimated 250 African Americans died in the riots—members of Atlanta's black middle class along with the poor and derelict. Professor William Crogman of Clark College noted the central irony of the riot: "Here we have worked and prayed and tried to make good men and women of our colored population," he observed, "and at our very doorstep the whites kill these good men." In Dark Town, a working-class neighborhood, blacks fought back to defend their homes, shooting into the white mob and driving off the attackers. In the aftermath of the riot, the city's leaders, black and white, managed to quash any nascent black unity by falling back on the old strategy of allying "the best white people and the best colored people" in the interest of peace and prosperity. But the riot caused many African Americans to question Washington's strategy of gradualism and accommodation.

Foremost among Washington's critics stood W. E. B. Du Bois, a Harvard graduate who urged African Americans to fight for civil rights and racial justice. In *The Souls of Black Folk* (1903), Du Bois attacked the "Tuskegee Machine," comparing Washington to a political boss who used his influence to silence his critics and reward his followers. Du Bois founded the Niagara movement in 1905, calling for universal male suffrage, civil rights, and leadership by a black intellectual elite. The Atlanta riot only bolstered his resolve. In 1909, the Niagara movement helped found the National Association for the Advancement of Colored People (NAACP), a coalition of blacks and whites that sought legal and political rights for African Americans through the courts. Like many progressive reform coalitions, the NAACP attracted a diverse group—social workers, socialists, and black intellectuals. In the decades that followed, the NAACP came to represent the future for African Americans, while Booker T. Washington, who died in 1915, represented the past.

▶**REVIEW**   How did race, class, and gender shape the limits of progressive reform?

Conclusion: The Transformation of the Liberal State

Progressivism was never a radical movement. Its goal remained to reform the existing system—by government intervention if necessary, but without uprooting any of the traditional American political, economic, or social institutions. As Theodore Roosevelt, the bellwether of the movement, insisted, "The only true conservative is the man who resolutely sets his face toward the future." Roosevelt was such a man, and progressivism was such a movement. But although progressivism was never radical, neither was it the laissez-faire liberalism of the previous century. Progressives' willingness to use the power of government to regulate business and achieve a measure of social justice redefined liberalism in the twentieth century, tying it to the expanded power of the state.

Progressivism contained many paradoxes. A diverse coalition of individuals and interests, the progressive movement began at the grass roots but left as its legacy a stronger presidency and unprecedented federal involvement in the economy and social welfare. A movement that believed in social justice, progressivism often promoted social control. And while progressives called for greater democracy, they fostered elitism with their worship of experts and efficiency.

Whatever its inconsistencies and limitations, progressivism took action to deal with the problems posed by urban industrialism. Progressivism saw grass-roots activists address social problems on the local and state levels and search for national solutions. By increasing the power of the presidency and expanding the power of the state, progressives worked to bring about greater social justice and to achieve a better balance between government and business. Jane Addams and Theodore Roosevelt could lay equal claim to the movement that redefined liberalism and launched the liberal state of the twentieth century. War on a global scale would provide progressivism with yet another challenge even before it had completed its ambitious agenda.

REVIEWING THE CHAPTER

Use the questions and timeline to review and strengthen your understanding of the chapter.

REVIEW QUESTIONS

1. What types of people were drawn to the progressive movement, and what motivated them? (pp. 650–55)

2. How did progressives justify their demand for more activist government? (pp. 655–58)

3. How did Roosevelt's foreign policy move the United States onto the world stage? (pp. 658–68)

4. Why did Roosevelt become the presidential nominee of the Progressive Party in 1912? (pp. 668–72)

5. How and why did Wilson's reform program evolve during his first term? (pp. 672–75)

6. How did race, class, and gender shape the limits of progressive reform? (pp. 675–81)

MAKING CONNECTIONS

1. Diverse approaches to reform came under the umbrella of progressivism. Discuss the work of three progressive reformers working at the grassroots or local government level. What do your examples reveal about progressivism? What characteristics connected their reform efforts? What separated them?

2. During the Gilded Age, industrial capitalism concentrated power in the hands of corporations. Americans searched for ways to shift the balance, including strikes, antitrust actions, and regulation. How did Theodore Roosevelt attempt to respond to this problem? How did his approach differ from earlier efforts? Was it effective?

3. Opponents on the campaign stump, Theodore Roosevelt and Woodrow Wilson shared a commitment to domestic reform. Compare their legislative programs, including the evolution of their policies over time and their ability to respond to shifting political circumstances. What do their policies reveal about their understandings of the roles of the executive and the federal government?

4. What contemporary movements lay beyond the limits of progressive reform? Why did progressive reform coincide with the restriction of minority rights? In your answer, discuss how radical movements provide insights into the character of progressivism itself.

TIMELINE

1889	• Jane Addams opens Hull House.	**1908**	• *Muller v. Oregon.* • Republican William Howard Taft elected president.
1895	• Booker T. Washington enunciates Atlanta Compromise.	**1909**	• Garment workers' strike in New York City. • National Association for the Advancement of Colored People (NAACP) formed.
1896	• *Plessy v. Ferguson.*		
1900	• Socialist Party founded.		
1901	• William McKinley assassinated; Theodore Roosevelt becomes president.	**1910**	• Hiram Johnson elected governor of California.
1902	• Antitrust lawsuit filed against Northern Securities Company. • Roosevelt mediates anthracite coal strike. • Newlands Reclamation Act.	**1911**	• Triangle fire in New York City. • Taft launches antitrust suit against U.S. Steel.
1903	• Women's Trade Union League founded. • United States begins construction of Panama Canal. • Elkins Act.	**1912**	• Roosevelt runs for president on Progressive Party ticket. • Democrat Woodrow Wilson elected president.
1904	• Roosevelt Corollary to Monroe Doctrine.	**1913**	• Suffragists march in Washington, D.C. • Federal Reserve Act.
1905	• Industrial Workers of the World founded. • W. E. B. Du Bois founds Niagara movement. • Roosevelt mediates at Algeciras conference.	**1914**	• Federal Trade Commission (FTC) created. • Clayton Antitrust Act.
1906	• Pure Food and Drug Act and Meat Inspection Act. • Atlanta race riot. • Hepburn Act.	**1916**	• Alice Paul launches National Woman's Party. • Margaret Sanger opens first U.S. birth control clinic. • Keating-Owen child labor law.
1907	• Panic on Wall Street. • Roosevelt signs "Gentlemen's Agreement" with Japan restricting immigration.	**1918**	• Supreme Court declares Keating-Owen unconstitutional.

▶ **For an online bibliography, practice quizzes, Web sites, images, and documents related to this chapter,** see the Book Companion Site at **bedfordstmartins.com/roark.**

▶ **For firsthand accounts of this period,** see Chapter 21 in Michael Johnson, ed., *Reading the American Past,* Fourth Edition.

22

CHAPTER

World War I:
The Progressive Crusade
at Home and Abroad

1914–1920

WHEN THE UNITED STATES entered World War I against Germany and its allies in 1917, it had neither a grand army nor a commander to lead one. But President Woodrow Wilson quickly tapped Major General John "Black Jack" Pershing, a ramrod-straight West Point graduate, to command the American Expeditionary Force (AEF) on the battlefields of France. Pershing had much to recommend him: He fought Apaches in the West in the 1880s, led a company of African American soldiers up San Juan Hill in Cuba in 1898 (hence his nickname "Black Jack"), overcame fierce resistance in the Philippine jungles in the first decade of the twentieth century, and headed Wilson's Punitive Expedition into Mexico in 1916 and 1917 in pursuit of the revolutionary bandit Pancho Villa. Pershing's courage and resilience had been severely tested in 1915 when he suffered the devastating loss of his wife and three daughters in a fire at their home in San Francisco.

On June 13, 1917, Pershing and his officer corps arrived in war-weary France, where huge crowds shouted "Vive l'Amérique!" and greeted the Americans as saviors. But Pershing knew that it would be months before America's disorganized war effort succeeded in supplying a steady stream of "doughboys," as American troops would be called. Pershing, who was responsible for organizing, training, and supplying this inexperienced force that eventually numbered two million,

Pershing Button
Steely-eyed and determined, General John J. Pershing, surrounded by the flags of the Allied nations, stares out at the viewer. The words circling the button declare that the Allies are "united in the cause of liberty," echoing President Woodrow Wilson's insistence that American democratic ideals were universal and could be achieved internationally through U.S. participation in the war. Collection of Janice L. and David J. Frent.

put his own stamp on the AEF. "The standards for the American Army will be those of West Point," he announced. "The upright bearing, attention to detail, uncomplaining obedience to instruction required of the cadet will be required of every officer and soldier of our armies in France." Hard and relentless, Pershing more than once chewed out an exhausted soldier for having mud on his boots and his collar unbuttoned.

Pershing found himself waging two wars, one against the Germans and the other against America's allies, as he constantly rebuffed French and British efforts to feed his fresh soldiers into their decimated and demoralized armies. Having seen too much of Europe's trench warfare, where enemies dug in, pounded one another with artillery, and squandered thousands of lives in hopeless assaults, Pershing insisted on keeping U.S. soldiers under his own command. He believed that the Americans could break the impasse by relying on the rifle and rapid-movement tactics taught at West Point to create "open warfare," an American style of warfare. But as a disgusted British journalist observed, "After eight months . . . you haven't really fired a damned shot!"

By the summer of 1918, when the Allied armies began preparing a massive attack against the Germans, Ferdinand Foch, head of the French army, rushed to Pershing's headquarters to "insist" once again that U.S. troops merge with his depleted divisions. Pershing responded: "Marshal Foch, you may insist all you please, but . . . our army will fight . . . only as an independent American Army." Foch stormed out, and Pershing readied his army to strike at the German forces dug in at St.-Mihiel and to begin what he was certain would be a victory march to Berlin. Assembling his officers, Pershing praised them for what they were about to do— break the stalemate of trench warfare. But U.S. troops met a storm of machine-gun and artillery fire, and it took forty days and 100,000 casualties for the Americans to reach the German border, something Pershing had thought his soldiers could do in a few days. Nevertheless, fresh American troops helped destroy the German will to continue the war. In November 1918, Berlin asked for an immediate armistice, and the "Great War," as participants called the conflict, ended.

Pershing's stubborn effort to protect the autonomy of his army was only part of the United States' tortuous struggle to identify its interests in World War I and to maintain its national independence. When Wilson entered the White House, he believed that war was an affliction that modern diplomacy would eventually eradicate. He proclaimed America's absolute neutrality when war erupted in Europe in 1914. By standing apart, Wilson explained, America could offer "impartial mediation" and broker a healing peace. But trade and principle soon entangled the United States in Europe's troubles. When the nation was finally drawn into the war in 1917, Wilson sought to maintain America's grand purpose. Clinging to his battered ideals, he hoped that America's participation would uplift both the United States and the entire world.

At home, the war helped reformers finally achieve their goals of national prohibition and woman **suffrage**, but it also promoted a vicious attack on Americans' civil liberties. Hyperpatriotism meant intolerance, repression, and vigilante violence. Overseas, Pershing's troops helped win the war in 1918, and in 1919 Wilson sailed for Europe to secure a just peace. Unable to dictate a settlement to the victors, Wilson accepted disappointing compromises. Upon his return to the United States, he met a crushing defeat that marked the end of Wilsonian internationalism. Crackdowns on dissenters, immigrants, racial and ethnic minorities, and unions signaled the end of the **Progressive** Era at home.

Woodrow Wilson and the World

Shortly after winning election to the presidency in 1912, Woodrow Wilson confided to a friend: "It would be an irony of fate if my administration had to deal with foreign affairs." Indeed, Wilson had focused his life and career on domestic concerns, seldom venturing far from home and traveling abroad only on brief vacations. As president of Princeton University and then governor of New Jersey, he had remained rooted in local affairs. In his campaign for the presidency, Wilson spoke passionately about domestic reform but hardly mentioned foreign affairs.

But Wilson could not avoid the world and the rising tide of militarism, **nationalism**, and violence that beat against American shores. Economic interests compelled the nation outward. Moreover, Wilson was drawn abroad by his own progressive political principles. He believed that the United States had a moral duty to champion national self-determination, peaceful free trade, and political **democracy**. "We have no selfish ends to serve," he proclaimed. "We desire no conquest, no dominion. . . . We are but one of the champions of the rights of mankind." Yet as president, Wilson revealed he was as ready as any American president to apply military solutions to problems of foreign policy.

Taming the Americas

When he took office, Wilson sought to distinguish his foreign policy from that of his Republican predecessors. To Wilson, Theodore Roosevelt's "big stick" and William Howard Taft's "dollar diplomacy" appeared a crude flexing of military and economic muscle. To signal a new direction, Wilson appointed William Jennings Bryan as secretary of state. A pacifist on religious grounds, Bryan immediately turned his attention to making agreements with thirty nations for the peaceful settlement of disputes.

But Wilson and Bryan, like Roosevelt and Taft, also believed that the **Monroe Doctrine** gave the United States special rights and responsibilities in the Western Hemisphere. Issued in 1823 to warn Europeans not to attempt to **colonize** the New World again, the doctrine had become a cloak for U.S. domination. Wilson thus authorized the 1912 occupation of Nicaragua by U.S. marines to thwart a radical revolution that threatened property owned by U.S. businesses. In 1915, he sent marines into Haiti to quell lawlessness and to protect U.S. interests, and in 1916 he followed a similar course in the Dominican Republic. Throughout the Western Hemisphere, U.S. military intervention paved the way for the financial domination of stateside banks and corporations. All the while, Wilson believed that U.S. actions were promoting order and democracy. "I am going to teach the South American Republics to elect good men!" he declared. He did not mention protecting the Panama Canal and U.S. investments.

Wilson's most serious involvement in Latin America came in Mexico. When General Victoriano Huerta seized power by violent means, most European nations promptly recognized Mexico's new government, but Wilson refused, declaring that he would not support a "government of butchers." In April 1914, when Huerta refused to apologize for briefly detaining American sailors in Tampico, Wilson sent 800 marines to seize the port of Veracruz to prevent the unloading of a large shipment of arms for Huerta, who was by then involved in a civil war of his own. Huerta fled to Spain, and the United States welcomed a more compliant government.

Wilson was not able to subdue Mexico that easily, however. A rebellion erupted among desperately poor farmers who believed that the new government of Venustiano Carranza, aided by U.S. business interests, had betrayed the revolution's promise to help the common people. In January 1916, the rebel army, commanded by Francisco "Pancho" Villa, seized a train carrying gold to Texas from an American-owned mine in Mexico and killed the 17 American engineers aboard. On March 9, a band of some 400 to 500 of Villa's men crossed the border for a predawn raid on Columbus, New Mexico. They stayed for less than two hours, but they burned much of Columbus and killed 18 Americans. Wilson promptly dispatched 12,000 troops, led by General John J. Pershing. The wily Villa avoided capture, and in January 1917, Wilson recalled Pershing so that he might prepare the army for the possibility of fighting in the Great War.

The European Crisis

Before 1914, Europe had enjoyed decades of peace, but just beneath the surface lay the potentially destructive forces of nationalism and **imperialism**. The consolidation of the German and Italian states into unified nations and the similar ambition of Russia to create a "Pan-Slavic" union initiated new rivalries throughout Europe. As the conviction spread that colonial possessions were a mark of national greatness, competition expanded onto the world stage. Most ominously, Germany's efforts under Kaiser Wilhelm II to challenge Great Britain's world supremacy by creating industrial muscle at home, an empire abroad, and a mighty navy threatened the balance of power and thus the peace.

European nations sought to avoid an explosion with a complex web of military and diplomatic alliances. By 1914, Germany, Austria-Hungary, and Italy (the Triple Alliance) stood opposed to Great Britain, France, and Russia (the Triple Entente, also known as "the Allies"). But in their effort to prevent war through a balance of power, Europeans had actually magnified the possibility of large-scale conflict by creating trip wires along the boundaries of two heavily armed power blocs (Map 22.1). Treaties, some of them secret, obligated members of the alliances to come to the aid of another member if attacked.

MAP 22.1   European Alliances after the Outbreak of World War I
With Germany and Austria-Hungary wedged between their Entente rivals and all parties fully armed, Europe was poised for war when Archduke Franz Ferdinand of Austria-Hungary was assassinated in Sarajevo in June 1914.

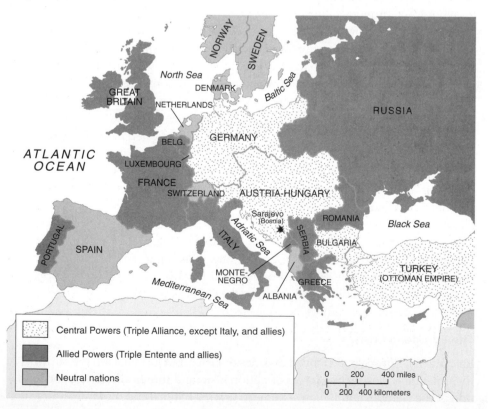

The fatal sequence began on June 28, 1914, in the Bosnian city of Sarajevo, when a Bosnian Serb terrorist assassinated Archduke Franz Ferdinand, heir to the Austro-Hungarian throne. On July 18, Austria-Hungary declared war on Serbia, holding it accountable for the killing. The elaborate **alliance system** meant that the war could not remain local. Russia announced that it would back the Serbs. Compelled by treaty to support Austria-Hungary, Germany on August 3 attacked Russia and France. In response, on August 4, Great Britain, upholding its pact with France, declared war on Germany. Within weeks, Europe was engulfed in war. The conflict became a world war when Japan, seeing an opportunity to rid itself of European competition in China, joined the cause against Germany.

Recognizing that war would devastate the civilization he knew, Britain's foreign secretary, Edward Grey, announced sadly: "The lamps are going out all over Europe. We shall not see them lit again in our lifetime." Indeed, the evenly matched alliances would fight a long and bloody war lasting more than four years, at a cost of 8.5 million soldiers' lives—an entire generation of young men. A war that started with a solitary murder proved impossible to stop.

The Ordeal of American Neutrality

Woodrow Wilson promptly announced that the war was purely a European matter. Because it engaged no vital American interest and involved no significant principle, he said, the United States would remain neutral and continue normal relations with the warring nations. America had traditionally insisted that "free ships made free goods"—that neutral nations were entitled to trade safely with all nations at war and to demand the safe passage of their citizens on the merchant and passenger ships of all belligerents. But more was involved than lofty principle. In the year before Europe went to war, the U.S. economy had slipped into a recession that wartime disruption of European trade could drastically worsen.

Although Wilson proclaimed neutrality, his sympathies, like those of many Americans, lay with Great Britain and France. Americans remembered gratefully crucial French assistance in the American Revolution. And they shared with the British a language, a **culture**, and a commitment to **liberty**. Germany, in contrast, was a monarchy with strong militaristic traditions. The British portrayed the German ruler, Kaiser Wilhelm II, as personally responsible for the war's atrocities, and before long American newspapers were labeling him "the Mad Dog of Europe" and "the Beast of Berlin." Still, Wilson insisted on neutrality, in part because he feared the conflict's effects on the United States as a nation of immigrants, millions of whom had only recently come from countries now at war. As he told the German ambassador, "We definitely have to be neutral, since otherwise our mixed populations would wage war on each other."

Britain's powerful fleet controlled the seas and quickly set up an economic blockade of Germany. The United States vigorously protested, but Britain refused to give up its naval advantage. The blockade actually had little economic impact on the United States. Between 1914 and the spring of 1917, while trade with Germany evaporated, war-related exports to Britain—food, clothing, steel, and munitions—escalated by some 400 percent, enough to pull the American economy out of its prewar slump. Although the British blockade bruised American feelings and clearly violated American neutrality, the Wilson administration gradually and reluctantly acquiesced, thus beginning the fateful process of alienation from Germany.

Germany retaliated with a submarine blockade of British ports. This terrifying new form of combat by *Unterseebooten*, or U-boats, threatened traditional rules of war. Unlike surface warships that could harmlessly stop freighters and prevent them from entering a war zone, submarines relied on surprising and sinking their quarry. And once they sank a ship, the tiny U-boats could not possibly pick up survivors. Britain portrayed the submarine as an outlaw weapon that violated notions of "civilized" warfare. Nevertheless, in February 1915, Germany announced that it intended to sink on sight enemy ships en route to the British Isles. On May 7, 1915, a German U-boat torpedoed the British passenger liner

Lusitania, killing 1,198 passengers, 128 of them U.S. citizens.

Front pages of American newspapers featured drawings of drowning women and children, and some demanded war. Others pointed out that Germany had warned prospective passengers and that the *Lusitania* carried millions of rounds of ammunition and so was a legitimate target.

"Enlist"
This poster depicting a young mother and her baby sinking beneath the cold waters of the Atlantic Ocean brought home the terrible cost of Germany's sinking of the British passenger liner *Lusitania* in 1915. Burned into American memory, the *Lusitania* remained a compelling reason to enlist in the armed forces after the United States entered the war in 1917.
Library of Congress.

Secretary of State Bryan resisted the hysteria and declared that a ship carrying war materiel "should not rely on passengers to protect her from attack—it would be like putting women and children in front of an army." He counseled Wilson to warn American citizens that they traveled on ships of belligerent countries at their own risk.

Wilson sought a middle course that would retain his commitment to peace and neutrality without condoning German attacks on passenger ships. On May 10, he distanced himself from the proponents of American intervention by declaring that "there is such a thing as a man being too proud to fight," which caused former president Theodore Roosevelt, who urged war, to label him a "flub dub and mollycoddle." But Wilson also rejected Bryan's position. Any further destruction of ships, Wilson declared, would be regarded as "deliberately unfriendly" and might lead the United States to break diplomatic relations with Germany. Wilson essentially demanded that Germany abandon unrestricted submarine warfare. Bryan resigned, predicting that the president had placed the United States on a collision course with Germany. Wilson's replacement for Bryan, Robert Lansing, was far from neutral. He announced that "the German Government is utterly hostile to all nations with democratic institutions." Because of Germany's "ambition for world dominance," it "must not be permitted to win this war or even to break even."

After Germany apologized for the civilian deaths on the *Lusitania*, tensions subsided. But in 1916, a German U-boat captain sank the British steamer *Sussex*, at the cost of two more American lives. To ensure continued U.S. neutrality, Germany went further, promising no more submarine attacks without warning and without provisions for the safety of civilians. Wilson's supporters celebrated the success of his middle-of-the-road strategy, which steered a course between belligerence and pacificism.

Wilson's diplomacy proved helpful in his bid for reelection in 1916. In the contest against Republican Charles Evans Hughes, the Democratic Party ran Wilson under the slogan "He kept us out of war." Wilson felt uneasy with the claim, recognizing that any "little German lieutenant can push us into the war at any time by some calculated outrage." But the Democrats' case for Wilson's neutrality appealed to enough of those in favor of peace to eke out a majority. Wilson won, but only by the razor-thin margins of 600,000 popular and 23 electoral votes.

The United States Enters the War

Step by step, the United States backed away from "absolute neutrality" and more forthrightly sided with the Allies (that is, with the Triple Entente). The consequence of protesting the German blockade of Great Britain but accepting the British blockade of Germany was that by 1916, the United States was supplying the Allies with 40 percent of their war materiel. When France and Britain ran short of money to pay for U.S. goods and asked for loans, Wilson argued that "loans by American bankers to any foreign government which is at war are inconsistent with the true spirit of neutrality." But rather than jeopardize America's wartime prosperity, Wilson relaxed his objections, and billions of dollars in loans kept American goods flowing to Britain and France.

In January 1917, Germany decided that it could no longer afford to allow neutral shipping to reach Great Britain while Britain's blockade gradually starved Germany. The German government announced that its navy would resume unrestricted submarine warfare and sink without warning any ship, enemy and neutral, found in the waters off Great Britain. Germany understood that the decision would probably bring the United States into the war but gambled that the submarines would strangle the British economy and allow German armies to win a military victory in France before American troops arrived in Europe.

Resisting demands for war, Wilson continued to hope for a negotiated peace and only broke off diplomatic relations with Germany. Then on February 25, 1917, British authorities informed Wilson of a secret telegram sent by the German foreign secretary, Arthur Zimmermann, to the German minister in Mexico. It promised that in the event of war between Germany and the United States, Germany would see that Mexico regained its "lost provinces" of Texas, New Mexico, and Arizona if Mexico would declare war against the United States. Wilson angrily responded to the Zimmermann telegram by asking Congress to approve a policy of "armed neutrality" that would allow merchant ships to fight back against any attackers. Germany's overture to Mexico convinced Wilson that the war was, indeed, a defense of democracy against German aggression.

In March, German submarines sank five American vessels off Britain, killing 66 Americans. On April 2, the president asked Congress to issue a declaration of war. No longer too proud to fight, he accused Germany of "warfare against all mankind." Still, he called for a "war without hate" and insisted that the destruction of Germany was not the goal of the United States. Rather, America fought to "vindicate the principles of peace and justice." He promised a world made "safe for democracy." On April 6, 1917, by majorities of 373 to 50 in the House and 82 to 6 in the Senate, Congress voted to declare war. Among those voting no was Representative Jeannette Rankin of Montana, the first woman elected to Congress.

Wilson continued to fear how the war would affect the nation at home. He said despairingly, "Once lead this people into war, and they'll forget there ever was such a thing as tolerance. To fight you must be brutal and ruthless, and the spirit of ruthless brutality will infect Congress, the courts, the policeman on the beat, the man in the street."

▶ R E V I E W   Why did President Wilson authorize repeated military interventions in the Americas?

"Over There"

American soldiers sailed for France with songwriter George M. Cohan's rousing "Over There" ringing in their ears:

> Over there, over there
> Send the word, send the word over there,
> That the Yanks are coming, the Yanks are coming
> The drums rum-tumming ev'rywhere.

Two million American troops eventually reached Europe, by far the largest military venture the United States had ever undertaken on foreign soil. Filled with a sense of democratic mission and trained to be morally upright as well as fiercely effective, some doughboys found the adventure exhilarating and maintained their idealism to the end. The majority, however, saw little that was gallant in rats, lice, and poison gas, and—despite the progressives' hopes—little to elevate the human soul in a landscape of utter destruction and death.

The Call to Arms

When America entered the war, Britain and France were nearly exhausted after almost three years of conflict. Hundreds of thousands of soldiers had perished; food and morale were dangerously low. Another Allied power, Russia, was in turmoil. In March 1917, a revolution had forced Czar Nicholas II to abdicate, and eight months later, in a separate peace with Germany, the Bolshevik revolutionary government withdrew Russia from the war.

On May 18, 1917, to meet the demand for fighting men, Wilson signed a sweeping Selective Service Act, authorizing a **draft** of all young men into the armed forces. **Conscription** soon transformed a tiny volunteer armed force into a vast army and navy. Although almost 350,000 inductees either failed to report or claimed conscientious objector status, draft boards eventually inducted 2.8 million men into the armed services, in addition to the 2 million who volunteered.

Among the 4.8 million men under arms, 370,000 were black Americans. Although African Americans remained understandably skeptical about President Wilson's war for democracy, most followed W. E. B. Du Bois's advice to "close ranks" and to temporarily "forget our special grievances" until the nation had won the war. During training, black recruits suffered the same prejudices that they encountered in civilian life. Rigidly segregated, they faced crude abuse and miserable conditions, and they were usually assigned to labor battalions, where they shouldered shovels more often than rifles.

Training camps sought to transform raw white recruits into fighting men. Progressives in the government were determined that American fighting men would emerge from training with the highest moral and civic values. Secretary of War Newton D. Baker, whose outlook had been shaped by his reform crusades as the progressive mayor of Cleveland, created the Commission on Training Camp Activities, staffed by YMCA workers and veterans of the settlement house and playground movements. Military training included games, singing, and college extension courses. The army asked soldiers to stop thinking about sex, explaining that a "man who is thinking below the belt is not efficient." The Military Draft Act of 1917 prohibited prostitution and alcohol near training camps. Wilson's choice to command the American Expeditionary Force (AEF), Major General John "Black Jack" Pershing, was as morally upright as he was militarily uncompromising. Described by one observer as "lean, clean, keen," he gave progressives perfect confidence.

The War in France

At the front, the AEF discovered a desperate situation. By mid-1917, the war had degenerated into a stalemate of armies dug defensively into hundreds of miles of trenches across France. Huddling in the mud among the corpses and rats, soldiers were separated from the enemy by only a few hundred yards of "no-man's-land." When ordered "over the top," troops raced desperately toward the enemy's trenches, only to be entangled in barbed wire, enveloped in poison gas, and mowed down by machine guns. The three-day battle of the Somme in 1916 cost the French and British forces 600,000 dead and wounded and the Germans 500,000. The deadliest battle of the war allowed the Allies to advance their trenches only a few meaningless miles across devastated land.

Still, U.S. troops saw almost no combat in 1917. The only exception was the 92nd Division of black troops. When Pershing received an urgent call for troops from the French, he sent the 92nd to the front to be integrated into the French army because he did not want to lose command over the white troops he valued more. In the 191 days they spent in battle—longer than any other American outfit—the 369th Regiment of the 92nd Division won more medals than any other American combat unit. Black soldiers recognized the irony of having to serve with the French to gain respect. Pershing told the French that their failure to draw the color line threatened Franco-American relations because it risked "spoiling the Negroes." German propagandists raised some painful questions. In a leaflet distributed to black troops, the Germans reminded them of their second-class citizenship and asked, "Why, then, fight the Germans, only for the benefit of the Wall Street robbers and to protect the millions they have loaned to the British, French, and Italians?"

White troops continued to train and used their free time to explore places that most of them otherwise could never have hoped to see. True to the crusader image, American officials allowed only uplifting tourism. Paris temptations were off-limits, and French premier Georges Clemenceau's offer to supply U.S. troops with licensed prostitutes was declined with the half-serious remark that if Wilson found out, he would stop the war.

Doughboys in France
Stretched out in the mud in the middle of what used to be a forest, men in the 23rd Infantry of the Second Division fire a 37 mm gun at German positions. By the time American doughboys arrived in Europe, hostile troops had faced each other for more than three years, burrowed into a double line of trenches protected by barbed wire, machine-gun nests, and mortars and backed by heavy artillery.
National Archives.

The sightseeing ended abruptly in March 1918. The Brest-Litovsk treaty signed that month by Germany and the Bolsheviks officially took Russia out of the war, and the Germans launched a massive offensive aimed at French ports on the Atlantic. After 6,000 cannons unleashed the heaviest barrage in history, a million German soldiers smashed a hole in the Allied lines at a cost of 250,000 casualties on each side. Pershing, who believed the right moment for U.S. action had finally come, visited Foch to ask for the "great honor" of becoming "engaged in the greatest battle in history." Foch agreed to Pershing's terms of a separate American command and in May assigned the Americans to the central sector.

In May and June, at Cantigny and then at Château-Thierry, the eager but green Americans checked the German advance with a series of dashing assaults (Map 22.2). Then they headed toward the forest stronghold of Belleau Wood, moving against streams of retreating Allied soldiers who cried defeat: "La guerre est finie!" (The war is over!). A French officer commanded American soldiers to retreat with them, but the American commander replied sharply, "Retreat, hell. We just got here." After charging through a wheat field against withering machine-gun fire, the marines plunged into hand-to-hand combat. Victory came

MAP 22.2   The American Expeditionary Force, 1918

In the last year of the war, the AEF joined the French army on the western front to respond to the final German offensive and pursue the retreating enemy until surrender.

hard, but a German report praised the enemy's spirit, noting that "the Americans' nerves are not yet worn out." Indeed, it was German morale that was on the verge of cracking.

In the summer of 1918, the Allies launched a massive counteroffensive that would end the war. A quarter of a million U.S. troops joined in the rout of German forces along the Marne River. In September, more than a million Americans took part in the assault that threw the Germans back from positions along the Meuse River. In November, a revolt against the German government sent Kaiser Wilhelm II fleeing to Holland. On November 11, 1918, a delegation from the newly established German republic met with the French high command to sign an armistice that brought the fighting to an end.

The adventure of the AEF was brief, bloody, and victorious. When Germany resumed unrestricted U-boat warfare in 1917, it was gambling that it could defeat Britain and France before the Americans could raise and train an army and ship it to France. The German military had miscalculated badly. By the end, 112,000 AEF soldiers perished from wounds and disease. Another 230,000 Americans suffered casualties but survived, many of them with permanent physical and psychological disabilities. Only the Civil War, which lasted much longer, had been more costly in American lives. European nations, however, suffered much greater losses: 2.2 million Germans, 1.9 million Russians, 1.4 million French, and 900,000 Britons. Where they had fought, the landscape was as blasted and barren as the moon.

▶**REVIEW**   How did the American Expeditionary Force contribute to the defeat of Germany?

The Crusade for Democracy at Home

Many progressives hoped that war would improve the quality of American life as well as free Europe from its bondage to tyranny and militarism. Mobilization helped propel the crusades for woman suffrage and prohibition to success. Progressives enthusiastically channeled industrial and agricultural production into the war effort. Labor shortages caused by workers entering the military provided new opportunities for women in the booming wartime economy. With labor at a premium, unionized workers gained higher pay and shorter hours. To instill loyalty in Americans whose ancestry was rooted in the belligerent nations, Wilson launched a campaign to foster patriotism. The campaign included the creation of a government agency to promote official propaganda, indoctrination in the schools, and parades, rallies, and films. But boosting patriotism led to suppressing dissent. When the government launched a harsh assault on civil liberties, mobs gained license to attack those whom they considered disloyal. As Wilson feared, the progressive ideals of rational progress and free expression took a beating at home when the nation undertook its foreign crusade for democracy.

The Progressive Stake in the War

The idea of the war as an agent of national improvement fanned the old zeal of the progressive movement. The influential philosopher-educator John Dewey urged Americans to recognize the "social possibilities of war." The Wilson administration realized that the federal government would have to assert greater control to mobilize the nation's human and physical resources. The nation's capital soon bristled with hastily created agencies charged with managing the war effort. Bernard Baruch headed the War Industries Board (WIB), created to stimulate and direct industrial production. At once a wealthy southern gentleman, a Jewish Wall Street stockbroker, and a reform Democrat, Baruch brought industrial management and labor together into a team that produced everything from boots to bullets and made U.S. troops the best-equipped soldiers in the world.

Herbert Hoover, a self-made millionaire engineer, headed the Food Administration. He led remarkably successful "Hooverizing" campaigns for "meatless" Mondays and "wheatless" Wednesdays and other ways of conserving resources. Guaranteed high prices, the American heartland not only supplied the needs of U.S. citizens and armed forces but also became the breadbasket of America's allies. Even Wilson's family did its part with a White House "victory garden" and sheep put out to graze on the White House lawn when the gardeners took war-related work.

Other wartime agencies abounded. The Railroad Administration directed railroad traffic, the Fuel Administration coordinated the coal industry and other fuel suppliers, the Shipping Board organized the merchant marine, and the National War Labor Policies Board resolved labor disputes. Their successes gave progressives reason to believe that the war promoted harmony between business and labor and progressive reform in general. Some progressives, however, stubbornly refused to accept the argument that war and reform marched together. Wisconsin senator Robert La Follette attacked the war unrelentingly, claiming that Wilson's promises of peace and democracy were a case of "the blind leading the blind," at home and abroad.

Industrial leaders found that wartime agencies and enforced efficiency helped corporate profits triple. Some working people also had cause to celebrate. Mobilization meant high prices for farmers and plentiful jobs at high wages in the new war industries. Because increased industrial production required peaceful labor relations, the National War Labor Policies Board enacted the eight-hour day, a living minimum wage, and **collective bargaining** rights in some industries. Wages rose sharply during the war (as did prices), and the American Federation of Labor (AFL) saw its membership soar from 2.7 million to more than 5 million.

The war also provided a huge boost to the stalled moral crusade to ban alcohol. By 1917, prohibitionists had convinced nineteen states to go dry. Liquor's opponents now argued that banning alcohol would make the cause of democracy powerful and pure. At the same time, shutting down the distilleries would save millions of bushels of grain that could feed the United States and its allies. "Shall the many have food or the few drink?" the drys asked. Prohibitionists added a patriotic twist by arguing that closing breweries with German names such as Schlitz, Pabst, and Anheuser-Busch would deal a blow to the German cause. In December 1917, Congress passed the Eighteenth Amendment, which banned the manufacture, transportation, and sale of alcohol. After swift ratification by the states, the amendment went into effect on January 1, 1920.

Women, War, and the Battle for Suffrage

Women had made real strides during the Progressive Era, but war presented new opportunities. More than 25,000 women served in France. About half were nurses. The others drove ambulances; ran canteens for the Salvation Army, Red Cross, and YMCA; worked with French civilians in devastated areas; and acted as telephone operators and war correspondents. Like the men who joined the war effort, they believed that they were taking part in a great national venture. "I am more than willing to live as a soldier and know of the hardships I would have to undergo," one canteen worker declared when applying to go overseas, "but I want to help my country. . . . I want . . . to do the *real* work." And like men, women struggled against disillusionment and depression in France. One woman explained: "Over in America,

U.S. Army Medical Corps Contract Surgeon's Uniform
About half of the 25,000 American women who served in France became nurses, who dealt with "a sea of stretchers, a human carpet." Women also drove ambulances, acted as social workers, and ran canteens for the Salvation Army, Red Cross, and YMCA. A handful of female physicians worked as contract surgeons for the U.S. army. Dr. Loy McAfee wore this uniform in France.
National Museum of American History, Smithsonian Institution, Washington, D.C.

we thought we knew something about the war . . . but when you get here the difference is [like the one between] studying the laws of electricity and being struck by lightning."

At home, long-standing barriers against hiring women fell when millions of workingmen became soldiers and few new immigrant workers crossed the Atlantic. The new Women's Bureau of the Department of Labor, along with the Women's Trade Union League (WTUL), helped open jobs to women, sometimes against the opposition of the major trade organization, the AFL. Tens of thousands of women found work in defense plants as welders, metalworkers, and heavy machine operators—jobs traditionally reserved for men—and with the railroads. A black woman who had worked before the war as a domestic explained why she wanted to keep her job as a laborer in a railroad yard: "We are making more money at this than any work we can get, and we do not have to work as hard as at housework which requires us to be on duty from six o'clock in the morning until nine or ten at night, with might[y] little time off and at very poor wages." Other women found white-collar work. Between 1910 and 1920, the number of women clerks doubled. Before the war ended, more than a million women had found work in war industries. "This is the women's age," exaggerated Margaret Dreier Robins, president of the WTUL. "At last . . . women are coming into the labor and festival of life on equal terms with men."

The most dramatic advance for women came in the political arena. Since the Seneca Falls convention of 1848, where women voiced their first formal demand for the ballot, the struggle for woman suffrage had inched forward. Adopting a state-by-state approach, suffragists had achieved some success, but before 1910 only four small western states had adopted woman suffrage. Elsewhere, voting rights for women met strong hostility and defeat. After 1910, suffrage leaders added a federal campaign to amend the Constitution, targeting Congress and the president, to the traditional state-by-state strategy for suffrage.

The radical wing of the suffragists, led by the indomitable Alice Paul, picketed the White House, where they unfurled banners that proclaimed: "America Is Not a Democracy. Twenty Million Women Are Denied the Right to Vote." They chained themselves to fences and went to jail, where many engaged in hunger strikes. "They seem bent on making their cause as obnoxious as possible," Woodrow Wilson declared. His wife, Edith, detested the idea of "masculinized" voting women. But membership in the mainstream organization, the National American Woman Suffrage Association (NAWSA), led by Carrie Chapman Catt, soared to some two million members. The NAWSA even accepted African American women into its ranks, though not on an equal basis. Seeing the handwriting on the wall, the Republican and Progressive parties endorsed woman suffrage in 1916.

In 1918, Wilson gave his support to suffrage, calling the amendment "vital to the winning of the war." He conceded that it would be wrong not to reward the wartime "partnership of suffering and sacrifice" with a "partnership of privilege and right." By linking their cause to the wartime emphasis on national unity, the advocates of woman suffrage finally triumphed. In 1919, Congress passed the Nineteenth Amendment, granting women the vote, and by August 1920, the required two-thirds of the states had ratified it. As Carrie Chapman Catt later recalled, "to get that word, male, out of the Constitution, cost the women of the country fifty-two years of campaigning." But rather than woman suffrage being the end of the long road to women's full equality, as some suffragists contended, it proved to be only the beginning.

Rally around the Flag—or Else

When Congress committed the nation to war, most peace advocates rallied around the flag. Several business and civic leaders who had been antiwar created the League to Enforce Peace in support of Wilson's insistence that military force had become the only means to peaceful ends. The Carnegie Endowment for International Peace adopted new stationery with the heading "Peace through Victory" and issued a resolution saying that "the most effectual means of promoting peace is to prosecute the war against the Imperial German Government."

Only a handful of reformers resisted the tide of patriotism. Soon after the guns began booming in 1914, a group of professional women, led by settlement house leader Jane Addams and economics professor Emily Greene Balch, denounced what Addams described as "the pathetic belief in the regenerative results of war." The Women's Peace Party that emerged in 1915 and its foreign affiliates in the Women's International League for Peace and Freedom (WILPF) led the struggle to persuade governments to negotiate peace and spare dissenters from harsh punishment. It proved discouraging, unpopular work, and after America entered the conflict, advocates for peace were routinely labeled cowards and traitors, their efforts crushed by the steamroller of conformity.

To suppress criticism of the war, Wilson stirred up patriotic fervor. In 1917, the president created the Committee on Public Information (CPI) under the direction of George Creel, a muckraking journalist who became the nation's cheerleader for war. He sent "Four-Minute Men," a squad of 75,000 volunteers, around the country to give brief pep talks that celebrated successes on the battlefields and in the factories. Posters, pamphlets (many written by respected journalists and professors), and cartoons depicted brave American soldiers and sailors defending freedom and democracy against the evil "Huns," the derogatory nickname applied to German soldiers.

America rallied around Creel's campaign. The film industry cranked out reels of melodrama about battle-line and home-front heroes and taught audiences to hiss at the German kaiser. A musical, *The Kaiser: The Beast of Berlin*, opened on Broadway in 1918. Colleges and universities generated war propaganda in the guise of scholarship, and some added courses depicting the war as a culmination of the age-old struggle for civilization. When Professor James McKeen Cattell of

Columbia University urged that America seek peace with Germany short of victory, university president Nicholas Murray Butler fired him on the grounds that "what had been folly is now treason."

A firestorm of anti-German passion erupted. Across the nation, "100% American" campaigns enlisted ordinary people to sniff out disloyalty. German, the most widely taught foreign language in 1914, practically disappeared from the nation's schools. Targeting German-born Americans, the *Saturday Evening Post* declared that it was time to rid the country of "the scum of the melting pot." The rabid attempt to punish Germans reached its extreme with the lynching of Robert Prager, a baker in Collinsville, Illinois. In the eyes of the mob, it was enough that Prager was German-born and had **socialist** leanings, even though he had not opposed American participation in the war. Persuaded by the defense lawyer who praised what he called a "patriotic murder," the jury at the trial of the killers took only twenty-five minutes to acquit.

As hysteria increased, the campaign reached absurd levels. In Montana, a school board barred a history text that had good things to say about medieval Germany. Menus across the nation changed German toast to French toast and sauerkraut to liberty cabbage. In Milwaukee, vigilantes mounted a machine gun outside the Pabst Theater to prevent the staging of Schiller's *Wilhelm Tell*, a powerful protest against tyranny. One vigilant citizen claimed to see a periscope in the Great Lakes, and the fiancée of one of the war's leading critics, caught dancing on the dunes of Cape Cod, was held on suspicion of signaling to German submarines.

The Wilson administration's zeal in suppressing dissent contrasted sharply with its war aims of defending democracy. In the name of self-defense, the Espionage Act (June 1917), the Trading with the Enemy Act (October 1917), and the Sedition Act (May 1918) gave the government sweeping powers to punish any opinion or activity it considered "disloyal, profane, scurrilous, or abusive." When Postmaster General Albert Burleson blocked mailing privileges for publications he considered disloyal, dozens of dissenting journals were forced to close down, including a leading literary magazine. Of the fifteen hundred individuals eventually charged with sedition, all but a dozen had merely spoken words the government found objectionable. One of them was Eugene V. Debs, the leader of the Socialist Party, who was convicted under the Espionage Act for speeches condemning the war as a capitalist plot and sent to the Atlanta penitentiary.

The president hoped that national commitment to the war would subdue partisan politics, but his Republican rivals used the war as a weapon against the Democrats. The trick was to oppose Wilson's conduct of the war but not the war itself. Republicans outshouted Wilson on the nation's need to mobilize for war but then complained that Wilson's War Industries Board was a tyrannical agency that crushed free enterprise. Such attacks appealed to widely diverse business, labor, and patriotic groups. As the war progressed, Republicans gathered power against the Democrats, who had narrowly reelected Wilson in 1916.

Wilson erred when he attempted to make the off-year congressional elections of 1918 a referendum on his leadership. Instead, amid criticism of the White House for playing politics with the war, Republicans gained a narrow majority in both the House and Senate. The end of Democratic control of Congress not only halted further domestic reform but also meant that the United States would advance toward military victory in Europe with political power divided between a Democratic president and a Republican Congress likely to challenge Wilson's plans for international cooperation.

> ▶REVIEW   How did progressive ideals fare during wartime?

A Compromised Peace

Wilson decided to reaffirm his noble war ideals by announcing his peace aims before the end of hostilities. He hoped the victorious Allies would adopt his plan for international democracy, but he was sorely disappointed. The leaders of Britain, France, and Italy (which joined the Allies in 1915 in hopes of postwar gains) understood that Wilson's principles jeopardized their own postwar plans for the acquisition of enemy territory, new colonial empires, and reparations. Wilson also faced strong opposition at home from those who feared that his enthusiasm for international cooperation would undermine American sovereignty.

Wilson's Fourteen Points

On January 8, 1918, President Wilson revealed to Congress his vision of a generous peace. Wilson's Fourteen Points provided a blueprint for a new democratic world order. The first five points affirmed basic liberal ideals: "open covenants of peace, openly arrived at"—that is, an end to secret treaties; freedom of the seas; removal of economic barriers to free trade; reduction of weapons of war; and recognition of the rights of colonized peoples. The next eight points supported the right to self-determination of European peoples who had been dominated by Germany or its allies. Wilson's fourteenth point called for a "general association of nations"—a League of Nations—to provide "mutual guarantees of political independence and territorial integrity to great and small states alike." The insistence on a League of Nations reflected Wilson's lifelong dream of a "parliament of man." Only such an organization of "peace-loving nations," he believed, could justify the war and secure a lasting peace. Wilson concluded his speech by pledging that the United States would welcome Germany into the family of "peace-loving nations" if it would renounce its militarism and imperialism.

Citizens of the United States and of every Allied country greeted the Fourteen Points enthusiastically. Wilson felt confident that he could prevail against undemocratic and selfish forces at the peace table. During the final year of the war, he pressured the Allies to accept the Fourteen Points as the basis of the postwar settlement. If necessary, Wilson was willing to speak over the heads of government leaders directly to the people and thus expand his role as spokesman for Americans to be the champion of all the world's people. The Allies had won the war; Wilson would win the peace.

The Paris Peace Conference

From January 18 to June 28, 1919, the eyes of the world focused on Paris. There, powerful men wrestled with difficult problems. Although no other American president had ever gone to Europe while in office, Wilson, inspired by his mission, decided to head the U.S. delegation. He believed he owed it to the American soldiers. "It is now my duty," he announced, "to play my full part in making good what they gave their life's blood to obtain." A dubious British diplomat retorted that Wilson was drawn to Paris "as a debutante is entranced by the prospect of her first ball." The decision to leave the country at a time when his political opponents challenged his leadership was risky enough, but his stubborn refusal to include prominent Republicans in the delegation proved foolhardy and eventually cost him his dream of a new world order with the United States at its center.

When Wilson and his entourage arrived on the French coast on Friday, December 13, Wilson joked that thirteen was his lucky number. Two million Parisians cheered the American president's motorcade as it entered France's capital city. After four terrible years of war, the common people of Europe almost worshipped Wilson, believing that he would create a safer, more decent world. When the conference convened at Louis XIV's magnificent palace at Versailles, however, Wilson encountered a different reception. Representing the Allies were the decidedly unidealistic David Lloyd George, prime minister of Britain; Georges Clemenceau, premier of France; and Vittorio Orlando, former prime minister of Italy. To the Allied leaders, Wilson appeared a naive and impractical moralist. His desire to gather former enemies within a new international democratic order showed how little he understood hard European realities. Clemenceau claimed that Wilson "believed you could do everything by formulas" and "empty theory." Disparaging the Fourteen Points, he added, "God himself was content with ten commandments."

The Allies wanted to fasten blame for the war on Germany, totally disarm it, and make it pay so dearly that it would never threaten its neighbors again. The French demanded retribution in the form of territory containing Germany's richest mineral resources. The British made it clear that they were not about to give up the powerful weapon of naval blockade for the vague principle of freedom of the seas.

The Allies forced Wilson to make drastic compromises. In return for France moderating its territorial claims, he agreed to support Article 231 of the peace treaty, assigning war guilt to Germany. Though saved from permanently losing Rhineland territory to the French, Germany was outraged at being singled out as the instigator of the war and saddled with more than $33 billion in damages. Many Germans felt that their nation had been betrayed. After agreeing to an armistice in the belief that peace terms would be based in Wilson's generous Fourteen Points, they faced hardship and humiliation instead.

Wilson had better success in establishing the principle of self-determination. But from the beginning, Secretary of State Robert Lansing knew that the president's concept of self-determination was "simply loaded with dynamite." Lansing wondered, "What unit has he in mind? Does he mean a race, a territorial area, or a community?" Even Wilson was vague about what self-determination actually meant. "When I gave utterance to those words," he admitted, "I said them without the knowledge that nationalities existed, which are coming to us day after day." Lansing suspected that the notion "will raise hopes which can never be realized. It will, I fear, cost thousands of lives. In the end it is bound to be discredited, to be called the dream of an idealist who failed to realize the danger until it was too late."

Yet partly on the basis of self-determination, the conference redrew the map of Europe and parts of the rest of the world. Portions of Austria-Hungary were ceded to Italy, Poland, and Romania, and the remainder was reassembled into Austria, Hungary, Czechoslovakia, and Yugoslavia—independent republics whose boundaries were drawn with attention to concentrations of major ethnic groups but which also included minorities. More arbitrarily, the Ottoman empire was carved up into small mandates (including Palestine) run by local leaders but under the control of France and Great Britain. The conference reserved the mandate system for those regions it deemed insufficiently "civilized" to have full independence. Thus, the reconstructed nations—each beset with ethnic and nationalist rivalries—faced the challenge of making a new democratic government work (Map 22.3, page 706). Many of today's bitterest disputes—in the Balkans and Iraq, between Greece and Turkey, between Arabs and Jews—have roots in the decisions made in Paris in 1919.

Wilson hoped that self-determination would also dictate the fate of Germany's colonies in Asia and Africa. But the Allies who had taken over the colonies during the war only allowed the League of Nations a mandate to administer them. Technically, the mandate system rejected imperialism, but in reality it only avoided the formality of imperialism while still allowing Europeans to maintain control. Because of mandates, Britain's empire grew by more than eight million people, while France added more than five million to its empire. Thus, while denying Germany its colonies, the Allies retained and added to their own far-flung territories.

The cause of democratic equality suffered another setback when the peace conference rejected Japan's call for inclusion of a principle of racial equality in the treaty. Wilson's belief in the superiority of whites, as well as his apprehension about how white Americans would respond to such a declaration, led him to

MAP 22.3   Europe after World War I
The post–World War I settlement redrew boundaries to create new nations based on ethnic group-ings. This outcome left within defeated Germany and Russia bitter peoples who resolved to recover the territory taken from them.

oppose the clause. To soothe hurt feelings, Wilson agreed to grant Japan a man-date over the Shantung Peninsula in northern China, which had formerly been controlled by Germany. The gesture mollified Japan's moderate leaders, but the military faction preparing to take over the country used bitterness toward racist Western colonialism to build support for expanding Japanese power throughout Asia.

Closest to Wilson's heart was finding a new way to manage international rela-tions. In Wilson's view, war had finally discredited the old strategy of balance of power. Instead, he proposed a League of Nations, which would provide **collective security** and order. The league would establish rules of international conduct and resolve conflicts between nations through rational and peaceful means. When the Allies agreed to the league, Wilson was overjoyed. He believed that the league would rectify the errors his colleagues had forced on him in Paris. The league would solidify and extend the noble work he had begun.

To many Europeans and Americans, the Versailles treaty came as a bitter disappointment. Wilson's admirers were shocked that the president dealt in compromise like any other politician. But without Wilson's presence, the treaty that was signed on June 28, 1919, surely would have been more vindictive. Wilson returned home in July 1919 consoled that, despite his frustrations, he had gained what he most wanted—a League of Nations. In Wilson's judgment, "We have completed in the least time possible the greatest work that four men have ever done."

The Fight for the Treaty

The tumultuous reception Wilson received when he arrived home persuaded him, probably correctly, that the American people supported the treaty. When the president submitted the treaty to the Senate in July 1919, he warned that failure to ratify it would "break the heart of the world." By then, however, criticism of the treaty was mounting, especially from Americans convinced that their countries of ethnic origin had not been given fair treatment. Irish Americans raged against the treaty's failure to grant Ireland independence from the British. Italian Americans complained that Italy had not gained all of the territory it deserved. And German Americans condemned the treaty as ferociously unfair to Germany. Others worried that the president's concessions at Versailles had jeopardized the treaty's capacity to provide a generous plan for rebuilding Europe and to guarantee world peace.

Some of the most potent critics were found in the Senate. Bolstered by a slight Republican majority in Congress, a group of Republican "irreconcilables," which included such powerful **isolationist** senators as Hiram Johnson of California and William Borah of Idaho, condemned the treaty for entangling the United States in world affairs. A larger group of Republicans did not object to American participation in world politics but feared that membership in the League of Nations would jeopardize the nation's ability to act independently. No Republican, in any case, was eager to hand Wilson and the Democrats a foreign policy victory with the 1920 presidential election little more than a year away.

At the center of Republican opposition was Wilson's archenemy, Senator Henry Cabot Lodge of Massachusetts. Lodge's hostility was in part personal. "I never thought I could hate a man as much as I hate Wilson," he once admitted. But Lodge also raised cogent objections to the treaty and the league. Lodge was no isolationist, but he thought that much of the Fourteen Points was a "general bleat about virtue being better than vice." Lodge expected the United States' economic and military power to propel the nation into a major role in world affairs. But he insisted that membership in the League of Nations, which would require collective action to maintain peace, threatened the nation's freedom of choice in foreign relations.

Lodge used his position as chairman of the Senate Foreign Relations Committee to air every sort of complaint. Out of the committee hearings came several amendments, or "reservations," that sought to limit the consequences of American membership in the league. For example, several reservations required approval of both the House and Senate before the United States could participate in league-sponsored economic sanctions or military action.

It gradually became clear that ratification of the treaty depended on acceptance of the Lodge reservations. Democratic senators, who overwhelmingly supported the treaty, urged Wilson to accept Lodge's terms, arguing that they left the essentials of the treaty intact. Wilson, however, insisted that the reservations cut "the very heart out of the treaty." He expressed personal hatred as well. "*Lodge* reservations?" he thundered. "Never! I'll never consent to adopt any policy with which that impossible name is so prominently identified."

Wilson decided to take his case directly to the people. On September 3, 1919, still exhausted from the peace conference and against the objections of his doctors, he set out by train on the most ambitious speaking tour ever undertaken by a president. He enjoyed some early success, but on September 25 in Pueblo, Colorado, Wilson collapsed and had to return to Washington. There, he suffered a massive stroke that partially paralyzed him. From his bedroom, Wilson sent messages instructing Democrats in the Senate to hold firm against any and all reservations. If the Senate approved the treaty with reservations, he said, he would not sign it. In the end, Wilson commanded enough loyalty to ensure a vote against the Lodge reservations. But when the treaty without reservations came before the Senate in March 1920, the combined opposition of the Republican irreconcilables and reservationists left Wilson six votes short of the two-thirds majority needed for passage.

The nations of Europe organized the League of Nations at Geneva, Switzerland, but the United States never became a member. Whether American membership could have prevented the world war that would begin in Europe in 1939 is highly unlikely, but the United States' failure to join certainly weakened the league from the start. In refusing to accept relatively minor compromises with Senate moderates, Wilson lost his treaty and American membership in the league. Woodrow Wilson and Henry Cabot Lodge both died in 1924, never seeing international order or security, never knowing the whirlwind of resentment and violence that would eventually follow the Great War's failure to make the world safe for democracy.

▶ **REVIEW**   Why did the Senate fail to ratify the Versailles treaty?

Democracy at Risk

The defeat of Wilson's idealistic plan for international democracy proved the crowning blow to progressives who had hoped that the war could boost reform at home. When the war ended, Americans wanted to demobilize swiftly. In the process, servicemen, defense workers, and farmers lost their war-related jobs.

The volatile combination—of unemployed veterans returning home, a stalled economy, and leftover wartime patriotism looking for a new cause—threatened to explode. Wartime anti-German passion was quickly followed by antiradicalism, a fevered campaign that ensnared unionists, socialists, dissenters, and African Americans and Mexicans who had committed no offense but to seek to escape rural poverty. The 1920 election marked the end of Wilson's two terms in the White House and his crusades.

Economic Hardship and Labor Upheaval

Americans greeted peace with a demand that the United States return to a peacetime economy. The government abruptly abandoned its wartime controls on the economy and canceled war contracts worth millions of dollars. In a matter of months, more than three million soldiers were mustered out of the military with only $60 and a one-way ticket home. When war production ceased and veterans flooded the job market, unemployment rose sharply. At the same time, consumers went on a postwar spending spree that drove inflation skyward. In 1919, prices rose 75 percent over prewar levels, and in 1920 prices rose another 28 percent.

Most of the gains workers had made during the war evaporated. Freed from wartime controls, business turned against the eight-hour day and attacked labor unions. With inflation eating up their paychecks, workers fought back. The year 1919 witnessed nearly 3,600 strikes involving 4 million workers. The most spectacular strike occurred in February 1919 in Seattle, where shipyard workers had been put out of work by demobilization. When a coalition of the radical Industrial Workers of the World (IWW, called Wobblies) and the moderate American Federation of Labor (AFL) called a general strike, the largest work stoppage in American history shut down the city. Newspapers across the nation claimed that the walkout was "a Bolshevik effort to start a revolution." The suppression of the strike by Seattle officials cost the AFL many of its wartime gains and contributed to the destruction of the IWW soon afterward.

A strike by Boston policemen in the fall of 1919 underscored postwar hostility toward labor militancy. Although the police had received no raise since before the war and were paid less than pick-and-shovel laborers, they won little sympathy. Once the officers stopped walking their beats, looters sacked the city. After two days of near anarchy, only slightly tamed by a volunteer police force of Harvard students and recently discharged soldiers, Massachusetts governor Calvin Coolidge called in the National Guard to restore order. The public, yearning for peace and security in the wake of war, welcomed Coolidge's anti-union assurance that "there is no right to strike against the public safety by anybody, anywhere, any time."

Labor strife climaxed in the grim steel strike of 1919. For decades, the steel industry had succeeded in beating back its workers' efforts to unionize. Faced with the industry's plan to revert to seven-day weeks, twelve-hour days, and weekly wages of about $20, the AFL determined to try again. When U.S. Steel and Bethlehem Steel refused to negotiate, Samuel Gompers, head of the AFL, called for a strike. In response, 350,000 workers in fifteen states walked out in September 1919. The steel industry hired 30,000 strikebreakers (many of them African Americans) and convinced the public that the strikers were radicals bent on subverting the Republic. State and federal troops protected scabs who crossed picket lines. In January 1920, after eighteen striking workers had been killed, the strike collapsed. That devastating defeat initiated a sharp decline in the fortunes of the labor movement, a trend that would continue for almost twenty years.

The Red Scare

Suppression of labor strikes was one response to the widespread fear of internal subversion that swept the nation in 1919. The "Red scare" ("Red" referred to the color of the Bolshevik flag), which far outstripped the assault on civil liberties during the war, had homegrown causes: the postwar recession, labor unrest, and the difficulties of reintegrating millions of returning veterans. But unsettling events abroad also added to Americans' anxieties.

Russian bolshevism became even more menacing in March 1919, when the new Soviet leaders created the Comintern, a worldwide association of **Communist** leaders intent on fomenting revolution in capitalist countries. A Communist revolution in the United States was extremely unlikely, but edgy Americans faced with a flurry of terrorist acts, most notably thirty-eight bombs mailed to prominent individuals, believed otherwise. Fear, anger, and uncertainty led swiftly to a hunt for terrorists, led by Attorney General A. Mitchell Palmer. Targeting men and women who harbored what Palmer considered ideas that could lead to violence, even though the individuals may not have done anything illegal, the Justice Department sought to purge the supposed enemies of America.

In January 1920, Palmer ordered a series of raids that netted 6,000 alleged subversives. Finding no revolutionary conspiracies, Palmer nevertheless ordered 500 noncitizen suspects deported. His action came in the wake of a campaign against the most notorious radical alien, Russian-born Emma Goldman. Before the war, Goldman's passionate support of labor strikes, women's rights, and birth control had made her a symbol of radicalism. Finally, after a stay in prison for attacking military conscription, she was ordered deported by J. Edgar Hoover, the eager director of the Justice Department's Radical Division. In December 1919, as Goldman and 250 others boarded a ship for exile in Russia, the defiant rebel turned on the gangplank to thumb her nose at a jeering crowd.

The effort to rid the country of alien radicals was matched by efforts to crush troublesome citizens. Law enforcement officials and vigilante groups joined hands against so-called Reds. In November 1919 in the rugged lumber town of Centralia, Washington, a menacing crowd gathered in front of the IWW hall. Nervous

Wobblies inside opened fire, killing three people. Three IWW members were arrested and later convicted of murder, but another, ex-soldier Wesley Everett, was carried off by the mob, which castrated him, hung him from a bridge, and then riddled his body with bullets. His death was officially ruled a suicide.

Public institutions joined the attack on civil liberties. Local libraries removed dissenting books. Schools fired unorthodox teachers. Police shut down radical newspapers. State legislatures refused to seat elected representatives who professed socialist ideas. And in 1919, Congress removed its lone socialist representative, Victor Berger, on the pretext that he was a threat to national safety.

That same year, the Supreme Court provided a formula for restricting free speech. In upholding the conviction of socialist Charles Schenck for publishing a pamphlet urging resistance to the draft during wartime (*Schenck v. United States*), the Court established a "clear and present danger" test. Such utterances as Schenck's during a time of national peril, Justice Oliver Wendell Holmes wrote, were equivalent to shouting "Fire!" in a crowded theater. But Schenck's pamphlet had little power to provoke a public firmly opposed to its message.

In time, the Red scare lost credibility. The lack of any real radical menace became clear after Attorney General Palmer warned in 1920 that radicals were planning to celebrate the Bolshevik Revolution with a nationwide wave of violence on May 1, international workers' day. Officials called out state militias, fortified public buildings and churches, mobilized bomb squads, and even placed machine-gun nests at major city intersections. When May 1 came and went without a single disturbance, the public mood turned from fear to scorn. The Red scare collapsed as a result of its excesses.

The Great Migrations of African Americans and Mexicans

Before the Red scare lost steam, the government raised alarms about the loyalty of African Americans. A Justice Department investigation concluded that Reds were fomenting racial unrest among blacks. Although the report was wrong about Bolshevik influence, it was correct in noticing a new stirring among African Americans, an assertiveness born of participation in the war effort and the massive migration out of the South.

In 1900, nine of every ten blacks still lived in the South, where poverty, **disfranchisement**, segregation, and violence dominated their lives. Thirty-five years after **emancipation**, African Americans had made little progress toward full citizenship. A majority of black men continued to toil in agriculture as dirt-poor tenants or sharecroppers, or they worked for wages of 60 cents a day. Black women worked in the homes of whites as domestics for $2 a week. Whites remained committed to keeping blacks down. "If we own a good farm or horse, or cow, or bird-dog, or yoke of oxen," a black sharecropper in Mississippi observed in 1913, "we are harassed until we are bound to sell, give away, or run away, before we can have any peace in our lives."

African Americans Migrate North
This southern family arrived in their new home in an unnamed northern city in 1912. Wearing their Sunday best, they carried the rest of what they owned in two suitcases. Several factors, including World War I and unemployment, combined to prompt the massive African American migration out of the South.

Photographs and Prints Division, Schomburg Center for Research in Black Culture, New York Public Library, Astor, Lenox and Tilden Foundations.

The First World War provided African Americans with the opportunity to escape the South's cotton fields and kitchens. War channeled almost 5 million American workers into military service. Moreover, it caused the number of European immigrants to fall from more than a million in 1914 to 31,000 in 1918. Deprived of their traditional sources of laborers just as production demands were increasing, northern industrialists turned to black labor. Lured north by labor recruiters, newspapers, and word of mouth, young black men, who made up the bulk of the early migrants, found work in steel mills, shipyards, munitions plants, railroad yards, automobile factories, and mines. From 1915 to 1920, a half million blacks (approximately 10 percent of the South's black population) boarded trains bound for Philadelphia, Detroit, Cleveland, Chicago, St. Louis, and other industrial cities.

Opportunities differed from city to city. In Detroit, for example, blacks found work in automobile factories. Ford and other companies established strong relations with urban black churches, which acted as recruiters for the labor-strapped industry. Workers at Ford wore badges to get in the gates, and black men were so proud of their jobs that they wore their badges to church on Sunday. Thousands of migrants wrote home to tell family and friends about their experiences in the North. One man announced proudly that he had recently been promoted to "first assistant to the head carpenter." He added, "I should have been here twenty years ago. I just begin to feel like a man. . . . My children are going to the same school with the whites and I don't have to [h]umble to no one. I have registered— will vote the next election and there ain't any 'yes sir'—it's all yes and no and Sam and Bill."

But the North was not the promised land. Black men stood on the lowest rungs of the labor ladder. Jobs of any kind proved scarce for black women. Limited by both race and sex, most worked as domestic servants as they did in the South. The existing black middle class sometimes shunned the less educated, less sophisticated rural southerners crowding into northern cities. Many whites, fearful of losing jobs and status, lashed out against the new migrants. Savage race riots ripped through two dozen northern cities. The worst occurred in July 1917 when a mob of whites invaded a section of East St. Louis, Illinois, crowded with blacks who had been recruited to help break a strike. The mob murdered at least 39 people and left most of the black district in flames. In 1918, the nation witnessed 96 lynchings of blacks, some of them returning war veterans still in uniform.

African Americans in the military also experienced racial violence. The worst episode occurred in August 1917 when a group of armed black soldiers in Houston, Texas, set out to avenge incidents of harassment by the police. In the clash that followed, thirteen whites, including several policemen, and one black soldier were killed. With vengeful swiftness that denied any appeal, a military court had thirteen black soldiers hanged and sentenced forty-one others to life imprisonment.

Still, most black migrants stayed in the North and encouraged friends and family to follow. By 1940, more than one million blacks had left the South, profoundly changing their own lives and the course of the nation's history. Black enclaves such as Harlem in New York and the South Side of Chicago, "cities within cities," emerged in the North. These assertive communities provided a foundation for black protest and political organization in the years ahead.

At nearly the same moment that black Americans streamed into northern cities, another migration was under way in the American Southwest. Between

1910 and 1920, the Mexican-born population in the United States soared from 222,000 to 478,000. Mexican immigration resulted from developments on both sides of the border. At the turn of the twentieth century, the Mexican dictator Porfirio Diaz initiated land policies that decimated poor farmers. When the Mexicans revolted against Diaz in 1910, initiating a ten-year civil war, the trickle of migration became a flood. North of the border, the Chinese Exclusion Act of 1882 and later the disruption of World War I cut off the supply of cheap foreign labor and caused western employers in the expanding rail, mining, construction, and agricultural industries to look south to Mexico for workers.

As a result of Americans' racial stereotyping of Mexicans—a U.S. government economist described them as "docile, patient, usually orderly in camp, fairly intelligent under competent supervision, obedient and cheap"—Mexicans were considered excellent prospects for manual labor but not for citizenship. Employers tried to dampen racial fears by stressing that the immigrants were only temporary residents, not a lasting threat. In 1917, when anti-immigration advocates convinced Congress to do something about foreigners coming into the United States, the restrictive legislation bowed to southwestern industry and exempted Mexicans. By 1920, ethnic Mexicans made up about three-fourths of California's farm laborers. They were also crucial to the Texas economy, accounting for three-fourths of laborers in the cotton fields and in construction there.

Like immigrants from Europe and black migrants from the South, Mexicans in the American Southwest dreamed of a better life. And like the others, they found both opportunity and disappointment. Wages were better than in Mexico, but life in the fields, mines, and factories was hard, and living conditions—in boxcars, labor camps, or urban barrios—often were dismal. Signs warning "No Mexicans Allowed" increased rather than declined. Mexican women nurtured families, but many also worked for wages. Thousands of women picked cotton, sometimes dragging hundred-pound cotton sacks with a baby perched on top. Among Mexican Americans, some of whom had lived in the Southwest for a century or more, *los recien llegados* (the recent arrivals) encountered mixed reactions. One Mexican American expressed this ambivalence: "We are all Mexicans anyway because the *gueros* [Anglos] treat us all alike." But he also called for immigration quotas because the recent arrivals drove down wages and incited white prejudice that affected all ethnic Mexicans. *Los recien llegados* also harbored mixed feelings, sometimes calling Mexican Americans *pochos* (faded or bleached ones).

Despite friction, large-scale immigration into the Southwest meant a resurgence of the Mexican cultural presence, which became the basis for greater solidarity and political action for the ethnic Mexican population. Shortly after World War I, Mexican Americans began organizing, a development that culminated with the formation of the League of United Latin American Citizens (LULAC) in Texas in 1929.

Postwar Politics and the Election of 1920

A thousand miles away in Washington, D.C., President Woodrow Wilson, bedridden and paralyzed, stubbornly ignored the mountain of domestic troubles—labor strikes, the Red scare, race riots, immigration backlash—and insisted that the 1920 election would be a "solemn referendum" on the League of Nations. Dutifully, the Democratic nominees for president, James M. Cox of Ohio, and for vice president, Franklin Delano Roosevelt of New York, campaigned on Wilson's international ideals. The Republican Party chose the handsome, gregarious Warren Gamaliel Harding, senator from Ohio. Harding's rise in Ohio politics was a tribute to his amiability, not his mastery of the issues.

Harding found the winning formula when he declared that "America's present need is not heroics, but healing; not nostrums [questionable remedies] but normalcy." But what was "normalcy"? Harding explained: "By 'normalcy' I don't mean the old order but a regular steady order of things. I mean normal procedure, the natural way, without excess." Eager to put wartime crusades and postwar strife behind them, voters responded by giving Harding the largest presidential victory ever: 60.5 percent of the popular vote and 404 out of 531 electoral votes. Once in office, Harding and his wife, Florence, threw open the White House gates, which had been closed since the declaration of war in 1917. Their welcome brought throngs of visitors and lifted the national pall, signaling a new, more easygoing era.

▶**REVIEW**   How did the Red scare contribute to the erosion of civil liberties after the war?

Conclusion: Troubled Crusade

America's experience in World War I was exceptional. For much of the world, the Great War produced great destruction, acres of blackened fields, ruined factories, and millions of casualties. But in the United States, war and prosperity marched hand in hand. America emerged from the war with the strongest economy in the world and a position of international preeminence.

Still, the nation paid a heavy price both at home and abroad. American soldiers and sailors encountered unprecedented horrors—submarines, poison gas, machine guns—and more than 100,000 died. On Memorial Day 1919, at the Argonne Cemetery, where 14,200 Americans lie, General John J. Pershing said: "It is not for us to proclaim what they did, their silence speaks more eloquently than words, but it is for us to uphold the conception of duty, honor and country for which they fought and for which they died. It is for the living to carry forward their purpose and make fruitful their sacrifice." Rather than redeeming their sacrifice, however, as Wilson promised, the peace that followed the armistice tarnished it. At home, rather than permanently improving working conditions, advancing public health, and spreading educational opportunity, as progressives had hoped, the war threatened to undermine the achievements of the previous two decades. Moreover, rather than promoting democracy in the United States, the war bred fear, intolerance, and repression that led to a crackdown on dissent and a demand for conformity. Reformers could count only woman suffrage as a permanent victory.

Woodrow Wilson had promised more than anyone could deliver. Progressive hopes of extending democracy and **liberal** reform nationally and internationally were dashed. In 1920, a bruised and disillusioned society stumbled into a new decade. The era coming to an end had called on Americans to crusade and sacrifice. The new era promised peace, prosperity, and a good time.

REVIEWING THE CHAPTER

Use the questions and timeline to review and strengthen your understanding of the chapter.

REVIEW QUESTIONS

1. Why did President Wilson authorize repeated military interventions in the Americas? (pp. 686–92)

2. How did the American Expeditionary Force contribute to the defeat of Germany? (pp. 693–97)

3. How did progressive ideals fare during wartime? (pp. 697–703)

4. Why did the Senate fail to ratify the Versailles treaty? (pp. 703–8)

5. How did the Red scare contribute to the erosion of civil liberties after the war? (pp. 708–15)

MAKING CONNECTIONS

1. Why did the United States at first resist intervening in World War I? Why did it later retreat from this policy and send troops? In your answer, discuss whether these decisions revised or reinforced earlier U.S. foreign policy.

2. Some reformers were optimistic that World War I would advance progressive ideals at home. Discuss specific wartime domestic developments that displayed progressivism's influence. How did war contribute to these developments? Did they endure in peacetime? Why or why not?

3. A conservative reaction in American politics followed peace, most vividly in the labor upheaval and Red scare that swept the nation. What factors drove these developments? How did they shape the postwar political spectrum?

4. During World War I, the nation witnessed important demographic changes. What drove African American and Mexican migration north? How did the war facilitate these changes? In your answer, explain the significance of these developments to the migrants and the nation.

TIMELINE

1914
- **April.** U.S. marines occupy Veracruz, Mexico.
- **June 28.** Assassination of Archduke Franz Ferdinand.
- **July 18.** Austria-Hungary declares war on Serbia.
- **August 3.** Germany attacks Russia and France.
- **August 4.** Great Britain declares war on Germany.

1915
- *Lusitania* sunk.
- Women's Peace Party formed.
- Italy joins Allies.

1916–1917
- General Pershing pursues Pancho Villa.
- Wilson reelected.

1917
- Zimmermann telegram intercepted.
- **April 6.** United States declares war on Germany.
- Committee on Public Information created.
- Selective Service Act.
- Espionage Act, Trading with the Enemy Act, and Sedition Act.
- East St. Louis, Illinois, race riot.
- Russia arranges separate peace with Germany.

1918
- **January 8.** President Wilson gives Fourteen Points speech.
- **May–June.** U.S. marines see first major combat at Cantigny and Château-Thierry.
- **November 11.** Armistice signed ending World War I.

1919
- **January.** Paris peace conference begins.
- **June.** Treaty of Versailles signed.
- **September.** Wilson undertakes speaking tour.
- Wave of labor strikes.

1920
- **January 1.** Prohibition begins.
- **January.** Palmer raids.
- **March.** Senate votes against ratification of Treaty of Versailles.
- **August 18.** Nineteenth Amendment ratified.
- **November.** Republican Warren G. Harding elected president.

▶ For an online bibliography, practice quizzes, Web sites, images, and documents related to this chapter, see the Book Companion Site at **bedfordstmartins.com/roark.**

▶ For firsthand accounts of this period, see Chapter 22 in Michael Johnson, ed., *Reading the American Past,* Fourth Edition.

CHAPTER

From New Era to Great Depression
1920–1932

A MERICANS IN THE 1920s cheered Henry Ford as an authentic American hero. When the decade began, he had already produced six million automobiles; by 1927, the figure reached fifteen million. In 1920, one car rolled off the Ford assembly line every minute; in 1925, one appeared every ten seconds. In 1920, a Ford car cost $845; in 1928, the price was less than $300, within range of most of the country's skilled workingmen. Henry Ford put America on wheels, and in the eyes of most Americans, he was an honest man who made an honest car: basic, inexpensive, and reliable. He became the greatest example of free enterprise's promise and achievement. But like the age in which he lived, Henry Ford was many-sided, more complex and contradictory than this simple image suggests.

Born in 1863 on a farm in Dearborn, Michigan, Ford hated the drudgery of farmwork and loved tinkering with machines. At sixteen, he fled rural life for Detroit, where he became a journeyman machinist and experimented with internal combustion engines. In 1893, he put together one of the first successful gasoline-driven carriages in the United States. His ambition, he said, was to "make something in quantity." The product he chose reflected American restlessness, the desire to be on the move. "Everybody wants to be someplace he ain't," Ford declared. "As soon as he gets there he wants to go right back." In 1903, with $28,000 from a few backers, Ford gathered twelve workers in a 250-by-50-foot shed and created the Ford Motor Company.

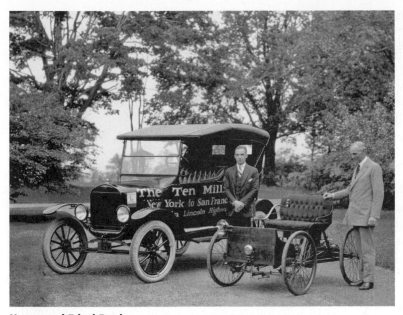

Henry and Edsel Ford
In this 1924 photograph, Henry Ford looks fondly at his first car while his son, Edsel,
stands next to the ten millionth Model T. An acute observer, Edsel Ford realized by
the mid-1920s that General Motors' more advanced Chevrolet was about to surpass
the Model T. Henry Ford stubbornly refused to change his automobile, but under
Edsel's leadership, the Ford Motor Company moved beyond the plain, boxy, black,
and fabulously successful Model T.
Henry Ford Museum and Greenfield Village.

Ford's early cars were custom-made one at a time. By 1914, his cars were
being built along a continuously moving assembly line; workers bolted on parts
brought to them by cranes and conveyor belts. Ford made only one kind of car,
the Model T, which became synonymous with mass production. A boxlike black
vehicle, it was cheap, easy to drive, and simple to repair. The Model T dominated
the market. Throughout the rapid expansion of the automotive industry, the Ford
Motor Company remained the industry leader, peaking in 1925, when it outsold
all its rivals combined.

Nobody entertained grander or more contradictory visions of the new
America he had helped to create than Henry Ford himself. When he began his
rise, **progressive** critics condemned the industrial giants of the nineteenth century as "robber barons" who lived in luxury while reducing their workers to
wage slaves. Ford, however, identified with the common folk and saw himself as
the benefactor of Americans yearning to be free and mobile.

Ford's automobile plants made him a billionaire, but their highly regimented
assembly lines reduced Ford workers to near robots. On the cutting edge of
modern technology, Ford nevertheless remained nostalgic about rural values. He

sought to revive the past in Greenfield Village, a museum outside Detroit, where he relocated buildings from a bygone era, including his parents' farmhouse. His museum contrasted sharply with the roaring Ford plant farther along the Detroit River at River Rouge. The African American and immigrant workers who worked there found no place in Greenfield Village. Yet all would be well, Ford insisted, if Americans remained true to their agrarian past and somehow managed to be modern and scientific at the same time.

Tension between traditional values and modern conditions lay at the heart of the conflicted 1920s. For the first time, more Americans lived in urban than in rural areas, yet Americans remained nostalgic about farms and small towns. Although the nation generally prospered, the new wealth widened the gap between rich and poor. While millions admired urban America's sophisticated new style and consumer products, others condemned postwar society for its vulgar materialism. A great outpouring of artistic talent led, ironically, to incessant critiques of America's artistic barrenness. The Ku Klux Klan and other champions of an idealized older America resorted to violence as well as words when they chastised the era's "new woman," "New Negro," and surging immigrant populations.

The public, disillusioned with the outcome of World War I, turned from the Christian moralism and idealism of the Progressive Era. In the twenties, Ford and businessmen like him replaced political reformers such as Theodore Roosevelt and Woodrow Wilson as the models of progress. The U.S. Chamber of Commerce crowed, "The American businessman is the most influential person in the nation." Social justice gave way to individual advancement. At the center of it all, President Calvin Coolidge spoke in praise of those in power when he declared, "The business of America is business." The fortunes of the era rose, then crashed, according to the values and practices of the business community.

The New Era

The rejection of progressives' pleas for government intervention and regulation in favor of the revival of free-enterprise individualism helped make the 1920s a time of contradiction and ambivalence. Once Woodrow Wilson left the White House, the energy generated by the crusade in Europe flowed away from civic reform and toward private economic endeavor. The rise of a freewheeling economy and a heightened sense of individualism caused Secretary of Commerce Herbert Hoover to declare that America had entered a "New Era," one of many labels used to describe the complex 1920s. Some terms focus on the decade's high-spirited energy and cultural changes: Roaring Twenties, Jazz Age, Flaming Youth, Age of the Flapper. Others echo the rising importance of money—Dollar Decade, Golden Twenties, Prosperity Decade—or reflect the sinister side of gangster profiteering—Lawless Decade. Still others emphasize the lonely confusion of the Lost Generation and the stress and anxiety of the Aspirin Age.

America in the twenties was many things, but there was no getting around the truth of Calvin Coolidge's insight: The business of America *was* business. Politicians and diplomats proclaimed business the heart of American civilization. Average men and women bought into the idea that business and its wonderful products were what made America great, as they snatched up the unprecedented flood of new consumer items American factories sent forth.

A Business Government

Republicans controlled the White House from 1921 to 1933. The first of the three Republican presidents was Warren Gamaliel Harding, the Ohio senator who in his 1920 campaign called for a "return to normalcy," by which he meant the end of public crusades and a return to private pursuits. Harding, who had few qualifications for the presidency, promised a government run by the best minds, and he appointed to his cabinet a few men of real stature. Herbert Hoover, the self-made millionaire and former head of the wartime Food Administration, became secretary of commerce and, according to one wag who testified to Hoover's ambition and energy, assistant secretary of everything else. But wealth also counted. Most significantly, Harding answered the call of **conservatives** and appointed Andrew Mellon, one of the richest men in America, secretary of the treasury. And friendship counted, too. Harding handed out jobs to his old "Ohio gang," whose only qualification was their friendship. This curious combination of merit and cronyism made for a disjointed administration in which a few "best minds" debated national needs, while much less qualified men looked for ways to advance their own interests.

When Harding was elected in 1920 in a landslide over Democratic opponent James Cox, the unemployment rate hit 20 percent, the highest ever up to that point. Farmers fared the worst, as their bankruptcy rate increased tenfold. Harding pushed measures to aid American enterprise and regain national prosperity—high tariffs to protect American businesses (the Fordney-McCumber tariff in 1922 raised duties to unprecedented heights), price supports for agriculture, and the dismantling of wartime government control over industry in favor of unregulated private business. "Never before, here or anywhere else," the U.S. Chamber of Commerce said proudly, "has a government been so completely fused with business."

Harding's policies to boost American enterprise made him very popular, but ultimately his small-town congeniality and trusting ways did him in. Some of his friends in the "Ohio gang" were up to their necks in lawbreaking. Three of Harding's appointees would go to jail, and others would be indicted. Interior Secretary Albert Fall was convicted of accepting bribes of more than $400,000 for leasing oil reserves on public land in Teapot Dome, Wyoming, and "Teapot Dome" became a synonym for political corruption.

Baffled about how to deal with "my God-damned friends," Harding in the summer of 1923 set off on a trip to Alaska to escape his troubles. But the president found no rest, and his health declined. On August 2, 1923, a shocked nation learned of the fifty-eight-year-old Harding's death from a heart attack.

Vice President Calvin Coolidge was vacationing at his family's farmhouse in Plymouth Notch, Vermont, when he was awakened during the night with the news of Harding's death. The family gathered in the parlor, where, by the flickering light of an oil lamp, Coolidge's father, a justice of the peace, swore his son in as president. This rustic drama had the intended effect of calming a nation confronting the death of a president and continuing scandal in Washington.

Coolidge once expressed his belief that "the man who builds a factory builds a temple, the man who works there worships there." Reverence for free enterprise meant that Coolidge continued and extended Harding's policies of promoting business and limiting government. With Coolidge's approval, Secretary of the Treasury Andrew Mellon reduced the government's control over the economy. Tax cuts for corporations and wealthy individuals sliced government tax revenue by about half. New rules for the Federal Trade Commission severely limited its power to regulate business. Secretary of Commerce Herbert Hoover limited government authority by encouraging trade associations that would keep business honest and efficient through voluntary cooperation.

Coolidge found a staunch ally in the Supreme Court. For many years, the Court had opposed federal regulation of hours, wages, and working conditions on the grounds that such legislation was the proper concern of the states. With Coolidge, the Court also found ways to curtail a state's ability to regulate business. It ruled against **closed shops**—businesses where only union members could be employed—while confirming the right of owners to form exclusive trade associations. In 1923, the Court declared unconstitutional the District of Columbia's minimum-wage law for women, asserting that the law interfered with the freedom of employer and employee to make labor contracts. On a broad front, the Court and the president attacked government intrusion in the free market, even when the prohibition of government regulation threatened the welfare of workers.

The election of 1924 confirmed the defeat of the progressive principle that the state should take a leading role in ensuring the general welfare. To oppose Coolidge, the Democrats nominated John W. Davis, a corporate lawyer whose conservative views differed little from Republican principles. Only the Progressive Party and its presidential nominee, Senator Robert La Follette of Wisconsin, offered a genuine alternative. When La Follette championed labor unions, regulation of business, and protection of civil liberties, Republicans coined the slogan "Coolidge or Chaos." By 1924, most Americans had turned their backs on what they considered labor radicalism and reckless reform, and Coolidge captured more votes than his two opponents put together. The election proved that Coolidge was right when he declared, "This is a business country, and it wants a business government." What was true of the government's relationship to business at home was also true abroad.

Promoting Prosperity and Peace Abroad

After orchestrating the Senate's successful effort to block U.S. membership in the League of Nations, Henry Cabot Lodge boasted, "We have torn Wilsonism up by the roots." But repudiation of Wilsonian internationalism and rejection of **collective security** through the League of Nations did not mean that the United States retreated into **isolationism**. The United States emerged from World War I with its economy intact and enjoyed a decade of stunning growth. Economic involvement in the world and the continuing chaos in Europe made withdrawal impossible. Corporate chieftain Owen Young observed: "Whether the United States will sit in the court of great economic movements throughout the world is not a question which the Senate, or even all of our people combined can decide. We are there . . . inescapably there." New York replaced London as the center of world finance, and the United States became the world's chief creditor. American banks poured billions into war-torn Europe's economic recovery. Europe not only absorbed American loans and products but also encountered a flood of American popular culture in the form of fashion, style, and Hollywood motion pictures.

One of the Republicans' most ambitious foreign policy initiatives was the Washington Disarmament Conference, which convened to establish a global balance of naval power. Secretary of State Charles Evans Hughes shaped the Five-Power Naval Treaty of 1922 committing Britain, France, Japan, Italy, and the United States to a proportional reduction of naval forces. The treaty led to the scrapping of more than two million tons of warships, by far the world's greatest success in disarmament. Americans celebrated President Harding for safeguarding the peace while remaining outside the League of Nations. By fostering international peace, he also helped make the world a safer place for American trade.

A second major effort on behalf of world peace came in 1928, when Secretary of State Frank Kellogg joined French foreign minister Aristide Briand to produce the Kellogg-Briand pact. Nearly fifty nations signed the solemn pledge to renounce war and settle international disputes peacefully. Most Americans considered the nation's signature an affirmation of its commitment to peace rather than to Wilson's foolish notion of a progressive, uplifting war.

But Republican administrations preferred private sector diplomacy to state action. With the blessing of the White House, a team of American financiers led by Chicago banker Charles Dawes swung into action when Germany suspended its war reparation payments in 1923. Impoverished, Germany was staggering under the massive bill of $33 billion presented by the victorious Allies in the Versailles treaty. When Germany failed to meet its annual payment, France sought to enforce the treaty by occupying Germany's industrial Ruhr Valley, creating the worst international crisis since the war. In 1924, American corporate leaders produced the Dawes Plan, which halved Germany's annual reparation payments, initiated fresh American loans to Germany, caused the French to retreat from the Ruhr, and got money flowing again in Germany's financial markets. Although the United States failed to join the league, it continued to exercise significant economic and diplomatic influence abroad. These Republican successes overseas helped fuel prosperity at home.

Automobiles, Mass Production, and Assembly-Line Progress

The automobile industry emerged as the largest single manufacturing industry in the nation. By the end of the decade, aided by the federal government's decision to spend more on roads than on anything else, cars, trucks, and buses surged past railroads as the primary haulers of passengers and freight. Henry Ford shrewdly located his company in Detroit. Key materials for the automobile were manufactured in nearby states, making their transport convenient. Keystone of the American economy, the automobile industry not only employed hundreds of thousands of workers directly but also brought whole industries into being—filling stations, garages, fast-food restaurants, and "guest cottages" (motels). The need for tires, glass, steel, highways, oil, and refined gasoline for automobiles provided millions of related jobs. By 1929, one American in four found employment directly or indirectly in the automobile industry. "Give us our daily bread" was no longer addressed to the Almighty, one commentator quipped, but to Detroit.

Automobiles altered the face of America. Cars changed where people lived, what work they did, how they spent their leisure, even how they thought. Hundreds of small towns decayed because the automobile enabled rural people to bypass them in favor of more distant cities and towns. The one-room schoolhouse and the crossroads church began to vanish from the landscape. Urban streetcars began to disappear as workers moved from the cities to the suburbs and commuted to work along crowded highways. In Los Angeles, which boasted of the nation's most extensive system of electric trolleys, almost a thousand miles of track suffered a slow death at the hands of the automobile. Nothing shaped modern America more than the automobile, and efficient mass production made the automobile revolution possible.

Mass production by the assembly-line technique had become standard in almost every factory, from automobiles to meatpacking to cigarettes. To improve efficiency, corporations reduced assembly-line work to the simplest, most repetitive tasks. They also established specialized divisions—procurement, production, marketing, and employee relations—each with its own team of professionally trained managers. Changes on the assembly line and in management, along with technological advances, significantly boosted overall efficiency. Between 1922 and 1929, productivity in manufacturing increased 32 percent. Average wages, however, increased only 8 percent. As assembly lines became standard, laborers lost many of the skills in which they had once taken pride, but corporations reaped great profits from these changes.

Industries also developed programs for workers that came to be called **welfare capitalism**. Some businesses improved safety and sanitation inside factories and instituted paid vacations and pension plans. Welfare capitalism purposely encouraged loyalty to the company and discouraged traditional labor unions. Not wanting to relive the chaotic strikes of 1919, industrialists sought to eliminate reasons for workers to join unions. One labor organizer in the steel industry bemoaned the success of welfare capitalism. "So many workmen here had been lulled to sleep by the company union, the welfare plans, the social organizations fostered by the employer," he declared, "that they had come to look upon the employer as their protector, and had believed vigorous trade union organization unnecessary for their welfare."

Consumer Culture

Mass production fueled corporate profits and national economic prosperity. Despite a brief postwar recession, the economy grew spectacularly during the 1920s. Per capita income increased by a third, the cost of living stayed the same, and unemployment remained low. But the rewards of the economic boom were not evenly distributed. Americans who labored with their hands inched ahead, while white-collar workers enjoyed significantly more spending money and more leisure time to spend it. Mass production of a broad range of new products—automobiles, radios, refrigerators, electric irons, washing machines—produced a consumer-goods revolution.

In this new era of abundance, more people than ever conceived of the American dream in terms of the things they could acquire. How the business boom and business values of the 1920s affected average Americans is revealed in the classic *Middletown* (1929), an analysis of the lives of the inhabitants of Muncie, Indiana. Muncie was, above all, "a culture in which everything hinges on money." Moreover, faced with technological and organizational change beyond their comprehension, many citizens had lost confidence in their ability to play an effective role in civic affairs. Instead, they deferred to the supposed expertise of leaders in politics and economics and so found themselves relegated to the role of more passive consumers.

The pied piper of these disturbing changes, according to *Middletown*, was the rapidly expanding business of advertising, which stimulated the desire for new products and hammered away at the traditional values of thrift and saving. Newspapers, magazines, radios, and billboards told Americans what they had to have in order to be popular, secure, and successful. Advertising linked material goods to the fulfillment of every spiritual and emotional need. Americans increasingly defined and measured their social status, and indeed their personal worth, on the yardstick of material possessions. Happiness itself rode on owning a car and choosing the right cigarettes and toothpaste.

By the 1920s, the United States had achieved the physical capacity to satisfy Americans' material wants (Figure 23.1). The economic problem shifted from production to consumption: Who would buy the goods flying off American assembly lines? One solution was to expand America's markets in foreign countries, and government and business joined in that effort. Another solution to the problem of consumption was to expand the market at home.

Henry Ford realized early on that "mass production requires mass consumption." He understood that automobile workers not only produced cars but would also buy them if they made enough money. "One's own employees ought to be one's own best customers," Ford said. In 1914, he raised wages in his factories to $5 a day, more than twice the going rate. High wages made for workers who were more loyal and more exploitable, and high wages returned as profits when workers bought Fords. Within twenty-four hours of Ford's announcement, ten thousand men had lined up outside his employment office in Detroit.

FIGURE 23.1   Production of Consumer Goods, 1920–1930
Transportation, communications, and entertainment changed the lives of consumers in the 1920s. Laborsaving devices for the home were popular, but the vastly greater sales of automobiles and radios showed that consumerism was powerful in moving people's attention beyond their homes.

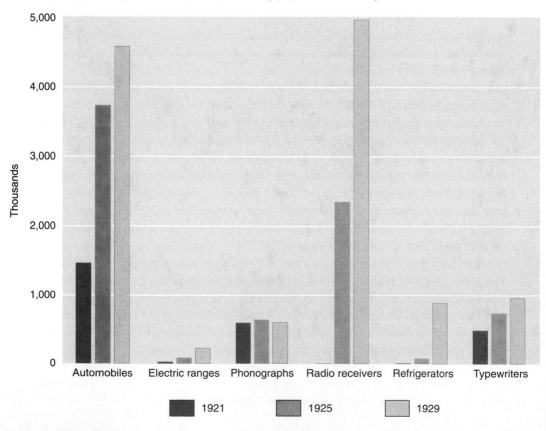

Not all industrialists were as farseeing as Ford. Because the wages of many workers barely edged upward, many people's incomes were too puny to satisfy the growing desire for consumer goods. Business supplied the solution: Americans could realize their dreams through credit. Installment buying—a little money down, a payment each month—allowed people to purchase expensive items they could not otherwise afford or purchase items before saving the necessary money. As one newspaper announced, "The first responsibility of an American to his country is no longer that of a citizen, but of a consumer." During the 1920s, America's motto became spend, not save. Old values—"Use it up, wear it out, make it do or do without"—seemed about as pertinent as a horse and buggy. American **culture** had shifted.

▶**REVIEW**   How did the spread of the automobile transform the United States?

The Roaring Twenties

By the beginning of the decade, psychoanalyst Sigmund Freud had become a household name. Most Americans knew little of the complexity of his pioneering work in the psychology of the unconscious because they learned about his therapies in popular magazines. Still, people realized that Freud offered a way of looking at the world that was as radically different and important to the twentieth century as Charles Darwin's theory of evolution had been to the century before. In the twenties, much to Freud's disgust, the American media turned his therapeutic wisdom about the sexual origins of behavior on its head. If it is wrong to deny that we are sexual beings, some reasoned, then the key to health and fulfillment must lie in following impulse freely. Those who doubted this reasoning were simply "repressed."

The new ethic of personal freedom excited a significant number of Americans to seek pleasure without guilt in a whirl of activity that earned the decade the name "Roaring Twenties." Prohibition made lawbreakers of millions of otherwise decent folk. Flappers and "new women" challenged traditional gender boundaries. Other Americans enjoyed the "Roaring Twenties" at a safe distance through the words and images of vastly expanded mass communication. Motion pictures, radio, and magazines marketed celebrities. In the freedom of America's big cities, particularly New York, a burst of creativity produced the "New Negro," who confounded and disturbed white Americans. The "Lost Generation" of writers, profoundly disillusioned with mainstream America's cultural direction, fled the country.

Prohibition

Republicans generally sought to curb the powers of government and liberate private initiative, but the twenties witnessed a great exception to this rule when the federal government implemented one of the last reforms of the Progressive Era: the Eighteenth Amendment, which banned the manufacture and sale of alcohol and took effect in January 1920 (see chapter 22) and made the United States the world's only society ever to outlaw its most popular intoxicant. Drying up the rivers of liquor that Americans consumed, supporters of prohibition declared, would boost production, eliminate crime, and lift the nation's morality. A powerful coalition supported prohibition, but women were particularly enthusiastic because heavy drinking was closely associated with domestic violence and poverty.

Charged with enforcing prohibition, the Treasury Department put more than 3,000 agents in the field, and in 1925 alone, they smashed more than 172,000 illegal stills. The annual per person consumption of alcoholic beverages declined from 2.60 gallons just before prohibition to less than a gallon in 1934, the year after prohibition ended. But Treasury agents faced a staggering task. Local resistance was intense. In 1929, an agent in Indiana reported, "Conditions in most important cities very bad. Lax and corrupt public officials great handicap . . . prevalence of drinking among minor boys and the . . . middle or better class of adults." The "speakeasy," a place where men (and, increasingly, women) drank publicly, became a common feature of the urban landscape. There, bootleggers, so named a century before because they put bottles in their tall boots to sneak past tax collectors, provided whiskey smuggled from Canada, tequila from Mexico, and liquor concocted in makeshift stills. Otherwise upright people discovered the thrill of breaking the law. One dealer, trading on common knowledge that whiskey still flowed in the White House, distributed cards advertising himself as the "President's Bootlegger."

Eventually, serious criminals took over the liquor trade. Alphonse "Big Al" Capone became the era's most notorious gang lord by establishing in Chicago a bootlegging empire that reputedly grossed more than $60 million in a single year. During the first four years of prohibition, Chicago witnessed more than two hundred gang-related killings as rival mobs struggled for control of the lucrative liquor trade. The most notorious event came on St. Valentine's Day 1929, when Capone's Italian-dominated mob machine-gunned seven members of a rival Irish gang. Federal authorities finally sent Capone to prison for income tax evasion. "I give the public what the public wants," Capone told a reporter, "and all I get is abuse." Capone was a gangster, but he portrayed himself as a resourceful entrepreneur and successful businessman.

Gang-war slayings prompted demands for the repeal of the Eighteenth Amendment. In 1931, a panel of distinguished experts reported that prohibition, which supporters had defended as "a great social and economic experiment," had failed. The social and political costs of prohibition outweighed the benefits. Prohibition caused ordinary citizens to disrespect the law, corrupted the police, and demoralized the judiciary. In 1933, after thirteen years, the nation ended prohibition, making the Eighteenth Amendment the only constitutional amendment to be subsequently repealed.

The New Woman

Of all the changes in American life in the 1920s, none sparked more heated debate than the alternatives offered to the traditional roles of women. Increasing numbers of women worked and went to college, defying older gender hierarchies and norms. Even mainstream magazines such as the *Saturday Evening Post* began publishing stories about young, college-educated women who drank gin cocktails, smoked cigarettes, wore skimpy dresses and dangly necklaces, daringly rolled their stockings at the knee, and enjoyed sex. Before the Great War, the "new woman" dwelt in New York City's bohemian Greenwich Village, but afterward the mass media brought her into middle-class America's living rooms.

Politically, women entered uncharted territory when the Nineteenth Amendment, ratified in 1920, granted them the vote. **Feminists** felt liberated and expected women to reshape the political landscape. Celebrating enfranchisement, a Kansas woman declared, "I went to bed last night a *slave*[;] I awoke this morning a *free woman*." Women began pressuring Congress to pass laws that especially concerned women, including measures to protect women in factories and grant federal aid to schools. Black women lobbied particularly for federal courts to assume jurisdiction over the crime of lynching. But women's only significant legislative success came in 1921 when Congress enacted the Sheppard-Towner Act, which extended federal assistance to states seeking to reduce shockingly high infant mortality rates. Rather than the beginning of women's political success, the act marked the high tide of women's influence in the 1920s.

A number of factors helped thwart women's political influence. Male domination of both political parties, the rarity of female candidates, and lack of experience in voting, especially among recent immigrants, kept many women away from the polls. In the South, poll taxes, literacy tests, and outright terrorism continued to decimate the vote of African Americans, men and women alike.

Most important, rather than forming a solid voting bloc, feminists divided. Some argued for women's right to special protection; others demanded equal protection. The radical National Woman's Party fought for an Equal Rights Amendment that stated flatly: "Men and women shall have equal rights throughout the United States." The more moderate League of Women Voters feared that the amendment's wording threatened state laws that provided women special protection, such as barring women from night work and preventing them from working on certain machines. Put before Congress in 1923, the Equal Rights Amendment went down to defeat, and radical women were forced to act within a network of private agencies and reform associations to advance the causes of birth control, legal equality for minorities, and the end of child labor.

Economically, women's relationship to paid work changed. More women worked for pay—approximately one in four by 1930—but they clustered in "women's jobs." The proportion of women working in manufacturing fell, while the number of women working as secretaries, stenographers, and typists skyrocketed. Women almost monopolized the occupations of librarian, nurse, elementary school teacher, and telephone operator. Women also represented 40 percent of salesclerks by 1930. More female white-collar workers meant fewer women were interested in protective legislation for women; new women wanted salaries and opportunities equal to men's.

Increased earnings gave working women more buying power and a special relationship with the new **consumer culture**. A stereotype soon emerged of the flapper, so called because of the short-lived fad of wearing unbuckled galoshes. The flapper had short "bobbed" hair and wore lipstick and rouge. She spent freely on the latest styles—dresses with short skirts and drop waists, bare arms, and no petticoats—and she danced all night to wild jazz.

The new woman both reflected and propelled the modern birth control movement. Margaret Sanger, the crusading pioneer for contraception during the Progressive Era, restated her principal conviction in 1920: "No woman can call herself free until she can choose consciously whether she will or will not be a mother." By shifting strategy in the twenties, Sanger courted the conservative American Medical Association; linked birth control with the eugenics movement, which advocated limiting reproduction among "undesirable" groups; and thus made contraception a respectable subject for discussion.

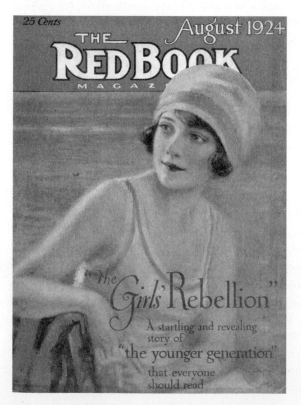

"The Girls' Rebellion"
The August 1924 cover of *Redbook*, a popular women's magazine, portrays the kind of postadolescent girl who was making respectable families frantic. Flappers scandalized their middle-class parents by flouting the old moral code. The cover promises a story inside about girls gone wild. Fictionalized, emotion-packed stories such as this brought the new woman into every woman's home.
Picture Research Consultants & Archives.

Flapper style and values spread from coast to coast through films, novels, magazines, and advertisements. New women challenged American convictions about **separate spheres** for women and men, the double standard of sexual conduct, and Victorian ideas of proper female appearance and behavior. Although only a minority of American women became flappers, all women, even those who remained at home, felt the great changes of the era.

The New Negro

The 1920s witnessed the emergence not only of the "new woman" but also of the "New Negro." Both new identities riled conservatives and reactionaries. African Americans who challenged the caste system that confined dark-skinned Americans to the lowest levels of society confronted whites who insisted that race relations would not change. Cheers for black soldiers quickly faded after their return from World War I, and African Americans soon faced grim days of economic hardship and race riots (see chapter 22).

During the 1920s, the prominent African American intellectual W. E. B. Du Bois and the National Association for the Advancement of Colored People (NAACP) aggressively pursued the passage of a federal antilynching law to counter mob violence against blacks in the South. Many poor blacks, however, disillusioned with mainstream politics, turned for new leadership to a Jamaican-born visionary named Marcus Garvey. Garvey urged African Americans to rediscover the heritage of Africa, take pride in their own culture and achievements, and maintain racial purity by avoiding **miscegenation**. In 1917, Garvey launched the Universal Negro Improvement Association (UNIA) to help African Americans gain economic and political independence entirely outside white society. In 1919, the UNIA created its own shipping company, the Black Star Line, to support the "Back to Africa" movement among black Americans. Garvey knew how to inspire followers, but he was no businessman, and the enterprise was an economic failure. In 1927, the federal government pinned charges of illegal practices on Garvey and deported him to Jamaica. Nevertheless, the issues Garvey raised about racial pride, black identity, and the search for equality persisted, and his legacy remains at the center of **black nationalist** thought.

Still, most African Americans maintained hope in the American promise. In New York City, hope and talent came together. Poor blacks from the South, as well as sophisticated immigrants from the West Indies, poured into Harlem in uptown Manhattan. New York City's black population increased 115 percent (from 152,000 to 327,000) in the 1920s, while its white population increased only 20 percent. Similar demographic changes occurred on a smaller scale throughout the urban North. Overcrowding and unsanitary housing accompanied this black population explosion, but so too did a new self-consciousness and self-confidence that fed into artistic accomplishment.

The extraordinary mix of black artists, sculptors, novelists, musicians, and poets in Harlem deliberately set out to create a distinctive African American culture that drew on their identities as Americans and Africans. As scholar Alain Locke put it in 1925, they introduced to the world the "New Negro," who rose from the ashes of slavery and segregation to proclaim African Americans' creative genius. The emergence of the New Negro came to be known as the Harlem Renaissance. Building on the independence and pride displayed by black soldiers during the war, black artists sought to defeat the fresh onslaught of racial discrimination and violence with poems, paintings, and plays. "We younger Negro artists . . . intend to express our individual dark-skinned selves without fear or shame," Langston Hughes, a determined young black poet, said of the Harlem Renaissance. "If white people are pleased, we are glad. If they are not, it doesn't matter. We know we are beautiful. And ugly, too."

The Harlem Renaissance produced dazzling talent. Black writer James Weldon Johnson, who in 1903 had written the Negro national anthem, "Lift Every Voice," wrote "God's Trombones" (1927), in which he expressed the wisdom and beauty of black folktales from the South. The poetry of Langston Hughes, Claude McKay, and Countee Cullen celebrated the vitality of life in Harlem. Zora Neale Hurston's novel *Their Eyes Were Watching God* (1937) explored the complex passions of black people in a southern community. Black painters, led by Aaron Douglas, linked African art, which had recently inspired European modernist artists, to the concept of the New Negro. In bold, colorful scenes, Douglas combined biblical and African myths in ways that expressed a powerful cultural heritage for African Americans.

Despite such vibrancy, Harlem for most whites remained a separate black ghetto known only for its lively nightlife. Fashionable whites crowded into Harlem's nightclubs, the most famous of which was the Cotton Club. There, whites believed they could hear "real" jazz, a relatively new musical form, in its "natural" surroundings. The vigor and optimism of the Harlem Renaissance left a powerful legacy for black Americans, but the creative burst did little in the short run to dissolve the prejudice of a white society not yet prepared to allow African Americans equal opportunities.

Mass Culture

By the late 1920s, jazz had captured the nation. Americans who clung to symphonic music called jazz "jungle music," but jazz giants such as Louis Armstrong, Jelly Roll Morton, and Duke Ellington, accompanied by singers such as Ma Rainey, Bessie Smith, and Ethel Waters, entertained huge audiences. Jazz was only one of the entertainment choices of Americans, however. In the twenties, popular culture, like consumer goods, was mass-produced and mass-consumed. Since politics was undemanding and uninteresting, Americans looked elsewhere for excitement. The proliferation of movies, radios, music, and sports meant that they found plenty to do, and in doing the same things, they helped create a national culture.

Nothing offered escapist delights like the movies. Admission was cheap, and in the dark, Americans of all classes could savor the same ideal of the good life. Blacks and whites, however, still entered theaters through separate entrances and sat separately. Hollywood, California, discovered the successful formula of combining opulence, sex, and adventure. By 1929, Hollywood was drawing more than 80 million people to the movies in a single week, as many as lived in the entire country. Rudolph Valentino, described as "catnip to women," and Clara Bow, the "It Girl" (everyone knew what *it* was), became household names. "America's Sweetheart," Mary Pickford, and her real-life husband, Douglas Fairbanks, offered more wholesome adventure. Most loved of all was the comic Charlie Chaplin, whose famous character, the wistful Little Tramp, showed an endearing inability to cope with the rules and complexities of modern life.

Americans also found heroes in sports. Baseball, professionalized since 1869 and segregated into white and black leagues, solidified its place as the national pastime in the 1920s. It remained essentially a game played by and for the working class, an outlet for raw energy with a tinge of rebelliousness. In George Herman "Babe" Ruth, baseball had the most cherished free spirit of the time. The "Sultan of Swat" mixed his record-setting home runs with rowdy escapades, demonstrating to fans that sports offered a way to break out of the ordinariness of everyday life. By "his sheer exuberance," one sportswriter declared, Ruth "has lightened the cares of the world."

The public also fell in love with a young boxer from the grim mining districts of Colorado. As a teenager, Jack Dempsey had made his living hanging around saloons betting he could beat anyone in the house. When he took the heavyweight crown just after World War I, he was revered as the people's champ, an American equalizer who was a stand-in for the average American who felt increasingly confined by bureaucracy and machine-made culture. In Philadelphia in 1926, a crowd of 125,000 fans saw challenger Gene Tunney carve up and defeat the people's champ.

Football, essentially a college sport, held greater sway with the upper classes. The most famous coach, Knute Rockne of Notre Dame, celebrated football for its life lessons of hard work and teamwork. Let the professors make learning as interesting and significant as football, Rockne advised, and the problem of getting young people to learn would disappear. But in keeping with the times, football moved toward a more commercial spectacle. Harold "Red" Grange, "the Galloping Ghost," led the way by going from stardom at the University of Illinois to the Chicago Bears in the new professional football league.

The decade's hero worship reached its zenith in the celebration of Charles Lindbergh, a young pilot who set out on May 20, 1927, from Long Island in his single-engine plane, *The Spirit of St. Louis*, to become the first person to fly nonstop across the Atlantic. Newspapers tagged Lindbergh "the Lone Eagle"—the perfect hero for an age that celebrated individual accomplishment. "Charles Lindbergh," one journalist proclaimed, "is the stuff out of which have been made the pioneers that opened up the wilderness. His are the qualities which we, as a people, must nourish." Lindbergh realized, however, that technical and organizational complexity was fast reducing chances for solitary achievement. Consequently, he titled his book about the flight *We* (1927) to include the machine that had made it all possible.

Another machine—the radio—became important to mass culture in the 1920s. The nation's first licensed radio station, KDKA in Pittsburgh, began broadcasting in 1920, and soon American airwaves buzzed with news, sermons, soap operas, sports, comedy, and music. Americans on the West Coast laughed at the latest jokes from New York. For the first time, citizens were able to listen to the voices of political candidates without leaving home. Because they could now reach prospective customers in their own homes, advertisers bankrolled radio's rapid growth. Between 1922 and 1929, the number of radio stations in the United States increased from 30 to 606. In just seven years, homes with radios jumped from 60,000 to a staggering 10.25 million.

Radio added to the spread of popular music, especially jazz. Jazz—with its energy and freedom—provided the sound track for a new, distinct social class of youths. As the traditional bonds of community, religion, and family loosened, the young felt less pressure to imitate their elders and more freedom to develop their own culture. An increasing number of college students helped the "rah-rah" style of college life become a fad promoted in movies, songs, and advertisements. The collegiate set was the vanguard of the decade's "flaming youth."

The Lost Generation

Some writers and artists felt alienated from America's mass-culture society, which they found shallow, anti-intellectual, and materialistic. Adoration of silly movie stars disgusted them. Moreover, they believed that business culture blighted American life. To their minds, Henry Ford made a poor hero. Young, white, and mostly college educated, these expatriates, as they came to be called, felt embittered by the war and renounced the progressives who had promoted it as a crusade. For them, Europe—not Hollywood or Harlem—seemed the place to seek their renaissance.

The American-born writer Gertrude Stein, long established in Paris, remarked famously as the young exiles gathered around her, "They are the lost generation." Most of the expatriates, however, believed to the contrary that they had finally found themselves. Far from the complications of home, the expatriates helped launch the most creative period in American art and literature in the twentieth century. The novelist whose spare, clean style best exemplified the expatriate efforts to make art mirror basic reality was Ernest Hemingway. Hemingway's experience in the Great War convinced him that the world in which he was raised, with its Christian moralism and belief in progress, was bankrupt. Admirers found the terse language and hard lessons of his novel *The Sun Also Rises* (1926) to be perfect expressions of a world stripped of illusions.

Many writers who remained in America were exiles in spirit. Before the war, intellectuals had eagerly joined progressive reform movements. Afterward, they were more likely to act as lonely critics of American cultural vulgarity. With prose dripping with scorn for conventional values, novelist Sinclair Lewis in *Main Street* (1920) and *Babbitt* (1922) satirized his native Midwest as a cultural wasteland. Humorists such as James Thurber created outlandish characters to poke fun at American stupidity and inhibitions. And southern writers, led by William Faulkner, explored the South's grim class and race heritage. Worries about alienation surfaced as well. Although F. Scott Fitzgerald gained fame and wealth as the chronicler of flaming youth, he spoke sadly in *This Side of Paradise* (1920) of a disillusioned generation "grown up to find all Gods dead, all wars fought, all faiths in man shaken."

▶ **REVIEW**   How did the new freedoms of the 1920s challenge older conceptions of gender and race?

Resistance to Change

Large areas of the country did not share in the wealth of the 1920s and had little confidence that they would anytime soon. By the end of the decade, 40 percent of the nation's farmers were landless, and 90 percent of rural homes had no indoor plumbing, gas, or electricity. Rural America's wariness and distrust of urban America turned to despair in the 1920s when the census reported that the majority of the population had shifted from the country to the city (Map 23.1, page 736). Urban domination over the nation's political and cultural life and sharply rising economic disparity drove rural Americans in often ugly, reactionary directions.

Cities seemed to stand for everything rural areas stood against. Rural America imagined itself as solidly Anglo-Saxon (despite the presence of millions of African Americans in the South and Mexican Americans, Native Americans, and Asian Americans in the West), and the cities seemed to be filled with undesirable immigrants. Rural America was the home of old-time **Protestant** religion, and the cities teemed with Catholics, Jews, liberal Protestants, and atheists. Rural America championed old-fashioned moral standards—abstinence and self-denial—while the cities spawned every imaginable vice. Once the "backbone of the Republic," rural Americans had become poor country cousins. In the 1920s, frustrated rural people sought to recapture their country by helping to push through prohibition, dam the flow of immigrants, revive the Ku Klux Klan, defend the Bible as literal truth, and defeat an urban Roman Catholic for president.

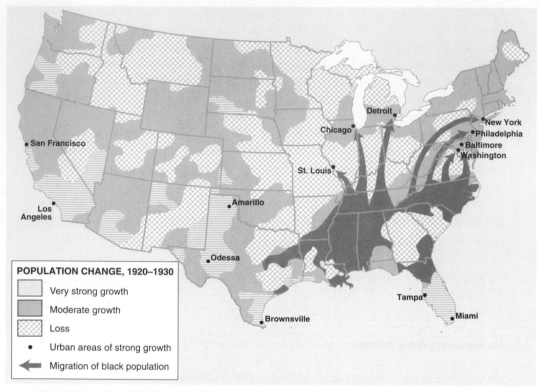

MAP 23.1   The Shift from Rural to Urban Population, 1920–1930
The movement of whites and Hispanics toward urban and agricultural opportunity made Florida, the West, and the Southwest the regions of fastest population growth. In contrast, large numbers of blacks left the rural South to find a better life in the North. Because most migrating blacks left the countryside for faraway cities, while white and Hispanic migrants tended to move shorter distances, the population shift brought more drastic overall change to blacks than to whites and Hispanics.

Rejecting the Undesirables

Before the war, when about a million immigrants arrived each year, some Americans warned that unassimilable foreigners were smothering the nation. War against Germany and its allies expanded **nativist** and antiradical sentiment. After the war, large-scale immigration resumed (another 800,000 immigrants arrived in 1921) at a moment when industrialists no longer needed new factory laborers. African American and Mexican migration had relieved labor shortages. Moreover, union leaders feared that millions of poor immigrants would undercut their efforts to organize American workers. Rural America's God-fearing Protestants were particularly alarmed that most of the immigrants were Catholic, Jewish, or atheist. In 1921, Congress responded by severely restricting immigration.

In 1924, Congress very nearly slammed the door shut. The Johnson-Reid Act limited the number of immigrants to no more than 161,000 a year and gave each European nation a quota based on 2 percent of the number of people from that country in America in 1890. The act revealed the fear and bigotry that fueled anti-immigration legislation. While it cut immigration by more than 80 percent, it squeezed some nationalities far more than others. Backers of Johnson-Reid openly declared that America had become the "garbage can and the dumping ground of the world," and they manipulated quotas to ensure entry only to "good" immigrants. By basing quotas on the 1890 census, in which western Europeans predominated, the law effectively reversed the trend toward immigration from southern and eastern Europe, which by 1914 had amounted to 75 percent of the yearly total. For example, the Johnson-Reid Act allowed Great Britain 62,458 entries, but Russia could send only 1,992.

The 1924 law reaffirmed the 1880s legislation barring Chinese immigrants and added Japanese and other Asians to the list of the excluded. But it left open immigration from the Western Hemisphere, and during the 1920s, some 500,000 Mexicans crossed the border. Farm interests preserved Mexican immigration because of Mexicans' value in southwestern agriculture.

Rural Americans, who had most likely never laid eyes on a Polish packing-house worker, a Slovak coal miner, an Armenian sewing machine operator, or a Chinese laundry worker, strongly supported the 1924 law, as did industrialists and labor leaders. The immigration restriction laws of the 1920s provided the basic framework for immigration policy until the 1960s. They marked the end of an era—the denial of the Statue of Liberty's open-arms welcome to Europe's "huddled masses yearning to breathe free."

Antiforeign hysteria climaxed in the trial of two **anarchist** immigrants from Italy, Nicola Sacco and Bartolomeo Vanzetti. Arrested in 1920 for robbery and murder in South Braintree, Massachusetts, the men were sentenced to death by a judge who openly referred to them as "anarchist bastards." In response to doubts about the fairness of the verdict, the governor of Massachusetts named a blue-ribbon review committee that found the trial judge guilty of a "grave breach of official decorum" but refused to recommend a motion for retrial. When Massachusetts executed Sacco and Vanzetti on August 23, 1927, fifty thousand mourners followed the caskets in the rain, convinced that the men had died because they were immigrants and radicals, not because they were murderers.

The Rebirth of the Ku Klux Klan

The nation's sour, antiforeign mood struck a responsive chord in members of the Ku Klux Klan. The Klan first appeared in the South during Reconstruction to thwart black freedom and expired with the reestablishment of white supremacy. In 1915, the Klan revived soon after D. W. Griffith's blockbuster

WKKK Badge

Some half a million women were members of the Women of the Ku Klux Klan (WKKK). Women fit perfectly within the KKK because the organization proclaimed itself the defender of the traditional virtues of pure womanhood and decent homes. This badge from Harrisburg, Pennsylvania, advertises the local WKKK's support for a home for "orphan and dependent children." Klanswomen also joined in boycotts of businesses owned by Jews and others whom they did not consider "100% American."

Collection of Janice L. and David J. Frent.

film *Birth of a Nation* celebrated earlier Klan racist violence as heroic and necessary. Reborn at Stone Mountain, Georgia, the new Klan extended its targets beyond black Americans and quickly spread beyond the South. Under a banner proclaiming "100 percent Americanism," the Klan promised to defend family, morality, and traditional American values against the threats posed by blacks, immigrants, radicals, feminists, Catholics, and Jews.

Building on the frustrations of rural America, the Klan attracted three million to four million members—women as well as men. Women members worked for prohibition, strong public schools, and traditional morality. By the mid-1920s, the Klan had spread throughout the nation, almost controlling Indiana and influencing politics in Illinois, California, Oregon, Texas, Louisiana, Oklahoma, and Kansas. The Klan's uniforms and rituals helped counter a sense of insignificance among people outside the new world of cities and corporations. In 1926, Klan imperial wizard Hiram Wesley Evans described the assault of modernity. "One by one all our traditional moral standards went by the boards or were so disregarded that they ceased to be binding," he explained. "The sacredness of our Sabbath, of our homes, of chastity, and finally even of our right to teach our own children in schools [were] fundamental facts and truth torn away from us." Americans "who maintained the old standards did so only in the face of constant ridicule," he said. The Klan offered a certain counterfeit dignity to old-stock, Protestant, white Americans who felt passed over, and its hoods allowed members to beat and intimidate their victims with little fear of consequences.

Eventually, social changes, along with lawless excess, crippled the Klan. Immigration restrictions eased the worry about invading foreigners, and sensational wrongdoing by Klan leaders cost it the support of traditional moralists. Grand Dragon David Stephenson of Indiana, for example, went to jail for the kidnapping and rape of a woman who subsequently committed suicide. Yet the social grievances, economic problems, and religious anxieties of the countryside and small towns remained, ready to be ignited.

The Scopes Trial

In 1925 in a steamy Tennessee courtroom, old-time religion and the new spirit of science went head-to-head. The confrontation occurred after several southern states passed legislation against the teaching of Charles Darwin's theory of evolution in the public schools. **Fundamentalist** Protestants insisted that the Bible's creation story be taught as the literal truth. In answer to a clamor from scientists and civil liberties organizations for a challenge to the law, John Scopes, a young biology teacher in Dayton, Tennessee, offered to test his state's ban on teaching evolution. When Scopes came to trial in the summer of 1925, Clarence Darrow, a brilliant defense lawyer from Chicago, volunteered to defend him. Darrow, an avowed agnostic, took on the prosecution's William Jennings Bryan, three-time Democratic nominee for president, symbol of rural America, and fervent fundamentalist, who was eager to defeat the proposition that humans had evolved from apes.

The Scopes trial quickly degenerated into a media circus. The first trial to be covered live on radio, it attracted an avid nationwide audience. Most of the reporters from big-city newspapers were hostile to Bryan, none more so than the cynical H. L. Mencken, who painted Bryan as a sort of Darwinian missing link ("a sweating anthropoid" and a "gaping primate"). When, under relentless questioning by Darrow, Bryan declared on the witness stand that he did indeed believe that the world had been created in six days and that Jonah had lived in the belly of a whale, his humiliation in the eyes of most urban observers was complete. Nevertheless, the Tennessee court upheld the law and punished Scopes with a $100 fine. Although fundamentalism won the battle, it lost the war. Mencken had the last word in a merciless obituary for Bryan, who died just a week after the trial ended. Portraying the "monkey trial" as a battle between the country and the city, Mencken flayed Bryan as a "charlatan, a mountebank, a zany without shame or dignity," motivated solely by "hatred of the city men who had laughed at him for so long."

As Mencken's acid prose indicated, Bryan's humiliation was not purely a victory of reason and science. It also revealed the disdain urban people felt for country people and the values they clung to. The Ku Klux Klan revival and the Scopes trial dramatized and inflamed divisions between city and country, intellectuals and the uneducated, the privileged and the poor, the scoffers and the faithful.

Al Smith and the Election of 1928

The presidential election of 1928 brought many of the developments of the 1920s—prohibition, immigration, religion, and the clash of rural and urban values—into sharp focus. Republicans emphasized the economic success of their party's pro-business government. But because both parties generally agreed that the American economy was basically sound, the campaign turned on social issues that divided Americans. Tired of the limelight, Calvin Coolidge chose not to seek reelection, and the Republicans turned to Herbert Hoover, the energetic secretary of commerce and the leading public symbol of 1920s prosperity.

The Democrats nominated four-time governor of New York Alfred E. Smith. Smith adopted "The Sidewalks of New York" as a campaign theme song and seemed to represent all that rural Americans feared and resented. A child of immigrants, Smith got his start in politics with the help of Tammany Hall, New York City's Irish-dominated political machine and the epitome of big-city corruption in many minds. He believed that immigration quotas were wrong, and he spoke out against restriction. He signed New York State's anti-Klan bill and condemned the decade's growing intolerance. Smith also opposed prohibition, believing that it was a nativist attack on immigrant customs. When Smith supposedly asked reporters in 1922, "Wouldn't you like to have your foot on the rail and blow the foam off some suds?" prohibition forces dubbed him "Alcohol Al."

Smith's greatest vulnerability in the heartland, however, was his religion. He was the first Catholic to run for president. A Methodist bishop in Virginia denounced Roman Catholicism as "the Mother of ignorance, superstition, intolerance and sin" and begged Protestants not to vote for a candidate who represented "the kind of dirty people that you find today on the sidewalks of New York." An editorial in the *Baptist and Commoner* argued that the election of Smith "would be granting the Pope the right to dictate to this government what it should do."

Hoover, who neatly combined the images of morality, efficiency, service, and prosperity, won the election by a landslide. He received nearly 58 percent of the vote and gained 444 electoral votes to Smith's 87. The Republicans' most notable success came in the previously solid Democratic South, where Smith's religion, views on prohibition, and big-city persona allowed them to take four states. Smith carried the Lower South, where the Democratic Party's identification with white supremacy prevailed. The Republican victory was marred only by the party's reduced support in the cities and among discontented farmers. The nation's largest cities voted Democratic in a striking reversal of 1924, indicating the rising strength of ethnic minorities, including Smith's fellow Catholics.

▶REVIEW   Why did the relationship between urban and rural America deteriorate in the 1920s?

The Great Crash

At his inauguration in 1929, Herbert Hoover told the American people, "Given a chance to go forward with the policies of the last eight years, we shall soon with the help of God be in sight of the day when poverty will be banished from this nation." Those words came back to haunt Hoover, for within eight months, the Roaring Twenties came to a crashing halt. The prosperity Hoover touted collapsed with the stock market, and the nation ended nearly three decades of barely interrupted economic growth. Like much of the world, the United States fell into the most serious economic depression of all time. Hoover and his reputation were among the first casualties, along with the reverence for business that had been the hallmark of the New Era.

Herbert Hoover: The Great Engineer

When Herbert Hoover became president in 1929, he seemed the perfect choice to lead a prosperous business nation. He personified America's rags-to-riches ideal, having risen from poor Iowa orphan to one of the world's most celebrated mining engineers by the time he was thirty. His success in managing efforts to feed civilian victims of the fighting during World War I won him acclaim as the "Great Humanitarian" and led Woodrow Wilson to name him head of the Food Administration once the United States entered the war. Hoover's reputation soared even higher as secretary of commerce in the Harding and Coolidge administrations.

Hoover was no old-fashioned pro-business advocate like most of the men who gathered in Washington during the 1920s. He belonged to the progressive wing of his party, and as early as 1909, he declared, "The time when the employer could ride roughshod over his labor is disappearing with the doctrine of '**laissez-faire**' on which it is founded." He urged a limited business-government partnership that would actively manage the sweeping changes Americans experienced. In his thoughtful book *American Individualism* (1922), Hoover sketched a picture of American individualism that was as much cooperative, mutual, and responsible as it was "rugged." When Hoover entered the White House, he brought a reform agenda: "We want to see a nation built of home owners and farm owners. We want to see their savings protected. We want to see them in steady jobs. We want to see more and more of them insured against death and accident, unemployment and old age. We want them all secure."

But Hoover also had ideological and political liabilities. Principles that appeared strengths in the prosperous 1920s—individual self-reliance, industrial self-management, and a limited federal government—became straitjackets when economic catastrophe struck. Moreover, Hoover had never held an elected public office, had a poor political touch, and was too thin-skinned to be an effective politician. Even so, most Americans considered him "a sort of superman" able to solve any problem. Prophetically, he confided to a friend his fear that "if some unprecedented calamity should come upon the nation . . . I would be sacrificed to the unreasoning disappointment of a people who expected too much." The distorted national economy set the stage for the calamity Hoover so feared.

The Distorted Economy

In the spring of 1929, the United States enjoyed a fragile prosperity. Although America had become the world's leading economy, it had done little to help rebuild Europe's shattered economy after World War I. Instead, the Republican administrations demanded that Allied nations repay their war loans. To repay, Allied governments insisted on large reparation payments from Germany. This tangled web of debts and reparations sapped Europe's economic vitality. Moreover, to boost American business, the United States enacted tariffs that prevented other nations from selling their goods to Americans. Fewer sales meant that foreign nations had less money to buy American goods, which were pouring out in record abundance. American banks propped up the nation's export trade by extending credit to foreign customers, and fresh debt piled onto existing debt in an absurd pyramid. By the end of the decade, the United States had acquired most of the world's gold in return for its exports.

The domestic economy was also in trouble. Wealth was badly distributed. Farmers continued to suffer from low prices and chronic indebtedness; the average income of families working the land amounted to only $240 per year. The wages of industrial workers, though rising during the decade, failed to keep up with productivity and corporate profits. Overall, nearly two-thirds of all American families lived on less than the $2,000 per year that economists estimated would "supply only basic necessities." In sharp contrast, the top 1 percent received 15 percent of the nation's income, an amount equal to that received by the bottom 42 percent of the population. The Coolidge administration worsened the deepening inequality by cutting taxes on the wealthy.

By 1929, the inequality of wealth produced a serious problem in consumption. The rich, brilliantly portrayed in F. Scott Fitzgerald's novel *The Great Gatsby* (1925), gilded the era with their lavish spending; but they could absorb only a tiny fraction of the nation's output. Ordinary folk, on whom the system ultimately depended, were unable to take up the slack. For a time, the new device of installment buying—buying on credit—kept consumer demand up. By the end of the decade, four out of five cars and two out of three radios were bought on credit. Personal indebtedness rose to an all-time high that could not be sustained.

Signs of economic trouble began to appear at mid-decade. New construction slowed down. Automobile sales faltered. With nearly thirty million cars on the road, demand had been met, and companies began cutting back production and laying off workers. Banks followed suit. Between 1921 and 1928, as investment and loan opportunities faded, five thousand banks failed, wiping out the life savings of thousands. Still, the boom seemed to roar on, muffling the sounds of economic distress just beneath the surface.

The Crash of 1929

Even as the economy faltered, America's faith in it remained unshaken. Hoping for even bigger slices of the economic pie, Americans speculated wildly in the stock market on Wall Street. Between 1924 and 1929, the values of stocks listed on the New York Stock Exchange increased by more than 400 percent. Buying stocks on margin—that is, putting up only part of the money at the time of purchase—grew rampant. Many people got rich this way, but those who bought on credit could finance their loans only if their stocks increased in value. Speculators could not imagine that the market might fall and they would be forced to meet their margin loans with cash they did not have.

Finally, in the autumn of 1929, the market hesitated. Sniffing danger, investors nervously began to sell their overvalued stocks. The dip quickly became a panic on October 24, the day that came to be known as Black Thursday. Brokers jammed the stock exchange desperately trying to unload shares. Stirred by the cries of "Sell! Sell!" outside their windows, the giants of finance gathered in the offices of J. P. Morgan Jr., son of the nineteenth-century Wall Street lion, to plot ways of restoring confidence. They injected $100 million of their assets to bolster the market and issued brave declarations of faith. But more panic selling came on Black Tuesday, October 29, the day the market suffered a greater fall than ever before. In the next six months, the stock market lost six-sevenths of its total value.

It was once thought that the crash alone caused the Great Depression. It did not. In 1929, the national and international economies were already riddled with severe problems. But the dramatic losses in the stock market crash, the sudden collapse of the mood of irrational exuberance, and the fear of risking what was left acted as a great brake on economic activity. The collapse on Wall Street shattered the New Era's aggressive confidence that America would enjoy perpetually expanding prosperity.

Hoover and the Limits of Individualism

At first, Americans expressed relief that Herbert Hoover resided in the White House when the bubble broke. Unlike some conservatives who believed that the government should do nothing during economic downturns, Hoover believed that "we should use the powers of government to cushion the situation" by preventing future financial panics and mitigating the hardships of farmers and the unemployed. Hoover was no do-nothing president, but there were limits to his activism.

In November 1929, to keep the stock market collapse from ravaging the entire economy, Hoover called a White House conference of business and labor leaders and urged them to join in a voluntary plan for recovery: Businesses would maintain production and keep their workers on the job; labor would accept existing wages, hours, and conditions. Within a few months, however, the bargain fell apart. As demand for their products declined, industrialists cut production, sliced wages, and laid off workers. Poorly paid or unemployed workers could not buy much, and their decreased spending led to further cuts in production and further loss of jobs. Thus began the terrible spiral of economic decline.

To deal with the problems of rural America, Hoover got Congress to pass the Agricultural Marketing Act in 1929. The act created the Farm Board, which used its budget of $500 million to buy up agricultural surpluses and thus, it was hoped, raise prices. But prices declined. To help end the decline, Hoover joined conservatives in urging protective tariffs on agricultural goods, and the Hawley-Smoot tariff of 1930 established the highest rates in history. The same year, Congress also authorized $420 million for public works projects to give the unemployed jobs and create more purchasing power. In three years, the Hoover administration nearly doubled federal public works expenditures.

But with each year of Hoover's term, the economy weakened. Tariffs did not end the suffering of farmers because foreign nations retaliated with increased tariffs of their own that crippled American farmers' ability to sell abroad. In 1932, Hoover hoped to help hard-pressed industry with the Reconstruction Finance Corporation (RFC), a federal agency empowered to lend government funds to endangered banks and corporations. The theory was **trickle-down economics**: Pump money into the economy at the top, and in the long run, the people at the bottom would benefit. Or as one wag put it, "Feed the sparrows by feeding the horses." In the end, very little of what critics of the RFC called a "millionaires' dole" trickled down to the poor.

And the poor multiplied. Hundreds of thousands of workers lost their jobs each month. By 1932, an astounding one-quarter of the American workforce—more than twelve million people—were unemployed. There was no direct federal assistance, and state services and private charities were swamped. The depression that began in 1929 devastated much of the world, but no other modern nation provided such feeble support to the jobless. Cries grew louder for the federal government to give hurting people relief.

In responding, Hoover revealed the limits of his conception of government's proper role. He compared direct federal aid to the needy to the "dole" in Britain, which he thought destroyed the moral fiber of the chronically unemployed. In 1931, he allowed the Red Cross to distribute government-owned agricultural surpluses to the hungry. In 1932, he relaxed his principles further to offer small federal loans, not gifts, to the states to help them in their relief efforts. But these concessions were no more than Band-Aids on deep wounds. Hoover's circumscribed notions of legitimate government action proved vastly inadequate to address the problems of restarting the economy and ending human suffering.

▶ **REVIEW**   Why did the American economy collapse in 1929?

Life in the Depression

In 1930, suffering on a massive scale set in. Despair settled over the land. Men and women hollow-eyed with hunger grew increasingly bewildered and angry in the face of cruel contradictions. They saw agricultural surpluses pile up in the countryside and knew that their children were going to bed hungry. They saw factories standing idle and knew that they and millions of others were willing to work. The gap between the American people and leaders who failed to resolve these contradictions widened as the depression deepened. By 1932, America's economic problems had created a dangerous social and political crisis.

The Human Toll

Statistics only hint at the human tragedy of the Great Depression. When Herbert Hoover took office in 1929, the American economy stood at its peak. When he left in 1933, it had reached its twentieth-century low. In 1929, national income was $88 billion. By 1933, it had declined to $40 billion. In 1929, unemployment was 3.1 percent, or 1.5 million workers. By 1933, unemployment stood at 25 percent, or 12.5 million workers. By 1932, more than 9,000 banks had shut their doors, and depositors had lost more than $2.5 billion. The nation's steel industry operated at only 12 percent of capacity.

   Jobless, homeless victims wandered in search of work, and the tramp, or hobo, became one of the most visible figures of the decade. Riding the rails or hitchhiking, a million vagabonds tended to move southward and westward, toward the sun and opportunities, they hoped, for seasonal agricultural work. Other unemployed men and women, sick or less hopeful, huddled in doorways, overcome, one man remembered, by "helpless despair and submission." Scavengers haunted alleys behind restaurants and picked over garbage dumps in search of food. One writer told of an elderly woman who always took off her glasses to avoid seeing the maggots crawling over the garbage

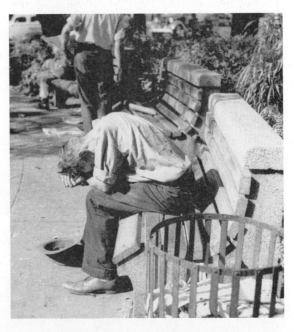

An Unemployed Youth
Brought up to believe that if you worked hard, you got ahead, the unemployed had difficulty seeing failure to find work as anything other than personal failure. Many slipped into despair and depression. We can only imagine this young man's story. Whether he found work, joined the throngs of beggars on the streets, or rode the rails as a hobo looking for something better is unknown.
Library of Congress.

she ate. Starvation claimed its victims, but enervating malnutrition posed the greater threat. The Children's Bureau announced that one in five schoolchildren did not get enough to eat. "I don't want to steal," a Pennsylvania man wrote to the governor in 1931, "but I won't let my wife and boy cry for something to eat. . . . How long is this going to keep up? I cannot stand it any longer."

Rural poverty was most acute. Tenant farmers and sharecroppers, mainly in the South, came to symbolize how poverty crushed the human spirit. Eight and a half million people, three million of them black, crowded into two- and three-room cabins lacking screens or even doors, without plumbing, electricity, running water, or sanitary wells. They subsisted—just barely—on salt pork, cornmeal, molasses, beans, peas, and whatever they could hunt or fish. All the diseases of dietary and vitamin deficiencies wracked them. When economist John Maynard Keynes was asked whether anything like this degradation had existed before, he replied, "Yes, it was called the Dark Ages and it lasted four hundred years."

There was no federal assistance to meet this human catastrophe, only a patchwork of strapped charities and destitute state and local agencies. For a family of four without any income, the best the city of Philadelphia could do was provide $5.50 per week. That was not enough to live on but was still comparatively generous. New York City, where the greatest number of welfare cases gathered, provided only $2.39 per week; and Detroit, devastated by the auto industry's failure, allotted 60 cents a week before the city ran out of money altogether.

The deepening crisis roused old fears and caused some Americans to look for scapegoats. Among the most thoroughly scapegoated were Mexican Americans. During the 1920s, cheap agricultural labor from Mexico flowed legally across the U.S. border, welcomed by the large farmers. In the 1930s, however, public opinion turned on the newcomers, denouncing them as dangerous aliens who took jobs from Americans. Government officials, most prominently those in Los Angeles County, targeted Mexican residents for deportation regardless of citizenship status. As many as half a million Mexicans and Mexican Americans were deported or fled to Mexico.

The depression deeply affected the American family. Young people postponed marriage. When they did marry, they produced few children. White women, who generally worked in low-paying service areas, did not lose their jobs as often as men who worked in steel, automobile, and other heavy industries. After a decade of rising consumption and conflating consumption with self-worth, idle men suffered a loss of self-esteem. "Before the depression," one unemployed father reported, "I wore the pants in this family, and rightly so." Jobless, he lost "self-respect" and also "the respect of my children, and I am afraid that I am losing my wife." Both government and private employers discriminated against married women workers, but necessity continued to drive women into the marketplace. As a result, by 1940 some 25 percent more women were employed for wages than in 1930.

Denial and Escape

To express his optimism about economic recovery, President Hoover maintained formal dress and manners in the White House, and at dinner, with or without guests, a retinue of valets and waiters attended him. No one was starving, he calmly assured the American people. Contradicting the president's message were makeshift shantytowns, called "Hoovervilles," that sprang up on the edges of America's cities. Newspapers used as cover by those sleeping on the streets were "Hoover blankets." An empty pocket turned inside out was a "Hoover flag," and jackrabbits caught for food were "Hoover hogs." Innumerable bitter jokes circulated about the increasingly unpopular president. One told of Hoover asking for a nickel to telephone a friend. Flipping him a dime, an aide said, "Here, call them both."

While Hoover practiced denial, other Americans sought refuge from reality at the movies. Throughout the depression, between 60 million and 75 million people (nearly two-thirds of the nation) managed to scrape together enough change to fill the movie palaces every week. Box office hits such as *Forty-second Street* and *Gold Diggers of 1933* capitalized on the hope that prosperity lay just around the corner. But a few filmmakers grappled with hard realities rather than escape them. *Our Daily Bread* (1932) expressed compassion for the down-and-out, while *The Public Enemy* (1931) taught hard lessons about gangsters' ill-gotten gains. Indeed, under the new production code of 1930, designed to protect public morals, all movies had to find some way to show that crime did not pay.

Despite Hollywood's efforts to keep Americans on the right side of the law, crime increased. Away from the movie palaces, out in the countryside, the plight of people who had lost their farms to bank foreclosures led to the romantic idea that bank robbers were only getting back what banks had stolen from the poor. Woody Guthrie, the populist folksinger from Oklahoma, captured the public's tolerance for outlaws in his widely admired tribute to a murderous bank robber with a choirboy face, "The Ballad of Pretty Boy Floyd":

> Yes, as through this world I ramble,
> I see lots of funny men,
> Some will rob you with a six-gun,
> Some will rob you with a pen.
> But as through your life you'll travel,
> Wherever you may roam,
> You won't never see an outlaw drive
> A family from their home.

Working-Class Militancy

Members of the nation's working class bore the brunt of the economic collapse. In Chicago, workingwomen received less than twenty-five cents an hour. Sawmill workers in the West got a nickel. Still, the labor movement, including the dominant American Federation of Labor (AFL), was slow to respond. By 1931, William Green, head of the AFL, had turned militant. "I warn the people who are exploiting the workers," he shouted, "that they can drive them only so far before they will turn on them and destroy them. They are taking no account of the history of nations in which governments have been overturned. Revolutions grow out of the depths of hunger."

Like labor leaders, the American people were slow to anger, then strong in protest. On the morning of March 7, 1932, several thousand unemployed auto workers massed at the gates of Henry Ford's River Rouge factory in Dearborn, Michigan, to demand work. Ford sent out his private security forces, and when the workers began throwing rocks, Ford's army responded with gunfire, killing four demonstrators and wounding dozens more. An outraged public—forty thousand strong—turned out for the unemployed men's funerals, while editorials and protest rallies across the country denounced Ford's callous resort to violence.

Farmers mounted uprisings of their own. When Congress refused to guarantee farm prices that would at least equal the cost of production, several thousand farmers created the National Farmers' Holiday Association in 1932, so named because its members planned to take a "holiday" from shipping crops to market. When some farmers persisted, militants barricaded roads and dumped thousands of gallons of milk in ditches. Farm militants also resorted to what they called "penny sales." When banks foreclosed and put farms up for auction, neighbors warned others not to bid, bought the foreclosed property for a few pennies, and returned it to the bankrupt owners. Under this kind of pressure, some states suspended debts or reduced mortgages. In California in 1933, when landowners cut their laborers' already substandard wages, more than 50,000 farmworkers, most of them Mexicans, went on strike. Militancy won farmers little in the way of long-term solutions, but one individual observed that "the biggest and finest crop of revolutions you ever saw is sprouting all over the country right now."

The Great Depression—the massive failure of Western capitalism—propelled the international Communist movement to new heights. In the United States, it brought **socialism** back to life and catapulted the **Communist Party** to its greatest size and influence in American history. Some 100,000 Americans—workers, intellectuals, college students—joined the Communist Party in the belief that only an overthrow of the capitalist system could save the victims of the depression. In 1931, the party, through its National Miners Union, carried its convictions into Harlan County, Kentucky, to support a strike by brutalized coal miners. Newspapers and newsreels provided graphic portrayals of the violence unleashed by mine

"Scottsboro Boys"
Nine black youths, ranging in age from thirteen to twenty-one, stand in front of rifle-bearing National Guard troops called up by Alabama governor B. M. Miller, who feared a mob lynching after two white women accused the nine of rape in March 1931. In less than two weeks, an all-white jury heard flimsy evidence, convicted the nine of rape, and sentenced them to death. Although none was executed, all nine spent years in jail. Eventually, the state dropped the charges against the youngest four and granted paroles to the others. The last "Scottsboro Boy" left jail in 1950.
© Bettmann/Corbis.

owners' thugs against the strikers. Eventually, the owners beat the miners down, but the Communist Party emerged from the coalfields with a reputation as the most dedicated and fearless champion of the union cause.

The left also led the fight against racism. Whereas both major parties refused to challenge segregation in the South, the Socialist Party, led by Norman Thomas, attacked the system of sharecropping that left many African Americans in near servitude. The Communist Party also took action. When nine young black men in Scottsboro, Alabama (the "Scottsboro Boys"), were arrested on trumped-up rape charges in 1931, a team of lawyers sent by the party saved the defendants from the electric chair. The party also opposed the efforts of Alabama plantation owners to evict their black tenants. Although Communists were unable to force much change in the deeply entrenched southern way of life, their efforts briefly attracted new recruits to the party. From only about 50 black members in 1930, party totals rose to 10,000 by the end of the decade.

Radicals on the left often sparked action, but protests by moderate workers and farmers occurred on a far greater scale. Breadlines, soup kitchens, foreclosures, unemployment, and cold despair drove patriotic men and women to question American capitalism. "I am as conservative as any man could be," a Wisconsin farmer explained, "but any economic system that has in its power to set me and my wife in the streets, at my age—what can I see but red?"

▶**REVIEW**   How did the depression reshape American politics?

Conclusion: Dazzle and Despair

In the aftermath of World War I, America turned its back on progressive crusades and embraced conservative Republican politics, the growing influence of corporate leaders, and business values. Changes in the nation's economy—Henry Ford's automobile revolution, advertising, mass production—propelled fundamental change throughout society. Living standards rose, economic opportunity increased, and Americans threw themselves into private pleasures—gobbling up the latest household goods and fashions, attending baseball and football games and boxing matches, gathering around the radio, and going to the movies. As big cities came to dominate American life, the culture of youth and flappers became the leading edge of what one observer called a "revolution in manners and morals." At home in Harlem and abroad in Paris, American literature, art, and music flourished.

For many Americans, however, none of the glamour and vitality had much meaning. Instead of seeking thrills at speakeasies, plunging into speculation on Wall Street, or escaping abroad, the vast majority struggled just to earn a decent living. Blue-collar America did not participate fully in white-collar prosperity. Rural America was almost entirely left out of the Roaring Twenties. Country folk, deeply suspicious and profoundly discontented, championed prohibition, revived the Klan, attacked immigration, and defended old-time Protestant religion.

Just as the dazzle of the Roaring Twenties hid deep divisions in society, extravagant prosperity masked structural flaws in the economy. The crash of 1929 and the depression that followed starkly revealed the economy's crises of international trade and consumption. Hard times swept high living off the front pages of the nation's newspapers. Different images emerged: hoboes hopping freight trains, strikers confronting police, malnourished sharecroppers staring blankly into the distance, empty apartment buildings alongside cardboard shantytowns, and mountains of food rotting in the sun while guards with shotguns chased away the hungry.

The depression hurt everyone, but the poor were hurt most. As farmers and workers sank into aching hardship, businessmen rallied around Herbert Hoover to proclaim that private enterprise would get the country moving again. But things fell apart, and Hoover faced increasingly more radical opposition. Membership in the Socialist and Communist parties surged, and more and more Americans contemplated desperate measures. By 1932, the depression had nearly brought the nation to its knees. America faced its greatest crisis since the Civil War, and citizens demanded new leaders who would save them from the "Hoover Depression."

REVIEWING THE CHAPTER

Use the questions and timeline to review and strengthen your understanding of the chapter.

REVIEW QUESTIONS

1. How did the spread of the automobile transform the United States? (pp. 720–27)

2. How did the new freedoms of the 1920s challenge older conceptions of gender and race? (pp. 727–35)

3. Why did the relationship between urban and rural America deteriorate in the 1920s? (pp. 735–40)

4. Why did the American economy collapse in 1929? (pp. 740–44)

5. How did the depression reshape American politics? (pp. 744–50)

MAKING CONNECTIONS

1. In the 1920s, Americans' wariness of the concentration of power in the hands of industrial capitalists gave way to unrestrained confidence in American business. What drove this shift in popular opinion? How did it influence Republicans' approach to governance and the development of the American economy in the 1920s?

2. Americans' encounters with the wealth and increased personal freedom characteristic of the 1920s varied greatly. Discuss the impact such variation had on Americans' responses to new circumstances. Why did some embrace the era's changes, while others resisted them? Ground your answer in a discussion of specific political, legal, or cultural conflicts.

3. How did shifting government policy contribute to both the boom of the 1920s and the bust of 1929? In your answer, consider the part domestic and international policy played in these developments, including taxation, tariffs, and international banking.

4. The Great Depression plunged the nation into a profound crisis with staggering personal and national costs. How did Americans attempt to lessen the impact of these circumstances? In your answer, discuss and compare the responses of individual Americans and the federal government.

TIMELINE

1920	• Eighteenth Amendment goes into effect. • Nineteenth Amendment ratified. • Republican Warren G. Harding elected president.
1921	• Sheppard-Towner Act. • Congress restricts immigration.
1922	• Fordney-McCumber tariff. • Five-Power Naval Treaty.
1923	• Equal Rights Amendment defeated in Congress. • Harding dies; Vice President Calvin Coolidge becomes president.
1924	• Dawes Plan. • Coolidge elected president. • Johnson-Reid Act.
1925	• Scopes trial.
1927	• Charles Lindbergh flies nonstop across the Atlantic. • Nicola Sacco and Bartolomeo Vanzetti executed.
1928	• Kellogg-Briand pact. • Republican Herbert Hoover elected president.
1929	• St. Valentine's Day murders. • Farm Board created. • Stock market collapses.
1930	• Congress authorizes $420 million for public works projects. • Hawley-Smoot tariff.
1931	• "Scottsboro Boys" arrested. • Harlan County, Kentucky, coal strike.
1932	• River Rouge factory demonstration. • Reconstruction Finance Corporation established. • National Farmers' Holiday Association formed.

▶ **For an online bibliography, practice quizzes, Web sites, images, and documents related to this chapter,** see the Book Companion Site at **bedfordstmartins.com/roark.**

▶ **For firsthand accounts of this period,** see Chapter 23 in Michael Johnson, ed., *Reading the American Past,* Fourth Edition.

24

CHAPTER

The New Deal Experiment

1932–1939

I N THE DEPTHS OF THE GREAT DEPRESSION, a Pennsylvania mother with three small children appealed to the Hoover administration for help for her husband, "who is a world war Veteran and saw active service in the trenches, became desperate and applied for Compensation or a pension from the Government and was turned down." With a weekly income of only $15.60, she and her family were suffering. There ought to be enough, she declared, "to pay all world war veterans a pension . . . and there by relieve a lot of suffering, and banish resentment that causes Rebellions and Bolshevism." She asked questions murmured by millions of other desperate Americans: "Oh why is it that it is always a bunch of overley rich, selfish, dumb ignorant money hogs that persist in being Senitors, legislatures, representitives? Where would they and their possessions be if it were not for the Common Soldier, the common laborer that is compelled to work for a starvation wage[?] . . . Right now our good old U.S.A. is sitting on a Seething Volcano."

This mother's plea echoed in the demands of tens of thousands of World War I veterans who gathered in Washington, D.C., during June and July 1932 to lobby for immediate payment of the pension (known as a "bonus"). The veterans came from every state and by nearly every means of transportation. The throng that congregated in a huge camp on the outskirts of Washington appeared "dusty, weary, and melancholy" to a Washington reporter, who noted that the veterans included jobless "truck drivers and blacksmiths, steel workers and coal miners, stenographers and common laborers," in all "a fair cross section" of the nation:

Attack on the Bonus Marchers
Washington police, led by five hundred army soldiers commanded by General Douglas MacArthur, participated in the attack on the Bonus Marchers in July 1932. Soldiers lobbed tear gas grenades toward the marchers, quickly breaking up skirmishes like the one shown here, then advanced into the veterans' camp and torched it.
National Archives.

immigrants and natives; whites, blacks, and Native Americans. The "one absentee," a black civil rights leader observed, was "James Crow." All the veterans, one journalist wrote, were "down at the heel."

Calling themselves Bonus Marchers or the Bonus Army, the veterans hoped their numbers, solidarity, and poverty would persuade Congress to give them the bonus they had been promised in 1924: $1 for every day they had been in uniform and a bit extra for time served overseas. Instead of cash payments, Congress decided to hand out promissory notes that veterans could not convert to cash until 1945. Bonus Marchers condemned this "tombstone bonus," which would not be paid until many of them were dead. Veterans from Utah and California emblazoned their truck with this message: "We Done a Good Job in France, Now You Do a Good Job in America—We Need the Bonus."

The veterans had supporters in Congress but not in the White House. President Herbert Hoover opposed the payment of an expensive bonus that would require the government to go into debt. Hoover refused to meet with representatives of the Bonus Army, who, his press secretary charged, were "communists or bums." The

House of Representatives, controlled by Democrats, voted to pay the promised bonus of $2.4 billion, but the Senate, dominated by Hoover's fellow Republicans, rejected the bonus. Upon hearing of their defeat in the Senate, the Bonus Marchers did not confirm Republican fears of a **Communist** mob but instead joined in singing "America" before slowly drifting back to their camp.

About twenty thousand veterans remained in Washington, determined, as one of them proclaimed, "to stay here until 1945 if necessary to get our bonus." While the Bonus Army hunkered down in their shanties, Hoover feared that the veterans would riot and spark uprisings throughout the country. He ordered General Douglas MacArthur to evict the Bonus Marchers from the city but not to invade their camp.

On July 28, MacArthur led an attack force of five tanks and five hundred soldiers armed with loaded weapons and fixed bayonets through the streets of Washington. Exceeding Hoover's orders, MacArthur pushed the Bonus Marchers back into their camp, where his soldiers torched the veterans' humble dwellings. While their camp burned, the Bonus Marchers raced away. MacArthur boasted that without his victory over the veterans, "the institutions of our Government would have been severely threatened."

MacArthur's expulsion of the Bonus Army undermined public support for the beleaguered, fearful Hoover. When the Democrats' recently nominated presidential candidate, Franklin Delano Roosevelt, heard about the attack, he correctly predicted that it "will elect me." Voters rejected Hoover, who seemed unsympathetic to the suffering caused by the Great Depression. In Roosevelt's inaugural address in March 1933, barely seven months after the expulsion of the Bonus Army, he proclaimed, "The only thing we have to fear is fear itself." Instead of succumbing to fear and suspicion, Roosevelt said, Americans should roll up their sleeves and find some way out of their present difficulties. Roosevelt's confidence that the government could help citizens energized **New Deal** policies and his presidency, the longest in American history.

When several thousand veterans reassembled in Washington to lobby again for the bonus a few months after Roosevelt's inauguration, the new president's hospitality contrasted with Hoover's hostility. Roosevelt arranged for the veterans to be housed in abandoned military barracks and fed at government expense. He invited a delegation of veterans to the White House, where he chatted casually with them, explaining that he could not support the bonus because he considered it too expensive, although he was determined to help them and other victims of the depression. And, to the veterans' surprise and delight, Eleanor Roosevelt slogged through rain and mud to talk personally with them, to express her sympathy, and to lead them in singing their favorite songs. As the veterans voluntarily left their encampment in Washington, one remarked, "Hoover sent the Army; Roosevelt sent his wife."

Unlike the Bonus Marchers, the tens of millions of other Americans suffering from the Great Depression did not flock to Washington to lobby the government.

But like the Bonus Marchers, they appreciated Roosevelt's optimism and expressions of concern. Even more, they welcomed government help from Roosevelt's New Deal initiatives to provide relief for the needy, to speed economic recovery, and to reform basic economic and governmental institutions. Roosevelt's New Deal elicited bitter opposition from critics on the right and left and failed to satisfy fully its own goals of relief, recovery, and reform. But within the Democratic Party, the New Deal energized a powerful political coalition that helped millions of Americans withstand the privations of the Great Depression. In the process, the federal government became a major presence in the daily lives of most American citizens.

Franklin D. Roosevelt: A Patrician in Government

Unlike the millions of Americans in 1932 who had no work, little food, and still less hope, Franklin Roosevelt came from a wealthy and privileged background that contributed to his optimism, self-confidence, and vitality. He constantly drew upon these personal qualities in his political career to bridge the economic, social, and cultural chasm that separated him from the struggles of ordinary Americans. During the twelve years he served as president (1933–1945), many elites came to hate him as a traitor to his class, while millions more Americans, especially the hardworking poor and dispossessed, revered him because he cared about them and their problems.

The Making of a Politician

Born in 1882, Franklin Delano Roosevelt grew up on his father's leafy estate at Hyde Park on the Hudson River, north of New York City. Insulated from the privations experienced by working people, Roosevelt was steeped at home and school in high-minded doctrines of public service and Christian duty to help the poor and weak. He prepared for a career in politics, hoping to follow in the political footsteps of his fifth cousin, Theodore Roosevelt. In 1905, when he married his distant cousin Eleanor Roosevelt, the current president of the United States, Theodore Roosevelt, gave the bride away—a sign of Franklin Roosevelt's gilt-edged political and familial connections.

Unlike cousin Teddy, Franklin Roosevelt sought his political fortune in the Democratic Party. After a two-year stint in the New York legislature, he ascended to national office when Woodrow Wilson appointed him assistant secretary of the navy. In 1920, he catapulted to the second spot on the national Democratic ticket as the vice presidential candidate of presidential nominee James M. Cox. Although Cox lost the election (see chapter 22), Roosevelt's energetic campaigning convinced Democratic leaders that he had a bright future in national politics.

In the summer of 1921, at the age of thirty-nine, his life took a painful detour. He became infected with the polio virus, which paralyzed both his legs. For the rest of his life, he could stand only with his legs encased in heavy steel braces, and he could walk a few awkward steps only by leaning on another person. Tireless physical therapy helped him regain his vitality and intense desire for high political office. But he had to recapture his political momentum mostly from a sitting position, although he studiously avoided being photographed in the wheelchair he used routinely.

After his polio attack, Roosevelt frequently visited a polio therapy facility at Warm Springs, Georgia. There, he combined the health benefits of the soothing waters with political overtures to southern Democrats, which helped make him a rare political creature: a New Yorker from the Democratic Party's urban and immigrant wing with whom whites from the Democratic Party's entrenched southern wing felt comfortable.

Roosevelt's chance to return to political office came in 1928. New York's Democratic governor, Al Smith, urged Roosevelt to succeed him. Smith, the Democrats' presidential nominee, hoped Roosevelt would help secure New York's electoral votes. Although Smith lost in both New York and the nation (see chapter 23), Roosevelt squeaked out a victory. As governor of the nation's most populous state, Roosevelt was poised to showcase his leadership and his suitability for a presidential campaign of his own. His activist policies as governor became a dress rehearsal for his subsequent career as president.

Deeply affected by the cascading woes of the Great Depression, Governor Roosevelt believed that government should intervene to protect citizens from economic hardships rather than do nothing but wait for the law of supply and demand to improve the economy. According to the **laissez-faire** views of many **conservatives**—especially Republicans, but also numerous Democrats—the depression represented the hard hand of the market winnowing the strong survivors from the weak losers. Unlike Roosevelt, conservatives believed that government help for the needy sapped individual initiative and impeded the self-correcting forces of the market by rewarding people for losing the economic struggle to survive. Roosevelt lacked a full-fledged counterargument to these conservative claims, but he sympathized with the plight of poor people. He proclaimed, "To these unfortunate citizens aid must be extended by governments, not as a matter of charity but as a matter of social duty. . . . [No one should go] unfed, unclothed, or unsheltered."

The highlight of Roosevelt's efforts to relieve the economic hardships of New Yorkers was the Temporary Emergency Relief Administration (TERA), created in 1931. It provided an unprecedented $20 million in aid for the poor, earning him the gratitude of needy New Yorkers and the attention of national politicians.

To his supporters, Roosevelt seemed to be a leader determined to attack the economic crisis without deviating from **democracy**—unlike **fascist** parties gaining strength in Europe—or from capitalism—unlike Communists in power in the Soviet Union. Roosevelt's ideas about precisely how to revive the economy were vague. A prominent journalist characterized Roosevelt in 1931 as "a kind of amiable boy scout . . . a pleasant man who, without any important qualifications for the office, would very much like to be president." Such sneering comments did not sway Roosevelt's many supporters, who appreciated his energy, activism, and belief that, as he put it, "the duty of the state towards its citizens is the duty of the servant to its master." Roosevelt's conviction that government could and should do something to help Americans climb out of the economic abyss propelled him into the front ranks of the national Democratic Party.

The Election of 1932

The Democrats who convened in Chicago in July 1932 to nominate their presidential candidate knew that Hoover's unpopularity gave them a historic opportunity to recapture the White House. In fifty-six of the seventy-two years since Abraham Lincoln's election, Republicans had occupied the White House. Now, with the nation gripped by the worst depression in its history, Democrats might reverse generations of Republican rule if they chose the right nominee.

Opposition to Republicans and hunger for office, but little else, united Democrats. Warring factions divided Democrats by region, religion, **culture**, and commitment to the status quo. Southern Democrats chaired powerful committees in Congress thanks to their continual reelection in the one-party South devoted to white supremacy. This southern, native-born, white, rural, **Protestant**, conservative wing of the Democratic Party found little common ground with the northern, immigrant, urban, disproportionately Catholic, **liberal** wing. Rural and native-born *drys* (supporters of prohibition) clashed with urban and foreign-born *wets* (opponents of prohibition). Eastern-establishment Democratic dignitaries shared few goals with angry farmers and factory workers. Still, this unruly coalition of constituencies finally agreed to nominate Franklin Roosevelt as the Democratic presidential candidate.

In his acceptance speech, Roosevelt vowed to help "the forgotten man at the bottom of the pyramid"—such as the Bonus Marchers then in Washington—with "bold, persistent experimentation." Highlighting his differences with Hoover and the Republicans, he proposed to lead the nation with "liberal thought, . . . planned action, . . . [an] enlightened international outlook, and . . . the greatest good to the greatest number of our citizens." He pledged "a new deal for the American people."

Few details about what Roosevelt meant by "a new deal" emerged in the presidential campaign. He declared that "the people of America want more than anything else . . . two things: work . . . with all the moral and spiritual values that go with work . . . and a reasonable measure of security . . . for themselves and for their wives and children." Although Roosevelt never explained exactly how the federal government could provide either work or security, voters decided that whatever his new deal might be, it was better than reelecting Hoover.

Roosevelt won the 1932 presidential election in a historic landslide. He received 57 percent of the nation's votes, the first time a Democrat had won a

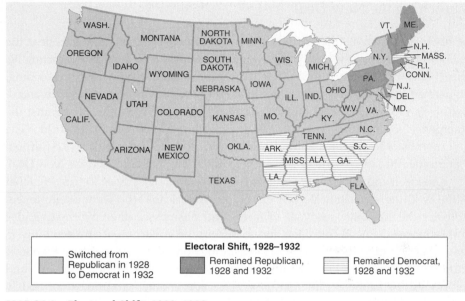

Electoral Shift, 1928–1932

Switched from Republican in 1928 to Democrat in 1932

Remained Republican, 1928 and 1932

Remained Democrat, 1928 and 1932

MAP 24.1   Electoral Shift, 1928–1932
The Democratic victory in 1932 signaled the rise of a New Deal coalition within which women and minorities, many of them new voters, made the Democrats the majority party for the first time in the twentieth century.

majority of the popular vote since 1852. Roosevelt amassed 472 electoral votes to Hoover's 59, carrying state after state that had voted Republican for years (Map 24.1). Roosevelt's coattails swept Democrats into control of Congress by large margins. The popular mandate for change was loud and clear.

Roosevelt's victory represented the emergence of what came to be known as the New Deal coalition. Attracting support from farmers, factory workers, immigrants, city folk, African Americans, women, and **progressive** intellectuals, Roosevelt launched a realignment of the nation's political loyalties. The New Deal coalition dominated American politics throughout Roosevelt's presidency and remained powerful long after his death in 1945. United less by ideology or support for specific policies, voters in the New Deal coalition instead expressed faith in Roosevelt's promise of a government that would, somehow, change things for the better. Nobody, including Roosevelt, knew exactly what the New Deal would change or whether the changes would revive the nation's ailing economy and improve Americans' lives. But Roosevelt and many others knew that the future of American capitalism and democracy was at stake.

▶**REVIEW**   Why did Franklin D. Roosevelt win the 1932 presidential election by such a large margin?

Launching the New Deal

At noon on March 4, 1933, Americans gathered around their radios to hear the inaugural address of the newly elected president. Roosevelt began by asserting his "firm belief that the only thing we have to fear is fear itself—nameless, unreasoning, unjustified terror which paralyzes needed efforts to convert retreat into advance." Roosevelt promised "direct, vigorous action" in order "to wage war against the emergency" confronting "a stricken Nation in the midst of a stricken world." The first months of Roosevelt's administration, termed "the Hundred Days," fulfilled that promise in a whirlwind of government initiatives that launched the New Deal.

Roosevelt and his advisers had three interrelated objectives: to provide relief to the destitute, especially the one out of four Americans who were unemployed; to foster the economic recovery of farms and businesses, thereby creating jobs and reducing the need for relief; and to reform the government and economy in ways that would reduce the risk of devastating consequences in future economic slumps. The New Deal never fully achieved these goals of relief, recovery, and reform. But by aiming for them, Roosevelt's experimental programs enormously expanded government's role in the nation's economy and society.

The New Dealers

To design and implement the New Deal, Roosevelt needed ideas and people. As governor of New York, he frequently hosted private, informal conversations about social and economic policy with a small group of professors from Columbia University. Dubbed the "Brains Trust," these men and others continued to advise the new president about the problems faced by the nation and how to deal with them.

Hundreds of other reformers rushed to join the Roosevelt administration. Among the most important were two veterans of Roosevelt's New York governorship: Harry Hopkins and Frances Perkins. Hopkins was a tough-talking, soft-hearted social worker devoted to the **social gospel** of moral and material uplift of the downtrodden. He administered New Deal relief efforts and served as one of the president's loyal confidants. Like Hopkins, Perkins embraced the social gospel tradition, having worked for a time in Jane Addams's Hull House in Chicago. She also had extensive experience trying to improve working conditions in shops and factories. In fact, she had directed New York's investigation of the 1911 Triangle Shirtwaist Factory fire that killed 146 women (see chapter 21). Roosevelt tapped Perkins to serve as secretary of labor, making her the first woman cabinet member in American history—an indication of her expertise and of the growing strength of women in the Democratic Party, which had an active Women's Division.

No New Dealers were more important than the president and his wife, Eleanor. The gregarious president radiated charm and good cheer, giving the New Deal's bureaucratic regulations a benevolent human face. Eleanor Roosevelt became the New Deal's unofficial ambassador. She served, she said, as "the eyes and ears of the New Deal" as she traveled throughout the nation connecting the corridors of power in Washington to Americans of all colors and creeds in church basements, meeting halls, and front parlors. A North Carolina women's rights activist recalled, "One of my great pleasures was meeting Mrs. Roosevelt. . . . [S]he was so free of prejudice . . . [and] she was always willing to take a stand, and there were stands to take about blacks and women."

As Roosevelt's programs swung into action, many Americans benefited directly through jobs and relief or indirectly through economic improvements. In time, the millions of beneficiaries of the New Deal became grassroots New Dealers who expressed their appreciation by voting Democratic on election day. A signal success of the New Deal was to create a durable political coalition of Democrats that would reelect Roosevelt in 1936, 1940, and 1944.

As Roosevelt and his advisers developed plans to meet the economic emergency, their watchwords were *action*, *experiment*, and *improvise*. Without a sharply defined template for how to provide relief, recovery, and reform, they moved from ideas to policies as quickly as possible, hoping to identify ways to help people and to boost the economy. But underlying New Dealers' experimentation and improvisation were four guiding ideas.

First, Roosevelt and his advisers sought capitalist solutions to the economic crisis. They believed that the depression had resulted from basic imbalances in the nation's capitalist economy—imbalances they wanted to correct. They had no desire to eliminate private property or impose **socialist** programs, such as public ownership of productive resources. Instead, they hoped to save the capitalist economy by remedying its flaws.

Second, Roosevelt's Brains Trust persuaded him that the greatest flaw of America's capitalist economy was underconsumption, the root cause of the current economic paralysis. Underconsumption, New Dealers argued, resulted from the gigantic productive success of capitalism. Factories and farms produced more than they could sell to consumers, causing factories to lay off workers and farmers to lose money on bumper crops. Workers without wages and farmers without profits shrank consumption and choked the economy. Somehow, the balance between consumption and production needed to be restored.

Third, New Dealers believed that the immense size and economic power of American corporations needed to be counterbalanced by government and by organization among workers and small producers. Unlike progressive trustbusters, New Dealers did not seek to splinter big businesses. Huge businesses had developed for good economic reasons and were here to stay. Roosevelt and his advisers hoped to counterbalance big economic institutions and their quest for profits with government programs focused on protecting individuals and the public interest.

Fourth, New Dealers felt that government must somehow moderate the imbalance of wealth created by American capitalism. Wealth concentrated in a few hands reduced consumption by most Americans and thereby contributed to the current economic gridlock. In the long run, government needed to find a way to permit ordinary working people to share more fully in the fruits of the economy. In the short term, New Dealers sought to lend a helping hand to poor people who suffered from the maldistribution of wealth.

Banking and Finance Reform

Roosevelt wasted no time making good on his inaugural pledge for "action now." As he took the oath of office on March 4, the nation's banking system was on the brink of collapse. Since 1930, more than five thousand banks had collapsed. Roosevelt immediately declared a four-day "bank holiday" in order to devise a plan to shore up banks and restore depositors' confidence. Working round the clock, New Dealers drafted the Emergency Banking Act, which gave the secretary of the treasury the power to decide which banks could be safely reopened and to release funds from the Reconstruction Finance Corporation (RFC) to bolster banks' assets. To secure the confidence of depositors, Congress passed the Glass-Steagall Banking Act, setting up the Federal Deposit Insurance Corporation (FDIC), which guaranteed bank customers that the federal government would reimburse them for deposits if their banks failed.

On Sunday night, March 12, while the banks were still closed, Roosevelt broadcast the first of what became a series of "fireside chats." Speaking in a friendly, informal manner, he addressed the millions of Americans who tuned their radios to hear the president explain these first New Deal initiatives. The new banking legislation, he said, made it "safer to keep your money in a reopened bank than under the mattress." With such plain talk, Roosevelt translated complex matters into common sense. This and subsequent fireside chats forged a direct connection—via radio waves—between Roosevelt and millions of Americans. Evidence of their link to Roosevelt piled up in the White House mail room. Millions shared the views of a man from Paris, Texas, who wrote to Roosevelt, "You are the one & only President that ever helped a Working Class of People. . . . Please help us some way I Pray to God for relief."

The banking legislation and fireside chat worked. Within a few days, most of the nation's major banks reopened, and they remained solvent as reassured depositors switched funds from their mattresses to their bank accounts. Some radical critics of the New Deal believed that Roosevelt should have nationalized the banks and made them a cornerstone of economic planning by the federal government. Instead, these first New Deal measures propped up the private banking system with federal funds and subjected banks to federal regulation and oversight. One adviser proclaimed, "Capitalism was saved in eight days," although in reality the rescue operation took much longer to succeed.

In his inaugural address, Roosevelt criticized financiers for their greed and incompetence. To prevent the fraud, corruption, insider trading, and other abuses that had tainted Wall Street and contributed to the crash of 1929, Roosevelt pressed Congress to regulate the stock market. Legislation in 1934 created the Securities and Exchange Commission (SEC) to oversee financial markets by licensing investment dealers, monitoring all stock transactions, and requiring corporate officers to make full disclosures about their companies. To head the SEC, Roosevelt named an abrasive and ambitious Wall Street financier, Joseph P. Kennedy, who had a somewhat shady reputation for stock manipulation. When critics complained about his selection, Roosevelt replied shrewdly, "Set a thief to catch a thief." Under Kennedy's leadership, the SEC helped a cleaned-up and regulated Wall Street to recover slowly, although the stock market stayed well below its frothy heights of the 1920s.

Relief and Conservation Programs

Patching the nation's financial structure provided little relief for the hungry and unemployed. A poor man from Nebraska asked Eleanor Roosevelt "if the folk who was borned here in America . . . are this Forgotten Man, the President had in mind, [and] if we are this Forgotten Man then we are still Forgotten." Since its founding, the federal government had never assumed responsibility for needy people, except in moments of natural disaster or emergencies such as the Civil War. Instead, churches, private charities, county and municipal governments, and occasionally states assumed the burden of poor relief, usually with meager payments. To persuade Americans that the depression necessitated unprecedented federal relief efforts, Harry Hopkins dispatched investigators throughout the nation to describe the plight of impoverished Americans. Reports filtered back to Washington of families surviving on "bull-dog gravy"—a thin paste of lard, flour, and water—along with news that the working hours of tens of thousands of Americans had been cut, reducing their wages to about $1.50 a day. As one New Yorker wrote the government, "We work, ten hours a day for six days. In the grime and dirt of a nation [for] . . . low pay [making us] . . . slaves—slaves of the depression!"

Hopkins's investigators galvanized support for the Federal Emergency Relief Administration (FERA), which provided $500 million to feed the hungry and create jobs. Established in May 1933, FERA supported four million to five million households with $20 or $30 a month. FERA also created jobs for the unemployed on thousands of public works projects, organized by Hopkins into the Civil Works Administration (CWA), which put paychecks worth more than $800 million into the hands of previously jobless workers. Earning wages between forty and sixty cents an hour, laborers renovated schools, dug sewers, and rebuilt roads and bridges. FERA extended the scope of relief to include health and education, providing vaccinations for millions and funding literacy classes.

The most popular work relief program was the Civilian Conservation Corps (CCC), established in March 1933. It offered unemployed young men a chance to earn wages while working to conserve natural resources, a long-standing interest of Roosevelt. Women were excluded from working in the CCC until Eleanor Roosevelt demanded that a token number of young women be hired. One of the three million young men who enlisted in the CCC, Blackie Gold, had been out of work and had to "beg for coal, [and] buy bread that's two, three days old" in order to help support his large family. After he joined the CCC, Gold earned $30 a month and was required to send all but $5 home to his family. By the end of the program in 1942, the three million CCC workers had checked soil erosion, tamed rivers, and planted more than two billion trees. CCC workers left a legacy of vast new recreation areas, along with roads that made those areas accessible to millions of Americans. Just as important, the CCC, CWA, and other work relief efforts replaced the stigma of welfare with the dignity of jobs. As one woman said about her husband's work relief job, "We aren't on relief anymore. My husband is working for the Government."

The New Deal also sought to harness natural resources for hydroelectric power. Continuing a project begun under Hoover, the New Deal completed the colossal Hoover Dam across the Colorado River in Nevada, providing not only electricity but also flood control and irrigation water for Arizona and southern

---

Civilian Conservation Corps Workers

The Civilian Conservation Corps employed these young men in 1933 to build a truck trail in a remote region of Snoqualmie National Forest in the state of Washington. Instead of using machinery for the heavy construction work, the CCC intentionally used the muscles of working men in order to maximize employment.

© Bettmann/Corbis.

California. In addition, building the dam provided badly needed jobs and wages for thousands of unemployed workers.

The New Deal's most ambitious and controversial natural resources development project was the Tennessee Valley Authority (TVA), created in May 1933 to build dams along the Tennessee River to supply impoverished rural communities with cheap electricity. The TVA planned model towns for power station workers and new homes for the farmers who would benefit from electricity and flood control. The most ambitious example of New Deal enthusiasm for planning, the TVA set out to demonstrate that a partnership between the federal government and local residents could overcome the barriers of state governments and private enterprises to make efficient use of abundant natural resources and break the ancient cycle of poverty. The TVA never fully realized these utopian ends, but it improved the lives of millions in the region with electric power, flood protection, soil reclamation, and jobs.

New sources of hydroelectric power helped the New Deal bring the wonders of electricity to country folk, fulfilling an old progressive dream. When Roosevelt became president, 90 percent of rural Americans lacked electricity. Private electric companies refused to build transmission lines into the sparsely settled countryside when they had a profitable market in more accessible and densely populated urban areas. Beginning in 1935, the Rural Electrification Administration (REA) made low-cost loans available to local cooperatives for power plants and transmission lines to serve rural communities. Within ten years, the REA delivered electricity to nine out of ten farms, giving rural Americans access for the first time to modern conveniences that urban people had enjoyed for decades.

Agricultural Initiatives

Farmers had been mired in a depression since the end of World War I. New Dealers diagnosed the farmers' plight as a classic case of overproduction and underconsumption. Following age-old practices, farmers tried to compensate for low crop prices by growing more crops, hoping to boost their earnings by selling larger quantities. Instead, producing more crops pushed prices lower still. Farm income sank from a disastrously low $6 billion in 1929 to a catastrophically low $2 billion in 1932. The median annual income among farm families plunged to $167, barely one-tenth of the national average.

New Dealers sought to cut agricultural production, thereby raising crop prices and farmers' income. With more money in their pockets, farm families—who made up one-third of all Americans—would then buy more goods and lift consumption in the entire economy. To reduce production, the Agricultural Adjustment Act (AAA) authorized the "domestic allotment plan," which paid farmers *not* to grow crops. Individual farmers who agreed not to plant crops on a portion of their fields (their "allotment") would receive a government payment compensating them for the crops they did not plant. Since crops were already in the ground by the time the act was passed in May 1933, drastic measures were necessary to reduce production immediately. While millions of Americans went to bed hungry, farmers slaughtered millions of cattle, hogs, sheep, and other livestock and destroyed millions of acres of crops in order to qualify for their allotment payments.

With the formation of the Commodity Credit Corporation, the federal government allowed farmers to hold their harvested crops off the market and wait for a higher price. In the meantime, the government stored the crop and gave farmers a "commodity loan" based on a favorable price. If the market price rose above that level, a farmer could sell the crop, repay the loan, and pocket the difference. If the market price never rose above the loan level, the farmer simply took the loan as payment, and the government kept the crop. In effect, commodity loans addressed the problem of underconsumption by making the federal government a major consumer of agricultural goods and reducing farmers' vulnerability to low prices. New Dealers also sponsored the Farm Credit Act (FCA) to provide long-term credit on mortgaged farm property, allowing debt-ridden farmers to avoid foreclosures that were driving thousands off their land.

Crop allotments, commodity loans, and mortgage credit made farmers major beneficiaries of the New Deal. Crop prices rose impressively, farm income jumped 50 percent by 1936, and FCA loans financed 40 percent of farm mortgage debt by the end of the decade. These gains were distributed fairly equally among farmers in the corn, hogs, and wheat region of the Midwest. In the South's cotton belt, however, landlords controlled the distribution of New Deal agricultural benefits and shamelessly rewarded themselves while denying benefits to many sharecroppers and tenant farmers—blacks and whites—by taking the land they had worked out of production and assigning it to the allotment program. Many such tenants and sharecroppers could no longer find work, and their privation worsened. The president of the Oklahoma Tenant Farmers' Union explained that large farmers who got "Triple-A" payments often used the money to buy tractors and then "forced their tenants and [share]croppers off the land," causing these "Americans to be starved and dispossessed of their homes in our land of plenty."

Industrial Recovery

Unlike farmers, industrialists cut production with the onset of the depression. Between 1929 and 1933, industrial production fell more than 40 percent to balance low demand with low supply and thereby maintain prices. But the industrialists' strategy created major economic and social problems for Roosevelt and his advisers, since falling industrial production meant that millions of working people lost their jobs. Unlike farmers, most working people lived in towns and cities and needed jobs to eat. Mass unemployment also reduced consumer demand for industrial products, contributing to a downward spiral in both production and jobs, with no end in sight. Industries responded by reducing wages for employees who still had jobs, further reducing demand—a trend made worse by competition among industrial producers. New Dealers struggled to find a way to break this cycle of unemployment and underconsumption—a way consistent with corporate profits and capitalism.

The New Deal's National Industrial Recovery Act (NIRA) opted for a government-sponsored form of industrial self-government through the National Recovery Administration (NRA), established in June 1933. The NRA encouraged industrialists in every part of the economy to agree on rules, known as codes, to define fair working conditions, to set prices, and to minimize competition. The idea behind codes was to stabilize existing industries and maintain their work-forces while avoiding what both industrialists and New Dealers termed "destruc-tive competition," which forced employers to cut wages and jobs. Industry after industry wrote elaborate codes addressing detailed features of production, pricing, and competition. In exchange for relaxing federal antitrust regulations that prohibited such business agreements, the NRA received a promise from participating businesses that they would recognize the right of working people to organize and engage in **collective bargaining**. To encourage consumers to patronize businesses participating in NRA codes, the New Deal mounted a public relations campaign that displayed the NRA's Blue Eagle in shop windows and on billboards throughout the nation.

New Dealers hoped that NRA codes would yield businesses with a social con-science, ensuring fair treatment of workers and consumers and promotion of the general economic welfare. Instead, NRA codes tended to strengthen conventional business practices. Large corporations wrote codes that served primarily their own interests rather than the needs of workers or the welfare of the national economy. The failure of codes to cover agricultural or domestic workers led one woman to complain to Roosevelt that the NRA "never mentioned the robbery of the Housewives" by the privations caused by the depression. Many business leaders criticized NRA codes as heavy-handed government regulation of private enterprise. Some even claimed that the NRA was a homegrown version of Benito Mussolini's corporate fascism taking shape in Italy. In reality, however, com-pliance with NRA codes was voluntary, and government enforcement efforts were weak to nonexistent. The NRA did little to reduce unemployment, raise consumption, or relieve the depression. In effect, it represented a peace offering to business leaders by Roosevelt and his advisers, conveying the message that the New Deal did not intend to wage war against profits or private enterprise. The peace offering failed, however. Most corporate leaders became active and often bitter opponents of Roosevelt and the New Deal.

▶**REVIEW**   How did New Dealers try to steer the nation toward recovery from the Great Depression?

Challenges to the New Deal

The first New Deal initiatives engendered fierce criticism and political opposition. From the right, Republicans and business people charged that New Deal programs were too radical, undermining private property, economic stability, and democracy. Critics on the left faulted the New Deal for its failure to allay the human suffering caused by the depression and for its timidity in attacking corporate power and greed.

Resistance to Business Reform

New Deal programs rescued capitalism, but business leaders lambasted Roosevelt, even though their economic prospects improved more than those of most other Americans during the depression. Republicans and business leaders fulminated against New Deal efforts to regulate or reform what they considered their private enterprises. Although concentrated corporate power avoided reform, business leaders still conducted stridently anti–New Deal campaigns that expressed their resentment and fear of regulations, taxes, and unions. One opponent called the president "Stalin Delano Roosevelt" and insisted that the New Deal was really a "Raw Deal."

By 1935, two major business organizations, the National Association of Manufacturers and the Chamber of Commerce, had become openly anti–New

Major Legislation of the New Deal's First Hundred Days

	Name of Act	Basic Provisions
March 9, 1933	Emergency Banking Act	Provides for reopening stable banks and authorizing the Reconstruction Finance Corporation (RFC) to supply funds.
March 31, 1933	Civilian Conservation Corps Act	Provides jobs for unemployed young men.
May 12, 1933	Agricultural Adjustment Act	Provides funds to pay farmers for not growing crops.
May 12, 1933	Federal Emergency Relief Act	Provides relief funds for the destitute.
May 18, 1933	Tennessee Valley Authority Act	Creates the TVA to bring electric power and conservation to the area.
June 16, 1933	National Industrial Recovery Act	Specifies cooperation among business, government, and labor in setting fair prices and working conditions.
June 16, 1933	Glass-Steagall Banking Act	Creates the Federal Deposit Insurance Corporation (FDIC) to insure bank deposits.

Deal. Their critiques were amplified by the American Liberty League, founded in 1934, which blamed the New Deal for betraying basic constitutional guarantees of freedom and individualism. To them, the AAA was a "trend toward fascist control of agriculture," relief programs marked "the end of democracy," and the NRA was a plunge into the "quicksand of visionary experimentation." Although Liberty League membership never exceeded 125,000, its well-financed publicity campaign widened the rift between Roosevelt and business people.

Economic planners who favored rational planning in the public interest and labor leaders who sought to influence wages and working conditions by organizing unions attacked the New Deal from the left. In their view, the NRA stifled enterprise by permitting **monopolistic** practices. They pointed out that industrial trade associations twisted NRA codes to suit their aims, thwarted competition, and engaged in price gouging. Labor leaders especially resented the NRA's willingness to allow businesses to form company-controlled unions while blocking workers from organizing genuine grassroots unions to bargain for themselves.

The Supreme Court stepped into this cross fire of criticisms in May 1935 and declared that the NRA unconstitutionally conferred powers reserved to Congress on an administrative agency staffed by government appointees. The NRA codes soon lost the little authority they had. The failure of the NRA demonstrated the depth of many Americans' resistance to economic planning and the stubborn refusal of business leaders to yield to government regulations or reforms.

Casualties in the Countryside

The AAA weathered critical battering by champions of the old order better than the NRA. Allotment checks for keeping land fallow and crop prices high created loyalty among farmers with enough acreage to participate. As a white farmer in North Carolina declared, "I stand for the New Deal and Roosevelt . . . , the AAA . . . and crop control." Agricultural processors and distributors, however, criticized the AAA. They objected that the program reduced the volume of crop production—the only source of their profits—while they paid a tax on processed crops that funded the very program that disadvantaged them. In 1936, the Supreme Court agreed with their contention that they were victims of an illegal attempt to tax one group (processors and distributors) to enrich another (farmers). Down but not out, the AAA rebounded from the Supreme Court ruling by eliminating the offending tax and funding allotment payments from general government revenues.

Protests stirred, however, among those who did not qualify for allotments. The Southern Farm Tenants Union argued passionately that the AAA enriched large farmers and impoverished small farmers who rented rather than owned their land. One black sharecropper explained why only $75 a year from New

Okie Family
This tenant farmer worked land near Eagleton, Oklahoma, but became sick with pneumonia and lost his farm. Accompanied by his five children, he carted all his possessions in a toy wagon along a highway while looking for work. Such poor, jobless migrants were common along America's roads during the 1930s.
Library of Congress.

Deal agricultural subsidies trickled down to her: "De landlord is landlord, de politicians is landlord, de judge is landlord, de shurf [sheriff] is landlord, ever'body is landlord, en we [sharecroppers] ain' got nothin'!" Such testimony showed that the AAA, like the NRA, tended to help most those who least needed help. Roosevelt's political dependence on southern Democrats caused him to avoid confronting such economic and racial inequities in the South's entrenched order.

Displaced tenants often joined the army of migrant workers who straggled across rural America during the 1930s, some to flee Great Plains dust storms. Many migrants came from Mexico to work Texas cotton, Michigan beans, Idaho sugar beets, and California crops of all kinds. But since the number of people willing to take agricultural jobs usually exceeded the number of jobs available, wages fell and native-born white migrants fought to reserve even these low-wage jobs for themselves. Hundreds of thousands of "Okies" streamed out of the Dust Bowl of Oklahoma, Kansas, Texas, and Colorado, where chronic drought and harmful agricultural practices blasted crops and hopes. Parched, poor, and wind-blown, Okies—like the Joad family immortalized in John Steinbeck's novel *The Grapes of Wrath* (1939)—migrated to the lush fields and orchards of California, congregating in labor camps and hoping to find work and a future. But migrant laborers seldom found steady or secure work. As one Okie said, "When they need us they call us migrants, and when we've picked their crop, we're bums and we got to get out."

Politics on the Fringes

Politically, the New Deal's staunchest opponents were in the Republican Party—organized, well-heeled, mainstream, and determined to challenge Roosevelt at every turn. But the New Deal also faced challenges from the political fringes, fueled by the hardship of the depression and the hope for a cure-all.

Socialists and Communists accused the New Deal of being the handmaiden of business elites and of rescuing capitalism from its self-inflicted crisis. Socialist author Upton Sinclair ran for governor of California in 1934 on a plan he called "End Poverty in California." Sinclair demanded that the state take ownership of idle factories and unused land and give them to cooperatives of working people, a first step toward what he envisioned as a "Cooperative Commonwealth" that would put the needs of people above profits. Sinclair lost the election, ending the most serious socialist electoral challenge to the New Deal.

Many intellectuals and artists sought to advance the cause of more radical change by joining left-wing organizations, including the American Communist Party. At its high point in the 1930s, the party had about thirty thousand members, the large majority of them immigrants, especially Scandinavians in the upper Midwest and eastern European Jews in major eastern and midwestern cities. Indi-vidual Communists worked to organize labor unions, protect the civil rights of black people, and help the destitute, but the party preached the overthrow of "bourgeois democracy" and the destruction of capitalism in favor of Soviet-style communism. Party spokesmen termed the NRA a "fascist slave program" and likened Roosevelt and the New Deal to Hitler and the Nazis. Such talk attracted few followers among the nation's millions of poor and unemployed. They wanted jobs and economic security within American capitalism and democracy, not violent revolution to establish a dictatorship of the Communist Party.

More powerful radical challenges to the New Deal sprouted from home-grown roots. Many Americans felt overlooked by New Deal programs that con-centrated on finance, agriculture, and industry but did little to produce jobs or aid the poor. The merciless reality of the depression also continued to erode the security of people who still had a job but worried constantly that they, too, might be pushed into the legions of the unemployed and penniless.

A Catholic priest in Detroit named Charles Coughlin spoke to and for many worried Americans in his weekly radio broadcasts, which reached a nationwide audience of 40 million. Father Coughlin expressed outrage at the suffering and inequities that he blamed on Communists, bankers, and "predatory capitalists," who, he claimed, were mostly Jews. In 1932, Coughlin applauded Roosevelt's election and declared, "The New Deal is Christ's deal." But Coughlin became frustrated by Roosevelt's refusal to grant him influence, turned against the New Deal, and in 1935 founded the National Union for Social Justice, or Union Party, to challenge Roosevelt in the 1936 presidential election. Tapping the popular appeal of anti-Semitism, Coughlin's Union Party called for an expanded money supply backed by silver so that the poor could be rescued from the "international bankers" responsible for the depression and coddled by Roosevelt.

Among those who answered Father Coughlin's call was Dr. Francis Townsend in Long Beach, California. Angry that many of his retired patients lived in misery, Townsend proposed in 1934 the creation of the Old Age Revolving Pension, which would pay every American over age sixty a pension of $200 a month. To receive the pension, senior citizens had to agree to spend the entire amount within thirty days, thereby stimulating the economy. Townsend organized pension clubs with more than two million paying members and petitioned the federal government to enact his scheme. When the major political parties rebuffed his impractical plan, Townsend merged his forces with Coughlin's Union Party in time for the 1936 election.

A more formidable challenge to the New Deal came from the powerful southern wing of the Democratic Party. Huey Long, son of a backcountry Louisiana farmer, was elected governor of the state in 1928 with his slogan "Every man a king, but no one wears a crown." Unlike nearly all other southern white politicians who harped on white supremacy, Long championed the poor over the rich, country people over city folk, and the humble over elites. As governor, "the Kingfish"—as he liked to call himself—delivered on his promises to provide jobs and build roads, schools, and hospitals, but he also behaved ruthlessly to achieve his goals. Journalists routinely referred to him as the "dictator of Louisiana." Swaggering and bullying to get his way, Long delighted his supporters, who elected him to the U.S. Senate in 1932. Senator Long introduced a sweeping "soak the rich" tax bill that would outlaw personal incomes of more than $1 million and inheritances of more than $5 million. When the Senate rejected his proposal, Long decided to run for president, mobilizing more than five million Americans behind his "Share Our Wealth" plan. Like Townsend's scheme, Long's program promised far more than it could deliver. The Share Our Wealth campaign died when Long was assassinated in 1935, but his constituency and the wide appeal of a more equitable distribution of wealth persisted.

The challenges to the New Deal from both Republicans and more radical groups stirred Democrats to solidify their winning coalition. In the midterm congressional elections of 1934—normally a time when a seated president loses support—voters gave New Dealers a landslide victory. Democrats increased their majority in the House of Representatives and gained a two-thirds majority in the Senate.

▶ **REVIEW**   Why did the New Deal face criticism from both ends of the political spectrum?

Toward a Welfare State

The popular mandate for the New Deal revealed by the congressional elections persuaded Roosevelt to press ahead with bold new efforts to achieve relief, recovery, and reform. Despite the initiatives of the Hundred Days, the depression still strangled the economy. Rumbles of discontent from Father Coughlin, Huey Long, and their supporters showed that New Deal programs had fallen far short of their goals. In 1935, Roosevelt capitalized on his congressional majorities to enact major new programs that signaled the emergence of an American **welfare state**.

Taken together, these New Deal efforts stretched a safety net under the lives of ordinary Americans. Although many citizens remained unprotected, New Deal programs helped millions with jobs, relief, and government support. Knitting together the safety net was the idea that the federal government bore responsibility for the welfare of individual Americans. When individuals suffered because of economic and social forces beyond their control—as in the Great Depression—the federal government had the duty to provide them with a measure of support and protection. The safety net of welfare programs tied the political loyalty of working people to the New Deal and the Democratic Party. As a North Carolina mill worker said, "Mr. Roosevelt is the only man we ever had in the White House who would understand that my boss is a sonofabitch."

Relief for the Unemployed

First and foremost, Americans still needed jobs. Since the private economy left eight million people jobless by 1935, Roosevelt and his advisers launched a massive work relief program. Roosevelt believed that direct government handouts crippled recipients with "spiritual and moral disintegration . . . destructive to the human spirit." Jobs, in contrast, bolstered individuals' "self-respect, . . . self-confidence, . . . courage, and determination." With a congressional appropriation of nearly $5 billion—more than all government revenues in 1934—the New Deal created the Works Progress Administration (WPA) to give unemployed Americans government-funded jobs on public works projects. The WPA put millions of jobless citizens to work on roads, bridges, parks, public buildings, and more. WPA paychecks pumped billions of dollars into the economy, boosting consumption along with what Roosevelt termed "the human spirit" of working people. In addition, Congress passed—over Roosevelt's veto—the bonus long sought by the Bonus Marchers, giving veterans an average of $580 and further stimulating the economy.

By 1936, WPA funds provided jobs for 7 percent of the nation's labor force. In effect, the WPA made the federal government the employer of last resort, creating useful jobs when the capitalist economy failed to do so. In hiring, WPA officials tended to discriminate in favor of white men and against women and racial minorities. But by the time the WPA ended in 1943—because mobilization for World War II created full employment—it had made major contributions to both relief and recovery. Overall, WPA jobs put thirteen million men and women to work and gave them paychecks worth $10 billion.

About three out of four WPA jobs involved construction and renovation of the nation's physical infrastructure. WPA workers built 572,000 miles of country roads, 78,000 bridges, 67,000 miles of city streets, 40,000 public buildings, 8,000 parks, 350 airports, and much else. In addition to work with picks, shovels, hammers, nails, bricks, and mortar, the WPA gave jobs to thousands of artists, musicians, actors, journalists, poets, and novelists. The WPA also organized sewing rooms for jobless women, giving them work and wages and allowing them to produce more than 100 million pieces of clothing that were then donated to the needy. One reporter observed that the women "come in [to the sewing rooms] sullen, dejected [and] half starved," but before long, "working in pleasant surroundings [and] having some money and food [do] wonders to restore their health and morale." The WPA reached the most isolated corners of the nation. For example, WPA-funded librarians and nurses on horseback delivered books and health care to remote cabins in Appalachia. Throughout the nation, WPA projects displayed tangible evidence of the New Deal's commitment to public welfare.

Empowering Labor

During the Great Depression, factory workers who managed to keep their jobs worried constantly about being laid off while their wages and working hours were cut. When workers tried to organize labor unions to protect themselves, municipal and state governments usually sided with employers. Since the Gilded Age, the state and federal governments had been far more effective at busting unions than at busting **trusts**. The New Deal dramatically reversed the federal government's stance toward unions. With legislation and political support, the New Deal encouraged an unprecedented wave of union organizing among the nation's working people. When the head of the United Mine Workers, John L. Lewis, told coal miners that "the President wants you to join a union," he exaggerated only a little. New Dealers believed that unions would counterbalance the organized might of big corporations by defending working people, maintaining wages, and replacing the bloody violence that often accompanied strikes with economic peace and commercial stability.

Violent battles on the nation's streets and docks showed the determination of militant labor leaders to organize unions that would protect jobs as well as wages. In 1934, striking workers in Toledo, Minneapolis, San Francisco, and elsewhere were beaten and shot by police and the National Guard. In Congress, labor leaders lobbied for the National Labor Relations Act (NLRA), a bill sponsored by Senator Robert Wagner of New York that authorized the federal government to intervene in labor disputes and supervise the organization of labor unions. Justly considered a "Magna Carta for labor," the Wagner Act, as it came to be called, guaranteed industrial workers the right to organize unions, putting the might of federal law behind the appeals of labor leaders. The Wagner Act created the National Labor Relations Board (NLRB) to sponsor and oversee elections for union representation. If the majority of workers at a company voted for a union, then the union became the sole bargaining agent for the entire workplace, and the employer was required to negotiate with the elected union leaders. Roosevelt signed the Wagner Act in July 1935, providing for the first time federal support for labor organization—the most important New Deal reform of the industrial order.

The achievements that flowed from the Wagner Act and renewed labor militancy were impressive. When Roosevelt became president in 1933, union membership—almost entirely composed of skilled workers in trade unions affiliated with the American Federation of Labor (AFL)—stood at three million, down by half since the end of World War I. With the support of the Wagner Act, union membership expanded almost fivefold, to fourteen million, by the time of Roosevelt's death in 1945. By then, 30 percent of the workforce was unionized, the highest union representation in American history.

Most of the new union members were factory workers and unskilled laborers, many of them immigrants, women, and African Americans. For decades, established AFL unions had no desire to organize factory and unskilled workers, who struggled along without unions. In 1935, under the aggressive leadership of the mine workers' John L. Lewis and the head of the Amalgamated Clothing Workers, Sidney Hillman, a coalition of unskilled workers formed the Committee for Industrial Organization (CIO; later the Congress of Industrial Organizations). The CIO, helped by the Wagner Act, mobilized organizing drives in major industries. The exceptional courage and organizing skill of labor militants, a few of them Communists, earned the CIO the leadership role in the campaign to organize the bitterly anti-union automobile and steel industries.

The bloody struggle by the CIO-affiliated United Auto Workers (UAW) to organize workers at General Motors climaxed in January 1937. Striking workers occupied the main assembly plant in Flint, Michigan, in a "sit-down" strike that slashed the plant's production of 15,000 cars a week to a mere 150. Stymied, General Motors eventually surrendered and agreed to make the UAW the sole bargaining agent for all the company's workers and to refrain from interfering with union activity. Having subdued the auto industry's leading producer, the

UAW expanded its campaign until, after much violence, the entire industry was unionized when the Ford Motor Company capitulated in 1941.

The CIO hoped to ride organizing success in auto plants to victory in the steel mills. But after unionizing the industry giant U.S. Steel, the CIO ran up against fanatic opposition from smaller steel firms. Following a police attack that killed ten strikers at Republic Steel outside Chicago in May 1937, the battered steel-workers halted their organizing campaign. In steel and other major industries, such as the stridently anti-union southern textile mills, organizing efforts stalled until after 1941, when military mobilization created labor shortages that gave workers greater bargaining power.

Social Security and Tax Reform

The single most important feature of the New Deal's emerging welfare state was Social Security. An ambitious, far-reaching, and permanent reform, Social Security was designed to provide a modest income to relieve the poverty of elderly people. Only about 15 percent of older Americans had private pension plans, and during the depression, corporations and banks often failed to pay the meager pensions they had promised. Corporations even fired or demoted employees to avoid or reduce pension payments. Prompted by the popular but impractical panaceas of Dr. Townsend, Father Coughlin, and Huey Long, Roosevelt became the first president to advocate protection for the elderly. He told Congress that "it is our plain duty to provide for that security upon which welfare depends . . . and undertake the great task of furthering the security of the citizen and his family through social insurance."

The political struggle for Social Security highlighted class differences among Americans. Support for the measure came from a coalition of advocacy groups for the elderly and the poor, traditional progressives, leftists, social workers, and labor unions. Arrayed against them were economic conservatives, including the American Liberty League, the National Association of Manufacturers, the Chamber of Commerce, and the American Medical Association. Enact the Social Security system, these conservatives and their representatives in the Republican Party warned, and the government will gain a whip hand over private property, destroy initiative, and reduce proud individuals to spineless loafers.

The large New Deal majority in Congress carried the day in August 1935. The Social Security Act required that pensions for the elderly be funded not by direct government subsidies, but instead by tax contributions from workers and their employers. Although this provision subtracted money from consumption—thus hindering economic recovery—it gave contributing workers a personal stake in the system and made it politically invulnerable. When eligible workers reached retirement age, they were not subject to a means test to prove that they were needy. Instead, they were entitled to receive benefits based on their contributions and years of work. Social Security also created unemployment insurance, paid

Social Security Card

The Social Security Act required each working American who participated in the system to register with the government and obtain a unique number inscribed on an identity card, making benefits portable from one job and one state to another. For the first time in the nation's history, millions of ordinary citizens were numbered, registered, and identified by the government. Administering the massive agency needed to collect and regulate this information and distribute the benefits gave government jobs to tens of thousands.

Picture Research Consultants & Archives.

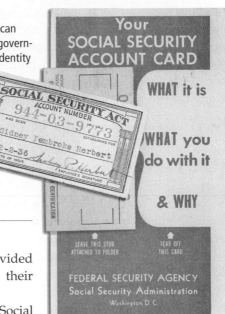

for by employers' contributions, that provided modest benefits for workers who lost their jobs.

Not all workers benefited from the Social Security Act. It excluded domestic and agricultural workers from receiving benefits, thereby making ineligible about half of all African Americans and more than half of all employed women—about five million people in all. In addition, the law excluded workers employed by religious and nonprofit organizations, such as schools and hospitals, rendering ineligible even more working women and minorities.

In a bow to traditional beliefs about local governments' responsibility for public assistance, Social Security issued multimillion-dollar grants to the states (rather than to individuals) to help support dependent children (a program expanded in 1950 to include Aid to Families with Dependent Children), public health services, and the blind. After the Supreme Court in 1937 upheld the right of Congress to require all citizens to pay for Social Security through federal taxes, the program was expanded to include benefits for dependent survivors of deceased recipients. Although the first Social Security check (for $41.30) was not issued until 1940, the system gave millions of working people the assurance that in the future, when they became too old to work, they would receive a modest income from the federal government. This safety net protected many ordinary working people from fears of a penniless and insecure old age.

Fervent opposition to Social Security struck New Dealers as evidence that the rich had learned little from the depression. Roosevelt had long felt contempt for the moneyed elite who ignored the sufferings of the poor. He looked for a way to redistribute wealth that would weaken conservative opposition, advance the cause of social equity, and defuse political challenges from Huey Long and Father Coughlin. In June 1935, as the Social Security Act was being debated, Roosevelt delivered a message to Congress outlining comprehensive tax reform. Charging that large fortunes put "great and undesirable concentration of control in [the hands of] relatively few individuals," Roosevelt urged a graduated tax on corporations, an inheritance tax, and an increase in maximum personal income taxes. Congress endorsed Roosevelt's basic principle by taxing those with higher incomes at a somewhat higher rate.

Neglected Americans and the New Deal

Although the WPA and other work relief programs aided working people, the average unemployment rate for the 1930s stayed high—17 percent, about one of every six workers. Even many working people remained more or less untouched by New Deal benefits. Workers in industries that resisted unions received little help from the Wagner Act or the WPA. Tens of thousands of women in southern textile mills, for example, commonly received wages of less than ten cents an hour and were fired if they protested. Domestic workers—almost all of them women—and agricultural workers—many of them African, Hispanic, or Asian Americans—were neither unionized nor eligible for Social Security. The patchwork of New Deal reforms erected a two-tier welfare state. In the top tier, organized workers in major industries were the greatest beneficiaries of New Deal initiatives. In the bottom tier, millions of neglected Americans—women, children, and old folks, along with the unorganized, unskilled, uneducated, and unemployed—often fell through the New Deal safety net.

The New Deal neglected few citizens more than African Americans. About half of black Americans in cities were jobless, more than double the unemployment rate among whites. In the rural South, where the vast majority of African Americans lived, conditions were worse. New Deal agricultural policies such as the AAA favored landowners and often resulted in black sharecroppers and tenants being pushed off the land they farmed. **Disfranchisement** by intimidation and legal subterfuge prevented southern blacks from protesting their plight at the ballot box. Protest risked vicious retaliation from local whites. After years of decline, lynching increased during the 1930s. In Georgia, radical black unionist Angelo Herndon was sentenced to the chain gang for trying to organize black workers. Only 11 of more than 10,000 WPA supervisors in the South were black, even though African Americans accounted for about a third of the region's population. Up north, a 1935 riot that focused on white-owned businesses in Harlem dramatized blacks' resentment and despair. Bitter critics charged that the New Deal's NRA stood for "Negro Run Around" or "Negroes Ruined Again."

Roosevelt responded to such criticisms with great caution, since New Deal reforms required the political support of powerful conservative, segregationist, southern white Democrats, who would be alienated by programs that aided blacks. A white Georgia relief worker expressed the common view that "any Nigger who gets over $8 a week is a spoiled Nigger, that's all." Stymied by the political clout of entrenched white racism, New Dealers still tried to attract political support from black leaders. Roosevelt's overtures to African Americans prompted northern black voters in the 1934 congressional elections to shift from the Republican to the Democratic Party, helping elect New Deal Democrats.

Eleanor Roosevelt sponsored the appointment of Mary McLeod Bethune— the energetic cofounder of the National Council of Negro Women—as head of the Division of Negro Affairs in the National Youth Administration. The highest-ranking black official in Roosevelt's administration, Bethune used her position to guide a small number of black professionals and civil rights activists to posts within New Deal agencies. Nicknamed the "Black Cabinet," these men and women composed the first sizable representation of African Americans in white-collar posts in the federal government, and they ultimately helped about one in four African Americans get access to New Deal relief programs.

Despite these gains, by 1940 African Americans still suffered severe handicaps. Most of the thirteen million black workers toiled at low-paying menial jobs, unprotected by the New Deal safety net. Infant mortality was 50 percent greater among blacks than among whites, and life expectancy was twelve years shorter. Making a mockery of the "separate but equal" doctrine, segregated black schools had less money and worse facilities than white schools, and only 1 percent of black students earned college degrees. In southern states, there were no black police officers or judges and hardly any black lawyers, and vigilante violence against blacks went unpunished. For these problems of black Americans, the New Deal offered few remedies.

Hispanic Americans fared no better. About a million Mexican Americans lived in the United States in the 1930s, most of them first- or second-generation immigrants who worked at stoop labor tending crops throughout the West. During the depression, field workers saw their low wages plunge lower still to about a dime an hour. Ten thousand Mexican American pecan shellers in San Antonio, Texas, earned only a nickel an hour. To preserve scarce jobs for U.S. citizens, the federal government choked off immigration from Mexico, while state and local officials prohibited the employment of aliens on work relief projects and deported tens of thousands of Mexican Americans, many with their American-born children. Local white administrators of many New Deal programs throughout the West discriminated against Hispanics and other people of color. When Mexican Americans managed to land jobs on government projects, they often received lower wages than their white counterparts. A New Deal study concluded that "the Mexican is . . . segregated from the rest of the community as effectively as the Negro . . . [by] poverty and low wages."

Asian Americans had similar experiences. Asian immigrants were still excluded from U.S. citizenship and in many states were not permitted to own land. By 1930, more than half of Japanese Americans had been born in the United States, but they were still liable to discrimination. Even college-educated Asian Americans worked in family shops, restaurants, and laundries. One young Asian American expressed the frustration felt by many others: "I am a fruitstand worker. I would much rather it were doctor or lawyer . . . but my aspirations [were] frustrated long ago by circumstances [and] I am only what I am, a professional carrot washer."

Native Americans also suffered neglect from New Deal agencies. As a group, they remained the poorest of the poor. Since the Dawes Act of 1887 (see chapter 17), the federal government had encouraged Native Americans to assimilate—to abandon their Indian identities and adopt the cultural norms of the majority society. Under the leadership of the New Deal's commissioner of Indian affairs, John Collier, the New Deal's Indian Reorganization Act (IRA) of 1934 largely reversed that policy. Collier claimed that "the most interesting and important fact about Indians" was that they "do not expect much, often they expect nothing at all; yet they are able to be happy." Given such views, the IRA provided little economic aid to Native Americans, but it did restore their right to own land communally and to have greater control over their own affairs, including a vote on whether they should live under the IRA, as more than two-thirds opted to do in special elections in 1934 and 1935. The IRA brought little immediate benefit to Native Americans and has remained a divisive issue for decades, but it provided an important foundation for Indians' economic, cultural, and political resurgence a generation later (see chapter 28).

The troubadour of working people, singer and songwriter Woody Guthrie, traveled the nation for eight years during the 1930s "by the thumb route . . . no job, no money, no home . . . no nothing." At night, he recalled, other rambling men told him "the story of their life, how it used to be," giving voice to experiences especially common among Americans neglected by the New Deal: "how the home went to pieces, how the young wife died or left, how the mother died in the insane asylum, how Dad tried twice to kill himself, and lay flat on his back for 18 months—and then the crops got to where they wouldn't bring nothing, work in factories would kill a dog . . . and—always, always [you] have to fight and argue and cuss and swear . . . to try to get a nickel more out of the rich bosses."

▶**REVIEW**   What features of a welfare state did the New Deal create and why?

The New Deal from Victory to Deadlock

To accelerate the sputtering economic recovery, Roosevelt shifted the emphasis of the New Deal in the mid-1930s. Instead of seeking cooperation from conservative business leaders, he decided to rely on the growing New Deal coalition to enact reforms over the strident opposition of the Supreme Court, Republicans, and corporate interests.

Added to New Deal strength in farm states and big cities were some new allies on the left. Throughout Roosevelt's first term, socialists and Communists denounced the slow pace of change and accused the New Deal of failing to serve the interests of the workers who produced the nation's wealth. But in 1935, the Soviet Union, worried about the threat of fascism in Europe, instructed Communists throughout the world to join hands with non-Communist progressives in a "Popular Front" to advance the fortunes of the working class. With varying degrees of enthusiasm, many radicals switched from opposing the New Deal to supporting its relief programs and encouragement of labor unions.

Roosevelt's conservative opponents reacted to the massing of New Deal force by intensifying their opposition to the welfare state. To Roosevelt, the situation seemed part of a drama that had played out since the nation's beginning, pitting a Hamiltonian faction of wealth and privilege against the heirs of Jefferson, who, like Roosevelt himself, favored a more equitable distribution of wealth and opportunity.

The Election of 1936

Roosevelt believed that the presidential election of 1936 would test his leadership and progressive ideals. The depression still had a stranglehold on the economy. Nearly eight million Americans remained jobless, and millions more were stuck in poverty. Conservative leaders believed that the New Deal's failure to lift the nation out of the depression indicated that Americans were ready for a change. Left-wing critics insisted that the New Deal had missed the opportunity to displace capitalism with a socialist economy and that voters would embrace candidates who recommended more radical remedies.

Republicans turned to the Kansas heartland to select Governor Alfred (Alf) Landon as their presidential nominee. A moderate who had supported some New Deal measures, Landon stressed mainstream Republican proposals to achieve a balanced federal budget and to ease the perils of illness and old age with old-fashioned neighborliness instead of faceless government bureaucracies such as Social Security.

Roosevelt put his faith in the growing coalition of New Deal supporters who, he believed, shared his conviction that the New Deal was the nation's liberator from a long era of privilege and wealth for a few and "economic slavery" for the rest. At the end of the campaign, Roosevelt assailed his "old enemies . . . business and financial monopoly, speculation, reckless banking, [and] class antagonism," and he proclaimed, "Never before in all our history have these forces been so united against one candidate as they stand today. They are unanimous in their hate for me—and I welcome their hatred."

Roosevelt triumphed spectacularly. He won 60.8 percent of the popular vote—11 million more votes than Landon—making it the widest margin of victory in a presidential election to date. He carried the electoral votes of every state except Maine and Vermont. Third parties—including the Socialist and Communist parties—fell pitifully short of the support they expected and never again mounted a significant challenge to the New Deal. Congressional results were equally lopsided, with Democrats outnumbering Republicans more than three to one in both houses. In northern cities with many immigrant voters, Democrats more than doubled their 1932 tallies.

In his inaugural address, Roosevelt pledged to use his mandate to help all citizens achieve a decent standard of living. He announced, "I see one third of a nation ill-housed, ill-clad, [and] ill-nourished," and he promised to devote his second term to alleviating their hardship.

Court Packing

In the afterglow of his reelection triumph, Roosevelt pondered how to remove the remaining obstacles to New Deal reforms. He decided to target the Supreme Court. Laden with conservative justices appointed by Republican presidents, the Court had invalidated eleven New Deal measures as unconstitutional interferences with free enterprise. Now, Social Security, the Wagner Act, the Securities and Exchange Commission, and other New Deal innovations were moving toward an ominous rendezvous with the justices.

Roosevelt concluded that he must do something to ensure that the Supreme Court's "horse and buggy" notions did not dismantle the New Deal. He proposed that one new justice be added for each existing judge who had served for ten years and was over the age of seventy. In effect, the proposed law would give Roosevelt the power to pack the Court with up to six New Dealers who could outvote the elderly, conservative, Republican justices.

But the president had not reckoned with Americans' deeply rooted deference to the independent authority of the Supreme Court. More than two-thirds of Americans believed that the Court should be free from political interference. Even New Deal supporters were disturbed by the "court-packing" scheme. The suggestion that individuals over age seventy had diminished mental capacity also offended many elderly members of Congress. Roosevelt insisted that the bill was intended to improve the efficiency of an "overworked" Court, but its real purpose was to make room for supporters of New Deal initiatives. A storm of public protest whipped up by conservatives prompted the heavily Democratic Senate to defeat the bill in 1937.

Although Roosevelt's court-packing plan failed, Supreme Court justices got the message. After the furor abated, Chief Justice Charles Evans Hughes and fellow moderate Owen Roberts moderated their views enough to keep the Court from invalidating the Wagner Act and Social Security. Then the most conservative of the elderly justices—the "four horsemen of reaction," one New Dealer called them—retired. Roosevelt eventually named eight justices to the Court—more than any other president. His choice of liberals to fill vacancies on the Court ultimately gave New Deal laws safe passage through the shoals of judicial review.

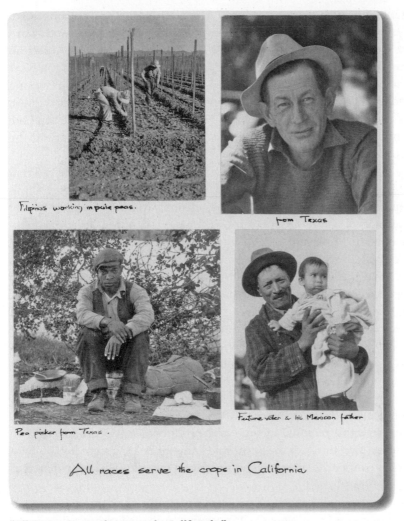

Filipinos working in pole peas.

from Texas

Pea picker from Texas.

Future voter & his Mexican father

All races serve the crops in California

"All Races Serve the Crops in California"
New Deal agencies dispatched dozens of photographers to document the lives
of Americans during the 1930s. This page from the 1935 journal of New Deal
photographer Dorothea Lange documents migrant workers whom she encountered
in California fields.
Library of Congress.

Reaction and Recession

Emboldened by their defeat of the court-packing plan, Republicans and southern
Democrats rallied around their common conservatism to obstruct additional
reforms. Former president Herbert Hoover proclaimed that "the New Deal repudiation of Democracy has left the Republican Party alone the guardian of the Ark

of the Covenant with its charter of freedom." The New Deal's acts, he continued, were "based upon the coercion and compulsory organization of men" and "born of a Roman despot[,] . . . Karl Marx[,] . . . a British professor[,] . . . American radicals . . . [and] Brain Trusters." Democrats' arguments over whether the New Deal needed to be expanded—and if so, how—undermined the consensus among reformers and sparked antagonism between Congress and the White House. The ominous rise of belligerent regimes in Germany, Italy, Japan, and elsewhere slowed reform as some Americans began to worry more about defending the nation than changing it.

Roosevelt himself favored slowing the pace of the New Deal. He believed that existing New Deal measures had steadily boosted the economy and largely eliminated the depression crisis. In fact, the gross national product in 1937 briefly equaled the 1929 level before dropping lower for the rest of the decade. Unemployment declined to 14 percent in 1937 but quickly spiked upward and stayed higher until 1940. Roosevelt's unwarranted optimism about the economic recovery persuaded him that additional deficit spending by the federal government was no longer necessary. He also worried that pump-priming deficits would cause inflation and reduce the value of hard-earned savings. Accordingly, he moved cautiously toward a balanced budget by cutting funds for relief projects, and he urged the Federal Reserve Board to raise interest rates to tamp down inflation.

Roosevelt's retrenchment soon backfired. The reduction in deficit spending reversed the improving economy. Roosevelt's worries about inflation failed to consider the stubborn realities of unemployment and poverty. Even at the high-water mark of recovery in the summer of 1937, seven million people lacked jobs. In the next few months, national income and production slipped backward so steeply that almost two-thirds of the economic gains since 1933 were lost by June 1938. Farm prices dropped 20 percent, and unemployment rose by more than two million.

This economic reversal hurt the New Deal politically. Conservatives argued that this recession proved that New Deal measures produced only an illusion of progress. The way to weather the recession was to tax and spend less and wait for the natural laws of supply and demand to restore prosperity. Many New Dealers insisted instead that the continuing depression demanded that Roosevelt revive federal spending and redouble efforts to stimulate the economy. In 1938, Congress heeded such pleas and enacted a massive new program of federal spending.

The New Deal's ad hoc methods received support from the brilliant English economist John Maynard Keynes. In his influential work *The General Theory of Employment, Interest, and Money* (1936), Keynes made a sophisticated, theoretical argument in favor of practices that New Deal relief agencies had developed in a commonsense way. Keynes declared that the depression illustrated that a nation's economic activity could become stalled at a level far short of its true potential. When that happened, only government intervention could pump enough money into the economy to restore prosperity.

Roosevelt never had the inclination or the time to follow his economic advisers into the thicket of **Keynesian** theory. But the recession scare of 1937–1938 taught the president the Keynesian lesson that economic growth had to be carefully nurtured. Escape from the depression required a plan for large-scale spending to alleviate distress and stimulate economic growth.

The Last of the New Deal Reforms

From the moment he was sworn in, Roosevelt sought to expand the powers of the presidency. He believed that the president needed more authority to meet emergencies such as the depression and to administer the sprawling federal bureaucracy. In September 1938, Congress passed the Administrative Reorganization Act, which gave Roosevelt (and future presidents) new influence over the bureaucracy. Combined with a Democratic majority in Congress, a now-friendly Supreme Court, and the revival of deficit spending, the newly empowered White House seemed to be in a good position to move ahead with a revitalized New Deal.

Resistance to further reform was also on the rise, however. Conservatives argued that the New Deal had pressed government centralization too far. Even the New Deal's friends became weary of one emergency program after another while economic woes continued to shadow New Deal achievements. By the midpoint of Roosevelt's second term, restive members of Congress balked at new initiatives. Clearly, the New Deal was losing momentum, but enough support remained for one last burst of reform.

Agriculture still had strong claims on New Deal attention in the face of drought, declining crop prices, and impoverished sharecroppers and tenants. In 1937, the Agriculture Department created the Farm Security Administration (FSA) to provide housing and loans to help tenant farmers become independent. A black tenant farmer in North Carolina who received an FSA loan told a New Deal interviewer, "I wake up in the night sometimes and think I must be half-dead and gone to heaven." But relatively few tenants received loans, because the FSA was starved for funds and ran up against the major farm organizations intent on serving their own interests. For those who owned farms, the New Deal offered renewed prosperity with a second Agricultural Adjustment Act (AAA) in 1938. To moderate price swings by regulating supply, the plan combined production quotas on five staple crops—cotton, tobacco, wheat, corn, and rice—with storage loans through its Commodity Credit Corporation. The most prosperous farmers benefited most, but the act's Federal Surplus Commodities Corporation added an element of charity by issuing food stamps so that the poor could obtain surplus food. The AAA of 1938 brought stability to American agriculture and ample food to most—but not all—tables.

Advocates for the urban poor also made modest gains after decades of neglect. New York senator Robert Wagner convinced Congress to pass the National Housing Act in 1937. By 1941, some 160,000 residences had been made available to poor people at affordable rents. The program did not come close to meeting the need for affordable housing, but for the first time, the federal government took an active role in providing decent urban housing.

The last major piece of New Deal labor legislation, the Fair Labor Standards Act of June 1938, reiterated the New Deal pledge to provide workers with a decent standard of living. After lengthy haggling and compromise that revealed the waning strength of the New Deal, Congress finally agreed to intervene in the long-sacrosanct realm of worker contracts. The new law set wage and hours standards and at long last curbed the use of child labor. The minimum-wage level was modest—twenty-five cents an hour for a maximum of forty-four hours a week. And, in order to attract enough conservative votes, the act exempted merchant seamen, fishermen, domestic help, and farm laborers—relegating most women and African Americans to lower wages. Enforcement of the minimum-wage standards was weak and haphazard. Thousands of workers petitioned the federal government for relief from their substandard wages. Among them were Bill Brown, who worked a forty-four-hour week in a box factory and got paid $8.80 instead of $11, and Minnie Smith, who sewed pockets on clothing for sixty hours a week and did not receive her required sixteen hours of time-and-a-half overtime wages. Nevertheless, the Fair Labor Standards Act slowly advanced Roosevelt's inaugural promise to improve the living standards of the poorest Americans.

The final New Deal reform effort failed to make much headway against the hidebound system of racial injustice. Although Roosevelt denounced lynching as murder, he would not jeopardize his vital base of southern political support by demanding antilynching legislation. In 1934 and 1935, Congress voted down attempts to make lynching a federal crime, and in 1938 the last antilynching bill of the decade died in the Senate. Laws to eliminate the poll tax—used to deny blacks the opportunity to vote—encountered the same overwhelming resistance. The New Deal refused to confront racial injustice with the same vigor it brought to bear on economic hardship.

By the end of 1938, the New Deal had lost steam and encountered stiff opposition. In the congressional elections of 1938, Republicans picked up seven seats in the Senate and eighty in the House, giving them more congressional influence than they had enjoyed since 1932. New Dealers could claim unprecedented and resounding achievements since 1933, but nobody needed reminding that those achievements had not ended the depression. In his annual message to Congress in January 1939, Roosevelt signaled a halt to New Deal reforms by speaking about preserving the progress already achieved rather than extending it. Overseas, nations with much weaker economies than the United States struggled to overcome the woes of the worldwide depression. Germany and Japan resorted to rapid military rearmament to boost their economies and to strengthen their campaigns for territorial conquest. Roosevelt pointed to the ominous threats posed by fascist aggressors in Germany and Japan, and he proposed defense expenditures that surpassed New Deal appropriations for relief and economic recovery.

▶ **REVIEW**   Why did political support for New Deal reforms decline?

Conclusion: Achievements and Limitations of the New Deal

The New Deal replaced the fear symbolized by Hoover's expulsion of the Bonus Army with Roosevelt's confidence, optimism, and energetic pragmatism. A growing majority of Americans agreed with Roosevelt that the federal government should help those in need, thereby strengthening the political coalition that propelled the New Deal. In the process of seeking relief for victims of the depression, recovery of the general economy, and basic reform of major economic institutions, the New Deal vastly expanded the size and influence of the federal government and changed the way the American people viewed Washington. New Dealers achieved significant victories, such as Social Security, labor's right to organize, and guarantees that farm prices would be maintained through controls on production and marketing. New Deal measures marked the emergence of a welfare state, but the New Deal's limited, two-tier character left many needy Americans with little aid.

Full-scale relief, recovery, and reform eluded New Deal programs. Even though millions of Americans benefited directly from the alphabet soup of agencies and programs, both relief and recovery were limited and temporary. In 1940, the depression still plagued the economy. The most durable New Deal achievements were reforms that stabilized agriculture, encouraged the organization of labor unions, and created the safety net of Social Security and fair labor standards. Perhaps the most impressive achievement of the New Deal was what did not happen. Although authoritarian governments and anticapitalist policies were common outside the United States during the 1930s, they were shunned by the New Deal coalition. The greatest economic crisis the nation had ever faced did not cause Americans to abandon democracy, as happened in Germany, where Adolf Hitler seized dictatorial power. Nor did the nation turn to radical alternatives such as socialism or communism.

Republicans and other conservatives claimed that the New Deal amounted to a form of socialism that threatened democracy and capitalism. But rather than attack capitalism, Franklin Roosevelt sought to save it, and he succeeded. That success also marked the limits of the New Deal's achievements. Like his cousin Teddy, Franklin Roosevelt understood that a strengthened national government was necessary to curb the destructive tendencies of concentrated economic power. A shift of authority toward the federal government, both Roosevelts believed, would allow capitalist enterprises to be balanced by the nation's democratic tradition. The New Deal stopped far short of challenging capitalism either by undermining private property or by imposing strict national planning.

New Dealers repeatedly described their programs as a kind of warfare against the economic adversities of the 1930s. In the next decade, with the depression only partly vanquished, the Roosevelt administration had to turn from the New Deal's war against economic crisis at home to participate in a worldwide conflagration to defeat the enemies of democracy abroad.

REVIEWING THE CHAPTER

Use the questions and timeline to review and strengthen your understanding of the chapter.

REVIEW QUESTIONS

1. Why did Franklin D. Roosevelt win the 1932 presidential election by such a large margin? (pp. 756–59)

2. How did the New Dealers try to steer the nation toward recovery from the Great Depression? (pp. 760–67)

3. Why did groups at both ends of the political spectrum criticize the New Deal? (pp. 768–73)

4. What features of a welfare state did the New Deal create and why? (pp. 773–80)

5. Why did political support for New Deal reforms decline? (pp. 780–87)

MAKING CONNECTIONS

1. Franklin Roosevelt's landslide victory in 1932 changed the political landscape. How did Roosevelt build an effective interregional political coalition for the Democratic Party? How did the challenges of balancing interests within the coalition shape the policies of the New Deal? In your answer, discuss the character of the coalition and specific reforms.

2. New Dealers experimented with varied solutions to the economic disorder of the 1930s. Compare reform efforts targeting rural and industrial America. Were they effective? Why or why not? What do they reveal about how the Roosevelt administration understood the underlying causes of the Great Depression?

3. Although the New Deal enjoyed astonishing popularity, some Americans were consistently critical of Roosevelt's reforms. Why? In your answer, discuss three opponents of the New Deal, being attentive to changes over time in their opinions. Were they able to influence the New Deal? If so, how?

4. Although the New Deal extended help to many Americans, all did not benefit equally from the era's reforms. Who remained outside the reach of New Deal assistance? Why? In your answer, consider how politics shaped the limits of reform, both in constituents' ability to demand assistance and in the federal government's response to their demands.

TIMELINE

1932	• Bonus Army marches on Washington.
1933	• Democrat Franklin D. Roosevelt becomes president. • **March–June.** Legislation of the Hundred Days establishes the New Deal. • Roosevelt closes the nation's banks for a four-day "bank holiday." • Federal Emergency Relief Administration (FERA) established.
1934	• Securities and Exchange Commission (SEC) created. • Upton Sinclair loses bid for governorship of California. • American Liberty League founded. • Dr. Francis Townsend devises Old Age Revolving Pension scheme. • Indian Reorganization Act.
1935	• Legislation creates Works Progress Administration (WPA). • Wagner Act. • Committee for Industrial Organization (CIO) founded. • Social Security Act. • Father Charles Coughlin begins National Union for Social Justice.

1936	• John Maynard Keynes publishes *The General Theory of Employment, Interest, and Money.* • Franklin Roosevelt elected to a second term by a landslide.
1937	• United Auto Workers stages successful sit-down strike at General Motors plant in Flint, Michigan. • Roosevelt's court-packing legislation defeated in the Senate.
1937–1938	• Economic recession slows recovery from depression.
1938	• Second Agricultural Adjustment Act and Fair Labor Standards Act. • Congress rejects administration's antilynching bill. • Administrative Reorganization Act.

▶ **For an online bibliography, practice quizzes, Web sites, images, and documents related to this chapter,** see the Book Companion Site at **bedfordstmartins.com/roark.**

▶ **For firsthand accounts of this period,** see Chapter 24 in Michael Johnson, ed., *Reading the American Past,* Fourth Edition.

25
CHAPTER

The United States and the Second World War
1939–1945

O N A SUN-DRENCHED FLORIDA AFTERNOON in January 1927, Paul Tibbets took his first airplane ride. Twelve-year-old Tibbets cinched on a leather helmet; clambered into the front seat of the open cockpit of a cloth-covered red, white, and blue biplane; and sailed aloft over Miami. While the barnstorming pilot sitting behind him brought the plane in low over the Hialeah racetrack, Tibbets pitched Baby Ruth candy bars tethered to small paper parachutes to racing fans in the grandstands below. After two more candy-bar drops over the racetrack, the pilot raced to the beach and swooped down to two hundred feet as Tibbets tossed out the remaining candy bars and watched the bathers scramble for chocolate from heaven. After Tibbets and the pilot repeated their stunt for a week, sales of Baby Ruths soared for Tibbets's father's candy business, and Tibbets was hooked on flying.

Born in Quincy, Illinois, in 1915, Tibbets entered the University of Florida in 1933 and took flying lessons at the Gainesville airport. He continued to fly in his spare time and in 1937 decided to join the Army Air Corps to become a military pilot.

Shortly after the Japanese attack on Pearl Harbor in December 1941, Tibbets led a squadron of airplanes flying antisubmarine patrol against German U-boats lurking along the East Coast. When the heavily armored B-17 Flying Fortress bombers began to come off American assembly lines early in 1942, he took a squadron of the new planes from the United States to England. On

August 17, 1942, he led the first American daytime bombing raid on German-occupied Europe, releasing 1,100 pounds of bombs from his B-17, nicknamed *Butcher Shop*, on the railroad yards of Rouen in northern France—the first of some 700,000 tons of explosives dropped by American bombers during the air war in Europe.

After numerous raids over Europe, Tibbets was reassigned to the North African campaign, where his duties included ferrying the American commander, General Dwight D. Eisenhower, into the battle zone. After eight months of combat missions, Tibbets returned to the United States and was ordered to test the new B-29 Super Fortress being built in Wichita, Kansas. The B-29 was much bigger than the B-17 and could fly higher and faster, making it ideal for the campaign against Japan. Tibbets's mastery of the B-29 caused him to be singled out in September 1944 to command a top-secret unit training for a special mission.

The mission, officials confided to Tibbets, was to be ready to drop on Japan a bomb that was so powerful it might bring the war to an end. No such bomb yet existed, but American scientists and engineers were working around the clock to build one. Tibbets kept this secret from his men but took them and his B-29s to Utah to develop a way to drop such a powerful weapon without getting blown up by it. Tibbets trained his pilots to fly at 31,000 feet, then execute a dangerous, sharp, diving turn of 155 degrees that tested the limits of the aircraft but moved it beyond the range of the expected blast.

In May 1945, Tibbets took his B-29s and men to Tinian Island in the Pacific, where they trained for

Colonel Paul Tibbets
Before taking off to drop the world's first atomic bomb on Hiroshima, Tibbets posed next to his B-29 bomber, named *Enola Gay* in honor of his mother. A crew of eleven airmen accompanied Tibbets on the top-secret mission. After the war, President Harry S. Truman told Tibbets, "Don't you ever lose any sleep over the fact that you planned and carried out that mission. It was my decision. You had no choice."
© Bettmann/Corbis.

their secret mission by flying raids over Japanese cities and dropping ordinary bombs. The atomic bomb arrived on Tinian on July 26, just ten days after the successful test explosion in the New Mexico desert. Nicknamed "Little Boy," the bomb packed the equivalent of 40 million pounds of TNT, or 200,000 of the 200-pound bombs Tibbets and other American airmen had dropped on Europe.

At 2:30 a.m. on August 6, 1945, Tibbets, his crew, and their atomic payload took off in the B-29 bomber *Enola Gay* and headed for Japan. Less than seven hours later, over the city of Hiroshima, Tibbets and his men released Little Boy from the *Enola Gay*'s bomb bay. The plane bucked upward after dropping the 4.5-ton explosive, while Tibbets banked the plane sharply to the right and struggled to maintain control as the shock wave from the explosion blasted past and a purple cloud mushroomed nearly ten miles into the air. For an hour and a half as Tibbets flew back toward Tinian, he could see the mushroom cloud of atomic destruction unleashed by Little Boy. Three days later, Tibbets's men dropped a second atomic bomb on Nagasaki, and within five days, Japan surrendered.

Paul Tibbets's experiences traced an arc followed by millions of Americans during World War II, from the innocence of bombarding Miami with candy bars to the deadly nuclear firestorms that rained down on Japan. Like Tibbets, Americans joined their allies to fight the Axis powers in Europe and Asia. Like his *Enola Gay* crewmen—who hailed from New York, Texas, California, New Jersey, New Mexico, Maryland, North Carolina, Pennsylvania, Michigan, and Nevada— Americans from all regions united to defeat the **fascist** aggressors. American industries mobilized to produce advanced bombers—like the ones Tibbets piloted over Europe, North Africa, and Japan—along with enough other military equipment to supply the American armed forces and their allies. At an enormous cost in human life and suffering, the war brought employment and prosperity to most Americans at home, ending the depression, providing new opportunities for women, and ushering the nation into the postwar world as a triumphant economic and—on the wings of Paul Tibbets's *Enola Gay*—atomic superpower.

Peacetime Dilemmas

The First World War left a dangerous and ultimately deadly legacy. The victors— especially Britain, France, and the United States—sought to avoid future wars at almost any cost. The defeated nations, as well as those who felt humiliated by the Versailles peace settlement—particularly Germany, Italy, and Japan—aspired to reassert their power and avenge their losses by means of renewed warfare. Japan invaded the northern Chinese province of Manchuria in 1931 with ambitions to expand throughout Asia. Italy, led by the fascist Benito Mussolini since 1922, hungered for an empire in Africa. In Germany, National Socialist Adolf Hitler rose to power in 1933 in a quest to dominate Europe and the world. These aggressive, militaristic, antidemocratic regimes seemed a smaller threat to most people in the United States during the 1930s than the economic crisis at home. Shielded from external threats by the Atlantic and Pacific oceans, Americans hoped to avoid entanglement in foreign woes and to concentrate on climbing out of the nation's economic abyss.

Roosevelt and Reluctant Isolation

Like most Americans during the 1930s, Franklin Roosevelt believed that the nation's highest priority was to attack the domestic causes and consequences of the depression. But unlike most Americans, Roosevelt had long advocated an active role for the United States in international affairs. As assistant secretary of the navy in Woodrow Wilson's administration, he championed the significance of naval strength in the global balance of power. After World War I, Roosevelt embraced Wilson's vision that the United States should take the lead in making the world "safe for democracy," and he continued to advocate American membership in the League of Nations during the **isolationist** 1920s. When he ran for governor of New York in 1928, he criticized Republican isolationists for subverting international peace by demanding that battered European nations pay off their wartime loans and reparations in full and on time.

The depression forced Roosevelt to retreat from his previous internationalism. He came to believe that energetic involvement in foreign affairs diverted resources and political support from domestic recovery. During his 1932 presidential campaign, he pulled back from his endorsement of the League of Nations and reversed his previous support for forgiving European war debts. Once in office, Roosevelt sought to combine domestic economic recovery with a low-profile foreign policy that encouraged free trade and disarmament. "Foreign markets must be regained if America's producers are to rebuild a full and domestic prosperity," he explained in 1935. In turn, free trade required international peace, the goal of disarmament.

In pursuit of international amity, Roosevelt was constrained by economic circumstances and American popular opinion. After an opinion poll demonstrated popular support for recognizing the Soviet Union—an international pariah since the Bolshevik Revolution in 1917—Roosevelt established formal diplomatic relations in 1933. But when the League of Nations condemned Japanese and German aggression, Roosevelt did not enlist the nation in the league's attempts to keep the peace because he feared jeopardizing isolationists' support for **New Deal** measures in Congress. America watched from the sidelines when Japan withdrew from the league and ignored the limitations on its navy imposed after World War I. The United States also looked the other way when Hitler rearmed Germany and recalled its representative to the league in 1933, declaring that the international organization sought to thwart Germany's national ambitions. Roosevelt worried that the league's inability to curb German and Japanese violations of league sanctions and the Versailles settlement threatened world peace. But he reassured Americans that the nation would not "use its armed forces for the settlement of any [international] dispute anywhere."

The Good Neighbor Policy

In his 1933 inaugural address, Franklin Roosevelt announced that the United States would pursue "the policy of the good neighbor" in international relations. A few weeks later, he emphasized that this policy applied specifically to Latin America, where U.S. military forces had often intervened in local affairs. Now, Roosevelt said, the old policy of arrogant intervention would be replaced by a "helping hand" extended in a desire for friendly cooperation to create "more order in this hemisphere and less dislike." In December 1933 at the Inter-American Conference in Montevideo, Uruguay, Secretary of State Cordell Hull formalized the good neighbor pledge that no nation had the right to intervene in the internal or external affairs of another.

The good neighbor policy did not indicate a U.S. retreat from empire in Latin America. Instead, it declared that the United States would not depend on military force to exercise its influence in the region. When Mexico nationalized American oil holdings and revolution boiled over in Nicaragua, Guatemala, and Cuba during the 1930s, Roosevelt refrained from sending in the marines to defend the interests of American corporations. In 1934, Roosevelt even withdrew American marines from Haiti, which they had occupied since 1916. Although nonintervention honored the principle of national self-determination, it also permitted the rise of dictators such as Anastasio Somoza in Nicaragua and Fulgencio Batista in Cuba, who exploited and terrorized their nations with private support from U.S. businesses and the hands-off policy of Roosevelt's administration.

Military nonintervention also did not prevent the United States from exerting its economic influence in Latin America. In 1934, Congress passed the Reciprocal Trade Agreements Act, which gave the president the power to reduce tariffs on goods imported into the United States from nations that agreed to lower their own tariffs on U.S. exports. By 1940, twenty-two nations had agreed to reciprocal tariff reductions, helping U.S. exports to Latin America double during Roosevelt's first two terms and contributing to the New Deal's goal of boosting the domestic economy through free trade. Although the economic power of the United States continued to overshadow that of its neighbors, the nonintervention policy planted seeds of friendship and hemispheric solidarity that grew in importance while events in Europe and Asia continued to erode international peace.

The Price of Noninvolvement

In Europe, fascist governments in Italy and Germany threatened military aggression. Italian dictator Benito Mussolini proclaimed, "War is to the man what maternity is to the woman. . . . Peace [is] . . . depressing and a negation of all the fundamental virtues of man." In Germany, Hitler made similar pronouncements and vigorously rebuilt Germany's military strength. German rearmament openly defied the terms of the Versailles peace treaty, but Britain and France only made verbal protests. The overwhelming desire to avoid conflict led Britain in 1935 to permit Germany to begin to rebuild its fleet of surface ships and submarines. Emboldened, Hitler plotted to avenge defeat in World War I by recapturing territories with German inhabitants, all the while accusing Jews of polluting the purity of the Aryan master race. The virulent anti-Semitism of Hitler and his Nazi Party unified non-Jewish Germans and attracted sympathizers among many other Europeans, even in France and Britain, thereby weakening support for opposing Hitler or defending the Jews.

In Japan, a stridently militaristic government planned to follow the invasion of Manchuria in 1931 with conquests extending throughout Southeast Asia. The Manchurian invasion bogged down in a long and vicious war when Chinese Nationalists rallied around their leader, Chiang Kai-shek, to fight against the Japanese. Preparations for new Japanese conquests continued, however. Early in 1936, Japan openly violated naval limitation treaties it had agreed to and began to build a battle-ready fleet to achieve naval superiority in the Pacific.

In the United States, the hostilities in Asia and Europe reinforced isolationist sentiments. Popular disillusionment with the failure of Woodrow Wilson's idealistic goals caused many Americans to question the nation's participation in World War I. In 1933, Gerald Nye, a Republican from North Dakota, chaired a Senate committee that investigated why the United States had gone to war in 1917. The Nye committee concluded that greedy "merchants of death"—American weapons makers, bankers, and financiers—dragged the nation into the war to line their own pockets. The Nye committee persuaded many Americans that war profiteers might once again push the nation into a world war.

International tensions and the Nye committee report prompted Congress to pass a series of neutrality acts between 1935 and 1937 in order to avoid the circumstances that, they believed, had caused the nation to abandon its isolationism and become a combatant in World War I. The neutrality acts prohibited making loans and selling arms to nations at war and authorized the president to warn Americans about traveling on ships belonging to belligerent countries.

By 1937, as the nation continued to struggle with the depression, the growing conflicts overseas caused some Americans to call for a total embargo on all trade with warring countries. Roosevelt and Congress worried that such an embargo would hurt the nation's economy by reducing production and boosting unemployment. The Neutrality Act of 1937 attempted to reconcile the nation's desire for both peace and foreign trade with a "cash-and-carry" policy that required warring nations to pay cash for nonmilitary goods and to transport them in their own ships. This policy supported foreign trade and thereby benefited the nation's economy, but it also helped foreign aggressors by supplying them with goods and thereby undermining peace.

The desire for peace in France, Britain, and the United States led Germany, Italy, and Japan to launch offensives on the assumption that the Western democracies lacked the will to oppose them. In March 1936, Nazi troops marched into the industry-rich Rhineland on Germany's western border, in blatant violation of the Treaty of Versailles. One month later, Italian armies completed their conquest of Ethiopia, projecting fascist power into Africa. In December 1937, Japanese invaders captured Nanking and celebrated their triumph in the "Rape of Nanking," a deadly rampage of murder, rape, and plunder that killed 200,000 Chinese civilians.

In Spain, a bitter civil war broke out in July 1936 when fascist rebels led by General Francisco Franco attacked the democratically elected Republican government. Both Germany and Italy reinforced Franco with soldiers, weapons, and aircraft, while the Soviet Union provided much less aid to the Republican Loyalists. The Spanish civil war seemed to many observers a dress rehearsal for a coming worldwide conflict, but it did not cause European democracies or the U.S. government to help the Loyalists, despite sympathizing with their cause. More than 3,000 individual Americans enlisted in the Russian-sponsored Abraham Lincoln Brigade to fight for the Loyalists. But, abandoned by the Western nations, the Loyalists and their allies were defeated in 1939, and Franco built a fascist bulwark in southern and western Europe.

Hostilities in Europe, Africa, and Asia alarmed Roosevelt and other Americans. The president sought to persuade most Americans to moderate their isolationism and find a way to support the victims of fascist aggression. Speaking in Chicago in October 1937, Roosevelt declared that the "epidemic of world lawlessness is spreading" and warned that "mere isolation or neutrality" offered no remedy for the "contagion" of war. Instead, he proposed that the United States "quarantine" aggressor nations and stop the spread of war's contagion.

Roosevelt's speech ignited a storm of protest from isolationists. The *Chicago Tribune* accused the president of seeking to replace "Americanism" with "internationalism." Disappointed by the strength of isolationism and the absence of congressional support for his quarantine policy, Roosevelt remarked, "It's a terrible thing to look over your shoulder when you are trying to lead and find no one there." The popularity of isolationist sentiment convinced Roosevelt that he needed to maneuver carefully if the United States were to help prevent fascist aggressors from conquering Europe and Asia, leaving the United States an isolated and imperiled island of **democracy**.

▶ REVIEW   Why did isolationism during the 1930s concern Roosevelt?

The Onset of War

Between 1939 and 1941, fascist victories overseas eventually eroded American isolationism. But initially, fascist anti-Semitism and military conquests in China, Ethiopia, and Spain failed to arouse many Americans, who were still mired in the depression. By 1939, however, continuing German and Japanese aggression caused more and more Americans to believe that it was time for the nation to take a stand. At first, taking a stand was limited to providing material support to the enemies of Germany and Japan, principally Britain, China, and the Soviet Union. But Japan's surprise attack on Pearl Harbor eliminated that restraint, and the nation began to mobilize for an all-out assault on foreign foes.

Nazi Aggression and War in Europe

Under the spell of isolationism, Americans passively watched Hitler's relentless campaign to dominate Europe. Hitler bullied Austria in 1938 into accepting incorporation—*Anschluss*—into the Nazi Third Reich, expanding the territory under Germany's control. Next, Hitler turned his attention to the German-speaking Sudetenland, granted to Czechoslovakia by the Versailles treaty. The Czechs were prepared to fight rather than surrender their territory, but Britain and France hoped to avoid war by making a deal with Hitler. British prime minister Neville Chamberlain went to Munich, Germany, in September 1938 and offered Hitler terms of "appeasement," as he called it, that would give the Sudetenland to Germany if Hitler agreed to leave the rest of Czechoslovakia alone. Hitler accepted Chamberlain's offer and solemnly promised that he would make no more territorial claims in Europe. Chamberlain returned to England proclaiming that his Munich agreement had achieved "peace in our time." But peace depended on Hitler's keeping a promise he never intended to honor, dooming appeasement from the outset. In March 1939, Hitler boldly marched the German army into Czechoslovakia and conquered it without firing a shot.

In April 1939, Hitler demanded that Poland return the German territory it had been awarded after World War I. Britain and France finally recognized that appeasement had failed and that Hitler would continue his aggression unless he was defeated by military might. Both Britain and France assured Poland that they would go to war with Germany if Hitler launched an eastward offensive across the Polish border. In turn, Hitler negotiated with his bitter enemy, Soviet premier Joseph Stalin, offering him concessions in order to prevent the Soviet Union from joining Britain and France in opposing a German attack on Poland. Despite the enduring hatred between fascist Germany and the **Communist** Soviet Union, the two powers signed the Nazi-Soviet treaty of nonaggression in August 1939, exposing Poland to an onslaught by the German Wehrmacht (army) and the Soviet Red Army.

At dawn on September 1, 1939, Hitler unleashed his attack on Poland, exhorting his generals to "close your hearts to pity! Act brutally!" German tanks and airplanes led the *blitzkrieg* (literally, "lightning war") that gave lethal mechanized support to the invading infantry. The attack triggered Soviet attacks on eastern Poland and declarations of war from France and Britain two days later, igniting a conflagration that raced around the globe. When it finally ended after Paul Tibbets's historic flight in August 1945, more than 60 million people were dead and untold millions more maimed. But in September 1939, Germany seemed invincible as its armies sped across Poland, causing many people to wonder if any nation could stop the Nazi war machine. Sooner or later, many people feared, all of Europe would share Poland's fate: defeat, German occupation, and vicious authoritarian government enforced by merciless repression and unblinking terror.

After the Nazis overran Poland, Hitler paused for a few months before launching a westward blitzkrieg. In April 1940, German forces smashed through Denmark and Norway. In May, Germany invaded the Netherlands, Belgium, Luxembourg, and France. The French believed that their Maginot Line, a concrete fortification built after World War I and stretching from the Swiss border to the forested Ardennes region on the edge of Belgium, would halt the German attack. But the Maginot Line proved little more than a detour for Hitler's mechanized divisions, which wheeled around the fortification's northern end and raced south toward Paris.

The speed of the German attack trapped more than 300,000 British and French soldiers, who retreated to the port of Dunkirk, where an improvised armada of British vessels hurriedly ferried them to safety across the English Channel, leaving the Dunkirk beaches strewn with thousands of tons of abandoned military gear. By mid-June 1940, France had surrendered the largest army in the world, signed an armistice that gave Germany control of the entire French coastline and nearly two-thirds of the countryside, and installed a collaborationist government at Vichy in southern France headed by Philippe Pétain. With an empire that stretched across Europe from Poland to France, Hitler seemed poised to vault the English Channel and attack Britain.

The new British prime minister, Winston Churchill, vowed that Britain, unlike France, would never accept a humiliating surrender to Hitler. "We shall fight on the seas and oceans [and] . . . in the air," he proclaimed, "whatever the cost may be, we shall fight on the beaches, . . . and in the fields and in the streets . . . [and] we shall never surrender." Churchill's defiance stiffened British resolve for a last-ditch defense against Hitler's attack, which began in mid-June 1940 when wave after wave of German bombers targeted British military installations and cities, killing tens of thousands of civilians. The undermanned and outgunned Royal Air Force fought as doggedly as Churchill had predicted and finally won the Battle of Britain by November, clearing German bombers from British skies and handing Hitler his first frustrating defeat. Churchill praised the valiant British pilots, declaring that "never . . . was so much owed by so many to so few." Advance knowledge of German plans made possible by British use of the new technology of radar and the ability to decipher Germany's top-secret military codes aided British pilots. Battered and exhausted, Britain could not hold out forever without American help, as Churchill repeatedly wrote Roosevelt in private.

From Neutrality to the Arsenal of Democracy

When the Nazi attack on Poland ignited the war in Europe, Roosevelt issued an official proclamation of American neutrality. Most Americans condemned German aggression and favored Britain and France, but isolationism remained powerful. Roosevelt feared that if Congress did not repeal the arms embargo mandated by the Neutrality Act of 1937, France and Britain would soon succumb to the Nazi onslaught. The president's request for repeal of the embargo provoked isolationists to protest that the United States had no business interfering in a European conflict. After heated debate, Congress voted in November 1939 to revise the neutrality legislation and allow belligerent nations to buy arms, as well as nonmilitary supplies, on a cash-and-carry basis.

In practice, the revised neutrality law permitted Britain and France to purchase American war materiel and carry it across the Atlantic in their own ships, thereby shielding American vessels from attack by German submarines lurking in the Atlantic. Roosevelt feared that such halfhearted support for the antifascist cause threatened the United States. He wrote to a friend, "What worries me is that public opinion . . . is patting itself on the back every morning and thanking God for the Atlantic Ocean (and the Pacific Ocean)" and underestimating "the serious implications" of the European war "for our own future."

Roosevelt searched for a way to aid Britain short of entering a formal alliance or declaring war against Germany. Churchill pleaded for American destroyers, aircraft, and munitions, but he had no money to buy them under the prevailing cash-and-carry neutrality law. In May 1940, Roosevelt asked Congress for almost $1.3 billion in defense spending to expand the navy and multiply the production of airplanes to 50,000 a year. By late summer, as the Battle of Britain raged in the skies over Britain, Roosevelt concocted a scheme to deliver fifty old destroyers to Britain in exchange for American access to British bases in the Western Hemisphere. Claiming the constitutional power to strengthen America's defenses by swapping destroyers for bases, Roosevelt took the first steps toward building a firm Anglo-American alliance against Hitler.

While German Luftwaffe (air force) pilots bombed Britain, Roosevelt decided to run for an unprecedented third term as president in 1940. He hoped to woo voters away from their complacent isolationism to back the nation's international interests as well as New Deal reforms. But the presidential election, which Roosevelt won handily, provided no clear mandate for American involvement in the European war. The Republican candidate, Wendell Willkie, a former Democrat who generally favored New Deal measures and Roosevelt's foreign policy, attacked Roosevelt as a warmonger. Willkie's accusations caused the president to promise voters, "Your boys are not going to be sent into any foreign wars," a pledge counterbalanced by his repeated warnings about the threats to America posed by Nazi aggression.

Empowered by the voters for another presidential term, Roosevelt maneuvered to support Britain in every way short of war. In a fireside chat shortly after Christmas 1940, he proclaimed that it was incumbent on the United States to become "the great arsenal of democracy" and send "every ounce and every ton of munitions and supplies that we can possibly spare to help the defenders who are in the front lines."

In January 1941, Roosevelt proposed the Lend-Lease Act, which allowed the British to obtain arms from the United States without paying cash but with the promise to reimburse the United States when the war ended. The purpose of Lend-Lease, Roosevelt proclaimed, was to defend democracy and human rights throughout the world, specifically the Four Freedoms: "freedom of speech and expression . . . freedom of every person to worship God in his own way . . . freedom from want . . . [and] freedom from fear." Congress passed the Lend-Lease Act in March 1941 and started a flow of support to Britain that totaled more than $50 billion during the war, far more than all federal expenditures combined since Roosevelt had become president in 1933.

Lend-Lease placed the United States on a collision course with Germany. Nazi U-boats (submarines) prowled the Atlantic, preying upon ships laden with supplies for Britain, making it only a matter of time before American citizens and their property would be attacked. Roosevelt provided naval escorts for Lend-Lease supplies and gave his commanders orders to "shoot on sight" menacing German submarines, thus edging the nation closer to all-out combat.

Stymied in his plans for an invasion of England, Hitler turned his massive army eastward and on June 22, 1941, sprang a surprise attack on the Soviet Union, his erstwhile ally in the 1939 Nazi-Soviet nonaggression pact. Neither Roosevelt nor Churchill had any love for Joseph Stalin or communism, but they both welcomed the Soviet Union to the anti-Nazi cause. Both Western leaders understood that Hitler's attack on Russia would provide relief for the hard-pressed British. Roosevelt quickly persuaded Congress to extend Lend-Lease to the Soviet Union, beginning the shipment of millions of tons of trucks, jeeps, locomotives, and other equipment that, in all, supplied about 10 percent of Russian war materiel.

As Hitler's Wehrmacht raced across the Russian plains and Nazi U-boats tried to choke off supplies to Britain and the Soviet Union, Roosevelt met with Churchill aboard a ship near Newfoundland to cement the Anglo-American alliance. In August 1941, the two leaders issued the Atlantic Charter, pledging the two nations to freedom of the seas and free trade as well as the right of national self-determination. Roosevelt told Churchill privately that the United States would continue to serve as the arsenal of democracy and that he would be watching for some incident that might trigger public support for full-scale American entry into the war against Germany.

Japan Attacks America

Although the likelihood of war with Germany preoccupied Roosevelt, Hitler exercised a measure of restraint in directly provoking America. Japanese ambitions in Asia clashed more openly with American interests and commitments, especially in China and the Philippines. And unlike Hitler, the Japanese high command planned to attack the United States if necessary to pursue their aspirations to rule an Asian empire they termed the Greater East Asia Co-Prosperity Sphere. Appealing to widespread Asian bitterness toward white colonial powers, such as the British in India and Burma, the French in Indochina (now Vietnam), and the Dutch in the East Indies (now Indonesia), the Japanese campaigned to preserve "Asia for the Asians." Japan's invasion of China—which had lasted for ten years by 1941—proved that its true goal was Asia for the Japanese. Japan coveted the raw materials available from China and Southeast Asia and ignored American demands to stop its campaign of aggression.

In 1940, Japan signaled a new phase of its **imperial** designs by entering a defensive alliance with Germany and Italy—the Tripartite Pact. In 1941, U.S. naval intelligence cracked the Japanese secret code and learned that Tokyo also planned to invade the resource-rich Dutch East Indies. To thwart these plans, in July 1941 Roosevelt announced a trade embargo that denied Japan access to oil, scrap iron, and other goods essential for its war machines. Roosevelt hoped the embargo would strengthen factions within Japan that opposed the militarists and sought to restore relations with the United States.

The American embargo played into the hands of Japanese militarists headed by General Hideki Tojo, who seized control of the government in October 1941 and persuaded other leaders, including Emperor Hirohito, that swift destruction of American naval bases in the Pacific would leave Japan free to follow its destiny. Decoded Japanese messages alerted American officials that an attack on U.S. forces was imminent somewhere in the Pacific, but no American knew where and when the attack would come until it was too late. Early on the morning of December 7, 1941, 183 attack aircraft lifted off six Japanese carriers that had secretly steamed within striking range of the U.S. Pacific Fleet at Pearl Harbor on the Hawaiian island of Oahu. At about eight o'clock, the Japanese planes streaked from the sky, bombing and torpedoing the American fleet riding serenely at anchor in the harbor and destroying hundreds of aircraft parked in neat rows on the runways of Hickam Field. The devastating surprise attack sank or disabled 18 ships, including all of the fleet's battleships; killed more than 2,400 Americans; and wounded more than 1,000, almost crippling U.S. war-making

Pearl Harbor Victims
Brothers Wesley and Edward Heidt from Los Angeles were one of thirty-four pairs of brothers killed when Japanese warplanes sank the battleship *Arizona* at Pearl Harbor.

U.S.S. *Arizona* Memorial, Hawaii, National Park Service/photo by Douglas Peebles.

capacity in the Pacific. Luckily for the United States, Japanese pilots failed to destroy the vital machine shops and oil storage facilities at Pearl Harbor, and none of the nation's aircraft carriers happened to be in port at the time of the attack.

The Japanese scored a stunning tactical victory at Pearl Harbor, but in the long run, the attack proved a colossal blunder. The victory made many Japanese commanders overconfident about their military prowess. Worse for the Japanese, Americans instantly united in their desire to fight and avenge the attack, which Roosevelt termed "dastardly and unprovoked." The president vowed that "this form of treachery shall never endanger us again." On December 8, Congress almost unanimously endorsed the president's call for a declaration of war. The only holdout was the pacifist Republican congresswoman Jeannette Rankin of Montana, who had also opposed U.S. entry into World War I. Neither Hitler nor Mussolini knew about the Japanese attack in advance, but they both declared war against America on December 11, bringing the United States into all-out war with the Axis powers in both Europe and Asia.

▶REVIEW   How did Roosevelt attempt to balance American isolationism with the increasingly ominous international scene of the late 1930s?

Mobilizing for War

The time had come, Roosevelt announced, for the prescriptions of "Dr. New Deal" to be replaced by the stronger medicines of "Dr. Win-the-War." Military and civilian leaders rushed to secure the nation against possible attacks, causing Americans of Japanese descent to be stigmatized and sent to internment camps. Roosevelt and his advisers lost no time enlisting millions of Americans in the armed forces to bring the isolationist-era military to fighting strength for a two-front war. The war emergency also required economic mobilization unparalleled in the nation's history. As Dr. Win-the-War, Roosevelt set aside the New Deal goal of reform and plunged headlong into transforming the American economy into the world's greatest military machine, thereby achieving full employment and economic recovery, goals that had eluded the New Deal.

Home-Front Security

Shortly after declaring war against the United States, Hitler dispatched German submarines to hunt American ships along the Atlantic coast from Maine to Florida, where Paul Tibbets and other American pilots tried to destroy them. But the U-boats had devastating success for about eight months, sinking hundreds of U.S. ships and threatening to disrupt the Lend-Lease lifeline to Britain and the Soviet Union. The submarines benefited from the failure of port cities such as New York and Miami to observe the rules requiring blackouts, allowing U-boats to spot vulnerable ships against the lighted horizon.

Hulks of destroyed vessels littered Atlantic beaches, but by mid-1942, the U.S. navy had chased German submarines away from the East Coast and into the mid-Atlantic, reducing the direct threat to the nation. Naval ships patrolled the nation's coasts, and fortifications were built to defend against seaborne assaults. These and other security measures raised popular awareness of the possibility of an attack on the U.S. mainland, but no such attack occurred.

Within the continental United States, Americans remained sheltered from the chaos and destruction the war was bringing to hundreds of millions in Europe and Asia. Nevertheless, the government worried constantly about espionage and internal subversion. Billboards and posters warned Americans that "Loose lips sink ships" and "Enemy agents are always near; if you don't talk, they won't hear." The campaign for patriotic vigilance focused on German and Japanese foes, but Americans of Japanese descent became targets of official and popular persecution because of Pearl Harbor and long-standing racial prejudice against people of Asian descent.

About 320,000 people of Japanese descent lived in the United States in 1941, two-thirds of them in Hawaii, where they largely escaped wartime persecution because they were essential and valued members of society. On the mainland, however, Japanese Americans were a tiny minority—even along the West Coast, where most of them worked on farms and in small businesses—subject to frenzied wartime suspicions and persecution. A prominent newspaper columnist echoed the widespread sentiment that "the Japanese . . . should be under armed guard to the last man and woman right now and to hell with habeas corpus until the danger is over." Although an official military survey concluded that Japanese Americans posed no danger, popular hostility fueled a campaign to round up all mainland Japanese Americans—two-thirds of them U.S. citizens. "A Jap's a

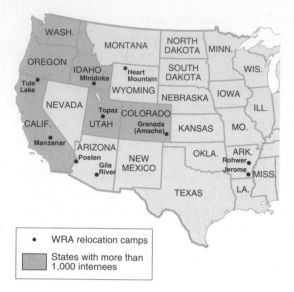

MAP 25.1   Western Relocation Authority Centers

Responding to prejudice and fear of sabotage, President Roosevelt authorized the roundup and relocation of all Americans of Japanese descent in 1942. Taken from their homes in the cities and fertile farmland of the far West, Japanese Americans were confined in desolate camps scattered as far east as the Mississippi River.

• WRA relocation camps

■ States with more than 1,000 internees

Jap. . . . It makes no difference whether he is an American citizen or not," one official declared.

On February 19, 1942, Roosevelt issued Executive Order 9066, which authorized sending all Americans of Japanese descent to ten makeshift prison (or internment) camps—euphemistically termed "relocation centers"—located in remote areas of the West (Map 25.1). Allowed little time to secure or sell their property, Japanese Americans lost homes and businesses worth about $400 million and lived out the war penned in by barbed wire and armed guards. Although several thousand Japanese Americans served with distinction in the U.S. armed forces and no case of subversion by a Japanese American was ever uncovered, the Supreme Court, in its 1944 *Korematsu* decision, upheld Executive Order 9066's blatant violation of constitutional rights as justified by "military necessity."

Building a Citizen Army

In 1940, Roosevelt encouraged Congress to pass the Selective Service Act to register men of military age who would be subject to a **draft** if the need arose. More than 6,000 local draft boards registered more than 30 million men and, when war came, rapidly inducted them into military service. In all, more than 16 million men and women served in uniform during the war, two-thirds of them draftees, mostly young men between the ages of eighteen and twenty-six. Although only about one family in five had a family member in the military, nearly everybody had friends and neighbors who had gone off to war. By the time the war ended, more than 10 million Americans had served in the army, nearly 4 million in the navy, 600,000 in the marines, and 240,000 in the coast guard. In addition, 350,000 women joined the Nurse's Corps and women's military units in the army, navy, and Marine Corps. Though barred from combat duty, these women worked at nearly every noncombatant assignment, eroding traditional barriers to women's military service.

The Selective Service Act prohibited discrimination "on account of race or color," and almost a million African American men and women donned uniforms, as did half a million Mexican Americans, 25,000 Native Americans, and 13,000 Chinese Americans. The racial insults and discrimination suffered by all people of color made some soldiers ask, as a Mexican American GI did on his way to the European front, "Why fight for America when you have not been treated as an American?" Only black Americans were trained in segregated camps, confined in segregated barracks, and assigned to segregated units. The Red Cross even segregated the blood it used to treat casualties, supposedly protecting wounded whites from contamination by black blood—needless to say, a practice with no scientific merit. Secretary of War Henry Stimson opposed any change in the segregation of blacks, declaring that the military should not serve as a "sociological laboratory." Accordingly, most black Americans were consigned to manual labor, and relatively few served in combat until late in 1944, when the need for military manpower in Europe intensified. Then, as General George Patton told black soldiers in a tank unit in Normandy, "I don't care what color you are, so long as you go up there and kill those Kraut sonsabitches."

Homosexuals also served in the armed forces, although in much smaller numbers than black Americans. Allowed to serve as long as their sexual preferences remained covert, gay Americans, like other minorities, sought to demonstrate their worth under fire. "I was superpatriotic," a gay combat veteran recalled. Another gay GI remarked, "Who in the hell is going to worry about [homosexuality]" in the midst of the life-or-death realities of war?

Conversion to a War Economy

In 1940, the American economy remained mired in the depression. Nearly one worker in seven was still without a job, factories operated far below their productive capacity, and the total federal budget was under $10 billion. Shortly after the attack on Pearl Harbor, Roosevelt announced the goal of converting the economy to produce "overwhelming . . . , crushing superiority of equipment in any theater of the world war." In a rush to produce military supplies, factories were converted from making passenger cars to assembling tanks and airplanes, and production was ramped up to record levels. By the end of the war, there were more jobs than workers, plants were operating at full capacity, and the federal budget topped $100 billion.

To organize and oversee this tidal wave of military production, Roosevelt called upon business leaders to come to Washington and, for the token payment of a dollar a year, head new government agencies such as the War Production Board, which, among other things, set production priorities and pushed for maximum output. Contracts flowed to large corporations such as General Electric, Ford, and U.S. Steel, often on a basis that guaranteed their profits. During the first half of 1942, the government issued contracts worth more than $100 billion, a sum greater than the entire gross national product in 1941.

Booming wartime employment swelled union membership. To speed production, the government asked unions to pledge not to strike. Despite the relentless pace of work, union members kept their no-strike pledge, with the important exception of members of the United Mine Workers, who walked out of the coal mines in 1943, demanding a pay hike and earning the enmity of many Americans.

Overall, conversion to war production achieved Roosevelt's ambitious goal of "overwhelming . . . , crushing superiority" in military goods. At a total cost of $304 billion during the war, the nation produced an avalanche of military equipment, including 300,000 airplanes, 88,000 tanks, 7,000 ships, 3 million vehicles, billions of bullets, and much more—in all, more than double the combined production of Germany, Japan, and Italy. In the last eighteen months of the war, for example, every American in the Pacific theater could draw upon 8,000 pounds of military supplies, in stark contrast with each Japanese soldier's access to only 2 pounds. Giving tangible meaning to the term "arsenal of democracy," this outpouring of military goods supplied not only U.S. forces but also America's allies.

> ▶**REVIEW**   How did the Roosevelt administration mobilize the human and industrial resources necessary to fight a two-front war?

Fighting Back

The United States confronted a daunting military challenge in December 1941. The attack on Pearl Harbor destroyed much of its Pacific Fleet, crippling the nation's ability to defend against Japan's massive offensive throughout the southern Pacific. In the Atlantic, Hitler's U-boats sank American ships, while German armies occupied most of western Europe and relentlessly advanced eastward into the Soviet Union. Roosevelt and his military advisers believed that defeating Germany took top priority. To achieve that victory required preventing Hitler from defeating America's allies, Britain and the Soviet Union. If they fell, Hitler would command all the resources of Europe in a probable assault on the United States. To fight back effectively against Germany and Japan, the United States had to coordinate military and political strategy with its allies and muster all its human and economic assets. But in 1941, nobody knew whether that would be enough.

Turning the Tide in the Pacific

In the Pacific theater, Japan's leading military strategist, Admiral Isoroku Yamamoto, ordered an all-out offensive throughout the southern Pacific. He believed that if his forces did not quickly conquer and secure the territories they targeted, Japan would eventually lose the war as a result of America's far

Japanese Pilot's Flag
Japanese pilots often carried small flags covered with admonitions to fight hard and well. This flag belonged to a pilot named Imano, whose relatives sent him aloft with an inscription that read, "Let your divine plane soar in the sky. We who are left behind pray only for your certain success in sinking an enemy ship." Notably, the inscription did not emphasize returning home safely.
U.S. Naval Academy Museum/photo by Richard D. Bond Jr.

greater resources. Swiftly, the Japanese assaulted American airfields in the Philippines and captured U.S. outposts on Guam and Wake Island. Singapore, the great British naval base in Malaya, surrendered to the Japanese in February 1942, and most of Burma had fallen by March. All that stood in the way of Japan's domination of the southern Pacific was the American stronghold in the Philippines.

The Japanese unleashed a withering assault against the Philippines in January 1942 (see Map 25.3, page 821). The American commander, General Douglas MacArthur, retreated to Australia in March, leaving General Jonathan Wainwright to hold out as long as possible. Wainwright surrendered to the Japanese in May, and the Japanese victors marched the weak and malnourished survivors sixty-five miles to a concentration camp. Thousands of captured American and Filipino soldiers died during the Bataan Death March, and 16,000 more perished in the camps. By the summer of 1942, the Japanese war machine had conquered the oil-rich Dutch East Indies and was poised to strike Australia and New Zealand.

The Japanese had larger, faster, and more heavily armed ships than the United States, and their airplanes outperformed anything the Americans could send up against them. But a daring raid on Tokyo in April 1942 by a squadron of carrier-based B-25 bombers led by Lieutenant Colonel James Doolittle boosted American morale and demonstrated that even the Japanese imperial capital lay within reach (barely) of American might.

In the spring of 1942, U.S. forces launched a major two-pronged counteroffensive that military officials hoped would reverse the Japanese advance. Forces led by General MacArthur moved north from Australia and attacked the Japanese in the Philippines. Far more decisively, Admiral Chester W. Nimitz sailed his battle fleet west from Hawaii to retake Japanese-held islands in the mid-Pacific. On May 7–8, 1942, in the Coral Sea just north of Australia, the American fleet and carrier-based warplanes defeated a Japanese armada that was sailing around the coast of New Guinea.

Nimitz then learned from an intelligence intercept that the Japanese were massing an invasion force aimed at Midway Island, an outpost guarding the Hawaiian Islands. Nimitz maneuvered his carriers and cruisers into the Central Pacific to surprise the Japanese. In a furious battle that raged June 3–6, American ships and planes delivered a devastating blow to the Japanese navy, sinking a heavy cruiser, two destroyers, and four of Japan's six aircraft carriers. The American fleet lost only one carrier and one destroyer in the fight. The Battle of Midway reversed the balance of naval power in the Pacific and put the Japanese at a disadvantage for the rest of the war. Japan managed to build only six more large carriers during the war, while the United States launched dozens, proving the wisdom of Yamamoto's prediction. The Battle of Midway turned the tide of Japanese advances in the Pacific but did little to dislodge the Japanese from the many places they had conquered and now stoutly defended.

The Campaign in Europe

In the dark months after Pearl Harbor, Hitler's eastern-front armies marched ever deeper into the Soviet Union while his western-front forces prepared to invade Britain. As in World War I, the Germans attempted to starve the British into submission by destroying their seaborne lifeline. Technological advances made German U-boats much more effective than they had been in World War I. In 1941 and 1942, they sank Allied ships faster than new ones could be built. Overall, the U-boat campaign sank 4,700 merchant vessels and nearly 200 warships and killed 40,000 Allied seamen.

Until mid-1943, the outcome of the war in the Atlantic remained in doubt. Then, newly invented radar detectors and production of sufficient destroyer escorts for merchant vessels allowed the Allies to prey upon the lurking U-boats. After suffering a 75 percent casualty rate among U-boat crews, Hitler withdrew German submarines from the North Atlantic in late May 1943. In the next four months, more than 3,500 American supply ships crossed the Atlantic without a single loss. Winning the battle of the Atlantic allowed the United States to continue to supply its British and Soviet allies for the duration of the war and to reduce the imminent threat of a German invasion of Britain.

The most important strategic question confronting the United States and its allies was when and where to open a second front against the Nazis. Stalin demanded that America and Britain mount an immediate and massive assault across the English Channel into western France. A cross-Channel invasion would force Hitler to divert his armies from the eastern front and relieve the pressure on the Soviet Union, which was fighting alone against the full strength of the German Wehrmacht. Churchill and Roosevelt instead delayed opening a second front, allowing the Germans and the Soviets to slug it out. This weakened both the Nazis and the Communists and made an eventual Allied attack on western France more likely to succeed. Churchill and Roosevelt promised Stalin that they would open a second front, but they decided to strike first in southern Europe and the Mediterranean, which Churchill termed Europe's "soft under-belly."

The plan targeted a region of long-standing British influence in the eastern Mediterranean. In October and November 1942, British forces at El-Alamein in Egypt halted German general Erwin Rommel's drive to capture the Suez Canal, Britain's lifeline to the oil of the Middle East and to British colonies in India and South Asia (see Map 25.2, page 818). In November, an American army under General Dwight D. Eisenhower landed far to the west, in French Morocco. Propelled by American tank units commanded by General George Patton, the Allied armies had defeated the Germans in North Africa by May 1943. The North African campaign killed and captured 350,000 Axis soldiers, pushed the Germans out of Africa, made the Mediterranean safe for Allied shipping, and opened the door for an Allied invasion of Italy.

In January 1943, while the North African campaign was still under way, Roosevelt traveled to the Moroccan city of Casablanca to confer with Churchill and other Allied leaders. Stalin did not attend but urged his allies to keep their promise of opening a major second front in western Europe. Roosevelt and Churchill announced that they would accept nothing less than the "unconditional surrender" of the Axis powers, ruling out peace negotiations. But Churchill and Roosevelt concluded that they needed more time to amass sufficient forces for the cross-Channel invasion of France that Stalin demanded. In the meantime, they planned to capitalize on their success in North Africa and strike against Italy, consigning the Soviet Union to bear the brunt of the Nazi war machine for another year.

On July 10, 1943, combined American and British amphibious forces landed 160,000 troops in Sicily. The badly equipped Italian defenders quickly withdrew to the mainland. Soon afterward, Mussolini was deposed in Italy, ending the reign of Italian fascism. Quickly, the Allies invaded the mainland, and the Italian government surrendered unconditionally. The Germans responded by rushing reinforcements to Italy and seizing control of Rome, turning the Allies' Italian campaign into a series of battles to liberate Italy from German occupation.

German troops dug into strong fortifications and fought to defend every inch of Italy's rugged terrain. Only after a long, deadly, and frustrating campaign up the Italian peninsula did the Allies finally liberate Rome in June 1944. Allied forces continued to push into northern Italy against stubborn German defenses for the remainder of the war, making the Italian campaign the war's deadliest for American infantrymen. One soldier wrote that his buddies "died like butchered swine."

The Italian campaign occupied numerous German divisions that Hitler might otherwise have deployed on the Russian front, but no German forces were actually taken away from the ongoing attack against the Soviet Union. Stalin denounced the Allies' Italian campaign because it left "the Soviet Army, which is fighting not only for its country, but also for its Allies, to do the job alone, almost single-handed." The Italian campaign exacted a high cost from the Americans and British, bringing the Nazis no closer to surrender and consuming men and materiel that might have been reserved for a second front in France.

▶ **REVIEW**   How did the United States seek to counter the Japanese in the Pacific and the Germans in Europe?

The Wartime Home Front

The war effort mobilized Americans as never before. Factories strained to churn out ever more bombs, bullets, tanks, ships, and airplanes, which workers rushed to assemble, leaving farms and small towns to congregate in cities. Women took jobs with wrenches and welding torches, boosting the nation's workforce and fraying traditional notions that a woman's place was in the home rather than on the assembly line. Despite rationing and shortages, unprecedented government expenditures for war production brought prosperity to many Americans after years of depression-era poverty. Although Americans in uniform risked their lives on battlefields in Europe and Asia, Americans on the U.S. mainland enjoyed complete immunity from foreign attack—in sharp contrast to their Soviet and British allies. The wartime ideology of human rights provided justification for the many sacrifices Americans were required to make in support of the military effort. It also established a standard of basic human equality that became a potent weapon in the campaign for equal rights at home and against the horrifying atrocities of the Holocaust perpetrated by the Nazis.

Women and Families, Guns and Butter

Millions of American women gladly left home toting a lunch pail and changed into overalls and work gloves to take their places on assembly lines in defense industries. At the start of the war, about a quarter of adult women worked outside the home, most as teachers, nurses, social workers, or domestic servants. Few women worked in factories, except for textile mills and sewing industries, because employers and male workers often discriminated against them. But wartime mobilization of the economy and the siphoning of millions of men into the armed forces left factories begging for women workers.

Government advertisements urged women to take industrial jobs by assuring them that their household chores had prepared them for work on the "Victory Line." One billboard proclaimed, "If you've sewed on buttons, or made buttonholes, on a [sewing] machine, you can learn to do spot welding on airplane parts. . . . If you've followed recipes exactly in making cakes, you can learn to load a shell." Millions of women responded, and by the end of the war, women working outside the home numbered 18 million, 50 percent more than in 1939. Contributing to the war effort also paid off in wages that averaged $31 for a forty-eight-hour week, more than the typical steelworker earned in 1941. A Kentucky woman remembered her job at a munitions plant, where she earned "the fabulous sum of $32 a week. To us it was an absolute miracle. Before that, we made nothing." Although men got paid an average of $54 for comparable wartime work, women accepted the pay differential and welcomed their chance to earn wages and help win the war at the same time.

The majority of married women remained at home, occupied with domestic chores and child care. But they, too, supported the war effort, planting Victory Gardens to provide homegrown vegetables, saving tin cans and newspapers for recycling into war materiel, and hoarding pennies and nickels to buy war bonds. Many families scrimped to cope with the 30 percent inflation during the war, but families supported by men and women in manufacturing industries enjoyed

Pitching In at Home
This poster adapts the standard children's book illustration style of the period to the war effort. White and middle-class all, mother and children collect old golf clubs, cocktail shakers, and trophies so that these symbols of American life can be recycled into armaments for defense.
Chicago Historical Society.

wages that grew twice as fast as inflation.

The war influenced how all families spent their earnings. Buying a new washing machine or car was out of the question, since factories that used to build them now made military goods. Many other consumer goods—such as tires, gasoline, shoes, and meat—were rationed at home to meet military needs overseas. But most Americans had more money in their pockets than ever before, and they readily found things to spend it on, including movie tickets, cosmetics, and music recordings. Spending for personal consumption rose by 12 percent during the war.

The wartime prosperity and abundance enjoyed by most Americans contrasted with the experiences of their hard-pressed allies. Personal consumption fell by 22 percent in Britain, and food output plummeted to just one-third of prewar levels in the Soviet Union, creating widespread hunger and even starvation. Few went hungry in the United States. New Deal restraints on agricultural production were lifted, and farm output grew by 25 percent each year during the war, providing an astonishing cornucopia of food to be exported to the Allies.

The Double V Campaign

Fighting against Nazi Germany and its ideology of Aryan racial supremacy, Americans were confronted with the extensive racial prejudice in their own country. Roosevelt declared that black Americans were in the war "not only to defend America but . . . to establish a universal freedom under which a new basis of security and prosperity can be established for all—regardless of station, race, or creed." The *Pittsburgh Courier*, a leading black newspaper, asserted that the wartime emergency called for a "Double V" campaign seeking "victory over our enemies at home and victory over our enemies on the battlefields abroad." It was time, the *Courier* proclaimed, "to persuade, embarrass, compel and shame our government and our nation . . . into a more enlightened attitude."

In 1941, black organizations demanded that the federal government require companies receiving defense contracts to integrate their workforces. A. Philip Randolph, head of the Brotherhood of Sleeping Car Porters, promised that 100,000 African American marchers would descend on Washington if the president did not eliminate discrimination in defense industries. Roosevelt decided to risk offending his white allies in the South and in unions and issued Executive Order 8802 in mid-1941. It authorized the Committee on Fair Employment Practices to investigate and prevent racial discrimination in employment. Civil rights champions hailed the act, and Randolph triumphantly called off the march.

Progress came slowly, however. In 1940, nine out of ten black Americans lived below the federal poverty line, and those who worked earned an average of 39 percent of whites' wages. In search of better jobs and living conditions, 5.5 million black Americans migrated from the South to centers of industrial production in the North and West, making a majority of African Americans city dwellers for the first time in U.S. history. Many discovered that unskilled jobs were available but that unions and employers often barred blacks from skilled trades. At least eighteen major unions—including the machinists, ironworkers, shipbuilders, and railway workers—explicitly prohibited black members. Severe labor shortages and government fair employment standards opened assembly-line jobs in defense plants to African Americans, causing black unemployment to drop by 80 percent during the war. But more jobs did not mean equal pay for blacks. The average income of black families rose during the war, but by the end of the conflict, it still stood at only half of what white families earned.

Blacks' migration to defense jobs intensified racial antagonisms, which boiled over in the hot summer of 1943, when 242 race riots erupted in 47 cities. In the "zoot suit riots" in Los Angeles, hundreds of white servicemen, claiming they were punishing draft dodgers, chased and beat young Mexican American men who dressed in distinctive broad-shouldered, peg-legged zoot suits. The worst mayhem occurred in Detroit, where a long-simmering conflict between whites and blacks over racially segregated housing ignited into a race war. Whites with clubs smashed through black neighborhoods, and blacks retaliated by destroying and looting white-owned businesses. In two days of violence, twenty-five blacks and nine whites were killed, and scores more were injured.

Racial violence created the impetus for the Double V campaign, officially supported by the National Association for the Advancement of Colored People (NAACP), which asserted black Americans' demands for the rights and privileges enjoyed by all other Americans—demands reinforced by the Allies' wartime ideology of freedom and democracy. While the NAACP focused on court challenges to segregation, a new organization founded in 1942, the Congress of Racial Equality (CORE), organized picketing and sit-ins against **Jim Crow** restaurants and theaters. The Double V campaign greatly expanded membership in the NAACP but achieved only limited success against racial discrimination during the war.

Wartime Politics and the 1944 Election

Americans rallied around the war effort in unprecedented unity. Despite the consensus on war aims, the strains and stresses of the nation's massive wartime mobilization made it difficult for Roosevelt to maintain his political coalition. Whites often resented blacks who migrated to northern cities, took jobs, and made themselves at home. Many Americans complained about government price controls and the rationing of scarce goods while the war dragged on. Military service overseas kept many Democratic voters from casting ballots in the 1942 congressional elections, and the low turnout helped Republicans make gains in Congress.

Republicans seized the opportunity to roll back New Deal reforms. A **conservative** coalition of Republicans and southern Democrats succeeded in abolishing several New Deal agencies in 1942 and 1943, including the Work Projects Administration and the Civilian Conservation Corps. But the Roosevelt administration fought back. Congress guaranteed absentee ballots for service members, strengthening Democrats at the polls in 1944.

In June 1944, Congress unanimously approved the landmark GI Bill of Rights, promising to give veterans government funds for education, housing, and health care and to provide loans to help them start businesses and buy homes. The GI Bill put the financial resources of the federal government behind the abstract goals of freedom and democracy for which veterans were fighting, and it empowered millions of GIs to better themselves and their families after the war.

After twelve turbulent years in the White House, Roosevelt was exhausted and gravely ill with heart disease, but he was determined to remain president until the war ended. "All that is within me cries out to go back to my home on the Hudson River," he declared. "But as a good soldier . . . I will accept and serve" if reelected president. Roosevelt's poor health made the selection of a vice presidential candidate unusually important. Convinced that many Americans had soured on **liberal** reform, Roosevelt chose Senator Harry S. Truman of Missouri as his running mate. A reliable party man from a southern border state, Truman satisfied urban Democratic leaders while not worrying white southerners who were nervous about challenges to racial segregation.

The Republicans, confident of a strong conservative upsurge in the nation, nominated as their presidential candidate the governor of New York, Thomas

E. Dewey, who had made his reputation as a tough crime fighter. In the 1944 presidential campaign, Roosevelt's failing health alarmed many observers, but his frailty was outweighed by Americans' unwillingness to change presidents in the midst of the war and by Dewey's failure to persuade most voters that the New Deal was a creeping **socialist** menace. Voters gave Roosevelt a 53.5 percent majority, his narrowest presidential victory, ensuring his continued leadership as Dr. Win-the-War.

Reaction to the Holocaust

The political crosscurrents in the United States were tame in comparison with the Holocaust, Hitler's vicious campaign to exterminate the Jews. Since the 1930s, the Nazis had persecuted the Jews in Germany and every German-occupied territory, causing many Jews to seek asylum beyond Hitler's reach. Millions of Jews from southern and eastern Europe had arrived in the United States during the late nineteenth and early twentieth centuries. But America's immigration restriction laws of the 1920s had slammed the door shut, allowing in only a small number of immigrants from each nation. Some Americans sought to make exceptions to the quotas for Jews fleeing Nazi persecution, but many Americans resisted. Roosevelt sympathized with the refugees' pleas for help, but he did not want to jeopardize his foreign policy or offend American voters. After Hitler's Anschluss in 1938, thousands of Austrian Jews sought to immigrate to the United States, but 82 percent of Americans opposed admitting them, and they were turned away. Roosevelt tried to persuade countries in Latin America and Africa to accept Jewish refugees, but none would do so. In 1939, friends of the refugees introduced legislation that would have granted asylum to 20,000 German refugee children, most of them Jewish. The bill was defeated in Congress, in large measure because of American anti-Semitism. In 1940, refugee British children—few of whom were Jewish—were welcomed into the United States without delay.

In 1942, numerous reports that Hitler was implementing a "final solution" filtered out of German-occupied Europe. Jews and other "undesirables"—such as Gypsies, religious and political dissenters, and homosexuals—were being sent to concentration camps. Old people, children, and others deemed too weak to work were systematically slaughtered and cremated, while the able-bodied were put to work at slave labor until they died of starvation and abuse. Despite such reports, skeptical U.S. State Department officials refused to grant asylum to Jewish refugees. The U.S. Office of War Information worried that charging Germans with crimes against humanity might incite them to greater resistance and prolong the war. Most Americans, including top officials, believed that reports of the killing camps were exaggerated. Only 152,000 of Europe's millions of Jews managed to gain refuge in the United States prior to America's entry into the war. Afterward, the number of refugees admitted dropped steadily, to just 2,400 by 1944. Those still trapped in Europe could only hope for rescue by the Allied armies.

Desperate to stem the killing, the World Jewish Congress appealed to the Allies to bomb the death camps and the railroad tracks leading to them in order to hamper the killing and block further shipments of victims. The proposals to bomb the camps got no farther than the desks of Assistant Secretary of War John J. McCloy in Washington and Foreign Secretary Anthony Eden in London. Intent on achieving military victory as soon as possible, they repeatedly turned down bombing requests, arguing that the air forces could not spare resources from their military missions. There was an element of moral indifference as well. An eloquent plea from Jewish leader Chaim Weizmann elicited a rejection letter from Eden's Foreign Office that ended with a tragic understatement: "I understand that this decision will be a disappointment to you, but be sure that the matter was considered exhaustively."

The nightmare of the Holocaust was all too real. When Russian troops arrived at Auschwitz in Poland in February 1945, they found emaciated prisoners, skeletal corpses, gas chambers, pits filled with human ashes, and loot the Nazis had stripped from the dead, including hair, gold fillings, and false teeth. At last, the truth about the Holocaust began to be known beyond the Germans who had perpetrated and tolerated these atrocities and the men, women, and children who had succumbed to the genocide. By then, it was too late for the 9 million victims—mostly Jews—of the Nazis' crimes against humanity.

▶**REVIEW** How did the war influence American society?

Toward Unconditional Surrender

By February 1943, Soviet defenders had finally defeated the massive German offensive against Stalingrad, turning the tide of the war in Europe. After gargantuan sacrifices in fighting that had lasted for eighteen months and killed more than 95 percent of the Russian soldiers and noncommissioned officers engaged at Stalingrad, the Red Army forced Hitler's Wehrmacht to turn back toward the west. Now the Soviets and their Western allies faced the task of driving the Nazis out of eastern and western Europe and forcing them to surrender. It was long past time, Stalin proclaimed, for Britain and the United States to open a second front in France, but that offensive was postponed for more than a year after the Red Army's victory at Stalingrad. In the Pacific, the Allies had halted the expansion of the Japanese empire but now had the deadly task of dislodging Japanese defenders from the far-flung outposts they still occupied. Allied military planners devised a strategy to annihilate Axis resistance by taking advantage of America's industrial superiority.

From Bombing Raids to Berlin

While the Allied campaigns in North Africa and Italy were under way, British and American pilots flew bombing missions from England to the continent as an airborne substitute for the delayed second front on the ground. During night raids, British bombers targeted general areas, hoping to hit civilians, create terror, and undermine morale. Beginning with Paul Tibbets's flight in August 1942, American pilots flew heavily armored B-17s from English airfields in daytime raids on industrial targets vital for the German war machine, especially oil refineries and ball bearing factories.

German air defenses took a fearsome toll on Allied pilots and aircraft. In 1943, two-thirds of American airmen did not survive to complete their twenty-five-mission tours of duty. In all, 85,000 American airmen were killed in the skies over Europe. Many others were shot down and held as prisoners of war. B-17 copilot Corbin B. Willis Jr. was shot down over Germany in 1944, and four of his five crew members who survived the crash were murdered by German civilians outraged by repeated Allied bombings. Willis, who spent the remainder of the war in prisoner of war camps, recalled, "You wouldn't really expect them to greet you with roses—so I understood their feeling—I'm sure my own family would be out there swinging and hitting in like circumstances." In February 1944, the arrival of America's durable and deadly P-51 Mustang fighter gave Allied bombers superior protection. The Mustangs slowly began to sweep the Luftwaffe from the skies, allowing bombers to penetrate deep into Germany and pound civilian and military targets around the clock. In April 1944, the Allies began to target bridges and railroads in northwestern Europe in preparation for their cross-Channel invasion.

In November 1943, Churchill, Roosevelt, and Stalin met in Teheran to discuss wartime strategy and the second front. Roosevelt conceded to Stalin that the Soviet Union would exercise de facto control of the eastern European countries that the Red Army occupied as it rolled back the still-potent German Wehrmacht. Stalin agreed to enter the war against Japan once Germany finally surrendered, in effect promising to open a second front in the Pacific theater. Roosevelt and Churchill promised that they would at last launch a massive second-front assault in northern France. Code-named Overlord, the offensive was scheduled to begin in May 1944 with the combined manpower of 4 million Americans massed in England, along with fourteen divisions from Britain, three from Canada, and one each from Poland and France.

General Eisenhower was assigned overall command of Allied forces and stockpiled mountains of military supplies in England. German defenders, directed by General Erwin Rommel, fortified the cliffs and mined the beaches of northwestern France. But the huge deployment of Hitler's armies in the east, which were trying to halt the Red Army's westward offensive, left too few German troops to stop the millions of Allied soldiers waiting to attack. More decisive, years of Allied air raids had decimated the German Luftwaffe, which could send aloft only 300 fighter planes against 12,000 Allied aircraft.

Diversionary bombing and false radio messages about armies that did not exist encouraged the Germans to expect an Allied invasion where the English Channel is narrowest. The actual invasion site was three hundred miles away, on the beaches of Normandy (Map 25.2). After frustrating delays caused by stormy

---

MAP 25.2   The European Theater of World War II, 1942–1945

The Russian reversal of the German offensive at Stalingrad and Leningrad, combined with Allied landings in North Africa and Normandy, trapped Germany in a closing vise of Allied armies on all sides.

weather, Eisenhower launched the largest amphibious assault in world history on D Day, June 6, 1944. Rough seas and deadly fire from German machine guns slowed the assault, but Allied soldiers finally succeeded in securing the beachhead. As naval officer Tracy Sugarman recalled, "What I thought were piles of cordwood [on the beach] I later learned were the bodies of 2,500 men killed by withering fire from the Nazi gun emplacements." Sugarman reported that he and the other GIs who made the landing "were exhausted and we were exultant. We had survived D-Day!"

Within a week, a flood of soldiers, tanks, and other military equipment swamped the Normandy beaches and propelled Allied forces toward Germany. On August 25, the Allies liberated Paris from four years of Nazi occupation. As the giant pincers of the Allied and Soviet armies closed on Germany in December 1944, Hitler ordered a counterattack to capture the Allies' essential supply port at Antwerp, Belgium. In the Battle of the Bulge (December 16, 1944, to January 31, 1945), as the Allies termed it, German forces drove fifty-five miles into Allied lines before being stopped at Bastogne. More than 70,000 Allied soldiers were killed, including more Americans than in any other battle of the war. The Nazis lost more than 100,000 men and hundreds of tanks, fatally depleting Hitler's reserves. Army lieutenant Alvin Dickson observed the macabre scene of "all the bodies . . . frozen stiff. . . . Many dead Americans and Germans are lying beneath the snow now . . . [many with] the ring finger . . . cut off in order to get the ring."

In February 1945, while Allied armies relentlessly pushed German forces backward, Churchill, Stalin, and Roosevelt met secretly at Yalta, a Russian resort town on the Black Sea, to discuss their plans for the postwar world. Seriously ill and noticeably frail, Roosevelt managed to secure Stalin's promise to permit votes of self-determination in the eastern European countries occupied by the Red Army. The Allies pledged to support Chiang Kai-shek as the leader of China. The Soviet Union obtained a role in the postwar governments of Korea and Manchuria in exchange for entering the war against Japan after the defeat of Germany.

The "Big Three" also agreed on the creation of a new international peacekeeping organization, the United Nations (UN). All nations would have a place in the UN General Assembly, but the Security Council would wield decisive power, and its permanent representatives from the Allied powers—China, France, Great Britain, the Soviet Union, and the United States—would possess a veto over UN actions. The American response to the creation of the UN reflected the triumph of internationalism during the nation's mobilization for war. The Senate ratified the United Nations Charter in July 1945 by a vote of 89 to 2.

While Allied armies sped toward Berlin, Allied warplanes dropped more bombs after D Day than in all the previous European bombing raids combined. In February 1945, Allied bombers rained a firestorm of death and destruction on Berlin and Dresden, killing 60,000 civilians. By April 11, Allied armies sweeping in from the west reached the banks of the Elbe River, the agreed-upon rendezvous with the Red Army, and paused while the Soviets smashed into Berlin.

In three weeks of vicious house-to-house fighting, the Red Army captured Berlin on May 2. Hitler had committed suicide on April 30, and the provisional German government surrendered unconditionally on May 7. The war in Europe was finally over, with the sacrifice of 135,576 American soldiers, nearly 250,000 British troops, and 9 million Russian combatants.

Roosevelt did not live to witness the end of the war. On April 12, while resting in Warm Springs, Georgia, the president suffered a fatal stroke. Americans grieved for the man who had led them through years of depression and world war, and they worried aloud about his successor, Vice President Harry Truman, who would have to steer the nation to victory over Japan and protect American interests in the postwar world.

The Defeat of Japan

After the punishing defeats in the Coral Sea and at Midway, Japan had to quell renewed resistance on the Asian mainland and to fend off Allied naval and air attacks. In 1943, British and American forces, along with Indian and Chinese allies, launched an offensive against Japanese outposts in southern Asia, pushing through Burma and into China, where the armies of Chiang Kai-shek continued to resist conquest. In the Pacific, Americans and their allies attacked Japanese strongholds by sea, air, and land, moving island by island toward the Japanese homeland (Map 25.3).

The island-hopping campaign began in August 1942, when American marines landed on Guadalcanal in the southern Pacific. For the next six months, a savage battle raged for control of the strategic area. Finally, during the night of February 8, 1943, Japanese forces withdrew. The terrible losses on both sides indicated to the marines how costly it would be to defeat Japan. After the battle, Joseph Steinbacher, a twenty-one-year-old from Alabama, sailed from San Francisco to New Guinea, where, he recalled, "all the cannon fodder waited to be assigned" to replace the killed and wounded.

In mid-1943, American, Australian, and New Zealand forces launched offensives in New Guinea and the Solomon Islands that gradually secured the South Pacific. In the Central Pacific, amphibious forces conquered the Gilbert and Marshall islands, which served as forward bases for decisive air assaults on the Japanese home islands. As the Allies attacked island after island, Japanese soldiers were ordered to refuse to surrender no matter how hopeless their plight. At Tarawa, a barren coral island of less than three square miles, 3,000 Japanese defenders battled American marines for three days, killing 1,000 Americans and wounding 2,000 until the 17 Japanese survivors finally succumbed. Such fierce Japanese resistance spurred remorseless Allied attacks on Japanese-occupied islands, usually begun with air and naval bombardment, followed by amphibious landings by marines and grinding, inch-by-inch combat to root Japanese

MAP 25.3   The Pacific Theater of World War II, 1941–1945
To drive the Japanese from their far-flung empire, the Allies launched two combined naval and military offensives—one to recapture the Philippines and then attack Japanese forces in China, the other to hop from island to island in the Central Pacific toward the Japanese mainland.

fighters out of bunkers and caves with grenades, flamethrowers, and anything else at hand.

While the island-hopping campaign kept pressure on Japanese forces, the Allies invaded the Philippines in the fall of 1944. In the four-day Battle of Leyte Gulf, the greatest naval encounter in world history, the American fleet crushed the Japanese armada, clearing the way for Allied victory in the Philippines. While the Philippine campaign was under way, American forces captured two crucial islands—Iwo Jima and Okinawa—from which they planned to launch an attack on the Japanese homeland. To defend Okinawa and prevent the American invaders from getting within close bombing range of their home islands, Japanese leaders ordered thousands of suicide pilots, known as *kamikaze*, to crash their bomb-laden planes into Allied ships. Like airborne torpedoes, kamikaze caused fearsome destruction. But instead of destroying the American fleet, they demolished the last vestige of the Japanese air force. By June 1945, the Japanese were nearly defenseless on the sea and in the air. Still, their leaders prepared to fight to the death for their homeland.

Joseph Steinbacher, now a sergeant, and other troops who had suffered "horrendous" casualties in the Philippines were told by their commanding officer, "Men, in a few short months we are going to invade the island of Kyushu, the southernmost Japanese island. We will be going in on the first wave and are expecting ninety percent casualties the first day. . . . For the few of us left alive [after reinforcements arrive] the war will be over." Steinbacher later recalled his "mental attitude at that moment. I know that I am now a walking dead man and will not have a snowball's chance in hell of making it through the last great battle to conquer the home islands of Japan."

Atomic Warfare

In mid-July 1945, as Allied forces prepared for the final assault on Japan, American scientists tested a secret weapon at an isolated desert site near Los Alamos, New Mexico. In 1942, Roosevelt had authorized the top-secret Manhattan Project to find a way to convert nuclear energy into a superbomb before the Germans added such a weapon to their arsenal. More than 100,000 Americans, led by scientists, engineers, and military officers at Los Alamos, worked frantically to win the fateful race for an atomic bomb. Germany surrendered two and a half months before the test on July 16, 1945, when scientists first witnessed an awesome explosion that sent a mushroom cloud of debris eight miles into the atmosphere.

A delegation of scientists and officials, troubled by the bomb's destructive force, secretly proposed that the United States give a public demonstration of the bomb's cataclysmic power, hoping to persuade Japan's leaders to surrender. With the Japanese incapable of offensive action and blockaded by the Allied fleet, proponents of a demonstration were encouraged because Japanese emissaries were already putting out feelers about peace negotiations. But U.S. government officials quickly rejected such a demonstration: Americans had enough nuclear material for only three bombs, the demonstration bomb might fail to explode, and the Japanese might not surrender even if it did. Also, despite numerous defeats, Japan still had more than 6 million reserves at home, fortified by more than 5,000 kamikaze aircraft stockpiled for a last-ditch defense against the anticipated Allied assault, which U.S. military advisers estimated would cost the lives of at least 250,000 Americans.

President Truman heard about the successful bomb test when he was in Potsdam, Germany, negotiating with Stalin about postwar issues. Truman realized that the atomic bomb could hasten the end of the war with Japan, perhaps before the Russians could attack the Japanese in Korea and Manchuria, as Stalin had pledged at Yalta. Within a few months after the defeat of Germany, Truman also recognized that the bomb gave the United States a devastating atomic **monopoly** that could be used to counter Soviet ambitions and advance American interests in the postwar world.

Truman, who had been a commander of combat troops in World War I, saw no reason not to use the atomic bomb against Japan if doing so would save American lives. But first he issued an ultimatum: Japan must surrender unconditionally or face utter ruin. When the Japanese failed to respond by the deadline given, Truman ordered that a bomb be dropped on a Japanese city not already heavily damaged by American raids. On August 6, Colonel Paul Tibbets piloted the *Enola Gay* over Hiroshima and released an atomic bomb, leveling the city and incinerating 78,000 people. Three days later, after the Japanese government still refused to surrender, Tibbets-trained airmen dropped a second atomic bomb on Nagasaki, killing more than 100,000 civilians.

At last, a peace faction took control of the Japanese government, and with American assurance that the emperor could retain his throne after the Allies took over, Japan surrendered on August 14. On a troop ship departing from Europe for

---

Hiroshima Bombing
This rare shot taken by a news photographer in Hiroshima immediately after the atomic bomb exploded on August 6, 1945, suggests the shock and incomprehension that survivors later described as their first reactions. On August 9, another atomic bomb created similar devastation in Nagasaki. UN photo.

what would have been the final assault on Japan, an American soldier spoke for millions of others when he heard the wonderful news that the killing was over: "We are going to grow to adulthood after all."

▶ **REVIEW**   Why did Truman elect to use the atomic bomb against Japan?

Conclusion: Allied Victory and America's Emergence as a Superpower

Shortly after Pearl Harbor, Hitler pronounced America "a decayed country" without "much future"; a country "half Judaized, and the other half Negrified"; a country "where everything is built on the dollar" and bound to fall apart. American mobilization for World War II disproved Hitler's arrogant prophecy, as Paul Tibbets's historic flight dramatized. At a cost of 405,399 American lives, the nation united with its allies to battle Axis aggressors in Europe and Asia and eventually to crush them into unconditional surrender. Almost all Americans believed they had won a "good war" against totalitarian evil. The Allies saved Asia and Europe from enslavement and finally halted the Nazis' genocidal campaign against the Jews and others whom the Nazis considered inferior. To secure human rights and protect the world against future wars, the Roosevelt administration took the lead in creating the United Nations.

Wartime production lifted the nation out of the Great Depression. The gross national product soared to four times what it had been when Roosevelt became president in 1933. Jobs in defense industries eliminated chronic unemployment, provided wages for millions of women workers and African American migrants from southern farms, and boosted Americans' prosperity. Ahead stretched the challenge of maintaining that prosperity while reintegrating millions of uniformed men and women.

By the end of the war, the United States had emerged as a global superpower. Wartime mobilization made the American economy the strongest in the world, buttressed by the military clout of the nation's nuclear monopoly. Although the war left much of the world a rubble-strewn wasteland, the American mainland had enjoyed immunity from attack. The Japanese occupation of China had left 50 million people without homes and millions more dead, maimed, and orphaned. The German offensive against the Soviet Union had killed more than 20 million Russian soldiers and civilians. Germany and Japan lay in ruins, their economies as shattered as their military forces. The Allies had killed more than 4 million Nazi soldiers and more than 1.2 million Japanese combatants, as well as hundreds of thousands of civilians. But in the gruesome balance sheet of war, the Axis powers had inflicted far more grief, misery, and destruction upon the global victims of their aggression than they had suffered in return.

As the dominant Western nation in the postwar world, the United States asserted its leadership in the reconstruction of Europe while occupying Japan and overseeing its economic and political recovery. America soon confronted new challenges in the tense aftermath of the war, as the Soviets seized political control of eastern Europe, a Communist revolution swept China, and national liberation movements emerged in the colonial empires of Britain and France. The surrender of the Axis powers ended the battles of World War II, but the forces unleashed by the war would shape the United States and the rest of the world for decades to come.

REVIEWING THE CHAPTER

Use the questions and timeline to review and strengthen your understanding of the chapter.

REVIEW QUESTIONS

1. Why did isolationism during the 1930s concern Roosevelt? (pp. 792–96)

2. How did Roosevelt attempt to balance American isolationism with the increasingly ominous international scene of the late 1930s? (pp. 797–802)

3. How did the Roosevelt administration mobilize the human and industrial resources necessary to fight a two-front war? (pp. 802–6)

4. How did the United States seek to counter the Japanese in the Pacific and the Germans in Europe? (pp. 806–10)

5. How did the war influence American society? (pp. 810–16)

6. Why did Truman elect to use the atomic bomb against Japan? (pp. 816–24)

MAKING CONNECTIONS

1. Does isolationism bolster or undermine national security and national economic interests? Discuss Roosevelt's evolving answer to this question as revealed in his administration's policies toward Europe. In your answer, consider how other constraints (such as politics, history, and ethics) affected administration policies.

2. World War II brought new prosperity to many Americans. Why did war succeed in creating the full economic recovery that the New Deal had pursued with more limited success? In your answer, discuss both the objectives of specific New Deal economic reforms and the needs of the wartime economy.

3. Japan's attack on Pearl Harbor plunged the United States into war with the Axis powers. How did the United States recover from this attack to play a decisive role in the Allies' victory? Discuss three American military or diplomatic actions and their contribution to the defeat of the Axis powers.

4. As the United States battled racist regimes abroad, the realities of discrimination at home came sharply into focus. How did minorities' contributions to the war effort as soldiers and laborers draw attention to these problems? What were the political implications of these developments? In your answer, consider both grassroots political action and federal policy.

TIMELINE

1935–1937	• Congress passes neutrality acts.
1936	• Nazi Germany occupies Rhineland. • Mussolini conquers Ethiopia. • Spanish civil war begins.
1937	• Japanese troops capture Nanking. • Roosevelt introduces his quarantine policy.
1938	• Hitler annexes Austria. • Munich agreement.
1939	• German troops occupy Czechoslovakia. • Nazi-Soviet nonaggression pact. • **September 1.** Germany's attack on Poland begins World War II.
1940	• Germany invades Denmark, Norway, France, Belgium, Luxembourg, and the Netherlands. • British and French evacuation from Dunkirk. • Vichy government installed in France. • Battle of Britain. • Tripartite Pact signed by Japan, Germany, and Italy.
1941	• Lend-Lease Act. • **June.** Germany invades Soviet Union. • **August.** Atlantic Charter issued. • **December 7.** Japanese attack Pearl Harbor.
1942	• Roosevelt authorizes internment of Japanese Americans. • Japan captures Philippines. • Congress of Racial Equality (CORE) founded. • Battles of Coral Sea and Midway. • Roosevelt authorizes Manhattan Project. • **November.** U.S. forces invade North Africa.
1943	• Allied leaders demand unconditional surrender of Axis powers. • Zoot suit riots. • U.S. and British forces invade Sicily.
1944	• **June 6.** D Day.
1945	• **February.** Yalta Conference. • **April 12.** Roosevelt dies; Vice President Harry Truman becomes president. • **April 30.** Hitler commits suicide. • **May 7.** Germany surrenders. • **July.** United States joins United Nations. • **August 6.** United States drops atomic bomb on Hiroshima. • **August 9.** United States drops atomic bomb on Nagasaki. • **August 14.** Japan surrenders, ending World War II.

▶ **For an online bibliography, practice quizzes, Web sites, images, and documents related to this chapter,** see the Book Companion Site at **bedfordstmartins.com/roark.**

▶ **For firsthand accounts of this period,** see Chapter 25 in Michael Johnson, ed., *Reading the American Past*, Fourth Edition.

Cold War Politics in the Truman Years

1945–1953

H EADS TURNED WHEN Congresswoman Helen Gahagan Douglas walked through the U.S. Capitol. From 1945 to 1951, when she represented California's Fourteenth Congressional District in Los Angeles, she had no more than 10 female colleagues at any one time in the 435-member House of Representatives. Not only did she stand out as a woman in a thoroughly masculine institution, but she also drew attention as a tall and strikingly attractive woman, a former Broadway star and opera singer of the 1920s and 1930s. She served in Congress when the fate of the **New Deal** was up for grabs and the nation charted a dramatic new course in foreign policy.

Born in 1900 to affluent parents, Helen Gahagan grew up in Brooklyn, New York. She was drawn to the theater as a child and defied her father to leave Barnard College for the stage after her sophomore year. She quickly won fame on Broadway, where she starred in show after show until she fell in love with one of her leading men, Melvyn Douglas. They married in 1931, and she followed him to Hollywood, where he hoped to advance his movie career. During the 1930s, she bore two children. She continued to appear in theater productions and concerts as well as in one movie, but her career was on the wane.

In contrast to her husband, who held liberal political views from his youth, Douglas abandoned the staunch Republicanism of her parents during the depression, when Franklin D. Roosevelt's leadership captured her admiration. As Hollywood became a hotbed of liberal and radical politics, the Douglases were

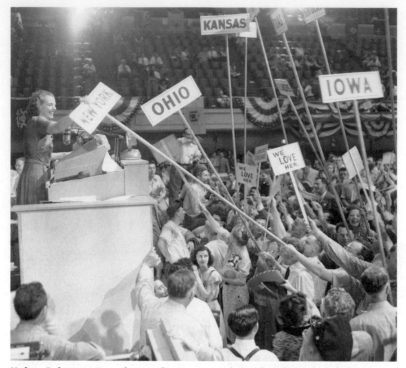

Helen Gahagan Douglas at the Democratic National Convention
The congresswoman from California was a popular campaigner for the Democrats
and a featured speaker at the Democratic National Conventions of 1944 and 1948
(shown here). Douglas's appeal sparked interest in her for higher office. The
Washington Post called it the "first genuine boom in history for a woman for vice-
president," but she made it clear that she was not in the running.
© Bettmann/Corbis.

drawn in. Both were shaken by the anti-Semitism and militarism that they
witnessed on a visit to Germany in 1937. "I was overwhelmed by horror and a
premonition of disaster," Helen later recalled, vowing never to perform there
again and subsequently joining the Anti-Nazi League in California. But migrant
workers aroused her greatest passion. Upon hearing of the desperate conditions
of tenant farmers moving to California from Oklahoma and other states, she "took
[her] first step into politics." Visiting migrant camps, she saw "faces stamped
with poverty and despair." "Haunted" by this "human calamity," she agreed to
become chair of the John Steinbeck Committee to Aid Migratory Workers.

Douglas's research, speaking, and organizing on behalf of migrant farmworkers brought her to President Roosevelt's attention. She testified before Congress
and became a guest at the White House, a friend of Eleanor Roosevelt's, and a
campaigner for the president in 1940. In California, she rose fast in party politics,

becoming vice chairman of the state Democratic Party and head of the Women's Division. All of these experiences contributed to her decision to run for Congress in 1944 and helped secure her election. She represented not the posh Hollywood district where she lived, but the Fourteenth Congressional District in downtown Los Angeles, with its multiethnic, multiracial population, which helped shape her progressive politics.

Like many other liberals who were devoted to Roosevelt, Douglas was devastated by his death and unsure of his successor, Harry S. Truman. "Who was Harry Truman anyway?" she said. "None of us knew much about him." A compromise choice for the vice presidency, this "accidental president" lacked the charisma, experience, and political skills with which Roosevelt had transformed both foreign and domestic policy, won four presidential elections, and forged a Democratic Party coalition that dominated national politics. Initially criticized and abandoned by many Roosevelt loyalists, Truman faced a resurgent Republican Party, which had gained strength in Congress during World War II, as well as revolts from within his own party. The new president confronted domestic problems that the New Deal had not solved—how to sustain economic growth and avoid another depression without the war to fuel the economy—and international challenges that threatened to undermine the nation's security and called for bold international initiatives.

As early as 1946, Truman and his advisers became convinced that the Soviet Union posed a major threat to the United States. The president gradually shaped a policy designed to contain and thwart Soviet power wherever it threatened to spread. By 1947, a new term had been coined to describe the intense rivalry between the superpowers—**cold war**. As a member of the House Foreign Affairs Committee, Douglas urged the administration to find ways to cooperate with the Soviet Union, and she voted against aid to Greece and Turkey, the first step in a new policy to contain the spread of **communism**. Thereafter, she was Truman's loyal ally, supporting the Marshall Plan, the creation of the **North Atlantic Treaty Organization (NATO)**, and the war in Korea. The **containment** policy achieved its goals in Europe, but communism spread in Asia, and at home a wave of anti-Communist hysteria—a second Red scare—harmed many Americans and stifled dissent and debate about U.S. policies.

Douglas's earlier links with leftist and liberal groups; her advocacy of civil rights, women's rights, and federal health, housing, and education programs; and her defense of civil liberties threatened by the crusade against supposed subversives made her and many other liberals easy targets for conservative politicians seeking to capitalize on the anti-Communist fervor. When she decided to run for the U.S. Senate in 1950, she faced Republican Richard M. Nixon. Her opponent had gained national attention as a member of the House Un-American Activities Committee, which sought to expose Communists in government and whose funding Douglas had voted to cut. Nixon's campaign put her on the defensive, labeling her as "pink right down to her underwear" and telephoning thousands of homes on election eve with the anonymous message, "I think you should know Helen Douglas is a Communist." Nixon won a decisive victory but carried throughout his life the appellation Douglas gave him, "Tricky Dick." Douglas's political career ended in defeat, just as much of Truman's domestic agenda fell victim to the Red scare.

From the Grand Alliance to Containment

With Japan's surrender in August 1945, Americans besieged the government for the return of their loved ones. Baby booties arrived at the White House with a note, "Please send my daddy home." Americans looked forward to the disman-tling of the large military establishment and expected the Allies, led by the United States and working within the United Nations, to cooperate in the management of international peace. Postwar realities quickly dashed these expectations. A dangerous new threat seemed to arise as the wartime alliance forged by the United States, Great Britain, and the Soviet Union crumbled, and the United States began to develop the means to contain the spread of Soviet power around the globe.

The Cold War Begins

"The guys who came out of World War II were idealistic," reported Harold Russell, a young paratrooper who had lost both hands in a training accident. "We felt the day had come when the wars were all over." Public opinion polls echoed the veterans' confidence in the promise of peace. But political leaders were less optimistic. Once the Allies had overcome a common enemy, the prewar mistrust and antagonism between the Soviet Union and the West resurfaced over their very different visions of the postwar world.

The Western Allies' delay in opening a second front in Western Europe aroused Soviet suspicions during the war. The Soviet Union made supreme wartime sacrifices, losing more than twenty million citizens and vast portions of its agricultural and industrial capacity. At the war's end, Soviet leader Joseph Stalin wanted to make Germany pay for the rebuilding of the Soviet economy and to expand Soviet influence in the world. Above all, he wanted friendly gov-ernments on the Soviet Union's borders in Eastern Europe, especially in Poland, through which Germany had attacked Russia twice within twenty-five years. A ruthless dictator, he also wanted to maintain his own power.

In contrast to the Soviet devastation, enemy fire had never touched the main-land of the United States, and its 405,000 dead amounted to just 2 percent of the Soviet loss. With a vastly expanded economy and a monopoly on atomic weapons, the United States was the most powerful nation on the planet. That sheer power, along with U.S. economic interests, policymakers' views about how the recent war might have been avoided, and a belief in the superiority of American institutions and intentions, all affected how American leaders approached the Soviet Union after the war.

Fearing a return of the depression, U.S. officials believed that a healthy economy depended on opportunities abroad. American companies needed access to raw materials, markets for their goods, and security for their investments overseas. These needs could be met best in countries with similar economic and political systems, not in those where government controls interfered with the free flow of products and dollars. As Truman put it in 1947, "The American system can survive in America only if it becomes a world system."

Yet both leaders and citizens regarded their foreign policy not as a self-interested campaign to guarantee economic interests, but as the means to preserve national security and bring freedom, **democracy**, and capitalism to the rest of the world. Laura Briggs spoke for many Americans who believed "it was our destiny to prove that we were the children of God and that our way was right for the world."

Recent history also shaped postwar foreign policy. Americans believed that Britain and France might have prevented World War II had they resisted rather than appeased Hitler's initial aggression. Navy Secretary James V. Forrestal, for example, argued against trying to "buy [the Soviets'] understanding and sympathy. We tried that once with Hitler." This "appeasement" analogy would be invoked repeatedly when the United States faced challenges to the international status quo.

The man with ultimate responsibility for U.S. policy was a keen student of history but came to the White House with little international experience. When Germany attacked the Soviet Union in 1941, then-Senator Truman expressed his hope that the two would kill each other off. As president, he envisioned Soviet-American cooperation, as long as the Soviet Union conformed to U.S. plans for the postwar world and restrained its expansionist impulses. Proud of his ability to make quick decisions, Truman determined to be firm with the Soviets, knowing well that America's nuclear monopoly gave him the upper hand.

Soviet and American interests clashed first in Eastern Europe. Stalin insisted that the Allies' wartime agreements gave him a free hand in the countries defeated or liberated by the Red Army, just as the United States was unilaterally reconstructing governments in Italy and Japan. The Soviet dictator used harsh methods to install Communist governments in neighboring Poland and Bulgaria. Elsewhere, the Soviets initially tolerated non-Communist governments in Hungary and Czechoslovakia. And in the spring of 1946, Stalin responded to pressure from the West and removed troops from Iran on the Soviet Union's southwest border, allowing U.S. access to the rich oil fields there.

Stalin considered U.S. officials hypocritical in demanding democratic elections in Eastern Europe while supporting dictatorships friendly to U.S. interests in Latin America. The United States clung to its sphere of influence while opposing Soviet efforts to create its own. But the Western Allies were unwilling to match tough words with military force against the largest army in the world. Under intense domestic pressure to demobilize their own troops, they issued sharp protests but failed to prevent the Soviet Union from establishing satellite countries in most of Eastern Europe.

In 1946, the wartime Allies contended over Germany's future. American policymakers wanted to demilitarize Germany, but they also sought rapid industrial revival there to foster European economic recovery and thus America's own long-term prosperity. By contrast, the Soviet Union wanted Germany weak militarily and economically, and Stalin demanded heavy reparations to help rebuild the devastated Soviet economy. Unable to settle their differences, the Allies divided Germany. The Soviet Union installed a puppet Communist government in the eastern section, and in December 1946, Britain, France, and the United States unified their occupation zones, beginning the process that established the Federal Republic of Germany—West Germany—in 1949 (Map 26.1).

The war of words escalated early in 1946. Boasting of the superiority of the Soviet system, Stalin told a Moscow audience in February that capitalism inevitably produced war. One month later, Truman traveled with Winston Churchill to Fulton, Missouri, where the former prime minister denounced Soviet suppression of the popular will in Eastern and central Europe. "From Stettin in the Baltic to Trieste in the Adriatic, an **iron curtain** has descended across the Continent," Churchill said. Although Truman did not officially endorse Churchill's iron curtain speech, his presence implied agreement with the idea of joint British-American action to combat Soviet aggression. Stalin regarded the speech as "a call to war against the USSR."

In February 1946, George F. Kennan, a career diplomat with experience in Eastern Europe and Moscow, wrote a comprehensive rationale for hard-line foreign policy. Downplaying the influence of Communist ideology in Soviet policy, he instead stressed the Soviets' insecurity and Stalin's need to maintain authority at home, which he believed prompted Stalin to exaggerate threats from abroad and to expand Soviet power. These circumstances, Kennan argued, made it impossible to negotiate with Stalin. Secretary of State James F. Byrnes and other key Truman advisers agreed with him.

Kennan predicted that the Soviet Union would retreat from its expansionist efforts "in the face of superior force," and he recommended that the United States respond with "unalterable counterforce"—the approach that came to be called containment. Kennan expected that containment would eventually end in "either the breakup or the gradual mellowing of Soviet power." This message reached a larger audience when Kennan's views were published in *Foreign Affairs* magazine in July 1947. Kennan later expressed dismay when his ideas were used to justify

MAP 26.1   The Division of Europe after World War II
The "iron curtain," a term coined by Winston Churchill to refer to the Soviet grip on Eastern and central Europe, divided the continent for nearly fifty years. Communist governments controlled the countries along the Soviet Union's western border. The only exception was Finland, which remained neutral.

what he considered an indiscriminate American response wherever communism seemed likely to arise. Nonetheless, his analysis marked a critical turning point in the development of the cold war, providing a compelling rationale for wielding U.S. power throughout the world.

Not all public figures accepted the toughening line. In September 1946, Secretary of Commerce Henry A. Wallace, Truman's predecessor as vice president, urged greater understanding of the Soviets' concerns about their nation's security, insisting that "we have no more business in the political affairs of Eastern Europe than Russia has in the political affairs of Latin America." State Department officials were furious, and when Wallace refused to be muzzled on foreign policy topics, Truman fired him.

The Truman Doctrine and the Marshall Plan

In 1947, the United States began to implement the doctrine of containment that would guide foreign policy for the next four decades. It was not an easy transition; Americans approved taking a hard line against the Soviet Union, but they wanted to keep their soldiers and tax dollars at home. In addition to selling containment to the public, Truman had to gain the support of a Republican-controlled Congress, which included a forceful bloc, led by Ohio senator Robert A. Taft, opposed to a strong U.S. presence in Europe.

Crises in two Mediterranean countries triggered the implementation of containment. In February 1947, Britain informed the United States that its crippled economy could no longer sustain military assistance either to Greece, where the autocratic government faced a leftist uprising, or to Turkey, which was trying to resist Soviet pressures. Truman promptly sought congressional authority to send military and economic missions, along with $400 million in aid, to the two countries. Meeting with congressional leaders, Undersecretary of State Dean Acheson predicted that if Greece and Turkey fell, communism would soon consume three-fourths of the world. After a stunned silence, Michigan senator Arthur Vandenberg, the Republican foreign policy leader and a recent convert from **isolationism**, warned that to get approval, Truman would have to "scare hell out of the country."

Truman did just that. Outlining what would later be called the **domino theory**, he warned that if Greece fell to the rebels, "confusion and disorder might well spread throughout the entire Middle East" and then create instability in Europe. Failure to act, he said, "may endanger the peace of the world—and shall surely endanger the welfare of the nation." According to what came to be called the **Truman Doctrine**, the United States would not only resist Soviet military power but also "support free peoples who are resisting attempted subjugation by armed minorities or by outside pressures."

The president failed to convince Helen Gahagan Douglas and some of her colleagues in Congress, who wanted the United States to try first to resolve the crises in Greece and Turkey through the United Nations before acting unilaterally and who opposed propping up the authoritarian Greek government. But the administration won the day, setting a standard for cold war interventions that would aid any kind of government if the only alternative appeared to be communism. Congress did not formally accept the Truman Doctrine when it approved aid for Greece and Turkey. Yet the assumption that national security depended on rescuing any anti-Communist government from internal rebels or outside pressure became the cornerstone of U.S. foreign policy until the end of the 1980s.

A much larger assistance program for Europe followed aid to Greece and Turkey. In May 1947, Acheson described a war-ravaged Western Europe, with "factories destroyed, fields impoverished, transportation systems wrecked, populations scattered and on the borderline of starvation." American citizens were sending generous amounts of private aid, but Europe needed large-scale assistance. It was "a matter of national self-interest," Acheson argued, for the United States to provide aid. Only economic recovery could halt the growth of **socialist** and Communist parties in France and Italy and confine Soviet influence to Eastern Europe.

In March 1948, Congress approved the European Recovery Program—known as the Marshall Plan, after retired general George C. Marshall, who as secretary of state proposed the plan—and over the next five years, the United States spent $13 billion to restore the economies of sixteen Western European nations. Marshall invited all European nations and the Soviet Union to cooperate in a request for aid, but as administration officials expected, the Soviets objected to the American terms of free trade and financial disclosure and ordered their Eastern European satellites likewise to reject the offer.

The Marshall Plan marked the first step toward the European Union. Humanitarian desires to help destitute Europeans, as well as the strategic goal of keeping Western Europe free of communism, drove the adoption of this enormous aid program. In addition, the assistance program helped boost the U.S. economy, because the European nations spent most of the dollars to buy American products, and Europe's economic recovery created new opportunities for American investment.

In February 1948, while Congress debated the Marshall Plan, the Soviets staged a brutal coup and installed a Communist regime in Czechoslovakia, the last democracy left in Eastern Europe. Next, Stalin threatened Western access to Berlin. That former capital of Germany lay within Soviet-controlled East Germany, but all four Allies jointly occupied Berlin, dividing it into separate administrative units. As the Western Allies moved to organize West Germany as a separate nation, the Soviets retaliated by blocking roads and rail lines between West Germany and the Western-held sections of Berlin, cutting off food, fuel, and other essentials to two million inhabitants.

"We stay in Berlin, period," Truman vowed. Yet he wanted to avoid a confrontation with Soviet troops. So for nearly a year, U.S. and British pilots airlifted 2.3 million tons of goods to sustain the West Berliners. Stalin hesitated to shoot down these cargo planes, and in 1949 he lifted the blockade. The city was then divided into East Berlin, under Soviet control, and West Berlin, which became part of West Germany. For many Americans, the Berlin airlift confirmed the wisdom of containment: When challenged, the Russians backed down, as Kennan had predicted. Moreover, the airlift changed the image of the United States in German eyes from an occupying force to a savior.

Building a National Security State

During the Truman years, advocates of the new containment policy fashioned a six-pronged defense strategy: (1) development of atomic weapons, (2) strengthening traditional military power, (3) military alliances with other nations, (4) military and economic aid to friendly nations, (5) an espionage network and secret means to subvert Communist expansion, and (6) a propaganda offensive to win popular admiration for the United States around the world.

In September 1949, the United States lost its nuclear monopoly when officials confirmed that the Soviets had detonated an atomic bomb. In an effort to keep the United States ahead, in January 1950 Truman approved the development of a hydrogen bomb, equivalent to five hundred atomic bombs, rejecting the arguments of several scientists who had worked on the atomic bomb and of George Kennan, who warned of an endless arms race. The "super bomb" was ready by 1954, but the U.S. advantage was brief. In November 1955, the Soviets exploded their own hydrogen bomb.

From the 1950s through the 1980s, **deterrence** formed the basis of American nuclear strategy. To deter the Soviet Union from attacking, the United States strove to maintain a nuclear force more powerful than the Soviets'. Because the Russians pursued a similar policy, the superpowers became locked in an ever-escalating nuclear weapons race, as Kennan had predicted. Albert Einstein, whose mathematical discoveries had laid the foundations for nuclear weapons, commented grimly on the enormous destructive force now possessed by the superpowers. The war that came after World War III, he warned, would "be fought with sticks and stones."

To implement the second component of its containment strategy, the United States beefed up its conventional military power to deter Soviet threats that might not warrant nuclear retaliation. The National Security Act of 1947 streamlined defense planning by uniting the military branches under a single secretary of defense and creating the National Security Council (NSC) to advise the president. With this legislation, the Department of War became the Department of Defense, a name change emphasizing the nation's growing militarization. "War" denoted a limited time of engagement, "Defense" a permanent, ongoing, and substantial undertaking.

During the Berlin crisis, Congress hiked military appropriations and enacted a peacetime **draft**. In addition, Congress granted permanent status to the women's military branches, though it limited their numbers and rank and banned them from combat. One of military women's staunchest supporters, General Dwight D. Eisenhower, had assured Congress "that after an enlistment or two women will ordinarily—and thank God—they will get married." With 1.5 million men and women in uniform in 1950, the military strength of the United States had quadrupled since the 1930s, and defense expenditures claimed one-third of the federal budget.

Collective security, the third prong of postwar military strategy, also developed during the Berlin showdown. In June 1948, the Senate approved the general principle of regional military alliances. One year later, the United States joined Canada and Western European nations in its first peacetime military alliance, the North Atlantic Treaty Organization (NATO), designed to counter a Soviet threat

Cold War Spying

The Central Intelligence Agency (CIA) became one of the most important tools for obtaining Soviet secrets, deceiving the enemy, countering subversive activities by Communists, and assisting local forces against leaders whom the United States wanted to oust. Secret agents operating behind the iron curtain gathered information with bugs and devices such as these cameras hidden in cigarette packs. Spying soon gained a prominent place in popular culture, most notably in more than a dozen movies featuring James Bond.

Jack Naylor Collection.

to Western Europe (see Map 26.1). For the first time in its history, the United States pledged to go to war if one of its allies was attacked.

The fourth element of defense strategy involved foreign assistance programs to strengthen friendly countries, such as aid to Greece and Turkey and the Marshall Plan. In addition, in 1949 Congress approved $1 billion of military aid to its NATO allies, and the government began economic assistance to nations in other parts of the world.

The fifth ingredient of containment improved the government's espionage capacities and ability to deter communism through covert activities. The National Security Act of 1947 created the Central Intelligence Agency (CIA) not only to gather information but also to perform any "functions and duties related to intelligence affecting the national security" that the NSC might authorize. Such activities included propaganda, sabotage, economic warfare, and support for "anti-communist elements in threatened countries of the free world." Secret operations by the CIA helped defeat Italy's Communist Party in the 1948 election there. Subsequently, CIA agents would help topple legitimate foreign governments and violate the rights of U.S. citizens. In many respects, the CIA was virtually unaccountable to Congress or the public.

Finally, the U.S. government sought, through cultural exchanges and propaganda, to win "hearts and minds" throughout the world. As the cold war intensified, the government expanded the Voice of America, created during World War II to broadcast U.S. propaganda abroad. In addition, the State Department sent books, exhibits, and performers to foreign countries. Jazz musicians were especially popular as "cultural ambassadors," tapping into the excitement in many foreign countries about this recognizably American creation.

By 1950, the United States had abandoned age-old tenets of foreign policy. Isolationism and neutrality had given way to a peacetime military alliance and efforts to control events far beyond U.S. borders. Short of war, the United States could not stop the descent of the iron curtain, but it aggressively and successfully promoted economic recovery and a military shield for the rest of Europe.

Superpower Rivalry around the Globe

Efforts to implement containment moved beyond Europe. In Africa, Asia, and the Middle East, World War II accelerated a tide of national liberation movements against war-weakened **imperial** powers. By 1960, forty countries, with more than a quarter of the world's people, had won their independence. These nations came to be referred to collectively, along with Latin America, as the **third world**, a term denoting countries outside the Western (first world) and Soviet (second world) orbits that had not yet developed industrial economies.

Like Woodrow Wilson during World War I, Roosevelt and Truman promoted the ideal of self-determination. The United States granted independence to the Philippines in 1946, applauded the British withdrawal from India, and encouraged France to relinquish its empire in Indochina. At the same time, both the United States and the Soviet Union cultivated in emerging nations governments that were friendly to their own interests.

Leaders of many liberation movements, impressed with the rapid economic growth of Russia, adopted socialist or Communist ideas. Although few had formal ties with the Soviet Union, American leaders saw these movements as a threatening extension of Soviet power. Seeking to hold communism at bay by fostering economic development and political stability, the Truman administration initiated the Point IV Program in 1949, providing technical aid to developing nations. These modest amounts of aid contrasted sharply with the huge sums provided to Europe, where the administration's priorities lay.

In Asia, civil war raged in China, where the Communists, led by Mao Zedong (Mao Tse-tung), fought the official Nationalist government under Chiang Kai-shek. While the Communists gained support among the peasants for their land reforms and valiant stand against the Japanese, Chiang's corrupt and incompetent government alienated much of the population. Failing in its efforts to promote negotiations between Chiang and Mao, the United States provided almost $3 billion in aid to the Nationalists during the civil war. Yet Truman and his advisers believed that to divert further resources from Europe to China would be futile, given the ineptness of Chiang's government.

In October 1949, Mao established the People's Republic of China (PRC), and the Nationalists fled to the island of Taiwan. Fearing a U.S.-supported invasion to recapture China for the Nationalists, Mao signed a treaty with the Soviet Union in which each nation pledged to defend the other in case of attack. The United States refused to recognize the PRC, blocked its admission to the United Nations, and supported the Nationalist government in Taiwan. Only a massive U.S. military commitment could have stopped the Chinese Communists, yet some Republicans cried that Truman and "the pro-Communists in the State Department" had "lost" China. China became a political albatross for the Democrats, who resolved never again to be vulnerable to charges of being soft on communism.

With China in turmoil, the administration reconsidered its plans for postwar Japan. Initially, the U.S. military occupation had aimed to reform the Japanese government, purge militarists from official positions, and decentralize the economy. But by 1948, U.S. policy had shifted to helping Japan rapidly reindustrialize and secure access to food, markets, and natural resources in Asia. In a short time, the Japanese economy was flourishing. American soldiers remained on military bases in Japan, but the official occupation ended when the two nations signed a peace treaty and a mutual security pact in September 1951. Like West Germany, Japan now sat squarely within the American orbit, ready to serve as an economic hub in a vital area.

The one place where cold war considerations did not control American policy was Palestine. In 1943, then-Senator Harry Truman spoke passionately about Nazi Germany's annihilation of the Jews, asserting, "This is not a Jewish problem, it is an American problem—and we must . . . face it squarely and honorably." As president, he had the opportunity to make good on his words. Jews had been migrating to Palestine, their biblical homeland, since the nineteenth century, resulting in tension and hostilities with the Palestinian Arabs. After World War II, as hundreds of thousands of European Jews sought refuge and the creation of a national homeland in Palestine, fighting devolved into brutal terrorism on both sides.

Truman's foreign policy experts sought American-Arab friendship as a critical barrier against Soviet influence in the Middle East and as a means to secure access to Arabian oil. Uncharacteristically defying his advisers, the president responded instead to pleas from Jewish organizations, his moral commitment to Holocaust survivors, and his interest in the American Jewish vote for the 1948 election. When Jews in Palestine declared the state of Israel in May 1948, Truman quickly recognized the new country and made its defense the cornerstone of U.S. policy in the Middle East.

▶ **REVIEW**   Why did relations between the United States and the Soviet Union deteriorate after World War II?

Truman and the Fair Deal at Home

Referring to the Civil War general who coined the phrase "War is hell," Truman said in December 1945, "Sherman was wrong. I'm telling you I find peace is hell." Challenged by crises abroad, Truman also faced shortages, strikes, inflation, and other problems attending the reconversion of the economy to peacetime production. At the same time, he tried to expand New Deal reform with his own "Fair Deal" agenda of initiatives in civil rights, housing, education, and health care— efforts hindered by the wave of anti-Communist hysteria sweeping the country. In sharp contrast to his success with Congress in foreign policy, Truman achieved but a modest slice of his domestic agenda.

Reconverting to a Peacetime Economy

Despite scarcities and deprivations during World War II, most Americans had enjoyed a higher standard of living than ever before. Economic experts as well as ordinary citizens worried about sustaining that standard and providing jobs for millions of returning soldiers. Truman wasted no time unveiling his plan, asking Congress to enact a twenty-one-point program of social and economic reforms. He wanted to maintain the government's power to regulate the economy while it adjusted to peacetime production, and he sought government programs to provide basic essentials such as housing and health care to those in need, programs that had been on the drawing board during the New Deal. "Not even President Roosevelt ever asked for as much at one sitting," exploded Republican leader Joseph W. Martin Jr.

Congress approved only one of Truman's key proposals—full-employment legislation—and even that was watered down. The Employment Act of 1946 invested the federal government with the responsibility "to promote maximum employment, production, and purchasing power," thereby formalizing what had been implicit in Roosevelt's actions to counter the depression—government's responsibility for maintaining a healthy economy. The law created the Council of Economic Advisors to assist the president, but it authorized no new powers to translate the government's obligation into effective action.

Inflation, not unemployment, turned out to be the most severe problem in the early postwar years. Unable to buy civilian goods during the war, consumers now had $30 billion in savings that they were itching to spend. But shortages of meat, automobiles, housing, and a host of other items persisted. Housing was so scarce that some veterans lived in basements and garages, and one newspaper ran the headline SLOGAN FOR 1946: TWO FAMILIES IN EVERY GARAGE. Until industry could convert fully to civilian production and make more goods available, consumer demand would continue to drive up prices. With a basket of groceries on her arm to dramatize rising costs, Helen Gahagan Douglas urged Congress to support Truman's efforts to maintain price and rent controls. Those efforts fell, however, to pressures from business groups and others determined to curb the growth of government powers.

Labor relations were another thorn in Truman's side. Organized labor survived the war stronger than ever, its 14.5 million members making up 35 percent of the civilian workforce. Yet union members feared the erosion of wartime gains.

Women's Role in Peacetime

Like many manufacturers forced to convert to war production during World War II, Proctor Electric Company hoped to profit after the war from pent-up consumer demand. Even before the company had fully reconverted its plants, ads tempted consumers with products soon to come and asked them to be patient until Proctor could meet their needs, as this 1946 ad indicates. Picture Research Consultants & Archives.

TRYING TO CATCH UP WITH YOUR DEMANDS...*THOUSANDS OF NEW PROCTOR IRONS AND TOASTERS*

Here they come!

PROCTOR
AUTOMATIC ELECTRIC APPLIANCES

PROCTOR ELECTRIC COMPANY, DIVISION OF PROCTOR & SCHWARTZ, INC., PHILADELPHIA 40, PENNSYLVANIA

With wages frozen during the war, the rising incomes of working-class families had come from the availability of higher-paying jobs and the chance to work longer hours. The end of overtime meant a 30 percent cut in take-home pay for most workers.

Women also saw their earnings decline. Polls indicated that as many as 68 to 85 percent wanted to keep their wartime jobs, but most who remained in the workforce had to settle for relatively low-paying jobs in light industry or the service sector. Displaced from her shipyard work, Marie Schreiber took a cashier's job, lamenting, "You were back to women's wages, you know . . . practically in half." Congresswoman Douglas sponsored bills to require equal pay for equal work, to provide child care for employed mothers, and to create a government commission to study the status of women, goals supported by a number of women's organizations and women in labor unions. Nonetheless, at a time when women were viewed primarily as wives and mothers and when a strong current of opinion resisted further expansion of federal powers, these initiatives got nowhere.

Nor could women expect much from most unions, although they supported equal pay legislation. Organized labor was now engaged in an intense struggle to preserve workers' wartime gains. They turned to the weapon they had set aside during the war as five million workers went out on strike in 1946, more than at any other time in U.S. history, affecting nearly every major industry. Workers saw corporate executives profiting at their expense. Shortly before voting to strike, a former marine and the men he carpooled with calculated that a lavish party given by a company executive had cost more than they would earn in a whole year at the steel mill. "That sort of stuff made us realize, hell we had to bite the bullet . . . the bosses sure didn't give a damn for us."

Although most Americans approved of unions in principle, they became fed up with strikes, blamed unions for rising prices and shortages of consumer goods, and called for government restrictions on organized labor. Truman, too, was dismayed that wartime unity had crumbled, but he spread the blame around, writing to his mother in October 1945: "The Congress [is] balking, labor has gone crazy, and management isn't far from insane in selfishness." When the massive wave of strikes subsided at the end of 1946, workers had won wage increases of about 20 percent, but the loss of overtime along with rising prices left their purchasing power only slightly higher than in 1942.

By 1947, the nation had survived the strains associated with the reconversion of the economy from wartime to peacetime. A number of factors enabled the country to elude the postwar depression that so many had feared. Wartime profits enabled businesses to invest in new plants and equipment. Consumers could now spend their wartime savings on houses, cars, and appliances that had lain beyond their reach during the depression and war. Defense spending and the $38 billion in aid that enabled war-stricken countries to purchase American products also stimulated the economy. A soaring birthrate further sustained consumer demand. Although prosperity was far from universal, the United States entered into a remarkable economic boom that lasted through the 1960s and led to a flood of new consumer goods. (See chapter 27.)

Another economic boost came from the only large welfare measure passed after the New Deal. The Servicemen's Readjustment Act (GI Bill), enacted in 1944, offered 16 million veterans job training and education; unemployment compensation while they looked for jobs; and low-interest loans to purchase homes, farms, and small businesses. By 1948, some 1.3 million veterans had bought houses with government loans. Helping 2.2 million ex-soldiers attend college, the subsidies sparked a boom in higher education. A drugstore clerk before his military service, Don Condren was able to get an engineering degree and buy his first house. "I think the GI Bill gave the whole country an upward boost economically," he said.

Condren overlooked the disparate ways in which the GI Bill operated. Both African Americans and women found themselves unwelcome in veterans groups that provided information about the new benefits. Like key New Deal programs such as unemployment insurance and aid to mothers with dependent children, GI programs were administered at the state and local levels, which especially in the South routinely discriminated against African Americans. Black veterans who sought jobs for which the military had trained them were shuttled into menial labor. One decorated veteran pointed out that the GI Bill "draws no color line," yet "my color bars me from most decent jobs, and if, instead of accepting menial work, I collect my $20 a week readjustment allowance, I am classified as a 'lazy nigger.'" Throughout the country, African Americans were denied Veterans

Administration and Federal Housing Administration loans when they sought to buy houses in poorer neighborhoods, because government agencies had designated homes in these areas as risky investments. Thousands of black veterans did benefit from the GI Bill, but it did not help all ex-soldiers equally.

Blacks and Mexican Americans Push for Their Civil Rights

"I spent four years in the army to free a bunch of Frenchmen and Dutchmen," an African American corporal declared, "and I'm hanged if I'm going to let the Alabama version of the Germans kick me around when I get home." Black veterans as well as civilians resolved that the return to peace would not be a return to the racial injustices of prewar America. Their political clout had grown with the migration of two million African Americans to northern and western cities, where they could vote and their ballots could make a difference. Even in the South, the proportion of blacks who could vote inched up from 2 percent to 12 percent in the 1940s. Pursuing civil rights through the courts and Congress, the National Association for the Advancement of Colored People (NAACP) counted half a million members.

In the postwar years, individual African Americans broke through the color barrier, achieving several "firsts." Jackie Robinson integrated major league baseball when he played for the Brooklyn Dodgers in 1947, braving abuse from fans and players to win the Rookie of the Year Award. In 1950, Ralph J. Bunche received the Nobel Peace Prize for his United Nations work, and Gwendolyn Brooks was awarded the Pulitzer Prize for poetry. Charlie "Bird" Parker, Ella Fitzgerald, and a host of other black musicians were hugely popular across racial lines.

Still, for most African Americans, little had changed, especially in the South, where violence greeted their attempts to assert their rights. Armed white men turned back Medgar Evers (who would become a key civil rights leader in the 1960s) and four other veterans trying to vote in Mississippi. A mob lynched Isaac Nixon for voting in Georgia, and an all-white jury acquitted the men accused of his murder. In the South, governors, U.S. senators, other politicians, and local vigilantes routinely intimidated potential black voters with threats of economic retaliation and violence.

The cold war heightened American leaders' sensitivity to racial issues, as the United States and Soviet Union vied for the allegiance of newly independent nations with nonwhite populations. Soviet propaganda pointed to racial injustice in the United States, and African Americans themselves petitioned the United Nations to pressure the government on their behalf. Republican senator Henry Cabot Lodge called race relations "our Achilles' heel before the world," while Secretary of State Dean Acheson noted that "hostile reaction to [segregation and discrimination] . . . is growing in alarming proportions," endangering "our moral leadership of the free and democratic nations of the world."

Segregation

The segregation visible on this bus was a feature of life in the South from the late nineteenth century until the 1960s. State and local laws mandated separation, denying African Americans the right to facilities such as white hospitals, cemeteries, schools, libraries, swimming pools, restrooms, and drinking fountains.

Stan Wayman/Time Life Pictures/Getty Images.

"My very stomach turned over when I learned that Negro soldiers just back from overseas were being dumped out of army trucks in Mississippi and beaten," wrote Truman, shaken by the violence and under pressure to act by civil rights leaders and **liberals**. Wrestling with the Democrats' need for northern black and liberal votes as well as southern white votes, Truman acted more boldly on civil rights than any previous president. In 1946, he created the President's Committee on Civil Rights, and in February 1948 he asked Congress to enact the committee's recommendations. The first president to address the NAACP, in June 1947, Truman asserted that all Americans should have equal rights to housing, education, employment, and the ballot.

As with much of his domestic program, the president failed to act aggressively on his bold words. Congress rebuffed Truman's proposals for civil rights legislation, but eleven states outlawed discrimination in employment, and eighteen states banned discrimination in public accommodations. Running for reelection in 1948 and pressured by civil rights activists, Truman issued an executive order to desegregate the armed services, but it lay unimplemented until the Korean War. A large gap loomed between what Truman said about civil rights and what his government accomplished, yet desegregation of the military and the administration's support of civil rights cases in the Supreme Court contributed to far-reaching changes, while his Committee on Civil Rights set an agenda for years to come. Breaking with the past, Truman used his office to set a moral agenda for the nation's longest unfulfilled promise.

Although discussion of race and civil rights usually focused on African Americans, Mexican Americans endured similar injustices. In 1929, they had formed the League of United Latin-American Citizens (LULAC) to combat discrimination and segregation in the Southwest. Like black soldiers after World War II, Mexican American veterans believed, as one of them insisted, that "we had earned our credentials as American citizens. We had paid our dues. . . . We were not about to take any crap." When Mexican Americans encountered difficulties in getting their veterans' benefits, in 1948 a group in Corpus Christi, Texas, led by Dr. Héctor Peréz García, a combat surgeon who had earned the Bronze Star, formed the American GI Forum. The organization took off when the wife of Felix Longoria, who had given his life in the Philippines, was refused the use of a white funeral chapel in Three Rivers, Texas, and was told that her husband would be buried in the Mexican section of the cemetery. With the help of Senator Lyndon Johnson, the GI Forum arranged for burial in Arlington National Cemetery. It went on to become a key national organization battling discrimination against Latinos and electing sympathetic officials.

"Education is our freedom," read the GI Forum's motto, signifying the importance of learning to Mexican Americans and indirectly their dismay at the routine segregation of children in the public schools. Parents filed a class action suit in Orange County, California, winning a federal court decision in 1947 that outlawed the practice of separating Mexican American and white children in the schools. In 1948, LULAC and the GI Forum persuaded a federal court to outlaw Texas school districts' practice of segregating Mexican American students in separate schools or classes. Such projects paralleled the efforts of the NAACP on behalf of African Americans that would culminate in the *Brown* decision in 1954 (see chapter 27). These efforts, along with challenges to discrimination in employment and efforts for political representation, demonstrated a growing mobilization of Mexican Americans in the Southwest.

The Fair Deal Flounders

Republicans capitalized on public frustrations with economic reconversion in the 1946 congressional election, accusing the administration of "confusion, corruption, and communism." Helen Gahagan Douglas hung on to her seat, but the Republicans captured control of Congress for the first time in fourteen years. Many had campaigned against New Deal "bureaucracy" and "radicalism" in 1946, and they succeeded in the Eightieth Congress to weaken some reform programs and enact tax cuts favoring higher-income groups.

Organized labor took the most severe attack when Congress passed the Taft-Hartley Act over Truman's veto in 1947. Called "Tuff-Heartless" by unions, the law reduced the power of organized labor and made it more difficult to organize workers. For example, states could now pass "right-to-work" laws, which banned the practice of requiring all workers to join a union once a majority had voted for it. Many states, especially in the South and West, rushed to enact such laws, encouraging industries to relocate there. Taft-Hartley maintained the New Deal principle of government protection for **collective bargaining**, but it put the government more squarely between labor and management.

As the 1948 elections approached, Truman faced not only a resurgent Republican Party headed by its nominee, Thomas E. Dewey, but also two revolts within his own party. On the left, Henry A. Wallace, whose foreign policy views had cost him his cabinet seat, led the new Progressive Party. On the right, South Carolina governor J. Strom Thurmond headed the States' Rights Party—the Dixiecrats— formed by southern Democrats who had walked out of the 1948 Democratic Party convention when it passed a liberal civil rights plank.

Almost alone in believing he could win, Truman crisscrossed the country by train, answering supporters' cries of "Give 'em hell, Harry." So bleak were Truman's prospects that the confident Dewey ran a low-key campaign, and on election night, the *Chicago Daily Tribune* printed its next day's issue with the headline DEWEY DEFEATS TRUMAN. But Truman took 303 electoral votes to Dewey's 189, and his party regained control of Congress. His unexpected victory attested to his skills as a campaigner, broad support for his foreign policy, the enduring popularity of New Deal reform, and appreciation of the booming economy.

Truman failed to turn his victory into success for his Fair Deal agenda. Congress made modest improvements in Social Security and raised the minimum wage, but it passed only one significant reform measure. Housing was a top priority for Congresswoman Douglas, who deplored the lack of adequate shelter, especially for veterans reduced to living in "hand-me-down houses for heroes." She was a passionate advocate for the Housing Act of 1949, which authorized 810,000 units of government-constructed housing over the next six years and represented a landmark commitment by the government to address the housing needs of the poor. Yet it fell far short of actual need—just 61,000 units had been built when Truman left office—and slum clearance frequently displaced the poor without providing decent alternatives.

With southern Democrats often joining the Republicans, Congress rejected Truman's civil rights measures and proposals for a federal health care program, aid to education, and a new agriculture program to benefit small farmers and consumers. His efforts to revise immigration policy produced the McCarran-Walter Act of 1952, ending the outright ban on immigration and citizenship for Japanese and other Asians. But the law also authorized the government to bar suspected Communists and homosexuals and maintained the discriminatory quota system established in the 1920s. Truman denounced that provision as "unworthy of our traditions and our ideals," but Congress overrode his veto.

Although he blamed political opponents for defeating his Fair Deal, Truman in fact devoted much more energy to foreign policy than to his domestic proposals. Moreover, by late 1950, the Korean War embroiled the president in controversy, diverted his attention from domestic affairs, and depleted his power as a legislative leader. His failure to make good on his domestic proposals set the United States apart from most European nations, which by the 1950s had in place comprehensive health, housing, and employment security programs to underwrite the material well-being of their populations.

The Domestic Chill: McCarthyism

Truman's domestic program also suffered from a wave of anti-Communist hysteria that weakened liberal and leftist forces. Both "Red-baiting" (attempts to discredit individuals or ideas by associating them with communism) and official retaliation against leftist critics of the government had flourished during the Red scare at the end of World War I (see chapter 22). A second Red scare convulsed the nation after World War II, born of partisan political maneuvering, collapse of the Soviet-American alliance, setbacks in U.S. foreign policy, and disclosures of Soviet espionage.

Republicans who had attacked the New Deal as a plot of radicals now jumped on cold war events, such as the Soviet takeover of Eastern Europe and the Communist triumph in China, to accuse Democrats of fostering internal subversion. Wisconsin senator Joseph R. McCarthy avowed that "the Communists within our borders have been more responsible for the success of Communism abroad than Soviet Russia." McCarthy's charges—such as the allegation that retired general George C. Marshall belonged to a Communist conspiracy—were reckless and often ludicrous, but the press covered him avidly, and **McCarthyism** became a term synonymous with the anti-Communist crusade.

Revelations of Soviet espionage gave some credibility to fears of internal communism. In 1945, for example, Igor Gouzenko defected from the Soviet Embassy in Ottawa and disclosed a Soviet spy ring. In the United States, a number of ex-Communists, including Whittaker Chambers and Elizabeth Bentley, testified that they and others had provided secret documents to the Soviets. Most alarming of all, in 1950 Klaus Fuchs, a British physicist working on the atomic bomb project, confessed that he was a spy and implicated several Americans, including Ethel and Julius Rosenberg. The Rosenbergs pleaded innocent but were convicted of conspiracy to commit espionage and electrocuted in 1953.

Records opened in the 1990s showed that the Soviet Union did receive secret documents from Americans that probably hastened its development of nuclear weapons by a year or two. Yet membership in the U.S. Communist Party had declined. At the peak of the hysteria, it had only about twenty thousand members, some of them undercover FBI agents. The vast majority of individuals hunted down in the Red scare had simply at one time joined the Communist Party, associated with Communists, or supported radical causes. And most of those activities had taken place long before the cold war had made the Soviet Union an enemy. Investigators often cared little for such distinctions, however.

In Washington, investigations went on in both Congress and the executive branch. Stung by charges of communism in the 1946 midterm elections, Truman issued Executive Order 9835 in March 1947, establishing loyalty review boards throughout the government to investigate every federal employee. "A nightmare from which there [was] no awakening" was how State Department employee Esther Brunauer described it when she and her husband, a chemist in the navy, both lost their jobs because he had joined a Communist youth organization in the 1920s and associated with suspected radicals. After he left office, Truman insisted to a friend, "I wanted security with the rights of individuals protected," but government investigators violated the **Bill of Rights** by allowing anonymous informers to make charges and placing the burden of proof on the accused. More than two thousand **civil service** employees lost their jobs, and another ten thousand resigned as the program continued into the mid-1950s.

At a time when homosexuality was widely considered to be abnormal and shameful, gay men and lesbians were particularly vulnerable to charges of disloyalty. In the first four years of the loyalty program, more than four hundred suspected homosexuals were fired or resigned over charges of "sexual perversion," and this number grew as the Red scare intensified in the 1950s. Years later, Truman admitted that the loyalty program had been a mistake.

Congressional committees, such as the House Un-American Activities Committee (HUAC), often pushed executive branch officials to go after suspicious employees even more avidly, and these committees also conducted their own investigations of individuals' past and present political associations. When those under scrutiny refused to name names, investigators charged that silence was tantamount to confession, and these "unfriendly witnesses" lost their jobs and suffered public ostracism. In 1947, HUAC investigated radical activity in Hollywood. Frank Sinatra protested, wondering if someone called for "a square deal for the underdog, will they call you a Commie? . . . Are they going to scare us into silence?" Some actors and directors cooperated, but ten refused, citing their First Amendment rights. The "Hollywood Ten" served jail sentences for contempt of Congress, a punishment that Helen Gahagan Douglas fought, and found themselves blacklisted in the movie industry.

The Truman administration also went directly after the Communist Party, prosecuting its leaders under the Smith Act, passed in 1940, which made it a crime to "advocate the overthrow and destruction of the Government of the United States by force and violence." Although civil libertarians argued that the guilty verdicts violated First Amendment rights to freedom of speech, press, and association, the Supreme Court ruled in 1951 (*Dennis v. United States*) that the Communist threat overrode constitutional guarantees.

The domestic cold war spread beyond the nation's capital. State and local governments investigated citizens, demanded loyalty oaths, fired individuals suspected of disloyalty, banned books from public libraries, and more. Universities dismissed professors, and public school teachers lost their jobs in New York, Los Angeles, and elsewhere. Because the Communist Party had helped organize unions and championed racial justice, labor and civil rights activists fell prey to McCarthyism as well. As African American activist Jack O'Dell remembered, "The segregationists defended segregation by saying they weren't against . . . equal rights for blacks—they were against communism. But their interpretation of Communist was anybody who supported the right of blacks to have civil rights."

McCarthyism caused untold economic and psychological harm to individuals innocent of breaking any law. Thousands of people were humiliated and discredited, hounded from their jobs, even in some cases imprisoned. The anti-Communist crusade violated fundamental constitutional rights of freedom of speech and association, stifled expression of dissenting ideas, and removed unpopular causes from public contemplation.

▶REVIEW   Why did Truman have limited success in implementing his domestic agenda?

The Cold War Becomes Hot: Korea

The cold war erupted into a shooting war in June 1950, when troops from Communist North Korea invaded South Korea. For the first time, Americans went into battle to implement containment. Confirming the global reach of the Truman Doctrine, U.S. involvement in Korea also marked the militarization of American foreign policy. The United States, in concert with the United Nations, ultimately held the line in Korea, but at a great cost in lives, dollars, and domestic unity.

Korea and the Military Implementation of Containment

The war grew out of the artificial division of Korea after World War II as well as long-standing divisions among the Korean people. Having expelled the Japanese, who had controlled Korea since 1904, the United States and the Soviet Union created two occupation zones separated by the thirty-eighth parallel (Map 26.2, page 850). The Soviets supported the Korean Communist Party in the North, while the United States backed the Korean Democratic Party in the South. With Moscow and Washington unable to agree on a unification plan, in July 1948 the United Nations sponsored elections in South Korea. The American-favored candidate, Korean nationalist Syngman Rhee, was elected president, and the United States withdrew most of its troops. In the fall of 1948, the Soviets established the People's Republic of North Korea under Kim Il-sung and also withdrew. Although doubting that

MAP 26.2   The Korean War, 1950–1953

Although each side had plunged deep into enemy territory, the war ended in 1953 with the dividing line between North and South Korea nearly where it had been before the fighting began.

Rhee's repressive government could sustain popular support, U.S. officials appreciated his staunch anticommunism and provided small amounts of economic and military aid to South Korea.

Insurgencies of workers and peasants against factory owners, landlords, and the Rhee government claimed 100,000 lives between 1946 and mid-1950, and skirmishes between North and South Korean troops at the thirty-eighth parallel occurred beginning in 1948. In June 1950, however, the civil war turned into an international war when 90,000 North Koreans swept into South Korea. Truman's advisers immediately assumed that the Soviet Union, China, or both had instigated the attack. Revelations decades later indicated that the Russians and the Chinese had acquiesced, but with little enthusiasm. Instead, Kim Il-sung had been the main instigator. Kim wanted to bolster his position by championing Korean unification, and the substantial opposition to Rhee suggested that many South Koreans would support the North Korean army.

On June 30, six days after learning of the attack, Truman decided to intervene, viewing Korea as "the Greece of the Far East." With the Soviet Union boycotting the UN Security Council to protest its refusal to seat a representative from the People's Republic of China, the United States obtained UN sponsorship of a collective effort to repel the attack. Authorized to appoint a commander for the UN force, Truman named General Douglas MacArthur, World War II hero and head of the postwar occupation of Japan.

Sixteen nations, including many NATO allies, sent troops to Korea, but the United States furnished most of the personnel and weapons, deploying almost 1.8 million troops and dictating military strategy. By failing to ask Congress for a declaration of war, Truman violated the spirit if not the letter of the Constitution. Moreover, although Congress authorized the mobilization of troops and appropriated funds to fight the war, the president's political opponents called it "Truman's war" when the military situation worsened.

The first American soldiers rushed to Korea unprepared and ill equipped, enduring severe defeats in the first three months of the war. The North Koreans took the capital of Seoul and drove deep into South Korea, forcing UN troops to retreat to Pusan by September. General MacArthur launched a bold counteroffensive at Inchon, 180 miles behind North Korean lines. By mid-October, UN forces had pushed the North Koreans back to the thirty-eighth parallel. Then came the momentous decision of whether to invade North Korea and seek to unify the country.

From Containment to Rollback to Containment

"Troops could not be expected . . . to march up to a surveyor's line and stop," remarked Secretary of State Dean Acheson, reflecting popular and official support for transforming the military objective from containment to elimination of the enemy and unification of Korea. Thus, for the only time during the cold war, the United States tried to roll back communism. With UN approval, on September 27, 1950, Truman authorized MacArthur to cross the thirty-eighth parallel. Concerned about possible intervention by China or the Soviet Union, the president directed the general to keep UN troops away from the Korean-Chinese border. Disregarding the order, MacArthur sent UN forces to within forty miles of China. When the troops approached the Yalu River separating China from Korea, one U.S. army officer recalled, "I thought we had won the war." But 300,000 Chinese soldiers waited on the other side. They stormed across the border, helping the North Koreans recapture Seoul by December.

Under the leadership of General Matthew B. Ridgway, the Eighth Army turned the tide again. During three months of grueling battle, UN forces fought their way back to the thirty-eighth parallel. At that point, Truman decided to seek a negotiated settlement. MacArthur was furious when the goal of the war reverted to containment, which to him represented defeat. Truman and his advisers, however, adamantly opposed a wider war in Asia. According to General Omar Bradley, chairman of the Joint Chiefs of Staff, MacArthur wanted to wage "the wrong war, at the wrong place, at the wrong time, with the wrong enemy."

MacArthur took his case to the public, in effect challenging both the president's authority to conduct foreign policy and the principle of civilian control of the military. Fed up with MacArthur's insubordination, Truman fired him in April 1951. Many Americans, however, sided with MacArthur. "Quite an explosion. . . . Letters of abuse by the dozens," Truman recorded in his diary. The general came home to a hero's welcome, while baseball fans booed the president when he appeared at Washington, D.C.'s Griffith Stadium on opening day.

The adulation for MacArthur reflected American frustrations with containment. Why should Americans die simply to preserve the status quo rather than destroy the enemy once and for all? Siding with MacArthur enabled Americans to hold on to their belief that the United States was all-powerful and to pin the Korean stalemate on the government's ineptitude or willingness to shelter subversives. Moreover, Truman's earlier success in "scaring the hell" out of the country over the threat of communism in Greece and Turkey came back to haunt him. If communism was so evil, why not stamp it out as MacArthur wanted? When Congress investigated MacArthur's firing, all of the top military leaders supported the president, yet Truman never recovered from the political fallout. Nor was he able to end the war. Cease-fire negotiations began in July 1951, but peace talks dragged on for two more years while twelve thousand more U.S. soldiers died.

Korea, Communism, and the 1952 Election

Popular discontent with President Truman's war boosted Republican candidates in the 1952 election. The Republicans' presidential nominee, General Dwight D. Eisenhower, had emerged from World War II with immense popularity. Reared in modest circumstances in Abilene, Kansas, Eisenhower attended West Point and rose steadily through the army ranks. As supreme commander in Europe, he won widespread acclaim for leading the Allied armies to victory over Germany. After the war, he served as army chief of staff and then as president of Columbia University. In 1950, Truman appointed Eisenhower the first supreme commander of NATO forces.

Both Republicans and Democrats had courted Eisenhower for the presidency in 1948. Although the general believed that professional soldiers should stay out of politics, he found compelling reasons to run in 1952. Eisenhower generally agreed with Democratic foreign policy, but he deplored the Democrats' propensity to solve domestic problems with costly new federal programs. He equally disliked the foreign policy views of the leading Republican presidential contender, Senator Robert A. Taft, who attacked containment and sought to cut defense spending. Eisenhower decided to run both to stop Taft and the **conservative** wing of the Republican Party and to turn the Democrats out of the White House.

Eisenhower defeated Taft for the nomination, but the old guard prevailed on the party platform. It excoriated containment as "negative, futile, and immoral"

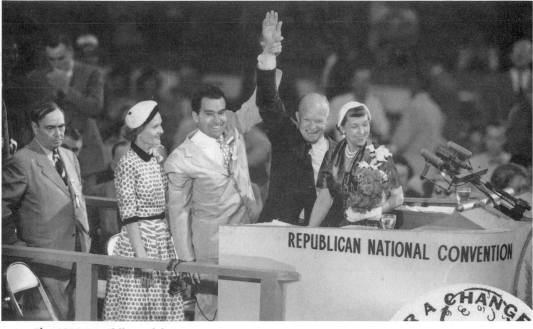

The 1952 Republican Ticket
At the Republican convention in 1952, presidential nominee Dwight D. Eisenhower stands with his wife, Mamie (right); his running mate, Richard Nixon; and Nixon's wife, Patricia (left), at the start of their campaign.
© Bettmann/Corbis.

and charged the Truman administration with shielding "traitors to the Nation in high places." By choosing thirty-nine-year-old Senator Richard M. Nixon for his running mate, Eisenhower helped to appease the right wing of the party and ensured that anticommunism would be a major theme of the campaign.

Richard Milhous Nixon grew up in southern California, worked his way through college and law school, served in the navy, and briefly practiced law. In 1946, he entered politics, helping the Republicans recapture Congress by defeating a liberal incumbent for a seat in the House of Representatives. Nixon quickly made a name for himself as a member of HUAC and a key anti-Communist, moving to the Senate with his victory over Helen Gahagan Douglas in 1950.

With his public approval ratings sinking, Truman decided not to run for reelection. The Democrats nominated Adlai E. Stevenson, the popular governor of Illinois, who was acceptable to both liberals and southerners. Stevenson could not escape the domestic fallout from the Korean War, however, nor could he match the widespread appeal of Eisenhower. While Eisenhower refrained from Red-baiting, Nixon reprised the anti-Communist tactics of his Senate campaign, calling Stevenson "Adlai the Appeaser" and saying that his opponent had a degree from the "cowardly college of Communist Containment."

The Republican campaign stumbled just once, over the last item of its "Korea, Communism, and Corruption" policy. When the press reported that Nixon had accepted money from a private political fund supported by wealthy Californians, Democrats jumped to the attack, even though such gifts were common and legal. While Eisenhower deliberated about whether to dump Nixon from the ticket, Nixon saved himself by making an emotional nationwide appeal on the new medium of television. He disclosed his finances and documented his modest standard of living. Conceding that the family pet, Checkers, could be considered an illegal gift (he had received the dog from a Texas salesman), Nixon refused to break his daughters' hearts by returning the cocker spaniel. The overwhelmingly positive response to the "Checkers speech" kept Nixon on the ticket.

Shortly before the election, Eisenhower announced dramatically, "I shall go to Korea," and voters registered their confidence in his ability to end the war. Cutting sharply into traditional Democratic territory, Eisenhower won several southern states and garnered 55 percent of the popular vote overall. His coattails carried a narrow Republican majority to Congress.

An Armistice and the War's Costs

Eisenhower made good on his pledge to end the Korean War. In July 1953, the two sides reached an armistice that left Korea divided, again roughly at the thirty-eighth parallel, with North and South separated by a two-and-one-half-mile-wide demilitarized zone (see Map 26.2). The war took the lives of 36,000 Americans and wounded more than 100,000. Nick Tosques, among thousands of U.S. soldiers who were taken prisoner, spent two and a half years in a prisoner of war camp. "They interrogated us every day," he recalled. "You never knew when they were coming for you. . . . Pretty soon I was telling them anything, just to keep from getting hit." South Korea lost more than 1 million people to war-related causes, and more than 1.8 million North Koreans and Chinese were killed or wounded.

The Truman administration judged the war a success for containment, since the United States had backed up its promise to help nations that were resisting communism. Both Truman and Eisenhower managed to contain what amounted to a world war—involving twenty nations altogether—within a single country. Moreover, despite both presidents' threats to use nuclear weapons, they authorized only conventional weapons in Korea.

The Korean War had an enormous effect on defense policy and spending. In April 1950, two months before the war began, the National Security Council completed a top-secret report on the United States' military strength. The document, known as NSC 68, warned that the survival of the nation required a massive military buildup and the tripling of the defense budget. Truman took no immediate action on these recommendations, but the Korean War brought about nearly all of the military expansion called for in NSC 68, vastly increasing U.S.

capacity to act as a global power. Using the Korean crisis to expand American clout elsewhere, Truman won congressional approval to rearm West Germany and commit troops to NATO. Military spending shot up from $14 billion in 1950 to $50 billion in 1953 and remained above $40 billion thereafter. By 1953, defense spending claimed 60 percent of the federal budget, and the size of the armed forces had tripled.

To General Matthew Ridgway, MacArthur's successor as commander of the UN forces, Korea taught the lesson that U.S. forces should never again fight a land war in Asia. Eisenhower concurred. Nevertheless, the Korean War induced the Truman administration to expand its role in Asia by increasing aid to the French, who were fighting to hang on to their colonial empire in Indochina. As U.S. marines retreated from a battle against Chinese soldiers in 1950, they sang, prophetically, "We're Harry's police force on call, / So put back your pack on, / The next step is Saigon, / Cheer up, me lads, bless 'em all."

▶ **REVIEW**   How did the Korean War shape American foreign policy in the 1950s?

Conclusion: The Cold War's Costs and Consequences

Helen Gahagan Douglas initially resisted designating the Soviet Union as an enemy and opposed the implementation of containment with aid to Greece and Turkey in 1947. By 1948, however, she had gotten behind Truman's decision to fight communism throughout the world, which marked the most momentous foreign policy initiative in the nation's history. More than any development in the postwar world, the cold war defined American politics and society for decades to come. It transformed the federal government, shifting its priorities from domestic to external affairs, greatly expanding its budget, and substantially increasing the power of the president. Military spending helped transform the nation itself, as defense contracts encouraged economic and population booms in the West and Southwest. The nuclear arms race put the people of the world at risk, consumed resources that might have been used to improve living standards, and skewed the economy toward dependence on military projects. While debate persisted about who was responsible for the cold war and whether it could have been avoided, no one could doubt its impact on American society or the world.

In sharp contrast to foreign policy, the domestic policies of the postwar years reflected continuity with the past. Most of the New Deal reforms remained in place despite Republicans' promises to turn back the clock. Helen Gahagan Douglas came to Congress hoping to expand the New Deal, to help find "a way by which all people can live out their lives in dignity and decency." She avidly supported Truman's proposals for new programs in education, health, agriculture, and civil rights, but a majority of her colleagues did not. Consequently, the poor and minorities suffered even while a majority of Americans enjoyed a higher standard of living in an economy boosted by cold war spending and the reconstruction of Western Europe and Japan.

Many Americans, not accustomed to paying sustained attention to the rest of the world or to fighting wars without total defeat of the enemy, had difficulty accepting the terms of the cold war. Consequently, another high cost of the cold war was the anti-Communist hysteria that swept the nation, costing Douglas a Senate seat and more generally stifling debate and narrowing the range of ideas acceptable for political discussion. Partisan politics and Truman's warnings about the Communist menace fueled McCarthyism, but the obsession with subversion also fed on popular frustrations over the failure of containment to produce clear-cut victories. Convulsing the nation in bitter disunity, McCarthyism reflected a loss of confidence in American power. And that frustration grew with the Korean War, which ended in stalemate rather than the defeat of communism. It would be a major challenge of the next administration to restore national unity and confidence.

REVIEWING THE CHAPTER

Use the questions and timeline to review and strengthen your understanding of the chapter.

REVIEW QUESTIONS

1. Why did relations between the United States and the Soviet Union deteriorate after World War II? (pp. 830–39)

2. Why did Truman have limited success in implementing his domestic agenda? (pp. 839–49)

3. How did the Korean War shape American foreign policy in the 1950s? (pp. 849–55)

MAKING CONNECTIONS

1. Containment shaped American actions abroad for almost half a century. Why did it become the dominant feature of American foreign policy after World War II? In your answer, discuss both proponents and opponents of the policy.

2. How did returning American servicemen change postwar domestic life in the areas of education and civil rights? In your answer, discuss how wartime experiences influenced their demands.

3. Why did anti-Communist hysteria sweep the country in the early 1950s? How did it shape domestic politics? In your answer, be sure to consider the influence of developments abroad and at home.

TIMELINE

1945	• Roosevelt dies; Vice President Harry S. Truman becomes president.
1946	• Postwar labor unrest. • President's Committee on Civil Rights created. • United States grants independence to Philippines. • Employment Act. • Republicans gain control of Congress.
1947	• George F. Kennan's article on containment policy published. • National Security Act: National Security Council (NSC) and Central Intelligence Agency (CIA) created. • Truman asks for aid to Greece and Turkey and announces Truman Doctrine. • Truman establishes loyalty program.
1948	• Congress approves Marshall Plan. • Women become permanent part of armed services. • Truman orders desegregation of armed services. • American GI Forum founded. • United States recognizes state of Israel. • Truman elected president.

1948–1949	• Berlin crisis and airlift.
1949	• Communists take over mainland China; Nationalists retreat to Taiwan. • North Atlantic Treaty Organization (NATO) formed. • Point IV technical aid program begins. • Soviet Union explodes atomic bomb.
1950	• Senator Joseph McCarthy begins to accuse U.S. government of harboring Communists. • Truman approves development of hydrogen bomb. • United States sends troops to South Korea.
1951	• Truman relieves General Douglas MacArthur of command in Korea. • United States ends occupation of Japan and signs peace treaty and mutual security pact.
1952	• Republican Dwight D. Eisenhower elected president.
1953	• Armistice halts Korean War.

▶ **For an online bibliography, practice quizzes, Web sites, images, and documents related to this chapter,** see the Book Companion Site at **bedfordstmartins.com/roark.**

▶ **For firsthand accounts of this period,** see Chapter 26 in Michael Johnson, ed., *Reading the American Past,* Fourth Edition.

27
CHAPTER

The Politics and Culture of Abundance

1952–1960

TRAILED BY REPORTERS, U.S. vice president Richard M. Nixon led Soviet premier Nikita Khrushchev through the American National Exhibition in Moscow in July 1959. The display of American consumer goods followed an exhibition of Soviet products in New York, part of a cultural exchange between the two superpowers that reflected a slight thaw in the **cold war** after Khrushchev replaced Stalin. Both Khrushchev and Nixon seized on the propaganda potential of the moment. As they made their way through the display, their verbal sparring turned into a slugfest of words and gestures that reporters dubbed the "kitchen debate."

Showing off a new color television set, Nixon said the Soviet Union "may be ahead of us . . . in the thrust of your rockets for . . . outer space," but he assured Khrushchev that the United States outstripped the Soviets in consumer goods. Nixon linked capitalism with democracy, asserting that the array of products represented "what freedom means to us . . . our right to choose." Moreover, "any steelworker could buy this house," Nixon boasted, as they walked through a six-room ranch-style model. Khrushchev retorted that in the Soviet Union, "you are entitled to housing," whereas in the United States the poor were reduced to sleeping on the pavement.

While the two men inspected appliances in the model kitchen, Nixon declared, "These are designed to make things easier for our women." Khrushchev responded that his country did not have "the capitalist attitude toward women"

The Kitchen Debate
Soviet premier Nikita Khrushchev (left) and Vice President Richard M. Nixon (center) debate the
relative merits of their nations' economies at the American National Exhibition held in Moscow
in 1959.
Howard Sochurek/TimePix/Getty.

and appreciated women's contributions to the economy, not their domesticity.
The Soviet leader found many of the items on display interesting, he said, but
added that "they are not needed in life. . . . They are merely gadgets." In reply,
Nixon insisted, "Isn't it far better to be talking about washing machines than
machines of war?" Khrushchev agreed, yet he affirmed the persistence of cold
war tensions when he later blustered, "We too are giants. You want to threaten—
we will answer threats with threats."

The Eisenhower administration (1953–1961) in fact had begun with threats to
the Soviet Union. During the 1952 campaign, Republicans had vowed to roll back
communism and liberate "enslaved" peoples under Soviet rule. In practice, however, President Dwight D. Eisenhower settled for a **containment** policy much like
that of his predecessor, Harry S. Truman, though Eisenhower relied more on
nuclear weapons and on secret actions by the Central Intelligence Agency (CIA)
against left-leaning governments. Yet, as Nixon's visit to Moscow demonstrated,
Eisenhower seized on political changes in the Soviet Union to reduce tensions in
Soviet-American relations.

Continuity with the Truman administration also characterized domestic policy. Although Eisenhower favored the business community with tax cuts and opposed strong federal efforts in health care, education, and race relations, he did not propose to roll back **New Deal** programs. He even extended the federal government with a massive highway program, and he remained immensely popular through his two terms in office. Most political leaders and experts believed that the stunning economic growth would enable the nation to overcome poverty without cost to the "haves," yet deprivation clung stubbornly to some 20 percent of the population, invisible amid the economic abundance.

The Moscow display testified to the unheard-of material gains savored by most Americans in the postwar era. Cold war weapons production spurred the economy, whose vitality stimulated suburban development, contributed to the burgeoning population and enterprise in the West and Southwest (the **Sun Belt**), and enabled millions of Americans to buy a host of new products. As new homes, television sets, and household appliances transformed their patterns of living, Americans took part in a **consumer culture** that also celebrated marriage, family, and traditional gender roles, even as more and more married women took jobs outside the home. Also challenging dominant norms were an emerging youth culture and dissenting writers known as the Beats.

The cold war and the economic boom helped African Americans mount the most dramatic movement of the 1950s, a struggle against the system of segregation and **disfranchisement** that had replaced slavery. Large numbers of African Americans took direct action against the institutions of injustice, developing the organizations, leadership, and strategies to mount a civil rights movement of unprecedented size and power.

Eisenhower and the Politics of the "Middle Way"

Moderation was the guiding principle of Eisenhower's domestic agenda and leadership style. In 1953, he pledged a "middle way between untrammeled freedom of the individual and the demands for the welfare of the whole Nation" and promised that his administration would "avoid government by bureaucracy as carefully as it avoids neglect of the helpless." Eisenhower generally resisted expanding the federal government's activities, he tried to stay on the sidelines when the Supreme Court ordered schools to desegregate, and his administration terminated the federal trusteeship of dozens of Indian tribes.

As an advocate of moderation, however, Eisenhower supported the continuation, and in some cases the expansion, of New Deal programs. He signed key legislation establishing a national highway system and enlarged the federal bureaucracy with a new Department of Health, Education, and Welfare. Nicknamed "Ike" by his friends and the public, the confident war hero remained popular throughout his presidency, but he was not able to lift the Republican Party to national dominance.

Modern Republicanism

In contrast to the old guard conservatives in his party who wanted to repeal much of the New Deal and preferred a unilateral approach to foreign policy, Eisenhower preached "modern Republicanism." This meant resisting additional federal intervention in economic and social life, but it did not mean turning the clock back to the 1920s. Democratic control of Congress after the elections of 1954 further contributed to the moderate approach of the Eisenhower administration, whose record overall maintained the course charted by Roosevelt and Truman.

The new president attempted to distance himself from the anti-Communist fervor that had plagued the Truman administration. Yet Eisenhower intensified Truman's loyalty program, allowing the head of any federal agency to dismiss an employee on grounds of loyalty, security, or "suitability." Thousands of civil servants charged with disloyalty lost their jobs. Reflecting his disinclination to involve himself in controversial issues, Eisenhower refused to denounce Senator Joseph McCarthy publicly. Instead, it was left to the senator to destroy himself.

In 1954, McCarthy tightened his own noose when he went after the army. As he hurled reckless charges of communism against military personnel during weeks of televised hearings, public opinion turned against him. When the army's lawyer demanded of McCarthy, "Have you left no sense of decency?" those in the hearing room applauded. A Senate vote to condemn McCarthy in December 1954 marked the end of his influence, but Eisenhower's inaction had allowed the senator to spread his poison longer than he might otherwise have done.

Eisenhower sometimes echoed the **conservative** Republicans' conviction that government was best left in the hands of state officials and that economic decisions were best left to private business. "If all Americans want is security, they can go to prison," Eisenhower commented about social welfare in 1949. Although **liberals** scorned the president's conservatism by calling him "Eisenhoover," the **welfare state** grew somewhat during his administration, and the federal government took on new projects. Eisenhower signed laws bringing ten million more workers into Social Security, increasing the minimum wage, and continuing the federal government's modest role in financing public housing. He enlarged the government with a new Department of Health, Education, and Welfare, naming former Women's Army Corps commander Oveta Culp Hobby to head it. (Hobby was only the second woman ever appointed to a U.S. cabinet post.) And when the spread of polio neared epidemic proportions and terrified parents, Eisenhower obtained funds from Congress to distribute a vaccine, even though conservatives preferred that states assume that responsibility.

Eisenhower's greatest domestic initiative was the Interstate Highway and Defense System Act of 1956. Promoted as essential to national defense and an impetus to economic growth, the act authorized the construction of a national highway system, with the federal government paying most of the costs through increased fuel and vehicle taxes. Road trips to new places became easier for

Americans, and goods moved more quickly around the nation. The new high-ways also spurred suburban expansion and growth in the fast-food and motel industries. And substantial gains went to the trucking, construction, and auto-mobile industries, which had lobbied hard for the law. The monumental highway project eventually exacted unforeseen costs in the form of air pollution, energy consumption, declining railroads and mass transportation in general, and decay of central cities.

In other areas, Eisenhower restrained federal activity in favor of state gov-ernments and private enterprise. His large tax cuts directed most benefits to business and the wealthy, and he stubbornly resisted national health insurance, federal aid to primary and secondary education, and White House leadership on behalf of civil rights. Moreover, whereas Democrats sought to keep nuclear power in government hands, Eisenhower signed legislation authorizing the private manufacture and sale of nuclear energy. Workers began building the first commercial nuclear power plant in Pennsylvania in 1954.

Termination and Relocation of Native Americans

Eisenhower's efforts to limit the activities of the federal government were consis-tent with a new direction in Indian policy, which reversed the emphasis on strengthening tribal governments and preserving Indian **culture** that had been established in the Indian Reorganization Act of 1934 (see chapter 24). After World War II, when some 25,000 Indians had left their homes for military service and another 40,000 for work in defense industries, policymakers began to favor assimilating Native Americans and ending their special relationships with the government.

To some officials, who reflected the cold war emphasis on conformity to dominant American values, the communal practices of Indians resembled social-ism and stifled individual initiative. Eisenhower's commissioner of Indian affairs, Glenn Emmons, expressed the pragmatic view that tribal lands could not produce income sufficient to lift Indians from poverty, but he also revealed the ethnocentrism of policymakers when he insisted that Indians wanted to "work and live like Americans."

By 1960, the government had implemented a three-part program of compen-sation, termination, and relocation. In 1946, Congress established the Indian Claims Commission to discharge outstanding claims by Native Americans for land taken by the government. When it closed in 1978, the commission had settled 285 cases, with compensation exceeding $800 million. Yet the awards were based on land values at the time the land was taken and did not include interest.

The second policy, termination, also originated in the Truman administra-tion, where Commissioner Dillon S. Myer asserted that his Bureau of Indian Affairs should "not do anything which others can do as well or better" and "nothing for Indians which Indians can do for themselves." Beginning in 1953,

Eisenhower signed bills transferring jurisdiction over tribal land to state and local governments and ending the trusteeship relationship between Indians and the federal government. The loss of federal hospitals, schools, and other special arrangements devastated Indian tribes. As had happened after passage of the Dawes Act in 1887 (see chapter 17), some corporate interests and individuals took advantage of the opportunity to purchase Indian land cheaply. An Indian leader reported that some of his people saw termination as the "severing of ties already loose and ineffective," but to the great majority, it was "like the strike of doom." The government abandoned termination in the 1960s after some 13,000 Indians and more than one million acres of their land had been affected. Decades later, the Menominee and Klamath tribes fought to reverse termination and secured restoration of their tribal status. Ada Deer led the Menominee restoration movement and later became the first Native American woman to head the Bureau of Indian Affairs.

Relocation, the third piece of Native American policy, began with a pilot program in 1948 and involved more than 100,000 Native Americans by 1973. The government encouraged Indians to move to cities and provided one-way bus tickets there. At the Indians' destinations, relocation centers were supposed to help with housing, job training, and medical care. To make it difficult to return home, government officials sent Indians far away from their reservations—South Dakota Sioux to California, for example, and Alaskan natives to Chicago. Still, about one-third of those who relocated went back to the reservation. Most who stayed in

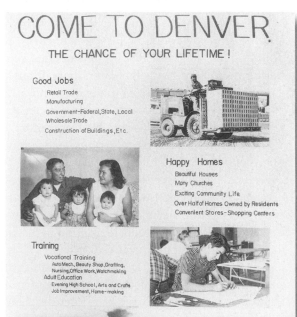

Indian Relocation

As part of its new emphasis on assimilation in the late 1940s and 1950s, the Bureau of Indian Affairs distributed this leaflet to entice Native Americans to move from their reservations to cities. Either with government assistance or on their own, thousands of Indians relocated in the years after World War II. In 1950, just 13.4 percent of Indians lived in urban areas. By 1970, 44 percent did so.

National Archives.

cities faced great difficulties: racism, lack of adequately paying jobs for which they had skills, poor housing in what became Indian ghettos, and the loss of their traditional culture. "I wish we had never left home," one woman said. "It's dirty and noisy, and people all around, crowded. . . . It seems like I never see the sky or trees." Her sons were headed for reform school, and her husband was out of work and drinking.

Reflecting long-standing disagreements among Indians themselves, some who overcame these obstacles applauded the program. One man did not mind that his grandchildren did not consider themselves Indians; he contrasted the urban jobs and educational opportunities with the reservations, where "I see no jobs, nothing to do, everyone just drinks." But most urban Indians remained in or near poverty, and even many who had welcomed relocation eventually determined that they must resist "assimilation to the degree that we would lose our identity as Indian people, lose our culture and our [way] of living." Within two decades, a national pan-Indian movement emerged to do just that and demand much more for Indians. The new militancy and connections across tribal lines that arose was a by-product of the urbanization of Native Americans (see chapter 28).

The 1956 Election and the Second Term

Not all citizens were living the American dream, but with the nation at peace and the economy booming, Eisenhower easily defeated Adlai Stevenson in 1956, doubling his margin of 1952. Yet Democrats kept control of Congress, and in the midterm elections two years later, they all but wiped out the Republican Party, gaining a 64–34 majority in the Senate and a 282–135 advantage in the House. Although Ike captured voters' hearts, a majority of Americans remained wedded to the programs and policies of the Democrats.

Eisenhower faced more serious leadership challenges in his second term. The economy plunged into a recession in late 1957, and unemployment rose to 7 percent. Eisenhower fought with Congress over the budget and vetoed bills to expand housing, urban development, and public works projects. The president and Congress did reach agreement in two key areas: enacting the first, though largely symbolic, civil rights legislation in a century and establishing a new role for the government in education.

In the end, the first Republican administration after the New Deal left the size and functions of the federal government intact, though it tipped policy some-what more in favor of corporate interests. Unparalleled prosperity graced the Eisenhower years, and inflation was kept low. The economy weathered two recessions without putting to the test the president's aversion to substantial federal intervention.

Eisenhower celebrated what he called the "wide diffusion of wealth and in-comes" across the United States. Yet neglected amid the remarkable abundance were some forty million Americans who lived below the income level designated by the government as the minimum necessary to provide a decent standard of living. Rural poverty was particularly pronounced, as was poverty among African Americans and other minorities. The widespread belief among liberals as well as conservatives that an expanding economy would end poverty was unfounded, yet it persisted because the one in five Americans who lived in deprivation were largely voiceless.

▶REVIEW   How did Eisenhower's domestic policies reflect his moderate political vision?

Liberation Rhetoric and the Practice of Containment

At his 1953 inauguration, Eisenhower warned that "forces of good and evil are massed and armed and opposed as rarely before in history." Like Truman, he saw communism as a threat to the nation's security and economic interests. Eisenhower's foreign policy differed from Truman's, however, in three areas: its rhetoric, its means, and—after Stalin's death in 1953—its movement toward accommodation with the Soviet Union.

Republican rhetoric, voiced most prominently by Secretary of State John Foster Dulles, deplored containment as "negative, futile, and immoral" because it accepted the existing Soviet sphere of control. Yet despite promises to roll back Soviet power, the Eisenhower administration continued the containment policy. The United States intervened at the margins of Communist power—in Asia, the Middle East, and Latin America—but not at its core in Europe. Eisenhower assigned nuclear weapons and CIA secret operations larger roles in defense strategy, and he took steps to ease tensions between the two superpowers.

The "New Look" in Foreign Policy

To meet his goals of balancing the budget and cutting taxes, Eisenhower was determined to control military expenditures. Moreover, he feared that massive defense spending would threaten the nation's economic strength. A state based on warfare could destroy the very society it was intended to protect. As he declared in 1953, "Every gun that is made, every warship launched, every rocket fired signifies, in the final sense, a theft from those who hunger and are not fed, those who are cold and not clothed."

Reflecting Americans' confidence in technology and opposition to a large peacetime army, Eisenhower's defense strategy concentrated U.S. military strength in nuclear weapons, along with the planes and missiles to deliver them. Instead of spending huge amounts for large ground forces of its own, the United States would give friendly nations American weapons and back them up with an ominous nuclear arsenal. This was Eisenhower's "New Look" in foreign policy.

Airpower and nuclear weapons provided, in Defense Secretary Charles Wilson's words, a "bigger bang for the buck." Secretary of State Dulles believed that America's willingness to "go to the brink" of war with its intimidating nuclear weapons—a strategy called **brinksmanship**—would block any Soviet efforts to expand.

Nuclear weapons could not stop a Soviet nuclear attack, but in response to one, they could inflict enormous destruction on the USSR. This certainty of "massive retaliation" was meant to deter the Soviets from launching an attack. Because the Soviet Union could respond similarly to an American first strike, this nuclear standoff became known as mutually assured destruction, or MAD. Winston Churchill called it a "mutual balance of terror." Yet leaders of each nation sought not just balance but nuclear superiority, and they pursued an ever-escalating arms race.

Nuclear weapons were useless, however, in rolling back the **iron curtain**, because they would destroy the very peoples whom the United States promised to liberate. When a revolt against the Soviet-controlled government began in Hungary in 1956, Dulles's liberation rhetoric proved to be empty. A radio plea from Hungarian freedom fighters cried, "SOS! They just brought us a rumor that the American troops will be here within one or two hours." But help did not come. Eisenhower was unwilling to risk U.S. soldiers and possible nuclear war, and Soviet troops soon suppressed the insurrection, killing thirty thousand Hungarians.

Applying Containment to Vietnam

A major challenge to the containment policy came in Southeast Asia. During World War II, a Vietnamese **nationalist** named Ho Chi Minh had founded a coalition called the Vietminh to fight both the occupying Japanese forces and the French colonial rulers. In 1945, the Vietminh declared Vietnam's independence from France, and when France fought to maintain its colony, the area plunged into war (see Map 29.2, page 941). Because Ho declared himself a Communist, the Truman administration quietly began to provide aid to the French. American principles of national self-determination took a backseat to the battle against communism.

Eisenhower viewed communism in Vietnam much as Truman had regarded it in Greece and Turkey, a view that became known as the **domino theory**. "You have a row of dominoes," Eisenhower explained, and "you knock over the first one, and what will happen to the last one is the certainty that it will go over very quickly." A Communist victory in Southeast Asia, he warned, could trigger the fall of Japan, Taiwan, and the Philippines. By 1954, the United States was contributing 75 percent of the cost of France's war, but Eisenhower resisted a larger role. When the French asked for troops and airplanes from the United States to avert almost certain defeat at Dien Bien Phu, Eisenhower firmly said no. Conscious of U.S. losses in the Korean War, he would not commit troops to another ground war in Asia.

Dien Bien Phu fell in May 1954 and with it the French colony of Vietnam. Two months later in Geneva, France signed a truce. The Geneva accords temporarily partitioned Vietnam at the seventeenth parallel, separating the Vietminh in the north from the puppet government established by the French in the south. Within two years, the Vietnamese people were to vote in elections for a unified government. The United States did not sign the accords but promised to support free elections.

Some officials warned against U.S. involvement in Vietnam. Defense Secretary Wilson could "see nothing but grief in store for us if we remained in that area." Eisenhower and Dulles nonetheless moved to prop up the dominoes with a new alliance. In September 1954, the United States joined with Britain, France, Australia, New Zealand, Thailand, Pakistan, and the Philippines in the Southeast Asia Treaty Organization (SEATO), committed to the defense of Cambodia, Laos, and South Vietnam. Shortly thereafter, the United States began to send weapons and military advisers to South Vietnam and put the CIA to work infiltrating and destabilizing North Vietnam. Fearing a Communist victory in the elections mandated by the Geneva accords, the United States supported South Vietnamese prime minister Ngo Dinh Diem's refusal to hold the vote.

Between 1955 and 1961, the United States provided $800 million to the South Vietnamese army (the Army of the Republic of Vietnam, or ARVN). Yet the ARVN proved grossly unprepared for the **guerrilla warfare** that began in the late 1950s. With military assistance from Ho Chi Minh's government in Hanoi, Vietminh rebels in the south stepped up their guerrilla attacks on the Diem government. The insurgents gained control over villages in part because the largely Buddhist peasants were outraged by the repressive regime of the Catholic, Westernized Diem. Unwilling to abandon containment, Eisenhower left his successor with the deteriorating situation and a firm commitment to defend South Vietnam against communism.

Interventions in Latin America and the Middle East

While trying to buttress friendly governments in Asia, the Eisenhower administration worked secretly to topple unfriendly ones in Latin America and the Middle East. Increasingly, officials saw internal civil wars in terms of the cold war conflict between the superpowers and tended to view nationalist uprisings as Communist threats to democracy. They acted against governments that not only seemed too leftist but also threatened U.S. economic interests. The Eisenhower administration took this course of action out of sight of Congress and the public, making the CIA an important arm of foreign policy in the 1950s.

The government of Guatemala, under the popularly elected reformist president Jacobo Arbenz, was not Communist or Soviet controlled, but it accepted support from the local Communist Party (see Map 29.1, page 935). In 1953, Arbenz moved to help landless, poverty-stricken peasants by nationalizing land owned but not cultivated by the United Fruit Company, a U.S. corporation whose annual profits were twice the size of the Guatemalan government's budget. United Fruit refused Arbenz's offer to compensate it at the value of the land the company had declared for tax purposes. Then, in response to the nationalization program, the CIA organized and supported an opposition army that overthrew the elected government and installed a military dictatorship in 1954. United Fruit kept its land, and Guatemala succumbed to a series of destructive civil wars that lasted through the 1990s.

When Cubans' desire for political and economic autonomy erupted in 1959, a CIA agent promised "to take care of Castro just like we took care of Arbenz." American companies had long controlled major Cuban resources—especially sugar, tobacco, and mines—and decisions made in Washington directly influenced the lives of the Cuban people. An uprising in 1959 led by Fidel Castro drove out the U.S.-supported dictator Fulgencio Batista and led the CIA to warn Eisenhower that "Communists and other extreme radicals appear to have penetrated the Castro movement." When the United States denied Castro's requests for loans, he turned to the Soviet Union. And when U.S. companies refused Castro's offer to purchase them at their assessed value, he began to nationalize their property. Many anti-Castro Cubans fled to the United States and reported his atrocities, including the execution of hundreds of Batista's supporters. Before leaving office, Eisenhower broke off diplomatic relations with Cuba and authorized the CIA to train Cuban exiles for an invasion.

In the Middle East, as in Guatemala, the CIA intervened to oust an elected government, support an unpopular dictatorship, and help American corporations (see Map 30.2, page 982). In 1951, the left-leaning prime minister of Iran, Mohammed Mossadegh, had nationalized oil fields and refineries, thereby threatening Western oil interests. While accepting support from the Iranian Communist Party, Mossadegh also challenged the power of Shah Mohammad Reza Pahlavi, Iran's hereditary leader, who favored foreign oil interests and the Iranian wealthy classes.

Eisenhower noted in his diary how important it was to keep oil-rich areas "under the control of people who are friendly . . . [or] suffer the most disastrous and doleful consequences." He authorized CIA agents to instigate a coup against Mossadegh by bribing army officers and paying Iranians to demonstrate against the government. In August 1953, Iranian army officers captured Mossadegh and reestablished the shah's power, whereupon Iran renegotiated its oil concessions, giving U.S. companies a 40 percent share. Although the intervention worked in the short run, Americans in 1979 would reap the fury of Iranian opposition to the repressive government that the United States helped reinstall. Resentment over this use of force would poison U.S.-Iranian relations into the twenty-first century.

Elsewhere in the Middle East, the Eisenhower administration continued Truman's support of Israel but also sought to foster friendships with Arab nations to secure access to oil and build a bulwark against communism. Hindering such efforts were U.S. demands that smaller nations take the American side in the cold war, even when those nations preferred neutrality and the opportunity for assistance from both Western and Communist nations. In 1955, as part of the U.S. effort to win Arab allies, Secretary of State Dulles began talks with Egypt about American support to build the Aswan Dam on the Nile River. The following year, Egypt's leader, Gamal Abdel Nasser, sought arms from Communist Czechoslovakia, formed a military alliance with other Arab nations, and recognized the People's Republic of China. Unwilling to tolerate such independence, Dulles called off the deal for the dam.

On July 26, 1956, Nasser responded by seizing the Suez Canal, then owned by Britain and France. Taking the canal advanced Nasser's prestige and power in the region because it coincided with nationalist aspirations in the Arab world and revenue from the canal could provide capital for constructing the dam. In response to the seizure, Israel, whose forces had been skirmishing with Egyptian troops along their common border since 1948, attacked Egypt with military help from Britain and France. Eisenhower opposed the intervention, recognizing that the Egyptians had claimed their own territory and that Nasser "embodie[d] the emotional demands of the people . . . for independence." He put economic pressure on Britain and France while calling on the United Nations to arrange a truce. The French and British soon pulled back, forcing Israel to retreat.

Despite staying out of the Suez crisis, Eisenhower made it clear that the United States would actively combat communism in the Middle East. In March 1957, Congress passed a joint resolution approving economic and military aid to any Middle Eastern nation "requesting assistance against armed aggression from any country controlled by international communism." The president invoked this "Eisenhower Doctrine" to send aid to Jordan in 1957 and troops to Lebanon in 1958 to counter anti-Western pressures on those governments.

The Nuclear Arms Race

While the Eisenhower administration moved against perceived Communist inroads abroad, a number of events encouraged the president to seek a reduction of superpower tensions. After Stalin's death in 1953, a more moderate leadership under Nikita Khrushchev emerged. The Soviet Union signed a peace treaty with Austria and removed its troops. Like Eisenhower, who remarked privately that the arms race would lead "at worst to atomic warfare, at best to robbing every people and nation on earth of the fruits of their own toil," Khrushchev wanted to reduce defense spending and the threat of nuclear devastation. Eisenhower and Khrushchev met in Geneva in 1955 at the first summit conference since the end of World War II. The meeting symbolized what Eisenhower called "a new spirit of conciliation and cooperation," but it produced no new agreements, and cold war competition persisted.

In August 1957, the Soviets test-fired their first intercontinental ballistic missile (ICBM) and two months later beat the United States into space by launching *Sputnik*, the first artificial satellite to circle the earth. After the first American satellite exploded—news headlines called it a "Flopnik"—the United States caught up, launching a successful satellite in January 1958. Nonetheless, *Sputnik* raised fears that the United States lagged behind the USSR not only in missile development and space exploration but also in science and education. Eisenhower insisted that the United States possessed nuclear superiority and tried to diminish public panic. He established the National Aeronautics and Space Administration (NASA) in July 1958, approved a gigantic budget increase for space research and development, and signed the National Defense Education Act, providing loans and scholarships for students in math, foreign languages, and science.

Yet even if the United States did possess nuclear superiority, it could not guarantee security, because both superpowers possessed sufficient nuclear weapons to devastate each other. Most Americans did not follow Civil Defense Administration recommendations to construct home bomb shelters, but they did realize how precarious nuclear weapons had made their lives. The Committee for a Sane Nuclear Policy, an organization founded to oppose the nuclear arms race, had 130 chapters by 1958. It ran one ad that was headlined FACING A DANGER UNLIKE ANY DANGER THAT HAS EVER EXISTED.

Even as the superpowers competed for nuclear dominance, they continued to talk. In 1959, Khrushchev visited the United States, and Nixon went to the Soviet Union, where he engaged in the famous kitchen debate. By 1960, the two sides were within reach of a ban on nuclear testing, and Khrushchev and Eisenhower agreed to meet again in Paris in May.

To avoid jeopardizing the summit, Eisenhower canceled espionage flights over the Soviet Union, but his order came one day too late. On May 1, 1960, a Soviet missile shot down a U-2 spy plane over Soviet territory. The State Department first denied that U.S. planes had been violating Soviet airspace, but the Soviets produced the pilot and the photos taken on his flight. Eisenhower and Khrushchev met briefly in Paris, but the U-2 incident dashed all prospects for a nuclear arms agreement.

Eisenhower's "more bang for the buck" defense budget enormously increased the U.S. nuclear capacity, more than quadrupling the stockpile of nuclear weapons. By the time he left office in 1961, the United States had installed ICBMs in the United States and Britain and was prepared to deploy more in Italy and Turkey. The first Polaris submarine carrying nuclear missiles was launched in November 1960.

As Eisenhower left office, he warned about the growing influence of the **military-industrial complex** in American government and life. To contain the defense budget, Eisenhower had struggled against persistent pressures from defense contractors, who, in tandem with the military, sought more dollars for newer, more powerful weapons systems. In his farewell address, he warned that the "conjunction of an immense military establishment and a large arms industry . . . exercised a total influence . . . in every city, every state house, every office of the federal government." The cold war had created a warfare state.

▶REVIEW   Where and how did Eisenhower practice containment?

New Work and Living Patterns in an Economy of Abundance

Stimulated in part by American military spending, economic productivity increased enormously in the 1950s. A multitude of new items came on the market, and consumption became the order of the day. Millions of Americans enjoyed

Poverty in an Era of Abundance
The Whiteheads, a coal-mining family in Kentucky, represented the hidden side of the affluent postwar era. Mrs. John Whitehead, shown here, lived with her husband, their six children, and their six grandchildren in this three-room house. It had neither running water nor electricity, and the only access to the house was over a mountain trail.
National Archives.

new homes in the suburbs, and higher education became the norm for the middle class. Although every section of the nation enjoyed the new abundance, the West and Southwest especially boomed in production, commerce, and population.

Work itself changed. Fewer people labored on farms, service sector employment overtook manufacturing jobs, and women's employment grew. These economic shifts disadvantaged some Americans, and they did little to help the forty million who lived in poverty. Most Americans, however, enjoyed a higher standard of living, leading economist John Kenneth Galbraith to call the United States "the affluent society."

Technology Transforms Agriculture and Industry

Between 1940 and 1960, agricultural output mushroomed while the number of farmworkers declined by almost one-third. Farmers achieved nearly miraculous productivity through greater crop specialization, more intensive use of fertilizers, and, above all, mechanization. Tractors, mechanical pickers, and other machines increasingly substituted for human and animal power. A single mechanical cotton picker replaced fifty people and cut the cost of harvesting a bale of cotton from $40 to $5.

The decline of family farms and the growth of large commercial farming, or **agribusiness**, were both causes and consequences of mechanization. Benefiting handsomely from federal price supports begun in the New Deal, larger farmers could afford technological improvements, whereas smaller producers lacked capital to invest in the machinery necessary to compete. Consequently, average farm size more than doubled between 1940 and 1964, and the number of farms fell by more than 40 percent.

Many small farmers who hung on constituted a core of rural poverty often overlooked in the celebration of affluence. Southern landowners replaced sharecroppers with machines, forcing them off the land. Hundreds of thousands of African Americans joined an exodus to cities, where racial discrimination and a lack of jobs for which they could qualify mired many in urban poverty. A Mississippi woman whose family had worked on a plantation since slavery reported that most of her relatives headed for Chicago when they heard that "it was going to be machines now that harvest the crops." Worrying that "it might be worse up there," she agonized, "I'm afraid to leave and I'm afraid to stay, and whichever I do, I think it might be real bad for my boys and girls."

New technology also increased industrial production. Between 1945 and 1960, for example, the automobile industry cut in half the number of labor-hours needed to manufacture a car. Technology also transformed industries such as electronics, chemicals, and air transportation and promoted the growth of television, plastics, computers, and other newer industries. American businesses enjoyed access to cheap oil, ample markets abroad, and little foreign competition.

Moreover, even with Eisenhower's conservative fiscal policies, government spending reached $80 billion annually and created new jobs.

Labor unions enjoyed their greatest success during the 1950s, and real earnings for production workers shot up 40 percent. The merger in 1955 of the American Federation of Labor (AFL) and the Congress of Industrial Organizations (CIO) improved labor's bargaining position. As one worker put it, "We saw continual improvement in wages, fringe benefits like holidays, vacation, medical plans . . . all sorts of things that provided more security for people." In most industrial nations, governments provided most of the benefits that underwrote workers' security, but the United States developed a mixed system in which company-funded programs won by unions through **collective bargaining** played a much larger role. This system resulted in wide disparities among workers, severely disadvantaging those not represented by unions.

While the absolute number of organized workers continued to grow, union membership peaked at 27.1 percent of the labor force in 1957. Technological advances chipped away at jobs in heavy industry, reducing the number of workers in the steel, copper, and aluminum industries by 17 percent. "You are going to have trouble collecting union dues from all of these machines," commented a Ford manager at a newly automated engine plant to union leader Walter Reuther. Moreover, the economy as a whole was shifting from production to service. Instead of making products, more workers distributed goods, performed services, kept records, provided education, or carried out government work. Unions made some headway in these fields, especially among government employees, but most service industries resisted unionization.

The growing clerical and service occupations swelled the demand for female workers. By the end of the 1950s, 35 percent of all women over age sixteen worked outside the home—twice as many as in 1940—and women held nearly one-third of all jobs. Women entered a sharply segregated workplace. The vast majority worked in clerical jobs, light manufacturing, domestic service, teaching, and nursing, and because these were female occupations, wages were relatively low. In 1960, the average full-time female worker earned just 60 percent of the average male worker's wages. At the bottom of the employment ladder, black women took home only 42 percent of what white men earned.

Burgeoning Suburbs and Declining Cities

Although suburbs had existed since the nineteenth century, nothing symbolized the affluent society more than their tremendous expansion in the 1950s. Eleven million of the thirteen million new homes built during that decade went up in the suburbs, and by 1960 one in four Americans lived there. As Nixon boasted to Khrushchev during the kitchen debate, the suburbs were accessible to families with modest incomes. Builder William J. Levitt modified the factory assembly-line process, planning nearly identical units so that individual construction workers could move from house to house and perform the same single operation in each one. In 1949, families could purchase these mass-produced houses in his 17,000-home development called Levittown, on Long Island, New York, for just under $8,000 each. Developments similar to Levittown, as well as more luxurious ones, quickly went up throughout the country.

The government underwrote home ownership with low-interest mortgage guarantees through the Federal Housing Administration and the Veterans Administration and by making interest on mortgages tax deductible. Thousands of miles of interstate highway running through urban areas indirectly subsidized suburban development. Without the automobile and the freeway, the suburban expansion could not have occurred.

The growing suburbs helped polarize society, especially along racial lines. Each Levittown homeowner signed a contract pledging not to rent or sell to a non-Caucasian. The Supreme Court declared such covenants unenforceable in 1948, but suburban America remained dramatically segregated. Levitt commented, "We can solve a housing problem, or we can try and solve a racial problem, but we cannot combine the two." Contemporary commentators pointed to other flaws of the suburbs. Social critic Lewis Mumford blasted the suburbs as "a multitude of uniform, unidentifiable houses, lined up inflexibly, at uniform distances, on uniform roads, in a treeless communal wasteland, inhabited by people of the same class, the same income, the same age group." By the 1960s, suburbs came under attack for bulldozing the natural environment, creating groundwater contamination, and disrupting wildlife patterns.

As white residents joined the suburban migration, blacks moved to cities in search of economic opportunity, increasing their numbers in most cities by 50 percent during the 1950s. Black migrants, however, came to cities that were already in decline, losing not only population but also commerce and industry to the suburbs or to southern and western states. "Detroit is in the doldrums," commented a social welfare worker, as the city lost 100,000 manufacturing jobs in the 1950s. New business facilities began to ring central cities, and shoppers gradually chose suburban malls over downtown department stores. Many of the new jobs lay beyond the reach of the recent black arrivals to the inner cities.

The Rise of the Sun Belt

Americans were on the move westward as well as to the suburbs. Architect Frank Lloyd Wright quipped, "Everything loose will land in Los Angeles." No regions experienced the postwar economic and population booms more intensely than the West and Southwest. After World War II, California's inhabitants more than doubled, and California overtook New York as the most populous state. Sports franchises followed fans: In 1958, the Brooklyn Dodgers moved to Los Angeles, joined by the Minneapolis Lakers three years later.

MAP 27.1   The Rise of the Sun Belt, 1940–1980
The growth of defense industries, a non-unionized labor force, and the spread of air-conditioning all helped spur economic development and population growth, which made the Sun Belt the fastest-growing region of the country between 1940 and 1980.

A pleasant natural environment drew new residents to the West and Southwest, but no magnet proved stronger than the promise of economic opportunity (Map 27.1). As railroads had fueled western growth in the nineteenth century, the automobile and airplane spurred the post–World War II surge. The technology of air-conditioning made possible industrial development and by 1960 cooled nearly eight million homes in the so-called Sun Belt, which stretched from Florida to California.

So important was the defense industry to the South and West that it was later referred to as the "Gun Belt." The aerospace industry boomed in Seattle–Tacoma, Los Angeles, Tucson, and Dallas–Fort Worth, and military bases helped underwrite prosperity in cities such as San Diego and San Antonio. Although defense dollars benefited other regions, the Sun Belt captured the lion's share of cold war spending for the research and production of bombers and missiles, other weapons, and satellites. By the 1960s, nearly one of every three California workers held a defense-related job.

The surging populations and industries soon raised environmental concerns. Providing sufficient water and power to cities and to agribusiness meant replacing free-flowing rivers in the West with a series of dams and reservoirs. Native Americans lost salmon fishing sites on the Columbia River, and dams on the Upper Missouri displaced nine hundred Indian families. Sprawling urban and suburban settlement without efficient public transportation contributed to blankets of smog over cities such as Los Angeles. Development began to degrade the very environment that people had come to the area to enjoy.

The high-technology basis of postwar economic development drew well-educated, highly skilled workers to the West. But the economic promise also attracted the poor. "We see opportunity all around us here. . . . We smell freedom here, and maybe soon we can taste it," commented a black mother in California. Between 1945 and 1960, more than one-third of the African Americans who left the South moved west, and more blacks moved to California than to any other state.

The Mexican American population also grew, especially in California and Texas. To supply California's vast agribusiness industry, the government continued the ***bracero* program** begun during World War II. Until the program ended in 1964, more than 100,000 Mexicans entered the United States each year to labor in the fields—and many of them stayed, legally or illegally. But permanent Mexican immigration was not as welcome as Mexicans' low-wage labor. The government launched a series of raids in 1954 called "Operation Wetback." More than one million Mexicans without documentation were deported, and the operation made U.S. citizens of Mexican descent feel unwelcome and threatened them with incidents of mistaken identity.

At the same time, Mexican American citizens gained a small victory in their ongoing struggle for civil rights in *Hernandez v. Texas*. When a Texas jury convicted Pete Hernandez of murder, lawyers from the American GI Forum and the League of United Latin-American Citizens (see chapter 26) appealed on the grounds that persons of Mexican origin had been routinely excluded from jury service. In 1954, the Supreme Court decided the first Mexican American civil rights case of the post–World War II era, ruling unanimously that Mexican Americans constituted a distinct group and that their systematic exclusion from juries violated the constitutional guarantee of equal protection.

Free of the discrimination faced by minorities, white Americans reaped the fullest fruits of prosperity in the West. In April 1950, when California developers advertised the opening of Lakewood, a large housing development in Los Angeles County, thirty thousand people lined up to purchase tract houses for $8,000 to $10,000 ($68,000 to $85,000 in 2007 dollars). Many of the new homeowners were veterans, blue-collar and lower-level white-collar workers whose defense-based jobs at McDonnell Douglas and other aerospace corporations enabled them to fulfill the American dream of the 1950s. A huge shopping mall, Lakewood Center, offered myriad products of the consumer culture. The workers' children also had access to community colleges and six state universities—all within easy reach of Lakewood.

The Democratization of Higher Education

California's university system was the most dramatic example of a spectacular transformation of higher education. Between 1940 and 1960, college enrollments in the United States leaped from 1.5 million to 3.6 million. More than 40 percent of young Americans attended college by the mid-1960s, up from 15 percent in the 1940s. More families could afford to keep their children in school longer, and the federal government subsidized the education of more than two million veterans. The cold war also sent millions of federal dollars to universities for defense-related research. Tax dollars spent on higher education more than doubled from 1950 to 1960, as state governments vastly expanded the number of public colleges and universities, and municipalities began to build two-year community colleges.

All Americans did not benefit equally from the democratization of higher education. Although the college enrollments of blacks surged from 37,000 in 1941 to 90,000 in 1961, African Americans constituted only about 5 percent of all college students, less than half their percentage of the population. Black men and women attended college in nearly equal numbers, but for a time, the educational gap between white men and women grew. Although the number of college women increased, it did not keep pace with the number of men. In 1940, women had earned 40 percent of undergraduate degrees, but as veterans flocked to college campuses, women's proportion fell to 25 percent in 1950 and rebounded to only 33 percent by 1960.

The large veteran enrollments did make the traditional student body more diverse along lines of class, age, and marital status. Colleges relaxed rules that had forbidden students to marry in order to accommodate the mature, war-tempered population. Unlike men, however, women tended to drop out of college after marriage and to take jobs so their husbands could stay in school. Reflecting gender norms of the 1950s, most college women responding to a survey agreed that "it is natural for a woman to be satisfied with her husband's success and not crave personal achievement." A decade later, many of these same women would resent their second-class status and become **feminists**.

> ▶ REVIEW   How did technology contribute to changes in the economy, suburbanization, and the growth of the Sun Belt?

The Culture of Abundance

The unprecedented prosperity of the 1950s intensified the transformation of the nation into a consumer society, changing the way Americans lived and converting the traditional work ethic into an ethic of consumption. Rising incomes enabled more people to marry earlier, the birthrate soared, and dominant values

celebrated family life and traditional gender roles. Religious observance expanded even as Americans sought satisfaction in material possessions. Television, entering the homes of most Americans, both reflected and helped promote a
consumer culture. Undercurrents of rebellion, especially among young people,
and women's increasing employment defied some of the dominant norms but
did not greatly disrupt the complacency of the 1950s.

Consumption Rules the Day

"If you grew up in the 1950s," journalist Robert Samuelson remembered, "you
were a daily witness to the marvels of affluence . . . [to] a seemingly endless
array of new gadgets and machines." Scorned by Khrushchev during the kitchen
debate as unnecessary gadgets, consumer items flooded American society in the
1950s. Although the purchase and display of consumer goods had always been
part of American life (see chapter 23), by the 1950s consumption had become
a reigning value, vital for economic prosperity and essential to individuals'
identity and status. In place of the traditional emphasis on work and savings, the
consumer culture encouraged satisfaction and happiness through the purchase
and use of new products.

The consumer culture rested on a firm material base. Between 1950 and 1960,
both the gross national product (the value of all goods and services produced
during a year) and median family income grew by 25 percent in constant dollars.
Economists claimed that 60 percent of Americans enjoyed middle-class incomes
in 1960. Referring to the popular ranch-style houses in the new suburbs, *House
Beautiful* magazine boasted, "Our houses are all on one level, like our class
structure." Though ignoring the one in five Americans who still lived in poverty,
the statement did reflect the increasing ability of people to consume products that
made class differences less visible. By 1960, four out of every five families owned
a television set, nearly all had a refrigerator, and most owned at least one car. The
number of shopping centers quadrupled between 1957 and 1963.

Several forces spurred this unparalleled abundance. A population surge—
from 152 million in 1950 to 180 million in 1960—expanded the demand for products and boosted industries ranging from housing to baby goods. Consumer
borrowing also fueled the economic boom, as people increasingly made purchases on installment plans. Diner's Club issued the first credit card in 1951, and
private debt more than doubled during the decade. In 1955, *Life* magazine noted
a "revolution in consumer purchasing." Instead of saving their money for future
purchases, Americans now bought on credit and enjoyed their possessions while
they paid for them.

Although the sheer need to support themselves and their families explained
most women's employment, a desire to secure some of the new abundance
pulled growing numbers of women out of the home. In fact, married women's
employment rose more than any other group in the 1950s. As one remarked,

"My Joe can't put five kids through college . . . and the washer had to be replaced, and Ann was ashamed to bring friends home because the living room furniture was such a mess, so I went to work." The standards for family happiness imposed by the consumer culture increasingly required a second income.

The Revival of Domesticity and Religion

Even as married women took jobs in unprecedented numbers, a dominant ideology celebrated traditional family life and conventional gender roles. Both popular culture and public figures defined the ideal family as a male breadwinner, a full-time homemaker, and three or four children in a new suburban home. The emphasis on home and family life reflected to some extent the desire for security amid anxieties about the cold war and nuclear menace. Like Nixon in the kitchen debate, one government official saw women's role in cold war terms, charging that the Soviet Union viewed women "first as a source of manpower, second as a mother," and insisting that "the highest calling of a woman's sex is the home."

Writer and feminist Betty Friedan gave a name to the idealization of women's domestic roles in the 1950s in her book *The Feminine Mystique*, published in 1963. Friedan criticized advertisers, social scientists, educators, women's magazines, and public officials for pressuring women to seek fulfillment in serving others. According to the feminine mystique that they promulgated, biological differences dictated entirely different roles for men and women. The ideal woman kept a spotless house, raised perfect children, served her husband's career, and provided him with emotional and sexual satisfaction. Not many women directly challenged the feminine mystique, but Edith Stern, a college-educated writer, maintained that "many arguments about the joys of housewifery have been advanced, largely by those who have never had to work at it."

Although the glorification of domesticity clashed with women's increasing employment, many Americans' lives did embody the family ideal. Postwar prosperity enabled people to marry earlier and to have more children. The American birthrate, in decline since the nineteenth century, soared between 1945 and 1965, peaking in 1957 with 4.3 million births and producing the "baby boom" generation. Experts such as the best-selling author Dr. Benjamin Spock encouraged mothers to devote even more attention to child rearing, while they also urged fathers to cultivate family "togetherness" by spending more time with their children.

Along with a renewed emphasis on family life, the 1950s witnessed a surge of interest in religion. By 1960, about 63 percent of Americans belonged to a church or synagogue, up from 50 percent in 1940. Polls reported that 95 percent of all Americans believed in God. Roman Catholic archbishop Fulton J. Sheen was so popular due to his books and TV shows that in 1952, he won an Emmy Award for "Most Outstanding Television Personality." Evangelism took on new life, most notably in the nationwide crusades of Baptist minister Billy Graham, whose powerful oratory moved mass audiences to accept Christ. Congress linked religion more closely to the state by adding "under God" to the pledge of allegiance in 1954 and by requiring in 1955 that "In God We Trust" be printed on all currency.

Eisenhower's pastor attributed the renewed interest in religion to the prosperous economy, which "provided the leisure, the energy, and the means for a level of human and spiritual values never before reached." Religion also calmed anxieties in the nuclear age, while ministers such as Graham made the cold war a holy war, labeling communism "a great sinister anti-Christian movement masterminded by Satan." Some critics questioned the depth of the religious revival, attributing the growth in church membership to a desire for conformity and a need for social outlets. One commentator, for example, noted that 53 percent of Americans could not name any book of the Christian Bible's New Testament.

Television Transforms Culture and Politics

Just as family life and religion offered a respite from cold war anxieties, so too did the new medium of television. In 1950, fewer than 10 percent of American homes boasted a television set, but by 1960 about 87 percent of all households owned one. On average, Americans spent more than five hours each day in front of the screen.

Viewers were especially attracted to situation comedies, which projected the family ideal and the feminine mystique into millions of homes. On TV, married women did not have paying jobs, and they deferred to their husbands, though they often got the upper hand through subtle manipulation. In the most popular television show of the early 1950s, *I Love Lucy*, the husband-and-wife team of Lucille Ball and Desi Arnaz played the couple Lucy and Ricky Ricardo. In step with the trends, they had a child and moved from an apartment in the city to a house in suburbia. Ricky would not let Lucy get a job, and many plots depicted her zany attempts to thwart his objections.

Television began to affect politics in the 1950s. Senator Joseph McCarthy's reckless attacks on army members were televised nationwide in 1954 and contributed to his downfall. Eisenhower's 1952 presidential campaign used TV ads for the first time, although he was not happy that "an old soldier should come to this." By 1960, television played a key role in election campaigns. Reflecting on his narrow victory in 1960, president-elect John F. Kennedy remarked, "We wouldn't have had a prayer without that gadget."

Television transformed politics in other ways. Money played a much larger role in elections because candidates needed to pay for expensive TV spots. The ability to appeal directly to voters in their living rooms put a premium on personal attractiveness and encouraged candidates to build their own campaign

The Made-for-TV Family

The Adventures of Ozzie and Harriet began as a radio program in the 1940s and ran on television from 1952 to 1966. Along with other family sitcoms, it idealized white family life, in which no one got divorced or became gravely ill, no one took drugs or seriously misbehaved, fathers held white-collar jobs, mothers did not work outside the home, and husbands and wives slept in twin beds. Picture Research Consultants & Archives.

organizations, relying less on political parties. The declining strength of parties and the growing power of money in elections were not new trends, but TV did much to accelerate them.

Unlike government-financed television in Europe, American TV was paid for by private enterprise. What NBC called a "selling machine in every living room" became the major vehicle for hawking the products of the affluent society and creating a consumer culture. In the mid-1950s, advertisers spent $10 billion to push their goods on TV, and they did not hesitate to interfere with shows that might jeopardize the sale of their products. The cigarette company that sponsored the *Camel News Caravan* banned any news film clips showing "No Smoking" signs. Television programs themselves, not just commercials, tantalized viewers with things to buy. On *Queen for a Day*, for example, the women with the most pitiful personal stories won fur coats, vacuum cleaners, and other merchandise prominently displaying sponsors' names.

In 1961, Newton Minow, chairman of the Federal Communications Commission, called television a "vast wasteland." While acknowledging some of TV's great achievements, particularly documentaries and drama, Minow depicted it as "a procession of game shows, . . . formula comedies about totally unbelievable families, blood and thunder, mayhem, violence, sadism, murder . . . and cartoons." But viewers kept tuning in. In little more than a decade, television came to dominate Americans' leisure time, influence their consumption patterns, and shape their perceptions of the nation's leadership.

Countercurrents

Pockets of dissent underlay the complacency of the 1950s. Some intellectuals took exception to the materialism and conformity of the era. In *The Lonely Crowd* (1950), sociologist David Riesman lamented a shift from the "inner-directed" to the "other-directed" individual. In contrast to the independent thinking that had characterized earlier Americans, Riesman found a regrettable eagerness to adapt to external standards of behavior and belief. Sharing that distaste for the importance of "belonging," William H. Whyte Jr., in his popular book *The Organization Man* (1956), blamed the modern corporation for making employees tailor themselves to the group, thus sacrificing risk taking and independence for dull conformity. Vance Packard's 1959 best seller, *The Status Seekers*, decried "the vigorous merchandising of goods as status-symbols" and argued that "class lines . . . appear to be hardening."

Implicit in much of the critique of consumer culture was concern about the loss of traditional masculinity. Consumption itself was associated with women and their presumed greater susceptibility to manipulation. Men, required to conform and get along in order to get ahead, moved farther away from the individualism and aggressiveness that had been associated with masculinity in the nineteenth century. Moreover, the increase in married women's employment compromised the male ideal of breadwinner, and experts were calling on men to spend more time with their families and practice togetherness in the domestic sphere.

Into this gender confusion came *Playboy*, which began publication in 1953 and quickly gained a circulation of one million. The new magazine idealized masculine independence in the form of bachelorhood, pitying men who were "trapped" in marriages and assaulting the reigning middle-class norms of domesticity and respectability. By associating the sophisticated bachelor with good wine, music, furnishings, and the like, the magazine made consumption more masculine. With photographs of naked young women, *Playboy* promoted sexual freedom, at least for men.

In fact, new research on Americans' sexual behavior disclosed that it often departed from the family ideal of the postwar era. Two books published by Alfred Kinsey and other researchers at Indiana University—*Sexual Behavior in the Human Male* (1948) and *Sexual Behavior in the Human Female* (1953)—uncovered a surprising range of sexual conduct. Surveying more than sixteen thousand individuals, Kinsey found that 85 percent of the men and 50 percent of the women had had sex before marriage, half of the husbands and a quarter of the wives had engaged in adultery, and one-third of the men and one-seventh of the women reported homosexual experiences.

Although Kinsey's sampling procedures later cast doubt on his ability to generalize across the population, the books became best sellers. They also drew a firestorm of outrage, especially because Kinsey insisted on the natural variability of human sexuality and refused to make moral judgments. Evangelist Billy Graham protested "the damage this book will do to the already deteriorating morals of America," and the Rockefeller Foundation stopped funding Kinsey's work.

Less direct challenges to mainstream standards appeared in the everyday behavior of young Americans. "Roll over Beethoven and tell Tchaikovsky the news!" belted out Chuck Berry in his 1956 hit record celebrating a new form of music that combined country sounds and black rhythm and blues—rock and roll. White teenagers lionized Elvis Presley, who shocked their parents with his tight pants, hip-rolling gestures, and sensuous rock-and-roll music. "Before there was Elvis . . . I started going crazy for 'race music,'" recalled a white man of his teenage years. "It had a beat. I loved it. . . . That got me into trouble with my parents and the schools." His recollection underscored African Americans' contributions to rock and roll, as well as the rebellion expressed by white youths' attraction to black music.

The most blatant revolt against conventionality came from the self-proclaimed Beat generation, a small group of primarily male literary figures based in New York City's Greenwich Village and in San Francisco. Rejecting nearly everything in mainstream culture—patriotism, consumerism, technology, conventional family life, discipline—the Beats celebrated spontaneity and absolute personal freedom, including drug consumption and freewheeling sex. In his landmark poem *Howl* (1956), Allen Ginsberg inveighed against "Robot apartments! invisible suburbs! skeleton treasuries! blind capitals! demonic industries! . . . monstrous bombs!" and denounced the social forces that "frightened me out of my natural ecstasy!" Jack Kerouac, who gave the Beat generation its name, published the best-selling novel *On the Road* (1957), whose energetic, stream-of-consciousness, bebop-style prose narrated the impetuous cross-country travels of two young men. "The only people for me," he wrote, "are the mad ones . . . desirous of everything at the same time, the ones who never yawn or say a commonplace thing, but burn, burn, burn like fabulous yellow roman candles exploding like spiders across the stars." The Beats' shocking lifestyles affronted "square" Americans, but their rebelliousness would provide a model for a much larger movement of youthful dissidents in the 1960s.

Bold new styles in the visual arts also showed the 1950s to be more than a decade of bland conventionality. An artistic revolution that flowered in New York City, known as "action painting" or "abstract expressionism," rejected the idea that painting should represent recognizable forms. Jackson Pollock and other abstract expressionists, emphasizing spontaneity, poured, dripped, and threw paint on canvases or substituted sticks and other implements for brushes. The new form of painting so captivated and redirected the Western art world that New York replaced Paris as its center.

► **REVIEW**   Why did American consumption expand so dramatically in the 1950s, and what aspects of society and culture did it influence?

Emergence of a Civil Rights Movement

Building on the civil rights initiatives begun during World War II and its after-math, African Americans posed the most dramatic challenge to the status quo of the 1950s as they sought to overcome the political and social barriers that had replaced the literal bonds of slavery. Every southern state mandated rigid segre-gation in public settings ranging from hospitals and schools to drinking fountains and restrooms. Voting laws and practices in the South disfranchised the vast majority of African Americans in that region; employment discrimina-tion kept them at the bottom of the economic ladder throughout the country.

Although black protest was as old as American racism, in the 1950s a grass-roots movement arose that attracted national attention and the support of white liberals. Pressed by civil rights groups, the Supreme Court delivered significant institutional reforms, but the most important changes of all occurred among blacks themselves. Ordinary African Americans in substantial numbers sought their own liberation, building a movement that would transform race relations in the United States.

African Americans Challenge
the Supreme Court and the President

Several factors spurred black protest in the 1950s. Between 1940 and 1960, more than three million African Americans moved from the South into areas where they could vote and exert political pressure. Black leaders made sure that for-eign policy officials realized how racist practices at home handicapped the United States in its competition with the Soviet Union for allies among newly independent nations. In the South, the very system of segregation meant that African Americans controlled certain organizational resources, such as churches and colleges, where leadership skills could be honed and networks developed.

The legal strategy of the major civil rights organization, the National Asso-ciation for the Advancement of Colored People (NAACP), reached its crowning achievement with the Supreme Court decision in *Brown v. Board of Education* in 1954. *Brown* consolidated five separate suits that reflected the growing determi-nation of black Americans to fight for their rights. Oliver Brown, a World War II veteran and welder in Topeka, Kansas, filed suit because his eight-year-old daughter had to pass by a white school just seven blocks from their home to at-tend a black school more than a mile away. In Virginia, sixteen-year-old Barbara Johns, angered at the wretched conditions in her black high school, came home one day and announced, "I walked out of school this morning and carried 450 students with me." The walkout Johns initiated resulted in another of the suits joined in *Brown*. The NAACP's lead lawyer, future Supreme Court justice

Thurgood Marshall, urged the Court to overturn the "separate but equal" precedent established in *Plessy v. Ferguson* in 1896 (see chapter 21). A unanimous Court, headed by Chief Justice Earl Warren, declared, "Separate educational facilities are inherently unequal" and thus violated the Fourteenth Amendment.

Ultimate responsibility for enforcement of the decision lay with President Eisenhower, but he refused to endorse *Brown*. He also kept silent in 1955 when whites murdered Emmett Till, a fourteen-year-old black boy who had allegedly whistled at a white woman in Mississippi. Reflecting his own racial prejudice, his preference for limited federal intervention in the states, and a leadership style that favored consensus and gradual progress, Eisenhower kept his distance from civil rights issues. Such inaction fortified southern resistance to school desegregation and contributed to the gravest constitutional crisis since the Civil War.

The crisis came in Little Rock, Arkansas, in September 1957. Local officials dutifully prepared for the integration of Central High School, but Governor Orval Faubus sent Arkansas National Guard troops to block the enrollment of nine black students, claiming that their presence would cause public disorder. Later, he agreed to allow them to enter but withdrew the National Guard, leaving the students to face an angry white mob. "During those years when we desperately needed approval from our peers," Melba Patillo Beals remembered, "we were victims of the most harsh rejection imaginable." As television cameras transmitted the ugly scene across the nation, Eisenhower was forced to send regular army troops to Little Rock, the first federal military intervention in the South since Reconstruction. Even though he took pains to explain that he had acted to preserve the law, not promote integration, southern leaders were outraged. To Georgia senator Richard Russell, the soldiers were like "Hitler's storm troops." Escorted by paratroopers, the black students stayed in school, and Eisenhower withdrew the army in November. Other southern cities avoided integration by closing public schools and using tax dollars to support private white-only schools. Seven years after *Brown*, only 6.4 percent of southern black students attended integrated schools.

Eisenhower did order the integration of public facilities in Washington, D.C., and on military bases, and he supported the first federal civil rights legislation since Reconstruction. Yet the Civil Rights Acts of 1957 and 1960 lacked effective enforcement mechanisms, a compromise to avoid a filibuster by southern senators, leaving southern blacks still unprotected in their basic rights. Baseball star Jackie Robinson spoke for many African Americans when he wired Eisenhower in 1957, "We disagree that half a loaf is better than none. Have waited this long for a bill with meaning—can wait a little longer." Eisenhower appointed the first black professional to the White House staff, E. Frederick Morrow, but Morrow confided in his diary, "I feel ridiculous . . . trying to defend the administration's record on civil rights."

Montgomery and Mass Protest

From slave revolts and individual acts of defiance through the legal and lobbying efforts of the NAACP, black protest had a long tradition. What set the civil rights movement of the 1950s and 1960s apart was the large number of people involved, their willingness to confront white institutions directly, and the use of nonviolent protest and **civil disobedience** to bring about change. The Congress of Racial Equality (CORE) and other groups had experimented with these tactics in the 1940s, and African Americans had boycotted the segregated bus system in Baton Rouge, Louisiana, in 1953, but the first sustained protest to claim national attention began in Montgomery, Alabama, on December 1, 1955.

On that day, police arrested Rosa Parks for violating a local segregation ordinance. Riding a crowded bus home from her job as a seamstress in a department store, she refused to give up her seat so that a white man could sit down. "People always say that I didn't give up my seat because I was tired, but that isn't true," Parks recalled. "I was not tired physically. . . . I was not old. . . . I was forty-two. No, the only tired I was, was tired of giving in." The bus driver called the police, who promptly arrested her.

Parks had long been active in the local NAACP, headed by E. D. Nixon. They had already talked about challenging bus segregation. So had the Women's Political Council (WPC), composed of black professional women and led by Jo Ann Robinson, an English professor at Alabama State College who had been humiliated by a bus driver when she had inadvertently sat in the white section of the bus. Such local individuals and organizations, long committed to improving conditions for African Americans, laid critical foundations for the black freedom struggle throughout the South.

When word came of Parks's arrest and decision to fight the case, WPC leaders immediately mobilized teachers and students to distribute fliers calling for Montgomery blacks to stay off the buses. E. D. Nixon called a mass meeting at the Holt Street Baptist Church, where a crowd of supporters stretched for blocks outside. Those assembled founded the Montgomery Improvement Association (MIA) to organize a bus boycott. The MIA arranged volunteer car pools and marshaled more than 90 percent of the black community to sustain the yearlong boycott.

Elected to head the MIA was twenty-six-year-old Martin Luther King Jr., the new pastor at the Dexter Avenue Baptist Church, who had a doctorate in theology from Boston University. A captivating speaker, King spoke to mass meetings at churches throughout the boycott, inspiring blacks' courage and commitment by linking racial justice to the redeeming power of Christian love. He promised, "If you will protest courageously and yet with dignity and Christian love . . . historians will have to pause and say, 'There lived a great people—a black people—who injected a new meaning and dignity into the veins of civilization.'"

Montgomery blacks summoned their courage and determination in abundance. They walked miles to get to work, contributed their meager financial

Montgomery Civil Rights Leaders
During the Montgomery bus boycott, local white officials sought to intimidate African Americans with arrests and lawsuits. Here Rosa Parks, one of ninety-two defendants, ascends the steps of the Montgomery County courthouse in March 1956, accompanied by longtime civil rights leader E. D. Nixon.
AP Images.

resources, and stood up with dignity to intimidation and police harassment. An older woman insisted, "I'm not walking for myself, I'm walking for my children and my grandchildren." Jo Ann Robinson, a cautious driver, got seventeen traffic tickets in the space of two months. Authorities arrested several leaders, and whites firebombed King's house. Yet the movement persisted until November 1956, when the Supreme Court declared unconstitutional Alabama's laws requiring bus segregation. Blacks had demonstrated that they could sustain a lengthy protest and would not be intimidated.

King's face on the cover of *Time* magazine in February 1957 marked the start of his rapid rise to national and international fame. In January, black clergy from across the South had chosen King to head the Southern Christian Leadership Conference (SCLC), newly established to coordinate local protests against segregation and disfranchisement. The prominence of King and other ministers obscured the substantial numbers and critical importance of black women in the movement. In fact, the SCLC owed much of its success to Ella Baker, a seasoned activist who came from New York to set up and run its office in Atlanta. Meanwhile, the SCLC, the NAACP, and CORE developed centers in several southern cities, paving the way for a mass movement that would revolutionize the racial system of the South.

▶ **REVIEW**   What were the goals and strategies of civil rights activists in the 1950s?

Conclusion: Peace and Prosperity Mask Unmet Challenges

At the American National Exhibition in Moscow in 1959, the consumer goods that Nixon proudly displayed to Khrushchev and the cold war competition that crackled through their dialogue reflected two dominant themes of the 1950s: the prosperity of the U.S. economy and the superpowers' success in keeping cold war competition within the bounds of peace. The tremendous economic growth of the 1950s, which raised the standard of living for most Americans, resulted in part from the cold war: One of every ten American jobs depended directly on defense spending.

Affluence changed the very landscape of the United States. Suburban housing developments sprang up, interstate highways began to divide cities and connect the country, farms declined in number but grew in size, and population and industry moved south and west. Daily habits and even values of ordinary people shifted as the economy became more service oriented, and the opportunity to buy a host of new products intensified the growth of a consumer culture.

The general prosperity and seeming conformity, however, masked a number of developments and problems that Americans would face head-on in later years: rising resistance to an unjust racial system, a 20 percent poverty rate, the movement of married women into the labor force, and the emergence of a self-conscious youth generation. Although the federal government's defense spending and housing, highway, and education subsidies played a large role in the economic boom, in general Eisenhower tried to curb domestic programs and let private enterprise have its way. His administration maintained the welfare state inherited from the Democrats but resisted substantial further reforms.

In global affairs, Eisenhower exercised restraint on large issues, recognizing the limits of U.S. power. In the name of **deterrence**, he promoted the development of more destructive atomic weapons, but he withstood pressures for even larger defense budgets. Still, Eisenhower took from Truman the assumption that the United States must fight communism everywhere, and when movements in Iran, Guatemala, Cuba, and Vietnam seemed too radical, too friendly to communism, or too inimical to American economic interests, he tried to undermine them, often with secret operations and severe consequences for native populations.

Although Eisenhower presided over eight years of peace and prosperity, his foreign policy inspired anti-Americanism, established dangerous precedents for the expansion of executive power, and forged commitments and interventions that future generations would deem unwise. As Eisenhower's successors took on the struggle against communism and grappled with the domestic challenges of race, poverty, and urban decay that he had avoided, the tranquility and consensus of the 1950s would give way to the turbulence and conflict of the 1960s.

REVIEWING THE CHAPTER

Use the questions and timeline to review and strengthen your understanding of the chapter.

REVIEW QUESTIONS

1. How did Eisenhower's domestic policies reflect his moderate political vision? (pp. 860–65)

2. Where and how did Eisenhower practice containment? (pp. 865–71)

3. How did technology contribute to changes in the economy, suburbanization, and the growth of the Sun Belt? (pp. 871–77)

4. Why did American consumption expand so dramatically in the 1950s, and what aspects of society and culture did it influence? (pp. 877–83)

5. What were the goals and strategies of civil rights activists in the 1950s? (pp. 884–88)

MAKING CONNECTIONS

1. Both President Truman and President Eisenhower perceived a grave threat in the Soviet Union and the spread of communism around the world. How did these two presidents approach foreign policy during the cold war? In your answer, consider their similarities and differences.

2. The 1950s brought significant changes to the everyday lives of many Americans. Discuss the economic and demographic changes that contributed to the growth of suburbs and the Sun Belt. How did these trends shape the culture of abundance? In your answer, consider both Americans who participated in these trends and those who did not.

3. During the 1950s, actions by the federal government and the courts had a significant impact on African Americans, Native Americans, and Mexican Americans. Discuss how new policies and court actions came about and how laws affected these groups for better and for worse.

4. Eisenhower was the first Republican president since the New Deal had transformed the federal government. How did his "modern Republicanism" address Roosevelt's legacy? How did the shape and character of government change or not change during Eisenhower's administration?

TIMELINE

1952	• Republican Dwight D. Eisenhower elected president.	**1955–1956**	• Montgomery, Alabama, bus boycott.
1953	• Termination of special status of American Indians and relocation of thousands off reservations. • CIA engineers coup against government of Iran.	**1956**	• Interstate Highway and Defense System Act. • Eisenhower reelected by landslide to second term. • *Howl* published.
1954	• CIA stages coup against government of Guatemala. • France signs Geneva accords, withdrawing from Vietnam. • United States organizes Southeast Asia Treaty Organization (SEATO) and begins aid to South Vietnam. • Government launches Operation Wetback. • Building of first commercial nuclear power plant begins. • *Hernandez v. Texas.* • *Brown v. Board of Education.* • Senate condemns Senator Joseph McCarthy.	**1957**	• Southern Christian Leadership Conference (SCLC) founded. • Soviets launch *Sputnik.* • Labor union membership peaks at 27.1 percent of labor force. • *On the Road* published.
		1958	• National Aeronautics and Space Administration (NASA) established.
		1959	• Kitchen debate between Nixon and Khrushchev.
		1960	• Soviets shoot down U.S. U-2 spy plane. • Thirty-five percent of women work outside the home. • One-quarter of Americans live in suburbs.
1955	• Eisenhower and Khrushchev meet in Geneva.		

▶ **For an online bibliography, practice quizzes, Web sites, images, and documents related to this chapter,** see the Book Companion Site at **bedfordstmartins.com/roark.**

▶ **For firsthand accounts of this period,** see Chapter 27 in Michael Johnson, ed., *Reading the American Past*, Fourth Edition.

28
CHAPTER

Reform, Rebellion, and Reaction

1960–1974

O N AUGUST 31, 1962, Fannie Lou Hamer boarded a bus carrying eighteen African Americans from Ruleville, Mississippi, to the county seat in Indianola, where they intended to register to vote. Blacks accounted for more than 60 percent of Sunflower County's population but only 1.2 percent of registered voters. Before young civil rights activists arrived in Ruleville to start a voter registration drive, Hamer recalled, "I didn't know that a Negro could register and vote." Her forty-five years of poverty, exploitation, and political **disfranchisement** typified the lives of most blacks in the rural South. The daughter of sharecroppers, Hamer began work in the cotton fields at age six, attending school in a one-room shack from December to March and only until she was twelve. She later married Perry Hamer and moved onto a plantation, where both she and her husband worked in the fields and she did domestic work for the owner and recorded the cotton that sharecroppers harvested.

At the Indianola County courthouse, Hamer and her companions had to pass through a hostile, white, gun-carrying crowd. Using a common practice to deny blacks the vote, the registrar tested Hamer on an obscure section of the state constitution, which had not been part of her schooling. She failed the test but resolved to try again. When the plantation owner ordered Hamer to withdraw her registration application or get off his land, she left the plantation. Ten days later, bullets flew into the home of friends who had taken her in. Refusing to be intimidated, she registered to vote on her third attempt, attended a civil rights leadership training conference, and began to mobilize others to vote. In 1963, she and other activists were arrested in Winona, Mississippi, and brutally beaten. Hamer went from jail to the hospital, where her sister could not recognize her battered face.

Fannie Lou Hamer's courage and determination made her a prominent figure in the black freedom struggle. Such activists shook the nation's conscience, provided a protest model for other groups, and pushed the government to enact not only civil rights legislation but also a host of other **liberal** policies. Although the federal government often tried to curb civil rights protest, the two Democratic presidents of the 1960s favored using government to ameliorate social and economic problems. After John F. Kennedy was assassinated in November 1963, Lyndon B. Johnson launched the **Great Society**—a multitude of efforts to promote racial justice, education, medical care, urban development, environmental

Mississippi Freedom Democratic Party Rally

Fannie Lou Hamer (left foreground) and other activists sing at a rally outside the Democratic National Convention in 1964, supporting the Mississippi Freedom Democratic Party (MFDP) in its challenge to the all-white delegation sent by the regular Mississippi Democratic Party. At the far right is Ella Baker, who helped organize the Southern Christian Leadership Conference.

Matt Herron/Take Stock.

and economic health, and more. Those who struggled for racial justice lost property and sometimes their lives, but by the end of the decade, American law had caught up with the American ideal of equality.

Yet legal change did not go far enough. Strong civil rights legislation and pathbreaking Supreme Court decisions did little to mitigate the deplorable economic conditions of African Americans nationwide, on which Hamer and others increasingly focused after 1965. Nor were liberal politicians consistently reliable supporters, as Hamer found out in 1964 when President Johnson and his allies rebuffed black Mississippi Democrats' efforts to be represented at the Democratic National Convention. "We followed all the laws that the white people themselves made," she said, only to find that "the white man is not going to give up his power to us. . . . We have to take [it] for ourselves." By 1966, a minority of African American activists were demanding black power; the movement soon splintered, and white support sharply declined. The war in Vietnam stifled liberal reform, while a growing number of **conservatives** protested that the Great Society went too far and condemned the challenge to American values and institutions mounted by blacks, students, and others.

Though disillusioned and often frustrated, Fannie Lou Hamer remained an activist until her death in 1977, participating in new social movements stimulated by the black freedom struggle. In 1969, she supported students at Mississippi Valley State College who demanded black studies courses and a voice in campus decisions. In 1972, she attended the first conference of the National Women's Political Caucus, established to achieve greater representation for women in government. The caucus was part of a diverse **feminist** movement that transformed women's legal status as well as the everyday relationships between women and men.

Feminists and other groups, including ethnic minorities, environmentalists, and gays and lesbians, carried the tide of reform into the 1970s. They pushed the Republican administration of Richard M. Nixon to sustain the liberalism of the 1960s, with its emphasis on a strong government role in regulating the economy, guaranteeing the welfare and rights of all individuals, and improving the quality of life. Despite its conservative rhetoric, the Nixon administration implemented school desegregation and **affirmative action** and adopted pathbreaking measures in environmental regulation, equality for women, and justice for Native Americans. The years between 1960 and 1974 contained the greatest efforts to reconcile America's promise with reality since the **New Deal**.

Liberalism at High Tide

At the Democratic National Convention in 1960, John F. Kennedy announced "a New Frontier" that would confront "unsolved problems of peace and war, unconquered pockets of ignorance and prejudice, unanswered questions of poverty and surplus." Four years later, Lyndon B. Johnson invoked the ideal of a "Great Society, [which] rests on abundance and liberty for all [and] demands an end to poverty and racial injustice."

Acting under the liberal faith that government should use its power to solve social and economic problems, end injustice, and promote the welfare of all citizens, the Democratic administrations of the 1960s won legislation on civil rights, poverty, education, medical care, housing, consumer protection, and environmental protection. These measures took up the unfulfilled agendas of the New Deal and Fair Deal, responded to new demands for rights from African Americans and other groups, and addressed new concerns growing out of the maturation of a consumer society and rapid economic growth.

The Unrealized Promise of Kennedy's New Frontier

John F. Kennedy grew up in privilege, the child of an Irish Catholic businessman who served in Franklin D. Roosevelt's administration and nourished political ambitions for his sons. Helped by a distinguished World War II navy record, Kennedy won election to the House of Representatives in 1946 and the Senate in 1952. His record in Congress was unremarkable, but with a powerful political machine, his family's fortune, and a dynamic personal appeal, Kennedy won the Democratic presidential nomination in 1960. He stunned many Democrats by choosing as his running mate Lyndon B. Johnson of Texas, a rival for the presidential nomination whom liberals disparaged as a typical southern conservative.

Kennedy defeated his Republican opponent, Vice President Richard M. Nixon, in an excruciatingly close election. African American voters contributed to his victory, helping to offset the 52 percent of the white vote cast for Nixon and contributing to Kennedy's 118,550-vote margin overall. Lyndon Johnson helped the ticket carry most of the South, and a rise in unemployment in 1960 also favored the Democrats. Finally, Kennedy benefited from the nation's first televised presidential debates, during which he appeared cool, confident, and handsome beside a nervous, sweaty, and pale Nixon.

The Kennedy administration projected energy, idealism, and glamour, although in fact Kennedy was in most ways a cautious, pragmatic politician. The first president to hold live televised press conferences, Kennedy charmed the audience with his grace, vigor, and self-mocking wit. He kept hidden from the public serious health problems and affairs with several women, making himself vulnerable to blackmail and risking the dignity of his office. Journalists turned a blind eye, instead projecting warm images of an energetic, youthful president with his chic and cultured wife, Jacqueline.

At his inauguration, the forty-three-year-old Kennedy declared that a "new generation" was assuming leadership, and he called on Americans to cast off complacency and self-indulgence and serve the common good. "Ask not what your country can do for you," he implored, "ask what you can do for your country." Although Kennedy's idealism inspired many, especially the young, he failed to redeem campaign promises to expand the **welfare state**. Two central items on the Democratic agenda since the Truman administration, federal aid for education and health care for the elderly, got nowhere. Moreover, he declined to assume leadership on behalf of racial justice until late in his term, when civil rights activists gave him no choice. But he did sign legislation making it illegal to pay women less than men for the same work (see page 921).

Moved by the desperate conditions he observed when he campaigned in Appalachia in 1960, Kennedy responded to a number of reformers concerned about rising rates of juvenile delinquency and seeking to push poverty onto the national agenda. For instance, in 1962, he read Michael Harrington's *The Other America*, which described the poverty that left more than one in five Americans "maimed in body and spirit, existing at levels beneath those necessary for human decency." By 1962, Kennedy had won support for a $2 billion urban renewal program; area redevelopment legislation that offered incentives to businesses to locate, and thereby provide jobs, in economically depressed areas; and a training program for the unemployed. In the summer of 1963, Kennedy asked aides to plan a full-scale attack on poverty, and he issued a dramatic call for a comprehensive civil rights bill, marking a turning point in his domestic agenda.

Kennedy had promised to make economic growth a key objective. "A rising tide lifts all boats" expressed his belief that economic growth could eradicate poverty and solve most social problems, as well as make the nation more competitive with the Soviet Union. Kennedy's economic advisers argued that reducing taxes would infuse money into the economy and thus increase demand, boost production, and decrease unemployment. To that end, he asked Congress to pass an enormous tax cut in 1963. This use of fiscal policy to stimulate the economy even when there was no recession was called the "new economics."

Kennedy did not live to see approval of his tax bill. Passed in February 1964, the law contributed to the greatest economic boom since World War II. Unemployment dropped to 4.1 percent, and the gross national product shot up by 7 to 9 percent annually between 1964 and 1966. Some liberal critics of the tax cut, however, pointed out that it favored those who were well-off and that economic growth alone would not eliminate poverty. They argued instead for increased spending on social programs.

Kennedy's economic efforts were in their infancy when he fell victim to an assassin's bullet on November 22, 1963. That event touched Americans as had no other since the end of World War II. Within minutes of the shooting—which occurred as Kennedy's motorcade passed through Dallas, Texas—radio and television broadcast the unfolding horror to the nation. Millions watched the return of *Air Force One* to Washington, bearing the president's coffin, his widow in her bloodstained suit, and the new president, Lyndon Baines Johnson.

Stunned Americans struggled with what had happened and why. Soon after the assassination, police arrested Lee Harvey Oswald and concluded that he had fired the shots from a nearby building. Two days later, as a television audience watched Oswald being transferred from one jail to another, a local nightclub operator, Jack Ruby, killed him. Suspicions arose that Ruby murdered Oswald to cover up a conspiracy by ultraconservative Texans who hated Kennedy, or by Communists who supported Castro's Cuba. To get at the truth, President Johnson appointed a commission headed by Chief Justice Earl Warren, which concluded in September 1964 that both Oswald and Ruby had acted alone. Although several experts pointed to errors and omissions in the report, and some contested the lone-killer explanation, most scholars agreed that no conspiracy had existed.

Debate continued over how to assess Kennedy's domestic record. It had been unremarkable in his first two years, but his proposals on taxes, civil rights, and poverty in 1963 suggested an important shift. Whether Kennedy could have persuaded Congress to enact his initiatives remained in question. In the words of journalist James Reston, "What was killed was not only the president but the promise. . . . He never reached his meridian: We saw him only as a rising sun."

Johnson Fulfills the Kennedy Promise

Lyndon B. Johnson assumed the presidency with a wealth of political experience. A self-made man from the Texas Hill Country, he had won election to the House of Representatives in 1937 and to the Senate in 1948. Although his Texas base required caution on civil rights and attention to the interests of oil and other big businesses, Johnson's growing desire for national leadership had led him to take more liberal stands. After 1955, he used his post as Senate majority leader brilliantly to force a consensus on civil rights legislation in 1957 and 1960. His own modest upbringing in an impoverished area, his admiration for Franklin Roosevelt, and his fierce ambition to outdo the New Deal president all spurred his commitment to reform. Equally compelling were external pressures generated by the black freedom struggle and the host of movements it helped inspire.

Johnson's coarse wit, extreme vanity, and Texas accent repulsed those who preferred the sophisticated Kennedy style. Lacking his predecessor's eloquence, Johnson excelled behind the scenes, where he could entice, maneuver, or threaten legislators to support his objectives. The famous "Johnson treatment" became legendary. In his ability to achieve consensus around his goals, he had few peers in American history.

"I had to take the dead man's program and turn it into a martyr's cause," Johnson declared, entreating Congress to act so that "John Fitzgerald Kennedy did not live or die in vain." He won over fiscal conservatives and signed Kennedy's tax cut bill in February 1964. Still more revolutionary was the passage

The "Johnson Treatment"
Abe Fortas, a distinguished lawyer who had argued a major criminal rights case, *Gideon v. Wainwright* (1963), before the Supreme Court, was a close friend and adviser of President Johnson. This photograph of the president and Fortas taken in July 1965 illustrates how Johnson used his body as well as his voice to bend people to his will.
Yoichi R. Okamoto/LBJ Library Collection.

of the Civil Rights Act in 1964, which Kennedy had proposed in response to the black freedom struggle. It was the strongest such measure since Reconstruction, and its passage required every ounce of Johnson's political skill to pry sufficient votes from Republicans to balance the "nays" of southern Democrats. Senate Republican leader Everett Dirksen's aide reported that Johnson "never left him alone for thirty minutes."

Antipoverty legislation followed fast on the heels of the Civil Rights Act. Johnson urged aides to "push ahead full tilt" on a poverty program that was still in an embryonic state when Kennedy died. Just two months after the president called for "an unconditional war on poverty" in his January 1964 State of the Union message, the administration rushed a draft bill to Congress, which responded with equal haste in August. The Economic Opportunity Act of 1964 authorized ten programs under the new Office of Economic Opportunity and allocated $800 million for the first year (about 1 percent of the federal budget). Many provisions targeted youths, including Head Start for preschoolers, work-study grants for college students, and the Job Corps for unemployed young people. There were also loans to businesses willing to hire the long-term unemployed; aid to small farmers; and the Volunteers in Service to America (VISTA) program, which paid modest wages to volunteers working with the disadvantaged. A legal services program provided lawyers for the poor, leading to lawsuits that enforced their rights to welfare programs.

The most novel and controversial part of the law, the Community Action Program (CAP), required "maximum feasible participation" of the poor themselves in antipoverty programs. This approach resembled the "participatory democracy" of young white and black activists and members of other social movements of the 1960s, encouraging ordinary people to challenge established leaders and institutions. Poor people began to organize local community action programs to take control of their neighborhoods and make welfare agencies, school boards, police departments, and housing authorities more accountable to the people they served.

When mayors complained that activists were causing trouble for local governments and "fostering class struggle," Johnson backed off from pushing genuine representation for the poor. Nonetheless, CAP gave people usually excluded from government an opportunity to act on their own behalf and to develop leadership skills. To a Mississippi sharecropper forced by poverty to leave school to work before he learned to read and write, a local CAP literacy program provided basic skills and self-respect. "It has meant more to me than I can express," he said. "I can now write my name and I will be able to help my younger children when they start school."

Policymaking for a Great Society

Having steered the nation through the assassination trauma and established his capacity for national leadership, Johnson projected stability and security in the midst of a booming economy. Few voters wanted to risk the dramatic change promised by his Republican opponent in the 1964 election, Arizona senator Barry M. Goldwater, who attacked the welfare state and suggested using nuclear weapons if necessary to crush **communism** in Vietnam. Although Goldwater captured five southern states, Johnson achieved a record-breaking landslide of 61 percent of the popular vote. Democrats won resounding majorities in the House (295–140) and Senate (68–32), yet, as we shall see in chapter 30, Goldwater's campaign aroused considerable grassroots support. A movement on the right grew alongside the more noticeable left and liberal movements, eventually attaining conservative ascendancy in national politics.

"I want to see a whole bunch of coonskins on the wall," Johnson told his aides, using a hunting analogy to stress his ambitious legislative goals that would usher in what he called the "Great Society." The large Democratic majorities in Congress and the political capital drawn from his landslide victory enabled Johnson to succeed mightily. He persuaded Congress to act on discrimination, poverty, education, medical care, housing, consumer and environmental protection, and more. Reporters called the legislation of the Eighty-ninth Congress (1965–1966) "a political miracle."

The Economic Opportunity Act of 1964 was the opening shot in the War on Poverty. Congress doubled the program's funding in 1965 and passed new initiatives to promote economic development. Targeting depressed regions that the general economic boom had bypassed, these measures—like the tax cut of

Reforms of the Great Society, 1964–1968

1964

Twenty-fourth Amendment	Abolishes poll tax as prerequisite for voting.
Tax Reduction Act	Provides $10 billion in tax cuts in 1964 and 1965.
Civil Rights Act	Bans discrimination in public accommodations, public education, and employment and extends protections to American Indians on reservations.
Economic Opportunity Act	Creates programs for the disadvantaged, including Head Start, VISTA, the Job Corps, and CAP.
Wilderness Preservation Act	Sets aside 9.1 million acres of national forest for protection.

1965

Elementary and Secondary Education Act	Provides $1.3 billion in aid to elementary and secondary schools.
Medical Care Act	Provides health insurance (Medicare) for all citizens age sixty-five and over. Extends federal health benefits to welfare recipients (Medicaid).
Voting Rights Act	Bans literacy tests and other voting tests and authorizes the federal government to act directly to enable African Americans to both register and vote.
Executive Order 11246	Bans discrimination on the basis of race, religion, and national origin by employers awarded government contracts and requires them to "take affirmative action to ensure equal opportunity."
Department of Housing and Urban Development (HUD)	Created to provide programs to address housing and community issues.
National Arts and Humanities Act	Creates National Endowment for the Arts (NEA) and Humanities (NEH) to support the work of artists, musicians, writers, and scholars.
Water Quality Act	Requires states to set and enforce water quality standards.
Immigration and Nationality Act	Abolishes fifty-year-old quotas based on national origins, increasing the number of non-Western and southern and eastern European immigrants.
Air Quality Act	Imposes air pollution standards for motor vehicles.
Higher Education Act	Expands federal assistance to colleges and universities.

1966

National Traffic and Motor Vehicle Safety Act	Establishes federal safety standards.
Highway Safety Act	Requires federally approved safety programs at the state level.
Department of Transportation	Created to administer transportation programs and policies.
Model Cities Act	Authorizes more than $1 billion to ameliorate the nation's slums.

1967

Executive Order 11375	Extends an earlier executive order banning discrimination and requiring affirmative action by federal contractors to cover women.

1968

Civil Rights Act of 1968	Bans discrimination in housing and jury service.
National Housing Act	Subsidizes the private construction of 1.7 million units of low-income housing.

1964—sought to help the poor indirectly by stimulating economic growth and providing jobs through road building and other public works projects. In addition, the Model Cities Act of 1966 authorized more than $1 billion to improve conditions in the nation's slums.

Other antipoverty efforts provided direct aid. A new food stamp program largely replaced the distribution of surplus commodities, giving poor people greater choice in obtaining food. Rent supplements also allowed more options, enabling some poor families to avoid public housing projects. Moreover, a movement of welfare mothers, the National Welfare Rights Organization, assisted by antipoverty lawyers, pushed administrators of Aid to Families with Dependent Children (AFDC) to ease restrictions on welfare recipients. The number of families receiving assistance jumped from less than one million in 1960 to three million by 1972, benefiting 90 percent of those eligible.

Central to Johnson's War on Poverty were efforts to equip the poor with the skills necessary to find jobs. A former schoolteacher, Johnson saw federal support for public education as a natural extension of the New Deal; it had been on the Democratic Party agenda for two decades. To Roosevelt's Four Freedoms (see chapter 25), Johnson added a fifth: "freedom from ignorance." His Elementary and Secondary Education Act of 1965 marked a turning point by involving the federal government in K–12 education. Combating poverty with federal funds, the measure sent dollars to local school districts based on the number of poor children educated therein, and it provided equipment and supplies to private and parochial schools to be used for poor children. That same year, Congress passed the Higher Education Act, vastly expanding federal assistance to colleges and universities for buildings, programs, scholarships, and low-interest student loans.

The federal government's responsibility for health care marked an even more significant watershed. Faced with a powerful medical lobby that opposed national health insurance as "socialized medicine," Johnson pared down Truman's proposed plan for government-sponsored universal care. Instead, he focused on the elderly, who constituted a large portion of the nation's poor. Congress responded with the Medicare program, providing the elderly with universal compulsory medical insurance financed largely through Social Security taxes. A separate program, Medicaid, authorized federal grants to supplement state-paid medical care for poor people.

Whereas federal aid to education, Medicare, and Medicaid fulfilled New Deal and Fair Deal promises, the Great Society's civil rights legislation represented a break with tradition and an expansion of liberalism. Racial minorities were neglected or discriminated against in such New Deal programs as old-age assistance and unemployment insurance. Moreover, Truman's call for measures to end racial discrimination bore few results. By contrast, the Civil Rights Act of 1964 made discrimination in employment, education, and public accommodations illegal. The Voting Rights Act of 1965 banned literacy tests like the one that stymied Fannie Lou Hamer and authorized federal intervention to ensure access to the voting booth.

Another form of discrimination fell with the Immigration and Nationality Act of 1965, which abolished fifty-year-old quotas based on national origins that were biased against immigrants from areas outside northern and western Europe. Signing the bill at the Statue of Liberty, Johnson proclaimed the end of "a cruel and enduring harm." The law maintained caps on the total number of immigrants and for the first time limited those from the Western Hemisphere; preference was now given to immediate relatives of U.S. citizens and to those with desirable skills. Senator Edward Kennedy predicted that "our cities will not be flooded with a million citizens annually," but the measure's unanticipated consequences did nearly that, triggering a surge of immigration near the end of the century (see chapter 31).

Great Society benefits reached well beyond victims of discrimination and the poor. Medicare, for example, covered the elderly, regardless of income. A surge of consumer activism fueled by Ralph Nader's exposé of the auto industry, *Unsafe at Any Speed* (1965), won legislation making cars safer and raising standards for the food, drug, and cosmetics industries.

Johnson himself insisted that the Great Society meet "not just the needs of the body but the desire for beauty and hunger for community" and that it enable Americans "to live the good life." In 1965, he became the first president to send Congress a special message on the environment, obtaining measures to control water and air pollution and to preserve the natural beauty of the American landscape. First Lady "Lady Bird" Johnson made beautification of the environment her primary public project. In addition, the National Arts and Humanities Act of 1965 funded artists, musicians, writers, and scholars and brought their work to public audiences.

The flood of reform legislation dwindled after 1966, when Democratic majorities in Congress diminished and a backlash against government programs arose. Some Americans expressed their opposition with buttons reading "I fight poverty—I work." The Vietnam War dealt the largest blow to Johnson's ambitions, diverting his attention from domestic affairs, spawning an antiwar movement that crippled his leadership, and devouring tax dollars that might have been used for reform (see chapter 29).

Against these odds, in 1968 Johnson pried out of Congress one more civil rights law, which banned discrimination in housing and jury service. He also signed the National Housing Act of 1968, which authorized an enormous increase in the construction of low-income housing—1.7 million units over three years—and, by leaving construction and ownership in private hands, a new way of providing it. Government-guaranteed low-interest loans spurred developers to build houses and enabled poor people to purchase those homes.

Assessing the Great Society

Measured by statistics, the reduction in poverty in the 1960s was considerable. The number of impoverished Americans fell from more than 20 percent of the population in 1959 to around 13 percent in 1968. Those who Johnson had said "lived on the outskirts of hope" gained more control of their circumstances and a sense of their right to a fairer share of America's bounty. Assessing what turned her family of longtime welfare recipients into tax-paying workers, Rosemary Bray concluded, "What fueled our dreams and fired our belief that our lives could change for the better was the promise of the civil rights movement and the war on poverty." A Mexican American beneficiary of a jobs program that trained him to be a sheet metal worker reported that his children "will finish high school and maybe go to college. . . . I see my family and I know the chains are broken."

Certain groups fared much better than others, however. Large numbers of the aged and male-headed families rose out of poverty, while the plight of female-headed families actually worsened. Whites escaped poverty at a faster rate than racial and ethnic minorities. Great Society programs contributed to a burgeoning black middle class, and the proportion of African Americans who were poor fell by 10 percentage points between 1966 and 1974. Still, one-third of them remained impoverished.

Conservative critics charged that Great Society programs discouraged initiative by giving the poor "handouts." Liberal critics claimed that the emphasis on training and education unjustly placed the responsibility for poverty on the poor themselves rather than on an economic system that could not provide enough adequately paying jobs. Most government training programs prepared graduates for low-skilled labor and could not guarantee employment. In contrast to the New Deal, the Great Society avoided structural reform of the economy and spurned public works projects as a means of providing jobs for the disadvantaged.

Who reaped the greatest advantages from Great Society programs? Programs such as Medicare and those addressing consumer safety and environmental reform benefited Americans across the board. Most of the funds for economically depressed areas built highways and thus helped the construction industry. Real estate developers, investors, and moderate-income families benefited most from the National Housing Act of 1968. Commercial development and high-income housing often relied on slum clearance programs, which displaced the poor and caused blacks to refer to urban renewal as "Negro removal." Physicians' fees and hospital costs soared after the enactment of Medicare and Medicaid, resulting in advantages for both health care providers and the elderly and poor.

Some critics argued that ending poverty required a redistribution of income—raising taxes and using those funds to create jobs, overhaul welfare systems, and rebuild slums. Great Society programs did invest more heavily in the public sector, but Johnson's efforts relied on economic growth for funding rather than on new taxes on the rich or middle class. There was no significant redistribution of income, despite large increases in subsidies for food stamps, housing, medical care, and AFDC. The poorest 20 percent of the population received 5.1 percent of total national income in 1964 and 5.4 percent in 1974. Economic prosperity allowed spending for the poor to rise and significantly improved the lives of millions, but that spending never approached the amounts necessary to claim victory in the War on Poverty.

The Judicial Revolution

A key element of liberalism's ascendancy emerged in the Supreme Court under Chief Justice Earl Warren (1953–1969). In contrast to the Progressive Era and the New Deal, when federal courts blocked reform, the Supreme Court in the 1960s proved a strong ally, often moving out in front of Congress and public opinion. Expanding the Constitution's promise of equality and individual rights, the Court's decisions supported an activist government to prevent injustice and provided new protections to disadvantaged groups and accused criminals.

Following the pathbreaking *Brown v. Board of Education* school desegregation decision of 1954 (see chapter 27), the Court ruled against all-white public facilities and struck down educational plans devised by southern states to avoid integration. In cases upholding the rights of freedom of assembly and speech, it enabled the black freedom struggle to continue sit-ins, marches, and other tactics crucial to its success. In addition, a unanimous Court in *Loving v. Virginia* (1967) struck down state laws banning interracial marriage. The justices' declaration that marriage was one of the "basic civil rights of man," a "fundamental freedom," would later be repeated by gay men and lesbians seeking the right to marry.

Chief Justice Warren considered *Baker v. Carr* (1963) his most important decision. The case grew out of a complaint that Tennessee electoral districts were drawn so inequitably that sparsely populated rural districts had far more representatives than densely populated urban areas. Using the Fourteenth Amendment guarantee of "equal protection of the laws," *Baker* established the principle of "one person, one vote" for both state legislatures and the House of Representatives. Most states had to redraw electoral districts, thus making state legislatures more responsive to metropolitan interests.

The egalitarian thrust of the Warren Court also reformed the criminal justice system as the justices used the Fourteenth Amendment to overturn a series of convictions on the grounds that the accused had been deprived of "life, liberty, or property, without due process of law." In decisions that dramatically altered law enforcement practices and the treatment of individuals accused of a crime, the Court declared that states, as well as the federal government, were subject to the **Bill of Rights**. For example, in *Gideon v. Wainwright* (1963), the Court ruled that when accused criminals could not afford to hire a lawyer, states must provide a lawyer without charge. In 1966, *Miranda v. Arizona* required police officers to inform suspects of their rights upon arrest. It also overturned convictions based on evidence obtained by unlawful arrest, by electronic surveillance, or without a search warrant.

As Supreme Court decisions overturned judicial precedents and often moved ahead of public opinion, critics accused the justices of obstructing law enforcement and letting criminals go free. The mayor of Los Angeles, for example, equated *Miranda* with "handcuffing the police." Liberals, however, argued that these rulings promoted equal treatment in the criminal justice system: The wealthy always had access to legal counsel, and practiced criminals were well aware of their right to remain silent. The beneficiaries of the decisions were the poor and the ignorant, as well as the general population, whose right to privacy was strengthened by the stricter guidelines for admissible evidence.

The Court's decisions on prayer and Bible reading in public schools provoked even greater outrage. *Abington School District v. Schempp* (1963) ruled that a Pennsylvania law requiring Bible reading and prayer in the schools violated the First Amendment principle of separation of church and state. Later decisions ruled against official prayer in public schools even if students were not required to participate. These decisions left students free to pray on their own, but an infuriated Alabama legislator complained, "They put Negroes in the schools and now they've driven God out." The Court's supporters, however, declared that the religion cases protected the rights of non-Christians and atheists.

Two or three justices who believed that the Court was overstepping its authority often issued sharp dissents. Outside the Court, opponents worked to pass laws or constitutional amendments that would upset despised decisions, and billboards demanded, "Impeach Earl Warren." Critics of the Court were part of a larger backlash mounting against Great Society liberalism. Nonetheless, the Court's major decisions withstood the test of time.

▶**REVIEW**   How did the Kennedy and Johnson administrations exemplify a liberal vision of the federal government?

The Second Reconstruction

As much as Supreme Court decisions, the black freedom struggle distinguished the liberalism of the 1960s from that of the New Deal. Before the Great Society reforms—and, in fact, contributing to them—African Americans had mobilized a movement that struck down legal separation and discrimination in the South. Whereas the first Reconstruction reflected the power of northern Republicans in the aftermath of the Civil War, the second Reconstruction depended heavily on the courage and determination of black people themselves. Sheyann Webb, one of the thousands of marchers in the 1965 Selma, Alabama, campaign for voting rights, recalled, "We were just people, ordinary people, and we did it."

The early black freedom struggle focused on legal rights in the South and won widespread acceptance. But when African Americans began to attack racial injustice in the rest of the country and to challenge the deplorable economic conditions that equal rights left untouched, a strong backlash developed as the movement itself lost cohesion.

The Flowering of the Black Freedom Struggle

The Montgomery bus boycott of 1955–1956 gave racial issues national visibility, produced a leader in Martin Luther King Jr., and demonstrated the effectiveness of mass organization. In the 1960s, protest expanded dramatically, mobilizing blacks into direct confrontation with the people and institutions that segregated and discriminated against them: retail establishments, public parks and libraries, buses and depots, voting registrars, and police forces.

Massive direct action began in February 1960, when four African American college students in Greensboro, North Carolina, requested service at the whites-only Woolworth's lunch counter. Within days, hundreds of young people joined them, and others launched sit-ins in thirty-one southern cities. At Southern Christian Leadership Conference (SCLC) headquarters, Ella Baker picked up the phone and challenged her young contacts at various colleges: "What are you going to do? It's time to move."

Baker organized a meeting of student activists in April 1960 and supported their decision to form a new organization, independent from the older generation. They founded the Student Nonviolent Coordinating Committee (SNCC, pronounced "snick") and initially embraced **civil disobedience** and the nonviolence principles of Martin Luther King Jr. Activists would directly confront their oppressors and stand up for their rights, but they would not respond if attacked. In the words of SNCC leader James Lawson, "Nonviolence nurtures the atmosphere in which reconciliation and justice become actual possibilities." Instead of the top-down leadership of King and established civil rights organizations, however, SNCC adopted a decentralized, nonhierarchical structure that fostered decision making and the development of leadership at the grassroots level.

The activists' optimism and commitment to nonviolence soon underwent severe testing. Although some cities quietly met student demands, more typically activists encountered violence. Hostile whites poured food over demonstrators, burned them with cigarettes, called them "niggers," and pelted them with rocks. Local police attacked protesters with dogs, clubs, fire hoses, and tear gas; they arrested more than 3,600 demonstrators in the year following the Greensboro sit-in.

Another wave of protest occurred in May 1961, when the Congress of Racial Equality (CORE) organized Freedom Rides to integrate interstate transportation in the South. When a group of six whites and seven blacks traveling from Washington, D.C., to New Orleans reached Alabama, whites bombed their bus and beat the riders with baseball bats so fiercely that an observer "couldn't see their faces through the blood." CORE rebuffed President Kennedy's pleas to call off the rides. But after a huge mob attacked the riders in Montgomery, Alabama, and injured a government observer, Attorney General Robert Kennedy dispatched federal marshals to restore order. Although violence against the riders abated, Freedom Riders arriving in Jackson, Mississippi, were promptly arrested, and several hundred spent part of the summer in jail. All told, more than four hundred blacks and whites participated in the Freedom Rides, which manifested the typical elements of the black freedom struggle: administration efforts to stop the protests, officials' reluctance to step in to protect demonstrators, and the steely courage of African Americans in the face of tremendous violence against them.

Encouraged by Kennedy administration officials who preferred voter registration to civil disobedience (it was more likely to benefit the Democratic Party), SNCC and other groups began the Voter Education Project in the summer of 1961. Seeking to register voters in the South, they, too, met violence. Whites bombed black churches, threw tenant farmers out of their homes, and beat and jailed activists such as Fannie Lou Hamer. In June 1963, a white man gunned down Mississippi NAACP leader Medgar Evers in front of his house in Jackson; the murderer eluded conviction until the 1990s. Similar violence met King's 1963 campaign in Birmingham, Alabama, to integrate public facilities and open jobs to blacks. The police attacked demonstrators with dogs, cattle prods, and fire hoses—brutalities that television broadcast around the world. Bombs exploded at the motel where King was staying and at his brother's house. Four months later, a bomb killed four black girls at a Birmingham Sunday school.

The largest demonstration drew 250,000 blacks and whites to the nation's capital in August 1963 in the March on Washington for Jobs and Freedom, inspired by the strategy of A. Philip Randolph in 1941 (see chapter 25). Speaking from the Lincoln Memorial, King put his indelible stamp on the day. He invoked the Bible, Negro spirituals, and patriotic anthems, drawing on all the passion and skills that made him the greatest orator of his day. "I have a dream," he repeated again and again, that "the sons of former slaves and the sons of former slave owners will be able to sit down together at the table of brotherhood." With the crowd roaring in support, he imagined the day "when all of God's children . . . will be able to join hands and sing . . . 'Free at last, free at last; thank God Almighty, we are free at last.'"

The euphoria of the March on Washington quickly faded as activists returned to continued violence in the South. In 1964, the Mississippi Freedom Summer Project mobilized more than a thousand northern black and white college students to conduct a voter registration drive. Resistance was fierce, inflamed by the sight of white activist women working alongside black men. By the end of the summer, only twelve hundred new voters had been allowed to register. Southern whites had killed several activists, beaten eighty, arrested more than a thousand, and burned thirty-five black churches. Hidden resistance came from the federal government itself, as the FBI spied on King and other leaders and expanded its activities to "expose, disrupt, misdirect, discredit, or otherwise neutralize" black protest.

Still, the movement persisted. In March 1965, Alabama state troopers used such fierce force to turn back a voting rights march from Selma to the state capitol in Montgomery that the incident earned the name "Bloody Sunday" and compelled President Johnson to call up the Alabama National Guard to protect the marchers. Before the Selma campaign was over, whites had killed three demonstrators. Battered and hospitalized on Bloody Sunday, John Lewis, chairman of SNCC (and later a congressman), managed to make the final march to the capitol, which he counted as one of his most meaningful experiences: "In October of that year the Voting Rights bill was passed and we all felt we'd had a part in it."

The Response in Washington

Civil rights leaders would have to wear sneakers, Lyndon Johnson said, if they were going to keep up with him. But both Kennedy and Johnson, reluctant to alienate crucial Democratic voters in the South and their representatives in Congress, acted less on their own initiative than in response to the black freedom struggle, moving only when events gave them little choice. Kennedy sent federal marshals to Montgomery to protect the Freedom Riders, dispatched troops to enable air force veteran James H. Meredith to enroll in the all-white University of Mississippi in 1962, and called up the Alabama National Guard during the Birmingham demonstrations. But, aware of the political costs of deploying federal force, he told activists pleading for more federal protection that law enforcement was a local matter.

In June 1963, Kennedy finally made good on his promise to seek strong antidiscrimination legislation. Pointing to the injustice suffered by blacks, Kennedy asked white Americans, "Who among us would then be content with the counsels of patience and delay?" Johnson took up Kennedy's commitment with passion, assisted by a number of factors. Scenes of violence against peaceful demonstrators appalled many television viewers across the nation. The resulting public support, the "Johnson treatment," and the president's appeal to memories of the martyred Kennedy all produced the most important civil rights law since Reconstruction.

The Civil Rights Act of 1964 guaranteed access for all Americans to public accommodations, public education, employment, and voting, thus sounding the death knell for the South's system of segregation and discrimination. The law also extended constitutional protections to Indians on reservations. Title VII of the measure, banning discrimination in employment, not only attacked racial discrimination outside the South but also outlawed job discrimination against women. Because Title VII applied to every aspect of employment, including wages, hiring, and promotion, it represented a giant step toward equal employment opportunity for white women as well as racial minorities.

Responding to black voter registration drives in the South, Johnson soon demanded legislation to remove "every remaining obstacle to the right and the opportunity to vote." In August 1965, he signed the Voting Rights Act, which empowered the federal government to intervene directly to enable African Americans to both register and vote, thereby launching a major transformation in southern politics. Implementation of the act depended on the efforts of blacks themselves, whose voting rates shot up dramatically (Map 28.1). In turn, the number of African Americans holding political office in the South increased from a handful in 1964 to more than a thousand by 1972. Gains at the local level

MAP 28.1   The Rise of the African American Vote, 1940–1976

Voting rates of southern blacks increased gradually in the 1940s and 1950s but shot up dramatically in the deep South after the Voting Rights Act of 1965 provided for federal agents to enforce African Americans' right to vote.

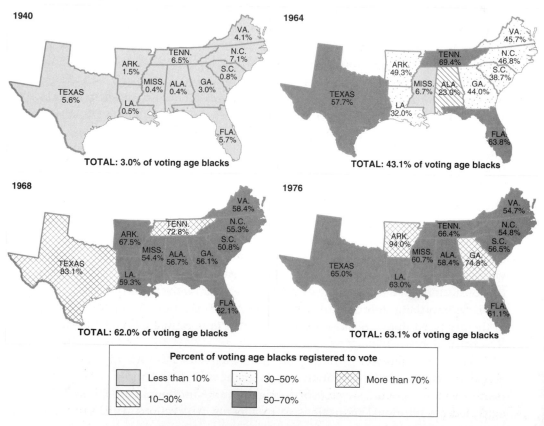

translated into tangible benefits as black officials upgraded public facilities, police protection, roads, and other basic services for their constituents.

Johnson had also declared the need "to move beyond opportunity to achievement," to realize "not just equality as a right and theory, but equality as fact and result." To this end, he issued an executive order in 1965 to require employers holding government contracts (affecting about one-third of the labor force) to take affirmative action to ensure equal opportunity. Extended to cover women in 1967, the controversial affirmative action program was called "reverse discrimination" by people who incorrectly thought that it required quotas and the hiring of unqualified candidates. In fact, it required employers to counter the effects of centuries of oppression by acting forcefully to align their labor force with the available pool of qualified candidates. Most corporations came to see affirmative action as a good employment practice.

In 1968, Johnson pried one final bill from a Congress increasingly resistant to calls for liberal reform. Opposition to civil rights outside the South had already appeared in 1963, when the California legislature passed a law banning discrimination in housing. Realtors led a repeal movement, which overturned the law in a statewide initiative and indicated that a majority of voters were more concerned with keeping the government out of their decisions to do as they pleased with their property than with the rights of minorities to be free of discrimination. And when Martin Luther King Jr. launched a campaign against de facto segregation in Chicago in 1966, demonstrators were met by jeers and stones thrown by thousands of whites. Johnson tried for two years to get a federal open-housing law, succeeding only in 1968 in the wake of King's assassination. The Civil Rights Act of 1968 banned racial discrimination in housing and jury selection and authorized federal intervention when states failed to protect civil rights workers from violence.

Black Power and Urban Rebellions

By 1966, civil rights activism had undergone dramatic changes. Black protest extended to the entire nation, demanding not just legal equality but also economic justice and no longer holding nonviolence as its basic principle. None of these developments was entirely new. Some African Americans had always armed themselves in self-defense, and even in the early 1960s, many activists doubted that demonstrators' passive suffering would change the hearts of racists. Still, the black freedom struggle began to appear more threatening to the white majority.

In part, the new emphases resulted from a combination of heightened activism and unrealized promise. Integration and legal equality did little to improve quickly the material conditions of blacks, and black rage at oppressive conditions erupted in waves of urban uprisings from 1965 to 1968. The Watts district of Los Angeles in August 1965, Newark and Detroit in July 1967, and the nation's capital in April 1968 saw the most looting and destruction of property, but violence visited hundreds of cities, usually after an incident between white police and local blacks. The Detroit riots ended in 43 deaths (30 at the hands of law enforcement officers, with most of the victims black), 7,000 arrests, and 1,300 destroyed buildings.

In the North, Malcolm X posed a powerful new challenge to the ethos of non-violence. In 1952, he went to work for the Nation of Islam, which drew on the long tradition of **black nationalism** and whose adherents called themselves Black Muslims. Calling for black pride and autonomy, separation from the "corrupt [white] society," and self-defense against white violence, Malcolm X attracted a large following, especially in urban ghettos. In 1964, he left the Nation of Islam, began to cultivate a wider constituency, and expressed an openness to working with black integrationists and with whites. At a Harlem rally in February 1965, three Black Muslims shot and killed him.

The ideas espoused by Malcolm X resonated with younger activists. At a June 1966 rally in Greenwood, Mississippi, SNCC chairman Stokely Carmichael gave those principles a new name when he shouted, "We want black power." Those words quickly became the rallying cry in SNCC and CORE, and the black power movement riveted national attention in the late 1960s. A young autoworker in Detroit enthused, "I dig what Stokely Carmichael said. . . . Whites appear to be friendly by passing a few laws, but my basic situation gets worse and worse."

Young black activists shared Fannie Lou Hamer's disillusion with white liberals, remembering how Democratic Party officials had sold out the Mississippi Freedom Democratic Party at the 1964 convention.

Carmichael called integration "a subterfuge for the maintenance of white supremacy" and rejected assimilation because it implied white superiority. African Americans were encouraged to develop independent businesses, control their own schools and communities, and form

Afro Rake

In a movement that paralleled the white counterculture in the 1960s and 1970s, young African Americans began to reject middle-class blacks' tendency to fashion their appearance after that of whites. They adopted African styles of dress and let their hair grow into a natural Afro style. African Americans used combs like this Afro rake, or pick, which makes further political statements with its clenched fist and peace symbol.

Salamandu, courtesy National Afro-American Museum and Cultural Center; Courtesy Antonio's Manufacturing Inc., Cresson, PA.

all-black political organizations. The phrase "Black is beautiful" emphasized pride in African American **culture** and connections to dark-skinned people around the world. According to black power advocates, nonviolence brought only more beatings and killings. After police killed an unarmed black teenager in San Francisco in 1966, Huey Newton and Bobby Seale organized the Black Panther Party for Self-Defense and armed its members to defend themselves against police brutality.

The press paid inordinate attention to black radicals, and the civil rights movement encountered a severe white backlash. Although the urban riots of the mid-1960s erupted spontaneously, triggered by specific incidents of police mistreatment, horrified whites blamed the riots on black power militants. By 1966, a full 85 percent of the white population—up from 34 percent two years earlier—thought that African Americans were pressing for too much too quickly. White autoworkers in St. Louis expressed their anxiety about equal opportunity for African Americans by setting a can of shoe polish next to a sign reading, "Paint your face black and you can get anything."

Agreeing with black power advocates about the need for "a radical reconstruction of society," Martin Luther King Jr. expanded the scope of the struggle. In 1965, he mounted a drive for better jobs, schools, and housing in Chicago, and in 1968 he planned a Poor People's March to Washington to seek greater antipoverty efforts. Yet he clung to nonviolence and integration as the means to this end. In April 1968, the thirty-nine-year-old leader went to Memphis to support striking municipal sanitation workers. There, on April 4, he was murdered by an escaped white convict.

Although black power organizations made most of the headlines, they failed to capture the massive support from African Americans that King and other earlier leaders had attracted. Nor could they alleviate the poverty and racism entrenched in the urban North and West. Black militants were harassed by the FBI and jailed; some encounters left both black militants and police dead. Yet black power's emphasis on racial pride and its critique of American institutions resonated loudly and helped shape the protest activities of other groups.

▶REVIEW   How did the civil rights movement change in the mid-1960s?

A Multitude of Movements

The civil rights movement's undeniable moral claims helped make protest more respectable, while its impact on public opinion and government policy encouraged other groups with grievances. Native Americans, Latinos, college students, women, gay men and lesbians, environmentalists, and others drew on the black freedom struggle for inspiration and models of activism. These groups engaged in direct-action protests, expressed their own cultural nationalism, and challenged dominant institutions and values. Like participants in the black freedom struggle, they met strong resistance, and their accomplishments fell far below their aims. Still, their grievances gained attention in the political arena, and they expanded justice and opportunity for many of their constituents.

Native American Protest

Native American activism took on fresh militancy and goals in the 1960s. The termination and relocation programs of the 1940s and 1950s, contrary to their intent, stirred Indian resistance, a sense of Indian identity across tribal lines, and a determination to preserve traditional culture. In 1961, a more militant generation of Native Americans expressed growing discontent with the government and with the older Indian leadership by forming the National Indian Youth Council (NIYC). The cry "red power" reflected the influence of black radicalism on Native Americans who rejected assimilation and sought the freedom to control their own circumstances.

Native Americans demonstrated and occupied land and public buildings, claiming rights to natural resources and territory they had owned collectively before European settlement. For example, beginning in 1963, Northwest Indians mounted "fish-ins" to enforce century-old treaty rights. In 1969, Native American militants captured world attention when several dozen seized Alcatraz Island, an abandoned federal prison in San Francisco Bay, claiming their right of "first discovery" of this land. They remained on the island for nineteen months, using the occupation to publicize injustices against Indians, promote pan-Indian cooperation, celebrate traditional cultures, and inspire other activists. One of the organizers, Dr. LaNada Boyer, a Shoshoni-Bannock Indian and the first Native American to attend the University of California, Berkeley, said of Alcatraz, "We were able to raise, not only the consciousness of other American people, but our own people as well, to reestablish our identity as Indian people, as a culture, as political entities."

In Minneapolis in 1968, two Chippewa Indians, Dennis Banks and George Mitchell, founded the American Indian Movement (AIM) to attack problems in cities, where about 300,000 Indians lived. AIM sought to protect Indians from police harassment, secure antipoverty funds, and establish "survival schools" to teach Indian history and values. The new movement's appeal quickly spread beyond urban areas and filled many Indians, especially young people, with a sense of purpose. AIM members did not have "that hangdog reservation look I was used to," Lakota activist and author Mary Crow Dog wrote, and their visit to her South Dakota reservation "loosened a sort of earthquake inside me."

AIM leaders helped organize the "Trail of Broken Treaties" caravan to the nation's capital in 1972, when some of the activists took over the Bureau of Indian

Occupation of the Bureau of Indian Affairs
The American Indian Movement (AIM) organized the "Trail of Broken Treaties" caravan to Washington, D.C., in 1972, and on November 2, hundreds of Indians occupied the Bureau of Indian Affairs. The occupiers agreed to leave after six days based on promises that the government would create a task force to study their grievances, that it would not prosecute them, and that it would finance their travels home. The demonstrators failed to win their demands but gained attention for their cause.
© Bettmann/Corbis.

Affairs to express their outrage at the bureau's paternalism, policies, and bureaucratic interference in Indians' lives. In 1973, a much longer siege occurred on the Lakota Sioux reservation in South Dakota. Conflicts there between AIM militants and older tribal leaders led AIM to take over for seventy-two days the village of Wounded Knee, where U.S. troops had massacred more than one hundred Sioux Indians in 1890.

Although these dramatic occupations failed to achieve their specific goals, Indians won the end of relocation and termination policies; greater tribal sovereignty and control over community services; enhanced health, education, and other services; and protection of Indian religious practices. A number of laws and court decisions restored rights to ancestral lands or compensated tribes for land seized in violation of treaties. Native Americans recovered a measure of respect and pride. In a special message on the "Forgotten American" in 1968, President Johnson recognized their assertion of "the right of the First Americans to remain Indians while exercising their rights as Americans."

Latino Struggles for Justice

The fastest-growing minority group in the 1960s was Latinos, or Hispanic Americans, an extraordinarily varied population encompassing people of Mexican, Puerto Rican, Caribbean, and other Latin American origins. (The term *Latino* stresses their common bonds as a minority group in the United States. The older, less political term *Hispanic* also includes those with origins in Spain.) People of Puerto Rican and Caribbean descent flocked to East Coast cities, but more than half of the nation's Latino population—including some six million Mexican Americans—lived in California, Texas, Arizona, New Mexico, and Colorado. In addition, thousands illegally crossed the two-thousand-mile border between Mexico and the United States in search of economic opportunity.

Political organization of Mexican Americans dated back to the League of United Latin-American Citizens (LULAC) in 1929, which aided newer immigrants and fought segregation and discrimination through litigation (see chapter 26). In the 1960s, however, young Mexican Americans, like African Americans and Native Americans, increasingly rejected traditional politics in favor of direct action. One symbol of this generational challenge was young activists' adoption of the term *Chicano* (from *mejicano*, the Spanish word for "Mexican").

Chicano protest drew national attention to California, where Cesar Chavez and Dolores Huerta organized a movement to improve the wretched conditions of migrant agricultural workers. As a child moving from farm to farm with his family, living in soggy tents, and exploited by labor contractors, Chavez changed schools frequently and encountered indifference and discrimination from teachers. One, he recalled, "hung a sign on me that said, 'I am a clown, I speak Spanish.'" After serving in World War II, Chavez began to organize voter registration drives among Mexican Americans. He also began to study labor history and the ideas of Catholic reformers and India's independence leader Mahatma Gandhi.

In contrast to Chavez, Dolores Huerta grew up in an integrated urban neighborhood where she avoided the farmworkers' grinding poverty but witnessed subtle forms of discrimination. Once, a high school teacher challenged her authorship of an essay because it was so well written. After completing community college and starting a family, she met Chavez. Believing that a labor union was the key to progress, they founded the United Farm Workers (UFW) in 1962. Although Chavez headed the union until his death in 1993, Huerta was indispensable to its vitality. One UFW leader described her as "a thirty-five-year-old firebrand in 1965 . . . commanding crusty macho *campesinos* twenty years her senior."

To gain leverage for striking workers, the UFW capitalized on consumer consciousness and mounted a nationwide boycott of California grapes. An estimated seventeen million Americans observed the boycott and helped win a wage increase for the workers in 1970. Although the UFW struggled and lost membership during the 1970s, it helped politicize Mexican Americans and improved farmworkers' lives.

Other Chicanos mobilized to force the Equal Employment Opportunity Commission (EEOC), the enforcement agency of Title VII of the Civil Rights Act of 1964, to act against job discrimination against Mexican Americans. LULAC, the American GI Forum (see chapter 26), and other groups picketed government offices. President Johnson responded in 1967 by appointing Vicente T. Ximenes as the first Mexican American to serve on the commission and by creating a special committee on Mexican American affairs.

Claiming "brown power," Chicanos organized to end discrimination in education, gain political power, and combat police brutality. In 1968, high school students in southwestern cities launched a wave of strikes called "Blow Outs" to protest racism in the public schools. In Denver, Rodolfo "Corky" Gonzales set up "freedom schools" where Chicano children studied the Spanish language and Mexican American history. The nationalist strains of Chicano protest were evident in La Raza Unida (the United Race), a political party founded in 1970 by José Angel Gutierrez in Texas and based on cultural pride and brotherhood. Along with blacks and Native Americans, Chicanos continued to be disproportionately represented among the poor, but they gradually won more political offices, more effective enforcement of antidiscrimination legislation, and greater respect for their culture.

Student Rebellion, the New Left, and the Counterculture

Although materially and legally more secure than their African American, Indian, and Latino counterparts, white youths also expressed dissent, supporting the black freedom struggle and launching student protests, the antiwar movement, and the new feminist and environmental movements. Challenging establishment institutions and traditional values, young activists helped change higher education, the family, the national government, and other key institutions. Young Americans were part of a larger, international phenomenon, as student movements arose in Mexico, Germany, Turkey, Czechoslovakia, Japan, and other nations around the globe.

The central organization of white student protest was Students for a Democratic Society (SDS), formed in 1960 from an older **socialist**-oriented organization. In 1962, the organizers wrote in their statement of purpose, "We are people of this generation, bred in at least modest comfort, housed now in universities, looking uncomfortably at the world we inherit." The idealistic students criticized the complacency of their elders, the remoteness of decision makers, and the powerlessness and alienation generated by a bureaucratic society. Their goal of "participatory democracy" echoed the antihierarchical and grassroots leadership style of Ella Baker and SNCC. SDS aimed to mobilize a "New Left" around the goals of civil rights, peace, and universal economic security. Other forms of student activism soon followed.

The first large-scale white student protest arose at the University of California, Berkeley, in 1964, when university officials banned students from setting up tables to recruit support for various causes. Led by whites back from civil rights work in the South, the students claimed the right to freedom of expression and political action. The "free speech" movement occupied the administration building, and more than seven hundred students were arrested before the California Board of Regents overturned the new restrictions.

Hundreds of student rallies and building occupations followed on campuses across the country, especially after 1965, when opposition to the Vietnam War mounted and students protested against universities' links to the military (see chapter 29). Students also changed the collegiate environment. Women at the University of Chicago, for example, charged in 1969 that all universities "discriminate against women, impede their full intellectual development, deny them places on the faculty, exploit talented women and mistreat women students." At Howard University, African American students called for a "Black Awareness Research Institute" and demanded that academic departments "place more emphasis on how these disciplines may be used to effect the liberation of black people." Across the country, students won curricular reforms such as black studies and women's studies programs, more financial aid for minority and poor students, independence from paternalistic rules, and a larger voice in campus decision making.

Student rebels came from the "baby boom" generation that swelled college enrollments in the 1960s and gave young people a sense of power and generational solidarity. Most white student activists came from middle-class families; with no immediate need to support themselves, they had the luxury of attacking the very system that made their rebellion possible. Such conduct bewildered and angered older Americans, even more so when it blended into a cultural revolution against nearly every conventional standard of behavior.

Drawing on the ideas of the Beats of the 1950s, the counterculture often overlapped the New Left and student movements. Cultural radicals, or "hippies," as they were called, rejected mainstream values such as the work ethic, materialism, rationality, order, and sexual control. Seeking personal rather than political change, they advocated "Do your own thing" and drew attention with their long hair and wildly colorful clothing. They sought to discard inhibitions and elevate their senses with illegal drugs such as marijuana and LSD. The Haight-Ashbury district of San Francisco harbored the most famous hippie community, but thousands of radicals established communes in cities or on farms, where they renounced private property and shared everything, often including sexual partners.

Rock and folk music defined both the counterculture and the political left. English groups such as the Beatles and the Rolling Stones and homegrown performers such as Bob Dylan, Janis Joplin, Jefferson Airplane, and Jerry Garcia's Grateful Dead took American youth by storm. Music during the 1960s often carried insurgent political and social messages that reflected radical youth culture.

Despairing of the violence around the world and the threat of nuclear annihilation, "Eve of Destruction," a top hit of 1965, reminded young men, "You're old enough to kill but not for votin'." The Woodstock Music Festival, which featured the greatest rock and folk musicians of the era and drew 400,000 young people to a farm in Bethel, New York, in 1969, epitomized the centrality of music to the youth rebellion.

The hippies faded away in the 1970s, but many elements of the counterculture—rock music, jeans, and long hair, as well as new social attitudes—filtered into the mainstream. More tolerant approaches to sexual behaviors spawned what came to be called the "sexual revolution," with help from the birth control pill, which became available in the 1960s. Self-fulfillment became a dominant concern of many Americans, and questioning of authority became more widespread.

Gay Men and Lesbians Organize

More permissive sexual norms did not stretch easily to include tolerance of homosexuality. Gay men and lesbians avoided the discrimination and segregation suffered by racial and ethnic minorities only by concealing their essential identities. Those who couldn't or wouldn't found themselves fired from jobs, arrested for their sexual activities, deprived of their children, denied admission to the United States as immigrants, or accused of being "perverted." While most kept their sexuality hidden, in the 1950s, some gays and lesbians began to organize.

Some of the first gay associations were founded in response to the government's aggressive efforts to keep homosexuals out of the **civil service**. Several gay men filed lawsuits against the government, and in October 1965, a picket line formed outside the White House with signs calling discrimination against homosexuals "as immoral as discrimination against Negroes and Jews." Not until ten years later, however, did the Civil Service Commission formally announce the end of its antigay policy.

The spark that ignited a larger movement was struck in 1969 when police raided a gay bar, the Stonewall Inn, in New York City's Greenwich Village, and gay men and lesbians fought back. "Suddenly, they were not submissive anymore," a police officer remarked. Energized by the defiance shown at the Stonewall riots, gay men and lesbians founded a host of new groups, often demonstrating the influence of other 1960s movements by choosing names such as Gay Liberation Front and slogans such as "Gay is good" and by showing up on college campuses. A more reformist organization, the National Gay and Lesbian Task Force, was founded in 1973 to ensure that sustained, national attention was given to gay issues.

The gay rights movement struggled much longer and harder to win recognition than did other social movements. In 1972, a gay man and a lesbian addressed the Democratic National Convention for the first time, but they took the podium at 2 a.m. Gay rights did not get into the party's platform until 1980. Also in 1972,

Ann Arbor, Michigan, passed the first antidiscrimination ordinance, and two years later, Elaine Noble's election to the Massachusetts legislature marked the first time an openly gay candidate won state office. In 1973, gay activists persuaded the American Psychiatric Association to remove its designation of homosexuality as a mental disease. It would take decades for these initial gains to improve conditions for most homosexuals, but by the mid-1970s, gay men and lesbians had established a movement through which they could claim equal rights and express pride in their sexual identities.

A New Movement to Save the Environment

Although environmentalism differed from other social movements in that it was organized around a cause rather than the particular identity of its members, it exhibited the influence of other movements and like them contributed to a redefinition of liberalism in the 1960s and beyond. One aspect of the new environmental movement resembled the conservation movement born in the **Progressive** Era to preserve portions of nature for recreational and aesthetic purposes and conserve it for future use (see chapter 21). Especially in the West, the post–World War II explosion of economic growth and mushrooming population, with the resulting demands for electricity and water, made such efforts seem even more critical. Environmental groups began mobilizing in the 1950s to stop the construction of dams that would disrupt national parks and wilderness areas.

The new environmentalists, however, went beyond conservationism to attack the ravaging effects of industrial development on human life and health. The polluted air and water and the spread of deadly chemicals attending economic growth threatened wildlife, plants, and the delicate ecological balance that sustained human life. To the leaders of a new organization, Friends of the Earth, unlimited economic growth was "no longer healthy, but a cancer."

Biologist Rachel Carson drew national attention to environmental concerns in 1962 with her best seller *Silent Spring*, which described the harmful effects of toxic chemicals such as the pesticide DDT. The Sierra Club and other older conservation organizations expanded their agendas, and a host of new groups arose. Millions of Americans expressed environmental concerns on the first observation of Earth Day in April 1970. Students distributed fliers encouraging recycling, Girl Scouts removed garbage from the Potomac River, African Americans in St. Louis demonstrated the effects of poisons in lead paint, and people across the country planted trees.

Responding to these concerns, the federal government staked out a broad role in environmental regulation. Lyndon Johnson sent the first presidential message on the environment to Congress and signed laws controlling air and water pollution and preserving the American landscape. Richard Nixon's 1970 State of the Union message called "clean air, clean water, open spaces . . . the birthright of every American," and that year he created the Environmental Protection Agency

(EPA) to enforce clean air and water policies and regulate pesticides. Congress also passed the Occupational Safety and Health Act (OSHA), protecting workers against workplace accidents and disease, and the Clean Air Act of 1970, setting national standards for air quality and restricting factory and automobile emissions of carbon dioxide and other pollutants. Even with lenient enforcement and substantial population and economic growth, air pollutants in major cities had decreased by one-third by 1990.

Nevertheless, the dominant value of economic growth often trumped environmental concerns, especially by the late 1970s, when antigovernment sentiment rose and the economy slumped. Corporations seeking to expand, apply new technologies, or exploit natural resources resisted restrictions. "If you're hungry and out of work, eat an environmentalist," read a union bumper sticker reflecting fears that regulations threatened jobs. Many Americans who wanted to protect the environment also valued economic expansion, personal acquisition, and convenience. Despite these conflicts, the environmental movement achieved cleaner air and water, a reduction in toxic wastes, and some preservation of endangered species and wilderness. And Americans now recognized that human beings had developed the power to destroy life on earth.

▶ **REVIEW**   How did the black freedom struggle influence other reform movements of the 1960s and 1970s?

The New Wave of Feminism

On August 26, 1970, fifty years after women won the right to vote, tens of thousands of women across the country took to the streets—radical women in jeans and conservatively dressed suburbanites, peace activists and politicians, and a sprinkling of women of color. They carried signs reading "Sisterhood Is Powerful" and "Don't Cook Dinner—Starve a Rat Today." Some of the banners opposed the war in Vietnam, others demanded racial justice, but women's own liberation stood at the forefront.

Becoming visible by the late 1960s, the women's movement reached its high tide in the 1970s and persisted in various forms into the twenty-first century. By that time, despite a powerful countermovement, women had experienced tremendous transformations in their legal status, public opportunities, and personal and sexual relationships, and popular expectations about appropriate gender roles had shifted dramatically.

A Multifaceted Movement Emerges

Beginning in the 1940s, large demographic changes laid the preconditions for a resurgence of feminism. As ever larger numbers of women took jobs, the

Founding the National Women's Political Caucus
In 1971, feminists created the National Women's Political Caucus, an organization with the goal of electing women to office and increasing their voice in political party affairs. The founders are shown here: from left to right, *Ms.* editor Gloria Steinem, Congresswoman Bella Abzug, Congresswoman Shirley Chisholm, and *The Feminine Mystique* author Betty Friedan.
AP Images.

importance of their paid work to the economy and to their families belied the idea of women as dependent, domestic beings and awakened many women in the labor force, especially labor union women, to the inferior conditions of their employment. The democratization of higher education brought more women to college campuses, where their aspirations exceeded the confines of domesticity and of routine, subordinate jobs.

Policy initiatives in the early 1960s reflected both these larger transformations and the efforts of small bands of women's rights activists. In 1961, Assistant Secretary of Labor Esther Peterson persuaded President Kennedy to create the President's Commission on the Status of Women (PCSW). Chaired by Eleanor Roosevelt, the commission reported its findings in October 1963, eight months after Betty Friedan attacked sex discrimination in *The Feminine Mystique* (see chapter 27). Though not challenging women's domestic roles, the commission

reported widespread discrimination against women and recommended remedies. Counterparts of the PCSW sprang up in every state, filled with women
eager for action.

The PCSW highlighted a practice that women's organizations and labor
unions had sought to eliminate for two decades: the age-old custom of paying
women less than men for the same work. Their efforts were rewarded when
Kennedy signed the Equal Pay Act in June 1963, making wage disparities based
on gender illegal. Within a few years, women began to win pay increases and
back pay worth millions of dollars, although four decades later, women still
had not closed the income gap.

Like other movements, the rise of feminism owed much to the black freedom
struggle, which created a moral climate sensitive to injustice and provided precedents and strategies that feminists followed. Women gained the ban against sex
discrimination in Title VII of the Civil Rights Act of 1964 and the extension of
affirmative action to women by piggybacking onto civil rights measures. They
soon grew impatient when the government failed to take these new policies
seriously and moved slowly to enforce them. The head of Title VII's enforcement
agency called the sex discrimination provision "a fluke . . . conceived out of
wedlock" and told reporters that men were entitled to have female secretaries.
Outraged and deciding they needed a "civil rights organization for women,"
Betty Friedan, civil rights activist Pauli Murray, several union women, and others
founded the National Organization for Women (NOW) in 1966.

Simultaneously, a more radical feminism grew among civil rights and New
Left activists. In 1965, two white women, Mary King and Casey Hayden, wrote
that their work in SNCC had taught them "to think radically about the personal
worth and abilities of people whose role in society had gone unchallenged before" and that "a lot of women in the movement have begun trying to apply those
lessons to their own relations with men." Although most black women did not
consider themselves to be marginalized in the movement, and in fact often led
local groups, King and Hayden presented their ideas to white male radicals in the
New Left, who responded with indifference or ridicule. By contrast, their message invigorated other white women who shared their frustration with subordinate roles. Many women walked out of New Left organizations, and by 1967 they
had created an independent women's liberation movement composed of small
groups across the nation.

Women's liberation began to gain public attention, especially when dozens of
women picketed the Miss America beauty pageant in 1968, protesting against
being forced "to compete for male approval [and] enslaved by ludicrous 'beauty'
standards." They crowned a sheep Miss America and invited women to throw
away their "bras, girdles, curlers, false eyelashes, wigs," and other "objects of
female torture." Women began to speak publicly about personal experiences that
had always been shrouded in secrecy, such as rape and abortion. Throughout the
country, women joined consciousness-raising groups, where they discovered

that what they had considered "personal" problems reflected an entrenched system of discrimination against and devaluation of women.

Radical feminists, who called their movement "women's liberation," differed from feminists in NOW and other more mainstream groups in several ways. NOW focused on equal treatment for women in the public sphere; women's liberation emphasized ending women's subordination in the family and in other personal relationships. Groups such as NOW wanted to integrate women into existing institutions; radical groups insisted that women's liberation required a total transformation of economic, political, and social institutions. Differences between these two strands of feminism blurred in the 1970s, as NOW and other mainstream groups embraced many of the issues raised by radicals.

Although NOW elected a black president, Aileen Hernandez, in 1970, the new feminism's leadership and constituency were predominantly white and middle-class. Women of color criticized white women's organizations for their frequent indifference to the disproportionate poverty experienced by minority women and their vulnerability to additional layers of discrimination based on race or ethnicity. One black woman said, "My mother took care of rich white kids. I didn't think they were oppressed." To black women, much more frequently compelled to work in the lowest-paying jobs for their families' survival, employment did not necessarily look like liberation. Cellestine Ware, an African American writer and a founder of New York Radical Feminists, insisted that black and white women could work together "only if the movement changes its priorities to work on issues that affect the lives of minority group women."

In addition to struggling with vast differences among women, feminism also contended with the refusal of the mass media to take women's grievances seriously. The press neglected or misreported on other movements, but it reserved its ridicule for feminism. When the Associated Press distributed a story on the marches and demonstrations of August 1970, for example, it used the headline IT'S WOMEN'S DAY TODAY—WATCH IT, BUB! The *Chicago Defender* titled its story on a local event "No Bra Burning in Rally," and when the House of Representatives passed an equal rights amendment to the U.S. Constitution in 1970, the *New York Times* criticized it in an editorial titled "The Henpecked House." After Gloria Steinem founded *Ms.: The New Magazine for Women* in 1972, feminists had their own mass-circulation periodical controlled by women. *Ms.* ignored the recipes and fashion tips of typical women's magazines and featured literature by women writers and articles on a broad range of feminist issues.

Ms. reported on a feminism that was exceedingly multifaceted. Most African American women worked through their own groups, such as the older National Council of Negro Women and the National Black Feminist Organization, founded in 1973. Similarly, in the early 1970s, American Indian women and Mexican American women founded national organizations, and Asian American women formed local movements. Labor union women had been fighting for workplace gender justice since the 1940s, and blue-collar women organized the National

Coalition of Labor Union Women in 1974. Lesbians established collectives throughout the country, as well as their own caucuses in organizations such as NOW. Welfare mothers formed the National Welfare Rights Organization, and religious women mobilized in the National Council of Churches of Christ to "place the question of women's liberation in the main stream of the church's concern." Women founded a host of other groups that focused on single issues such as health, abortion rights, education, and violence against women. In addition, U.S. feminists interacted with women abroad, joining a movement that crossed national boundaries.

Common threads underlay the great diversity of organizations, issues, and activities. Above all, feminism represented the belief that women were barred from, unequally treated in, or poorly served by the male-dominated public arena, encompassing politics, medicine, law, education, and religion. Many feminists also sought equality in the private sphere, challenging traditional norms that identified women primarily as wives and mothers or sex objects, subservient to men.

Feminist Gains Spark a Countermovement

Although more an effect than a cause of women's rising employment, feminism lifted female aspirations and helped lower barriers to posts monopolized by men. Women made some inroads into skilled crafts and management positions. Between 1970 and 2000, their share of law degrees shot up from 5 percent to nearly 50 percent, and their proportion of medical degrees from less than 10 percent to more than 35 percent. Women gained political offices very slowly; yet by 2006, they constituted about 15 percent of Congress and more than 20 percent of all state executives and legislators.

Feminists also encountered frustrations along with achievements. Despite some inroads into male-dominated occupations, most women still worked in low-paying, traditionally female jobs. Employed women continued to bear primary responsibility for their homes and families, thereby working a "double day." Congress attempted to ease this burden with a comprehensive child care bill in 1971, but President Nixon vetoed it.

Despite this setback, during the 1970s women gained the most sweeping changes in laws and policies since they won the right to vote in 1920. In 1972, Congress passed the Equal Rights Amendment (ERA), which would outlaw differential treatment of men and women under all state and federal laws.

Although public opinion polls registered support for most feminist goals, by the mid-1970s a strong countermovement focused on preventing ratification of the ERA arose. Phyllis Schlafly, a conservative activist in the Republican Party, mobilized thousands of women at the grassroots level who believed that traditional gender roles were God given and feared that feminism would devalue their own roles as wives and mothers. These women, marching on state capitols, persuaded some male legislators to block ratification. When the time limit ran out in 1982, only thirty-five states had ratified the amendment, three short of the necessary three-fourths majority.

Along with groups of doctors and lawyers who had sought abortion law reform since the 1950s, feminists pressured state legislatures to end restrictions on abortion. "Without the full capacity to limit her own reproduction," abortion rights activist Lucinda Cisler insisted, "a woman's other 'freedoms' are tantalizing mockeries that cannot be exercised." In 1973, the Supreme Court issued the landmark *Roe v. Wade* decision, ruling that the Constitution protects the right to abortion, which states cannot prohibit in the early stages of pregnancy.

This decision spurred even more intense opposition than the ERA. Many Americans believed that human life begins with conception and equated abortion with murder. The Catholic Church and other religious organizations provided institutional support for their protest; conservative politicians and their supporters constituted another segment of the right-to-life movement. Like ERA opponents with whom they often overlapped, the right-to-life movement mobilized thousands of women who believed that abortion disparaged motherhood and that feminism threatened their traditional roles. Beginning in 1977, abortion foes got Congress to restrict the right to abortion by denying coverage under Medicaid and other government-financed health programs, and the Supreme Court allowed states to impose other obstacles. These restraints especially disadvantaged poor and rural women.

Despite resistance, feminists won other lasting gains. Title IX of the Education Amendments Act of 1972 banned sex discrimination in all aspects of education, such as admissions, athletics, and faculty hiring. Congress also outlawed sex discrimination in credit in 1974, opened U.S. military academies to women in 1976, and prohibited discrimination against pregnant workers in 1978. Moreover, the Supreme Court struck down laws that treated men and women differently in Social Security, welfare and military benefits, and workers' compensation.

At the state and local levels, women saw reforms in areas that radical feminists had first brought attention to. They won laws forcing police departments and the legal system to treat rape victims more justly and humanely. No longer did a woman have to prove that she had put up a fight against a rapist or see her sexual history paraded before the courtroom; rape was now a crime even when it was committed by a husband against his wife. Activists also pushed domestic violence onto the public agenda. They obtained government financing for shelters for battered women and laws ensuring both greater protection for victims of domestic violence and more effective prosecution of abusers.

▶REVIEW   Why did a strong countermovement emerge to oppose feminist reform?

Liberal Reform in the Nixon Administration

Feminism was not the only movement to arouse strong antagonism. Opposition to civil rights measures, Great Society reforms, and protest groups—along with frustrations surrounding the war in Vietnam (see chapter 29)—delivered the White House to Republican Richard M. Nixon in 1968. As presidential candidate, Nixon attacked the Great Society for "pouring billions of dollars into programs that have failed," and he promised to represent the "forgotten Americans, the non-shouters, the non-demonstrators."

Yet despite Nixon's desire to attract southern whites and other Democrats disaffected by Johnson's reforms and by protesters, liberal policies persisted into the early 1970s. The Nixon administration either promoted or accepted substantially greater federal assistance to the poor; new protections for African Americans, Native Americans, women, and other groups; major environmental regulations; and financial policies deviating sharply from traditional Republican economics.

Extending the Welfare State and Regulating the Economy

A number of factors shaped the liberal policies of the Nixon administration. Not only did the Democrats continue to control Congress, but Nixon also wanted to preserve support from moderates in his party and increase Republican ranks by attracting some traditional Democrats. He could not entirely ignore grassroots movements, and several of his advisers were sympathetic to particular concerns, such as environmentalism and Native American rights. Serious economic problems also compelled new approaches, and although Nixon's real passion lay in foreign policy, he knew that history's approving gaze would depend in part on how he handled problems at home.

Under Nixon, government assistance programs grew. Congress resisted his attempts to eliminate the Office of Economic Opportunity. Key programs such as Medicaid, Head Start, Legal Services, and job training remained intact. Social Security benefits—now required to rise with the cost of living—increased; subsidies for low-income housing tripled; and a new billion-dollar program provided Pell grants for low-income students to attend college. In response to growing public concern about undernourishment, Nixon supported a huge expansion of the food stamp program, which benefited 12.5 million recipients. Noting the disparity between Nixon's political speeches and his practice as president, one of his speechwriters, the archconservative Pat Buchanan, grumbled, "Vigorously did we inveigh against the Great Society, enthusiastically did we fund it."

Nixon also acted contrary to his antigovernment rhetoric when economic crises and energy shortages induced him to increase the federal government's power in the marketplace. By 1970, both inflation and unemployment had surpassed 6 percent. This unprecedented combination of a stagnant economy and inflation was dubbed "stagflation." Domestic troubles were compounded by the decline of American dominance in the international economy. Fully recovered from World War II, the economies of Japan and Western Europe grew faster than the U.S. economy in the 1970s. Foreign cars, electronic equipment, and other products competed favorably with American goods throughout the world. In 1971, for the first time in decades, the United States imported more than it exported. Because the amount of dollars in foreign hands exceeded U.S. gold reserves, the nation could no longer back up its currency with gold.

With an eye to the 1972 election, Nixon abandoned the convertibility of dollars into gold and devalued the dollar to increase exports by making American goods cheaper in foreign markets. To protect domestic manufacturers, he imposed a 10 percent surcharge on most imports, and he froze wages and prices, thus enabling the government to stimulate the economy without fueling inflation. In the short run, these policies worked, and Nixon was resoundingly reelected in 1972. Yet by 1974, unemployment had crept back up and inflation soared, leaving to Nixon's successor the most severe economic crisis since the depression of the 1930s.

Soaring energy prices intensified stagflation. Throughout the post–World War II economic boom, the nation's abundant oil deposits and access to cheap Middle Eastern oil had encouraged the building of large cars and glass-enclosed skyscrapers with no concern for fuel efficiency. By the 1970s, the United States, with just 6 percent of the world's population, was consuming one-third of its fuel resources.

In the fall of 1973, the United States faced its first energy crisis. Arab nations, furious at the administration's support of Israel during the Yom Kippur War (see chapter 29), cut off oil shipments to the United States. As oil supplies fell in the winter of 1973–74, long lines formed at gas stations, where prices had nearly doubled, and many homes were cold. In response, Nixon authorized temporary emergency measures allocating petroleum and establishing a national 55-mile-per-hour speed limit to save gasoline. The energy crisis eased, but the nation had yet to come to grips with its seemingly unquenchable demand for fuel and dependence on foreign oil.

More permanently, Nixon expanded the government's regulatory role with a host of environmental protection measures. He proclaimed in 1970 that the nation must make "reparations for the damage we have done to our air, to our land and to our water" and urged Congress to "end the plunder of America's natural heritage." In addition to establishing the Environmental Protection Agency, he signed strong clean air legislation and measures to regulate noise pollution, oil spill cleanup, and the dumping of pesticides into the oceans. Environmentalists claimed that Nixon failed to do enough, pointing particularly to his veto—for budgetary reasons—of the Clean Water Act of 1972, which Congress overrode. Yet Nixon's environmental initiatives surpassed those of previous administrations.

Responding to Demands for Social Justice

To woo white southerners and northern workers away from the Democratic Party, Nixon's 1968 campaign had exploited hostility to black protest and new civil rights policies, but his administration had to answer to the courts and to Congress. In 1968, fourteen years after the *Brown* decision, school desegregation had barely touched the South: Two-thirds of African American children did not have a single white schoolmate. Like Eisenhower, Nixon was reluctant to use federal power to compel integration, but the Supreme Court overruled administration efforts to delay court-ordered desegregation and compelled it to enforce the law. By the time Nixon left office, fewer than one in ten southern black children attended totally segregated schools.

Nixon also began to implement affirmative action among federal contractors and unions and awarded more government contracts and loans to minority businesses. Congress took the initiative in other areas. In 1970, it extended the Voting Rights Act of 1965 by five years, and in 1972 it strengthened the Civil Rights Act of 1964 by enlarging the powers of the Equal Employment Opportunity Commission and authorizing the commission to initiate lawsuits against employers suspected of discrimination.

Women as well as minority groups benefited from the implementation of affirmative action and the strengthened EEOC, but several measures of the Nixon administration also specifically attacked sex discrimination. The president privately expressed patronizing attitudes about women, who he thought were more "erratic" and "emotional" than men. "Thank God we don't have any in the Cabinet," he told aides. Yet again, he confronted a growing popular movement and listened to more open-minded advisers and Republican feminists. Nixon vetoed a child care bill and publicly opposed abortion, but he signed the pathbreaking Title IX, guaranteeing equality in all aspects of education, and allowed his Labor Department to push affirmative action.

President Nixon gave more public support for justice to Native Americans than to any other protest group. While not bowing to radical demands, the administration dealt cautiously with extreme protests, such as the occupation of the Bureau of Indian Affairs in Washington, D.C., and the village of Wounded Knee, South Dakota. Nixon signed measures recognizing claims of Alaskan and New Mexican Indians and restoring tribal status to the Menominee, whose status had been terminated in 1961. He also set in motion legislation restoring additional tribal lands and granting Indians more control over their schools and other service institutions.

▶ **REVIEW**   Why and how did Republican president Richard Nixon expand the liberal reforms of previous administrations?

Conclusion: Achievements and Limitations of Liberalism

Senate majority leader Mike Mansfield was not alone in concluding that Lyndon Johnson "has done more than FDR ever did, or ever thought of doing." The Great Society had expanded the New Deal's focus on economic security, refashioning liberalism to embrace individual rights and to extend material well-being to groups neglected by or discriminated against in New Deal programs. Yet opposition to Johnson's leadership grew so strong by 1968 that he abandoned hopes for reelection. As his liberal vision lay in ruins, he asked, "How was it possible that all these people could be so ungrateful to me after I have given them so much?"

Fannie Lou Hamer could have provided a number of reasons. Support from the federal government was minimal when her efforts and those of others to help southern blacks obtain their rights met with violence. Moreover, her attempts to use Johnson's antipoverty programs to help poor blacks in Mississippi eventually ended in failure. Internal problems hampered her projects, but they also reflected some of the more general shortcomings of the War on Poverty. Hastily planned and inadequately funded, many antipoverty programs significantly benefited industry and the nonpoor. The War on Poverty focused more on remediating individual shortcomings than on economic and political reforms that would ensure adequately paying jobs for all. Because Johnson launched an all-out war in Vietnam and refused to ask for sacrifices from prosperous Americans, the Great Society never commanded the resources necessary for victory over poverty.

Furthermore, black aspirations exceeded white Americans' commitment to genuine equality. When the civil rights movement moved to attack racial barriers long entrenched throughout the nation and sought equality in fact as well as in law, it faced a powerful backlash. By the end of the 1960s, the revolution in the legal status of African Americans was complete, but the black freedom struggle had lost much of its momentum, and African Americans remained, with Native Americans and Chicanos, at the bottom of the economic ladder.

Critics of Johnson's Great Society overlooked its more successful and lasting elements. Medicare and Medicaid provided access to health care for the elderly and the poor and contributed to a sharp decline in poverty among aged Americans. Federal aid for education and housing became permanent elements of national policy. Moreover, Richard Nixon's otherwise conservative administration implemented school desegregation in the South and affirmative action, expanded government assistance to the disadvantaged, initiated substantial environmental regulations, and secured new rights for Native Americans and women. Women especially benefited from the decline of discrimination, and significant numbers of African Americans and other minority groups began to enter the middle class.

Yet the perceived shortcomings of government programs contributed to social turmoil and fueled the resurgence of conservative politics. Young radicals launched direct confrontations with the government and universities that, together with racial conflict, escalated into political discord and social disorder. The war in Vietnam polarized American society as much as did racial issues or the behavior of young people, and it devoured resources that might have been used for social reform and undermined faith in presidential leadership.

REVIEWING THE CHAPTER

Use the questions and timeline to review and strengthen your understanding of the chapter.

REVIEW QUESTIONS

1. How did the Kennedy and Johnson administrations exemplify a liberal vision of the federal government? (pp. 893–904)

2. How did the civil rights movement change in the mid-1960s? (pp. 904–11)

3. How did the black freedom struggle influence other reform movements of the 1960s and 1970s? (pp. 911–19)

4. Why did a strong countermovement emerge to oppose feminist reform? (pp. 919–24)

5. Why and how did Republican president Richard Nixon expand the liberal reforms of previous administrations? (pp. 925–27)

MAKING CONNECTIONS

1. Both Franklin Roosevelt's New Deal and Lyndon Johnson's Great Society attacked poverty. How was Johnson's approach different from Roosevelt's? Which was more successful, and what contributed to the relative successes and failures of each approach?

2. During the 1960s, African Americans made substantial gains in asserting their freedoms and rights. Discuss how the civil rights movement produced significant social change. Were there limits to its success? What part did government play in this process?

3. Women participated in various ways in the feminism that emerged in the 1960s. How can we explain the rise of this movement? What assumptions and goals were held in common in this diverse movement?

4. Most of the reform movements of the 1960s sought equality as one of their key priorities, but significant differences existed among Americans in general about what equality meant. Should equality be limited to equal treatment under the law, or should it extend to economic welfare, education, sexual relations, and other aspects of life? Examining two reform movements, discuss how different ideas of equality contributed to the accomplishments and disappointments of each movement.

TIMELINE

1960
- Lunch counter sit-ins.
- Democrat John F. Kennedy elected president.
- Student Nonviolent Coordinating Committee (SNCC) established.
- Students for a Democratic Society (SDS) founded.
- FDA approves birth control pill.

1961
- Congress of Racial Equality (CORE) sponsors Freedom Rides.

1962
- United Farm Workers (UFW) founded.

1963
- *The Feminine Mystique* published.
- President's Commission on the Status of Women issues report.
- Equal Pay Act.
- *Baker v. Carr.*
- *Abington School District v. Schempp.*
- March on Washington.
- President Kennedy assassinated; Lyndon B. Johnson becomes president.

1964
- Civil Rights Act.
- Economic Opportunity Act.
- Tax cuts enacted.

1965
- Selma-to-Montgomery march.
- Voting Rights Act.

1965–1966
- Congress passes most of Johnson's Great Society domestic programs.

1966
- Black Panther Party for Self-Defense founded.
- *Miranda v. Arizona.*
- National Organization for Women (NOW) founded.

1967
- Detroit riots.
- *Loving v. Virginia.*

1968
- Martin Luther King Jr. assassinated.
- American Indian Movement (AIM) founded.
- Republican Richard M. Nixon elected president.

1969
- Stonewall riots.

1970
- First Earth Day celebrated.
- Occupational Safety and Health Act.
- Environmental Protection Agency established.
- Clean Air Act.

1971
- Nixon takes United States off gold standard and freezes prices and wages.

1972
- Title IX of Education Amendments Act.
- Congress passes Equal Rights Amendment; sends it to states for ratification.
- American Indians' "Trail of Broken Treaties" caravan to Washington, D.C.

1973
- AIM members occupy Wounded Knee, South Dakota.
- *Roe v. Wade.*

▶ **For an online bibliography, practice quizzes, Web sites, images, and documents related to this chapter,** see the Book Companion Site at **bedfordstmartins.com/roark.**

▶ **For firsthand accounts of this period,** see Chapter 28 in Michael Johnson, ed., *Reading the American Past,* Fourth Edition.

29
CHAPTER

Vietnam and the Limits of Power

1961–1975

A S A PLANELOAD OF SOLDIERS prepared to land, the pilot announced, "Gentlemen, we'll be touching down in Da Nang, Vietnam, in about ten minutes. . . . On behalf of the entire crew and staff, I'd like to say we've enjoyed having you with us . . . and we hope to see all of you again next year on your way home. Goodbye and good luck." As the number of U.S. soldiers fighting in Vietnam soared, after 1966 most went to war on commercial airliners, complete with stewardesses (as they were called then) in miniskirts.

The picture of military personnel traveling to battle like business executives or tourists only hints at how different the Vietnam War was from America's previous wars. Marine infantry officer Philip Caputo landed at Da Nang in March 1965 confident, as were many soldiers in previous wars, that the enemy "would be quickly beaten and that we were doing something altogether noble and good." But in just a few months, "what had begun as an adventurous expedition had turned into an exhausting, indecisive war of attrition in which we fought for no other cause than our own survival."

Another soldier discovered even more quickly that "something was wrong." Wondering about the wire mesh that wrapped the military bus he boarded just after landing, he was told, "The gooks will throw grenades through the windows." Soldiers in Vietnam initially used the racist word *gook* to refer to the enemy—the North Vietnamese or their supporters in the South—but it soon became a term used for any Vietnamese. One American reported on the "changes coming over guys on our side—decent fellows, who wouldn't dream of calling an Oriental a 'gook' back home." The problem was that "they couldn't tell who was their friend and who wasn't. Day after day, out on patrol we'd come to . . . a shabby village, and the elders would welcome us and the children come running with smiles on

American Soldiers Confront the South Vietnamese

The unconventional nature of the Vietnam War often resulted in U.S. soldiers harming the very people they were sent to save. In this photo, a trooper of the U.S. First Cavalry stands guard while a medic treats South Vietnamese civilians who had been wounded during a search-and-destroy mission near Da Nang in October 1967. The mission destroyed their hamlet.

© Bettmann/Corbis.

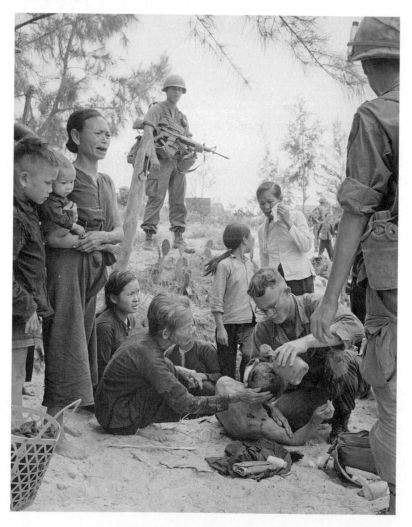

their faces, waiting for the candy we'd give them. But . . . just as we were leaving the village behind, the enemy would open up on us, and there was bitterness among us that the villagers hadn't given us warning."

Americans' horrifying and bewildering experiences in Vietnam grew out of **cold war** commitments made in the 1940s and 1950s by Presidents Harry S. Truman and Dwight D. Eisenhower. John F. Kennedy wholeheartedly took on those commitments, promising more flexible and vigorous efforts to thwart **communism**. The most memorable words of his 1961 inaugural address declared that the United States would "pay any price, bear any burden, meet any hardship, support any friend, oppose any foe to assure the survival and the success of liberty." Philip Caputo joined the Marine Corps to gain independence and adventure, but he also reported being "seduced into uniform by Kennedy's challenge . . . and by the missionary idealism he had awakened in us."

Vietnam became the foremost test of John F. Kennedy's anticommunism. He sent increasing amounts of American arms and personnel to sustain the South Vietnamese government, but it was Lyndon B. Johnson who dramatically escalated that commitment in 1965 and turned a civil war among the Vietnamese into America's war. At peak strength in 1968, 543,000 U.S. military personnel served in Vietnam; all told, some 2.6 million saw duty there throughout the war. Yet this massive intervention not only failed to defeat North Vietnam but also created intense discord at home. It cost President Johnson another term in office and contributed to the political demise of his Republican successor, Richard M. Nixon. Some Americans lauded the government's goal in Vietnam and decried only its failure to pursue it effectively. Others believed that preserving a non-Communist South Vietnam was neither in the best interests of the United States nor within its capacity or moral right to achieve.

But none could deny the war's enormous costs. Lieutenant Caputo lamented that "our idealism was lost, our morals corrupted, and the purpose forgotten." Martin Luther King Jr. mourned "the promises of the Great Society . . . shot down on the battlefield of Vietnam." In addition to derailing domestic reform, the war exacted a heavy toll in American lives and dollars, disrupted the economy, kindled internal conflict, and led to the violation of protesters' rights, leaving a deep and lasting mark on the nation.

As the United States fought communism in Vietnam and, on a much smaller scale, in other **third world** countries, American leaders moved to ease cold war tensions with the major Communist powers. After a dramatic standoff with the Soviet Union during the Cuban missile crisis, the United States began to cooperate with its cold war enemy to limit nuclear testing and the spread of nuclear weapons. In 1972, the two superpowers agreed for the first time to restrict the development of new nuclear weapons. In addition, Nixon's historic visit to China in 1972 marked the abandonment of the policy of isolating China and paved the way for normal diplomatic relations by the end of the 1970s.

New Frontiers in Foreign Policy

John F. Kennedy moved quickly to fulfill his promise to pursue **containment** more aggressively and with more flexible means. In contrast to the Eisenhower administration's emphasis on nuclear weapons, Kennedy was determined to expand not only the nation's nuclear capacity but also its ability to fight conventional battles and to engage in **guerrilla warfare**. To ensure U.S. superiority over the Soviet Union in every domain, Kennedy accelerated the nation's space exploration program and increased attention to the third world. To deny the Soviets a nuclear outpost in the Western Hemisphere, he took the United States to the brink of nuclear war during the 1962 Cuban missile crisis. Less dramatically but no less tenaciously, Kennedy sent increasing amounts of American arms and personnel to South Vietnam in an effort to save the government from Communist insurgents.

Meeting the "Hour of Maximum Danger"

Underlying Kennedy's foreign policy was an assumption that the United States had "gone soft—physically, mentally, spritually soft," as he put it in 1960. He called the Eisenhower era "years of drift and impotency," and he associated that administration with femininity when he mocked Nixon's kitchen debate with Soviet premier Nikita Khrushchev as well as Nixon's celebration of American consumer goods. "I would rather take my television black and white and have the largest rockets in the world," Kennedy declared. Often photographed engaging in vigorous sports, he and his closest advisers projected a masculine style that was tough, competitive, and hard-driving.

Having campaigned against the Eisenhower administration for relying too heavily on nuclear weapons, Kennedy moved to build up conventional ground forces, to provide a **flexible response** to Communist expansion. He also charged that limits on defense spending had caused the United States to fall behind even in nuclear capability. In January 1961, Kennedy warned that the nation faced a grave peril: "Each day the crises multiply. . . . Each day we draw nearer the hour of maximum danger."

Although the president exaggerated the threat to national security, several developments in 1961 heightened the sense of crisis and provided a rationalization for his military buildup. Shortly before Kennedy's inauguration, Khrushchev publicly encouraged "wars of national liberation," thereby aligning the Soviet Union with independence movements in the third world that were often anti-Western. His statement reflected in part the Soviet competition with China for the allegiance of emerging nations, but U.S. officials saw in his words a threat to the status quo of containment.

Cuba, just ninety miles off the Florida coast, posed the most immediate threat to the United States. Fidel Castro's revolution had already moved Cuba into the Soviet orbit, and Eisenhower's CIA had been planning an invasion of the island by Cuban exiles living in the United States. Kennedy ordered the invasion to proceed even though his military advisers gave it only a fair chance of success. To do otherwise, the president believed, would create an appearance of weakness.

On April 17, 1961, about 1,400 anti-Castro exiles trained and armed by the CIA landed at the Bay of Pigs on the south shore of Cuba (Map 29.1). Contrary to U.S. expectations, no popular uprising materialized to support the anti-Castro brigade. Kennedy refused to provide direct military support, and the invaders quickly fell to Castro's forces. The disaster humiliated Kennedy and the United States, posing a stark contrast to the president's inaugural promise of a new, more effective foreign policy. The attempted armed interference evoked memories of **Yankee imperialism** among Latin Americans, aligned Cuba even more closely with the Soviet Union, and helped Castro consolidate his power.

Days before the Bay of Pigs invasion, the Soviet Union delivered a psychological blow when a Soviet astronaut became the first human being to orbit the

---

MAP 29.1 U.S. Involvement in Latin America and the Caribbean, 1954–1994
During the cold war, the United States frequently intervened in Central American and Caribbean countries to suppress Communist or leftist movements.

earth. In May 1961, Kennedy called for a huge new commitment to the space program, with the goal of sending a man to the moon by 1970. Responding to his call to "win the battle that is now going on around the world between freedom and tyranny," Congress authorized the Apollo program and boosted appropriations for space exploration. John H. Glenn orbited the earth in 1962, and seven years later, in July 1969, two U.S. astronauts landed on the moon.

Early in his presidency, Kennedy sought a meeting with Khrushchev to show him "that we can be as tough as he is." But when the two met in June 1961 in Vienna, Austria, Khrushchev was belligerent and shook the president's confidence. The stunned Kennedy reported privately, "He just beat [the] hell out of me. . . . If he thinks I'm inexperienced and have no guts . . . we won't get anywhere with him." Khrushchev demanded an agreement recognizing the existence of two Germanys. Otherwise, he warned, the Soviets would sign a separate treaty with East Germany, a move that would threaten America's occupation rights in and access to West Berlin, which lay some one hundred miles within East Germany.

Khrushchev was concerned about the massive exodus of East Germans into West Berlin, a major embarrassment for the Communists. To stop this flow of escapees from behind the **iron curtain**, in August 1961 East Germany shocked the world by erecting a wall between East and West Berlin. With the Berlin Wall stemming the tide of migration and Kennedy insisting that West Berlin was "the great testing place of Western courage and will," Khrushchev backed off from his threats. But not until 1972 did the superpowers recognize East and West Germany as separate nations and guarantee Western access to West Berlin.

Kennedy used the Berlin crisis to add $3.2 billion to the defense budget. He increased draft calls and mobilized the reserves and National Guard, adding 300,000 troops to the military. By providing for a "flexible response" strategy, this buildup of conventional forces met his demand for "a wider choice than humiliation or all-out nuclear action." Nonetheless, Kennedy also pushed for the development of new nuclear weapons and delivery systems, more than doubling the nation's nuclear force within three years.

New Approaches to the Third World

Complementing Kennedy's hard-line policy toward the Soviet Union were fresh approaches to the **nationalist** movements that had convulsed the world since the end of World War II. In 1960 alone, seventeen African nations gained their independence. Much more than his predecessors, the president publicly supported third world aspirations, believing that the United States could win the hearts and minds of people in developing nations by helping to fulfill hopes for autonomy and **democracy**.

To that end, in 1961 Kennedy created the Alliance for Progress, promising $20 billion in aid for Latin America over the next decade. Like the Marshall Plan (see chapter 26), the Alliance for Progress was designed to thwart communism and hold nations within the American sphere by fostering economic development. Likewise, the new Agency for International Development (AID) emphasized economic over military aid in foreign assistance programs.

Also in 1961, Kennedy launched his most dramatic third world initiative with an idea borrowed from Senator Hubert H. Humphrey: the Peace Corps. The program recruited young men and women to work in developing countries, many of them responding to Kennedy's appeal for idealism and sacrifice in his inaugural address. One volunteer spoke of his service as a way to ease his guilt at having been "born between clean sheets when others were issued into the dust with a birthright of hunger." After studying a country's language and **culture**, Peace Corps volunteers went to work directly with its people, opening schools, providing basic health care, and assisting with agriculture, nutrition, and small economic enterprises. By the mid-1970s, more than 60,000 volunteers had served two-year stints in Latin America, Africa, and Asia.

Nevertheless, Kennedy's foreign aid initiatives fell far short of their objectives. Though generally welcomed, Peace Corps projects did not address the receiving countries' larger economic and political structures, and they numbered too few to make a dent in the poverty and suffering in third world countries. By 1969, the United States had provided only half of the $20 billion promised to the Alliance for Progress, much of which went to military projects or into the pockets of corrupt ruling elites. In addition, a soaring birthrate in Latin America counteracted economic gains, and these nations increasingly bore heavy foreign debt.

Kennedy also used direct military means to bring political stability to the third world. He rapidly expanded the "special forces" corps that had been established under Eisenhower to aid groups sympathetic to the United States and fighting against Communist-leaning national liberation movements. These counterinsurgency forces, including the army's Green Berets and the navy SEALs, constituted elite military corps trained to wage guerrilla warfare and equipped with the latest technology. They would get their first test in Vietnam.

The Arms Race and the Nuclear Brink

The final piece of Kennedy's defense strategy was to strengthen American nuclear dominance. The president realized quickly that the "missile gap" he had decried during the 1960 campaign was a myth, but that did not lessen his determination to make the United States even stronger. He upped the number of nuclear weapons based in Europe from 2,500 to 7,200 and multiplied fivefold the supply of intercontinental ballistic missiles (ICBMs). Concerned that this buildup would enable the United States to launch a first strike and wipe out Soviet missile sites before they could respond, the Soviet Union stepped up its own ICBM program. Thus began the most intense arms race in history.

The superpowers came perilously close to using their weapons of terror in 1962, when Khrushchev decided to install nuclear missiles in Cuba, while

Preparing for the Worst
Waiting out the tense days of the Cuban missile crisis, many Americans tried to prepare for the worst possible outcome. Owners of Chalet Suzanne, a hotel in Lake Wales, Florida, canned several thousand cases of well water, labeled "NASK" for Nuclear Attack Survival Kit. Courtesy Chalet Suzanne Foods, Inc., Lake Wales, Florida. Photo by David Woods.

insisting to Kennedy that he had no intention to do so. Khrushchev wanted to protect Cuba from further U.S. attempts at intervention, and he sought to balance the U.S. missiles aimed at the Soviet Union from Britain, Italy, and Turkey. On October 16, the CIA showed Kennedy aerial photographs of missile launching sites under construction in Cuba. Considering this an intolerable threat to the United States, the president met daily in secret with a small group of advisers to manage the ensuing thirteen-day Cuban missile crisis. Rather than conducting quiet negotiations with the Soviets, Kennedy launched a public showdown. On October 22, he announced to a television audience that the military was on full alert and that the navy would turn back any Soviet vessel suspected of carrying offensive missiles to Cuba. (Only later did the United States find out that offensive missiles were already there.) Kennedy warned Khrushchev that any attack launched from Cuba would trigger a full nuclear assault against the Soviet Union.

Projecting the appearance of toughness was paramount to President Kennedy. Although the missiles did not "alter the strategic balance in fact," according to one of his aides, "that balance would have been substantially altered in appearance; and in matters of national will and world leadership such appearances contribute to reality." Kennedy feared that Soviet missiles in Cuba would intimidate other Latin American governments. "Communism and Castroism are going to be spread . . . as governments frightened by this new evidence of power [fall]."

But if Kennedy was willing to risk nuclear war for appearances, he also exercised caution, refusing advice from the military to bomb the missile sites. On October 24, Russian ships carrying nuclear warheads toward Cuba suddenly turned back. When one ship crossed the blockade line, Kennedy matched Khrushchev's restraint, ordering the navy to follow the ship rather than attempt to stop it.

While Americans experienced the cold war's most fearful days, Kennedy and Khrushchev negotiated an agreement. Ultimately, the Soviets removed the missiles and pledged not to introduce new offensive weapons into Cuba. The

United States promised not to invade the island. Secretly, Kennedy also agreed to remove the U.S. missiles from Turkey. The Cuban crisis led to Khrushchev's fall from power two years later, and Kennedy emerged triumphant. "I cut his balls off," Kennedy rejoiced in private, reflecting considerations of manhood that helped shape his foreign policy. The image of an inexperienced president fumbling the Bay of Pigs invasion gave way to that of a brilliant leader combining firmness with restraint, bearing the United States through its "hour of maximum danger."

Having proved his toughness, Kennedy worked with Khrushchev to prevent future confrontations by installing a special "hot line" to speed top-level communication at critical moments. In a major speech at American University in June 1963, Kennedy called for a reexamination of cold war assumptions, asking Americans "not to see conflict as inevitable." Acknowledging the superpowers' immense differences, Kennedy stressed what they had in common: "We all breathe the same air. We all cherish our children's future and we are all mortal." Kennedy also called for an end to "a vicious cycle" in which "new weapons beget counterweapons." In August 1963, the United States, the Soviet Union, and Great Britain signed a limited test ban treaty, reducing the threat of radioactive fallout from nuclear testing and raising hopes for further superpower accord.

A Growing War in Vietnam

In his speech at American University, Kennedy criticized the idea of "a Pax Americana enforced on the world by American weapons of war," but he increased the flow of those weapons into South Vietnam. The foreign policy setbacks during his early months in office suggested the need to make a stand somewhere. "There are just so many concessions that one can make to the Communists in one year and survive politically," he said, recognizing the blows to the Democratic Party when China was "lost" to communism in 1949.

Kennedy's strong anticommunism and attachment to a vigorous foreign policy prepared him to expand the commitment in Vietnam that he had inherited from Eisenhower. Foreign policy experts of Kennedy's generation took from the Munich agreement in 1938—when Britain and France acceded to Germany's annexation of part of Czechoslovakia—the lesson that appeasement didn't work. Convinced that China and the Soviet Union were behind Ho Chi Minh's efforts to unify Vietnam under his leadership, Kennedy's key military adviser, General Maxwell Taylor, argued that holding firm in Vietnam would show the Soviets and Chinese that wars of national liberation were not "cheap, safe, and disavowable [but] costly, dangerous, and doomed to failure." The new counterinsurgency program could provide the means to do just that.

By the time Kennedy took office, more than $1 billion in aid and seven hundred U.S. military advisers had failed to stabilize South Vietnam. Two major obstacles stood in the way of this objective. First, the South Vietnamese insurgents—whom Americans called Vietcong, short for *Vietnam Cong-san* ("Vietnamese Communists")—were an indigenous force whose initiative came from within, not from the Soviet Union or China. Because the Saigon government refused to hold the elections promised in the 1954 Geneva accords, the rebels saw no choice but to take up arms. Increasingly, Ho Chi Minh's Communist government in North Vietnam supplied them with weapons and soldiers.

Second, the South Vietnamese government and army (the Army of the Republic of Vietnam, or ARVN) refused to satisfy the demands of the insurgents but could not defeat them militarily. Ngo Dinh Diem, South Vietnamese premier from 1954 to 1963, chose self-serving military leaders for their personal loyalty rather than for their effectiveness. Many South Vietnamese, the majority of whom were Buddhists, saw the Catholic Diem as a tool of the West. His government's corruption and brutal repression of opponents alienated many South Vietnamese, not just the Communists. Even Secretary of State Dean Rusk called him "an oriental despot."

The growing intervention by North Vietnam made matters worse. In 1960, the Hanoi government established the National Liberation Front (NLF), composed of South Vietnamese rebels but directed by the northern army. In addition, Hanoi constructed a network of infiltration routes (called the "Ho Chi Minh Trail") in neighboring Laos and Cambodia, through which it sent people and supplies to help liberate the South (Map 29.2). Violence escalated between 1960 and 1963, bringing the Saigon government close to collapse.

Kennedy responded to the deteriorating situation with measured steps. Some advisers called for an all-out effort, using any force necessary to save South Vietnam from communism. Others questioned whether such a victory was either necessary or possible. Undersecretary of State Chester Bowles, for example, warned that the American effort was "headed full blast up a dead end street," while W. Averell Harriman, foreign policy adviser to Roosevelt and Truman, warned that the United States should not "stake its prestige" on a government that he deemed unsalvageable.

Taking the middle ground, Kennedy gradually escalated the U.S. commitment, nonetheless worrying that each step was "like taking a drink. . . . The effect wears off, and you have to take another." By the spring of 1963, military aid had doubled, and the 9,000 Americans serving in Vietnam as military advisers occasionally participated in actual combat. Although the United States extracted new promises of reform from Diem, the South Vietnamese government never made good on them.

Reflecting racist attitudes of American superiority over nonwhite populations, officials assumed that the U.S. military's technology and sheer power could win in Vietnam. Soldiers such as Philip Caputo carried to Vietnam "the pride and overpowering self-assurance" that victory was inevitable. Yet advanced weapons were ill suited to the guerrilla warfare practiced by the enemy, whose surprise attacks were designed to weaken support for the South Vietnamese government. In addition, U.S. weapons and strategy harmed the very people they were

MAP 29.2   The Vietnam War, 1964–1975

The United States sent 2.6 million soldiers to Vietnam and spent more than $150 billion on the longest war in American history, but it was unable to prevent the unification of Vietnam under a Communist government.

intended to save. Thousands of peasants were uprooted and resettled in "strategic hamlets," supposedly secure from the Communists. Those left in the countryside fell victim to bombs—containing the highly flammable substance napalm—dropped by the U.S.-backed ARVN to quell the Vietcong. In January 1962, U.S. planes began to spray herbicides such as Agent Orange to destroy the Vietcong's jungle hideouts and food supply.

With tacit permission from Washington, South Vietnamese military leaders executed a coup against Diem and his brother, who headed the secret police, on November 2, 1963. Kennedy expressed shock that the two were murdered but indicated no change in policy. In a speech to be given on the day he was assassinated, he called Americans to their responsibilities as "the watchmen on the walls of world freedom." Referring specifically to Southeast Asia, his undelivered speech warned, "We dare not weary of the task." At his death, 16,000 Americans had served in Vietnam, and 100 had died there.

▶REVIEW   Why did Kennedy believe that engagement in Vietnam was crucial to his foreign policy?

Lyndon Johnson's War against Communism

The cold war assumptions that had shaped Kennedy's foreign policy underlay his successor's approach to Southeast Asia and Latin America. Retaining Kennedy's key advisers—most importantly, Secretary of State Rusk, Secretary of Defense Robert McNamara, and National Security Adviser McGeorge Bundy—Lyndon Johnson continued the massive buildup of nuclear weapons and conventional and counterinsurgency forces. In 1965, when the South Vietnamese government approached collapse, Johnson made the fateful decisions to order U.S. troops into combat and to initiate sustained bombing of the North. That same year, Johnson sent U.S. marines to the Dominican Republic to crush a leftist rebellion.

An All-Out Commitment in Vietnam

The president who wanted to make his mark on domestic policy was compelled to face the excruciating dilemma inherited from his predecessors, who had committed the United States to stopping communism in Vietnam. Early in his administration, the general public paid little attention to Vietnam and seemed willing to follow the administration's lead. Yet some advisers, politicians, and international leaders raised questions about the wisdom of a greater commitment in Vietnam, viewing the situation there as a civil war rather than Communist aggression. Only French president Charles de Gaulle openly challenged U.S. policy, but most international leaders did not consider Vietnam crucial to containing communism and were not prepared to share the military burden in more than token ways. Several leading Democrats, including Senate majority leader Mike Mansfield, privately argued that a stable South Vietnam was unlikely. Mansfield wondered whether Vietnam could be won with a "limited expenditure of American lives and resources somewhere commensurate with our national interests." Senate Armed Services Committee member Richard Russell warned, "It'd take a half million men. They'd be bogged down there for ten years." Although critics expressed their own ambivalence and did not offer any clear-cut solutions, they urged the administration to pursue a face-saving way out, such as reconvening the Geneva conference that had partitioned Vietnam in 1954.

Johnson ignored the opportunity for disengagement that these critics saw in 1964 and expanded the United States' military involvement. Along with most of his advisers, he believed that the long-standing commitment to South Vietnam put American credibility on the line. Moreover, the president's own credibility also came into play. Like Kennedy, he feared the domestic political repercussions and especially what disengagement without victory might do to his ability to achieve his Great Society (see chapter 28). His own insecurities, fear of being compared unfavorably with Kennedy, and concern for his "manliness" precluded a course that might make him appear soft or cowardly. Mansfield's views, he said, were those of a "milquetoast."

Chemical Weapons

The U.S. military began to use the tear gas CS (o-chlorobenzylidenemalononitrile) in grenades in Vietnam in 1964 and was discharging more than two million pounds of CS a year by 1969. It was used in operations such as the one shown here. Military planes also dropped or sprayed CS from the air to rid large areas of enemy forces. CS is usually not lethal but has incapacitating effects. Nonetheless, its use evoked criticism both at home and abroad.

James H. Pickerell/Stock Connection.

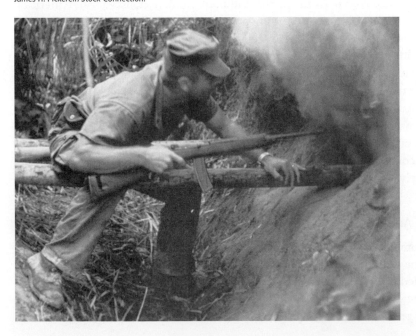

Johnson understood the ineffectiveness of his South Vietnamese allies and agonized over sending young men into combat. Yet he continued to dispatch more military advisers, weapons, and economic aid, and in August 1964, he seized an opportunity to increase the pressure on North Vietnam. During a routine espionage mission in the Gulf of Tonkin, off the coast of North Vietnam, two U.S. destroyers reported that North Vietnamese gunboats had fired on them on August 2 and 4 (see Map 29.2). Johnson quickly ordered air strikes on North Vietnamese torpedo bases and oil storage facilities, and he sought authority from Congress to take "all necessary measures to repel any armed attacks against the forces of the United States and to prevent further aggression." By covering up uncertainty about whether the second attack had even occurred and the provocative U.S. actions of staging covert raids and operating close to the North Vietnamese coast, he misled Congress and the public about the situation. As a result, Congress supported Johnson's strategy with the Gulf of Tonkin Resolution on August 7, 1964, with just two senators voting against it.

The president's tough stance only two months before the 1964 election helped counter the charges made by his opponent, Arizona senator Barry Goldwater, that he was "soft on communism." Yet Johnson also presented himself as the peace candidate. When Goldwater proposed massive bombing of North Vietnam, Johnson assured Americans that "we are not going to send American boys nine or ten thousand miles away from home to do what Asian boys ought to be doing for themselves."

Soon after winning reelection, however, Johnson did widen the war. He rejected peace overtures from North Vietnam, which insisted on American withdrawal and a coalition government in South Vietnam as steps toward ultimate unification of the country. Instead, he accepted the advice of McNamara and other aides to begin a bombing campaign against the North. Operation Rolling Thunder, a strategy of gradually intensified bombing of North Vietnam, began in February 1965. Less than a month later, Johnson ordered the first U.S. combat troops to South Vietnam, and in July he shifted U.S. troops from defensive to offensive operations, dispatching 50,000 more soldiers. Although the administration downplayed the import of these decisions in order to maintain public and congressional support, they marked a critical turning point. Now it was genuinely America's war.

Preventing Another Castro in Latin America

Closer to home, Johnson faced persistent problems in Latin America despite the efforts of the Alliance for Progress. Thirteen times during the 1960s, military coups toppled Latin American governments, and local insurgencies grew apace. The administration's response varied from case to case but centered on the determination to prevent any more Castro-type revolutions.

In 1964, riots erupted in the Panama Canal Zone, which the United States had seized and made a U.S. territory early in the century (see chapter 21). Instigated by Panamanians who viewed the United States as a colonial power, the riots left four U.S. soldiers and more than twenty Panamanians dead. Johnson sent troops to quell the disturbance, but he also initiated negotiations that eventually led to the transfer of the canal to Panamanian authority in 2000.

Elsewhere, Johnson's Latin American policy generated new cries of "Yankee imperialism." In 1961, voters in the Dominican Republic ousted a long-standing dictator and elected a constitutional government headed by reformist Juan Bosch, who was overthrown by a military coup two years later. In 1965, when Bosch supporters launched an uprising against the military government, Johnson sent more than 20,000 soldiers to quell what he perceived to be a leftist revolt and take control of the island. A truce was arranged, and in 1966 Dominicans voted in a constitutional government under a moderate rightist.

This first outright show of Yankee force in Latin America in four decades damaged the administration at home and abroad. Although it had justified intervention on the grounds that Communists were among the rebels, it quickly became clear that they had played no significant role, and U.S. actions kept the reform-oriented Boschists from returning to power. Moreover, the president had not consulted the Dominicans or the Organization of American States (OAS), to which the United States had pledged that it would respect national sovereignty in Latin America. Only after the troops had already landed in the Dominican Republic did Johnson ask for approval from the OAS. Several nations, including Mexico, Chile, and Venezuela, refused to grant it.

The Americanized War

The military success in the Dominican Republic no doubt encouraged the president to press on in Vietnam. During Operation Rolling Thunder from 1965 to early 1968, the United States gradually escalated attacks against the North Vietnamese and their Vietcong allies, endeavoring to break their will without provoking intervention by the Chinese, as they had done in Korea. Johnson himself scrutinized military plans, boasting, "They can't even bomb an outhouse without my approval."

Over the course of the war, U.S. pilots dropped 3.2 million tons of explosives, more than the United States had dropped in all of World War II. Claiming monthly death tolls of more than 2,000 North Vietnamese, the intensive bombing nonetheless failed to dampen the Hanoi government's commitment. In the South, the United States rained down more than twice the tonnage of bombs dropped on North Vietnam.

General William Westmoreland's strategy of attrition was designed to search out and kill the Vietcong and North Vietnamese regular army. The military used helicopters extensively to conduct offensives all over South Vietnam. Because there was no battlefront as in previous wars, officials calculated progress not in territory seized but in "body counts" and "kill ratios"—the number of enemies killed relative to the cost in American and ARVN lives. According to U.S. army officer Colin Powell, who served two tours in Vietnam and later served as U.S. secretary of state under George W. Bush, "The Army desperately needed some-thing to measure. What military objectives could we claim in this week's report? A hill? A valley? A hamlet? Rarely. Consequently, bodies became the measure." In this situation, American soldiers did not always distinguish between military combatants and civilians; according to Lieutenant Philip Caputo, the operating rule was "If it's dead and Vietnamese, it's VC [Vietcong]."

Teenagers fought the Vietnam War, in contrast to World War II, where the average soldier was twenty-six years old. Until the voting age dropped from twenty-one to eighteen in 1971, most soldiers, whose average age was nineteen, could not even vote for the officials who sent them to war. Men of all classes had fought in World War II, but Vietnam was the war of the poor and working class, who constituted about 80 percent of the troops. More privileged youths avoided the **draft** by using college deferments or family connections to get into the National Guard. Sent from Plainville, Kansas, to Vietnam in 1965, Mike Clodfelter could not recall "a single middle-class son of the town's businessmen, lawyers, doctors, or ranchers from my high school graduating class who experienced the Armageddon of our generation."

Much more than World War II, Vietnam was a men's war. Because the United States did not undergo full mobilization for Vietnam, officials did not seek women's sacrifices for the war effort. In response to a reporter who said that some military women were distressed at not being called to serve in Vietnam, Johnson joked, "Well there is always a chance of anything taking place when our women are sufficiently distressed." Still, between 7,500 and 10,000 women served in Vietnam, the vast majority of them nurses. Although women were not allowed to carry weapons, they did come under enemy fire, and eight lost their lives. Many more struggled with their helplessness in the face of the dead and maimed bodies they tended. "When you finally saved a life," said Peggy DuVall, "you wondered what kind of life you had saved."

Early in the war, African Americans constituted 31 percent of combat troops, often choosing the military over the meager opportunities in the civilian econ-omy. Special forces ranger Arthur E. Woodley Jr. recalled, "I was just what my country needed. A black patriot. . . . The only way I could possibly make it out of the ghetto was to be the best soldier I possibly could." Death rates among black soldiers were disproportionately high until 1966, when the military adjusted per-sonnel assignments to achieve a better racial balance.

The young troops faced extremely difficult conditions. Soldiers fought in thick jungles and swamps filled with leeches, in oppressive heat, rain, and humidity. Lieutenant Caputo remembered "weeks of expectant waiting and, at random intervals, conducting vicious manhunts through jungles and swamps where snipers harassed us constantly and booby traps cut us down one by one." Soldiers in previous wars had served "for the duration," but each Vietnam warrior served a one-year tour of duty. A commander called it "the worst personnel policy in history," because men had less incentive to fight near the end of their tours, wanting merely to stay alive and whole. The U.S. military inflicted great losses on the enemy, yet the war remained a stalemate. As infantryman Tim O'Brien reported, "We slay one of them, hit a mine, kill another, hit another mine. . . . And each piece of ground left behind is his [the enemy's] from the moment we are gone on our next hunt."

The South Vietnamese government was an enormous obstacle to victory, even though in 1965 it settled into a period of stability led by Air Marshal Nguyen Cao Ky and General Nguyen Van Thieu. Graft and corruption continued to flourish, and Ky and Thieu failed to rally popular support. In the intensified fighting and inability to distinguish friend from foe, ARVN and American troops killed and wounded thousands of South Vietnamese civilians and destroyed their villages. By 1968, five million people, nearly 30 percent of the population, had become refugees. Huge infusions of American dollars and goods to the South Vietnamese government produced prostitution and rampant inflation, hurt local industries, and increased dependence on foreign aid. The failure to stabilize South Vietnam even as the U.S. military presence expanded enormously created grave challenges for the administration at home.

> ▶ **REVIEW**   How did American troops serving in Vietnam differ from those who served in World War II, and how were their experiences different?

A Nation Polarized

Soon President Johnson was fighting a war on two fronts. Domestic opposition to the war in Southeast Asia grew significantly after 1965 as daily television broadcasts of the carnage of Vietnam made it the first "living-room war." In March 1968, torn between his domestic critics and the military's clamor for more troops, Johnson announced restrictions on the bombing, a new effort at negotiations, and his decision not to pursue reelection. Throughout 1968, demonstrations, violence, and assassinations convulsed the nation. Vietnam took center stage in the election, and voters narrowly favored the Republican candidate, former vice president Richard Nixon, who promised to achieve "peace with honor."

The Widening War at Home

Johnson's authorization of Operation Rolling Thunder swelled the previously quiet doubts and criticism into a mass movement against the war. In April 1965,

Students for a Democratic Society (SDS) recruited 20,000 people for a demonstration in Washington, D.C., and SDS chapters sprang up on more than 300 college campuses. Thousands of students joined campus protests against Reserve Officers Training Corps (ROTC) programs, CIA recruiters, manufacturers of war materiel, and university research for the Department of Defense. Martin Luther King Jr. deployed his moral authority against the war, rebuking the U.S. government in 1967 as "the greatest purveyor of violence in the world today" and calling opposition to the war "the privilege and burden of all of us who deem ourselves bound by allegiances and loyalties which are broader and deeper than nationalism." Environmentalists attacked the use of chemical weapons, such as the deadly dioxin product Agent Orange, which the military used to destroy foliage where the enemy might hide. A new draft policy in 1967 ended defer-ments for postgraduate education and upped male students' stake in ending the war. In the spring of 1968, as many as one million college and high school students participated in a nationwide strike.

Antiwar sentiment also entered society's mainstream. The *New York Times* began questioning administration policy in 1965, and by 1968 media critics included the *Wall Street Journal, Life* magazine, and popular TV anchorman Walter Cronkite. Clergy, business people, scientists, and physicians formed their own groups to pressure Johnson to stop the bombing and start negotiations. An increasing number of prominent Democratic senators, including J. William Fulbright, George McGovern, and majority leader Mike Mansfield, urged Johnson to substitute negotiation for force. Fulbright's book *The Arrogance of Power* warned against the "tendency of great nations to equate power with virtue" and urged American leaders not to think of the country as "God's chosen savior of mankind."

Opposition to the war took diverse forms: letter-writing campaigns to offi-cials, teach-ins on college campuses, mass marches, student strikes, withhold-ing of federal taxes, draft card and flag burnings, **civil disobedience** against military centers and producers of war materiel, and attempts to stop trains carrying troops. Although the peace movement never claimed a majority of the population, it focused media attention on the war and severely limited the administration's options. The twenty-year-old consensus around cold war for-eign policy had broken down.

Many would not fight in the war. The World Boxing Association stripped Muhammad Ali of his world heavyweight title when he refused to serve in what he called a "white man's war." More than 170,000 men who opposed the war on moral or religious grounds gained conscientious objector status and performed nonmilitary duties at home or in Vietnam. About 60,000 fled the country to escape the draft, and more than 200,000 were accused of failing to register or of committing other draft offenses.

When he got his induction notice in 1968, Tim O'Brien agonized over what to do. He opposed the war, but avoiding the draft would subject his family to criticism and embarrassment in his small Minnesota town, where young men

African American Antiwar Protest

The first expression of African American opposition to the war in Vietnam occurred in Mississippi in July 1965 when a group of civil rights workers called for draft resistance. Blacks should not fight for freedom in Vietnam "until all the Negro People are free in Mississippi," the activists said, and they should not risk their lives "and kill other Colored People in Santo Domingo and Viet Nam." This protester on the West Coast expresses similar sentiments in April 1967.

Joe Flowers / Black Star / Stockphoto.com.

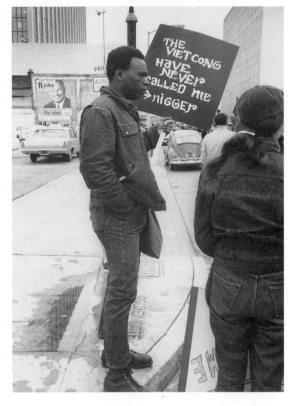

were expected to serve their country. In addition, he said, "I owed the prairie something. For twenty-one years I'd lived under its laws, accepted its education . . . wallowed in its luxuries, played on its Little League teams." In the end, he could not bring himself to desert his country. Although he held to his belief that "the war was wrong," O'Brien went to Vietnam with the army.

Opponents of the war held far from unanimous views. Those who saw the conflict in moral terms wanted total withdrawal, insisting that their country had no right to interfere in a civil war in another country and stressing the suffering of the Vietnamese people. A larger segment of antiwar sentiment reflected practical considerations—the belief that the war could not be won at a bearable cost. Not demanding total withdrawal, those activists wanted Johnson to stop bombing North Vietnam and seek negotiations.

Working-class people were no more antiwar than other groups, but they recognized the class dimensions of the war and the public opposition to it. A firefighter whose son had died in Vietnam said bitterly, "It's people like us who give up our sons for the country. The business people, they run the country and make money from it. The college types . . . go to Washington and tell the government what to do. . . . But their sons don't end up in the swamps over there, in Vietnam."

The antiwar movement outraged millions of Americans who supported the war. Some members of the generation who had fought against Hitler could not understand younger men's refusal to support their government. "How can Americans take sides against their own young men sent to Vietnam to fight and perhaps to die?" asked supporters of government policy. They expressed their anger at war protesters with bumper stickers that read "America: Love It or Leave It."

By 1967, the administration realized that "discontent with the war is now wide and deep," as McGeorge Bundy put it. Recognizing public opinion as a critical weapon in the war effort, President Johnson used various means to silence critics. He equated opposition to the war with communism and assistance to the enemy. To avoid focusing attention on the war's costs, he eschewed price and wage controls to control inflation and delayed asking for a tax increase to pay for the war. Not until June 1968 did Congress pass a 10 percent income tax surcharge, after Johnson promised to cut domestic spending. Great Society programs suffered, but the surcharge failed to reverse the inflationary surge.

The administration also deceived the public by making optimistic statements about the war's progress and concealing ever-graver doubts within the administration about the possibility of success in Vietnam. Johnson tried to discredit war critics, calling them "Nervous Nellies" or Communists, and he ordered the CIA to spy on peace advocates, resulting in CIA files on more than 7,000 citizens. Without the president's specific authorization, the FBI infiltrated the peace movement, disrupted its work, and spread false information about activists. Even the resort to illegal measures failed to subdue the opposition.

1968: Year of Upheaval

The year 1968 was a year of violent confrontations around the world. Protests against governments erupted from Mexico City to Paris to Tokyo, usually led by students in collaboration with workers. American society also became increasingly polarized. On one side were the so-called **hawks**, who charged that the United States was fighting with one hand tied behind its back and called for intensification of the war. The **doves** wanted de-escalation or withdrawal. As U.S. troop strength neared half a million and military deaths approached 20,000 by the end of 1967, most people were torn between weariness with the war and worry about reneging on the Americans' commitment. As one woman said to a pollster, "I want to get out but I don't want to give up."

Grave doubts penetrated the administration itself in 1967. Secretary of Defense Robert McNamara, a principal architect of U.S. involvement, now believed that the North Vietnamese "won't quit no matter how much bombing we do." And he feared for the image of the United States, "the world's greatest superpower, killing or seriously injuring 1,000 noncombatants a week, while trying to pound a tiny, backward nation into submission on an issue whose merits are hotly disputed." McNamara did not publicly oppose the war, but in early 1968 he left the administration.

A critical turning point came with the Tet Offensive, which began on January 30, 1968. Just a few weeks after General Westmoreland reported that "the enemy has been driven away from the population centers [and] compelled to disperse," the North Vietnamese and Vietcong attacked key cities and every major American base in South Vietnam. This was the biggest surprise of the war, and not simply because both sides had customarily observed a truce during the Vietnamese New Year holiday (called Tet). The offensive displayed the Communists' vitality and refusal to be intimidated by the presence of half a million American soldiers. Militarily, the enemy suffered a defeat, losing more than 30,000 men, ten times as many as ARVN and U.S. forces. Psychologically, however, Tet was devastating to the United States.

The Tet Offensive underscored the credibility gap between official statements and the war's actual progress. TV anchorman Walter Cronkite wondered, "What the hell is going on? I thought we were winning the war." The attacks created a million more South Vietnamese refugees as well as widespread destruction. Explaining how he had defended a village, a U.S. army official said, "We had to destroy the town to save it." The statement epitomized for more and more Americans the brutality and senselessness of the war. Public approval of Johnson's handling of it dropped to 26 percent.

In the aftermath of Tet, Johnson considered a request from Westmoreland for 200,000 more troops. He conferred with advisers in the Defense Department and an unofficial group of foreign policy experts who had been key architects of cold war policies for two decades. Dean Acheson, Truman's secretary of state, summarized their conclusion: "We can no longer do the job we set out to do in the time we have left and we must begin to take steps to disengage."

On March 31, 1968, Lyndon Johnson announced in a televised speech that the United States would reduce its bombing of North Vietnam and that he was prepared to begin peace talks. Then he made the stunning declaration that he would not run for reelection. The gradual escalation of the war was over, and military strategy shifted from "Americanization" to "Vietnamization" of the war. But this was not a shift in policy. The goal remained a non-Communist South Vietnam; the United States would simply rely more heavily on the South Vietnamese to achieve it.

Negotiations began in Paris in May 1968. The United States would not agree to recognition of the Hanoi government's National Liberation Front, to a coalition government, or to American withdrawal. The North Vietnamese would agree to nothing less. Although the talks continued, so did the fighting.

Meanwhile, violence escalated at home. Some two hundred protests on college campuses occurred in the spring of 1968. In the bloodiest action, students occupied buildings at Columbia University in New York City, with demands related to the university's war-related research and to its treatment of African Americans. When negotiations failed, university officials called in the city police, who cleared the buildings, injuring scores of demonstrators and arresting more than seven hundred. An ensuing student strike prematurely ended the academic year.

In June, two months after the murder of Martin Luther King Jr. and the riots that followed, another assassination shook the nation. Senator Robert F. Kennedy, campaigning in California for the Democratic Party's presidential nomination, was shot by a Palestinian Arab refugee who was outraged by Kennedy's support for Israel.

In August, protesters battled the police in Chicago, where the Democratic Party had convened to nominate its presidential ticket. Several thousand demonstrators came to the city, some to support the peace candidate Senator Eugene McCarthy, others to act more aggressively. Many of the latter had been mobilized by the Youth International Party (Yippies), a splinter group of SDS. Its leaders, Abbie Hoffman and Jerry Rubin, urged protesters to demonstrate their hatred of the establishment by provoking the police and creating chaos. They expressed their disdain for the Democratic Party and liberal politics by bringing a live pig as their candidate.

Chicago's Democratic mayor Richard J. Daley issued a ban on rallies and marches, ordered a curfew, and mobilized thousands of police. On August 25, demonstrators responded to police orders to disperse with insults and jeers, whereupon police attacked protesters with tear gas and clubs. Street battles continued for three days, culminating in a police riot on the night of August 28. Taunted by the crowd, the police used mace and nightsticks, clubbing not only those who had come to provoke violence but also reporters, peaceful demonstrators, and convention delegates.

Although the bloodshed in Chicago horrified those who saw it on television, it had little effect on the outcome of either major party's convention. An assassin had ended Robert Kennedy's promising campaign in June, and Vice President Hubert H. Humphrey trounced the remaining antiwar candidate, Eugene McCarthy, by nearly three to one for the Democratic nomination. McCarthy's refusal to share the podium with Humphrey as the convention ended underscored the bitter split within the party. In contrast, the Republican convention nominated former vice president Richard Nixon on the first ballot. For his running mate, Nixon chose Maryland governor Spiro T. Agnew, hoping to gather southern support.

For the first time in nearly fifty years, a strong third party also entered the electoral scene. Former Alabama governor George C. Wallace, a staunch segregationist, ran on the ticket of the American Independent Party. Wallace appealed to Americans nationwide who were disenchanted with the reforms and rebellions of the 1960s and outraged by assaults on traditional values. Nixon guardedly played on resentments that fueled the Wallace campaign, calling for "law and order" and attacking liberal Supreme Court decisions, busing for school desegregation, and protesters of all sorts.

The two major-party candidates differed little on the central issue of Vietnam. Nixon promised to "bring an honorable end" to the war but did not indicate how he would do it. Humphrey had strong reservations about U.S. policy in Vietnam, yet as vice president he wanted to avoid a break with Johnson. The president boosted Humphrey's campaign at the end of October when he announced a halt to the bombing of North Vietnam, but it was not enough. With nearly ten million votes (13 percent of the total), the American Independent Party produced the strongest third-party finish since 1924. Nixon edged out Humphrey by just half a million popular votes but garnered 301 electoral college votes to Humphrey's 191 and Wallace's 46. The Democrats lost a few seats in Congress but kept control of both houses.

The 1968 election revealed deep cracks in the coalition that had kept the Democrats in power for most of the previous thirty years. Johnson's liberal policies on race shattered a century of Democratic Party dominance in the South, which delivered all its electoral votes to Wallace or Nixon. Elsewhere, large numbers of blue-collar workers broke union ranks to vote for Wallace or Nixon, along with other groups that associated the Democrats with racial turmoil, poverty programs, inflation, changing sexual mores, and failure to turn the tide in Vietnam. These resentments would soon be mobilized into a resurging right in American politics (see chapter 30).

►**REVIEW**   How did the Vietnam War shape the election of 1968?

Nixon, Détente, and the Search for Peace in Vietnam

Nixon assumed the presidency with ambitious foreign policy goals, hoping to make his mark on history by applying his broad understanding of international relations to a changing world. Diverging from Republican orthodoxy, his dramatic overtures to the Soviet Union and China reduced decades-old hostilities. Yet anticommunism remained central to U.S. policy. In Latin America, Africa, and the Middle East, Nixon backed repressive regimes when the alternatives suggested victories for the left. Relying on public deception, secrecy, and silencing of opponents even more than his predecessor, Nixon aggressively pursued the war in Vietnam, expanding the conflict into Cambodia and Laos and ferociously bombing North Vietnam. Yet in the end, he was forced to settle for peace without victory.

Moving toward Détente with the Soviet Union and China

In Nixon's view, the "rigid and bipolar world of the 1940s and 1950s" was giving way to "the fluidity of a new era of multilateral diplomacy." Well aware of the increasing conflict between the Soviet Union and China that escalated into military skirmishes along their common border in 1969, he worked with National Security Adviser Henry A. Kissinger, his key foreign policy adviser, to exploit the situation. Nixon and Kissinger believed that if these two nations checked each other's power, their threat to the United States would lessen. According to Nixon, Soviet-Chinese hostility "served our purpose best if we maintained closer relations with each side than they did with each other." In addition, these two nations might be used to help the United States extricate itself from Vietnam.

Following two years of secret negotiations, in February 1972 Nixon became the nation's first president to set foot on Chinese soil—an astonishing act by a man who had climbed the political ladder as a fervent anti-Communist. Recognizing that his anti-Communist credentials were what enabled him to conduct this shift in U.S.-Chinese relations with no significant domestic repercussions, Nixon remarked to Chinese leader Mao Zedong, "Those on the right can do what those on the left only talk about." Although the act was largely symbolic, cultural and scientific exchanges followed, and American manufacturers began to find markets in China—small steps in the process of **globalization** that would take giant strides in the 1990s (see chapter 31).

As Nixon and Kissinger had hoped, the warming of U.S.-Chinese relations increased Soviet responsiveness to their strategy of **détente**, their term for easing conflict with the Soviet Union. Détente meant not abandoning containment but instead focusing on issues of common concern, such as arms control and trade. Containment would be achieved not only by military threat but also by ensuring that Soviet and Chinese stakes in a stable international order would restrain the leaders of those countries from precipitating crises. Nixon's goal was "a stronger healthy United States, Europe, Soviet Union, China, Japan, each balancing the other."

Arms control, trade, and stability in Europe were three areas where the United States and the Soviet Union had common interests. In May 1972, three months after his return from China, Nixon visited Moscow, signing several agreements on trade and cooperation in science and space. Most significantly, Soviet and U.S. leaders concluded arms limitation treaties that had grown out of the Strategic Arms Limitation Talks (SALT) begun in 1969. Both sides agreed to limit antiballistic missiles (ABMs) to two each. Giving up pursuit of a defense against nuclear weapons was a move of crucial importance, because it prevented either nation from building so secure an ABM defense against a nuclear attack that it would risk a first strike.

Gerald Ford, who became president when Nixon resigned in 1974 (see chapter 30), failed to sustain détente. The secrecy of the Nixon-Kissinger initiatives had alienated legislators, and some Democrats charged that détente ignored Soviet violations of human rights. Members of both parties worried that Soviet strength was overtaking that of the United States. In response, Congress derailed trade agreements with the Soviet Union, refusing economic favors unless the Soviets stopped their harsh treatment of internal dissidents and Jews.

Nonetheless, U.S., Soviet, and European leaders signed a historic agreement in 1975 in Helsinki, Finland, formally recognizing the post–World War II boundaries in Europe. Members of both major American political parties objected to the Helsinki accords because they acknowledged Soviet domination over Eastern Europe—a condition that had triggered the cold war thirty years earlier. To get

Western consent to the accords, the Soviets had to accept a clause stating that the signing countries recognized "the universal significance of human rights and fundamental freedoms." Dissidents in the Soviet Union and its Eastern European satellites soon used this official promise of rights to mount challenges to the Soviet dictatorship that would culminate in its overthrow fifteen years later.

Shoring Up Anticommunism in the Third World

Nixon promised in 1973, "The time has passed when America will make every other nation's conflict our own . . . or presume to tell the people of other nations how to manage their own affairs." Yet in Vietnam and elsewhere, Nixon and Kissinger continued to equate Marxism with a threat to U.S. interests and actively resisted social revolutions that might lead to communism.

Consequently, the Nixon administration helped to overthrow Salvador Allende, a self-proclaimed Marxist who was elected president of Chile in 1970. Since 1964, the Central Intelligence Agency (CIA) and U.S. corporations concerned about nationalization of their Chilean properties had assisted Allende's opponents. After Allende became president, Nixon ordered the CIA director to make the Chilean economy "scream" and thus destabilize his government. In 1973, with the help of the CIA, the Chilean military engineered a coup, killed Allende, and established a brutal dictatorship under General Augusto Pinochet, ending decades of democracy in Chile. Representative government was reestablished in 1990, and in 2006 a Chilean court charged Pinochet with torture, kidnapping, and murder.

In other parts of the world, too, the Nixon administration stood by repressive regimes. In southern Africa, it eased pressures on white minority governments that tyrannized blacks. The National Security Council assumed that the "whites are here to stay. . . . There is no hope for the blacks to gain the political rights they seek through violence, which will lead only to chaos and increased opportunities for Communists." In the Middle East, the United States sent secret, massive arms shipments to support the shah of Iran's harsh regime because Iran had enormous petroleum reserves and seemed a stable anti-Communist ally. Unnoticed by most Americans, the administration cemented a relationship that turned many Iranians against the United States and would ignite a new crisis when the shah was overthrown in 1979 (see chapter 30).

Like his predecessors, Nixon pursued a delicate balance between defending Israel's security and seeking the goodwill of Arab nations strategically and economically important to the United States. Conflict between Israel and the Arab nations had escalated into the Six-Day War in 1967, when Israel attacked Egypt after that nation had massed troops on its border and cut off the sea passage to Israel's southern port. Although Syria and Jordan joined the war on Egypt's side, Israel won a stunning victory, seizing territory that amounted to twice its original size. Israeli forces took control of the Sinai Peninsula and Gaza Strip from

Egypt, the Golan Heights from Syria, and the West Bank (which included the Arab sector of Jerusalem, a city sacred to Jews, Christians, and Muslims alike) from Jordan.

That decisive victory did not quell Middle Eastern turmoil. In October 1973, on the Jewish holiday Yom Kippur, Egypt and Syria surprised Israel with a full-scale attack. When the Nixon administration sided with Israel in the Yom Kippur War, Arab nations retaliated with an oil embargo that created severe shortages in the United States. After Israel repulsed the attack, Kissinger attempted to mediate between Israel and the Arab nations, efforts that continued for more than three decades with only limited success. The Arab countries refused to recognize Israel's right to exist, Israel began to settle its citizens in territories occupied during the Six-Day War, and no solution could be found for the Palestinian refugees who had been displaced by the creation of Israel in the late 1940s. The simmering conflict contributed to anti-American sentiment among Arabs who viewed the United States as Israel's supporter.

Vietnam Becomes Nixon's War

"I'm not going to end up like LBJ, holed up in the White House afraid to show my face on the street," the new president asserted. "I'm going to stop that war. Fast." Nixon gradually withdrew U.S. ground troops, but he was no more willing than Eisenhower, Kennedy, or Johnson to be the president who allowed South Vietnam to fall to the Communists. To Nixon and Kissinger, that goal was tied to the larger objective of maintaining American credibility. Regardless of the wisdom of the initial intervention, Kissinger asserted, "the commitment of 500,000 Americans has settled the importance of Vietnam. For what is involved now is confidence in American promises."

From 1969 to 1972, Nixon and Kissinger pursued a four-pronged approach. First, they tried to strengthen the South Vietnamese military and government. Second, to disarm the antiwar movement at home, Nixon gradually replaced U.S. forces with South Vietnamese soldiers and American technology and bombs. Third, Nixon and Kissinger negotiated with both North Vietnam and the Soviet Union. Fourth, the military applied intensive bombing to persuade Hanoi to accept American terms at the bargaining table.

As part of the Vietnamization of the war, ARVN forces grew to more than a million, and the South Vietnamese air force became the fourth largest in the world. U.S. advisers and funds also promoted land reform, village elections, and the building of schools, hospitals, and transportation facilities. Meanwhile, U.S. forces withdrew, decreasing from 543,000 in 1968 to 140,000 by the end of 1971, a move that critics called merely "changing the color of the corpses." Despite reduced draft calls and a decrease in the number of American deaths from nearly 800 a month in 1969 to 352 in 1970, more than 20,000 Americans perished in Vietnam during the last four years of the war.

In the spring of 1969, Nixon began a ferocious air war in Cambodia, carefully hiding it from Congress and the public for more than a year. Seeking to knock out North Vietnamese sanctuaries in Cambodia, Americans dropped more than 100,000 tons of bombs but succeeded only in sending the North Vietnamese to other hiding places. Echoing Johnson, Kissinger believed that a "fourth-rate power like North Vietnam" had to have a "breaking point," but the hundreds of thousands of tons of bombs delivered by U.S. pilots failed to find it.

To support a new, pro-Western Cambodian government installed through a military coup in 1970 and "to show the enemy that we were still serious about our commitment in Vietnam," Nixon ordered a joint U.S.-ARVN invasion of Cambodia in April 1970. That order made Vietnam "Nixon's war" and provoked outrage at home. Nixon made a belligerent speech defending his move and emphasizing the importance of U.S. credibility: "If when the chips are down, the world's most powerful nation acts like a pitiful helpless giant, the forces of totalitarianism and anarchy will threaten free nations" everywhere. Upon reading a draft of the speech, a cabinet member predicted, "This will make the students puke."

They did more. In response, more than 100,000 people protested in Washington, D.C., and students boycotted classes on hundreds of campuses. At Kent State University in Ohio, National Guard troops were dispatched after protesting students burned an old ROTC building. Then, at a rally there on May 4, when some students threw rocks at the troops, they fired at the students, killing four and wounding ten others. "They're starting to treat their own children like they treat us," commented a black woman in Harlem. In a confrontation at Jackson State College in Mississippi on May 14, police shot into a dormitory, killing two black students. And in August, police in Los Angeles used tear gas and clubs against Chicano antiwar protesters.

Congressional reaction to the invasion of Cambodia revealed increasing concern about abuses of presidential power. In the name of national security, presidents since Franklin Roosevelt had conducted foreign policy without the consent or sometimes even the knowledge of Congress—for example, Eisenhower in Iran and Johnson in the Dominican Republic. But in their determination to win the war in Vietnam, Johnson and Nixon had taken extreme measures to deceive the public and silence their critics. The bombing and invasion of Cambodia infuriated enough legislators that the Senate voted to terminate the Gulf of Tonkin Resolution, which had given the president virtually a blank check in Vietnam, and to cut off funds for the Cambodian operation. The House refused to go along, but by the end of June, Nixon had pulled all U.S. troops out of Cambodia.

The Cambodian invasion failed to break the will of North Vietnam, but it set in motion a terrible tragedy for the Cambodian people. The North Vietnamese moved further into Cambodia and strengthened the Khmer Rouge, Communist insurgents attempting to overthrow the U.S.-supported government of Lon Nol. A brutal civil war raged until 1975, when the Khmer Rouge triumphed and imposed a savage rule, slaughtering millions of Cambodians and giving the name "killing fields" to the land of a historically peaceful people.

In 1971, Vietnam veterans themselves became a visible part of the peace movement, the first men in U.S. history to protest a war in which they had fought. Veterans held a public investigation of "war crimes" in Vietnam, rallied in front of the Capitol, and cast away their war medals. In May 1971, veterans numbered among the 40,000 protesters who engaged in civil disobedience in an effort to shut down Washington. Officials made more than 12,000 arrests, which courts later ruled violations of protesters' rights.

After the spring of 1971, there were fewer massive antiwar demonstrations, but protest continued. Public attention focused on the court-martial of Lieutenant William Calley, which began in November 1970 and resulted in his conviction. During the trial, Americans learned that in March 1968, Calley's company had systematically killed every inhabitant of the hamlet of My Lai, nearly all of whom were old men, women, and children. Estimates put the death toll at more than 400 villagers. The Americans had encountered no enemy forces there. The military covered up the atrocity for more than a year before a journalist exposed it. Eventually, twelve officers and enlisted men were charged with murder or assault to commit murder, but only Calley was convicted.

Administration policy suffered another blow in June 1971 with the publication of the *Pentagon Papers*, secret government documents consisting mostly of a study that Defense Secretary Robert McNamara had ordered in 1967. The *New York Times* got the material from Daniel Ellsberg, who had worked on the study and whose attempts to persuade officials of the war's futility had been unsuccessful. Even though the study did not cover the Nixon administration, government lawyers went to court to stop further publication, in part out of fear that other information would be leaked. The Supreme Court, however, was more concerned about freedom of the press, arguing that the attempt to stop publication was a "flagrant, indefensible" violation of the First Amendment. Subsequent circulation of the *Pentagon Papers*, which revealed considerable pessimism among officials during the early years of the war even as they made rosy promises, heightened disillusionment with the war by casting doubts on the government's credibility. More than 60 percent of Americans polled in 1971 considered it a mistake to have sent American troops to Vietnam; 58 percent believed the war to be immoral.

Military morale sank in the last years of the war. Having been exposed to the antiwar movement at home, many of the remaining soldiers had less faith in the war than their predecessors had had. Racial tensions among soldiers mounted, many soldiers sought escape in illegal drugs, and they committed hundreds of "fraggings," attacks on officers by enlisted men. In a 1971 report, "The Collapse of the Armed Forces," a retired Marine Corps colonel described the lack of discipline: "Our army that now remains in Vietnam [is] near mutinous."

The Peace Accords and the Legacy of Defeat

Nixon and Kissinger continued to believe that intensive firepower could bring the North Vietnamese to their knees, and they combined that force with negotiation. In March 1972, responding to a strong North Vietnamese offensive, the United States resumed sustained bombing of the North, mined Haiphong and other harbors for the first time, and announced a naval blockade. With peace talks stalled, in December Nixon ordered the most devastating bombing of North Vietnam yet.

The intense bombing, called "jugular diplomacy" by Kissinger, was costly to both sides, but it brought renewed negotiations. On January 27, 1973, representatives of the United States, North Vietnam, South Vietnam, and the Vietcong (now called the People's Revolutionary Government) signed a formal accord in Paris. The agreement required removal of all U.S. troops and military advisers but allowed North Vietnamese forces to remain. Both sides agreed to return prisoners of war. Nixon called the agreement "peace with honor," but it in fact allowed only a face-saving withdrawal for the United States.

Fighting resumed immediately among the Vietnamese. Nixon's efforts to support the South Vietnamese government, and indeed his ability to govern at all, were increasingly eroded by what came to be known as the Watergate scandal (see chapter 30). Nixon had been forced to give up his office by 1975, when North Vietnam launched a new offensive. On May 1, it occupied Saigon and renamed it

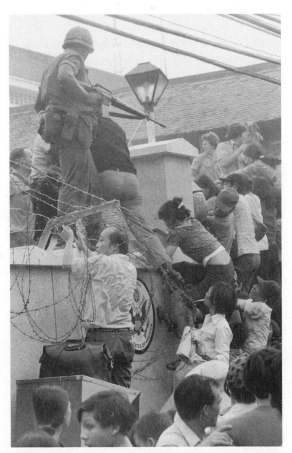

Evacuating South Vietnam
As Communist troops rolled south toward Saigon in the spring of 1975, desperate South Vietnamese attempted to flee along with the departing Americans. These South Vietnamese attempt to scale the wall of the U.S. Embassy to reach evacuation helicopters. Thousands of Vietnamese who wanted to be evacuated were left behind.
AP Images.

Ho Chi Minh City to honor the Communist leader. The Americans hastily evacuated, along with 150,000 of their South Vietnamese allies.

Confusion, humiliation, and tragedy marked the rushed departure. The United States lacked sufficient transportation capabilities and time to evacuate all those South Vietnamese who wanted to leave. U.S. marines beat back desperate Vietnamese trying to escape through the U.S. Embassy. Former lieutenant Philip Caputo, who had returned to South Vietnam as a journalist and got out at the last minute, felt "like a deserter." His helicopter "took some ground fire from South Vietnamese soldiers who probably felt that the Americans had betrayed them."

During the four years it took Nixon to end the war, he had expanded the conflict into Cambodia and Laos and had launched massive bombing campaigns in Vietnam. Although increasing numbers of legislators criticized the war, Congress never denied the president the funds to fight it and never rescinded the Gulf of Tonkin Resolution. Only after the peace accords did the legislative branch stiffen its constitutional authority in the making of war, passing the War Powers Act in November 1973. The law required the president to report to Congress within forty-eight hours of deploying military forces abroad. If Congress failed to endorse the president's action within sixty days, the troops would have to be withdrawn. The new law, however, did little to dispel the distrust of and disillusionment with the government that had swelled with Americans' realization that their leaders had not told the truth about Vietnam.

The disorder that had accompanied antiwar protests and bitter divisions among Americans were other legacies of the war. Even children of Nixon administration officials protested the war that their fathers were waging. Vietnam diverted money from domestic programs and sounded the death knell of Johnson's Great Society. It created federal budget deficits and triggered inflation that contributed to ongoing economic crises throughout the 1970s (see chapter 30).

Four presidents had declared that the survival of South Vietnam was essential for the United States to prevail in the cold war, but their dire predictions that a Communist victory in South Vietnam would set the dominoes cascading did not materialize. Although Vietnam, Laos, and Cambodia all fell within the Communist camp in the spring of 1975, Thailand, Burma, Malaysia, and the rest of Southeast Asia did not. When China and Vietnam reverted to their historically hostile relationship, the myth of a monolithic Communist power overrunning Asia evaporated.

The long pursuit of victory in Vietnam complicated the United States' relations with other nations, as even its staunchest ally, Britain, doubted the wisdom of the war. The spectacle of terrifying American power used against a small Asian country alienated many in the third world and compromised efforts to win the hearts and minds of people in developing nations through initiatives such as the Peace Corps and the Alliance for Progress.

The cruelest legacy of Vietnam fell on those who had served. "We would not return to cheering crowds, parades, and the pealing of great cathedral bells," wrote Philip Caputo. The failure of the United States to win the war, its unpopularity at home, and its character as a guerrilla war denied veterans the traditional homecoming of returning soldiers. Veterans themselves expressed two kinds of reactions to the defeat. Many believed in the war's purposes and felt betrayed by the government for not letting them and their now-dead comrades win it. Other veterans blamed the government for sacrificing the nation's youth in an immoral, unnecessary, or useless war, expressing their sense of the war's futility by referring to their dead comrades as having been "wasted." Sometimes identifying with the Vietnamese more than with their white comrades, veterans belonging to minority groups had more reason to doubt the nobility of their purpose. A Native American soldier assigned to resettle Vietnamese civilians found it to be "just like when they moved us to the rez [reservation]. We shouldn't have done that."

Because the Vietnam War was a civil, guerrilla war, combat was especially brutal. The terrors of conventional warfare were multiplied, and so were the motivations to commit atrocities. The massacre at My Lai was only the most widely publicized war crime. To demonstrate the immorality of the war, peace advocates stressed the atrocities, contributing to a distorted image of the Vietnam veteran as dehumanized and violent.

Most veterans came home to public neglect; some faced harassment from antiwar activists who failed to distinguish the war from the warriors. A veteran remembered the "feelings of rejection and scorn that a bunch of depressed and confused young men experienced when they returned home from doing what their country told them to do." Government benefits were less generous to Vietnam veterans than they had been to those of the past two wars. Yet two-thirds of Vietnam veterans said that they would serve again, and most veterans readjusted well to civilian life.

Nonetheless, some suffered long after the war ended. The Veterans Administration (VA) estimated that nearly one-sixth of the veterans suffered from post-traumatic stress disorder, with its symptoms of fear, recurring nightmares, feelings of guilt and shame, violence, drug and alcohol abuse, and suicidal tendencies. Thirty years after performing army intelligence work in Saigon, Doris Allen "still hit the floor sometimes when [she heard] loud bangs." In the late 1970s, many of those who had served in Vietnam began to produce deformed children and fell ill themselves with cancer, severe skin disorders, and other ailments. Veterans claimed a link between those illnesses and Agent Orange, an herbicide that contained the deadly poison dioxin, which the military had sprayed by the millions of gallons over Vietnam. Not until 1991 did Congress provide assistance to veterans with diseases linked to the poison.

By then, the climate had changed. The war began to enter the realm of popular culture, with novels, TV shows, and hit movies depicting a broad range of military experience—from soldiers reduced to brutality to men and women serving with courage and integrity. The incorporation of the Vietnam War into the collective experience was symbolized most dramatically in the Vietnam Veterans

Memorial unveiled in Washington, D.C., in November 1982. Designed by Yale architecture student Maya Lin, the black, V-shaped wall inscribed with the names of 58,200 men and women lost in the war became one of the most popular sites in the nation's capital. In an article describing the memorial's dedication, a Vietnam combat veteran spoke to and for his former comrades: "Welcome home. The war is over."

▶ **REVIEW**   How did Nixon try to bring American involvement in Vietnam to a close?

Conclusion: An Unwinnable War

Vietnam was America's longest war. The United States spent more than $150 billion (nearly $600 billion in 2007 dollars) and sent 2.6 million young men and women to Vietnam. Of those, 58,200 never returned, and 150,000 suffered serious injury. The war shattered consensus at home, increased presidential power at the expense of congressional authority and public accountability, weakened the economy and domestic reform, and contributed to the downfall of two presidents.

Even as Nixon and Kissinger took steps to ease cold war tensions with the major Communist powers—the Soviet Union and China, which were also the main suppliers of the North Vietnamese—they also acted vigorously throughout the third world to install or prop up anti-Communist governments. They embraced their predecessors' commitment to South Vietnam as a necessary cold war engagement because they believed that to do otherwise would threaten American credibility and make the United States appear weak. Defeat in Vietnam did not make the United States the "pitiful helpless giant" predicted by Nixon, but it did mark the relative decline of U.S. power and the impossibility of containment on a global scale.

One of the constraints on U.S. power was the tenacity of revolutionary movements determined to achieve national independence. Marine lieutenant Philip Caputo recalled his surprise at discovering "that the men we had scorned as peasant guerrillas were, in fact, a lethal, determined enemy." Overestimating the effectiveness of American technological superiority, U.S. officials badly underestimated the sacrifices that the enemy was willing to make and failed to realize how easily the United States could be perceived as a colonial intruder.

A second constraint on Eisenhower, Kennedy, Johnson, and Nixon was their resolve to avoid a major confrontation with the Soviet Union or China. For Johnson, who conducted the largest escalation of the war, caution was especially critical so as not to provoke direct intervention by the Communist superpowers. After China exploded its first atomic bomb in 1964, the potential heightened for the Vietnam conflict to escalate into worldwide disaster.

Third, in Vietnam the United States sought to prop up an extremely weak ally engaged in a civil war. The South Vietnamese government never won the support of its people, and the intense devastation the war brought to civilians only made things worse. Short of taking over the South Vietnamese government and military, the United States could do little to strengthen South Vietnam's ability to resist communism.

Finally, domestic opposition to the war, which by 1968 included significant portions of mainstream America, constrained the options of Johnson and Nixon. As the war dragged on, with increasing American casualties and growing evidence of the damage being inflicted on innocent Vietnamese, more and more civilians wearied of the conflict. Even some who had fought in the war joined the movement, including Philip Caputo, who sent his campaign ribbons and a bitter letter of protest to the White House. In 1973, Nixon and Kissinger bowed to the resolution of the enemy and the limitations of U.S. power. As the war wound down, passions surrounding it contributed to a rising conservative movement that would substantially alter the post–World War II political order.

REVIEWING THE CHAPTER

Use the questions and timeline to review and strengthen your understanding of the chapter.

REVIEW QUESTIONS

1. Why did Kennedy believe that engagement in Vietnam was crucial to his foreign policy? (pp. 934–42)

2. How did American troops serving in Vietnam differ from those who served in World War II, and how were their experiences different? (pp. 942–47)

3. How did the Vietnam War shape the election of 1968? (pp. 947–53)

4. How did Nixon try to bring American involvement in Vietnam to a close? (pp. 953–62)

MAKING CONNECTIONS

1. Cuba featured prominently in the most dramatic foreign policy actions of the Kennedy administration. Citing specific events, discuss why Cuba was an area of great concern to the administration. How did Cuba figure into Kennedy's cold war policies? Were his actions in regard to Cuba effective?

2. Explain the Gulf of Tonkin incident and its significance to American foreign policy. How did President Lyndon Johnson respond to the incident? What considerations, domestic and international, contributed to his course of action?

3. The United States' engagement in Vietnam divided the nation. Discuss the range of American responses to the war. How did they change over time? How did domestic political concerns shape the country's response to the war? How did the war shape domestic politics in the 1960s and early 1970s?

4. What was détente, and how did it affect the United States' cold war foreign policy? What were its achievements and limitations? In your answer, discuss how Nixon's approach to communism built on and departed from the previous two administrations' approaches.

TIMELINE

1961	• Bay of Pigs invasion. • Berlin Wall erected. • Kennedy administration increases military aid to South Vietnam. • Alliance for Progress established. • Peace Corps created.	**1969**	• American astronauts land on moon. • Nixon orders secret bombing of Cambodia.
1962	• Cuban missile crisis.	**1970**	• Nixon orders invasion of Cambodia. • Students killed during protests at Kent State and Jackson State.
1963	• Limited nuclear test ban treaty signed. • President Kennedy assassinated; Lyndon B. Johnson becomes president.	**1971**	• *New York Times* publishes *Pentagon Papers*.
1964	• Anti-American rioting in Panama Canal Zone. • Gulf of Tonkin Resolution.	**1972**	• Nixon becomes first U.S. president to visit China. • Nixon visits Moscow to sign arms limitation treaties with Soviets.
1965	• First major demonstration against Vietnam War. • Operation Rolling Thunder begins. • Johnson orders first combat troops to Vietnam. • U.S. troops invade Dominican Republic.	**1973**	• Paris Peace Accords. • War Powers Act. • CIA-backed military coup in Chile. • Arab oil embargo following Yom Kippur War.
1967	• Arab-Israeli Six-Day War.	**1975**	• North Vietnam takes over South Vietnam, ending the war. • Helsinki accords.
1968	• Hundreds of thousands of Americans demonstrate against Vietnam War. • Tet Offensive. • Johnson decides not to seek second term. • Police and protesters clash near Democratic convention in Chicago. • Republican Richard Nixon elected president.		

▶ **For an online bibliography, practice quizzes, Web sites, images, and documents related to this chapter,** see the Book Companion Site at **bedfordstmartins.com/roark.**

▶ **For firsthand accounts of this period,** see Chapter 29 in Michael Johnson, ed., *Reading the American Past,* Fourth Edition.

30
CHAPTER

America Moves to the Right
1969–1989

P HYLLIS SCHLAFLY experienced "one of the most exciting days of my life" when she heard **conservative** Republican Barry Goldwater address the National Federation of Republican Women in 1963. Like Goldwater, she opposed the moderate stance of the Eisenhower administration and current Republican leadership. Both Schlafly and Goldwater wanted the United States to go beyond merely containing **communism** and to eliminate that threat entirely. They also wanted to cut back the government in Washington, especially its role in providing social welfare and enforcing civil rights. Disappointed by Goldwater's loss to Lyndon Johnson in 1964, Schlafly nevertheless took heart in the conservatives' ability to engineer his nomination. She assailed the policy innovations and turmoil of the 1960s, adding new issues to the conservative agenda and helping to build a grassroots movement that would redefine the Republican Party and American politics into the twenty-first century.

Phyllis Stewart was born in St. Louis in 1924, attended Catholic schools, and worked her way through Washington University testing ammunition at a World War II defense plant. She earned an M.A. in government from Radcliffe College in 1945 and went to work at the American Enterprise Institute, where she imbibed the think tank's conservatism. Returning to the Midwest, she married Fred Schlafly, an Alton, Illinois, attorney whose anticommunism and antigovernment passions equaled hers. The mother of six children, Schlafly claimed, "I don't think there's anything as much fun as taking care of a baby," and she asserted that she would "rather scrub bathroom floors" than write political articles.

Yet while insisting that caring for home and family was women's most important career, Schlafly spent much of her time on the road—writing, speaking, leading Republican women's organizations, and testifying before legislative committees. She lost two bids for Congress in her heavily Democratic district in Illinois, in 1952 and again in 1970. Her book, *A Choice Not an Echo*, which she self-published in 1964, pushed Barry Goldwater for president and sold more than a

---

The Phyllis Schlafly Report
Phyllis Schlafly's monthly newsletter for members of her conservative Eagle Forum began in 1967 with articles attacking federal social programs and calling for stronger measures and weapons to fight communism. When Congress passed the Equal Rights Amendment in 1972, the *Report* began to add antifeminism and other concerns of the New Right to its agenda, including opposition to abortion rights, to sex education, and to protections for gays and lesbians.
Courtesy of Phyllis Schlafly.

The Phyllis Schlafly Report

VOL. 5, NO. 10, SECTION 2   Box 618, ALTON, ILLINOIS 62002   MAY, 1972

The Fraud Called The Equal Rights Amendment

If there ever was an example of how a tiny minority can cram its views down the throats of the majority, it is the Equal Rights Amendment, called ERA. A noisy claque of women's lib agitators rammed ERA through Congress, intimidating the men into voting for it so they would not be labeled "anti-woman."

The ERA passed Congress with big majorities on March 22, 1972 and was sent to the states for ratification. When it is ratified by 38 states, it will become the law of the land. Within two hours of Senate passage, Hawaii ratified it. New Hampshire and Nebraska, both anxious to be second, rushed their approval the next day. Then in steady succession came Iowa, Idaho, Delaware, Kansas, Texas, Maryland, Tennessee, Alaska, Rhode Island, and New Jersey. As this goes to press, 13 states have ratified it and others are on the verge of doing so.

Three states have rejected it: Oklahoma, Vermont and Connecticut.

What is ERA? The Amendment reads: "Equality of rights under the law shall not be denied or abridged by the United States or by any state on account of sex."

Does that sound good? Don't kid yourself. This innocuous-sounding amendment will take away far more important rights than it will ever give. This was made abundantly clear by the debate in Congress. Senator Sam Ervin (D., N.C.) called it "the most drastic measure in Senate history." He proved this by putting into the *Congressional Record* an article from the *Yale Law Journal* of April 1971.

The importance of this *Yale Law Journal* article is that both the proponents and the opponents of ERA agree that it is an accurate analysis of the consequences of ERA. Congresswoman Martha Griffiths, a leading proponent of ERA, sent a copy of this article to every member of Congress, stating that "It will help every member of Congress to understand the purposes and effects of the Equal Rights Amendment.... The article makes clear how ERA will work in many situations."

An analysis of what the ERA will do to the laws which now protect women reveals that women will be the big losers. ERA will absolutely and positively make women subject to the draft and to combat duty.

the most important of all women's rights.

"In all states husbands are primarily liable for the support of their wives and children.... The child support sections of the criminal nonsupport laws ... could not be sustained where only the male is liable for support." (*YLJ*, pp. 944-945)

"The Equal Rights Amendment would bar a state from imposing greater liability for support on a husband than on a wife merely because of his sex." (*YLJ*, p. 945)

"Like the duty of support during marriage and the obligation to pay alimony in the case of separation or divorce, nonsupport would have to be eliminated as a ground for divorce against husbands only...." (*YLJ*, p. 951)

"The Equal Rights Amendment would not require that alimony be abolished but only that it be available equally to husbands and wives." (*YLJ*, p. 952)

2. **ERA will wipe out the laws which protect only women against sex crimes such as rape.**

"Courts faced with criminal laws which do not apply equally to men and women would be likely to invalidate the laws rather than extending or rewriting them to apply to women and men alike." (*YLJ*, p. 966)

"Seduction laws, statutory rape laws, laws prohibiting obscene language in the presence of women, prostitution and 'manifest danger' laws ... The Equal Rights Amendment would not permit such laws, which base their sex discriminatory classification on social stereotypes." (*YLJ*, p. 954)

"The statutory rape laws, which punish men for having sexual intercourse with any woman under an age specified by law ... suffer from a similar defect under the Equal Rights Amendment....

"To be valid, a criminal law singling out

million copies. In 1967, she began publishing *The Phyllis Schlafly Report*, a monthly newsletter about current political issues. Throughout the 1950s and 1960s, Schlafly called for stronger efforts to combat communism at home and abroad, a more powerful military, and a less active government in domestic affairs—all traditional conservative goals.

In the 1970s, Schlafly began to address new issues, including **feminism** and the Equal Rights Amendment, abortion, gay rights, busing for racial integration, and religion in the schools. Her positions resonated with many Americans fed up with the protest movements, expansion of government, challenges to authority, and loosening of moral standards that seemed to define the 1960s. And the votes of those Americans began to reshape American politics—in Richard Nixon's victories in the presidential elections of 1968 and 1972; in the presidency of Jimmy Carter, whose policies stood substantially to the right of his Democratic predecessors; and in conservative Ronald Reagan's capture of the Republican Party, the presidency, and the political agenda in 1980.

Although Richard Nixon did not embrace the entire conservative agenda, he sought to make the Republicans the dominant party by appealing to disaffected blue-collar and southern white Democrats. The Watergate revelations forced Nixon to leave the presidency in disgrace in 1974, and his Republican successor, Gerald Ford, occupied the Oval Office for little more than two years; but the shift of the political spectrum to the right continued even when Democrat Jimmy Carter captured the White House in 1976. Antigovernment sentiment grew out of the deceptions of the Johnson administration, Nixon's abuse of presidential powers, and the inability of Presidents Ford and Carter to resolve domestic and foreign crises. As Americans saw surging unemployment and inflation—an unprecedented combination called stagflation—shrink their incomes, their confidence in government and willingness to pay taxes eroded.

In 1980, Phyllis Schlafly's call for "a choice not an echo" was realized when Ronald Reagan won the presidency. Cutting taxes and government regulations, attacking social programs, expanding the nation's military capacity, and pressuring the Soviet Union and communism in the **third world**, Reagan addressed the hopes of traditional conservatives. Like Schlafly, he also championed the concerns of the **New Right**, opposing abortion and sexual permissiveness and supporting a larger role for religion in public life. Reagan's goals encountered resistance from feminists, civil rights groups, environmentalists, and others who fought to keep what they had won in the 1960s and 1970s. Although his administration failed to enact the entire conservative agenda, enormously increased the national debt, and engaged in illegal activities to thwart communism in Latin America, Reagan's popularity helped send his vice president, George H. W. Bush, to the White House at the end of his second term. And Reagan's determined optimism and spirited leadership contributed to a revival in national pride and confidence.

Nixon and the Rise of Postwar Conservatism

As we saw in chapter 28, Nixon acquiesced in the continuation of most **Great Society** programs and even approved pathbreaking environmental and minority and women's rights measures. Yet his public rhetoric and certain of his actions signaled the country's rightward move in both politics and sentiment. Whereas Kennedy had appealed to Americans to contribute to the common good, Nixon invited Americans to "let each of us ask—not just what will government do for me, but what can I do for myself?" His words invoked individualism and reliance on the market and private enterprise rather than on government, preferences that would grow stronger in the nation during the 1970s and beyond.

During Nixon's presidency, a new strand of conservatism joined the older movement that focused on anticommunism, a strong national defense, and a limited federal role in domestic affairs. New conservatives, whom Phyllis Schlafly helped mobilize, wanted to restore what they considered traditional moral values by increasing the presence of Christianity in public life and opposing sex education, feminism, abortion, homosexuality, and sexual permissiveness.

Emergence of a Grassroots Movement

Although Lyndon Johnson's landslide victory over Barry Goldwater in 1964 seemed to mark the triumph of **liberalism**, the election results actually concealed a rising conservative movement. Defining his purpose as "enlarging freedom at home and safeguarding it from the forces of tyranny abroad," Goldwater, an Arizona senator, echoed the ideas of conservative intellectuals who argued that government intrusions into economic life hindered prosperity, stifled personal responsibility, and interfered with individuals' rights to determine their own values. Conservatives assailed big government in domestic affairs but demanded a strong military to eradicate "Godless communism."

Behind Goldwater's nomination was a growing grassroots movement. Vigorous especially in the South and West, it included middle-class suburban women and men, members of the rabidly anti-Communist John Birch Society, and college students in the new Young Americans for Freedom (YAF). They did not give up when he lost the election. Margaret Minek, a community organizer for Goldwater, insisted, "We have a . . . flame . . . burning and the energy it gives off needs to be utilized." In California, newly energized conservatives like Minek helped Ronald Reagan defeat the incumbent liberal governor, Edmund Brown, in 1966, another sign of the right's rising strength. Reagan linked Brown with the Watts riot and student disruptions at the University of California at Berkeley, exploiting popular fears about rising taxes, student rebellion, and black demands for justice.

Grassroots conservatism was not limited to the West and South, but a number of **Sun Belt** characteristics made it especially strong in places such as Orange County, California; Dallas, Texas; Scottsdale, Arizona; and Jefferson Parish,

Louisiana. Such predominantly white areas contained relatively homogeneous, skilled, and economically comfortable populations, as well as military bases and defense production facilities. The West harbored a long-standing tradition of **Protestant** morality, individualism, and opposition to interference by a remote federal government. That tradition continued with the emergence of the New Right, even though it was hardly consistent with the Sun Belt's economic dependence on defense spending and on huge federal projects that provided water and power for the burgeoning population and its economy.

The South, which also benefited from military bases, the space program, and other federal projects, shared the West's antipathy toward the federal government. Hostility to racial change, however, was much more central to the South's conservatism. After signing the Civil Rights Act of 1964, President Lyndon Johnson remarked privately, "I think we just delivered the South to the Republican Party." Indeed, Barry Goldwater carried five southern states in 1964. Even though Goldwater had voted against the law because he saw it as an unwarranted expansion of federal power, not because he favored segregation and discrimination, a southern White Citizens' Council leader said, "He voted against the Civil Rights Act, and we just showed our appreciation."

Grassroots movements emerged around what conservatives believed marked the "moral decline" of their nation. In 1962, Mel and Norma Gabler began scrutinizing school textbooks under consideration by the Texas board of education. They were able to torpedo many of the books that they found not in conformity with "the Christian-Judeo morals, values, and standards as given to us by God through . . . the Bible," and they lent their expertise to like-minded citizens throughout the country. Sex education roused the ire of Eleanor Howe in Anaheim, California, who felt that "nothing [in the sex education curriculum] depicted my values. . . . It wasn't so much the information. It was the shift in values." The Supreme Court's liberal decisions on issues such as school prayer, obscenity, and birth control also galvanized conservatives to restore "traditional values" to the nation.

In the 1970s, grassroots protests against taxes grew alongside concerns about morality. As inflation and unemployment threatened Americans' economic security, many also found themselves paying higher taxes, especially in the form of property taxes as the value of their homes increased. In 1978, Californians revolted in a popular referendum reducing property taxes by more than one-half and limiting the state legislature's ability to raise taxes. What a newspaper called a "primal scream by the People against Big Government" spread to similar antitax crusades in other states.

Nixon Courts the Right

In his 1968 presidential campaign, Richard Nixon exploited hostility to black protest and new civil rights policies, wooing white southerners and a considerable number of northern voters away from the Democratic Party. As president, he used this "southern strategy" to make further inroads into traditional Democratic strongholds in the 1972 election.

The Nixon administration reluctantly enforced court orders to achieve high degrees of integration in southern schools, but it resisted efforts to deal with segregation outside the South. In northern and western cities, where segregation resulted from residential patterns as well as decisions by school district officials, half of all African American children attended nearly all-black schools. After courts began to order the transfer of students between schools in white and black neighborhoods to achieve desegregation and the Supreme Court assented in *Swann v. Charlotte-Mecklenburg Board of Education* in 1971, busing became "political dynamite," according to a Gallup poll. "We've had all we can take of judicial interference with local schools," Phyllis Schlafly railed in 1972.

Children had been riding buses to school for decades, but busing for racial integration provoked fury. Violence erupted in Boston in 1974 when a district judge ruled for the National Association for the Advancement of Colored People (NAACP) in its suit against the Boston school committee. The judge found that school officials had maintained what amounted to a dual system and ordered busing "if necessary to achieve a unitary school system." When black students began to attend the formerly all-white South Boston High School, white students boycotted classes and angry whites threw rocks at black students disembarking from buses. White parents blasted the judge as a privileged liberal residing in the suburbs, where residents would not be touched by busing. As was true elsewhere, the whites most affected came from working-class families who remained in cities abandoned by the more affluent and whose children often rode buses to predominantly black, overcrowded schools with deficient facilities. Clarence McDonough decried the liberal officials who bused his "kid half way around Boston so that a bunch of politicians can end up their careers with a clear conscience."

African Americans themselves were conflicted about sending their children on long rides to schools where teachers might not welcome or respect them. Democratic congresswoman Shirley Chisholm saw busing as an artificial solution to residential segregation and inadequate school financing. Still, she knew that when white children were bused into black schools, "the school board would suddenly see the wisdom of improving those schools and giving them a fair share of the annual budget."

White parents and students eventually became more accepting of integration, especially after the creation of magnet schools and other new mechanisms for desegregation offered more choice. Nonetheless, integration propelled white flight to the suburbs. The number of white students in Boston public schools by 1987 was just one-third of what it had been in 1974.

Nixon failed to persuade Congress to end court-ordered busing, but after he had appointed four new justices, the Supreme Court moved in his direction in the

1974 case *Milliken v. Bradley*, imposing strict limits on the use of busing to achieve racial balance. Nixon's judicial appointments also reflected the southern strategy. He criticized the Supreme Court under Chief Justice Earl Warren for being "unprecedentedly politically active . . . using their interpretation of the law to remake American society according to their own social, political, and ideological precepts." When Warren resigned in 1969, Nixon replaced him with Warren E. Burger, a federal appeals court judge who was a **strict constructionist**—someone inclined to interpret the Constitution narrowly and to limit government intervention on behalf of individual rights.

Unions and civil rights groups, however, mounted strong campaigns against Nixon's next two nominees, both conservative southern judges, and the Senate forced him to settle on more moderate candidates. The Burger Court proved more sympathetic than the Warren Court to the president's agenda, restricting somewhat the protections of individual rights established by the previous Court, but continuing to uphold many of the liberal programs of the 1960s. For example, the Court limited the range of **affirmative action** in *Regents of the University of California v. Bakke* (1978), but it allowed affirmative action programs to attack the results of past discrimination if they avoided strict quotas or racial classifications.

Nixon's southern strategy and other repercussions of the civil rights revolution of the 1960s ended the Democratic hold on the "solid South." In 1964, Senator Strom Thurmond of South Carolina, leader of the Dixiecrat challenge to Truman in 1948, changed his party affiliation to Republican. North Carolina senator Jesse Helms followed suit in 1971, and aspirants for office throughout the South began to realize that the future for Democratic candidates had darkened there. By 2005, Republicans held the majority of southern seats in both houses of Congress and governorships in seven southern states.

In addition to capitalizing on racial issues, Nixon aligned himself with those fearful about women's changing roles and new demands. In 1971, he vetoed a bill providing federal funds for day care centers with a message that combined the old and new conservatism. Parents should purchase child care services "in the private, open market," he insisted, not through government programs. He played to concerns of social conservatives by warning about the measure's "family-weakening implications." In response to the movement to liberalize abortion laws, Nixon sided with "defenders of the right to life of the unborn." He did not comment publicly on *Roe v. Wade* (1973), but his earlier stance against abortion anticipated the Republican Party's eventual embrace of this as a key issue for the New Right.

▶ **REVIEW**   How did Nixon's policies reflect the increasing influence of conservatives on the Republican Party?

Constitutional Crisis and Restoration

Nixon's ability to attract Democrats resulted in his resounding victory in the 1972 election. Two years later, however, the so-called Watergate scandal caused him to abandon his office. Nixon's abuse of power and efforts to cover up crimes committed by subordinates betrayed the public trust and forced the first presidential resignation in history. His handpicked successor, Gerald Ford, helped restore confidence in the presidency, but the aftermath of Watergate and severe economic problems returned the White House to the Democrats in 1976. Nonetheless, so robust was the conservative tide that it not only survived the temporary setback when Nixon resigned the presidency but also quickly challenged the Democratic administration that followed.

The Election of 1972

Nixon's ability to appeal to concerns about Vietnam, race, law and order, and traditional morality heightened his prospects for reelection in 1972. Although the war in Vietnam continued, antiwar protests diminished with the decrease in American ground forces and casualties. Nixon's economic initiatives had temporarily checked inflation and unemployment, and his attacks on busing and antiwar protesters had appealed to the right, positioning him favorably for the 1972 election.

A large field of contenders vied for the Democratic nomination, including New York representative Shirley Chisholm, the first African American to make a serious bid for the presidency. On the right, Governor George Wallace of Alabama resurfaced to capture a series of southern primaries as well as those of Michigan and Maryland, but his campaign was cut short when a shot fired by a deranged man left him paralyzed below the waist. South Dakota senator George S. McGovern came to the Democratic convention as the clear leader, and the composition of the convention delegates made his position even stronger.

After the bitter 1968 convention, the Democrats had reformed their rules, requiring delegations to represent the proportions of minorities, women, and youths in their states. These newcomers displaced many regular Democrats—officeholders, labor leaders, and representatives of entrenched ethnic groups. One labor leader thought that "the Democratic party was taken over by the kooks," referring to the considerable numbers of young people and women among these newcomers who were to the left of party regulars. Though easily nominated, McGovern struggled against Nixon from the outset. Republicans portrayed him as a left extremist, and his support for busing, a generous welfare program, immediate withdrawal from Vietnam, and deep cuts in the Pentagon's budget alienated conservative Democrats.

Seeing a parallel with Goldwater in 1964, a Nixon speechwriter called McGovern "Nixon's gift from the gods." Indeed, Nixon achieved a landslide victory second only to Johnson's, winning 60.7 percent of the popular vote and every state except Massachusetts. Although the Democrats maintained control of Congress, Nixon won majorities among traditional Democrats—southerners, Catholics, urbanites, and blue-collar workers. The president, however, had little time to savor his triumph, as revelations began to emerge about crimes committed to ensure the victory.

Watergate

During the early-morning hours of June 17, 1972, five men working for Nixon's reelection campaign crept into Democratic Party headquarters in the Watergate complex in Washington, D.C. Intending to repair a bugging device installed in an earlier break-in, they were discovered and arrested on the scene. Nixon and his aides then tried to cover up the intruders' connection to administration officials, setting in motion the most serious constitutional crisis since the Civil War. Reporters dubbed the scandal "Watergate."

Over the next two years, Americans learned that Nixon and his associates had engaged in other abuses, such as accepting illegal campaign contributions, using so-called dirty tricks to sabotage Democratic candidates, and unlawfully attempting to silence critics of the Vietnam War. Nixon was not the first president to lie to the public or to misuse power. Every president since Franklin D. Roosevelt had enlarged the powers of his office, justifying his actions as necessary to protect national security. This expansion of executive powers, often called the "imperial presidency," weakened the traditional **checks and balances** on the executive branch and opened the door to abuses.

No president, however, had dared to go as far as Nixon, who saw opposition to his policies as a personal attack and was willing to violate the Constitution to stop it. The Watergate scandal began when White House adviser Charles Colson established a secret unit nicknamed the "plumbers" to stop the kinds of "leaks" that had led to publication of the *Pentagon Papers* in 1971 (see chapter 29). These men soon turned to projects to disrupt and discredit Democrats, and in 1972 they broke into Watergate to bug the Democratic Party's phones.

Upon the arrest of the Watergate burglars, Nixon plotted to conceal links between the burglars and the White House while publicly denying any connection. In April 1973, after investigations by a grand jury and the Senate suggested that White House aides had been involved, Nixon accepted official responsibility for Watergate but denied any knowledge of the break-in or cover-up. He also announced the resignations of three White House aides and the attorney general. In May, he authorized the appointment of an independent special prosecutor, Archibald Cox, to conduct an investigation.

Meanwhile, sensational revelations exploded in the Senate investigating committee, headed by Democrat Samuel J. Ervin of North Carolina. White House counsel John Dean described projects to harass "enemies" through tax audits

The Gap in the Watergate Tapes

Franklin Roosevelt installed the first recording apparatus in the White House under his desk in 1940, but Richard Nixon was the first to use a voice-activated system. This system taped about 2,800 hours of conversations, which most participants did not know were being recorded. When Nixon turned over the tapes during the Watergate investigation, an eighteen-and-a-half-minute gap was discovered in a conversation between Nixon and his chief of staff just three days after the Watergate break-in. Nixon's secretary said that her foot must have slipped on the controls while she was transcribing the tape with the machine pictured here.

Nixon Presidential Materials Project, National Archives and Records Administration.

and other illegal means and implicated the president in efforts to cover up the Watergate break-in. The most damaging blow struck when a White House aide disclosed that all conversations in the Oval Office were taped. Both Cox and the Ervin committee immediately asked for the tapes related to Watergate. When Nixon refused, citing executive privilege and separation of powers, Cox and Ervin took their case to court.

Additional disclosures exposed Nixon's misuse of federal funds and tax evasion. In August 1973, Vice President Spiro Agnew resigned after an investigation revealed that he had taken bribes while governor of Maryland. Although Nixon's choice of House minority leader Gerald Ford of Michigan to succeed Agnew won widespread approval, Agnew's resignation further tarnished the administration.

On October 19, 1973, Nixon ordered special prosecutor Cox to stop trying to obtain the Oval Office tapes. When Cox refused, Nixon directed Attorney General Elliot Richardson to fire Cox. Richardson instead resigned, as did the next man in line at the Justice Department. Finally, the solicitor general, Robert Bork, agreed to carry out the president's order and fire Cox. The press called the series of dismissals and resignations the "Saturday night massacre." Soon 250,000 telegrams condemning Nixon's action flooded the White House, and his popular support plummeted to 27 percent.

In a famous televised speech, Nixon insisted, "I am not a crook," but in February 1974, the House of Representatives voted to begin an **impeachment** investigation. In April, Nixon began to release edited transcripts of the tapes. As the public read passages sprinkled with "expletive deleted," House Republican leader Hugh Scott of Pennsylvania abandoned his support of the president, calling the transcripts a "deplorable, shabby, disgusting, and immoral performance by all." The transcripts revealed Nixon's orders to aides in March 1973: "I don't give a shit what happens. I want you all to stonewall it, let them plead the Fifth Amendment, cover up or anything else, if it'll save it—save the plan."

In July 1974, the House Judiciary Committee began debate over specific charges for impeachment: (1) obstruction of justice, (2) abuse of power, (3) contempt of Congress, (4) unconstitutional waging of war by the secret bombing of Cambodia, and (5) tax evasion and the selling of political favors. The committee voted to take the first three charges to the House, where a vote of impeachment seemed certain. Ordered by a unanimous Supreme Court to hand over the remaining tapes, Nixon released transcripts on August 5 that contained his conversations about how to use the CIA to hinder the FBI's investigation of the break-in. This was sufficient evidence to seal his fate.

Nixon announced his resignation to a national television audience on August 8, 1974. Acknowledging some incorrect judgments, he insisted that he had always tried to do what was best for the nation. The next morning, Nixon ended a rambling, emotional farewell to his staff with some advice: "Always give your best, never get discouraged, never get petty; always remember, others may hate you, but those who hate you don't win unless you hate them, and then you destroy yourself." Had he practiced that advice, he might have saved his presidency.

The Ford Presidency and the 1976 Election

Gerald R. Ford, who had represented Michigan in the House of Representatives since 1948, had built a reputation as a conservative party loyalist. Not a brilliant thinker, he was known for his integrity, humility, and dedication to public office. "I'm a Ford, not a Lincoln," he acknowledged. Most of official Washington and the American public looked favorably on his succession as president.

Upon taking office, Ford announced, "Our long nightmare is over," but he shocked many Americans one month later when he ended the particular nightmare of the former president. On September 8, 1974, he granted Nixon a pardon "for all offenses against the United States which he . . . has committed or may have committed or taken part in" during his presidency. This most generous presidential pardon ever issued saved Nixon from nearly certain indictment and trial. The pardon provoked a tremendous outcry from Congress and the public. Democratic senator Mike Mansfield declared, "All men are created equal," and "that includes presidents and plumbers." Democrats made impressive gains in the November congressional elections, while Ford's action gave Nixon a new political life. Having gained a pardon without having to admit that he had broken the law, violated his oath of office, and betrayed the public trust, he rebuilt his image over the next two decades into that of an elder statesman. Thirty of his associates ultimately pleaded guilty to or were convicted of crimes related to Watergate.

Congress moved to guard against the types of abuses revealed in the Watergate investigations. The Federal Election Campaign Act of 1974, for example, established public financing of presidential campaigns and imposed some restrictions on contributions to help prevent the selling of political favors. Yet politicians found other ways of raising money, for example through political action committees (PACs) of interest groups, to which individuals could contribute more than they could to individual candidates. Moreover, in the 1976 case *Buckley v. Valeo*, the Supreme Court struck down limitations on campaign spending by equating such spending with freedom of speech, guaranteed by the First Amendment. Ever-larger campaign donations flowed to candidates from interest groups, corporations, labor unions, and wealthy individuals. In 1978, Congress established a nonpartisan procedure for appointing special prosecutors. The law was used to investigate possible criminal actions by Presidents Reagan and Clinton (see chapter 31), as well as several lesser officials, before it expired in 1998.

Special investigating committees in Congress discovered a host of illegal FBI and CIA activities stretching back to the 1950s, including harassment of political dissenters and plots to assassinate Fidel Castro and other foreign leaders. In response to these revelations, President Ford established new controls on covert operations, and Congress created permanent committees to oversee the intelligence agencies. Yet these measures did little to diminish the public's cynicism and lack of trust in government that had been developing since the 1960s.

Disillusionment with government grew as the Ford administration seemed unable to resolve serious economic problems: a low growth rate, high unemployment, a foreign trade deficit, and soaring energy prices tied to dependence on oil from abroad. Ford carried these burdens into the election campaign of 1976, while contending with a major challenge from the Republican right. Blasting Nixon's and Ford's foreign policy of **détente** for causing the "loss of U.S. military supremacy," California governor Ronald Reagan came close to capturing the nomination.

The Democrats nominated James Earl "Jimmy" Carter Jr., former governor of Georgia. A graduate of the U.S. Naval Academy, Carter spent seven years as a nuclear engineer in the navy before returning to Plains, Georgia, to run the family peanut farming business. Carefully prepared on policy issues, the soft-spoken candidate appealed to the rise of **evangelical** religion and alienation from government by stressing his profound faith as a "born-again Christian" and his distance from the government in Washington. Although he selected liberal senator Walter F. Mondale of Minnesota as his running mate and accepted a platform compatible with traditional Democratic principles, Carter's nomination nonetheless marked a decided rightward turn in the party.

In light of the revelations of corruption in the Nixon administration, Carter had considerable appeal as a candidate who carried his own bags, lived modestly, and taught a Bible class at his Baptist church. He also benefited from Ford's failure to solve the country's economic problems, which helped him win the traditional Democratic coalition of blacks, organized labor, and ethnic groups, and even recapture some of the white southerners who had voted for Nixon in 1972. Yet although Democrats retained substantial margins in Congress, Carter received just 50 percent of the popular vote to Ford's 48 percent.

> ▶REVIEW   Why did Nixon resign the presidency in August 1974?

The "Outsider" Presidency of Jimmy Carter

Carter promised a government that was "competent" as well as "honest, decent, open, fair, and compassionate." He also warned Americans "that even our great Nation has its recognized limits, and that we can neither answer all questions nor solve all problems." Carter's humility, personal honesty, and decency helped revive trust in the presidency but did not inspire confidence in his ability to lead the nation through domestic and foreign crises.

Energy shortages and stagflation worsened, exposing Carter's deficiencies in working with Congress and rallying the public to his objectives. His administration achieved notable advances in environmental and energy policies, and he oversaw foreign policy successes concerning the Panama Canal, China, and the Middle East. Yet near the end of his term, Soviet-American relations deteriorated, new crises emerged in the Middle East, and the economy plummeted, all costing him a second term.

Retreat from Liberalism

Jimmy Carter vowed "to help the poor and aged, to improve education, and to provide jobs," but at the same time "not to waste money." When his desire to help conflicted with his goal to limit spending, Carter's commitment to reform took second place. Increasing numbers of Americans unhappy about their tax dollars being used to benefit the disadvantaged while stagflation eroded their own material status welcomed Carter's approach. But his fiscal stringency frustrated liberal Democrats pushing for major welfare reform and a national health insurance program. They accused him of deserting the Democratic reform tradition stretching back to Franklin D. Roosevelt.

A number of factors hindered Carter's ability to lead. His outsider status had helped him win office but left him without strong ties to party leaders in Congress, who often found him self-righteous, overly self-confident, and not inclined to compromise. Democrats complained of inadequate consultation and Carter's tendency to flood them with comprehensive proposals when they were more accustomed to incremental reforms. In addition, Carter refused to offer simple solutions to the American people, who had a short attention span and were impatient for quick action against the forces that were squeezing their pocketbooks. Moreover, even though the Democrats continued to control Congress, party leaders were hard-pressed to deliver a united front. Reforms in response to highly publicized scandals that had touched congressional leaders in the 1960s had reduced the power of committee chairs and decentralized the decision-making process.

Even an expert in the art of persuasion might not have done much better than Carter. The economic problems he inherited from the Nixon and Ford administrations—unemployment, inflation, and sluggish economic growth—confounded economic doctrine, which assumed that when unemployment was high, inflation would be low, and vice versa. Usually, rising prices accompanied a humming economy with a strong demand for labor. Now, however, the nation faced steep inflation and high unemployment at the same time.

Carter first targeted unemployment. Although liberals complained that his programs did not do enough, Carter signed bills pumping $14 billion into the economy through public works and public service jobs programs and cutting taxes by $34 billion over a three-year period. Unemployment, which had hovered near 8 percent in late 1976, fell below 6 percent in 1978. But then inflation surged. Working people, wrote one journalist, "winced and ached. . . . Promises had been made to all of them over the two decades; but now the promises were being re- deemed in money which might become as worthless as Confederate dollars." To curb inflation, Carter curtailed federal spending, and the Federal Reserve Board tightened the money supply. Not only did these measures fail to halt inflation, which surpassed 13 percent in 1980, but they also contributed to rising unem- ployment, reversing the gains made in Carter's first two years.

Long-standing liberal objectives made little headway under Carter. His com- mitment to holding down the federal budget frustrated Democrats pushing for comprehensive welfare reform, national health insurance, and a wide-ranging program to create jobs for all by making the government the employer of last resort. Carter did sign legislation to ensure solvency in the Social Security system, but the measure increased both employer and employee contributions, thereby increasing the tax burden of lower- and middle-income Americans.

By contrast, corporations and wealthy individuals gained from new legisla- tion, such as a sharp cut in the capital gains tax. When the Chrysler Corporation approached bankruptcy in 1979, Congress provided $1.5 billion in loan guarantees to ensure the survival of the tenth-largest corporation in the country. Congress also acted on Carter's proposals to give greater rein to free enterprise, deregulat- ing airlines in 1978 and the banking, trucking, and railroad industries in 1980. Carter's successor would move much further, implementing conservatives' attachment to a free market and unfettered private enterprise.

Energy and Environmental Reform

Complicating the government's efforts to deal with stagflation was the nation's enormous consumption of energy and its dependence on foreign nations to fill one-third of its energy demands. Fuel shortages and skyrocketing oil prices threatened the entire economy, just as they had during the energy crisis of 1973. Consequently, Carter proposed a comprehensive program to conserve energy, and he elevated its importance by establishing the Department of Energy. Beset with competing demands among energy producers and consumers, Congress picked Carter's program apart. The National Energy Act of 1978 penalized man-ufacturers of gas-guzzling automobiles and provided other incentives for conservation and the development of alternative fuels, but the act fell far short of a long-term, comprehensive program.

In 1979, a new upheaval in the Middle East, the Iranian revolution, created the most severe energy crisis yet. In midsummer, 60 percent of gasoline stations closed down because of shortages; frustrated drivers sat in long lines at stations that were open, where they paid unprecedentedly high prices for gas. "We are struggling with a profound transition from a time of abundance to a time of growing scarcity in energy," Carter told the nation, and he asked Congress for additional measures to address this problem. Congress reduced controls on oil and gas to stimulate American production and imposed a windfall profits tax on producers to redistribute some of the profits that would accrue to them as a result of deregulation.

All of Carter's energy measures failed to reduce American dependence on foreign oil. European nations shared that dependence but more successfully con-trolled consumption. They levied high taxes on gasoline, causing people to rely more on public transportation and manufacturers to produce more energy-efficient cars, in the process also limiting the release of carbon gases into the atmosphere. In the automobile-dependent United States, however, where public transit was poor, people were accustomed to driving long distances, and many were seething over what they considered high taxes, politicians dismissed that approach. By the end of the century, the United States, with 6 percent of the world's population, would consume more than 25 percent of global oil produc-tion (Map 30.1, page 980).

One source of alternative fuel, nuclear energy, aroused opposition from a vig-orous environmental movement. Activists warned of radiation leakage, potential accidents, and the hazards of radioactive wastes from nuclear power plants, which provided about 10 percent of the nation's electricity in the 1970s. In 1976, hundreds of members of the Clamshell Alliance went to jail for attempting to block construction of a nuclear power plant in Seabrook, New Hampshire. Groups such as the Abalone Alliance in California and SHAD (Sound and Hudson against Atomic Development) on Long Island, New York, sprang up across the United States to demand an environment safe from nuclear radiation and waste.

The perils of nuclear energy claimed international attention in March 1979, when an accident occurred at the Three Mile Island nuclear facility near Harrisburg, Pennsylvania. Technicians worked for days to prevent a meltdown of the reactor core. Popular opposition and the great expense of building nuclear

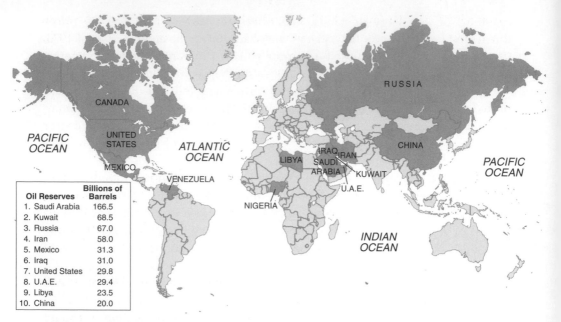

Oil Reserves	Billions of Barrels
1. Saudi Arabia	166.5
2. Kuwait	68.5
3. Russia	67.0
4. Iran	58.0
5. Mexico	31.3
6. Iraq	31.0
7. United States	29.8
8. U.A.E.	29.4
9. Libya	23.5
10. China	20.0

MAP 30.1 Worldwide Oil Reserves, 1980

Data produced by geologists and engineers enable experts to estimate the size of "proved oil reserves," quantities that are recoverable with existing technology and prices. The recovery of reserves depends on many factors, including the precise location of the oil. Large portions of the U.S. reserves, for example, lie under deep water in the Gulf of Mexico, where it is expensive to drill and where operations can be disrupted by hurricanes.

power plants stalled further development of the industry. The explosion of a nuclear reactor and the spread of deadly radiation in Chernobyl, Ukraine, in 1986 further solidified antinuclear concerns as part of the environmental movement.

A disaster at Love Canal in Niagara Falls, New York, advanced other environmental goals by underscoring the human costs of unregulated development. Residents there suffering high rates of serious illness noted that their homes sat amid highly toxic waste products from a nearby chemical company. One Love Canal resident, Lois Gibbs, who eventually headed a national movement against toxic wastes, explained how she and many other women were galvanized to become environmentalists: "I never thought of myself as an activist or organizer. I was a housewife, a mother, but all of a sudden it was my family, my children, and my neighbors." Finally responding to the activists in 1978, the State of New York agreed to help families relocate, and the Carter administration sponsored legislation in 1980 that created the so-called Superfund, $1.6 billion for the cleanup of hazardous wastes left by the chemical industry.

Carter's environmental legislation did not stop there. He signed bills to improve clean air and water programs; to expand the Arctic National Wildlife Refuge preserve (ANWR) in Alaska; and to control strip-mining, which left destructive scars on the land. During the 1979 gasoline crisis, Carter attempted to balance the development of domestic fuel sources with environmental concerns. Acknowledging that "some of the new technologies we will need to develop pose environmental risks," he upset some environmental activists. But he also won legislation to conserve energy and to provide incentives for the development of environmentally friendly alternative fuels, such as solar energy.

Promoting Human Rights Abroad

Campaigning in 1976, Jimmy Carter charged that his predecessors' foreign policy violated the nation's principles of freedom and human dignity. "We're ashamed of what our government is as we deal with other nations around the world," he said. Carter promised to reverse the cynical support of dictators, secret diplomacy, interference in the internal affairs of other countries, and excessive reliance on military solutions.

Human rights formed the cornerstone of his approach. Carter administration officials chastised governments that denied their citizens basic rights, and they applied economic pressure, denying aid or trading privileges to nations such as Argentina, Chile, and El Salvador, as well as to the white minority governments of Rhodesia and South Africa, which brutally violated the rights of their black majorities. Yet in other instances, Carter sacrificed human rights ideals in favor of strategic and security considerations. He invoked no sanctions against repressive governments in Iran, South Korea, and the Philippines, for example, and he established formal diplomatic relations with the People's Republic of China in 1979, even though the Chinese government blatantly refused to grant its people **democratic** rights.

Carter's human rights principles faced another test when a popular movement overthrew an oppressive dictatorship in Nicaragua. U.S. officials were uneasy about the leftist Sandinistas who led the rebellion and had ties to Cuba. Once they assumed power in 1979, however, Carter recognized the new government and sent economic aid, signaling that the way a government treated its citizens was as important as how anti-Communist and friendly to American interests it was.

Applying moral principles to relations with Panama, Carter sped up negotiations over control of the Panama Canal and in 1977 obtained a treaty providing for joint control of the canal until 2000, when Panama would take over. Supporters viewed the treaty as recompense for the blatant use of U.S. power to obtain the canal in 1903. Opponents insisted on retaining the vital waterway. "We bought it, we paid for it, it's ours," claimed Ronald Reagan during the presidential primaries of 1976. It took a massive effort by the administration to get Senate ratification of the treaty.

Seeking to promote peace in the Middle East, Carter seized on the courage of Egyptian president Anwar Sadat, the first Arab leader to risk his political career

MAP 30.2   The Middle East, 1948–1989
Determination to preserve access to the rich oil reserves of the Middle East and commitment to the security of Israel were the fundamental—and often conflicting—principles of U.S. foreign policy in that region.

by talking directly with Israeli officials. Carter invited Sadat and Israeli prime minister Menachem Begin to the presidential retreat at Camp David, Maryland, where he applied his tenacious diplomacy, mediating between the two for thirteen days. These talks led to an agreement—the Camp David accords—that Begin and Sadat signed at the White House in March 1979. Egypt became the first Arab state to recognize Israel, and Israel agreed to gradual withdrawal from the Sinai Peninsula, which it had seized in the 1967 Six-Day War (Map 30.2). Although the issues of Palestinian self-determination in other Israeli-occupied territories (the West Bank and Gaza) and the plight of Palestinian refugees remained unresolved, Carter had facilitated the first meaningful steps toward peace in the Middle East.

The Cold War Intensifies

Consistent with his human rights approach, Carter preferred to pursue national security through nonmilitary means and initially sought accommodation with the Soviet Union. But in 1979, he abandoned efforts to obtain Senate ratification of a new strategic arms limitation treaty and began development of an enormous new missile system and intermediate-range missiles to be deployed in Western Europe.

Carter's decision to pursue a military buildup came in 1979 when the Soviet Union invaded neighboring Afghanistan, whose recently installed Communist government was threatened by Muslim opposition (see Map 30.2). Insisting that the Soviet aggression "could pose the greatest threat to peace since the Second World War," Carter also imposed economic sanctions on the Soviet Union, barred U.S. participation in the 1980 Summer Olympic Games in Moscow, and obtained legislation requiring all nineteen-year-old men to register for the **draft**.

Claiming that Soviet actions jeopardized oil supplies from the Middle East, the president announced the "Carter Doctrine," threatening the use of any means necessary to prevent an outside force from gaining control of the Persian Gulf. His human rights policy fell by the wayside as the United States stepped up aid to the military dictatorship in Afghanistan's neighbor, Pakistan. Carter authorized the CIA to provide aid secretly to the Afghan rebels, which it funneled through Pakistan. Finally, Carter called for hefty increases in defense spending.

Events in Iran also encouraged this reversion to a hard-line, militaristic approach. All the U.S. arms and aid had not enabled the shah to crush Iranian dissidents who still resented the CIA's role in the overthrow of the Mossadegh government in 1953 (see chapter 27), condemned the shah's savage attempts to silence opposition, and detested his adoption of Western **culture** and values. These grievances erupted into a revolution in 1979 that forced the shah out of Iran. Just two years earlier, Carter had pronounced the shah's government "an island of stability," and the revolution shocked U.S. officials who failed to detect the growing hostility toward American support for dictators in the Middle East. The new provisional government began talks with the United States, but it soon gave way to Shiite Islamic **fundamentalists** led by Ayatollah Ruholla Khomeini, whom the shah had exiled in 1964.

Carter's decision to allow the shah into the United States for medical treatment intensified anti-Americanism among Iranians, who believed that the United States would put the shah back in power as it had done in 1953. Demonstrations against the United States escalated in the capital city of Teheran. On November 4, 1979, a crowd broke into the U.S. Embassy and seized sixty-six U.S. diplomats, CIA officers, citizens, and military attachés (who were ordered not to fire). Refusing their demands that the shah be returned to Iran for trial, Carter froze Iranian assets in U.S. banks and placed an embargo on Iranian oil. In April 1980, he sent a small military operation into Iran, but the rescue mission failed.

The disastrous rescue attempt and scenes of blindfolded and cuffed U.S. citizens paraded before TV cameras fed Americans' feelings of impotence, simmering since the defeat in Vietnam. These frustrations in turn increased support for a more militaristic foreign policy. Opposition to Soviet-American détente, combined with the Soviet invasion of Afghanistan, nullified the thaw in relations that had begun in the 1960s. The American hostages in Iran filled the news during the 1980 presidential campaign and contributed to Carter's defeat. Iran freed the hostages the day he left office, but relations with the United States remained tense.

> ▶REVIEW   How did Carter attempt to balance his commitment to human rights and anticommunism in his foreign policy?

Ronald Reagan and the Conservative Ascendancy

Ronald Reagan's election in 1980 marked the most important turning point in politics since Franklin D. Roosevelt won the presidency in 1932. Eisenhower and Nixon were middle-of-the-road Republicans, but Reagan's victory established conservatism's dominance in the Republican Party. Since the 1930s, the Democrats had defined the major issues. In the 1980s, the Republicans assumed that initiative, while Democrats searched for voter support by moving toward the right. The United States was not alone in this political shift. Conservatives rose to power in Britain with Prime Minister Margaret Thatcher, and they led governments in Germany, Canada, and Sweden, while socialist and social democratic governments in France and elsewhere trimmed their welfare states.

On the domestic front, the Reagan administration embraced the conservative Christian values of the New Right, but it left its most important mark on the economy: victory over inflation, deregulation of industry, a moratorium on social spending, enormous tax cuts, and a staggering **federal budget deficit**. Economic expansion, which took off after 1983, helped the middle class and brought great wealth to some, but the percentage of poor Americans increased, and income distribution became more unequal. Although the Reagan era did not see a policy revolution comparable to that of the **New Deal**, it dealt a sharp blow to the liberalism that had informed American politics since that time.

Appealing to the New Right and Beyond

The oldest candidate ever nominated for the presidency, Ronald Reagan was born in Tampico, Illinois, in 1911. After attending a small religious college, he worked as a sportscaster before becoming a movie actor. He initially shared the politics of his staunchly Democratic father but moved to the right in the 1940s and 1950s and campaigned for Goldwater in 1964.

Reagan's political career took off when he was elected governor of California in 1966. He ran as a conservative, but in office he displayed considerable flexibility, approving a major tax increase, a strong water pollution bill, and a liberal abortion law. Displaying similar agility in the 1980 presidential campaign, he softened earlier attacks on programs such as Social Security and chose the moderate George H. W. Bush as his running mate.

Ronald Reagan Nominated for President

Nancy and Ronald Reagan respond to cheers at the 1980 Republican National Convention, where he was nominated for president. Reagan became one of the most popular presidents of the twentieth century.

Lester Sloan/Woodfin Camp & Associates.

Despite his move to the center, some Republicans balked at his nomination and at the party platform, which reflected the concerns of the party's right wing. For example, after Phyllis Schlafly persuaded the party to reverse its forty-year support for the Equal Rights Amendment, moderate and liberal Republican women protested outside the convention hall. Some Republicans found a more acceptable presidential candidate in Illinois representative John B. Anderson, who deserted his party to run as an independent.

Reagan's campaign capitalized on the economic recession and the international challenges symbolized by the Americans held hostage in Iran. Repeatedly, Reagan asked voters, "Are you better off now than you were four years ago?" He promised to "take government off the backs of the people" and to restore Americans' morale and other nations' respect. A narrow majority of voters, 51 percent, responded to Reagan's upbeat message. Carter won 41 percent of the vote, and 7 percent went to Anderson. The 1980 election also delivered control of the Senate to the Republicans for the first time since the 1950s.

While the economy and Iran sealed Reagan's victory, he also benefited from the burgeoning grassroots conservative movements. An extraordinarily adept politician, Reagan appealed to a wide spectrum of groups and sentiments: free-market advocates, militant anti-Communists, fundamentalist Christians, white southerners, and white working-class Democrats—the so-called "Reagan Democrats," disenchanted with the Great Society and suffering from the high inflation and unemployment rates of the 1970s.

A critical bloc of Reagan's support came from religious conservatives, predominantly Protestants, who constituted a relatively new phenomenon in politics known as the New Right or New Christian Right. During the 1970s, evangelical and fundamentalist Christianity claimed thousands of new adherents, making adept use of sophisticated mass-mailing techniques and the "electronic ministry." Evangelical ministers such as Pat Robertson preached to huge television audiences, attacking feminism, abortion, and homosexuality and calling for the restoration of old-fashioned "family values." They wanted prayer back in the schools and sex education out of them. A considerable number of Catholics, such as Phyllis Schlafly, shared the fundamentalists' goal of a return to their version of "Christian values."

Conservatives created a raft of political organizations, such as the Moral Majority, founded by minister Jerry Falwell in 1979 to fight "left-wing, social-welfare bills, . . . pornography, homosexuality, [and] the advocacy of immorality in school textbooks." The Christian Coalition, created by Pat Robertson in 1989, claimed 1.6 million members and control of the Republican Party in more than a dozen states. The instruments of more traditional conservatives, who advocated limited government at home and militant anticommunism abroad, likewise flourished. These included publications such as the *National Review*, founded in the 1950s and edited by William F. Buckley Jr., and conservative think tanks such as the American Enterprise Institute. The monthly *Phyllis Schlafly Report* merged the sentiments of the old and new right, which were also manifest in its publisher's organization, Eagle Forum.

Reagan embraced the full spectrum of conservatism, including its inconsistencies. For example, the New Right's demand for government intervention into private matters to stop abortion and homosexuality conflicted with the traditional conservative attachment to **laissez-faire**. Reagan avowed agreement on abortion, school prayer, and other New Right issues, but he did not push hard for so-called moral or social policies. Instead, his major achievements lay in areas most important to the older right—strengthening the nation's anti-Communist posture and reducing taxes and government restraints on free enterprise. "In the present crisis," Reagan declared, "government is not the solution to our problem, government is the problem."

Reagan's admirers stretched far beyond conservatives. The extraordinarily popular president was liked even by Americans who opposed his policies and even when he made glaring mistakes. At one meeting, he failed to recognize his secretary of housing and urban development, the only African American in his cabinet. On another occasion, he proclaimed that vegetation caused 90 percent of all air pollution, prompting student environmentalists to adorn a tree with a sign reading, "Chop me down before I kill again." Reagan made so many misstatements that aides tried to keep him away from reporters, and they carefully scripted the former actor's public appearances.

Reagan's optimism, confidence, and easygoing humor formed a large part of his appeal. Ignoring the darker moments of the American past, he presented a version of history that Americans could feel good about. Listeners understood his declaration that it was "morning in America" as a promise that the best was yet to come. Reagan also gained public sympathy after being shot by a would-be assassin in March 1981. Just before surgery to remove the bullet, Reagan joked to physicians, "I hope you're Republicans." His tremendous popularity helped him withstand serious charges of executive branch misconduct in his second term.

Unleashing Free Enterprise

Reagan's first domestic objective was a massive tax cut. Although tax reduction in the face of a large budget deficit contradicted traditional Republican economic doctrine, Reagan relied on a new theory called **supply-side economics**, which held that cutting taxes would actually increase revenue. Supply-siders insisted that lower taxes would enable businesses to expand, encourage individuals to work harder because they could keep more of their earnings, and increase the production of goods and services—the supply—which in turn would boost demand. Reagan promised that the economy would grow so much that the government would recoup the lost taxes, but instead it incurred a galloping deficit.

In the summer of 1981, Congress passed the Economic Recovery Tax Act, the largest tax reduction in U.S. history. Rates of individuals with the lowest incomes fell from 14 percent to 11 percent, while those of individuals with the highest incomes dropped from 70 percent to 50 percent. The law gave corporations tax breaks and cut taxes on capital gains, gifts, and inheritances. A second measure, the Tax Reform Act of 1986, reduced taxes even more, lowering the maximum rate on individual income to 28 percent and on business income to 35 percent. Although the 1986 law narrowed loopholes used primarily by the wealthy, affluent Americans saved far more on their tax bills than did average taxpayers, and the distribution of wealth tipped further in favor of the rich.

"Hack, chop, crunch!" were *Time* magazine's words for Reagan's efforts to free private enterprise from government restraints. Carter had confined deregulation to particular industries, such as air transportation and banking, while increasing health, safety, and environmental regulations. The Reagan administration, by contrast, pursued across-the-board deregulation. It declined to enforce the Sherman Antitrust Act (see chapter 18), which was designed to limit **monopoly**, against an unprecedented number of business mergers and takeovers. Reagan also loosened regulations protecting employee health and safety, and he weakened labor unions. When thousands of members of the Professional Air Traffic Controllers Organization (PATCO) struck in 1981, Reagan fired them, destroying their union (which had supported his election) and intimidating organized labor.

Ronald Reagan loved the outdoors and his remote ranch in southern California, where all told he spent nearly a year of his two-term presidency. Yet he blamed environmental laws for the nation's sluggish economic growth and targeted them for deregulation. His first secretary of the interior, James Watt, declared, "We will mine more, drill more, cut more timber," and he released federal lands to private exploitation. Meanwhile, the head of the Environmental Protection Agency relaxed enforcement of air and water pollution standards. Of environmentalists, Reagan wisecracked, "I don't think they'll be happy until the White House looks like a bird's nest," but their numbers grew in opposition to his administration's policies. Popular support for environmental protection forced several environmental officials to resign and blocked full realization of Reagan's deregulatory goals.

Deregulation of the banking industry, begun under Carter with bipartisan support, created a crisis in the savings and loan industry. Some of the newly deregulated savings and loan institutions (S&Ls) extended enormous loans to real estate developers and invested in other high-yield but risky ventures. S&L owners reaped lavish profits, and their depositors enjoyed high interest rates. But when real estate values began to plunge, hundreds of S&Ls went bankrupt. After Congress voted to bail out the S&L industry in 1989, the burden of the largest financial scandal in U.S. history, estimated at more than $100 billion, fell on American taxpayers.

The S&L crisis deepened the federal deficit, which soared despite Reagan's pledge to pare federal spending. When the administration cut funds for food stamps, job training, aid to low-income students, and other social welfare programs, hundreds of thousands of people lost benefits. Increases in defense spending, however, far exceeded the budget cuts, and the deficit continued to climb: from $74 billion in 1981 to a high of $220 billion in 1986. Under Reagan, the nation's debt tripled to $2.3 trillion, and interest on the debt consumed one-seventh of all federal expenditures. And despite all of his antigovernment rhetoric, the number of federal employees actually grew from 2.9 million to 3.1 million during his presidency.

It took the severest recession since the 1930s to squeeze inflation out of the U.S. economy. Unemployment approached 11 percent late in 1982, and record numbers of banks and businesses closed. The threat of unemployment further undermined organized labor, forcing unions to make concessions that management insisted were necessary for industry's survival. In 1983, the economy recovered and entered a period of unprecedented growth.

That economic upswing and Reagan's own popularity posed a formidable challenge to the Democrats in the 1984 election. They nominated Carter's vice president, Walter F. Mondale, to head the ticket, but even his precedent-breaking move in choosing a woman as his running mate (New York representative Geraldine A. Ferraro) did not save the Democrats from a humiliating defeat. Reagan charged his opponents with concentrating on America's failures, while he emphasized success and possibility. Democrats, he claimed, "see an America where every day is April 15th [the due date for income tax returns] . . . we see an America where every day is the Fourth of July."

Voters responded to the president's sunny vision and the economic comeback, giving him a landslide victory with 59 percent of the popular vote and a 523-to-13 margin in the electoral college. Winning only Mondale's home state of Minnesota, the Democrats pondered how to stem the exodus of longtime loyalists— particularly southern white males—to the Republican Party. Stung by Republican charges that the Democratic Party was captive to "special interests" such as labor, women, and minorities, some Democratic leaders, including the young Arkansas governor, Bill Clinton, urged a further party shift toward the right.

Winners and Losers in a Flourishing Economy

After the economy took off in 1983, some Americans won great fortunes as popular culture celebrated making money and displaying wealth. Books by business wizards topped best seller lists, the press described lavish million-dollar parties, and a new television show, *Lifestyles of the Rich and Famous*, drew large audiences. College students listed making money as their primary ambition.

Participating conspicuously in the new affluence were members of the baby boom generation, known popularly as "yuppies," short for "young urban professionals." These mostly white, well-educated young men and women lived in urban condominiums and pursued fast-track careers. They also consumed lavishly—fancy cars, health clubs, expensive vacations, and electronic gadgets. Though definitely a minority, they established consumption standards that many tried to emulate. And, in fact, millions of Americans enjoyed larger houses that they filled with such new products as VCRs, microwave ovens, and personal computers.

Many of the newly wealthy got rich from moving assets around rather than from producing goods. Notable exceptions included Steven Jobs, who invented the Apple computer in his garage; Bill Gates, who transformed the software industry; and Liz Claiborne, who turned a $250,000 investment into a billion-dollar fashion enterprise. But many others made money by manipulating debt and restructuring corporations through mergers and takeovers. Most financial wizards operated within the law, but occasionally greed led to criminal convictions. Michael Milken took home well over $50 million a year before he landed in jail for using insider information to maximize his financial manipulations.

Other economic problems remained. The U.S. steel, automobile, and electronics industries were surpassed by those of Germany and Japan. Americans bought more Volkswagens and Hondas and fewer Fords and Chevrolets. With Americans purchasing more foreign-made goods than domestic producers were able to sell abroad, the nation's trade deficit (the difference between imports and exports) soared.

International competition forced the collapse of some older companies. Others moved factories and jobs abroad to be closer to foreign markets or to benefit from the low wages in countries such as Mexico and Korea. Service industries expanded during this process of **de-industrialization** and created new jobs at home, but these jobs paid substantially lower wages. When David Ramos was laid off in 1982 from his $12.75-an-hour job in a steel plant, his wages fell to $5 an hour as a security guard, forcing his family to rely on food stamps. The number of full-time workers earning wages below the poverty level ($12,195 for a family of four in 1990) rose from 12 percent to 18 percent of all workers in the 1980s.

The weakening of organized labor combined with the decline in manufacturing to erode the position of blue-collar workers. Chicago steelworker Ike Mazo, who contemplated the $6-an-hour jobs available to him, fumed, "It's an attack on the living standards of workers." Increasingly, a second income was needed to stave off economic decline. By 1990, nearly 60 percent of married women with young children worked outside the home. Yet even with two incomes, fewer young families could afford a home or provide a good life for their children. "I worry about their future every day," Mazo's wife confessed. "Will we be able to put them through college? . . . Will they be out in the workforce working for four dollars an hour?" The average $10,000 disparity between men's and women's annual earnings made things even harder for the nearly 20 percent of families headed by women.

In keeping with conservative philosophy, Reagan adhered to **trickle-down economics**, insisting that a booming economy would benefit everyone. Average personal income did rise during his tenure, but the trend toward greater economic inequality that had begun in the 1970s intensified in the 1980s, encouraged in part by his tax policies. The rich got richer, a portion of the middle class did well, and the poor got poorer. Personal income shot up sharply for the wealthiest 20 percent of Americans, while it fell for the poorest by 9.8 percent between 1979 and 1987.

Poverty statistics, too, revealed a reversal of the trend toward greater equality. Between 1980 and 1988, poor people increased from 11.7 percent to 13.5 percent of the total U.S. population—the highest poverty rate in the industrialized world. Social Security and Medicare helped keep the poverty rate among the elderly relatively low. Less fortunate were other groups that the economic boom had bypassed: racial minorities, female-headed families, and children. One child in five lived in poverty. Although overall unemployment fell below 6 percent after 1983, more than 10 percent of black men could not find a job.

Even as the economy boomed, affluent urbanites walked past men and women sleeping in subway stations and on park benches. Experts debated the total number of homeless Americans—estimates ranged from 350,000 upward—but no one doubted that homelessness had increased. Those without shelter included the victims of long-term unemployment, the erosion of welfare benefits, and slum clearance, as well as Vietnam veterans and individuals suffering from mental illness, drug addiction, and alcoholism.

▶ **REVIEW**   Why did economic inequality increase during the Reagan administration?

Continuing Struggles over Rights

The rise of conservatism put liberal social movements on the defensive, as the Reagan administration moved away from the national commitment to equal opportunity undertaken in the 1960s and the president's federal court appointments reflected that shift. Feminists and minority groups fought to defend protections they had recently won, and they achieved some limited gains. The gay and lesbian rights movement actually grew in numbers, edging attitudes toward greater tolerance and winning important protections at the state and local levels.

Battles in the Courts and Congress

President Reagan agreed with conservatives that the nation had moved too far in guaranteeing rights to minority groups. Crying "reverse discrimination," they maintained that affirmative action unfairly hurt whites. Instead they called for "color-blind" policies, ignoring statistics showing that minorities and white women still lagged far behind white men in opportunities and income. Intense mobilization by civil rights groups, educational leaders, and even corporate America prevented the administration from abandoning affirmative action, and the Supreme Court upheld important antidiscrimination policies. Moreover, although Reagan wanted to allow the Voting Rights Act to expire, Congress voted to extend it with veto-proof majorities. The administration did, however, put the brakes on civil rights enforcement by appointing conservatives to the Justice Department, the Civil Rights Commission, and other agencies and by slashing their budgets.

Congress stepped in to defend antidiscrimination programs after the Justice Department persuaded the Supreme Court to severely weaken Title IX of the Education Amendments Act of 1972, a key law promoting equal opportunity in education. *Grove City v. Bell* (1984) allowed the Justice Department to abandon dozens of civil rights cases against schools and colleges, which in turn galvanized a coalition of civil rights organizations and groups representing women, the aged, and the disabled, along with their allies. In 1988, Congress passed the Civil Rights Restoration Act, which reversed the administration's victory in *Grove City* and banned any organization that practiced discrimination on the basis of race, color, national origin, sex, disability, or age from receiving government funds.

The *Grove City* decision reflected a rightward movement in the federal judiciary, upon which liberals had counted as a powerful ally in their struggles for civil rights and social justice. President Reagan encouraged this trend by taking advantage of the opportunity to appoint half of the 761 federal court judges and three new Supreme Court justices. By carefully selecting conservative candidates, he turned the tide in favor of strict construction—the literal interpretation of the Constitution that narrowly adheres to the words of its authors, thereby limiting judicial power to protect individual rights.

Reagan's first Supreme Court appointment was Sandra Day O'Connor, a moderate conservative. Liberals defeated his nomination of ultraconservative Robert Bork in a bitter contest, but the appointments of Antonin Scalia and Anthony M. Kennedy gave strict constructionists a slim majority. The full impact of these appointments became clear after Reagan left office, as the Court allowed states to impose restrictions that weakened access to abortion for poor and uneducated women, reduced protections against employment discrimination, and whittled down legal safeguards against the death penalty.

Feminism on the Defensive

One of the signal achievements of the New Right was capturing the Republican Party's position on women's rights. For the first time in its history, the Republican Party took an explicitly antifeminist tone, opposing both the Equal Rights Amendment (ERA) and a woman's right to abortion, key goals of women's rights activists. When the time limit for ratification of the ERA ran out in 1982, Phyllis Schlafly celebrated victory on the issue that had first galvanized her antifeminist campaign, while amendment supporters looked for the silver lining. Sonia Johnson, who was excommunicated by the Mormon Church for her feminism in 1979, exaggerated only somewhat when she called the ratification struggle "the greatest political training ground for women in the history of the world." (See chapter 28.)

Cast on the defensive, feminists began to focus even more on women's economic and family problems, where they found some common ground with the Reagan administration. The Child Support Enforcement Amendments Act helped single and divorced mothers to collect court-ordered child support payments from absent fathers. The Retirement Equity Act of 1984 benefited divorced and older women by strengthening their claims to their husbands' pensions and enabling women to qualify more easily for private retirement pensions.

The Reagan administration had its own concerns about women, specifically about the **gender gap**—women's tendency to vote for liberal and Democratic candidates in larger numbers than men did. (Party leaders welcomed the opposite element of that trend: white men's movement into Republican ranks.) Reagan eventually appointed three women to cabinet posts and, in 1981, selected the first woman, Sandra Day O'Connor, for the Supreme Court, despite the Christian Right's objection to her support of abortion. But these actions accompanied a general decline in the number of women and minorities in high-level government positions. And with higher poverty rates than men, women suffered most from Reagan's cuts in social programs.

Although court decisions placed restrictions on women's ability to obtain abortions, feminists fought successfully to retain the basic principles of *Roe v. Wade*. Moreover, they won a key decision from the Supreme Court ruling that sexual harassment in the workplace constituted sex discrimination. However, the women's movement hit a stone wall in efforts to improve day care services and promote pay equity—

Confrontations over Abortion

Failing to win a constitutional amendment banning abortion, some groups in the right-to-life movement adopted more militant tactics in the late 1970s and 1980s, picketing abortion clinics, yelling at patients and employees, and trying to block entrance into clinics. Here police outside a clinic in Silver Spring, Maryland, remove protesters, arresting more than twenty of them. © Bettmann/Corbis.

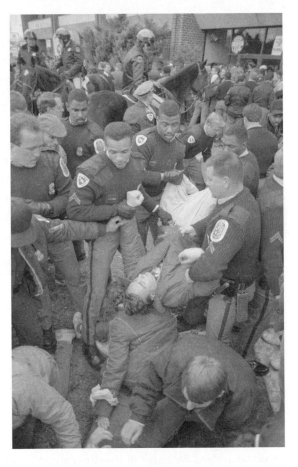

equal pay for traditionally female jobs that were comparable in worth to jobs held primarily by men. The women's movement pursued locally what it failed to achieve at the federal level. The pay equity movement took hold in several states, and many states strengthened their laws against rape. States also increased funding for domestic violence programs and stepped up efforts to protect victims and prosecute abusers.

The Gay and Lesbian Rights Movement

In contrast to feminism and other social movements, gay and lesbian rights activism grew during the 1980s, galvanized in part by the discovery in 1981 of a devastating new disease, acquired immune deficiency syndrome (AIDS). Because initially the disease disproportionately affected male homosexuals, as the epidemic swept through communities of gay men in New York and San Francisco, activists mobilized to promote public funding for AIDS education, prevention, and treatment.

The gay and lesbian rights movement helped closeted homosexuals experience the relief of "coming out." Their visibility increased awareness, if not always acceptance, of homosexuality among the larger population. Beginning with the election of Elaine Noble to the Massachusetts legislature in 1974, several openly gay politicians won offices from mayor to member of Congress, and the Democrats began to include gay rights in their party platforms. Activists organized gay rights marches throughout the country, turning out half a million people in New York City in 1987.

Popular attitudes about homosexuality moved toward greater tolerance but remained complex, leading to uneven changes in policies. Dozens of cities banned job discrimination against homosexuals, and beginning with Wisconsin in 1982, eleven states made sexual orientation a protected category under civil rights laws. Local governments and large corporations began to offer health insurance and other benefits to same-sex domestic partners.

Yet a strong countermovement challenged the drive for recognition of gay rights. The Christian Right targeted gays and lesbians as symbols of national immorality and succeeded in overturning some homosexual rights measures, which already lagged far behind antidiscrimination guarantees for minorities and women. Many states removed antisodomy laws from the books, but the conservative position won out in a 1986 Supreme Court decision that upheld the constitutionality of such laws. Until the Court reversed that opinion in 2003, more than a dozen states retained laws that left homosexuals vulnerable to criminal charges for private consensual behavior.

> ▶ **REVIEW**   What gains and setbacks did minorities, feminists, and gays and lesbians experience during the Reagan years?

Ronald Reagan Confronts an "Evil Empire"

Running for president in the wake of the Soviet invasion of Afghanistan and the Iranian hostage crisis, Reagan accused Carter of weakening the military and losing the confidence of the nation's allies and the respect of its enemies. As president, he accelerated the arms buildup begun by Carter and harshly censured the Soviet Union, calling it "an evil empire." Yet despite the new aggressiveness—or, as some argued, because of it—Reagan presided over the most impressive thaw in superpower conflict since the **cold war** had begun. On the periphery of the cold war, however, Reagan practiced militant anticommunism, authorizing aid to antileftist movements in Asia, Africa, and Central America and dispatching troops to the Middle East and the Caribbean. When Congress blocked Reagan's efforts to assist opponents of the leftist government in Nicaragua, administration officials resorted to secret and illegal means to effect their agenda.

Militarization and Interventions Abroad

Reagan expanded the military with new bombers and missiles, an enhanced nuclear force in Europe, a larger navy, and a rapid-deployment force. Despite the growing budget deficit, Congress approved most of these programs, and military expenditures shot up by one-third in the first half of the 1980s. Throughout Reagan's presidency, defense spending averaged $216 billion a year, up from $158 billion in the Carter years and higher even than in the Vietnam era.

Reagan justified the military buildup as a means to negotiate with the Soviets from a position of strength, but it provoked an outburst of pleas to halt the arms race. A rally demanding a freeze on additional nuclear weapons drew 700,000 people in New York City in 1982. Hundreds of thousands demonstrated across Europe, stimulated by fears of new U.S. missiles scheduled for deployment in **North Atlantic Treaty Organization (NATO)** countries in 1983.

Reagan startled many of his own advisers in March 1983 by announcing plans for research on the Strategic Defense Initiative (SDI). Immediately dubbed "Star Wars" by critics who doubted its feasibility, the project would deploy lasers in space to destroy enemy missiles before they could reach their targets. Reagan conceded that SDI could appear as "an aggressive policy" allowing the United States to strike first and not fear retaliation. The Soviets reacted angrily because SDI violated the 1972 Antiballistic Missile Treaty and would require huge investments to develop their own Star Wars technology. Future administrations continued to spend billions on SDI research, but without producing a working system.

The U.S. military buildup could not extinguish a newer threat to international stability—force or violence initiated by nonstate organizations and designed to gain political objectives by frightening civilian populations. Such terrorism had a long history throughout the world, but in the 1970s and 1980s, Americans saw it escalate in the Middle East, used by Palestinians after the Israeli occupation of the West Bank and by other groups hostile to Western policies. A new terrorist organization, Hezbollah, composed of Shiite Muslims and backed by Iran and Syria, was founded in Lebanon in 1982 after Israeli forces invaded that country to stop the Palestine Liberation Organization (PLO) from using sanctuaries in Lebanon to launch attacks on Israel.

Reagan's effort to stabilize Lebanon by sending 2,000 marines to join an international peacekeeping mission failed. In April 1983, a suicide attack on the U.S. Embassy in Beirut killed 63 people, and in October a Hezbollah fighter drove a bomb-filled truck into a U.S. marine barracks there, killing 241 marines (see Map 30.2). The attack prompted the withdrawal of U.S. troops, and Lebanon remained in chaos, while incidents of murder, kidnapping, and hijacking by various Middle Eastern extremist groups continued. Reagan adamantly proclaimed his refusal to negotiate, insisting that to bargain with terrorists would only encourage more assaults.

Following a cold war pattern begun under Eisenhower, the Reagan administration sought to contain leftist movements close to home and across the globe. In October 1983, 5,000 U.S. troops invaded Grenada, a small island nation in the Caribbean that had succumbed to a left-wing, Marxist coup. In Asia, the United States moved more quietly, aiding the Afghan rebels' war against Afghanistan's Soviet-backed government. In the African nation of Angola, the United States armed rebel forces against the government supported by both the Soviet Union and Cuba. Reagan also sided with the South African government, which was brutally suppressing black protest against apartheid, forcing Congress to override his veto in order to impose economic sanctions against South Africa.

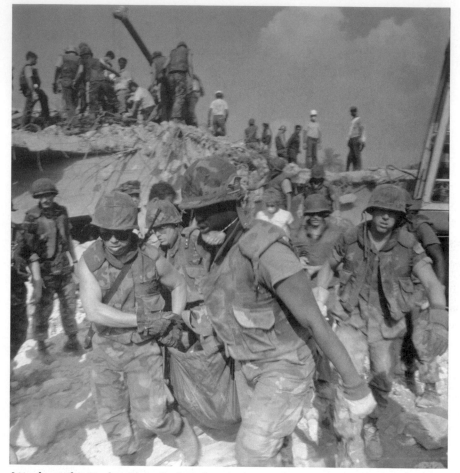

Attack on the Marine Barracks in Beirut
On October 23, 1983, members of Islamic Jihad, an anti-Israel, anti-Western terrorist group
sponsored by Iran, demonstrated their hostility toward the U.S. troops stationed in Lebanon by
exploding a car bomb outside the U.S. marine compound and killing 241 Americans. Shown here
are military personnel searching for and removing bodies of their dead comrades.
© Bettmann/Corbis.

Administration officials were most fearful of left-wing movements in Central
America, which Reagan claimed could "destabilize the entire region from the
Panama Canal to Mexico." When a leftist uprising occurred in El Salvador in
1981, the United States sent money and military advisers to prop up the authoritarian government even though it had committed murderous human rights violations. In neighboring Nicaragua, where Reagan aimed to unseat the left-wing
Sandinistas, who had toppled a long-standing dictatorship, the administration
aided the Contras (literally, "opposers"), a coalition of armed opposition to the
Sandinistas.

The Iran-Contra Scandal

The Reagan administration's commitment to the Contras revealed that the War Powers Act had not settled the question of presidential versus congressional authority in using force abroad. Fearing another Vietnam, many Americans opposed aligning the United States with reactionary forces not supported by the majority of Nicaraguans. Congress strongly and repeatedly instructed the president to stop aid to the Contras, but the administration continued to secretly provide them with weapons and training. Through legal and illegal means, the Reagan administration sustained the Contras and helped wreck the Nicaraguan economy, thereby undermining support for the Sandinista government. After nine years of civil war, Nicaragua's president, Daniel Ortega, agreed to a political settlement, and when he was defeated by a coalition of all the opposition groups, he stepped aside.

Secret aid to the Contras was part of a larger project that came to be known as the Iran-Contra scandal. It began in 1985, when leaders of the National Security Council, NSC aide marine lieutenant colonel Oliver North, and CIA director William Casey arranged to sell arms to Iran, then in the midst of an eight-year war with neighboring Iraq. They did so, even while the United States supplied Iraq with funds and weapons, to get Iran to pressure Hezbollah to release seven American hostages being held in Lebanon (see Map 30.2). Funds from the arms sales were then channeled through Swiss bank accounts to aid the Nicaraguan Contras. Over the objections of his secretary of state, who called it "a very bad idea," and his secretary of defense, Reagan approved the arms sales, but the three subsequently denied knowing that the proceeds were diverted to the Contras.

When news of the affair surfaced in November 1986, the Reagan administration faced serious charges. The president's aides had bargained with terrorists, which Reagan had vowed never to do, and, more seriously, had defied Congress's express ban on military aid for the Contras. Investigations by an independent prosecutor appointed by Reagan led to a trial that aired live on the relatively new medium of cable television. Seven individuals pleaded guilty or were convicted of lying to Congress and destroying evidence. North's felony conviction was later overturned on a technicality, and President George H. W. Bush pardoned the other six officials in December 1992. The independent prosecutor's final report found no evidence that Reagan had broken the law, but it concluded that both Reagan and Vice President Bush had known about the diversion of funds to the Contras and that Reagan had "knowingly participated or at least acquiesced" in covering up the scandal—the most serious case of executive branch misconduct since Watergate.

A Thaw in Soviet-American Relations

A momentous reduction in cold war tensions soon overshadowed the Iran-Contra scandal. The new Soviet-American accord depended both on Reagan's flexibility and on an innovative Soviet head of state who recognized that his country's domestic problems demanded an easing of cold war antagonism. Mikhail Gorbachev assumed power in 1985 determined to revitalize an inefficient Soviet economy incapable of delivering basic consumer goods. Hoping to stimulate production and streamline distribution, Gorbachev introduced some elements of free enterprise and proclaimed a new era of *glasnost* (greater freedom of expression), eventually allowing new political parties, contested elections, and challenges to Communist rule.

Concerns about immense defense budgets moved both Reagan and Gorbachev to the negotiating table. Enormous military expenditures stood between the Soviet premier and his goal of economic revival. With growing popular support for arms reductions, along with a push from his wife, Nancy, Reagan made disarmament a major goal in his last years in office and readily responded when Gorbachev took the initiative. A positive personal chemistry developed between them, and they met four times between 1985 and 1988. Although Reagan's insistence on proceeding with SDI nearly killed the talks, by December 1987 the superpowers had completed an intermediate-range nuclear forces (INF) agreement. The treaty eliminated all short- and medium-range missiles from Europe and provided for on-site inspection for the first time. This was also the first time either nation had pledged to eliminate weapons already in place.

In 1988, Gorbachev further reduced tensions by announcing a gradual withdrawal from Afghanistan, which had become the Soviet equivalent of America's Vietnam. In addition, the Soviet Union, the United States, and Cuba agreed on a political settlement for the civil war in the African nation of Angola. And in the Middle East, both superpowers supported a cease-fire and peace talks in the eight-year war between Iran and Iraq. Within three years, the cold war that had defined the world for nearly half a century would be history.

▶**REVIEW**   How did anticommunism shape Reagan's foreign policy?

Conclusion: Reversing the Course of Government

"Ours was the first revolution in the history of mankind that truly reversed the course of government," boasted Ronald Reagan in his farewell address in 1989. The word *revolution* exaggerated the change, but his administration did mark the slowdown or reversal of expanding federal budgets, programs, and regulations that had taken off in the 1930s. Although he did not deliver on the social or moral issues dear to the heart of the New Right, Reagan represented the "choice not an echo" that Phyllis Schlafly had called for in 1964, as he used his skills as "the Great Communicator" to cultivate antigovernment sentiment and undo the liberal assumptions of the New Deal.

Distrust of the federal government grew along with the backlash against the reforms of the 1960s and the conduct of the Vietnam War. Watergate and other misdeeds of the Nixon administration further disillusioned Americans. Presidents Ford and Carter restored morality to the White House, but neither could solve the gravest economic problems since the Great Depression—a low rate of economic growth, stagflation, and an increasing trade deficit. Even the Democrat Carter gave higher priority to fiscal austerity than to social reform, and he began the government's retreat from regulation of key industries.

A new conservative movement helped Reagan win the presidency and flourished during his administration. Reagan's tax cuts, combined with hefty increases in defense spending, created a federal deficit crisis that justified cuts in social welfare spending and made new federal initiatives unthinkable. Many Americans continued to support specific federal programs—especially those, such as Social Security and Medicare, that reached beyond the poor—but public sentiment about the government in general had taken a U-turn from the Roosevelt era. Instead of seeing the government as a helpful and problem-solving institution, many believed that not only was it ineffective at solving national problems, but it often made things worse. As Reagan appointed new Supreme Court justices, the Court retreated from liberalism, restricting the government's authority to protect individual rights and regulate the economy.

With the economic recovery that set in after 1982 and his optimistic rhetoric, Reagan lifted the confidence of Americans about their nation and its promise— confidence that had eroded with the economic and foreign policy blows of the 1970s. Beginning his presidency with harsh rhetoric against the Soviet Union and a huge military buildup, Reagan helped move the two superpowers to the highest level of cooperation since the cold war began. Although that accord was not welcomed by strong anti-Communist conservatives like Phyllis Schlafly, it signaled developments that would transform American-Soviet relations—and the world—in the next decade.

REVIEWING THE CHAPTER

Use the questions and timeline to review and strengthen your understanding of the chapter.

REVIEW QUESTIONS

1. How did Nixon's policies reflect the increasing influence of conservatives on the Republican Party? (pp. 968–71)

2. Why did Nixon resign the presidency in August 1974? (pp. 972–77)

3. How did Carter attempt to balance his commitment to human rights and anti-communism in his foreign policy? (pp. 977–84)

4. Why did economic inequality increase during the Reagan administration? (pp. 984–90)

5. What gains and setbacks did minorities, feminists, and gays and lesbians experience during the Reagan years? (pp. 991–94)

6. How did anticommunism shape Reagan's foreign policy? (pp. 994–98)

MAKING CONNECTIONS

1. What was Watergate's legacy for American politics in the following decade? In your answer, explain what led to Nixon's resignation. How did Congress try to prevent such abuses of power in the future?

2. Both ends of the American political spectrum changed significantly in the 1970s and 1980s. Describe these changes and discuss how they shaped contemporary American politics. In your answer, be sure to cite specific political developments.

3. Recent experiences in Vietnam hung over the foreign policy decisions of Presidents Carter and Reagan. How did each president try to reconcile the lessons of that conflict and the ongoing cold war? In your answer, be sure to discuss the legacy of the Vietnam War in the United States in the 1970s and 1980s.

4. American regional politics shifted in significant ways during the 1970s and 1980s. Why was grassroots conservatism particularly strong in the Sun Belt? What was its relationship to the civil rights and equal opportunity developments of the 1960s?

TIMELINE

1966	• Republican Ronald Reagan elected governor of California.	**1979**	• Camp David accords signed. • Carter establishes formal diplomatic relations with China. • Soviet Union invades Afghanistan. • Hostage crisis in Iran begins. • Moral Majority founded.
1968	• Republican Richard Nixon elected president.		
1969	• Warren E. Burger appointed chief justice of U.S. Supreme Court.		
1971	• Nixon vetoes comprehensive child care bill.	**1980**	• Congress deregulates banking, trucking, and railroad industries. • Congress passes Superfund legislation. • Republican Ronald Reagan elected president.
1972	• Nixon campaign aides arrested at Watergate complex.		
1974	• Nixon resigns; Gerald Ford becomes president. • Ford pardons Nixon of any crimes he may have committed while president. • *Milliken v. Bradley.*	**1981**	• Researchers identify AIDS virus. • Economic Recovery Tax Act.
		1982	• Large demonstrations against nuclear weapons.
		1983	• Terrorist bomb kills 241 U.S. marines in Beirut, Lebanon. • Reagan announces plans for Strategic Defense Initiative ("Star Wars").
1976	• Democrat Jimmy Carter elected president.		
1977	• United States signs Panama Canal Treaty.	**1986**	• Iran-Contra scandal.
1978	• *Regents of University of California v. Bakke.* • Congress deregulates airlines.	**1987**	• INF agreement signed.
		1988	• Civil Rights Restoration Act.

▶ **For an online bibliography, practice quizzes, Web sites, images, and documents related to this chapter,** see the Book Companion Site at **bedfordstmartins.com/roark.**

▶ **For firsthand accounts of this period,** see Chapter 30 in Michael Johnson, ed., *Reading the American Past,* Fourth Edition.

31
CHAPTER

The End of the Cold War and the Challenges of Globalization

Since 1989

N HIS MOSCOW HOTEL ROOM on April 22, 1988, Ronald Reagan's national security adviser, army general Colin L. Powell, contemplated the plans that Premier Mikhail Gorbachev had just announced, which would dramatically alter the Soviet Union's government and economy. "Lying there in bed," Powell recalled, "I realized that one phase of my life had ended, and another was about to begin. Up until now, as a soldier, my mission had been to confront, contain, and if necessary, combat **communism**. Now I had to think about a world without a **Cold War**." For the next sixteen years, Powell would have a central place in redefining his country's role in a world transformed.

Colin Powell was born in Harlem in 1937 and grew up in the Bronx, the son of parents who had emigrated from Jamaica in 1920. His father headed the shipping department in a garment factory, where his mother worked as a seamstress. After attending public schools, Powell enrolled in City College of New York, where he joined the army's Reserve Officers Training Corps (ROTC) program, the defining experience of his college years. "The discipline, the structure, the camaraderie, the sense of belonging," he said, "were what I craved." Commissioned as a lieutenant when he graduated in 1958, Powell began a lifelong career in military and public service, rising to the highest rank of four-star general. He

Secretary of State Colin Powell
The decision by George W. Bush to invade Iraq in March 2003 ran counter to Colin Powell's commitment to acting through the international community and sacrificing American lives only when a vital
interest was at stake and a plan for ending the intervention had been established. Although Powell's
position lost out to that of the more hawkish Vice President Dick Cheney and Secretary of Defense
Donald Rumsfeld, Powell stayed in his job until 2005. In this photo taken in February 2003, he listens
to Rumsfeld. National Security Adviser Condoleezza Rice stands behind them.
Charles Ommanney/Contact Press Images for Newsweek.

chose to stay in the army primarily because "I loved what I was doing." But he
also recognized that "for a black, no other avenue in American society offered so
much opportunity."

Powell's two tours of duty in Vietnam taught him that "you do not squander
courage and lives without clear purpose, without the country's backing, and
without full commitment." In his subsequent capacities as national security adviser to Ronald Reagan, chairman of the Joint Chiefs of Staff in the George H. W.
Bush and Bill Clinton administrations, and secretary of state under George W.
Bush, Powell endeavored to keep his country out of "halfhearted warfare for
half-baked reasons that the American people could not understand or support."

Powell's sense that Gorbachev's reforms would bring about the end of the
cold war became a reality more quickly than anyone anticipated. Eastern Europe
broke free from Communist control in 1989, and the Soviet Union disintegrated in
1991. As the lone superpower, the United States deployed both military and
diplomatic power throughout the 1990s during episodes of instability in Latin
America, the Middle East, eastern Europe, and Asia, almost always in concert

with the major nations of Europe and Asia. In 1991, in its first full-fledged war since Vietnam, the United States led a United Nations–authorized force of twenty-eight nations to repel Iraq's invasion of Kuwait.

During his temporary retirement from public service in the 1990s, Powell remarked that "neither of the two major parties fits me comfortably." Many Americans seemed to agree: They turned Republican George H. W. Bush out of office in 1992 but elected Republican Congresses during Democrat Bill Clinton's administration. When Republican George W. Bush (son of George H. W. Bush) entered the White House in 2001, he faced a nearly evenly divided Congress. Between 1989 and 2000, domestic policies reflected a slight retreat from the **conservatism** of the Reagan years. The first Bush administration approved tighter environmental protections and new rights for people with disabilities, and President Clinton signed measures strengthening gun control and aiding low-wage earners. But the pendulum swung back to the right in the second Bush presidency.

All three presidents shared a commitment to hastening the **globalization** processes that were linking nations together in an increasingly connected economy. As capital, products, information, and people crossed national boundaries at greater speed, the United States experienced a surge of immigration rivaling that of a century earlier, which had brought Powell's parents to the United States. Powell cheered globalization, predicting that the world would become "defined by trade relations, by the flow of information, capital, technology, and goods, rather than by armies glaring at each other across borders."

He was not so naive as to anticipate a world "without war or conflict," recognizing challenges such as nuclear proliferation, **nationalist** passions in areas of former Soviet dominance, civil wars in Africa, and Islamic **fundamentalism**. But he shared other Americans' shock when in September 2001 deadly terrorist attacks in New York City and Washington, D.C., exposed American vulnerability to new and horrifying threats. The administration's response to terrorism overwhelmed Secretary of State Powell's commitments to internationalism, multilateralism, and military restraint as George W. Bush began a second war against Iraq, implementing a distinct shift to a foreign policy based on preemptive attacks against presumed threats and going it alone if necessary.

Domestic Stalemate and Global Upheaval: The Presidency of George H. W. Bush

Vice President George H. W. Bush announced his bid for the presidency in the 1988 election, declaring, "We don't need radical new directions." Generally satisfied with the agenda set by Ronald Reagan and facing a Democratic-controlled Congress, Bush proposed few domestic initiatives. His dispatch of troops to oust the corrupt dictator of Panama, Manuel Noriega, represented a much longer continuity, following a century of U.S. intervention in Latin America.

Yet as the most dramatic changes since the 1940s swept through the world, Bush confronted situations that did not fit the simpler free world versus communism framework that had guided foreign policy since World War II. Most Americans approved of Bush's handling of two challenges to U.S. foreign policy and military capacity: the disintegration of the Soviet Union and its hold over Eastern Europe, and Iraq's invasion of neighboring Kuwait. But voters' concern over a sluggish economy and other domestic problems limited Bush to one term in the White House.

Gridlock in Government

The son of a wealthy New England senator, George Herbert Walker Bush fought in World War II, earned a degree from Yale, and then settled in Texas to make his own way in the oil industry and politics. He served in Congress during the 1960s and headed the CIA during the Nixon and Ford years. When Ronald Reagan achieved a commanding lead in the 1980 presidential primaries, Bush put his own ambitions on hold, adjusted his more moderate policy positions to fit Reagan's conservative agenda, and accepted second place on the Republican ticket. At the end of Reagan's second term, Republicans rewarded him with the presidential nomination.

Several candidates competed for the Democratic nomination in 1988. The Reverend Jesse Jackson—whose Rainbow Coalition campaign centered on the needs of minorities, women, the working class, and the poor—made an impressive bid, winning several primaries and seven million votes. But a more centrist candidate, Massachusetts governor Michael Dukakis, won the nomination. On election day, half the eligible voters stayed home, indicating their disgust with the negative campaigning or their satisfaction with the Republican record on peace and prosperity. Divided government would remain, however, as 54 percent of the voters chose Bush but the Democrats gained seats in the House and Senate.

Although President Bush saw himself primarily as guardian and beneficiary of the Reagan legacy, he promised "a kinder, gentler nation" and was more inclined than Reagan to approve government activity in the private sphere. For example, he signed the Clean Air Act of 1990, the strongest, most comprehensive environmental law in history. It required power plants to cut sulfur dioxide emissions by more than half in ten years and oil companies to develop cleaner-burning gasoline.

Some forty million Americans reaped the benefits of a second regulatory measure, the Americans with Disabilities Act (1990). Job discrimination against people with disabilities was now illegal, and private businesses, public accommodations, and transportation facilities had to be made handicapped accessible. Cynthia Jones, publisher of a magazine on disability politics, noticed a breeze that stirred over the White House lawn at the signing of the bill. She said, "It was kind of like a new breath of air was sweeping across America. . . . People knew they had rights. That was wonderful."

Yet Bush also needed to satisfy party conservatives. His most famous campaign pledge had been "Read my lips: No new taxes," and he opposed most proposals requiring additional federal funds. "If you're looking for George Bush's domestic program, and many people are, this is it: the veto pen," charged Democratic House majority leader Richard Gephardt. Bush vetoed thirty-six bills, including those that would have lifted abortion restrictions, extended unemployment benefits, raised taxes, mandated family and medical leave for workers, and reformed campaign financing. Press reports increasingly used the words *stalemate*, *gridlock*, and *divided government*.

Continuing a trend begun during the Reagan years, states tried to compensate for this paralysis, becoming more innovative than Washington. "Our federal politics are gridlocked, and governors have become the ones who have to have the courage to put their necks out," said a spokesperson for the governors. States passed bills to block corporate takeovers, establish parental leave policies, require equal pay for jobs of equal worth, improve food labeling, and protect the environment. Beginning in the 1980s, a few states began to pass measures guaranteeing gay and lesbian rights. In the 1990s, dozens of cities passed ordinances requiring businesses receiving tax abatements or other city benefits to pay wages well above the federal minimum wage. And in 1999, California passed a gun control bill with much tougher restrictions on assault weapons than reformers had been able to get through Congress.

A huge **federal budget deficit** inherited from the Reagan administration impelled the president in 1990 to abandon his "no new taxes" pledge, a move that outraged advocates of **supply-side economics** and other conservatives. The new law, which Bush depended on Democrats to pass, authorized modest tax increases for high-income Americans and higher taxes on gasoline, cigarettes, alcohol, and luxury items. Despite criticism from many Republicans, the taxes had little effect on the massive tax reductions of the early 1980s, leaving intact a key element of Reagan's legacy. Neither the new revenues nor controls on spending curbed the deficit, which was boosted by rising costs for Social Security and Medicare/Medicaid, as well as by spending on war and natural disasters.

Bush also continued Reagan's efforts to create a more conservative Supreme Court. His first nominee, federal appeals court judge David Souter, won easy confirmation by the Senate. But in 1991, when the only African American on the Court, Justice Thurgood Marshall, retired, Bush set off a national controversy. He nominated Clarence Thomas, a conservative black appeals court judge, who had opposed **affirmative action** as head of the Equal Employment Opportunity Commission (EEOC) under Reagan. Charging that Thomas would not protect minority rights, the National Association for the Advancement of Colored People (NAACP) and other **liberal** organizations fought the nomination. Then Anita Hill, a black law professor and former EEOC employee, shook the confirmation process by accusing Thomas of sexual harassment.

Before the Senate Judiciary Committee, Thomas angrily denied the charges, claiming that he was the victim of a "high-tech lynching for uppity blacks." Hill's testimony failed to sway the Senate, which voted narrowly to confirm him. The hearings angered many women, who noted that only two women sat in the Senate and none on the Judiciary Committee and denounced the male senators for failing to take sexual harassment seriously. **Feminists** complained that men "still don't get it" and redoubled their efforts to get more women into office, making 1992 a banner year for women elected to office. Thomas's confirmation solidified the Supreme Court's shift to the right.

Going to War in Central America and the Persian Gulf

President Bush won greater support for his actions abroad, and he twice sent U.S. soldiers into battle. Nearly every cold war president before him had dispatched aid or troops to Central America and the Caribbean in the name of suppressing communism, but Bush intervened in Panama for different reasons. The United States had tolerated and, in fact, paid Panamanian dictator Manuel Noriega when he had helped the Contras in Nicaragua and served as a CIA informer about Communist activities in the region. But in 1989, after Noriega was indicted for drug trafficking by a grand jury in Miami, Florida, and after his troops killed an American marine, President Bush ordered 25,000 military personnel into Panama. In an invasion labeled "Operation Just Cause," U.S. forces quickly overcame Noriega's troops, sustaining 23 deaths, while hundreds of Panamanians died, many of them civilians. Chairman of the Joint Chiefs of Staff Colin Powell noted that "our euphoria over our victory in Just Cause was not universal." Both the United Nations and the Organization of American States censured the unilateral action by the United States.

If the invasion of Panama fit within the century-old tradition of **Yankee imperialism**, Bush's second military engagement rested solidly on international approval. Considering Iran America's major enemy in the Middle East, U.S. officials had quietly assisted the Iraqi dictator Saddam Hussein in his war against neighboring Iran, which he began in 1980 and which ended inconclusively in 1988 with heavy losses on both sides. In August 1990, Hussein sent troops into the small, oil-rich country of Kuwait to the south (Map 31.1), and within days the invasion neared the Saudi Arabian border, threatening the world's largest oil reserves. President Bush reacted quickly, ordering a massive mobilization of American forces and assembling an international coalition to stand up to Iraq. He invoked principles of national self-determination and international law, but long-standing interests in Middle Eastern oil also drove the U.S. response. As the largest importer of oil, the United States consumed one-fourth of the world's supply, 20 percent of which came from Iraq and Kuwait.

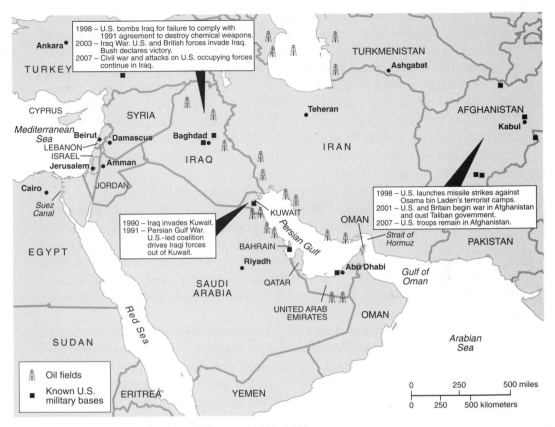

1998 – U.S. bombs Iraq for failure to comply with 1991 agreement to destroy chemical weapons.
2003 – Iraq War. U.S. and British forces invade Iraq. Bush declares victory.
2007 – Civil war and attacks on U.S. occupying forces continue in Iraq.

1990 – Iraq invades Kuwait.
1991 – Persian Gulf War. U.S.-led coalition drives Iraqi forces out of Kuwait.

1998 – U.S. launches missile strikes against Osama bin Laden's terrorist camps.
2001 – U.S. and Britain begin war in Afghanistan and oust Taliban government.
2007 – U.S. troops remain in Afghanistan.

Oil fields

Known U.S. military bases

0   250   500 miles
0   250   500 kilometers

MAP 31.1   Events in the Middle East, 1989–2007
During the Persian Gulf War of 1991, Egypt, Syria, and other Middle Eastern nations joined the coalition against Iraq, and the twenty-two-member Arab League supported the war as a means to liberate Kuwait. After September 11, 2001, the Arab League approved of U.S. military operations in Afghanistan because the attacks "were an attack on the common values of the world." Yet, except for the countries where the United States had military bases—Bahrain, Kuwait, Qatar, and Saudi Arabia—no Arab country supported the American invasion and occupation of Iraq in 2003.

Reflecting the easing of cold war tensions, the Soviet Union joined the United States in condemning Hussein and cut off arms shipments to Iraq. The UN declared an embargo on Iraqi oil and authorized the use of force if Iraq did not withdraw from Kuwait by January 15, 1991. By then the United States had deployed 400,000 soldiers to Saudi Arabia; they were joined by 265,000 troops from some two dozen other nations, including Egypt, Syria, and several other Arab states. "The community of nations has resolutely gathered to condemn and repel lawless aggression," Bush announced. "With few exceptions, the world now stands as one."

With Iraqi forces still in Kuwait, in January 1991 Bush asked Congress to approve war. Considerable sentiment favored waiting to see if the embargo and other means would force Hussein to back down, a position quietly urged within the administration by Colin Powell. Linking the crisis to the failure of U.S. energy conservation, Democratic senator Edward M. Kennedy insisted, "Not a single American life should be sacrificed in a war for the price of oil." Congress debated for three days and then authorized war by a margin of five votes in the Senate and sixty-seven in the House. On January 17, 1991, the U.S.-led coalition launched Operation Desert Storm, a forty-day air war against Iraq that entailed bombing military targets, power plants, oil refineries, and transportation networks. Having severely crippled Iraq by air, the coalition then stormed into Kuwait with massive ground forces on February 23. Within one hundred hours, Hussein announced that he would withdraw from Kuwait (see Map 31.1).

"By God, we've kicked the Vietnam syndrome once and for all," President Bush exulted on March 1. Most Americans found no moral ambiguity in the Persian Gulf War and took pride in the display of military competence. In contrast to the loss of 58,000 American lives in Vietnam, 270 U.S. service members perished in Desert Storm. The United States stood at the apex of global leadership, steering a coalition in which Arab nations fought beside their former colonial rulers.

Some Americans criticized the Bush administration for ending the war without deposing Hussein. But Bush pointed out that the UN mandate limited the mission to driving Iraqi forces out of Kuwait, and he recognized the fear among Middle Eastern leaders that an effort to oust Hussein would destabilize the region. His secretary of defense Richard Cheney questioned the ability of coalition forces to secure a stable government to replace Hussein and considered the price of a long occupation too high. Administration officials believed that the war had crippled Iraq's military power and that economic sanctions and Hussein's pledges not to rearm or develop weapons of mass destruction, secured by a system of UN inspections, would contain the dictator.

Yet Middle Eastern stability remained elusive. Israel, which had endured Iraqi missile attacks, was more secure, but the Israeli-Palestinian conflict remained intractable. Despite military losses, Saddam Hussein remained in power and turned his war machine on Iraqi Kurds and Shiite Muslims whom the United States had encouraged to rebel. Iraqi citizens suffered malnutrition, disease, and death caused by the continuing embargo and the destruction of the nation's infrastructure. And Hussein found ways to conceal arms from UN weapons inspectors before he threw them out in 1998.

The End of the Cold War

Soviet support in the war to turn back Iraqi aggression marked how greatly relations between the United States and the USSR had changed in just a few years. The forces of change that Gorbachev had encouraged in the Communist world (see chapter 30) swept through Eastern Europe in 1989, where popular uprisings

0   250   500 miles

0   250   500 kilometers

Communist regimes overthrown since 1989

Republics of the former Soviet Union joining new Commonwealth of Independent States

Republics of the former Soviet Union not joining Commonwealth of Independent States

ATLANTIC OCEAN

FORMER SOVIET UNION

Nov. 1989 – Berlin Wall falls.
Oct . 1990 – East and West Germany reunified.

1985 – Gorbachev comes to power.
Aug. 1991 – Moscow coup fails and USSR dissolves.

June 1989 – Solidarity Party wins elections.

Nov. 1989 – Communist leadership ousted.
Dec. 1989 – Vaclav Havel named president.
1993 – Splits into the Czech Republic and Slovakia.

Moscow

April 1990 – Free elections sweep non-Communists into power.

Dec.1989 – Communist dictator overthrown and executed.
May 1990 – Salvation Front wins elections.

1991 – Dissolves in civil war; truce in 1995.

Nov. 1989 – Communist leader ousted.
Aug. 1990 – Free elections held.

North Sea

NETH.
UNITED KINGDOM
IRELAND
BEL.
FRANCE
SWITZ.
PORT.
SPAIN
MOROCCO   ALGERIA   TUNISIA   *Mediterranean Sea*
DEN.
Berlin   POLAND
GERMANY
LUX.
CZECH.
AUS.   HUN.
YUGOSLAVIA
ITALY
ALB.
GREECE
EST.
LAT.
LITH.
Baltic Sea
BELARUS
UKRAINE
MOLDOVA
ROMANIA
BULG.
Black Sea
TURKEY
ARMENIA
AZER.
GEORGIA
Caspian Sea
Aral Sea
KAZAKHSTAN
KYRGYZSTAN
UZBEKISTAN
TURKMENISTAN
TAJIKISTAN
AFGHANISTAN
PAKISTAN
IRAN
IRAQ

MAP 31.2   Events in Eastern Europe, 1989–2002
The overthrow of Communist governments throughout Eastern Europe and the splintering of the Soviet Union into more than a dozen separate nations were among the most momentous changes in world history since World War II.

demanded an end to state repression, official corruption, and economic bureau-cracies unable to deliver an acceptable standard of living. Communist govern-ments toppled like dominoes (Map 31.2), virtually without bloodshed, because Gorbachev refused to prop them up with Soviet armies, a stand that won him the Nobel Peace Prize in 1990. East Germany opened its border with West Germany, and in November 1989, ecstatic Germans danced on the Berlin Wall, which had separated East and West since 1961, using whatever was at hand to demolish that dominant symbol of the cold war. An amazed East Berliner crossed over the line exclaiming, "They just let us go. I can't believe it."

Promoted by President Bush, unification of East and West Germany sped to completion in 1990, and former **iron curtain** countries such as the Czech Repub-lic, Hungary, and Poland were lining up to join **NATO**. Although U.S. military forces remained in Europe as part of NATO, Europe no longer depended on the

United States for its security. Its economic clout also grew as Western Europe, including unified Germany, formed a common economic market in 1992. The destiny of Europe, to which the United States and the Soviet Union had held the key for forty-five years, now lay in European hands.

Inspired by the liberation of Eastern Europe, republics within the Soviet Union soon sought their own independence, while Gorbachev's efforts at economic change brought widespread destitution. According to one Muscovite, "Gorbachev knew how to bring us freedom but he did not know how to make sausage." In December 1991, Boris Yeltsin, president of the Russian Republic, announced that Russia and eleven other republics had formed a new entity, the Commonwealth of Independent States (CIS), and other former Soviet states declared their independence. With nothing left to govern, Gorbachev resigned. The Soviet Union had dissolved, and with it the cold war tensions that had defined U.S. foreign policy for decades.

China and North Korea resisted the liberalizing tides sweeping the world. In 1989, Chinese soldiers killed hundreds of pro-**democracy** demonstrators in Tiananmen Square in Beijing, and the Communist government cracked down on advocates of reform, arresting some ten thousand citizens. North Korea remained under a Communist dictatorship committed to developing nuclear weapons.

"The post–cold war world is decidedly not postnuclear," declared one U.S. official. In 1990, the United States and Soviet Union had signed the Strategic Arms Reduction Talks (START) treaty, which cut about 30 percent of each superpower's nuclear arsenal. And in 1996, the UN General Assembly overwhelmingly approved a total nuclear test ban treaty. Yet India and Pakistan, hostile neighbors, refused to sign the treaty, and both exploded atomic devices in 1998, increasing the nuclear risk in South Asia. Moreover, in a highly partisan vote, the Republican-controlled Senate defeated U.S. ratification of the test ban treaty in October 1999, halting a decade of progress on nuclear weapons control. In 2006, North Korea exploded a nuclear device, a reminder that the potential for rogue nations and terrorist groups to develop nuclear weapons threatened international peace and security.

The 1992 Election

Despite ongoing instability in the Middle East, in March 1991 Bush's chances for reelection in 1992 looked golden. The Gulf War victory catapulted his approval rating to 88 percent, causing the most prominent Democrats to opt out of the presidential race. But that did not deter William Jefferson "Bill" Clinton, who at age forty-five had served as governor of Arkansas for twelve years. Like Jimmy Carter in 1976 and Michael Dukakis in 1988, Clinton and his running mate, Tennessee senator Albert Gore Jr., presented themselves as "New Democrats." Both belonged to the Democratic Leadership Council, which Clinton had helped found in 1985 to rid the party of its liberal image.

Clinton and Gore on Tour
During the 1992 presidential campaign, Bill Clinton and his wife, Hillary—accompanied by running mate Al Gore and his wife, Tipper—went out on several bus tours as a way of demonstrating the Democrats' connection to ordinary people. Not far from this campaign stop in Sylvester, Georgia, the bus caravan passed by a handmade sign that read "Bubbas for Clinton/Gore."
© Ira Wyman/Sygma/Corbis.

In an approach reminiscent of Richard Nixon's appeal to "forgotten Americans" in 1968, Clinton promised to work for the "forgotten middle class," who "do the work, pay the taxes, raise the kids, and play by the rules." Disavowing the "tax and spend" label that Republicans pinned on his party, he promised a tax cut for the middle class and pledged to reinvigorate government and the economy. Moreover, Clinton claimed, "we're going to put an end to welfare as we know it."

With no new crises to display his foreign policy talents, Bush was vulnerable to voters' concerns about the ailing economy and to the Clinton campaign's emphasis on bread-and-butter issues. As foreign competition drove businesses to trim budgets, victims of corporate downsizing and outsourcing worried about finding new jobs, while other workers worried about keeping theirs. Unemployment edged over 7 percent in 1992.

The popularity of a third candidate, self-made Texas billionaire H. Ross Perot, revealed Americans' frustrations with government and the major parties. Although Perot gave no press conferences, he used television extensively and attracted a sizable grassroots movement with his down-to-earth personality and appeals to voters' disgust with Washington. Perot's candidacy hurt the president more than it hurt Clinton, and it established the federal budget deficit as a key campaign issue.

Fifty-five percent of those eligible showed up at the polls, just barely reversing the thirty-year decline in voter turnout. Clinton won 43 percent of the popular vote, Bush 38 percent, and Perot 19 percent—the strongest third-party finish in eighty years. By casting two-thirds of their votes against Bush, voters suggested a mandate for change but not the direction that change should take.

▶ **REVIEW**   Why did George H. W. Bush lose the presidency in 1992?

The Clinton Administration's Search for the Middle Ground

The president who asserted that "the era of big government is over" was not Ronald Reagan but Bill Clinton, reflecting the Democratic Party's move to the right that had begun with Jimmy Carter in the 1970s. Clinton did not completely abandon liberal principles. He signed important measures benefiting the working poor; delivered incremental reforms to feminists, environmentalists, and other groups; and spoke out in favor of affirmative action and gay rights. Yet his administration attended more to the concerns of middle-class Americans than to the needs of the poor, and it restrained federal programs and appropriations for the disadvantaged.

Clinton's eight-year presidency witnessed the longest economic boom in history and ended with a budget surplus. Although various factors generated the prosperity, many Americans identified Clinton with the buoyant economy, elected him to a second term, and continued to support him even when his reckless sexual behavior resulted in **impeachment**. The Senate did not find sufficient cause to remove him from office, but the scandal crippled Clinton's leadership in his last years in office.

Clinton's Promise of Change

Clinton wanted to restore confidence in government as a force for good but also to avoid alienating antigovernment voters. The huge budget deficit that he inherited—$4.4 trillion in 1993—further precluded substantial federal initiatives. Moreover, just as Clinton was short on cash, he also lacked political capital. Perot's challenges denied Clinton a majority of the popular vote in both 1992 and 1996, and the Republicans controlled Congress for all but his first two years in office. Throughout most of his presidency, he was burdened by investigations into past financial activities and private indiscretions. While the president had an extraordinary knack for appealing to voters, making them feel that he liked and understood them, he could not translate that attraction into gains for his party.

Despite these obstacles, Clinton achieved a number of incremental reforms. Using his executive authority, he eased restrictions on abortion and signed several bills that Republicans had previously blocked. In 1993, Congress enacted gun control legislation and the Family and Medical Leave Act, which entitled workers in larger companies to unpaid leave for childbirth, adoption, and family medical emergencies. Another goal of the women's movement, the Violence against Women Act of 1994, authorized $1.6 billion and new remedies for combating sexual assault and domestic violence. Clinton won stricter air pollution controls and greater protection for wilderness areas and national forests and parks. Other liberal measures of the Clinton administration included an increase in the minimum wage, expansion of aid to low- and moderate-income college students, and the creation of AmeriCorps, a program enabling students to pay for their education with community service.

Most significantly, Clinton pushed through a substantial increase in the Earned Income Tax Credit (EITC) for low-wage earners, a program begun under Ford in 1975. The EITC gave tax cuts to people who worked full-time at meager wages or, if they paid no taxes, a subsidy to lift their family income above the poverty line. By 2003, some fifteen million low-income families were benefiting from the EITC, almost half of them minorities. One expert called it "the largest antipoverty program since the **Great Society**."

Shortly before Clinton took office, the economy had begun to rebound, and the boom that followed helped boost his popularity through the 1990s. Economic expansion, along with budget cuts, tax increases, and declining unemployment, produced in 1998 the first budget surplus since 1969. Despite the biggest tax cut since 1981—a 1997 law reducing taxes on estates and capital gains and providing tax credits for families with children and for higher education—the surplus grew. The seemingly inexorable growth of government debt had turned around.

Clinton stumbled badly, however, in his efforts to provide universal health insurance and curb skyrocketing medical costs. Under the direction of First Lady Hillary Rodham Clinton and with very little congressional consultation, the administration proposed an ambitious, complicated plan that much of the health care industry charged would mean higher taxes and government interference in medical decisions. Congress enacted piecemeal reform enabling workers who changed jobs to retain health insurance and underwriting health care for five million uninsured children, but affordable health care for all remained elusive.

Along with efforts to promote government as a positive force, Clinton used his appointing powers to change its face to one that "looked like America," building on the gradual progress women and minorities had made during the previous decades. For example, African Americans and women had become mayors in major cities from New York to San Francisco. Virginia had elected the first black governor since Reconstruction, and Florida the first Latino. In the executive branch, Clinton appointed the most diverse group of department heads ever assembled, including six women, three African Americans, and two Latinos.

Secretary of Commerce Norman Y. Mineta became the first Asian American to hold a cabinet post. Janet Reno became the first female attorney general and Madeleine K. Albright the first female secretary of state. Clinton's judicial appointments had a similar cast. Of his first 129 appointments to federal courts, nearly one-third were women, 31 were black, and 11 were Latino. In 1993, he named the second woman to the Supreme Court, Ruth Bader Ginsburg, whose arguments had won key women's rights rulings from the Supreme Court before she became an appeals court judge in 1980.

The Clinton Administration Moves Right

Although parts of Clinton's agenda fell within the liberal tradition, his presidency overall moved the Democratic Party to the right. The $4.4 trillion deficit he inherited precluded significant federal spending, and the 1994 elections swept away the Democratic majorities in both houses of Congress, encouraging Clinton to embrace more strongly Republican issues such as reforming welfare and downsizing government. Led by Representative Newt Gingrich of Georgia, Republicans claimed the 1994 election as a mandate for their "contract with America," a conservative platform to end "government that is too big, too intrusive, and too easy with the public's money" and to elect "a Congress that respects the values and shares the faith of the American family." Most voters did not know the details of the "contract," and opposition from Democrats and moderate Republicans blocked passage of most of the pledges, but Gingrich succeeded in moving the debate to the right.

The most extreme antigovernment sentiment developed far from Washington in the form of grassroots armed militias. Their stance celebrated white Christian supremacy and reflected conservatives' hostility to such diverse things as taxes and the United Nations. Claiming the need to defend themselves from government tyranny, they stockpiled weapons and anticipated government repression. Their ranks grew with passage of gun control legislation and after government agents stormed the headquarters of an armed religious cult in Waco, Texas, in April 1993, resulting in more than 80 deaths. On the second anniversary of that event, a bomb leveled a federal building in Oklahoma City, taking 169 lives in the worst terrorist attack in the nation's history up to that point. Authorities quickly arrested two militia members, who were tried and convicted in 1997.

Clinton bowed to conservative views on gay and lesbian rights, backing away from a campaign promise to lift the ban on gays in the military. Homosexuals served in the military in many other nations, including France and Israel, but U.S. military leaders and key legislators objected. Instead, in 1993 he announced the "don't ask, don't tell" policy, forbidding officials from asking military personnel about their sexuality but allowing the dismissal of men and women who said they were gay or engaged in homosexual behavior. Eventually, more than ten thousand homosexuals were discharged, one of whom was army Arabic linguist Cathleen Glover. "The military preaches integrity, integrity, integrity," she said, "but asks you to lie to everyone around you." In 1996, Clinton also signed the Defense of Marriage Act, prohibiting the federal government from recognizing state-licensed marriages between same-sex couples.

Nonetheless, gays and lesbians continued to make strides as attitudes about homosexuality became more tolerant. By 2006, more than half of the five hundred largest companies provided health benefits to same-sex domestic partners and included sexual orientation in their nondiscrimination policies. More than twenty-five states banned discrimination in public employment, and many of those laws extended to private employment, housing, and education. In 2000, the Vermont legislature created a category called "civil unions" for same-sex couples, which entitled them to rights available to married couples in legal matters such as inheritance, taxation, and medical decisions. Most states banned gay marriage, but by 2006 five states offered gays the opportunity to legalize their relationships with civil unions.

Clinton's efforts to cast himself as a centrist were apparent in his handling of the **New Deal** program Aid to Families with Dependent Children (AFDC), which most people called welfare. Public sentiment about poverty had been shifting since the 1960s. Instead of blaming poverty on the lack of adequate jobs or other external circumstances, more people blamed the poor themselves and believed that welfare programs trapped the poor in cycles of dependency. Many questioned why they should be subsidizing poor mothers now that so many women had joined the labor force. Nearly everyone considered work better than welfare, but supporters of AFDC doubted that the economy could provide sufficient jobs at decent wages. Moreover, most estimates showed that welfare cost less than government job training, child care, and other assistance poor people needed for the transition from welfare to work.

By vetoing two measures on welfare reform, Clinton forced a less punitive bill, which he signed as the 1996 election approached. The Personal Responsibility and Work Opportunity Reconciliation Act abolished AFDC and with it the nation's fifty-year pledge to provide a minimum level of subsistence for all children. The law provided grants to the states in a program called Temporary Assistance for Needy Families (TANF), but it limited welfare payments to two years, regardless of whether the recipient could find a job, and it set a lifetime limit of aid at five years. Reflecting growing controversy over immigration, TANF also barred legal immigrants who had not become citizens from obtaining food stamps and other benefits and allowed states to stop Medicaid for legal immigrants.

Marian Wright Edelman, president of the Children's Defense Fund, called Clinton's signing of the bill a "moment of shame." In its first decade, the law produced neither the horrors predicted by its critics nor the successes promised by its advocates. As intended, it did force single mothers to seek employment, cutting welfare rolls from 12.5 million to 4.5 million between 1996 and 2006. Yet not all former welfare recipients became self-supporting. Forty percent of former welfare mothers were not working regularly after being cut from the rolls, and those who did find jobs earned on average only about $12,000 a year. More than one-third of children living in female-headed families still lived in poverty.

Clinton's signature on the new law denied Republicans a partisan issue in the 1996 presidential campaign. The president ran as a moderate who would save the country from extremist Republicans, while the Republican Party also moved to the center, passing over conservatives to nominate Kansan Robert Dole, a World War II hero and former Senate majority leader. Clinton won 49 percent of the votes; 41 percent went to Dole and 9 percent to third-party candidate Ross Perot. In the largest **gender gap** to date, women gave 54 percent of their votes to Clinton and 38 percent to Dole, while men split their votes nearly evenly. Although Clinton won reelection with room to spare, voters sent a Republican majority back to Congress.

Impeaching the President

Clinton's genial and articulate style, his ability to capture the middle ground of the electorate, and the nation's economic resurgence enabled the self-proclaimed "comeback kid" to survive scandals and an impeachment trial in 1998. Early in his presidency, charges of illegal activities related to firings of White House staff, political use of FBI records, and "Whitewater"—the nickname for real estate dealings that the Clintons had conducted in Arkansas—led to an official investigation by an independent prosecutor. The president also faced a sexual harassment lawsuit filed in 1994 by a state employee claiming that Clinton had made unwanted sexual advances while he was governor. A federal court threw out the case in 1998, but another sexual scandal more seriously threatened Clinton's presidency.

In January 1998, Kenneth Starr, independent prosecutor for Whitewater, began to investigate the charge that Clinton had had sexual relations with a twenty-one-year-old White House intern, Monica Lewinsky, and then lied about it to a federal grand jury. At first, Clinton vehemently denied the charge, but subsequently he bowed to the mounting evidence against him. Starr took his case for impeachment to the House of Representatives, which in December 1998 voted, mostly along party lines, to impeach the president on two counts: perjury and obstruction of justice. Clinton became the second president (the first was Andrew Johnson, in 1868) to be impeached by the House and tried by the Senate.

Most Americans condemned the president's private behavior but approved of the job he was doing and thus opposed impeachment. Some saw Starr as a fanatic invading individuals' privacy. One man said, "Let him get a divorce from his wife. Don't take him out of office and disrupt the country." Those favoring impeachment insisted that the president must set a high moral standard for the nation and that lying to a grand jury, even over a private matter, was a serious offense.

The Senate trial, held in early 1999, was less partisan. A number of senators believed Clinton to be guilty of perjury and obstruction of justice but did not believe that those actions constituted the high crimes and misdemeanors required by the Constitution for removal from office. With a two-thirds majority needed for that result, the Senate voted 45 to 55 on the perjury count and 50 to 50 on the obstruction of justice count. A majority, including some Republicans, seemed to agree with a Clinton advocate that the president's behavior, though "indefensible, outrageous, unforgivable, shameless," did not warrant his removal from office.

The investigation that triggered events leading up to impeachment ended in 2000 when the independent prosecutor reported insufficient evidence of illegalities related to the Whitewater land deals. The probe had cost taxpayers almost $60 million. In the face of widespread dissatisfaction with Whitewater and other investigations by special prosecutors, Congress let the independent counsel act expire in 1998. Although more than 60 percent of Americans gave Clinton high marks on his job performance throughout the scandal, it distracted him from domestic and international problems and precluded significant policy advances in his last years in office.

The Booming Economy of the 1990s

Clinton's ability to weather the impeachment crisis owed much to the prosperous economy, which in 1991 began its longest period of expansion in U.S. history. During the 1990s, the gross domestic product grew by more than one-third, thirteen million new jobs were created, inflation remained in check, unemployment reached 4 percent (its lowest point in twenty-five years), and the stock market soared.

The president eagerly took credit for the thriving economy, and his policies did contribute to the boom. He made deficit reduction a priority, and in exchange the Federal Reserve Board and bond market traders lowered interest rates, which in turn encouraged economic expansion by making money easier to borrow. Businesses also prospered because they had squeezed down their costs through restructuring and laying off workers. Economic problems in Europe and Asia helped American firms become more competitive in the international market. And the computer revolution and the application of information technology boosted productivity.

People at all income levels benefited from the economic boom, but it had uneven effects. Gaps between rich and poor, as well as between the wealthy and the middle class, which had been growing since the 1970s, failed to narrow. This persistence of inequality in a rising economy was linked in part to the growing use of information technology, which increased demand for highly skilled workers, while the movement of manufacturing jobs abroad lessened opportunities and wages for the less skilled. In addition, deregulation and the continuing decline of unions hurt lower-skilled workers, and the national minimum wage failed to keep up with inflation.

Although more minorities than ever attained middle-class status, in general people of color remained lowest on the economic ladder, reflecting Colin Powell's observation that "race still casts a shadow over our society." For instance, in 2005 the median income for white households surpassed $50,000, but it stood at only $31,000 and $36,000 for African American and Latino households, respectively. Median family income for Asian Americans exceeded that of whites, primarily because Asian families had more education and more wage earners. That year, poverty afflicted about 25 percent of blacks, 22 percent of Latinos, and 11.1 percent of Asian Americans, in contrast to 8.3 percent of whites.

> ▶**REVIEW**   What policies of the Clinton administration reflect the president's efforts to move his party to the right?

The United States in a Globalizing World

America's economic success in the 1990s was linked to its dominance in the world economy. From that position, President Clinton tried to shape the tremendous transformations occurring in a process that came to be called globalization—the growing integration and interdependence of national citizens and economies. Building on the initiatives of the Bush administration, Clinton lowered a number of barriers to trade across national borders, despite stiff opposition from critics who emphasized the economic deprivation and environmental devastation that often resulted. Debates likewise arose over the large numbers of immigrants entering the United States.

Clinton agreed with Bush that the United States must retain its economic and military dominance over all other nations. The president took military action in Somalia, Haiti, the Middle East, and eastern Europe, and he pushed hard to ease the conflict between Israel and the Palestinians. Yet no new global strategy emerged to replace the **containment** of communism as the decisive factor in the exercise of American power abroad.

Defining America's Place in a New World Order

In 1991, President George H. W. Bush declared a "new world order" emerging from the ashes of the cold war. As the sole superpower, the United States was determined to let no nation challenge its military superiority or global leadership. Bush and Clinton alike pushed for an open world, with the United States at the apex serving as a model of capitalism, freedom, and democracy. Yet policymakers struggled to define guiding principles for deciding when and how to use the nation's military and diplomatic power in a post–cold war world of some 190 nations. Combating Saddam Hussein's naked aggression and threat to vital oil reserves seemed the obvious course to Bush and his advisers in 1991. Determining the appropriate action in other areas of instability, however, proved much more difficult, and the United States under Clinton applied its force inconsistently throughout the 1990s.

Africa was a case in point, where civil wars, famine, and extreme human suffering rarely evoked a strong American response. In 1991, President Bush ended economic sanctions against South Africa as it began to recognize the rights of its black majority. In 1992, guided largely by humanitarian concern, Bush had attached U.S. forces to a UN operation in the small northern African country of Somalia, where famine and civil war raged. In 1993, President Clinton allowed the humanitarian mission in Somalia to turn into "nation building"—an effort to establish a stable government—and eighteen U.S. soldiers were killed. The outcry at home, after Americans saw film of Somalis dragging a soldier's corpse through the streets, suggested that most citizens were unwilling to sacrifice lives when no vital economic or political interest seemed threatened. Indeed, both the United States and the United Nations stood by in 1994 when more than half a million people were massacred in a brutal civil war in the central African nation of Rwanda.

As always, the United States was more inclined to use force nearer its borders, but in the case of the Caribbean country of Haiti, it gained international support for intervention. In 1991, after a military coup overthrew Jean-Bertrand Aristide, the democratically elected president of Haiti, thousands of Haitians tried to escape political violence and poverty, many on flimsy boats heading for Florida. In 1994, Clinton got the United Nations to impose economic sanctions on Haiti and to authorize intervention by U.S. troops. Hours before twenty thousand troops were to invade Haiti, the military leaders promised to step down. U.S. forces peacefully landed and began disarming Haitian soldiers, and Aristide was restored to power. Initially a huge success, U.S. policy continued to be tested as Haiti faced grave economic challenges and a new rebellion in 2004.

In eastern Europe, the collapse of communism ignited the most severe crisis on the continent since the 1940s. During the cold war, the Communist government of Yugoslavia, a federation of six republics, had held ethnic tensions in check, and many Muslims, Croats, and Serbs had grown accustomed to living and working together. After the Communists were swept out in 1989, Yugoslavia splintered into separate states and fell into civil war as ruthless leaders exploited ethnic differences to bolster their power.

The Serbs' aggression under President Slobodan Milosevic against Bosnian Muslims in particular horrified much of the world, but both European and U.S. leaders hesitated to use military force. As reports of terror, rape, and torture in

Bosnia increased, American leaders worried about the image of the world's strongest nation unwilling to use its power to stop the violence.

Finally, in 1995, Clinton ordered U.S. fliers to join NATO forces in intensive bombing of Serbian military concentrations. That effort and successful offensives by the Croatian and Bosnian armies forced Milosevic to the bargaining table. In November 1995, the United States brought representatives from Serbia, Croatia, and Bosnia to Dayton, Ohio, where they hammered out a peace treaty. President Clinton then agreed to send twenty thousand American troops to Bosnia as part of a NATO peacekeeping mission.

In 1998, new fighting broke out in the southern Serbian province of Kosovo, where ethnic Albanians, who constituted 90 percent of the population, were making a bid for independence. The Serbian army brutally retaliated, driving out one-third of Kosovo's 1.8 million Albanian Muslims. In 1999, NATO launched a U.S.-led bombing attack on Serbian military and government targets that, after three months, forced Milosevic to agree to a peace settlement. Serbians voted Milosevic out of office in October 2000, and he died in 2006 while on trial for genocide by a UN war crimes tribunal.

Elsewhere, Clinton remained willing to deploy U.S. power when he could send missiles rather than soldiers, and he was prepared to act without international support or UN sanction. In August 1998, bombs exploded at the U.S. embassies in Kenya and Tanzania, killing 12 Americans and more than 250 Africans. Clinton retaliated with missile attacks on terrorist training camps in Afghanistan and facilities in Sudan controlled by Osama bin Laden, a Saudi-born millionaire who financed the Islamic-extremist terrorist network linked to the embassy attacks.

Clinton also launched air strikes against Iraq in 1993 when a plot to assassinate former president Bush was uncovered; in 1996 after Saddam Hussein attacked the Kurds in northern Iraq; and repeatedly between 1998 and 2000 after Hussein expelled UN weapons inspectors. The attacks, from bases in Turkey, Kuwait, and Saudi Arabia, sent thousands of bombs and missiles against Iraqi military installations and research facilities but failed to make Hussein more compliant. Whereas Bush had acted in the Gulf War with the support of an international force that included Arab states, Clinton acted unilaterally and in the face of Arab opposition.

To ameliorate the Israeli-Palestinian conflict, a major source of Arab hostility toward the West, Clinton used diplomatic rather than military power. In 1993, due largely to the efforts of the Norwegian government, Yasir Arafat, head of the Palestine Liberation Organization (PLO), and Yitzhak Rabin, Israeli prime minister, recognized the existence of each other's states for the first time and agreed to Israeli withdrawal from the Gaza Strip and Jericho, allowing for Palestinian self-government there. In July 1994, Clinton presided over another turning point as Rabin and King Hussein of Jordan signed a declaration of peace. Yet difficult issues remained to be settled: control of Jerusalem, with sites sacred to Christians, Jews, and Muslims alike; the fate of Palestinian refugees; and the more than 200,000 Israeli settlers living in the West Bank, the land seized by Israel in 1967, where 3 million Palestinians were determined to establish their own state. Clinton's last effort to broker negotiations between the PLO and Israel failed in 2000, and violence between Israelis and Palestinians consumed the area, strengthening anti-American sentiment among Arabs, who saw the United States as Israel's ally.

Debates over Globalization

The Clinton administration moved energetically on the economic side to speed up the growth of a "global marketplace." The process of globalization had begun in the fifteenth century, when Europeans began to trade with and populate other parts of the world. Between the U.S. Civil War and World War I, products, capital, and labor crossed national boundaries in ever-larger numbers. In that era, globalization was based on **imperialism**, as Western nations took direct control of foreign territories, extracted their natural resources, and restricted manufacturing. Late-twentieth-century globalization, in contrast, advanced among sovereign nations and involved the industrialization of less developed areas, such as Korea and China. Other distinguishing marks of the more recent globalization were its scope and intensity: New communications technologies such as the Internet and cell phones connected nations, corporations, and individuals—nearly the entire planet—at much greater speed and much less cost than ever before.

Building on efforts by Presidents Reagan and Bush, Clinton sought to speed up globalization, seeking new measures to ease restrictions on international commerce. In November 1993, he won congressional approval of the North American Free Trade Agreement (NAFTA). Organized labor and others fearing loss of jobs and industries to Mexico lobbied vigorously against NAFTA, and a majority of Democrats opposed it, but Republican support ensured approval. The agreement eliminated all tariffs and trade barriers among the United States, Canada, and Mexico, making the NAFTA trio the second-largest trading bloc in the world after the European Union. In 1994, the Senate ratified the General Agreement on Tariffs and Trade (GATT), establishing the World Trade Organization (WTO) to enforce among some 135 member nations substantial tariff reductions, the elimination of import quotas, and other provisions of the GATT treaty. And in 2005, Clinton's successor, George W. Bush, got Congress to lower more trade barriers with the passage of the Central American–Dominican Republic Free Trade Agreement (CAFTA-DR).

As Clinton worked to ease restrictions on the free flow of products and capital across national borders, debates about globalization raged. Much of corporate America welcomed the elimination of trade barriers. "Ideally, you'd have every plant you own on a barge," remarked Jack Welch, CEO of General Electric. Critics linked globalization to the weakening of unions, the erosion of the social safety net provided for workers since the 1930s, and the growing gap between rich and poor. Demanding "fair trade" rather than simply free trade, they wanted trade treaties requiring other countries to enforce decent wage and labor standards. Environmentalists similarly wanted countries seeking increased commerce with the United States to adopt measures that would eliminate or reduce pollution and prevent the destruction of endangered species.

In November 1999, tens of thousands of activists dramatized the globalization debate when they gathered in Seattle, Washington, to protest a meeting of the WTO. Protesters charged the WTO with promoting a global economy that destroyed the environment, devastated poorer developing nations, and undercut living standards and wages for workers. At the Seattle demonstrations and elsewhere, U.S. labor unions emphasized the flight of factory jobs to developing nations as corporate executives sought cheaper labor to lower production costs. Tico Almeida, fresh out of college, was thrilled to hear "workers and unions from rich and poor countries alike stand together and say, 'We want rules for workers' rights to be integrated into the global economy.'"

Globalization controversies often centered on relationships between the United States, which dominated the world's industrial core, and the developing nations on the periphery, whose cheap labor and lax environmental standards caught the eye of investors. United Students against Sweatshops, for example, attacked the international conglomerate Nike, which paid Chinese workers $1.50 to produce a pair of shoes selling for more than $100 in the United States. Yet many leaders of developing nations actively sought foreign investment, insisting that wages deemed pitiful by Americans offered people in poor nations a much better living than they could otherwise obtain. At the same time, developing countries often pointed to the hypocrisy of the United States in advocating free trade in industry while heavily subsidizing its own agricultural sector. "When countries like America, Britain and France subsidize their farmers," complained John Nagenda, a grower in Uganda, "we get hurt."

The demonstrations in Seattle and protests that followed in Washington, D.C., and other parts of the world also targeted international financial institutions such as the World Bank and International Monetary Fund (IMF). Activists charged that the IMF forced devastating regulations on developing nations, which had little voice in trade policy decisions. For example, the IMF often required poor nations to privatize state industries, deregulate their economies, and cut social welfare spending in order to obtain loans. Whereas globalization's cheerleaders argued that in the long run, everyone would benefit, critics focused on the short-term victims. "International trade and global financial markets are very good at generating wealth," conceded American businessman George Soros, "but they cannot take care of other social needs, such as the preservation of peace, alleviation of poverty, protection of the environment, labor conditions, or human rights."

Critics of globalization enjoyed a few successes. In 2000, President Clinton signed an executive order requiring an environmental impact review before the signing of any trade agreement. Beyond the United States, officials from the World Bank and the IMF, along with representatives from wealthy economies, promised in 2000 to provide poor nations more debt relief and a greater voice in decisions about loans and grants. According to World Bank president James D. Wolfensohn, "Our challenge is to make globalization an instrument of opportunity and inclusion—not fear."

The Internationalization of the United States

Globalization was typically associated with the expansion of American enterprise and **culture** to other countries, yet the United States experienced within its own borders the dynamic forces of globalization. Already in the 1980s, Japanese, European, and Middle Eastern investors had purchased American stocks and bonds, real estate, and corporations such as Firestone, Brooks Brothers, and 20th Century Fox. Local communities welcomed foreign capital, and states competed to recruit foreign automakers to establish plants within their boundaries. American non-union workers began to produce Hondas in Marysville, Ohio, and BMWs in Spartanburg, South Carolina. By 2002, the paychecks of nearly 4 million American workers came from European-owned companies.

Globalization was transforming not just the economy but American society as well, as the United States experienced a tremendous surge of immigration in the late twentieth century. By 2006, the nation housed 35.7 million immigrants, who constituted 12.4 percent of the population. The 20 million who arrived between 1980 and 2005 surpassed the previous peak immigration of the first two decades of the twentieth century and exhibited a striking difference in country of origin. Eighty-five percent of the earlier immigrants had come from Europe; by the 1980s, almost half of the new arrivals were Asians, and nearly 40 percent came from Latin America and the Caribbean. Consequently, immigration changed the racial and ethnic composition of the nation. By 2004, the Asian and Pacific Islander population had grown to 13 million, and the number of Latinos had increased to more than 41 million, becoming—at 14 percent—the largest minority group in the nation.

The promise of economic opportunity, as always, lured immigrants to America, and the Immigration and Nationality Act of 1965 enabled them to come. Although the law set an annual ceiling of 270,000 immigrants, it allowed close relatives of U.S. citizens to enter above the ceiling, thus creating migration chains by which once newcomers became citizens, their spouses, children, and parents also gained entry. In addition, the cold war had sent U.S. military and other personnel around the world, enabling foreigners to learn about the nation and make personal contacts with citizens. And during the cold war, U.S. immigration policy was generous to people who wished to escape communism, welcoming more than 800,000 Cubans after Castro's revolution in 1959 and more than

Immigrant Labor

Large farms depended on Latino workers, who constituted more than 45 percent of agricultural labor in 2002. A majority of these workers were citizens, but growers insisted that they could not supply Americans with fresh produce without immigrant labor, legal and illegal. The dependence of agriculture and service industries on this labor helped block movements for greater immigration restrictions. The workers here are harvesting strawberries near Carlsbad, California.

Sandy Huffaker/Getty Images.

600,000 Vietnamese, Laotians, and Cambodians in the years following the Vietnam War.

The racial composition of the new immigration heightened the century-old wariness of native-born Americans toward recent arrivals. Pressure for more restrictive policies stemmed from beliefs that immigrants took jobs from the native-born, suppressed wages by accepting low-paying employment, or eroded the dominant culture and language. Americans expressed particular hostility toward the millions of immigrants who entered the country illegally—an estimated 4.4 million between 2000 and 2005—even though the economy depended on their cheap labor. The Immigration Reform and Control Act of 1986, which penalized employers who hired undocumented aliens but also granted amnesty to some 2 million illegal immigrants who had been in the country before 1982, did little to stem the tide.

The new immigration was once again making America an international, interracial society. The largest numbers of immigrants flocked to California, New York, Texas, Florida, New Jersey, and Illinois, but new immigrants dispersed much more throughout the country than did those of the early twentieth century. Taquerias, sushi bars, and Vietnamese restaurants appeared in southeastern and midwestern towns; cable TV companies added Spanish-language stations; and the international sport of soccer soared in popularity. Mixed marriages also displayed the growing fusion of cultures, recognized by the Census Bureau in 2000 when it let Americans check more than one racial category on their forms. Only half-joking, the famous golfer Tiger Woods called himself a "Cablinasian" to reflect his mixed heritage of Caucasian, black, American Indian, and Asian. Demographers predicted that by 2050, the U.S. population would be just over 50 percent white, 16 percent black, 24 percent Latino, and 9 percent Asian.

Like their predecessors a hundred years earlier, the majority of post-1965 immigrants were unskilled and poor. They took the lowest-paying jobs, including farm and yard work, child and elder care, and cleaning services—work that employers insisted they could not get enough native-born Americans to perform. Yet a significant number of immigrants were highly skilled workers, sought after by burgeoning high-tech industries. For example, in 1999 about one-third of the scientists and engineers who worked in California's Silicon Valley had been born abroad. A majority of the thirty-one employees of UroGenesys, a California biotech company, were immigrants from countries such as Vietnam, Poland, Lebanon, China, India, Israel, Scotland, and Peru. The company's owner boasted, "I cannot think of another country in the world where you could so easily put such a team together."

▶REVIEW   Who criticized free trade agreements and why?

President George W. Bush: Conservatism at Home and Radical Initiatives Abroad

The second son of a former president to gain the White House, George W. Bush pushed an agenda that was closer to Ronald Reagan's than that of his father, George H. W. Bush. The younger Bush signed key legislation to improve public school education and to subsidize prescription drugs for elderly citizens. But he also persuaded Congress to pass enormous tax cuts that favored the wealthy, reduced environmental protections, and tipped the balance on the Supreme Court with two conservative appointments. The tax cuts, along with spending on new international and domestic crises, turned the substantial budget surplus that Bush had inherited into the largest deficit in the nation's history.

As Islamist terrorism replaced communism as the primary threat to U.S. security, the Bush administration launched a war in Afghanistan in 2001 and expanded the federal government's powers to investigate and detain individuals. In distinct contrast to his father's multilateral and cautious approach to foreign policy, George W. Bush adopted a policy of unilateralism and preemption by going to war against Iraq in 2003. The president was reelected by a majority of voters in 2004, but even at huge costs, the Iraq War failed to secure American objectives, and Bush confronted serious foreign and domestic crises in his second term.

The Disputed Election of 2000

Even though Clinton's presidency ended with a flourishing economy, Albert Gore, his vice president, failed to retain the White House for the Democrats in the election of 2000. Gore's running mate, Connecticut senator Joseph Lieberman, was the first Jewish American to run on a major-party ticket, and public opinion polls indicated that a majority of Americans agreed with the Democratic nominees on most issues. Yet many voters found Gore's style stiff and pompous and considered him too willing to change his positions for political advantage. He was further burdened with the taint of Clinton administration scandals.

George W. Bush emerged as the Republican nominee from a series of bountifully funded, hard-fought primaries. The oldest son of former president George H. W. Bush, he had attended Yale and Harvard, worked in the oil industry and as managing partner of the Texas Rangers baseball team, and served as governor of Texas since 1994. Inexperienced in national and international affairs, Bush chose for his running mate a seasoned official, Richard B. Cheney, who had served in the Nixon, Ford, and first Bush administrations.

Both candidates ran cautious campaigns, accommodating their positions to what polls indicated voters wanted. Bush's strategy mirrored Clinton's in 1992. Calling himself a "compassionate conservative," Bush separated himself from the extreme right wing of his party and tried to co-opt Democratic issues such as education. Like Republicans before him, he promised substantial cuts in taxes and federal spending.

Many observers predicted that the amazingly strong economy would give Gore the edge, and he did surpass Bush by more than half a million votes. Once the polls closed, however, it became clear that Florida's 25 electoral college votes would decide the presidency. Bush's margin was so tiny in Florida, where his brother served as governor, that it prompted an automatic recount of the votes, which eventually gave Bush an edge of 537 votes.

Meanwhile, the Democrats asked for hand-counting of Florida ballots in several heavily Democratic counties where voting machine errors and confusing ballots may have left thousands of Gore votes unrecorded. The Republicans, in turn, went to court to try to stop the hand-counts. The outcome of the 2000 election hung in the balance for more than a month as cases went all the way to the Supreme Court. Finally, a bitterly divided Supreme Court ruled five to four against further recounts, and Gore conceded the presidency to Bush on December 13, 2000. For the first time since 1888, a president who failed to win the popular

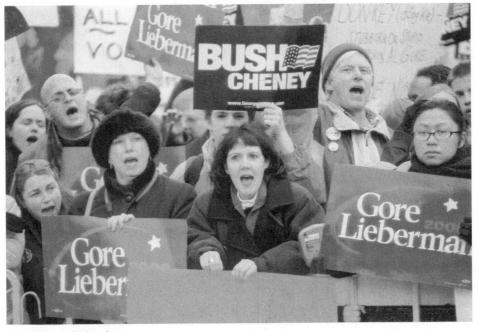

The Disputed Election
While attorneys representing presidential candidates George W. Bush and Al Gore pursued lawsuits over the counting of ballots that would determine who won Florida's electoral college votes, backers of both sides rallied outside the Supreme Court in Washington, D.C., on December 11, 2000, the day before the Court issued its five-to-four ruling that ended the ballot recounts and consequently secured the presidency for Bush. Critics charged that the five justices who voted to stop the recounts had applied partisanship rather than objectivity to the case, pointing out that if those justices had followed their custom of favoring state over federal authority, they would have allowed Florida to continue the recounts.
AP Images.

vote took office. Despite the lack of a popular mandate, the Bush administration set out to make dramatic policy changes.

The Domestic Policies of a "Compassionate Conservative"

As was the case with his predecessor, Bush's appointments brought significant diversity to the executive branch. He chose African Americans Colin Powell as secretary of state and Condoleezza Rice first as national security adviser and subsequently as secretary of state, when Powell left that office in January 2005. Five of Bush's top-level appointees were women, including Secretary of Labor Elaine L. Chao, the first Asian American woman to serve in the cabinet. In 2005, Alberto R. Gonzales, a Latino, became attorney general.

Bush moved quickly on his domestic agenda, building on his campaign promise to govern as a "compassionate conservative." A devout born-again

Christian, he immediately established the White House Office of Faith-Based and Community Initiatives to encourage religious and community groups to participate in government programs aimed at prison inmates, drug addicts, the unemployed, and other groups. The religious right praised the initiatives, but others charged that they violated the constitutional separation of church and state, and federal courts ruled in more than a dozen cases that faith ministries were using government funds to indoctrinate the people they served.

Bush's fiscal policies were more conservative and more compassionate toward the rich than toward average Americans. In 2001, he signed a bill reducing taxes over the next ten years by $1.35 trillion. A 2003 tax law slashed another $320 billion. The laws heavily favored the rich by reducing income taxes, phasing out estate taxes, and cutting tax rates on capital gains and dividends. They also provided benefits for married couples and families with children, offered tax deductions for college expenses, and gave an immediate rebate of up to $300 to each taxpayer.

The administration insisted that the tax cuts would promote economic growth and jolt the economy out of the recession that had begun in 2000, when the dot-com stock bubble burst. Opponents stressed inequities in the tax cuts and pointed to a mushrooming federal deficit—the highest in U.S. history—that surpassed $400 billion in 2004. Senator Joseph Lieberman charged that Bush's tax cuts were "giving the most to those who need it least, piling more debt on the backs of our children and robbing Social Security and Medicare to pay for it." Republicans had traditionally railed against budget deficits, but now they saw them as a way to limit the size of the federal government. "Anything that will help us stop spending money, I'm in favor of," declared Representative Sue Myrick from North Carolina. "And if there's a deficit, that may help us." The economy did recover, and the deficit dropped to $250 billion in 2006; but the national debt had grown from $5.7 trillion in 2000 to $8.3 trillion in 2006, costing the government $406 billion in interest payments that year. The United States became increasingly dependent on China and other foreign investors, who held more than half of the debt.

As Clinton had done, Bush altered environmental policy by issuing regulations that did not require congressional approval. But whereas Clinton had imposed greater controls, Bush weakened environmental protection to benefit his larger goals of reducing government regulation, promoting economic growth, and increasing energy production. The Senate blocked Bush's efforts to allow drilling for oil in the Arctic National Wildlife Refuge, but elsewhere the administration opened millions of wilderness acres of public land to the mining, oil, and timber industries. Bush imposed new restrictions on diesel pollutants and relaxed environmental requirements under the Clean Air Act and Clean Water Act. To worldwide dismay, the administration withdrew from the Kyoto Protocol on global warming, signed in 1997 by 178 nations to reduce greenhouse gas emissions. "Shame on Bush," chanted protesters when Secretary of State Powell addressed the Earth Summit in 2002.

While environmentalists pushed for measures to limit American energy consumption, the administration called for more rapid development of energy resources. During his second term, as gasoline prices reached all-time highs in 2005, Bush signed the Energy Policy Act, a compromise bill providing $14 billion in subsidies to producers of oil, coal, nuclear power, and alternative sources of energy. After Hurricanes Katrina and Rita ravaged oil and natural gas production in the Gulf of Mexico in 2005, Bush asked Americans to conserve energy but proposed no new regulations.

Conservatives hailed Bush's appointment of two new Supreme Court justices. In 2005, John Roberts, who had served in the Reagan and George H. W. Bush administrations, was named chief justice. The president faced a stiffer challenge in finding a successor to the moderate Sandra Day O'Connor, who retired shortly thereafter. His first choice, Harriet Miers, had questionable credentials— she had never served as a judge—and drew opposition from both the right and the left before eventually stepping aside. Bush then nominated Samuel A. Alito, a staunch conservative who won confirmation by a narrow and mostly partisan margin of 58 to 42.

In contrast to the partisan conflict that attended judicial appointments and tax and environmental policy, Bush mobilized bipartisan support behind the No Child Left Behind (NCLB) Act of 2002. The law marked the greatest change in federal education policy since the 1960s, substantially extending the role of the federal government in public education, a realm historically left to the state and local governments. Promising to end, in Bush's words, "the story of children being just shuffled through the system," the law required every school to meet annual testing standards, provided penalties for failing schools, and allowed parents to transfer their children out of such schools. It authorized an increase in federal aid aimed primarily at the poorest districts, but not enough for Senator Paul Wellstone of Minnesota, one of the few critics of the education bill, who asked, "How can you reach the goal of leaving no child behind on a tin cup budget?" This query anticipated problems that states would face in implementing the legislation, because only 7 percent of their education budgets came from the federal government. By 2004, most states were straining to meet the demands of the new education standards as they struggled with severe budget crises.

The Bush administration's second major effort to co-opt Democratic Party issues constituted what the president hailed as "the greatest advance in health care coverage for America's seniors" since the start of Medicare in 1965. In December 2003, the president signed a bill authorizing prescription drug benefits for the elderly and at the same time expanding the role of private insurers in the Medicare system. Most Democrats opposed the legislation, charging that it left big gaps in coverage, subsidized private insurers with federal funds to compete with Medicare, banned imports of low-priced drugs, and prohibited the government from negotiating with drug companies to reduce prices. Legislators of both parties worried about the cost of the new drug benefit, estimated to surpass $500 billion after it took effect in 2006. Although the law's requirement that beneficiaries choose from dozens of private insurance plans made the program confusing, more than 80 percent of the elderly who signed up for the benefit were at least "somewhat satisfied" with the program. Medical costs overall continued to soar, and the number of uninsured Americans reached 46.6 million in 2006.

Hurricane Katrina
Residents of the poverty-stricken Lower Ninth Ward of New Orleans cry for help after floods submerged 80 percent of the city in the wake of Hurricane Katrina in August 2005. The boat was useless to these people because it had lost its motor. Some residents waited as long as five days to be rescued.
AP Images/David J. Phillip.

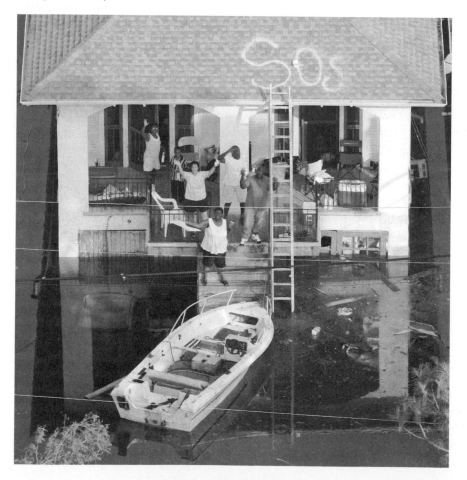

One domestic undertaking of the Bush administration found little approval anywhere: its handling of Hurricane Katrina, which in August 2005 devastated the coasts of Alabama, Louisiana, and Mississippi and ultimately resulted in some fifteen hundred deaths. Dodging the worst of the storm itself, residents of New Orleans suffered catastrophe when some of the levees broke, flooding 80 percent of the city. What happened next shook a deeply rooted assumption held by Americans, even conservatives who were devoted to limited government: that government owed its citizens protection from natural disasters. Federal, state, and local officials failed the citizens of New Orleans in two ways: They had not built the levees to withstand such a deluge, and they failed to rescue citizens when the levees broke and flooded their homes.

Although most New Orleans residents left the city before the hurricane hit, some decided to ride it out, and others were too old, too poor, or too sick to flee. More than one-fourth of all households did not own a car, and others could not afford alternative housing. One man responsible for thirteen relatives later said, "I'd like to ask the mayor how you take fourteen people with no finances and book them in a hotel. It's not that we didn't leave. It's that we couldn't leave." Thousands abandoned in the city spent anguished days waiting on rooftops for help; wading in filthy, toxic water; and enduring the heat, stench, disorder, and lack of basic necessities at the convention center and Superdome, where they had been told to go for safety and protection.

"How can we save the world if we can't save our own people?" wondered a Louisianan whose home escaped damage. He was one of hundreds of people with small boats who rushed to rescue people from their rooftops. Thousands of other volunteers helped evacuees in distant cities and a year later were still traveling to the Gulf Coast to assist with reconstruction. Millions more opened their pocketbooks to aid the victims. Yet the immense private generosity and the superb response of a few groups, such as the U.S. coast guard and the Louisiana Department of Wildlife and Fisheries, could not make up for the feeling that the nation had failed some of its citizens when they needed it most. A year later, only 40 percent of the population had returned home, and restoration of the city lay years in the future. Moreover, since so many of Katrina's hardest-hit victims were poor and black (the poverty rate among children in New Orleans exceeded 40 percent before the storm), the disaster highlighted the severe injustices and deprivations remaining in American society.

The Globalization of Terrorism

The response to Hurricane Katrina contrasted sharply with the Bush administration's decisive reaction to the horror that had unfolded four years earlier on the morning of September 11, 2001. In the most deadly attack ever launched on American soil, nineteen terrorists hijacked four planes and flew three of them into the twin towers of New York City's World Trade Center and the Pentagon in

Washington, D.C.; the fourth crashed in a field in Pennsylvania. The attacks took nearly 2,800 lives, including U.S. citizens and people from ninety countries. The nation, indeed the world, was stunned.

The hijackers were members of Osama bin Laden's Al Qaeda international terrorist network, some of whom had been living in the United States for several years. Organized from bin Laden's sanctuaries in Afghanistan, where the radical Muslim Taliban government had taken control, the attacks reflected several elements of globalization. The technological advances and increased mobility accompanying globalization facilitated bin Laden's worldwide coordination of Al Qaeda and aided the hijackers' activities. Moreover, Islamic extremists were enraged by the spread of Western goods, culture, and values into the Muslim world, as well as by the 1991 Persian Gulf War against Iraq and the stationing of American troops in Saudi Arabia, bin Laden's homeland. Acting on a distorted interpretation of one of the world's great religions, bin Laden sought to rid the Middle East of Western influence and install puritanical Muslim control. Whether poor or middle-class, living in Middle Eastern homelands governed by undemocratic and corrupt governments or in Western cities where they felt alienated and despised, the 9/11 terrorists and others who came after them saw the West, and especially the United States, as the evil source of their humiliation and the supporter of Israel's oppression of Palestinian Muslims.

In the wake of the September 11 attacks, President Bush's public approval rating skyrocketed as he sought a global alliance against terrorism and won at least verbal support from most governments. On October 11, the United States and Britain began bombing Afghanistan, and American special forces aided the Northern Alliance, the Taliban government's main opposition. By December, the Taliban government was destroyed, but bin Laden had not been captured, and numerous Al Qaeda forces had escaped or remained in hiding throughout the world. Afghans elected a new national government, but although the United States still had 27,000 troops in Afghanistan seven years later, economic stability and physical security remained out of reach.

At home, the balance between **liberty** and security tilted. Throughout the country, anti-immigrant sentiment revived, and anyone appearing to be Middle Eastern or practicing Islam was likely to arouse suspicion. Authorities arrested more than a thousand Arabs and Muslims, and an internal study by the Justice Department later reported that many people with no connection to terrorism spent months in jail, denied their rights. "I think America overreacted . . . by singling out Arab-named men like myself," said Shanaz Mohammed, who was jailed for eight months for an immigration violation.

"The smoke was still coming out of the rubble in New York City when we passed the law," said C. L. Otter, Republican representative from Idaho, referring to the USA Patriot Act, which Congress approved by huge margins in October 2001. The law gave the government new powers to monitor suspected terrorists and their associates, including the ability to pry personal information about individuals from libraries, universities, and businesses, while allowing more exchange of information between criminal investigators and those investigating foreign threats. It soon provoked calls for revision from both conservatives and liberals. Kathleen MacKenzie, a councilwoman in Ann Arbor, Michigan, explained why the council passed a resolution opposing the Patriot Act: "[A]s awful as we feel about September 11 and as concerned as we were about national safety, we felt that giving up [rights] was too high a price to pay." A security official countered, "If you don't violate someone's human rights some of the time, you probably aren't doing your job."

Insisting that presidential powers were virtually limitless in times of national crisis, Bush stretched his powers as commander in chief until he met resistance from the courts and Congress. In 2001, the administration established special military commissions to try prisoners captured in Afghanistan and taken to the U.S. military base at Guantánamo, Cuba. But in 2006, responding to a suit filed by one of the some five hundred detainees who had languished there for years, the Supreme Court ruled five to three that Congress had not authorized such tribunals and that they violated international law. In 2006, congressional leaders became openly critical of the administration for wiretapping phone calls made and received by U.S. residents without obtaining the warrants required by law, and a federal district court ruled that the wiretapping program violated privacy, free speech, and the separation of powers.

The government also sought to protect Americans from future terrorist attacks through the greatest reorganization of the executive branch since 1948. In November 2002, Congress authorized the new Department of Homeland Security (DHS), combining 170,000 federal employees from twenty-two agencies through which responsibilities for different aspects of domestic security had been dispersed. Chief among the department's duties were intelligence analysis; immigration and border security; chemical, biological, and nuclear countermeasures; and emergency preparedness and response. During the new department's first five years, no terrorist attacks were launched in the United States, but doubts were raised about its effectiveness when its subagency, the Federal Emergency Management Agency (FEMA), failed so badly in response to Hurricane Katrina.

Unilateralism, Preemption, and the Iraq War

The Bush administration sought collective action against the Taliban, but on most other international issues, it adopted a go-it-alone approach. In addition to withdrawing from the Kyoto Protocol on global warming and violating international rules about the treatment of military prisoners, it scrapped the 1972 Antiballistic Missile Treaty in order to develop the space-based Strategic Defense Initiative (SDI) first proposed by Ronald Reagan. Bush also withdrew the United States from the UN's International Criminal Court, and he rejected an agreement to enforce bans on the development and possession of biological weapons—an agreement signed by all of America's European allies.

Nowhere was the new policy of unilateralism more striking than in a new war against Iraq, a war pushed by Vice President Dick Cheney and Secretary of Defense Donald H. Rumsfeld, but not Secretary of State Colin Powell. In his State of the Union message in January 2002, Bush identified Iraq, Iran, and North Korea as an "axis of evil." His words alarmed political leaders in both Europe and Asia, who insisted that those three nations posed entirely different challenges. Preferring to emphasize diplomacy rather than confrontation, Bush's opponents in Europe and Asia objected to his unilateral assessment.

Nonetheless, addressing West Point graduates in June, President Bush proclaimed a new policy for American security based not on containment but on preemption: "Traditional concepts of deterrence will not work against a terrorist enemy whose avowed tactics are wanton destruction and the targeting of innocents; whose so-called soldiers seek martyrdom in death and whose most potent protection is statelessness." Because nuclear, chemical, and biological weapons enabled "even weak states and small groups [to] attain a catastrophic power to strike great nations," the United States had to "be ready for preemptive action." For a century, the United States had intervened militarily and unilaterally in the affairs of small nations, but it had not gone to war except to repel aggression against itself or its allies. The president's claim that the United States had the right to start a war was at odds with international law and with many Americans' understanding of their nation's ideals. It distressed most of America's great-power allies.

Nonetheless, the Bush administration moved deliberately to apply the doctrine of preemption to Iraq, whose dictator, Saddam Hussein, appeared to be in violation of UN resolutions from the 1991 Gulf War requiring Iraq to destroy and stop further development of nuclear, chemical, and biological weapons. In November 2002, the United States persuaded the UN Security Council to pass a resolution requiring Iraq to disarm or face "serious consequences." When Iraq failed to comply fully with new UN inspections, the Bush administration decided on war. Making (now widely disputed) claims that Hussein had links to Al Qaeda and harbored terrorists and that Iraq possessed weapons of mass destruction, the president insisted that the threat was immediate and great enough to justify preemptive action. Despite opposition from the Arab world and most major nations—including France, Germany, China, and Russia—which preferred to give the UN inspectors more time, the United States and Britain invaded Iraq on March 19, 2003, supported by some thirty nations (see Map 31.1). This coalition included Australia, Italy, Japan, and Spain but few major powers or traditional allies. The coalition forces won an easy and decisive victory, and Bush declared the end of the war on May 1. Saddam Hussein remained at large until December 2003.

Arabs were glad to see the end of Hussein, but many did not welcome the presence of American troops in Iraq. As the publisher of a Lebanese newspaper put it, "[Iraqis] have to choose between the night of tyranny and the night of humiliation stemming from foreign occupation." Moreover, damage from U.S. bombing and widespread looting resulting from the failure of U.S. troops to secure order and provide basic necessities left Iraqis wondering how much they had gained. "With Saddam there was tyranny, but at least you had a salary to put food on your family's table," said a young father from Hussein's hometown of Tikrit. Tha'ar Abdul Qader, who worked at a children's hospital in Baghdad, complained, "They can take our oil, but at least they should let us have electricity and water." In March 2003, President Bush promised that the lives of Iraqis would "dramatically improve," but four years later Iraqis had less electricity than they had had before the war, and a majority lacked access to clean water. Continuing violence had caused 2 million to flee their country and displaced 1.9 million within Iraq.

The administration had not planned adequately for the occupation and sent far fewer forces to Iraq than it had deployed in 1991 in response to Iraq's invasion of Kuwait. The 140,000 American forces in Iraq came under attack almost daily from remnants of the former Hussein regime, religious extremists, and hundreds of foreign terrorists now entering the chaotic country. Seeking to divide Iraqis and undermine the occupation, terrorists launched deadly assaults on such targets as the UN mission in Baghdad and Red Cross headquarters, as well as on major mosques and Iraqi citizens, resulting in tens of thousands dead. L. Paul Bremer, who headed the Iraqi occupation for fourteen months, believed that U.S. forces were "spread too thin on the ground. During my morning intelligence briefings, I would sometimes picture an understrength fire crew racing from one blaze to another."

The war became an issue in the presidential campaign of 2004, which registered the highest voter turnout since 1968. Massachusetts senator John Kerry, the Democratic nominee, criticized Bush's unilateralist foreign policy and the administration's conduct of the war. A slim majority of voters, however, indicated their belief that Bush would better protect American security from terrorist threats than Kerry. Once again, the election turned on a single state. This time it was Ohio, which gave Bush a 286 to 252 victory in the electoral college. The president won 50.7 percent of the popular vote to Kerry's 48.3 percent and carried Republican majorities into Congress.

In June 2004, the United States transferred sovereignty to an interim Iraqi government, and in January 2005, about 58 percent of Iraqis eligible to vote risked their safety to elect a national assembly. The daunting challenges facing the national assembly were to write a constitution, satisfy Iraq's sharply divided political blocs, and decide to what extent Islamic religious law would shape the new government. Violence escalated against government officials, Iraqi civilians, and occupation forces. A nineteen-year-old Iraqi, confined to his house by his parents, who feared he could be killed or lured into terrorist activities, said, "If I'm killed, it doesn't even matter because I'm dead right now." Some observers spoke of **guerrilla warfare**, "quagmire," and civil war, evoking comparisons with the U.S. experience in Vietnam. By 2006, when U.S. military deaths approached 3,000 and Iraqi civilian casualties reached tens of thousands, public opinion polls in the United States found that a majority of Americans believed that the Iraq War was a mistake.

The president's father, George H. W. Bush, had refused to invade Iraq at the end of the 1991 Gulf War. He explained that Colin Powell, Dick Cheney, and other advisers agreed that "unilaterally exceeding the United Nations' mandate would have destroyed the precedent of international response to aggression that we hoped to establish." The first Bush administration resisted making the nation "an occupying power in a bitterly hostile land," refusing to incur the "incalculable human and political costs" that such an invasion would produce.

By 2006, his son's very different approach was subject to criticism that crossed party lines and included leading military figures. Critics acknowledged that the U.S. military had felled a brutal dictator, but coalition forces were not sufficiently numerous or prepared for the turmoil that followed the invasion, nor did they find the weapons of mass destruction or links to Osama bin Laden that administration officials had insisted made the war necessary. Rather, in the chaos induced by the invasion of Iraq, more than a thousand terrorists entered Iraq—the place, according to one expert, "for fundamentalists to go . . . to stick it to the West."

The war and occupation exacted a steep price not only in dollars but also in American and Iraqi lives, U.S. relations with the other great powers, and the nation's reputation in the world, especially among Arab nations. Revelations of prisoner abuse in the Abu Ghraib prison in Iraq and in the Guantánamo detention camp housing captives from the Afghan war further tarnished the U.S. image. Anti-Americanism around the world rose to its highest point in history. The budget deficit swelled, and resources were diverted to Iraq from other national security challenges, including the stabilization of Afghanistan, the elimination of bin Laden and Al Qaeda, and the threats posed by North Korea's and Iran's pursuit of nuclear weapons.

Voters registered their dissatisfaction with the war in the 2006 congressional elections, turning control of both houses over to the Democrats for the first time since 1994. President Bush replaced Secretary of Defense Donald Rumsfeld, and the administration displayed more willingness to work with other nations in dealing with Iraq, Iran, and North Korea. Yet Bush clung to the goal of bringing democracy to the Middle East, even as the situation in Iraq deteriorated. Despite opposition from the Democratic-controlled Congress, who wanted a timetable for withdrawal from Iraq and turning over responsibility for security to the Iraqi government, in 2007 the administration began a troop surge that increased U.S. forces in Iraq to 160,000. Officials made no promises about how long the U.S. military would be needed, and the conflict over the war at home intensified.

> ▶REVIEW   Why did the United States invade Iraq in March 2003?

Conclusion: Defining the Government's Role at Home and Abroad

On March 21, 2003, some 225 years after the birth of the United States, Colin Powell referred to the unfinished nature of the American promise when he declared that the question of America's role in the world "isn't answered yet." In fact, the end of the cold war, the rise of international terrorism, and the George W. Bush administration's doctrines of preemption and unilateralism sparked new debates over the long-standing question of how the United States should act beyond its borders.

Nor had Americans set to rest questions about the role of government at home. In a population so greatly derived from people fleeing oppressive governments, Americans had debated for more than two centuries what responsibilities the government could or should shoulder and what was best left to private enterprise, families, churches, and other voluntary institutions. Far more than other democracies, the United States had taken the path of private rather than public obligation, individual rather than collective solutions. In the twentieth century, Americans had significantly enlarged the federal government's powers and responsibilities, but the last three decades of the twentieth century had seen a decline of trust in government's ability to improve people's lives, even as a poverty rate of 20 percent among children and a growing gap between rich and poor survived the economic boom of the 1990s.

The shifting of control of the government back and forth between Republicans and Democrats from 1989 to 2006 revealed a dynamic debate over the role of government in domestic affairs. The protections enacted for people with disabilities during the first Bush administration and Bill Clinton's incremental reforms in some social areas built on a deep-rooted tradition that sought to realize the American promise of justice and human well-being. Those who mobilized against the ravages of globalization worked internationally for what **populists, progressives,** New Deal reformers, and many activists of the 1960s had sought for the domestic population: protection of individual rights, curbs on **laissez-faire** capitalism, assistance for victims of rapid economic change, and fiscal policies that placed greater responsibility on those best able to pay for the collective good. The second Bush administration, however—with a few exceptions, such as the No Child Left Behind Act and the prescription drug program for the elderly—advocated a more limited role for the federal government.

As the United States entered the twenty-first century, it became ever more deeply embedded in the global economy as products, information, and people crossed borders with amazing speed and frequency. Although the end of the cold war brought about unanticipated cooperation between the United States and its former enemies, globalization also contributed to international instability and the threat of deadly terrorism to a nation unaccustomed to foreign attacks within its own borders. In response to those dangers, the second Bush administration began to chart a departure from the multilateral approach to foreign policy that had been built up by Republican and Democratic administrations alike since World War II. Yet as the United States became mired in reconstruction efforts in Iraq, Americans continued to debate how the nation could best maintain domestic security while still exercising its economic and military power on a rapidly changing planet.

REVIEWING THE CHAPTER

Use the questions and timeline to review and strengthen your understanding of the chapter.

REVIEW QUESTIONS

1. Why did George H. W. Bush lose the presidency in 1992? (pp. 1003–12)

2. What policies of the Clinton administration reflect the president's efforts to move his party to the right? (pp. 1012–18)

3. Who criticized free trade agreements and why? (pp. 1018–25)

4. Why did the United States invade Iraq in March 2003? (pp. 1025–37)

MAKING CONNECTIONS

1. How did George H. W. Bush continue the policies of his predecessor, Ronald Reagan? How did he depart from them?

2. President Bill Clinton called himself a "New Democrat." How did his policies and goals differ from those of Democrats in the past?

3. In the late twentieth century, economic globalization transformed the United States. Explain what globalization is and describe how it affected the U.S. economy and population in the 1990s.

4. The terrorist attacks of September 11, 2001, were unprecedented. What gave rise to the attacks? How did the nation respond?

TIMELINE

1988	• Republican George H. W. Bush elected president.	**1999**	• Senate trial fails to approve articles of impeachment.
1989	• Communism collapses in Eastern Europe; Berlin Wall falls.		• United States, with NATO, bombs Serbia.
	• United States invades Panama.	**2000**	• Republican George W. Bush elected president.
1990	• Americans with Disabilities Act.	**2001**	• **September 11.** Terrorists attack World Trade Center and Pentagon.
1991	• Persian Gulf War.		• United States attacks Afghanistan, driving out Taliban government.
1992	• Democrat William Jefferson "Bill" Clinton elected president.		• USA Patriot Act.
1993	• Israel and PLO sign peace accords.		• $1.35 trillion tax cut.
	• North American Free Trade Agreement (NAFTA).	**2002**	• No Child Left Behind Act.
	• Clinton announces policy for gays in military.		• Department of Homeland Security established.
	• Family and Medical Leave Act.	**2003**	• United States attacks Iraq, driving out Saddam Hussein.
1994	• United States sends troops to Haiti.		• Prescription drug coverage added to Medicare.
	• General Agreement on Tariffs and Trade (GATT) establishes World Trade Organization (WTO).	**2004**	• George W. Bush reelected president.
1995	• Bombing of federal building in Oklahoma City.	**2005**	• Hurricane Katrina.
			• Central American–Dominican Republic Free Trade Agreement (CAFTA-DR).
1996	• Personal Responsibility and Work Opportunity Reconciliation Act.	**2006**	• Majority of Americans believe Iraq War was a mistake.
	• President Clinton reelected.		
1997	• Tax cut enacted.	**2007**	• Bush begins troop surge in Iraq.
1998	• United States bombs terrorist sites in Afghanistan and Sudan.		
	• United States bombs Iraq.		
	• President Clinton impeached.		

▶ **For an online bibliography, practice quizzes, Web sites, images, and documents related to this chapter,** see the Book Companion Site at **bedfordstmartins.com/roark.**

▶ **For firsthand accounts of this period,** see Chapter 31 in Michael Johnson, ed., *Reading the American Past*, Fourth Edition.

For additional documents, see the DocLinks feature at **bedfordstmartins.com/roark**.

THE DECLARATION OF INDEPENDENCE

In Congress, July 4, 1776,

THE UNANIMOUS DECLARATION
OF THE THIRTEEN UNITED STATES OF AMERICA

When in the course of human events, it becomes necessary for one people to dissolve the political bands which have connected them with another, and to assume, among the powers of the earth, the separate and equal station to which the laws of nature and of nature's God entitle them, a decent respect to the opinions of mankind requires that they should declare the causes which impel them to the separation.

We hold these truths to be self-evident, that all men are created equal; that they are endowed by their Creator with certain unalienable rights; that among these, are life, liberty, and the pursuit of happiness. That, to secure these rights, governments are instituted among men, deriving their just powers from the consent of the governed; that, whenever any form of government becomes destructive of these ends, it is the right of the people to alter or to abolish it, and to institute a new government, laying its foundation on such principles, and organizing its powers in such form, as to them shall seem most likely to effect their safety and happiness. Prudence, indeed, will dictate that governments long established, should not be changed for light and transient causes; and, accordingly, all experience hath shown, that mankind are more disposed to suffer, while evils are sufferable, than to right themselves by abolishing the forms to which they are accustomed. But, when a long train of abuses and usurpations, pursuing invariably the same object, evinces a design to reduce them under absolute despotism, it is their right, it is their duty, to throw off such government and to provide new guards for their future security. Such has been the patient sufferance of these colonies, and such is now the necessity which constrains them to alter their former systems of government. The history of the present King of Great Britain is a history of repeated injuries and usurpations, all having, in direct object, the establishment of an absolute tyranny over these States. To prove this, let facts be submitted to a candid world:

He has refused his assent to laws the most wholesome and necessary for the public good.

He has forbidden his governors to pass laws of immediate and pressing importance, unless suspended in their operation till his assent should be obtained; and, when so suspended, he has utterly neglected to attend to them.

He has refused to pass other laws for the accommodation of large districts of people, unless those people would relinquish the right of representation in the legislature; a right inestimable to them, and formidable to tyrants only.

He has called together legislative bodies at places unusual, uncomfortable, and distant from the depository of their public records, for the sole purpose of fatiguing them into compliance with his measures.

He has dissolved representative houses repeatedly for opposing, with manly firmness, his invasions on the rights of the people.

He has refused, for a long time after such dissolutions, to cause others to be elected; whereby the legislative powers, incapable of annihilation, have returned to the people at large for their exercise; the state remaining in the mean-time exposed to all the danger of invasion from without, and convulsions within.

He has endeavoured to prevent the population of these States; for that purpose, obstructing the laws for naturalization of foreigners, refusing to pass others to encourage their migration hither, and raising the conditions of new appropriations of lands.

He has obstructed the administration of justice, by refusing his assent to laws for establishing judiciary powers.

He has made judges dependent on his will alone, for the tenure of their offices, and the amount and payment of their salaries.

He has erected a multitude of new offices, and sent hither swarms of officers to harass our people, and eat out their substance.

He has kept among us, in times of peace, standing armies, without the consent of our legislature.

He has affected to render the military independent of, and superior to, the civil power.

He has combined, with others, to subject us to a jurisdiction foreign to our Constitution, and unacknowledged by our laws; giving his assent to their acts of pretended legislation:

For quartering large bodies of armed troops among us:

For protecting them by a mock trial, from punishment, for any murders which they should commit on the inhabitants of these States:

For cutting off our trade with all parts of the world:

For imposing taxes on us without our consent:

For depriving us, in many cases, of the benefit of trial by jury:

For transporting us beyond seas to be tried for pretended offences:

For abolishing the free system of English laws in a neighboring province, establishing therein an arbitrary government, and enlarging its boundaries, so as to render it at once an example and fit instrument for introducing the same absolute rule into these colonies:

For taking away our charters, abolishing our most valuable laws, and altering, fundamentally, the powers of our governments:

For suspending our own legislatures, and declaring themselves invested with power to legislate for us in all cases whatsoever.

He has abdicated government here, by declaring us out of his protection, and waging war against us.

He has plundered our seas, ravaged our coasts, burnt our towns, and destroyed the lives of our people.

He is, at this time, transporting large armies of foreign mercenaries to complete the works of death, desolation, and tyranny, already begun, with circumstances of cruelty and perfidy scarcely paralleled in the most barbarous ages, and totally unworthy the head of a civilized nation.

He has constrained our fellow citizens, taken captive on the high seas, to bear arms against their country, to become the executioners of their friends, and brethren, or to fall themselves by their hands.

He has excited domestic insurrections amongst us, and has endeavored to bring on the inhabitants of our frontiers, the merciless Indian savages, whose known rule of warfare is an undistinguished destruction of all ages, sexes, and conditions.

In every stage of these oppressions, we have petitioned for redress; in the most humble terms; our repeated petitions have been answered only by repeated injury. A prince, whose character is thus marked by every act which may define a tyrant, is unfit to be the ruler of a free people.

Nor have we been wanting in attention to our British brethren. We have warned them, from time to time, of attempts made by their legislature to extend an unwarrantable jurisdiction over us. We have reminded them of the circumstances of our emigration and settlement here. We have appealed to their native justice and magnanimity, and we have conjured them, by the ties of our common kindred, to disavow these usurpations, which would inevitably interrupt our connections and correspondence. They, too, have been deaf to the voice of justice and consanguinity. We must, therefore, acquiesce in the necessity which denounces our separation, and hold them as we hold the rest of mankind, enemies in war, in peace, friends.

We, therefore, the representatives of the United States of America, in general Congress assembled, appealing to the Supreme Judge of the world for the rectitude of our intentions, do, in the name, and by authority of the good people of these colonies, solemnly publish and declare, that these united colonies are, and of right ought to be, free and independent states: that they are absolved from all allegiance to the British Crown, and that all political connection between them and the state of Great Britain is, and ought to be, totally dissolved; and that, as free and independent states, they have full power to levy war, conclude peace, contract alliances, establish commerce, and to do all other acts and things which independent states may of right do. And, for the support of this declaration, with a firm reliance on the protection of Divine Providence, we mutually pledge to each other our lives, our fortunes, and our sacred honor.

The foregoing Declaration was, by order of Congress, engrossed, and signed by the following members:

John Hancock

New Hampshire
Josiah Bartlett
William Whipple
Matthew Thornton

Massachusetts Bay
Samuel Adams
John Adams
Robert Treat Paine
Elbridge Gerry

Rhode Island
Stephen Hopkins
William Ellery

Connecticut
Roger Sherman
Samuel
    Huntington
William Williams
Oliver Wolcott

New York
William Floyd
Phillip Livingston
Francis Lewis
Lewis Morris

New Jersey
Richard Stockton
John Witherspoon
Francis Hopkinson
John Hart
Abraham Clark

Pennsylvania
Robert Morris
Benjamin Rush
Benjamin Franklin
John Morton
George Clymer
James Smith
George Taylor
James Wilson
George Ross

Delaware
Caesar Rodney
George Read
Thomas M'Kean

Maryland
Samuel Chase
William Paca
Thomas Stone
Charles Carroll,
    of Carrollton

North Carolina
William Hooper
Joseph Hewes
John Penn

South Carolina
Edward Rutledge
Thomas
    Heyward, Jr.
Thomas Lynch, Jr.
Arthur Middleton

Virginia
George Wythe
Richard Henry Lee
Thomas Jefferson
Benjamin Harrison
Thomas Nelson, Jr.
Francis Lightfoot
    Lee
Carter Braxton

Georgia
Button Gwinnett
Lyman Hall
George Walton

Resolved, That copies of the Declaration be sent to the several assemblies, conventions, and committees, or councils of safety, and to the several commanding officers of the continental troops; that it be proclaimed in each of the United States, at the head of the army.

THE ARTICLES OF CONFEDERATION AND PERPETUAL UNION

Agreed to in Congress, November 15, 1777.
Ratified March 1781.

BETWEEN THE STATES OF NEW HAMPSHIRE, MASSACHUSETTS BAY, RHODE ISLAND AND PROVIDENCE PLANTATIONS, CONNECTICUT, NEW YORK, NEW JERSEY, PENNSYLVANIA, DELAWARE, MARYLAND, VIRGINIA, NORTH CAROLINA, SOUTH CAROLINA, GEORGIA.*

Article 1

The stile of this confederacy shall be "The United States of America."

Article 2

Each State retains its sovereignty, freedom and independence, and every power, jurisdiction, and right, which is not by this confederation expressly delegated to the United States, in Congress assembled.

Article 3

The said states hereby severally enter into a firm league of friendship with each other for their common defence, the security of their liberties and their mutual and general welfare; binding themselves to assist each other against all force offered to, or attacks made upon them, or any of them, on account of religion, sovereignty, trade, or any other pretence whatever.

Article 4

The better to secure and perpetuate mutual friendship and intercourse among the people of the different states in this union, the free inhabitants of each of these states, paupers, vagabonds, and fugitives from justice excepted, shall be entitled to all privileges and immunities of free citizens in the several states; and the people of each State shall have free ingress and regress to and from any other State, and shall enjoy therein all the privileges of trade and commerce, subject to the same duties, impositions, and restrictions, as the inhabitants thereof respectively; provided, that such restrictions shall not extend so far as to prevent the removal of property, imported into any State, to any other State of which the owner is an inhabitant; provided also, that no imposition, duties, or restriction, shall be laid by any State on the property of the United States, or either of them.

If any person guilty of, or charged with treason, felony, or other high misdemeanor in any State, shall flee from justice and be found in any of the United States, he shall, upon demand of the governor or executive power of the State from which he fled, be delivered up and removed to the State having jurisdiction of his offence.

Full faith and credit shall be given in each of these states to the records, acts, and judicial proceedings of the courts and magistrates of every other State.

---

*This copy of the final draft of the Articles of Confederation is taken from the *Journals,* 9:907–925, November 15, 1777.

Article 5

For the more convenient management of the general interests of the United States, delegates shall be annually appointed, in such manner as the legislature of each State shall direct, to meet in Congress, on the 1st Monday in November in every year, with a power reserved to each State to recall its delegates, or any of them, at any time within the year, and to send others in their stead for the remainder of the year.

No State shall be represented in Congress by less than two, nor by more than seven members; and no person shall be capable of being a delegate for more than three years in any term of six years; nor shall any person, being a delegate, be capable of holding any office under the United States, for which he, or any other for his benefit, receives any salary, fees, or emolument of any kind.

Each State shall maintain its own delegates in a meeting of the states, and while they act as members of the committee of the states.

In determining questions in the United States, in Congress assembled, each State shall have one vote.

Freedom of speech and debate in Congress shall not be impeached or questioned in any court or place out of Congress: and the members of Congress shall be protected in their persons from arrests and imprisonments, during the time of their going to and from, and attendance on Congress, except for treason, felony, or breach of the peace.

Article 6

No State, without the consent of the United States, in Congress assembled, shall send any embassy to, or receive any embassy from, or enter into any conference, agreement, alliance, or treaty with any king, prince, or state; nor shall any person, holding any office of profit or trust under the United States, or any of them, accept of any present, emolument, office or title, of any kind whatever, from any king, prince, or foreign state; nor shall the United States, in Congress assembled, or any of them, grant any title of nobility.

No two or more states shall enter into any treaty, confederation, or alliance, whatever, between them, without the consent of the United States, in Congress assembled, specifying accurately the purposes for which the same is to be entered into, and how long it shall continue.

No state shall lay any imposts or duties which may interfere with any stipulations in treaties entered into by the United States, in Congress assembled, with any king, prince, or state, in pursuance of any treaties already proposed by Congress to the courts of France and Spain.

No vessels of war shall be kept up in time of peace by any State, except such number only as shall be deemed necessary by the United States, in Congress assembled, for the defence of such State or its trade; nor shall any body of forces be kept up by any State, in time of peace, except such number only as, in the judgment of the United States, in Congress assembled, shall be deemed requisite to garrison the forts necessary for the defence of such State; but every State shall always keep up a well regulated and disciplined militia, sufficiently armed and accoutred, and shall provide, and constantly have ready for use, in public stores, a due number of field pieces and tents, and a proper quantity of arms, ammunition and camp equipage.

No State shall engage in any war without the consent of the United States, in Congress assembled, unless such State be actually invaded by enemies, or shall have received certain advice of a resolution being formed by some nation of Indians to invade such State, and the danger is so imminent as not to admit of a delay till the United States, in Congress assembled, can be consulted; nor shall any State grant commissions to any ships or vessels of war, nor letters of marque or reprisal, except it be after a declaration of war by the United States, in Congress assembled, and then only against the kingdom or state, and the subjects thereof, against which war has been so declared, and under such regulations as shall be established by the United States, in Congress assembled, unless such State be infested by pirates, in which case vessels of war may be fitted out for that occasion, and kept so long as the danger shall continue, or until the United States, in Congress assembled, shall determine otherwise.

Article 7

When land forces are raised by any State for the common defence, all officers of or under the rank of colonel, shall be appointed by the legislature of each State respectively, by whom such forces shall be raised, or in such manner as such State shall direct; and all vacancies shall be filled up by the State which first made the appointment.

Article 8

All charges of war and all other expences, that shall be incurred for the common defence or general welfare, and allowed by the United States, in Congress assembled, shall be defrayed out of a common treasury, which shall be supplied by the several states, in proportion to the value of all land within each State, granted to or surveyed for any person, as such land and the buildings and improvements thereon shall be estimated according to such mode as the United States, in Congress assembled, shall, from time to time, direct and appoint.

The taxes for paying that proportion shall be laid and levied by the authority and direction of the legislatures of the several states, within the time agreed upon by the United States, in Congress assembled.

Article 9

The United States, in Congress assembled, shall have the sole and exclusive right and power of determining on peace and war, except in the cases mentioned in the 6th article; of sending and receiving ambassadors; entering into treaties and alliances, provided that no treaty of commerce shall be made, whereby the legislative power of the respective states shall be restrained from imposing such imposts and duties on foreigners as their own people are subjected to, or from prohibiting the exportation or importation of any species of goods or commodities whatsoever; of establishing rules for deciding, in all cases, what captures on land or water shall be legal, and in what manner prizes, taken by land or naval forces in the service of the United States, shall be divided or appropriated; of granting letters of marque and reprisal in times of peace; appointing courts for the trial of piracies and felonies committed on the high seas, and establishing courts for receiving and determining, finally, appeals in all cases of captures; provided, that no member of Congress shall be appointed a judge of any of the said courts.

The United States, in Congress assembled, shall also be the last resort on appeal in all disputes and differences now subsisting, or that hereafter may arise between two or more states concerning boundary, jurisdiction or any other cause whatever; which authority shall always be exercised in the manner following: whenever the legislative or executive authority, or lawful agent of any State, in controversy with another, shall present a petition to Congress, stating the matter in question, and praying for a hearing, notice thereof shall be given, by order of Congress, to the legislative or executive authority of the other State in controversy, and a day assigned for the appearance of the parties by their lawful agents, who shall then be directed to appoint, by joint consent, commissioners or judges to constitute a court for hearing and determining the matter in question; but, if they cannot agree, Congress shall name three persons out of each of the United States, and from the list of such persons each party shall alternately strike out one, the petitioners beginning, until the number shall be reduced to thirteen; and from that number not less than seven, nor more than nine names, as Congress shall direct, shall, in the presence of Congress, be drawn out by lot; and the persons whose names shall be so drawn, or any five of them, shall be commissioners or judges to hear and finally determine the controversy, so always as a major part of the judges who shall hear the cause shall agree in the determination; and if either party shall neglect to attend at the day appointed, without shewing reasons which Congress shall judge sufficient, or, being present, shall refuse to strike, the Congress shall proceed to nominate three persons out of each State, and the secretary of Congress shall strike in behalf of such party absent or refusing; and the judgment and sentence of the court to be appointed, in the manner before prescribed, shall be final and conclusive; and if any of the parties shall refuse to submit to the authority of such court, or to appear or defend their claim or cause, the court shall nevertheless proceed to pronounce sentence or judgment, which shall, in like manner, be final and decisive, the judgment or sentence and other proceedings begin, in either case, transmitted to Congress, and lodged among the acts of Congress for the security of the parties concerned: provided, that every commissioner, before he sits in judgment, shall take an oath, to be administered by one of the judges of the supreme or superior court of the State where the cause shall be tried, "well and truly to hear and determine the matter in question, according to the best of his judgment, without favour, affection, or hope of reward:" provided, also, that no State shall be deprived of territory for the benefit of the United States.

All controversies concerning the private right of soil, claimed under different grants of two or more states, whose jurisdictions, as they may respect such lands and the states which passed such grants, are adjusted, the said grants, or either of them, being at the same time claimed to have originated antecedent to such settlement of jurisdiction, shall, on the petition of either party to the Congress of the United States, be finally determined, as near as may be, in the same manner as is before prescribed for deciding disputes respecting territorial jurisdiction between different states.

The United States, in Congress assembled, shall also have the sole and exclusive right and power of regulating the alloy and value of coin struck by their own authority, or by that of the respective states; fixing the standard of weights and measures throughout the United States; regulating the trade and managing all affairs with the Indians not members of any of the states; provided that the legislative right of any State within its own limits be not infringed or violated; establishing and regulating post offices from one State to another throughout all the United States, and exacting such postage on the papers passing through the same as may be requisite to defray the expences of the said office; appointing all officers of the land forces in the service of the United States, excepting regimental officers; appointing all the officers of the naval forces, and commissioning all officers whatever in the service of the United States; making rules for the government and regulation of the said land and naval forces, and directing their operations.

The United States, in Congress assembled, shall have authority to appoint a committee to sit in the recess of Congress, to be denominated "a Committee of the States," and to consist of one delegate from each State, and to appoint such other committees and civil officers as may be necessary for managing the general affairs of the United States, under their direction; to appoint one of their number to preside; provided that no person be allowed to serve in the office of president more than one year in any term of three years; to ascertain the necessary sums of money to be raised for the service of the United States, and to appropriate and apply the same for defraying the public expences; to borrow money or emit bills on the credit of the United States, transmitting, every half year, to the respective states, an account of the sums of money so borrowed or emitted; to build and equip a navy; to agree upon the number of land forces, and to make requisitions from each State for its quota, in proportion to the number of white inhabitants in such State; which requisitions shall be binding; and thereupon, the legislature of each State shall appoint the regimental officers, raise the men, and cloathe, arm, and equip them in a soldier-like manner, at the expence of the United States; and the officers and men so cloathed, armed, and equipped, shall march to the place appointed and within the time agreed on by the United States, in Congress assembled; but if the United States, in Congress assembled, shall, on consideration of circumstances, judge proper that any State should not raise men, or should raise a smaller number than its quota, and that any other State should raise a greater number of men than the quota thereof, such extra number shall be raised, officered, cloathed, armed, and equipped in the same manner as the quota of such State, unless the legislature of such State shall judge that such extra number cannot be safely spared out of the same, in which case they shall raise, officer, cloathe, arm, and equip as many of such extra number as they judge can be safely spared. And the officers and men so cloathed, armed, and equipped, shall march to the place appointed and within the time agreed on by the United States, in Congress assembled.

The United States, in Congress assembled, shall never engage in a war, nor grant letters of marque and reprisal in time of peace, nor enter into any treaties or alliances, nor coin money, nor regulate the value thereof, nor ascertain the sums and expences necessary for the defence and welfare of the United States, or any of them: nor emit bills, nor borrow money on the credit of the United States, nor appropriate money, nor agree upon the number of vessels of war to be built or purchased, or the number of land or sea forces to be raised, nor appoint a commander in chief of the army or navy, unless nine states assent to the same; nor shall a question on any other point, except for adjourning from day to day, be determined, unless by the votes of a majority of the United States, in Congress assembled.

The Congress of the United States shall have power to adjourn to any time within the year, and to any place within the United States, so that no period of adjournment be for a longer duration than the space of six months, and shall publish the journal of their proceedings monthly, except such parts thereof, relating to treaties, alliances or military operations, as, in their judgment, require secrecy; and the yeas and nays of the delegates of each State on any question shall be entered on the journal, when it is desired by any delegate; and the delegates of a State, or any of them, at his, or their request, shall be furnished with a transcript of the said journal, except such parts as are above excepted, to lay before the legislatures of the several states.

Article 10

The committee of the states, or any nine of them, shall be authorized to execute, in the recess of Congress, such of the powers of Congress as the United States, in Congress assembled, by the consent of nine states, shall, from time to time, think expedient to vest them with; provided, that no power be delegated to the said committee, for the exercise of which, by the articles of confederation, the voice of nine states, in the Congress of the United States assembled, is requisite.

Article 11

Canada acceding to this confederation, and joining in the measures of the United States, shall be admitted into and entitled to all the advantages of this union; but no other colony shall be admitted into the same, unless such admission be agreed to by nine states.

Article 12

All bills of credit emitted, monies borrowed and debts contracted by, or under the authority of Congress before the assembling of the United States, in pursuance of the present confederation, shall be deemed and considered as a charge against the United States, for payment and satisfaction whereof the said United States and the public faith are hereby solemnly pledged.

Article 13

Every State shall abide by the determinations of the United States, in Congress assembled, on all questions which, by this confederation, are submitted to them. And the articles of this confederation shall be inviolably observed by every State, and the union shall be perpetual; nor shall any alteration at any time hereafter be made in any of them, unless such alteration be agreed to in a Congress of the United States, and be afterwards confirmed by the legislatures of every State.

These articles shall be proposed to the legislatures of all the United States, to be considered, and if approved of by them, they are advised to authorize their delegates to ratify the same in the Congress of the United States; which being done, the same shall become conclusive.

THE CONSTITUTION OF THE UNITED STATES*

Agreed to by Philadelphia Convention, September 17, 1787.
Implemented March 4, 1789.

Preamble

We the people of the United States, in order to form a more perfect union, establish justice, insure domestic tranquility, provide for the common defense, promote the general welfare, and secure the blessings of liberty to ourselves and our posterity, do ordain and establish this Constitution for the United States of America.

Article I

Section 1   All legislative powers herein granted shall be vested in a Congress of the United States, which shall consist of a Senate and a House of Representatives.

Section 2   The House of Representatives shall be composed of members chosen every second year by the people of the several States, and the electors in each State shall have the qualifications requisite for electors of the most numerous branch of the State Legislature.

No person shall be a Representative who shall not have attained to the age of twenty-five years, and been seven years a citizen of the United States, and who shall not, when elected, be an inhabitant of that State in which he shall be chosen.

Representatives and direct taxes shall be apportioned among the several States which may be included within this Union, according to their respective numbers, *which shall be determined by adding to the whole number of free persons, including those bound to service for a term of years and excluding Indians not taxed, three-fifths of all other persons.* The actual enumeration shall be made within three years after the first meeting of the Congress of the United States, and within every subsequent term of ten years, in such manner as they shall by law direct. The number of Representatives shall not exceed one for every thirty thousand, but each State shall have at least one Representative; *and until such enumeration shall be made, the State of New Hampshire shall be entitled to choose three, Massachusetts eight, Rhode Island and Providence Plantations one, Connecticut five, New York six, New Jersey four, Pennsylvania eight, Delaware one, Maryland six, Virginia ten, North Carolina five, South Carolina five, and Georgia three.*

---

*Passages no longer in effect are in italic type.

When vacancies happen in the representation from any State, the Executive authority thereof shall issue writs of election to fill such vacancies.

The House of Representatives shall choose their Speaker and other officers; and shall have the sole power of impeachment.

Section 3   The Senate of the United States shall be composed of two Senators from each State, *chosen by the legislature thereof,* for six years; and each Senator shall have one vote.

Immediately after they shall be assembled in consequence of the first election, they shall be divided as equally as may be into three classes. The seats of the Senators of the first class shall be vacated at the expiration of the second year, of the second class at the expiration of the fourth year, and of the third class at the expiration of the sixth year, so that one-third may be chosen every second year; *and if vacancies happen by resignation or otherwise, during the recess of the legislature of any State, the Executive thereof may make temporary appointments until the next meeting of the legislature, which shall then fill such vacancies.*

No person shall be a Senator who shall not have attained to the age of thirty years, and been nine years a citizen of the United States, and who shall not, when elected, be an inhabitant of that State for which he shall be chosen.

The Vice-President of the United States shall be President of the Senate, but shall have no vote, unless they be equally divided.

The Senate shall choose their other officers, and also a President *pro tempore*, in the absence of the Vice-President, or when he shall exercise the office of President of the United States.

The Senate shall have the sole power to try all impeachments. When sitting for that purpose, they shall be on oath or affirmation. When the President of the United States is tried, the Chief Justice shall preside: and no person shall be convicted without the concurrence of two-thirds of the members present.

Judgment in cases of impeachment shall not extend further than to removal from the office, and disqualification to hold and enjoy any office of honor, trust or profit under the United States: but the party convicted shall nevertheless be liable and subject to indictment, trial, judgment and punishment, according to law.

Section 4   The times, places and manner of holding elections for Senators and Representatives shall be prescribed in each State by the legislature thereof; but the Congress may at any time by law make or alter such regulations, except as to the places of choosing Senators.

The Congress shall assemble at least once in every year, and such meeting *shall be on the first Monday in December, unless they shall by law appoint a different day.*

Section 5   Each house shall be the judge of the elections, returns and qualifications of its own members, and a majority of each shall constitute a quorum to do business; but a smaller number may adjourn from day to day, and may be authorized to compel the attendance of absent members, in such manner, and under such penalties, as each house may provide.

Each house may determine the rules of its proceedings, punish its members for disorderly behavior, and with the concurrence of two-thirds, expel a member.

Each house shall keep a journal of its proceedings, and from time to time publish the same, excepting such parts as may in their judgment require secrecy; and the yeas and nays of the members of either house on any question shall, at the desire of one-fifth of those present, be entered on the journal.

Neither house, during the session of Congress, shall, without the consent of the other, adjourn for more than three days, nor to any other place than that in which the two houses shall be sitting.

Section 6   The Senators and Representatives shall receive a compensation for their services, to be ascertained by law and paid out of the treasury of the United States. They shall in all cases except treason, felony and breach of the peace, be privileged from arrest during their attendance at the session of their respective houses, and in going to and returning from the same; and for any speech or debate in either house, they shall not be questioned in any other place.

No Senator or Representative shall, during the time for which he was elected, be appointed to any civil office under the authority of the United States, which shall have been created, or the emoluments whereof shall have been increased, during such time; and no person holding any office under the United States shall be a member of either house during his continuance in office.

Section 7   All bills for raising revenue shall originate in the House of Representatives; but the Senate may propose or concur with amendments as on other bills.

Every bill which shall have passed the House of Representatives and the Senate, shall, before it become a law, be presented to the President of the United States; if he approve he shall sign it, but if not he shall return it with objections to that house in which it shall have originated, who shall enter the objections at large on their journal, and proceed to reconsider it. If after such reconsideration two-thirds of that house shall agree to pass the bill, it shall be sent, together with the objections, to the other house, by which it shall likewise be reconsidered, and, if approved by two-thirds of that house, it shall become a law. But in all such cases the votes of both houses shall be determined by yeas and nays, and the names of the persons voting for and against the bill shall be entered on the journal of each house respectively. If any bill shall not be returned by the President within ten days (Sundays excepted) after it shall have been presented to him, the same shall be a law, in like manner as if he had signed it, unless the Congress by their adjournment prevent its return, in which case it shall not be a law.

Every order, resolution, or vote to which the concurrence of the Senate and House of Representatives may be necessary (except on a question of adjournment) shall be presented to the President of the United States; and before the same shall take effect, shall be approved by him, or being disapproved by him, shall be repassed by two-thirds of the Senate and House of Representatives, according to the rules and limitations prescribed in the case of a bill.

Section 8   The Congress shall have power

To lay and collect taxes, duties, imposts, and excises, to pay the debts and provide for the common defense and general welfare of the United States; but all duties, imposts and excises shall be uniform throughout the United States;

To borrow money on the credit of the United States;

To regulate commerce with foreign nations, and among the several States, and with the Indian tribes;

To establish an uniform rule of naturalization, and uniform laws on the subject of bankruptcies throughout the United States;

To coin money, regulate the value thereof, and of foreign coin, and fix the standard of weights and measures;

To provide for the punishment of counterfeiting the securities and current coin of the United States;

To establish post offices and post roads;

To promote the progress of science and useful arts by securing for limited times to authors and inventors the exclusive right to their respective writings and discoveries;

To constitute tribunals inferior to the Supreme Court;

To define and punish piracies and felonies committed on the high seas and offences against the law of nations;

To declare war, grant letters of marque and reprisal, and make rules concerning captures on land and water;

To raise and support armies, but no appropriation of money to that use shall be for a longer term than two years;

To provide and maintain a navy;

To make rules for the government and regulation of the land and naval forces;

To provide for calling forth the militia to execute the laws of the Union, suppress insurrections and repel invasions;

To provide for organizing, arming, and disciplining the militia, and for governing such part of them as may be employed in the service of the United States, reserving to the States respectively the appointment of the officers, and the authority of training the militia according to the discipline prescribed by Congress;

To exercise exclusive legislation in all cases whatsoever, over such district (not exceeding ten miles square) as may, by cession of particular States, and the acceptance of Congress, become the seat of the government of the United States, and to exercise like authority over all places purchased by the consent of the legislature of the State, in which the same shall be, for erection of forts, magazines, arsenals, dock-yards, and other needful buildings;—and

To make all laws which shall be necessary and proper for carrying into execution the foregoing powers, and all other powers vested by this Constitution in the government of the United States, or in any department or officer thereof.

Section 9   *The migration or importation of such persons as any of the States now existing shall think proper to admit shall not be prohibited by the Congress prior to the year one thousand eight hundred and eight; but a tax or duty may be imposed on such importation, not exceeding ten dollars for each person.*

The privilege of the writ of habeas corpus shall not be suspended, unless when in cases of rebellion or invasion the public safety may require it.

No bill of attainder or ex post facto law shall be passed.

No capitation, or other direct, tax shall be laid, unless in proportion to the census or enumeration herein before directed to be taken.

No tax or duty shall be laid on articles exported from any State.

No preference shall be given by any regulation of commerce or revenue to the ports of one State over those of another; nor shall vessels bound to, or from, one State be obliged to enter, clear, or pay duties in another.

No money shall be drawn from the treasury, but in consequence of appropriations made by law; and a regular statement and account of the receipts and expenditures of all public money shall be published from time to time.

No title of nobility shall be granted by the United States: and no person holding any office of profit or trust under them, shall, without the consent of the Congress, accept of any present, emolument, office, or title, of any kind whatever, from any king, prince, or foreign state.

Section 10   No State shall enter into any treaty, alliance, or confederation; grant letters of marque and reprisal; coin money; emit bills of credit; make anything but gold and silver coin a tender in payment of debts; pass any bill of attainder, ex post facto law, or law impairing the obligation of contracts, or grant any title of nobility.

No State shall, without the consent of Congress, lay any imposts or duties on imports or exports, except what may be absolutely necessary for executing its inspection laws: and the net produce of all duties and imposts, laid by any State on imports or exports, shall be for the use of the treasury of the United States; and all such laws shall be subject to the revision and control of the Congress.

No State shall, without the consent of Congress, lay any duty of tonnage, keep troops, or ships of war in time of peace, enter into any agreement or compact with another State, or with a foreign power, or engage in war, unless actually invaded, or in such imminent danger as will not admit of delay.

Article II

Section 1   The executive power shall be vested in a President of the United States of America. He shall hold his office during the term of four years, and, together with the Vice-President, chosen for the same term, be elected as follows:

Each State shall appoint, in such manner as the legislature thereof may direct, a number of electors, equal to the whole number of Senators and Representatives to which the State may be entitled in the Congress; but no Senator or Representative, or person holding an office of trust or profit under the United States, shall be appointed an elector.

The electors shall meet in their respective States, and vote by ballot for two persons, of whom one at least shall not be an inhabitant of the same State with themselves. And they shall make a list of all the persons voted for, and of the number of votes for each; which list they shall sign and certify, and transmit sealed to the seat of government of the United States, directed to the President of the Senate. The President of the Senate shall, in the presence of the Senate and House of Representatives, open all the certificates, and the votes shall then be counted. The person having the greatest number of votes shall be the President, if such number be a majority of the whole number of electors appointed; and if there be more than one who have such majority, and have an equal number of votes, then the House of Representatives shall immediately choose by ballot one of them for President; and if no person have a majority, then from the five highest on the list said house shall in like manner choose the President. But in choosing the President the votes shall be taken by States, the representation from each State having one vote; a quorum for this purpose shall consist of a member or members from two-thirds of the States, and a majority of all the States shall be necessary to a choice. In every case, after the choice of the President, the person having the greatest number of votes of the electors shall be the Vice-President. But if there should remain two or more who have equal votes, the Senate shall choose from them by ballot the Vice-President.

The Congress may determine the time of choosing the electors, and the day on which they shall give their votes; which day shall be the same throughout the United States.

No person except a natural-born citizen, *or a citizen of the United States at the time of the adoption of this Constitution,* shall be eligible to the office of President; neither shall any person be eligible to that office who shall not have attained to the age of thirty-five years, and been fourteen years a resident within the United States.

In cases of the removal of the President from office or of his death, resignation, or inability to discharge the powers and duties of the said office, the same shall devolve on the Vice-President, and the Congress may by law provide for the case of removal, death, resignation, or inability, both of the President and Vice-President, declaring what officer shall then act as President, and such officer shall act accordingly, until the disability be removed, or a President shall be elected.

The President shall, at stated times, receive for his services a compensation, which shall neither be increased nor diminished during the period for which he shall have been elected, and he shall not receive within that period any other emolument from the United States, or any of them.

Before he enter on the execution of his office, he shall take the following oath or affirmation:—"I do solemnly swear (or affirm) that I will faithfully execute the office of the President of the United States, and will to the best of my ability preserve, protect and defend the Constitution of the United States."

Section 2   The President shall be commander in chief of the army and navy of the United States, and of the militia of the several States, when called into the actual service of the United States; he may require the opinion, in writing, of the principal officer in each of the executive departments, upon any subject relating to the duties of their respective offices, and he shall have power to grant reprieves and pardons for offenses against the United States, except in cases of impeachment.

He shall have power, by and with the advice and consent of the Senate, to make treaties, provided two-thirds of the Senators present concur; and he shall nominate, and by and with the advice and consent of the Senate, shall appoint ambassadors, other public ministers and consuls, judges of the Supreme Court, and all other officers of the United States, whose appointments are not herein otherwise provided for, and which shall be established by law: but Congress may by law vest the appointment of such inferior officers, as they think proper, in the President alone, in the courts of law, or in the heads of departments.

The President shall have power to fill up all vacancies that may happen during the recess of the Senate, by granting commissions which shall expire at the end of their next session.

Section 3   He shall from time to time give to the Congress information of the state of the Union, and recommend to their consideration such measures as he shall judge necessary and expedient; he may, on extraordinary occasions, convene both houses, or either of them, and in case of disagreement between them, with respect to the time of adjournment, he may adjourn them to such time as he shall think proper; he shall receive ambassadors and other public ministers; he shall take care that the laws be faithfully executed, and shall commission all the officers of the United States.

Section 4   The President, Vice-President and all civil officers of the United States shall be removed from office on impeachment for, and on conviction of, treason, bribery, or other high crimes and misdemeanors.

Article III

Section 1   The judicial power of the United States shall be vested in one Supreme Court, and in such inferior courts as the Congress may from time to time ordain and establish. The judges, both of the Supreme and inferior courts, shall hold their offices during good behavior, and shall, at stated times, receive for their services a compensation which shall not be diminished during their continuance in office.

Section 2   The judicial power shall extend to all cases, in law and equity, arising under this Constitution, the laws of the United States, and treaties made, or which shall be made, under their authority;—to all cases affecting ambassadors, other public ministers and consuls;—to all cases of admiralty and maritime jurisdiction;—to controversies to which the United States shall be a party;—to controversies between two or more States;—*between a State and citizens of another State;*—between citizens of different States;—between citizens of the same State claiming lands under grants of different States, and between a State, or the citizens thereof, and foreign states, citizens or subjects.

In all cases affecting ambassadors, other public ministers and consuls, and those in which a State shall be party, the Supreme Court shall have original jurisdiction. In all the other cases before mentioned, the Supreme Court shall have appellate jurisdiction, both as to law and fact, with such exceptions, and under such regulations, as the Congress shall make.

The trial of all crimes, except in cases of impeachment, shall be by jury; and such trial shall be held in the State where said crimes shall have been committed; but when not committed within any State, the trial shall be at such place or places as the Congress may by Law have directed.

Section 3 Treason against the United States shall consist only in levying war against them, or in adhering to their enemies, giving them aid and comfort. No person shall be convicted of treason unless on the testimony of two witnesses to the same overt act, or on confession in open court.

The Congress shall have power to declare the punishment of treason, but no attainder of treason shall work corruption of blood, or forfeiture except during the life of the person attainted.

Article IV

Section 1 Full faith and credit shall be given in each State to the public acts, records, and judicial proceedings of every other State. And the Congress may by general laws prescribe the manner in which such acts, records, and proceedings shall be proved, and the effect thereof.

Section 2 The citizens of each State shall be entitled to all privileges and immunities of citizens in the several States.

A person charged in any State with treason, felony, or other crime, who shall flee from justice, and be found in another State, shall on demand of the executive authority of the State from which he fled, be delivered up, to be removed to the State having jurisdiction of the crime.

No Person held to service or labor in one State, under the laws thereof, escaping into another, shall, in consequence of any law or regulation therein, be discharged from such service or labor, but shall be delivered up on claim of the party to whom such service or labor may be due.

Section 3 New States may be admitted by the Congress into this Union; but no new State shall be formed or erected within the jurisdiction of any other State; nor any State be formed by the junction of two or more States, or parts of States, without the consent of the legislatures of the States concerned as well as of the Congress.

The Congress shall have power to dispose of and make all needful rules and regulations respecting the territory or other property belonging to the United States; and nothing in this Constitution shall be so construed as to prejudice any claims of the United States, or of any particular State.

Section 4 The United States shall guarantee to every State in this Union a republican form of government, and shall protect each of them against invasion; and on application of the legislature, or of the executive (when the legislature cannot be convened), against domestic violence.

Article V

The Congress, whenever two-thirds of both houses shall deem it necessary, shall propose amendments to this Constitution, or, on the application of the legislatures of two-thirds of the several States, shall call a convention for proposing amendments, which, in either case, shall be valid to all intents and purposes, as part of this Constitution, when ratified by the legislatures of three-fourths of the several States, or by conventions in three-fourths thereof, as the one or the other mode of ratification may be proposed by the Congress; provided *that no amendments which may be made prior to the year one thousand eight hundred and eight shall in any manner affect the first and fourth clauses in the ninth section of the first article*; and that no State, without its consent, shall be deprived of its equal suffrage in the Senate.

Article VI

All debts contracted and engagements entered into, before the adoption of this Constitution, shall be as valid against the United States under this Constitution, as under the Confederation.

This Constitution, and the laws of the United States which shall be made in pursuance thereof; and all treaties made, or which shall be made, under the authority of the United States, shall be the supreme law of the land; and the judges in every State shall be bound thereby, anything in the Constitution or laws of any State to the contrary notwithstanding.

The Senators and Representatives before mentioned, and the members of the several State legislatures, and all executive and judicial officers, both of the United States and of the several States, shall be bound by oath or affirmation to support this Constitution; but no religious test shall ever be required as a qualification to any office or public trust under the United States.

Article VII

The ratification of the conventions of nine States shall be sufficient for the establishment of this Constitution between the States so ratifying the same.

Done in convention by the unanimous consent of the States present, the seventeenth day of September in the year of our Lord one thousand seven hundred and eighty-seven and of the Independence of the United States of America the twelfth. In witness whereof we have hereunto subscribed our names.

George Washington
PRESIDENT AND DEPUTY FROM VIRGINIA

New Hampshire
John Langdon
Nicholas Gilman

Massachusetts
Nathaniel Gorham
Rufus King

Connecticut
William Samuel
   Johnson
Roger Sherman

New York
Alexander
   Hamilton

New Jersey
William Livingston
David Brearley
William Paterson
Jonathan Dayton

Pennsylvania
Benjamin Franklin
Thomas Mifflin
Robert Morris
George Clymer
Thomas
   FitzSimons
Jared Ingersoll
James Wilson
Gouverneur Morris

Delaware
George Read
Gunning
   Bedford, Jr.
John Dickinson
Richard Bassett
Jacob Broom

Maryland
James McHenry
Daniel of St.
   Thomas Jenifer
Daniel Carroll

Virginia
John Blair
James Madison, Jr.

North Carolina
William Blount
Richard Dobbs
   Spaight
Hugh Williamson

South Carolina
John Rutledge
Charles
   Cotesworth
   Pinckney
Charles Pinckney
Pierce Butler

Georgia
William Few
Abraham Baldwin

AMENDMENTS TO THE CONSTITUTION

(including the six unratified amendments)

Although the first ten amendments to the Constitution are commonly known as the Bill of Rights, only Amendments 1–8 actually provide guarantees of individual rights. Amendments 9 and 10 deal with the structure of power within the constitutional system. The Bill of Rights was promised to appease Antifederalists who refused to ratify the Constitution without guarantees of individual liberties and limitations to federal power. After studying more than two hundred amendments recommended by the ratifying conventions of the states, Federalist James Madison presented a list of seventeen to Congress, which used Madison's list as the foundation for the twelve amendments that were sent to the states for ratification. Ten of the twelve were adopted in 1791. The first on the list of twelve, known as the Reapportionment Amendment, was never adopted (see page A-18). The second proposed amendment was adopted in 1992 as Amendment 27 (see page A-26).

Amendment I

Congress shall make no law respecting an establishment of religion, or prohibiting the free exercise thereof; or abridging the freedom of speech, or of the press; or the right of the people peaceably to assemble, and to petition the government for a redress of grievances.

Amendment II

A well-regulated militia being necessary to the security of a free State, the right of the people to keep and bear arms shall not be infringed.

Amendment III

No soldier shall, in time of peace, be quartered in any house without the consent of the owner, nor in time of war, but in a manner to be prescribed by law.

Amendment IV

The right of the people to be secure in their persons, houses, papers, and effects, against unreasonable searches and seizures, shall not be violated, and no warrants shall issue but upon probable cause, supported by oath or affirmation, and particularly describing the place to be searched, and the persons or things to be seized.

Amendment V

No person shall be held to answer for a capital, or otherwise infamous crime, unless on a presentment or indictment of a grand jury, except in cases arising in the land or naval forces, or in the militia, when in actual service in time of war or public danger; nor shall any person be subject for the same offence to be twice put in jeopardy of life or limb; nor shall be compelled in any criminal case to be a witness against himself, nor be deprived of life, liberty, or property, without due process of law; nor shall private property be taken for public use without just compensation.

Amendment VI

In all criminal prosecutions, the accused shall enjoy the right to a speedy and public trial, by an impartial jury of the State and district wherein the crime shall have been committed, which district shall have been previously ascertained by law, and to be informed of the nature and cause of the accusation; to be confronted with the witnesses against him; to have compulsory process for obtaining witnesses in his favor, and to have the assistance of counsel for his defence.

Amendment VII

In suits at common law, where the value in controversy shall exceed twenty dollars, the right of trial by jury shall be preserved, and no fact tried by a jury shall be otherwise reexamined in any court of the United States, than according to the rules of the common law.

Amendment VIII

Excessive bail shall not be required, nor excessive fines imposed, nor cruel and unusual punishments inflicted.

Amendment IX

The enumeration in the Constitution, of certain rights, shall not be construed to deny or disparage others retained by the people.

Amendment X

The powers not delegated to the United States by the Constitution, nor prohibited by it to the States, are reserved to the States respectively, or to the people.

Unratified Amendment

Reapportionment Amendment (proposed by Congress September 25, 1789, along with the Bill of Rights)

After the first enumeration required by the first article of the Constitution, there shall be one Representative for every thirty thousand, until the number shall amount to one hundred, after which the proportion shall be so regulated by Congress, that there shall be not less than one hundred Representatives, nor less than one Representative for every forty thousand persons, until the number of Representatives shall amount to two hundred; after which the proportion shall be so regulated by Congress, that there shall not be less than two hundred Representatives, nor more than one Representative for every fifty thousand persons.

Amendment XI

[Adopted 1798]

The judicial power of the United States shall not be construed to extend to any suit in law or equity, commenced or prosecuted against one of the United States by citizens of another State, or by citizens or subjects of any foreign state.

Amendment XII

[Adopted 1804]

The electors shall meet in their respective States, and vote by ballot for President and Vice-President, one of whom, at least, shall not be an inhabitant of the same State with themselves; they shall name in their ballots the person voted for as President, and in distinct ballots the person voted for as Vice-President, and they shall make distinct lists of all persons voted for as President, and of all persons voted for as Vice-President, and of the number of votes for each, which lists they shall sign and certify, and transmit sealed to the seat of government of the United States, directed to the President of the Senate;—the President of the Senate shall, in the presence of the Senate and House of Representatives, open all the certificates and the votes shall then be counted;—the person having the greatest number of votes for President shall be the President, if such number be a majority of the whole number of electors appointed; and if no person have such majority, then from the persons having the highest numbers not exceeding three on the list of those voted for as President, the House of Representatives shall choose immediately, by ballot, the President. But in choosing the President, the votes shall be taken by States, the representation from each State having one vote; a quorum for this purpose shall consist of a member or members from two-thirds of the States, and a majority of all the States shall be necessary to a choice. And if the House of Representatives shall not choose a President whenever the right of choice shall devolve upon them, before *the fourth day of March* next following, then the Vice-President shall act as President, as in the case of the death or other constitutional disability of the President.

The person having the greatest number of votes as Vice-President shall be the Vice-President, if such number be a majority of the whole number of electors appointed; and if no person have a majority, then from the two highest numbers on the list the Senate shall choose the Vice-President; a quorum for the purpose shall consist of two-thirds of the whole number of Senators, and a majority of the whole number shall be necessary to a choice. But no person constitutionally ineligible to the office of President shall be eligible to that of Vice-President of the United States.

Unratified Amendment

Titles of Nobility Amendment (proposed by Congress May 1, 1810)

If any citizen of the United States shall accept, claim, receive or retain any title of nobility or honor or shall, without the consent of Congress, accept and retain any present, pension, office or emolument of any kind whatever, from any emperor, king, prince or foreign power, such person shall cease to be a citizen of the United States, and shall be incapable of holding any office of trust or profit under them or either of them.

The Civil War and Reconstruction Amendments (Thirteenth, Fourteenth, and Fifteenth Amendments)

In the four months between the election of Abraham Lincoln and his inauguration, more than 200 proposed constitutional amendments were presented to Congress as part of a desperate attempt to hold the rapidly dissolving Union together. Most of these were efforts to appease the southern states by protecting the right to own slaves or by disfranchising African Americans through constitutional amendment. None were able to win the votes required from Congress to send them to the states. The relatively innocuous Corwin Amendment seemed to be the only hope for preserving the Union by amending the Constitution.

The northern victors in the Civil War tried to restructure the Constitution just as the war had restructured the nation. Yet they were often divided in their goals. Some wanted to end slavery; others hoped for social and economic equality regardless of race; others hoped that extending the power of the ballot box to former slaves would help create a new political order. The debates over the Thirteenth, Fourteenth, and Fifteenth Amendments were bitter. Few of those who fought for these changes were satisfied with the amendments themselves; fewer still were satisfied with their interpretation. Although the amendments put an end to the legal status of slavery, it took nearly a hundred years after the amendments' passage before most of the descendants of former slaves could begin to experience the economic, social, and political equality the amendments had been intended to provide.

Unratified Amendment

Corwin Amendment (proposed by Congress March 2, 1861)

No amendment shall be made to the Constitution which will authorize or give to Congress the power to abolish or interfere, within any State, with the domestic institutions thereof, including that of persons held to labor or service by the laws of said State.

Amendment XIII

[Adopted 1865]

Section 1   Neither slavery nor involuntary servitude, except as a punishment for crime whereof the party shall have been duly convicted, shall exist within the United States, or any place subject to their jurisdiction.

Section 2   Congress shall have power to enforce this article by appropriate legislation.

Amendment XIV

[Adopted 1868]

Section 1   All persons born or naturalized in the United States, and subject to the jurisdiction thereof, are citizens of the United States and of the State wherein they reside. No State shall make or enforce any law which shall abridge the privileges or immunities of citizens of the United States; nor shall any State deprive any person of life, liberty, or property, without due process of law; nor deny to any person within its jurisdiction the equal protection of the laws.

Section 2   Representatives shall be appointed among the several States according to their respective numbers, counting the whole number of persons in each State, excluding Indians not taxed. But when the right to vote at any election for the choice of Electors for President and Vice-President of the United States, Representatives in Congress, the executive and judicial officers of a State, or the members of the legislature thereof, is denied to any of the male inhabitants of such State, being twenty-one years of age and citizens of the United States, or in any way abridged, except for participation in rebellion, or other crime, the basis of representation therein shall be reduced in the proportion which the number of such male citizens shall bear to the whole number of male citizens twenty-one years of age in such State.

Section 3   No person shall be a Senator or Representative in Congress, or Elector of President and Vice-President, or hold any office, civil or military, under the United States, or under any State, who, having previously taken an oath, as a member of Congress, or as an officer of the United States, or as a member of any State legislature, or as an executive or judicial officer of any State, to support the Constitution of the United States, shall have engaged in insurrection or rebellion against the same, or given aid or comfort to the enemies thereof. Congress may, by a vote of two-thirds of each house, remove such disability.

Section 4   The validity of the public debt of the United States, authorized by law, including debts incurred for payment of pensions and bounties for services in suppressing insurrection or rebellion, shall not be questioned. But neither the United States nor any State shall assume or pay any debt or obligation incurred in aid of insurrection or rebellion against the United States, or any claim for the loss or emancipation of any slave; but all such debts, obligations, and claims shall be held illegal and void.

Section 5   The Congress shall have power to enforce, by appropriate legislation, the provisions of this article.

Amendment XV

[Adopted 1870]

Section 1   The right of citizens of the United States to vote shall not be denied or abridged by the United States or by any State on account of race, color, or previous condition of servitude.

Section 2   The Congress shall have power to enforce this article by appropriate legislation.

The Progressive Amendments (Sixteenth–Nineteenth Amendments)

No amendments were added to the Constitution between the Civil War and the Progressive Era. America was changing, however, in fundamental ways. The rapid industrialization of the United States after the Civil War led to many social and economic problems. Hundreds of amendments were proposed, but none received enough support in Congress to be sent to the states. Some scholars believe that regional differences and rivalries were so strong during this period that it was almost impossible to gain a consensus on a constitutional amendment. During the Progressive Era, however, the Constitution was amended four times in seven years.

Amendment XVI

[Adopted 1913]

The Congress shall have power to lay and collect taxes on incomes, from whatever source derived, without apportionment among the several States, and without regard to any census or enumeration.

Amendment XVII

[Adopted 1913]

Section 1   The Senate of the United States shall be composed of two Senators from each State, elected by the people thereof, for six years; and each Senator shall have one vote. The electors in each State shall have the qualifications requisite for electors of [voters for] the most numerous branch of the State legislatures.

Section 2   When vacancies happen in the representation of any State in the Senate, the executive authority of such State shall issue writs of election to fill such vacancies: Provided, that the Legislature of any State may empower the executive thereof to make temporary appointments until the people fill the vacancies by election as the Legislature may direct.

Section 3   This amendment shall not be so construed as to affect the election or term of any Senator chosen before it becomes valid as part of the Constitution.

Amendment XVIII

[Adopted 1919; repealed 1933 by Amendment XXI]

Section 1   After one year from the ratification of this article the manufacture, sale, or transportation of intoxicating liquors within, the importation thereof into, or the exportation thereof from the United States and all territory subject to the jurisdiction thereof, for beverage purposes, is hereby prohibited.

Section 2   The Congress and the several States shall have concurrent power to enforce this article by appropriate legislation.

Section 3   This article shall be inoperative unless it shall have been ratified as an amendment to the Constitution by the legislatures of the several States, as provided by the Constitution, within seven years from the date of the submission thereof to the States by the Congress.

Amendment XIX

[Adopted 1920]

Section 1   The right of citizens of the United States to vote shall not be denied or abridged by the United States or by any State on account of sex.

Section 2   Congress shall have the power to enforce this article by appropriate legislation.

Unratified Amendment

Child Labor Amendment (proposed by Congress June 2, 1924)

Section 1   The Congress shall have power to limit, regulate, and prohibit the labor of persons under eighteen years of age.

Section 2   The power of the several States is unimpaired by this article except that the operation of State laws shall be suspended to the extent necessary to give effect to legislation enacted by Congress.

Amendment XX

[Adopted 1933]

Section 1   The terms of the President and Vice-President shall end at noon on the 20th day of January, and the terms of Senators and Representatives at noon on the 3rd day of January, of the years in which such terms would have ended if this article had not been ratified; and the terms of their successors shall then begin.

Section 2   The Congress shall assemble at least once in every year, and such meeting shall begin at noon on the 3rd day of January, unless they shall by law appoint a different day.

Section 3   If, at the time fixed for the beginning of the term of the President, the President-elect shall have died, the Vice-President-elect shall become President. If a President shall not have been chosen before the time fixed for the beginning of his term, or if the President-elect shall have failed to qualify, then the Vice-President-elect shall act as President until a President shall have qualified; and the Congress may by law provide for the case wherein neither a President-elect nor a Vice-President-elect shall have qualified, declaring who shall then act as President, or the manner in which one who is to act shall be selected, and such person shall act accordingly until a President or Vice-President shall have qualified.

Section 4   The Congress may by law provide for the case of the death of any of the persons from whom the House of Representatives may choose a President whenever the right of choice shall have devolved upon them, and for the case of the death of any of the persons from whom the Senate may choose a Vice-President whenever the right of choice shall have devolved upon them.

Section 5   Sections 1 and 2 shall take effect on the 15th day of October following the ratification of this article.

Section 6   This article shall be inoperative unless it shall have been ratified as an amendment to the Constitution by the Legislatures of three-fourths of the several States within seven years from the date of its submission.

Amendment XXI

[Adopted 1933]

Section 1   The eighteenth article of amendment to the Constitution of the United States is hereby repealed.

Section 2   The transportation or importation into any State, Territory, or Possession of the United States for delivery or use therein of intoxicating liquors, in violation of the laws thereof, is hereby prohibited.

Section 3   This article shall be inoperative unless it shall have been ratified as an amendment to the Constitution by conventions in the several States, as provided in the Constitution, within seven years from the date of the submission thereof to the States by the Congress.

Amendment XXII

[Adopted 1951]

Section 1   No person shall be elected to the office of the President more than twice, and no person who has held the office of President, or acted as President, for more than two years of a term to which some other person was elected President shall be elected to the office of President more than once. But this article shall not apply to any person holding the office of President when this Article was proposed by the Congress, and shall not prevent any person who may be holding the office of President, or acting as President, during the term within which this Article becomes operative from holding the office of President or acting as President during the remainder of such term.

Section 2   This article shall be inoperative unless it shall have been ratified as an amendment to the Constitution by the legislatures of three-fourths of the several States within seven years from the date of its submission to the States by the Congress.

Amendment XXIII

[Adopted 1961]

Section 1   The District constituting the seat of Government of the United States shall appoint in such manner as the Congress may direct: A number of electors of President and Vice-President equal to the whole number of Senators and Representatives in Congress to which the District would be entitled if it were a State, but in no event more than the least populous State; they shall be in addition to those appointed by the States, but they shall be considered for the purposes of the election of President and Vice-President, to be electors appointed by a State; and they shall meet in the District and perform such duties as provided by the twelfth article of amendment.

Section 2   The Congress shall have the power to enforce this article by appropriate legislation.

Amendment XXIV

[Adopted 1964]

Section 1   The right of citizens of the United States to vote in any primary or other election for President or Vice-President, for electors for President or Vice-President, or for Senator or Representative in Congress, shall not be denied or abridged by the United States or any State by reason of failure to pay any poll tax or other tax.

Section 2   The Congress shall have the power to enforce this article by appropriate legislation.

Amendment XXV

[Adopted 1967]

Section 1   In case of the removal of the President from office or of his death or resignation, the Vice-President shall become President.

Section 2   Whenever there is a vacancy in the office of the Vice-President, the President shall nominate a Vice-President who shall take office upon confirmation by a majority vote of both Houses of Congress.

Section 3   Whenever the President transmits to the President pro tempore of the Senate and the Speaker of the House of Representatives his written declaration that he is unable to discharge the powers and duties of his office, and until he transmits to them a written declaration to the contrary, such powers and duties shall be discharged by the Vice-President as Acting President.

Section 4   Whenever the Vice-President and a majority of either the principal officers of the executive departments or of such other body as Congress may by law provide, transmit to the President pro tempore of the Senate and the Speaker of the House of Representatives their written declaration that the President is unable to discharge the powers and duties of his office, the Vice-President shall immediately assume the powers and duties of the office as Acting President.

Thereafter, when the President transmits to the President pro tempore of the Senate and the Speaker of the House of Representatives his written declaration that no inability exists, he shall resume the powers and duties of his office unless the Vice-President and a majority of either the principal officers of the executive department[s] or of such other body as Congress may by law provide, transmit within four days to the President pro tempore of the Senate and the Speaker of the House of Representatives their written declaration that the President is unable to discharge the powers and duties of his office. Thereupon Congress shall decide the issue, assembling within forty-eight hours for that purpose if not in session. If the Congress, within twenty-one days after receipt of the latter written declaration, or, if Congress is not in session, within twenty-one days after Congress is required to assemble, determines by two-thirds vote of both Houses that the President is unable to discharge the powers and duties of his office, the Vice-President shall continue to discharge the same as Acting President; otherwise, the President shall resume the powers and duties of his office.

Amendment XXVI

[Adopted 1971]

Section 1   The right of citizens of the United States, who are eighteen years of age or older, to vote shall not be denied or abridged by the United States or by any State on account of age.

Section 2   The Congress shall have power to enforce this article by appropriate legislation.

Unratified Amendment

Equal Rights Amendment (proposed by Congress March 22, 1972;
seven-year deadline for ratification extended to June 30, 1982)

Section 1   Equality of rights under the law shall not be denied or abridged by the United States or by any State on account of sex.

Section 2   The Congress shall have the power to enforce, by appropriate legislation, the provisions of this article.

Section 3   This amendment shall take effect two years after the date of ratification.

Unratified Amendment

D.C. Statehood Amendment (proposed by Congress August 22, 1978)

Section 1   For purposes of representation in the Congress, election of the President and Vice-President, and article V of this Constitution, the District constituting the seat of government of the United States shall be treated as though it were a State.

Section 2   The exercise of the rights and powers conferred under this article shall be by the people of the District constituting the seat of government, and as shall be provided by Congress.

Section 3   The twenty-third article of amendment to the Constitution of the United States is hereby repealed.

Section 4   This article shall be inoperative, unless it shall have been ratified as an amendment to the Constitution by the legislatures of three-fourths of the several states within seven years from the date of its submission.

Amendment XXVII

[Adopted 1992]

No law, varying the compensation for the services of the Senators and Representatives, shall take effect, until an election of Representatives shall have intervened.

A Note to Students: This list of terms is provided to help you with historical and economic vocabulary. Many of these terms refer to broad, enduring concepts that you may encounter not only in further studies of history but also when following current events. The terms appear in bold at their first use in each chapter. In the glossary, the page numbers of those chapter-by-chapter appearances are provided so you can look up the terms' uses in various periods and contexts. For definitions and discussions of words not included here, consult a dictionary and the book's index, which will point you to topics covered at greater length in the book.

affirmative action   Policies established in the 1960s and 1970s by governments, businesses, universities, and other institutions to overcome the effects of past discrimination against specific groups such as racial and ethnic minorities and women. Measures to ensure equal opportunity include setting goals for admission, hiring, and promotion; considering minority status when allocating resources; and actively encouraging victims of past discrimination to apply for jobs and other resources. (pp. 893, 971, 1005)

agribusiness   Farming on a large scale, using the production, processing, and distribution methods of modern business. Farming became a big business, not just a way to feed a family and make a living, in the late nineteenth century as farms got larger and more mechanized. In the 1940s and 1950s, specialized commercial farms replaced many family-run operations and grew to an enormous scale. (pp. 535, 872)

alliance system   The military and diplomatic system formulated in an effort to create a balance of power in pre–World War I Europe. Nations were bound together by rigid and comprehensive treaties that promised mutual aid in the case of attack by specific nations. The system swung into action after the Austrian archduke Franz Ferdinand was assassinated in Sarajevo on June 28, 1914, dragging most of Europe into war. (p. 689)

anarchist   A person who rebels against established order and authority. An anarchist is someone who believes that government of any kind is unnecessary and undesirable and should be replaced with voluntary cooperation and free association. Anarchists became increasingly visible in the United States in the late nineteenth and early twentieth centuries. They advocated revolution and grew in numbers through appeals to discontented laborers. Anarchists frequently employed violence in an attempt to achieve their goals. In 1901, anarchist Leon Czolgosz assassinated President William McKinley. (pp. 593, 622, 658, 737)

antebellum   A term that means "before a war" and commonly refers to the period prior to the Civil War. (pp. 354, 375, 463, 479)

antinomian   A person who does not obey societal or religious laws. In colonial Massachusetts, Puritan authorities accused Anne Hutchinson of antinomianism because she believed that Christians could achieve salvation by faith alone. They further asserted, incorrectly, that Hutchinson also held the belief that it was not necessary to follow God's laws as set forth in the Bible. (p. 96)

archaeology   A social science devoted to learning about people who lived in the past through the study of physical artifacts created by humans. Most but not all archaeological study focuses on the history of people who lived before the use of the written word. (p. 2)

Archaic   A term applied to various hunting and gathering cultures that descended from Paleo-Indians. The term also refers to the period of time when these cultures dominated ancient America, roughly from 8000 BP to between 2000 and 1000 BP. (p. 9)

artifacts   Material remains studied and used by archaeologists and historians to support their interpretations of human history. Examples of artifacts include bones, pots, baskets, jewelry, furniture, tools, clothing, and buildings. (p. 2)

artisan   A term commonly used prior to 1900 to describe a skilled craftsman, such as a cabinetmaker. (pp. 45, 104, 118, 183, 233, 365, 382, 588)

Bill of Rights   The commonly used term for the first ten amendments to the U.S. Constitution. The Bill of Rights (the last of which was ratified in 1791) guarantees individual liberties and defines limitations to federal power. Many states made the promise of the prompt addition of a bill of rights a precondition for their ratification of the Constitution. (pp. 240, 246, 848, 904)

black nationalism   A term linked to several African American movements emphasizing racial pride, separation from whites and white institutions, and black autonomy. Black nationalism gained in popularity with the rise of Marcus Garvey and the Universal Negro Improvement Association (1917–1927) and later with the Black Panther Party, Malcolm X, and other participants of the black power movements of the 1960s. (pp. 731, 910)

bloody shirt   A refrain used by Republicans in the late nineteenth century to remind the voting public that the Democratic Party, dominated by the South, was largely responsible for the Civil War and that the Republican Party had led the victory to preserve the Union. Republicans urged their constituents to "vote the way you shot." (pp. 497, 588)

***bracero* program**   A policy begun during World War II to help with wartime agriculture in which Mexican laborers (*braceros*) were permitted to enter the United States and work for a limited period of time but not to gain citizenship or permanent residence. The program officially ended in 1964. (p. 876)

brinksmanship   A cold war practice of appearing willing and able to resort to nuclear war in order to make an enemy back down. Secretary of State John Foster Dulles was the foremost proponent of this policy. (p. 866)

Calvinism   The religious doctrine of which the primary tenet is that salvation is predestined by God. Founded by John Calvin of Geneva during the Protestant Reformation, Calvinism required its adherents to live according to a strict religious and moral code. The Puritans who settled in colonial New England were devout Calvinists. (p. 92) *See also* predestination.

checks and balances   A system in which the executive, legislative, and judicial branches of the government curb each other's power. Checks and balances were written into the U.S. Constitution during the Constitutional Convention of 1787. (pp. 241, 973)

civil disobedience   The public and peaceful violation of certain laws or government orders on the part of individuals or groups who act out of a profound conviction that the law or directive is unjust or immoral and who are prepared to accept the consequences of their actions. Civil disobedience was practiced most famously in U.S. history in the black freedom struggle of the 1960s. (pp. 678, 886, 905, 948)

civil service The administrative service of a government. This term often applies to reforms following the passage of the Pendleton Act in 1883, which set qualifications for U.S. government jobs and sought to remove such jobs from political influence. (pp. 317, 498, 564, 848, 917) *See also* spoils system.

closed shop An establishment in which every employee is required to join a union in order to obtain a job. (p. 722)

cold war The hostile and tense relationship that existed between the Soviet Union on the one hand and the United States and other Western nations on the other from 1947 to 1989. This war was said to be "cold" because the hostility stopped short of armed (hot) conflict, which was warded off by the strategy of nuclear deterrence. (pp. 829, 858, 933, 994, 1001) *See also* deterrence.

collective bargaining Negotiation by a group of workers (usually through a union) and their employer concerning rates of pay and working conditions. (pp. 698, 767, 846, 873)

collective security An association of independent nations that agree to accept and implement decisions made by the group, including going to war in defense of one or more members. The United States resolutely avoided such alliances until after World War II, when it created the North Atlantic Treaty Organization (NATO) in response to the threat posed by the Soviet Union. (pp. 706, 723, 836) *See also* North Atlantic Treaty Organization.

colonization The process by which a country or society gains control over another, primarily through settlement. (pp. 31, 54, 88, 329, 457, 635, 687)

Columbian exchange The transatlantic exchange of goods, peoples, and ideas that began when Columbus arrived in the Caribbean in 1492, ending the age-old separation of the hemispheres. (p. 37)

communism (Communist Party) A system of government and political organization, based on Marxist-Leninist ideals, in which a single authoritarian party controls the economy through state ownership of production, as a means toward reaching the final stage of Marxist theory in which the state dissolves and economic goods are distributed evenly for the common good. Communists around the globe encouraged the spread of communism in other nations in hopes of fomenting worldwide revolution. At its peak in the 1930s, the Communist Party of the United States worked closely with labor unions and insisted that only the overthrow of the capitalist system by its workers could save the victims of the Great Depression. After World War II, the Communist power and aspirations of the Soviet Union were held to be a direct threat to American democracy, prompting the cold war. (pp. 710, 748, 755, 797, 829, 859, 898, 933, 965, 1001) *See also* cold war.

conscription Compulsory military service. Americans were first subject to conscription during the Civil War. The Selective Service Act of 1940 marked the first peacetime use of conscription. (pp. 460, 581, 693) *See also* draft.

conservatism A political and moral outlook dating back to Alexander Hamilton's belief in a strong central government resting on a solid banking foundation. Currently associated with the Republican Party, conservatism today places a high premium on military preparedness, free market economics, low taxes, and strong sexual morality. (pp. 429, 458, 482, 553, 619, 662, 721, 757, 814, 852, 861, 893, 965, 1003)

consumer culture (consumerism) A society that places a high value on, and devotes substantial resources to, the purchase and display of material goods. Elements of American consumerism were evident in the nineteenth century but really took hold in the twentieth century with installment buying and advertising in the 1920s and again with the postwar prosperity of the 1950s. (pp. 542, 593, 730, 860)

containment The U.S. foreign policy developed after World War II to hold in check the power and influence of the Soviet Union and other groups or nations espousing communism. The strategy was first fully articulated by diplomat George F. Kennan in 1946–1947. (pp. 829, 859, 934, 1018)

covenant An agreement or pact; in American history, this refers to a religious agreement. The Pilgrims used this term in the Mayflower Compact to refer to the agreement among themselves to establish a law-abiding community in which all members would work together for the common good. Later, New England Puritans used this term to refer to the agreement they made with God and each other to live according to God's will as revealed through Scripture. (pp. 84, 117) *See also* Halfway Covenant.

cult of domesticity The nineteenth-century belief that women's place was in the home, where they should create a haven for harried men working in the outside world. This ideal was made possible by the separation of the workplace and the home and was used to sentimentalize the home and women's role in it. (pp. 600, 629) *See also* separate spheres.

culture A term used here to connote what is commonly called "way of life." It refers not only to how a group of people supplied themselves with food and shelter but also to their family relationships, social groupings, religious ideas, and other features of their lives. (pp. 3, 32, 55, 82, 127, 264, 280, 307, 350, 375, 434, 462, 510, 557, 583, 593, 689, 727, 758, 911, 983, 1023)

de-industrialization A long period of decline in the industrial sector. The term often refers specifically to the decline of manufacturing and the growth of the service sector of the economy in post–World War II America. This shift and the loss of manufacturing resulting from it were caused by more efficient and automated production techniques at home, increased competition from foreign-made goods, and the use of cheap labor abroad by U.S. manufacturers. (p. 989)

democracy A system of government in which the people have the power to rule, either directly or indirectly, through their elected representatives. Believing that direct democracy was dangerous, the framers of the Constitution created a government that gave direct voice to the people only in the House of Representatives and that placed a check on that voice in the Senate by offering unlimited six-year terms to senators, elected by the state legislatures to protect them from the whims of democratic majorities. The framers further curbed the perceived dangers of democracy by giving each of the three branches of government (legislative, executive, and judicial) the ability to check the power of the other two. (pp. 184, 217, 245, 292, 314, 399, 409, 443, 487, 541, 597, 615, 657, 686, 757, 796, 831, 936, 981, 1010) *See also* checks and balances.

détente French for "loosening." The term refers to the easing of tensions between the United States and the Soviet Union during the Nixon administration. (pp. 954, 976)

deterrence The linchpin of U.S. military strategy during the cold war. The strategy of deterrence dictated that the United States would maintain a nuclear arsenal so substantial that the Soviet Union would refrain from attacking the United States and its allies out of fear that the United States would retaliate in devastating proportions. The Soviets pursued a similar strategy. (pp. 836, 888)

disfranchisement The denial of suffrage to a group or individual through legal or other means. Beginning in 1890, southern progressives preached the disfranchisement of black voters as a "reform" of the electoral system. The most common means of eliminating black voters were poll taxes and literacy tests. (pp. 219, 296, 321, 422, 486, 679, 711, 778, 860, 891)

domino theory   The assumption underlying U.S. foreign policy from the early cold war until the end of the Vietnam War. The theory was that if one country fell to communism, neighboring countries also would fall under Communist control. (pp. 834, 866)

doves   Peace advocates, particularly during the Vietnam War. (p. 950)

draft (draftee)   A system for selecting individuals for compulsory military service. A draftee is an individual selected through this process. (pp. 187, 458, 693, 804, 836, 946, 983) *See also* conscription.

emancipation   The act of freeing from slavery or bondage. The emancipation of American slaves, a goal shared by slaves and abolitionists alike, occurred with the passage of the Thirteenth Amendment in 1865. (pp. 222, 297, 329, 393, 437, 475, 711)

English Reformation   *See* Reformation.

Enlightenment   An eighteenth-century philosophical movement that emphasized the use of reason to reevaluate previously accepted doctrines and traditions. (p. 134)

evangelicalism   The trend in Protestant Christianity stressing salvation through conversion, repentance of sin, adherence to Scripture, and the importance of preaching over ritual. During the Second Great Awakening in the 1830s, evangelicals worshipped at camp meetings and religious revivals led by exuberant preachers. (pp. 307, 365, 390, 563, 976) *See also* Second Great Awakening.

fascism   An authoritarian system of government characterized by dictatorial rule, disdain for international stability, and a conviction that warfare is the only means by which a nation can attain greatness. Nazi Germany and Mussolini's Italy are the prime examples of fascism. (pp. 757, 792)

federal budget deficit   The situation resulting when the government spends more money than it takes in. (pp. 984, 1005)

feminism   The belief that men and women have the inherent right to equal social, political, and economic opportunities. The suffrage movement and second-wave feminism of the 1960s and 1970s were the most visible and successful manifestations of feminism, but feminist ideas were expressed in a variety of statements and movements as early as the late eighteenth century and continue to be expressed in the twenty-first. (pp. 490, 677, 729, 877, 893, 967, 1006)

finance capitalism   Refers to investment sponsored by banks and bankers and the profits garnered from the sale of financial assets such as stocks and bonds. The decades at the end of the twentieth century are known as a period of finance capitalism because banks and financiers increasingly took on the role of stabilizing markets and reorganizing industries. (p. 552)

flexible response   Military strategy employed by the Kennedy and Johnson administrations designed to match a wide range of military threats by complementing nuclear weapons with the buildup of conventional and special forces and using them all in a gradual and calibrated way as needed. Flexible response was a departure from the strategy of massive retaliation used by the Eisenhower administration. (p. 934)

franchise   The right to vote. The franchise was gradually widened in the United States to include groups such as women and African Americans, who had no vote when the Constitution was ratified. (pp. 370, 490, 628) *See also* suffrage.

free labor   Work conducted free from constraint and in accordance with the laborer's personal inclinations and will. Prior to the Civil War, free labor became an ideal championed by Republicans (who were primarily Northerners) to articulate individuals' right to work how and where they wished and to accumulate property in their own name. The ideal of free labor lay at the heart of the North's argument that slavery should not be extended into the western territories. (pp. 330, 346, 378, 408, 477)

free silver   The late-nineteenth-century call by silver barons and poor American farmers for the widespread coinage of silver and for silver to be used as a base upon which to expand the paper money supply. The coinage of silver created a more inflationary monetary system that benefited debtors. (pp. 568, 619) *See also* gold standard.

free soil   The idea advanced in the 1840s that Congress should prohibit slavery within the western territories. "Free soil, free speech, free labor, and free men" became the rallying cry of the short-lived Free-Soil Party. (pp. 408, 455)

frontier   A borderland area. In U.S. history, this refers to the borderland between the areas primarily inhabited by Europeans or their descendants and the areas solely inhabited by Native Americans. (pp. 32, 67, 97, 117, 145, 185, 284, 305, 349, 407, 510)

fundamentalism   Strict adherence to core, often religious beliefs. The term has varying meanings for different religious groups. Protestant fundamentalists adhere to a literal interpretation of the Bible and thus deny the possibility of evolution. Muslim fundamentalists believe that traditional Islamic law should govern nations and that Western influences should be banned. (pp. 739, 983, 1003)

gag rule   A procedural rule invoked to prohibit discussion or debate on a particular subject in a legislative body. From 1836 to 1844, a series of gag rules prevented the House of Representatives from discussing the large number of antislavery petitions from abolitionist groups that flooded that chamber. (p. 333)

gender gap   An electoral phenomenon that became apparent in the 1980s when men and women began to display different preferences in voting. Women tended to favor liberal candidates, and men tended to support conservatives. The key voter groups contributing to the gender gap were single women and women who worked outside the home. (pp. 992, 1016)

globalization   The spread of political, cultural, and economic influences and connections among countries, businesses, and individuals around the world through trade, immigration, communication, and other means. In the late twentieth century, globalization was intensified by new communications technology that connected individuals, corporations, and nations with greater speed at low prices. This led to an increase in political and economic interdependence and mutual influence among nations. (pp. 954, 1003)

gold standard   A monetary system in which any circulating currency was exchangeable for a specific amount of gold. Advocates for the gold standard believed that gold alone should be used for coinage and that the total value of paper banknotes should never exceed the government's supply of gold. The triumph of gold standard supporter William McKinley in the 1896 presidential election was a big victory for supporters of this policy. (pp. 570, 616) *See also* free silver.

gospel of wealth   The idea that wealth garnered from earthly success should be used for good works. Andrew Carnegie promoted this view in an 1889 essay in which he maintained that the wealthy should serve as stewards and act in the best interests of society as a whole. (pp. 556, 651)

government bonds Promissory notes issued by a government in order to borrow money from members of the public. Such bonds are redeemable at a set future date. Bondholders earn interest on their investments. (p. 196)

Great Awakening The widespread movement of religious revitalization in the 1730s and 1740s that emphasized vital religious faith and personal choice. It was characterized by large, open-air meetings at which emotional sermons were given by itinerant preachers. (p. 135)

Great Society President Lyndon Johnson's domestic program, which included civil rights legislation, antipoverty programs, government subsidy of medical care, federal aid to education, consumer protection, and aid to the arts and humanities. (pp. 892, 968, 1013)

guerrilla warfare Fighting carried out by an irregular military force usually organized into small, highly mobile groups. Guerrilla combat was common in the Vietnam War and during the American Revolution. Guerrilla warfare is often effective against opponents who have greater material resources. (pp. 179, 424, 441, 519, 639, 867, 934, 1036)

Halfway Covenant A Puritan compromise that allowed the unconverted children of the "visible saints" to become "halfway" members of the church and to baptize their own children even though they were not full members of the church themselves because they had not experienced full conversion. Massachusetts ministers accepted this compromise in 1662, but the compromise remained controversial throughout the seventeenth century. (p. 99)

hard currency (hard money) Money coined directly from, or backed in full by, precious metals (particularly gold). (pp. 196, 224, 251, 312)

hawks Advocates of aggressive military action or all-out war, particularly during the Vietnam War. (p. 950) *See also* War Hawks.

holding company A system of business organization whereby competing companies are combined under one central administration in order to curb competition and ensure profit. Pioneered in the late 1880s by John D. Rockefeller, holding companies, such as Standard Oil, exercised monopoly control even as the government threatened to outlaw trusts as a violation of free trade. (p. 549) *See also* monopoly; trust.

horizontal integration A system in which a single person or corporation creates several subsidiary businesses to sell a product in different markets. John D. Rockefeller pioneered the use of horizontal integration in the 1880s to control the refining process, giving him a virtual monopoly on the oil-refining business. (p. 549) *See also* vertical integration; monopoly.

impeachment The process by which formal charges of wrongdoing are brought against a president, a governor, or a federal judge. (pp. 487, 974, 1012)

imperialism The system by which great powers gain control of overseas territories. The United States became an imperialist power by gaining control of Puerto Rico, Guam, the Philippines, and Cuba as a result of the Spanish-American War. (pp. 499, 615, 687, 801, 838, 1012)

indentured servitude A system that committed poor immigrants to four to seven years of labor in exchange for passage to the colonies and food and shelter after they arrived. An indenture is a type of contract. (pp. 56, 116)

iron curtain A metaphor coined by Winston Churchill during his commencement address at Westminster College in Fulton, Missouri, in 1946, to refer to the political, ideological, and military barriers that separated Soviet-controlled Eastern Europe from the rest of Europe and the West following World War II. (pp. 832, 866, 936, 1009)

isolationism   A foreign policy perspective characterized by a desire to have the United States withdraw from the conflicts of the world and enjoy the protection of two vast oceans. (pp. 635, 707, 723, 793, 834)

Jim Crow   The system of racial segregation that developed in the post–Civil War South and extended well into the twentieth century; it replaced slavery as the chief instrument of white supremacy. Jim Crow laws segregated African Americans in public facilities such as trains and streetcars and denied them basic civil rights, including the right to vote. It was also at this time that the doctrine of "separate but equal" became institutionalized. (pp. 495, 583, 679, 814)

Keynesian economics   A theory developed by economist John Maynard Keynes that guided U.S. economic policy from the New Deal to the 1970s. According to Keynesians, the federal government has a duty to stimulate and manage the economy by spending money on public works projects and by making general tax cuts in order to put more money into the hands of ordinary people, thus creating demand. (p. 785)

laissez-faire   The doctrine, based on economic theory, that government should not interfere in business or the economy. Laissez-faire ideas guided American government policy in the late nineteenth century and conservative politics in the twentieth century. Business interests that supported laissez-faire in the late nineteenth century accepted government interference when it took the form of tariffs or subsidies that worked to their benefit. A broader use of the term refers to the simple philosophy of abstaining from interference. (pp. 556, 615, 649, 741, 757, 986, 1037)

land grant   A gift of land from a government, usually intended to encourage settlement or development. The British government issued several land grants to encourage development in the American colonies. In the mid-nineteenth century, the U.S. government issued land grants to encourage railroad development and, through the passage of the Land-Grant College Act (also known as the Morrill Act) in 1862, set aside public land to support universities. (pp. 57, 101, 146, 187, 345, 525, 544)

liberalism   The political doctrine that government rests on the consent of the governed and is duty-bound to protect the freedom and property of the individual. In the twentieth century, liberalism became associated with the idea that government should regulate the economy and ensure the material well-being and individual rights of all people. (pp. 615, 649, 716, 758, 814, 844, 861, 892, 968, 1005)

liberty   The condition of being free or enjoying freedom from control. This term also refers to the possession of certain social, political, or economic rights, such as the right to own and control property. Eighteenth-century American colonists invoked the principle to argue for strict limitations on government's ability to tax its subjects. (pp. 84, 145, 184, 217, 248, 276, 307, 378, 421, 443, 480, 689, 1032)

manifest destiny   A term coined by journalist John O'Sullivan in 1845 to express the popular nineteenth-century belief that the United States was destined to expand westward to the Pacific Ocean and had an irrefutable right and God-given responsibility to do so. This idea provided an ideological shield for westward expansion and masked the economic and political motivations of many of those who championed it. (pp. 350, 416, 636)

McCarthyism   The practice of searching out suspected Communists and others outside mainstream American society, discrediting them, and hounding them from government and other employment. The term derives from Senator Joseph McCarthy, who gained notoriety for leading such repressive activities from 1950 to 1954. (p. 847)

mercantilism   A set of policies that regulated colonial commerce and manufacturing for the enrichment of the mother country. Mercantilist policies ensured that the American colonies in the mid-seventeenth century produced agricultural goods and raw materials to be shipped to England, where they would increase wealth in the mother country through reexportation or manufacture into finished goods that would then be sold to the colonies and elsewhere. (p. 71)

Middle Passage   The crossing of the Atlantic (as a slave destined for auction) in the hold of a slave ship in the eighteenth and nineteenth centuries. Conditions were unimaginably bad, and many slaves died during these voyages. (p. 127)

military-industrial complex   A term first used by President Dwight D. Eisenhower to refer to the aggregate power and influence of the armed forces in conjunction with the aerospace, munitions, and other industries that produced supplies for the military in the post–World War II era. (p. 870)

miscegenation   The sexual mixing of races. In slave states, despite the social stigma and legal restrictions on interracial sex, masters' almost unlimited power over their female slaves meant that liaisons inevitably occurred. Many states maintained laws against miscegenation into the 1950s. (pp. 378, 560, 731)

monopoly   Exclusive control and domination by a single business entity over an entire industry through ownership, command of supply, or other means. Gilded Age businesses monopolized their industries quite profitably, often organizing holding companies and trusts to do so. (pp. 29, 308, 504, 535, 549, 615, 660, 769, 823, 987) *See also* holding company; trust.

Monroe Doctrine   President James Monroe's 1823 declaration that the Western Hemisphere was closed to any further colonization or interference by European powers. In exchange, Monroe pledged that the United States would not become involved in European struggles. Although Monroe could not back his policy with action, it was an important formulation of national goals. (pp. 299, 636, 665, 687)

nationalism   A strong feeling of devotion and loyalty toward one nation over others. Nationalism encourages the promotion of the nation's common culture, language, and customs. (pp. 289, 358, 461, 686, 866)

nativism   Bias against immigrants and in favor of native-born inhabitants. American nativists especially favor persons who come from white, Anglo-Saxon, Protestant lines over those from other racial, ethnic, and religious heritages. Nativists may include former immigrants who view new immigrants as incapable of assimilation. Many nativists, such as members of the Know-Nothing Party in the nineteenth century and the Ku Klux Klan through the contemporary period, voice anti-immigrant, anti-Catholic, and anti-Semitic sentiments. (pp. 419, 528, 652, 736)

New Deal   The group of social and economic programs that President Franklin Roosevelt developed to provide relief for the needy, speed economic recovery, and reform economic and government institutions. The New Deal was a massive effort to bring the United States out of the Great Depression and ensure its future prosperity. (pp. 619, 755, 793, 827, 860, 893, 984, 1015)

New Right   Politically active religious conservatives who became particularly vocal in the 1980s. The New Right criticized feminism, opposed abortion and homosexuality, and promoted "family values" and military preparedness. (p. 967)

New South   A vision of the South, promoted after the Civil War by Henry Grady, editor of the *Atlanta Constitution*, that urged the South to abandon its dependence on agriculture and use its cheap labor and natural resources to compete with northern industry. Many Southerners migrated from farms to cities in the late nineteenth century, and Northerners and foreigners invested a significant amount of capital in railroads, cotton and textiles, mining, lumber, iron, steel, and tobacco in the region. (pp. 475, 558)

North Atlantic Treaty Organization (NATO)   A post–World War II alliance that joined the United States, Canada, and Western European nations into a military coalition designed to counter the Soviet Union's efforts to expand. Each NATO member pledged to go to war if any member was attacked. Since the end of the cold war, NATO has been expanding to include the formerly Communist countries of Eastern Europe. (pp. 829, 995, 1009)

nullification   The idea that states can disregard federal laws when those laws represent an overstepping of congressional powers. The controversial idea was first proposed by opponents of the Alien and Sedition Acts of 1798 and later by South Carolina politicians in 1828 as a response to the Tariff of Abominations. (pp. 269, 278, 322, 410)

oligopoly   A competitive system in which several large corporations dominate an industry by dividing the market so each business has a share of it. More prevalent than outright monopolies during the late 1800s, the oligopolies of the Gilded Age successfully muted competition and benefited the corporations that participated in this type of arrangement. (pp. 523, 555)

paternalism   The idea that slavery was a set of reciprocal obligations between masters and slaves, with slaves providing labor and obedience and masters providing basic care and direction. The concept of paternalism denied that the slave system was brutal and exploitative. Although paternalism did provide some protection against the worst brutality, it did not guarantee decent living conditions, reasonable work, or freedom from physical punishment. (p. 382)

planters   Owners of large farms (or, more specifically, plantations) that were worked by twenty or more slaves. By 1860, planters had accrued a great deal of local, statewide, and national political power in the South despite the fact that they represented a minority of the white electorate. Planters' dominance of southern politics demonstrated both the power of tradition and stability among southern voters and the planters' success at convincing white voters that the slave system benefited all whites, even those without slaves. (pp. 63, 105, 127, 154, 181, 262, 285, 329, 379, 410, 444, 478, 558)

plutocracy   A society ruled by the richest members. The excesses of the Gilded Age and the fact that just 1 percent of the population owned more than half the real and personal property in the country led many to question whether the United States was indeed a plutocracy. (p. 587)

pogrom   An organized and often officially encouraged massacre of an ethnic minority; usually used in reference to attacks on Jews. (p. 582)

popular sovereignty   The idea that government is subject to the will of the people. Before the Civil War, this was the idea that the residents of a territory should determine, through their legislatures, whether to allow slavery. (pp. 295, 409)

Populism   A political movement that led to the creation of the People's Party, primarily comprising southern and western farmers who railed against big business and advocated business and economic reforms, including government ownership of the railroads. The movement peaked in the late nineteenth century. The Populist ticket won more than 1 million votes in the presidential election of 1892 and 1.5 million in the congressional elections of 1894. The term *populism* has come to mean any political movement that advocates on behalf of the common person, particularly for government intervention against big business. (pp. 615, 656, 1037)

pragmatism   A philosophical movement whose American proponents, William James and John Dewey, stated that there were no eternal truths and that the real worth of any idea lay in its consequences. Dewey tested his theories in the classroom, pioneering in American education the role of process over content and encouraging students to learn by doing. American pragmatists championed social experimentation, providing an important impetus for progressive reform in the early part of the twentieth century. (p. 655)

predestination   The idea that individual salvation or damnation is determined by God at, or just prior to, a person's birth. The concept of predestination invalidated the idea that salvation could be obtained through either faith or good works. (p. 92) *See also* Calvinism.

progressivism (progressive movement)   A wide-ranging twentieth-century reform movement that advocated government activism to mitigate the problems created by urban industrialism. Progressivism reached its peak in 1912 with the creation of the Progressive Party, which ran Theodore Roosevelt for president. The term *progressivism* has come to mean any general effort advocating for social welfare programs. (pp. 587, 619, 649, 686, 719, 759, 918, 1037)

Protestantism   A powerful Christian reform movement that began in the sixteenth century with Martin Luther's critiques of the Roman Catholic Church. Over the centuries, Protestantism has taken many different forms, branching into numerous denominations with differing systems of worship. (pp. 49, 68, 86, 117, 168, 291, 324, 349, 375, 420, 588, 651, 735, 758, 969)

Protestant Reformation   *See* Reformation.

Puritanism   The ideas and religious principles held by dissenters from the Church of England, including the belief that the church needed to be purified by eliminating the elements of Catholicism from its practices. (pp. 68, 85, 117)

Reformation   The reform movement that began in 1517 with Martin Luther's critiques of the Roman Catholic Church, which led to the formation of Protestant Christian groups. The English Reformation began with Henry VIII's break with the Roman Catholic Church, which established the Protestant Church of England. Henry VIII's decision was politically motivated; he had no particular quarrel with Catholic theology and remained an orthodox Catholic in most matters of religious practice. (pp. 49, 85)

reform Darwinism   A social theory, based on Charles Darwin's theory of evolution, that emphasized activism, arguing that humans could speed up evolution by altering the environment. A challenge to social Darwinism, reform Darwinism condemned laissez-faire and demanded that the government take a more active approach to solving social problems. It became the ideological basis for progressive reform in the late nineteenth and early twentieth centuries. (p. 655) *See also* laissez-faire; social Darwinism.

republicanism   The belief that the unworkable model of European-style monarchy should be replaced with a form of government in which supreme power resides in the hands of citizens with the right to vote and is exercised by a representative government answerable to this electorate. In Revolutionary-era America, republicanism became a social philosophy that embodied a sense of community and called individuals to act for the public good. (pp. 183, 213, 246, 274, 400)

scientific management   A system of organizing work, developed by Frederick Winslow Taylor in the late nineteenth century, to increase efficiency and productivity by breaking tasks into their component parts and training workers to perform specific parts. Labor resisted this effort because it de-skilled workers and led to the speedup of production lines. Taylor's ideas were most popular at the height of the Progressive Era. (p. 655)

Second Great Awakening   A popular religious revival that preached that salvation was available to anybody who chose to take it. The revival peaked in the 1830s, and its focus on social perfection inspired many of the reform movements of the Jacksonian era. (p. 324) *See also* evangelicalism.

separate spheres   A concept of gender relations that developed in the Jacksonian era and continued well into the twentieth century, holding that women's proper place was in the world of hearth and home (the private sphere) and men's was in the world of commerce and politics (the public sphere). The doctrine of separate spheres eroded slowly over the nineteenth and twentieth centuries as women became more and more involved in public activities. (pp. 325, 559, 600, 731) *See also* cult of domesticity.

social Darwinism   A social theory, based on Charles Darwin's theory of evolution, that argued that all progress in human society came as the result of competition and natural selection. Gilded Age proponents such as William Graham Sumner and Herbert Spencer claimed that reform was useless because the rich and poor were precisely where nature intended them to be and intervention would retard the progress of humanity. (pp. 555, 583, 630, 651) *See also* reform Darwinism.

social gospel movement   A religious movement in the late nineteenth and early twentieth centuries founded on the idea that Christians have a responsibility to reform society as well as individuals. Social gospel adherents encouraged people to put Christ's teachings to work in their daily lives by actively promoting social justice. (pp. 650, 760)

socialism   A governing system in which the state owns and operates the largest and most important parts of the economy. (pp. 597, 619, 653, 702, 748, 761, 815, 835, 915)

social purity movement   A movement to end prostitution and eradicate venereal disease, often accompanied by the censorship of materials deemed "obscene." (p. 650)

spoils system   An arrangement in which party leaders reward party loyalists with government jobs. This slang term for *patronage* comes from the saying "To the victor go the spoils." Widespread government corruption during the Gilded Age spurred reformers to curb the spoils system through the passage of the Pendleton Act in 1883, which created the Civil Service Commission to award government jobs on the basis of merit. (pp. 317, 498, 557) *See also* civil service.

state sovereignty   A state's autonomy or freedom from external control. The federal system adopted at the Constitutional Convention in 1787 struck a balance between state sovereignty and national control by creating a strong central government while leaving the states intact as political entities. The states remained in possession of many important powers on which the federal government cannot intrude. (p. 446)

states' rights   A strict interpretation of the Constitution that holds that federal power over the states is limited and that the states hold ultimate sovereignty. First expressed in 1798 through the passage of the Virginia and Kentucky Resolutions, which were based on the assumption that the states have the right to judge the constitutionality of federal laws, the states' rights philosophy became a cornerstone of the South's resistance to federal control of slavery. (pp. 233, 299, 321, 460, 480, 671)

strict constructionism　An approach to constitutional law that attempts to adhere to the original intent of the writers of the Constitution. Strict construction often produces Supreme Court decisions that defer to the legislative branch and to the states and restrict the power of the federal government. Opponents of strict construction argue that the Constitution is an organic document that must be interpreted to meet conditions unimagined when it was written. (p. 971)

suffrage　The right to vote. The term *suffrage* is most often associated with the efforts of American women to secure voting rights. (pp. 219, 324, 368, 400, 477, 559, 613, 649, 686) *See also* franchise.

Sun Belt　The southern and southwestern regions of the United States, which grew tremendously in industry, population, and influence after World War II. (pp. 860, 968)

supply-side economics　An economic theory based on the premise that tax cuts for the wealthy and for corporations encourage investment and production (supply), which in turn stimulate consumption. Embraced by the Reagan administration and other conservative Republicans, this theory reversed Keynesian economic policy, which assumes that the way to stimulate the economy is to create demand through federal spending on public works and general tax cuts that put more money into the hands of ordinary people. (pp. 987, 1005) *See also* Keynesian economics.

temperance movement　The reform movement to end drunkenness by urging people to abstain from the consumption of alcohol. Begun in the 1820s, this movement achieved its greatest political victory with the passage of a constitutional amendment in 1919 that prohibited the manufacture, sale, and transportation of alcohol. That amendment was repealed in 1933. (pp. 329, 365, 562, 628, 651)

third world　Originally a cold war term linked to decolonization, *third world* was first used in the late 1950s to describe newly independent countries in Africa and Asia that were not aligned with either Communist nations (the second world) or non-Communist nations (the first world). Later, the term was applied to all poor, nonindustrialized countries, in Latin America as well as in Africa and Asia. Many international experts see *third world* as a problematic category when applied to such a large and disparate group of nations, and they criticize the discriminatory hierarchy suggested by the term. (pp. 838, 933, 967)

trickle-down economics　The theory that financial benefits and incentives given to big businesses in the top tier of the economy will flow down to smaller businesses and individuals and thus benefit the entire nation. President Herbert Hoover unsuccessfully used the trickle-down strategy in his attempt to pull the nation out of the Great Depression, stimulating the economy through government investment in large economic enterprises and public works such as construction of the Hoover Dam. In the late twentieth century, conservatives used this economic theory to justify large tax cuts and other financial benefits for corporations and the wealthy. (pp. 744, 990)

Truman Doctrine　President Harry S. Truman's assertion that American security depended on stopping any Communist government from taking over any non-Communist government—even nondemocratic and repressive dictatorships—anywhere in the world. Beginning in 1947 with American aid to help Greece and Turkey stave off Communist pressures, this approach became a cornerstone of American foreign policy during the cold war. (p. 834)

trust   A corporate system in which corporations give shares of their stock to trustees, who coordinate the industry to ensure profits to the participating corporations and curb competition. Pioneered by Standard Oil, such business practices were deemed unfair, were moderated by the Sherman Antitrust Act (1890), and were finally abolished by the combined efforts of Presidents Theodore Roosevelt and William Howard Taft and the sponsors of the 1914 Clayton Antitrust Act. The term *trust* is also loosely applied to all large business combinations. (pp. 549, 649, 774) *See also* holding company.

vertical integration   A system in which a single person or corporation controls all processes of an industry from start to finished product. Andrew Carnegie first used vertical integration in the 1870s, controlling every aspect of steel production from the mining of iron ore to the manufacturing of the final product, thereby maximizing profits by eliminating the use of outside suppliers or services. (p. 547)

virtual representation   The notion, propounded by the British Parliament in the eighteenth century, that the House of Commons represented all British subjects—wherever they lived and regardless of whether they had directly voted for their representatives. Prime Minister George Grenville used this idea to argue that the Stamp Act and other parliamentary taxes on British colonists did not constitute taxation without representation. The American colonists rejected this argument, insisting that political representatives derived authority only from explicit citizens' consent (indicated by elections) and that members of a distant government body were incapable of adequately representing their interests. (p. 155)

War Hawks   Young Republicans elected to the U.S. Congress in the fall of 1810 who were eager for war with Britain in order to legitimize attacks on Indians, end impressment, and avenge foreign insults. (p. 285) *See also* hawks.

welfare capitalism   The idea that a capitalistic, industrial society can operate benevolently to improve the lives of workers. The notion of welfare capitalism became popular in the 1920s as industries extended the benefits of scientific management to improve safety and sanitation in the workplace as well as institute paid vacations and pension plans. (p. 725) *See also* scientific management.

welfare state   A nation or state in which the government assumes responsibility for some or all of the individual and social welfare of its citizens. Welfare states commonly provide education, health care, food programs for the poor, unemployment compensation, and other social benefits. The United States dramatically expanded its role as a welfare state with the provisions of the New Deal in the 1930s. (pp. 773, 861, 895)

Yankee imperialism   A cry raised in Latin American countries against the United States when it intervened militarily in the region without invitation or consent from those countries. (pp. 935, 1006)

yeoman   A farmer who owned a small plot of land that was sufficient to support a family and was tilled by family members and perhaps a few servants. (pp. 69, 131, 324, 394, 459, 491, 536)

A note about the index:

Names of individuals appear in boldface.

Letters in parentheses following pages refer to:
(i)   illustrations, including photographs and artifacts, as well as information in picture captions
(f)   figures, including charts and graphs
(m) maps
(t)   tables

Antislavery movement, 330–332, 411. *See also*
    Abolition and abolitionism
  in election of 1848, 410
  free blacks in, 370
  in South, 402
Antisodomy laws, 994
Antitrust activities
  Roosevelt, Theodore, and, 660
  Taft and, 670
  U.S. Steel and, 663–664
  of Wilson, 673–674
Antiwar protests, during Vietnam War, 915,
    947–952, 957, 958
Apache Indians, 19, 355, 519–520, 525
Apartheid, in South Africa, 995
Apartments, residential, 605
Appalachian Mountains, movement to west
    of, 152–153
Appeal . . . to the Coloured Citizens of the World,
    An (Walker), 330, 374
Appeasement, before World War II, 797
Appliances, 725, 878
Appomattox Court House, Virginia, Lee's
    surrender at (1865), 470
Apportionment, by population, 233, 234
Apprenticeship laws, in black codes, 482
Arab-Israeli wars, 955–956
Arab League, 1007(m)
Arab world
  Clinton and, 1018
  Eisenhower and, 868–869
  Nixon and, 955–956
Arafat, Yasir, 1020
Arapaho Indians, 352, 515, 517, 520
Arbella (ship), 89
Arbenz, Jacobo, 867–868
Archaeology, 2, 3–4
Archaic hunters and gatherers, 9–12
Architecture
  Chicago school of, 605
  skyscrapers, 604
Arctic National Wildlife Refuge, 980, 1028
Ardennes forest region, 798
Argonne Cemetery, 715
Arikara Indians, 518
Aristide, Jean-Bertrand, 1019
Aristocracy, vs. democracy, 314
Arizona, 416, 512
Arizona (ship), 802(i)
Ark (ship), 69
Arkansas, 441, 477
Armed forces. *See also* Military; Militia;
    specific forces
  African Americans in, 458–459
  British, 136, 189
  Carter and, 983

  in Civil War, 446, 447, 448–449, 463
  in cold war, 836
  Continental army as, 177–178, 186–188
  desegregation of, 844
  Hamilton and, 267
  homosexuals in, 805
  Jefferson and, 277
  in Little Rock, 885
  McCarthy and, 861
  Reagan and, 994–995
  in Seven Years' War, 151–152
  in Shays's Rebellion, 229–230
  strikes and, 595–596, 661
  in Vietnam War, 946
  women's, 836
  in World War I, 684–685, 690(i), 693–694
  in World War II, 804–805
Armenian immigrants, 581
Armistice
  after Korean War, 854–855
  after World War I, 704–707
Armour, Philip, 550
Arms and armaments. *See also* Weapons
  "cash-and-carry" policy and, 795–796
  embargo on sales, 799
  Lend-Lease Act and, 800
Arms control, 954, 998, 1010
Arms race. *See* Nuclear arms race
Armstrong, Louis, 732
Army-McCarthy hearings, 861, 880
Army of Northern Virginia, 449, 451
Army of the Potomac, 448, 468
Army of the Republic of Vietnam (ARVN),
    867, 940, 956
Arnold, Benedict, 189, 198, 204
Arrogance of Power, The (Fulbright), 948
"Arsenal of democracy," U.S. as, 800, 806
Art(s). *See also* specific arts and artists
  funding for, 901
  in Harlem Renaissance, 732
  Lost Generation and, 727
  in 1950s, 883
Arthur, Chester A., 565
Articles of Confederation (1781–1789), 212,
    213–217, 223–231
  congress under, 214, 226–228, 229–230
  economy and finances under, 224–225
  equality and slavery under, 220–221
Artifacts, 2
  Chumash, 11(i)
  from Folsom site, 1–3
  of Woodland Indians, 15–16
Artisans, 118, 183, 588
  at Constitutional Convention, 233
  in Pennsylvania, 104
  on plantations, 382

ATLAS OF THE TERRITORIAL GROWTH OF THE UNITED STATES

Lake Superior

Lake Huron

Lake Michigan

Lake Ontario

Lake Erie

St. Lawrence R.

N.H.

MASS.

NEW YORK

Connecticut R.

Hudson R.

RHODE ISLAND

CONNECTICUT

PENN.

Delaware R.

NEW JERSEY

Susquehanna R.

DELAWARE

MARYLAND

Potomac R.

Chesapeake Bay

Missouri R.

Proclamation Line of 1763

THE ORIGINAL THIRTEEN COLONIES

James R.

VIRGINIA

Ohio R.

NORTH CAROLINA

Cumberland R.

Tennessee R.

Cape Fear R.

ATLANTIC OCEAN

Arkansas R.

SOUTH CAROLINA

Mississippi R.

Savannah R.

GEORGIA

THE ORIGINAL THIRTEEN COLONIES IN 1776

0   150   300 miles

0   150   300 kilometers

Gulf of Mexico

M-2

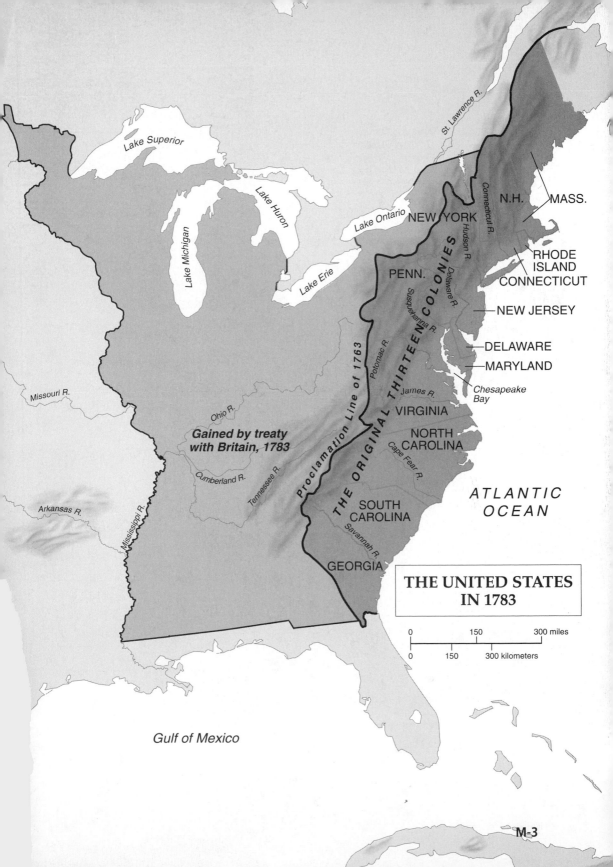

Lake Superior

Lake Huron

Lake Michigan

Lake Ontario

Lake Erie

St. Lawrence R.

N.H.

MASS.

NEW YORK

Hudson R.

Connecticut R.

RHODE
ISLAND

CONNECTICUT

PENN.

Delaware R.

NEW JERSEY

Susquehanna R.

DELAWARE

MARYLAND

THE ORIGINAL THIRTEEN COLONIES

Potomac R.

*Chesapeake
Bay*

James R.

VIRGINIA

Proclamation Line of 1763

NORTH
CAROLINA

Cape Fear R.

**Gained by treaty
with Britain, 1783**

Missouri R.

Ohio R.

Cumberland R.

Tennessee R.

SOUTH
CAROLINA

*ATLANTIC
OCEAN*

Arkansas R.

Savannah R.

Mississippi R.

GEORGIA

THE UNITED STATES
IN 1783

0	150	300 miles
0	150	300 kilometers

Gulf of Mexico

M-3

Area ceded by
Great Britain,
1818

Area ceded by
the United States
to Great Britain,
1818

Missouri R.

Columbia R.

Snake R.

LOUISIANA
PURCHASE
from France, 1803

N. Platte R.

Platte R.

S. Platte R.

Sacramento R.

San Joaquin R.

Colorado R.

Red R.

PACIFIC
OCEAN

Rio Grande

M-4

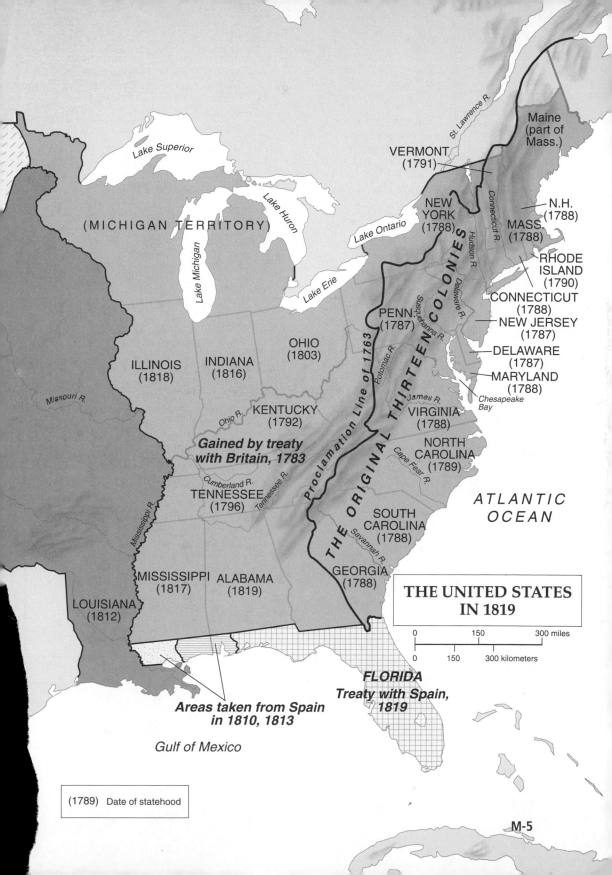

Lake Superior

Lake Huron

(MICHIGAN TERRITORY)

Lake Michigan

Lake Erie

Lake Ontario

St. Lawrence R.

Maine
(part of
Mass.)

VERMONT
(1791)

NEW
YORK
(1788)

Connecticut R.

Hudson R.

N.H.
(1788)

MASS.
(1788)

RHODE
ISLAND
(1790)

CONNECTICUT
(1788)

NEW JERSEY
(1787)

DELAWARE
(1787)

MARYLAND
(1788)

PENN.
(1787)

Susquehanna R.

Delaware R.

OHIO
(1803)

ILLINOIS
(1818)

INDIANA
(1816)

Missouri R.

Ohio R.

KENTUCKY
(1792)

**Gained by treaty
with Britain, 1783**

Cumberland R.

TENNESSEE
(1796)

Tennessee R.

Mississippi R.

Proclamation Line of 1763

THE ORIGINAL THIRTEEN COLONIES

Potomac R.

James R.

Chesapeake
Bay

VIRGINIA
(1788)

NORTH
CAROLINA
(1789)

Cape Fear R.

SOUTH
CAROLINA
(1788)

Savannah R.

ATLANTIC
OCEAN

MISSISSIPPI
(1817)

ALABAMA
(1819)

GEORGIA
(1788)

LOUISIANA
(1812)

**THE UNITED STATES
IN 1819**

| 0 | 150 | 300 miles |
| 0 | 150 | 300 kilometers |

**Areas taken from Spain
in 1810, 1813**

FLORIDA
**Treaty with Spain,
1819**

Gulf of Mexico

(1789)   Date of statehood

M-5

Area ceded by
Great Britain,
1818

Area ceded by
the United States
to Great Britain,
1818

Missouri R.

Columbia R.

OREGON COUNTRY
Agreement with Britain,
1846

(OREGON TERRITORY)

Snake R.

LOUISIANA

PURCHASE

from France, 1803

N. Platte R.

Platte R.

S. Platte R.

Sacramento R.

(UTAH TERRITORY)

San Joaquin R.

MEXICAN CESSION,
1848

Colorado R.

CALIFORNIA
(1850)

(NEW MEXICO TERRITORY)

(Claim waived
by Texas, 1850)

Red R.

TEXAS

Annexed, 1845

TEXAS
(1845)

GADSDEN PURCHASE
from Mexico, 1853

PACIFIC
OCEAN

Rio Grande

M-6

Areas ceded by Britain, 1842
(Webster-Ashburton Treaty)

Lake Superior

St. Lawrence R.

MAINE
(1820)

VERMONT
(1791)

Connecticut R.

NEW
YORK
(1788)

Hudson R.

N.H.
(1788)

MASS.
(1788)

Lake Ontario

RHODE
ISLAND
(1790)

(MINNESOTA
TERRITORY)

WISCONSIN
(1848)

Lake Michigan

Lake Huron

MICHIGAN
(1837)

Lake Erie

CONNECTICUT
(1788)

NEW JERSEY
(1787)

Delaware R.

DELAWARE
(1787)

IOWA
(1846)

ILLINOIS
(1818)

INDIANA
(1816)

OHIO
(1803)

PENN.
(1787)

Susquehanna R.

Potomac R.

THE ORIGINAL THIRTEEN COLONIES

MARYLAND
(1788)

*Chesapeake
Bay*

James R.

VIRGINIA
(1788)

Proclamation Line of 1763

Missouri R.

Ohio R.

KENTUCKY
(1792)

Gained by treaty
with Britain, 1783

MISSOURI
(1821)

Cumberland R.

Tennessee R.

TENNESSEE
(1796)

NORTH
CAROLINA
(1789)

Cape Fear R.

ARKANSAS
(1836)

Mississippi R.

SOUTH
CAROLINA
(1788)

Savannah R.

ATLANTIC
OCEAN

(INDIAN
TERRITORY)

MISSISSIPPI
(1817)

ALABAMA
(1819)

GEORGIA
(1788)

LOUISIANA
(1812)

**THE UNITED STATES
IN 1853**

| 0 | 150 | 300 miles |
| 0 | 150 | 300 kilometers |

FLORIDA
(1845)

Areas taken from Spain
in 1810, 1813

FLORIDA
Treaty with Spain,
1819

Gulf of Mexico

(1789) Date of statehood

M-7

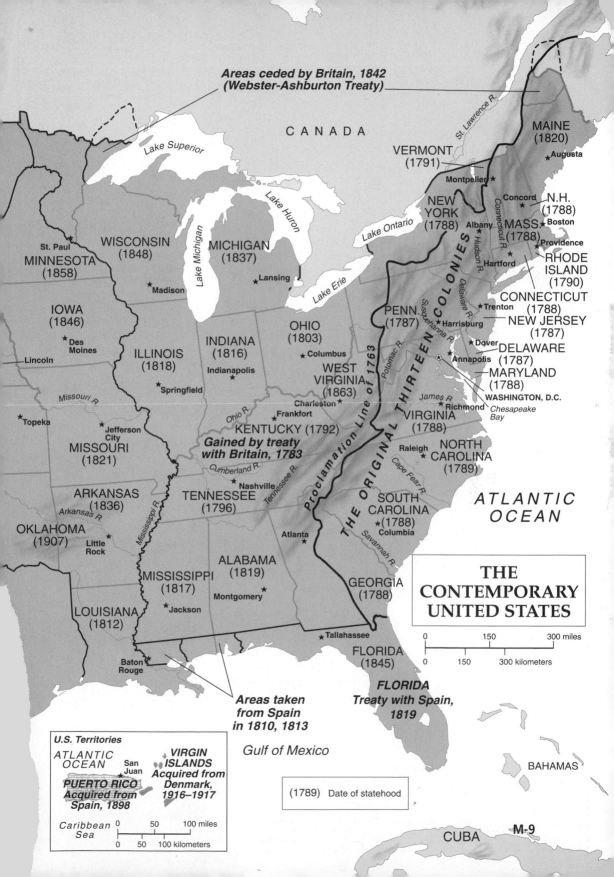

Areas ceded by Britain, 1842
(Webster-Ashburton Treaty)

CANADA

Lake Superior

*Areas taken
from Spain
in 1810, 1813*

**THE
CONTEMPORARY
UNITED STATES**

MINNESOTA
(1858)
★ St. Paul

WISCONSIN
(1848)

MICHIGAN
(1837)
★ Lansing

Lake Michigan

Lake Huron

Lake Erie

Lake Ontario

VERMONT
(1791)

MAINE
(1820)
★ Augusta

Montpelier ★

NEW
YORK
(1788)

★ Albany

Concord ★ N.H.
(1788)

MASS. ★ Boston
(1788)

Providence ★

RHODE
ISLAND
(1790)

Hartford ★

CONNECTICUT
(1788)

★ Trenton

NEW JERSEY
(1787)

IOWA
(1846)

★ Des
Moines

Lincoln ★

ILLINOIS
(1818)

INDIANA
(1816)

★ Indianapolis

OHIO
(1803)

★ Columbus

PENN.
(1787)

★ Harrisburg

★ Dover DELAWARE
(1787)

Annapolis ⊛ MARYLAND
(1788)

WASHINGTON, D.C.

★ Madison

★ Springfield

Missouri R.

WEST
VIRGINIA
(1863)

Charleston ★

Frankfort ★

★ Richmond

Chesapeake
Bay

Topeka ★

Jefferson
City ★

MISSOURI
(1821)

KENTUCKY (1792)

*Gained by treaty
with Britain, 1783*

Cumberland R.

VIRGINIA
(1788)

James R.

Ohio R.

THE ORIGINAL THIRTEEN COLONIES

Proclamation Line of 1763

Susquehanna R.

Hudson R.

Connecticut R.

Delaware R.

Potomac R.

Raleigh ★

NORTH
CAROLINA
(1789)

Cape Fear R.

ARKANSAS
(1836)

Arkansas R.

TENNESSEE
(1796)

★ Nashville

Tennessee R.

SOUTH
CAROLINA
(1788)
★ Columbia

OKLAHOMA
(1907)

Little
Rock ★

Mississippi R.

Atlanta ★

Savannah R.

ATLANTIC
OCEAN

LOUISIANA
(1812)

MISSISSIPPI
(1817)

★ Jackson

ALABAMA
(1819)

Montgomery ★

GEORGIA
(1788)

★ Tallahassee

FLORIDA
(1845)

*FLORIDA
Treaty with Spain,
1819*

Baton
Rouge ★

Gulf of Mexico

BAHAMAS

CUBA

| 0 | 150 | 300 miles |
| 0 | 150 | 300 kilometers |

U.S. Territories

ATLANTIC
OCEAN

San
Juan ★

*VIRGIN
ISLANDS
Acquired from
Denmark,
1916–1917*

PUERTO RICO
*Acquired from
Spain, 1898*

Caribbean
Sea

| 0 | 50 | 100 miles |
| 0 | 50 | 100 kilometers |

(1789) Date of statehood

M-9